T0340784

Oxford
Compact
ENGLISH-ENGLISH-
ODIA
Dictionary

ଇଂରାଜୀ-ଇଂରାଜୀ-ଓଡ଼ିଆ
ଶବ୍ଦକୋଷ

Oxford Compact ENGLISH-ENGLISH-ODIA Dictionary

ଇଂରାଜୀ-ଇଂରାଜୀ-ଓଡ଼ିଆ ଶବ୍ଦକୋଷ

Editor

B.K. TRIPATHY

Oxford University Press is a department of the University of Oxford. It furthers the University's objective of excellence in research, scholarship, and education by publishing worldwide. Oxford is a registered trade mark of Oxford University Press in the UK and in certain other countries.

Published in India by
Oxford University Press
22 Workspace, 2nd Floor, 1/22 Asaf Ali Road, New Delhi 110 002

This edition published in 2016
Ninth impression 2024
This edition is published by arrangement with
Oxford University Press, Oxford
for sale throughout the world.

ISBN-13: 978-0-19-947224-6
ISBN-10: 0-19-947224-6

Typeset by Computer Club, Kolkata 700 073td
Printed in India by Thomson Press, (India) Ltd.

Illustrations by Tapas Guha

ବିଷୟ-ସୂଚୀ

ଭୂମିକା

ଏହି ଶବ୍ଦକୋଷର ସଙ୍କଳନ ସେହି ଛାତ୍ର ଓ ଛାତ୍ରୀଙ୍କ ପାଇଁ କରାଯାଉଛି ଯେଉଁମାନଙ୍କ ମାତୃଭାଷା ଓଡ଼ିଆ ଅଟେ ତଥା ଯେଉଁମାନେ ଇଂରାଜୀକୁ ଦ୍ୱିତୀୟ ଭାଷା ରୂପେ ଶିଖୁଛନ୍ତି। ଏହି ଶବ୍ଦକୋଷ ବିଶେଷ ଭାବେ ଆଠ ବର୍ଷରୁ ଅଧିକ ଆୟୁର ଛାତ୍ର-ଛାତ୍ରୀଙ୍କ ପାଇଁ ପ୍ରସ୍ତୁତ କରାଯାଇଛି। ଏହା ଏକ ଇଂରାଜୀ-ଇଂରାଜୀ-ଓଡ଼ିଆ ଶବ୍ଦକୋଷ ଅଟେ ଓ ଏଥିରେ ଶବ୍ଦର ଅର୍ଥ ପ୍ରଥମେ ଇଂରାଜୀରେ ଓ ତା'ପରେ ଓଡ଼ିଆରେ ଲେଖାଯାଇଛି। ଏହାର ରଚନା ଦୁଇଟି ଉଦ୍ଦେଶ୍ୟକୁ ନେଇ କରାଯାଇଛି (କ) ଇଂରାଜୀ ଶବ୍ଦର ଅର୍ଥ ବିବରଣୀ ଦେବା ଓ (ଖ) ଇଂରାଜୀ ଭାଷାର ପ୍ରୟୋଗ ଓ ବ୍ୟାକରଣ ଜ୍ଞାନ ବର୍ଦ୍ଧନ କରିବା।

ଏହି ଶବ୍ଦକୋଷରେ 12,000 ରୁ ଅଧିକ ବିବରଣୀ ନାମ ଦିଆଯାଇଛି, ଯେଉଁଥିରେ ଶୀର୍ଷ ଶବ୍ଦ, ଉପଶୀର୍ଷ ଶବ୍ଦ, ଢ଼ଗ ଓ ଉପବାକ୍ୟ ଅଛି। ଶବ୍ଦାବଳୀର ସଂକଳନ ଛାତ୍ର-ଛାତ୍ରୀମାନଙ୍କର ଆବଶ୍ୟକତା ପ୍ରତି ଧ୍ୟାନ ରଖି କରାଯାଇଛି ଓ ଏହି ଶବ୍ଦକୋଷରେ ନୂତନ ତଥା ବର୍ତ୍ତମାନ ବିଷୟ ସମ୍ବନ୍ଧୀତ ଶବ୍ଦର ସମାବେଶ ମଧ୍ୟ କରାଯାଇଛି। ଓଡ଼ିଆ ମାଧ୍ୟମରେ ପଢ଼ାପଢ଼ି କରୁଥିବା ବିଦ୍ୟାର୍ଥୀଙ୍କୁ ଏହି ଶବ୍ଦକୋଷ ଅତ୍ୟନ୍ତ ଉପଯୋଗୀ ହେବ।

ଶବ୍ଦକୋଷର ପ୍ରୟୋଗବିଧି

ଶବ୍ଦ ଖୋଜିବାର ବିଧି

ଶବ୍ଦକୋଷରେ ଶବ୍ଦ ବର୍ଣ୍ଣମାଳା ଅନୁଯାୟୀ ସ୍ଥିତ ଥାନ୍ତି। ଏହି ଶବ୍ଦକୋଷରେ ଶବ୍ଦ ଇଂରାଜୀ ବର୍ଣ୍ଣମାଳା ଅନୁସାରେ କ୍ରମଶଃ ଅଛି ଓ ବଡ଼ ଅକ୍ଷରରେ ଦିଆଯାଇଛି। ଇଂରାଜୀ ବର୍ଣ୍ଣମାଳା —

a b c d e f g h i j k l m n o p q r s t u v w x y z

ଶବ୍ଦକୋଷରେ ଶବ୍ଦ ଖୋଜିବା ପାଇଁ ଉକ୍ତ ଶବ୍ଦର ପ୍ରଥମ ଅକ୍ଷର ଦେଖନ୍ତୁ। ଉଦାହରଣ ସ୍ୱରୂପ ଶବ୍ଦ **bake** ନିଜର ପ୍ରଥମ ଅକ୍ଷର **b** ରୁ ଆରମ୍ଭ ହେଉଥିବା ବିବରଣୀରେ ମିଳିବ। ବର୍ତ୍ତମାନ **bake** ର ଦ୍ୱିତୀୟ ଅକ୍ଷର **a** ଦେଖନ୍ତୁ। ଶବ୍ଦ **bake** କୁ ଛାଡ଼ି **ba** ରୁ ଆରମ୍ଭ ହେଉଥିବା ଆହୁରି ଅତିରିକ୍ତ ଶବ୍ଦ ଅଛି। ଯଥା **baby** ଓ **back** ଏଥି ନିମନ୍ତେ **bake** ର ତୃତୀୟ ଅକ୍ଷର **k** ଦେଖନ୍ତୁ। ଏହିପରି ଆଗକୁ ବଢ଼ିଲେ **bake** ଶବ୍ଦ ମିଳିଯିବ।

ଏହି କୋଷରେ ଉପଶୀର୍ଷପଦ (ଶୀର୍ଷପଦରୁ ଉତ୍ପନ୍ନ ଶବ୍ଦ) ମଧ୍ୟ ଶୀର୍ଷଶବ୍ଦର ତଳେ ଦିଆଯାଇଛି। ଉଦାହରଣ ସ୍ୱରୂପ **confused, confusing** ଓ **confusion** ଶୀର୍ଷଶବ୍ଦ **confuse** ତଳେ ଦିଆଯାଇଛି।

ଉଚ୍ଚାରଣ

ଏହି ଶବ୍ଦକୋଷରେ ସମସ୍ତ ଶୀର୍ଷଶବ୍ଦ ଓ କଠିନ ଉପଶୀର୍ଷଶବ୍ଦର ଉଚ୍ଚାରଣ ସେହି ଶୀର୍ଷଶବ୍ଦର (ଅଥବା ଉପଶୀର୍ଷଶବ୍ଦ) ଠିକ୍ ପରେ ଉଚ୍ଚାରଣ ଓଡ଼ିଆ ଲିପିରେ ଅଛି ଓ International Phonetic Alphabet (IPA) ଶୈଳୀ, ଅନୁଯାୟୀ ଅଛି। ଉଚ୍ଚାରଣ ଶୈଳୀରେ ଚିହ୍ନର ପୂର୍ଣ୍ଣସୂଚୀ ପୃଷ୍ଠା xii ରେ ଦିଆଯାଇଛି।

ବ୍ୟାକରଣ ଶ୍ରେଣୀ ଅଥବା ଶବ୍ଦ–ପ୍ରକାର

ଉଚ୍ଚାରଣର ଠିକ୍ ପରେ ଶୀର୍ଷଶବ୍ଦ ଅଥବା ଉପଶୀର୍ଷଶବ୍ଦର ବ୍ୟାକରଣ ଶ୍ରେଣୀ (ଯଥା *noun*, *adjective*, *adverb* ଓ *verb*) ଇଟାଲିକ୍ସ ଅକ୍ଷରରେ ଦିଆଯାଇଛି।

ବେଳେବେଳେ ଗୋଟିଏ ଶୀର୍ଷଶବ୍ଦ ଦୁଇ କିମ୍ବା ଅଧିକ ଶବ୍ଦ–ପ୍ରକାର ରୂପରେ ଥାଏ। ଯଥା **coil** *noun* ଓ **coil** *verb*। ଏହି ଶବ୍ଦ–ପ୍ରକାରକୁ ପୃଥକ୍ କରାଯାଇଛି। ଯେଉଁଠାରେ ଯେଉଁ ଶବ୍ଦ–ପ୍ରକାର ଅର୍ଥ ସମ୍ପୂର୍ଣ୍ଣ ଭିନ୍ନ ଥାଏ। ସେହିଠାରେ ତା'ର ସ୍ୱତନ୍ତ୍ର ବିଭାଗ ପ୍ରସ୍ତୁତ କରାଯାଇଛି ଓ ତା'ଉପରେ ସଂଖ୍ୟା ଦିଆଯାଇଛି ଯଥା **row^1**, **row^2** ଓ **row^3** ।

ଶବ୍ଦର ବ୍ୟାକରଣ ରୂପ

କ୍ରିୟାର ରୂପରେ ପରିବର୍ତ୍ତନ ସ୍ୱରୂପ ଉତ୍ପନ୍ନ ସମସ୍ତ ରୂପ ବନ୍ଧନୀ ମଧ୍ୟରେ ଦିଆଯାଇଛି। ବିଶେଷଣ ଓ କ୍ରିୟା ବିଶେଷଣର ତୁଳନାତ୍ମକ ରୂପ ଓ ବିଶେଷ୍ୟର ବହୁବଚନ ରୂପ ମଧ୍ୟ ବନ୍ଧନୀରେ ଦିଆଯାଇଛି।

rise /raɪz/ *verb* (**rises, rising, rose** /rəʊz/, **has risen** /ˈrɪzn/)
pretty /ˈprɪti/ *adjective* (**prettier, prettiest**)
laboratory /ləˈbɒrətri/ *noun* (*plural* **laboratories**)

କିଛି ବିଶେଷ୍ୟର ବହୁବଚନ ରୂପ ଅନେକ ଏକବଚନ ରୂପଠାରୁ ଅଲଗା ନଥାନ୍ତି। ଏହି ସୂଚନା ବନ୍ଧନୀରେ ଦିଆଯାଇଛି —

headquarters /ˌhedˈkwɔːtəz/ *noun* (*plural* **headquarters**)

ଅର୍ଥ

ଇଂରାଜୀ ଓ ଓଡ଼ିଆ ଉଭୟ ଭାଷାରେ ଅର୍ଥ ସରଳ ଶବ୍ଦରେ ଦିଆଯାଇଛି। ଓଡ଼ିଆ ଭାଷାରେ ଅର୍ଥ ଅଧିକ ସ୍ଥାନରେ ବର୍ଣ୍ଣନ ଓ ବ୍ୟାଖ୍ୟା ଦ୍ୱାରା ବର୍ଣ୍ଣନା କରାଯାଇଛି। ଯେଉଁଠାରେ ସମ୍ଭବ ହେଉଛି, ସେଠାରେ ଗୋଟିଏ ଶବ୍ଦରେ ମଧ୍ୟ ଅର୍ଥ ବ୍ୟକ୍ତ କରାଯାଇଛି। କେବଳ ଗୋଟିଏ ଶବ୍ଦରେ ଅର୍ଥ ସେହି ସ୍ଥାନରେ ବ୍ୟକ୍ତ କରାଯାଇଛି ଯେତେବେଳେ ଗୋଟିଏ ଶବ୍ଦରେ ଅର୍ଥ ସେହି ସ୍ଥାନରେ ବ୍ୟକ୍ତ କରାଯାଇଛି ଯେତେବେଳେ ଏହି ଅର୍ଥର ଭାବ ଇଂରାଜୀ ଅର୍ଥ ଭାବ ସହ ପୁରା ରୂପେ ମିଳୁଥାଏ। ଗୋଟିଏ ଶବ୍ଦର ଏକରୁ ଅଧିକ ଅର୍ଥକୁ 1, 2, 3, ... ସଂଖ୍ୟା ଦେଇ କରି ଅଲଗା କରାଯାଇଛି। ଯେଉଁ ଅର୍ଥର ପ୍ରୟୋଗ ଅଧିକ ହେଉଥାଏ। ସେହି ଅର୍ଥକୁ ପ୍ରଥମରେ ଦିଆଯାଇଛି —

centre /ˈsentə(r)/ *noun* **1** the part in the middle ମଧ୍ୟବିନ୍ଦୁ, କେନ୍ଦ୍ରବିନ୍ଦୁ *The carpet is in the centre of the room.* **2** a place where people come to do something special କେନ୍ଦ୍ରସ୍ଥଳ, ମୁଖ୍ୟ ସ୍ଥାନ *a shopping centre*

ଉଦାହରଣ

ଶବ୍ଦର ଉଚିତ୍ ପ୍ରୟୋଗକୁ ଇଂରାଜୀ ଉଦାହରଣ ଦ୍ୱାରା ସ୍ପଷ୍ଟ କରାଯାଇଛି। ଉଦାହରଣ ଇଟାଲିକ୍ସ ଅକ୍ଷରରେ ଦିଆଯାଇଛି। ଦୁଇଟି ଅଥବା ଅଧିକ ଉଦାହରଣକୁ ○ ଚିହ୍ନ ଦ୍ୱାରା ପୃଥକ କରାଯାଇଛି —

begin /bɪˈgɪn/ *verb* (**begins, beginning, began** /bɪˈgæn/, **has begun** /bɪˈgʌn/) start to do something or start to happen ଆରମ୍ଭ କରିବା; ଆରମ୍ଭ ହେବା *The film begins at 7.30 p.m.* ○ *I'm beginning to feel cold.*

ଢ଼ଗ ଓ ଅନ୍ୟ ଉପବାକ୍ୟ

ଶୀର୍ଷଶବ୍ଦ ସମ୍ପର୍କୀୟ ଢ଼ଗ ଓ ଅନ୍ୟ ଉପବାକ୍ୟ ଶୀର୍ଷଶବ୍ଦର ତଳେ ବଡ଼ ଅକ୍ଷରରେ ଦିଆଯାଇଛି। ଏହାର ଅର୍ଥ ଓ ଉଦାହରଣ ମଧ୍ୟ ଦିଆଯାଇଛି —

fool[1] /fu:l/ *noun* a person who is silly or who does something silly ବୋକା, ନିର୍ବୋଧ ବ୍ୟକ୍ତି

make a fool of yourself do something that makes you look silly ନିଜକୁ ବୋକା ବନେଇବା *He always makes a fool of himself at parties.*

bend[1] /bend/ *verb* (**bends, bending, bent** /bent/, **has bent**) become curved; make something that was straight into a curved shape ବଙ୍କେଇବା, ନଇଁବା *She couldn't bend the metal bar.*

bend down, bend over move your body forward and down ନଇଁବା *She bent down to put on her shoes.*

ଶବ୍ଦ ପ୍ରୟୋଗ ଉପରେ ଟିପ୍ପଣୀ (ନୋଟ୍)

ଶବ୍ଦ ପ୍ରୟୋଗ ବିଷୟରେ ସୂଚନା ବନ୍ଧନୀରେ ଦିଆଯାଇଛି। ଏହା (1) ଭ୍ରମ ସୃଷ୍ଟି କରୁଥିବା ଏକା ପରି ଲାଗୁଥିବା ଶବ୍ଦ (2) ବ୍ୟାକରଣ ବିଷୟ ଯଥା **modal verbs** ଓ (3) ଉଚ୍ଚାରଣ ଓ ଶବ୍ଦ ଉତ୍ପତ୍ତି —

for or **since**?

ଆମେ ଘଟଣାର ସମୟକାଳ ସୂଚାଇବା ପାଇଁ **for** ବ୍ୟବହାର କରୁ, ଯଥା — ସମୟ, ଦିନ ଗୁଡ଼ିକ ବା ବର୍ଷ

*She has been ill **for** three days.*
*I have lived in London **for** ten months.*
*We have been married **for** thirty years.*

ଆମେ ଅତୀତର ନିର୍ଦ୍ଦିଷ୍ଟ ତାରିଖ (date), ସମୟ (time) ବା ଘଟଣା (event) ସୂଚାଇବା ପାଇଁ **since** ବ୍ୟବହାର କରୁ ଯଥା —

*I have been here **since** six o'clock.*
*She has been alone **since** her son moved to Mumbai.*
*We have been married **since** 1965.*

ସମ୍ବନ୍ଧୀୟ ଶବ୍ଦ ବିଷୟରେ ସୂଚନା

ସମ୍ବନ୍ଧୀୟ ଶବ୍ଦ ବିଷୟରେ ମଧ୍ୟ ବିସ୍ତୃତ ସୂଚନା ଦିଆଯାଇଛି —

✪ ବ୍ୟାଙ୍କ୍‌ରେ **account** ଖୋଲିଲେ ଟଙ୍କା ଜମା **(deposit)** କରିପାରିବ ବା **(withdraw)** କାଢ଼ି ପାରିବ, ଆଉ ମଧ୍ୟ ବ୍ୟାଙ୍କରେ ଗୋଟିଏ ଦେଶର ଟଙ୍କାକୁ **exchange** କରି ଅନ୍ୟ ଦେଶର ମୁଦ୍ରା ପାଇପାରିବେ। ଏହା ବ୍ୟତୀତ ବ୍ୟାଙ୍କରୁ ଋଣ **(loan)** ମଧ୍ୟ ନେଇପାରିବେ।

ଏହା ସହ, ବିପରୀତ ଶବ୍ଦ ଓ ସଂଦର୍ଭ ଶବ୍ଦ ମଧ୍ୟ ବ୍ୟାପକ ରୂପେ ଦିଆଯାଇଛି —

certain[1] /ˈsɜːtn/ *adjective* without any doubt; sure ନିଃସନ୍ଦେହ, ନିଶ୍ଚିତ *I am certain that I have seen her before*. ✪ ବିପରୀତ **uncertain**

bear[1] /beə(r)/ *noun* a big wild animal with thick fur ଭାଲୁ, ଭଲ୍ଲୁକ ➪ **teddy bear** ବି ଦେଖନ୍ତୁ ।

ଚିତ୍ର

ଏହି ଶବ୍ଦକୋଷରେ 300 ରୁ ଅଧିକ ଚିତ୍ର ଦିଆଯାଇଛି । ଏହି ଚିତ୍ର ଅର୍ଥକୁ ଅଧିକ ସ୍ପଷ୍ଟ କରିବାରେ ସହାୟତା କରିବ —

ଶବ୍ଦ କୋଷର ମୂଳ ତତ୍ତ୍ୱ

ଶୀର୍ଷଶବ୍ଦ: ଶିରୋନାମା ଇଂରାଜୀରେ ବଡ଼ ଅକ୍ଷରରେ ଦିଆଯାଇଛି।

ବ୍ୟାକରଣ ଶୈଳୀ: ଶବ୍ଦର ବ୍ୟାକରଣ ଶୈଳୀ ଇଂରାଜୀରେ ଇଟାଲିକ୍ସ ଅକ୍ଷରରେ ଦିଆଯାଇଛି।

ଶିରୋନାମାର ଉପରେ ମୁଦ୍ରିତ ଅଙ୍କ: କିଛି ଶବ୍ଦ ଏକାପରି ଦୃଷ୍ଟିଗୋଚର ହୋଇଥାନ୍ତି, ମାତ୍ର ଅର୍ଥ ବ୍ୟାକରଣ, ଉଚ୍ଚାରଣ ଆଦିର ଦୃଷ୍ଟିରୁ ଭିନ୍ନ ଥାନ୍ତି। ଯଥା **back**[1], **back**[2], **back**[3], **back**[4] ଏହି ଶବ୍ଦ ଗୁଡ଼ିକର ପୃଥକ୍ ଶିରୋନାମା ଦିଆଯାଇଛି ଓ ସଂଖ୍ୟା ଦିଆଯାଇଛି।

ଢ଼ଗ: ଶିରୋନାମା ସମ୍ପର୍କୀୟ ଢ଼ଗକୁ ଶିରୋ-ନାମାର ତଳେ ବଡ଼ ଅକ୍ଷରରେ ଅର୍ଥ ଓ ଉଦାହରଣ ସହ ଦିଆ-ଯାଇଛି।

ଅର୍ଥ: ଅର୍ଥକୁ ଇଂରାଜୀ ଓ ଓଡ଼ିଆ ଉଭୟ ଭାଷାରେ ବୁଝାଇ ଦିଆଯାଇଛି, ଯେଉଁଠାରେ ଗୋଟିଏରୁ ଅଧିକ ଅର୍ଥ ଅଛି। ଅର୍ଥକୁ 1, 2, 3 ଆଦି ସଂଖ୍ୟା ଦେଇ ଅଲଗା କରାଯାଇଛି।

ଉଚ୍ଚାରଣ: ଶିରୋନାମାର ଠିକ୍ ପରେ ତା'ର ଉଚ୍ଚାରଣ IPA ଲିପିରେ ଦିଆଯାଇଛି।

back[1] /bæk/ *noun* **1** the part that is behind or farthest from the front ପଛପଟ, ଦେହର ପଛଭାଗ, ପିଠି *The answers are at the back of the book.* ✪ ବିପରୀତ **front** **2** the part of a person or an animal between the neck and the bottom ମଣିଷ ବା ପଶୁର ପଛପଟ *He lay on his back and looked up at the sky.* ➪ ଚିତ୍ର ପାଇଁ **body** ଦେଖନ୍ତୁ।

behind somebody's back when somebody is not there, so that they do not know about it କାହାର ଅନୁପସ୍ଥିତିରେ *Don't talk about Shruti behind her back.*

back[2] /bæk/ *adjective* away from the front ପଛ *the back door*

back[3] /bæk/ *adverb* **1** away from the front ପଛକୁ, ପଛପଟେ *I looked back to see if she was coming.* **2** in or to the place where somebody or something was before ପୂର୍ବସ୍ଥାନକୁ, ପୂର୍ବସ୍ଥାନରେ *I'll be back at six o'clock.* **3** as a way of returning or answering something ଉତ୍ତରରେ, ପ୍ରତ୍ୟୁତ୍ତରରେ *I wrote her a letter, but she didn't write back.*

back[4] /bæk/ *verb* (**backs, backing, backed**) **1** move backwards or make something move backwards ପଛକୁ ଯିବା, ପଛକୁ ନେବା *She backed the car out of the garage.* **2** say that you think somebody or something is right or the best ସମର୍ଥନ ଦେବା।

ଉପବାକ୍ୟ: ଶିରୋନାମା ସମ୍ପର୍କୀୟ ଉପବାକ୍ୟ ଶିରୋନାମାର ତଳେ ବଡ଼ ଅକ୍ଷରରେ ଅର୍ଥ ଓ ଉଦାହରଣ ସହିତ ଦିଆଯାଇଛି ।

ଉଦାହରଣ: ଶିରୋନାମାର ପ୍ରୟୋଗକୁ ଇଂରାଜୀ ଉଦାହରଣ ଦ୍ୱାରା ସ୍ପଷ୍ଟ କରାଯାଇଛି ।

back out not do something that you promised or agreed to do ପ୍ରତିଶ୍ରୁତିରୁ ପଛେଇଯିବା *Rajiv backed out of the game, so we only had ten players.*

ବିଶେଷଣ ରୂପ: ବିଶେଷଣର ତୁଳନାତ୍ମକ ରୂପ ବନ୍ଧନୀରେ ଓ ବଡ଼ ଅକ୍ଷରରେ ଦିଆଯାଇଛି ।

deep /di:p/ *adjective* (**deeper, deepest**) **1** something that is deep goes down a long way ଗଭୀର, ଗହିରିଆ *Be careful—the water is very deep.* ✪ ବିପରୀତ **shallow** ✪ ଏହାର ବିଶେଷ୍ୟ ହେଲା **depth** । **2** a deep colour is strong and dark ଗାଢ଼ (ରଙ୍ଗ ଇତ୍ୟାଦି) *She has deep blue eyes.* ✪ ବିପରୀତ **pale 2** ବା **light² 1** **3** a deep sound is low and strong ଗମ୍ଭୀର *He has a deep voice*. **4** if you are in a deep sleep, it is difficult for somebody to wake you up ଗଭୀର, ଗାଢ଼ *She was in such a deep sleep that she didn't hear me calling her.*

ଉପ ଶିରୋନାମା ଶବ୍ଦ: ଶିରୋନାମା ଶବ୍ଦରୁ ସୃଷ୍ଟି ହୋଇଥିବା ଶବ୍ଦକୁ ଉପଶିରୋନାମା କହନ୍ତି । ଏହାକୁ ଶିରୋନାମା ପରେ ବର୍ଣ୍ଣମାଳାକ୍ରମ ଅନୁଯାୟୀ ଦିଆଯାଇଛି ।

deeply *adverb* strongly or completely ଗଭୀର ଭାବରେ, ପ୍ରଗାଢ଼ ଭାବରେ *He is sleeping very deeply.*

ସମ୍ବନ୍ଧୀୟ ଶବ୍ଦ: ବିପରୀତ ଶବ୍ଦ, ସମ୍ବନ୍ଧୀୟ ଶବ୍ଦ ସମ୍ପର୍କରେ ଟିପ୍ପଣୀ ବ୍ୟାପକ ରୂପେ ଦିଆଯାଇଛି । ଏହି ଶବ୍ଦ ପାଠକଙ୍କର ଶବ୍ଦ ଭଣ୍ଡାରକୁ ବଢ଼ାଇବାରେ ସହାୟକ ସିଦ୍ଧ ହେବ ।

ଚିତ୍ର: ପାଠକଙ୍କର ଶବ୍ଦ ଭଣ୍ଡାରକୁ ବିକଶିତ କରିବା ପାଇଁ ନାମାଙ୍କିତ ଚିତ୍ର ବ୍ୟବହାର କରାଯାଇଛି ।

deer /dɪə(r)/ *noun* (*plural* **deer**) a wild animal that eats grass and can run fast ହରିଣ, ମୃଗ, କୁରଙ୍ଗ

✪ ମାଈ ହରିଣକୁ **doe** କୁହାଯାଏ ଏବଂ ଅଣ୍ଡିରା ହରିଣକୁ **stag** କୁହାଯାଏ । ହରିଣ ଛୁଆକୁ **fawn** କୁହାଯାଏ ।

goose /gu:s/ *noun* (*plural* **geese** /gi:s/) a bird like a large duck that has a long neck ଲମ୍ବା ବେକ ଥିବା ବଡ଼ ବତକ ପରି ପକ୍ଷୀ, ଗୁଜ୍

ବିଶେଷ୍ୟ ରୂପ: ବିଶେଷ୍ୟର ସବୁ ଅନିୟମିତ ରୂପ ବନ୍ଧନୀରେ ଦିଆଯାଇଛି।

hear /hɪə(r)/ *verb* (**hears, hearing, heard** /hɜ:d/, **has heard**) **1** take in sounds through your ears ଶୁଣିବା *Can you hear that noise?*

କ୍ରିୟା ରୂପ: କ୍ରିୟାକୁ ନିମ୍ନଲିଖିତ ରୂପ ଦିଆଯାଇଛି — present tense ଓ past participle.

hear or **listen**?

Hear ବା **listen** ର ପ୍ରୟୋଗ ଭିନ୍ନ ଭିନ୍ନ ଭାବରେ ବ୍ୟବହୃତ ହୁଏ ଯେତେବେଳେ ଆମେ **hear** କରୁ ଶବ୍ଦ ଆମ କାନକୁ ଆସେ — *I **heard** the door close.*
ଯେତେବେଳେ କୌଣସି ଧ୍ୱନିର ପ୍ରୟାସ ଦ୍ୱାରା ଶୁଣାଯାଏ, ତେବେ **listen** ଶବ୍ଦର ପ୍ରୟୋଗ କରାଯାଏ —
*I **listen to** the radio every morning.*

ଶବ୍ଦ ପ୍ରୟୋଗ ସମ୍ପର୍କୀୟ ନୋଟ: ବିଭିନ୍ନ ଶବ୍ଦଙ୍କର ଠିକ୍ ପ୍ରୟୋଗର ଉପଯୋଗୀ ଟିପ୍ପଣୀ ଦିଆଯାଇଛି।

a /eɪ/ *article* **1** one or any ଏକ, ଗୋଟିଏ, ଜଣେ, ଯେକୌଣସି *A dog has four legs.* ○ *He's a teacher.* **2** each, or for each ପ୍ରତି, ପ୍ରତ୍ୟେକ *She phones her mother three times a week.* ○ *This juice costs Rs 10 a bottle.*

a or **an**?

ସ୍ୱରବର୍ଣ୍ଣ ଧ୍ୱନି (**a, e, i, o, u**) ରୁ ଆରମ୍ଭ ହେଉଥିବା ଶବ୍ଦ ପୂର୍ବରୁ **an** ବ୍ୟବହୃତ ହୁଏ। ବ୍ୟଞ୍ଜନବର୍ଣ୍ଣ ଧ୍ୱନିରୁ ଆରମ୍ଭ ଶବ୍ଦ ପୂର୍ବରୁ **a** ବ୍ୟବହୃତ ହୁଏ। ମନେ ରଖନ୍ତୁ ଶବ୍ଦର ପ୍ରାରମ୍ଭିକ ଅକ୍ଷର ମୁଖ୍ୟ ନୁହେଁ। ଶବ୍ଦର ଧ୍ୱନି ଅନୁସାରେ **'a'** ବା **'an'** ବ୍ୟବହାର କରାଯାଏ।

a *box*	**an** *apple*
a *singer*	**an** *hour*
a *university*	**an** *MP*

ବ୍ୟାକରଣ ଟିପ୍ପଣୀ: ବ୍ୟାକରଣ ସମ୍ବନ୍ଧୀୟ ଟିପ୍ପଣୀ ଅନେକ ସ୍ଥାନରେ ବିସ୍ତୃତ ରୂପରେ ଦିଆଯାଇଛି।

ଉଚ୍ଚାରଣ ଶୈଳୀ

ଏହି ଶବ୍ଦକୋଷ ଦିଆଯାଇଥିବା ଉଚ୍ଚାରଣ ଶୈଳୀ International Phonetic Alphabet (IPA) ଶୈଳୀ ଅନୁଯାୟୀ ଆଧାରିତ ଅଟେ। ଏହି ଶୈଳୀରେ ପ୍ରତ୍ୟେକ ଧ୍ୱନି ପାଇଁ ଏକ ବିଶେଷ ଚିହ୍ନର ପ୍ରୟୋଗ କରାଯାଏ। ଏହି ଚିହ୍ନର ଓଡ଼ିଆ ଲିପିରେ ଅନୁବାଦ କରାଯାଇଛି ଓ ବିସ୍ତୃତ ସୂଚୀ ନିମ୍ନରେ ଦିଆଯାଇଛି।

Consonants

IPA symbol	Usage
p	cap /kæp/
b	rub /rʌb/
t	fit /fɪt/
d	red /red/
k	break /breɪk/
g	flag /flæg/
tʃ	rich /rɪtʃ/
dʒ	badge /bædʒ/
f	life /laɪf/
v	wave /weɪv/
θ	myth /mɪθ/
ð	bathe /beɪð/
s	fuss /fʌs/
z	railings /ˈreɪlɪŋz/
ʃ	fish /fɪʃ/
ʒ	vision /ˈvɪʒn/
h	hat /hæt/
m	fame /feɪm/
n	fin /fɪn/
ŋ	ring /rɪŋ/
l	file /faɪl/
r	run /rʌn/
(r)	for /fɔ:(r)/
j	young /jʌŋ/
w	won /wʌn/

Vowels and dipthongs

IPA symbol	Usage
i	happy /ˈhæpi/
ɪ	fig /fɪg/
i:	see /si:/
e	ten /ten/
æ	cat /kæt/
ɑ:	far /fɑ:(r)/
ɒ	lot /lɒt/
ɔ:	saw /sɔ:/
ʊ	put /pʊt/
u	actual /ˈæktʃuəl/
u:	too /tu:/
ʌ	cut /kʌt/
ɜ:	bird /bɜ:d/
ə	about; paper /əˈbaʊt; ˈpeɪpə(r)/
eɪ	fade /feɪd/
əʊ	go /gəʊ/
aɪ	five /faɪv/
ɔɪ	boy /bɔɪ/
aʊ	now /naʊ/
ɪə	near /nɪə(r)/
eə	chair /tʃeə(r)/
ʊə	pure /pjʊə(r)/

ସ୍ୱର ଉପରେ ଜୋର୍ (ଉଚ୍ଚାରଣ ସମୟରେ)

|ˈ| ଏହି ଚିହ୍ନ ପରେ ଥିବା ଅକ୍ଷର ଗୁଡ଼ିକ ଉପରେ ଅଧିକ ଜୋର୍ ଦିଆଯାଇଛି। (syllable) ଉଦାହରଣ ସ୍ୱରୂପ, **demand** /dɪˈma:nd/ ରେ ଆଉ ଅକ୍ଷର ସମୁହ /ˈma:nd/ ଉପରେ ଜୋର୍ ଦିଆଯାଇଥାଏ। ଯେତେବେଳେ **digit** /ˈdɪdʒɪt/ ରେ ପ୍ରଥମ ଅକ୍ଷର ସମୁହ (ˈdɪ) ଉପରେ (ସ୍ୱର) ଜୋର୍ ଦିଆଯାଇଥାଏ।

|ˌ| ଏହି ଚିହ୍ନ ପରେ କୁହାଯାଉଥିବା ଅକ୍ଷର ଉପରେ ଅନ୍ୟ ଅକ୍ଷର ସମୁହ ଠାରୁ ଅଧିକ ଜୋର୍ ଦିଆଯାଇଥାଏ। ମାତ୍ର ଏତେ ନାହିଁ ଯେତେ |ˈ| ଚିହ୍ନ ପରେ କୁହାଯାଉଥିବା ଅକ୍ଷର ସମୁହ ଉପରେ ଜୋର୍ ଦିଆଯାଏ। ଉଦାହରଣ ସ୍ୱରୂପ ଶବ୍ଦ **agitation** /ˌædʒɪˈteɪʃn/ ରେ ପ୍ରାଥମିକ ଜୋର୍ ତୃତୀୟ ଅକ୍ଷର-ସମୂହ (ˈte) ଓ ଗୌଣ ଜୋର୍ ପ୍ରଥମ ଅକ୍ଷର ସମୁହ (ˌæ) ଉପରେ ଦିଆଯାଇଥାଏ।

A a

a /eɪ/ *article* **1** one or any ଏକ, ଗୋଟିଏ, ଜଣେ, ଯେକୌଣସି *A dog has four legs.* ○ *He's a teacher.* **2** each, or for each ପ୍ରତି, ପ୍ରତ୍ୟେକ *She phones her mother three times a week.* ○ *This juice costs Rs 10 a bottle.*

a or **an**?	
ସ୍ୱରବର୍ଣ୍ଣ ଧ୍ୱନି (**a, e, i, o, u**) ରୁ ଆରମ୍ଭ ହେଉଥିବା ଶବ୍ଦ ପୂର୍ବରୁ **an** ବ୍ୟବହୃତ ହୁଏ। ବ୍ୟଞ୍ଜନବର୍ଣ୍ଣ ଧ୍ୱନିରୁ ଆରମ୍ଭ ଶବ୍ଦ ପୂର୍ବରୁ **a** ବ୍ୟବହୃତ ହୁଏ। ମନେ ରଖନ୍ତୁ ଶବ୍ଦର ପ୍ରାରମ୍ଭିକ ଅକ୍ଷର ମୂଖ୍ୟ ନୁହେଁ। ଶବ୍ଦର ଧ୍ୱନି ଅନୁସାରେ **'a'** ବା **'an'** ବ୍ୟବହାର କରାଯାଏ।	
a *box*	**an** *apple*
a *singer*	**an** *hour*
a *university*	**an** *MP*

abacus /ˈæbəkəs/ *noun* (*plural* **abacuses**) a frame with wires or rods on which beads can slide ଗଣିବା ପାଇଁ ଏକ ଉପକରଣ (ଯଥା: ପିଲାଙ୍କ ସ୍ଲେଟ୍ ସହିତ ଗଣିବା ପାଇଁ ଥିବା ତାର ଗଳା ମାଳି); ଆବାକସ୍ *An abacus is used for counting.*

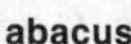

abandon /əˈbændən/ *verb* (**abandons, abandoning, abandoned**) **1** leave somebody or something completely କୌଣସି ଲୋକ ବା ପଦାର୍ଥକୁ ପରିତ୍ୟାଗ କରିବା; ଛାଡ଼ିଦେବା *He abandoned his car in the snow.* **2** stop doing something before it is finished କୌଣସି କାମ ସମ୍ପୂର୍ଣ୍ଣ ହେବା ପୂର୍ବରୁ କାମ ବନ୍ଦ କରିଦେବା, ଛାଡ଼ିଦେବା *When the rain started, we abandoned our game.*

abandoned /əˈbændənd/ *adjective* left completely and no longer used or wanted ପରିତ୍ୟକ୍ତ, ବର୍ଜିତ (ଘର, ବ୍ୟକ୍ତି ଇତ୍ୟାଦି) *an abandoned ship*

abbreviation /əˌbriːviˈeɪʃn/ *noun* a short form of a word କୌଣସି ଶବ୍ଦର ସଂକ୍ଷିପ୍ତ ରୂପ *TV is an abbreviation for 'television'.*

abdomen /ˈæbdəmən/ *noun* **1** the part of the human body below the chest that contains the stomach and intestines (ମଣିଷ ଦେହର) ପେଟ, ତଳିପେଟ, ଉଦର **2** the end part of an insect's body (କୀଟ ଦେହର) ପଛପଟ, ଶେଷ ଭାଗ ➪ ଚିତ୍ର ପାଇଁ **insect** ଦେଖନ୍ତୁ।

abide /əˈbaɪd/ *verb* (**abides, abiding, abided**) if you abide by a law or an agreement, you accept it and follow it ନିୟମ ମାନିବା, ପ୍ରତିଶ୍ରୁତି ରକ୍ଷା କରିବା *abide by the laws of a country*

ability /əˈbɪləti/ *noun* (*plural* **abilities**) the power and knowledge to do something (କୌଣସି କାମ କରିବାର) ଶକ୍ତି, ସାମର୍ଥ୍ୟ, ଜ୍ଞାନ *She has the ability to pass the exam, but she must work harder.*

able /ˈeɪbl/ *adjective*

be able to have the power, skill or knowledge to do something (କୌଣସି କାମ କରିବାପାଇଁ) ଦକ୍ଷ, ସମର୍ଥ *Will you be* *able to do this sum?* ➪ **can**[1] ଦେଖନ୍ତୁ।

abnormal /æb'nɔ:ml/ *adjective* different from the usual or the normal ଅସ୍ୱାଭାବିକ *abnormal behaviour*

aboard /ə'bɔ:d/ *adverb, preposition* on or onto a ship, train, bus or an aeroplane ଜାହାଜରେ, ରେଳଗାଡ଼ିରେ, ବସ୍‌ରେ, ଉଡ଼ାଜାହାଜରେ (ଆରୋହଣ ବା ଆରୋହିତ) *Welcome aboard this flight to Chennai.*

abolish /ə'bɒlɪʃ/ *verb* (**abolishes**, **abolishing**, **abolished**) stop or end something by law (ପ୍ରଥା, ଅନୁଷ୍ଠାନ ଇତ୍ୟାଦି) ଆଇନ୍ ଅନୁସାରେ ବନ୍ଦ କରିବା, ଲୋପ କରିବା। *The Americans abolished slavery in 1863.*

abolition /ˌæbə'lɪʃn/ *noun* (*no plural*) ବନ୍ଦ କରିବା ପ୍ରକ୍ରିୟା, ବିଲୋପନ *the abolition of hunting*

about /ə'baʊt/ *preposition, adverb* **1** a little more or less than; a little before or after ପ୍ରାୟ; ଠିକ୍ ପରିମାଣ ବା ସମୟର ପାଖାପାଖି *She's about 50 years old.* ○ *I arrived at about two o'clock.* **2** of; on the subject of ସମ୍ପର୍କରେ, ସମ୍ବନ୍ଧରେ, ବିଷୟରେ *a book about cats* **3** in or to different places or in different directions ଚାରିପଟେ, ଏଣେତେଣେ, ନିକଟରେ *There were books lying about on the floor.*

be about to be going to do something very soon ଅତି ଶୀଘ୍ର କରିବାକୁ ବା ହେବାକୁ ଯାଉଥିବା *The film is about to start.*

above /ə'bʌv/ *preposition, adverb* **1** in or to a higher place; higher than somebody or something ଉପରେ, ଊର୍ଦ୍ଧ୍ୱରେ; ଉପରକୁ, ଊର୍ଦ୍ଧ୍ୱକୁ; କୌଣସି ବ୍ୟକ୍ତି ବା ପଦାର୍ଥର ଉପର ପଦବି ବା ସ୍ଥାନରେ *I looked up at the sky above.* **2** more than a number or price (ସଂଖ୍ୟା ବା ଦର) ଅଧିକ *children aged ten and above*
✪ ବିପରୀତ **below**

abridged /ə'brɪdʒd/ *adjective* (play, novel, etc.) made shorter by removing some parts ସଂକ୍ଷିପ୍ତ କରାଯାଇଥିବା (ନାଟକ, ଉପନ୍ୟାସ ଇତ୍ୟାଦି) *an abridged version of* David Copperfield

abroad /ə'brɔ:d/ *adverb* in or to another country ଅନ୍ୟ ଦେଶରେ ବା ଦେଶକୁ *Are you going abroad this summer?*

abrupt /ə'brʌpt/ *adjective* **1** sudden and unexpected, often in an unpleasant way ହଠାତ୍; ଆକସ୍ମିକ, ଅତର୍କିତ *an abrupt change of plans* **2** unfriendly and rude ରୁକ୍ଷ (ବ୍ୟବହାର) *an abrupt manner*

absence /'æbsəns/ *noun* (*no plural*) a time when a person or thing is not there ଅନୁପସ୍ଥିତି, ଉପସ୍ଥିତ ନଥିବା ଅବସ୍ଥା *I am doing Manju's job in her absence.* ✪ ବିପରୀତ **presence**

absent /'æbsənt/ *adjective* not there; away ଅନୁପସ୍ଥିତ; ନାହିଁ *He was absent from school yesterday because he was ill.* ✪ ବିପରୀତ **present**[1] **1**

absent-minded *adjective* if you are absent-minded, you often forget or do not notice certain things because you are thinking about something else ଭୁଲାମନ, ଅନ୍ୟମନସ୍କ

absolute /ˈæbsəluːt/ *adjective* complete ସମ୍ପୂର୍ଣ୍ଣ, ପୂରା *I've never played chess before. I'm an absolute beginner.*

absolutely *adverb* completely ସମ୍ପୂର୍ଣ୍ଣ ଭାବରେ, ପୂରାପୂରି *You're absolutely right.*

absorb /əbˈzɔːb/ *verb* (**absorbs, absorbing, absorbed**) take in something like liquid or heat, and hold it (ତରଳ ପଦାର୍ଥକୁ) ଅବଶୋଷଣ କରିବା; (ଉତ୍ତାପ) ଗ୍ରହଣ ଓ ଧାରଣ କରିବା *The dry ground absorbed all the rain.*

absurd /əbˈsɜːd/ *adjective* something that is absurd is so silly that it makes you laugh ଉଦ୍‌ଭଟ; ଅସଙ୍ଗତ; ଅଯୌକ୍ତିକ, ହାସ୍ୟାସ୍ପଦ *You look absurd in that hat!*

absurdity *noun* (*plural* **absurdities**) ଅସଙ୍ଗତି; ଅଯୌକ୍ତିକତା

abundant /əˈbʌndənt/ *adjective* present in very large quantities or numbers ପ୍ରଚୁର, ବହୁତ, ପ୍ରଭୂତ *This year we have had abundant rainfall.*

abundance /əˈbʌndəns/ *noun* ପ୍ରାଚୁର୍ଯ୍ୟ, ବହୁଳତା *Fruit and vegetables grow here in abundance.*

abuse[1] /əˈbjuːs/ *verb* (**abuses, abusing, abused**) **1** use something in a wrong or bad way ଅପବ୍ୟବହାର କରିବା; ଭୁଲ ଭାବେ ବ୍ୟବହାର କରିବା **2** be cruel or unkind to somebody ନିଷ୍ଠୁର ହେବା **3** say rude things to somebody ଖରାପ ବ୍ୟବହାର କରିବା, ଗାଳି ଦେବା

abuse[2] /əˈbjuːs/ *noun* (*no plural*) **1** the act of using something in a wrong or bad way ଅପବ୍ୟବହାର **2** the act of being cruel or unkind to somebody ନିଷ୍ଠୁରତା, ଦୟାହୀନ ବ୍ୟବହାର **3** rude words ଅପମାନଜନକ ଭାଷା

accent /ˈæksənt/ *noun* the way a person from a certain place or country speaks a language କୌଣସି ସ୍ଥାନ, ଅଞ୍ଚଳ ବା ଦେଶର ଶବ୍ଦ ଉଚ୍ଚାରଣ ଢଙ୍ଗ *She speaks English with an American accent.*

accept /əkˈsept/ *verb* (**accepts, accepting, accepted**) **1** say 'yes' when somebody asks you to have or do something ଇଚ୍ଛାପୂର୍ବକ ଗ୍ରହଣ କରିବା; 'ହଁ' କରିବା ବା ମାନିଯିବା *I accepted the invitation to his party.* ✪ ବିପରୀତ **reject** **2** agree that something is true or right ଠିକ୍ ବୋଲି ମାନିବା *She accepted that she had made a mistake.*

give **accept**

acceptable /əkˈseptəbl/ *adjective* allowed by most people; good enough ଗ୍ରହଣୀୟ, ଗ୍ରହଣଯୋଗ୍ୟ *It's not acceptable to make so many mistakes.*

access[1] /ˈækses/ *noun* (*plural* **accesses**) **1** a way to enter a place ପ୍ରବେଶ ପଥ **2** an opportunity to use something ବ୍ୟବହାର କରିବାର ଅଧିକାର ବା ସୁଯୋଗ *have access to computers*

access² /'ækses/ *verb* (**accesses**, **accessing, accessed**) open a computer file କମ୍ପ୍ୟୁଟର୍ ଫାଇଲ୍ ଖୋଲିବା

accessible /ək'sesəbl/ *adjective* that which can be easily reached ପହଞ୍ଚିବା ବା ପାଇବା ପାଇଁ ସହଜ ହୋଇଥିବା। ✪ ବିପରୀତ **inaccessible**

accessory /ək'sesəri/ *noun* (*plural* **accessories**) a thing that is used for decorating something but is not an important part of it ଅତ୍ୟାବଶ୍ୟକ ନ ହୋଇଥିବା ସଜାସଜି କରିବା ଜିନିଷ *car accessories*

accident /'æksɪdənt/ *noun* something, often bad, that happens by chance ଆକସ୍ମିକ ଦୁର୍ଘଟଣା; ଅପ୍ରତ୍ୟାଶିତ ଘଟଣା *I had an accident when I was driving to work—my car hit a tree.*

accidental *adjective* if something is accidental, it happens by chance ଆକସ୍ମିକ, ଅପ୍ରତ୍ୟାଶିତ *an accidental meeting*

accidentally *adverb* ଆକସ୍ମିକ ଭାବେ, ଅପ୍ରତ୍ୟାଶିତ ଭାବେ (ଇଚ୍ଛାକୃତ ଭାବେ ନୁହେଁ) *He accidentally broke the window.*

accommodate /ə'kɒmədeɪt/ *verb* (**accommodates**, **accommodating**, **accommodated**) give someone a place to stay or live in ରହିବାକୁ ସ୍ଥାନ ଦେବା, ଘର ବା ଆବାସ ଦେବା

accommodation /əˌkɒmə'deɪʃn/ *noun* (*no plural*) a place to stay or live in ରହିବା ବା ବସବାସ କରିବା ସ୍ଥାନ, ଘର ଇତ୍ୟାଦି *It's difficult to find cheap accommodation in Mumbai.*

accompany /ə'kʌmpəni/ *verb* (**accompanies**, **accompanying**, **accompanied**) **1** go with somebody to a place ସାଙ୍ଗରେ ଯିବା *Three teachers accompanied the students on their trip to Jaipur.* **2** happen at the same time as something else ଏକା ସାଙ୍ଗରେ ଘଟିବା *Thunder is usually accompanied by lightning.*

according to *preposition* as somebody or something says or states (କାହାରି କଥା ବା ମତ) ଅନୁସାରେ *According to Mini, this book is really good.* ○ *According to the report, the project would not be delayed.*

account /ə'kaʊnt/ *noun* **1** words that somebody says or writes about something that happened (କୌଣସି ଘଟଣାର) ବିବରଣ, ବର୍ଣ୍ଣନା *He gave the police an account of the car accident.* **2** an arrangement you have with a bank to deposit or take out money ବ୍ୟାଙ୍କରେ ଟଙ୍କା ରଖିବା ଓ କାଢ଼ିବା ବ୍ୟବସ୍ଥା *I paid the money into my bank account.* **3 accounts** (*no singular*) lists of all the money that a person or business receives and pays ଆୟ ଓ ବ୍ୟୟର ବିବରଣ, ହିସାବ *Who keeps the accounts for your business?*

accountant /ə'kaʊntənt/ *noun* a person whose job is to make lists of all the money that people or businesses receive and pay ହିସାବରକ୍ଷକ, ଆୟ ବ୍ୟୟର ହିସାବ ରଖୁଥିବା ବ୍ୟକ୍ତି

accurate /'ækjərət/ *adjective* exactly right, with no mistakes ନିର୍ଭୁଲ, ସଠିକ୍;

ଅବିକଳ *He gave an accurate description of the house.* ✪ ବିପରୀତ **inaccurate**

accurately *adverb* ସଠିକ୍ ଭାବରେ, ନିର୍ଭୁଲ ଭାବରେ; ଅବିକଳ ଭାବରେ *The map was accurately drawn.*

accuse /əˈkjuːz/ *verb* (**accuses**, **accusing**, **accused**) say that somebody has done something wrong ଦୋଷୀ ବୋଲି ଅଭିଯୋଗ କରିବା, ଦୋଷାରୋପ କରିବା, ଅଭିଯୁକ୍ତ କରିବା *The police accused the woman of stealing.*

accusation /ˌækjuˈzeɪʃn/ *noun* ଦୋଷାରୋପଣ, ଅଭିଯୋଗ, ଅପବାଦ *The accusations were not true.*

accustomed /əˈkʌstəmd/ *adjective* **accustomed to** being used to (କୌଣସି ବିଷୟରେ ବା କୌଣସି ପଦାର୍ଥର ବ୍ୟବହାରରେ) ଅଭ୍ୟସ୍ତ *She's not accustomed to eating rice every day.*

ache[1] /eɪk/ *verb* (**aches**, **aching**, **ached**) feel pain ଦରଜ ବା ଯନ୍ତ୍ରଣା ଅନୁଭବ କରିବା; କାଟିବା, ବିନ୍ଧିବା *My legs ached after the long walk.*

ache[2] /eɪk/ *noun* a pain that lasts for a long time ବହୁ ସମୟ ରହୁଥିବା ଯନ୍ତ୍ରଣା, ଦରଜ ବା ବିନ୍ଧା *I've got a headache.* ○ *She's got toothache.*

achieve /əˈtʃiːv/ *verb* (**achieves**, **achieving**, **achieved**) do or finish something well after trying hard କଷ୍ଟକରି କୌଣସି କାମ ଶେଷ କରିବା; ଲକ୍ଷ ସାଧନ କରିବା; କାମରେ ସିଦ୍ଧି ଲାଭ କରିବା *She has achieved a lot since taking up this job six months ago.*

achievement *noun* something that somebody has done after trying hard କାର୍ଯ୍ୟସିଦ୍ଧି; କୃତି, କୀର୍ତ୍ତି *Climbing Mount Everest was his greatest achievement.*

acid /ˈæsɪd/ *noun* a liquid that can burn things ଅନ୍ୟ ପଦାର୍ଥକୁ ପୋଡ଼ି ଦେଇପାରୁଥିବା ତରଳ ପଦାର୍ଥ, ଏସିଡ୍ ବା ଅମ୍ଳ

acid rain *noun* (*no plural*) rain that has chemicals in it from factories, for example. It can damage trees, rivers and buildings କଳକାରଖାନାର ବିନିଷ୍କକାରୀ ବାଷ୍ପ ବା ରାସାୟନିକ ପଦାର୍ଥ ମିଶିଥିବା ବର୍ଷା ଯାହା ଘରଦ୍ୱାର; ଗଛପତ୍ରକୁ ନଷ୍ଟ କରେ ଓ ନଈନାଳକୁ ପ୍ରଦୂଷିତ କରେ

acknowledge /əkˈnɒlɪdʒ/ *verb* (**acknowledges**, **acknowledging**, **acknowledged**) **1** agree that something is true ସତ ବୋଲି ମାନିବା ବା ସ୍ୱୀକାର କରିବା *He acknowledged that he had made a mistake.* **2** say or write that you have received something (ଚିଠି ଇତ୍ୟାଦିର) ପ୍ରାପ୍ତି ସ୍ୱୀକାର କରିବା *She never acknowledged my letter.*

acknowledgement *noun* **1** a letter, etc. that is written to say that something has been received (ଚିଠି ଇତ୍ୟାଦିର) ପ୍ରାପ୍ତି ସ୍ୱୀକାର ପତ୍ର ବା ରସିଦ୍ *I still haven't received an acknowledgement of my subscription cheque.* **2 acknowledgements** (*plural*) a short piece of writing at the beginning of a book in which the author thanks all the people who helped him or her to write the book ବହିର ଆରମ୍ଭରେ ଥିବା କୃତଜ୍ଞତା ପତ୍ର (ଯେଉଁଥିରେ ଲେଖାରେ ସାହାଯ୍ୟ କରିଥିବା ସମସ୍ତଙ୍କୁ ଧନ୍ୟବାଦ ଅର୍ପଣ କରାଯାଇଥାଏ।)

acorn /ˈeɪkɔːn/ *noun* a small nut that is the fruit of an oak tree ଓକ ଗଛର ବାଦାମ ପରି ଫଳ

acquire /əˈkwaɪə(r)/ *verb* (**acquires**, **acquiring**, **acquired**) get or buy something ପାଇବା, ଲାଭ କରିବା, ଅର୍ଜନ କରିବା ବା କିଣିବା *He has acquired a house in Delhi.*

acrobat /ˈækrəbæt/ *noun* a person who does difficult movements of the body, for example in a **circus** ଶାରୀରିକ କୌଶଳ (ଖେଳ କସରତ୍) ଦେଖାଉଥିବା ବ୍ୟକ୍ତି

across /əˈkrɒs/ *adverb*, *preposition* **1** from one side to the other side of something ଏ ପଟରୁ ସେ ପଟ ପର୍ଯ୍ୟନ୍ତ *We walked across the field.* **2** on the other side of something ଆରପଟେ, ଆର ପାଖରେ *There is a bank across the road.*

act[1] /ækt/ *verb* (**acts**, **acting**, **acted**) **1** do something, or behave in a certain way କାମ କରିବା; ନିର୍ଦ୍ଦିଷ୍ଟ ପ୍ରକାର ବ୍ୟବହାର ପ୍ରଦର୍ଶନ କରିବା *Doctors acted quickly to save the boy who was injured in the accident.* **2** pretend to be somebody else in a play, film or television programme ନାଟକ, ଚଳଚ୍ଚିତ୍ର ଅଥବା ଦୂରଦର୍ଶନ କାର୍ଯ୍ୟକ୍ରମରେ ଅଭିନୟ କରିବା

act[2] /ækt/ *noun* **1** something that you do କାର୍ଯ୍ୟ, କୃତି *an act of kindness* **2** one part of a play (ନାଟକର) ଅଙ୍କ *This play has five acts.* **3** a law that a government makes ଆଇନ୍

acting[1] /ˈæktɪŋ/ *noun* (*no plural*) being in plays or films ଅଭିନୟ କରିବା କାମ

acting[2] /ˈæktɪŋ/ *adjective* doing the work of somebody else for a short time ଅସ୍ଥାୟୀ ଭାବେ ଆଉ ଜଣଙ୍କ ସ୍ଥାନ ବା ପଦବୀରେ କାମ କରୁଥିବା *Mr Baruah will be the acting president while Mr Malhotra is away.*

action /ˈækʃn/ *noun* **1** (*plural* **actions**) something that you do କାର୍ଯ୍ୟ, କାମ *The little girl copied her mother's actions.* **2** (*no plural*) doing things କାମ କରିବା *Now is the time for action!*

activate /ˈæktɪveɪt/ *verb* (**activates**, **activating**, **activated**) make something start working ସକ୍ରିୟ କରିବା; ଚାଳନ ଶକ୍ତି ଦେବା; କ୍ରିୟାଶୀଳ କରିବା *The smoke activated the fire alarm.*

active /ˈæktɪv/ *adjective* if you are active, you are always busy and able to do a lot of things କ୍ରିୟାଶୀଳ, ସକ୍ରିୟ, ଚଳଚଞ୍ଚଳ *My grandmother is 75 but she's still very active.*

actively *adverb* ସକ୍ରିୟ ଭାବରେ *She is actively involved in preparing the annual report of the company.*

active voice *noun* (*no plural*) the form of the verb in which the subject is the person or thing that performs the action କର୍ତ୍ତୃବାଚ୍ୟ ➪ **passive voice** ଦେଖନ୍ତୁ ।

activity /ækˈtɪvəti/ *noun* **1** (*no plural*) a lot of things happening and people doing things କାମଦାମ, ଗହଳି ଚହଳି *On the day of the festival there was a lot of activity in the streets.* **2** (*plural* **activities**) something that you do କାମ, ଧନ୍ଦା *Swimming is one of his favourite activities.*

actor /ˈæktə(r)/ *noun* a person who acts in plays, films or television programmes ଅଭିନେତା

actress /ˈæktrəs/ *noun* (*plural* **actresses**) a woman who acts in plays, films or television programmes ଅଭିନେତ୍ରୀ

actual /ˈæktʃuəl/ *adjective* that really happened; real ପ୍ରକୃତ; ବାସ୍ତବ *The actual cost of the car was higher than what he had expected.*

actually *adverb* really; in fact ପ୍ରକୃତରେ, ବାସ୍ତବରେ *We thought it was going to rain, but actually it was sunny all day.*

acute /əˈkju:t/ *adjective* very serious, grave ତୀବ୍ର, ପ୍ରଖର; ଗମ୍ଭୀର, ଗୁରୁତର *acute water shortage* ○ *acute pain*

AD /ˌeɪˈdi:/ *abbreviation* used in dates, AD shows the number of years it has been after the birth of Jesus Christ ଖ୍ରୀଷ୍ଟ ପର; ଯୀଶୁଖ୍ରୀଷ୍ଟଙ୍କ ଜନ୍ମଠାରୁ ଗଣାଯାଉଥିବା ବର୍ଷ *AD 1066* ➪ **BC** ଦେଖନ୍ତୁ।

ad /æd/ *noun* public notice advertising something (goods for sale, house to let etc.) ବିଜ୍ଞାପନ, ବିଜ୍ଞପ୍ତି (ଜିନିଷ ବିକ୍ରି, ଘର ଭଡ଼ା ଇତ୍ୟାଦି ପାଇଁ)

adapt /əˈdæpt/ *verb* (**adapts**, **adapting**, **adapted**) change the way that you do things because you are in a new situation ନୂତନ ଅବସ୍ଥା ଅନୁସାରେ ନିଜ କାମରେ ପରିବର୍ତ୍ତନ ଆଣିବା *He has adapted quickly to his new school.*

add /æd/ *verb* (**adds**, **adding**, **added**) **1** put something with something else ମିଶାଇବା, ସଂଯୋଗ କରିବା *Mix the flour with the milk and then add the eggs.* **2** put numbers together ମିଶାଣ ବା ଯୋଗ କରିବା *If you add 2 and 5 together, you get 7.* ✪ ବିପରୀତ **subtract** **3** say something more ଆହୁରି କହିବା ବା ଲେଖିବା

addition /əˈdɪʃn/ *noun* **1** (*no plural*) putting numbers together ମିଶାଣ, ଯୋଗ, ସମଷ୍ଟି *We learnt addition and subtraction at primary school.* ➪ **subtraction** ଦେଖନ୍ତୁ। **2** (*plural* **additions**) a thing or person that you add to other things or people ଅଧିକ ଭାବେ ଦିଆଯାଉଥିବା ସାମଗ୍ରୀ ବା ଲୋକ; ସମ୍ମିଳିତ ବ୍ୟକ୍ତି ବା ପଦାର୍ଥ *They have a new addition to their family.*

in addition to something as well as something ଏହାଛଡ଼ା, ଆହୁରି ମଧ୍ୟ *Raghav speaks five languages in addition to Hindi.*

additional *adjective* extra; more than what was expected ଅତିରିକ୍ତ, ଅଧିକ। *additional expenses*

address[1] /ə'dres/ *noun* (*plural* **addresses**) **1** the number of the house and the name of the street and town where somebody lives or works ଠିକଣା **2** a set of words and symbols that shows where you can find a piece of information using the computer, for example on the Internet କମ୍ପ୍ୟୁଟର୍ ଜରିଆରେ ଇଣ୍ଟରନେଟ୍‌ରେ କୌଣସି ବିଷୟ ଜାଣିବା ପାଇଁ ଥିବା ସାଙ୍କେତିକ ଠିକଣା ବା ଚିହ୍ନ *I gave him my new email address.* **3** a speech given to a gathering ବକ୍ତୃତା

address[2] /ə'dres/ *verb* (**addresses**, **addressing**, **addressed**) **1** write a name and address on a letter, etc. ଚିଠି ଇତ୍ୟାଦିରେ ଠିକଣା ଲେଖିବା *The letter was wrongly addressed to our old home.* **2** speak to someone, especially a gathering ସଭା ସମିତିରେ କାହାରିକୁ କହିବା *The chairman will now address the meeting.*

adequate /'ædɪkwət/ *adjective* enough for your need ଯଥେଷ୍ଟ, ପର୍ଯ୍ୟାପ୍ତ *They are very poor and do not have adequate food or clothing.* ✪ ବିପରୀତ **inadequate**

adequately *adverb* ପର୍ଯ୍ୟାପ୍ତ ଭାବରେ *The project was not adequately funded.*

adjacent /ə'dʒeɪsnt/ *adjective* next to or near to something ପାଖରେ ଥିବା, ନିକଟବର୍ତ୍ତୀ *We work in adjacent rooms.*

adjective /'ædʒɪktɪv/ *noun* a word that you use with a noun, that tells you more about it (ବ୍ୟାକରଣରେ) ବିଶେଷଣ *'This soup is hot'* ଏହି ବାକ୍ୟରେ *hot* ବିଶେଷଣ।

adjust /ə'dʒʌst/ *verb* (**adjusts**, **adjusting**, **adjusted**) make a small change to something to make it more suitable ସ୍ଥିତି ଅଳ୍ପ ବଦଳାଇ ଉପଯୁକ୍ତ ଅବସ୍ଥାକୁ ଆଣିବା; ମେଳ ଖୁଆଇବା *You can adjust the height of this chair.*

administer /əd'mɪnɪstə(r)/ *verb* (**administers**, **administering**, **administered**) control and manage a country, business or an organization ପରିଚାଳନା କରିବା; ଶାସନ ଚଳାଇବା *administer a school*

administration /əd,mɪnɪ'streɪʃn/ *noun* (*no plural*) controlling or managing something, for example a business, an office or a school ପ୍ରଶାସନ, ପରିଚାଳନା

admiral /'ædmərəl/ *noun* a very senior officer in the navy ନୌସେନାଧ୍ୟକ୍ଷ

admire /əd'maɪə(r)/ *verb* (**admires**, **admiring**, **admired**) think or say that somebody or something is very good ପ୍ରଶଂସା ଦୃଷ୍ଟିରେ ଦେଖିବା; ସମ୍ମାନ କରିବା *I really admire you for doing such a difficult job.*

admiration /,ædmə'reɪʃn/ *noun* (*no plural*) ସମ୍ମାନ ଶ୍ରଦ୍ଧା *I have great admiration for her work.*

admission /əd'mɪʃn/ *noun* (*no plural*) the act of letting somebody enter a place or join a school, college, etc. ପ୍ରବେଶାନୁମତି; ସ୍କୁଲ, କଲେଜ୍ ଇତ୍ୟାଦିରେ ଯୋଗଦାନ

admit /əd'mɪt/ *verb* (**admits**, **admitting**, **admitted**) **1** say that you have done something wrong ମାନିଯିବା, ସ୍ୱୀକାର କରିବା *I admit that I made a mistake.* ✪ ବିପରୀତ **deny** **2** let somebody or something go into a place କୌଣସି ସ୍ଥାନରେ ଅନୁମତି ସହ ପ୍ରବେଶ କରିବାକୁ ଦେବା *This ticket admits one person to the museum.*

adopt /ə'dɒpt/ *verb* (**adopts**, **adopting**, **adopted**) legally take the child of another person into your family as your own child ପୋଷ୍ୟ ସନ୍ତାନ ଭାବେ ଗ୍ରହଣ କରିବା *They adopted Srilata after her parents died.*

adore /ə'dɔ:(r)/ *verb* (**adores**, **adoring**, **adored**) love somebody or something very much ଅତି ଆଦର କରିବା; ଶ୍ରଦ୍ଧା କରିବା *She adores her grandchildren.*

adult /'ædʌlt/ *noun* a person or an animal that has grown to the full size; not a child ପରିଣତ ବୟସର ବ୍ୟକ୍ତି, ବୟସ୍କ ବ୍ୟକ୍ତି *Adults as well as children will enjoy this film.*

advance[1] /əd'vɑ:ns/ *adjective* something that is given or happens before another thing ଅଗ୍ରିମ, ଆଗତୁରା ଦିଆ ଯାଇଥିବା ବା ହେଉଥିବା *The weather office gave advance warning of the cyclone.*

advance[2] /əd'vɑ:ns/ *verb* (**advances**, **advancing**, **advanced**) **1** make progress or improvement ଉନ୍ନତି କରିବା, ପ୍ରଗତି କରିବା, ଆଗେଇବା *The country has advanced a lot in the last ten years.* **2** move forward in a threatening way ଡରେଇଲା ପରି ଆଗେଇବା *The army advanced into the city.* ✪ ବିପରୀତ **retreat**

advance[3] /əd'vɑ:ns/ *noun* **1** progress in something ଅଗ୍ରଗତି, ଉନ୍ନତି *advances in the medical field* **2** an amount of money that is paid for work before it has begun ଅଗ୍ରିମ ପାଉଣା, କାମ ହେବା ପୂର୍ବରୁ ଦିଆଯାଇଥିବା ଟଙ୍କା

in advance before something happens ଆଗରୁ, ପୂର୍ବରୁ, ଆଗତୁରା *We paid for the tickets in advance.*

advanced /əd'vɑ:nst/ *adjective* of or for somebody who is really good at something; of a higher level ଆଗୁଆ, ଉନ୍ନତ, ଉଚ୍ଚସ୍ତରୀୟ *an advanced Maths class*

advantage /əd'vɑ:ntɪdʒ/ *noun* something that helps you or that is useful ସୁବିଧା, ସୁଯୋଗ *It's an advantage if you speak both languages.* ✪ ବିପରୀତ **disadvantage**

adventure /əd'ventʃə(r)/ *noun* something exciting that you do or that happens to you ଉଦ୍ଦୀପକ ବା ଆନନ୍ଦଦାୟକ ଅସାଧାରଣ ଅନୁଭୂତି; ଦୁଃସାହସିକ କାମ *She wrote a book about her adventures in Africa.*

adventurous /əd'ventʃərəs/ *adjective* an adventurous person likes to do exciting, dangerous things ଦୁଃସାହସୀ (ବ୍ୟକ୍ତି); ଦୁଃସାହସିକ (କାମ)

adverb /'ædvɜ:b/ *noun* a word that tells you how, when or where something happens (ବ୍ୟାକରଣରେ) କ୍ରିୟା ବିଶେଷଣ, କ୍ରିୟାକୁ ବର୍ଣ୍ଣନା କରୁଥିବା ଶବ୍ଦ *'She spoke slowly'* ରେ *'slowly'* ହେଉଛି କ୍ରିୟା ବିଶେଷଣ

advertise /ˈædvətaɪz/ *verb* (**advertises, advertising, advertised**) use posters, newspapers or television to give people information about jobs, things to buy or events to go to ବିଜ୍ଞାପନ ଦେବା *I saw those shoes advertised on TV.*

advertisement /ədˈvɜːtɪsmənt/ *noun* information on a poster, in a newspaper or on television that tells you about a job, something to buy or an event to go to ବିଜ୍ଞାପନ *I saw an advertisement on TV for a new kind of chocolate bar.* ✪ ଏହାର ସଂକ୍ଷିପ୍ତ ରୂପ ହେଲା **ad**।

advice /ədˈvaɪs/ *noun* (*no plural*) words that you say to help somebody decide what to do ଉପଦେଶ, ପରାମର୍ଶ *He will give you advice about where to go.* ✪ ଧ୍ୟାନ ଦିଅନ୍ତୁ ! ଇଂରାଜୀରେ 'an advice' କହିବା ଠିକ୍ ହେବନାହିଁ। 'some advice' ବା 'a piece of advice' ବ୍ୟବହାର କରାଯାଏ — *I need some advice.* ○ *Let me give you a piece of advice.*

advise /ədˈvaɪz/ *verb* (**advises, advising, advised**) tell somebody what you think they should do ଉପଦେଶ ଦେବା, ପରାମର୍ଶ ଦେବା *The doctor advised him to stop smoking.*

adviser /ədˈvaɪzə(r)/ *noun* a person who gives advice ପରାମର୍ଶଦାତା

advocate /ˈædvəkeɪt/ *noun* **1** a lawyer who speaks in a court ଓକିଲ, ଆଡ୍‌ଭୋକେଟ୍ **2** someone who supports a cause, an idea or an action (କୌଣସି ମତ ବା ନୀତିର) ପ୍ରବକ୍ତା ବା ସମର୍ଥକ

aerated /ˈeəreɪtid/ *adjective* with a lot of bubbles of gas ଅଙ୍ଗାରକାମ୍ଳ ବାଷ୍ପ ଭର୍ତ୍ତି ହୋଇଥିବା (ତରଳ ପଦାର୍ଥ) *aerated water*

aerial /ˈeəriəl/ *noun* a metal rod or wire that receives radio or television signals ରେଡ଼ିଓ ବା ଟିଭି. ସଂଚାର ଗ୍ରହଣ କରିବାକୁ ଥିବା ତାର ବା ଧାତୁ କାଠି, ଏରିଆଲ୍

aerobics /eəˈrəʊbɪks/ *noun* a form of physical exercise consisting of energetic movements that is performed with music ସଙ୍ଗୀତ ସହ ନାଚିକୁଦି କରାଯାଉଥିବା ବ୍ୟାୟମ

aerobics

aeroplane /ˈeərəpleɪn/ *noun* a machine that has wings and can fly ଉଡ଼ାଜାହାଜ, ବ୍ୟୋମଯାନ ➪ ଚିତ୍ର ପାଇଁ **aircraft** ଦେଖନ୍ତୁ।

aerosol /ˈeərəsɒl/ *noun* a metal container from which a liquid comes out in a spray ବାୟୁଚାପ ଦିଆ ଡବା ବା

aerosols

ବୋତଲ ଯେଉଁଥିରୁ କୌଣସି ତରଳ ପଦାର୍ଥ ଚାପଦ୍ୱାରା ସୂକ୍ଷ୍ମ ଭାବରେ ବିଚ୍ଛୁରିତ କରାଯାଏ

afar /əˈfɑ:(r)/ *adverb*

from afar from a long distance away ଦୂରକୁ, ଦୂରରେ

affair /əˈfeə(r)/ *noun* **1** something that happens; an event ଘଟଣା *The wedding was a very quiet affair.* **2** something that you, an organization or the government must deal with or think about; business ବିଷୟ, ବ୍ୟାପାର *foreign affairs*

affect /əˈfekt/ *verb* (**affects**, **affecting**, **affected**) make a difference to something or someone ପ୍ରଭାବ ପକାଇବା, ପ୍ରତିକ୍ରିୟା ସୃଷ୍ଟିକରିବା *Smoking can affect your health badly.*

affection /əˈfekʃn/ *noun* (*no plural*) the feeling of loving or liking somebody ଅନୁରାଗ, ସ୍ନେହ, ଆଦର *She has great affection for her aunt.*

affectionate /əˈfekʃənət/ *adjective* feeling or showing love ସ୍ନେହଶୀଳ, ଅନୁରାଗ ପୂର୍ଣ୍ଣ *She gave him an affectionate hug.*

afford /əˈfɔ:d/ *verb* (**affords**, **affording**, **afforded**)

can afford something if you can afford something, you have enough money to pay for it ବ୍ୟୟ କରିପାରିବା, ଖର୍ଚ୍ଚସାପେକ୍ଷ *I can't afford a holiday right now.*

affordable /əˈfɔ:dəbl/ *adjective* something that is affordable can be bought without spending a lot of money ବେଶୀ ଟଙ୍କା ଖର୍ଚ୍ଚ ନକରି କିଣି ହେଉଥିବା ବା କରି ହେଉଥିବା

afforestation /əˌfɒrɪˈsteɪʃn/ *noun* (*no plural*) the process of planting trees in areas where there aren't many trees ବନୀକରଣ, ଗଛ ନଥିବା ବା ଅଳ୍ପ ଗଛ ଥିବା ଅଞ୍ଚଳରେ ଗଛଲଗାଇବା ✪ ବିପରୀତ **deforestation**

afraid /əˈfreɪd/ *adjective* if you are afraid of something, it frightens you ଭୟଭୀତ, ତ୍ରସ୍ତ, ଶଙ୍କିତ *Most people are afraid of snakes.*

I'm afraid ... a polite way of saying that you are sorry ମୁଁ ଦୁଃଖିତ ଯେ... *I'm afraid I can't come to your party.*

after[1] /ˈɑ:ftə(r)/ *preposition* **1** later than somebody or something ପରେ, ପରବର୍ତ୍ତୀ ସମୟରେ *Maya arrived after dinner.* **2** behind or following somebody or something ପଛରେ *Ten comes after nine.* ✪ ବିପରୀତ **before[1]**

after[2] /ˈɑ:ftə(r)/ *conjunction, adverb* at a time later than somebody or something ପରେ, ପରବର୍ତ୍ତୀ କାଳରେ *We arrived after the film had started.* ○ *Sudha left at five o'clock and I left soon after.*

afternoon /ˌɑ:ftəˈnu:n/ *noun* the part of a day between midday and about 5 o'clock in the evening ଅପରାହ୍ନ; ମଧ୍ୟାହ୍ନ ଠାରୁ ସନ୍ଧ୍ୟା ୫ଟା ମଧ୍ୟର ସମୟ *Yesterday afternoon I went shopping.*

afterwards /ˈɑ:ftəwədz/ *adverb* later ପରେ, ପରବର୍ତ୍ତୀ ସମୟରେ *We had dinner and went to see a film afterwards.*

again /əˈgen/ *adverb* **1** one more time; once more ଆଉଥରେ, ପୁଣି, ପୁନର୍ବାର *Could you say that again,* *please?* **2** in the way that somebody or something was before ପୁଣି, ପୁନର୍ବାର *You'll soon feel well again.* **again and again** many times ଥରକୁ ଥର, ବାରମ୍ବାର *I've told you again and again not to do that!*

against /əˈgenst/ *preposition* **1** on the other side in a game, fight, etc. ବିପକ୍ଷରେ *They played against a football team from another town.* **2** if you are against something, you do not like it ବିରୁଦ୍ଧରେ *Many people are against the plan.* **3** next to and touching somebody or something ଲାଗିକରି, ଆଉଜାଇ *Put the ladder against the wall.*

age /eɪdʒ/ *noun* **1** the amount of time that somebody or something has been in the world ବୟସ *She is seven years of age.* ○ *I started work at the age of 21.* ✪ 'How old are you?' — କାହାରି ବୟସ ଜାଣିବାକୁ ହେଲେ ସାଧାରଣତଃ ପଚରାଯାଏ। **2** a certain time in history ଇତିହାସର କୌଣସି ବିଶେଷ କାଳ ବା ଯୁଗ *the Stone Age* **3 ages** (*plural*) a very long time ବହୁସମୟ, ବହୁ କାଳ *She's lived here for ages.*

aged /eɪdʒd/ *adjective* very old ବୟୋବୃଦ୍ଧ, ବୃଦ୍ଧ, ବୁଢ଼ା *He took good care of his aged parents.*

the aged *noun* (*plural*) old people ବୟୋବୃଦ୍ଧ ଲୋକ *a home for the aged*

agency /ˈeɪdʒənsi/ *noun* (*plural* **agencies**) the work or office of somebody who does business for others ଅନ୍ୟ ସଂସ୍ଥାମାନଙ୍କର ପ୍ରତିନିଧି ଭାବେ କରାଯାଉଥିବା କାମ ବା ଏହି କାମର କାର୍ଯ୍ୟାଳୟ *A travel agency plans holidays for people.*

agent /ˈeɪdʒənt/ *noun* a person who does business for another person or for a company ପ୍ରତିନିଧି, ଅଭିକର୍ତ୍ତା *a travel agent*

aggressive /əˈgresɪv/ *adjective* if you are aggressive, you are ready to argue or fight ଲଢୁଆ, ଆକ୍ରମଣଶୀଳ, ଆକ୍ରମଣାତ୍ମକ

aghast /əˈgɑːst/ *adjective*

aghast at something shocked at something terrible you have just seen ଭୟାଭିଭୂତ, ବିସ୍ମିତ ବା ହତୋସାହିତ ହୋଇ *I was aghast at the way she treated her kitten.*

agile /ˈædʒaɪl/ *adjective* someone who is agile can move quickly and easily କ୍ଷିପ୍ର, ଚଞ୍ଚଳ, କର୍ମତତ୍ପର

agitate /ˈædʒɪteɪt/ *verb* (**agitates**, **agitating**, **agitated**) **1** upset or disturb someone ଗୋଳମାଳ କରିବା, ଉତ୍ତେଜନା ସୃଷ୍ଟିକରିବା **2** speak strongly against something that you feel is wrong ଉତ୍ତେଜିତ ଭାବରେ ପ୍ରତିବାଦ କରି କହିବା *The students agitated against the fee hike.*

agitation /ˌædʒɪˈteɪʃn/ *noun* ଆନ୍ଦୋଳନ, ଆଲୋଡ଼ନ *a nationwide agitation*

ago /əˈgəʊ/ *adverb* before now; in the past ପୂର୍ବକାଳରେ, ବହୁଦିନ ପୂର୍ବେ *I learnt to drive a long time ago.*

agony /ˈægəni/ *noun* (*plural* **agonies**) very great pain ଅତି ବେଶୀ ମାନସିକ ବା ଶାରୀରିକ ଯନ୍ତ୍ରଣା *He screamed in agony.*

agree /ə'gri:/ *verb* (**agrees**, **agreeing**, **agreed**) **1** have the same idea as another person about something ସହମତ ହେବା *I agree with you.* ✪ ବିପରୀତ **disagree** **2** say 'yes' when somebody asks you to do something 'ହଁ' କହିବା *Anu agreed to come to the party.*

agreement /ə'gri:mənt/ *noun* **1** (*plural* **agreements**) a plan or decision that two or more people or countries have made together ଦେଶ ବା ବ୍ୟକ୍ତିଙ୍କ ମଧ୍ୟରେ ପରସ୍ପର ବୁଝାମଣା; ସହମତି ବା ଚୁକ୍ତି *There is a trade agreement between the two countries.* **2** (*no plural*) having the same ideas as somebody ସହମତ ବା ଏକମତ ହେବା *We are in agreement about buying a house.*

agriculture /'ægrɪkʌltʃə(r)/ *noun* (*no plural*) keeping animals and growing plants for food; farming କୃଷି ଓ ପଶୁପାଳନ

agricultural *adjective* କୃଷି ସମ୍ବନ୍ଧୀୟ; କୃଷିଯୋଗ୍ୟ *agricultural land*

ahead /ə'hed/ *adverb* **1** in front of somebody or something ଆଗରେ, ଆଗୁଆ, ସମ୍ମୁଖରେ *We could see a light ahead of us.* **2** into the future ଭବିଷ୍ୟତକୁ *We must look ahead and make a plan.*

go ahead start to do something when you have been given the permission ଅନୁମତି ନେଇ ଆଗେଇବା ବା କରିବା *'Can I borrow your bicycle?' 'Yes, go ahead.'*

ahimsa *noun* (*no plural*) the belief in non-violence ଅହିଂସା *Both Gautama Buddha and Mahatma Gandhi believed in ahimsa.*

aid[1] /eɪd/ *noun* (*no plural*) help, or something that gives help ସାହାଯ୍ୟ *The government sent medical aid to the flood-affected people.*

aid[2] /eɪd/ *verb* (**aids, aiding, aided**) help someone ସାହାଯ୍ୟ କରିବା

AIDS /eɪdz/ *noun* (*no plural*) a serious illness that stops the body from protecting itself against diseases ଦେହରେ ରୋଗନିରୋଧ ଶକ୍ତିର ହ୍ରାସ କରାଉଥିବା ମାରାତ୍ମକ ରୋଗ ✪ AIDS ର ପୁରା ଆଖ୍ୟା ହେଲା **Acquired Immune Deficiency Syndrome**।

aim[1] /eɪm/ *verb* (**aims, aiming, aimed**) **1** point something, for example a gun, at somebody or something that you want to hit (ବନ୍ଧୁକ ଇତ୍ୟାଦିରେ) ଲକ୍ଷ୍ୟ କରିବା *The farmer aimed his gun at the rabbit.* **2** want or plan to do something ଅଭିପ୍ରାୟ କରିବା; ଯୋଜନା କରିବା *He's aiming to leave at nine o'clock.*

aim[2] /eɪm/ *noun* something that you want and plan to do ଉଦ୍ଦେଶ୍ୟ, ଲକ୍ଷ୍ୟ, ଯୋଜନା *Ketan's aim is to find a good job.*

air[1] /eə(r)/ *noun* (*no plural*) **1** what you take in through your nose and mouth when you breathe ବାୟୁ, ପବନ **2** the space around and above things ବାୟୁମଣ୍ଡଳ; ପୃଥିବୀ ପୃଷ୍ଠର ଉପରକୁ ଥିବା ସ୍ଥାନ *He threw the ball up in the air.*

by air in an aircraft ଉଡ଼ାଜାହାଜରେ *It's more expensive to travel by air than by train.*

air² /eə(r)/ *verb* (**airs**, **airing**, **aired**) broadcast or telecast a programme on radio or television ରେଡ଼ିଓ ବା ଟିଭି ପାଇଁ କାର୍ଯ୍ୟକ୍ରମ ସଞ୍ଚାର କରିବ

air-conditioning *noun* (*no plural*) a way of keeping the air in a building dry and cool କୋଠା ଇତ୍ୟାଦିରେ ଶୀତ, ତାପ ଓ ଆଦ୍ରତାର ନିୟନ୍ତ୍ରଣ

air-conditioned *adjective* with air-conditioning ଶୀତତାପ ନିୟନ୍ତ୍ରିତ *an air-conditioned office*

aircraft /ˈeəkrɑːft/ *noun* (*plural* **aircraft**) a machine that can fly, for example an aeroplane or a helicopter ଉଡ଼ାଜାହାଜ ବା ହେଲିକେପ୍ଟର୍

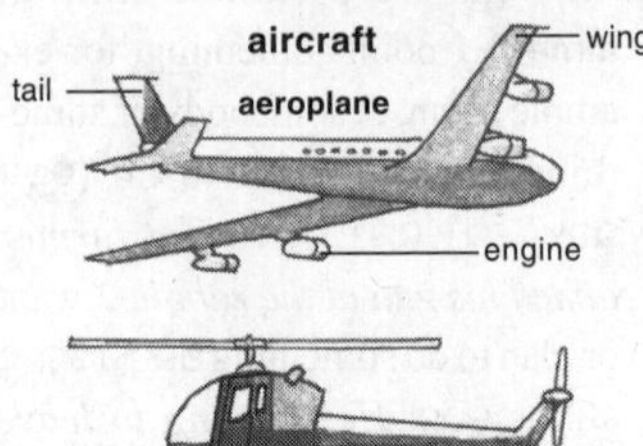

air force *noun* the part of a country's **armed forces** that uses aircraft for fighting ଦେଶର ବାୟୁସେନାର ବିମାନ ବାହିନୀ

air-hostess *noun* (*plural* **air-hostesses**) a woman whose job is to look after people on an aeroplane ଯାତ୍ରୀ ବିମାନରେ କାମ କରୁଥିବା ଅତିଥି ସେବିକା ବିମାନ ସେବିକା

airline /ˈeəlaɪn/ *noun* a company with aeroplanes that carry people or goods ଯାତ୍ରୀ ବା ମାଲ ନିଆଅଣା କରୁଥିବା ବିମାନ ସଂସ୍ଥା *Lufthansa is a German airline.*

airmail /ˈeəmeɪl/ *noun* (*no plural*) a way of sending letters and parcels by aeroplane ବିମାନ ଦ୍ୱାରା ପଠାଯାଉଥିବା ଡାକ *Send the letter by airmail.*

airport /ˈeəpɔːt/ *noun* a place where people get on and off aero-planes, with buildings where passengers can wait ବିମାନ ବନ୍ଦର *I'll meet you at the airport.*

airy /ˈeəri/ *adjective* having plenty of fresh air ବାୟୁମୟ, ବାୟୁ ସଞ୍ଚାଳିତ

aisle /aɪl/ *noun* a way between rows of seats, for example in a church, theatre or an aeroplane ଦୁଇ ପାଖର ବସିବା ଜାଗା ମଝିରେ ଥିବା ଯିବା ଆସିବା ବାଟ

alarm¹ /əˈlɑːm/ *noun* **1** (*no plural*) a sudden feeling of fear ହଠାତ୍ ହୋଇଥିବା ଭୟ ବା ଆତଙ୍କ *He heard a noise and jumped out of bed in alarm.* **2** (*plural* **alarms**) something that tells you about danger, for example by making a loud noise ବିପଦ ସଙ୍କେତ ଯନ୍ତ୍ର *Does your car have an alarm?*

alarm² /əˈlɑːm/ *verb* (**alarms**, **alarming**, **alarmed**) make somebody or something suddenly feel afraid or worried ଭୟ ସୃଷ୍ଟି କରିବା; ବିପଦର ଆଶଙ୍କା ଜନ୍ମାଇବା *The noise alarmed the bird and it flew away.*

alarm clock *noun* (*plural* **alarm clocks**) a clock that can be set to wake you up at a fixed time ଘଣ୍ଟି ବଜେଇ ସଜାଗ କରିବା ଘଣ୍ଟା

album /ˈælbəm/ *noun* **1** a book with empty pages where you can put photographs or stamps, for example ଫଟ, ପୁରୁଣାଡାକ ଟିକଟ ଇତ୍ୟାଦି ରଖିବା ପାଇଁ ବହି **2** a collection of music recorded on a cassette, compact disc or record କ୍ୟାସେଟ୍, କମ୍ପ୍ୟାକ୍ଟ ଡିସ୍କ ବା ରେକର୍ଡ଼ରେ ରେକର୍ଡ଼ କରାଯାଇଥିବା ଗୀତ ସମୂହ *Have you heard this album?*

albumen /ˈælbjumɪn/ *noun* the white part of an egg ଅଣ୍ଡାର ଧଳା ଅଂଶ, ଆଲ୍‌ବୁମେନ୍

alcohol /ˈælkəhɒl/ *noun* (*no plural*) **1** the liquid in drinks, for example wine, beer or whisky, that can make people feel drunk ସୁରା, ବିଅର୍, ହ୍ୱିସ୍କି ଇତ୍ୟାଦିରେ ଥିବା ତରଳ ପଦାର୍ଥ ଯାହା ପିଇଲେ ନିଶା ହୁଏ, ଆଲ୍‌କୋହଲ୍ **2** drinks like wine, beer or whisky ମଦ, ମଦ୍ୟ

alcoholic *adjective* ଆଲ୍‌କୋହଲ୍ ଥିବା *an alcoholic drink*

alert[1] /əˈlɜːt/ *adjective* awake and ready to do things ସଜାଗ, ସତର୍କ, ସାବଧାନ *A good driver is always alert.*

alert[2] /əˈlɜːt/ *noun* a warning of danger ବିପଦର ସଙ୍କେତ ବା ଚେତାବନୀ *There was a bomb alert at the station.*

algae /ˈældʒiː; ˈælgiː/ *noun* (*plural*) very simple plants with no roots or leaves. Algae live in or near water ପାଣିରେ ବା ଓଦା ଜାଗାରେ ହେଉଥିବା ନିଷ୍ଫଳା ଉଦ୍ଭିଦ; ଶିଉଳି, ଶୈବାଳ ✪ Algae ର ଏକ ବଚନ ହେଲା **alga** /ˈælgə/।

algebra /ˈældʒɪbrə/ *noun* (*no plural*) a form of mathematics in which numbers are represented by letters and symbols ବୀଜଗଣିତ

alien /ˈeɪliən/ *noun* **1** a foreigner ବିଦେଶୀ ବ୍ୟକ୍ତି **2** a person or an animal that comes from another planet in space ଅନ୍ୟ ଗ୍ରହରୁ ଆସିଥିବା ବ୍ୟକ୍ତି ବା ପଶୁ

align /əˈlaɪn/ *verb* (**aligns**, **aligning**, **aligned**) arrange things in a straight line or parallel to something else ଏକ ଧାଡ଼ିରେ ରଖିବା ବା ଅନ୍ୟ କାହା ସହ ସମାନ୍ତରାଳ ଭାବେ ରଖିବା *Align the books on the shelf.*

alignment *noun* ସମାନ ରେଖାରେ ରଖିବା କାମ *Check the alignment of the wheels.*

alike /əˈlaɪk/ *adjective* almost the same; not different ସଦୃଶ, ଅନୁରୂପ, ଏକାପରି *The two sisters are very alike.*

alive /əˈlaɪv/ *adjective* living; not dead ଜୀବିତ, ସଜୀବ *Are your grandparents alive?*

all[1] /ɔːl/ *adjective*, *pronoun* **1** every one of a group ସବୁଲୋକ, ସମସ୍ତେ *Are you all listening?* **2** every part of something; the whole of something ସମୁଦାୟ, ସବୁ *She's eaten all the bread.*

all[2] /ɔːl/ *adverb* completely ସମ୍ପୂର୍ଣ୍ଣ ଭାବରେ, ପୁରା *She lives all alone.*

all along from the beginning ଆରମ୍ଭରୁ *I knew all along that she was going to win.*

allergy /ˈælədʒi/ *noun* (*plural* **allergies**) an illness that is caused when you eat, breathe or touch a particular substance କିଛି ପଦାର୍ଥ ଖାଇଲେ, ଛୁଇଁଲେ

ବା ପ୍ରଶ୍ୱାସରେ ନେଲେ ଦେହରେ ହେଉଥିବା ପ୍ରତିକୂଳ ପ୍ରତିକ୍ରିୟା ବା ରୋଗ; ଆଲର୍ଜି *an allergy to milk*

allergic /əˈlɜːdʒɪk/ *adjective* **1** having an allergy to something କୌଣସି ପଦାର୍ଥ ପ୍ରତି ଆଲର୍ଜି ଥିବା *I'm allergic to milk.* **2** caused by an allergy ଆଲର୍ଜି ଦ୍ୱାରା ହୋଇଥିବା *an allergic reaction*

alley /ˈæli/ *noun* (*plural* **alleys**) a narrow path between two buildings ସରୁ ଗଳି ବା ପଥ (ଦୁଇ କୋଠା ମଧ୍ୟରେ)

alligator /ˈælɪgeɪtə(r)/ *noun* a big long **reptile** with sharp teeth, that is similar to a crocodile. Alligators live in rivers and lakes in America and China ଆମେରିକା ଓ ଚାଇନାରେ ରହୁଥିବା ଏକ ପ୍ରକାର ବୃହତାକାର କୁମ୍ଭୀର

alliteration /əˌlɪtəˈreɪʃn/ *noun* repetition of a letter or a sound at the beginning of words in a set of words, for example the sound 's' in *'sing a song of sixpence'* ଜମକ, ଅନୁପ୍ରାସ, ଏକ ଧ୍ୱନିର ବାରମ୍ବାର ବ୍ୟବହାର

allow /əˈlaʊ/ *verb* (**allows, allowing, allowed**) say that somebody can have or do something ଅନୁମତି ଦେବା *You're not allowed to smoke here.*

allowance /əˈlaʊəns/ *noun* **1** the amount of money that you get regularly ନିର୍ଦ୍ଦିଷ୍ଟ ଭତ୍ତା, ନିର୍ଦ୍ଦିଷ୍ଟ ସମୟରେ ମିଳୁଥିବା ଟଙ୍କା *monthly allowance* **2** the amount of something you are allowed ଜିନିଷପତ୍ର ନେବାପାଇଁ ଅନୁମତିପ୍ରାପ୍ତ ପରିମାଣ *20 kg baggage allowance*

alloy /ˈælɔɪ/ *noun* a metal formed by mixing two metals together ମିଶ୍ରଧାତୁ, ସଙ୍କର ଧାତୁ *Brass is an alloy of copper and zinc.*

all right *adjective* **1** good or good enough ଠିକ୍; ଠାକ୍, ସନ୍ତୋଷଜନକ *Is everything all right?* **2** well; not hurt ଭଲ, ଅକ୍ଷତ, ନିରୋଗ *I was ill, but I'm all right now.* **3** yes, I agree ହଁ, ହଉ *'Let's go home.' 'All right.'*

ally /ˈælaɪ/ *noun* (*plural* **allies**) a person or country that agrees to help another person or country, for example in a war ମିତ୍ରରାଷ୍ଟ୍ର; ସହାୟକ ବ୍ୟକ୍ତି, ସହଯୋଗୀ

almond /ˈɑːmənd/ *noun* an oval-shaped nut that you can eat ବାଦାମ୍ ➪ ଚିତ୍ର ପାଇଁ **nut** ଦେଖନ୍ତୁ।

almost /ˈɔːlməʊst/ *adverb* nearly; not quite ପ୍ରାୟ *It's almost three o'clock.* ○ *I almost fell into the river!*

alms /ɑːmz/ *noun* (*plural*) money, food and clothes given to a beggar ଭିକ୍ଷା, ଭିକ

alone /əˈləʊn/ *adverb* **1** without any other person ଏକା, ଏକୁଟିଆ, ଏକାକୀ *My grandmother lives alone.* **2** only କେବଳ *You alone can help me.*

along[1] /əˈlɒŋ/ *preposition* **1** from one end of something towards the other end ଏପଟରୁ ସେପଟ ପର୍ଯ୍ୟନ୍ତ *We walked along the road.* **2** in a line next to something long କଡ଼େ କଡ଼େ, ପାର୍ଶ୍ୱରେ *There are trees along the river bank.*

along² /əˈlɒŋ/ *adverb* **1** forward ଆଗକୁ *He drove along very slowly.* **2** with me, you, etc. ସାଙ୍ଗରେ, ସାଥିରେ *We're going to the cinema. Why don't you come along too?*

aloud /əˈlaʊd/ *adverb* speaking so that other people can hear ବଡ଼ ପାଟିରେ, ଅନ୍ୟମାନେ ଶୁଣିଲା ପରି *I read the story aloud to my sister.*

alphabet /ˈælfəbet/ *noun* all the letters of a language ବର୍ଣ୍ଣମାଳାର ନିର୍ଦ୍ଦିଷ୍ଟଭାବେ ସଜ୍ଜିତ ଅକ୍ଷରସବୁ *The English alphabet starts with A and ends with Z.*

alphabetical *adjective* in the order of the alphabet ବର୍ଣ୍ଣମାଳା ଅନୁକ୍ରମରେ ସଜ୍ଜିତ *Put these words in alphabetical order.*

already /ɔːlˈredi/ *adverb* before now or before then ନିର୍ଦ୍ଦିଷ୍ଟ ସମୟ ପୂର୍ବରୁ *We ran to the station but the train had already left.*

already and yet

Yet ଏବଂ **already** ର ଅର୍ଥ ଏକା ଅଟେ, କିନ୍ତୁ **yet** ର ପ୍ରୟୋଗ କେବଳ ନାସ୍ତିବାଚକ ଏବଂ ପ୍ରଶ୍ନବାଚକ ବାକ୍ୟରେ ବ୍ୟବହାର କରାଯାଏ —
I have finished this book ***already.***
I haven't finished this book ***yet.***
Have you finished this book ***yet****?*

also /ˈɔːlsəʊ/ *adverb* as well; too ଆଉ ମଧ୍ୟ, ଅଧିକନ୍ତୁ *She speaks Gujarati and she is also learning Tamil.*

alter /ˈɔːltə(r)/ *verb* (**alters**, **altering**, **altered**) become different; change something ବଦଳିଯିବା; ବଦଳାଇବା, ପରିବର୍ତ୍ତନ କରିବା *These trousers are too long—I'm going to alter them.*

alteration /ˌɔːltəˈreɪʃn/ *noun* a small change ଅଳ୍ପ ପରିବର୍ତ୍ତନ

alternate /ɔːlˈtɜːnət/ *adjective* **1** first one and then the other ଏକାନ୍ତରୀକ, ଗୋଟିଏ ଛାଡ଼ି ଆଉ ଗୋଟିଏ *At school we have English and Hindi lessons on alternate days.* **2** one of every two ଦୁଇଟିରୁ ଗୋଟିଏ, ଗୋଟିଏ ଛାଡ଼ି ଗୋଟିଏ *I visit him on alternate Sundays.*

alternative /ɔːlˈtɜːnətɪv/ *noun* a thing that you can choose instead of another thing ବିକଳ୍ପ; କୌଣସି ଜିନିଷ ବା ବିଷୟ ବଦଳରେ ନେଇ ହେଉଥିବା ଅନ୍ୟ ଜିନିଷ ବା ବିଷୟ *We could go by train—the alternative is to take the car.*

although /ɔːlˈðəʊ/ *conjunction* in spite of something; though ଯଦିଓ *Although she was ill, she went to work.*

altitude /ˈæltɪtjuːd/ *noun* the height above sea level ସମୁଦ୍ର ପତ୍ତନ ଠାରୁ (କୌଣସି ସ୍ଥାନ ବା ଜିନିଷର) ଉଚ୍ଚତା *At an altitude of 8,848 metres, Mount Everest is the highest mountain in the world.*

altogether /ˌɔːltəˈgeðə(r)/ *adverb* counting everything or everybody ମୋଟ ଉପରେ, ସବୁ ମିଶାଇ *Karan gave me Rs 50 and Sunil gave me Rs 75, so I've got Rs 125 altogether.*

aluminium /ˌæləˈmɪnɪəm/ *noun* (*no plural*) a light metal often used for making cooking utensils ରୂପା ପରି ଦିଶୁଥିବା ହାଲୁକା ଓ ନମନୀୟ ଧାତୁ (ଯେଉଁଥିରେ ବାସନ ଇତ୍ୟାଦି ତିଆରି ହୁଏ)

always /ˈɔːlweɪz/ *adverb* **1** at all times; every time ସବୁବେଳେ *I have always lived in Kolkata.* ○ *The train is always late.* **2** for ever ସଦା ସର୍ବଦା *I will always remember that day.*

am ଶବ୍ଦ **be** ର ଏକ ଧାତୁରୂପ

a.m. /ˌeɪˈem/ *abbreviation* you use 'a.m.' after a time to show that it is between midnight and midday ରାତି ୧୨ଟାରୁ ଦିନ ୧୨ଟା ପର୍ଯ୍ୟନ୍ତ ସମୟ *I start work at 9.30 a.m.* ➪ **p.m.** ଦେଖନ୍ତୁ।

amateur /ˈæmətə(r)/ *noun* a person who does something because he/she enjoys it, but does not get money for it ସୌଖୀନ କର୍ମୀ (ଟଙ୍କା ନ ନେଇ ଖୁସିରେ କାମ କରୁଥିବା ବ୍ୟକ୍ତି)

amateur *adjective* ସୌଖୀନ, ଅପେଷାଦାର *an amateur photographer* ➪ **professional** ଦେଖନ୍ତୁ।

amaze /əˈmeɪz/ *verb* (**amazes**, **amazing**, **amazed**) make somebody very surprised ବିସ୍ମିତ କରିବା, ଆଶ୍ଚର୍ଯ୍ୟାନ୍ୱିତ କରିବା *Matthew amazed me by remembering my birthday.*

amazement *noun* (*no plural*) great surprise ବିସ୍ମୟ *She looked at me in amazement.*

ambassador /æmˈbæsədə(r)/ *noun* an important person who goes to another country and works there for the government of his/her own country ରାଜଦୂତ, ରାଷ୍ଟ୍ରଦୂତ *the Indian Ambassador to Germany* ➪ **embassy** ଦେଖନ୍ତୁ।

amber /ˈæmbə(r)/ *noun* (*no plural*) **1** a yellowish-brown colour ନାରଙ୍ଗି ବା ହଳଦିଆ ମାଟିଆ ରଙ୍ଗ *The traffic lights turned to amber.* **2** a hard clear yellow-brown substance used for making objects for decoration or jewellery ହଳଦିଆ ମାଟିଆ ରଙ୍ଗଶକ୍ତ ସ୍ୱଚ୍ଛ ପଦାର୍ଥ ଯାହାକି ଅଳଙ୍କାରରେ ବ୍ୟବହାର କରାଯାଏ।

ambition /æmˈbɪʃn/ *noun* something that you want to do very much ଉଚ୍ଚାଭିଳାସ, ଉଚ୍ଚାକାଙ୍କ୍ଷା *My ambition is to become a doctor.*

ambitious /æmˈbɪʃəs/ *adjective* a person who is ambitious wants to do well ଉଚ୍ଚାଭିଳାଷୀ

ambulance /ˈæmbjələns/ *noun* a special van that takes people who are ill or hurt to hospital ଅସୁସ୍ଥ ବା ଆହତ ଲୋକଙ୍କୁ ଡାକ୍ତରଖାନାକୁ ନେବା ପାଇଁ ଥିବା ମଟର ଗାଡ଼ି, ଆମ୍ବୁଲାନ୍ସ୍

amenity /əˈmiːnəti/ *noun* (*plural* **amenities**) a thing or facility that is useful and makes life more comfortable ସୁରୁଖୁରୁରେ ଚଳିବା ପାଇଁ ଥିବା ସୁବିଧା ବା ସୁବିଧା ଯୋଗାଉଥିବା ପଦାର୍ଥ

ammunition

ammunition /ˌæmjuˈnɪʃn/ *noun* (*no plural*) things that you fire from a gun or throw to hurt people or damage things ବନ୍ଧୁକଗୁଳି, ବୋମା, ଗୋଳା ଇତ୍ୟାଦି

ଅସ୍ତ୍ରଶସ୍ତ୍ର *The plane was carrying ammunition to the soldiers.*

amoeba /ə'mi:bə/ *noun* (*plural* **amoebas** ବା **amoebae** /ə'mi:bi:/ a very tiny living thing that is made of one cell ସୂକ୍ଷ୍ମ ଏକକୋଷୀ ଜୀବାଣୁ, ଆମିବା

among /ə'mʌŋ/, **amongst** /ə'mʌŋst/ *preposition* **1** in the middle of ମଧ୍ୟରେ, ଗହଣରେ *The house stands among the trees.* **2** for or by more than two things or people ଦୁଇରୁ ଅଧିକ ବ୍ୟକ୍ତି ବା ପଦାର୍ଥ ଭିତରେ *He divided the money amongst his six children.*

> **among** or **between**?
>
> **Among** ବା **amongst** ର ବ୍ୟବହାର ଦୁଇରୁ ଅଧିକ ବ୍ୟକ୍ତି ବା ବସ୍ତୁ ପାଇଁ ବ୍ୟବହାର କରାଯାଏ ଯେଉଁଠି କେବଳ ଦୁଇ ବ୍ୟକ୍ତି ବା ବସ୍ତୁ ଥାଏ, ସେଠି **between** ର ବ୍ୟବହାର କରାଯାଇ ଥାଏ — *Shikha and I divided the cake between us.*
> *I was standing between Chetna and Puja.*

amount /ə'maʊnt/ *noun* how much there is of something ପରିମାଣ *He spent a large amount of money.*

amphibian /æm'fɪbiən/ *noun* an animal that can live both on land and in water ଉଭୟ ଜଳ ଓ ସ୍ଥଳରେ ରହିପାରୁଥିବା ପ୍ରାଣୀ, ଉଭୟଚର ପ୍ରାଣୀ *Frogs and toads are amphibians.*

amuse /ə'mju:z/ *verb* (**amuses, amusing, amused**) make somebody smile or laugh ଅନ୍ୟକୁ ହସାଇବା, ଆମୋଦିତ କରିବା *Ravi's jokes always amused his friends.*

amusement /ə'mju:zmənt/ *noun* (*no plural*) the feeling that you have when you think something is funny ଆମୋଦ, କୌତୁକ *We watched in amusement as the dog chased its tail.*

amusing /ə'mju:zɪŋ/ *adjective* something that is amusing makes you smile or laugh ଆନନ୍ଦଦାୟକ, କୌତୁକିଆ *an amusing story*

an /ən/ *article* **1** one or any ଏକ, ଗୋଟିଏ, ଜଣେ; ଯେ କୌଣସି *I ate an apple.* **2** each, or for each ପ୍ରତି, ପ୍ରତ୍ୟେକ *It costs Rs 10 an hour to park your car here.* ➪ **a** ରେ ଟିପ୍ପଣୀ ଦେଖନ୍ତୁ ।

anaemia /ə'ni:miə/ *noun* (*no plural*) a condition in which there are not enough red cells in the blood ରକ୍ତହୀନତା, ଲାଲ୍ ରକ୍ତ କଣିକା ହ୍ରାସ ହେବା ଅବସ୍ଥା

analyse /'ænəlaɪz/ *verb* (**analyses, analysing, analysed**) study something in detail by examining its parts to understand it ବିଶ୍ଳେଷଣ କରିବା, ତନ୍ନତନ୍ନ କରି ପରୀକ୍ଷା କରିବା *His job is to analyse the data collected every day.*

analysis /ə'næləsɪs/ *noun* (*plural* **analyses** /ə'næləsi:z/) ବିଶ୍ଳେଷଣ *He's going to do an analysis of the election results.*

ancestor /'ænsestə(r)/ *noun* your ancestors are the people in your family who lived a long time before you ପୂର୍ବପୁରୁଷ *My ancestors came from Iran.*

ancestral /æn'sestrəl/ *adjective* ପୈତୃକ, ପୂର୍ବପୁରୁଷ ପ୍ରଦତ୍ତ *ancestral property*

anchor /ˈæŋkə(r)/ *noun* a heavy metal thing that you drop into the water from a ship or boat to keep it in one place ଲଙ୍ଗର, ଜାହାଜକୁ ଗୋଟିଏ ଜାଗାରେ ସ୍ଥିର ରଖିବା ପାଇଁ ଥିବା ଭାରୀ ଲୁହାଖଣ୍ଡ ଯାହା ଶିକୁଳି ଦ୍ୱାରା ପାଣିତଳକୁ ପକାଯାଏ

ancient /ˈeɪnʃənt/ *adjective* very old; from a time long ago ପ୍ରାଚୀନ, ଅତି ପୁରାତନ କାଳ ସମ୍ବନ୍ଧୀୟ *an ancient city*

and /ənd; ænd; ən/ *conjunction* a word that joins words or parts of sentences together ଓ, ଏବଂ *salt and pepper* ○ *They sang and danced all evening.*

anger /ˈæŋgə(r)/ *noun* (*no plural*) the strong feeling that you have when you are not pleased about something ରାଗ, କ୍ରୋଧ *He was filled with anger when he saw a man trying to steal his car.*

angle /ˈæŋgl/ *noun* the space between two lines that meet (ଡିଗ୍ରୀରେ ପରିମାପିତ) କୋଣ *an angle of 90°* ✪ କୋଣ ମାପିବାର ଏକକକୁ **degree** କୁହାଯାଏ। ➪ ଚିତ୍ର ପାଇଁ **shape** ଦେଖନ୍ତୁ।

angry /ˈæŋgri/ *adjective* (**angrier**, **angriest**) if you are angry, you feel or show anger କ୍ରୁଦ୍ଧ, ରାଗିଯାଇଥିବା

angrily /ˈæŋgreli/ *adverb* ରାଗିଯାଇ, କ୍ରୁଦ୍ଧ ଭାବରେ *'Somebody has taken my book!' she shouted angrily.*

animal /ˈænɪml/ *noun* **1** any living thing (including humans) that is not a plant ଜୀବ, ଯେକୌଣସି ଜୀବନ୍ତ ପଦାର୍ଥ (ଗଛପତ୍ର ନୁହେଁ) **2** any living thing that is not a bird, fish, insect, reptile or human ପଶୁ (ପକ୍ଷୀ, ମାଛ, ପୋକ, ସରୀସୃପ ବା ମଣିଷ ନୁହେଁ) *Cats, horses and rats are animals.*

animation /ˌænɪˈmeɪʃn/ *noun* the process of making films, computer games, etc. with pictures that seem to move କ୍ରମରେ ଅଙ୍କିତ ଚିତ୍ରମାନଙ୍କରୁ ଚଳଚ୍ଚିତ୍ର କରିବା ପଦ୍ଧତି *cartoon animation*

ankle /ˈæŋkl/ *noun* the part of your leg where it joins your foot ବଳାଗଣ୍ଠି, ପାଦ ଓ ଗୋଡ଼କୁ ସଂଯୋଗ କରୁଥିବା ଖଞ୍ଜ ➪ ଚିତ୍ର ପାଇଁ **body** ଦେଖନ୍ତୁ।

annex /əˈneks/ *verb* (**annexes, annexing, annexed**) take control of another country or region by force ବଳପୂର୍ବକ ଅନ୍ୟ ଦେଶ ବା ଅଞ୍ଚଳ ଅଧିକାର କରିବା *The British annexed several parts of India between 1848 and 1854.*

anniversary /ˌænɪˈvɜːsəri/ *noun* (*plural* **anniversaries**) a day when you remember something special that happened on the same day in another year ବାର୍ଷିକ ଉତ୍ସବର ଦିନ, ସାମ୍ବତ୍ସରିକ ଉତ୍ସବ *Today is their 25th wedding anniversary.*

announce /əˈnaʊns/ *verb* (**announces, announcing, announced**) tell a lot of people about something important ଘୋଷଣା କରିବା

The teacher announced the winner of the competition.

announcement *noun* telling people about something ଘୋଷଣା *I have an important announcement to make.*

announcer /əˈnaʊnsə(r)/ *noun* a person whose job is to tell us about programmes on radio or television ଘୋଷଣାକାରି ବ୍ୟକ୍ତି

annoy /əˈnɔɪ/ *verb* (**annoys, annoying, annoyed**) make somebody a little angry ବିରକ୍ତ କରିବା *My brother annoys me when he leaves his clothes all over the floor.*

annoyed *adjective* a little angry ବିରକ୍ତ *I was annoyed when he forgot to phone me.*

annual /ˈænjuəl/ *adjective* that happens or comes once every year ବାର୍ଷିକ, ବର୍ଷକୁ ଥରେ ହେଉଥିବା *There is an annual meeting in June.*

anon /əˈnɒn/ **1** *abbreviation* ର ସଂକ୍ଷିପ୍ତ ରୂପ **anonymous** **2** *adverb* soon ଶୀଘ୍ର, ଅଳ୍ପ ସମୟରେ *See you anon.*

anonymous /əˈnɒnɪməs/ *adjective* if something is anonymous, you do not know who did, gave or made it ବେନାମୀ *She received an anonymous letter.*

another /əˈnʌðə(r)/ *adjective, pronoun* **1** one more thing or person ଆଉ ଗୋଟିଏ (ଅଧିକା) *Would you like another sandwich?* **2** a different thing or person ଭିନ୍ନ (ବ୍ୟକ୍ତି ବା ପଦାର୍ଥ) *I've read this book. Do you have another?*

answer[1] /ˈɑːnsə(r)/ *verb* (**answers**, **answering**, **answered**) **1** say or write something when somebody has asked a question ଉତ୍ତର ଦେବା *I asked him if he was hungry but he didn't answer.* **2** write a letter to somebody who has written to you ଚିଠିର ଉତ୍ତର ଦେବା *She didn't answer my letter.*

answer the telephone pick up the telephone when it rings, and speak ଟେଲିଫୋନ୍ ବାଜିଲେ ତାକୁ ଉଠାଇ କଥା କହିବା

answer[2] /ˈɑːnsə(r)/ *noun* something that you say or write when somebody asks you something ଉତ୍ତର; ଜବାବ୍ *I asked Lucy a question but she didn't give me an answer.*

ant /ænt/ *noun* a very small insect that lives in big groups ପିମ୍ପୁଡ଼ି, ପିପୀଲିକା ➪ ଚିତ୍ର ପାଇଁ **insect** ଦେଖନ୍ତୁ।

Antarctic /ænˈtɑːktɪk/ *noun* (*no plural*) (**the Antarctic**) the permanently frozen region around the South Pole ଦକ୍ଷିଣ ମେରୁ ବା କୁମେରୁ ର ବରଫାବୃତ ଅଞ୍ଚଳ ➪ **Arctic** ଦେଖନ୍ତୁ।

anteater /ˈæntiːtə(r)/ *noun* an animal with a long tongue that eats **ants** ଗୋଜିଆ ମୁହଁ ଓ ଲମ୍ବା ଜିଭଥିବା ପିମ୍ପୁଡ଼ିଖିଆ ଜନ୍ତୁ

anteater

antelope /ˈæntɪləʊp/ *noun* (*plural* **antelope** ବା **antelopes**) a deer-like wild animal with horns and long thin legs. It can run fast ସରୁ ଓ ଲମ୍ବା ଗୋଡ଼ଥିବା କ୍ଷିପ୍ର ଗତିରେ ଦୌଡ଼ି ପାରୁଥିବା ହରିଣ ପରି ପଶୁ; କୃଷ୍ଣସାର ମୃଗ

antenna /æn'tenə/ *noun* (*plural* **antennae** /æn'təni/) **1** one of the two long, thin and tube-like structures on the heads of some insects and sea animals for feeling things କିଛି କୀଟ ଓ ସମୁଦ୍ର ଜୀବଙ୍କ ମୁଣ୍ଡରେ ଥିବା ସ୍ପର୍ଶକାରୀ ଶୃଙ୍ଗ ବା ଶୁଣ୍ଢ ➪ ଚିତ୍ର ପାଇଁ **insect** ଦେଖନ୍ତୁ। **2** an aerial ରେଡ଼ିଓ, ଟିଭି ଇତ୍ୟାଦିର ସଞ୍ଚାର ଗ୍ରହଣ କରିବା ପାଇଁ ବ୍ୟବହୃତ ଆକାଶତାର।

anthem /'ænθəm/ *noun* the official song of a country or an organization, sung to express loyalty towards that country or organization ପ୍ରଶଂସାସୂଚକ ସଙ୍ଗୀତ (ବିଶେଷତଃ ଦେଶ ବା ଜାତି ପ୍ରତି); ଜାତୀୟ ସଙ୍ଗୀତ *the national anthem*

anti- *prefix*
Anti- at the beginning of a word often means 'against' (ଶବ୍ଦର ଆରମ୍ଭରେ ଯୋଡ଼ାଯାଉଥିବା) ବିପରୀତାର୍ଥ ସୂଚକ ଶବ୍ଦ *an anti-smoking campaign*

antibiotic /ˌæntibaɪ'ɒtɪk/ *noun* a type of medicine like penicillin that kills bacteria and cures infections ରୋଗର ଜୀବାଣୁଙ୍କୁ ନଷ୍ଟ କରିବା ପାଇଁ ବ୍ୟବହୃତ ଔଷଧ (ଯଥା: ପେନିସିଲିନ୍)

anticipate /æn'tɪsɪpeɪt/ *verb* (**anticipates**, **anticipating**, **anticipated**) think that something may happen and be ready for it ପୂର୍ବାନୁମାନ କରି ପ୍ରସ୍ତୁତ ରହିବା *We didn't anticipate so many problems.*

anticlockwise /ˌænti'klɒkwaɪz/ *adjective*, *adverb* when something moves anticlockwise, it moves in the opposite direction to the hands of a clock ଘଣ୍ଟା କଣ୍ଟା ଚାଲୁଥିବାର ବିପରୀତ ଦିଗରେ ✪ ବିପରୀତ **clockwise**

antique /æn'ti:k/ *noun* an old thing that is worth a lot of money ପୁରୁଣା ଜିନିଷ ଯାହା ପୁରୁଣା ହୋଇଥିବାରୁ ମୂଲ୍ୟବାନ *These chairs are antiques.*

antique *adjective* ପୁରୁଣାକାଳିଆ *an antique vase*

antiseptic /ˌænti'septɪk/ *noun* a substance that prevents infection on a wound by killing bacteria ଜୀବାଣୁନାଶକ ପଦାର୍ଥ

antiseptic *adjective* ଜୀବାଣୁନାଶକ *an antiseptic cream*

antler /'æntlə(r)/ *noun* one of the two branching horns that grow on the head of male deer ହରିଣ ମୁଣ୍ଡର କେନାକେନା ହୋଇଉଠିଥିବା ଶୃଙ୍ଗ ➪ ଚିତ୍ର ପାଇଁ **deer** ଦେଖନ୍ତୁ।

anxiety /æŋ'zaɪəti/ *noun* (*plural* **anxieties**) a feeling of worry and fear ଉଦ୍‌ବେଗ, ଉତ୍କଣ୍ଠା, ଚିନ୍ତାଗ୍ରସ୍ତ ଅବସ୍ଥା

anxious /'æŋkʃəs/ *adjective* worried and afraid ଉତ୍କଣ୍ଠିତ, ଆତୁର, ଅଧୀର *She's anxious because her daughter hasn't come back yet.*

anxiously *adverb* ଉତ୍କଣ୍ଠିତ ହୋଇ *We waited anxiously.*

any /'eni/ *adjective*, *pronoun* **1** a word that you use in questions and after 'not' and 'if'; some ଗୋଟିଏ ବା କିଛି; କିଛିବି, ଆଦୌ *Have you got any money?* ○ *I don't speak any*

Spanish. ○ *She asked if I had any milk.* **2** no special one ଯେ କୌଣସି *Take any book you want.*

any *adverb* at all କିଛି ମାତ୍ରାରେ, ଟିକିଏବି *I can't walk any faster.*

anybody /ˈenibɒdi/, **anyone** /ˈeniwʌn/ *pronoun* any person ଯେକୌଣସି ଲୋକ *Did you see anyone you know?*

anything /ˈeniθɪŋ/ *pronoun* a thing of any kind ଯେ କୌଣସି ଜିନିଷ, ଯାହା କିଛି *Is there anything in that box?*

anything else something more ଆଉ କିଛି *'Would you like anything else?' asked the waiter.*

anyway /ˈeniweɪ/, **anyhow** /ˈenihaʊ/ *adverb* no matter what is true ଯାହା ହେଉନା କାହିଁକି, ତାସତ୍ତ୍ୱେ, ଯେକୌଣସି ପ୍ରକାରେ *It was very expensive but she bought it anyway.*

anywhere /ˈeniweə(r)/ *adverb* at, in or to any place ଯେକୌଣସି ସ୍ଥାନକୁ ବା ସ୍ଥାନରେ *Are you going anywhere this summer?* ○ *I can't find my pen anywhere.*

apart /əˈpɑːt/ *adverb* **1** away from the others; away from each other ଅଲଗା, ଦୂରରେ *The two houses are 500 metres apart.* **2** into parts ଅଂଶଗୁଡ଼ିକ ଅଲଗା କରିବା *He took my radio apart to repair it.*

apart from somebody or **something** if you do not count somebody or something ତାଙ୍କଛଡ଼ା, ତା'ଛଡ଼ା *There were ten people in the room, apart from me.*

apartment /əˈpɑːtmənt/ *noun* ➪ **flat**[1] ଦେଖନ୍ତୁ।

ape /eɪp/ *noun* an animal like a big monkey with no tail ଲାଙ୍ଗୁଡ଼ ନଥିବା ବାନର ସଦୃଶ ପ୍ରାଣୀମାନବ *Gorillas and chimpanzees are apes.*

chimpanzee

apologize /əˈpɒlədʒaɪz/ *verb* (**apologizes**, **apologizing**, **apologized**) say that you are sorry about something that you have done କ୍ଷମା ମାଗିବା *I apologized to Jatin for losing his book.*

apology /əˈpɒlədʒi/ *noun* (*plural* **apologies**) words that you say or write to show that you are sorry about something you have done ଭୁଲ୍ ପାଇଁ କ୍ଷମା ପ୍ରାର୍ଥନା *Please accept my apologies.*

apostrophe /əˈpɒstrəfi/ *noun* the sign (') that you use in writing. You use it to show that you have left a letter out of a word, for example in the word *I'm* (I am). You also use it to show that something belongs to somebody or something, as in *my son's room* ବର୍ଣ୍ଣଲୋପର ବା ସମ୍ବନ୍ଧ ପଦର ଚିହ୍ନ

apparatus /ˌæpəˈreɪtəs/ *noun* (*plural* **apparatuses**) the tools or pieces of equipment that are required to do a particular task ବୈଜ୍ଞାନିକ ବା ବୈଷୟିକ ଯନ୍ତ୍ର, ଉପକରଣ ବା ସରଞ୍ଜାମ *laboratory apparatus*

apparent /ə'pærənt/ *adjective* easy to see or understand; clear ସହଜରେ ଦିଶୁଥିବା ବା ଜାଣି ହେଉଥିବା *It was apparent that she didn't like him.*

apparently *adverb* according to the way something seems or appears, although you may not be completely sure about it ଦୃଶ୍ୟମାନ ଭାବରେ, ଜଣା ଯାଉଥିବା ଭାବେ *He has gone to school today, so he's apparently feeling better.*

appeal[1] /ə'pi:l/ *verb* (**appeals**, **appealing**, **appealed**) ask in a serious way for something that you need very much ପ୍ରାର୍ଥନା କରିବା, ଆବେଦନ କରିବା, ନିବେଦନ କରିବା *They appealed for food and clothing.*

appeal[2] /ə'pi:l/ *noun* the act of asking for something in a serious way ପ୍ରାର୍ଥନା, ଆବେଦନ, ନିବେଦନ *They made an appeal for help.*

appear /ə'pɪə(r)/ *verb* (**appears**, **appearing**, **appeared**) **1** come and be seen ଦେଖାଦେବା, ଦେଖାଯିବା *The sun suddenly appeared from behind a cloud.* ✪ ବିପରୀତ **disappear** **2** seem ଜଣାପଡୁଥିବା, ଲାଗୁଥିବା *It appears that I was wrong.*

appearance /ə'pɪərəns/ *noun* **1** what somebody or something looks like ବାହ୍ୟରୂପ *Her new glasses have changed her appearance.* **2** the coming of somebody or something; when somebody or something is seen ଆବିର୍ଭାବ, ଉପସ୍ଥିତ *Jaya's appearance at the party surprised everybody.* ✪ ବିପରୀତ **disappearance**

appetite /'æpɪtaɪt/ *noun* the feeling that you want to eat ଭୋକ, କ୍ଷୁଧା *Swimming always gives me an appetite.*

applaud /ə'plɔ:d/ *verb* (**applauds**, **applauding**, **applauded**) clap your hands to show that you like something ତାଳିମାରି ପ୍ରଶଂସା ଜଣାଇବା *We all applauded at the end of the song.*

applause /ə'plɔ:z/ *noun* (*no plural*) when a lot of people clap their hands to show that they like something ସମ୍ମିଳିତ କରତାଳି ଦ୍ୱାରା ପ୍ରଶଂସା ଜ୍ଞାପନ *loud applause*

apple /'æpl/ *noun* a hard round juicy fruit that is red, yellow or green in colour when ripe ସେଓ, ଆପ୍ଲ୍ ➪ ଚିତ୍ର ପାଇଁ **fruit** ଦେଖନ୍ତୁ ।

appliance /ə'plaɪəns/ *noun* a useful machine for doing something in the house ଘର କାମରେ ବ୍ୟବହୃତ ଉପକରଣ ବା ଯନ୍ତ୍ର *Washing machines and irons are electrical appliances.*

applicant /'æplɪkənt/ *noun* a person who asks for a job or a place at a university, for example (ଚାକିରି, ନାମଲେଖା ଇତ୍ୟାଦି ପାଇଁ) ଦରଖାସ୍ତକାରୀ ବା ପଦପ୍ରାର୍ଥୀ ବ୍ୟକ୍ତି *There were six applicants for the job.*

application /ˌæplɪ'keɪʃn/ *noun* writing to ask for something, for example a job ଦରଖାସ୍ତ

application form *noun* (*plural* **application forms**) a special piece of paper that you write on when you are trying to get something, for example a telephone connection ଦରଖାସ୍ତ ଫର୍ମ

apply /əˈplaɪ/ *verb* (**applies, applying, applied, has applied**) **1** write to ask for something ଦରଖାସ୍ତ ଦେବା *Sunil has applied for a place at the university.* **2** be about or be important to somebody or something ପ୍ରଯୁଜ୍ୟ ହେବା *This notice applies to all children over the age of twelve.*

appoint /əˈpɔɪnt/ *verb* (**appoints, appointing, appointed**) choose somebody for a job ନିଯୁକ୍ତ କରିବା *The bank has appointed a new manager.* ✪ ବିପରୀତ **dismiss 2**

appointment /əˈpɔɪntmənt/ *noun* a time that you have fixed to meet somebody ନିଯୁକ୍ତି *I've got an appointment with the doctor at ten o'clock.*

appreciate /əˈpriːʃieɪt/ *verb* (**appreciates, appreciating, appreciated**) **1** understand and enjoy something ପସନ୍ଦ କରିବା, ପ୍ରଶଂସା କରିବା *His paintings were appreciated by many people.* **2** be pleased about something that somebody has done for you କୃତଜ୍ଞ ହେବା *Thank you for your help. I appreciate it.*

appreciation /əˌpriːʃiˈeɪʃn/ *noun* (*no plural*) ଅନୁକୂଳ ମତ, ପସନ୍ଦ *We gave her some flowers to show our appreciation for her hard work.*

apprehensive /ˌæprɪˈhensɪv/ *adjective* if you are apprehensive, you are worried that something bad will happen ଶଙ୍କା, ଆଶଙ୍କା, ଭୟ

approach[1] /əˈprəʊtʃ/ *verb* (**approaches, approaching, approached**) come near or nearer to somebody or something ପାଖକୁ ଯିବା, ପାଖକୁ ଆସିବା *The board exams are approaching.*

approach[2] /əˈprəʊtʃ/ *noun* **1** (*no plural*) coming nearer to somebody or something ପାଖେଇ ଆସିବା ପ୍ରକ୍ରିୟା *the approach of winter* **2** (*plural* **approaches**) a way of doing something କାର୍ଯ୍ୟ ସମ୍ପାଦନର ପନ୍ଥା *This is a new approach to language learning.*

appropriate /əˈprəʊpriət/ *adjective* right for that time or place; suitable ଉପଯୁକ୍ତ, ସମୁଚିତ *The book was written in a style appropriate to the age of the children.* ✪ ବିପରୀତ **inappropriate**

approval /əˈpruːvl/ *noun* (*no plural*) showing or saying that somebody or something is good or right ଅନୁମୋଦନ, ଅନୁକୂଳ ମତ, ସମ୍ମତି *Tania's parents gave the marriage their approval.*

approve /əˈpruːv/ *verb* (**approves, approving, approved**) think or say that something or somebody is good or right ଅନୁମୋଦନ କରିବା, ସମ୍ମତି ଦେବା *She doesn't approve of smoking.* ✪ ବିପରୀତ **disapprove**

approximate /əˈprɒksɪmət/ *adjective* almost correct but not exact ପ୍ରାୟ

ଠିକ୍, ଆନୁମାନିକ *The approximate time of arrival is three o'clock.*

approximately *adverb* about; not exactly ପ୍ରାୟ *I live approximately two kilometres from the station.*

apricot /ˈeɪprɪkɒt/ *noun* a small soft yellow fruit ଏକ ଛୋଟ, ନରମ, ହଳଦିଆ ଫଳ।

April /ˈeɪprəl/ *noun* the fourth month of the year ଇଂରାଜୀ ବର୍ଷର ୪ର୍ଥ ମାସ।

apron /ˈeɪprən/ *noun* a thing that you wear over the front of your clothes to keep them clean, for example when you are cooking ରାନ୍ଧିଲାବେଳେ ଲୁଗା ସାମନାରେ ପିନ୍ଧାଯାଉଥିବା ଏକ ବସ୍ତ୍ର।

apt /æpt/ *adjective* suitable in a particular situation ଉପଯୁକ୍ତ, ଉଚିତ *an apt reply*

aquarium /əˈkweəriəm/ *noun* a glass container that is used to keep fish and other water animals and plants in homes and offices ପାଣିର ଉଦ୍ଭିଦ, ପ୍ରାଣୀ ଓ ମାଛ ରଖିବା ପାଇଁ ଥିବା ପାଣିଭରା କାଚ ବାକ୍ସ। କୃତ୍ରିମ ଜଳାଶୟ

aquarium

Aquarius /əˈkweəriəs/ *noun* the eleventh sign of the **zodiac** ରାଶି ଚକ୍ରର ଏକାଦଶ ରାଶି, କୁମ୍ଭ ରାଶି; କୁମ୍ଭ ନକ୍ଷତ୍ରପୁଞ୍ଜ

aquatic /əˈkwætɪk/ *adjective* **1** (of plants and animals) that live or grow in or near water ପାଣିରେ ବା ପାଣି ପାଖରେ ରହୁଥିବା (ତୃଣ ବା ଜୀବ); ଜଳଜ **2** (of games) played in water ପାଣିରେ ଖେଳା ଯାଉଥିବା (ଖେଳ)

arc /ɑːk/ *noun* a small curved part of a circle ବଳୟ, ଚାପ, ବୃତ୍ତାଂଶ ➪ ଚିତ୍ର ପାଇଁ **circle** ଦେଖନ୍ତୁ।

arch /ɑːtʃ/ *noun* (*plural* **arches**) a part of a bridge, building or wall that is in the shape of a half circle ଅର୍ଦ୍ଧଗୋଲାକୃତି ଖିଲାଣ, ତୋରଣ ➪ ଚିତ୍ର ପାଇଁ **bridge** ଦେଖନ୍ତୁ।

arch *verb* (**arches, arching, arched**) form a curve ଧନୁ ପରି ବଙ୍କାଇବା *The cat arched its back when it saw the dog.*

archaeology /ˌɑːkiˈɒlədʒi/ *noun* (*no plural*) the study of very old things like buildings and objects that are found in the ground ପ୍ରତ୍ନତତ୍ତ୍ୱ ବିଦ୍ୟା, ପୁରାତତ୍ତ୍ୱ

archaeologist /ˌɑːkiˈɒlədʒɪst/ *noun* a person who studies or knows a lot about archaeology ପ୍ରତ୍ନତତ୍ତ୍ୱ ବିଶାରଦ

archery /ˈɑːtʃəri/ *noun* (*no plural*) the sport of shooting arrows with a bow ଧନୁର୍ବିଦ୍ୟା

archer *noun* a person who shoots arrows with a bow ଧନୁର୍ଦ୍ଧର, ତୀରନ୍ଦାଜ

architect /ˈɑːkɪtekt/ *noun* a person whose job is to plan buildings ଘର, ପୋଲ ଇତ୍ୟାଦି ନିର୍ମାଣ ପାଇଁ ନକ୍ସା କରିବା ବ୍ୟକ୍ତି, ଶିଳ୍ପୀ-ଯନ୍ତ୍ରୀ, ସ୍ଥାପିତବିଦ୍ୟାବିତ୍

architecture /ˈɑːkɪtektʃə(r)/ *noun* (*no plural*) **1** planning and making buildings ନିର୍ମାଣ ପ୍ରକଳ୍ପର କଳା ଓ ବିଜ୍ଞାନ, ସ୍ଥାପିତବିଦ୍ୟା **2** the shape of buildings

ଗୃହନିର୍ମାଣ ଶୈଳୀ *Do you like modern architecture?*

Arctic /ˈɑːktɪk/ *noun* (*no plural*) (**the Arctic**) the permanently frozen region around the North Pole ସୁମେରୁ ବା ଉତ୍ତର ମେରୁର ବରଫାବୃତ ଅଞ୍ଚଳ ➪ **Antarctic** ଦେଖନ୍ତୁ ।

are ଶବ୍ଦ **be** ର ଏକ ଧାତୁରୂପ

area /ˈeəriə/ *noun* **1** a part of town, country or the world ଅଞ୍ଚଳ *Do you live in this area?* **2** the size of a flat space. If a room is three metres wide and four metres long, it has an area of twelve square metres ପରିସର, କ୍ଷେତ୍ର, ବିସ୍ତାର

aren't = **are not**

argue /ˈɑːgjuː/ *verb* (**argues, arguing, argued**) talk angrily with somebody because you do not agree ତର୍କବିତର୍କ କରିବା, ବାଦାନୁବାଦ କରିବା *I often argue with my brother about music.*

argument /ˈɑːgjumənt/ *noun* an angry talk between people with different ideas ତର୍କବିତର୍କ, ବାଦାନୁବାଦ *They had an argument about where to go on holiday.*

arid /ˈærɪd/ *adjective* hot and dry ଶୁଷ୍କ, ଗରମ, ମରୁଡ଼ିଗ୍ରସ୍ତ *arid climate*

Aries /ˈeərɪːz/ the first sign of the **zodiac** ରାଶିଚକ୍ରର ପ୍ରଥମ ସ୍ଥାନ, ମେଷ ରାଶି

arithmetic /əˈrɪθmətɪk/ *noun* (*no plural*) working with numbers to find an answer ସଂଖ୍ୟାଶାସ୍ତ୍ର, ଅଙ୍କବିଦ୍ୟା, ପାଟୀଗଣିତ

arm /ɑːm/ *noun* the part of your body from your shoulder to your hand ବାହୁ ଭୁଜ *He was carrying a book under his arm.* ➪ ଚିତ୍ର ପାଇଁ **body** ଦେଖନ୍ତୁ ।

armchair /ˈɑːmtʃeə(r)/ *noun* a comfortable chair with parts where you can put your arms ଆରାମ୍ ଚଉକି, ହାତଥିବା ଆଉଜିବା ଚଉକି *She was asleep in an armchair.*

armed /ɑːmd/ *adjective* with a weapon, for example a gun ସଶସ୍ତ୍ର, ଅସ୍ତ୍ରଶସ୍ତ୍ର ଧରିଥିବା *an armed robber*

the armed forces *noun* (*plural*) the army, air force and navy ସେନାବାହିନୀ (ସ୍ଥଳସେନା, ବାୟୁସେନା ଓ ନୌସେନା)

armour /ˈɑːmə(r)/ *noun* (*no plural*) metal clothes that men wore long ago to protect their bodies when they were fighting ଆତ୍ମରକ୍ଷା ପାଇଁ ପୂର୍ବକାଳରେ ଯୋଦ୍ଧାମାନେ ପିନ୍ଧୁଥିବା ଚର୍ମ ବା କବଚ *a suit of armour*

arms /ɑːmz/ *noun* (*plural*) guns, bombs and other weapons for fighting ବନ୍ଧୁକ, ଗୋଳାବାରୁଦ, ବୋମା ଇତ୍ୟାଦି ଅସ୍ତ୍ରଶସ୍ତ୍ର

army /ˈɑːmi/ *noun* (*plural* **armies**) a large group of soldiers who fight on land in a war ସୈନ୍ୟବାହିନୀ *He joined the army when he was eighteen.*

aroma /ə'rəʊmə/ *noun* a pleasant smell ସୁଗନ୍ଧ, ଭଲ ବାସ୍ନା *I love the aroma of freshly baked cakes.*

around /ə'raʊnd/ *preposition, adverb* **1** in or to different places or in different directions ଚାରିଆଡ଼େ, ବିଭିନ୍ନ ଦିଗରେ *His clothes were lying around the room.* **2** on or to all sides of something, often in a circle ଚାରିପଟେ *He ran around the track.* **3** in the opposite direction or in another direction ଭିନ୍ନଆଡ଼କୁ, ବିପରୀତ ଦିଗରେ *Turn around and go back the way you came.* **4** a little more or less than; a little before or after ଅଳ୍ପେ ବହୁତେ; ପାଖାପାଖି ସମୟରେ *I'll be meeting her at around seven o'clock.*

arrange /ə'reɪndʒ/ *verb* (**arranges, arranging, arranged**) **1** make a plan for the future ବ୍ୟବସ୍ଥା କରିବା, ଯୋଗାଡ଼ କରିବା *We arranged a big party for Deepa's birthday.* **2** put things in a certain order or place ଶ୍ରେଣୀବଦ୍ଧ ଭାବେ ରଖିବା, ସଜାଇ ରଖିବା *Arrange the chairs in a circle.*

arrangement /ə'reɪndʒmənt/ *noun* **1** something that you plan or agree for the future ବ୍ୟବସ୍ଥା, ବନ୍ଦୋବସ୍ତ *They are making the arrangements for their wedding.* **2** a group of things put together so that they look nice ସଜାଣ, ସାଜସଜ୍ଜା, ବିନ୍ୟାସ *a flower arrangement*

arrest[1] /ə'rest/ *verb* (**arrests, arresting, arrested**) when the police arrest somebody, they make that person a prisoner because they think that he/she has done something wrong ଗିରଫ କରିବା *The thief was arrested yesterday.*

arrest[2] /ə'rest/ *noun* the act of arresting somebody ଗିରଫ *The police made five arrests.*

be under arrest be a prisoner of the police ପୁଲିସ୍ ଗିରଫରେ ରହିବା

arrival /ə'raɪvl/ *noun* the act of coming to a place ପହଞ୍ଚିବା *My sister met me at the airport on my arrival.*
✪ ବିପରୀତ **departure**

arrive /ə'raɪv/ *verb* (**arrives, arriving, arrived**) come to a place ପହଞ୍ଚିବା *What time does the train arrive in Delhi?* ○ *Has my letter arrived?*

arrogant /'ærəgənt/ *adjective* a person who is arrogant thinks that he or she is better or more important than other people ଉଦ୍ଧତ, ଅହଙ୍କାରୀ

arrow /'ærəʊ/ *noun* **1** a long thin piece of wood or metal with a point at one end. You shoot an arrow from a **bow** ଶର, ତୀର **2** a sign in the shape of an arrow (→) that shows where something is or where you should go ଦିଗ ଇତ୍ୟାଦି ଦେଖାଇବାକୁ ଥିବା ତୀର ଚିହ୍ନ (→)

art /ɑːt/ *noun* (*no plural*) beautiful things like paintings and drawings that somebody has made କଳା, ଚାରୁକଳା *modern art*

artery /ˈɑːtəri/ *noun* (*plural* **arteries**) one of the many tubes that carry blood from the heart to other parts of the body ଧମନୀ ➪ **vein** ଦେଖନ୍ତୁ

article /ˈɑːtɪkl/ *noun* **1** a piece of writing in a newspaper or magazine ଖବରକାଗଜ, ପତ୍ରିକା ଇତ୍ୟାଦିରେ ପ୍ରକାଶିତ ଲେଖା, ପ୍ରବନ୍ଧ *Did you read the article about Bangalore in yesterday's newspaper?* **2** a thing ଦ୍ରବ୍ୟ, ଜିନିଷ *articles of clothing* **3** in grammar, the words **a**, **an** and **the** are called articles ଇଂରାଜୀ ବ୍ୟାକରଣରେ ବ୍ୟବହୃତ ହେଉଥିବା ଏକ, ଟି

artificial /ˌɑːtɪˈfɪʃl/ *adjective* made by people; not natural କୃତ୍ରିମ, ଅପ୍ରାକୃତିକ *artificial flowers*

artist /ˈɑːtɪst/ *noun* a person who paints or draws pictures କଳାକାର, ଶିଳ୍ପୀ, ଚିତ୍ରକର, କଳାବିତ୍

artistic /ɑːˈtɪstɪk/ *adjective* good at painting, drawing or making beautiful things କଳାନିପୁଣ, କଳାରୁଚି ସମ୍ପନ୍ନ *He's very artistic.*

as /əz/ *conjunction, preposition* **1** while; at the same time that something is happening ଯେତେବେଳେ, ବେଳକୁ *As I was going out, the telephone rang.* **2** because କାରଣ, ଯେହେତୁ *She didn't go to school as she was ill.* **3** in the same way; like ଯେମିତି *Please do as I tell you!* **4** in the job of ଭାବରେ, ପଦରେ *She works as a secretary for a big company.*

as ... as words that you use to compare people or things; the same amount ଯେତିକି ... ସେତିକ *Raghu is as tall as his father.*

ascend /əˈsend/ *verb* (**ascends**, **ascending**, **ascended**) go up, rise ଉପରକୁ ଉଠିବା, ଆରୋହଣ କରିବା, ଚଢ଼ିବା ✪ ବିପରୀତ **descend**

ascending *adjective* ଉପରକୁ ଉଠୁଥିବା, ଆରୋହଣ କରୁଥିବା *ascending order* ✪ ବିପରୀତ **descending**

ash /æʃ/ *noun* (*plural* **ash** ବା **ashes**) the grey stuff that you see after something has burned ପାଉଁଶ, ଭସ୍ମ *cigarette ash*

ashamed /əˈʃeɪmd/ *adjective* sorry and unhappy about something that you have done, or unhappy because you are not as good as other people in some way ଲଜ୍ଜିତ *I was ashamed about lying to my friends.*

ashore /əˈʃɔː(r)/ *adverb* onto the land ଜଳରୁ ସ୍ଥଳକୁ, କୂଳକୁ, ତଟକୁ *We left the boat and went ashore.*

aside /əˈsaɪd/ *adverb* on or to one side; away ଏକ ପାଖକୁ ବା ଏକ ପାଖରେ *He put the letter aside while he did his homework.*

ask /ɑːsk/ *verb* (**asks**, **asking**, **asked**) **1** try to get an answer by using a question ପଚାରିବା *I asked him what the time was.* ○ *'What's your name?' she asked.* **2** say that you would like somebody to do something for you (କିଛି କରିବାକୁ) କହିବା, ଅନୁରୋଧ କରିବା *I asked Sarita to drive me to the station.* **3** invite somebody ନିମନ୍ତ୍ରଣ କରିବା *Irfan has asked me to a party on Saturday.*

asleep /əˈsliːp/ *adjective* sleeping ନିଦ୍ରିତ, ସୁପ୍ତ, ଶୋଇଥିବା *The baby is* *asleep in the bedroom.* ✪ ବିପରୀତ **awake**

fall asleep start sleeping ଶୋଇପଡ଼ିବା *He fell asleep in front of the TV.*

aspect /ˈæspekt/ *noun* one part of a problem, idea, etc. କୌଣସି ବିଷୟର ଗୋଟିଏ ପଟ ବା ଦିଗ *Pronunciation is one of the most difficult aspects of learning English.*

assassinate /əˈsæsɪneɪt/ *verb* (**assassinates**, **assassinating**, **assassinated**) kill an important or a famous person ବିଶିଷ୍ଟ ବ୍ୟକ୍ତିଙ୍କୁ ହତ୍ୟା କରିବା *Mahatma Gandhi was assassinated in 1948.*

assassination /əˌsæsɪˈneɪʃn/ *noun* the act of killing an important or famous person (ବିଶିଷ୍ଟ ବ୍ୟକ୍ତିଙ୍କ) ହତ୍ୟା

assemble /əˈsembl/ *verb* (**assembles**, **assembling**, **assembled**) come together or bring people or things together ଏକାଠି ହେବା

assembly /əˈsembli/ *noun* (*plural* **assemblies**) a meeting of a big group of people for a special reason ଲୋକମାନଙ୍କର ସମାବେଶ *Our school assembly is at 8.30 in the morning.*

assignment /əˈsaɪnmənt/ *noun* a particular job that you have been asked to do ନିର୍ଦ୍ଦିଷ୍ଟକାମ, ଭାରାର୍ପିତ ବା ଦିଆଯାଇଥିବା କାମ *Her new assignment will take her to Mumbai.*

assist /əˈsɪst/ *verb* (**assists**, **assisting**, **assisted**) help somebody ସାହାଯ୍ୟ କରିବା *Nitin assisted her with her project.*

assistance *noun* (*no plural*) help ସାହାଯ୍ୟ, ସହାୟତା *I can't move this piano without your assistance.* ✪ ସାଧାରଣତଃ କଥାବାର୍ତ୍ତାରେ ଆମେ **help** ବ୍ୟବହାର କରିଥାଉଁ।

assistant /əˈsɪstənt/ *noun* a person who helps ସହାୟକ, ସହକାରୀ *Ms Dixit is not here today. Would you like to speak to her assistant?*

associate /əˈsəʊsiət/ *verb* (**associates**, **associating**, **associated**) put two ideas together in your mind ଦୁଇଟି ଭାବନାକୁ ମନରେ ସଂଯୋଗ କରିବା *We usually associate mangoes with summer.*

association /əˌsəʊsiˈeɪʃn/ *noun* a group of people who join or work together for a special reason ସଂଘ, ସମାଜ *the Football Association*

assume /əˈsjuːm/ *verb* (**assumes**, **assuming**, **assumed**) think that something is true when you are not completely sure ସତ ବୋଲି ଧରିନେବା *Jaya was ill yesterday, so I assumed that she would not come today.*

assure /əˈʃɔː(r)/ *verb* (**assures**, **assuring**, **assured**) tell somebody what is true or certain so that they feel less worried ଠିକ୍ କଥା କହି ନିଶ୍ଚିନ୍ତ କରିବା *I assure you that the dog isn't dangerous.*

asterisk /ˈæstərɪsk/ *noun* a star-shaped sign (*) ତାରକାଚିହ୍ନ

asteroid /ˈæstərɔɪd/ *noun* one of the many large irregular-shaped bodies that is found between the orbits of

Mars and **Jupiter** କ୍ଷୁଦ୍ରଗ୍ରହ (ଯାହାର ଏକ ବଳୟ ମଙ୍ଗଳ ଓ ବୃହସ୍ପତି ଗ୍ରହଙ୍କ ମଧ୍ୟରେ ଦେଖାଯାଏ)

astonish /ə'stɒnɪʃ/ *verb* (**astonishes**, **astonishing**, **astonished**) surprise somebody very much ବିସ୍ମିତ କରିବା *The news astonished everyone.*

astonishment *noun* (*no plural*) great surprise ବିସ୍ମୟ *He looked at me in astonishment when I told him the news.*

astounding /ə'staʊndɪŋ/ *adjective* something that is astounding surprises you greatly ଖୁବ୍, ବିସ୍ମିତ କରୁଥିବା, ବିସ୍ମୟକର *an astounding performance*

astray /ə'streɪ/ *adverb* (go) away from one's path ଭୁଲ୍ ବାଟରେ; ବିପଥରେ, କୁପଥରେ ।

astrology /ə'strɒlədʒi/ *noun* (*no plural*) the study of the position and movement of stars and planets in the belief that they affect people's lives ଫଳିତ ଜ୍ୟୋତିଷଶାସ୍ତ୍ର, ଭବିଷ୍ୟତ ଗଣନା ପଦ୍ଧତି

astronaut /'æstrənɔ:t/ *noun* a person who travels in a spaceship ମହାଶୂନ୍ୟ ଯାତ୍ରୀ

astronomy /ə'strɒnəmi/ *noun* (*no plural*) the study of the sun, moon, planets and stars ଜ୍ୟୋତିର୍ବିଜ୍ଞାନ, ଗଣିତ ଜ୍ୟୋତିଷ

astronomer /ə'strɒnəmə(r)/ *noun* a person who studies or knows a lot about astronomy ଜ୍ୟୋତିର୍ବିଜ୍ଞାନୀ

at /ət; æt/ *preposition* **1** a word that shows where ଠାରେ, ରେ *They are at school.* ○ *The answer is at the back of the book.* **2** a word that shows when ରେ, ସମୟରେ *I go to bed at ten o'clock.* **3** towards somebody or something ଆଡ଼କୁ *Look at the picture.* **4** a word that shows how much, how fast, etc. ରେ, ବେଗରେ *He usually drives at 60 km/hr.* **5** a word that shows how well somebody or something does something ରେ, ବିଷୟରେ *I'm not very good at maths.*

ate ଶବ୍ଦ **eat** ର ଏକ ଧାତୁରୂପ

athlete /'æθli:t/ *noun* a person who is good at sports like running, jumping or throwing ଖେଳ କସରତରେ ନିପୁଣ ବ୍ୟକ୍ତି *Athletes from all over the world go to the Olympic Games.*

athlete

athletics /æθ'letɪks/ *noun* (*plural*) sports like running, jumping or throwing ଦୌଡ଼, ଡିଆଁ, କୁଦା, ଫୋପଡ଼ା ଇତ୍ୟାଦି ଖେଳ ।

atlas /'ætləs/ *noun* (*plural* **atlases**) a book of maps ମାନଚିତ୍ର *a world atlas*

ATM /'ei ti: ˌem/ *noun* a machine in which you insert a special kind of plastic card to take out money from your **bank** account ବ୍ୟାଙ୍କ ପ୍ରଦତ୍ତ ପ୍ଲାଷ୍ଟିକ୍ କାର୍ଡ଼ ପୂରାଇ ନିଜ ଟଙ୍କା ନେଇ ହେଉଥିବା ଯନ୍ତ୍ର

✪ ATM **Automated Teller Machine** ର ସଂକ୍ଷିପ୍ତ ନାମ।

atmosphere /ˈætməsfɪə(r)/ *noun* **1** (*no plural*) all the gases around the earth ବାୟୁମଣ୍ଡଳ **2** (*plural* **atmospheres**) the feeling that places or people give you ସ୍ଥାନ ବା ଲୋକ ସୃଷ୍ଟିକରୁଥିବା ମାନସିକ ବା ନୈତିକ ବାତାବରଣ *The atmosphere in the office was very friendly.*

atom /ˈætəm/ *noun* the smallest part into which an **element** can be divided ପରମାଣୁ; ରାସାୟନିକ ଉପାଦାନର କ୍ଷୁଦ୍ରତମ ଅଂଶ ଯାହା ରାସାୟନିକ ପ୍ରକ୍ରିୟାରେ ଭାଗ ନେଇପାରେ *Water is made of atoms of hydrogen and oxygen.*

atomic *adjective* of or about atoms ପରମାଣୁ ସମ୍ବନ୍ଧୀୟ, ପରମାଣୁଜାତ, ପାରମାଣବିକ *atomic energy*

attach /əˈtætʃ/ *verb* (**attaches**, **attaching**, **attached**) join or fix one thing to another thing ଯୋଡ଼ିବା, ସଂଲଗ୍ନ କରିବା; ଯୋଖିବା, ଲଗାଇବା *I attached the photo to the letter.*

be attached to somebody or **something** like somebody or something very much ଆଦର କରିବା, ଭଲ ପାଇବା *He's very attached to you.*

attack /əˈtæk/ *verb* (**attacks**, **attacking**, **attacked**) start fighting against somebody or start damaging something ଆକ୍ରମଣ କରିବା *The army attacked the town.*

attack *noun* the act of trying to hurt somebody or damage something ଆକ୍ରମଣ *There was an attack on the President.*

attempt /əˈtempt/ *verb* (**attempts**, **attempting**, **attempted**) try to do something (କିଛି କରିବାକୁ) ଚେଷ୍ଟା କରିବା *He attempted to swim from England to France.* ✪ ସାଧାରଣତଃ କଥାବାର୍ତ୍ତାରେ ଆମେ **try** ବ୍ୟବହାର କରିଥାଉଁ।

attempt *noun* ଉଦ୍ୟମ, ଚେଷ୍ଟା *She made no attempt to help me.*

attend /əˈtend/ *verb* (**attends**, **attending**, **attended**) go to or be at a place where something is happening ଉପସ୍ଥିତ ହେବା, ଯୋଗଦେବା *Did you attend the meeting?*

attendance /əˈtendəns/ *noun* the act of being present at a place ଉପସ୍ଥିତି

attention /əˈtenʃn/ *noun* (*no plural*) looking or listening carefully and with interest ଧ୍ୟାନ, ମନୋଯୋଗ *Can I have your attention, please?*

pay attention look or listen carefully ଧ୍ୟାନ ଦେବା, ମନୋଯୋଗ ପୂର୍ବକ ଦେଖିବା ବା ଶୁଣିବା *Please pay attention to what I'm saying.*

attentive /əˈtentɪv/ *adjective* if you are attentive, you watch, hear or think about something very carefully ମନୋଯୋଗୀ, ନିବିଷ୍ଟ, ସତର୍କ *an attentive audience*

attic /ˈætɪk/ *noun* the room or space under the roof of a house ଅାଟୁ ତଳେ ଥିବା ସ୍ଥାନ ବା କୋଠରି *My old clothes are in a box in the attic.*

attitude /ˈætɪtjuːd/ *noun* the way you think or feel about something ମନୋଭାବ, ଭାବଧାରା *What's your attitude to education?*

attract /əˈtrækt/ *verb* (**attracts**, **attracting**, **attracted**) **1** make somebody or something come nearer ଆକର୍ଷଣ କରିବା, ପାଖକୁ ଟାଣିନେବା *The birds were attracted by the smell of fish.* **2** make somebody like somebody or something (କାହାରିପ୍ରତି) ସ୍ପୃହା ଜାତ କରାଇବା

attraction /əˈtrækʃn/ *noun* **1** (*plural* **attractions**) something that people like and feel interested in ଭଲ ଲାଗିଲାପରି ସ୍ଥାନ ବା ପଦାର୍ଥ, ଆକର୍ଷଣ *Delhi has a lot of tourist attractions, like the Qutub Minar and the Red Fort.* **2** (*no plural*) liking somebody or something very much; being liked very much ସ୍ପୃହାଜାତ କରିବା ଶକ୍ତି ବା ଗୁଣ

attractive /əˈtræktɪv/ *adjective* pretty, nice to look at; interesting ସୁନ୍ଦର, ଆକର୍ଷଣୀୟ *She's very attractive.* ✪ ବିପରୀତ **unattractive**

auction /ˈɔːkʃn/ *noun* a sale where each thing is sold to the person who will give the most money for it ନିଲାମ

audience /ˈɔːdiəns/ *noun* all the people who are watching or listening to a film, play, concert or the television ଦର୍ଶକ, ଦେଖଣାହାରି

audio /ˈɔːdiəʊ/ *adjective* connected with the recording of sound ଶବ୍ଦ ବା ଧ୍ୱନି ଆଲେଖନ (ରେକର୍ଡ଼ିଂ) ବା ପୁନରୁତ୍ପାଦ ସମ୍ବନ୍ଧୀୟ *audio tapes*

audio-visual *adjective* using both sound and pictures ଉଭୟ ଦୃଶ୍ୟ ଓ ଧ୍ୱନି ବ୍ୟବହାର କରୁଥିବା, ଦୃଶ୍ୟ-ଶ୍ରାବ୍ୟ

August /ˈɔːgəst/ *noun* the eighth month of the year ଇଂରାଜୀ ବର୍ଷର ଅଷ୍ଟମ ମାସ

aunt /ɑːnt/ *noun* the sister of your mother or father, or the wife of your uncle ମାଉସୀ, ପିଉସୀ, ମାଇଁ ବା ଖୁଡ଼ି *Aunt Mary* ➪ ଚିତ୍ର ପାଇଁ **family** ଦେଖନ୍ତୁ।

auntie, **aunty** /ˈɑːnti/ *noun* aunt ମାଉସୀ, ପିଉସୀ, ଖୁଡ଼ି, ମାଇଁ

auspicious /ɔːˈspɪʃəs/ *adjective* something that is auspicious is likely to bring success in future ଶୁଭ, ଅନୁକୂଳ *an auspicious date for the wedding* ✪ ବିପରୀତ **inauspicious**

author /ˈɔːθə(r)/ *noun* a person who writes books or stories ଲେଖକ *Who is your favourite author?*

authority /ɔːˈθɒrəti/ *noun* **1** (*no plural*) the power to tell people what they must do କ୍ଷମତା, ପ୍ରଭୁତ୍ୱ *The police have the authority to stop cars.* **2** (*plural* **authorities**) a group of people who tell other people what they must do କ୍ଷମତା ପ୍ରାପ୍ତ ବ୍ୟକ୍ତି, ବ୍ୟକ୍ତିସମୂହ ବା ସଂସ୍ଥା *the city authorities.*

autobiography /ˌɔːtəbaɪˈɒgrəfi/ *noun* (*plural* **autobiographies**) a book that a person has written about his/her life ଆତ୍ମଜୀବନୀ, ଆତ୍ମଚରିତ ➪ **biography** ଦେଖନ୍ତୁ।

autograph /ˈɔːtəgrɑːf/ *noun* a famous person's signature, that he/she has written especially for you ବିଶିଷ୍ଟ ବ୍ୟକ୍ତି କାହାରି ପାଇଁ ବିଶେଷଭାବେ ଦେଇଥିବା ଦସ୍ତଖତ *He asked Sachin for his autograph.*

automatic /ɔːtəˈmætɪk/ *adjective* **1** if a machine is automatic, it can work by itself, without people controlling it ସ୍ୱୟଂଚାଳିତ, ସ୍ୱନିୟନ୍ତ୍ରିତ *an auto-*

matic washing machine **2** that you do without thinking ସ୍ୱତଃ ସ୍ଫୂର୍ତ୍ତ *Breathing is automatic.*

automatically *adverb* ସ୍ୱୟଂଚାଳିତ ଭାବରେ; ସ୍ୱତଃସ୍ଫୂର୍ତ୍ତ ଭାବରେ *The door closed automatically behind her.*

autumn /ˈɔːtəm/ *noun* the season between summer and winter ଶରତଋତୁ, ଗ୍ରୀଷ୍ମ ଓ ଶୀତର ମଧ୍ୟବର୍ତ୍ତୀ ଋତୁ

available /əˈveɪləbl/ *adjective* ready for you to use, have or see ସହଜରେ ମିଳୁଥିବା, ସହଜପ୍ରାପ୍ତ, ସୁଲଭ *I phoned the hotel to ask if there were any rooms available.*

avalanche /ˈævəlɑːnʃ/ *noun* a large mass of ice and snow that slides down a mountain ପାହାଡ଼ରୁ ଖସୁଥିବା ତୁଷାର ଅତଡ଼ା; ତୁଷାରସ୍ଖଳନ

avenue /ˈævənjuː/ *noun* a wide road or street often with trees on each side ପ୍ରଶସ୍ତ ରାସ୍ତା (ବିଶେଷତଃ ଦୁଇ ପଟରେ ଗଛ ଲାଗିଥିବା)

average /ˈævərɪdʒ/ *noun* **1** (*plural* **averages**) a word that you use when you work with numbers ହାରାହାରି *The average of 2, 3 and 7 is 4* (2 + 3 + 7 = 12, and 12 ÷ 3 = 4). **2** (*no plural*) what is ordinary or usual ସାଧାରଣ *Tipu's work at school is above average.*

avoid /əˈvɔɪd/ *verb* (**avoids**, **avoiding**, **avoided**) **1** stop something from happening; try not to do something ନକରିବା; ଘଟାଇ ନଦେବା, ବର୍ଜନ କରିବା *You should avoid eating too much chocolate.* **2** stay away or go away from somebody or something ଦୂରରେ ରହିବା *We crossed the road to avoid our teacher.*

awake /əˈweɪk/ *adjective* not sleeping ଶୋଇ ନଥିବା, ଜାଗ୍ରତ *The children are still awake.* ✪ ବିପରୀତ **asleep**

award[1] /əˈwɔːd/ *noun* a prize of money, etc. that you give to somebody who has done something very well ପୁରସ୍କାର *She won the award for best actress.*

award[2] /əˈwɔːd/ *verb* (**awards**, **awarding**, **awarded**) give a prize or money to somebody ପୁରସ୍କାର ଦେବା *He was awarded first prize in the painting competition.*

aware /əˈweə(r)/ *adjective* if you are aware of something, you know about it ଅବଗତ, ଜାଣିଥିବା *I was aware that somebody was watching me.* ✪ ବିପରୀତ **unaware**

away /əˈweɪ/ *adverb* **1** to or in another place ଦୂରକୁ, ଦୂରରେ; ଅନ୍ୟସ୍ଥାନରେ *She ran away.* ○ *He put his books away.* **2** from a place ଦୂରରେ *The sea is two kilometres away.*

awe /ɔː/ *noun* (*no plural*) a mixed feeling of respect, admiration and fear ଭକ୍ତି ଓ ଭୟ ମିଶ୍ରିତ ପ୍ରଶଂସା ଭାବ *We were in awe of the Principal.*

awful /ˈɔːfl/ *adjective* very bad ଖୁବ୍ ଖରାପ; କଷ୍ଟଦାୟକ *The pain was awful.* ○ *What awful weather!*

awfully /ˈɔːfli/ *adverb* very ଖୁବ୍, ଅତି ବେଶୀ *It was awfully hot.*

awkward /ˈɔːkwəd/ *adjective* **1** not comfortable ଅଖାଡୁଆ, ଅସ୍ୱସ୍ତିକର, ଅଡୁଆ, ଅସୁବିଧା *I felt awkward at the party because I didn't know anybody.* **2** difficult to do or use, for example କଷ୍ଟକର, ଅସୁବିଧା *This big box will be awkward to carry.*

axe /æks/ *noun* a tool for cutting wood କୁରାଢ଼ି, କୁଠାର *He chopped down the tree with an axe.*

axis /ˈæksɪs/ *noun* (*plural* **axes**) an imaginary line that passes through the centre of a circular spinning body ଅକ୍ଷ; ଏକ କଳ୍ପିତ ମଧ୍ୟରେଖା ଯାହା ଚାରିପଟେ କୌଣସି ଗୋଲକ ଘୂରିପାରେ *the axis of the earth*

axle /ˈæksl/ *noun* a bar that connects two wheels in a vehicle ଅକ୍ଷଦଣ୍ଡ, ଦୁଇଟି ଚକକୁ ଯୋଖି ରଖିଥିବା ଦଣ୍ଡ ବା ବାଡ଼ି

B b

baby /ˈbeɪbi/ *noun* (*plural* **babies**) a very young child ପିଲା, ସାନ ପିଲା, ଛୁଆ *She's going to have a baby.*

back[1] /bæk/ *noun* **1** the part that is behind or farthest from the front ପଛପଟ, ଦେହର ପଛଭାଗ, ପିଠି *The answers are at the back of the book.* ✪ ବିପରୀତ **front** **2** the part of a person or an animal between the neck and the bottom ମଣିଷ ବା ପଶୁର ପଛପଟ *He lay on his back and looked up at the sky.* ➪ ଚିତ୍ର ପାଇଁ **body** ଦେଖନ୍ତୁ ।

behind somebody's back when somebody is not there, so that they do not know about it କାହାର ଅନୁପସ୍ଥିତିରେ *Don't talk about Shruti behind her back.*

back[2] /bæk/ *adjective* away from the front ପଛ *the back door*

back[3] /bæk/ *adverb* **1** away from the front ପଛକୁ, ପଛପଟେ *I looked back to see if she was coming.* **2** in or to the place where somebody or something was before ପୂର୍ବସ୍ଥାନକୁ, ପୂର୍ବସ୍ଥାନରେ *I'll be back at six o'clock.* **3** as a way of returning or answering something ଉତ୍ତରରେ, ପ୍ରତ୍ୟୁତ୍ତରରେ *I wrote her a letter, but she didn't write back.*

back[4] /bæk/ *verb* (**backs, backing, backed**) **1** move backwards or make something move backwards ପଛକୁ ଯିବା, ପଛକୁ ନେବା *She backed the car out of the garage.* **2** say that you think somebody or something is right or the best ସମର୍ଥନ ଦେବା। *They're backing their school team.*

back out not do something that you promised or agreed to do ପ୍ରତିଶ୍ରୁତିରୁ ପଛେଇଯିବା *Rajiv backed out of the game, so we only had ten players.*

backbone /ˈbækbəʊn/ *noun* the line of bones down the back of your body ମେରୁଦଣ୍ଡ

background /ˈbækgraʊnd/ *noun* **1** the details about a person's family, education, etc. କୌଣସି ବ୍ୟକ୍ତିଙ୍କର ଶିକ୍ଷାଗତ ଯୋଗ୍ୟତା ଓ ସାମାଜିକ ଅବସ୍ଥା **2** the things at the back in a picture (ଚିତ୍ର ଇତ୍ୟାଦିର) ପୃଷ୍ଠଭୂମି *This is a photo of my house with the mountains in the background.*

backward /ˈbækwəd/ *adjective* **1** towards the back ପଛ ପଟକୁ, ପଛୁଆ, ପଶ୍ଚାଦ୍‌ବର୍ତ୍ତୀ *a backward step* **2** slow to learn or change ଧୀର ବିକାଶ କରୁଥିବା; ଅନୁନ୍ନତ *They live in a backward part of the country, where there is no electricity.*

backwards /ˈbækwədz/, **backward** /ˈbækwəd/ *adverb* **1** away from the front; towards the back ପଛକୁ, ପଛଆଡ଼କୁ *He fell backwards and hit the back of his head.* ✪ ବିପରୀତ **forwards, forward**[1] **1** **2** with the back or the end first ପଛପଟୁଆ, ଓଲଟାପଟୁ *If you say the alphabet backwards, you start with 'Z'.*

bacteria /bæk'tɪəriə/ *noun* (*plural*) very small things that live in air, water, soil, plants and animals. Some bacteria can make us ill ଜୀବାଣୁ (ପବନ, ପାଣି, ମାଟି, ଗଛ ଓ ଜୀବଙ୍କ ମଧ୍ୟରେ ରହୁଥିବା ଅତି ସୂକ୍ଷ୍ମ ତୃଣକୋଷ ରୋଗ ଯାହା ରୋଗ ସୃଷ୍ଟି କରିପାରେ)

bad /bæd/ *adjective* (**worse** /wɜːs/, **worst** /wɜːst/) **1** not good or nice ଖରାପ *The weather was very bad.* ○ *a bad smell* **2** serious ଗୁରୁତର; ମାରାତ୍ମକ *She had a bad accident.* **3** too old to be eaten; not fresh ପଚା, ସଢ଼ା (ଖାଦ୍ୟ) *This fish has gone bad.*

badge /bædʒ/ *noun* a small thing made of metal, plastic or cloth that you wear on your clothes. A badge can show that you belong to a school or club, for example, and it can have words or a picture on it ବ୍ୟାଜ୍; ପରିଚୟ ଫଳକ (ପରିଚୟ ଲେଖାଥିବା ମୋହର ପରି ଛୋଟ ଫଳକ ବା ସଂସ୍ଥାର ସଭ୍ୟ ଭାବରେ ପରିଚିତ ହେବାର ସଂକେତ ଥିବା ଫଳକ) *His jacket had his school badge on the pocket.*

badly /'bædli/ *adverb* (**worse** /wɜːs/, **worst** /wɜːst/) **1** in a bad way; not well ଖରାପ, ମନ୍ଦ ଭାବରେ *She played badly.* **2** very much ଅତିଶୟ ଭାବରେ, ଖୁବ୍‌ବେଶି *I badly need a holiday.* ✪ ବିପରୀତ **well[2] 1**

badminton /'bædmɪntən/ *noun* (*no plural*) a game for two or four players who try to hit a kind of light ball with feathers on it (called a **shuttlecock**) over a high net, using **rackets** ବ୍ୟାଡ୍‌ମିଣ୍ଟନ୍ (ଦୁଇ ବା ଚାରିଜଣଙ୍କ ମଧ୍ୟରେ ର୍‍ୟାକେଟ୍ ଓ ପରଲଗା ସଟ୍ଲକକ୍ ନେଇ ଖେଳାଯାଉଥିବା ଖେଳ)

bad-tempered *adjective* often angry ଚିଡ଼ିଚିଡ଼ା, ରାଗି *He's bad-tempered in the mornings.*

bag /bæg/ *noun* a thing made of cloth, paper, leather, etc. for holding and carrying things ବ୍ୟାଗ୍, ଥଳି, ମୁଣା *a large shopping bag* ➪ **handbag** ଦେଖନ୍ତୁ ।

baggage /'bægɪdʒ/ *noun* (*no plural*) bags and suitcases that you take with you when you travel କୁଆଡ଼େ ଯିବାବେଳେ ସାଙ୍ଗରେ ନିଆଯାଉଥିବା ଜିନିଷପତ୍ର *We put all our baggage in the car.*

bail[1] /beɪl/ *noun* **1** the amount of money paid to a court to allow a person who is under arrest to be set free until the trial ଜାମିନ୍‌ରେ ଅଦାଲତକୁ ଦିଆଯାଉଥିବା ଟଙ୍କା; ଜାମିନ୍ **2** (usually **bails**) in cricket, one of the two small pieces of wood that are placed over the **stumps** ବେଏଲ୍ (କ୍ରିକେଟ୍ ଖେଳରେ ଷ୍ଟମ୍ପ୍ ଉପରେ ରଖାଯାଉଥିବା ଗିଲି ପରି କାଠି)

bail[2] /beɪl/ *verb*

bail somebody out release someone or get someone released on bail

ଜାମିନ୍‌ରେ ମୁକୁଳାଇବା *His lawyer bailed him out.*

bait /beɪt/ *noun* (*no plural*) the food that is put on a hook or in a trap to catch fish, birds or animals ଥୋପ (ମାଛ ଇତ୍ୟାଦି ଧରିବା ପାଇଁ ଦିଆଯାଉଥିବା ଖାଦ୍ୟ ପ୍ରଲୋଭନ)

bake /beɪk/ *verb* (**bakes, baking, baked**) cook food in an oven ଅଭେନ୍ (ବନ୍ଦଚୁଲି) ରେ ଗରମ ଧାସରେ ସେକି ରାନ୍ଧିବା (କେକ୍ ଇତ୍ୟାଦି) *My brother baked a cake for my birthday.*

baker /ˈbeɪkə(r)/ *noun* a person who makes and sells bread and cakes ପାଉଁରୁଟି, କେକ୍ ଇତ୍ୟାଦି ତିଆରି କରି ବିକୁଥିବା ଲୋକ ✪ **Baker's** ବା **bakery** ପାଉଁରୁଟି, କେକ୍ ଇତ୍ୟାଦି ତିଆରି କରି ବିକୁଥିବା ଦୋକାନ।

balance[1] /ˈbæləns/ *verb* (**balances, balancing, balanced**) **1** make yourself or something stay without falling to one side or the other ଭାରସାମ୍ୟ ରଖିବା, ସମତୁଲ ରଖିବା; ପଡ଼ି ନଗଲା ପରି ରଖିବା *He balanced the bag on his head.* **2** give equal importance to two different things ଦୁଇଟି ବିଷୟ ମଧ୍ୟରେ ଭାରସାମ୍ୟ ରଖିବା *balance work and play*

balance[2] /ˈbæləns/ *noun* **1** (*no plural*) a steady position, with weight or amount equally distributed ଭାରସାମ୍ୟ (ଓଜନ, ପରିମାଣ ବା ସଂଖ୍ୟା ମଧ୍ୟରେ) *He tried to keep his balance while skating.* **2** (*no plural*) a position where two things are the same, so that one is not bigger or more important, for example ଭାରସାମ୍ୟ, ସନ୍ତୁଳନ *You need a balance between work and play.* ✪ ବିପରୀତ **imbalance 3** (*plural* **balances**) the amount of money you have or must pay after you have spent or paid some ଋଣ ଇତ୍ୟାଦି ସୁଝିଲା ପରେ ରହିଥିବା ବଳକା ଅର୍ଥ, ଅବଶିଷ୍ଟାଂଶ *The jacket costs Rs 500. You can pay Rs 100 now and the balance next week.* **4** (*plural* **balances**) an instrument for weighing things, with one plate hanging on each end of a bar ତରାଜୁ, ନିକିତି, ତୁଳାଦଣ୍ଡ

balanced diet *noun* meals that contain all the necessary nutrients that are required to keep your body healthy ଦେହପାଇଁ ସବୁ ଦରକାରୀ ଉପାଦାନ ଥିବା ଖାଦ୍ୟ, ସନ୍ତୁଳିତ ଆହାର

balcony /ˈbælkəni/ *noun* (*plural* **balconies**) a small place on the outside wall of a building, above the ground, where you can stand or sit ଘର ଉପର ମହଲାରୁ ବାହାରିଥିବା ଘେରା ବାରଣ୍ଡା

bald /bɔːld/ *adjective* with no hair or not much hair ଚନ୍ଦା, ଟାଙ୍ଗରା *My dad is going bald.*

bale /beɪl/ *noun* a large quantity of something that is tied tightly so that it can be transported ଗଣ୍ଠିଲି, ଗଣ୍ଠିରା, ବୋଝ୍, ବିଡ଼ା *a bale of cotton*

ball /bɔːl/ *noun* **1** a round thing that you use in games and sports ବଲ୍, ପେଣ୍ଡୁ, କନ୍ଦୁକ *Throw the ball to me.* **2** any round thing ଗୋଲିଆ ବା ବର୍ତ୍ତୁଳାକାର ପଦାର୍ଥ *a ball of string* **3** a big formal party where people dance ଆନୁଷ୍ଠାନିକ ନାଚ ପାଇଁ ଆୟୋଜିତ ବନ୍ଧୁମିଳନ

ballet /ˈbæleɪ/ *noun* a kind of dancing that tells a story with music but no words ସଙ୍ଗୀତ ସହ ଏକ ନିର୍ଦ୍ଦିଷ୍ଟ ଶୈଳୀରେ କରାଯାଉଥିବା ନାଟକୀୟ ନୃତ୍ୟ ଓ ଅଭିନୟ

balloon /bəˈluːn/ *noun* **1** a small thing like a bag made of coloured rubber. You fill it with air or gas to make it big and round ବେଲୁନ୍ **2** a very big bag that you fill with gas or air so that it can fly. People ride in a basket under it ଗରମ୍ ପବନ ବା ହାଲୁକା ବାଷ୍ପରେ ଭର୍ତ୍ତି ବଡ଼ ଗୋଲ୍ ମୁଣା ଯାହା ଉପରକୁ ଉଡ଼ିପାରେ ଓ ଯେଉଁଥିରେ ଲୋକ ବି ଉଡ଼ି ପାରନ୍ତି *I would like to go up in a balloon.*

ballpoint /ˈbɔːlpɔɪnt/ *noun* a pen that has a very small ball at the end or tip ବଲ୍ ପେନ୍, ବଲ୍ କଲମ

balm /bɑːm/ *noun* a usually pleasant-smelling cream or liquid that is applied on skin to relieve pain or make it softer ଆରୋଗ୍ୟଜନକ ସୁରଭିତ ମଲମ

bamboo /ˌbæmˈbuː/ *noun* a tall plant of the grass family that grows in hot countries ବାଉଁଶଗଛ, ବାଉଁଶ *Bamboo is used for making furniture.* ➪ ଚିତ୍ର ପାଇଁ **tree** ଦେଖନ୍ତୁ।

ban /bæn/ *verb* (**bans, banning, banned**) say that something must stop or must not happen ନିଷେଧ କରିବା, କଟକଣା ଜାରି କରିବା *The film was banned.*

ban *noun* ସିମାବନ୍ଧନ, ନିଷେଧ *There is a ban on smoking in public places.*

banana /bəˈnɑːnə/ *noun* a soft long yellow fruit କଦଳୀ, କଦଳୀଗଛ ➪ ଚିତ୍ର ପାଇଁ **fruit** ଦେଖନ୍ତୁ।

band /bænd/ *noun* **1** a thin flat piece of material that you put around something (ଶୋଭା ପାଇଁ ବା ଚିହ୍ନ ସ୍ୱରୂପ ବ୍ୟବହୃତ) ବନ୍ଧନୀ, ପଟି *I put a rubber band round the letters to keep them together.* **2** a group of people who do something together like play music or help other people କୌଣସି ଉଦ୍ଦେଶ୍ୟ ପାଇଁ ବା ସଙ୍ଗୀତ ପରିବେଷଣ ପାଇଁ ଏକ ଗୋଷ୍ଠୀ ବା ଦଳ *a rock band* ○ *a band of volunteers*

bandage /ˈbændɪdʒ/ *noun* a long piece of cloth that you put around a part of the body that is hurt କ୍ଷତ ଉପରେ ବନ୍ଧା ଯାଉଥିବା କନା ପଟି, ବ୍ୟାଣ୍ଡେଜ୍

bandit /ˈbændɪt/ *noun* a person who attacks and robs people who are travelling ଦସ୍ୟୁ, ଡକାୟତ, ଖଣ୍ଟ

bang[1] /bæŋ/ *noun* a sudden very loud noise ବାଡ଼େଇ ହେବାର ବା ବିସ୍ଫୋରଣର ଜୋର ଶବ୍ଦ *He shut the door with a bang.*

bang[2] /bæŋ/ *verb* (**bangs, banging, banged**) make a loud noise by hitting something hard or by closing something ଜୋର୍ ଶବ୍ଦ କରି କୌଣସି ଜନିଷ ବାଡ଼େଇବା ବା ବନ୍ଦ କରିବା *Don't bang the door!*

bangle /ˈbæŋɡl/ *noun* a large pretty ring of metal, glass or plastic that you wear around your wrist ଚୁଡ଼ି, କାଚ, ଖଡ୍ତୁ, ବଳା

banish /ˈbænɪʃ/ *verb* (**banishes, banishing, banished**) send someone out of their country as a punishment ନିର୍ବାସିତ କରିବା, ବିତାଡ଼ନ କରିବା, ଦେଶାନ୍ତର କରିବା *The men who* *killed the royal deer were banished from the kingdom.*

banisters /ˈbænɪstə(r)z/ *noun* (*plural*) a thing like a fence at the side of stairs that you hold on to when you go up or down ପାହାଚ ବାଡ଼

bank¹ /bæŋk/ *noun* **1** a place that keeps money safe for people ଲୋକଙ୍କ ଟଙ୍କା ନିରାପଦରେ ରଖୁଥିବା ସଂସ୍ଥା, ବ୍ୟାଙ୍କ *I've got Rs 3,000 in the bank.*

> ✪ ବ୍ୟାଙ୍କରେ **account** ଖୋଲିଲେ ଟଙ୍କା ଜମା **(deposit)** କରିପାରିବ ବା **(withdraw)** କାଢ଼ି ପାରିବ, ଆଉ ମଧ୍ୟ ବ୍ୟାଙ୍କରେ ଗୋଟିଏ ଦେଶର ଟଙ୍କାକୁ **exchange** କରି ଅନ୍ୟ ଦେଶର ମୁଦ୍ରା ପାଇପାରିବେ। ଏହା ବ୍ୟତୀତ ବ୍ୟାଙ୍କରୁ ଋଣ **(loan)** ମଧ୍ୟ ନେଇପାରିବେ।

bank² /bæŋk/ *noun* the land along the side of a river ନଈକୂଳର ଗଡ଼ାଣିଆଭୂମି *I climbed out of the boat onto the bank.*

banknote /ˈbæŋknəʊt/ *noun* a piece of paper money କାଗଜ ଟଙ୍କା, ନୋଟ୍ *These are German banknotes.*

bankrupt /ˈbæŋkrʌpt/ *adjective* not able to pay the money that you should pay to people ଦେଓ୍ୱାଳିଆ, ଋଣ ସୁଝିବାକୁ ଅକ୍ଷମ *His business went bankrupt.*

banner /ˈbænə(r)/ *noun* a long piece of cloth with a message on it. People carry banners to show what they think ମତାମତ ଲେଖାଯାଇଥିବା ଲମ୍ବା କନା *The banner said 'Stop the war'.*

banquet /ˈbæŋkwɪt/ *noun* a formal meal for many people ଆନୁଷ୍ଠାନିକ ଭୋଜି *a wedding banquet*

banyan /ˈbænjən/ *noun* an Indian tree with long branches that sends out shoots to the soil. These shoots form new roots and trunks that support the main trunk of the tree ବରଗଛ (ଯାହାର ଶାଖାରୁ ଓହଳ ବାହାରି ମାଟିରେ ପଶି ଚେର ଧରେ) ➪ ଚିତ୍ର ପାଇଁ **tree** ଦେଖନ୍ତୁ।

bar¹ /bɑː(r)/ *noun* **1** (*plural* **bars**) a piece of something hard ଖଣ୍ଡ *a bar of soap* ○ *a bar of chocolate* **2** (*plural* **bars**) a long piece of metal ବାଡ଼ି, ଦଣ୍ଡ *an iron bar* **3** (*plural* **bars**) a place where people can buy and have drinks and sometimes food ପାନୀୟ ଓ ଖାଦ୍ୟ ପରିବେଷଣ କରାଯାଉଥିବା ସ୍ଥାନ *There's a bar in the hotel.* **4 the bar** (*no plural*) the profession of a **barrister** ଓକିଲଗଣ, ଓକିଲାତି ବୃତ୍ତି *be called to the Bar*

bar² /bɑː(r)/ *verb* (**bars, barring, barred**) put something across a place so that people cannot pass ପ୍ରତିବନ୍ଧ ଦେବା, ଆଗୋଳିବା *A line of police barred the road.*

barbed wire *noun* (*no plural*) wire with a lot of sharp points on it. Some fences are made of barbed wire ତୀକ୍ଷ୍ଣ ମୁନ ଲଗାଯାଇଥିବା ତାର

barber /ˈbɑːbə(r)/ *noun* a person whose job is to cut men's hair ଭଣ୍ଡାରୀ, ବାରିକ, ନାପିତ *I went to the barber's to have my hair cut.*

bare /beə(r)/ *adjective* **1** without any covering ଖୋଲା, ଫୁଙ୍ଗୁଳା, ଅନାବୃତ *He had bare feet.* **2** empty ଖାଲି *a bare cupboard*

barefoot /ˈbeəfʊt/ *adjective, adverb* with no shoes or socks on your feet ଖାଲିପାଦ; ଖାଲି ପାଦରେ *The children ran barefoot along the beach.*

barely /ˈbeəli/ *adverb* almost not; only just ନହେଲା ପରି; ଅତି ଅଳ୍ପ *She barely ate anything.*

bargain[1] /ˈbɑːgən/ *noun* something that is cheaper than usual ଶସ୍ତା ଦରରେ କିଣିଥିବା ପଦାର୍ଥ *This dress was a bargain—it only cost Rs 100.*

bargain[2] /ˈbɑːgən/ *verb* (**bargains, bargaining, bargained**) talk with somebody about the right price for something ଦର କଷାକଷି କରିବା *I think he'll sell the car for less if you bargain with him.*

bark[1] /bɑːk/ *noun* (*no plural*) the substance that covers the outside of a tree ଗଛର ଛେଲି, ବକଳା

bark[2] /bɑːk/ *noun* a loud noise that a dog makes କୁକୁର ଭୁକା

bark *verb* (**barks, barking, barked**) make this noise ଭୁକିବା *The dog always barks at people it doesn't know.*

barley /ˈbɑːli/ *noun* (*no plural*) a plant that we use for food and for making beer and some other drinks ବାର୍ଲି ଗଛ ଓ ତାର ମଞ୍ଜି (ଯାହାକୁ ଖିରି କରି ଖିଆଯାଏ ଯେଉଁଥିରୁ ବିଅର ମଦ ତିଆରି କରାଯାଏ) ➪ ଚିତ୍ର ପାଇଁ **grain** ଦେଖନ୍ତୁ ।

barn /bɑːn/ *noun* a large building on a farm where you keep crops or animals ଶସ୍ୟ ଓ ପଶୁ ରଖାଯାଉଥିବା ବଡ଼ ଆକାରର କୋଠରି; ଶସ୍ୟାଗାର ବା ପଶୁଶାଳା

barracks /ˈbærəks/ *noun* (*plural*) a building or group of buildings where soldiers live ସେନାନିବାସ *the army barracks*

barrage /ˈbærɑːʒ/ *noun* **1** a wall built across a river to stop floods or store water ଆନିକଟ, ନଦୀର ଜଳରୋଧୀ ବନ୍ଧ **2** a large number of questions asked very quickly ଏକ ସମୟରେ ବହୁ ପ୍ରଶ୍ନର ଉତ୍ଥାପନ, ପ୍ରଶ୍ନବାଣ *a barrage of questions*

barrel /ˈbærəl/ *noun* **1** a big container for liquids, with round sides and flat ends ପିମ୍ପା, ପିପା *a barrel of oil* **2** the long metal part of a gun that a bullet goes out through ବନ୍ଧୁକର ନଳୀ

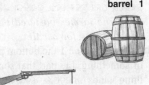

barren /ˈbærən/ *adjective* if a piece of land is barren, it is not good for growing crops ଅନୁର୍ବର, ନିଷ୍ଫଳ

barricade[1] /ˌbærɪˈkeɪd/ *noun* a thing or set of things placed across a road, etc. to stop people from passing through ପ୍ରତିବନ୍ଧ, ଲୋକଙ୍କ ଯିବା ଆସିବା ରୋକିବା ପାଇଁ ରାସ୍ତାଘାଟରେ ଲଗା- ଯାଉଥିବା ବାଡ଼

barricade[2] /ˌbærɪˈkeɪd/ *verb* (**barricades, barricading, barricaded**) stop people from going somewhere by setting up a barricade (ବାଡ଼ ବା ପ୍ରତିବନ୍ଧ ଲଗାଇ ଲୋକଙ୍କୁ) ଅବରୋଧ କରିବା *He barricaded the door to keep the reporters out.*

barrier /ˈbæriə(r)/ *noun* a fence or gate that stops you from going somewhere ବାଡ଼ ବା ଫାଟକ *You must show your ticket at the barrier before you get on the train.*

barrister /ˈbærɪstə(r)/ *noun* a lawyer ଓକିଲ

barrow /ˈbærəʊ/ *noun* a small cart that you can push or pull by hand ଦୁଇଚକିଆ ଠେଲା ଗାଡ଼ି

barter /ˈbɑːtə(r)/ *verb* (**barters, bartering, bartered**) when you barter, you exchange goods that you have for goods you do not have, without using money ଟଙ୍କା ବ୍ୟବହାର ନକରି ଦ୍ରବ୍ୟ ବଦଳରେ ଅନ୍ୟ ଦ୍ରବ୍ୟ ଦେଇ କିଣାବିକା କରିବା, ବାର୍ଟର୍ *The farmer bartered three sacks of rice for a calf.*

base[1] /beɪs/ *noun* **1** the bottom part of something; the part that something stands on ସବୁଠାରୁ ତଳେ ଥିବା ଅଂଶ; ମୂଳଦୁଆ, ପଉନ, ଭିତ୍ତି *The lamp has a flat base.* **2** the place that you start from and go back to ମୁଖ୍ୟସ୍ଥାନ *an army base*

base[2] /beɪs/ *verb* (**bases, basing, based**)

base something on something make something, using another thing as an important part ପ୍ରତିଷ୍ଠା କରିବା, ଆଧାରିତ କରିବା *The film is based on a true story.*

basement /ˈbeɪsmənt/ *noun* the rooms of a building that are below the level of the street ଘରର ସର୍ବନିମ୍ନ (ମାଟି ତଳେ ଥିବା) ମହଲା

basic /ˈbeɪsɪk/ *adjective* most important and necessary; simple ମୌଳିକ; ସାଧାରଣ *A person's basic needs are food, clothes and a place to live.*

basically *adverb* mostly; mainly ମୁଖ୍ୟତଃ *Basically I like her, but I don't always agree with what she says.*

basics /ˈbeɪsɪks/ *noun* (*no singular*) the most important details that you should know about something ମୌଳିକ ତଥ୍ୟ ବା ନୀତିନିୟମ *the basics of the game of chess*

basin /ˈbeɪsn/ *noun* **1** ⇨ **washbasin** ଦେଖନ୍ତୁ। **2** a large flat region where small rivers join a large one ନଦୀର ଅବବାହିକା *the Congo Basin*

basis /ˈbeɪsɪs/ *noun* (*plural* **bases** /ˈbeɪsiːz/) the most important part or idea, from which something grows ଭିତ୍ତି, ଆଧାର *Her notes formed the basis of a book.*

bask /bɑːsk/ *verb* (**basks, basking, basked**) sit or lie under the sun enjoying its warmth ଖରା ପୁଇଁବା, ସୂର୍ଯ୍ୟତାପ ଉପଭୋଗ କରିବା *The crocodiles were basking under the sun.*

basket /ˈbɑːskɪt/ *noun* a container made of thin sticks or thin pieces of plastic or metal, that you use for holding or carrying things ଟୋକେଇ, ବାଉଁଶିଆ, ପାଛିଆ, ଝୁଡ଼ି *a shopping basket* ➪ **waste-paper basket** ଦେଖନ୍ତୁ ।

basketball /ˈbɑːskɪtbɔːl/ *noun* (*no plural*) a game for two teams of five players who try to throw a ball so that it drops through a high ring into a net ବାସ୍କେଟ୍‌ବଲ୍ ଖେଳ ଯେଉଁଥିରେ ଦୁଇଟି ପାଞ୍ଚଜଣିଆ ଦଳ ଉଚ୍ଚସ୍ଥାପିତ ଗୋଲ ମଧ୍ୟଦେଇ ବଲ ଗଳାଇ ପଏଣ୍ଟ ପାଆନ୍ତି

bat[1] /bæt/ *noun* **1** an animal like a mouse with wings. Bats come out and fly at night ବାଦୁଡ଼ି **2** a piece of wood for hitting the ball in a game like cricket or table tennis କ୍ରିକେଟ୍ ବା ଟେବୁଲ୍ ଟେନିସ୍ ଖେଳରେ ବ୍ୟବହୃତ ବେଣ୍ଟଥିବା କାଠ ପଟା, ବ୍ୟାଟ୍

bat[1] **1**

bat[2] /bæt/ *verb* (**bats, batting, batted**) hit a ball with a bat in a game like cricket କ୍ରିକେଟ୍ ଖେଳରେ ବ୍ୟାଟ୍ ଧରି ବଲ୍‌କୁ ମାରିବା

batch /bætʃ/ *noun* (*plural* **batches**) a group of people or things ଦଳେ ବ୍ୟକ୍ତି ବା ପଦାର୍ଥ ସମୂହର ଏକ ଛେକ *a batch of students*

bath /bɑːθ/ *noun* the action of washing your body ଗାଧୁଆ *I had a bath this morning.*

bathtub *noun* a large thing that you fill with water and sit in to wash your body ଗାଧୁଆକୁଣ୍ଡ

bathe /beɪð/ *verb* (**bathes, bathing, bathed**) wash a part of your body carefully ଗାଧୋଇବା; ଧୋଇବା। *He bathed the cut on his finger.*

bathroom /ˈbɑːθruːm/ *noun* a room where you can wash and have a bath or shower ଗାଧୁଆଘର ➪ **toilet** ଦେଖନ୍ତୁ ।

baton /ˈbætɒn/ *noun* **1** a stick used by the leader of an orchestra to conduct music ବାଦ୍ୟବୃନ୍ଦର ପରିଚାଳକ ବ୍ୟବହାର କରୁଥିବା ଏକ ଛୋଟ ନିର୍ଦ୍ଦେଶକ ବାଡ଼ି **2** a short stick which a runner in a **relay race** passes on to the next runner in the team ରିଲେ ଦୌଡ଼ରେ ଦୌଡ଼ାଳି ନେଉଥିବା ଛୋଟ ବାଡ଼ି

batsman /ˈbætsmən/ *noun* (*plural* **batsmen**) the player who hits the ball in a game of cricket କ୍ରିକେଟ୍ ଖେଳରେ ବ୍ୟାଟିଂ କରୁଥିବା ଖେଳାଳି

batter /ˈbætə(r)/ *noun* **1** a thick mixture made by mixing flour, water and spices to coat vegetables, cheese or fish before frying them ପିଠୋଉ (ପରିବା, ଛେନା, ମାଛ ଇତ୍ୟାଦି ଏଥିରେ ବୁଡ଼ାଇ ଭାଜିବା ପାଇଁ ବା ପିଠା କରିବା ପାଇଁ) **2** a thick mixture of flour, sugar, eggs, etc. for making cakes ପିଠୋଉ (କେକ୍ କରିବା ପାଇଁ)

battery /ˈbætri/ *noun* (*plural* **batteries**) a thing that gives electricity. You put batteries inside things like torches and radios to make them work ବ୍ୟାଟେରି, ବିଦ୍ୟୁତ୍ ଧାରକ ଓ

ବିତରକ ଉପକରଣ *The car needs a new battery.*

battle /ˈbætl/ *noun* **1** a fight between armies in a war ଯୁଦ୍ଧ, ରଣ, ସମର *Who won the battle?* **2** trying very hard to fight something difficult କଷ୍ଟକର ସଂଘର୍ଷ

battle *verb* (**battles, battling, battled**) try very hard to do something difficult ସଂଘର୍ଷ କରିବା *The doctors battled to save her life.*

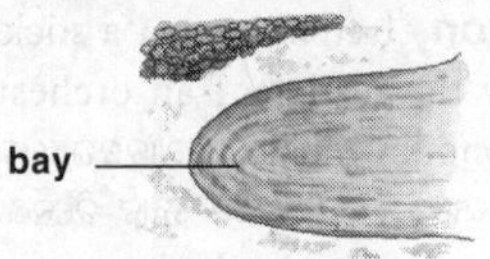

bay /beɪ/ *noun* (*plural* **bays**) a place where the land goes inwards and the sea fills the space ଉପସାଗର *the Bay of Bengal*

BC /ˌbiːˈsiː/ *abbreviation* BC in a date shows it was at a time before Christ was born ଖ୍ରୀଷ୍ଟପୂର୍ବ (ଯୀଶୁଙ୍କ ଜନ୍ମ ପୂର୍ବର ସମୟ) *Julius Caesar died in 44 BC.* ⇨ **AD** ଦେଖନ୍ତୁ।

be /bi/ *verb* **1** a word that you use when you name or describe somebody or something ଅଟେ; ଅଟ; ହେବା; ଥିବା *I'm Ravi.* ○ *Grass is green.* ○ *Are you hot?* ○ *Where were you yesterday?* **2** happen ଘଟିବା *Her birthday was in May.* **3** a word that you use with another verb ସହାୟକ କ୍ରିୟା *'What are you doing?' 'I am reading.'* **4** a word that you use with part of another verb to show that something happens to somebody or something ସହାୟକ କ୍ରିୟା *The house was built in 1910.*

 କ୍ରିୟା **be** ର ରୂପ

present tense		*short forms*	*negative short forms*
I	**am**	I'**m**	I'**m not**
you	**are**	you'**re**	you **aren't**
he/she/it	**is**	he'**s**/she'**s**/it'**s**	he/she/it **isn't**
we	**are**	we'**re**	we **aren't**
you	**are**	you'**re**	you **aren't**
they	**are**	they'**re**	they **aren't**
past tense			
I	**was**	*present participle* **being**	
you	**were**	*past participle* **been**	
he/she/it	**was**		
we	**were**		
you	**were**		
they	**were**		

beach /bi:tʃ/ *noun* (*plural* **beaches**) a piece of land next to the sea that is covered with sand or stones ବାଲୁକାମୟ ସମୁଦ୍ର ତଟ *a sandy beach*

bead /bi:d/ *noun* a small ball of wood, glass or plastic with a hole in the middle. Beads are put on a string to make a necklace କଣାଥିବା କଣ୍ଢି, ମାଳି, ଗୁଲି

beak /bi:k/ *noun* the hard pointed part of a bird's mouth ଥଣ୍ଟ, ଚଞ୍ଚୁ ➪ ଚିତ୍ର ପାଇଁ **bird** ଦେଖନ୍ତୁ।

beaker /'bi:kə(r)/ *noun* a glass cup having straight sides, used especially in scientific experiments ତରଳ ପଦାର୍ଥ ଢ଼ାଳି ପାରିବା ପାଇଁ ଚଞ୍ଚୁମୁଖ କାଚ ପାତ୍ର *Pour the water out from the beaker.*

beam¹ /bi:m/ *noun* **1** a long heavy piece of wood that holds up a roof or ceiling (କାଠ ବା ଲୁହାର) କଡ଼ି **2** a line of light ଆଲୋକ ରେଖା *sunbeams*

beam² /bi:m/ *verb* (**beams, beaming, beamed**) **1** smile very happily ଆନନ୍ଦପୂର୍ଣ୍ଣ ସ୍ମିତହାସ୍ୟ କରିବା **2** send out a beam of light, or radio or television signals ଆଲୋକରେଖା ପକାଇବା; ରେଡ଼ିଓ ବା ଟେଲିଭିଜନ୍ ତରଙ୍ଗ ବିକିରଣ କରିବା

bean /bi:n/ *noun* the long thin part of some plants, or the seeds inside it, that we use as food ଶିମ୍ବଛୁଇଁ, ଶିମ୍ବମଞ୍ଜି *French beans* ➪ ଚିତ୍ର ପାଇଁ **vegetable** ଦେଖନ୍ତୁ।

bear¹ /beə(r)/ *noun* a big wild animal with thick fur ଭାଲୁ, ଭଲ୍ଲୁକ ➪ **teddy bear** ବି ଦେଖନ୍ତୁ।

bear² /beə(r)/ *verb* (**bears, bearing, bore**/bɔ:(r)/, **has borne** /bɔ:n/) **1** accept something unpleasant without complaining ସହିଯିବା, ସହନ କରିବା *The pain was difficult to bear.* **2** hold somebody or something up so that they do not fall ବହନ କରିବା *The ice is too thin to bear your weight.*

can't bear something hate something ସହି ନପାରିବା; ଘୃଣା କରିବା *I can't bear this music.*

beard /bɪed/ *noun* the hair on a man's chin and cheeks ଦାଢ଼ି

beast /bi:st/ *noun* **1** a big animal ବଡ଼ ଜନ୍ତୁ ✪ ଆମେ ସାଧାରଣତଃ **animal** ଶବ୍ଦ ବ୍ୟବହାର କରୁ। **2** an unkind or cruel person ନିର୍ଦ୍ଦୟ ବା ନିଷ୍ଠୁର ବ୍ୟକ୍ତି

beat¹ /bi:t/ *noun* a sound that comes again and again (ସଙ୍ଗୀତର) ତାଳ; (ହୃଦୟର) ସ୍ପନ୍ଦନ *Can you feel the beat of your heart?*

beat² /bi:t/ *verb* (**beats, beating, beat, has beaten** /bi:tn/) **1** win a fight or game against a person or group of people ହରାଇବା, ପରାସ୍ତ କରିବା *Dev always beats me at tennis.* **2** hit somebody or something very hard many times ବାରମ୍ବାର ମାରିବା ବା ପିଟିବା *He was beating his drum very fast.* **3** make the same sound or movement many times ବାରମ୍ବାର ଏକା ପରି ଶବ୍ଦ କରିବା, ସ୍ପନ୍ଦିତ ହେବା *His heart was beating fast.* **4** mix food quickly with a fork, for example (ଅଣ୍ଡା ଇତ୍ୟାଦି) ଫେଣ୍ଟିବା, ଫେଣେଇବା *Beat the eggs and sugar together.*

beautiful /ˈbjuːtɪfl/ *adjective* very nice to see, hear or smell; lovely ସୁନ୍ଦର, ମନୋହର *Those flowers are beautiful.*

✪ ନାରୀ ବା ଝିଅଙ୍କୁ ବର୍ଣ୍ଣନା କଲାବେଳେ **beautiful** ଓ **pretty** ପ୍ରୟୋଗ କରାଯାଏ ଏବଂ ପୁରୁଷ ବା ପୁଅପିଲାଙ୍କୁ ବର୍ଣ୍ଣନା କଲାବେଳେ **handsome** ଓ **good-looking** କୁହାଯାଏ।

beautifully *adverb* ସୁନ୍ଦର ଭାବରେ *Rina sang beautifully.*

beauty /ˈbjuːti/ *noun* (*no plural*) being beautiful ସୌନ୍ଦର୍ଯ୍ୟ *She was a woman of great beauty.*

beauty parlour *noun* (*plural* **beauty parlours**) a place where you pay to get beauty treatments for your hair, skin, nails, etc. ଯେଉଁ ସ୍ଥାନରେ ପଇସା ଦେଇ ବାଳ, ତ୍ୱଚା, ନଖ ଇତ୍ୟାଦିର ପ୍ରସାଧନ ବା ସୌନ୍ଦର୍ଯ୍ୟ ବର୍ଦ୍ଧନ କରାଯାଏ

beaver

beaver /ˈbiːvə(r)/ *noun* an animal with a wide flat tail and strong teeth which it uses to make dams across rivers with wood and mud ବିଭର୍; ତୀକ୍ଷ୍ଣ ଦାନ୍ତ, କୋମଳ ମାଟିଆ ରଙ୍ଗର ଲୋମ ଓ ଚଉଡ଼ା ଲାଞ୍ଜଥିବା ଉଭୟଚର ମୂଷାଜାତୀୟ ପଶୁ ଯିଏ ଗଛକାଟି ନଈନାଳରେ ବନ୍ଧ ତିଆରି କରିପାରେ

because /bɪˈkɒz/ *conjunction* for the reason that କାରଣ, ଯେହେତୁ *He was angry because I was late.*

because of something as a result of something କୌଣସି କାରଣରୁ *We stayed at home because of the rain.*

become /bɪˈkʌm/ *verb* (**becomes, becoming, became** /bɪˈkeɪm/, **has become**) grow or change and begin to be something ହେବା; ଘଟିବା *She became a doctor in 2003.*

bed /bed/ *noun* **1** a thing that you sleep on ଖଟ *I was tired, so I went to bed.* ○ *The children are in bed.* **2** the bottom of a river or the sea ସମୁଦ୍ର, ନଈ ଇତ୍ୟାଦିର ଶଯ୍ୟା

make the bed put the covers on a bed so that it is tidy and ready for somebody to sleep on ଖଟ ବା ବିଛଣା ସଜାଡ଼ିବା

bedroom /ˈbedruːm/ *noun* a room where you sleep ଶୋଇଲାଘର, ଶୟନ କକ୍ଷ

bedtime /ˈbedtaɪm/ *noun* the time when you go to sleep every night ରାତିରେ ଶୋଇବା ସମୟ

bee /biː/ *noun* a small insect that flies and makes honey ମହୁମାଛି, ମଧୁମକ୍ଷିକା

beehive /ˈbiːhaɪv/ *noun* a box-like structure made for bees to live in ମହୁଫେଣା, ମଧୁଚକ୍ର; ମହୁମାଛି ରହିବା ପାଇଁ ତିଆରି ହୋଇଥିବା ବାକ୍ସ ପରି ଆଧାର

bee

been 1 ଶବ୍ଦ **be** ର ଏକ ଧାତୁରୂପ **2** ଶବ୍ଦ **go** ର ଏକ ଧାତୁରୂପ

have been to have gone to a place and come back ଯାଇଥିଲି, ଯାଇଥିଲ; ଯାଇଛି, ଯାଇଛି *Have you ever been to Assam?* ➪ **go** ଶବ୍ଦ ଠାରେ ଟିପ୍ପଣୀ ଦେଖନ୍ତୁ ।

beep /bi:p/ *noun* the short deep sound made by the horn of a vehicle or by some electronic machines ଇଲେକ୍ଟ୍ରନିକ୍ ଯନ୍ତ୍ର, ମଟର ହର୍ଣ୍ଣ ଇତ୍ୟାଦିର କ୍ଷଣିକ ତୀବ୍ର ଶବ୍ଦ *Please record your message after the beep.*

beer /bɪə(r)/ *noun* (*no plural*) an alcoholic drink made from grain ବିଅର୍; ଶସ୍ୟରୁ ତିଆରି ଏକ ପ୍ରକାର ହାଲୁକା ମଦ *three bottles of beer*

beetle /bi:tl/ *noun* an insect with hard wings and a shiny body ଗୋବର ପୋକ ପରି ପୋକ; ଭଅଁର ପରି ପୋକ ➪ ଚିତ୍ର ପାଇଁ **insect** ଦେଖନ୍ତୁ ।

beetroot /ˈbi:tru:t/ *noun* a round dark-red vegetable ବିଟ୍; ଏକ ଗୋଲିଆ ଗାଢ଼ଲାଲ୍ ପରିବା ➪ ଚିତ୍ର ପାଇଁ **vegetable** ଦେଖନ୍ତୁ ।

before[1] /bɪˈfɔ:(r)/ *preposition* **1** earlier than somebody or something ଆଗରୁ, ପୂର୍ବରୁ *He arrived before me.* **2** in front of somebody or something ସାମନାରେ, ସମ୍ମୁଖରେ *B comes before C in the alphabet.* ✪ ବିପରୀତ **after[1]**

before[2] /bɪˈfɔ:(r)/ *adverb* at an earlier time; in the past ଆଗରୁ, ପୂର୍ବରୁ *I've seen this film before.*

before[3] /bɪˈfɔ:(r)/ *conjunction* earlier than the time that ପୂର୍ବରୁ *I said goodbye before I left.*

beforehand /bɪˈfɔ:hænd/ *adverb* at an earlier time than something ପୂର୍ବରୁ, ଆଗରୁ *Tell me beforehand if you are going to be late.*

beg /beg/ *verb* (**begs, begging, begged**) **1** ask for money or food because you are very poor ମାଗିବା **2** ask somebody for something in a very strong way ଅନୁନୟ କରିବା; ଅନୁଗ୍ରହ ପ୍ରାର୍ଥନା କରିବା *She begged me to stay with her.* ○ *He begged for help.*

I beg your pardon 1 I am sorry କ୍ଷମା କରନ୍ତୁ *'You've taken my seat.' 'Oh, I beg your pardon.'* **2** What did you say? କ'ଣ କହିଲେ ?

beggar /ˈbegə(r)/ *noun* a person who asks other people for money or food ଭିକାରି, ଭିକ୍ଷୁକ

begin /bɪˈgɪn/ *verb* (**begins, beginning, began** /bɪˈgæn/, **has begun** /bɪˈgʌn/) start to do something or start to happen ଆରମ୍ଭ କରିବା; ଆରମ୍ଭ ହେବା *The film begins at 7.30 p.m.* ○ *I'm beginning to feel cold.*

beginner /bɪˈgɪnə(r)/ *noun* a person who is starting to do or learn something ନୂଆ କରି କିଛି କାମ ଆରମ୍ଭ କରୁଥିବା ବା ଶିଖୁଥିବା ବ୍ୟକ୍ତି; ଅନଭିଜ୍ଞ ବ୍ୟକ୍ତି; ଶିକ୍ଷାର୍ଥୀ

beginning /bɪˈgɪnɪŋ/ *noun* the time or place where something starts; the first part of something ଆରମ୍ଭ (ସ୍ଥାନ ବା ସମୟ); ପ୍ରଥମ ଭାଗ *I didn't see the beginning of the film.*

begun ଶବ୍ଦ **begin** ର ଏକ ଧାତୁରୂପ

behalf /bɪˈhɑ:f/ *noun*

on behalf of somebody, on somebody's behalf for somebody; in the place of somebody କାହା ପକ୍ଷରୁ କାହା ବଦଳରେ *Ms Mehta is away, so I am writing on her behalf.*

behave /bɪˈheɪv/ *verb* (**behaves, behaving, behaved**) do and say things in a certain way when you are with other people ଏକ ନିର୍ଦ୍ଦିଷ୍ଟ ଆଚରଣ ବା ବ୍ୟବହାର ପ୍ରଦର୍ଶନ କରିବା *They behaved very kindly towards me.* ✪ ବିପରୀତ **misbehave**

behave yourself be good; do and say the right things ଭଲ ବା ଉଚିତ୍ ଆଚରଣ ପ୍ରଦର୍ଶନ କର *Did the children behave themselves?*

behaviour /bɪˈheɪvjə(r)/ *noun* (*no plural*) the way you are; the way that you do and say things when you are with other people ଆଚରଣ, ବ୍ୟବହାର, ଚାଲିଚଳଣ *The teacher was pleased with the children's good behaviour.*

behind /bɪˈhaɪnd/ *preposition, adverb* **1** at or to the back of somebody or something ପଛରେ, ପଛକୁ *I hid behind the wall.* **2** in the place where you were before ପଛରେ; ଆଗରୁ ଯେଉଁଠି ଥିଲ ସେଠି *I got off the train but left my suitcase behind.*

behind the wall

behold /bɪˈhəʊld/ *verb* (**beholds, beholding, beheld** /bɪˈheld/) look at something rare or special ଦେଖିବା, ଚାହିଁବା *The view from the top of the mountain is a sight to behold.*

being[1] ଶବ୍ଦ **be** ର ଏକ ଧାତୁରୂପ

being[2] /ˈbiːɪŋ/ *noun* a living thing ଜୀବନ୍ତ ପ୍ରାଣୀ, ମଣିଷ ବା ପଶୁ *a human being*

belief /bɪˈliːf/ *noun* a sure feeling that something is true or real ବିଶ୍ୱାସ, ଦୃଢ଼ ଧାରଣା *his belief in God*

believe /bɪˈliːv/ *verb* (**believes, believing, believed**) feel sure that something is true or right; feel sure that what somebody says is true ସତ ବୋଲି ବିଶ୍ୱାସ କରିବା *Long ago, people believed that the earth was flat.*

believe in somebody or **something** feel sure that somebody or something is real ସତ ବୋଲି ଭାବିବା ବା ବିଶ୍ୱାସ କରିବା (କୌଣସି ବ୍ୟକ୍ତି ବା ପଦାର୍ଥକୁ) *Do you believe in ghosts?*

bell /bel/ *noun* a metal or electronic thing that makes a sound when something hits or touches it ଘଣ୍ଟି, ବେଲ୍ *I rang the bell and he answered the door.* ○ *The church bells were ringing.*

belong /bɪˈlɒŋ/ *verb* (**belongs, belonging, belonged**) have its right or usual place ଉପଯୁକ୍ତ ସ୍ଥାନରେ ରହିବା *That chair belongs in my room.*

belong to something be in a group, club, etc. (କୌଣସିସଂସ୍ଥା ଇତ୍ୟାଦିର) ସଭ୍ୟ ହେବା *She belongs to the tennis club.*

belongings /bɪˈlɒŋɪŋz/ *noun* (*no singular*) the things that you own ବ୍ୟକ୍ତିଙ୍କ ନିଜସ୍ୱ ଜିନିଷପତ୍ର *They lost all their belongings in the fire.*

beloved /bɪˈlʌvd/ *adjective* loved by someone ଅତିପ୍ରିୟ, ଅତି ଆଦରଣୀୟ *Shah Jahan built the Taj Mahal in memory of his beloved wife Mumtaz Mahal.*

below /bɪˈləʊ/ *preposition, adverb* **1** in or to a lower place than somebody or something ତଳରେ; ତଳକୁ; ତଳର *From the plane we could see the mountains below.* **2** less than a number or price (ସଂଖ୍ୟା ବା ଦରରେ) କମ୍ *The temperature was below zero.* ✪ ବିପରୀତ **above**

belt /belt/ *noun* a long piece of cloth or leather that you wear around your waist ବେଲ୍ଟ, କଟିବନ୍ଧ, କମରବନ୍ଧ ➪ **seat belt** ଦେଖନ୍ତୁ ।

bench /bentʃ/ *noun* (*plural* **benches**) a long seat made of wood or metal, for two or more people ବେଞ୍ଚ; ପଥର, ଧାତୁ ବା କାଠ ନିର୍ମିତ ଏକ ଲମ୍ବା ବସିବା ସ୍ଥାନ *a park bench*

bend[1] /bend/ *verb* (**bends, bending, bent** /bent/, **has bent**) become curved; make something that was straight into a curved shape ବଙ୍କେଇବା, ନଇଁବା *She couldn't bend the metal bar.*

bend down, bend over move your body forward and down ନଇଁବା *She bent down to put on her shoes.*

bend[2] /bend/ *noun* a part of a road or river that is not straight ବାଙ୍କ, ମୋଡ଼ (ନଈ, ରାସ୍ତା ଇତ୍ୟାଦିର) *Drive slowly—there's a bend in the road.*

beneath /biˈni:θ/ *preposition, adverb* in or to a lower place than somebody or something କୌଣସି ବ୍ୟକ୍ତି, କିମ୍ବା ବସ୍ତୁଠାରୁ ତଳେ, ନିମ୍ନ ସ୍ଥାନରେ; ତଳର, ତଳେଥିବା *From the tower, they looked down on the city beneath.* ✪ ଆମେ ସାଧାରଣତଃ **under** ବା **below** ବ୍ୟବହାର କରିଥାଉଁ ।

benefit /ˈbenɪfɪt/ *verb* (**benefits, benefiting** ବା **benefitting, benefited** ବା **benefitted**) be good or helpful in some way ଉପକାର କରିବା, ସାହାଯ୍ୟ କରିବା *Good education has benefited her.*

benefit *noun* something that is good or helpful ଉପକାର, ସୁବିଧା, ହିତ *What are the benefits of having a computer?*

bent ଶବ୍ଦ **bend**[1] ର ଏକ ଧାତୁରୂପ

berry /ˈberi/ *noun* (*plural* **berries**) a small soft fruit with seeds in it କୋଳି *a strawberry*

berth /bɜ:θ/ *noun* a bed for sleeping on a train or a ship ରେଳଗାଡ଼ି ବା ଜାହାଜରେ ଥିବା ଶୋଇବା ସ୍ଥାନ

beside /bɪˈsaɪd/ *preposition* at the side of somebody or something; next to somebody or something ପାଖରେ, ନିକଟରେ *Come and sit beside me.*

besides[1] /bɪˈsaɪdz/ *preposition* as well as somebody or something; if you do not count somebody or something ଆହୁରି ମଧ୍ୟ; ଏହା ଛଡ଼ା *There were four people in the room, besides me and Jayant.*

besides[2] /bɪˈsaɪdz/ *adverb* also ବ୍ୟତୀତ, ଅଧିକନ୍ତୁ *I don't like this shirt. Besides, it's too expensive.*

besiege /bɪˈsiːdʒ/ *verb* (**besieges**, **besieging**, **besieged**) surround a place in large numbers, especially to force the people inside to surrender ଅବରୋଧ କରିବା; ବେଷ୍ଟନ କରିବା, ଘେରିଯିବା *The enemy besieged the fort.*

best[1] /best/ *adjective* (**good** /gʊd/, **better** /ˈbetə(r)/, **best** /best/) most good ଶ୍ରେଷ୍ଠତମ, ସବୁଠୁଁ ଭଲ, ସର୍ବଶ୍ରେଷ୍ଠ, ସର୍ବୋତ୍ତମ *This is the best ice cream I have ever eaten!*

best[2] /best/ *adverb* **1** most well ସବୁଠୁଁ ଭଲ *I work best in the morning.* **2** more than all others; most ସବୁଠୁଁ, ସବୁଠାରୁ *Which picture do you like best?*

best[3] /best/ *noun* (*no plural*) the most good person or thing ସର୍ବଶ୍ରେଷ୍ଠ ବ୍ୟକ୍ତି ବା ପଦାର୍ଥ *Tina and Tara are good at tennis but Kiran is the best.*

all the best words that you use when you say goodbye to somebody, to wish them success ସର୍ବଶୁଭ ହେଉ (ବିଦାୟ ବେଳର ସଂଭାଷଣ)

bet /bet/ *verb* (**bets, betting, bet** ବା **betted, has bet** ବା **has betted**) say what you think will happen. If you are right, you win money, but if you are wrong, you lose money ବାଜିମାରିବା *I bet you Rs 50 that our team will win.*

bet *noun* ବାଜି *I lost the bet.*

betray /bɪˈtreɪ/ *verb* (**betrays, betraying, betrayed**) do something that harms somebody who trusts you ପ୍ରତାରଣା କରିବା, ଦଗାଦେବା *The guards betrayed the king and let the enemy into the castle.*

better /ˈbetə(r)/ *adjective* (**good** /gʊd/, **better** /ˈbetə(r)/, **best** /ˈbest/) **1** more good ଶ୍ରେଷ୍ଠତର *This book is better than that one.* **2** less ill ଟିକିଏ ଭଲ, ଅପେକ୍ଷାକୃତ ଭଲ *I was ill yesterday, but I feel better now.*

better *adverb* more well ଅପେକ୍ଷାକୃତ ଭଲ *You speak Tamil better than I do.*

had better ought to; should ବିଜ୍ଞତା ଦୃଷ୍ଟିରୁ; ଉଚିତ *You'd better leave now if you want to catch the train.*

between /bɪˈtwiːn/ *preposition* **1** in the space in the middle of two things or people (ଦୁଇଟି ପଦାର୍ଥ ବା ଲୋକ) ମଝିରେ *The letter B comes between A and C.* ○ *I sat between Sheila and Amit.* **2** after one time and before the next time (ଦୁଇଟି ସମୟର) ମଧ୍ୟରେ *I'll meet you between 4 and 4.30 p.m.* **3** more than one thing but less than another thing (ଦୁଇଟି ସଂଖ୍ୟା, ପରିମାଣ ଇତ୍ୟାଦି) ମଧ୍ୟରେ, ଭିତରେ *The meal will cost between Rs 100 and Rs 150.* **4** to and from two places (ଦୁଇସ୍ଥାନ)ମଧ୍ୟରେ *the flights between Delhi and Kolkata* **5** a word that you use when you compare two people or things ଭିନ୍ନତା *What is the difference between the two hotels?* ⇨ **among** ଶବ୍ଦଠାରେ ଟିପ୍ପଣୀ ଦେଖନ୍ତୁ।

beverage /ˈbevərɪdʒ/ *noun* any kind of drink other than water (ପାଣିଛଡ଼ା ଅନ୍ୟ ଯେକୌଣସି) ପାନୀୟ *alcoholic beverages*

beware /bɪˈweə(r)/ *verb*

beware of somebody or **something** be careful because somebody or something is dangerous ସାବଧାନ ରୁହ *Beware of the dog!*

bewildered /bɪˈwɪldə(r)d/ *adjective* if you are bewildered, you do not understand something or you do not know what to do ବିଭ୍ରାନ୍ତ, ବିଚଳିତ, କିଂକର୍ତ୍ତବ୍ୟବିମୂଢ଼ *He was bewildered by all the noises of the big city.*

bewildering /bɪˈwɪldərɪŋ/ *adjective* very confusing ବିଭ୍ରାନ୍ତିକର, ବାଉଳା କଲାପରି *There is a bewildering range of shampoos available now.*

beyond /bɪˈjɒnd/ *preposition, adverb* on the other side of something; further than something ଆର ପାଖରେ, ଅନ୍ୟପଟେ, ଦୂରରେ *There's a park beyond the school.*

bias /ˈbaɪəs/ *noun* a strong feeling for or against someone or something, that is not based on reason or facts ପକ୍ଷପାତ, କୌଣସି ବ୍ୟକ୍ତି ସପକ୍ଷ ବା ବିପକ୍ଷରେ ଅନାଧାରିତ ଭାବେ ଭଲ ବା ମନ୍ଦ ମତ ପୋଷଣ *My mother has a bias against men with long hair.*

biased /ˈbaɪəst/ *adjective* unfairly influenced in favour of or against someone or something ପକ୍ଷପାତୀ *biased news reports*

bib /bɪb/ *noun* a piece of cloth or plastic that a baby wears under its chin when it is eating ଶିଶୁର ଖାଇବା ବେଳେ ତା'ର ଛାତି ଉପରେ ଲଗାଯାଉଥିବା ବସ୍ତ୍ରଖଣ୍ଡ, ଜିପ୍

biceps /ˈbaɪseps/ *noun* (*plural* **biceps**) a large muscle at the front of the top part of the arm ଦ୍ୱିଶିରସ୍କ ପେଶୀ, କହୁଣି ଓ କାଖ ମଝିରେ ହାତର ଉପର ଭାଗର ପେଶୀ *bulging biceps*

bicycle /ˈbaɪsɪkl/ *noun* a machine with two wheels. You sit on a bicycle and push the pedals with your feet to make the wheels turn ସାଇକେଲ୍ *Can you ride a bicycle?* ✪ **Bicycle** ର ସଂକ୍ଷିପ୍ତ ଶବ୍ଦ ହେଲା **bike**। Bicycle ବଦଳରେ **cycle** ଶବ୍ଦ ମଧ୍ୟ ବ୍ୟବହୃତ ହୁଏ।

big /bɪg/ *adjective* (**bigger, biggest**) **1** not small; large ବଡ଼, ବୃହତ୍ *Delhi is a big city.* ○ *This shirt is too big for me.* ✪ ବିପରୀତ **small 1** **2** great or important ପ୍ରଧାନ, ବଡ଼ *a big problem* **3** older ବୟସ୍କ *Arti is my big sister.*

bike /baɪk/ *noun* a bicycle or a motorcycle ସାଇକେଲ୍ ବା ମଟରସାଇକେଲ୍

bill /bɪl/ *noun* a piece of paper that shows how much money you must pay for something (ଦ୍ରବ୍ୟ ବା ସେବା ପାଇଁ) ପାଉଣାର ଦାବି ପତ୍ର, ବିଲ୍ *Can I have the bill, please?*

billiards /ˈbɪliədz/ *noun* (*no plural*) a game for two people that is played around a long table. The two players try to hit the balls into pockets at the corners of the table with long sticks called cues ବିଲିୟାର୍ଡ୍ସ; ଦୁଇ ବ୍ୟକ୍ତିଙ୍କ ମଧ୍ୟରେ ଟେବୁଲ୍ ଉପରେ ଗୁଡ଼ିଏ ବଲ୍‌କୁ ବାଡ଼ିରେ ଖେଞ୍ଚି ଟେବୁଲ୍‌ର ଛ'ଟି ପକେଟ୍‌ରେ ପକାଇବା ଖେଳ।

billion /ˈbɪljən/ *number* one thousand million; 1,000,000,000 ଶହେକୋଟି, ହଜାରେ ନିୟୁତ *There are billions of people in the world.* ➪ **million** ଦେଖନ୍ତୁ।

bin /bɪn/ *noun* a container for storing things or throwing your rubbish into ବାଜେ ଜିନିଷ ରଖିବା ପାଇଁ ବଡ଼ ଡବା *I threw the empty bag into the bin.* ➪ **dustbin** ଦେଖନ୍ତୁ।

binary /ˈbaɪnəri/ *adjective* (a system of numbers in computers and mathematics) using only the digits 0 and 1 ଦ୍ୱିସଂଖ୍ୟକ; କେବଳ ୦ ଓ ୧ ବ୍ୟବହୃତ ହେଉଥିବା (ଗଣିତ ଓ କମ୍ପ୍ୟୁଟର୍ ପଦ୍ଧତି)

bind /baɪnd/ *verb* (**binds, binding, bound**/baʊnd/, **has bound**) tie string or rope round something to hold it firmly ବାନ୍ଧିବା *They bound the prisoner's arms and legs together.*

binoculars /bɪˈnɒkjələz/ *noun* (*no singular*) special glasses that you use to see things that are far away (ଦୂର ଜିନିଷ ଦେଖିବା ପାଇଁ) ଦୁଇ ଆଖିଆ ଦୂରବୀକ୍ଷଣ ଯନ୍ତ୍ର ➪ **telescope** ଦେଖନ୍ତୁ।

biodegradable /ˌbaɪəʊdɪˈgreɪdəbl/ *adjective* if something is biodegradable, it decays naturally and does not harm the environment ବ୍ୟାକ୍ଟେରିଆ, ଜୀବାଣୁ ବା ଅନ୍ୟ ଜୈବ ପଦାର୍ଥ ଦ୍ୱାରା ସଢ଼ି ଅବକର୍ଷିତ ହୋଇ ପାରୁଥିବା *Paper, dead leaves and kitchen waste are biodegradable.*

biogas /ˈbaɪəʊgæs/ *noun* (*no plural*) a gas produced by dead plants and rotting animal dung that can be used to cook food and light up homes ଜୈବବାଷ୍ପ, ସଢ଼ାଗଛ, ମଳ ଇତ୍ୟାଦି ବ୍ୟବହାର ଦ୍ୱାରା ପ୍ରସ୍ତୁତ ବାଷ୍ପ ଯାହାକୁ ଜଳାଇ ରାନ୍ଧି ହୁଏ ଓ ଘର ଆଲୋକିତ କରାଯାଏ

biography /baɪˈɒgrəfi/ *noun* (*plural* **biographies**) the story of a person's life written by another person ଜୀବନୀ, ଜୀବନ ବୃତ୍ତାନ୍ତ, ଜୀବନଚରିତ *the biography of Nehru by S. Gopal* ➪ **autobiography** ଦେଖନ୍ତୁ।

biology /baɪˈɒlədʒi/ *noun* (*no plural*) the study of the life of animals and plants ଜୀବ ବିଜ୍ଞାନ, ଉଦ୍ଭିଦ ଓ ପ୍ରାଣୀ ସମ୍ବନ୍ଧୀୟ ବିଜ୍ଞାନ *Biology is my favourite subject.* ➪ **botany** ଓ **zoology** ଦେଖନ୍ତୁ।

biosphere /ˈbaɪəʊsfɪə(r)/ *noun* the part of the earth's surface and the atmosphere where plants and animals can live ଜୀବମଣ୍ଡଳ, ପୃଥିବୀ ପୃଷ୍ଠର ଓ ବାୟୁମଣ୍ଡଳର ସେଇ ଅଂଶ ଯେଉଁଥିରେ ଗଛପତ୍ର ଓ ଜୀବଜନ୍ତୁ ବଞ୍ଚିପାରନ୍ତି

bird /bɜ:d/ *noun* an animal with feathers and wings ଚଢ଼େଇ, ପକ୍ଷୀ, ବିହଙ୍ଗ *Sparrows and parrots are birds.*

birth /bɜ:θ/ *noun* the time when a baby is born; being born ଜନ୍ମ; ଉତ୍ପତ୍ତି *the birth of a baby* ○ *What's your date of birth?*

give birth have a baby ପିଲାଜନ୍ମ କରିବା *My sister gave birth to her second child last week.*

birthday /ˈbɜ:θdeɪ/ *noun* (*plural* **birthdays**) the day each year that is the same as the date on which you were born ଜନ୍ମଦିନ *My birthday is on 2nd April.* ✪ ଆମେ କୌଣସି ବ୍ୟକ୍ତିର ଜନ୍ମଦିନରେ **Happy Birthday**! ବା **Many Happy Returns (of the day)**! କହି ଶୁଭକାମନା କରିଥାଉ ।

biscuit /ˈbɪskɪt/ *noun* a kind of small thin dry cake ବିସ୍କୁଟ୍ *a packet of biscuits*

bisect /baɪˈsekt/ *verb* (**bisects, bisecting, bisected**) divide something into two equal parts ସମବିଭାଜନ କରିବା, ଦୁଇ ସମାନ ଭାଗରେ ବିଭକ୍ତ କରିବା *A diametre bisects a circle into two equal parts.* ○ *This river bisects the city.*

bison /ˈbaɪsn/ *noun* a large hairy wild buffalo, found especially in North America and Europe ଉତ୍ତର ଆମେରିକା ଓ ୟୁରୋପର ପିଠିରେ କୁଜଥିବା ଲୋମଶ ବନ୍ୟ ମଇଁଷି

bit[1] /bɪt/ *noun* a small piece or amount of something ଛୋଟଖଣ୍ଡ, ଟୁକୁରା, ଅଳ୍ପ ପରିମାଣ *Some bits of the film were very funny.*

a bit 1 a little ଅଳ୍ପ, ସ୍ୱଳ୍ପ, ଟିକିଏ *You look a bit tired.* **2** a short time ଅଳ୍ପ ସମୟ *Let's wait a bit.*

bit[2] /bɪt/ *noun* the smallest unit of information that is used by a computer କମ୍ପ୍ୟୁଟର୍‌ରେ ବ୍ୟବହୃତ ସର୍ବନିମ୍ନ ପରିମାଣର ତଥ୍ୟ

bite[1] /baɪt/ *verb* (**bites, biting, bit** /bɪt/, **has bitten** /bɪtn/) **1** cut something with your teeth କାମୁଡ଼ିବା, କାମୁଡ଼ି ଛିଣ୍ଡାଇବା *The mice have bitten into the bread.* **2** if an insect or snake bites you, it hurts you by pushing a

birds

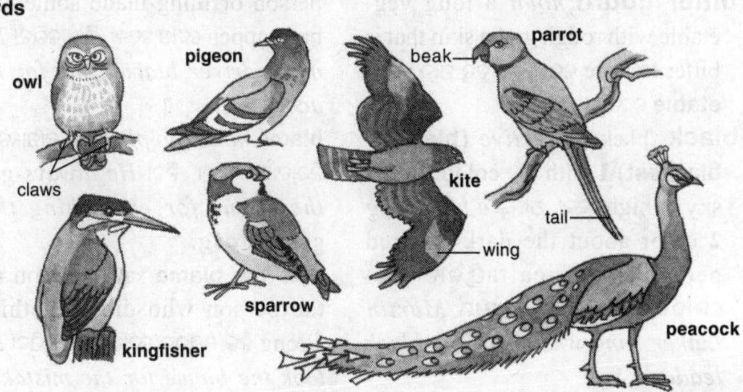

small sharp part into your skin ବିନ୍ଧିବା, କାମୁଡ଼ିବା *I've been bitten by mosquitoes.*

bite[2] /baɪt/ *noun* **1** a piece of food that you can put in your mouth ଖାଦ୍ୟର ଏକ ଗ୍ରାସ *He took a bite of his sandwich.* **2** a wound on your skin made by an insect or dog, for example ଦନ୍ତାଘାତ, କାମୁଡ଼ା *an insect bite*

bitter /ˈbɪtə(r)/ *adjective* **1** with a sharp unpleasant taste, like very strong coffee; not sweet ପିତା, କଷା, ତିକ୍ତ **2** very cold ଅତିଥଣ୍ଡା ବା ଶୀତ *a bitter wind* **3** angry and sad about something that has happened କ୍ରୋଧ ବା ଦୁଃଖ ଜାତ କରାଉଥିବା, ତିକ୍ତ *He felt very bitter about losing his job.*

bitterly *adverb* **1** in an unhappy and angry way କଟୁ ଭାବରେ, ଦୁଃଖ ଓ କ୍ରୋଧରେ, ତିକ୍ତ ଭାବରେ *'I don't want your help,' she replied bitterly.* **2** (about cold weather, wind, etc.) extremely ଅତିବେଶୀ (ଥଣ୍ଡା ପାଗ, ପବନ, ଇତ୍ୟାଦି) *a bitterly cold winter*

bitter gourd *noun* a long vegetable with rough green skin that is bitter to taste କଲରା ➪ ଚିତ୍ର ପାଇଁ **vegetable** ଦେଖନ୍ତୁ ।

black /blæk/ *adjective* (**blacker, blackest**) **1** with the colour of the sky at night କଳା, ଅନ୍ଧାର *a black dog* **2** of or about the dark-skinned people of Africa ଆଫ୍ରିକାର କଳା ଲୋକଙ୍କର ବା ତାଙ୍କ ସମ୍ବନ୍ଧୀୟ *Martin Luther King was a famous black leader.*

black *noun* **1** (*no plural*) the colour of the sky at night କଳା, ଅନ୍ଧାର *She was dressed in black.* **2** (*plural* **blacks**) a dark-skinned person from Africa ଆଫ୍ରିକୀୟ କଳା ଲୋକ

blackboard /ˈblækbɔːd/ *noun* a dark board that a teacher writes on with chalk କଳାପଟା, ବ୍ଲାକ୍‌ବୋର୍ଡ଼

blackmail /ˈblækmeɪl/ *noun* (*no plural*) saying that you will tell something bad about somebody if they do not give you money or do something for you ଗୁପ୍ତ କଥା କହିବାର ଭୟ ଦେଖାଇ ଅର୍ଥ ଆଦାୟ

blacksmith /ˈblæksmɪθ/ *noun* a person who makes things from iron କମାର, ଲୁହାର, ଲୌହକାର

blade /bleɪd/ *noun* **1** the flat sharp part of a knife, sword or another thing that cuts ଛୁରୀ, ଖଣ୍ଡା ଇତ୍ୟାଦିର ଫଳକ ବା ତୀକ୍ଷ୍ଣ ଅଂଶ **2** a flat thin leaf of grass ଘାସର ଏକ ପତ୍ର, କୁଶ *a blade of grass*

blame /bleɪm/ *verb* (**blames, blaming, blamed**) say that a certain person or thing made something bad happen ଦୋଷ ଦେବା, ନିନ୍ଦା କରିବା *The other driver blamed me for the accident.*

blame *noun* (*no plural*) ଦୋଷାରୋପ, ନିନ୍ଦାବାଦ, ଦୋଷ, ନିନ୍ଦା *He always gets the blame for everything that goes wrong.*

take the blame say that you are the person who did something wrong ନିଜ ଉପରକୁ ଦୋଷଟା ନେଇଯିବା *Ira took the blame for the mistake.*

blank /blæŋk/ *adjective* **1** with no writing, pictures or anything else on it ଅଲେଖା, ସାଦା *a blank piece of paper* **2** if your face is blank, it shows no feelings or understanding ଆଗ୍ରହ ବା ଅଭିବ୍ୟକ୍ତି ନଥିବା *I asked her a question, but she just gave me a blank look.*

blanket /ˈblæŋkɪt/ *noun* a thick cover that you use on a bed to keep yourself warm କମ୍ବଳ, ମୋଟା ଘୋଡ଼େଇ ହେଲା

blast /blɑːst/ *noun* **1** the action of a bomb exploding ବିସ୍ଫୋରଣ *Two people were killed in the blast.* **2** a sudden movement of air ବତାସ *a blast of cold air*

blast off *noun* (*no plural*) the time when a spacecraft leaves the ground କ୍ଷେପଣାସ୍ତ୍ର ବା ମହାକାଶଯାନର ଉତ୍‌କ୍ଷେପଣ

blaze /bleɪz/ *noun* a large strong fire ଉଜ୍ଜ୍ୱଳ ଅଗ୍ନିଶିଖା *The firefighter put out the blaze.*

blaze *verb* (**blazes, blazing, blazed**) burn strongly and brightly ପ୍ରଜ୍ୱଳିତ ହେବା *a blazing fire*

blazer /ˈbleɪzə(r)/ *noun* a jacket. Blazers sometimes show which school or club you belong to (ବିଦ୍ୟାଳୟ, କ୍ଲବ ଇତ୍ୟାଦିର) ସ୍ୱତନ୍ତ୍ର ପୋଷାକ ଭାବେ ପିନ୍ଧୁଥିବା କୋଟ୍ ➪ ଚିତ୍ର ପାଇଁ **badge** ଦେଖନ୍ତୁ ।

bleak /bliːk/ *adjective* (**bleaker, bleakest**) **1** cold and unpleasant ଥଣ୍ଡା ଓ ଧୂସର *It was a bleak winter's day.* **2** if a situation is bleak, it is in a very bad state and there is no hope of any improvement ନିରାଶାମୟ

bleat /bliːt/ *verb* (**bleats, bleating, bleated**) make the sound of a goat or a sheep ମେଣ୍ଢା, ଛେଳି ବା ବାଛୁରି ପରି ବୋବାଇବା

bleed /bliːd/ *verb* (**bleeds, bleeding, bled** /bled/, **has bled**) lose blood ରକ୍ତ ବହିବା *I have cut my hand and it's bleeding.*

blend /blend/ *verb* (**blends, blending, blended**) **1** mix ମିଶାଇବା, ଗୋଳେଇବା, ଫେଣ୍ଟିବା *Blend the sugar and the butter together.* **2** look or sound good together ମିଶିଯିବା, ଖାପ ଖାଇବା *These colours blend very well.*

bless /bles/ *verb* (**blesses, blessing, blessed**) ask for God's help and protection for somebody or something ଆଶିର୍ବାଦ ଦେବା *The priest blessed the young couple.*

blew ଶବ୍ଦ **blow**[1] ର ଏକ ଧାତୁରୂପ

blind /blaɪnd/ *adjective* not able to see ଅନ୍ଧ, ଚକ୍ଷୁହୀନ *The blind man had a dog to help him.*

the blind *noun* (*plural*) people who are blind ଅନ୍ଧ ଲୋକ

blindness *noun* (*no plural*) being blind ଅନ୍ଧତ୍ୱ, ଚକ୍ଷୁହୀନତା

blindfold /ˈblaɪndfəʊld/ *noun* a piece of cloth that you put over somebody's eyes so that they cannot see ଅନ୍ଧପୁଟୁଳି, ଆଖିପଟି

blink /blɪŋk/ *verb* (**blinks, blinking, blinked**) shut and open your eyes very quickly ଆଖି ମିଟିମିଟି କରିବା, ଆଖି ପିଛୁଳା ପକାଇବା

bliss /blɪs/ *noun* (*no plural*) perfect happiness, joy or enjoyment ପରମାନନ୍ଦ ବା ପରମ ସୁଖ *It was bliss to eat home-made food again.*
blissful *adjective* extremely happy or enjoyable ଆନନ୍ଦଦାୟକ, ସୁଖକର *She spent two blissful weeks away on holiday.*

blister /ˈblɪstə(r)/ *noun* a small painful swelling on your skin, that is full of liquid. Rubbing or burning can cause blisters ଫୋଟକା *My new shoes gave me blisters.*

blizzard /ˈblɪzəd/ *noun* a very bad storm with snow and strong winds ପ୍ରବଳ ତୁଷାର ଝଡ଼

blizzard

blob /blɒb/ *noun* a small drop of a thick liquid (ତରଳ ପଦାର୍ଥର) ଏକ ଟୋପା, ବୁନ୍ଦ *There are blobs of paint on the floor.*

block[1] /blɒk/ *noun* **1** a big heavy piece of something, with flat sides ଚଟକା କଡ଼ଥିବା ଭାରୀ ପଦାର୍ଥର ବଡ଼ ଖଣ୍ଡ *a block of wood* **2** a big building with a lot of offices or flats inside ବହୁ ବାସଗୃହ ବା ଅଫିସ୍ ଥିବା କୋଠା *a block of flats* **3** a thing that stops somebody or something from moving forward ପ୍ରତିବନ୍ଧ *The police have put up roadblocks around the town.*

block[2] /blɒk/ *verb* (**blocks, blocking, blocked**) stop somebody or something from moving forward ନିରୋଧ କରିବା, ରୋକିବା, ଓଗାଳିବା *A fallen tree blocked the road.*

blood /blʌd/ *noun* (*no plural*) the thick red liquid inside your body ରକ୍ତ, ଶୋଣିତ

bloody /ˈblʌdi / *adjective* (**bloodier, bloodiest**) **1** covered with blood ରକ୍ତାକ୍ତ, ରକ୍ତରଞ୍ଜିତ *a bloody nose* **2** with a lot of killing ବହୁ ଲୋକ ମରୁଥିବା *It was a bloody war.*

bloom /blu:m/ *verb* (**blooms, blooming, bloomed**) have flowers (ଫୁଲ) ପ୍ରସ୍ଫୁଟିତ ହେବା, ଫୁଟିବା *Roses are blooming now.*

blossom /ˈblɒsəm/ *verb* (**blossoms, blossoming, blossomed**) have flowers (ଫୁଲ) ପ୍ରସ୍ଫୁଟିତ ହେବା, ଫୁଟିବା *The gulmohar trees are blossoming now.*

blouse /blaʊz/ *noun* a piece of clothing like a shirt that a woman or girl wears on the top part of her body ବ୍ଲାଉଜ୍, କାଞ୍ଚୁଲା, ନାରୀମାନଙ୍କର ଛାତିପିନ୍ଧା ଜାମା

blow[1] /bləʊ/ *verb* (**blows, blowing, blew** /blu:/, **has blown** /bləʊn/) **1** when air or wind blows, it moves ପବନ ବହିବା *The wind was blowing from the sea.* **2** move something through the air ପବନ ସ୍ରୋତରେ ଉଡ଼ିଯିବା ବା ଉଡ଼ାଇନେବା *The wind blew my cap off.* **3** send air out from your mouth ଫୁଙ୍କିବା

blow up 1 explode; make something explode, for example with a bomb ବିସ୍ଫୋରଣ ହେବା ବା କରିବା *The plane blew up.* **2** fill something with air ପବନ ଭର୍ତ୍ତିକରିବା, ଫୁଲାଇବା *We blew up some balloons for the party.*

blow² /bləʊ/ *noun* hitting somebody or something hard; being hit hard ମାଡ଼, ପ୍ରହାର, ପାହାର *He felt a blow on the back of his head and he fell.*

blue /bluː/ *adjective* (**bluer, bluest**) having the colour of a clear sky on a sunny day ନୀଳ, ଆକାଶବର୍ଣ୍ଣର *He wore a blue shirt.* ○ *Her eyes are bright blue.*

blue *noun* ନୀଳବର୍ଣ୍ଣ, ଆକଶବର୍ଣ୍ଣ *She was dressed in blue.*

blunt /blʌnt/ *adjective* **1** with an edge or point that is not sharp ଦଣ୍ଡରା *This pencil is blunt.* ✪ ବିପରୀତ **sharp 1 2** if you are blunt, you say what you think in a way that is not polite ସ୍ପଷ୍ଟବାଦୀ *She was very blunt and told me that she didn't like my plan.*

blur /blɜː(r)/ *verb* (**blurs, blurring, blurred**) make something less clear ଅସ୍ପଷ୍ଟ କରିବା ବା ହେବା *If you move while you are taking a photo, it will get blurred.*

blush /blʌʃ/ *verb* (**blushes, blushing, blushed**) if you blush, your face suddenly becomes red because you are shy, for example ଲାଜରେ ମୁହଁ ଲାଲ୍ ହୋଇ ଯିବା, ଲଜ୍ଜିତ ହେବା *She blushed when he looked at her.*

boar /bɔː(r)/ *noun* **1** a male pig ଅଣ୍ଡିରା ଘୁସୁରି ବା ଶୂକର **2** a wild pig ବାରହା, ବନ୍ୟ ଶୂକର

board¹ /bɔːd/ *noun* **1** a long thin flat piece of wood ପଟା, କାଠପଟା *I nailed a board across the broken window.* **2** a flat piece of wood, for example, that you use for a special purpose କୌଣସି ନିର୍ଦ୍ଦିଷ୍ଟ କାମରେ ବ୍ୟବହୃତ ପଟା ବା କାଠ ଫଳକ *There is a list of names on the noticeboard.* ○ *a chessboard* ➪ **blackboard** ଓ **noticeboard** ବି ଦେଖନ୍ତୁ । **3** a group of people who control or run a company or an organization ସମିତି, କାର୍ଯ୍ୟପରିଚାଳକ ଗୋଷ୍ଠୀ *the board of directors*

on board on a ship or an aeroplane ଜାହାଜ ବା ଉଡ଼ାଜାହାଜରେ ଚଢ଼ିଥିବା *How many passengers are on board?*

board² /bɔːd/ *verb* (**boards, boarding, boarded**) get on a ship, bus, train or an aeroplane ଜାହାଜ, ଉଡ଼ାଜାହାଜ, ରେଳଗାଡ଼ି ବା ବସ୍‌ରେ ଚଢ଼ିବା *We boarded the plane at five o'clock in the morning.*

boarding school *noun* a school where children live during term time ଆବାସିକ ବିଦ୍ୟାଳୟ

boast /bəʊst/ *verb* (**boasts, boasting, boasted**) talk in a way that shows you are too proud of something you have or something you can do ନିଜର ଅଛି ବୋଲି ଗର୍ବ କରିବା, ବଡ଼େଇ କରିବା *He boasted that he was the fastest runner in the school.*

boat /bəʊt/ *noun* a small ship for travelling on water ଡଙ୍ଗା, ନୌକା, ଛୋଟ ଜାହାଜ *a fishing boat*

body /ˈbɒdi/ *noun* **1** (*plural* **bodies**) all of a person or an animal, but not the mind ଦେହ, ଶରୀର *Arms, legs, hands and feet are all parts of the human body.* **2** (*plural* **bodies**) all of a person or animal, but not the legs, arms or head ଦେହର ଗଣ୍ଡି (ହାତ, ଗୋଡ଼, ମୁଣ୍ଡ ଛାଡ଼ି) **3** (*plural* **bodies**) a dead person ମଲା ମଣିଷ, ମୃତ ଶରୀର *The police found a body in the river.* **4** (*no plural*) the main or central part of something ଯେକୌଣସି ପଦାର୍ଥର ମୁଖ୍ୟ ଅଂଶ *the body of the car* **5** (*plural* **bodies**) a group of people working together for a particular job ଗୋଷ୍ଠୀ *the governing body of the school*

the human body

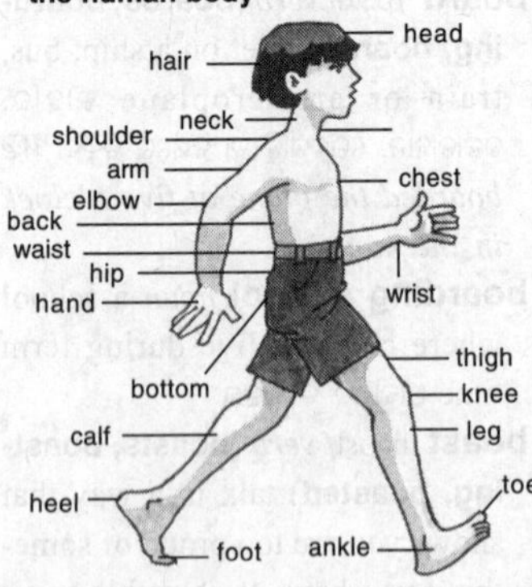

bodyguard /ˈbɒdiɡɑːd/ *noun* a person or group of people whose job is to keep an important person safe ଦେହରକ୍ଷୀ *All the President's bodyguards carry guns.*

boil[1] /bɔɪl/ *verb* (**boils, boiling, boiled**) **1** when a liquid boils, it becomes very hot and makes steam and bubbles (ତରଳ ପଦାର୍ଥ) ଫୁଟେଇବା *Water boils at 100°C.* **2** cook something in very hot water ସିଝାଇବା *Boil the rice in a pan.*

boil[2] /bɔɪl/ *noun* a painful swelling under the skin ବଥ, ବ୍ରଣ

boiling /ˈbɔɪlɪŋ/ *adjective* very hot ତାତି ଫୁଟୁଥିବା, ବହୁତ ଗରମ *Add the tea leaves to the boiling water.*

boiling point *noun* the temperature at which a liquid boils ସ୍ଫୁଟନାଙ୍କ, ତରଳ ପଦାର୍ଥର ବାଷ୍ପହେବା ଉତ୍ତାପ *The boiling point of water is 100°C.*

bold /bəʊld/ *adjective* (**bolder, boldest**) brave and not afraid ସାହସୀ, ନିର୍ଭୀକ *It was very bold of you to ask for more money.*

boldly *adverb* ନିର୍ଭୀକଭାବରେ *He boldly said that he disagreed.*

bolt /bəʊlt/ *noun* **1** a piece of metal that you move across to lock a door କିଳିଣୀ **2** a thick metal pin that you use with another piece of metal (called a **nut**) to fix things together ମୁଦିଆ ପେଞ୍ଚ, ନଟ୍‌ରେ ଲାଗୁଥିବା ➪ ଚିତ୍ର ପାଇଁ **nut** ଦେଖନ୍ତୁ।

bolt *verb* (**bolts, bolting, bolted**) lock a door by putting a bolt across it କିଳିଣୀ ବନ୍ଦ କରି ଦୁଆର କିଳିବା

bomb /bɒm/ *noun* a thing that explodes and hurts people or damages things ବୋମା *Aircraft dropped bombs on the city.*

bomb *verb* (**bombs, bombing, bombed**) attack people or a place with bombs ବୋମା ପକାଇ ଆକ୍ରମଣ କରିବା *The city was bombed during the war.*

bond /bɒnd/ *noun* something that unites two or more people together ବନ୍ଧନ, ସଂଯୋଗ, ସଂଯୁକ୍ତ କରିବା ପଦାର୍ଥ ବା ଶକ୍ତି *a bond of friendship*

bone /bəʊn/ *noun* one of the hard white parts inside the body of a person or an animal ହାଡ଼, ଅସ୍ଥି *She broke a bone in her foot.* ○ *This fish has a lot of bones in it.*

bone marrow *noun* a soft substance found inside the bones ହାଡ଼ର ମଜ୍ଜା, ଶସ

bonfire /ˈbɒnfaɪə(r)/ *noun* a big fire that you make outside ଅଗ୍ନିଉତ୍ସବ, ଖୋଲା ଜାଗାରେ ଜଳା ଯାଉଥିବା ନିଆଁ

bonnet /ˈbɒnɪt/ *noun* **1** the front part of a car that covers the engine ମଟରଗାଡ଼ି ଇଞ୍ଜିନ୍‌ର ଆବରଣ ବା ଢ଼ାଙ୍କୁଣୀ ➪ ଚିତ୍ର ପାଇଁ **car** ଦେଖନ୍ତୁ। **2** a soft hat that you tie under your chin ଶିଶୁ ବା ସ୍ତ୍ରୀଲୋକଙ୍କର ଓଠ ତଳେ ଫିତାବନ୍ଧା ନରମ ଟୋପି

bonus /ˈbəʊnəs/ *noun* (*plural* **bonuses**) **1** an amount of money or reward that is received in addition to the salary ବୋନସ୍, ଅଧିଲଭ୍ୟ ଟଙ୍କା (ଦରମା ଛଡ଼ା) **2** something extra that you receive which was not expected ଅଧିକା ପାଉଣା *Free lunch is a bonus of the new job.*

book[1] /bʊk/ *noun* a thing that you read or write in, that has lots of pieces of paper joined together inside a cover ବହି, ପୁସ୍ତକ; ଖାତା *I'm reading a book by Ruskin Bond.* ○ *an exercise book*

book[2] /bʊk/ *verb* (**books, booking, booked**) ask somebody to keep something for you so that you can use it later (ପରେ ବ୍ୟବହାର କରିବା) ସଂରକ୍ଷଣ କରିବା *We booked a room for two nights at a hotel in Shimla.*

booking /ˈbʊkɪŋ/ *noun* asking somebody to keep something for you so that you can use it later ଆଗୁଆ ସଂରକ୍ଷଣ, ଆରକ୍ଷଣ *When did you make your booking?*

booking-office *noun* a place where you buy tickets ଟିକଟ କିଣିବା ସ୍ଥାନ

booklet /ˈbʊklət/ *noun* a small thin book ଛୋଟ ସରୁ ବହି

bookshop /ˈbʊkʃɒp/ *noun* a shop that sells books ବହିଦୋକାନ

boom /buːm/ *verb* (**booms, booming, boomed**) make a loud deep sound ଗୁରୁ ଗମ୍ଭୀର ଧ୍ୱନି କରିବା *We heard the guns booming in the distance.*

boost /buːst/ *verb* (**boosts, boosting, boosted**) increase the power or value of something ଶକ୍ତି, ମୂଲ୍ୟ, ଖ୍ୟାତି ଇତ୍ୟାଦି ବୃଦ୍ଧି କରିବା *The success of the film boosted the actor's career.*

boost *noun* ବୃଦ୍ଧି *His career got a boost last year.*

boot /buːt/ *noun* **1** a shoe that covers your foot and ankle and sometimes part of your leg ବଳାଗଣ୍ଠି ପର୍ଯ୍ୟନ୍ତ ପାଦ ଆବରଣ କରୁଥିବା ଜୋତା, ବୁଟ୍ **2** the part of a car where you can put bags and boxes, usually at the back ମଟରଗାଡ଼ିର ସାଧାରଣତଃ ପଛପଟେଥିବା ଜିନିଷ ରଖିବା ସ୍ଥାନ ➪ ଚିତ୍ର ପାଇଁ **car** ଦେଖନ୍ତୁ।

booty /ˈbu:ti / *noun* (*no plural*) things of value stolen by thieves or captured by soldiers in a time of war ଲୁଣ୍ଠିତ ଧନ ବା ଯୁଦ୍ଧଲବ୍ଧ ଦ୍ରବ୍ୟ

border /ˈbɔ:də(r)/ *noun* **1** a line between two countries ଦୁଇ ଦେଶ ମଧ୍ୟରେ ଥିବା ସୀମାରେଖା *You need a passport to cross the border.* **2** a line along the edge of something ଧଡ଼ି *a white tablecloth with a blue border*

bore[1] ଶବ୍ଦ **bear**[2] ର ଅନ୍ୟ ଧାତୁରୂପ

bore[2] /bɔ:(r)/ *verb* (**bores, boring, bored**) if something bores you, it makes you feel tired because it is not interesting ଇଆଡୁ ସିଆଡୁ ଗପି ବିରକ୍ତ କରିବା *He bores everyone with his long stories.*

bored *adjective* not interested; unhappy because you have nothing interesting to do ବିରକ୍ତ ଓ ଅନୁରକ୍ତ *She had a bored expression on her face.*

boring *adjective* not interesting ବିରକ୍ତିକର *That lesson was boring!*

bore[3] /bɔ:(r)/ *verb* (**bores, boring, bored**) make a thin round hole in something ଘୁରୁଥିବା ଯନ୍ତ୍ର ସାହାଯ୍ୟରେ ବା ଶୁଣ୍ଢ ଇତ୍ୟାଦିରେ ସରୁଗୋଲ କଣା କରିବା *The insects bored holes into the wood.*

born /bɔ:n/ *adjective*

be born start your life ଜନ୍ମ ହେବା *I was born in 1995.*

borne ଶବ୍ଦ **bear**[2] ର ଏକ ଧାତୁରୂପ

borrow /ˈbɒrəʊ/ *verb* (**borrows, borrowing, borrowed**) take and use something that you will give back after a short time ଧାର ନେବା, ଉଧାରରେ ଆଣିବା *I borrowed some books from the library.*

boss /bɒs/ *noun* (*plural* **bosses**) a person who controls a place where people work and tells people what they must do ମାଲିକ, ହାକିମ, ନିଯୋକ୍ତା, ପରିଚାଳକ *I asked my boss for a day's leave.*

botany /ˈbɒtəni/ *noun* (*no plural*) the study of plants ଉଦ୍ଭିଦବିଦ୍ୟା ➪ **biology** ଓ **zoology** ବି ଦେଖନ୍ତୁ।

both /bəʊθ/ *adjective*, *pronoun* the two; not only one but also the other ଉଭୟ, ଦୁହେଁ, ଦୁଇଟି *Hold it in both hands.* ○ *Both her brothers are doctors.*

both *adverb* ଉଭୟ, ଦୁହେଁ *We were both tired.*

both ... and not only ... but also କେବଳ (ଏହା) ନୁହେଁ ଆହୁରି ମଧ୍ୟ *She is both rich and intelligent.*

bother /ˈbɒðə(r)/ *verb* (**bothers, bothering, bothered**) **1** worry somebody; stop somebody from doing something, for example thinking, working or sleeping ହଇରାଣ କରିବା, ବିରକ୍ତ କରିବା *Is this music bothering you?* **2** spend extra time and energy on doing something ଅଧିକ ସମୟ ବା ଶକ୍ତି ଖଟେଇବା *Don't bother to dust the shelf—I'll do it later.*

bottle /ˈbɒtl/ *noun* a tall round glass or plastic container for liquids, with a narrow part at the top ବୋତଲ *They drank two bottles of water.*

bottom /ˈbɒtəm/ *noun* **1** the lowest part of something (କୌଣସି ପଦାର୍ଥର) ତଳଭାଗ ବା ଅଂଶ *They live at the bottom of the hill.* ○ *Look at the picture at the bottom of the page.* ✪ ବିପରୀତ **top**[1] **2** the part of your body that you sit on ପିଚା, ନିତମ୍ବ *She fell on her bottom.* ➪ ଚିତ୍ର ପାଇଁ **body** ଦେଖନ୍ତୁ ।

bottom *adjective* lowest ସବୁଠାରୁ ତଳେ ଥିବା *Put the book on the bottom shelf.* ✪ ବିପରୀତ **top**[2]

bough /baʊ/ *noun* a large branch of a tree ଗଛର ବଡ଼ ଡାଳ ବା ଶାଖା

bought ଶବ୍ଦ **buy** ର ଏକ ଧାତୁରୂପ

boulder /ˈbəʊldə(r)/ *noun* a very big rock ବଡ଼ ପଥର ଖଣ୍ଡ

bounce /baʊns/ *verb* (**bounces, bouncing, bounced**) **1** when a ball bounces, it moves away quickly after it hits something hard ପ୍ରତିକ୍ଷିପ୍ତ ହେବା, କେଉଁଥିରେ ବାଜି ଲେଉଟି ଆସିବା (ବଲ୍ ପରି) *The ball bounced off the wall.* **2** make a ball do this ବଲ୍‌କୁ ଏହିପରି ଡିଆଁଇବା *The boy was bouncing a basketball.*

bound[1] ଶବ୍ଦ **bind** ର ଏକ ଧାତୁରୂପ

bound[2] /baʊnd/ *adjective* **bound to** certain to do something ନିଶ୍ଚିତ ଭାବେ *She works very hard, so she is bound to pass the exam.*

bound[3] /baʊnd/ *adjective*

bound for going to a place (କୌଣସି) ଆଡ଼କୁ ଯାଉଥିବା *This ship is bound for Goa.*

bound[4] /baʊnd/ *verb* (**bounds, bounding, bounded**) jump, or run with small jumps ଡେଇଁ ଡେଇଁ ଦୌଡ଼ିବା *The dog bounded up the steps.*

boundary /ˈbaʊndri/ *noun* (*plural* **boundaries**) a line between two places ସୀମା, ପରିସୀମା, ସରହଦ *This fence is the boundary between the two gardens.*

bouquet /buˈkeɪ/ *noun* a bunch of flowers that you give or get as a present ପୁଷ୍ପଗୁଚ୍ଛ, ଫୁଲତୋଡ଼ା *She gave me a bouquet of roses.*

bow[1] /baʊ/ *verb* (**bows, bowing, bowed**) bend your head or body forward to show respect ସମ୍ମାନାର୍ଥେ ମୁଣ୍ଡ ନୁଆଁଇବା, ନତମସ୍ତକ ହେବା *The actors bowed at the end of the play.*

bow *noun* ନତମସ୍ତକ *He gave a bow and left the room.*

bow[2] /bəʊ/ *noun* a kind of knot with two round parts, that you use when you are tying shoes, ribbons, etc. ପ୍ରଜାପତିର ମେଲା ଡେଣା ପରି ବନ୍ଧା ଯାଇଥିବା ଜୋତା ଫିତା, ରିବନ୍ ଇତ୍ୟାଦି

bow[3] /bəʊ/ *noun* a curved piece of wood with a string between the two ends. You use a bow to send **arrows** through the air ଧନୁ ➪ ଚିତ୍ର ପାଇଁ **arrow** ଦେଖନ୍ତୁ ।

bowl[1] /bəʊl/ *noun* a deep round dish or container କଂସା, ଗିନା, ତାଟିଆ *a sugar bowl* ○ *a bowl of soup*

bowl[2] /bəʊl/ *verb* (**bowls, bowling, bowled**) throw a ball so that somebody can hit it in a game of cricket କ୍ରିକେଟ୍ ଖେଳରେ ବ୍ୟାଟ୍ସମ୍ୟାନ୍ ଖେଳିବା ପାଇଁ ବଲ ନିକ୍ଷେପ କରିବା

bowler /ˈbəʊlə(r)/ *noun* a player who throws the ball to a batsman in cricket କ୍ରିକେଟ୍ ଖେଳରେ ବ୍ୟାଟ୍ସମ୍ୟାନ୍ ଖେଳିବା ପାଇଁ ବଲ୍ ନିକ୍ଷେପ କରୁଥିବା ଖେଳାଳୀ

box[1] /bɒks/ *noun* (*plural* **boxes**) a container with straight sides. A box often has a lid ବାକ୍ସ, ପେଡ଼ି *Put the books in a cardboard box.* ○ *a box of chocolates* ○ *a box of matches*

box[2] /bɒks/ *verb* (**boxes, boxing, boxed**) fight with your hands, wearing thick gloves, as a sport ମୁଷ୍ଟିଯୁଦ୍ଧ କରିବା

boxer *noun* a person who boxes as a sport ମୁଷ୍ଟିଯୁଦ୍ଧ, ବକ୍ସର୍

boxing *noun* (*no plural*) the sport of fighting with your hands, wearing thick gloves ହାତମୁଣା (ଗ୍ଲୋଭ୍ସ) ପିନ୍ଧି କରାଯାଉଥିବା ମୁଷ୍ଟି ଯୁଦ୍ଧ

boy /bɔɪ/ *noun* (*plural* **boys**) a male child; a young man ବାଳକ

boycott /ˈbɔɪkɒt/ *verb* (**boycotts, boycotting, boycotted**) refuse to buy, use or take part in something because you do not approve of it ବାସନ୍ଦ କରିବା, ସମ୍ପର୍କ କାଟି ଦେବା *During the freedom struggle, many Indians boycotted foreign goods.*

boycott *noun* (*no plural*) ବାସନ୍ଦ *the boycott of foreign goods*

Boy Scout

Boy Scout *noun* a member of a special club for boys ବୟ୍ ସ୍କାଉଟ୍, ବାଳକମାନଙ୍କର ଏକ ବିଶେଷ ସଂସ୍ଥାର ସଦସ୍ୟ

brace /breɪs/ *noun* a connected set of wires fixed to the teeth to make them straight ଦାନ୍ତ ସଳଖିବା ପାଇଁ ବ୍ୟବହୃତ ଏକ ତାର ଢାଞ୍ଚା

bracelet /ˈbreɪslət/ *noun* a pretty piece of metal, wood or plastic that you wear around your wrist ଚୁଡ଼ି, କଙ୍କଣ, ବଳା; ହାତ ଚେନ୍

brackets /ˈbrækɪts/ *noun* (*plural*) marks like these ( ), [ ] that you use in writing; ( ), [ ] ବନ୍ଧନୀ ଚିହ୍ନ

Braille /breɪl/ *noun* (*no plural*) a special printing system for the blind people in which words, etc. are printed as raised dots that can be read by touching them ଅନ୍ଧଲୋକଙ୍କ ପାଇଁ ଲେଖିବା ଓ ଛାପିବା ପଦ୍ଧତି ଯେଉଁଥିରେ ଫୁଟୁଫୁଟିକିଆ ଉଦ୍‌ଗତ ଅକ୍ଷର ଛୁଇଁ ପଢ଼ାଯାଏ ✪ ଫରାସୀ ଶିକ୍ଷାବିତ **Louis Braille** (ଲୁଇ ବ୍ରେଏଲ୍) ଏହି **Braille** (ବ୍ରେଏଲ୍) ପଦ୍ଧତି ଉଦ୍ଭାବନ କରିଥିଲେ। ସେ ତିନି ବର୍ଷ ବୟସରୁ ଅନ୍ଧ ହୋଇ ଯାଇଥିଲେ।

brain /breɪn/ *noun* the part inside the head of a person or an animal that controls the body, thoughts and feelings ମସ୍ତିଷ୍କ, ମଗଜ

brake /breɪk/ *noun* a thing that you move to make a car, bicycle, etc. go slower or stop ବ୍ରେକ୍, ଗାଡ଼ି ଇତ୍ୟାଦିର ଗତି କମାଇବା ବା ରୋକିବା ଉପକରଣ *I put my foot on the brake.*

brake *verb* (**brakes, braking, braked**) use a brake ବ୍ରେକ୍ ମାରିବା *The driver braked suddenly when a goat ran onto the road.*

branch /brɑ:ntʃ/ *noun* (*plural* **branches**) **1** one of the parts of a tree that grow out from the **trunk** ଗଛର ଶାଖା ବା ଡାଳ ➪ ଚିତ୍ର ପାଇଁ **plant** ଓ **tree** ଦେଖନ୍ତୁ। **2** an office or a shop that is part of a big company (ବ୍ୟାଙ୍କ, ବ୍ୟବସାୟ ପ୍ରତିଷ୍ଠାନ ଇତ୍ୟାଦିର) ସ୍ଥାନୀୟ କାର୍ଯ୍ୟାଳୟ *This bank has branches all over the country.*

brand /brænd/ *noun* the name of a thing you buy that a certain company makes ନିର୍ଦ୍ଦିଷ୍ଟ ଉତ୍ପାଦନର ଦ୍ରବ୍ୟ *'Nescafe' is a well-known brand of coffee.*

brass /brɑ:s/ *noun* (*no plural*) a yellow metal made from copper and zinc ପିତ୍ତଳ

brave /breɪv/ *adjective* (**braver, bravest**) ready to do dangerous or difficult things without fear ସାହସୀ, ନିର୍ଭୀକ *It was brave of her to go into the burning building.*

bravely *adverb* ସାହସର ସହିତ *He fought bravely in the war.*

bravery *noun* (*no plural*) being brave ସାହସ, ବୀରତ୍ୱ

bray /breɪ/ *noun* the loud harsh sound made by a donkey ଗଧରଡ଼ି

bray *verb* (**brays, braying, brayed**) make the sound made by a donkey ଗଧରଡ଼ି କରିବା

bread /bred/ *noun* (*no plural*) food made from flour and baked in an oven ପାଉଁରୁଟି *I bought a loaf of bread.* ○ *a slice of bread and butter*

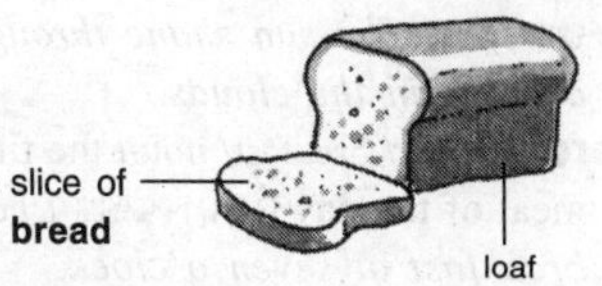

breadth /bredθ/ *noun* how far it is from one side of something to the other ପ୍ରସ୍ଥ, ଓସାର, ଚଉଡ଼ା ✪ ଏହାର ବିଶେଷଣ ହେଲା **broad**।

break¹ /breɪk/ *verb* (**breaks, breaking, broke** /brəʊk/, **has broken** /'brəʊkən/) **1** make something go into pieces by dropping it or hitting it, for example ଭାଙ୍ଗିବା, ଖଣ୍ଡ ଖଣ୍ଡ କରିବା *He broke the window.* **2** go into pieces by falling or hitting, for example ଭାଙ୍ଗିଯିବା, ଖଣ୍ଡଖଣ୍ଡ ହେବା। *I dropped the cup and it broke.*

break down if a machine or car breaks down, it stops working ଅକାମି ହେବା, ଅଚଳ ହେଇଯିବା *We were late because our car broke down.*

break off take away a piece of something by breaking it ଛିନ୍ନ କରିବା, ଛିଣ୍ଡାଇବା *He broke off a piece of chocolate for me.*

break out 1 start suddenly ହଠାତ୍ ଆରମ୍ଭ ହେବା *A fire broke out last night.* **2** escape from a place like a prison କାରାବାସରୁ ଖସି ପଳାଇବା *Four prisoners broke out of the jail last night.*

break² /breɪk/ *noun* **1** a short time when you stop doing something ବିରାମ, ବିରତି *We worked all day without a break.* **2** a place where something opens or has broken

ଫାଙ୍କ, ଫାଟ *The sun shone through a break in the clouds.*

breakfast /ˈbrekfəst/ *noun* the first meal of the day ସକାଳ ଜଳଖିଆ *I had breakfast at seven o'clock.*

breakthrough /ˈbreɪkθruː/ *noun* an important development ବଡ଼ ରକମର ଅଗ୍ରଗତି ବା ଉଦ୍ଭାବନ

breast /brest/ *noun* **1** one of the two soft round parts of a woman's body that can give milk ସ୍ତନ **2** the front part of a bird's body ଚଢ଼େଇର ଛାତିପଟ

breath /breθ/ *noun* taking in or letting out air through your nose and mouth ନିଃଶ୍ୱାସ ଓ ପ୍ରଶ୍ୱାସ *Take a deep breath.*

hold your breath stop breathing for a short time ନିଃଶ୍ୱାସ ପ୍ରଶ୍ୱାସ ରୋକିବା

out of breath breathing very quickly ଧଇଁସଇଁ *She was out of breath after climbing the stairs.*

breathe /briːð/ *verb* (**breathes, breathing, breathed**) take in and let out air through your nose and mouth ନିଃଶ୍ୱାସ ଛାଡ଼ିବା ଓ ପ୍ରଶ୍ୱାସ ନେବା *The doctor told me to breathe in and then breathe out again slowly.*

breathless /ˈbreθləs/ *adjective* if you are breathless, you are breathing quickly or with difficulty ରୁଦ୍ଧଶ୍ୱାସ, ଧଇଁସଇଁ

breed[1] /briːd/ *verb* (**breeds, breeding, bred** /bred/, **has bred**) make young animals ପଶୁପକ୍ଷୀ ଜନ୍ମ କରିବା *Birds breed in the spring.*

breed[2] /briːd/ *noun* a particular variety of similar animals ଏକା ପ୍ରକାର ପଶୁ ବା ଉଦ୍ଭିଦ

breeze /briːz/ *noun* a light wind ମୃଦୁ ବା ହାଲ୍କା ପବନ

brick /brɪk/ *noun* a small block made of hard clay, with two long sides and two short sides. Bricks are used for building ଇଟା *a brick wall*

bride /braɪd/ *noun* a woman on the day of her wedding କନ୍ୟା, ବଧୂ

bridegroom /ˈbraɪdgruːm/ *noun* a man on the day of his wedding ବର, ବରପାତ୍ର

bridge /brɪdʒ/ *noun* a thing that is built over a road, railway or river so that people, trains or cars can cross it ପୋଲ, ସେତୁ *We walked over the bridge.*

bridge

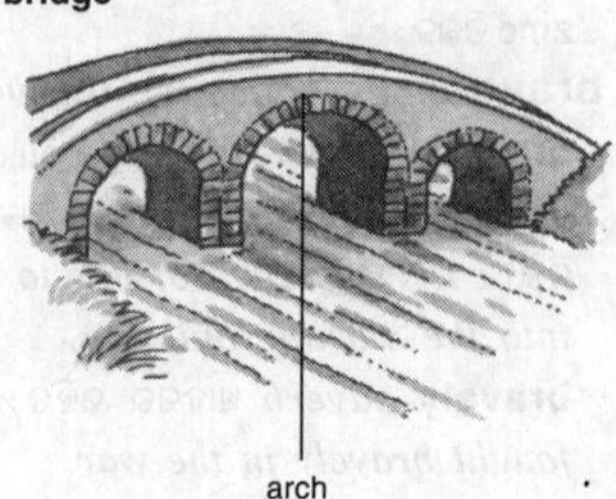

brief /briːf/ *adjective* (**briefer, briefest**) short or quick ସ୍ୱଳ୍ପକାଳର *a brief telephone call*

in brief in a few words ସଂକ୍ଷେପରେ *Here is the news in brief.*

briefly *adverb* ଅଳ୍ପ ସମୟ ପାଇଁ *We stopped work briefly for lunch.*

briefcase /ˈbriːfkeɪs/ *noun* a flat case for carrying papers in ଦଲିଲ୍‌ପତ୍ର ରଖିବା ବାକ୍ସ, ବ୍ରିଫ୍‌କେଶ୍

brigade /brɪˈgeɪd/ *noun* **1** a group of soldiers that forms a unit in the army (ତିନି ବ୍ୟାଟାଲିଅନ୍ ବିଶିଷ୍ଟ) ସୈନ୍ୟଦଳ **2** a group of people in uniform working together for something ଏକ ନିର୍ଦ୍ଦିଷ୍ଟ କାମ ପାଇଁ ସଂଗଠିତ ବ୍ୟକ୍ତିବୃନ୍ଦ *the fire brigade*

bright /braɪt/ *adjective* (**brighter, brightest**) **1** with a lot of light ଉଜ୍ଜ୍ୱଳ *It was a bright sunny day.* **2** with a strong colour ଉଜ୍ଜ୍ୱଳ ରଙ୍ଗର *a bright yellow shirt* **3** clever ଚାଲାକ୍, ଚତୁର, ବୁଦ୍ଧିମାନ *She is the brightest child in the class.*

brightly *adverb* ଉଜ୍ଜ୍ୱଳ ଭାବରେ *brightly coloured clothes*

brightness *noun* (*no plural*) ଉଜ୍ଜ୍ୱଳତା, ଓଜଲ୍ୟ *the brightness of the sun*

brighten /ˈbraɪtn/, **brighten up** *verb* (**brightens, brightening, brightened**) become brighter or happier; make something brighter ଉଜ୍ଜ୍ୱଳ କରିବା ବା ହେବା *These flowers will brighten up the room.*

brilliant /ˈbrɪliənt/ *adjective* **1** with a lot of light; very bright ଉଜ୍ଜ୍ୱଳ, ଦୀପ୍ତିମାନ୍ *brilliant sunshine* **2** very intelligent ଅତି ବୁଦ୍ଧିମାନ୍ *a brilliant student* **3** very good; excellent ଚମତ୍କାର, ଅତି ଭଲ *The film was brilliant!*

brilliantly *adverb* ଚମତ୍କାର ଭାବରେ *She played brilliantly.*

brim /brɪm/ *noun* the edge around the top of something like a cup, bowl or glass ପାତ୍ରର ଉପର ଧାର, ମଙ୍ଗ ବା ଫନ୍ଦ

bring /brɪŋ/ *verb* (**brings, bringing, brought** /brɔːt/, **has brought**) **1** come to a place with somebody or something ଆଣିବା *Can I bring a friend to the party?* ○ *Can you bring me a glass of water?* **2** make something happen ପ୍ରବର୍ତ୍ତିତ କରିବା *Money doesn't always bring happiness.*

bring back return something ପଛକୁ ଆଣିବା *I have brought back the book you lent me.*

brinjal /ˈbrɪndʒl/ *noun* a vegetable with shiny purple skin and soft white flesh with a lot of small seeds ବାଇଗଣ ➪ ଚିତ୍ର ପାଇଁ **vegetable** ଦେଖନ୍ତୁ।

brisk /brɪsk/ *adjective* (**brisker, briskest**) quick and using a lot of energy ଚଞ୍ଚଳ, ଶକ୍ତି ସମ୍ପନ୍ନ *We went for a brisk walk.*

bristle /ˈbrɪsl/ *noun* a short thick hair like the hair on a brush ଛୋଟ ଟାଣ ଲୋମ (ଯାହା ବ୍ରସ୍‌ରେ ବ୍ୟବହୃତ ହୁଏ) ➪ ଚିତ୍ର ପାଇଁ **brush** ଦେଖନ୍ତୁ।

brittle /ˈbrɪtl/ *adjective* something that is brittle is hard but breaks easily ଟାଣ ଓ ଭଙ୍ଗୁର *Her nails are very brittle.*

broad /brɔːd/ *adjective* (**broader, broadest**) **1** large from one side to the other; wide ଓସାରିଆ, ଚଉଡ଼ା, ପ୍ରଶସ୍ତ *a broad river* ✪ ଏହାର ବିଶେଷ୍ୟ ହେଲା **breadth**। ✪ ବିପରୀତ **narrow** **2** covering a range of people or things ବ୍ୟାପକ ପରିସରର *a broad survey of the reading habits of students*

3 general; not in detail ସାଧାରଣ, ସବିଶେଷ ତଥ୍ୟ ନଥିବା *a broad description of the new course*

broadly *adverb* in a general way, not covering too many details ସାଧାରଣ ଭାବରେ *The students were asked to broadly describe the effects of pollution.*

broadcast /ˈbrɔːdkɑːst/ *verb* (**broadcasts, broadcasting, broadcast, has broadcast**) send out sound or pictures by radio or television ରେଡ଼ିଓ ବା ଟେଲିଭିଜନ୍ କାର୍ଯ୍ୟକ୍ରମ ସଂଚାର କରିବା *The English news is broadcast at 9 p.m.*

broadcast *noun* something that is sent out by radio or television ରେଡ଼ିଓ ବା ଟେଲିଭିଜନ୍ ସଂଚାର ବା ପ୍ରସାରଣ *a news broadcast*

broccoli /ˈbrɒkəli/ *noun* a vegetable that looks like a cauliflower but has a green part in the middle ଏକପ୍ରକାର ସବୁଜ ବର୍ଣ୍ଣର ଫୁଲକୋବି ➪ ଚିତ୍ର ପାଇଁ **vegetable** ଦେଖନ୍ତୁ ।

broke, broken ଶବ୍ଦ **break**[1] ର ଏକ ଧାତୁରୂପ

broken /ˈbrəʊkən/ *adjective* in pieces or not working ଭଙ୍ଗା *a broken window*

bronze /brɒnz/ *noun* (*no plural*) a brown metal made from copper and tin ତମ୍ବା ଓ ଟିଣର ମିଶ୍ରଧାତୁ, କଂସା *a bronze medal*

brooch /brəʊtʃ/ *noun* (*plural* **brooches**) a pretty thing with a pin at the back that you wear on your clothes ସ୍ତ୍ରୀଲୋକଙ୍କର ବସ୍ତ୍ର ଉପରେ ବ୍ୟବହୃତ ପିନ୍ ପରି ଅଳଙ୍କାର

brood[1] /bruːd/ *verb* (**broods, brooding, brooded**) **1** think a lot about what is worrying you ଚିନ୍ତା କରିବା, ଉଦ୍‌ବିଗ୍ନ ହେବା *She was brooding about her son's poor performance in the exams.* **2** when a bird broods, it sits on its eggs so that they can hatch ଚଢ଼େଇ ଅଣ୍ଡା ଉଷୁମାଇବା

brood[2] /bruːd/ *noun* all the young birds born at the same time to the same mother ଏକା ସମୟ ଜନ୍ମର ପକ୍ଷୀ ବା ପଶୁ ଛୁଆ

brook /brʊk/ *noun* a small stream ଛୋଟନଈ, ଝରଣା

broom /bruːm/ *noun* a brush with a long handle that you use for sweeping ଲମ୍ବା ଝାଡୁ

brother /ˈbrʌðə(r)/ *noun* your brother is a man or a boy who has the same parents as you ଭାଇ, ଭ୍ରାତା *My younger brother is called Manav.* ➪ ଚିତ୍ର ପାଇଁ **family** ଦେଖନ୍ତୁ ।

brother-in-law *noun* (*plural* **brothers-in-law**) **1** the brother of your wife or husband ସ୍ୱାମୀଙ୍କ ଭାଇ, ଦିଅର, ଦେଢ଼ଶୁର, ସ୍ତ୍ରୀଙ୍କ ଭାଇ, ଶଳା **2** the husband of your sister ଭଉଣୀଙ୍କ ସ୍ୱାମୀ, ଭିଣୋଇ ➪ ଚିତ୍ର ପାଇଁ **family** ଦେଖନ୍ତୁ ।

brought ଶବ୍ଦ **bring** ର ଏକ ଧାତୁରୂପ

brow /braʊ/ *noun* the part of your face above your eyes ଭ୍ରୂଲତା

brown /braʊn/ *adjective* (**browner, brownest**) with the colour of coffee ପିଙ୍ଗଳ ବର୍ଣ୍ଣ *brown eyes*

brown *noun* the colour of coffee ମାଟିଆ ବା ବାଦାମି ରଙ୍ଗ

bruise /bruːz/ *noun* a dark mark on your skin that appears after something hits it ଆଘାତଜନିତ କ୍ଷତ, ଖଣ୍ଡିଆ ଖାବରା

brush /brʌʃ/ *noun* (*plural* **brushes**) a thing that you use for cleaning, painting or making your hair tidy (ସଫାକରିବା ବା ମୁଣ୍ଡ କୁଣ୍ଡାଇବା) ବ୍ରସ୍, (ଚିତ୍ରାଙ୍କନର) ତୂଳି ➪ **hairbrush, paintbrush** ଓ **toothbrush** ବି ଦେଖନ୍ତୁ।

brush *verb* (**brushes, brushing, brushed**) use a brush to do something ଘସି ସଫା କରିବା *I brush my teeth twice a day.*

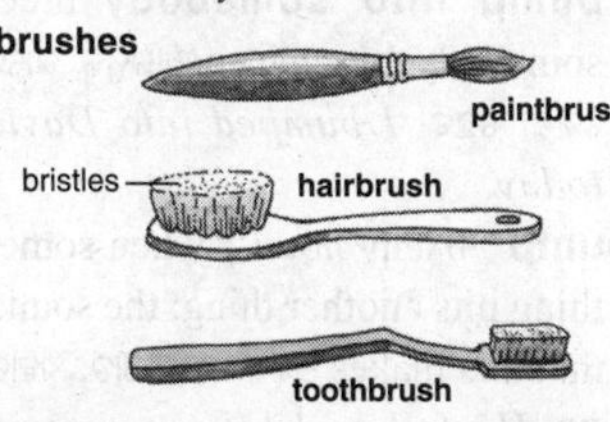

bubble /ˈbʌbl/ *noun* a small ball of air or gas inside a liquid ପାଣି ଫୋଟକା, ବୁଦ୍‌ବୁଦ *You can see bubbles in a glass of Coke.*

bucket /ˈbʌkɪt/ *noun* a round metal or plastic container with a handle. You use a bucket for carrying or storing water, for example ବାଲ୍ଟି

buckle /ˈbʌkl/ *noun* a metal or plastic thing on the end of a belt or strap that you use for joining it to the other end ଅଣ୍ଟାରେ ବେଲ୍ଟ୍ ସ୍ଥିର ରଖୁଥିବା ବକ୍‌ଲିସ୍

bud /bʌd/ *noun* a leaf or flower before it opens କଢ଼, କଳିକା, ଅଙ୍କୁର *There are many buds on the jasmine tree.* ➪ ଚିତ୍ର ପାଇଁ **plant** ଦେଖନ୍ତୁ।

Buddhism *noun* (*no plural*) a religion that is based on the teachings of the Buddha ବୌଦ୍ଧଧର୍ମ

Buddhist *noun* a person who follows the religion of **Buddhism** ବୌଦ୍ଧ ଧର୍ମାବଲମ୍ବୀ ବ୍ୟକ୍ତି

Buddhist *adjective* ବୌଦ୍ଧ *a Buddhist temple*

budge /bʌdʒ/ *verb* (**budges, budging, budged**) move a little or make something move a little ସାମାନ୍ୟ ଘୁଞ୍ଚିବା ବା ଘୁଞ୍ଚାଇବା *He pushed the door with all his strength but it wouldn't budge.*

budget /ˈbʌdʒɪt/ *noun* a plan of how you will spend the money that is available to you or your organization ବ୍ୟୟ ଓ ଆୟର ଅଟକଳ *We have a weekly budget for food.*

buffalo /ˈbʌfələʊ/ *noun* (*plural* **buffalo** ବା **buffaloes**) a large animal found in Asia and Africa that looks like a cow but has black skin. It usually has long curved horns ମଇଁଷି

bug /bʌg/ *noun* a small insect ପୋକ, କୀଟ

build /bɪld/ *verb* (**builds, building, built** /bɪlt/, **has built**) make something by putting parts together ତିଆରି କରିବା, ନିର୍ମାଣ କରିବା, ଗଢ଼ିବା *He built a wall in front of the house.*

builder /ˈbɪldə(r)/ *noun* a person whose job is to make buildings ଘର ଇତ୍ୟାଦି ନିର୍ମାଣକାରୀ ବ୍ୟକ୍ତି

building /ˈbɪldɪŋ/ *noun* a thing with a roof and walls. Houses, schools and shops are all buildings ଘର, କୋଠା

bulb /bʌlb/ *noun* the glass part of an electric lamp that gives light ବଲ୍ବ୍, ବିଜୁଳିବତୀର କାଚ ଆଧାର

bulbul *noun* a bird that is known for its singing, found in Africa and South Asia ବୁଲ୍‌ବୁଲ୍ ଚଢ଼େଇ

bulge /bʌldʒ/ *verb* (**bulges, bulging, bulged**) become bigger than usual; go out in a round shape from something that is usually flat ଫୁଲିବା, ଫୁଲି ଉଠିବା *My stomach is bulging—I have eaten too much.*

bulge *noun* a round part that goes out from something that is usually flat ଫୁଲା, ସ୍ଫୀତି *a bulge in the stomach*

bull /bʊl/ *noun* the male of the cow and of some other animals ଷଣ୍ଢ, ବୃଷଭ; ଅଣ୍ଡିରା ହାତୀ, ତିମି ଇତ୍ୟାଦି ➪ ଚିତ୍ର ପାଇଁ **cow** ଦେଖନ୍ତୁ ।

bulldozer /ˈbʊldəʊzə(r)/ *noun* a big heavy machine that moves earth and makes land flat ଭୂମିସୋଧକ ବଡ଼ କଳଲଙ୍ଗଳ ପରି ଯନ୍ତ୍ର

bullet /ˈbʊlɪt/ *noun* a small piece of metal that shoots out of a gun ବନ୍ଧୁକର ଗୁଳି ➪ ଚିତ୍ର ପାଇଁ **ammunition** ଦେଖନ୍ତୁ ।

bulletin /ˈbʊlətɪn/ *noun* **1** a short news report on television or radio ଖବରର ଏକ ଏକ ସଂକ୍ଷିପ୍ତ ବିବରଣ *the evening news bulletin* **2** a report printed by an organization or a club to give news about its activities କୌଣସି ସଂସ୍ଥାର ଖବର ବା ଘୋଷଣାପତ୍ର

bully /ˈbʊli/ *noun* (*plural* **bullies**) a person who hurts or frightens a weaker person ଅନ୍ୟମାନଙ୍କୁ ଭୟଭୀତ କରାଉଥିବା ବ୍ୟକ୍ତି

bully *verb* (**bullies, bullying, bullied, has bullied**) hurt or frighten a weaker person ଡରାଇବା (ବିଶେଷତଃ ଦୁର୍ବଳଙ୍କୁ) *She was bullied by the older girls at school.*

bump[1] /bʌmp/ *verb* (**bumps, bumping, bumped**) hit somebody or something when you are moving ବାଡ଼େଇ ହେବା, ଧକ୍କା ହେବା *She bumped into a chair.*

bump into somebody meet somebody by chance ଆକସ୍ମିକ ଭାବେ ଦେଖା ହେବା *I bumped into David today.*

bump[2] /bʌmp/ *noun* **1** when something hits another thing; the sound that this makes ଧକ୍କା ବା ଆଘାତ; ଏହାର ଶବ୍ଦ *He fell and hit the ground with a bump.* **2** a small part on something flat that is higher than the rest ଢିପ *The car hit a bump in the road.*

bumper /ˈbʌmpə(r)/ *noun* a bar on the front and back of a car, lorry, etc. The bumper helps to protect the car if it hits something ମଟର ଗାଡ଼ିର ଆଗ ଓ ପଛପଟର ଧକ୍କାରୋଧକ ଉପକରଣ ➪ ଚିତ୍ର ପାଇଁ **car** ଦେଖନ୍ତୁ ।

bumpy /ˈbʌmpi/ *adjective* (**bumpier, bumpiest**) with a lot of bumps ଖାଲ ଢିପଥିବା, ବନ୍ଧୁର *a bumpy road*

bun /bʌn/ *noun* a small round cake or piece of bread ଛୋଟ ଗୋଲିଆ ପାଉଁରୁଟି ବା କେକ୍

bunch /bʌntʃ/ *noun* (*plural* **bunches**) a group of things that grow together or that you tie or hold together ଗୁଚ୍ଛ, ଗୋଛା, ପେଣ୍ଡା *a bunch of grapes* ○ *a bunch of flowers*

bundle /ˈbʌndl/ *noun* a group of things that you tie or wrap together ଗଣ୍ଠିଲି, ପୁଟୁଳି, ଗୋଛା, ବିଡ଼ା *a bundle of old newspapers*

bungalow /ˈbʌŋgələʊ/ *noun* a house that has only one floor, with no upstairs rooms ଏକ ମହଲା ଘର

bunk /bʌŋk/ *noun* a narrow bed that is fixed to a wall, on a ship or train, for example କାନ୍ଥ ସଂଲଗ୍ନ ଥାକ ପରିଶଜ୍ୟା (ଜାହାଜ, ରେଳଗାଡ଼ି ଇତ୍ୟାଦିର)

bunny /ˈbʌni/ *noun* (*plural* **bunnies**) a child's word for **rabbit** (ପିଲାଙ୍କ ଭାଷାରେ) ଠେକୁଆ

buoy /bɔɪ/ *noun* (*plural* **buoys**) a thing that floats in the sea to show ships where there are dangerous places ଜାହାଜ ଯାତାୟତ ପାଇଁ ବିପଜ୍ଜନକ ସ୍ଥାନ ସୂଚାଉଥିବା ଭାସମାନ ବସ୍ତୁ

buoy

burden /ˈbɜːdn/ *noun* a responsibility that worries you or is difficult to carry out ଗୁରୁ ଦାୟିତ୍ୱ, ବୋଝ

burger /ˈbɜːgə(r)/ *noun* meat or vegetables cut into very small pieces and made into a flat round-shaped cutlet, that you eat between two pieces of bread ଛୋଟ ଛୋଟ କଟା ପରିବା ବା ମାଂସର ଏକ ଚଟକା ଆରିସା ପିଠା ପରି ଖଣ୍ଡ ଯାହାକୁ ଦୁଇଖଣ୍ଡ ପାଉଁରୁଟି ମଝିରେ ରଖି ଖିଆଯାଏ

burglar /ˈbɜːglə(r)/ *noun* a person who goes into a building to steal things ଘରପଶା ଚୋର

burglary *noun* (*plural* **burglaries**) the crime of going into a house to steal things ଲୁଚିଛପି ଘରେ ପଶି କରାଯାଉଥିବା ଚୋରି *There were two burglaries in this street last week.*

burial /ˈberiəl/ *noun* the time when a dead body is put in the ground ଶବକୁ ପୋତିବା ବା କବର ଦେବା କାମ ✪ ଏହାର କ୍ରିୟାପଦ ହେଲା **bury**।

buried, buries ଶବ୍ଦ **bury** ର ଏକ ଧାତୁରୂପ

burn[1] /bɜːn/ *verb* (**burns, burning, burnt** /bɜːnt/ ବା **burned, has burnt has burned**) **1** make flames and heat; be on fire ଜଳାଇବା, ଜଳିବା *Paper burns easily.* **2** harm or destroy somebody or something with fire or heat ନିଆଁ ଲଗାଇ ଧ୍ୱଂସ କରିବା ବା କ୍ଷତି କରିବା, ପୋଡ଼ି ଦେବା, ପୋଡ଼ିଯିବା *I burned my fingers on a match.*

burn down burn, or make a building burn, until there is nothing left ଘର ଇତ୍ୟାଦି ପୋଡ଼ି ଧ୍ୱଂସ କରିବା ବା ହେବା *Their house burned down.*

burn[2] /bɜːn/ *noun* a place on your body where fire or heat has hurt it ପୋଡ଼ା କ୍ଷତ, ଚିଆଁ, ଫୋଟକା *She's got a burn on her hand.*

burrow /ˈbʌrəʊ/ *noun* a hole in the ground where some animals, for example rabbits, live କୋକିଶିଆଳି, ଠେକୁଆ ଇତ୍ୟାଦି ରହିବା ପାଇଁ ଭୂଇଁରେ ଖୋଳିଥିବା ଗାତ

burst[1] /bɜːst/ *verb* (**bursts, bursting, burst, has burst**) break open suddenly because there is too much inside; make something break open suddenly ଫୁଟିବା, ହଠାତ୍ ଖଣ୍ଡ ଖଣ୍ଡ ହୋଇ ଭାଙ୍ଗିଯିବା; ଫାଟିଯିବା। *The bag was so full that it burst.*

burst into something start doing something suddenly ହଠାତ୍ ଆରମ୍ଭ କରିବା ବା ହେବା। *He read the letter and burst into tears.* ○ *The car burst into flames.*

burst[2] /bɜːst/ *noun* something that happens suddenly and quickly ହଠାତ୍ ଘଟିଥିବା ଘଟଣା *a burst of laughter*

bury /ˈberi/ *verb* (**buries, burying, buried, has buried**) **1** put a dead body in the ground ଶବକୁ ପୋଡ଼ିବା ବା କବର ଦେବା। ✪ ଏହାର ବିଶେଷ୍ୟ ହେଲା **burial**। **2** put something in the ground or under something ପୋତିବା *The dog buried a bone in the garden.*

bus /bʌs/ *noun* (*plural* **buses**) a thing like a big car, that carries a lot of people ବସ୍, ଯାତ୍ରୀବାହୀ ବଡ଼ ମଟର ଗାଡ଼ି *Where do you get off the bus?*

bus stop *noun* a place where buses stop and people get on and off ବସ୍ ରହିବା ସ୍ଥାନ

bush /bʊʃ/ *noun* (*plural* **bushes**) a plant like a small tree with a lot of branches ବୁଦା, ବହୁ ଶାଖାଥିବା ଛୋଟ ଗଛ *a rose bush*

business /ˈbɪznəs/ *noun* (*no plural*) buying and selling things ବ୍ୟବସାୟ, କିଣାବିକା *I want to go into business when I leave school.*

businessman /ˈbɪznəsmæn/ *noun* (*plural* **businessmen**) a man who deals in buying and selling things ବ୍ୟବସାୟୀ

businesswoman /ˈbɪznəswʊmən/ *noun* (*plural* **businesswomen**) a woman who deals in buying and selling things ବ୍ୟବସାୟିନୀ

busy /ˈbɪzi/ *adjective* (**busier, busiest**) **1** with a lot of things that you must do; working or not free ବହୁ କାମ ଥିବା, ବ୍ୟସ୍ତ, କାର୍ଯ୍ୟବ୍ୟସ୍ତ *Mr Jain can't see you now—he's busy.* **2** with a lot of things happening କର୍ମମୁଖର, କାର୍ଯ୍ୟବ୍ୟସ୍ତ *The shops are always busy at Diwali.*

but[1] /bət/ *conjunction* a word that you use to show something different କିନ୍ତୁ, ପରନ୍ତୁ *My sister speaks Marathi but I don't.*

but[2] /bət/ *preposition* except ଛଡ଼ା, ବ୍ୟତୀତ *She eats nothing but rice.*

butcher /ˈbʊtʃə(r)/ *noun* a person who cuts and sells meat କଂସାଇ, ପଶୁମାରି ମାଂସ ବିକୁଥିବା ବ୍ୟକ୍ତି

butter /ˈbʌtə(r)/ *noun* (*no plural*) soft yellow food that is made from milk. You put it on bread or use it in cooking ଲହୁଣି *She spread butter on the bread.*

butterfly /ˈbʌtəflaɪ/ *noun* (*plural* **butterflies**) an insect with big coloured wings ପ୍ରଜାପତି ➪ ଚିତ୍ର ପାଇଁ **caterpillar** ଓ **insect** ଦେଖନ୍ତୁ।

button /ˈbʌtn/ *noun* **1** a small round thing on clothes. You push it through a small hole (a **buttonhole**) to fasten clothes together ବୋତାମ **2** a small thing on a machine, that you push ଯନ୍ତ୍ରକୁ ସଚଳ କରିବା ପାଇଁ ଥିବା ବୋତାମ ପରିସ୍ୱିଚ୍ *Press this button to ring the bell.*

buy /baɪ/ *verb* (**buys, buying, bought** /bɔːt/, **has bought**) give money to get something କିଣିବା, କ୍ରୟକରିବା *I bought a new watch.* ✪ ବିପରୀତ **sell**

buyer /ˈbaɪə(r)/ *noun* a person who buys something କ୍ରେତା, କିଣିବା ବାଲା ✪ ବିପରୀତ **seller**

buzz /bʌz/ *verb* (**buzzes, buzzing, buzzed**) make a sound like bees ମହୁମାଛି ପରି ପରି ଶବ୍ଦ କରିବା, ଗୁଣୁଗୁଣୁ ଶବ୍ଦ କରିବା

by[1] /baɪ/ *preposition* **1** very near ପାଖରେ, ନିକଟରେ *They live by the sea.* **2** not later than ସୁଦ୍ଧା, ପରେ ନୁହେଁ *I must finish this work by six o'clock.* **3** a word that shows who or what did something ଦ୍ୱାରା କୃତ *a painting by M.F. Husain* **4** using something ଦ୍ୱାରା *He paid by cheque.* **5** a word that shows how ଦ୍ୱାରା *You turn the computer on by pressing this button.*

by[2] /baɪ/ *adverb* past ପାଖଦେଇ *She drove by without stopping.*

bye /baɪ/, **bye-bye** *interjection* goodbye ବିଦାୟ, ଯିବା ବେଳର ସଂଭାଷଣ

byte /baɪt/ *noun* a unit of information that is stored in a computer as a letter or a number and is equal to eight **bits** କମ୍ପ୍ୟୁଟର୍ ଆଲିଖନର ଆଠଟି ଖଣ୍ଡ ବା ଚିହ୍ନ (ବିଟ୍) ଯାହା ଦ୍ୱାରା ଗୋଟିଏ ଅକ୍ଷର ବା ସଂଖ୍ୟା ହୁଏ

C c

C /si:/ *abbreviation, symbol* **1 celsius, centigrade** ର ସଂକ୍ଷିପ୍ତ ରୂପ **2** the number 100 in Roman numerals ରୋମାନ୍ ସଂଖ୍ୟାରେ ଶତକ ଚିହ୍ନ (୧୦୦)

cab /kæb/ *noun* **taxi** ଯାତ୍ରୀବାହୀ ଭଡ଼ା ମଟର ଗାଡ଼ି

cabbage /ˈkæbɪdʒ/ *noun* a large round vegetable with thick green leaves ବନ୍ଧାକୋବି ➪ ଚିତ୍ର ପାଇଁ **vegetable** ଦେଖନ୍ତୁ ।

cabin /ˈkæbɪn/ *noun* **1** a small room on a ship or a plane ଜାହାଜ ବା ଉଡ଼ାଜାହାଜର ଛୋଟ କୋଠରି **2** a small simple house made of wood କାଠରେ ତିଆରି ଛୋଟ ଘର *a log cabin at the edge of the lake*

cabinet /ˈkæbɪnət/ *noun* **1** (*plural* **cabinets**) a small cupboard with shelves, drawers and doors ଥାକ, ଡ୍ର ଓ ଦ୍ୱାର ଥିବା ଛୋଟ ଆଲମାରି *a bathroom cabinet* **2 the Cabinet** (*no plural*) a group of the most important people in the government ମନ୍ତ୍ରୀମଣ୍ଡଳ

cable /ˈkeɪbl/ *noun* a very strong thick rope made of metal or wires ତାର ତିଆରି ଶକ୍ତ ଦଉଡ଼ି

cable television *noun* (*no plural*) a way of sending pictures and sound along wires (ଗ୍ରାହକମାନଙ୍କ ପାଇଁ) ତାର ଦ୍ୱାରା ସଂଚାରିତ ଟେଲିଭିଜନ୍ କାର୍ଯ୍ୟକ୍ରମ

cactus /ˈkæktəs/ *noun* (*plural* **cactuses** ବା **cacti** /ˈkæktaɪ/) a plant with a lot of sharp points that grows in hot dry places ନାଗଫେଣୀ ଗଛ, କ୍ୟାକ୍‌ଟସ୍

cafe /ˈkæfeɪ/ *noun* a small restaurant ଛୋଟ ଭୋଜନାଳୟ

cafeteria /ˌkæfəˈtɪəriə/ *noun* a place where people pay for their meals at a counter and carry the food to their tables themselves ନିଜେ ବାଢ଼ି ଖାଇବା ବ୍ୟବସ୍ଥାଥିବା ଭୋଜନାଳୟ

cage /keɪdʒ/ *noun* a place with bars round it where animals or birds are kept so that they cannot escape ପିଞ୍ଜରା, ଯନ୍ତା

cake /keɪk/ *noun* **1** a sweet food that is made from flour, eggs, sugar and butter and is baked in the oven ମଇଦା, ଦୁଧ, ଚିନି, ଅଣ୍ଡା ଇତ୍ୟାଦି ଫେଣ୍ଟି ଓଭେନ (ବନ୍ଦଚୁଲି) ରେ ଗରମ ଧାସରେ ସେକି କରାଯାଉଥିବା ପୋଡ଼ପିଠା, ପିଠା, କେକ୍ *Would you like a piece of cake?* **2** a small flat round piece of something ଖଣ୍ଡ, ଟୁକୁରା *a cake of soap*

calamity /kəˈlæməti/ *noun* (*plural* **calamities**) a terrible thing that causes great harm or damage ଦୁର୍ବିପାକ, ଦୁର୍ଦ୍ଦଶା

calcium /ˈkælsiəm/ *noun* (*no plural*) a soft white element that is found in teeth and bones. It is also found in milk and cheese ଚୂନ, ଚକ୍, ହାଡ଼, ଦାନ୍ତ, ଦୁଧ, ଛେନା ଇତ୍ୟାଦିରେ ଥିବା ଏକ ଧାତବ ଉପାଦନ

calculate /ˈkælkjuleɪt/ *verb* (**calculates, calculating, calculated**) find the answer by using mathematics ଗଣିବା, ହିସାବ କରିବା *Can you calculate how much the holiday will cost?*

calculation /ˌkælkjuˈleɪʃn/ *noun* the act of finding an answer by using mathematics ଗଣନ, ହିସାବ *I need to do a few calculations to find out the total expenditure.*

calculator /ˌkælkjuleɪtə(r)/ *noun* an electronic instrument that adds, subtracts, multiplies and divides ଗଣନା ଯନ୍ତ୍ର, କାଲ୍‌କୁଲେଟର୍

calendar /ˈkælɪndə(r)/ *noun* a list of the days, weeks and months of one year ବର୍ଷକର ମାସ, ଦିନ, ବାର, ଋତୁ ଇତ୍ୟାଦି ଥିବା ସାରଣୀ, କ୍ୟାଲେଣ୍ଡର୍ *Look at the calendar and tell me what day of the week December 2nd is this year.*

calf[1] /kɑːf/ *noun* (*plural* **calves** /kɑːvz/) a young cow ବାଛୁରି ଦେଖନ୍ତୁ

calf[2] /kɑːf/ *noun* (*plural* **calves** /kɑːvz/) the back of your leg, below your knee ମଣିଷ ଗୋଡ଼ର ପେଣ୍ଡା ➪ ଚିତ୍ର ପାଇଁ **body** ଦେଖନ୍ତୁ ।

call[1] /kɔːl/ *noun* **1** a loud cry or shout ଉଚ୍ଚ ସ୍ୱରର ଡାକ, ଚିତ୍କାର *a call for help* **2** the act of using the telephone ଟେଲିଫୋନ୍ ଡାକ *I received a call from Jyoti yesterday.*

call[2] /kɔːl/ *verb* (**calls, calling, called**) **1** speak loudly and clearly so that somebody who is far away can hear you ବଡ଼ ପାଟିରେ କହିବା, ଚିତ୍କାର କରିବା *She called out the names of the winners.* **2** ask somebody to come ଡାକିବା, ଡକାଇବା *He was so ill that we had to call the doctor.* **3** give a name to somebody or something ନାମକରଣ କରିବା *They called the baby Sonia.* **4** telephone somebody ଟେଲିଫୋନ୍‌ରେ କଥାବାର୍ତ୍ତା ହେବା *I'll call you later.*

calm[1] /kɑːm/ *adjective* (**calmer, calmest**) **1** quiet, and not excited or afraid ଶାନ୍ତ, ପ୍ରଶାନ୍ତ, ଧୀର *Try to keep calm—there's no danger.* **2** without much wind ବେଶୀ ପବନ ବହୁ ନଥିବା *calm weather*

calmly *adverb* ଶାନ୍ତ ଭାବରେ *He spoke calmly about the accident.*

calm[2] /kɑːm/ *verb* (**calms, calming, calmed**)

calm down become less afraid or excited; make somebody less afraid or excited ଶାନ୍ତ ହେବା, ଧୀର ହେବା *Calm down and tell me what happened.*

calorie /ˈkæləri/ *noun* a measure of the amount of energy food gives you ଖାଦ୍ୟରେ ଥିବା ଶକ୍ତି ବା ଏହାର ପରିମାପ *A banana milkshake is high in calories.*

calves ଶବ୍ଦ **calf** ର ବହୁବଚନ

came ଶବ୍ଦ **come** ର ଏକ ଧାତୁରୂପ

camel /ˈkæml/ *noun* a large animal with one or two round parts (called **humps**) on its back. Camels carry people and things in the desert ଏକ ବା ଦୁଇ କୁଜଥିବା ଓଟ

camel

camera /ˈkæmərə/ *noun* a thing that you use for taking photographs or moving pictures କ୍ୟାମେରା, ଫଟୋ ବା

ଚଳଚ୍ଚିତ୍ର ଉଠା ଯନ୍ତ୍ର *I need a new film for my camera.*

camouflage /ˈkæməflɑːʒ/ *noun* (*no plural*) a kind of pattern or colour that helps a human being, an animal or insect to blend with its surroundings ମଣିଷ, ସୈନ୍ୟସାମନ୍ତ, ପଶୁ ବା କୀଟଙ୍କର ପରିବେଶ ସାଙ୍ଗେ ମିଶିଗଲା ପରି ରଙ୍ଗରୂପ ଧାରଣ *The tiger's stripes act as an excellent camouflage.*

camouflage

camp /kæmp/ *noun* a place where people live in tents for a short time ଶିବିର, ଛାଉଣୀ

camp *verb* (**camps, camping, camped**) live in a tent for a short time ଅଳ୍ପ ସମୟ ପାଇଁ ଶିବିରରେ ବା ତମ୍ବୁରେ ରହିବା

camping *noun* (*no plural*) living in a tent for a short time ଶିବିରବାସ, ତମ୍ବୁରହଣି *Camping isn't much fun when it rains.*

campsite /ˈkæmpsaɪt/ *noun* (*plural* **campsites**) a place where you can camp ଶିବିର ସ୍ଥାନ

campaign /kæmˈpeɪn/ *noun* a plan to get a special result ବିଶେଷ ଉଦ୍ଦେଶ୍ୟରେ ଅଭିଯାନ *an election campaign*

can[1] /kən; kæn/ *modal verb* **1** be able to; be strong enough, clever enough, etc. ସମର୍ଥହେବା, ପାରିବା *She can speak three languages.* ○ *Can you swim?* **2** be allowed to ଅନୁମତି ପାଇବା *You can go now.* **3** a word that you use when you ask somebody to do something (ପ୍ରଶ୍ନ ବା ଅନୁରୋଧଭାବରେ) ପାରିବକି ? କରି ପାରିବକି ? *Can you help me finish the work, please?*

> ✪ **Can** ର ନାସ୍ତିବାଚକ ପଦ ହେଲା **cannot** ବା ସଂକ୍ଷେପରେ **can't** — *She can't swim.*
>
> **Can** ର ଅତୀତକାଳ **could** ଭବିଷ୍ୟତ କାଳ **(future tense)** ଓ ସମାପ୍ତ କାଳ **(perfect tense)** ପାଇଁ **can** ସ୍ଥାନରେ **be able to** ବ୍ୟବହାର କରିବା ବିଧେୟ । — *I* **can** *see it.* ○ *You* **will be able to** *see it if you stand on this chair.*
>
> ➪ **modal verb** ପାଇଁ ଟିପ୍ପଣୀ ଦେଖନ୍ତୁ ।

can[2] /kən/ *noun* a metal container for food, drinks or certain liquids like paint (ଖାଦ୍ୟ, ପାନୀୟ, ରଙ୍ଗ ଇତ୍ୟାଦିର) ଧାତୁନିର୍ମିତ ଡବା *a can of paint* ➪ ଚିତ୍ର ପାଇଁ **container** ଦେଖନ୍ତୁ ।

canal /kəˈnæl/ *noun* a path that is made through land and filled with water so that boats can travel through it କେନାଲ୍, ନାଳ, କୁଲ୍ୟା, ପ୍ରଣାଳୀ *the Suez Canal*

cancel /ˈkænsl/ *verb* (**cancels, cancelling, cancelled**) say that something you have planned will not happen ବାତିଲ୍, କରିବା, ରଦ୍ଦ କରିବା, ପ୍ରତ୍ୟାହାର କରିବା *The singer was ill, so the concert was cancelled.*

cancellation /ˌkænsəˈleɪʃn/ *noun* ବାତିଲ୍ କରିବା ପ୍ରକ୍ରିୟା; ରଦ୍ଦ *the cancellation of the President's visit*

cancer[1] /ˈkænsə(r)/ *noun* a very dangerous illness that makes some **cells**

(very small parts in the body) grow too fast କର୍କଟରୋଗ, କିଛି ଜୀବ — କୋଷକୁ ଅତି ମାତ୍ରାରେ ବଢ଼ାଉଥିବା ମାରାତ୍ମକ ରୋଗ *Smoking can cause cancer.*

Cancer² /ˈkænsə(r)/ *noun* the fourth sign of the **Zodiac** ରାଶିଚକ୍ରର ଚତୁର୍ଥରାଶି, କର୍କଟ ରାଶି; କର୍କଟ କ୍ଷେତ୍ରପୁଞ୍ଜ

candidate /ˈkændɪdət/ *noun* a person who wants to be chosen for something like a job or who is standing for an election (ଚାକିରି, ନିର୍ବାଚନ ଇତ୍ୟାଦିର) ପ୍ରାର୍ଥୀ *finding a suitable candidate for the job*

candle /ˈkændl/ *noun* a long round piece of wax with a string in the middle that burns to give light ମହମବତୀ

candlestick /ˈkændlstɪk/ *noun* a thing that holds a candle ମହମବତୀ ରଖିବା ଆଧାର

candy /ˈkændi/ *noun* (*plural* **candies**) a sweet or a toffee ମିଶ୍ରି ପରି ମିଠେଇ

cane /keɪn/ *noun* **1** the slender, strong and often flexible stem of some plants ବେତ ବା ବେତ ପରି ପଦାର୍ଥ (ଯଥା: ଆଖୁ) *sugar cane* **2** a long thin stick ସରୁ ଲମ୍ବା ବାଡ଼ି

canine /ˈkeɪnaɪn/ *noun* one of the four sharp pointed teeth in our mouth ଶ୍ୱାନଦାନ୍ତ, ମୁନିଆ ଦାନ୍ତ ➪ **incisor, molar** ଓ **premolar** ଦେଖନ୍ତୁ । ➪ ଚିତ୍ର ପାଇଁ **tooth** ଦେଖନ୍ତୁ ।

cannon /ˈkænən/ *noun* a big gun on wheels that fires heavy metal balls ତୋପ, କମାଣ

cannot = **can not**

canoe /kəˈnuː/ *noun* a light narrow boat that you use on rivers. You move it through the water with a piece of wood (called a **paddle**) ସରୁଆ ହାଲ୍କା ଆହୁଲାମରା ଡଙ୍ଗା

canopy /ˈkænəpi/ *noun* (*plural* **canopies**) **1** a piece of cloth, canvas, plastic, etc. that covers something from above ଚାନ୍ଦୁଆ **2** something that forms a cover by spreading over an area like the branches of a tree ଚାନ୍ଦୁଆ ବା ବିସ୍ତାରିତ ଗଛଡାଳ ପରି ଆବରଣ, ସାମିଆନା

can't = **can not**

canteen /kænˈtiːn/ *noun* the place where people eat when they are at school or work ସ୍କୁଲ, କଲେଜ୍ ବା କାର୍ଯ୍ୟାଳୟର ଭୋଜନାଳୟ

canvas /ˈkænvəs/ *noun* (*no plural*) strong heavy cloth. Tents and sails are often made of canvas, and it is also used for painting pictures on (ପୋଲ, ତମ୍ବୁ, ତୈଳ ଚିତ୍ର ପାଇଁ ବ୍ୟବହୃତ) ଶକ୍ତ ମୋଟା କନା

cap /kæp/ *noun* **1** a soft hat ଟୋପି *a baseball cap* **2** a thing that covers the top of a bottle or tube ଠିପି *Put the cap back on the bottle.*

capable /ˈkeɪpəbl/ *adjective* **1** able to do something ସମର୍ଥ *You are capable of passing the exam if you work harder.* **2** able to do things well ଦକ୍ଷ *a capable student* ✪ ବିପରୀତ **incapable**

capacity /kəˈpæsəti/ *noun* (*plural* **capacities**) the amount a container can hold ଧାରଣଶକ୍ତି *a tank with a capacity of 1,000 litres*

cape /keɪp/ *noun* **1** a piece of clothing like a coat without sleeves ହାତ ନଥିବା କୋଟ୍ **2** a high part of the land that goes out into the sea ଅନ୍ତରୀପ *Cape of Good Hope*

capital /ˈkæpɪtl/ *noun* **1** the most important city in a country or state, where the government is ରାଜଧାନୀ *New Delhi is the capital of India.* **2** (**capital letter** ମଧ୍ୟ) a big letter of the alphabet ଇଂରାଜୀ ବର୍ଣ୍ଣମାଳାର ବଡ଼ ଅକ୍ଷର *A, B and C are capitals; a, b and c are not.* ○ *Names of people and places begin with a capital letter.* ➪ **small 3** ଦେଖନ୍ତୁ। **3** money that is put into a business or bank to produce more money ମୂଳଧନ, ମୂଳପାଣ୍ଠି (ବ୍ୟବସାୟ ଇତ୍ୟାଦିର)

Capricorn /ˈkæprɪkɔ:n/ *noun* the tenth sign of the **zodiac** ମକର ରାଶି

capsize /kæpˈsaɪz/ *verb* (**capsizes, capsizing, capsized**) turn over in the water (ପାଣିରେ ଜାହାଜ ଇତ୍ୟାଦି) ଓଲଟି ପଡ଼ିବା *During the storm, the boat capsized.*

capsule /ˈkæpsju:l/ *noun* a very small container with medicine inside it ଛୋଟ କୋଷ ବା ଆବରଣରେ ଆବୃତ ଔଷଧ

captain /ˈkæptɪn/ *noun* **1** the person who is in charge of a ship or an aircraft ଜାହାଜ ବା ଉଡ଼ାଜାହାଜର ଅଧକ୍ଷ *The captain sent a message by radio for help.* **2** the leader of a group of people ଖେଳାଳି ଦଳର ଅଧିନାୟକ *He's the captain of the school football team.*

caption /ˈkæpʃn/ *noun* the words above or below a picture in a book or newspaper, that tell you about it (ବହି ବା ଖବର କାଗଜରେ ଥିବା ଚିତ୍ରର ଉପରେ ବା ତଳେ ଥିବା) ଆଖ୍ୟା ଲେଖ

captive /ˈkæptɪv/ *noun* a person who is not free; a prisoner ବନ୍ଦୀ

capture /ˈkæptʃə(r)/ *verb* (**captures, capturing, captured**) catch somebody and keep them somewhere so that they cannot escape ବନ୍ଦୀ କରିବା *The police captured the robbers.* ✪ ବିପରୀତ **release 1**

capture *noun* (*no plural*) ବନ୍ଦୀକରଣ, ଧରିନେବା, ଧରାପଡ଼ିବା *the capture of the escaped prisoners*

car /kɑ:(r)/ *noun* a vehicle with four wheels, usually with enough space for four or five people କାର୍, ମଟରଗାଡ଼ି *She travels to work by car.*

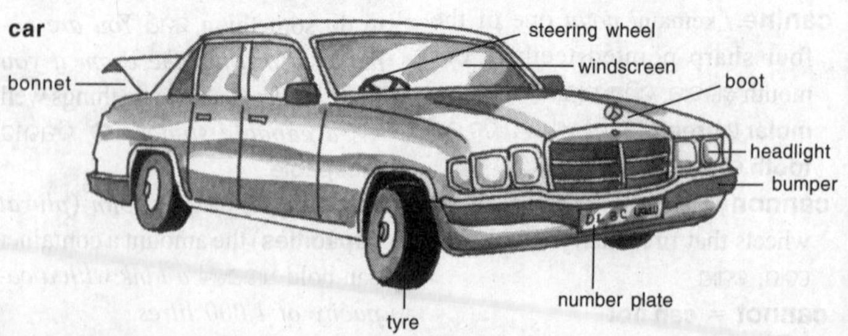

car park *noun* (*plural* **car parks**) a piece of land or a building where you can leave your car for some time ବହୁ ମଟରଗାଡ଼ି ରଖିବା ସ୍ଥାନ ବା କୋଠାର ତଳ

caravan /ˈkærəvæn/ *noun* **1** a small house on wheels, that a car or a truck can pull (ଶୋଇବା, ବସିବା, ରୋଷେଇ କରିବା ଇତ୍ୟାଦିର ସୁବିଧାଥିବା) ଚକଲଗା ଯାନ (ଯାହା କାର୍ ବା ଟ୍ରକ୍ ଦ୍ୱାରା ଟାଣି ନିଆଯାଏ) **2** a group of people travelling together across a desert and mostly with animals ଏକାଠି ହୋଇ ଯାଉଥିବା ଯାତ୍ରୀଦଳ

carbohydrate /ˌkɑːbəʊˈhaɪdreɪt/ *noun* a substance present in sugar and potatoes which gives energy to the body ଶ୍ୱେତସାର, କାର୍ବୋହାଇଡ୍ରେଟ୍, ଚିନି, ଆଳୁ ଇତ୍ୟାଦିରେ ଥିବା ଶର୍କରା ଜାତୀୟ ପଦାର୍ଥ

carbon /ˈkɑːbən/ *noun* (*no plural*) the element that coal and diamonds are made of and that is found in all living things ଅଙ୍ଗାରକ, କାର୍ବନ୍, କୋଇଲା, ଗ୍ରାଫାଇଟ୍, ହୀରା ଇତ୍ୟାଦି ରୂପରେ ପ୍ରକୃତିରେ ମିଳୁଥିବା ପଦାର୍ଥ

carbon dioxide *noun* (*no plural*) a gas with no colour or smell that human beings and animals breathe out ଅଙ୍ଗାରକାମ୍ଳ, ନିଃଶ୍ୱାସରେ ଛଡ଼ା ଯାଉଥିବା ବାଷ୍ପ

card /kɑːd/ *noun* **1** a piece of thick stiff paper that is folded in the middle with writing or pictures on it ମୋଟା କାଗଜ ଖଣ୍ଡ (ଲେଖିବା ବା ଛାପିବା ପାଇଁ); ଲେଖା ବା ଚିତ୍ର ଥିବା ଏହିପରି କାଗଜ *We send birthday cards, Christmas cards and postcards to our friends.* ➪ **credit card** ଦେଖନ୍ତୁ । **2** a playing card; one of a set of 52 cards called a **pack of cards** that you use to play games. A pack has four groups of thirteen cards — **hearts, clubs, diamonds** and **spades** ତାସ୍ (ବାଉନପଟ ତାସ୍ ଯେଉଁଥିରେ ଲାଲିପାନ, ଚିଡ଼ିଆ, ଠିକିରି ଓ କଳାପାନର ତେର ତେରପଟ ତାସ୍ଥାଏ) *Let's have a game of cards.*

cardboard /ˈkɑːdbɔːd/ *noun* (*no plural*) very thick paper that is used for making boxes, etc. କାର୍ଡ଼ବୋର୍ଡ଼, କାଗଜପଟା (ମୋଟା ଟାଣ କାଗଜ ଯେଉଁଥିରେ ବାକ୍ସ ଇତ୍ୟାଦି ତିଆରି ହୁଏ)

cardiac /ˈkɑːdiæk/ *adjective* related to the heart or to heart diseases ହୃତ୍ପିଣ୍ଡ ବା ହୃଦ୍‌ରୋଗ ସମ୍ବନ୍ଧୀୟ

cardigan /ˈkɑːdɪgən/ *noun* a knitted woollen jacket ଉଲ୍ ବା ପଶମ ଜାମା, କୋଟ୍ ବା ଜ୍ୟାକେଟ୍

cardinal number *noun* a whole number like 1, 2 and 3 that tells you the quantity of something rather than its order ପୂର୍ଣ୍ଣସଂଖ୍ୟା, ଗଣନ ସଂଖ୍ୟା ବା ମୌଳିକ ସଂଖ୍ୟା (୧,୨,୩,୪ ଇତ୍ୟାଦି) ➪ **ordinal number** ଦେଖନ୍ତୁ ।

care[1] /keə(r)/ *noun* (*no plural*) thinking about what you are doing so that you do not make a mistake or damage something ଯତ୍ନ, ସତର୍କତା *Wash these glasses with care!*

take care be careful ଯତ୍ନନିଅ; ଯତ୍ନନେବା, ସାବଧାନ ରହିବା *Take care when you cross the road.*

take care of somebody or **something** look after somebody or something; do what is necessary କାହାରି ଯତ୍ନ ନେବା, ଦେଖାଶୁଣା କରିବା *Anju is taking care of her sister's baby today.*

care² /keə(r)/ *verb* (**cares, caring, cared**) **1** think that it is important ଗୁରୁତ୍ୱପୂର୍ଣ୍ଣ ବୋଲି ଭାବିବା; ଖାତିର କରିବା *He doesn't care what others think of him.* **2** like somebody or something ଖାତିର କରିବା, ପ୍ରାଧାନ୍ୟ ଦେବା *He cares a lot for his parents.*

career /kəˈrɪə(r)/ *noun* a job that you learn to do and then do for many years ବୃତ୍ତି, ପେସା ଓ ଏହାର ଦୀର୍ଘକାଳ *a career in teaching*

careful /ˈkeəfl/ *adjective* if you are careful, you think about what you are doing so that you do not make a mistake or have an accident ସାବଧାନ, ସତର୍କ *Careful! The plate is very hot.* ✪ ବିପରୀତ **careless**

carefully *adverb* ସାବଧାନ ଭାବରେ, ସତର୍କତା ସହ, ମନ ଦେଇ *Please listen carefully.*

careless /ˈkeələs/ *adjective* if you are careless, you do not think enough about what you are doing, and as a result you make mistakes ଅସାବଧାନ, ଅମନଯୋଗୀ *Careless drivers can cause accidents.* ✪ ବିପରୀତ **careful**

carelessly *adverb* ଅସାବଧାନ ଭାବେ *She carelessly threw her coat on the floor.*

carelessness *noun* (*no plural*) the act of being careless ଅସାବଧାନତା

caretaker /ˈkeəteɪkə(r)/ *noun* a person whose job is to look after a large building like a school or a block of flats ରକ୍ଷଣା ବେକ୍ଷଣକାରୀ, ତତ୍ତ୍ୱାବଧାୟକ

cargo /ˈkɑːgəʊ/ *noun* (*plural* **cargoes** ବା **cargos**) the things that a ship or an aeroplane carries ଜାହାଜ ବା ବିମାନରେ ନିଆଯାଉଥିବା ମାଲ୍ ବା ଦ୍ରବ୍ୟ *a cargo of wheat*

caring /ˈkeərɪŋ/ *adjective* being helpful and kind to someone because you care about them ଯତ୍ନଶୀଳ *caring parents*

carnival /ˈkɑːnɪvl/ *noun* a public celebration where people wear colourful clothes, take out processions and dance in the streets ମେଳା, ଆନନ୍ଦୋତ୍ସବ *the Goa carnival*

carnivore /ˈkɑːnɪvɔː(r)/ *noun* an animal that eats other animals for food ମାଂସାଶୀ ପ୍ରାଣୀ ➪ **herbivore, insectivore** ଓ **omnivore** ଦେଖନ୍ତୁ।

carnivorous /kɑːˈnɪvərəs/ *adjective* ମାଂସାଶୀ, ମାଂସଖିଆ *carnivorous animals*

carol /ˈkærəl/ *noun* a religious song that people sing at Christmas ବଡ଼ଦିନ ବା କ୍ରିସମାସ୍ ଗୀତ

carpenter /ˈkɑːpəntə(r)/ *noun* a person who makes things from wood ବଢ଼େଇ

carpentry /ˈkɑːpəntri/ *noun* (*no plural*) the skill of making things from wood ବଢ଼େଇକାମ, କାଠକାମ

carpet /ˈkɑːpɪt/ *noun* a covering for the floor. Carpets are often made of wool and are sometimes the same size as the floor ଗାଲିଚା, ଦରି

carriage /ˈkærɪdʒ/ *noun* **1** one of the parts of a train where people sit ଯାତ୍ରୀ ବସୁଥିବା ରେଳଡବା *The carriages at the back of the train were empty.* **2** a vehicle that is pulled by horses and is used at special times ଘୋଡ଼ାଗାଡ଼ି

carried, carries ଶବ୍ଦ **carry** ର ଏକ ଧାତୁରୂପ

carrot /ˈkærət/ *noun* a long thin orange root which is used as a vegetable ଗାଜର (ପରିବା) ➪ ଚିତ୍ର ପାଇଁ **vegetable** ଦେଖନ୍ତୁ।

carry /ˈkæri/ *verb* (**carries, carrying, carried, has carried**) **1** hold something and take it to another place or keep it with you ବହନ କରିବା, ବୋହିବା *He carried the suitcase to my room.* **2** move people or things ବହନ କରିବା, ନେବାଆଣିବା କରିବା *Special fast trains carry people to the capital city.*

carry on continue doing something କ୍ରମାଗତ ଚଳାଇବା; କରି ଚାଲ *Carry on with your work.*

cart /kɑːt/ *noun* **1** a wooden vehicle with two or four wheels that is usually pulled by a horse ଚାରିଚକିଆ ବା ଦୁଇ ଚକିଆ ମାଲବାହୀ ଘୋଡ଼ାଗାଡ଼ି **2** a small light vehicle with wheels that can be pushed or pulled by hands ହାତଟଣା ଛୋଟ ଗାଡ଼ି ବା ଠେଲାଗାଡ଼ି, ଠେଲା

carton /ˈkɑːtn/ *noun* a container made of cardboard or plastic କାର୍ଡ଼ବୋର୍ଡ଼ ବା ପ୍ଲାଷ୍ଟିକ୍ ଡବା *a carton of milk* ➪ ଚିତ୍ର ପାଇଁ **container** ଦେଖନ୍ତୁ।

cartoon /kɑːˈtuːn/ *noun* **1** a funny drawing, for example in a newspaper ବ୍ୟଙ୍ଗଚିତ୍ର **2** a television or cinema film made with drawings, not pictures of real people and places ଅଙ୍କିତ ଚିତ୍ରରୁ ପ୍ରସ୍ତୁତ ଟେଲିଭିଜନ୍ ଗପ ବା ଚଳଚ୍ଚିତ୍ର *a Mickey Mouse cartoon*

cartoon film

cartridge /ˈkɑːtrɪdʒ/ *noun* a small tube-like shell containing explosive powder along with a bullet ବନ୍ଧୁକ ଗୁଳିର ଆଧାର ବା ଖୋଳ, ଟୋଟା

carve /kɑːv/ *verb* (**carves, carving, carved**) cut wood or stone to make a picture or shape କାଠ ବା ପଥର କାଟି ଚିତ୍ର ବା ମୂର୍ତ୍ତିର ଆକାର ଦେବା *Sheeba's father carved a little horse for her out of wood.*

case /keɪs/ *noun* **1** a container like a box for keeping something in ଖୋଳ, ବାକ୍ସ, ପେଡ଼ି, ଡବା *Put the camera back in its case.* ➪ **briefcase** ଓ **suitcase** ବି ଦେଖନ୍ତୁ। **2** an example of something ଘଟଣା *There were four cases of this disease in the school last month.* **3** a question that people in a court of law must decide about ମକଦ୍ଦମା, ମାମଲା *a divorce case*

in case because something might happen କାଳେ, ଯଦି *Take an umbrella in case it rains.*

cash /kæʃ/ *noun* (*no plural*) money in coins and notes ନଗଦ ଟଙ୍କା *How would you like to pay—cash or cheque?*

cash crop *noun* (*plural* **cash crops**) a crop that is grown to be sold and not to be used or eaten by the people who grow it ବିକ୍ରିପାଇଁ ଉଦ୍ଦିଷ୍ଟ ଫସଲ, ଅର୍ଥକାରୀ ଫସଲ

cashier /kæ'ʃɪə(r)/ *noun* the person who gives or takes money in a bank ବ୍ୟାଙ୍କ ବା ଅଫିସ୍‌ର ଟଙ୍କା ପଇସା ଦିଆନିଆ କରୁଥିବା କର୍ମଚାରୀ, କ୍ୟାସିଅର୍

cassette /kə'set/ *noun* a plastic box with special tape inside for storing and playing sound, music or moving pictures ଚୁମ୍ବକୀୟ ଫିତା (ଟେପ୍) ବା ଆଲୋକଚିତ୍ର (ଫିଲ୍ମ) ଟେପ୍ ରହିଥିବା ଏକ ନିବୁଜ ଆଧାର, କ୍ୟାସେଟ୍ *a video cassette*

cassette player, cassette recorder *noun* a machine that can put (**record**) sound or music on tape and play it again later କ୍ୟାସେଟ୍ ବଜାଇବା ଯନ୍ତ୍ର; କ୍ୟାସେଟ୍‌ରେ ରେକର୍ଡ଼ (ଆଲିଖନ) କରି ବଜାଇ ପାରୁଥିବା ଯନ୍ତ୍ର

cast[1] /kɑ:st/ *verb* (**casts, casting, cast, has cast**) **1** when you cast a glance at someone or something, you look in their direction very quickly (ଦୃଷ୍ଟି) ନିକ୍ଷେପ କରିବା ବା ପକାଇବା, ଚାହିଁବା **2** when you cast something, you throw it away or into another thing using force ଫୋପାଡ଼ିବା, ଫିଙ୍ଗିବା, ପକାଇବା *The fisherman cast his net into the lake.* **3** when an object casts a shadow, it causes some portion of another object to darken (ଛାଇ) ପକାଇବା, ନିକ୍ଷେପ କରିବା, ପଡ଼ିବା *During a solar eclipse, the moon casts a shadow on the earth.* **4** when someone is cast in a movie or play, they have been chosen to play a role in it (ନାଟକ, ଚଳଚ୍ଚିତ୍ର ଇତ୍ୟାଦିରେ) ଭୂମିକା ବଣ୍ଟନ କରିବା, ରୋଲ୍ ଦେବା *She was cast as a lawyer in the movie.*

cast[2] /kɑ:st/ *noun* all the actors in a play or film ନାଟକ ବା ଚଳଚ୍ଚିତ୍ର ଅଭିନେତା ଅଭିନେତ୍ରୀ ବୃନ୍ଦ

castle /'kɑ:sl/ *noun* a large old building that was built to keep people safe from their enemies ଦୁର୍ଗପରି ପ୍ରାସାଦ; ଦୁର୍ଗ *Windsor Castle*

casual /'kæʒuəl/ *adjective* **1** not planned ଆପାତିକ, ସାମୟିକ, ଅପରିକଳ୍ପିତ **2** not for serious or important times ସାଧାରଣ *Jeans and T-shirts are casual clothes.*

casualty /'kæʒuəlti/ *noun* (*plural* **casualties**) a person who is hurt or killed in an accident or a war ଦୁର୍ଘଟଣା ବା ଯୁଦ୍ଧରେ ଆହତ ବା ମୃତବ୍ୟକ୍ତି

casualty department, casualty *noun* the place in a hospital where doctors help people who have been hurt in an accident ଦୁର୍ଘଟଣାରେ ଆହତ ବ୍ୟକ୍ତିଙ୍କ ଚିକିତ୍ସା ପାଇଁ ଚିକିତ୍ସାଳୟରେ ଥିବା ସ୍ଥାନ, ଆହତ ଚିକିତ୍ସା ବିଭାଗ

cat /kæt/ *noun* **1** a small furry animal that people sometimes keep as a pet. Cats catch mice and birds ବିଲେଇ, ବିରାଡ଼ି, ମାର୍ଜାର ✪ ବିଲେଇ ଛୁଆକୁ **kitten** କହନ୍ତି। **2** the name of a group of large wild animals. Tigers and lions are cats ବାଘ, ସିଂହ ଇତ୍ୟାଦି ବିଲେଇ ଜାତିର ବନ୍ୟ ଜନ୍ତୁ

catastrophe /kə'tæstrəfi/ *noun* a sudden disaster that causes a large number of people to suffer ଦୁର୍ବିପାକ, ଆକସ୍ମିକ ବିପତ୍ତି

catch /kætʃ/ *verb* (**catches, catching, caught** /kɔːt/, **has caught**) **1** take and hold something that is moving ହାତରେ ଧରି ପକାଇବା, ଧରିବା *He threw the ball to me and I caught it.* **2** find and hold somebody or something ଧରିଆଣି ରଖିବା *How many fish did you catch last week?* **3** be early enough for a bus, train, etc. that is going to leave (ରେଳ, ବସ୍ ଇତ୍ୟାଦି) ଧରିବା, ଠିକ୍ ସମୟରେ ପହଞ୍ଚି-ଚଢ଼ିବା *You should run if you want to catch the bus.* ✪ ବିପରୀତ **miss 3** **4** get an illness ରୋଗଧରିବା, ରୋଗଗ୍ରସ୍ତ ହେବା *She caught a cold.*

catch fire start to burn ନିଆଁ ଲାଗିବା *The house caught fire.*

catch somebody red-handed find someone in the act of doing something wrong ହାତାହାତି ଧରିବା, ଖରାପ କାମ କରୁଥିବା ସମୟରେ ଧରିବା

categorize /ˈkætəgəraɪz/ *verb* (**categorizes, categorizing, categorized**) divide people or things into groups according to what they have in common ନିର୍ଦ୍ଦିଷ୍ଟ ଶ୍ରେଣୀଭୁକ୍ତ କରିବା, ଶ୍ରେଣୀ ବିଭାଜନ କରିବା *The students were categorized according to the languages known to them.*

categorization /ˌkætəgəraɪzeɪʃən/ *noun* ଶ୍ରେଣୀଭୁକ୍ତ, ଶ୍ରେଣୀବିଭାଜନ *categorization according to age*

category /ˈkætəgəri/ *noun* (*plural* **categories**) a group of people or things of the same kind ଶ୍ରେଣୀ ବା ବିଭାଗ, ଏକ ମଛା ବା ଶ୍ରେଣୀର ଲୋକ ବା ପଦାର୍ଥ

caterpillar /ˈkætəpɪlə(r)/ *noun* a thing like a long hairy worm that will become a butterfly or moth ପ୍ରଜାପତିର ପୂର୍ବରୂପ, ଶୂକ; ସାଁବାଳୁଆ ପରି କୀଟ

life cycle of a butterfly

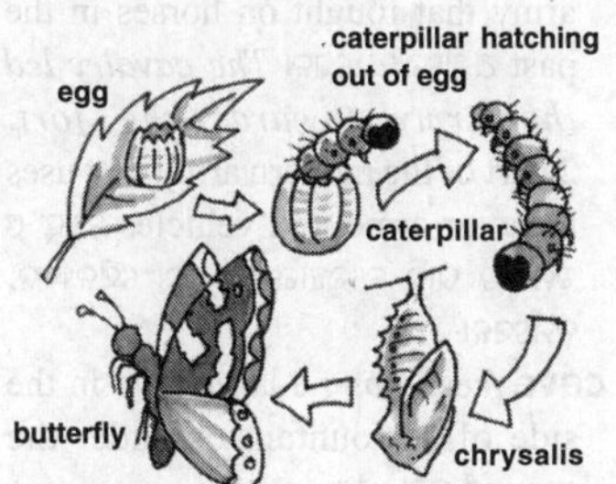

cattle /ˈkætl/ *noun* (*plural*) cows and bulls ଗୋରୁ, ଗାଈ, ଷଣ୍ଢ; ଗୋମହିଷାଦି ଗୃହପାଳିତ ପଶୁ *a herd of cattle*

caught ଶବ୍ଦ **catch** ର ଏକ ଧାତୁରୂପ

cauliflower /ˈkɒliflaʊə(r)/ *noun* a large vegetable with green leaves outside and a hard white part in the middle ଫୁଲ କୋବି ➪ ଚିତ୍ର ପାଇଁ **vegetable** ଦେଖନ୍ତୁ।

cause[1] /kɔːz/ *noun* the thing or person that makes something happen କାରଣ, ହେତୁ *Bad driving is the cause of most road accidents.*

cause[2] /kɔːz/ *verb* (**causes, causing, caused**) be the reason why something happens ଘଟାଇବା, ଭିଆଇବା, କାରଣହେବା *Who caused the accident?*

caution /ˈkɔːʃn/ *noun* (*no plural*) great care taken to avoid danger ସାବଧାନତା, ସତର୍କତା *Caution! Wet floor.*

cautious /ˈkɔ:ʃəs/ *adjective* careful because there may be danger ସତର୍କ, ହୁସିଆର, ସାବଧାନ *They were cautious while crossing the bridge.*

cavalry /ˈkævlri/ *noun* **1** part of the army that fought on horses in the past ଅଶ୍ୱାରୋହୀ ସେନା *The cavalry led the army towards the fort.* **2** part of the modern army that uses tanks or armoured vehicles ଟ୍ୟାଙ୍କ୍ ଓ ବର୍ମାବୃତ ଗାଡ଼ି ବ୍ୟବହାର କରୁଥିବା ସୈନ୍ୟଦଳ, ବର୍ମସେନା

cave /keɪv/ *noun* a large hole in the side of a mountain or under the ground ଗୁହା, ଗୁମ୍ଫା

CD /ˌsi:ˈdi:/ *noun* **compact disc** ର ସଂକ୍ଷିପ୍ତ ରୂପ

cease /si:s/ *verb* stop or end something ବନ୍ଦ କରିବା, ଶେଷ କରିବା, ବନ୍ଦ ହେବା *The two sides ceased hostilities at midnight.*

ceiling /ˈsi:lɪŋ/ *noun* the part of a room over your head ଛାତର ଭିତର ପାଖ, ଛାତ ତଳ

celebrate /ˈselɪbreɪt/ *verb* (**celebrates, celebrating, celebrated**) enjoy yourself because you have a special reason to be happy ଉତ୍ସବ ପାଳନ କରିବା, ଖୁସି ମନାଇବା *If you pass your exams, we'll have a party to celebrate.*

celebration /ˌselɪˈbreɪʃn/ *noun* a party that you have for a special reason ଉତ୍ସବ, ସମାରୋହ *birthday celebrations*

celebrity /səˈlebrəti/ *noun* (*plural* **celebrities**) a famous person ବିଖ୍ୟାତ ବ୍ୟକ୍ତି, ପ୍ରସିଦ୍ଧ ବ୍ୟକ୍ତି *film celebrities*

cell /sel/ *noun* **1** the smallest part of any living thing ଜୀବକୋଷ, ଜୀବନ୍ତ ବସ୍ତୁର କ୍ଷୁଦ୍ରତମ କାର୍ଯ୍ୟକାରୀ ଅଂଶ **2** a small room where a prisoner lives ବନ୍ଦୀଶାଳାର ଛୋଟ କୋଠରୀ

cellar /ˈselə(r)/ *noun* a room in the part of a building that is under the ground and that is used for storing things ଜିନିଷପତ୍ର (ବା ମଦ) ରଖିବା ପାଇଁ ଘର ତଳେ ଥିବା ପ୍ରକୋଷ୍ଠ *a coal cellar*

cellphone /ˈselfəʊn/ *noun* ଛୋଟ ଫୋନ୍ (ମଧ୍ୟ **mobile phone**) a small phone that can be carried along ସାଙ୍ଗରେ ନେଇ ହେଉଥିବା ଛୋଟ ଫୋନ୍

Celsius /ˈselsiəs/ *noun* (*no plural*) a measure of temperature. Water freezes at 0°Celsius and boils at 100°Celsius ତାପର ସେଣ୍ଟିଗ୍ରେଡ୍ ମାପକ ଯେଉଁଥିରେ ପାଣିର ହିମାଙ୍କ 0° ଓ ସ୍ଫୁଟନାଙ୍କ ୧୦୦°, ସେଲ୍‌ସିଅସ୍ ✪ Celsius ର ସଂକ୍ଷିପ୍ତ ରୂପ **C** *52°C*

cement /sɪˈment/ *noun* (*no plural*) grey powder that becomes hard like stone when you mix it with water and leave it to dry. Cement is used in building ସିମେଣ୍ଟ

cemetery /ˈsemətri/ *noun* (*plural* **cemeteries**) an area of ground where dead people are put under the earth ସମାଧି କ୍ଷେତ୍ର, କବର ଦେବା ସ୍ଥାନ

census /ˈsensəs/ *noun* (*plural* **censuses**) the official count of all the people living in a country along with other facts and information ଜନ ଗଣନା

cent /sent/ *noun* a small coin that people use in the USA and some other countries. There are 100 cents in a **dollar** ଯୁକ୍ତରାଷ୍ଟ୍ରର ମୁଦ୍ରା ଡଲାରର ଶହେ ଭାଗରୁ ଏକଭାଗ 100

centigrade /ˈsentɪɡreɪd/ *noun* **celsius** ସେଣ୍ଟିଗ୍ରେଡ୍, ସେଲସିଅସ୍‌ର ଅନ୍ୟନାମ

centimetre /ˈsentɪmiːtə(r)/ *noun* a measure of length. There are 100 centimetres in a **metre** ଲମ୍ବର ମେଟ୍ରିକ୍ ମାପ, ମିଟର୍‌ର ୧୦୦ ଭାଗରୁ ଭାଗେ ✪ Centimetre ର ସଂକ୍ଷିପ୍ତ ରୂପ ହେଲା **cm** ଯଥା *55 cm*

centipede /ˈsentɪpiːd/ *noun* a small creature with a long thin body and many legs ଶତପଦୀ କୀଟ, ବହୁପଦୀ କୀଟ (ତେଲୁଣିପୋକ, ତେନ୍ତୁଳିଆ ବିଛା ଇତ୍ୟାଦି)

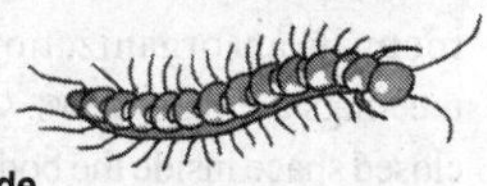

centipede

centre /ˈsentə(r)/ *noun* **1** the part in the middle ମଧ୍ୟବିନ୍ଦୁ, କେନ୍ଦ୍ରବିନ୍ଦୁ *The carpet is in the centre of the room.* **2** a place where people come to do something special କେନ୍ଦ୍ରସ୍ଥଳ, ମୁଖ୍ୟ ସ୍ଥାନ *a shopping centre*

central /ˈsentrəl/ *adjective* **1** in the middle part କେନ୍ଦ୍ରୀୟ, କେନ୍ଦ୍ରସ୍ଥ *Central Asia* **2** chief; basic ପ୍ରଧାନ; ମୌଳିକ *central issue; central question.*

century /ˈsentʃəri/ *noun* (*plural* **centuries**) **1** hundred years ଶହେବର୍ଷ **2** a time of hundred years, that we use in dates ଶତାବ୍ଦୀ *We are living at the beginning of the twenty-first century*. **3** hundred runs in cricket scored by a batsman in a single game କ୍ରିକେଟ୍ ଖେଳରେ ଏକା ପାଳିରେ ଶହେରନ୍, ଶତକ

ceramics /səˈræmɪks/ *noun* (*plural*) objects made of clay that have been baked to make them hard ମାଟିଗଢ଼ା ଓ ପୋଡ଼ା ପଦାର୍ଥ, ମୃଣ୍ମୟପାତ୍ର ଇତ୍ୟାଦି; ଏହା ତିଆରି କରିବାର କଳା ବା କାରିଗରି

ceramic *adjective* ପୋଡ଼ାମାଟିରେ ତିଆରି, ମୃଣ୍ମୟ ପାତ୍ର ସମ୍ବନ୍ଧୀୟ *ceramic cups*

cereal /ˈsɪəriəl/ *noun* a plant that farmers grow so that we can eat the seeds ଖାଦ୍ୟଶସ୍ୟ (ଧାନ, ଗହମ, ଡାଲି ଇତ୍ୟାଦି) *Wheat and rice are cereals.*

ceremony /ˈserəməni/ *noun* (*plural* **ceremonies**) a time when you do something special and important ବିଶେଷ କାର୍ଯ୍ୟର ସମାରୋହ ବା ଉତ୍ସବ *the opening ceremony of the Olympic Games* ○ *a wedding ceremony*

certain[1] /ˈsɜːtn/ *adjective* without any doubt; sure ନିଃସନ୍ଦେହ, ନିଶ୍ଚିତ *I am certain that I have seen her before.* ✪ ବିପରୀତ **uncertain**

make certain check something so that you are sure about it ନିଶ୍ଚିତ କରିବା *Please make certain that the window is closed before you leave.*

certain[2] /ˈsɜːtn/ *adjective* one or some that can be named କୌଣସି କୌଣସି *It's cheaper to telephone at certain times of the day.*

certainly /ˈsɜːtnli/ *adverb* without any doubt ନିଶ୍ଚିତ ଭାବେ *She is certainly the best swimmer in the team.*

certificate /səˈtɪfɪkət/ *noun* an important piece of paper that shows that something is true ନିଦର୍ଶନ ପତ୍ର, ପ୍ରମାଣପତ୍ର, ସାର୍ଟିଫିକେଟ୍ *Your birth certificate* *shows when and where you were born.*

CFC /ˌsiː ef ˈsiː/ *noun* a type of gas that is present in **aerosol** cans and causes harm to the **ozone layer** ଏକ ପ୍ରକାର ବାଷ୍ପ (କ୍ଲୋରଫ୍ଲୋର କାର୍ବନ: ଅଙ୍ଗାର, ଉଦ୍‌ଜାନ ଓ ଫ୍ଲୋରିନ୍‌ର ମିଶ୍ରବାଷ୍ପ) ଯାହା ବାୟୁମଣ୍ଡଳର ଓଜୋନ୍ ସ୍ତରକୁ ନଷ୍ଟ କରେ ✪ **Chlorofluorocarbon** ର ସଂକ୍ଷିପ୍ତ ରୂପ CFC।

chain[1] /tʃeɪn/ *noun* **1** metal rings that are joined together ଶିକୁଳି, ଚେନ୍ *She wore a gold chain round her neck.* ○ *My bicycle chain is broken.* **2** a group of things or people that are connected in a particular way ଗୁଡ଼ିଏ ଲୋକ ବା ବସ୍ତୁର ଶ୍ରେଣୀ, ଧାଡ଼ି ବା ମାଳ *a chain of mountains* **3** a group of stores or hotels having the same owner ଏକ ବ୍ୟବସାୟ ସଂସ୍ଥାର ବିଭିନ୍ନ ସ୍ଥାନରେ ଥିବା ଦୋକାନ, ହୋଟେଲ୍ ଇତ୍ୟାଦି, ଗୁଚ୍ଛ *a chain of restaurants*

chain[2] /tʃeɪn/ *verb* (**chains, chaining, chained**) attach somebody or something to a place with a chain ଶିକୁଳିରେ ବାନ୍ଧିବା *The dog was chained to the fence.*

chair /tʃeə(r)/ *noun* **1** a piece of furniture with four legs, a seat and a back that one person can sit on ଚଉକି, ଚୌକି *a table and four chairs* **2** a person who is in charge of a meeting ସଭାପତି ✪ ସଭାପତି ପାଇଁ **chairman, chairwoman** ବା **chairperson** ଶବ୍ଦର ବ୍ୟବହାର କରାଯାଇଥାଏ।

chalk /tʃɔːk/ *noun* a piece of soft white stick that you use for writing on a **blackboard** ଚକ୍, ଚକ୍‌ଖଡ଼ି, ଖଡ଼ି

challenge /ˈtʃælɪndʒ/ *verb* (**challenges, challenging, challenged**) ask somebody to play a game with you or fight with you to see who wins (ଖେଳ ବା ଲଢ଼େଇରେ ହାର୍‌ଜିତ୍ ଫଇସଲା ପାଇଁ) ଆହ୍ୱାନ, ଚ୍ୟାଲେଞ୍ଜ୍ *The boxer challenged the world champion to a fight.*

challenge *noun* a new or difficult thing that makes you try hard କୌଶଳ ବା ଉଦ୍ୟମ ଦରକାର କରୁଥିବା କାମ, କଷ୍ଟକର କାମ, ଦୁଃସାଧ କାମ *Climbing the mountain will be a real challenge.*

chamber /ˈtʃeɪmbə(r)/ *noun* **1** a room in an organization where meetings are held ପ୍ରକୋଷ୍ଠ, ସଭାଗୃହ **2** a closed space inside the body, a plant or a machine (ପଶୁ ବା ଉଦ୍ଭିଦ ଶରୀର ବା ଯନ୍ତ୍ର ମଧ୍ୟସ୍ଥ) ଗହ୍ୱର *the four chambers of the heart*

chameleon /kəˈmiːliən/ *noun* a lizard-like creature with large eyes and a long tail that can change its colour according to its surroundings ବହୁରୂପୀ ଏଣ୍ଡୁଅ

champion /ˈtʃæmpiən/ *noun* a person who is the best at a sport or game (ଖେଳକସରତରେ) ସର୍ବୋତ୍କୃଷ୍ଟ ପ୍ରତିଦ୍ୱନ୍ଦୀ *a chess champion*

championship *noun* a competition to find the champion ସର୍ବୋତ୍କୃଷ୍ଟ ଖେଳାଳି ବାଛିବା ପାଇଁ ପ୍ରତିଯୋଗିତା

chance /tʃɑːns/ *noun* **1** (*plural* **chances**) a time when you can do something ସୁଯୋଗ *It was their last chance to escape.* **2** (*no plural*)

something that happens which you cannot control; luck ଭାଗ୍ୟ, ଅଦୃଷ୍ଟ
by chance not because you have planned it ଆକସ୍ମିକ ଭାବରେ *We met by chance at the station.*

change[1] /tʃeɪndʒ/ *verb* (**changes, changing, changed**) **1** become different ବଦଳିବା, ପରିବର୍ତ୍ତିତ ହେବା *Water changes into ice when it gets very cold.* **2** put or take something in place of another thing ବଦଳାଇବା, ପରିବର୍ତ୍ତନ କରିବା *My new watch didn't work, so I took it back to the shop and changed it.* **3** put on different clothes ପୋଷାକ ବଦଳାଇବା *I must change before I go out.*

change[2] /tʃeɪndʒ/ *noun* **1** (*no plural*) money that you get back when you have paid too much ବଳକା ପଇସା *I gave the shopkeeper Rs 50. The sweets cost Rs 45, so he gave me Rs 5 as change.* **2** (*no plural*) small pieces of money; coins ଖୁଚୁରା ପଇସା, ରେଜା *I haven't got any change.* **3** (*plural* **changes**) a thing that is different now ପରିବର୍ତ୍ତନ, ଅଦଳବଦଳ *The new government has made a lot of changes.*

channel /ˈtʃænl/ *noun* **1** a narrow passage where water or other liquids can go ପାଣିଯିବା ନାଳ, ନଳା *drainage channels* **2** a passage of water connecting two larger bodies of water, especially seas ଦୁଇଟି ସମୁଦ୍ରକୁ ସଂଯୋଗ କରୁଥିବା (ପ୍ରଣାଳୀ ଠାରୁ ଚଉଡ଼ା ଜଳପଥ) *the English Channel* **3** one of the things you can choose on television ଟେଲିଭିଜନ୍‌ରେ ଭିନ୍ନ ଭିନ୍ନ ପ୍ରସାରଣ ସଂସ୍ଥାର କାର୍ଯ୍ୟକ୍ରମ ଆସୁଥିବା ପଥ, ଚ୍ୟାନେଲ୍ *Which channel are you watching?*

chant[1] /tʃɑːnt/ *noun* words or phrases spoken aloud or sung again and again by a group of people. A chant is usually a prayer or a religious song (କୌଣସି ଶବ୍ଦ ବା ପଂକ୍ତିର) ଗାଇଲା ପରି କଥନ; ସ୍ତୋତ୍ରପାଠ, ମନ୍ତ୍ରୋଚ୍ଚାରଣ

chant[2] /tʃɑːnt/ *verb* (**chants, chanting, chanted**) speak aloud or sing the same words or phrases again and again ଆବୃତ୍ତି କରିବା *'We won! We won!' they chanted happily.*

chaos /ˈkeɪɒs/ *noun* (*no plural*) a state of complete disorder ବିଶୃଙ୍ଖଳା, ବିଭ୍ରାଟ

chap /tʃæp/ *noun* fellow, lad ପୁରୁଷ, ବାଳକ, ଲୋକ *He's such a friendly chap!*

chapter /ˈtʃæptə(r)/ *noun* one of the parts of a book (ବହିର) ଅଧ୍ୟାୟ *That book has twelve chapters.*

character /ˈkærəktə(r)/ *noun* **1** (*plural* **characters**) a person in a play, book or film (ନାଟକ, ବହି ବା ଚଳଚ୍ଚିତ୍ରର) ଚରିତ୍ର *Tom and Jerry are famous cartoon characters.* **2** (*no plural*) the way a person or thing is (ବ୍ୟକ୍ତିଙ୍କ) ଚରିତ୍ର, ବ୍ୟକ୍ତିତ୍ୱ *He has a strong character.*

characteristic /ˌkærəktəˈrɪstɪk/ *noun* a feature which makes someone or something different from other people or things ବିଶେଷତ୍ୱ

charcoal /ˈtʃɑːkəʊl/ *noun* (*no plural*) a black substance that is made by burning wood. Charcoal is used as a fuel ଅଙ୍ଗାର, କାଠ କୋଇଲା

charge[1] /tʃɑ:dʒ/ *verb* (**charges, charging, charged**) **1** ask somebody to pay a certain price for something ନିର୍ଦ୍ଦିଷ୍ଟ ମୂଲ୍ୟ ମାଗିବା *The garage charged me Rs 200 for the repairs*. **2** say that somebody has done something wrong ଦୋଷାରୋପ କରିବା, ଅଭିଯୋଗ କରିବା *The police have charged him with murder*. **3** move quickly and with a lot of force ଆକ୍ରମଣ ପାଇଁ ଦୌଡ଼ିବା *The bull charged.*

charge[2] /tʃɑ:dʒ/ *noun* **1** the money that you must pay for something ମୂଲ୍ୟ, ଦର **2** a statement that somebody has done something wrong ଅଭିଯୋଗ, ଦୋଷାରୋପ *a charge of murder*

be in charge of somebody or **something** look after or control somebody or something (ବ୍ୟକ୍ତି ବା ପଦାର୍ଥର) ଦାୟିତ୍ୱ ନେବା, ଦେଖାଶୁଣା କରିବା *Raghu will be in charge of his baby brother when his mother goes out.*

chariot /ˈtʃæriət/ *noun* a small open vehicle drawn by horses in ancient times ପ୍ରାଚୀନ କାଳର ଘୋଡ଼ାଟଣା ରଥ

charity /ˈtʃærəti/ *noun* (*plural* **charities**) a group of people who collect money to help people who need it ଅଭାବଗ୍ରସ୍ତ ଲୋକଙ୍କୁ ସାହାଯ୍ୟ କରିବା ପାଇଁ ଟଙ୍କା ସଂଗ୍ରହ କରି ବାଣ୍ଟୁଥିବା ସଂସ୍ଥା *Many charities raised money for the flood affected people.*

charm /tʃɑ:m/ *noun* **1** (*no plural*) the power of quality of delighting people ଆନନ୍ଦଦାୟକ ଶକ୍ତି ବା ଗୁଣ *Anita has a lot of charm*. **2** (*plural* **charms**) a small thing that you wear because you think it will bring good luck ତେଉଁରିଆ, କବଚ, ତାବିଜ *She wears a necklace with a lucky charm on it.*

charm *verb* (**charms, charming, charmed**) make somebody like you ମୁଗ୍ଧ କରିବା *The baby charmed everybody with her smile.*

charming /ˈtʃɑ:mɪŋ/ *adjective* lovely; beautiful ସୁନ୍ଦର, ମନମୋହକ *a charming little village*

chart /tʃɑ:t/ *noun* **1** a drawing that gives information about something ତଥ୍ୟ ସୂଚାଉଥିବା ରେଖାଚିତ୍ର *a temperature chart* **2** a map of the sea that sailors use ନୌଚାଳନ ପାଇଁ ପଥନିର୍ଦ୍ଦେଶକ ମାନଚିତ୍ର

chase /tʃeɪs/ *verb* (**chases, chasing, chased**) run behind somebody or something and try to catch them ଗୋଡ଼ାଇବା, ଅନୁଧାବନ କରିବା *The dog chased the cat around the garden.*

chase *noun* ଅନୁଧାବନ *In that film, there is an exciting car chase.*

chat /tʃæt/ *noun* a friendly talk ଗପସପ, ଖୁସିଗପ, କଥାବାର୍ତ୍ତା *Let's have a chat about it later.*

chat *verb* (**chats, chatting, chatted**) talk in a friendly way ଗପସପ କରିବା, କଥାବାର୍ତ୍ତା କରିବା

chatter /ˈtʃætə(r)/ *verb* (**chatters, chattering, chattered**) **1** talk quickly about things that are not very important ବକବକ ହେବା *Stop chat-*

tering and finish your work. **2** when birds and monkeys chatter, they make short high sounds (ଚଢ଼େଇ ବା ମାଙ୍କଡ଼) ଚେଚାଁ, କଟରମଟର ହେବା

cheap /tʃi:p/ *adjective* (**cheaper, cheapest**) something that is cheap does not cost a lot of money ଶସ୍ତା *Tomatoes are cheaper in summer than in winter.* ✪ ବିପରୀତ **expensive** ବା **dear 3**

cheat /tʃi:t/ *verb* (**cheats, cheating, cheated**) do something that is not honest or fair ଠକିବା, ପ୍ରତାରଣା କରିବା *She cheated in the exam—she copied her friend's work.*

cheat *noun* a person who cheats ଠକ, ଶଠ, ପ୍ରତାରକ; ବ୍ୟକ୍ତି

check[1] /tʃek/ *verb* (**checks, checking, checked**) look at something to see that it is right, good, safe, etc. (ଅବସ୍ଥା, ସଠିକତା ଇତ୍ୟାଦି) ତନଖି କରିବା, ଯାଞ୍ଚ କରିବା, ପରୀକ୍ଷା କରିବା *Do the sums and then use a calculator to check your answers.* ○ *Check that all the windows are closed before you leave.*

check in tell the person at the desk in a hotel or an airport that you have arrived (ହୋଟେଲ୍ ବା ବିମାନ ବନ୍ଦରରେ) ପହଞ୍ଚି ତାଲିକାଭୁକ୍ତ ହେବା

check out pay your bill at a hotel, and leave ହିସାବ ତୁଟାଇ ହୋଟେଲ୍ ଛାଡ଼ିବା

check[2] /tʃek/ *adjective* a pattern of squares ଛକିକଟା ଡିଜାଇନ୍ ବା ଢ଼ାଞ୍ଚା

checked /tʃekt/ *adjective* with a pattern of squares ଛକିକଟା ଡିଜାଇନ୍ ବା ଢ଼ାଞ୍ଚା ଥିବା *a checked shirt*

check-up *noun* an examination by a doctor to see if you are well ସ୍ୱାସ୍ଥ୍ୟର ସମ୍ପୂର୍ଣ୍ଣ ଡାକ୍ତରୀ ମାଇନା ବା ପରୀକ୍ଷା

cheek /tʃi:k/ *noun* one of the two round parts of your face under your eyes ଗାଲ ➪ ଚିତ୍ର ପାଇଁ **face** ଦେଖନ୍ତୁ।

cheeky /tʃi:ki/ *adjective* (**cheekier, cheekiest**) not polite ଉଦ୍ଧତ *Don't be so cheeky!* ○ *She was scolded for being cheeky to the teacher.*

cheer /tʃɪə(r)/ *verb* (**cheers, cheering, cheered**) shout to show that you are pleased ପ୍ରଶଂସାଧ୍ୱନି କରିବା *The crowd cheered loudly when the President arrived.*

cheer up make somebody happier; become happier ଆନନ୍ଦିତ କରାଇବା, ଉତ୍ସାହିତ କରିବା *We gave Shelly some flowers to cheer her up.*

cheerful /ˈtʃɪəfl/ *adjective* happy ପ୍ରଫୁଲ୍ଲ, ପ୍ରସନ୍ନ *a cheerful smile*

cheerfully *adverb* ଆନନ୍ଦରେ, ଖୁସିରେ *He made tea for all of us cheerfully.*

cheese /tʃi:z/ *noun* a type of yellow or white food made from milk ଛେନା *bread and cheese*

cheetah /ˈtʃi:tə/ *noun* (*plural* **cheetahs**) a large wild animal of the cat family with black spots that can run very fast ଚିତାବାଘ

chef /ʃef/ *noun* the head cook in a restaurant ଭୋଜନାଳୟର ମୁଖ୍ୟ ରୋଷେଇଆ

chemical[1] /ˈkemɪkl/ *noun* a substance that is used in chemistry or is made by a chemical process ରାସାୟନିକ ପ୍ରକ୍ରିୟାରେ ବ୍ୟବହୃତ ଦ୍ରବ୍ୟ

chemical[2] /ˈkemɪkl/ *adjective* of chemistry or used in chemistry ରାସାୟନିକ *a chemical element*

chemist /ˈkemɪst/ *noun* **1** a person who makes and sells medicines ଔଷଧ ବିକ୍ରେତା ✪ **chemist** କର୍ମସ୍ଥାନକୁ **chemist's** କହନ୍ତି। ସେଠାରେ ଔଷଧ, ସାବୁନ୍, ଅତର ଇତ୍ୟାଦି ବିକ୍ରିହୁଏ। **2** a person who studies chemistry or who makes chemicals ରସାୟନବିତ୍

chemistry /ˈkemɪstri/ *noun* (*no plural*) the science that studies gases, liquids and solids to find out what they are and what they do ରସାୟନଶାସ୍ତ୍ର, ରସାୟନବିଦ୍ୟା

cheque /tʃek/ *noun* a piece of paper from a bank that you can write on and use to pay for things or draw money ବ୍ୟାଙ୍କରୁ ଟଙ୍କା କାଢ଼ିବା ପାଇଁ ବା କାହାରିକୁ ଟଙ୍କା ଦେବା ପାଇଁ ଲେଖୁଥିବା ବ୍ୟାଙ୍କ ପ୍ରଦତ୍ତ କାଗଜ, ଚେକ୍

cherry /ˈtʃeri/ *noun* (*plural* **cherries**) a small round red or black fruit with a hard seed inside ଭିତରେ ମଞ୍ଜିଥିବା ଏକ ଲାଲ୍ ବା କଳା ମିଠା କୋଳି ➪ ଚିତ୍ର ପାଇଁ **fruit** ଦେଖନ୍ତୁ।

chess /tʃes/ *noun* (*no plural*) a game that two people play with pieces called **chessmen** on a board that has black and white squares on it (called a **chessboard**) ସତରଞ୍ଚ ଖେଳ, ଚତୁଃରଙ୍ଗ ଖେଳ, ଚେସ୍

chest[1] /tʃest/ *noun* the front part of your body below your shoulders and above your waist ଛାତି, ବକ୍ଷ ➪ ଚିତ୍ର ପାଇଁ **body** ଦେଖନ୍ତୁ।

chest[2] /tʃest/ *noun* a large strong box with a lid ସିନ୍ଦୁକ, ବଡ଼ ବାକ୍ସ

chest of drawers *noun* (*plural* **chests of drawers**) a piece of furniture like a box with parts that you can pull out (**drawers**). It is usually used for keeping clothes in ଡ୍ରୟର୍, ଦରାଜ ବା ଡାଲାଥିବା କ୍ୟାବିନେଟ୍ ବା ଆଲମାରୀ

chew /tʃuː/ *verb* (**chews, chewing, chewed**) use your teeth to make food soft ଚୋବାଇବା, ଚର୍ବଣ କରିବା

chick /tʃɪk/ *noun* a young bird, especially a young chicken ଚଢ଼େଇଛୁଆ, ପକ୍ଷୀଶାବକ, (ବିଶେଷତଃ) କୁକୁଡ଼ାଛୁଆ

chicken /ˈtʃɪkɪn/ *noun* **1** (*plural* **chickens**) a bird that people keep on farms for its eggs and meat କୁକୁଡ଼ା ✪ ମାଈ କୁକୁଡ଼ାକୁ **hen** କହନ୍ତି ଓ ଅଣ୍ଡିରା କୁକୁଡ଼ାକୁ **cock** କହନ୍ତି। କୁକୁଡ଼ା ଛୁଆକୁ **chick** କୁହାଯାଏ। **2** (*no plural*) meat from a chicken କୁକୁଡ଼ାମାଂସ *roast chicken*

chief[1] /tʃiːf/ *adjective* most important; main ମୁଖ୍ୟ, ପ୍ରଧାନ *Careless driving is one of the chief causes of road accidents.*

chiefly *adverb* mostly; mainly ମୁଖ୍ୟତଃ, ପ୍ରଧାନତଃ।

chief[2] /tʃiːf/ *noun* the leader or ruler of a group of people ମୁଖିଆ, ମୁଖ୍ୟ ବ୍ୟକ୍ତି *the chief of an African tribe*

chief minister *noun* (*plural* **chief ministers**) the elected leader of the government in a state in India (ଭାରତରେ ରାଜ୍ୟ ସରକାରଙ୍କର) ମୁଖ୍ୟମନ୍ତ୍ରୀ

chieftain /ˈtʃiːftən/ *noun* the head of a tribe ମୁଖିଆ

child /tʃaɪld/ *noun* (*plural* **children** /ˈtʃɪldrən/) **1** a boy or girl ପିଲା (ବାଳକ ବା ବାଳିକା) *There are 30 children in the class.* **2** a daughter or son ପୁଅ ବା ଝିଅ *One of her children got married last year.*

childhood *noun* (*no plural*) the time when you are a child ବାଲ୍ୟାବସ୍ଥା, ଶୈଶବ *She had a happy childhood.*

chilli /ˈtʃɪli/ *noun* (*plural* **chillies**) a small green or red fruit of a plant that is used to give a hot taste to food ଲଙ୍କାମରିଚ

chillies

chilly /ˈtʃɪli/ *adjective* (**chillier, chilliest**) cold ଖୁବ୍ ଥଣ୍ଡା (ପାଗ ଇତ୍ୟାଦି) *a chilly morning* ମନେ ରଖନ୍ତୁ ! ଉଭୟ

> **chilli** ଓ **chilly** ର ଉଚ୍ଚାରଣ ଏକାପରି କିନ୍ତୁ ଅର୍ଥ ଅଲଗା ।
>
> **Chilli** (ଲଙ୍କାମରିଚ) ହେଲା ବିଶେଷ୍ୟ ଓ ଏହାକୁ ଖାଦ୍ୟ ପଦାର୍ଥରେ ରାଗ କରିବାକୁ ପକାଯାଏ । **Chilly** (ଖୁବ୍‌ଥଣ୍ଡା) ହେଲା ବିଶେଷଣ ଓ ଏହା ଥଣ୍ଡା ଜିନିଷକୁ ବର୍ଣ୍ଣନା କରିବା ପାଇଁ ବ୍ୟବହାର କରାଯାଏ ।

chime /tʃaɪm/ *verb* (**chimes, chiming, chimed**) make the sound that a bell makes ଘଣ୍ଟି ବାଜିବା ବା ବଜାଇବା *The clock chimed midnight.*

chimney /ˈtʃɪmni/ *noun* (*plural* **chimneys**) a large pipe over a fire that lets smoke go outside into the air ଘରୁ, ଫାୟାର୍‌ପ୍ଲେସରୁ, କାରଖାନାରୁ ଧୂଆଁ ବାହାରକୁ ଯିବା ପାଇଁ ଲମ୍ବା ନଳୀ, ଚିମ୍‌ନି ➪ ଚିତ୍ର ପାଇଁ **house** ଦେଖନ୍ତୁ ।

chimpanzee /ˌtʃɪmpænˈziː/ *noun* an African animal like a monkey with long arms and no tail (ଆଫ୍ରିକା ମହାଦେଶର) ଛୋଟ ଲାଙ୍ଗୁଳବିହୀନ ବାନର, ସିମ୍ପାଞ୍ଜି ➪ ଚିତ୍ର ପାଇଁ **ape** ଦେଖନ୍ତୁ ।

chin /tʃɪn/ *noun* the part of your face below your mouth ଚିବୁକ ➪ ଚିତ୍ର ପାଇଁ **face** ଦେଖନ୍ତୁ ।

chip¹ /tʃɪp/ *noun* **1** a thin slice of potato cooked in oil ସରୁ ଆଳୁ ଖଣ୍ଡର ଛଣାଭଜା *We had fish and chips for lunch.* **2** a microchip; a very small thing made of metal or plastic inside a computer, for example, that makes it work ବହୁ ବିଦ୍ୟୁତ୍ ପଥ ବା ସର୍କିଟ୍ ପରିବହନ କରୁଥିବା ଧାତୁ, ସିଲିକନ୍, ପ୍ଲାଷ୍ଟିକ ଇତ୍ୟାଦିର କ୍ଷୁଦ୍ର ଅର୍ଦ୍ଧଖଣ୍ଡ, ଚିପ୍, ମାଇକ୍ରୋଚିପ୍

chip² /tʃɪp/ *verb* (**chips, chipping, chipped**) break a small piece from something ଖଣ୍ଡଖଣ୍ଡ କରିବା, ଛୋଟ ଖଣ୍ଡ କରିବା, ଛୋଟ ଖଣ୍ଡ ଭାଙ୍ଗିଯିବା *Mother's cup has got chipped.*

chirp /tʃɜːp/ *noun* the short high sound that a small bird makes ଚଢ଼େଇର ରାବ

chirp *verb* (**chirps, chirping, chirped**) make this sound (ଚଢ଼େଇ) ଚେଁ ଚେଁ ରାବ କରିବା

chlorophyll /ˈklɒrəfɪl/ *noun* (*no plural*) the green substance in plants that helps them use sunlight to make their own food ପତ୍ରହରିତ୍; ଗଛପତ୍ରରେ ଥିବା ସବୁଜ ପଦାର୍ଥ (ଯାହା ସୂର୍ଯ୍ୟକିରଣରୁ ଗଛ ପାଇଁ ଖାଦ୍ୟ ତିଆରିରେ ସାହାଯ୍ୟ କରେ

ଆପଣ ଜାଣନ୍ତି କି ?
Chlorophyll ଦୁଇଟି ଗ୍ରୀକ୍ ଶବ୍ଦରୁ ତିଆରି —*chloro* (ସବୁଜ) ଏବଂ *phyll* (ପତ୍ର)

chocolate /ˈtʃɒklət/ *noun* a dark-brown sweet food that is made from cocoa କୋକୋ ମଞ୍ଜିର ଚୂନାରେ ତିଆରି ମିଠା, ଚକୋଲେଟ୍ *a bar of chocolate*

choice /tʃɔɪs/ *noun* **1** deciding which one; the act of choosing ବାଛିବା କାମ, ଚୟନ, ମନୋନୟନ *You made the right choice.* **2** a number of things that you can choose from ବାଛିବା ପାଇଁ ଥିବା ଜିନିଷସମୂହ *There is a big choice of vegetables in the market.*

choir /ˈkwaɪə(r)/ *noun* a big group of people who sing together ସମ୍ମିଳିତଗାୟନ ପାଇଁ ଏକ ବଡ଼ ଗୋଷ୍ଠୀ *a school choir*

choke /tʃəʊk/ *verb* (**chokes, choking, choked**) not be able to breathe because something is in your throat ଶ୍ୱାସରୋଧ କରିବା, ଶ୍ୱାସରୁଦ୍ଧ ହେବା

choose /tʃu:z/ *verb* (**chooses, choosing, chose** /tʃəʊz/, **has chosen** /ˈtʃəʊzn/) take the thing or person that you like best from the ones that are available ବାଛିବା, ଚୟନ କରିବା, ମନୋନୟନ କରିବା *Anita chose the biggest cake.*

chop /tʃɒp/ *verb* (**chops, chopping, chopped**) cut something with a knife or an axe ଛୁରୀ, କୁରାଢ଼ି ଇତ୍ୟାଦିର ଚୋଟରେ କାଟିବା *We chopped some wood for the fire.*

chord /kɔ:d/ *noun* a line that meets at two points on a circle ଜ୍ୟା, ବୃତ୍ତାଂଶର ଦୁଇ ସ୍ପର୍ଶକୁ ସଂଯୋଗ କରୁଥିବା ରେଖା ➪ **circle** ଦେଖନ୍ତୁ।

chore /tʃɔ:(r)/ *noun* a task that you have to do regularly ଦୈନନ୍ଦିନ କାମ, ତିନିଦିନିଆ କାମ *household chores like washing and cooking*

chorus /ˈkɔ:rəs/ *noun* (*plural* **choruses**) **1** a part of a song that you repeat ଗୀତର ଘୋଷା **2** music that is sung or words that are spoken by a group of people together ବହୁ ଲୋକଙ୍କର ଏକକାଳୀନ ଗାୟନ ବା କଥନ **3** a group of people singing or speaking together ମିଳିତ ସଂଗୀତର ଗାୟକ ଦଳ

chose, chosen ଶବ୍ଦ **choose** ର ଏକ ଧାତୁରୂପ

Christian /ˈkrɪstʃən/ *noun* a person who believes in Jesus Christ and what He taught ଖ୍ରୀଷ୍ଟଧର୍ମାବଲମ୍ବୀ ବ୍ୟକ୍ତି **Christian** *adjective* ଖ୍ରୀଷ୍ଟଧର୍ମ ସମ୍ବନ୍ଧୀୟ *Christian customs*

Christianity /ˌkrɪstiˈænəti/ *noun* (*no plural*) the religion that follows what Jesus Christ taught ଖ୍ରୀଷ୍ଟଧର୍ମ, ଯିଶୁଖ୍ରୀଷ୍ଟଙ୍କ ଦ୍ୱାରା ଦୀକ୍ଷିତ ଧର୍ମ

Christmas /ˈkrɪsməs/ *noun* 25 December, the day on which Jesus Christ's birthday is celebrated, 25 ଯିଶୁଖ୍ରୀଷ୍ଟଙ୍କ ଜନ୍ମଦିନ (ଡିସେମ୍ବର ୨୫) ରେ ପାଳିତ ଉତ୍ସବ

chrysalis /ˈkrɪsəlɪs/ *noun* the stage in the life cycle of a butterfly or moth where it encloses itself in a hard case and emerges after some time as an adult ପ୍ରଜାପତି ବା ମଥ୍ (ଏକ କୀଟ) ର ପ୍ୟୁପା ବା ମଧ୍ୟାବସ୍ଥାର ଆବରଣ ➪ ଚିତ୍ର ପାଇଁ **caterpillar** ଦେଖନ୍ତୁ।

chubby /ˈtʃʌbi/ *adjective* plump in a pleasant, healthy-looking way ହୃଷ୍ଟପୁଷ୍ଟ, ଗୋଲ୍‌ଗାଲ୍, ମୋଟାସୋଟା *chubby cheeks*

chuckle /ˈtʃʌkl/ *verb* (**chuckles, chuckling, chuckled**) laugh quietly ମନେମନେ ବା ପାଟିଚିପି ହସିବା, ଓଠଚିପି ହସିବା

church /tʃɜːtʃ/ *noun* (*plural* **churches**) a building where Christians go to pray ଗୀର୍ଜା, ଖ୍ରୀଷ୍ଟୀୟ ଉପାସନା ଗୃହ *They go to church every Sunday.*

cigarette /ˌsɪɡəˈret/ *noun* small pieces of tobacco in a tube of paper for smoking ସିଗାରେଟ୍

cinema /ˈsɪnəmə/ *noun* **1** a place where you go to see a film ସିନେମାଘର, ଚଳଚ୍ଚିତ୍ର ପ୍ରଦର୍ଶନଗୃହ *Let's go to the cinema tonight.* **2** the film industry in general ଚଳଚ୍ଚିତ୍ର ଶିଳ୍ପ *the Indian cinema*

circle[1] /ˈsɜːkl/ *noun* a round shape; a ring ବୃତ୍ତ

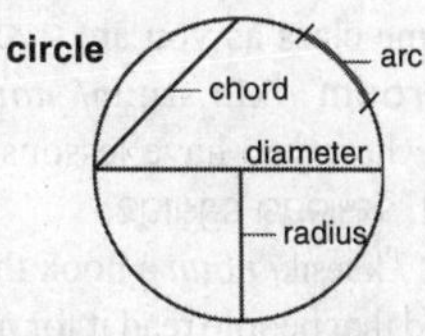

circle[2] /ˈsɜːkl/ *verb* (**circles, circling, circled**) go around something in a circle ଚାରିପଟେ ବୁଲି ଆସିବା, ବୃତ୍ତାକାରରେ ଗତି କରିବା *The plane circled the airport twice before landing.*

circuit /ˈsɜːkɪt/ *noun* the complete path through which an electric current can flow around ବିଦ୍ୟୁତ୍‌ପଥ, ବିଦ୍ୟୁତ ପ୍ରବାହର ପରିପଥ

circular /ˈsɜːkjələ(r)/ *adjective* with the shape of a circle; round ଗୋଲାକାର, ମଣ୍ଡଳାକାର, ବୃତ୍ତାକାର, ବର୍ତ୍ତୁଳ *a circular path*

circulate /ˈsɜːkjəleɪt/ *verb* (**circulates, circulating, circulated**) move round ସଂଚାଳନ କରିବା, ସଂଚାଳିତ ହେବା *Blood circulates in our bodies.*

circulation /ˌsɜːkjəˈleɪʃn/ *noun* **1** the movement of blood from the heart to the different parts of the body and back to the heart (ଶରୀରରେ) ରକ୍ତ ସଂଚାଳନ, ରକ୍ତ ପ୍ରବାହ **2** the movement of something from place to place or person to person (ତଥ୍ୟ, ଖବର ଇତ୍ୟାଦିର) ପ୍ରସାର

circulatory /ˌsɜːkjəˈleɪtəri/ *adjective* of or about blood circulation ରକ୍ତ ସଂଚାଳନ ସମ୍ବନ୍ଧୀୟ

circumference /səˈkʌmfərəns/ *noun* the distance around a circle (ବୃତ୍ତର) ପରିଧି

circumstances /ˈsɜːkəmstənsɪz/ *noun* (*plural*) the facts that are connected to an event or a person କୌଣସି ଘଟଣା ସହ ସମ୍ପୃକ୍ତ ବିଷୟ ବା ତଥ୍ୟ, ପରିସ୍ଥିତି; ବ୍ୟକ୍ତିଙ୍କ ଅବସ୍ଥା (ବିଶେଷତଃ ସ୍ୱଚ୍ଛଳତା ସମ୍ବନ୍ଧୀୟ) *financial circumstances*

circus /ˈsɜːkəs/ *noun* (*plural* **circuses**) a show in a big tent, with clowns, acrobats and animals ସର୍କସ୍

citizen /ˈsɪtɪzn/ *noun* a person who belongs to a country or a town ନାଗରିକ, ଦେଶବାସୀ, ବାସିନ୍ଦା *She became an Indian citizen.* ○ *the citizens of Delhi*

city /ˈsɪti/ *noun* (*plural* **cities**) a big and important town ବଡ଼ ସହର, ନଗର

civil /ˈsɪvl/ *adjective* of the people of a country ନାଗରିକମାନଙ୍କ ସମ୍ବନ୍ଧୀୟ *civil rights*

the Civil Service *noun* (*no plural*) the officials who work for the government, except for those belonging to the armed forces ସରକାରଙ୍କର ପ୍ରଶାସନିକ ସେବା ଓ ଏଥିରେ ନିୟୋଜିତ କର୍ମଚାରୀ

civilian /səˈvɪliən/ *noun* a person who is not a soldier ବେସାମରିକ ବ୍ୟକ୍ତି

civilization /ˌsɪvəlaɪˈzeɪʃn/ *noun* the way people live together in a particular place at a particular period of time ସଭ୍ୟତା *ancient civilizations*

claim /kleɪm/ *verb* (**claims, claiming, claimed**) **1** ask for something because it is yours ନିଜର ସମ୍ପତ୍ତି ବୋଲି ଦାବି କରିବା *If nobody claims the camera you found, you can have it.* **2** say that something is true ସତ ବୋଲି କହିବା *Amit claims that he did the work without help.*

clap /klæp/ *verb* (**claps, clapping, clapped**) hit your hands together to make a noise, usually to show that you like something ତାଳି ମାରିବା, କରତାଳି ଦେବା *At the end of the concert, the audience clapped loudly.*

clap *noun* the sound that you make when you hit your hands together ତାଳି, କରତାଳି

clash /klæʃ/ *verb* (**clashes, clashing, clashed**) **1** fight or argue ଲଢ଼େଇ ବା ଯୁକ୍ତିତର୍କ କରିବା, ବିବାଦ କରିବା *Police clashed with football fans outside the stadium last Saturday.* **2** be at the same time ସମକାଳୀନ ଘଟିବା *The match clashed with my swimming lesson, so I couldn't watch it.*

clasp /klɑːsp/ *verb* (**clasps, clasping, clasped**) when you clasp something, you hold it tightly ଭିଡ଼ିଧରିବା, ଜଡ଼େଇ ଧରିବା *The mother clasped her baby in her arms.*

class /klɑːs/ *noun* (*plural* **classes**) **1** a group of children or students who learn together ବିଦ୍ୟାଳୟର ଶ୍ରେଣୀ, କ୍ଲାସ୍ *The whole class passed the exam.* **2** the time when you learn something with a teacher ବିଦ୍ୟାଳୟରେ ଶିକ୍ଷକ ପଢ଼ାଉଥିବା ସମୟ *Classes begin at nine o'clock.* **3** a group of people or things that are the same in some way (ପ୍ରାଣୀ ବା ପଦାର୍ଥର) ଶ୍ରେଣୀ, ବର୍ଗ, ବିଭାଗ *There are many different classes of animals.*

classmate /ˈklɑːsmeɪt/ *noun* Your classmate is the person who is in the same class as you are ସହପାଠୀ

classroom /ˈklɑːsruːm/ *noun* a room where you have lessons in a school ବିଦ୍ୟାଳୟର ଶ୍ରେଣୀଗୃହ

classic /ˈklæsɪk/ *noun* a book that is so good that people read it for many years after it was written ଉଚ୍ଚଶ୍ରେଣୀର ଲେଖା ଯାହା ବହୁକାଳ ପଢ଼ାହୁଏ Alice in Wonderland *is a children's classic.*

classical /ˈklæsɪkl/ *adjective* in a style that people have used for a long time because they think it is good ପୁରାତନ କାଳର ରୀତି ଉପରେ ଆଧାରିତ *classical music*

classify /ˈklæsɪfaɪ/ *verb* (**classifies, classifying, classified, has classified**) divide things into groups according to the features that they have in common ଶ୍ରେଣୀ ବିଭାଗ କରିବା

classification /ˌklæsɪfɪˈkeɪʃn/ *noun* the division of something into groups according to the features that they have in common ଶ୍ରେଣୀବିଭାଗ *classification of animals into vertebrates and invertebrates*

clatter /ˈklætə(r)/ *noun* (*no plural*) a loud noise that hard things make when they hit each other ଖଡ୍‌ଖଡ୍ ଧଡ୍ ଧଡ୍ ଶବ୍ଦ *the clatter of knives and forks*

clause /klɔːz/ *noun* a part of a sentence that has a subject and a verb in it ବାକ୍ୟାଂଶ, ଖଣ୍ଡବାକ୍ୟ *If he leaves for home tonight, he will have to return on Sunday.* ଏଥିରେ ବାକ୍ୟାଂଶ ହେଲେ *If he leaves for home tonight* ଏବଂ *he will have to return on Sunday.*

claw /klɔː/ *noun* one of the hard pointed parts on the feet of some animals and birds (ପଶୁ, ପକ୍ଷୀ–ବାଘ, ଚିଲ ପ୍ରଭୃତିର) ମୁନିଆ ନଖ ଯାହାଦ୍ୱାରା ଶିକାରୀ ଜୀବ ଶିକାର କରିଥାଏ ଓ ସ୍ଥାନାନ୍ତର ମଧ୍ୟ କରିଥାଏ; ପଞ୍ଝା *Cats have sharp claws.*

clay /kleɪ/ *noun* (*no plural*) a kind of heavy earth that becomes hard when it is baked. Clay is used to make things like pots and tiles ପଶୁ ବା ପକ୍ଷୀର ମୁନିଆ ନଖ

clean¹ /kliːn/ *adjective* (**cleaner, cleanest**) not dirty ସଫାସୁତୁରା, ନିର୍ମଳ, ପରିଷ୍କୃତ *clean clothes* ○ *clean air* ✪ ବିପରୀତ **dirty** ବା **unclean**

clean² /kliːn/ *verb* (**cleans, cleaning, cleaned**) take away the dirt or marks from something; make something clean ସଫା କରିବା, ପରିଷ୍କାର କରିବା *Rohan helped his mother to clean the kitchen.*

cleanliness /ˈklenlinəs/ *noun* (*no plural*) the habit of being clean and tidy ପରିଚ୍ଛନ୍ନତା, ସଫାସୁତୁରା

clear¹ /klɪə(r)/ *adjective* (**clearer, clearest**) **1** easy to see, hear or understand ଦେଖିବା, ଶୁଣିବା ବୁଝିବା ପାଇଁ ସହଜ, ସୁସ୍ପଷ୍ଟ *She spoke in a loud clear voice.* ○ *This photograph is very clear.* **2** bright; without clouds ଉଜ୍ଜ୍ୱଳ, ମେଘ ନଥିବା *a clear day*

clear² /klɪə(r)/ *verb* (**clears, clearing, cleared**) **1** take things away from a place because you do not need them there ସଫା, କରିବା, ଅଦରକାରୀ ଜିନିଷ କାଢ଼ି ନେବା *When you have finished your meal, clear the table.* **2** become clear (ପାଗ ଇତ୍ୟାଦି) ପରିଷ୍କାର ହେବା *It rained in the morning, but in the afternoon the sky cleared.*
clear up make a place clean and tidy ସ୍ଥାନ ସଫାସୁତୁରା କରିବା *She helped me to clear up after the party.*

clearly /ˈklɪəli/ *adverb* **1** in a way that is easy to see, hear or understand ସ୍ପଷ୍ଟ ଭାବରେ *The notes explain* *very clearly what you have to do.* **2** without any doubt ପ୍ରକୃତରେ, ନିଃସନ୍ଦେହରେ, ନିଦ୍ୱନ୍ଦ୍ୱରେ *She is clearly very intelligent.*

clerk /klɑ:k/ *noun* a person in an office or bank who does things like writing letters କିରାଣୀ

clever /ˈklevə(r)/ *adjective* (**cleverer, cleverest**) able to learn, understand or do something quickly and well ଚାଲାକ, ଚତୁର, ଦକ୍ଷ, ବୁଦ୍ଧିମାନ୍ *a clever student*

cleverly *adverb* ଚତୁର ଭାବରେ, ଦକ୍ଷତାର ସହିତ *The book is cleverly written.*

cleverness *noun* (*no plural*) ଚତୁରତା, ବୁଦ୍ଧିମତା, ଦକ୍ଷତା *His cleverness helped him when he got locked outside the house.*

click /klɪk/ *noun* a short sharp sound ଟିକ୍ ବା ଖଟ୍ ଶବ୍ଦ *I heard a click as someone switched the light on.*

click *verb* (**clicks, clicking, clicked**) make this sound ଟିକ୍ ବା ଖଟ୍ ଶବ୍ଦ କରିବା *The door clicked shut.*

client /ˈklaɪənt/ *noun* a person who pays another person, for example a lawyer or an accountant, for help or advice (ଓକିଲ ବା ଅନ୍ୟ ଦକ୍ଷ ବ୍ୟକ୍ତିଙ୍କ) ମହକିଲ

cliff /klɪf/ *noun* the high steep side of a hill by the sea ତୀକ୍ଷଣ ଭାବେ ଉପରକୁ ଉଠିଥିବା ପାହାଡ଼ର ପାର୍ଶ୍ୱ ବା ଶୀର୍ଷ

climate /ˈklaɪmət/ *noun* the sort of weather that a place has ପାଣିପାଗ, ଜଳବାୟୁ, ପାଗ *Mangoes do not grow in cold climates.*

climb /klaɪm/ *verb* (**climbs, climbing, climbed**) **1** go up or down, walking or using your hands and feet (ଗଛ ବା ପାହାଡ଼ ପ୍ରଭୃତି ଉଚ୍ଚ ସ୍ଥାନକୁ ଚଢ଼ିବା ବା ଓହ୍ଲାଇବା **2** move to a higher place ଉଚ୍ଚାଜାଗାକୁ ଯିବା *The road climbs steeply.*

climb *noun* (*no plural*) ଆରୋହଣ *It was a long climb from the village to the top of the mountain.*

climbing *noun* (*no plural*) the sport of climbing mountains or rocks ପାହାଡ଼ ପଥର ଚଢ଼ା ଖେଳ

climber /ˈklaɪmə(r)/ *noun* a person who goes up and down mountains or rocks as a sport ପର୍ବତ ଆରୋହୀ

cling /klɪŋ/ *verb* (**clings, clinging, clung** /klʌŋ/, **has clung**) hold or stick tightly to somebody or something ଲାଖିଯିବା, ଜଡ଼େଇ ଧରିବା *The small child was crying and clinging to her mother.*

clinic /ˈklɪnɪk/ *noun* a place where you can go to get special help from a doctor ଘରୋଇ ଚିକିତ୍ସାଳୟ

clip[1] /klɪp/ *noun* a small piece of metal or plastic for holding things together ଧାରକ, କ୍ଲିପ୍ (କାଗଜ ଇତ୍ୟାଦି ଚାପି ଧରିବା ପାଇଁ ଧାତୁ ବା ପ୍ଲାଷ୍ଟିକର କ୍ଲିପ୍) *a paper clip*

clip *verb* (**clips, clipping, clipped**) join something to another thing with a clip କ୍ଲିପ୍ ଦ୍ୱାରା ଯୋଖି ଧରିବା *I clipped the photo to the letter.*

clip[2] /klɪp/ *verb* (**clips, clipping, clipped**) cut something in small parts to make it tidy ପରିଷ୍କାର କରିବା ପାଇଁ ଅଳ୍ପଅଳ୍ପ କାଟିବା *clip the bushes*

cloak /kləʊk/ *noun* a very loose coat that has no sleeves ଢ଼ିଲା ବାହାରପିନ୍ଧା ହାତ ନଥିବା ଲମ୍ବା କୋଟ୍

clock /klɒk/ *noun* a thing that shows you what time it is. It stands in a room or hangs on a wall (ଘରେ ଥୁଆ ହେବା କାନ୍ଥରେ ଝୁଲାହେବା) କାନ୍ଥ ଘଣ୍ଟା, ଏଲ୍‌ରାମ୍ ଘଣ୍ଟା *an alarm clock* ✪ ହାତ ବନ୍ଧା ଘଣ୍ଟାକୁ **watch** କହନ୍ତି।

> ✪ ପ୍ରକୃତ ସମୟ ଠାରୁ ଆଗୁଆ ସମୟ ଦେଖାଉଥିବା ଘଣ୍ଟା ବା ୱାଚ୍‌କୁ **fast** ଚାଲୁଛି ବୋଲି କହନ୍ତି। ପଛୁଆ ସମୟ ଦେଖାଇଲେ ତାକୁ **slow** କହନ୍ତି।

clockwise /ˈklɒkwaɪz/ *adjective, adverb* in the direction that the hands of a clock move ଘଣ୍ଟାକଣ୍ଟାର ଗତି ଦିଗରେ, ବାମରୁ ଡାହାଣକୁ *Turn the handle clockwise.* ✪ ବିପରୀତ **anticlockwise**

close[1] /kləʊz/ *adjective, adverb* (**closer, closest**) **1** near ନିକଟ, ନିକଟବର୍ତ୍ତୀ; ପାଖରେ, ନିକଟରେ *We live close to the station.* ✪ ବିପରୀତ **far**[1] **2** if people are close, they like or love each other very much ଘନିଷ୍ଠ, ନିକଟ ସମ୍ପର୍କୀୟ *I'm very close to my sister.*

closely *adverb* in a close way ନିକଟରୁ, ପୁଙ୍ଖାନୁପୁଙ୍ଖ ଭାବେ *We watched her closely.* ○ *Paul entered, closely followed by Mike.*

close[2] /kləʊz/ *verb* (**closes, closing, closed**) **1** shut ବନ୍ଦ କରିବା *Please close the window.* ○ *Close your eyes!* **2** stop being open, so that people cannot go there ବନ୍ଦ ହେବା *The banks close at 4.30 p.m.* ✪ ବିପରୀତ **open**[2]

closed *adjective* not open; shut ବନ୍ଦ *The shops are closed on Sundays.*

cloth /klɒθ/ *noun* **1** (*no plural*) material that is made of wool, cotton, etc. and that we use for making clothes and other things କପା, ପଶମ, ରେଶମ ଇତ୍ୟାଦିର କନା, ଲୁଗା ✪ ସାଧାରଣତଃ **material** ଶବ୍ଦ ବ୍ୟବହାର କରାଯାଏ। **2** a piece of cloth that you use for a special job (ବିଶେଷ କାମରେ ବ୍ୟବହୃତ) ଖଣ୍ଡେ କନା *a tablecloth*

clothe /kləʊð/ *verb* (**clothes, clothing, clothed**) if you clothe someone, you give them clothes to wear ପୋଷାକ ଯୋଗାଇବା ବା ପିନ୍ଧାଇବା; ଜାମାପଟା ପିନ୍ଧିବା *to feed and clothe an orphan*

clothes /kləʊðz/ *noun* (*plural*) things like dresses, shirts and trousers, that you wear to cover your body ଜାମାପଟା, ପିନ୍ଧିବା ଲୁଗାପଟା, ପୋଷାକ ପରିଚ୍ଛଦ *She was wearing new clothes.*

clothes line *noun* (*plural* **clothes lines**) the rope on which you hang out your wet clothes to dry ଲୁଗାଶୁଖା ଦଉଡ଼ି

cloud /klaʊd/ *noun* **1** a white or grey shape in the sky that is made of small drops of water ମେଘ, ଜଳଦ *Look at those dark clouds. It's going to rain.* **2** dust or smoke that looks like a cloud ଧୂଳି ବା ଧୂଆଁର ମେଘ ପରି ଆଚ୍ଛାଦନ *clouds of smoke*

cloudy *adjective* (**cloudier, cloudiest**) with a lot of clouds ମେଘୁଆ, ମେଘପୂର୍ଣ୍ଣ *a cloudy sky*

clove /kləʊv/ *noun* **1** a small dried flower of a tree that grows in hot countries and is used to add a special flavour to food ଲବଙ୍ଗ **2** one of the small separate parts of garlic ରସୁଣର କୋଳା

clove 1

garlic

clove 2

clown /klaʊn/ *noun* a person in a circus who wears funny clothes and makes people laugh ହସାଉଥିବା ଅଭିନୟକାରୀ (ବିଶେଷତଃ ସର୍କସ୍‌ରେ), ଜୋକର୍

club /klʌb/ *noun* **1** a group of people who do something together, or the place where they meet ସମିତି, ସଂଘ, କ୍ଲବ୍ *I belong to the tennis club.* **2** a heavy stick with a thick end ମୋଟା ମୁଣ୍ଡଥିବା ଭାରି ବାଡ଼ି, ଗଦା **3 clubs** (*plural*) the playing cards that have the shape ♣ on them ତାସ୍ ମୁଠାର ଚିଡ଼ିଆ ଘର *the three of clubs*

cluck /klʌk/ *verb* (**clucks, clucking, clucked**) make a noise like a hen କୁକୁଡ଼ାର ରାବ ପରି କ୍ଲକ୍ କ୍ଲକ୍ ଧ୍ୱନି ➪ **crow**[2] ବି ଦେଖନ୍ତୁ।

clue /klu:/ *noun* something that helps to find the answer to a problem, or to know the truth ରହସ୍ୟ ଉଦ୍‌ଘାଟନର ସୂତ୍ର, ଅନୁସନ୍ଧାନର ବାଟ ଦେଖାଉଥିବା ପଦାର୍ଥ *The police have found a clue that may help them to catch the burglar.*

clumsy /ˈklʌmzi/ *adjective* (**clumsier, clumsiest**) if you are clumsy, you often drop things or do things badly because you do not move in an easy or careful way (ଚଲାବୁଲା ବା କାମରେ) ବେଢ଼ଙ୍ଗିଆ, ଅବାଗିଆ, ଅଡୁଆ, ଅଳିଆ

clung ଶବ୍ଦ **cling** ର ଏକ ଧାତୁରୂପ

cluster /ˈklʌstə(r)/ *noun* a group of things of the same kind standing, growing or appearing together ସମଜାତୀୟ ଲୋକ, ପଶୁ ବା ପଦାର୍ଥର ଦଳ, ଗୁଚ୍ଛ ବା ପୁଞ୍ଜ *a cluster of stars*

clutch /klʌtʃ/ *verb* (**clutches, clutching, clutched**) hold something tightly ଜାବୁଡ଼ି ଧରିବା, ଦୃଢ଼ ଭାବରେ ଧରିରଖିବା। *The child clutched his mother's hand.*

cm *abbreviation* ହେଲା **centimetre** ମିଟରର ଶତତମ ଅଂଶ

c/o *abbreviation* ହେଲା **care of** ର ସଂକ୍ଷିପ୍ତ ରୂପ ✪ **c/o** (ଅନ୍ୟର) ମାରଫତରେ, ଜରିଆରେ (ଚିଠି ଇତ୍ୟାଦିରେ ବା ଠିକଣାରେ) *Mrs Usha Roy, c/o Mrs Varsha Mehta*

coach[1] /kəʊtʃ/ *noun* (*plural* **coaches**) **1** one of the parts of a train where people sit ରେଳଗାଡ଼ିର ଯାତ୍ରୀଡବା **2** a vehicle with four wheels that is pulled by horses ଚାରିଚକିଆ ଘୋଡ଼ାଗାଡ଼ି **3** a bus for taking people on long journeys ଦୂରଗାମୀ ବସ୍

coach[2] /kəʊtʃ/ *noun* (*plural* **coaches**) a person who teaches a sport ଖେଳ ଶିଖାଉଥିବା ବ୍ୟକ୍ତି, କୋଚ୍ *a football coach*

coach *verb* (**coaches, coaching, coached**) teach somebody ଶିଖାଇବା,

ପଢ଼ାଇବା, ଶିକ୍ଷା ଦେବା *She is coaching the Indian team for the Olympics.*

coal /kəʊl/ *noun* (*no plural*) hard black substance that is found below the ground and produces heat when you burn it କୋଇଲା, ଖଣିଜ କୋଇଲା

coarse /kɔːs/ *adjective* (**coarser, coarsest**) made of large thick pieces so that it is not smooth; rough ଖଦଡ଼ା, ଅମସୃଣ, ଚିକ୍କଣ ହୋଇ ନଥିବା *coarse sand* ○ *coarse material* ✪ ବିପରୀତ **fine**[1] **5**

coast /kəʊst/ *noun* the part of the land that is next to the sea ସମୁଦ୍ର ଉପକୂଳ ଓ ତାହାର ତଟଭୂମି, ବେଳାଭୂମି *the east coast of India*

coastline /ˈkəʊstlaɪn/ *noun* the edge of the land next to the sea ସମୁଦ୍ର ଧାର *a rocky coastline*

coat[1] /kəʊt/ *noun* **1** a piece of clothing that you wear over your other clothes when you go outside in cold weather or rain କୋଟ୍, ଜ୍ୟାକେଟ୍ *Put your coat on—it's cold today.* ○ *a raincoat* **2** the hair or fur that covers an animal ପଶୁର ଲୋମଶ ଆବରଣ *A tiger has a striped coat.*

coat[2] /kəʊt/ *verb* (**coats, coating, coated**) apply a layer of something over another thing (ରଙ୍ଗ ଇତ୍ୟାଦି) ବୋଳିବା, ଲେପନ କରିବା *Coat the cutlets with bread crumbs.*

cobbler /ˈkɒblə(r)/ *noun* a person who mends shoes ମୋଚି

cobra /ˈkəʊbrə/ *noun* a poisonous snake found in Asia and Africa, that can spread out the skin at the back of its head to make itself look bigger when attacked ନାଗ ସାପ, ଗୋଖର ସାପ, ମଣିନାଗ, ଫଣାଥିବା ନାଗ

cobweb /ˈkɒbweb/ *noun* a net that a spider makes to catch insects ବୁଢ଼ିଆଣୀ ଜାଲ

cock /kɒk/ *noun* a male chicken ଗଞ୍ଜା, ଅଣ୍ଡିରା କୁକୁଡ଼ା

cockpit /ˈkɒkpɪt/ *noun* the part of a plane where the pilot sits ଉଡ଼ାଜାହାଜରେ ବିମାନଚାଳକ (ପାଇଲଟ୍) ର ବସିବା ପ୍ରକୋଷ୍ଠ

cockroach /ˈkɒkrəʊtʃ/ *noun* (*plural* **cockroaches**) a large brown insect that lives in dirty places ଅସରପା । ➪ ଚିତ୍ର ପାଇଁ **invertebrates** ଦେଖନ୍ତୁ ।

cocoa /ˈkəʊkəʊ/ *noun* (*no plural*) a brown powder from the beans of a tree, that is used in making chocolate କୋକୋ ମଞ୍ଜିର ଚୂନା

coconut /ˈkəʊkənʌt/ *noun* a very large brown nut that grows on trees near the coasts of hot countries like India. Coconuts are hard and hairy on the outside, and they have sweet white food and liquid inside ନଡ଼ିଆ।

cocoon /kəˈkuːn/ *noun* a small cover of thin silken threads that a silkworm makes to protect itself before it is ready to become an adult butterfly or moth ପ୍ରଜାପତି, ମଥ୍ ଇତ୍ୟାଦି କୀଟ ପ୍ରଥମାବସ୍ଥାରେ ନିଜ ଚାରିପଟେ ବୁଣିଥିବା ଖୋଷା ➪ **caterpillar** ଦେଖନ୍ତୁ ।

code /kəʊd/ *noun* **1** a way of writing secret messages, using letters, numbers or special signs ସାଙ୍କେତିକ ଅକ୍ଷର, ସଂଖ୍ୟା ବା ଚିହ୍ନ ଦ୍ୱାରା ଗୋପନ ବାର୍ତ୍ତା ଲେଖିବା ପଦ୍ଧତି *The list of names was written in code.* **2** a group of numbers or letters that helps you find something କୌଣସି ଜିନିଷ ପାଇବା ପାଇଁ ସାଙ୍କେତିକ ଅକ୍ଷର, ସଂଖ୍ୟା ବା ଚିହ୍ନ *What's the telephone code for Delhi?*

coffee /ˈkɒfi/ *noun* (*no plural*) a drink of hot water mixed with a brown powder made from the beans of a tree that grows in hot countries କଫି (ଗ୍ରୀଷ୍ମମଣ୍ଡଳୀୟ ଏକ ପ୍ରକାର ବୁଦାଳିଆ ଗଛର ମଞ୍ଜି ବା ଏଥିରେ ତିଆରି ପାନୀୟ) *Would you like coffee or tea?* ○ *a cup of coffee*

coffin /ˈkɒfɪn/ *noun* a box that you put a dead person's body in କବରବାକ୍ସ, କଫିନ୍

coil /kɔɪl/ *noun* a long piece of rope or wire that goes round in circles କୁଣ୍ଡଳାକାରରେ ଗୁଡ଼ା ଯାଇଥିବା ଦଉଡ଼ି ବା ତାର, କଏଲ୍ *a coil of rope*

coil *verb* (**coils, coiling, coiled**) make something into a lot of circles that are joined together କୁଣ୍ଡଳାକାରରେ ଗୁଡ଼ାଇବା। *The snake coiled itself round a branch.*

coin /kɔɪn/ *noun* a round piece of money made of metal ଗୋଲାକାର ଧାତୁ ନିର୍ମିତ ମୁଦ୍ରା *a five-rupee coin*

coincide /ˌkəʊɪnˈsaɪd/ *verb* (**coincides, coinciding, coincided**) be or happen at the same time ଏକା ସମୟରେ ଘଟିବା *My parents' wedding anniversary coincides with Diwali this year.*

coincidence /kəʊˈɪnsɪdəns/ *noun* when things happen at the same time or in the same place by chance ଆକସ୍ମିକ ଭାବେ ଏକ ସମୟରେ ବା ସ୍ଥାନରେ ଘଟୁଥିବା ଘଟଣା, ସମସଂପାତ, କାକତାଳୀୟ *What a coincidence! I was thinking about you when you phoned!*

coir /ˈkɔɪə(r)/ *noun* (*no plural*) a rough material that is made from the fibres on the shell of a coconut ନଡ଼ିଆ କତା *a coir mattress*

cold[1] /kəʊld/ *adjective* (**colder, coldest**) not hot or warm; with a low temperature. Ice and snow are cold ଥଣ୍ଡା, ଶୀତ *Put your coat on—it's cold outside.* ○ *cold water*

cold[2] /kəʊld/ *noun* **1** (*no plural*) cold weather ଥଣ୍ଡା ପାଗ, କୋହଲା ପାଗ *Don't go out in the cold.* **2** (*plural* **colds**) an illness that makes you sneeze and cough ସର୍ଦ୍ଦି, ଥଣ୍ଡା, ଶ୍ଳେଷ୍ମା *I've caught a cold.*

cold-blooded *adjective* a cold-blooded animal has a body temperature that changes with the temperature of the surroundings ବାହାର ଉତ୍ତାପ ସାଙ୍ଗେ ନିଜ ରକ୍ତ ଥଣ୍ଡା ବା ଗରମ କରି ପାରୁଥିବା (ଜୀବ) *Reptiles and fish are cold-blooded animals.* ✪ ବିପରୀତ **warm-blooded**

coldly /ˈkəʊldli/ *adverb* in an unfriendly and unkind way ଉଦାସୀନ ବା ଦୟାହୀନ ଭାବରେ ✪ ବିପରୀତ **warmly**

collapse /kəˈlæps/ *verb* (**collapses, collapsing, collapsed**) fall down suddenly ହଠାତ୍ ପଡ଼ିଯିବା ବା ଭାଙ୍ଗିଯିବା *The building collapsed in the earthquake.*

collapse *noun* ହଠାତ୍ ପଡ଼ିଯିବା ବା ଭାଙ୍ଗିଯିବା ପ୍ରକ୍ରିୟା, ହଠାତ୍ ପତନ *the collapse of the bridge*

collar /ˈkɒlə(r)/ *noun* **1** the part of your clothes that goes round your neck ଜାମା ଇତ୍ୟାଦିର ଗଳାବନ୍ଧ, କଲାର୍ **2** a band that you put round the neck of a dog or cat କୁକୁର ବା ବିଲେଇଙ୍କ ଗଳାବନ୍ଧନ ପଟି ବା ବେଲ୍ଟ୍

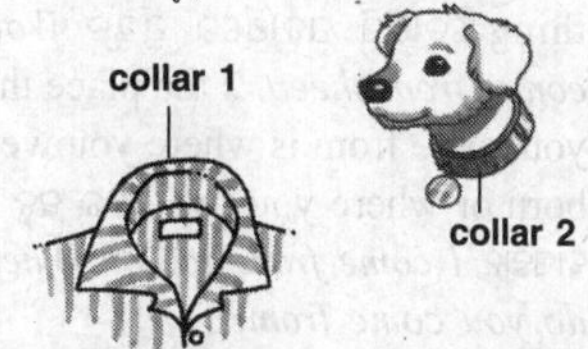

colleague /ˈkɒli:g/ *noun* a person who works with you ସହକର୍ମୀ

collect /kəˈlekt/ *verb* (**collects, collecting, collected**) **1** take things from different people or places and put them together ସଂଗ୍ରହ କରି କାମ କରିବା; ଏକାଠି ହେବା *My son collects stamps.* **2** go and bring somebody or something from a place ଆଣିବା *She collects her children from school at 3.30 p.m.*

collection /kəˈlekʃn/ *noun* a group of things that somebody has brought together ସଂଗୃହୀତ ବସ୍ତୁ *a coin collection*

collector /kəˈlektə(r)/ *noun* a person who collects things as a hobby or as a job ସଂଗ୍ରାହକ *a stamp collector* ○ *a ticket collector at a railway station*

college /ˈkɒlɪdʒ/ *noun* a place where people go to study more difficult subjects after they have left school କଲେଜ୍, ମହାବିଦ୍ୟାଳୟ *She's going to college next year.*

collide /kəˈlaɪd/ *verb* (**collides, colliding, collided**) move towards each other and hit each other ଧକ୍କା ଲାଗିବା *The two lorries collided.*

collision /kəˈlɪʒn/ *noun* when things or people collide ଧକ୍କା

colon /ˈkəʊlən/ *noun* a mark (:) that you use in writing, for example before a list ସ୍ଥୂଳାନ୍ତ୍ର, ବୃହଦନ୍ତ୍ର

colonel /ˈkɜ:nl/ *noun* an officer in the army କର୍ଣ୍ଣେଲ୍ (ମେଜର ଓ ବ୍ରିଗେଡ଼ିୟର୍ଙ୍କ ମଧ୍ୟସ୍ଥ ସେନାନାୟକ)

colony /ˈkɒləni/ *noun* (*plural* **colonies**) a country that is ruled by another country ଉପନିବେଶ *Kenya was once a British colony.*

colour /ˈkʌlə(r)/ *noun* Red, blue, yellow and green are all colours ରଙ୍ଗ ବର୍ଣ୍ଣ, *'What colour are your new shoes?' 'Black.'* ○ *The leaves change colour in autumn.*
✪ **Light, pale, dark, deep** ବା **bright** ଭଳି କିଛି ଶବ୍ଦ ଯାହା ଆମେ ରଙ୍ଗ ବର୍ଣ୍ଣନା କଲାବେଳେ ବ୍ୟବହାର କରୁ।

colour *verb* (**colours, colouring, coloured**) put colours on something ରଙ୍ଗ ଲଗାଇବା, ରଙ୍ଗାଇବା *The children coloured their pictures with crayons.*

colourful /ˈkʌləfl/ *adjective* with a lot of bright colours ରଙ୍ଗବେରଙ୍ଗ, ରଙ୍ଗରଞ୍ଜିତ *The garden is very colourful in the spring.*

column /ˈkɒləm/ *noun* **1** a tall post made of stone that is part of a building ଗୋଲାକାର ସ୍ତମ୍ଭ, ଖମ୍ବ **2** a long thin piece of writing on one side or part of a page (ଖବରକାଗଜ ଓ କିଛି ବହିରେ ଥିବା) ଲେଖାର ସ୍ତମ୍ଭ *Each page of this dictionary has two columns.*

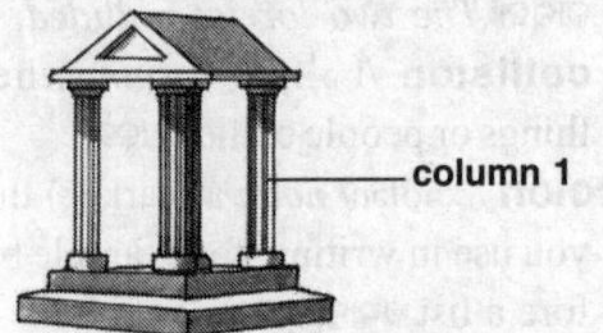

comb /kəʊm/ *noun* a flat piece of metal or plastic with a line of thin parts like teeth. You use it to make your hair tidy ପାନିଆ, ଚିରୁଣୀ

comb *verb* (**combs, combing, combed**) make your hair tidy with a comb ପାନିଆରେ ବାଳ କୁଣ୍ଡାଇବା *Have you combed your hair?*

combat /ˈkɒmbæt/ *noun* a fight, especially during a war ଯୁଦ୍ଧ, ଯୁଦ୍ଧକାଳୀନ ଲଢ଼େଇ

combination /ˌkɒmbɪˈneɪʃn/ *noun* two or more things mixed together ସଂଯୋଗ, ସମ୍ମିଳନ *The building is a combination of new and old styles.*

combine /kəmˈbaɪn/ *verb* (**combines, combining, combin- ed**) join or mix together ଯୋଡ଼ିବା ବା ମିଶାଇବା, ମିଳିତ କରିବା ବା ହେବା *The two schools combined and moved to a larger building.*

come /kʌm/ *verb* (**comes, coming, came** /keɪm/, **has come**) **1** move towards the person who is speaking or the place that you are talking about ଆସିବା *Come here, please.* ○ *The dog came when I called him.* **2** arrive ପହଞ୍ଚିବା *A letter came for you this morning.*

come back return ଫେରିବା; ଫେରିଆସ *I'm going to Italy tomorrow and I'm coming back in January.*

come from 1 be made from something କୌଣସି ପଦାର୍ଥରେ ପ୍ରସ୍ତୁତ *Wool comes from sheep.* **2** the place that you come from is where you were born or where you live ନିଜର ଜନ୍ମ ବା ବାସସ୍ଥାନ *I come from Japan. Where do you come from?*

come out appear ବାହାରି ଆସିବା *The rain stopped and the sun came out.*

comedian /kəˈmiːdiən/ *noun* a person whose job is to make people laugh ହାସ୍ୟ ସୃଷ୍ଟିକାରୀ ବ୍ୟକ୍ତି ବା ଅଭିନେତା

comedy /ˈkɒmədi/ *noun* (*plural* **comedies**) a funny play or film ହାସ୍ୟରସାତ୍ମକ ନାଟକ ବା ଚଳଚ୍ଚିତ୍ର

comet /ˈkɒmɪt/ *noun* a heavenly body made up of ice and dust that moves around the sun and looks like a very bright star with a tail ସୂର୍ଯ୍ୟ ଚାରିପଟେ ଘୁରୁଥିବା ଧୂମକେତୁ, ଲଞ୍ଜାତାରା *Halley's Comet*

comfort /ˈkʌmfət/ *noun* (*no plural*) having everything your body needs; being without pain or problems ମାନ ଓ ଦେହର ଆନନ୍ଦ ଅବସ୍ଥା, ଆରାମ୍ *They have enough money to live in comfort.*

comfortable /ˈkʌmftəbl/ *adjective* nice to sit in, to be in, or to wear ଆରାମ୍‌ଦାୟକ, ସୁଖଦ, ତୃପ୍ତିକର *This is a very comfortable bed.* ○ *comfortable shoes* ✪ ବିପରୀତ **uncomfortable**

comfortably *adverb* ଆରାମ୍‌ରେ *Are you sitting comfortably?*

comic[1] /ˈkɒmɪk/ **comical** /ˈkɒmɪkl/ *adjective* funny ହସାଉଥିବା, କୌତୁକିଆ, ନବଳିଆ, ମଜାଳିଆ

comic[2] /ˈkɒmɪk/ *noun* a magazine, especially for children, with pictures that tell a story ଚିତ୍ରଦ୍ୱାରା ଗପ ସୂଚାଉଥିବା ପତ୍ରିକା (ବିଶେଷତଃ ପିଲାମାନଙ୍କ ପାଇଁ)

comma /ˈkɒmə/ *noun* (*plural* **commas**) a mark (,) that you use in writing to make a short stop in a sentence ବିରାମଚିହ୍ନ, କମା, ବାକ୍ୟର ପ୍ରଥମଛେଦ (,)

command /kəˈmɑːnd/ *noun* **1** (*plural* **commands**) words that tell you that you must do something ଆଦେଶ, ନିର୍ଦ୍ଦେଶ *The soldiers must obey their general's commands*. **2** (*no plural*) being in charge of something ଅଧିକାର *Who is in command of this ship?*

command *verb* (**commands, commanding, commanded**) tell somebody that they must do something ଆଦେଶ ଦେବା *He commanded us to leave immediately.* ✪ ଆମେ ସାଧାରଣତଃ **order** ଶବ୍ଦର ବ୍ୟବହାର କରୁ ।

commander /kəˈmɑːndə(r)/ *noun* a person who is in charge of something, especially in the army ଅଧିପତି; ସେନାଧକ୍ଷ

comment[1] /ˈkɒment/ *noun* words that you say about something to show what you think ମନ୍ତବ୍ୟ, ଟିକା, ଟିପ୍ପଣୀ *She made some interesting comments about the film.*

comment[2] /ˈkɒment/ *verb* (**comments, commenting, commented**) when you comment on something, you say or write what you think about it ମନ୍ତବ୍ୟ ଦେବା ବା ଲେଖିବା

commentary /ˈkɒməntri/ *noun* (*plural* **commentaries**) words that somebody says about something that is happening କୌଣସି ଘଟଣା ଘଟୁଥିବା ସମୟରେ ଏହାର ଧାରାବାହିକ ବର୍ଣ୍ଣନା ବା ବିବରଣ କମେଣ୍ଟାରୀ *We listened to the radio commentary on the cricket match.*

commentator /ˈkɒmənteɪtə(r)/ *noun* a person who gives a commentary on radio or television ରେଡ଼ିଓ ବା ଟେଲିଭିଜନରେ ଘଟଣାର ଧାରାବାହିକ ବିବରଣ ପ୍ରଦାନକାରୀ

commercial /kəˈmɜːʃl/ *adjective* for or about buying and selling things ବ୍ୟବସାୟିକ, ବାଣିଜ୍ୟ ସମ୍ବନ୍ଧୀୟ *a commercial complex*

commercial *noun* a short film on television or radio that helps to sell something ରେଡ଼ିଓ ବା ଟେଲିଭିଜନ୍‌ରେ ଜିନିଷପତ୍ରର ବିକ୍ରି ବଢ଼ାଇବା ପାଇଁ ପ୍ରସାରିତ ଛୋଟ କାର୍ଯ୍ୟକ୍ରମ ବା ଚଳଚ୍ଚିତ୍ର ➪ **advertisement** ଦେଖନ୍ତୁ ।

commission /kəˈmɪʃn/ *noun* **1** a group of people appointed by the government to find out about something ନିର୍ଦ୍ଦିଷ୍ଟ କାମ ପାଇଁ ସରକାରଙ୍କ ଦ୍ୱାରା ନିଯୁକ୍ତ କିଛି ଲୋକଙ୍କ ଦ୍ୱାରା ଗଠିତ ଏକ ସମିତି, କମିଶନ୍ *A commission has been set up to investigate the riots*. **2** the amount of money that you pay someone for selling your goods ଜିନିଷ ବିକ୍ରି କରିବା ପାଇଁ ଦିଆଯାଉଥିବା ପାରିଶ୍ରମିକ, ଦସ୍ତୁରୀ, କମିସନ୍

a commission of 10 per cent on the total sales

commissioner /kəˈmɪʃənə(r)/ *noun* the head of a police or government department ପୁଲିସ୍ ବା ପ୍ରସାଶନର ବିଭାଗୀୟ ମୁଖ୍ୟ

commit /kəˈmɪt/ *verb* (**commits, committing, committed**) **1** do something bad (ଖରାପ୍ କାମ) କରିବା *This man has committed a very serious crime.* **2** promise to do something or fulfil a responsibility (କୌଣସି କାମ କରିବା ପାଇଁ) ପ୍ରତିଶ୍ରୁତି ବଦ୍ଧ ହେବା *She has committed herself to helping me prepare for the exams.*

commitment *noun* **1** a promise to do something ପ୍ରତିଶ୍ରୁତି *a commitment to complete the work in two months* **2** being fully involved in something you think is right or important ଠିକ୍ ବା ଭଲ କାମ ପାଇଁ ସ୍ୱତଃ ପ୍ରତିଜ୍ଞାବଦ୍ଧ *commitment to the preservation of nature*

committee /kəˈmɪti/ *noun* a group of people chosen by other people to plan or organize something ସମିତି, କମିଟି *The members of the housing society choose a new committee every year.*

commodity /kəˈmɒdəti/ *noun* (*plural* **commodities**) a thing that you can buy କିଣାଯାଉଥିବା ସାମଗ୍ରୀ, ପଣ୍ୟଦ୍ରବ୍ୟ *The prices of basic commodities like rice, wheat and oil have been rising in the last two months.*

common /ˈkɒmən/ *adjective* (**commoner, commonest**) **1** that you often see or that often happens ସାଧାରଣ, ମାମୁଲି, ବହୁବାର ଘଟୁଥିବା *Sanjay is a common name in India.* ✪ ବିପରୀତ **uncommon 2** that everybody in a group has or does; belonging to all ସର୍ବସାଧାରଣଙ୍କ ଅଧିକାରଭୁକ୍ତ *The two schools have a common playground.*

commonly *adverb* usually; normally ସାଧାରଣତଃ

commotion /kəˈməʊʃn/ *noun* confusion or excitement କୋଳାହଳ, ଗୋଳମାଳ, ବିଶୃଙ୍ଖଳା *There was a commotion outside the stadium when the players arrived.*

communicable /kəˈmjuːnɪkəbl/ *adjective* that can spread from one person or animal to another ସଂକ୍ରମଣଶୀଳ (ରୋଗ ଇତ୍ୟାଦି) *communicable diseases*

communicate /kəˈmjuːnɪkeɪt/ *verb* (**communicates, communicating, communicated**) talk or write to somebody (କହି ବା ଲେଖି, ଖବର, ତଥ୍ୟ ଇତ୍ୟାଦି) ଜଣାଇବା, ଆଦାନପ୍ରଦାନ କରିବା, ଯୋଗାଯୋଗ କରିବା *The pilots communicate with the airport by radio.*

communication /kəˌmjuːnɪˈkeɪʃn/ *noun* **1** (*no plural*) the act of talking or writing to somebody ଯୋଗାଯୋଗ, ଆଦାନ ପ୍ରଦାନ *Communication is difficult when two people don't speak the same language.* **2 communications** (*plural*) ways of sending information or moving from one place to another ଖବର ପଠାଇବା ବା ଯାତାୟତ ବ୍ୟବସ୍ଥା, ଯୋଗାଯୋଗ

community /kəˈmju:nəti/ *noun* (*plural* **communities**) the people who live in a place ଏକା ସ୍ଥାନ, ଅଞ୍ଚଳ ବା ଦେଶରେ ରହୁଥିବା ଲୋକସମୂହ, ସମ୍ପ୍ରଦାୟ *Life in a small fishing community is very different from life in a big city.*

commute /kəˈmju:t/ *verb* (**commutes, commuting, commuted**) travel a long way from home to work every day ଦୂରରେ ଥିବା କର୍ମସ୍ଥାନକୁ ପ୍ରତିଦିନ ଯିବା ଓ ସେଠାରୁ ଫେରିବା *She lives in Meerut and commutes to Delhi every day.*

commuter *noun* a person who commutes କାମ ପାଇଁ ପ୍ରତିଦିନ ଦୂରକୁ ଯିବାଆସିବା କରୁଥିବା ବ୍ୟକ୍ତି

compact disc *noun* a small disc that can store sound or information. You play it on a special machine called a **compact disc player** ଏକ ଛୋଟ ଡିସ୍କ ବା ଚକତି ଯାହା ଉପରେ ତଥ୍ୟ ବା ଧ୍ୱନି ଡିଜିଟାଲ୍ ପ୍ରକ୍ରିୟାରେ ରେକର୍ଡ଼ କରାଯାଏ ଓ କମ୍ପାକ୍ଟ ଡିସ୍କ ପ୍ଲେୟାର୍‌ରେ ପୁନରୁଦ୍ଧାର କରାଯାଏ ✪ ଏହାର ସଂକ୍ଷିପ୍ତ ରୂପ ହେଲା **CD** କମ୍ପ୍ୟୁଟର୍‌ରେ ଏହାକୁ କହନ୍ତି **CD-ROM** ।

companion /kəmˈpæniən/ *noun* a person who is with another person ସାଙ୍ଗ, ସାଥି, ସହଚର

company /ˈkʌmpəni/ *noun* **1** (*plural* **companies**) a group of people who work to make or sell things ବ୍ୟବସାୟିକ ସଂସ୍ଥା, କମ୍ପାନୀ *a television company* **2** (*no plural*) being with other people ସାଙ୍ଗ, ସାହଚର୍ଯ୍ୟ, ସାଙ୍ଗସାଥି *She lives alone so she likes company at weekends.*

comparative /kəmˈpærətɪv/ *noun* the form of an adjective or adverb that shows more of something ତୁଳନାତ୍ମକ ବିଶେଷଣ ବା କ୍ରିୟାବିଶେଷଣ *The comparative of 'bad' is 'worse'.*

compare /kəmˈpeə(r)/ *verb* (**compares, comparing, compared**) think about or look at people or things together so that you can see how they are different ତୁଳନା କରିବା *I've compared the prices in the two shops and the prices here are cheaper.*

comparison /kəmˈpærɪsn/ *noun* the act of seeing or understanding how things are different or the same ତୁଳନା, ତୁଳନାତ୍ମକ ବିଚାର *We made a comparison of prices in three different shops.*

compartment /kəmˈpɑ:tmənt/ *noun* **1** a small room in a train ରେଳଡବା *The first-class compartments are at the front of the train.* **2** a separate part inside a box or bag ବାକ୍ସ, ବ୍ୟାଗ୍ ଇତ୍ୟାଦିର ଅଲଗା ଖୋପ *The suitcase had a secret compartment at the back.*

compass /ˈkʌmpəs/ *noun* (*plural* **compasses**) **1** an instrument with a needle that always shows where north is ଚୁମ୍ବକ ଦ୍ୱାରା ଉତ୍ତର ମେରୁ ଦେଖାଉଥିବା ଯନ୍ତ୍ର, ଦିଗନିର୍ଣ୍ଣୟ ଯନ୍ତ୍ର, ଦିଗ୍‌ବାରଣଯନ୍ତ୍ର ➪ ଚିତ୍ର ପାଇଁ **needle** ଦେଖନ୍ତୁ । **2** (**compasses** ମଧ୍ୟ) an instrument with two thin parts that are joined at the top and which you use for drawing circles ଗୋଟିଏ ପଟେ ଯୋଡ଼ି ହୋଇଥିବା ଦୁଇ କଣ୍ଟା ବିଶିଷ୍ଟ ବୃତ୍ତାଙ୍କନ ଯନ୍ତ୍ର *a pair of compasses*

compass 2

compassion /kəmˈpæʃn/ *noun* (*no plural*) having a strong feeling of helping those who are in need or are suffering କରୁଣା, ଦୟା, ଅନୁକମ୍ପା

compatible /kəmˈpætəbl/ *adjective* suitable for living, working or being together ସହାବସ୍ଥାନକ୍ଷମ, ସାଙ୍ଗ ହୋଇ ରହିବା, କାମ କରିବା ଇତ୍ୟାଦି ଭଲ ପାଉଥିବା *compatible features*

compère[1] /ˈkɒmpeə(r)/ *noun* the person who conducts a television or radio show and introduces the guests or the performers of the show ମନୋରଞ୍ଜନ କାର୍ଯ୍ୟକ୍ରମରେ କଳାକାରମାନଙ୍କୁ ପରିଚୟ କରାଉଥିବା ଓ କାର୍ଯ୍ୟକ୍ରମ ପରିଚାଳନା କରୁଥିବା ବ୍ୟକ୍ତି, କମ୍ପିୟର୍, ସୂତ୍ରଧର

compère[2] /ˈkɒmpeə(r)/ *verb* (**compères, compèring, compèred**) act as the compère for a television or radio show କମ୍ପିୟର୍ ବା ସୂତ୍ରଧର ଭାବେ କାମ କରିବା (ରେଡ଼ିଓ ବା ଟେଲିଭିଜନ କାର୍ଯ୍ୟକ୍ରମରେ)

compete /kəmˈpi:t/ *verb* (**competes, competing, competed**) try to win a race or competition ପ୍ରତିଦ୍ୱନ୍ଦିତା କରିବା (ପ୍ରତିଯୋଗିତାରେ) *Teams from many countries compete in the World Cup.*

competition /ˌkɒmpəˈtɪʃn/ *noun* a game or test that people try to win ପ୍ରତିଯୋଗିତା *I won the first prize in the painting competition held last month.*

competitor /kəmˈpetɪtə(r)/ *noun* a person who is trying to win a competition ପ୍ରତିଦ୍ୱନ୍ଦୀ, ପ୍ରତିଯୋଗୀ

complain /kəmˈpleɪn/ *verb* (**complains, complaining, complained**) say that you do not like something; say that you are unhappy or angry about something ଅସନ୍ତୋଷ ପ୍ରକାଶ କରିବା, ଅଭିଯୋଗ କରିବା, ଆପତ୍ତି କରିବା *He complained to the waiter that the soup was cold.*

complaint /kəmˈpleɪnt/ *noun* **1** a statement that tells someone that you are not satisfied with something ଅଭିଯୋଗ ଆପତ୍ତି *The principal received a complaint from the students about the food served at the school canteen.* **2** an illness or disease that affects only a particular part of the body ରୋଗ, ଶରୀରର ଏକ ଅଙ୍ଗର ଅସୁସ୍ଥତା *a skin complaint*

complete[1] /kəmˈpli:t/ *adjective* **1** with none of its parts missing ସମ୍ପୂର୍ଣ୍ଣ, ପୂରା, ପୂର୍ଣ୍ଣାଙ୍ଗ *I've got a complete set of cards.* **2** finished ସମାପ୍ତ *The work is complete.* ✪ ବିପରୀତ **incomplete**

complete[2] /kəmˈpli:t/ *verb* (**completes, completing, completed**) finish doing or making something ସମାପ୍ତ କରିବା

completely /kəmˈpli:tli/ *adverb* totally; in every way ପୂରା, ସମ୍ପୂର୍ଣ୍ଣଭାବରେ

I completely forgot that it was your birthday!

complex[1] /ˈkɒmpleks/ *adjective* difficult to understand because it has a lot of different parts ଜଟିଳ *a complex problem*

complex[2] /ˈkɒmpleks/ *noun* (*plural* **complexes**) a group of buildings ଏକା ଜାଗାରେ ଥିବା ଏକା ଉଦ୍ଦେଶ୍ୟରେ ବ୍ୟବହୃତ ବହୁ କୋଠା *a sports complex*

complicated /ˈkɒmplɪkeɪtɪd/ *adjective* difficult to understand because it has a lot of different parts ଜଟିଳ *I can't explain how to play the game. It's too complicated.*

compliment /ˈkɒmplɪment/ *noun* **pay somebody a compliment** say something nice about somebody ପ୍ରଶଂସା କରିବା *Sunil paid her a compliment on her speech.*

complimentary /ˌkɒmplɪˈmentri/ *adjective* something that is complimentary comes free with another thing ବିନା ମୂଲ୍ୟରେ ଦିଆଯାଇଥିବା, ଲାଭ *We got a complimentary shirt when we bought three trousers.*

component /kəmˈpəʊnənt/ *noun* one of the different parts which make up a thing (କୌଣସି ପୂର୍ଣ୍ଣାଙ୍ଗ ଯନ୍ତ୍ର ବା ସଂସ୍ଥାର) ଅଙ୍ଗ ବା ଅଂଶ *the components of a radio*

composed /kəmˈpəʊzd/ *adjective* **1** made up of several different parts, things or people ଗଠିତ *The Lok Sabha is composed of MPs from the different states and union territories of India.* **2** calm and in control of one's feelings and emotions ଶାନ୍ତ, ସ୍ଥିରଚିତ୍ତ

composer /kəmˈpəʊzə(r)/ *noun* a person who writes music (ସଙ୍ଗୀତର) ରଚୟିତା *My favourite composer is A.R. Rahman.*

composition /ˌkɒmpəˈzɪʃn/ *noun* **1** the different parts that make up something କୌଣସି ପଦାର୍ଥର ବିଭିନ୍ନ ଉପାଦାନ *the composition of the earth's atmosphere* **2** a short text that has to be written in school as an exercise ପ୍ରବନ୍ଧ, ରଚନା *Write a composition of 300 words on any one of the topics given below.* ➪ **essay** ଦେଖନ୍ତୁ।

compost /ˈkɒmpɒst/ *noun* (*no plural*) a mixture of rotting plants, kitchen waste, etc. that is added to the soil to help plants grow well ଖତ, କୌଣସି ଜୈବ ପଦାର୍ଥ ସଢ଼ିବା ପ୍ରକ୍ରିୟାରୁ ପ୍ରସ୍ତୁତ ସାର

compound /ˈkɒmpaʊnd/ *noun* **1** something that is made up of two or more parts ଯୌଗିକ ବସ୍ତୁ, ଦୁଇ ବା ଅଧିକ ଦ୍ରବ୍ୟର ମିଶ୍ରଣ *Salt is a chemical compound.* **2** a word that is made from two or more words ଏକାଧିକ ଶବ୍ଦ ଦ୍ୱାରା ଗଠିତ ଶବ୍ଦ, ସମାସ *'Fingernail' and 'waiting-room' are compounds.* **3** an area with buildings, surrounded by walls ହତା

comprehension /ˌkɒmprɪˈhenʃn/ *noun* **1** (*no plural*) the ability to understand ବୁଝିବା ଶକ୍ତି, ଧୀଶକ୍ତି, ବୋଧଶକ୍ତି *His behaviour was beyond comprehension.* **2** (*plural* **comprehensions**) an exercise that tests how well you understand something that you hear or read ବୁଝିପାରିବା ଶକ୍ତିର ପରୀକ୍ଷା ପାଇଁ ଉଦ୍ଦିଷ୍ଟ ଲେଖା *a test in listening comprehension*

comprehensive /ˌkɒmprɪˈhensɪv/ *adjective* including all or almost all the facts, information and details connected to something ସବୁ ତଥ୍ୟ ଥିବା, ସର୍ବତଥ୍ୟ ସମ୍ବଳିତ *a comprehensive book on mammals*

compromise /ˈkɒmprəmaɪz/ *noun* an agreement with another person or group, when you both do part of what the other person or group wants ଆପୋଷ ସମାଧାନ

compromise *verb* (**compromises, compromising, compromised**) ଆପୋଷ ସମାଧାନ କରିବା *The workers compromised by agreeing to longer working hours.*

compulsory /kəmˈpʌlsəri/ *adjective* if something is compulsory, you must do it ବାଧ୍ୟତାମୂଳକ *School is compulsory for all children between the ages of five and sixteen.*

computer

computer /kəmˈpjuːtə(r)/ *noun* a machine that stores information and finds answers very quickly କମ୍ପ୍ୟୁଟର୍, ଇଲେକ୍‌ଟ୍ରୋନିକ୍ ଯନ୍ତ୍ର ଯାହାଦ୍ୱାରା ଗଣନା, ଯନ୍ତ୍ରଚାଳନ, ତଥ୍ୟ ସମୀକ୍ଷା ଓ ତଥ୍ୟ ସଂକଳନ କରାଯାଇପାରେ

computer program *noun* information that tells a computer what to do କମ୍ପ୍ୟୁଟର୍ କାର୍ଯ୍ୟକ୍ରମ

concave /kɒnˈkeɪv/ *adjective* (an outline or a surface) curved inwards ଦୃତ୍ତିର-ଭିତର ପଟ ପରି ବଙ୍କା, ଅନ୍ତବର୍ତ୍ତୁଳ, ଅବତଳ *concave lenses/mirrors*

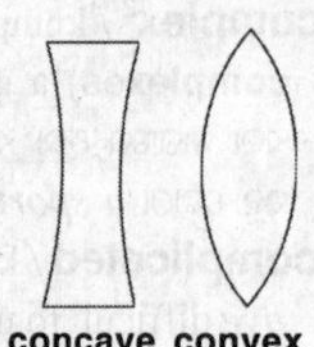

concave convex

⇨ **convex** ଦେଖନ୍ତୁ।

conceited /kənˈsiːtɪd/ *adjective* too proud of yourself and what you can do ଗର୍ବୀ, ଅହଂକାରୀ *It is very conceited of you to think that you are the best.*

concentrate /ˈkɒnsntreɪt/ *verb* (**concentrates, concentrating, concentrated**) think only about what you are doing and not about anything else ଏକାଗ୍ର ଚିତ୍ତରେ କୌଣସି ବିଷୟରେ ମନୋନିବେଶ କରିବା

concentration /ˈkɒnsnˈtreɪʃn/ *noun* (*no plural*) ଏକାଗ୍ରତା, ମନୋନିବେଶ *This work requires total concentration.*

concept /ˈkɒnsept/ *noun* an idea or a basic principle of something ଧାରଣା, ଚିନ୍ତାକଳ୍ପ *concepts of marketing*

concern[1] /kənˈsɜːn/ *verb* (**concerns, concerning, concerned**) **1** be important or of interest to somebody ପ୍ରଯୁଜ୍ୟ ବା ଦରକାରୀ ହେବା *This notice concerns all passengers travel-*

ling to Bangalore. **2** worry somebody ଚିନ୍ତାର ବିଷୟ ହେବା, ଚିନ୍ତିତ ହେବା *It concerns me that she hasn't reached as yet.* **3** be about something ବିଷୟକ ହେବା *The story concerns a young boy and his parents.*

concerned *adjective* worried about the safety or welfare of someone ଚିନ୍ତିତ, ଉଦ୍‌ବିଗ୍ନ

concern[2] /kən'sɜ:n/ *noun* **1** (*no plural*) worry ଚିନ୍ତା, ଉଦ୍‌ବେଗ *There is a lot of concern about this problem.* **2** (*plural* **concerns**) something that is important or interesting to somebody ଗୁରୁତ୍ୱ ଥିବା ବିଷୟ *Her problems are not my concern.*

concerning /kən'sɜ:nɪŋ/ *preposition* about ବିଷୟରେ *Thank you for your letter concerning the date of the next meeting.*

concert /'kɒnsət/ *noun* music played for a lot of people ବହୁ ଲୋକଙ୍କ ପାଇଁ ପରିବେଷିତ ସଙ୍ଗୀତ *a rock concert*

conch /kɒntʃ/ *noun* (*plural* **conches**) the shell of a sea animal. In India, certain kinds of conches are played by blowing into them. This is done on **auspicious** occasions like marriages ଶଙ୍ଖ

conclude /kən'klu:d/ *verb* (**concludes, concluding, concluded**) when something concludes, it ends ସମାପ୍ତ କରିବା ବା ହେବା *The annual function concluded with the chief guest's speech.*

conclusion /kən'klu:ʒn/ *noun* **1** what you believe or decide after thinking carefully ଭାବିଚିନ୍ତି ନିଆଯାଇଥିବା ସିଦ୍ଧାନ୍ତ *We came to the conclusion that you were right.* **2** the ending of something ସମାପ୍ତି, ଶେଷ

concrete[1] /'kɒŋkri:t/ *noun* (*no plural*) hard grey material made by mixing cement, sand, water, pebbles, etc. that is used in building (ଘର ତିଆରିରେ ବ୍ୟବହୃତ) ସିମେଣ୍ଟ, ବାଲି, ଗୋଡ଼ି ଓ ପାଣିର ମିଶ୍ରଣରେ ପ୍ରସ୍ତୁତ ପଦାର୍ଥ, କଂକ୍ରିଟ୍ *a building made of concrete*

concrete[2] /'kɒŋkri:t/ *adjective* true and based on facts and evidence ତଥ୍ୟ ଉପରେ ଆଧାରିତ *concrete proof*

condemn /kən'dem/ *verb* (**condemns, condemning, condemned**) say strongly that somebody or something is bad or wrong ନିନ୍ଦା କରିବା *Many people condemned the government's decision.*

condense /kən'dens/ *verb* (**condenses, condensing, condensed**) **1** change a gas into a liquid ବାଷ୍ପକୁ ତରଳ ପଦାର୍ଥରେ ପରିଣତ କରିବା **2** reduce or make something smaller ସଂକ୍ଷିପ୍ତ କରିବା *Sheila condensed the four-page story into one page.*

condensation /ˌkɒnden'seɪʃn/ *noun* **1** a process in which a gas changes into a liquid ବାଷ୍ପକୁ ତରଳ ପଦାର୍ଥରେ ପରିଣତ କରିବା ପ୍ରକ୍ରିୟା *condensation of water vapour* **2** the process of reducing something in size, usually a book (ବହି ଇତ୍ୟାଦିକୁ) ସଂକ୍ଷିପ୍ତ କରିବା ପ୍ରକ୍ରିୟା *condensation of a scientific report*

condition /kən'dɪʃn/ *noun* **1** (*no plural*) how a person, animal or thing is ଅବସ୍ଥା *The car was cheap and in good condition, so I bought it.* **2** (*plural* **conditions**) something that must happen before another thing can happen କୌଣସି କାମ ଯାହା ଉପରେ ଅନ୍ୟ କାମ ନିର୍ଭର କରେ; ସର୍ତ୍ତ *One of the conditions of the job is that you agree to work on Saturdays.*

conduct[1] /kən'dʌkt/ *verb* (**conducts, conducting, conducted**) **1** manage or organize something ପରିଚାଳନା କରିବା, ନିର୍ବାହ କରିବା *conduct a city tour* **2** stand in front of a group of musicians and direct them ସାମନାରେ ଠିଆ ହୋଇ ବାଦ୍ୟକାର ବୃନ୍ଦକୁ ପରିଚାଳନା କରିବା **3** (of a substance) allow heat or electricity to pass through (ଉତ୍ତାପ, ବିଦ୍ୟୁତ୍ ଇତ୍ୟାଦି) ପରିବହନ କରିବା **4** behave in a particular manner (ଏକ ପ୍ରକାର) (ଆଚରଣ ଦେଖାଇବା) *She conducted herself well.*

conduct[2] /'kɒndʌkt/ *noun* the manner in which a person behaves ଆଚରଣ, ବ୍ୟବହାର *The head boy was praised for his responsible conduct during his term.*

conductor /kən'dʌktə(r)/ *noun* **1** a person who sells tickets on a bus ବସ୍‌ର ଟିକଟ ଜାଞ୍ଚ କରୁଥିବା ବ୍ୟକ୍ତି, କଣ୍ଡକ୍ଟର୍ **2** a person who stands in front of a group of musicians and controls what they do ସାମନାରେ ଠିଆ ହୋଇ ବାଦ୍ୟବୃନ୍ଦକୁ ପରିଚାଳନା କରୁଥିବା ବ୍ୟକ୍ତି **3** a substance that allows heat or electricity to pass through it ଉତ୍ତାପ ବା ବିଦ୍ୟୁତଶକ୍ତି ପରିବାହୀ ପଦାର୍ଥ *a good conductor of heat*

cone /kəʊn/ *noun* **1** a shape with one flat round end and one pointed end ଶଙ୍କୁ, ଗୋଟିଏ ପଟ ବୃତ୍ତାକାର ଓ ଅନ୍ୟପଟ କ୍ରମଶଃ ସରୁ ହୋଇ ମୁନିଆଁ ହୋଇଥିବା ଆକାର ବା ବସ୍ତୁ *an ice-cream cone* ➪ ଚିତ୍ର ପାଇଁ **shape** ଦେଖନ୍ତୁ। **2** the hard fruit of a **pine** or **fir tree** ପାଇନ୍ ବା ଫର୍ ଗଛର ଶଙ୍କୁ ଆକାରର ଶୁଖିଲା ଫଳ *a pine cone* ➪ ଚିତ୍ର ପାଇଁ **pine** ଦେଖନ୍ତୁ।

conference /'kɒnfərəns/ *noun* a time when many people meet to talk about a special thing ସମ୍ମିଳନୀ, ସଭା, ଆଲୋଚନାଚକ୍ର *an international conference on peace*

confess /kən'fes/ *verb* (**confesses, confessing, confessed**) say that you have done something wrong (ଦୋଷ ଇତ୍ୟାଦି) ସ୍ୱୀକାର କରିବା, ମାନିଯିବା *He confessed that he had stolen the money.*

confession /kən'feʃn/ *noun* something that you confess (ଦୋଷ ଇତ୍ୟାଦିର) ସ୍ୱୀକାରୋକ୍ତି

confidence /'kɒnfɪdəns/ *noun* (*no plural*) the feeling that you can do something well ଦୃଢ଼ବିଶ୍ୱାସ *She answered the questions with confidence.*

confident /'kɒnfɪdənt/ *adjective* sure that you can do something well, or that something will happen ଆତ୍ମବିଶ୍ୱାସୀ *I'm confident that our team will win.*

confidently *adverb* ଗଭୀର ବିଶ୍ୱାସ ସହିତ

confidential /ˌkɒnfɪ'denʃl/ *adjective* if something is confidential, it is a secret and others should not or do not know about it ଗୁପ୍ତ, ଗୋପନୀୟ *confidential letters*

confine /kən'faɪn/ *verb* (**confines, confining, confined**) keep someone or something in a small place and not allow them to move freely ଆବଦ୍ଧ କରିବା, ସୀମାବଦ୍ଧ କରିବା *The princess was confined to the palace.*

confirm /kən'fɜ:m/ *verb* (**confirms, confirming, confirmed**) say that something is true or that something will happen କୌଣସି କଥା ବା କାମର ସତ୍ୟତାର ସମର୍ଥନ କରିବା, ଅନୁମୋଦନ କରିବା *Please write and confirm the date of your arrival.*

conflict /'kɒnflɪkt/ *noun* a fight or an argument ସଂଘର୍ଷ ବା ଯୁକ୍ତିତର୍କ

confuse /kən'fju:z/ *verb* (**confuses, confusing, confused**) **1** mix up somebody's ideas, so that they cannot think clearly or understand ବିଭ୍ରାନ୍ତ କରିବା, ବାଉଳା କରିବା *They confused me by asking so many questions.* **2** think that one thing or person is another thing or person ଗୋଟିଏ ଜିନିଷ ବା ବ୍ୟକ୍ତିକୁ ଅନ୍ୟ ଜିନିଷ ବା ବ୍ୟକ୍ତି ବୋଲି ଭାବିବା *Don't confuse the word 'weather' with 'whether'.*

confused *adjective* not able to think clearly ବାଉଳା, ବିଭ୍ରାନ୍ତ *The waiter got confused and brought everybody the wrong drink!*

confusing *adjective* difficult to understand ଗୋଳମାଳିଆ, ବୁଝି ନହେଲା ପରି *This map is very confusing.*

confusion /kən'fju:ʒn/ *noun* (*no plural*) the state of being confused ବିଭ୍ରାନ୍ତି, ବିଶୃଙ୍ଖଳା, ବୁଝି ନପାରିବା ଅବସ୍ଥା *He didn't speak any English, so he looked at me in confusion when I asked him a question in English.*

congested /kən'dʒestɪd/ *adjective* full of things, people or vehicles (ଲୋକ, ଗାଡ଼ି ଇତ୍ୟାଦି) ଦ୍ୱାରା ଭରପୂର ହୋଇଥିବା, ଅତି ଗହଳି ହୋଇଥିବା *congested roads*

congestion /kən'dʒestʃən/ *noun* (*no plural*) in a state of being congested ଭରପୁର ଅବସ୍ଥା, ଅତି ଗହଳି ହୋଇଥିବା ଅବସ୍ଥା *traffic congestion*

congratulate /kən'grætʃuleɪt/ *verb* (**congratulates, congratulating, congratulated**) tell somebody that you are pleased about something that they have achieved (ବ୍ୟକ୍ତିଙ୍କୁ) ଅଭିନନ୍ଦନ କରିବା, ବାହାବା ଦେବା *I congratulated Sachi on passing her exam.*

congratulations /kən,grætʃu'leɪʃnz/ *noun* (*plural*) a word that shows you are pleased about something that somebody has achieved ଅଭିନନ୍ଦନ, ବାହାବା *Congratulations on your new job!*

conifer /'kɒnɪfə(r)/ *noun* a kind of tree that produces hard dry fruit called cones. This tree has needle-like leaves that remain on the tree all through the year ଶଙ୍କୁଧାରୀ ଗଛ (ଯାର ପତ୍ର ମୁନିଆଁ ଓ ବର୍ଷସାରା ରହିଥାଏ)

conifer

coniferous *adjective* ଶଙ୍କୁ ଧାରୀ; ଶଙ୍କୁଧାରୀ ଗଛଥିବା *Pine and fir trees are coniferous trees.*

conjunction /kən'dʒʌŋkʃn/ *noun* a word that joins other words or parts of a sentence ସଂଯୋଜକ ଅବ୍ୟୟ ପଦ (ବ୍ୟାକରଣ) *'And', 'or' and 'but' are conjunctions.*

connect /kə'nekt/ *verb* (**connects, connecting, connected**) join one thing to another thing ସଂଯୁକ୍ତ ହେବା, ସଂଯୋଗ କରିବା *This wire connects the video recorder to the television.* ✪ ବିପରୀତ **disconnect**

connection /kə'nekʃn/ *noun* the way that one thing is joined to another (ଗୋଟିଏ ପଦାର୍ଥର ଅନ୍ୟ ପଦାର୍ଥ ସହ) ସଂଯୋଗ *We had a bad connection on the phone so I couldn't hear him very well.*

conquer /'kɒŋkə(r)/ *verb* (**conquers, conquering, conquered**) **1** win over a country or an opponent in a war, game or competition (ଯୁଦ୍ଧ, ଖେଳ ଇତ୍ୟାଦିରେ) ପରାସ୍ତ କରିବା, ଅଧିକୃତ କରିବା *The enemy forces conquered the capital.* **2** achieve a difficult task ଉଦ୍ୟମ ଦ୍ୱାରା କଷ୍ଟକର କାମ ସମ୍ପାଦନ କରିବା *Mount Everest was conquered by Tenzing Norgay and Edmund Hillary.*

conquest /'kɒŋkwest/ *noun* the act of winning over something ବିଜୟପ୍ରାପ୍ତି, ବିଜୟ *the conquest of Mount Everest*

conscience /'kɒnʃəns/ *noun* the feeling inside you about what is right and wrong ବିବେକ, ହିତାହିତ ଜ୍ଞାନ

conscious /'kɒnʃəs/ *adjective* awake and able to think ସଚେତ *The patient was conscious during the operation.* ✪ ବିପରୀତ **unconscious**

consciousness *noun* (*no plural*) ଚେତନା, ଚେତା *regain consciousness*

consent /kən'sent/ *noun* (*no plural*) agreeing to let somebody do something ଇଚ୍ଛାକୃତ ସମ୍ମତି, ସହମତି *His parents gave their consent to the marriage.*

consequence /'kɒnsɪkwəns/ *noun* that which happens because of something କାର୍ଯ୍ୟର ଫଳାଫଳ, ଅବସ୍ଥାର ପରିଣତି *I've just bought a car and as a consequence I have no money.* ○ *The mistake had terrible consequences.*

conservation /ˌkɒnsə'veɪʃn/ *noun* (*no plural*) taking good care of the world and its forests, lakes, plants and animals ପ୍ରାକୃତିକ ପରିବେଶର ସଂରକ୍ଷଣ *the conservation of the rainforests*

consider /kən'sɪdə(r)/ *verb* (**considers, considering, considered**) think carefully about something ବିଚାର କରିବା, ମନୋଯୋଗ ପୂର୍ବକ ଭାବିବା *I'm considering going to Rajasthan on holiday.*

considerable /kən'sɪdərəbl/ *adjective* great or large ଯଥେଷ୍ଟ (ପରିମାଣ ବା ମାତ୍ରା) *The car cost a considerable amount of money.*

considerably *adverb* ଯଥେଷ୍ଟ ଭାବରେ *My flat is considerably smaller than yours.*

considerate /kənˈsɪdərət/ *adjective* a person who is considerate is kind, and thinks and cares about other people (ଅନ୍ୟମାନଙ୍କ ପ୍ରତି) ବିଚାରଶୀଳ, (ଅନ୍ୟମାନଙ୍କ) ଭଲମନ୍ଦ ଭାବୁଥିବା *Please be more considerate and don't play loud music late at night.* ✪ ବିପରୀତ **inconsiderate**

consideration /kənˌsɪdəˈreɪʃn/ *noun* (*no plural*) being kind, and caring about other people's feeling ସହାନୁଭୂତିପୂର୍ଣ୍ଣ ବିଚାରଶୀଳତା

consist /kənˈsɪst/ *verb* (**consists, consisting, consisted**)

consist of something be made of something; have something as parts ଗଠିତ ହେବା *Jam consists of fruit and sugar.*

console /kənˈsəʊl/ *verb* (**consoles, consoling, consoled**) comfort someone because they are suffering, sad or disappointed (ଅନ୍ୟର ଦୁଃଖ ବା ନୈରାଶ୍ୟ ସମୟରେ) ସାନ୍ତ୍ୱନା ଦେବା

consolation /ˌkɒnsəˈleɪʃn/ *noun* if a person or thing is a consolation, they make you feel better when you are unhappy ସାନ୍ତ୍ୱନା ବା ଆଶ୍ୱସ୍ତି ଦେଉଥିବା ବ୍ୟକ୍ତି ବା ବିଷୟ; ସାନ୍ତ୍ୱନା

consonant /ˈkɒnsənənt/ *noun* any letter of the alphabet that is not *a*, *e*, *i*, *o* or *u*, or the sound that you make when you say it ବ୍ୟଞ୍ଜନବର୍ଣ୍ଣ ➪ **vowel** ଦେଖନ୍ତୁ।

conspiracy /kənˈspɪrəsi/ *noun* (*plural* **conspiracies**) a secret plan between people to do something wrong or illegal ଚକ୍ରାନ୍ତ, ଷଡ଼ଯନ୍ତ୍ର *a conspiracy to rob the bank*

conspire /kənˈspaɪə(r)/ *verb* (**conspires, conspiring, conspired**) secretly plan something with other people to do something wrong or illegal ଚକ୍ରାନ୍ତ କରିବା

constable /ˈkʌnstəbl/ *noun* an ordinary police officer ପୋଲିସ୍ ବିଭାଗର ନିମ୍ନ ଅଧିକାରୀ, ସିପାହି

constant /ˈkɒnstənt/ *adjective* something that is constant happens all the time ଅବିରତ; ଅପରିବର୍ତ୍ତନୀୟ, ସ୍ଥିର, ସ୍ଥାୟୀ *the constant noise of traffic*

constantly *adverb* ଅବିରତ ଭାବରେ *She talked constantly all evening.*

constellation /ˌkɒnstəˈleɪʃn/ *noun* a group of stars that make a distinct pattern in the sky ନକ୍ଷତ୍ର ମଣ୍ଡଳ, ନକ୍ଷତ୍ର ପୁଞ୍ଜ *the stars in the Great Bear constellation*

constituency /kənˈstɪtjuənsi/ *noun* (*plural* **constituencies**) a town or an area that chooses one **Member of Parliament** (a person in the government) ନିର୍ବାଚନମଣ୍ଡଳୀ

constituent /kənˈstɪtjuənt/ *noun* one of the many parts that make up something କୌଣସି ପଦାର୍ଥର ଉପାଦାନ *The constituents of water are hydrogen and oxygen.*

constitution /ˌkɒnstɪˈtjuːʃn/ *noun* the principles of a country by which its laws are guided; the document containing this ସଂବିଧାନ *the Indian Constitution*

construct /kənˈstrʌkt/ *verb* (**constructs, constructing, constructed**) build something ନିର୍ମାଣ କରିବା, ତିଆରି କରିବା। *The bridge was con-*

structed twenty years ago. ✪ ଚିତ୍ର ପାଇଁ **build** ଦେଖନ୍ତୁ ।

construction /ˌkənˈstrʌkʃn/ *noun* (*no plural*) building something ନିର୍ମାଣ *the construction of a new highway*

consult /kənˈsʌlt/ *verb* (**consults, consulting, consulted**) ask somebody or look in a book when you want to know something ପରାମର୍ଶ କରିବା *If the pain doesn't go away, you should consult a doctor.*

consume /kənˈsjuːm/ *verb* (**consumes, consuming, consumed**) eat, drink or use something ଖାଇବା, ପିଇବା ବା ବ୍ୟବହାର କରି ଶେଷ କରିବା *This car consumes a lot of petrol.*

consumer *noun* a person who buys or uses something ଉପଭୋକ୍ତା, ଖାଉଟିଆ *There are laws to protect consumers.*

consumption /kənˈsʌmpʃn/ *noun* (*no plural*) eating, drinking or using something ଖାଇବା, ପିଇବା ବା ବ୍ୟବହାର କରିବା ପ୍ରକ୍ରିୟା *This car has a high petrol consumption.*

contact[1] /ˈkɒntækt/ *noun* (*no plural*) meeting, talking to or writing to somebody (କାହାରି ସହ) ସଂଯୋଗ, ଯୋଗାଯୋଗ *Are you still in contact with the people you met on holiday?*

contact[2] /ˈkɒntækt/ *verb* (**contacts, contacting, contacted**) telephone or write to somebody, or go to see them (ଟେଲିଫୋନ୍ କରି, ଲେଖି ବା ଦେଖା କରି) ସଂଯୋଗ ସ୍ଥାପନ କରିବା

contact lens *noun* (*plural* **contact lenses**) a small round piece of plastic that you wear in your eye so that you can see better (ଚଷମା ବଦଳରେ) ଆଖି ଡୋଳାରେ ଲଗାଯାଉଥିବା ପ୍ଲାଷ୍ଟିକ୍ ଲେନ ➪ **lens** ଦେଖନ୍ତୁ ।

contain /kənˈteɪn/ *verb* (**contains, containing, contained**) have something inside it ଧାରଣ କରିବା *This box contains pens and pencils.*

container /kənˈteɪnə(r)/ *noun* a thing that you can put other things in. Boxes, bottles, bags and jars are all containers ବାକ୍ସ, ବୋତଲ, ବ୍ୟାଗ୍, ଡବା ଇତ୍ୟାଦି ଯେଉଁଥିରେ ଜିନିଷପତ୍ର ରଖାଯାଇ ପାରେ

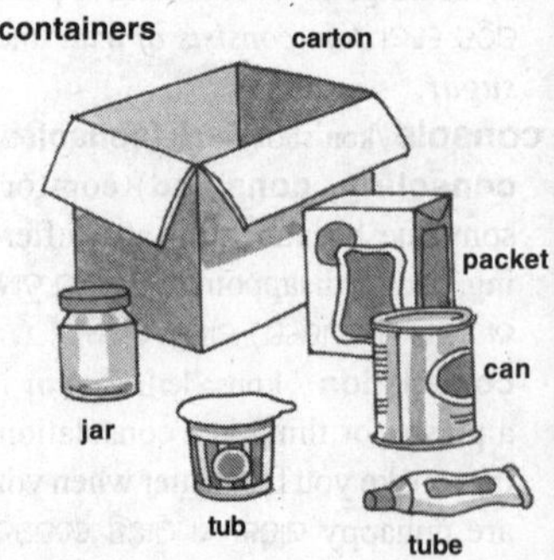

contaminate /kənˈtæmɪneɪt/ *verb* (**contaminates, contaminating, contaminated**) pollute or make something dirty and impure ପ୍ରଦୂଷିତ କରିବା, ଦୂଷଣ କରିବା *Emptying waste from factories into rivers contaminates them.*

contamination /kənˌtæmɪˈneɪʃn/ *noun* (*no plural*) ପ୍ରଦୂଷଣ *nuclear contamination*

content /kən'tent/ *adjective* satisfied with what one has ତୃପ୍ତ, ସନ୍ତୁଷ୍ଟ

contented *adjective* happy ତୃପ୍ତ, ସୁଖୀ, ଖୁସି *a contented smile* ✪ ବିପରୀତ **discontented**

contentment *noun* (*no plural*) the state of being content ସନ୍ତୋଷ, ତୃପ୍ତି ✪ ବିପରୀତ **discontentment**

contents /'kɒntents/ *noun* (*plural*) what is inside something (ବୋତଲ, ବାକ୍ସ, ଘର ଇତ୍ୟାଦି) ଭିତରେ ଥିବା ପଦାର୍ଥ; ବହିର ସୂଚୀପତ୍ର *I poured the contents of the bottle into a bowl.* ○ *The contents page of a book tells you what is in it.*

contest /'kɒntest/ *noun* a game or competition that people try to win ପ୍ରତିଯୋଗିତା *a boxing contest*

contestant *noun* a person who tries to win a contest ପ୍ରତିଦ୍ୱନ୍ଦୀ, ପ୍ରତିଯୋଗୀ *There are six contestants in the race.*

continent /'kɒntɪnənt/ *noun* one of the seven big pieces of land in the world, for example Africa, Asia or Europe ମହାଦେଶ

contingent /kən'tɪndʒənt/ *noun* a group of children or people of the same school or country who are taking part in an event (ସ୍କୁଲ୍, କଲେଜ୍ ବା ଦେଶ ଇତ୍ୟାଦିରୁ ବିଶେଷ କାମ ପ୍ରଦର୍ଶନ ପାଇଁ ପଠାଯାଇଥିବା) ଦଳ ବା ଗୋଷ୍ଠୀ

continue /kən'tɪnju:/ *verb* (**continues, continuing, continued**) **1** not stop happening or doing something କ୍ରମାଗତ ଚାଲିବା, କରିଚାଲିବା, ଅବିରତ ଭାବେ ଚାଲିବା *The rain continued all afternoon.* **2** start again after stopping ପୁଣି ଆରମ୍ଭ କରିବା *Let's have lunch now and continue the meeting this afternoon.*

continuous /kən'tɪnjuəs/ *adjective* something that is continuous goes on and does not stop ଅବିଚ୍ଛନ୍ନ, ନିରବଚ୍ଛିନ୍ନ, ଅବିରତ *a continuous line* ○ *a continuous noise*

continuously *adverb* ଅବିରତ ଭାବେ, ବନ୍ଦ ନହୋଇ *It rained continuously for five hours.*

contract /'kɒntrækt/ *noun* a piece of paper that says that somebody agrees to do something ଚୁକ୍ତି; ଚୁକ୍ତିପତ୍ର *The company has signed a contract to build the new road.*

contradict /ˌkɒntrə'dɪkt/ *verb* (**contradicts, contradicting, contradicted**) say that something is wrong or not true (କାହାରି କଥାକୁ) ଖଣ୍ଡନ କରିବା, ଭୁଲ୍ ବୋଲି କହିବା, ବିରୋଧୋକ୍ତି କରିବା *I said we didn't have any coffee yesterday evening, but Jaya contradicted me.*

contrary[1] /'kɒntrəri/ *noun*

on the contrary the opposite is true ଅପର ପକ୍ଷରେ, ବରଂ *'You look ill, Radha.' 'On the contrary, I feel fine.'*

contrary[2] /'kɒntrəri/ *adjective*

contrary to something very different from something; opposite to something ଭିନ୍ନ; ବିପରୀତ *He didn't stay in bed, contrary to the doctor's orders.*

contrast /ˈkɔntrɑːst/ *noun* a difference between things that you can see clearly ବୈଷମ୍ୟ, ବୈସାଦୃଶ୍ୟ, ଅସମତା *There is a big contrast between the weather in Rajasthan and in Kerala.*

contrasting /kənˈtrɑːstɪŋ/ *adjective* ବିଷମ, ମେଳ ଖାଉନଥିବା, ବିଯୋଡ଼ *contrasting colours*

contribute /kənˈtrɪbjuːt/ *verb* (**contributes, contributing, contributed**) **1** give money, things, etc. to help people in trouble (କାହାରି ଦୁର୍ଦ୍ଦଶାରେ ଟଙ୍କାପଇସା, ଜିନିଷପତ୍ର ଇତ୍ୟାଦି) ଦାନ କରିବା **2** be the cause of something ଘଟାଇବା

contribution /ˌkɒntrɪˈbjuːʃn/ *noun* money, clothes, etc. that you give to a person or an organization to help them (କୌଣସି ବ୍ୟକ୍ତି ବା ଅନୁଷ୍ଠାନକୁ ଟଙ୍କାପଇସା, ଜିନିଷପତ୍ର ଇତ୍ୟାଦିର) ଦାନ *We are sending contributions of food and clothing to people in poor countries.*

control[1] /kənˈtrəʊl/ *noun* (*no plural*) the power to make people or things do what you want ନିୟନ୍ତ୍ରଣ କ୍ଷମତା, ନିର୍ଦ୍ଦେଶ କ୍ଷମତା *Who has control of the government?*

lose control not be able to make people or things do what you want ନିୟନ୍ତ୍ରଣ କରିବା ଶକ୍ତି ହରାଇବା *The driver lost control and the bus went into the river.*

under control if something is under control, it is doing what you want it to do ନିୟନ୍ତ୍ରଣ କରିବା ଶକ୍ତି ହରାଇବା *The firemen have the fire under control.*

control[2] /kənˈtrəʊl/ *verb* (**controls, controlling, controlled**) make people or things do what you want ନିୟନ୍ତ୍ରଣ କରିବା *This switch controls the heating.*

controversy /ˈkɒntrəvɜːsi/ *noun* (*plural* **controversies**) something that causes a lot of argument, strong public disapproval or shock ବାଦାନୁବାଦ, ବିତର୍କ, ବିବାଦ *The film has caused a lot of controversy.*

controversial /ˌkɒntrəˈvɜːʃl/ *adjective* ବିବାଦମୂଳକ *a controversial film*

convenient /kənˈviːniənt/ *adjective* **1** easy for somebody or something; suitable ସୁବିଧାଜନକ, ଉପଯୁକ୍ତ *Let's meet on Friday. What's the most convenient time for you?* **2** easy to use or go to ଉପଯୁକ୍ତ, ସୁବିଧାଜନକ, ସହଜରେ ବ୍ୟବହାର ଯୋଗ୍ୟ *This station is very convenient for us.* ✪ ବିପରୀତ **inconvenient**

convent /ˈkɒnvənt/ *noun* **1** a place where religious women, called **nuns**, live, work and pray ଖ୍ରୀଷ୍ଟିଆନ୍ ସନ୍ୟାସିନୀଙ୍କ ବାସ ସ୍ଥାନ ବା ମଠ **2** (**convent school** ମଧ୍ୟ) a school run by **nuns** ଖ୍ରୀଷ୍ଟିଆନ୍ ସନ୍ୟାସିନୀଙ୍କ ଦ୍ୱାରା ଚାଳିତ ବିଦ୍ୟାଳୟ

conversation /ˌkɒnvəˈseɪʃn/ *noun* an informal talk କଥାବାର୍ତ୍ତା, ବାର୍ତ୍ତାଳାପ, କଥୋପକଥନ *She had a long conversation with her friend on the phone.*

convert /kənˈvɜːt/ *verb* (**converts, converting, converted**) change into another thing ପରିବର୍ତ୍ତନ କରିବା, ରୂପାନ୍ତର କରିବା *They converted the house into two flats.*

convex /ˈkɒnveks/ *adjective* (an outline or a surface) curved outwards ବୃତ୍ତର ବାହାର ପଟ ପରିବଙ୍କା, ବହିର୍ବର୍ତ୍ତୁଳ *a convex lens* ➪ **concave** ଦେଖନ୍ତୁ। ➪ ଚିତ୍ର ପାଇଁ **concave** ଦେଖନ୍ତୁ।

convey /kənˈveɪ/ *verb* (**conveys, conveying, conveyed**) make your feelings, ideas, etc. known to someone (ଭାବନା, ମତାମତ ଇତ୍ୟାଦି ଅନ୍ୟକୁ) ଜଣାଇବା, ଅବଗତ କରାଇବା *convey the happy news over the phone*

convict[1] /kənˈvɪkt/ *verb* (**convicts, convicting, convicted**) decide in a court of law that somebody has done something wrong ଅଦାଲତରେ ଦୋଷୀ ସାବ୍ୟସ୍ତ କରିବା *He was convicted of murder.*

convict[2] /ˈkɔnvɪkt/ *noun* a person who is put in prison because he has been found responsible for something bad that has happened କଇଦୀ, କାରାଦଣ୍ଡପ୍ରାପ୍ତ ଅପରାଧୀ

convince /kənˈvɪns/ *verb* (**convinces, convincing, convinced**) make somebody believe something ହୃଦ୍‌ବୋଧ କରାଇବା, ମନାଇବା *I couldn't convince him that I was right.*

convinced /kənˈvɪnst/ *adjective* certain ନିଶ୍ଚିତ *I'm convinced that I have seen her somewhere before.*

cook[1] /kʊk/ *verb* (**cooks, cooking, cooked**) make food ready to eat by heating it ରାନ୍ଧିବା *My father cooked the dinner.* ✪ ରନ୍ଧା ବିଷୟରେ ବହୁତ ଶବ୍ଦ ଅଛି **bake, boil, fry, grill, roast, stew** ଓ **toast** ଦେଖନ୍ତୁ।

cooking *noun* (*no plural*) the process of preparing food ରନ୍ଧନ, ରନ୍ଧା, ରାନ୍ଧିବା ପ୍ରକ୍ରିୟା, ରୋଷେଇ କରିବା *Who does the cooking in your family?*

cook[2] /kʊk/ *noun* a person who cooks ରାନ୍ଧୁଣିଆ, ପୂଝାରୀ *He is a good cook.*

cookery /ˈkʊkəri/ *noun* (*no plural*) the skill of preparing food, often as a subject that you can study ରନ୍ଧନ ବିଦ୍ୟା, ରାନ୍ଧିବା ପ୍ରଣାଳୀ *cookery lessons*

cookie /ˈkʊki/ *noun* a kind of **biscuit** (ଆମେରିକୀୟ) ମିଠା ବିସ୍କୁଟ୍

cool[1] /ku:l/ *adjective* (**cooler, coolest**) **1** a little cold; not warm ଶୀତଳ, ଥଣ୍ଡା *a cool breeze* **2** calm; not excited ଶାନ୍ତ, ପ୍ରଶାନ୍ତ, ସ୍ଥିର

cool[2] /ku:l/ *verb* (**cools, cooling, cooled**) make something less hot; become less hot ଥଣ୍ଡା କରିବା, ଶୀତଳେଇବା *Take the cake out of the oven and leave it to cool.*

cool down 1 become less hot ଥଣ୍ଡା ହେବା **2** become less excited or angry ଉତ୍ତେଜନା ବା କ୍ରୋଧ ଶାନ୍ତହେବା

coop /ku:p/ *noun* a cage for chickens କୁକୁଡ଼ା ରଖିବା ଟୋକେଇ ବା ପଞ୍ଜୁରୀ

cooperate /kəʊˈɒpəreɪt/ *verb* (**cooperates, cooperating, cooperated**) work together with someone in a helpful way ସହଯୋଗ କରିବା, ଅନ୍ୟସହ ମିଶି କାମ କରିବା *The two companies are cooperating with each other.*

cooperation /kəʊˌɒpəˈreɪʃn/ *noun* (*no plural*) help ସହଯୋଗ, ସାହାଯ୍ୟ *Thank you for your cooperation.*

coordinate /kəʊˈɔːdɪneɪt/ *verb* (**coordinates, coordinating, coordinated**) organize different groups of people or things so that they work together ବିଭିନ୍ନ ଗୋଷ୍ଠୀ, ଅଙ୍ଗପ୍ରତ୍ୟଙ୍ଗ ବା ଯନ୍ତ୍ରପାତି ମଧ୍ୟରେ ସମନ୍ୱୟ ରକ୍ଷା କରି କାମ କରାଇବା *Nitu coordinated the working of the team members.*

coordination /kəʊˌɒːdɪˈneɪʃn/ *noun* when you work in coordination, you work together with many people in an organized way ସମନ୍ୱୟ, ତାଳମେଳ

cope /kəʊp/ *verb* (**copes, coping, coped**)

cope with somebody or **something** do something well although it is difficult ପରିସ୍ଥିତି ବୁଝି ପାରିବା, ଠିକ୍ ଭାବରେ ପରିଚାଳନା କରିବା, ସମ୍ଭାଳିବା *She has four young children. I don't know how she copes with them!*

copied ଶବ୍ଦ **copy**[2] ର ଏକ ଧାତୁରୂପ

copies 1 ଶବ୍ଦ **copy**[1] ର ଏକ ବହୁବଚନ 2 ଶବ୍ଦ **copy**[2] ର ଏକ ଧାତୁରୂପ

copper /ˈkɒpə(r)/ *noun* (*no plural*) a metal with a colour between brown and red ତମ୍ବା, ତାମ୍ର *copper wire*

copy[1] /ˈkɒpi/ *noun* (*plural* **copies**) 1 a thing that is made to look exactly like another thing କୌଣସି ଜିନିଷର ଅବିକଳ ନକଲ (ବିଶେଷତଃ ଲେଖାର) *The secretary made two copies of the letter.* 2 one example of a book or newspaper ବହି, ପତ୍ରିକା ଇତ୍ୟାଦିର ଏକ ଖଣ୍ଡ *Two million copies of the newspaper are sold every day.*

copy[2] /ˈkɒpi/ *verb* (**copies, copying, copied, has copied**) 1 write or draw something so that it is exactly the same as another thing ନକଲ କରିବା, ପ୍ରତିଲିପି କରିବା *The teacher asked us to copy the list of words into our notebooks.* 2 try to look or do the same as another person ଅନୁକରଣ କରିବା *Tarun always copies what his brother does.*

core /kɔːr/ *noun* 1 the middle part of some kinds of fruit, where the seeds are କେତେକ ଫଳର ମଝିରେ ଥିବା ମଞ୍ଜିଆ ଅଂଶ *an apple core* 2 the central and most important part of something କୌଣସି ଜିନିଷର କେନ୍ଦ୍ରଭାଗ ବା ପ୍ରଧାନ ଅଂଶ, ମଞ୍ଜ *the earth's core*

cork /kɔːk/ *noun* 1 (*no plural*) a light but strong substance that comes from the bark of a special tree ସୋଲ, ଏକ ପ୍ରକାର ଗଛର ଛେଲିରୁ ପ୍ରସ୍ତୁତ ଭାସମାନ ପଦାର୍ଥ 2 (*plural* **corks**) a piece of cork that you put in a bottle to close it ବୋତଲର ସୋଲ ଠିପି

corn /kɔːn/ *noun* (*no plural*) the seeds of plants like wheat or maize ଶସ୍ୟ (ଧାନ, ଗହମ, ମକା ଇତ୍ୟାଦି)

corner /ˈkɔːnə(r)/ *noun* a place where two lines, walls or roads meet କଣ, କୋଣ

corporation /ˌkɔːpəˈreɪʃn/ *noun* 1 a large company ବଡ଼ ବ୍ୟବସାୟିକ ସଂସ୍ଥା

ବା କମ୍ପାନୀ **2** a group of people who meet to decide things କୌଣସି ନିର୍ଦ୍ଦିଷ୍ଟ କାମ ପାଇଁ ଅଧିକାରପ୍ରାପ୍ତ ଗୋଷ୍ଠୀ, ନିଗମ *a municipal corporation*

corpse /kɔ:ps/ *noun* the body of a dead person ମୃତଦେହ, ଶବ, ମଢ଼ା, ମୁର୍ଦାର

correct[1] /kəˈrekt/ *adjective* right or true; with no mistakes ସତ; ନିର୍ଭୁଲ୍, ସଠିକ୍ *All your answers were correct.* ✪ ବିପରୀତ **incorrect**

correctly *adverb* ସଠିକ୍ ଭାବରେ *Have I spelt your name correctly?*

correct[2] /kəˈrekt/ *verb* (**corrects, correcting, corrected**) show where the mistakes are in something and make it right ଭୁଲ୍, ଦେଖାଇ ତାକୁ ଠିକ୍ କରିବା

correction /kəˈrekʃn/ *noun* the right word or answer that is put in the place of what was wrong ସଂଶୋଧନ, ଭୁଲ୍ ସ୍ଥାନରେ ଠିକ୍ ଶବ୍ଦ ବା ଉତ୍ତର ସୂଚାଇବା

correspondence /ˌkɒrəˈspɒndəns/ *noun* (*no plural*) the act of writing letters; the letters that somebody writes or receives ଚିଠିପତ୍ର ଲେଖିବା ପ୍ରକ୍ରିୟା; ଚିଠିପତ୍ର

correspondent /ˌkɒrəˈspɒndənt/ *noun* a person who reports news from a particular place for a newspaper, radio or television company (ଖବରକାଗଜ, ରେଡ଼ିଓ ବା ଟେଲିଭିଜନର) ସଂବାଦଦାତା *NDTV's correspondent in Chennai*

corridor /ˈkɒrɪdɔ:(r)/ *noun* a long narrow part inside a building with rooms on each side of it ଘର ଭିତରେ ଦୁଇ ପଟେ ଥିବା କୋଠରିକୁ ଯିବା ପାଇଁ ସରୁ ଲମ୍ବା ମଝିବାଟ

corrosion /kəˈrəʊʒn/ *noun* a chemical process by which a metal becomes weak or is completely destroyed ଧାତବ ପଦାର୍ଥରେ କଳଙ୍କି ଲାଗି ନଷ୍ଟ ହେବାର ରାସାୟନିକ ପ୍ରକ୍ରିୟା *corrosion of iron by rust*

corrupt /kəˈrʌpt/ *adjective* dishonest in one's dealings ଅସାଧୁ, ଦୁର୍ନିତିଗ୍ରସ୍ତ *a corrupt police officer*

corruption /kəˈrʌpʃn/ *noun* (*no plural*) dishonest behaviour or dealings ଦୁର୍ନିତି *take measures against corruption*

cosmetics /kɒzˈmetɪks/ *noun* (*plural*) special powders, creams, etc. that you use on your face or hair to make yourself more beautiful ପାଉଡର, କ୍ରିମ୍ ଇତ୍ୟାଦି ସୌନ୍ଦର୍ଯ୍ୟ ବର୍ଦ୍ଧକ ଦ୍ରବ୍ୟ ବା ପ୍ରସାଧନ

cosmos /ˈkɒzmɒs/ *noun* the universe ବିଶ୍ୱବ୍ରହ୍ମାଣ୍ଡ

cost[1] /kɒst/ *noun* the money that you must pay to have something ମୂଲ୍ୟ, ଦାମ୍, ଦର *The cost of the repairs was very high.*

cost[2] /kɒst/ *verb* (**costs, costing, cost, has cost**) **1** have the price of ମୂଲ୍ୟ ବା ଦାମ୍ ଧାର୍ଯ୍ୟ ହେବା *This plant costs Rs 25.* **2** make you lose something କ୍ଷତି ହେବା *One mistake cost him his job.*

costly /ˈkɒstli/ *adjective* (**costlier, costliest**) expensive ଦାମିକା, ବହୁମୂଲ୍ୟ, ବ୍ୟୟସାପେକ୍ଷ *The repairs were very costly.*

costume /ˈkɒstju:m/ *noun* the special clothes that people wear in a country or at a certain time ବିଶେଷ ଢଙ୍ଗର ପୋଷାକ (ବିଶେଷତଃ କୌଣସି ସ୍ଥାନ ବା ସମୟର) *The actors wore beautiful costumes.*

cosy /ˈkəʊzi/ *adjective* (**cosier, cosiest**) warm and comfortable ଉଷୁମ୍ ଓ ଆରାମ୍ ଦାୟକ *a cosy room*

cottage /ˈkɒtɪdʒ/ *noun* a small house in the countryside ଗ୍ରାମାଞ୍ଚଳର କୁଟୀର ବା ଛୋଟଘର, କୁଡ଼ିଆ

cotton /ˈkɒtn/ *noun* (*no plural*) **1** a plant grown in hot countries which has soft white stuff around its seeds କପା ଗଛ ବା କପା, ତୁଳା **2** cloth or thread that is made from this soft white stuff ତୁଳାରୁ ତିଆରି ସୂତା ବା ଲୁଗା

cotton wool *noun* (*no plural*) soft light stuff made from cotton ତୁଳା ପଟି *The nurse cleaned the cut with cotton wool.*

couch /kaʊtʃ/ *noun* (*plural* **couches**) a long seat that you can sit or lie down on ବସିବା ପାଇଁ ନରମ୍ ଗଦି ଥିବା ଏକ ଲମ୍ବା ଚଉକି, କାଉଚ୍

couch

cough /kɒf/ *verb* (**coughs, coughing, coughed**) send air out of your throat with a sudden loud noise କାଶିବା *The smoke made me cough.*

cough *noun* କାଶ *a dry cough*

could /kəd; kʊd/ *modal verb* **1** the past tense of 'can', 'can' ର ଅତୀତ କାଳ *He could run very fast when he was young.* **2** a word that shows what will perhaps happen or what is possible ଭବିଷ୍ୟତରେ ଘଟିବାର ସମ୍ଭାବନା ସୂଚାଉଥିବା ଶବ୍ଦ *It could rain tomorrow.* **3** a word that you use to ask something in a polite way ପ୍ରଶ୍ନ କରିବାର ଏକ ଶିଷ୍ଟାଚାର ସୂଚକ ଶବ୍ଦ *Could you open the door?*

> ✪ Could ର ବିପରୀତ ହେଲା **could not** ବା ସଂକ୍ଷେପରେ **couldn't** ନପାରିବା — *It was dark and I couldn't see anything.*
>
> ⇨ **modal verb** ପାଇଁ ଟିପ୍ପଣୀ ଦେଖନ୍ତୁ ।

council /ˈkaʊnsl/ *noun* a group of people who are chosen to work together and to make rules and decide things (ଉପଦେଶ ଦେବାପାଇଁ, ନୀତି ନିର୍ଦ୍ଧାରଣ ପାଇଁ ବା ପ୍ରଶାସନ ପାଇଁ ଗଠିତ) ପରିଷଦ *The city council is planning to build a new swimming pool.*

count[1] /kaʊnt/ *verb* (**counts, counting, counted**) **1** say numbers one after the other in the right order ଗୋଟିଏ ପରେ ଗୋଟିଏ ଠିକ୍ କ୍ରମରେ ସଂଖ୍ୟା କହିବା *The children are learning to count from one to ten.* **2** look at people or things to see how many there are ଗଣିବା *I have counted the chairs—there are 32.*

count[2] /kaʊnt/ *noun* a man in some European countries who has a special title କିଛି ୟୁରୋପୀୟ ଦେଶର କିଛି ସଂଭ୍ରାନ୍ତ ଲୋକଙ୍କର ବିଶେଷ ଉପାଧି, କାଉଣ୍ଟ

countdown /ˈkaʊntdaʊn/ *noun* (*no plural*) the action of saying numbers backwards to zero, especially before an important event ଅବଗଣନା,

କିଛି ବିଶେଷ ଘଟଣାର ଆରମ୍ଭ ପାଇଁ ପଛୁଆ ଗଣି ଶୂନ୍ୟରେ ପହଞ୍ଚିବା *the countdown to the rocket's lift-off*

counter /ˈkaʊntə(r)/ *noun* **1** a long high table in a shop, bank or bar, that is between the people who work there and the customers who come in ଦୋକାନ, ବ୍ୟାଙ୍କ ଇତ୍ୟାଦିରେ ଗରାଖଙ୍କ ସହ କାରବାର କରିବା ପାଇଁ ଖଞ୍ଜା ହୋଇଥିବା ଲମ୍ବା ସମତଳ ଟେବୁଲ୍‌ର ଉପରିଭାଗ **2** a small round thing that you use when you play some games (କ୍ୟାରମ୍, ଲୁଡୋ ଇତ୍ୟାଦି ଖେଳର) ଗୋଟି

counterfeit /ˈkaʊntəfɪt/ *adjective* not real, but copied so well that it looks almost real କୃତ୍ରିମ, ନକଲି *counterfeit money*

countess /ˈkaʊntəs/ *noun* (*plural* **countesses**) **1** a woman who has a special title ବିଶେଷ ଉପାଧି ପ୍ରାପ୍ତ ୟୁରୋପୀୟ ମହିଳା; କାଉଣ୍ଟ ଉପାଧିପ୍ରାପ୍ତ ବ୍ୟକ୍ତିଙ୍କ ସ୍ତ୍ରୀ **2** the wife of a **count** କାଉଣ୍ଟର ସ୍ତ୍ରୀ

countless /ˈkaʊntləs/ *adjective* very many ଅଗଣିତ, ଅସଂଖ୍ୟ, ବହୁତ *I have tried to telephone him countless times.*

country /ˈkʌntri/ *noun* (*plural* **countries**) an area of land with its own people and government ଦେଶ

countryside /ˈkʌntrisaɪd/ *noun* (*no plural*) land with fields, woods, farms, etc. that is away from towns ଗ୍ରାମାଞ୍ଚଳ

couple /ˈkʌpl/ *noun* two people who are married, for example ଯୁଗଳ, ଯୋଡ଼ି, ଯଥାଃ ସ୍ୱାମୀ ଓ ସ୍ତ୍ରୀ, ଦମ୍ପତି *A young couple live next door.*

a couple of 1 two ହଳେ **2** a few ଅଳ୍ପ *I'll be back in a couple of minutes.*

couplet /ˈkʌplət/ *noun* two lines of poetry, equal in length and one following the other କବିତାରେ ଥିବା ଦୁଇ ଧାଡ଼ିର ପଂକ୍ତି *rhyming couplets*

courage /ˈkʌrɪdʒ/ *noun* (*no plural*) not being afraid, or not showing that you are afraid when you do something dangerous or difficult ସାହସ, ନିର୍ଭୀକତା *She showed great courage when she went into the burning building to save the child.*

courageous /kəˈreɪdʒəs/ *adjective* brave ସାହସୀ, ନିର୍ଭୀକ *a courageous young man*

courier /ˈkʊriə(r)/ *noun* a person or company whose job is to deliver important letters and parcels within a very short time ଶୀଘ୍ର ଡାକ ବଣ୍ଟନ କରୁଥିବା ବ୍ୟକ୍ତି ବା ସଂସ୍ଥା

course /kɔːs/ *noun* **1** a set of lessons on a certain subject ପାଠ୍ୟକ୍ରମ *He's taking a course in computer programming.* **2** a piece of ground for some kinds of sport ଗଲ୍ଫ ଖେଳ ବା ଦୌଡ଼ ପ୍ରତିଯୋଗିତାର ନିର୍ଦ୍ଦିଷ୍ଟ ପଡ଼ିଆ ବା ସ୍ଥାନ *a golf course* **3** the direction that something moves in ଅଗ୍ରଗତି, ଗତିପଥ *We followed the course of the river.*

of course certainly ଅବଶ୍ୟ, ନିଶ୍ଚିତଭାବେ *Of course I'll help you.*

court /kɔːt/ *noun* **1** (ମଧ୍ୟ **court of law**) a place where people (a **judge** or **jury**) decide if a person has done something wrong, and what the punishment will be ବିଚାରାଳୟ, ଅଦାଲତ, କୋର୍ଟ୍ *The man will appear in court tomorrow.* **2** a piece of ground where you can play a certain sport (ଟେନିସ୍ ବ୍ୟାଡ୍‌ମିଣ୍ଟନ୍ ଇତ୍ୟାଦି ଖେଳର) ଖେଳ ପଡ଼ିଆ *a tennis court* **3** a king or queen, their family and all the people who look after them ରାଜ ପରିବାର ଓ ପରିଷଦବର୍ଗ, ରାଜସଭା *the court of Emperor Akbar*

courteous /ˈkɜːtiəs/ *adjective* polite and showing respect ଭଦ୍ର, ଶିଷ୍ଟ *Be courteous to elders.*

courtesy /ˈkɜːtəsi/ *noun* (*plural* **courtesies**) polite and respectful behaviour ଭଦ୍ର ଆଚରଣ, ଶିଷ୍ଟତା, ଭଦ୍ରତା

courtier /ˈkɔːtie(r)/ *noun* a person who worked in the royal courts in the past (ପୂର୍ବ କାଳର) ରାଜାଙ୍କ ସହଚର ଓ ପରାମର୍ଶଦାତା; ପରିଷଦ, ସଭାସଦ୍

courtyard /ˈkɔːtjɑːd/ *noun* an open space without a roof, inside a building or between buildings ଅଗଣା

courtyard

cousin /ˈkʌzn/ *noun* the child of your aunt or uncle ମାମୁଁ, ମାଉସୀ, କକେଇ ବା ଦଦେଇଙ୍କ ପିଲା ➪ ଚିତ୍ର ପାଇଁ **family** ଦେଖନ୍ତୁ।

cover¹ /ˈkʌvə(r)/ *verb* (**covers, covering, covered**) put one thing over another thing to hide it or to keep it safe or warm ଘୋଡ଼ାଇବା, ଢ଼ାଙ୍କିବା, ଆବୃତ କରିବା *Cover the floor with a newspaper before you start painting.*

cover² /ˈkʌvə(r)/ *noun* **1** a thing that you put over another thing, for example to keep it safe ଆବରଣ, ଢ଼ାଙ୍କୁଣୀ, ଘୋଡ଼ଣୀ, ଲଫାପା ଇତ୍ୟାଦି *The computer has a plastic cover.* **2** the outside part of a book or magazine (ବହି, ପତ୍ରିକା ଇତ୍ୟାଦିର) ମଲାଟ *The book had a picture of a footballer on the cover.*

coverage /ˈkʌvərɪdʒ/ *noun* (*no plural*) the amount of reporting of a news item in a newspaper, on radio or television ଖବରକାଗଜ, ରେଡ଼ିଓ ବା ଟେଲିଭିଜନ୍‌ରେ ପରିବେଷଣ କରାଯାଉଥିବା ଖବର *Did you watch the live coverage of yesterday's match?*

covering /ˈkʌvərɪŋ/ *noun* something that covers another thing ଆବରଣ *There was a thick covering of snow on the ground.*

cow /kaʊ/ *noun* a big female farm animal that gives milk ଗାଈ ✪ **Bull** ଅଣ୍ଡିରା ଗୋରୁକୁ କହନ୍ତି ଏବଂ ବାଛୁରୀକୁ କହନ୍ତି **calf**।

coward /ˈkaʊəd/ *noun* a person who is afraid when there is danger or a problem ଭୀରୁ, ଡରୁଆ, ସହଜରେ ଡରି ଯାଉଥିବା ବ୍ୟକ୍ତି

cowboy /ˈkaʊbɔɪ/ *noun* a man who rides a horse and looks after cows on big farms in the USA (ଯୁକ୍ତରାଷ୍ଟ୍ର ଆମେରିକାର ବଡ଼ ବଡ଼ ପଶୁପାଳନ କ୍ଷେତ୍ରରେ) ଗାଈଗୋରୁଙ୍କ ଦାୟିତ୍ୱରେ ଥିବା ଘୋଡ଼ାଚଢ଼ା ପୁରୁଷ ପଶୁ ରକ୍ଷକ।

CPU /ˌsiː piː ˈjuː/ *noun* a part of computer which controls all the other parts of the computer କମ୍ପ୍ୟୁଟରର ମୂଳ ନିୟନ୍ତ୍ରକ ଯନ୍ତ୍ର ✪ CPU ହେଲା **Central Processing Unit** ର ସଂକ୍ଷିପ୍ତ ରୂପ ।

crab /kræb/ *noun* an animal that lives in and near the sea. It has a hard shell, eight legs and two big claws କଙ୍କଡ଼ା ➪ ଚିତ୍ର ପାଇଁ **sea** ଦେଖନ୍ତୁ ।

crack¹ /kræk/ *noun* a thin line on something where it is nearly broken ଫାଟ, ଫାଙ୍କ *There's a crack in this glass.*

crack² /kræk/ *verb* (**cracks, cracking, cracked**) break, but not into pieces ଖଣ୍ଡଖଣ୍ଡ ନହୋଇ ଖାଲି ଫାଟ ପଡ଼ିଲା ପରି ଭାଙ୍ଗିବା *The glass will crack if you pour boiling water into it.*

cracker /ˈkrækə(r)/ = **firecracker**

crackle /ˈkrækl/ *verb* (**crackles, crackling, crackled**) make a lot of short sharp sounds (ଶୁଖିଲା କାଠରେ ନିଆଁ ଲଗେଇଲେ ହେଉଥିବା) କଡ଼କଡ଼ ଚଡ଼ଚଡ଼ ଶବ୍ଦ *Dry wood crackles when you burn it.*

cradle /ˈkreɪdl/ *noun* a small bed for a baby ପିଲାଙ୍କ ଦୋଳିଖଟ (ଯେଉଁଥିରେ ବାଡ଼ ଲାଗିଥାଏ)

craft /krɑːft/ *noun* (*plural* **crafts**) a job in which you make things carefully and cleverly with your hands ହସ୍ତଶିଳ୍ପ, କାରିଗରି *Pottery and weaving are crafts.*

craftsman /ˈkrɑːftsmən/ *noun* (*plural* **craftsmen**) a person who has the skill to make things with his hands ହସ୍ତଶିଳ୍ପୀ, କାରିଗର *The craftsmen wove beautiful shawls.*

crafty /ˈkrɑːfti/ *adjective* someone who is crafty is clever and gets things done by using unfair or dishonest means ଧୂର୍ତ୍ତ, ସିଆଣିଆ, ଶଠ, ଚାଲାକ୍ କପଟୀ, ଧୂରୀଣ

cramp /kræmp/ *noun* a sudden pain caused by the pulling of muscles ଅଙ୍ଗଗ୍ରହ, ପେଶୀର ଆକସ୍ମିକ ଯନ୍ତ୍ରଣାଦାୟକ ଆକୁଞ୍ଚନ

cramped /kræmpt/ *adjective* in an uncomfortable condition (ସ୍ଥାନ ସମ୍ପର୍କରେ) ଅତି ସଂକୀର୍ଣ୍ଣ, ଚାପି ହେଲାପରି *He sat in a cramped position in the crowded bus.*

crane¹ /kreɪn/ *noun* a big machine with a long part for lifting or moving heavy things ବକଯନ୍ତ୍ର, ଉତ୍ତୋଳନ ଯନ୍ତ୍ର, କ୍ରେନ୍ (ଭାରୀ ପଦାର୍ଥ ଟେକି ଅନ୍ୟ ସ୍ଥାନରେ ରଖିପାରୁଥିବା ଯନ୍ତ୍ର)

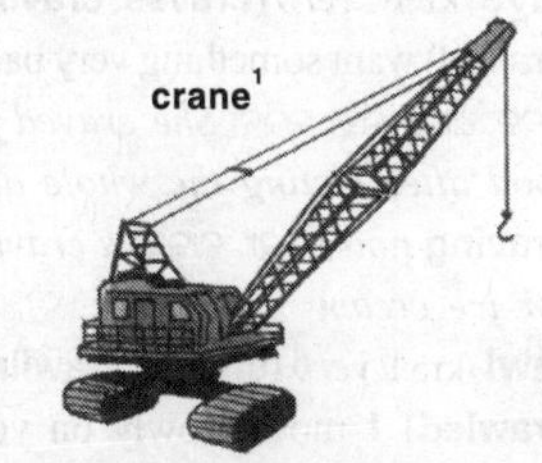

crane² /kreɪn/ *noun* a large waterbird with a long neck and long legs ବଗ, ବକ, କ୍ରୌଞ୍ଚ ।

crash¹ /kræʃ/ *noun* (*plural* **crashes**) **1** a loud noise when something falls or hits another thing ଭାରୀ ଜିନିଷ ପଡ଼ିଯିବା ବା ଭାଙ୍ଗିଯିବାର ଉଚ୍ଚଶବ୍ଦ *I heard a crash as the tree fell.* **2** an accident when something that is moving hits another thing ଧକ୍କା *a plane crash*

crash² /kræʃ/ *verb* (**crashes, crashing, crashed**) **1** fall or hit something with a loud noise ଉଚ୍ଚ ଶବ୍ଦ କରି ଧକ୍କା

ଲାଗିବା ବା ପଡ଼ିଯିବା *A tree crashed through the window.* **2** have an accident; hit something (ଯାନ, ବିମାନ ଇତ୍ୟାଦି) ଧକ୍କା ହେବା, ପଡ଼ିଯିବା *The bus crashed into a tree.*

crate /kreɪt/ *noun* a big box for carrying bottles or other things (ବୋତଲ ବା ଅନ୍ୟଜିନିଷ ନେଉଥିବା) ବଡ଼ ବାକ୍ସ, ଡ଼ାବଲ

crater /ˈkreɪtə(r)/ *noun* **1** a large hole in the top of a volcano through which hot liquid material (called **lava**) and gases come out ଆଗ୍ନେୟଗିରିରୁ ଉତ୍ତପ୍ତ ଲାଭା ବା ବାହାରୁଥିବା ମୁଖ ବା ଗହ୍ୱର। ➪ **volcano** ଦେଖନ୍ତୁ। **2** a huge hole in the ground ଗହ୍ୱର, ବଡ଼ ଖାଲ *craters on the moon*

crave /kreɪv/ *verb* (**craves, craving, craved**) want something very badly ପ୍ରବଳ ଭାବେ ଇଚ୍ଛା କରିବା *She craved for food after fasting the whole day.*

craving *noun* ଇଚ୍ଛା, ଲାଳସା *a craving for ice cream*

crawl /krɔːl/ *verb* (**crawls, crawling, crawled**) **1** move slowly on your hands and knees ଗୁରୁଣ୍ଡିବା; ଘୁଷୁରି ଘୁଷୁରି ଯିବା *Babies crawl before they can walk.* **2** move slowly with the body close to the ground ଚଟାଣ ସହିତ ଘୋଷାରୀ ହୋଇ ଧିରେ ଗତି କରିବା *An ant crawled across the floor.*

crayon /ˈkreɪən/ *noun* a soft thick stick of coloured wax or chalk ଲାଖ ବା ଚକ୍‌ର ରଙ୍ଗ ବେରଙ୍ଗ ଖଡ଼ି ବା ପେନ୍‌ସିଲ୍ *The children were drawing pictures with crayons.*

crazy /ˈkreɪzi/ *adjective* (**crazier, craziest**) mad or very stupid ପାଗଳ, ବାଉଳା ବା ଭାରି ବୋକା *You must be crazy to ride a bike at night with no lights.*

creak /kriːk/ *verb* (**creaks, creaking, creaked**) make a noise like a door that needs oil, or like an old wooden floor when you walk on it କର୍କଶ ଶବ୍ଦ, କଟ୍‌କଟ୍ ଶବ୍ଦ

cream[1] /kriːm/ *noun* **1** (*no plural*) the thick liquid that rises to the top of milk ଦୁଧର ସର *Do you want cream in your coffee?* **2** (*plural* **creams**) a thick liquid that you put on your skin to keep it soft ଦେହ ବା ମୁହଁରେ ଲଗାଇବା ସୌନ୍ଦର୍ଯ୍ୟବର୍ଦ୍ଧକ ଲହୁଣି ପରି ପ୍ରସାଧନ ଦ୍ରବ୍ୟ, କ୍ରିମ୍

cream[2] /kriːm/ *adjective* with a colour between white and yellow ଧଳା-ହଳଦିଆ ରଙ୍ଗ *She was wearing a cream dress.*

creamy /ˈkriːmi/ *adjective* with cream in it ସର ପଡ଼ିଥିବା ବା ସର ପରି *a creamy sauce*

crease /kriːs/ *verb* (**creases, creasing, creased**) make untidy lines in paper or cloth by not being careful with it କାଗଜ ବା ଲୁଗାପଟାର ଲୋଚାକୋଚା ଦାଗ *Don't sit on my jacket—you'll crease it.*

crease *noun* **1** a line in paper or cloth made by folding or pressing କାଗଜ ବା ଲୁଗା ଚଉତା ଭାଙ୍ଗ **2** a white line on the cricket field near each wicket. The crease marks the position of the bowler and the batsman କ୍ରିକେଟ୍ ଖେଳରେ ବୋଲର୍ ଓ ବ୍ୟାଟ୍ସମ୍ୟାନଙ୍କ ଅବସ୍ଥିତି ନିର୍ଣ୍ଣୟ କରୁଥିବା ଧଳା ଗାର

create /kri'eɪt/ *verb* (**creates, creating, created**) make something new ସୃଷ୍ଟି କରିବା, ନୂଆକରି ତିଆରି କରିବା *The company has created a new kind of engine.*

creation /kri'eɪʃn/ *noun* **1** (*no plural*) making something new ନୂଆ ଜିନିଷର ସୃଜନା *the creation of another state* **2** (*plural* **creations**) a new thing that somebody has made ନୂଆ ସୃଜନା, ନୂଆ କରି ତିଆରି ହୋଇଥିବା ପଦାର୍ଥ *the designer's latest creations*

creative /kri'eɪtɪv/ *adjective* a person who is creative has a lot of new ideas or is good at making new things ସୃଜନଶକ୍ତି ସମ୍ପନ୍ନ

creator /kri'eɪtə(r)/ *noun* a person who makes something new ସୃଷ୍ଟିକର୍ତ୍ତା *Walt Disney was the creator of Mickey Mouse.*

creature /'kri:tʃə(r)/ *noun* any living thing that is not a plant ପ୍ରାଣୀ (ବିଶେଷତଃ ପଶୁ) *birds, fish and other creatures*

credit[1] /'kredɪt/ *noun* (*no plural*) buying something and paying for it later ବର୍ତ୍ତମାନ ଜିନିଷ କିଣି ପରେ ଟଙ୍କା ଦେବା ପଦ୍ଧତି, ଉଧାର, ବାକିଆ ଖରିଦ

credit card *noun* (*plural* **credit cards**) a plastic card from a bank that you can use to buy something and pay for it later ବ୍ୟାଙ୍କ ଦେଉଥିବା ଉଧାର କାର୍ଡ଼ ଯାହା ଦେଖାଇ ଜିନିଷପତ୍ର କିଣି ପରେ ବ୍ୟାଙ୍କୁ ଟଙ୍କା ଦିଆଯାଏ

credit[2] /'kredɪt/ *noun* (*no plural*) saying that somebody or something is good ସୁନାମ, ବାହାବା, ବାହାଦୁରି *I did all the work but Jaya got all the credit for it!*

creek /kri:k/ *noun* **1** a narrow stream of water that flows from a sea into the land ସ୍ଥଳଭାଗକୁ ପଶି ଆସିଥିବା ସାଗରଶାଖା, ସଂକୀର୍ଣ୍ଣ ଉପସାଗର *a shallow creek* **2** a small stream or river ଛୋଟ ସରୁ ନଦୀ, ଜଳଧାର ବା ନଦୀ ଶାଖା

creep /kri:p/ *verb* (**creeps, creeping, crept** /krept/, **has crept**) move quietly and carefully so that nobody hears or sees you; move along close to the ground ଛପି ଛପି କେହି ନଜାଣିଲା ପରି ଯିବା, ଗୁରୁଣ୍ଡିଲା ପରି ଯିବା *The cat crept towards the bird.*

crescent /'kresnt/ *noun* the shape of the moon when it is less than half a circle ବୃତ୍ତାର୍ଦ୍ଧ ଠାରୁ କମ୍ ଆକାରର ଚନ୍ଦ୍ର

crew /kru:/ *noun* all the people who work on a ship or an aeroplane ଜାହାଜ ବା ବିମାନର ସମସ୍ତ କର୍ମଚାରୀ

crib /krɪb/ *noun* a baby's bed that has high sides ଶିଶୁମାନଙ୍କର ଉଚ୍ଚ ବାଡ଼ ଥିବା ଖଟ, ଖଟୁଲି

cricket[1] /'krɪkɪt/ *noun* (*no plural*) a game for two teams of eleven players who try to hit a small hard ball with a **bat** on a large field କ୍ରିକେଟ୍ ଖେଳ *We watched a cricket match.*

cricketer *noun* a person who plays cricket କ୍ରିକେଟ୍ ଖେଳାଳି

cricket[2] /'krɪkɪt/ *noun* a small brown insect that makes a loud noise ଝିଣ୍ଟିକା

cricket[2]

cried ଶବ୍ଦ **cry**[1] ର ଏକ ଧାତୁରୂପ

cries **1** ଶବ୍ଦ **cry**[1] ର ଏକ ଧାତୁରୂପ **2** ଶବ୍ଦ **cry**[2] ର ବହୁବଚନ

crime /kraɪm/ *noun* something somebody does that is against the law ଅପରାଧ *Murder and robbery are serious crimes.*

criminal /ˈkrɪmɪnl/ *noun* a person who does something that is against the law ଅପରାଧୀ

cripple /ˈkrɪpl/ *verb* (**cripples, crippling, crippled**) hurt your legs or back badly so that you cannot walk ଆଘାତ ଦ୍ୱାରା ଆର୍ଥିକ ବା ପଙ୍ଗୁ ହୋଇଯିବା ବା କରିଦେବା *She was crippled in an accident.*

crisis /ˈkraɪsɪs/ *noun* (*plural* **crises** /ˈkraɪsiːz/) a time when something very dangerous or serious happens ସଙ୍କଟକାଳ, ବିପଦ ସମୟ, ବିପତ୍ତି *a political crisis*

crisp /krɪsp/ *adjective* (**crisper, crispest**) hard and dry ମସକା, ମୁସୁମୁସିଆ, କଡ଼ମଡ଼ିଆ *If you keep the chips in a tin, they will stay crisp.*

critic /ˈkrɪtɪk/ *noun* a person who says what is good or bad about somebody or something ସମାଲୋଚକ, ସମୀକ୍ଷକ *a film critic*

critical /ˈkrɪtɪkl/ *adjective* **1** if you are critical of somebody or something, you say that they are wrong or bad ସମାଲୋଚନାମୂଳକ, ତ୍ରୁଟି ପ୍ରଦର୍ଶନ *They were very critical of my work.* **2** very serious or dangerous ଗୁରୁତର, ମାରାତ୍ମକ *a critical illness*

criticize /ˈkrɪtɪsaɪz/ *verb* (**criticizes, criticizing, criticized**) say that somebody or something is wrong or bad ତ୍ରୁଟି ପ୍ରଦର୍ଶନ କରିବା, ଦୋଷ କାଢ଼ିବା, ସମାଲୋଚନା କରିବା *He criticizes everything I do!*

croak /krəʊk/ *noun* the noise that a frog makes ବେଙ୍ଗର ବୋବାଇବା ଶବ୍ଦ, ଭେକରାବ

croak *verb* (**croaks, croaking, croaked**) make a noise like a frog makes ବେଙ୍ଗବୋବାଇଲା ପରି ଶବ୍ଦ କରିବା, କର୍କଶ ସ୍ୱରରେ କହିବା

crockery /ˈkrɒkəri/ *noun* (*no plural*) plates, cups and dishes ଚିନା ମାଟି ବାସନକୁସନ (ଥାଳି, ଥାଳିଆ, କପ୍, ଗିନା ଇତ୍ୟାଦି)

crocodile /ˈkrɒkədaɪl/ *noun* a big long reptile with sharp teeth. Crocodiles live in rivers in some hot countries କୁମ୍ଭୀର (କୁମ୍ଭୀର ଗ୍ରୀଷ୍ମ ମଣ୍ଡଳର ନଦୀରେ ରହନ୍ତି)

crooked /ˈkrʊkɪd/ *adjective* **1** not straight ବଙ୍କା, ବକ୍ର **2** dishonest; not straightforward ଅସାଧୁ କୁଟିଳ

crop /krɒp/ *noun* all the plants of one kind that a farmer grows at one time ଫସଲ, କୃଷିଜାତ ଶସ୍ୟ *There was a good crop of potatoes last year.* ○ *Rain is good for the crops.*

cross[1] /krɒs/ *noun* (*plural* **crosses**) a mark like + or × ଛକି ଚିହ୍ନ (+ ବା ×) *The cross on the map shows where I live.*

cross[2] /krɒs/ *verb* (**crosses, crossing, crossed**) **1** go from one side of something to the other ସଡ଼କ, ନଦୀ, ସମୁଦ୍ର ଇତ୍ୟାଦି ପାରହେବା *Be careful when you cross the road.* **2** put one thing over another thing ଗୋଟିଏ ଉପରେ ଆଉଗୋଟିଏ ରଖିବା *She sat down and crossed her legs.*

cross[3] /krɒs/ *adjective* angry ବିରକ୍ତ, କ୍ରୁଧ, କ୍ଷୁବ୍ଧ *I was cross with her because she was late.*

crossing /ˈkrɒsɪŋ/ *noun* a place where you can safely cross a road, railway tracks, etc. ଛକ ଜାଗା, ରାସ୍ତା, ରେଳଲାଇନ ଇତ୍ୟାଦି ସୁରକ୍ଷିତ ଭାବେ ପାର ହେବା ଜାଗା

crossroads /ˈkrɒsrəʊdz/ *noun* (*plural* **crossroads**) a place where two roads cross each other ରାସ୍ତାର ଛକ, ଚାରିଛକ, ଦୁଇ ବା ଅଧିକ ରାସ୍ତାର ମିଳନ ସ୍ଥଳ

crossword puzzle, crossword /ˈkrɒswɜːd/ *noun* a game on paper where you write words in squares ଶବ୍ଦ ଧନ୍ଦା, କ୍ରସ୍‌ୱାର୍ଡ଼

crossword

crouch /kraʊtʃ/ *verb* (**crouches, crouching, crouched**) bend your legs under you so that your body is close to the ground ନଇଁ ପଡ଼ି ଆଣ୍ଠୁକୁ ଛାତିରେ ଲଗାଇବା *I crouched under the table to hide.*

crow[1] /krəʊ/ *noun* a large black bird that makes a loud noise କୁଆ, କାଉ, କାକ, ବାୟସ

crow[2] /krəʊ/ *verb* (**crows, crowing, crowed**) make a loud noise like a male chicken (a **cock**) makes early in the morning କୁକୁଡ଼ା ବୋବାଇବା ➪ **cluck** ବି ଦେଖନ୍ତୁ।

crowd /kraʊd/ *noun* a lot of people together ଗହଳି, ଜନଗହଳି

crowded *adjective* full of people ଜନପୂର୍ଣ୍ଣ, ଜନାକୀର୍ଣ୍ଣ, ଗହଳି *The streets were very crowded.* ○ *a crowded bus*

crown /kraʊn/ *noun* a special circular ornament that a king or queen wears on his or her head at important times ମୁକୁଟ, କିରୀଟ (ରାଜା ବା ରାଣୀଙ୍କର)

crown *verb* (**crowns, crowning, crowned**) put a crown on the head of a new king or queen ମୁକୁଟ ପିନ୍ଧାଇବା (ରାଜା ବା ରାଣୀଙ୍କୁ) ରାଜ ଗାଦିର ବସାଇବା ବା ରାଜପଦାଭିଷିକ୍ତ କରିବା *Elizabeth II was crowned in 1952.*

crucial /ˈkruːʃl/ *adjective* very important ଅତିଗୁରୁତ୍ୱପୂର୍ଣ୍ଣ *The next few days are going to be crucial.*

crucify /ˈkruːsɪfaɪ/ *verb* (**crucifies, crucifying, crucified**) kill someone by fastening them onto a cross as punishment କ୍ରୁଶବିଦ୍ଧ କରି ମୃତ୍ୟୁ ଘଟାଇବା *It was common practice to crucify criminals in ancient times.*

crude /kruːd/ *adjective* (**cruder, crudest**) **1** rough or rude ଅଭଦ୍ର, ଅସଭ୍ୟ **2** in its natural state, before it is treated and purified ଅବିଶୁଦ୍ଧ, ଅଶୋଧିତ, ପ୍ରାକୃତିକ ଅବସ୍ଥାରେ ଥିବା *crude oil*

cruel /kruːəl/ *adjective* (**crueller, cruellest**) a person who is cruel is unkind and likes to hurt other people or animals ନିଷ୍ଠୁର, ନିର୍ଦ୍ଦୟ, ନିର୍ମମ, କ୍ରୁର ✪ ବିପରୀତ **kind**[1]

cruelty /ˈkruːəlti/ *noun* (*no plural*) being cruel ନିଷ୍ଠୁରତା, କ୍ରୁରତା, ନିର୍ଦ୍ଦୟତା *cruelty to animals*

crumb /krʌm/ *noun* a very small piece of bread, cake or biscuit ପାଉଁରୁଟି, କେକ୍, ବିସ୍କୁଟ୍ ଇତ୍ୟାଦିର ଟୁକୁରା ବା ଛୋଟ ଖଣ୍ଡ

crumble /ˈkrʌmbl/ *verb* (**crumbles, crumbling, crumbled**) break into very small pieces ଖଣ୍ଡ ଖଣ୍ଡ ହୋଇ ଭାଙ୍ଗିଯିବା ବା ଭାଙ୍ଗିପଡ଼ିବା *The old castle walls are crumbling.*

crunch /krʌntʃ/ *verb* (**crunches, crunching, crunched**) make a loud noise when you eat something that is hard କଡ଼ କଡ଼ କରି ଚୋବାଇବା *The dog was crunching a bone.*

crush /krʌʃ/ *verb* (**crushes, crushing, crushed**) press something very hard so that you break or damage it ଚାପି ବା ଛେଚି ଭାଙ୍ଗିଦେବା *She sat on my hat and crushed it.*

crust /krʌst/ *noun* **1** the hard part on the outside of bread ପାଉଁରୁଟି ବାହାରପଟର ଟାଣୁଆ ଅଂଶ **2** the hard layer that forms the earth's surface ଭୂପୃଷ୍ଠର ପଥରପରି ଟାଣୁଆ ପରସ୍ତ

crutch /krʌtʃ/ *noun* (*plural* **crutches**) a long stick that you put under your arm to help you walk when you have hurt your leg ଗୋଡ଼ ଆହତ ହେବା ବେଳେ ଚାଲିବା ପାଇଁ ସାହାଯ୍ୟ କରୁଥିବା କାଖତଳେ ଜକା ବାଡ଼ି *He broke his leg and now he's on crutches.*

cry[1] /kraɪ/ *verb* (**cries, crying, cried, has cried**) **1** have drops of water falling from your eyes, usually because you are unhappy କାନ୍ଦିବା। **2** shout or make a loud noise ଚିତ୍କାର କରିବା, ବଡ଼ ପାଟି କରିବା *She cried out in pain.*

cry[2] /kraɪ/ *noun* (*plural* **cries**) a loud noise that you make to show pain, fear or excitement, for example ଚିତ୍କାର, ଉଚ୍ଚ ସ୍ୱରର ଡାକ *We heard her cries and ran to help.*

crystal /ˈkrɪstl/ *noun* a kind of rock that looks like glass ସ୍ଫଟିକ, କାଚ ପରି ସ୍ୱଚ୍ଛ ବର୍ଣ୍ଣହୀନ ଖଣିଜ ପଦାର୍ଥ

cub /kʌb/ *noun* a young lion, bear, wolf, fox or tiger ବାଘ, ସିଂହ, ଭାଲୁ, ହେଟା ବା ବିଲୁଆଙ୍କ ଛୁଆ

cube /kju:b/ *noun* a shape like a box with six equal square sides ଘନକ୍ଷେତ୍ର, ଛଅଟି ସମପାର୍ଶ୍ୱ ଦ୍ୱାରା ଆବଦ୍ଧ ସମତଳ କ୍ଷେତ୍ର *an ice-cube* ➪ ଚିତ୍ର ପାଇଁ **shape** ଦେଖନ୍ତୁ।

cuckoo /ˈkʊku:/ *noun* (*plural* **cuckoos**) a bird that makes a sound like its name କୋଇଲି, କୋକିଳ

cucumber /ˈkju:kʌmbə(r)/ *noun* a long vegetable with a green skin. You often eat it in salads କାକୁଡ଼ି ➪ ଚତ୍ର ପାଇଁ **vegetable** ଦେଖନ୍ତୁ।

cuff /kʌf/ *noun* the end part of a sleeve, near your hand ପୂରାହାତ କାମିଜ୍‌ର ହାତର ଶେଷ ଅଂଶ

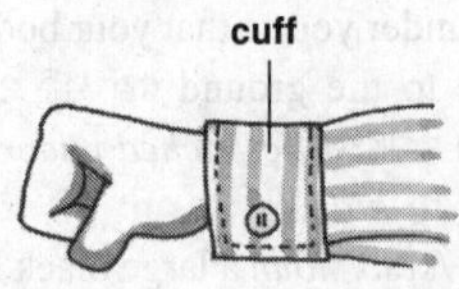

culprit /ˈkʌlprɪt/ *noun* someone who has done something wrong ଅପରାଧି, ଆସାମୀ, ଦୋଷୀ

cultivate /ˈkʌltɪveɪt/ *verb* (**cultivates, cultivating, cultivated**) use land for growing plants ଚାଷ କରିବା, ଶସ୍ୟ ଉତ୍ପାଦନ ପାଇଁ ଜମି ପ୍ରସ୍ତୁତ ଓ ବ୍ୟବହାର କରିବା *Only a* *small area of the island was cultivated.*

cultivation /ˌkʌltɪˈveɪʃn/ *noun* (*no plural*) ଚାଷ *cultivation of the land*

culture /ˈkʌltʃə(r)/ *noun* the art, ideas and way of life of a group of people ସଂସ୍କୃତି, ନିର୍ଦ୍ଦିଷ୍ଟ ଗୋଷ୍ଠୀର କଳା, ରୀତି ଓ ସଭ୍ୟତା *She is studying Indian culture.*

cultural *adjective* about things like art, music or theatre ସାଂସ୍କୃତିକ *cultural activities*

cunning /ˈkʌnɪŋ/ *adjective* clever; good at making people believe something that is not true ଚାଲାକ୍; ଧୂର୍ତ୍ତ, ଶଠ

cup /kʌp/ *noun* **1** a small round container with a handle, that you can drink from କପ୍ *a cup and saucer* **2** a large metal thing like a cup, that you get for winning in a competition ପ୍ରତିଯୋଗିତାର ବିଜେତାଙ୍କୁ ଦିଆଯାଉଥିବା କପ୍

cupboard /ˈkʌbəd/ *noun* a piece of furniture with shelves and doors, where you keep things like clothes or food ଜିନିଷପତ୍ର ରଖିବା ଆଲମାରି ବା କାନ୍ଥ ଆଲମାରି

curd /kɜːd/ *noun* a soft white thick substance that is formed when milk turns sour ଦହି, ଦଧି

cure /kjʊə(r)/ *verb* (**cures, curing, cured**) make an ill person well again ଆରୋଗ୍ୟ କରିବା, ରୋଗମୁକ୍ତ କରିବା

curiosity /ˌkjʊəriˈɒsəti/ *noun* (*no plural*) wanting to know about things କୌତୁହଳ, ଜାଣିବାର ଆଗ୍ରହ, ଅନୁସନ୍ଧିତ୍ସା *I was full of curiosity about the letter.*

curious /ˈkjʊəriəs/ *adjective* if you are curious, you want to know about something ଜାଣିବାକୁ ଆଗ୍ରହ ଥିବା, ଅନୁସନ୍ଧିତ୍ସୁ *I am curious to know where she found the money.*

curiously *adverb* ଜାଣିବାକୁ ଆଗ୍ରହ କରି, ଅନୁସନ୍ଧିତ୍ସୁ ଭାବରେ *'Where are you going?' she asked curiously.*

curl¹ /kɜːl/ *noun* a piece of hair in a round shape କୁଞ୍ଚିତ କେଶ, ବାଳର ଗୋଲିଆ କୁଞ୍ଚ

curly *adjective* (**curlier, curliest**) with a lot of curls କୁଞ୍ଚକୁଞ୍ଚିଆ *He's got curly hair.*

curl² /kɜːl/ *verb* (**curls, curling, curled**) bend into a round or curved shape କୁଣ୍ଡଳାକାରରେ ବଙ୍କାଇବା *The leaves were brown and curled.*

curl up put your arms, legs and head close to your body ଆଣ୍ଠୁ ଛାତି ଉପରକୁ ଟାଣି ଆଣି ବସିବା ବା ଶୋଇବା *The cat curled up by the fire.*

currant /ˈkʌrənt/ *noun* a small dried grape ଶୁଖିଲା ଅଙ୍ଗୁର, କିସ୍‌ମିସ୍

currency /ˈkʌrənsi/ *noun* (*plural* **currencies**) the money that a country uses ଦେଶର ପ୍ରଚଳିତ ମୁଦ୍ରା *The currency of the USA is the dollar.*

current¹ /ˈkʌrənt/ *noun* **1** air or water that is moving ପବନ ବା ପାଣିର ସ୍ରୋତ, ସୁଅ *It is dangerous to swim here because of the strong current.* **2** electricity that is going through a wire ବିଦ୍ୟୁତ୍ ପ୍ରବାହ

current² /ˈkʌrənt/ *adjective* something that is current is happening or being used now ସାମ୍ପ୍ରତିକ, ବର୍ତ୍ତମାନ ଘଟୁଥିବା *current fashions*

currently *adverb* now ବର୍ତ୍ତମାନ, ଏବେ *We are currently living in Delhi.*

curriculum /kə'rɪkjələm/ *noun* (*plural* **curriculums** ବା **curricula** /kə'rɪkjələ/ the subjects that are taught in a school or college (ସ୍କୁଲ୍, କଲେଜ୍ ଇତ୍ୟାଦିର) ପାଠ୍ୟକ୍ରମ *the school curriculum*

curry /'kʌri/ *noun* (*plural* **curries**) meat or vegetables cooked with spices. You often eat curry with rice ତରକାରୀ, ଝୋଳ (ମାଛ, ମାଂସ, ପରିବା ଇତ୍ୟାଦିର)

curse /kɜ:s/ *noun* words that wish for something bad to happen to somebody ଅଭିଶାପ

curtain /'kɜ:tn/ *noun* a piece of cloth that you move to cover a window ପରଦା, ପର୍ଦା (ଦୁଆର, ଝରକା ଇତ୍ୟାଦିର)

curve /kɜ:v/ *noun* a line that is not straight; a bend ବକ୍ରରେଖା; ବୁଲାଣି

curve *verb* (**curves, curving, curved**) bend; make a round shape ବଙ୍କା କରିବା ବା ହେବା, ବଙ୍କେଇବା *The road curves to the right.*

curved *adjective* ବଙ୍କା, ବକ୍ର *a table with curved legs*

cushion /'kʊʃn/ *noun* a bag filled with something soft. You put it on a chair and sit on it or rest your body against it ଗଦି, ତକିଆ ପରି ଗଦି ➪ **pillow** ବି ଦେଖନ୍ତୁ।

custard /'kʌstəd/ *noun* (*no plural*) a sweet yellow sauce made with milk. You eat it with fruit or puddings ଦୁଧ, ଚିନି, ଅଣ୍ଡା, ମକାଚୂନା ଓ ଫଳ ଇତ୍ୟାଦି ଫେଣ୍ଟି ରାନ୍ଧି କରାଯାଇଥିବା ବହଳିଆ ଖିରି ବା ମିଠା

custard apple *noun* (*plural* **custard apples**) a fruit with a dark rough skin and creamy pulp ଆତ, ଶିତାଫଳ।

custom /'kʌstəm/ *noun* something that a group of people usually do ଗତାନୁଗତିକ ପ୍ରଥା *It is a custom to light lamps at Diwali.*

customer /'kʌstəmə(r)/ *noun* a person who buys things from a shop ଗରାଖ, ଗ୍ରାହକ, କିଣିବା ଲୋକ।

customs /'kʌstəmz/ *noun* (*plural*) the place at an airport or a port where you must show what you have brought with you from another country ବନ୍ଦର ବା ବିମାନ ବନ୍ଦରରେ ବିଦେଶରୁ ଆସୁଥିବା ଜିନିଷର ଯାଞ୍ଚ କରିବା ସ୍ଥାନ; ଏହି ବିଭାଗ *a customs officer*

cut[1] /kʌt/ *verb* (**cuts, cutting, cut, has cut**) **1** break or make a hole in something with a knife or with scissors, for example କାଟିବା, ଛେଦନ କରିବା *I cut the string and opened the parcel.* ○ *I cut the apple in half.* **2** take one piece from something bigger କାଟି ଛୋଟ ଖଣ୍ଡେ ନେବା *Can you cut me a piece of cake, please?* **3** make something shorter କାଟି ଛୋଟ କରିବା *Have you had your hair cut?*

cut off stop something ବନ୍ଦ କରିବା *The workmen cut off the electricity.*

cut out take something from the place where it was by using scissors, etc. କଇଁଚି ଇତ୍ୟାଦିରେ କାଟି ବାହାର କରିବା *I cut the picture out of the newspaper.*

cut² /kʌt/ *noun* a place where something has made a cut କର୍ତ୍ତନ, କାଟିବା *I have a cut on my finger.*

cute /kjuːt/ *adjective* (**cuter, cutest**) pretty ସୁନ୍ଦର, ମନୋହର *What a cute little puppy!*

cutlery /ˈkʌtləri/ *noun* (*no plural*) knives, forks and spoons ଖାଇବା ଓ କାଢ଼ିବା ପାଇଁ ବ୍ୟବହୃତ ଚାମୁଚି, କଣ୍ଟା, ଛୁରୀ ଇତ୍ୟାଦି

cybercafe /ˈsaɪbəkæfeɪ/ *noun* a place where people pay to use the Internet ପଇସା ଦେଇ ଇଣ୍ଟରନେଟ୍ ଓ କମ୍ପ୍ୟୁଟର୍ ବ୍ୟବହାର କରିବା ସ୍ଥାନ

cycle /ˈsaɪkl/ *noun* **1** a bicycle ସାଇକେଲ୍ **2** a certain number of things happening regularly and repeatedly in a particular order ନିର୍ଦ୍ଦିଷ୍ଟ କ୍ରମରେ ବାରଂବାର ଘଟୁଥିବା ଘଟଣାବଳୀ

cycle *verb* (**cycles, cycling, cycled**) ride a bicycle ସାଇକେଲ୍ ଚଲାଇବା *I cycle to school every day.*

cyclist *noun* a person who rides a bicycle ସାଇକେଲ୍ ଚାଳକ

cyclone /ˈsaɪkləʊn/ *noun* a violent storm that brings fierce winds and heavy rainfall to hot countries like India and Bangladesh ପ୍ରବଳ ଝଡ଼, ବାତ୍ୟା

cygnet /ˈsɪgnət/ *noun* a young swan ରାଜ ହଂସର ଛୁଆ ➪ ଚିତ୍ର ପାଇଁ **swan** ଦେଖନ୍ତୁ ।

cylinder /ˈsɪlɪndə(r)/ *noun* **1** a long round shape, like a tube or a tin of food ଗୋଲ ଓ ଲମ୍ବା ନଳ ପରି ବା ଡବା ପରି ବସ୍ତୁ, ସିଲିଣ୍ଡର୍ ➪ ଚିତ୍ର ପାଇଁ **shape** ଦେଖନ୍ତୁ । **2** a large red metal container in which gas used for cooking is kept ରନ୍ଧନବାଷ୍ପ ରହୁଥିବା ଲାଲ୍ ରଙ୍ଗର ମୋଟା ଧାତୁର ଡବା, ଗ୍ୟାସ୍ ସିଲିଣ୍ଡର୍ ➪ ଚିତ୍ର ପାଇଁ **kitchen** ଦେଖନ୍ତୁ ।

D d

D /diː/ *symbol* the number 500 in Roman numerals ରୋମୀୟ ସଂଖ୍ୟା ୫୦୦

dacoit *noun* a word for an armed robber ଡକାୟତ, ଅସ୍ତ୍ରଧାରୀ ଚୋର

dad /dæd/ *noun* father ବାପା, ନନା, ପିତା *Hello, Dad.*

daddy /ˈdædi/ *noun* (*plural* **daddies**) a word for 'father' that children use ପିଲାମାନଙ୍କର ବାପାଙ୍କ ପ୍ରତି ସଂବୋଧନ ଶବ୍ଦ; ଡ୍ୟାଡି

daffodil /ˈdæfədɪl/ *noun* a yellow flower that grows in spring, mostly in Europe ଏକ ୟୁରୋପୀୟ ହଳଦିଆ ଫୁଲ

dagger /ˈdægə(r)/ *noun* a short pointed knife that people use as a weapon ଭୁଷା ଛୁରି, ଛୁରା ➪ **sword** ମଧ୍ୟ ଦେଖନ୍ତୁ ।

daily /ˈdeɪli/ *adjective, adverb* that happens or comes every day or once a day ଦୈନିକ, ପ୍ରତିଦିନ *a daily newspaper* ○ *The museum is open daily from 9 a.m. to 5 p.m.*

dairy /ˈdeəri/ *noun* (*plural* **dairies**) a place where milk is kept or where food like butter and cheese is made ଦୁଧ ଓ ଦୁଧରୁ ତିଆରି ଲହୁଣି, ଛେନା, ଦହି ଇତ୍ୟାଦି ପ୍ରସ୍ତୁତ ହୋଇ ମିଳୁଥିବା ସ୍ଥାନ

> **dairy** or **diary**?
>
> ମନେ ରଖନ୍ତୁ ! **Dairy** ଓ **diary** ଦୁଇଟା ଅଲଗା ଅଲଗା ଶବ୍ଦ । ଏହି ଦୁଇ ଶବ୍ଦର ଉଚ୍ଚାରଣ ଓ ଅର୍ଥ ଭିନ୍ନଭିନ୍ନ—
>
> **dairy**— ˈdeəri
>
> **diary**— ˈdaɪəri
>
> ପ୍ରତିଦିନର ଘଟଣା ଲେଖିବା ପାଇଁ ଏକ ତାରିଖ ଥିବା ଖାତା ବା ବହିକୁ **diary** କହନ୍ତି ।

daisy /ˈdeɪzi/ *noun* (*plural* **daisies**) a small flower with white petals and a yellow middle ଏକ ହଳଦିଆ କେଶର ଥିବା ଛୋଟ ଧଳା ଫୁଲ; ଡେଇଜି

dam /dæm/ *noun* a wall that is built across a river to hold the water back ନଦୀବନ୍ଧ; ନଦୀର ଜଳ ପ୍ରବାହକୁ ରୋକିବା ପାଇଁ ନିର୍ମିତ ବନ୍ଧ

damage /ˈdæmɪdʒ/ *verb* (**damages, damaging, damaged**) break or harm something ଭାଙ୍ଗିବା, କ୍ଷତି କରିବା *The house was badly damaged by fire.*

damage *noun* (*no plural*) କ୍ଷତି, ହାନି *He had an accident, but there wasn't much damage to his car.*

damp /dæmp/ *adjective* (**damper, dampest**) a little wet ଅଳ୍ପ ଓଦା, ଅଳ୍ପ ଆର୍ଦ୍ର, ସନ୍ତସନ୍ତିଆ *a cold damp house*

dampen /ˈdæmpən/ *verb* (**dampens, dampening, dampened**) **1** put some water on something to make it a little wet ଅଳ୍ପଓଦା, ଅଳ୍ପ ଓଦା କରିବା *Dampen the clothes before ironing them.* **2** make something less strong ହତୋତ୍ସାହ କରିବା *Even the bad weather did not dampen her spirits yesterday.*

dance[1] /dɑːns/ *verb* (**dances, dancing, danced**) move your body to music ନାଚିବା, ନୃତ୍ୟ କରିବା *Neetu dances well.*

dancer *noun* a person who dances ନର୍ତ୍ତକ, ନର୍ତ୍ତକୀ

dance[2] /dɑːns/ *noun* movements that you do to music ନାଚ, ନୃତ୍ୟ *folk dances of India*

danger /ˈdeɪndʒə(r)/ *noun* **1** (*no plural*) the possibility that something bad may happen ବିପଦ, ଆପଦ *You may be in danger if you travel alone late at night*. **2** (*plural* **dangers**) a person or thing that may bring harm or trouble ବିପଜ୍ଜନକ ବ୍ୟକ୍ତି ବା ପଦାର୍ଥ *Smoking is a danger to health.*

dangerous /ˈdeɪndʒərəs/ *adjective* a person or thing that is dangerous may hurt you ବିପଜ୍ଜନକ, ବିପଦପୂର୍ଣ୍ଣ *It's dangerous to drive a car at night without any lights.*

dangerously *adverb* ବିପଜ୍ଜନକ ଭାବରେ *She drives dangerously.*

dare /deə(r)/ *verb* (**dares, daring, dared**) **1** be brave enough to do something ସାହସ କରି କହିବା ବା କରିବା *I daren't tell Deepa that I've lost her book.* **2** ask somebody to do something dangerous or silly to see if they are brave enough କାହାରିକୁ କିଛି ବିପଜ୍ଜନକ ବା ହାସ୍ୟାସ୍ପଦ କାମ କରିବାକୁ ଆହ୍ୱାନ କରିବା *I dare you to jump off that wall!*

daring /ˈdeərɪŋ/ *adjective* not afraid to do dangerous things ସାହସୀ, ନିର୍ଭୀକ

dark[1] /dɑːk/ *adjective* (**darker, darkest**) **1** with no light, or not much light ଅନ୍ଧାର, ଅନ୍ଧକାର, ଅନ୍ଧାରୁଆ *It gets dark very early in winter*. **2** a dark colour is nearer to black than to white କଳା ଆସିଆ *a dark-green shirt* ✪ ବିପରୀତ **light[2] 1** ବା **pale 2** **3** a person who is dark has brown or black skin or hair (ମଣିଷ ବିଷୟରେ) କଳା ବା ବାଦାମୀ ବର୍ଣ୍ଣର ବା କଳା ବାଳଥିବା *a thin, dark woman* ✪ ବିପରୀତ **fair[1] 2**

dark[2] /dɑːk/ *noun* (*no plural*) when or where there is no light ଅନ୍ଧାର, ଅନ୍ଧକାର *Cats can see in the dark.*

darkness /ˈdɑːknəs/ *noun* (*no plural*) when or where there is no light ଅନ୍ଧାର, ଅନ୍ଧକାର, ଅନ୍ଧାରୁଆ *The whole house was in darkness.*

dart /dɑːt/ *verb* (**darts, darting, darted**) move quickly and suddenly (ତୀରପରି) କ୍ଷିପ୍ର ଗତିରେ ଯିବା, ତୀର ପରି ଛୁଟିଯିବା *He darted across the road.*

dash[1] /dæʃ/ *verb* (**dashes, dashing, dashed**) run quickly କ୍ଷିପ୍ର ବା ଦ୍ରୁତ ଗତିରେ ଯିବା *I dashed into a shop when it started to rain.*

dash[2] /dæʃ/ *noun* (*plural* **dashes**) a mark (—) that you use in writing to show a short stop or to separate two parts of a sentence ଲେଖା ବା ଛପାରେ ବ୍ୟବହୃତ ଏକ ଆନୁଭୂମିକ ଚିହ୍ନ (—)

data /ˈdeɪtə/ *noun* (*plural*) facts or information ତଥ୍ୟ *We are studying the data that we have collected.*

date[1] /deɪt/ *noun* the number of the day, the month and sometimes the year ତାରିଖ *What's the date today?* ○ *What is your date of birth?*

out of date not modern ପୁରୁଣାକାଳିଆ *The machinery they use is completely out of date.*

up to date 1 modern ଆଧୁନିକ **2** with the newest information ବର୍ତ୍ତମାନ ପର୍ଯ୍ୟନ୍ତ ସମୟର ତଥ୍ୟ ଥିବା *Is this list of names up to date?*

date² /deɪt/ *noun* a small sweet brown fruit ଖଜୁରି, ଖଜୁରି କୋଳି ➪ ଚିତ୍ର ପାଇଁ **fruit** ଦେଖନ୍ତୁ ।

daughter /ˈdɔːtə(r)/ *noun* a girl or woman who is somebody's child ଝିଅ, କନ୍ୟା, ପୁତ୍ରୀ, ଦୁହିତା *My oldest daughter is a doctor.* ➪ ଚିତ୍ର ପାଇଁ **family** ଦେଖନ୍ତୁ ।

daughter-in-law *noun* (*plural* **daughters-in-law**) the wife of your son ବୋହୂ, ପୁତ୍ରବଧୂ ➪ ଚିତ୍ର ପାଇଁ **family** ଦେଖନ୍ତୁ ।

dawn /dɔːn/ *noun* the time of the day when the sun comes up ଭୋର, ପ୍ରତ୍ୟୁଷ, ଉଷା, ପ୍ରଭାତ, ପ୍ରାତଃକାଳ ➪ **dusk** ଦେଖନ୍ତୁ ।

day /deɪ/ *noun* (*plural* **days**) **1** a time of 24 hours from midnight to the next midnight ଦିନ, ଦିବସ (ପାଶ୍ଚାତ୍ୟ ଦେଶରେ ଅଧ ରାତିର ପରିଦିନ ଅଧରାତି; ଭାରତରେ ସୂର୍ଯ୍ୟୋଦୟରୁ ପରଦିନ ସୂର୍ଯ୍ୟୋଦୟ) *There are seven days in a week.* **2** the time when it is light outside ଦିନ, ଦିବା, ସୂର୍ଯ୍ୟୋଦୟରୁ ସୂର୍ଯ୍ୟାସ୍ତ ପର୍ଯ୍ୟନ୍ତ ଆଲୋକିତ ସମୟ *Most people work during the day and sleep at night.*

one day 1 on a certain day in the past ଦିନେ *One day, a letter arrived.* ✪ ସାଧାରଣତଃ ଆମେ କୌଣସି କାହାଣୀର ଆରମ୍ଭରେ **one day** ର ବ୍ୟବହାର କରୁଁ । **2** at some time in the future (ଭବିଷ୍ୟତରେ), ଆଗାମୀ ଦିନରେ, ଦିନେନା ଦିନେ *I hope to visit Japan one day.*

some day at some time in the future କେବେ ଦିନେ, ଦିନେ ନା ଦିନେ *Some day I'll be rich and famous.*

the day after tomorrow not tomorrow, but the next day ପରଦିନ

the day before yesterday not yesterday, but the day before ଗଲା କାଲିର ପୂର୍ବଦିନ

the other day a few days ago କିଛି ଦିନ ତଳେ *I went to Chennai the other day.*

these days now ଏବେ, ବର୍ତ୍ତମାନ, ସଂପ୍ରତି *A lot of people work with computers these days.*

daylight /ˈdeɪlaɪt/ *noun* (*no plural*) the light from the sun during the day ସୂର୍ଯ୍ୟାଲୋକ, ଦିନ ବେଳ, ଦିବାଲୋକ *These colours look different in daylight.*

daytime /ˈdeɪtaɪm/ *noun* (*no plural*) the time when it is day and not night ଦିନ, ଦିବା, ଦିନ ବେଳ *I prefer to study in the daytime and go out in the evening.*

daze /deɪz/ *noun* when you are in a daze, you are not able to think clearly କାବା, ହତବୁଦ୍ଧି ଅବସ୍ଥା, ସ୍ତବ୍ଧ ଅବସ୍ଥା, ଚିନ୍ତାଶୂନ୍ୟ ଅବସ୍ଥା, ଅକଲଶୂନ୍ୟ ଅବସ୍ଥା

dazed /deɪzd/ *adjective* unable to think clearly because you are confused କାବା, ହତବାକ୍, ସ୍ତବ୍ଧ *He had a dazed and frightened look on his face.*

dazzle /ˈdæzl/ *verb* (**dazzles, dazzling, dazzled**) if a light dazzles you, it shines brightly in your eyes so that you cannot see for a short time ଆଖି ଝଲସିଯିବା ବା ଝଲସାଇବା *I was dazzled by the car's lights.*

DDT /ˌdi: di: ˈti:/ *noun* (*no plural*) a substance that is used to kill insects that are harmful to crops ଡିଡିଟି (ଡାଇକ୍ଲୋରୋ ଡାଇଫିନାଇଲ୍ ଟ୍ରାଇକ୍ଲୋରୋ-ଇଥେନ୍), ଏକ ପୋକମରା ରସାୟନ ଯାହା ଜୀବ ଓ ଶସ୍ୟ ପାଇଁ ମଧ୍ୟ କ୍ଷତିକାରକ

dead /ded/ *adjective* not living ମୃତ, ନିର୍ଜୀବ, ଜୀବଶୂନ୍ୟ, ମଲା *All my grandparents are dead.* ✪ ବିପରୀତ **living**[1] ବା **alive**

the dead *noun* (*plural*) dead people ମୃତ ଲୋକମାନେ ✪ ବିପରୀତ **the living**

deadly /ˈdedli/ *adjective* (**deadlier, deadliest**) something that is deadly may kill people or other living things ମାରାତ୍ମକ, ପ୍ରାଣହାନି କରାଇଲା ପରି, ସାଂଘାତିକ *a deadly snake*

deaf /def/ *adjective* not able to hear କାଲ, ବଧିର

the deaf *noun* (*plural*) people who are deaf କାଲ ବା ବଧିର ବ୍ୟକ୍ତି

deafness *noun* (*no plural*) being deaf ବଧିରତା

deal[1] /di:l/ *noun* an agreement, usually about buying, selling or working ବ୍ୟବସାୟିକ ଚୁକ୍ତି *Let's make a deal—I'll help you today if you help me tomorrow.*

deal[2] /di:l/ *noun*

a good deal or **a great deal** a lot; much ବହୁତ, ବହୁଭାଗ, ବହୁତ୍ କିଛି *We saw a good deal of Australia on our holiday.* ○ *We ate a great deal.*

deal[3] /di:l/ *verb* (**deals, dealing, dealt** /delt/, **has dealt**)

deal in something buy and sell something in business କିଣାବିକା କରିବା, କାରବାର କରିବା *We deal in property.*

deal out give something to each person ସମସ୍ତଙ୍କୁ ଦେବା, ବାଣ୍ଟିବା *I dealt out the cards for the next game.*

deal with somebody or **something** look after something and do what is necessary (ସମସ୍ୟା, ବ୍ୟକ୍ତି ଇତ୍ୟାଦି ବିଷୟରେ) ପଦକ୍ଷେପ ନେବା *I am too busy to deal with this problem now.*

dealer *noun* a person who buys and sells things ବେପାରୀ, ବ୍ୟବସାୟୀ *a property dealer*

dear /dɪə(r)/ *adjective* (**dearer, dearest**) **1** a word that you use before a person's name at the beginning of a letter ଚିଠି ଆରମ୍ଭରେ ଲେଖାଯାଉଥିବା ସଂବୋଧନ (ପ୍ରିୟ, ଶ୍ରଦ୍ଧେୟ, ଶଦ୍ଧେୟା ଇତ୍ୟାଦି) *Dear Mr Roy ...* ○ *Dear Sir or Madam* **2** much loved ପ୍ରିୟ, ପ୍ରିୟତମ, ପ୍ରିୟତମା *She was a dear friend.* **3** that costs a lot of money ଦାମିକା *Those apples are too dear.* ✪ ବିପରୀତ **cheap**

death /deθ/ *noun* the end of life ମୃତ୍ୟୁ; ଜୀବନର ସମାପ୍ତି *He became manager of the company after his father's death.*

debate /dɪˈbeɪt/ *noun* a discussion where two or more people speak in favour of or against a view (କୌଣସି ମତର) ସପକ୍ଷ ବା ବିପକ୍ଷରେ ଯୁକ୍ତିତର୍କ, ତର୍କ *a debate on the construction of dams*

debris /ˈdebri:/ *noun* (*no plural*) the broken pieces of something that has been destroyed in an accident ଭଗ୍ନାବଶେଷ, ଭଗ୍ନସ୍ତୁପ *There were many teams rescuing people buried un-*

der the debris of the buildings that fell in yesterday's earthquake.

debt /det/ *noun* money that you must pay back to somebody କରଜ, ଋଣ, ଦାୟ *The company has returned a lot of money but it still has debts.*

decade /ˈdekeɪd/ *noun* a period of ten years, especially a period such as 1990–1999 ଦଶନ୍ଧି, ଦଶାବ୍ଦୀ, ଦଶ ବର୍ଷର ସମୟ

decay /dɪˈkeɪ/ *verb* (**decays, decaying, decayed**) become bad or fall to pieces ସଢ଼ିଯିବା, ଭାଙ୍ଗିଯିବା, କ୍ଷୟ, ନଷ୍ଟ ହୋଇଯିବା *If you don't clean your teeth, they will decay.*

decay *noun* (*no plural*) କ୍ଷୟ, ଅବନତି, ନଷ୍ଟ *tooth decay*

deceit /dɪˈsiːt/ *noun* (*no plural*) the action of making somebody believe something that is not true ପ୍ରତାରଣା, ଠକାମି, ଚଞ୍ଚକତା

deceitful *adjective* dishonest ପ୍ରତାରଣାପୂର୍ଣ୍ଣ, ଶଠ, ପ୍ରବଞ୍ଚକ

deceive /dɪˈsiːv/ *verb* (**deceives, deceiving, deceived**) make somebody believe something that is not true ଠକିବା, ପ୍ରତାରଣା କରିବା *She deceived me into thinking she was a police officer.*

December /dɪˈsembə(r)/ *noun* the twelfth month of the year (ପାଶ୍ଚାତ୍ୟ ଗଣନାରେ) ବର୍ଷର ଶେଷ ବା ଦ୍ୱାଦଶ ମାସ; ଡିସେମ୍ବର

decent /ˈdiːsnt/ *adjective* **1** good enough; right ଭଲ, ଠିକ୍‌ଠାକ୍, ସଚ୍ଚା **2** honest and good ସଚ୍ଚୋଟ, ଭଦ୍ର *decent people*

decide /dɪˈsaɪd/ *verb* (**decides, deciding, decided**) choose something after thinking ବିଚାର କରି ନିଷ୍ପତ୍ତି ନେବା *We've decided to go to France for our holidays.*

deciduous /dɪˈsɪdʒuəs/ *adjective* used to describe a tree that sheds its leaves annually before winter sets in ବାର୍ଷିକ ପତ୍ରଝଡ଼ା ବା ପର୍ଣ୍ଣପାତ ହେଉଥିବା ଗଛ, ପର୍ଣ୍ଣମୋଚି ➪ **evergreen** ଦେଖନ୍ତୁ।

decimal /ˈdesɪml/ *noun* a part of a number, written after a dot (called a **decimal point**), for example 0.75 ଦଶମିକ ସଂଖ୍ୟା 0.75 ✪ '0.75' କୁ ଇଂରାଜୀରେ 'ଜୀରୋ ପଏଣ୍ଟ ସେଭନ ଫାଇଭ' ଓ ହିନ୍ଦୀରେ 'ଶୂନ୍ୟ ଦଶମଲଓ ସାତ ପାଞ୍ଚ ପଢ଼ାଯାଏ।

decipher /dɪˈsaɪfə(r)/ *verb* (**deciphers, deciphering, deciphered**) try to understand a difficult message or piece of writing ପଢ଼ି ବା ବୁଝି ନ ହେଉଥିବା ବାର୍ତ୍ତା ବା ଲେଖାର ଅର୍ଥ ବୁଝିବାର ଚେଷ୍ଟା କରିବା *It's difficult to decipher his handwriting.*

decision /dɪˈsɪʒn/ *noun* the act of choosing or deciding something after thinking ଭାବିଚିନ୍ତି ନିଆଯାଉଥିବା ବା ନିଷ୍ପତ୍ତି ବା ସିଦ୍ଧାନ୍ତ *I must make a decision about what I'm going to do when I leave school.*

deck /dek/ *noun* the floor of a ship or bus ଜାହାଜ ବା ବସ୍‌ର ଚଟାଣ ବା ମହଲା

declare /dɪˈkleə(r)/ *verb* (**declares, declaring, declared**) say very clearly what you think or what you will do, often to a lot of people ଘୋଷଣା କରିବା *The country declared war on its enemy.*

declaration /ˌdekləˈreɪʃn/ *noun* ଘୋଷଣା, ଘୋଷଣାନାମା *a declaration of independence*

decline /dɪˈklaɪn/ *verb* (**declines, declining, declined**) **1** become less or weaker; decrease କମିଯିବା, ଶକ୍ତିକ୍ଷୟ ହେବା, ହ୍ରାସ ହେବା *The population of tigers is declining rapidly.* **2** politely refuse to do something (କିଛି କରିବାକୁ) ଭଦ୍ର ଭାବରେ ମନା କରି ଦେବା *We declined their invitation to a vacation.*

decline *noun* a decrease in something ହ୍ରାସ, କ୍ଷୟ *a decline in profit over the years*

decompose /ˌdiːkəmˈpəʊz/ *verb* (**decomposes, decomposing, decomposed**) if something decomposes, it is destroyed by very tiny **organisms** ପଚିଯିବା, ସଢ଼ିଯିବା, ଖତ ହୋଇଯିବା *When dead plants and animals decompose, they make the soil fertile.*

decorate /ˈdekəreɪt/ *verb* (**decorates, decorating, decorated**) make something look nicer by adding beautiful things to it ସଜାଇବା *We decorated the room with flowers.*

decorations /ˌdekəˈreɪʃnz/ *noun* (*plural*) beautiful things that you add to something to make it look nicer ଶୋଭା ବଢ଼ାଉଥିବା ପଦାର୍ଥ, ସାଜସଜ୍ଜାର ସୁନ୍ଦର ଜିନିଷ *Christmas decorations*

decrease /dɪˈkriːs/ *verb* (**decreases, decreasing, decreased**) become smaller or less; make something smaller or less ସାନ ହୋଇଯିବା ବା କମିଯିବା; ସାନ କରିବା ବା କମାଇବା; ହ୍ରାସ ପାଇଯିବା *The number of people in the village has decreased from 200 to 150.*
✪ ବିପରୀତ **increase**

decrease *noun* ହ୍ରାସପ୍ରାପ୍ତି *There was a decrease in the number of people living in the village.*
✪ ବିପରୀତ **increase**

dedicate /ˈdedɪkeɪt/ *verb* (**dedicates, dedicating, dedicated**) when you dedicate yourself to some work, you put in a lot of your time and effort because you love doing it (କୌଣସି କାମ ପାଇଁ ନିଜକୁ) ଉତ୍ସର୍ଗ କରିବା; ମନ ଧ୍ୟାନ ଦେଇ ଲାଗିଯିବା *Mahatma Gandhi dedicated his life to the country.*

dedicated *adjective* if you are dedicated, you put in a lot of time and effort to do something well ଉତ୍ସର୍ଗୀକୃତ, ଏକାଗ୍ର *dedicated teachers*

dedication /ˌdedɪˈkeɪʃn/ *noun* **1** (*no plural*) the act of giving someone your time and energy because you love it ଉତ୍ସର୍ଗ, ସମର୍ପଣ, ଏକନିଷ୍ଠତା *Mother Teresa's dedication to help the poor has inspired many.* **2** (*plural* **dedications**) the message at the beginning of a book or a film naming somebody to whom it is dedicated as a mark of respect or love ଉତ୍ସର୍ଗୀକୃତ ଶ୍ରଦ୍ଧା ଦେଖାଇବା ପାଇଁ ବହି, ସିନେମା ଇତ୍ୟାଦିର ଆରମ୍ଭରେ ଦିଆଯାଇଥିବା ଉତ୍ସର୍ଗ ଲେଖା

deed /di:d/ *noun* something that somebody does; an action ଗୁରୁତ୍ୱପୂର୍ଣ୍ଣ କାମ *a brave deed* ○ *good/bad deed*

deep /di:p/ *adjective* (**deeper, deepest**) **1** something that is deep goes down a long way ଗଭୀର, ଗହିରିଆ *Be careful—the water is very deep.* ✪ ବିପରୀତ **shallow** ✪ ଏହାର ବିଶେଷ୍ୟ ହେଲା **depth** । **2** a deep colour is strong and dark ଗାଢ଼ (ରଙ୍ଗ ଇତ୍ୟାଦି) *She has deep blue eyes.* ✪ ବିପରୀତ **pale 2** ବା **light**[2] **1** **3** a deep sound is low and strong ଗମ୍ଭୀର *He has a deep voice.* **4** if you are in a deep sleep, it is difficult for somebody to wake you up ଗଭୀର, ଗାଢ଼ *She was in such a deep sleep that she didn't hear me calling her.*

deeply *adverb* strongly or completely ଗଭୀର ଭାବରେ, ପ୍ରଗାଢ଼ ଭାବରେ *He is sleeping very deeply.*

deer /dɪə(r)/ *noun* (*plural* **deer**) a wild animal that eats grass and can run fast ହରିଣ, ମୃଗ, କୁରଙ୍ଗ

> ✪ ମାଈ ହରିଣକୁ **doe** କୁହାଯାଏ ଏବଂ ଅଣ୍ଡିରା ହରିଣକୁ **stag** କୁହାଯାଏ । ହରିଣ ଛୁଆକୁ **fawn** କୁହାଯାଏ ।

default /dɪˈfɔ:lt/ *noun* **1** a failure to do something that the law says you must, like pay back a loan କର୍ତ୍ତବ୍ୟ ପାଳନ, ପ୍ରାପ୍ୟଦାନ ଦେବା ଇତ୍ୟାଦିରେ ବିଚ୍ୟୁତି ବା ବିଫଳତା **2** something that a computer does by itself when it is not given any command ଆଦେଶ ନ ପାଇବା ଅବସ୍ଥାରେ କମ୍ପ୍ୟୁଟର୍ ମନକୁମନ କରୁଥିବା କାମ

by default something that happens by chance and not because of one's efforts କୌଣସି କିଛି (ଘଟଣା ଇତ୍ୟାଦି) ସ୍ୱତଃ ପ୍ରଣୋଦିତ ଭାବେ ହେବା, କାହାରି ଅନୁପସ୍ଥିତି ଯୋଗୁଁ ବା ବିରୋଧ ନ ହେବା ଯୋଗୁଁ ଘଟିବା *The team won by default because the other team did not play.*

defeat /dɪˈfi:t/ *verb* (**defeats, defeating, defeated**) win a fight or game against a person or group of people ହରାଇଦେବା, ପରାଜିତ ବା ପରାସ୍ତ କରିବା *Their team was defeated in the finals by ten runs.*

defeat *noun* losing a game, fight or war ପରାଜୟ ✪ ବିପରୀତ **victory**

defect /ˈdi:fekt/ *noun* a fault in something ତ୍ରୁଟି, ଦୋଷ *You cannot find any defects in these saris.*

defective *adjective* having a fault ତ୍ରୁଟିପୂର୍ଣ୍ଣ, ଦୋଷଯୁକ୍ତ *defective saris*

defence /dɪˈfens/ *noun* (*no plural*) the act of fighting against people who attack, or keeping away dangerous people or things ପ୍ରତିରକ୍ଷା, ପ୍ରତିରୋଧ; ଆକ୍ରମଣ ପ୍ରତିରୋଧକ ବ୍ୟବସ୍ଥା *They fought the war in defence of their country.*

defend /dɪˈfend/ *verb* (**defends, defending, defended**) **1** fight to keep away people or things that attack ଆକ୍ରମଣର ପ୍ରତିରୋଧ କରିବା, ଆକ୍ରମଣରୁ ରକ୍ଷା କରିବା *They defended the city against the enemy.* **2** say that somebody has not done something wrong ସପକ୍ଷରେ କହିବା *My sister defended me when my father said I was lazy.*

deficiency /dɪˈfɪʃnsi/ *noun* (*plural* **deficiencies**) the lack of something ଅଭାବ, ସ୍ୱଳ୍ପତା *Vitamin A deficiency causes night blindness.*

define /dɪˈfaɪn/ *verb* (**defines, defining, defined**) **1** say what a word means (ଶବ୍ଦ ଇତ୍ୟାଦିର) ସଠିକ୍ ଅର୍ଥ ପ୍ରଦାନ କରିବା, ସଂଜ୍ଞା ଦେବା *How do you define 'rich'?* **2** describe clearly and exactly କୌଣସି ବିଷୟ ସ୍ପଷ୍ଟ ଓ ସଠିକ୍ ଭାବରେ ବର୍ଣ୍ଣନା କରିବା *Your responsibilities have been defined in your appointment letter.*

definite /ˈdefɪnət/ *adjective* sure; certain ସ୍ପଷ୍ଟ ଓ ନିର୍ଦ୍ଦିଷ୍ଟ; ନିଶ୍ଚିତ *I want a definite answer, 'yes' or 'no'.* ✪ ବିପରୀତ **indefinite**

definitely *adverb* certainly ନିଶ୍ଚିତ ଭାବରେ *I am definitely going to the theatre this evening.*

definition /ˌdefɪˈnɪʃn/ *noun* a group of words that tell you what another word means ସଂଜ୍ଞା; ଶବ୍ଦ ବା ଭାବର ସଠିକ୍ ଅର୍ଥ

deflate /dɪˈfleɪt/ *verb* (**deflates, deflating, deflated**) take the air out of something ପବନ ବାହାର କରିଦେବା; (ବେଲୁନ୍, ଚକ ଇତ୍ୟାଦିରୁ) *One of the front tyres got deflated when a nail pierced it.* ✪ ବିପରୀତ **inflate**

deflection /dɪˈflekʃn/ *noun* a sudden change in direction after hitting against something କୌଣସି ଜିନିଷରେ ବାଜିବା ହେତୁ ଗତିପଥର ବିଚ୍ୟୁତି; ବିକ୍ଷେପଣ *angle of deflection*

deforestation /diːˌfɒrɪˈsteɪʃn/ *noun* (*no plural*) the act of cutting down trees in a large area, like a forest ଜଙ୍ଗଲ ବିନାଶ ✪ ବିପରୀତ **afforestation**

deformity /dɪˈfɔːməti/ *noun* (*plural* **deformities**) a condition in which a part of the body is of an unusual shape because of injury or disease ବିକଳାଙ୍ଗତା, ଶରୀରର ବା ଅଙ୍ଗର ବିରୂପତା (ରୋଗ ବା ଦୁର୍ଘଟଣା ଯୋଗୁଁ)

degree /dɪˈgriː/ *noun* **1** a unit for measurement of temperature ତାପ ମାପର ଏକକ *Water boils at 100 degrees Celsius (100°C).* **2** a unit for measurement of angles କୋଣର ମାପାଙ୍କ *There are 90 degrees (90°) in a right angle.* **3** the amount or level of something; extent ପରିମାଣ, ମାତ୍ରା *This work requires a high degree of skill.* **4** universities and colleges give degrees to students who have completed special courses there ବିଶ୍ୱବିଦ୍ୟାଳୟରୁ ପ୍ରଦତ୍ତ ଉପାଧି; ଡିଗ୍ରୀ *a master's degree*

dehydrate /diːˈhaɪdreɪt/ *verb* (**dehydrates, dehydrating, dehydrated**) **1** dry something by removing water from it ଶୁଖାଇବା; ନିର୍ଜଳ କରିବା **2** when your body gets dehydrated, you become ill because you lose a lot of water in the form of **sweat** ବେଶି ଝାଳ ବହିବା ହେତୁ ଶରୀରରୁ ପାଣି ଅଂଶ କମିଯିବା ଓ ଏଥିଯୋଗୁଁ ଅସୁସ୍ଥ ହେବା

dehydration *noun* (*no plural*) the loss of water and salts from the body making a person ill ନିର୍ଜଳୀକରଣ, ନିର୍ଜଳୀୟନ; ଦେହରୁ ପାଣି ଓ ଲବଣ କମିଯିବା ହେତୁ ହେଉଥିବା ରୋଗ

deity /ˈdeɪəti/ *noun* (*plural* **deities**) a god or goddess ଦେବତା ବା ଦେବୀ *Greek/Hindu deities*

delay[1] /dɪˈleɪ/ *noun* (*plural* **delays**) a time when somebody or something is late ଡେରି, ବିଳମ୍ବ *There was a long delay at the airport.*

delay[2] /dɪˈleɪ/ *verb* (**delays, delaying, delayed**) **1** make somebody or something late ଡେରି କରିବା ବା ହେବା; ବିଳମ୍ବ କରିବା ବା ହେବା *My train was delayed for two hours because of the bad weather.* **2** not do something until a later time ଡେରି କରିବା, ସମୟ ଗଡ଼େଇବା *I delayed my holiday because I was ill.*

delegation /ˌdelɪˈgeɪʃn/ *noun* a group of people who have been chosen to speak for their country or organization (ଦେଶ ବା ସଂସ୍ଥାର) ପ୍ରତିନିଧି ଦଳ

delete /dɪˈliːt/ *verb* (**deletes, deleting, deleted**) remove something that is written or something that is stored on a computer ଅକ୍ଷର, ବାକ୍ୟ ଇତ୍ୟାଦି ବାଦ୍‌ଦେବା, କାଟିଦେବା; କମ୍ପ୍ୟୁଟରରେ ଥିବା ତଥ୍ୟ କାଢ଼ି ଦେବା, ଅପସାରଣ କରିବା *His name has been deleted from the list of voters.*

deliberate /dɪˈlɪbərət/ *adjective* **1** (something) that you want and plan to do, and do not do by mistake ଉଦ୍ଦେଶ୍ୟମୂଳକ ଓ ସୁଚିନ୍ତିତ **2** done slowly and carefully ଧିରେ କରିବା ବା ଯତ୍ନସହକାରେ କରିବା

deliberately *adverb* ଇଛା କରି, ଉଦ୍ଦେଶ୍ୟମୂଳକ ଭାବରେ *I didn't break the vase deliberately. It was an accident.*

delicacy /ˈdelɪkəsi/ *noun* **1** (*plural* **delicacies**) a type of food that is considered special in a particular place ସୁଖାଦ୍ୟ **2** (*no plural*) the quality of being delicate କୋମଳତା, ସୂକ୍ଷ୍ମତା

delicate /ˈdelɪkət/ *adjective* **1** if something is delicate, you can break or damage it very easily ସହଜରେ, ଭାଙ୍ଗିଯାଉଥିବା ବା ନଷ୍ଟ ହେଉଥିବା *I've got delicate skin, so I use special soap.* **2** pretty and fine ସୁନ୍ଦର ଓ ସୂକ୍ଷ୍ମ *delicate colours like pale pink and pale blue* **3** not strong ଦୁର୍ବଳ (ସ୍ୱାସ୍ଥ୍ୟ) *delicate health*

delicious /dɪˈlɪʃəs/ *adjective* very good to eat ସୁସ୍ୱାଦୁ *This soup is delicious.*

delight[1] /dɪˈlaɪt/ *verb* (**delights, delighting, delighted**) make somebody very pleased or happy ଅତି ଆନନ୍ଦିତ ବା ସନ୍ତୁଷ୍ଟ କରିବା

delighted *adjective* very pleased or happy ଅତି ଆନନ୍ଦିତ *I'm delighted to meet you.*

delight[2] /dɪˈlaɪt/ *noun* (*no plural*) great happiness ଆନନ୍ଦ, ଉଲ୍ଲାସ, ଖୁସି

delightful *adjective* very nice; lovely ଆନନ୍ଦଦାୟକ, ସୁଖପ୍ରଦ *We stayed in a delightful little hotel.*

deliver /dɪˈlɪvə(r)/ *verb* (**delivers, delivering, delivered**) take something to the place where it must go (ଚିଠି; ଜିନିଷପତ୍ର ଇତ୍ୟାଦି) ନେଇ ଯଥା ସ୍ଥାନରେ ଦେଇ ଦେବା; ପହଞ୍ଚାଇ ଦେବା *The postman delivered two letters this morning.*

delivery *noun* (*plural* **deliveries**) ପହଞ୍ଚାଇବା ବା ଦେଇ ଦେବା କାମ *We are waiting for a delivery of bread.*

delta /ˈdeltə/ *noun* a piece of land shaped like a triangle, where a river branches into smaller parts before entering the sea ନଦୀ ମୁହାଣରେ ଥିବା ତ୍ରିକୋଣଭୂମି *The rivers Ganga and Brahmaputra form the largest delta in the world.*

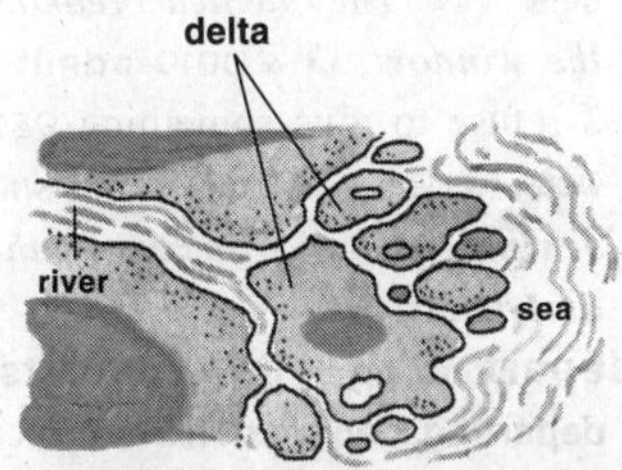

demand[1] /dɪˈmɑːnd/ *verb* (**demands, demanding, demanded**) say strongly that you must have something ଚାହିଁବା *The workers are demanding more money.*

demand[2] /dɪˈmɑːnd/ *noun* saying strongly that you must have something ଦାବି

democracy /dɪˈmɒkrəsi/ *noun* (*plural* **democracies**) a system of government where the people choose their leader (by **voting**) ଗଣତନ୍ତ୍ର, ପ୍ରଜାତନ୍ତ୍ର; ଲୋକତନ୍ତ୍ର (ଲୋକମାନଙ୍କ ନିର୍ବାଚିତ ପ୍ରତିନିଧିଙ୍କ ଦ୍ୱାରା ଦେଶ ପରିଚାଳନା ପଦ୍ଧତି); ଏହିପରି ପରିଚାଳିତ ଦେଶ

democratic /ˌdeməˈkrætɪk/ *adjective* if a country, etc. is democratic, all the people in it can choose its leaders or decide about the way it is organized ଗଣତାନ୍ତ୍ରିକ

demolish /dɪˈmɒlɪʃ/ *verb* (**demolishes, demolishing, demolished**) break a building so that it falls down (ଘର ଇତ୍ୟାଦି) ଭାଙ୍ଗିଦେବା, ଭୂପତିତ କରିବା *They demolished six houses and built a supermarket in their place.*

demolition /ˌdeməˈlɪʃn/ *noun* (ଘର ଇତ୍ୟାଦି) ଭାଙ୍ଗିଦେବା କାମ ବା ପ୍ରକ୍ରିୟା *the demolition of illegal buildings*

demon /ˈdiːmən/ *noun* an evil spirit; a devil ଭୂତ, ପ୍ରେତ, ଦାନବ

demonstrate /ˈdemənstreɪt/ *verb* (**demonstrates, demonstrating, demonstrated**) **1** show something clearly ପ୍ରଦର୍ଶନ କରିବା; ପ୍ରମାଣ କରିବା *He demonstrated how to operate the machine.* **2** walk or stand in public with a group of people to show that you have strong feelings about something ବିକ୍ଷୋଭ ପ୍ରଦର୍ଶନ କରିବା *Thousands of people demonstrated against the war.*

demonstration /ˌdemənˈstreɪʃn/ *noun* **1** showing how to do something, or how something works ପ୍ରଦର୍ଶନ, ପ୍ରତିପାଦନ; କୌଣସି ଜିନିଷ ଦେଖାଇବା ବା ଏହାର ପ୍ରୟୋଗ ପଦ୍ଧତି ବୁଝାଇଦେବା *He gave us a cookery demonstration.* **2** a group of people walking or standing together in public to show that they have strong feelings about something ସାମୂହିକ ମତାମତର ପ୍ରକାଶ

ପାଇଁ ସଭା; ଶୋଭାଯାତ୍ରା ଇତ୍ୟାଦି *There were peaceful demonstrations all over the country to protest against rising prices.*

demonstrative /dɪˈmɒnstrətɪv/ *adjective* openly showing your feelings, especially affection ମନୋଭାବ ସ୍ପଷ୍ଟ ଭାବରେ ପ୍ରକାଶ କରୁଥିବା *demonstrative behaviour*

den /den/ *noun* the place where a wild animal lives ବନ୍ୟ ପଶୁର ରହିବା ସ୍ଥାନ *a lion's den*

denied, **denies** ଶବ୍ଦ **deny** ର ଅନ୍ୟ ଧାତୁରୂପ

denomination /dɪˌnɒmɪˈneɪʃn/ *noun* a unit of value, especially of money (ମୁଦ୍ରା) ର ଭିନ୍ନଭିନ୍ନ ଏକକ ମୂଲ୍ୟ *coins of various denominations*

denominator /dɪˈnɒmɪneɪtə(r)/ *noun* the number written below the line in a fraction which tells you into how many parts the number is divided, for example 6 in $\frac{1}{6}$ ହର, ଭାଜକ ସଂଖ୍ୟା, ଯଥା: $\frac{1}{6}$ ରେ 6 ➪ **numerator** ଦେଖନ୍ତୁ।

dense /dens/ *adjective* with a lot of things, people or plants close together ଖୁନ୍ଦାଖୁନ୍ଦି, ଗହଳିଆ, ଘନ *dense forests*

densely *adverb* thickly; close together ଖୁନ୍ଦାଖୁନ୍ଦି ହୋଇ, ଘନ ଭାବରେ *Kerala is a densely populated state.*

density /ˈdensəti/ *noun* (*plural* **densities**) the relation between the number of people or things in a place and the area they occupy ଘନତ୍ୱ; ସ୍ଥାନର ଆୟତନ ତୁଳନାରେ ଜନସଂଖ୍ୟାର ଅନୁପାତ *density of population*

dent /dent/ *noun* a hollow place in something flat, that comes when you hit it or press it hard ଚେପା ହୋଇଥିବା ଜାଗା, ଟୋଲା ହୋଇଥିବା ଜାଗା ଆଘାତ ପାଇ ବା ପିଟି ହେବା ଦ୍ୱାରା ଭିତରକୁ ଦବି ଯାଇଥିବା ଜାଗା *There's a big dent in the side of my car.*

dentist /ˈdentɪst/ *noun* a person whose job is to look after people's teeth ଦାନ୍ତ ଡାକ୍ତର, ଡେଣ୍ଟିଷ୍ଟ ✪ ଦାନ୍ତ ଡାକ୍ତର ପାଖକୁ ଯିବାକୁ ହେଲେ ଆମେ କହିବା **go to the dentist's** ର ବ୍ୟବହାର କରାଯାଏ।

deny /dɪˈnaɪ/ *verb* (**denies, denying, denied, has denied**) **1** say that something is not true ନ ମାନିବା; ଅସତ୍ୟ ବୋଲି କହିବା *They denied breaking the window.* ✪ ବିପରୀତ **admit 1** **2** refuse to give something ବଞ୍ଚିତ କରିବା, ମନା କରିବା, କରାଇ ନଦେବା *The students were denied access to the library last week.*

depart /dɪˈpɑːt/ *verb* (**departs, departing, departed**) leave a place ଚାଲିଯିବା, ପ୍ରସ୍ଥାନ କରିବା *The next train to Lucknow departs from platform 3.* ✪ ସାଧାରଣତଃ ଆମେ **leave** ଶବ୍ଦ ବ୍ୟବହାର କରୁ।

department /dɪˈpɑːtmənt/ *noun* one of the parts of a university, school, government, shop, big company, etc. (ବିଶ୍ୱବିଦ୍ୟାଳୟ, ବିଦ୍ୟାଳୟ, ସରକାର, ଦୋକାନ, ବଡ଼ ସଂସ୍ଥା ଇତ୍ୟାଦିର) ବିଭାଗ *Professor Chatterjee is the head of the English department.*

department store *noun* a big shop that sells a lot of different things ବହୁତ ପ୍ରକାର ଜିନିଷ ବିକ୍ରି କରୁଥିବା ବଡ଼ ଦୋକାନ; ଡିପାର୍ଟମେଣ୍ଟ ଷ୍ଟୋର

departure /dɪˈpɑːtʃə(r)/ *noun* the act of leaving a place ପ୍ରସ୍ଥାନ *A board inside the airport shows arrivals and departures.* ✪ ବିପରୀତ **arrival**

depend /dɪˈpend/ *verb* (**depends, depending, depended**)

depend on somebody or **something 1** need somebody or something ନିର୍ଭର କରିବା *She still depends on her parents for money because she hasn't got a job.* **2** trust somebody; feel sure that somebody or something will do what you want ବିଶ୍ୱାସ କରିବା, ଆସ୍ଥା ରଖିବା *I know I can depend on my friends to help me.*

dependant /dɪˈpendənt/ *noun* a person who needs somebody to take care of them ଆଶ୍ରିତ ବ୍ୟକ୍ତି, ପରିପୋଷିତ ବ୍ୟକ୍ତି *His dependants included his mother, wife and two children.*

dependent /dɪˈpendənt/ *adjective* if you are dependent on somebody or something, you need them ନିର୍ଭରଶୀଳ, ଆଶ୍ରିତ *A baby is completely dependent on its parents.* ✪ ବିପରୀତ **independent**

depict /dɪˈpɪkt/ *verb* (**depicts, depicting, depicted**) **1** show something with the help of a painting, drawing or sculpture ଅଙ୍କନ ବା ଚିତ୍ରଣରେ ଦେଖାଇବା *The Buddha's life is depicted on the walls of the Ajanta and Ellora Caves.* **2** describe something in words ବର୍ଣ୍ଣନା କରିବା

deposit /dɪˈpɒzɪt/ *noun* money that you pay into a bank ବ୍ୟାଙ୍କରେ ରଖିବା ଟଙ୍କା

deposit *verb* (**deposits, depositing, deposited**) put something somewhere to keep it safe କୌଣସି ଜିନିଷ କୌଣସି ସ୍ଥାନରେ ନିରାପଦରେ ରଖିବା; ଗଚ୍ଛିତ କରି ରଖିବା *The money was deposited in the bank.*

depot /ˈdepəʊ/ *noun* **1** a place where buses are kept and repaired ବସ୍ ରଖିବା ଓ ମରାମତି କରିବା ସ୍ଥାନ **2** a place where large amounts of food are stored ଖାଦ୍ୟ, ଜିନିଷପତ୍ର ବା ଯନ୍ତ୍ରପାତି ରଖିବା ସ୍ଥାନ; ଗୋଦାମ *a milk depot*

depress /dɪˈpres/ *verb* (**depresses, depressing, depressed**) make somebody feel unhappy ଅବସନ୍ନ କରିବା, ବିଷାଦଗ୍ରସ୍ତ କରିବା, ଦୁଃଖୀ କରିବା *This cold winter weather really depresses me.*

depressed /dɪˈprest/ *adjective* if you are depressed, you are very unhappy ଅବସନ୍ନ, ବିଷାଦଗ୍ରସ୍ତ, ଅସୁଖୀ

depressing *adjective* something that is depressing makes you very unhappy ଅବସାଦ ଆଣୁଥିବା, ଦୁଃଖୀ କରାଉଥିବା

depression /dɪˈpreʃn/ *noun* (*no plural*) a feeling of unhappiness ଦୁଃଖପୂର୍ଣ୍ଣ ଅବସ୍ଥା

deprive /dɪˈpraɪv/ *verb* (**deprives, depriving, deprived**) take away something from someone that actually belongs to them (ନିଜ ଜିନିଷ, ପ୍ରାପ୍ୟ ଇତ୍ୟାଦିରୁ) ବଞ୍ଚିତ କରିବା, ଛଡ଼ାଇ ନେବା *He was deprived of his father's property by his uncle.*

depth /ˈdepθ/ *noun* how deep something is; how far it is from the top of something to the bottom ଗଭୀରତା *What is the depth of the swimming pool?*

descend /dɪˈsend/ *verb* (**descends, descending, descended**) go down ଅବତରଣ କରିବା, ତଳକୁ ଖସିବା, ଓହ୍ଲାଇବା *The plane started to descend.* ✪ ବିପରୀତ **ascend**

descendant /dɪˈsendənt/ *noun* your descendants are your children, grandchildren and everybody in your family who lives after you ଦାୟାଦ, ଉତ୍ତରାଧିକାରୀ, ପିଲାପିଲି

descending /dɪˈsendɪŋ/ *adjective* going down from a higher to a lower level ନିମ୍ନାଭିମୁଖୀ, ଉଚ୍ଚ ସ୍ତରରୁ ନିଚ ସ୍ତରକୁ ଖସୁଥିବା *descending order* ✪ ବିପରୀତ **ascending**

describe /dɪˈskraɪb/ *verb* (**describes, describing, described**) say what somebody or something is like or what happened ବର୍ଣ୍ଣନା କରିବା *Can you describe the place you went to last summer?*

description /dɪˈskrɪpʃn/ *noun* words that tell what somebody or something is like or what happened ବର୍ଣ୍ଣନା *The book gives a description of life in ancient India.*

desert[1] /ˈdezət/ *noun* a large area of land that is usually covered with sand. Deserts are very dry and not many plants can grow there ଶୁଷ୍କ; ଅନୁର୍ବର ଓ ବାଲୁକାମୟ ଅଞ୍ଚଳ; ମରୁଭୂମି *the Thar Desert in Rajasthan*

desert[2] /dɪˈzɜːt/ *verb* (**deserts, deserting, deserted**) to leave somebody or something, usually for ever ସବୁ ଦିନ ପାଇଁ ଛାଡ଼ିଦେବା *He deserted her in the middle of the forest.*

desert or **dessert**?
ମନେରଖ ! **Desert** ଓ **dessert** ଦୁଇଟା ଅଲଗ ଅଲଗ ଶବ୍ଦ । ଏ ଦୁଇ ଶବ୍ଦର ଉଚ୍ଚାରଣ ଓ ଅର୍ଥ ମଧ୍ୟ ଭିନ୍ନ **desert** — ˈdezət **dessert** — dɪˈzɜːt ଖାଇବା ଶେଷରେ ଖିଆଯାଉଥିବା ମିଠାକୁ **dessert** କୁହାଯାଏ ।

deserted /dɪˈzɜːtɪd/ *adjective* empty, because all the people have left ଖାଲି, ନିର୍ଜନ, ପରିତ୍ୟକ୍ତ *At night the streets are deserted.*

deserve /dɪˈzɜːv/ *verb* (**deserves, deserving, deserved**) be good or bad enough to have something ପାଇବା ଯୋଗ୍ୟ ହେବା *You have worked very hard and you deserve a rest.*

design[1] /dɪˈzaɪn/ *verb* (**designs, designing, designed**) draw a plan that shows how to make something ନକ୍ସା ଆଙ୍କିବା; ପରିକଳ୍ପିତ ରୂପ ଓ ଗଠନର ନକ୍ସା ଆଙ୍କିବା *The hotel was designed by a French architect.*

design[2] /dɪˈzaɪn/ *noun* **1** lines, shapes and colours on something ଅଙ୍କିତ ରୂପରେଖ ବା ଢାଞ୍ଚା *The tablecloth has a design of blue and green squares on it.* **2** a drawing that shows how to make something କୌଣସି ଜିନିଷ ତିଆରି କରିବା ପାଇଁ ଆବଶ୍ୟକ ହେଉଥିବା ରେଖାଚିତ୍ର; ପରିକଳ୍ପନାର ରେଖାଚିତ୍ର; ଡିଜାଇନ୍ *Have you seen the design for the new shopping centre?*

designer /dɪˈzaɪnə(r)/ *noun* a person whose job is to make drawings that show how something will be made କୌଣସି ଜିନିଷର ରୂପରେଖ ପରିକଳ୍ପନା କରି ତା'ର ରେଖାଚିତ୍ର ଆଙ୍କୁଥିବା ବ୍ୟକ୍ତି; ନକ୍ସାକାର ବା ରୂପକାର *a fashion designer*

desirable /dɪˈzaɪərəbl/ *adjective* something that is desirable is needed or is worth having ବାଞ୍ଛନୀୟ, କାମ୍ୟ *desirable qualifications for a secretary* ✪ ବିପରୀତ **undesirable**

desire / dɪˈzaɪə(r)/ *noun* a feeling of wanting something very much ଇଚ୍ଛା, ବାସନା, କାମନା *a desire for peace*

desk /desk/ *noun* a table with drawers, where you sit to read, write or work ମେଜ, ଲେଖା ପଢ଼ା କରିବା ପାଇଁ ଦରାଜ ଥିବା ମେଜ ବା ଡେସ୍କ

desktop /ˈdesktɒp/ *noun* **1** the top of a desk ଟେବୁଲ୍; ଡେସ୍କ ବା ମେଜର ଉପର ପିଠି **2** the screen of a computer on which the symbols of various programs are displayed ଟେବୁଲ୍ ଉପରେ ରଖିବା ପାଇଁ ଉଦ୍ଦିଷ୍ଟ କମ୍ପ୍ୟୁଟର୍, କମ୍ପ୍ୟୁଟର୍ ମନିଟର; ପର୍ଦା ଯାହା ଉପରେ କାର୍ଯ୍ୟକ୍ରମର ସଂକେତ ଥାଏ

desktop publishing *noun* the process of using a small computer, printer, etc. for publishing a small book or magazine ଛୋଟ ବହି ବା ପତ୍ରିକାର କମ୍ପ୍ୟୁଟର୍ ଓ ପ୍ରିଣ୍ଟର୍ ସାହାଯ୍ୟରେ ପ୍ରକାଶନ

desolate /ˈdesələt/ *adjective* where no person lives ନିର୍ଜନ, ଜନଶୂନ୍ୟ *a desolate area*

despair /dɪˈspeə(r)/ *noun* (*no plural*) a feeling of not having hope ନୈରାଶ୍ୟ, ଆଶାଶୂନ୍ୟ ଅବସ୍ଥାନ, ହତାଶା *He was in despair because he had no money and nowhere to live.*

despatch /dɪˈspætʃ/ (**dispatch** ମଧ୍ୟ) *verb* (**despatches, despatching, despatched**) send someone or something from one place to another ପଠାଇବା, ପ୍ରେରଣ କରିବା *The parcel was despatched a fortnight ago by my friend but it has still not reached me.*

desperate /ˈdespərət/ *adjective* if you are desperate, you have no hope and you are ready to do anything to get what you want ହତାଶ, ବିହ୍ୱଳ; ହତାଶା ଯୋଗୁଁ କିଛି ବି କରିବାକୁ ପ୍ରସ୍ତୁତ *She is so desperate for a job that she will work anywhere.*

despise /dɪˈspaɪz/ *verb* (**despises, despising, despised**) hate somebody or something very much ଘୃଣା କରିବା *I despise people who tell lies.*

despite /dɪˈspaɪt/ *preposition* although something is true; not noticing or not caring about something ସତ୍ତ୍ୱେ, ସୁଦ୍ଧା *We decided to go out despite the bad weather.*

desserts

dessert /dɪˈzɜːt/ *noun* something sweet that you eat at the end of a meal ଖାଇବା ଶେଷରେ ଦିଆଯାଉଥିବା ମିଠା *We had ice cream for dessert.*
⇨ **desert** ପାଇଁ ଟିପ୍ପଣୀ ଦେଖନ୍ତୁ।

destination /ˌdestɪˈneɪʃn/ *noun* the place where somebody or something is going ଗନ୍ତବ୍ୟ ସ୍ଥାନ, ଲକ୍ଷ୍ୟସ୍ଥଳ *They were very tired when they finally reached their destination.*

destiny /ˈdestəni/ *noun* (*plural* **destinies**) the things that happen to a person and cannot be controlled by anyone ଭାଗ୍ୟ *It was her destiny to become a well-known singer.*

destined *adjective* if something is destined, it has been decided for someone (especially by fate) and cannot be changed ଭାଗ୍ୟନିରୂପିତ

destroy /dɪˈstrɔɪ/ *verb* (**destroys, destroying, destroyed**) break something completely so that you cannot use it again or so that it is gone ଧ୍ୱଂସ କରିବା *The house was destroyed by fire.*

destruction /dɪˈstrʌkʃn/ *noun* (*no plural*) breaking something completely so that you cannot use it again or so that it is gone ଧ୍ୱଂସପ୍ରାପ୍ତି, ଧ୍ୱଂସ *the destruction of the city by bombs*

detach /dɪˈtætʃ/ *verb* (**detaches, detaching, detached**) separate two things that are joined ଅଲଗା କରିବା, ପୃଥକ୍ କରିବା *Can you detach the handle from the bag?*

detail /ˈdi:teɪl/ *noun* one of the many pieces of information about something କୌଣସି ବିଷୟ ବା ତଥ୍ୟର ଗୋଟିଏ ଛୋଟ ଅଂଶ *Give me all the details of tomorrow's event.*

in detail with all the small facts or features ସବିଶେଷ, ପୁଙ୍ଖାନୁପୁଙ୍ଖ *Tell me about your plan in detail.*

detect /dɪˈtekt/ *verb* (**detects, detecting, detected**) notice something that is difficult to find or see ସହଜରେ ଜାଣି ବା ଦେଖି ନ ହେଉଥିବା ପଦାର୍ଥ ବା ବିଷୟ ଖୋଜି ବାହାର କରିବା *The new machine is able to detect even minor earthquakes.*

detection /dɪˈtekʃn/ *noun* (*no plural*) the act of finding out something ଖୋଜି ବାହାର କରିବା କାମ *Police dogs are used for the detection of explosives at airports.*

detective /dɪˈtektɪv/ *noun* a person whose job is to find out who did a crime. Detectives are usually police officers ଅନୁସନ୍ଧାନକାରୀ, ଗୁଇନ୍ଦା, ଡିଟେକ୍ଟିଭ୍ *Sherlock Holmes is a famous detective in stories.*

deter /dɪˈtɜ:(r)/ *verb* (**deters, deterring, deterred**) discourage someone from doing something ନିରୁତ୍ସାହ କରିବା

detergent /dɪˈtɜ:dʒənt/ *noun* a powder or liquid that you use for washing things like clothes and dishes ଲୁଗାପଟା, ବାସନକୁସନ ଇତ୍ୟାଦି ସଫା କରିବା ପାଇଁ ଗୁଣ୍ଡ ବା ପାଣି ସବୁନ

deteriorate /dɪˈtɪəriəreɪt/ *verb* (**deteriorates, deteriorating, deteriorated**) become worse ଖରାପ ହୋଇଯିବା, ଅବନତି ଘଟିବା *Her health is continuously deteriorating.*

determination /dɪˌtɜ:mɪˈneɪʃn/ *noun* (*no plural*) the quality of being certain that you want to do something, even if it is difficult ମନର ଦୃଢ଼ତା, ଦୃଢ଼ ସଂକଳ୍ପ *She has shown great determination to succeed.*

determine /dɪˈtɜːmɪn/ *verb* (**determines, determining, determined**) **1** find out the cause of or facts about something ନିର୍ଦ୍ଧାରଣ କରିବା, ନିର୍ଣ୍ଣୟ କରିବା *medical tests to determine the cause of the illness* **2** decide or settle something officially ନିଷ୍ପତ୍ତି ନେବା, ସ୍ଥିର କରିବା *determine the winner of the race by replaying the recordings* **3** influence or be the cause of something ନିର୍ଭର କରିବା *Your performance will determine your salary.*

determined /dɪˈtɜːmɪnd/ *adjective* very certain that you want to do something ଦୃଢ଼ ପ୍ରତିଜ୍ଞା, ବଦ୍ଧ ପରିକର, ନିଶ୍ଚିତ *She is determined to win the match.*

detest /dɪˈtest/ *verb* (**detests, detesting, detested**) hate somebody or something very much ଘୃଣା କରିବା, ଖୁବ୍ ହତାଦର କରିବା *I detest spiders.*

devastating /ˈdevəsteɪtɪŋ/ *adjective* **1** causing a lot of destruction ଧ୍ୱଂସକାରୀ, ବିଧ୍ୱଂସୀ, ସର୍ବନାଶୀ, ପ୍ରଳୟଙ୍କରୀ *devastating floods* **2** something which is devastating shocks and upsets you ମର୍ମାହତ କଲାପରି *The news of the accident was devastating.*

devastation /ˌdevəˈsteɪʃn/ *noun* (*no plural*) the act of damaging or destroying a large area of land ବିଧ୍ୱଂସ, ଛାରଖାର ଅବସ୍ଥା, ବିଧ୍ୱସ୍ତ ଅବସ୍ଥା, ସର୍ବନାଶ *The earthquake caused a lot of devastation.*

develop /dɪˈveləp/ *verb* (**develops, developing, developed**) **1** become bigger or more complete; make something bigger or more complete, ବଡ଼ କରିବା ବା ହେବା, ପୂର୍ଣ୍ଣାଙ୍ଗ କରିବା ବା ହେବା, ବିକାଶ କରିବା *She's developing into one of the country's best athletes.* **2** when a photograph is developed, special chemicals are used on the film so that you can see the picture (ଆଲୋକ ଚିତ୍ର; ଫିଲ୍ମ ଇତ୍ୟାଦି) ପ୍ରକ୍ରିୟାକରଣ କରି ଚିତ୍ରକୁ ଦୃଶ୍ୟମାନ କରାଇବା

development /dɪˈveləpmənt/ *noun* **1** (*no plural*) becoming bigger or more complete; growing କ୍ରମୋନ୍ନତି, ବିକାଶ, ବୃଦ୍ଧି *We studied the development of babies in their first year of life.* **2** (*plural* **developments**) something new that happens ନୂଆ କଥା ଘଟିବା, ନୂଆ ଜିନିଷ ମିଳିବା, ନୂଆ ବିଷୟ ଜଣା ପଡ଼ିବା *There are new developments in science almost every day.*

device /dɪˈvaɪs/ *noun* a tool or machine that you use for doing a special job ଯନ୍ତ୍ର, ଉପକରଣ *a device for opening tins*

devil /ˈdevl/ *noun* an evil being or spirit ଖଳ ପ୍ରକୃତିର ଲୋକ ବା ପ୍ରେତ

devote /dɪˈvəʊt/ *verb* (**devotes, devoting, devoted**) give a lot of time or energy to something କୌଣସି ବିଶେଷ କାମ ବା ଉଦ୍ଦେଶ୍ୟରେ ଉତ୍ସର୍ଗ କରିବା *She devoted her life to helping the poor.*

devoted *adjective* if you are devoted to somebody or something, you love them very much (କୌଣସି ବ୍ୟକ୍ତି ବା ଉଦ୍ଦେଶ୍ୟପ୍ରତି) ଆସକ୍ତ ବା ନିଷ୍ଠାବାନ; ବିଶ୍ୱସ୍ତ, ଉତ୍ସର୍ଗୀକୃତ ଭାବେ *Rahul is devoted to his wife and children.*

devotee /ˌdevəˈtiː/ *noun* **1** a person who has a strong belief in religion ଧର୍ମନିଷ୍ଠ ବ୍ୟକ୍ତି, ଧାର୍ମିକବ୍ୟକ୍ତି, ଭକ୍ତ **2** a person who gives lots of time and energy to something ଅନୁରାଗୀ, ଉତ୍ସାହୀ ବ୍ୟକ୍ତି

devour /dɪˈvaʊə(r)/ *verb* (**devours, devouring, devoured**) eat something very quickly because you are very hungry ଶୀଘ୍ର ଶୀଘ୍ର ଖାଇଯିବା, ଗ୍ରାସ କରିବା, ଗିଳିଦେବା *The children devoured the sandwiches after returning from school.*

devout /dɪˈvaʊt/ *adjective* believing strongly in a religion ଧାର୍ମିକ, ଧର୍ମନିଷ୍ଠ *devout Christians*

dew /djuː/ *noun* (*no plural*) small drops of water that form on plants and grass in the night ଶିଶିର, କାକର *In the morning, the grass was wet with dew.*

diagnosis /ˌdaɪəgˈnəʊsɪs/ *noun* (*plural* **diagnoses** /ˌdaɪəgˈnəʊsiːz) what the doctor says about your illness after he/she has examined you and done certain tests (ଡାକ୍ତର ପରୀକ୍ଷା ଦ୍ୱାରା କରୁଥିବା) ରୋଗନିର୍ଣ୍ଣୟ; ନିଦାନ

diagonal /daɪˈægənl/ *adjective* when you draw a diagonal line from one corner of a square to the opposite corner, you make two triangles କର୍ଣ୍ଣ, କର୍ଣ୍ଣରେଖା, ତିର୍ଯ୍ୟକ୍ ସରଳରେଖା

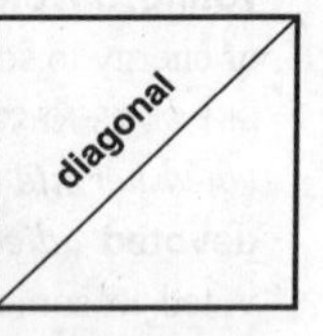

diagram /ˈdaɪəgræm/ *noun* a simple drawing that tells you what something is made up of or how it works କୌଣସି ପଦାର୍ଥର ରୂପରେଖ ଦେଖାଉଥିବା ରେଖାଚିତ୍ର *a diagram of the digestive system of the body*

dial /ˈdaɪəl/ *noun* a circle with numbers or letters on it. Some telephones, radios, clocks and watches have dials ସଂଖ୍ୟା ବା ଅକ୍ଷର ଲେଖା ଗୋଲାକାର ଚକତି; ଘଣ୍ଟା; ରେଡ଼ିଓ ଓ କିଛି ଟେଲିଫୋନ୍‌ର ମୁହଁ ପଟେ ଥିବା ପ୍ରଦର୍ଶନ ବା ଚାଳକ ଫଳକ; ଡାୟଲ୍

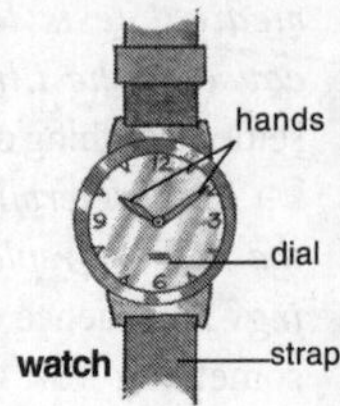

dial *verb* (**dials, dialling, dialled**) make a telephone call by moving a dial or pushing buttons ଟେଲିଫୋନ ଚକତି (ଡାୟାଲ) ଘୂରାଇ ବା ବୋତାମ ଚିପି ଅନ୍ୟ ଟେଲିଫୋନ୍ ସାଙ୍ଗେ ସଂଯୋଗ କରିବା *You have dialled the wrong number.*

dialogue /ˈdaɪəlɒg/ *noun* words that people say to each other in a book, play or film ବହି, ନାଟକ ବା ଚଳଚ୍ଚିତ୍ରରେ ଚରିତ୍ର ମାନଙ୍କର ପରସ୍ପର, କଥୋପକଥନ ବା କଥାବାର୍ତ୍ତା

diameter /daɪˈæmɪtə(r)/ *noun* a straight line across a circle, through the centre (ବୃତ୍ତର) ବ୍ୟାସ, ବ୍ୟାସରେଖା

diamond /ˈdaɪəmənd/ *noun* **1** a hard stone that looks like clear glass and is very expensive ହୀରା, ହୀରକ *The ring has a large diamond in it.* **2** the shape ♦ ଏହିଭଳି ଆକୃତି **3 diamonds** (*plural*) the playing cards that have red shapes like diamonds on them ତାସ୍‌ମୁଠାର ଠିକିରି ତାସ୍ *the eight of diamonds*

diary /ˈdaɪəri/ *noun* (*plural* **diaries**) a notebook where you write what you are going to do or what you have done each day ଦୈନନ୍ଦିନ ଘଟଣା ଲେଖାଯାଉଥିବା ଖାତା ➪ **dairy** ର ଟିପ୍ପଣୀ ଦେଖନ୍ତୁ ।

dice /daɪs/ *noun* (*plural* **dice**) a small piece of wood or plastic with spots on the sides for playing games ଲୁଡୁ ଇତ୍ୟାଦି ଖେଳରେ ଗଡ଼ାଯାଉଥିବା ଗୋଟି *Throw the dice.*

dictate /dɪkˈteɪt/ *verb* (**dictates, dictating, dictated**) **1** say words aloud so that another person can write or type them ଅନ୍ୟ ଜଣେ ଲେଖିବା ବା ଟାଇପ୍ କରିବା ପାଇଁ ଉଚ୍ଚ ସ୍ୱରରେ କହିବା; ବୟାନ କରିବା *She dictated a letter to her secretary.* **2** tell somebody that they must do something ନିର୍ଦ୍ଦେଶଦେବା, ଆଦେଶ ଦେବା *You can't dictate to me where I should go.*

dictation /dɪkˈteɪʃn/ *noun* words that you say aloud so that another person can write or type them ଅନ୍ୟ ଜଣେ ଲେଖିବା ବା ଟାଇପ୍ କରିବା ପାଇଁ କୁହାଯାଉଥିବା କଥା; ଶ୍ରୁତିଲିଖନ *We had a dictation in English today.*

dictator /dɪkˈteɪtə(r)/ *noun* a person who has complete control of a country ଏକଚ୍ଛତ୍ରବାଦୀ ଶାସକ

dictionary /ˈdɪkʃənri/ *noun* (*plural* **dictionaries**) a book that gives words from A to Z, explains what each word means and shows how to use these words ଅଭିଧାନ, ଶବ୍ଦକୋଷ, ଭାଷାକୋଷ

did ଶବ୍ଦ **do** ର ଏକ ଧାତୁରୂପ

didn't = **did not**

die /daɪ/ *verb* (**dies, dying, died, has died**) stop living ମରିଯିବା, ପ୍ରାଣତ୍ୟାଗ କରିବା, ମୃତ୍ୟୁଘଟିବା *People, animals and plants die if they don't have water.*

diesel /ˈdiːzl/ *noun* (*no plural*) oil, not petrol, that is used in diesel engines ଡିଜେଲ୍ ଇଞ୍ଜିନ୍‌ରେ ବ୍ୟବହାର ହେଉଥିବା ତେଲ, ଡିଜେଲ୍ *Some cars have diesel engines.*

diet /ˈdaɪət/ *noun* **1** the food that you usually eat ସ୍ୱାଭାବିକ ଖାଦ୍ୟ, ଖୋରାକ, ନିତିଦିନିଆ ଖାଦ୍ୟ *It is important to have a healthy diet.* **2** special foods that you eat when you are ill or when you want to get thinner ରୋଗାବସ୍ଥାରେ ବା ଝଡ଼ିବା ପାଇଁ ଦିଆଯାଉଥିବା ଖାଦ୍ୟ; ପଥ୍ୟ

difference /ˈdɪfrəns/ *noun* the way that one thing is not the same as another thing ପ୍ରଭେଦ, ତଫାତ୍, ପାର୍ଥକ୍ୟ ବୈସାଦୃଶ୍ୟ *What are the differences between humans and animals?*

✪ ବିପରୀତ **similarity**

make a difference have an effect on something ଫରକ ପକେଇବା, ପରିବର୍ତ୍ତନ ଆଣିବା *Your help has made a big difference—I understand the work much better now.*

different /ˈdɪfrənt/ *adjective* **1** not the same ଭିନ୍ନ *Cricket is different from baseball.* **2** many and not the same ଭିନ୍ନ ଭିନ୍ନ, ଅଲଗା *They sell thirty different sorts of ice cream.*

✪ ବିପରୀତ **similar**

differently *adverb* ଭିନ୍ନ ଭାବରେ *He's very quiet at school but he behaves very differently at home.*

differentiate /ˌdɪfəˈrenʃieɪt/ *verb* (**differentiates, differentiating, differentiated**) notice or tell how two or more things are different from each other ପାର୍ଥକ୍ୟ ସୂଚାଇବା, ତଫାତ୍ ବାରିବା *Can you differentiate between the twins?*

difficult /ˈdɪfɪkəlt/ *adjective* not easy to do or understand କଷ୍ଟକର, ଅସୁବିଧା ଜନକ (କାମ); ଦୁର୍ବୋଧ୍ୟ, ସହଜରେ ବୁଝି ହେଉନଥିବା (ବିଷୟ) *The exam was very difficult.* ✪ ବିପରୀତ **easy**

difficulty /ˈdɪfɪkəlti/ *noun* (*plural* **difficulties**) a problem; something that is not easy to do or understand ସମସ୍ୟା; ସହଜରେ କରି ହେଉନଥିବା କାମ; ଦୁର୍ବୋଧ ବିଷୟ; କଷ୍ଟକର *My grandfather walks with difficulty now.*

diffusion /dɪˈfjuːʒn/ *noun* the process of spreading or getting spread in all directions ପ୍ରସାରଣ, ବିକ୍ଷେପଣ *diffusion of gases*

dig /dɪɡ/ *verb* (**digs, digging, dug** /dʌɡ/, **has dug**) move some soil away and make a hole in the ground ଖୋଳିବା, ଗାତ କରିବା *You need to dig the garden before you plant the seeds.*

digest /daɪˈdʒest/ *verb* (**digests, digesting, digested**) when food is digested by your body, the food is changed into substances that your body can use ହଜମ କରିବା, ଜୀର୍ଣ୍ଣ କରିବା, ପରିପାକ କରିବା

digestion /daɪˈdʒestʃən/ *noun* (*no plural*) the process of changing food into substances that your body can use ହଜମ ପ୍ରକ୍ରିୟା, ପରିପାକ ପ୍ରକ୍ରିୟା, ପାଚନ

digestive /daɪˈdʒestɪv/ *adjective* connected with or related to the digestion of food ହଜମ ସମ୍ବନ୍ଧୀୟ; ଜୀର୍ଣ୍ଣକାରକ *the digestive system*

digit /ˈdɪdʒɪt/ *noun* any number between 0 and 9; 0 ଠାରୁ ୯ ପର୍ଯ୍ୟନ୍ତ ସଂଖ୍ୟା *The number 276 has three digits.*

digital /ˈdɪdʒɪtl/ *adjective* that which gives information in numbers ସଂଖ୍ୟା ପଂକ୍ତି ତଥ୍ୟ ଦେଖାଉଥିବା *a digital watch*

dignified /ˈdɪɡnɪfaɪd/ *adjective* calm, quiet and serious ଧୀର, ସ୍ଥିର ଓ ଗମ୍ଭୀର; ମର୍ଯ୍ୟାଦା ସମ୍ପନ୍ନ *a dignified old lady*

dignity /ˈdɪɡnəti/ *noun* calm and serious behaviour that makes people respect you ଶାନ୍ତ ଓ ଗମ୍ଭୀର ବ୍ୟବହାର; ମର୍ଯ୍ୟାଦା *The leaders behaved with dignity at the meeting.*

dilute /daɪˈluːt/ *verb* (**dilutes, diluting, diluted**) make a liquid thinner by adding water or another liquid (ତରଳ ପଦାର୍ଥରେ) ପାଣି ଇତ୍ୟାଦି ମିଶାଇ ପତଳା କରିବା *You need to dilute this paint before you use it.*

dim /dɪm/ *adjective* (**dimmer, dimmest**) not bright or clear (ଅଳ୍ପ ଆଲୋକ ଯୋଗୁ) ଅନ୍ଧାରୁଆ, ଅସ୍ପଷ୍ଟ, କମ୍ ଆଲୋକ ଥିବା *The light was so dim that we couldn't see anything.*

dimension /daɪˈmenʃn/ *noun* something that tells you how long, wide or deep a thing is କୌଣସି ଜାଗା ବା ପଦାର୍ଥର ପରିସର (ଦୈର୍ଘ୍ୟ, ପ୍ରସ୍ଥ, ଗଭୀରତା) *We wrote down the dimensions of the bedroom.*

dining room *noun* a room that is used mainly for eating meals in ଖାଇବା ଘର, ଭୋଜନ ପ୍ରକୋଷ୍ଠ

dinner /ˈdɪnə(r)/ *noun* the main meal of the day. You usually have dinner in the evening ଦିନର ପ୍ରଧାନ ଭୋଜନ; (ସାଧାରଣତଃ) ରାତ୍ରିଭୋଜନ *What time do you usually have dinner?* ⇨ **lunch** ଦେଖନ୍ତୁ ।

dinosaur /ˈdaɪnəsɔː(r)/ *noun* a big wild animal that lived a very long time ago ଅତି ପୁରାତନ କାଳର ଏକ ବିରାଟକାୟ ପ୍ରାଣୀ; ଡାଇନୋସୋର୍

ଆପଣ ଜାଣନ୍ତି କି?

Dinosaur ଶବ୍ଦ ଦୁଇଟି ଗ୍ରୀସୀୟ ଶବ୍ଦରୁ ଗଠିତ — **deinos** ଏବଂ **saurus, deinos** ର ଅର୍ଥ ଭୟଙ୍କର ଓ **saurus** ର ଅର୍ଥ ଗୋଧି ଜାତୀୟ ପ୍ରାଣୀ

dip /dɪp/ *verb* (**dips, dipping, dipped**) put something into a liquid for a short time and then take it out again ତରଳ ପଦାର୍ଥରେ ବୁଡ଼ାଇ ଉଠାଇବା *Dip your finger in the water to see how hot it is.*

diplomat /ˈdɪpləmæt/ *noun* a person whose job is to speak and do things for his/her country in another country କୁଟନୈତିକ ଚାକିରିରେ ନିୟୋଜିତ ଉଚ୍ଚାଧିକାରୀ

direct[1] /dəˈrekt/ *adjective, adverb* **1** as straight as possible, without turning or stopping ସିଧା, ସଳଖ *We flew direct from Delhi to Chennai.* **2** from one person or thing to another person or thing with nobody or nothing between them ସିଧାସଳଖ, ଅବାଧିତ; ଉନ୍ମୁକ୍ତ (ଦୁଇ ପଦାର୍ଥ ବା ବ୍ୟକ୍ତି ମଧ୍ୟରେ କୌଣସି ଅନ୍ୟ ପଦାର୍ଥ ବା ବ୍ୟକ୍ତି ନଥିବା) *You should keep this plant out of direct sunlight.* **3** in a clear and honest way ସ୍ପଷ୍ଟ, ଅକପଟ *The interviewer asked the politician some direct questions.* ✪ ବିପରୀତ **indirect**

direct[2] /dəˈrekt/ *verb* (**directs, directing, directed**) **1** tell somebody how to get to a place ଯିବା ବାଟ ବତାଇବା *Can you direct me to the station, please?* **2** tell or show somebody how to do something; control somebody or something ନିର୍ଦ୍ଦେଶ ଦେବା, ପରିଚାଳନା କରିବା *He has directed many plays at the National Theatre.*

direction /dəˈrekʃn/ *noun* where a person or thing is going or looking ଦିଗ *They got lost because they went in the wrong direction.*

directions /dəˈrekʃns/ *noun* (*plural*) words that tell you how to get to a place or how to do something ନିର୍ଦ୍ଦେଶ *I couldn't find the school, so I asked a woman for directions.*

directly /dəˈrektli/ *adverb* exactly; in a direct way ଠିକ୍ *The post office is directly opposite the bank.*

director /dəˈrektə(r)/ *noun* **1** a person who controls a business or a group of people ନିର୍ଦ୍ଦେଶକ, ନିୟନ୍ତ୍ରକ **2** a person who controls a film or play, for example by telling the actors what to do (ସିନେମା, ନାଟକ ଇତ୍ୟାଦିର) ନିର୍ଦ୍ଦେଶକ

dirt /dɜ:t/ *noun* (*no plural*) a substance that makes something dirty, for example mud or dust ଧୂଳି, ମଇଳା ପଦାର୍ଥ *The children came in from the garden covered in dirt.*

dirty /ˈdɜ:ti/ *adjective* (**dirtier, dirtiest**) not clean ମଇଳା *I washed the dirty clothes yesterday.* ✪ ବିପରୀତ **clean**[1]

dis- *prefix*
ଆମେ କୌଣସି ଶବ୍ଦର ଆରମ୍ଭରେ **dis-** ଲଗାଇଲେ ବିପରୀତ ଅର୍ଥ ପାଇବା ଯେପରି — **dis**agree = ଅସମ୍ମତ **dis**honest = ଅସାଧୁ, କପଟୀ, ମିଛ

disabled /dɪsˈeɪbld/ *adjective* not able to use a part of your body well ଅକ୍ଷମ ଶରୀରାଙ୍ଗ ଥିବା

the disabled *noun* (*plural*) people who are disabled ଅକ୍ଷମ ଶରୀରାଙ୍ଗ ଥିବା ବ୍ୟକ୍ତି

disadvantage /ˌdɪsədˈvɑ:ntɪdʒ/ *noun* a problem that makes something difficult or less good ଅସୁବିଧା, ପ୍ରତିକୂଳ ଅବସ୍ଥା *One of the disadvantages of living in this area is that there are no markets.* ✪ ବିପରୀତ **advantage**

disagree /ˌdɪsəˈgri:/ *verb* (**disagrees, disagreeing, disagreed**) say that another person's idea is wrong; not agree ମତାମତ ନ ହେବା, ଅସମ୍ମତ ହେବା *I said it was a good film, but Madhu disagreed with me.* ✪ ବିପରୀତ **agree 1**

disagreement /ˌdɪsəˈgri:mənt/ *noun* a situation when people have different ideas; an argument ମତଭେଦ, ମତାନ୍ତର, ଯୁକ୍ତିତର୍କ

disappear /ˌdɪsəˈpɪə(r)/ *verb* (**disappears, disappearing, disappeared**) if a person or thing disappears, they go away so people cannot see them ଅଦୃଶ୍ୟ ହେବା, ଅନ୍ତର୍ଦ୍ଧାନ ହେବା *The sun disappeared behind the clouds.* ✪ ବିପରୀତ **appear 1**

disappearance *noun* ଅଦୃଶ୍ୟ ବା ଅନ୍ତର୍ଦ୍ଧାନ ହେବା। *Everybody was worried about the child's disappearance.* ✪ ବିପରୀତ **appearance**

disappoint /ˌdɪsəˈpɔɪnt/ *verb* (**disappoints, disappointing, disappointed**) make you sad because what you wanted did not happen ହତାଶ କରିବା ବା ହେବା; ନିରାଶ କରିବା ବା ହେବା *I'm sorry to disappoint you, but I can't come to your party.*

disappointed *adjective* if you are disappointed, you feel sad because what you wanted did not happen ହତାଶ, ନିରାଶ *Sheela was disappointed when she didn't win the prize.*

disappointing *adjective* if something is disappointing, it makes you feel sad because it is not as good as you had hoped ହତାଶ ବା ନିରାଶ କଲାପରି, ଦୁଃଖଦ *disappointing exam results*

disappointment /ˌdɪsəˈpɔɪntmənt/ *noun* a feeling of sadness because what you wanted did not happen ହତାଶ, ନିରାଶା, ଦୁଃଖ *He couldn't hide his disappointment when he lost the match.*

disapprove /ˌdɪsəˈpruːv/ *verb* (**disapproves, disapproving, disapproved**) think that somebody or something is wrong ପ୍ରତିକୂଳ ମତ ପୋଷଣ କରିବା ବା ଦେବା ✪ ବିପରୀତ **approve**

disarm /dɪsˈɑːm/ *verb* (**disarms, disarming, disarmed**) take a weapon or weapons away from someone ଅସ୍ତ୍ର ଛଡ଼ାଇ ନେବା, ନିରସ୍ତ୍ର କରିବା *The police captured and disarmed the robber.*

disaster /dɪˈzɑːstə(r)/ *noun* something very bad that happens and that may hurt a lot of people ଆକସ୍ମିକ ଦୁର୍ଦ୍ଦଶା, ଘୋର ବିପତ୍ତି *Floods and earthquakes are natural disasters.*

disc /dɪsk/ *noun* **1** a round flat thing ଚକତି, ପତଳା ଚଟକା ଗୋଲିଆ ପଦାର୍ଥ **2** a round flat thing that makes music when you play it on a record player ପତଳା ଚଟକା ଗ୍ରାମୋଫୋନ୍ ରେକର୍ଡ଼ ➪ **compact disc**, **floppy disk** ଓ **hard disk** ଦେଖନ୍ତୁ ।

discharge[1] /ˈdɪstʃɑːdʒ/ *noun* **1** the act of sending out or releasing gas, liquid, etc.; the substance that is sent out in this way (ବାଷ୍ପ, ତରଳ ପଦାର୍ଥ ଇତ୍ୟାଦି) ନିର୍ଗତ କରିବା କାମ; ଏହି ନିର୍ଗତ ପଦାର୍ଥ *harmful discharge from factory chimneys* **2** allowing somebody to go away, especially a patient from the hospital or a soldier from the army, etc. ରୋଗୀକୁ ଡାକ୍ତରଖାନା ଛାଡ଼ି ଯିବାର ଅନୁମତି; ସୈନିକ ଇତ୍ୟାଦିଙ୍କୁ ସେନାବାହାନିରୁ ଅବ୍ୟାହତ

discharge[2] /dɪsˈtʃɑːdʒ/ *verb* (**discharges, discharging, discharged**) **1** send out or release gas, liquid, etc. (ବାଷ୍ପ, ତରଳ ପଦାର୍ଥ ଇତ୍ୟାଦି) ନିର୍ଗତ କରିବା *factories discharging harmful gases into the atmosphere* **2** allow a person to go away, especially a patient from the hospital or a soldier from the army, etc. ରୋଗୀକୁ ଡାକ୍ତରଖାନା ଛାଡ଼ି ଯିବାକୁ ଅନୁମତି ଦେବା; ସୈନିକ ଇତ୍ୟାଦିଙ୍କୁ କାର୍ଯ୍ୟରୁ ଅବ୍ୟାହତି ଦେବା *His mother was discharged from the hospital after her condition improved.*

disciple /dɪˈsaɪpl/ *noun* a person who follows a religious or political leader ଶିଷ୍ୟ, ଚେଲା, ଭକ୍ତ, ଛାତ୍ର

discipline /ˈdɪsəplɪn/ *noun* (*no plural*) teaching you to control yourself and follow rules ଆତ୍ମସଂଯମ ଓ ନିୟମ ପାଳନର ଶିକ୍ଷା

discipline *verb* (**disciplines, disciplining, disciplined**) ଆତ୍ମସଂଯମ ଓ ନିୟମପାଳନ କରାଇବା; ସଂଯତ କରିବା; ଶାସ୍ତି ଦେବା *You must discipline yourself to work harder.*

disc jockey *noun* a person who plays records on the radio or at discos or nightclubs ରେଡ଼ିଓ ବା ଡିସ୍କୋ, ରାତ୍ରି କ୍ଲବରେ ଜନପ୍ରିୟ ସଂଗୀତର ରେକର୍ଡ଼ ବଜାଉଥିବା ବ୍ୟକ୍ତି ✪ **DJ** ହେଲା disc jockey ର ସଂକ୍ଷିପ୍ତ ରୂପ ।

disco /ˈdɪskəʊ/ *noun* (*plural* **discos**) a place where people dance and listen to pop music ନାଚିବା ଓ ଜନପ୍ରିୟ ସଂଗୀତ ଶୁଣିବା ସ୍ଥାନ

disconnect /ˌdɪskəˈnekt/ *verb* (**disconnects, disconnecting, disconnected**) stop electricity, gas, etc. ବିଦ୍ୟୁତ; ରନ୍ଧା ଗ୍ୟାସ୍ ଇତ୍ୟାଦିର ଯୋଗାଣ ଲାଇନ୍ ବନ୍ଦ କରି ଦେବା *Your phone will be disconnected if you don't pay the bill.* ✪ ବିପରୀତ **connect**

discontent /ˌdɪskənˈtent/, **discontentment** /ˌdɪskənˈtentmənt/ *noun* (*no plural*) the state of being unhappy with what one has ଅସନ୍ତୋଷ, ଦୁଃଖ, କଷ୍ଟ, ଅଶାନ୍ତି *There was discontentment among the people because of the increase in petrol prices.* ✪ ବିପରୀତ **contentment**

discontented *adjective* ଅଶାନ୍ତ ଭାବ *feel discontented* ✪ ବିପରୀତ **contented**

discount /ˈdɪskaʊnt/ *noun* an amount of money that somebody takes away from the price of something to make it cheaper ଦାମ୍‌ରେ ରିହାତି, ଛାଡ଼ *Students often get a discount on travel.*

discourage /dɪsˈkʌrɪdʒ/ *verb* (**discourages, discouraging, discouraged**) make somebody not want to do something ନିରୁତ୍ସାହ କରିବା, ହତୋତ୍ସାହ କରିବା, ଆଶା ନ ଦେବା *Jyoti's parents tried to discourage her from leaving school.* ✪ ବିପରୀତ **encourage**

discover /dɪˈskʌvə(r)/ *verb* (**discovers, discovering, discovered**) find or learn something for the first time ଆବିଷ୍କାର କରିବା *Who discovered Australia?*

discovery *noun* (*plural* **discoveries**) finding or learning something for the first time ଆବିଷ୍କାର *Scientists have made an important new discovery.*

discrimination /dɪˌskrɪmɪˈneɪʃn/ *noun* (*no plural*) treating one person or a group in a different way from others ପକ୍ଷପାତ, ପାତର ଅନ୍ତର *discrimination against the poor*

discuss /dɪˈskʌs/ *verb* (**discusses, discussing, discussed**) talk about something ଆଲୋଚନା କରିବା *He discussed his problem with his friends.*

discussion /dɪˈskʌʃn/ *noun* ଆଲୋଚନା *We had an interesting discussion about politics.*

disease /dɪˈziːz/ *noun* an illness ରୋଗ; ଶାରୀରିକ ବା ମାନସିକ ଅସୁସ୍ଥତା *Chickenpox and measles are diseases.*

disgrace /dɪsˈɡreɪs/ *noun* (*no plural*) when other people stop thinking well of you, because you have done something bad ଲଜ୍ୟା, ଅପମାନ, ଅପଯଶ *He's in disgrace because he stole money from his brother.*

disgraceful /dɪsˈɡreɪsfl/ *adjective* something that is disgraceful is very bad and makes you feel ashamed ଲଜ୍ୟାଜନକ, ଅପମାନଜନକ *The way the football fans behaved was disgraceful.*

disguise /dɪsˈɡaɪz/ *verb* (**disguises, disguising, disguised**) make somebody or something different so that people will not know who or what they are ଛଦ୍ମବେଶରେ ରହିବା *They* *disguised themselves as guards and escaped from the prison.*

disguise *noun* things that you wear so that people do not know who you are ଛଦ୍ମବେଶ *We went to the party in disguise.*

disgust /dɪsˈɡʌst/ *noun* (*no plural*) a strong feeling of not liking something ବିରକ୍ତି, ଘୃଣା *They left the restaurant in disgust because the food was so bad.*

disgusted *adjective* if you are disgusted, you have a strong feeling of not liking something ବିରକ୍ତ, ଅତି ଅସନ୍ତୁଷ୍ଟ *I was disgusted to find a fly in my soup.*

disgusting *adjective* very bad ବିରକ୍ତିକର, ଖୁବ୍‌ଖରାପ *What a disgusting smell!*

dish /dɪʃ/ *noun* (*plural* **dishes**) **1** a container for food. You can use a dish to cook food in an **oven**, or to put food on the table (ରାନ୍ଧିବା ଖାଇବା ଓ ଖାଦ୍ୟ ପରିବେଷଣ କରିବା; ବାସନକୁସନ, ଥାଳି, ଗିନା, ପାତ୍ର ଇତ୍ୟାଦି **2** a part of a meal ପରିବେଷିତ ବହୁ ପ୍ରକାର ଖାଦ୍ୟରୁ ଗୋଟିଏ ପ୍ରକାର *We had a fish dish and a vegetable dish.*

dishonest /dɪsˈɒnɪst/ *adjective* a person who is dishonest says things that are not true, or steals or cheats ଶଠ, ଠକ, ମିଛୁଆ, ଅସାଧୁ ✪ ବିପରୀତ **honest**

disinfect /ˌdɪsɪnˈfekt/ *verb* (**disinfects, disinfecting, disinfected**) clean something with a special liquid that kills bacteria and germs. This special liquid is called a **disinfectant** ଏକ ବିଶେଷ ତରଳ ପଦାର୍ଥ ଦ୍ୱାରା ସଫାକରି ଜୀବାଣୁ ନାଶ କରିବା ଏହି ତରଳ ପଦାର୍ଥକୁ disinfectant କୁହାଯାଏ

disk /dɪsk/ *noun* a flat thing that stores information for computers ଏକ ପ୍ରକାର ଚକତି ଯେଉଁଥିରେ କମ୍ପ୍ୟୁଟର୍ ପାଇଁ ତଥ୍ୟ ରଖାଯାଏ *a floppy disk* ○ *a hard disk*

disk drive *noun* the part of a computer where you can put **floppy disks** ଫ୍ଲପି ଡିସ୍କ ଚାଳନ ପାଇଁ କମ୍ପ୍ୟୁଟରର ଏକ ଯନ୍ତ୍ର ➪ ଚିତ୍ର ପାଇଁ **computer** ଦେଖନ୍ତୁ।

dislike /dɪsˈlaɪk/ *verb* (**dislikes, disliking, disliked**) not like somebody or something ପସନ୍ଦ ନକରିବା, ଘୃଣା କରିବା ହତାଦର କରିବା *I dislike getting up early.* ✪ ବିପରୀତ **like**[1]

dislike *noun* (*no plural*) a feeling of not liking somebody or something (କୌଣସି ବ୍ୟକ୍ତି ବା ପଦାର୍ଥ ପ୍ରତି) ଅନାଦର ମନୋଭାବ, ବିତୃଷ୍ଣା *I have a strong dislike of hospitals.*

dismay /dɪsˈmeɪ/ *noun* (*no plural*) a strong feeling of surprise and worry ତୀବ୍ର ହତାଶ ବା ନିରାଶ ଭାବ *Nitin looked at me in dismay when I told him about the accident.*

dismiss /dɪsˈmɪs/ *verb* (**dismisses, dismissing, dismissed**) **1** allow somebody to leave a place କୌଣସି ସ୍ଥାନରୁ ଛାଡ଼ିଦେବା *The lesson finished and the teacher dismissed the class.* **2** make somebody leave their job କାମରୁ ବା ଚାକିରୀରୁ କାଢ଼ିଦେବା, ବରଖାସ୍ତ କରିବା *He was dismissed for stealing money from the company.* ✪ ସାଧାରଣତଃ ଆମେ **sack** ଓ **fire** ଶବ୍ଦକୁ ବ୍ୟବହାର କରାଯାଏ। ✪ ବିପରୀତ **appoint**

dismount /dɪsˈmaʊnt/ *verb* (**dismounts, dismounting, dismounted**) get off from a horse, cycle or motorcycle ଘୋଡ଼ା, ସାଇକେଲ୍ ବା ମଟର ସାଇକେଲ୍‌ରୁ ଓହ୍ଲାଇବା ✪ ବିପରୀତ **mount**

disobey /ˌdɪsəˈbeɪ/ *verb* (**disobeys, disobeying, disobeyed**) not do what somebody tells you to do ଅବଜ୍ଞା କରିବା, କଥା ନମାନିବା, ଅମାନ୍ୟ କରିବା ✪ ବିପରୀତ **obey**

disobedience /ˌdɪsəˈbiːdɪəns/ *noun* (*no plural*) not doing what somebody tells you to do ଅବାଧ୍ୟତା, ଆଦେଶ ଲଙ୍ଘନ ✪ ବିପରୀତ **obedience**

disobedient /ˌdɪsəˈbiːdɪənt/ *adjective* a person who is disobedient does not do what somebody tells them to do ଅବାଧ୍ୟ, ଅମାନିଆ ✪ ବିପରୀତ **obedient**

dispensary /dɪˈspensəri/ *noun* (*plural* **dispensaries**) **1** a place from where one can buy medicines ଔଷଧାଳୟ **2** a place where patients are treated for free ମାଗଣା ଚିକିତ୍ସାଳୟ

disperse /dɪˈspɜːs/ *verb* (**disperses, dispersing, dispersed**) separate and go or separate and send in different directions ଗୋଟିଏ ଜାଗାରେ ଏକାଠି ଥିବା ଅବସ୍ଥାରୁ ବିଭିନ୍ନ ଦିଗରେ ବିଛୁରିତ ହେବା ବା ଚାଲି ଯିବା *The seeds of the poppy plant are dispersed by wind.* ○ *The children dispersed after the assembly.*

dispersal /dɪˈspɜːsl/ *noun* the act of spreading and going in different directions ବିଭିନ୍ନ ଦିଗରେ ବିଛୁରଣ ବା ପ୍ରସ୍ଥାନ *Wind, water, birds and animals help in the dispersal of seeds.*

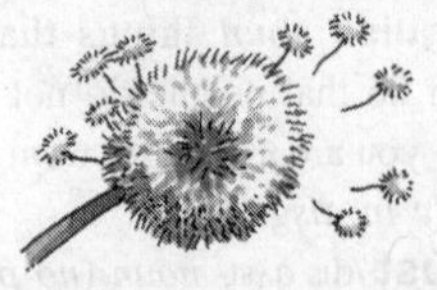
dispersal of seeds by wind

displace /dɪsˈpleɪs/ *verb* (**displaces, displacing, displaced**) remove something or someone and take their place ସ୍ଥାନାନ୍ତର କରିବା; ସ୍ଥାନଚ୍ୟୁତ ବ୍ୟକ୍ତିଙ୍କ ଜାଗାରେ ରହିବା

displacement *noun* ସ୍ଥାନଚ୍ୟୁତି, ଅପସାରଣ

display /dɪˈspleɪ/ *verb* (**displays, displaying, displayed**) show something so that people can see it ଲୋକେ ଦେଖିଲାପରି ଦେଖାଇବା; ପ୍ରଦର୍ଶନ କରିବା *All kinds of toys were displayed in the shop window.*

dispose /dɪˈspəʊz/ *verb* (**disposes, disposing, disposed**)

dispose of something throw something away or give something away because you do not want it ଅଦରକାରୀ ଜିନିଷ ଫୋପାଡ଼ି ଦେବା ବା ଦେଇଦେବା *Where can I dispose of this rubbish?*

disposal /dɪˈspəʊzl/ *noun* (*no plural*) ଅଦରକାରୀ ଜିନିଷର ନିଷ୍କାସନ ବ୍ୟବସ୍ଥା *the disposal of nuclear waste*

dispute /dɪˈspjuːt/ *noun* an angry talk between people with different ideas ବିବାଦ, ବାଦାନୁବାଦ, କଳି *There was a dispute about which driver caused the accident.*

dissatisfied /dɪsˈsætɪsfaɪd/ *adjective* not pleased with something ଅସନ୍ତୁଷ୍ଟ *I am very dissatisfied with your work.*

dissolve /dɪˈzɒlv/ *verb* (**dissolves, dissolving, dissolved**) when something dissolves, it mixes well with a liquid and becomes a part of it ମିଳେଇଯିବା; ତରଳ ପଦାର୍ଥରେ ଦ୍ରବୀଭୂତ କରିବା ବା ହେବା *Sugar and salt dissolve in water.*

distance /ˈdɪstəns/ *noun* how far it is from one place to another place ଦୂରତା, ଦୂରତ୍ୱ, ବ୍ୟବଧାନ *It's a short distance from my house to the station.*

distant /ˈdɪstənt/ *adjective* far away in space or time ଦୂର, ସୁଦୂର (ସ୍ଥାନ ବା ସମୟ) *distant countries*

distillation /ˌdɪstɪˈleɪʃn/ *noun* (*no plural*) the process of making a liquid pure by heating it till it becomes a gas and then cooling the gas to get back the liquid କୌଣସି ତରଳ ପଦାର୍ଥକୁ ଉତ୍ତାପ ଦ୍ୱାରା ବାଷ୍ପ କରି ଓ ଏହି ବାଷ୍ପକୁ ଥଣ୍ଡା କରି ବିଶୋଧିତ ତରଳ ପଦାର୍ଥ ପାଇବା ପ୍ରକ୍ରିୟା

distinct /dɪˈstɪŋkt/ *adjective* **1** easy to hear, see or smell; clear ସ୍ପଷ୍ଟ *There is a distinct smell of burning in this room.* **2** clearly different ଅଲଗା, ପୃଥକ୍, ଭିନ୍ନ *English and Hindi are two distinct languages.*

distinctly *adverb* clearly ସ୍ପଷ୍ଟଭାବରେ *I distinctly heard her say that her name was Sangeeta.*

distinction /dɪˈstɪŋkʃn/ *noun* **1** something that helps you tell the difference between things ପାର୍ଥକ୍ୟ; ଭିନ୍ନତା ସୂଚାଉଥିବା ଚିହ୍ନ ବା ଗୁଣ *distinctions between Eastern and Western cultures* **2** a special grade or mark that a student gets for performing well in any examination ପରୀକ୍ଷାରେ ଭଲ କଲେ ମିଳୁଥିବା ଉତ୍କର୍ଷତାମାନ *Payal got a distinction in Science.*

distinguish /dɪˈstɪŋgwɪʃ/ *verb* (**distinguishes, distinguishing, distinguished**) see, hear, etc. the difference between two things or people ପ୍ରଭେଦ ଜାଣିବା *Some people can't distinguish between my twin sister and me.*

distinguished /dɪˈstɪŋgwɪʃt/ *adjective* famous or important ପ୍ରସିଦ୍ଧ, ସଂଭ୍ରାନ୍ତ *a distinguished actor*

distract /dɪˈstrækt/ *verb* (**distracts, distracting, distracted**) if a person or thing distracts you, they stop you thinking about what you are doing ଅନ୍ୟମନସ୍କ କରିବା; ମନ ଇଆଡ଼େ ସିଆଡ଼େ ଟାଣିବା *The noise distracted me from my homework.*

distress /dɪˈstres/ *noun* (*no plural*) a strong feeling of pain or sadness; needing help ମାନସିକ ଯନ୍ତ୍ରଣା, ଦୁଃଖ, ବିହ୍ୱଳିତା; ଅସହାୟ ଅବସ୍ଥା

distribute /dɪˈstrɪbjuːt/ *verb* (**distributes, distributing, distributed**) give or send things to each person belonging to a large group ବାଣ୍ଟିବା, ବିତରଣ କରିବା *New books are distributed on the first day of school.*

distribution /ˌdɪstrɪˈbjuːʃn/ *noun* (*no plural*) ବଣ୍ଟନ, ବିତରଣ *the distribution of newspapers*

district /ˈdɪstrɪkt/ *noun* a part of a country or town ଜିଲ୍ଲା, ଅଞ୍ଚଳ

disturb /dɪˈstɜːb/ *verb* (**disturbs, disturbing, disturbed**) **1** stop somebody doing something, for example thinking, working or sleeping ଭାବିବା ବା କାମ କରିବା ବେଳେ ମନୋଯୋଗ ଭାଙ୍ଗିଦେବା; ନିଦ ଭାଙ୍ଗିଦେବା *My brother always disturbs me when I'm trying to do my homework.* **2** worry somebody ବିରକ୍ତ କରିବା; ବିବ୍ରତ କରିବା *We were disturbed by the news that Swati was ill.*

disturbance /dɪˈstɜːbəns/ *noun* **1** a thing that stops you doing something, for example thinking, working or sleeping ମନୋନିବେଶ ଭାଙ୍ଗୁଥିବା ବା ନିଦଭାଙ୍ଗିଦେଉଥିବା ଘଟଣା *disturbance caused by loud music* **2** when a group of people fight or make a lot of noise and trouble ପାଟିତୁଣ୍ଡ, ହଟ୍ଟଗୋଳ, ଗୋଳମାଳ *The cricket fans were causing a lot of disturbance outside the stadium.*

ditch /dɪtʃ/ *noun* (*plural* **ditches**) a long narrow channel at the side of a road or field that carries away water ଖାତ; ପାଣିବା ମଇଳା ନିଷ୍କାସନ ପାଇଁ ରାସ୍ତା ବା ପଡ଼ିଆ କଡ଼ରେ ଥିବା ନାଳ

dive /daɪv/ *verb* (**dives, diving, dived**) **1** jump into water with your arms and head first ମୁଣ୍ଡ ତଳକୁ କରି ପାଣିକୁ ଡେଇଁବା, ଡାଇଭ୍ ମାରିବା; ଗୋଡି ମାରିବା, କୁଦିପଡ଼ିବା *Sheila dived into the pool.* **2** go underwater ପାଣି ତଳକୁ ଯିବା, ବୁଡ଼ବୁଡ଼ି ମାରିବା, ବୁଡ଼ିଯିବା *The birds were diving for fish.*

diver *noun* a person who works underwater ବୁଡ଼ାଳି, ପାଣିରେ ବୁଡ଼ି କାମ କରୁଥିବା ଲୋକ

diving *noun* (*no plural*) the act of jumping into water or swimming underwater ଡାଇଭ୍ ବା ଗୋଡି ମାରିବା ପଦ୍ଧତି ବା ପ୍ରକ୍ରିୟା

diverge /daɪˈvɜːdʒ/ *verb* (**diverges, diverging, diverged**) separate and go in different directions କେନ୍ଦ୍ରୀୟ ସ୍ଥାନରୁ ଭିନ୍ନ ଭିନ୍ନ ଦିଗକୁ ପ୍ରସାରିତ ହେବା ବା ଯିବା; ଅଲଗା ହେବା *We went to school together but then our paths diverged.*

diverse /daɪˈvɜːs/ *adjective* very different from each other ବିଭିନ୍ନ ପ୍ରକାରର, ବିବିଧ *people from diverse cultures*

diversity /daɪˈvɜːsəti/ *noun* (*plural* **diversities**) a group of people or things who are very different from each other ବିଭିନ୍ନତା, ବିବିଧତା *India is a land of cultural diversities.*

divert /daɪˈvɜːt/ *verb* (**diverts, diverting, diverted**) make something go a different way ଅନ୍ୟ ଆଡ଼କୁ ନେବା, ସ୍ଥାନାନ୍ତର କରିବା *Our plane was diverted to another airport because of the bad weather.*

divide /dɪˈvaɪd/ *verb* (**divides, dividing, divided**) **1** share or cut something into smaller parts ଭାଗ କରିବା; କାଟି

ଖଣ୍ଡ ଖଣ୍ଡ କରିବା *The book is divided into ten chapters.* **2** find out how many times one number goes into a bigger number (ସଂଖ୍ୟାକୁ) ବିଭାଜନ କରିବା, ହରିବା, ହରଣ କରିବା *36 divided by 4 is 9* (36 ÷ 4 = 9).

dividend /ˈdɪvɪdend/ *noun* **1** the number that is being divided (ସଂଖ୍ୟାର) ଭାଜ୍ୟ **2** a share of a company's profit କମ୍ପାନୀ ଠାରୁ କିଣିଥିବା ସେୟାର ବା ଅଂଶ ଉପରେ ମିଳୁଥିବା ଲାଭାଂଶ

dividers /dɪˈvaɪdez/ *noun* (*plural*) a mathematical instrument similar to a compass but with both legs equal in length and used for measuring lines and angles ଏକ ପଟେ ସଂଲଗ୍ନ ଦୁଇଟି ମୁନିଆ ଚଳନକ୍ଷମ ଗୋଡ଼ ଥିବା ଜ୍ୟାମିତିକ ମାପକ ଯନ୍ତ୍ର (କୋଣ ଓ ରେଖା ମାପିବା ପାଇଁ); ଡିଭାଇଡର୍‌

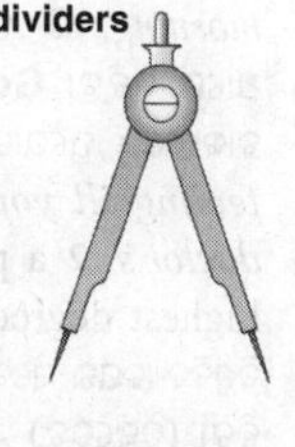

divine /dɪˈvaɪn/ *adjective* of, like or from God or a god ଈଶ୍ୱର ସମ୍ବନ୍ଧୀୟ, ଈଶ୍ୱରଦତ୍ତ, ଐଶ୍ୱରିକ, ଦୈବ *a divine message*

divisible /dɪˈvɪzəbl/ *adjective* if a number is divisible, it can be divided by another number without leaving a **remainder** ଭାଗଶେଷ ନ ରହି ବିଭାଜିତ ହୋଇ ପାରୁଥିବା; ବିଭାଜ୍ୟ *10 is divisible by 2* (10 ÷ 2 = 5, ଭାଗଶେଷ = 0).

division /dɪˈvɪʒn/ *noun* **1** (*no plural*) finding out how many times one number goes into a bigger number ବିଭାଜନ, ହରଣ **2** (*no plural*) sharing or cutting something into parts ଭାଗବାଣ୍ଟିବା ବା ଖଣ୍ଡ ଖଣ୍ଡ କରିବା ପ୍ରକ୍ରିୟା, ବିଭାଜନ, ବିଖଣ୍ଡନ *the division of Germany after the Second World War* **3** (*plural* **divisions**) one of the parts of a big organization କୌଣସି ବଡ଼ ସଂସ୍ଥାର ଏକ ବିଭାଗ

divisor /dɪˈvaɪzər/ *noun* a number which divides another number (ହରଣରେ) ଭାଜକ

divorce /dɪˈvɔːs/ *noun* the end of a marriage by law ଛାଡ଼ପତ୍ର

divorce *verb* (**divorces, divorcing, divorced**) ଛାଡ଼ପତ୍ର ଦେବା *He divorced his wife.*

Diwali *noun* the Indian festival of lights that is celebrated in October or November every year କାର୍ତ୍ତିକମାସରେ ଭାରତରେ ହେଉଥିବା ଦୀପାବଳି ଉତ୍ସବ

dizzy /ˈdɪzi/ *adjective* (**dizzier, dizziest**) if you feel dizzy, you feel that everything is turning round and round and that you are going to fall ମୁଣ୍ଡ ଘୁରେଇ ହେବା ପରି, ଘୂର୍ଣ୍ଣିତ ମସ୍ତକ *The room was very hot and I started to feel dizzy.*

DJ ହେଲା **disc jockey** ର ସଂକ୍ଷିପ୍ତ ରୂପ

do[1] /du; duː/ *verb* **1** a word that you use with another verb to make a question ସହାୟକ କ୍ରିୟା ଭାବେ ପ୍ରଶ୍ନବାଚକ ବାକ୍ୟରେ ବ୍ୟବହୃତ ଶବ୍ଦ *Do you want an apple?* **2** a word that you use with another verb when you are saying 'not' ସହାୟକ କ୍ରିୟା ଭାବରେ ନକାରାତ୍ମକ ବାକ୍ୟରେ ବ୍ୟବହୃତ ଶବ୍ଦ ('not' ସହ ସଂଯୁକ୍ତ କରି) *I like football but I don't like*

do¹ କ୍ରିୟାର ରୂପ				
present tense		*negative short forms*		*past tense* **did**
I	**do**	I	**don't**	*present participle* **doing**
you	**do**	you	**don't**	*past participle* **done**
he/she/it	**does**	he/she/it	**doesn't**	
we	**do**	we	**don't**	
you	**do**	you	**don't**	
they	**do**	they	**don't**	

tennis. **3** a word that you use in place of saying something again କୌଣସି ଖଣ୍ଡବାକ୍ୟ ପୁନରାବୃତ୍ତି କରିବା ବଦଳରେ ବ୍ୟବହୃତ ଶବ୍ଦ *She doesn't speak English, but I do.*

do² /du; duː/ *verb* (**does** /dʌz/, **doing, did** /dɪd/, **has done** /dʌn/) **1** carry out an action କରିବା *What are you doing?* ○ *He did the cooking.* **2** finish something; find the answer ସମାପ୍ତ କରିବା *I have done my homework.* **3** have a job or study something କାମ କରିବା ବା ପଢ଼ିବା *What does he do for a living?* ○ *She's doing Economics at Delhi University.*

be or **have to do with somebody** or **something** be connected with somebody or something କୌଣସି ବ୍ୟକ୍ତି; ବିଷୟ ବା ପଦାର୍ଥ ସହ ସମ୍ପୃକ୍ତ ରହିବା *I'm not sure what his job is—I think it's something to do with computers.*

do up fasten something (ବୋତାମ ଇତ୍ୟାଦି) ଲଗାଇବା *Do up the buttons on your shirt.* ✪ ବିପରୀତ **undo**

dock /dɒk/ *noun* a place by the sea or a river where ships go so that people can move things on and off them or repair them ପ୍ରୋତାଶ୍ରୟ, ଜାହାଜ ରହିବା ଓ ଜିନିଷପତ୍ର ଲଦା ଓହ୍ଲାଇବା କରାଇବା ପାଇଁ ସ୍ଥିର ଜଳ ଥିବା ସ୍ଥାନ, ଜାହାଜ ମରାମତି ସ୍ଥାନ

doctor /ˈdɒktə(r)/ *noun* **1** a person whose job is to make sick people well again ଡାକ୍ତର, ବୈଦ୍ୟ, ଚିକିତ୍ସକ *Doctor Chatterjee sees patients every morning.* ✪ ଡାକ୍ତର ପାଖକୁ ଯିବାକୁ ହେଲେ ଆମେ କହିବା **Go to the doctor's** ବାକ୍ୟାଂଶର ପ୍ରୟୋଗ କରାଯାଏ। *If you're feeling ill you should go to the doctor's.* **2** a person who has the highest degree from a university ବିଶ୍ୱବିଦ୍ୟାଳୟର ସର୍ବୋଚ୍ଚ ସ୍ନାତକୋତ୍ତର ଉପାଧି ବା ଡିଗ୍ରୀ (ଡକ୍ଟରେଟ୍) ✪ କାହାରି ନାମ ଆଗରେ 'Doctor' ଲେଖିବା ପାଇଁ ଏହାର ସଂକ୍ଷିପ୍ତ ରୂପ ହେଲା **Dr** ।

document /ˈdɒkjumənt/ *noun* a paper with important information on it ଦଲିଲ୍, ଦରକାରୀ ତଥ୍ୟ ଲେଖାଥିବା ଦସ୍ତାବିଜ ବା କାଗଜ *a legal document*

dodge /dɒdʒ/ *verb* (**dodges, dodging, dodged**) move quickly to avoid something or somebody ଧକ୍କା ନ ଲାଗିବା ପାଇଁ ସତ୍ୱର ଘୁଞ୍ଚିଯିବା *He ran across the busy road, dodging the cars.*

doe /dəʊ/ *noun* (*plural* **does** /dəʊz/) a female deer, rabbit or hare ମାଈ ହରିଣ ବା ଠେକୁଆ ➪ **deer** ଚିତ୍ର ପାଇଁ ଟିପ୍ପଣୀ ଦେଖନ୍ତୁ।

does 1 ଶବ୍ଦ **do** ର ଏକ ଧାତୁରୂପ 2 ଶବ୍ଦ **doe** ର ବହୁବଚନ

doesn't = **does not**

dog /dɒg/ *noun* an animal that many people keep as a pet or to guard their homes କୁକୁର, ଶ୍ୱାନ ✪ କୁକୁର ଛୁଆକୁ **puppy** କୁହାଯାଏ ।

doll /dɒl/ *noun* a toy like a very small person କଣ୍ଢେଇ

dollar /ˈdɒlə(r)/ *noun* money that people use in the USA and some other countries ଯୁକ୍ତରାଷ୍ଟ୍ର ଆମେରିକା ଅନ୍ୟ କିଛି ଦେଶର ମୁଦ୍ରା; ଡଲାର

dolphin /ˈdɒlfɪn/ *noun* an intelligent sea animal with a pointed mouth ମଧ୍ୟମ ଆକାରର ଗୋଳିଆ ଥୋମଣି ଥିବା ସାମୁଦ୍ରିକ ମାଛ; ଭୁଆସୁଣୀ ମାଛ; ଡଲଫିନ୍ ➪ ଚିତ୍ର ପାଇଁ **diver** ଦେଖନ୍ତୁ ।

dome /dəʊm/ *noun* the round roof of a building ଗୋଲିଆ ଛାତ, ଗମ୍ବୁଜ *Gol Gumbaz in Bijapur is the largest dome in India.*

domestic /dəˈmestɪk/ *adjective* 1 of or about the home or family ପରିବାର ସମ୍ବନ୍ଧୀୟ, ପାରିବାରିକ, ଘରୋଇ *domestic help* 2 of or inside a country ସ୍ୱଦେଶୀୟ, ଦେଶ ଭିତରର *a domestic flight* ➪ **international** ଦେଖନ୍ତୁ । 3 (of animals) kept on farms or as pets ଗୃହପାଳିତ, ପୋଷା ପଶୁ *domestic animals*

domesticate /dəˈmestɪkeɪt/ *verb* (**domesticates, domesticating, domesticated**) make a wild animal obey and work for you (ବନ୍ୟଜନ୍ତୁକୁ) ପୋଷାମନେଇବା, ମଣାଯାଇଥିବା ଜୀବ *Dogs were first domesticated about 10,000 years ago.*

domesticated *adjective* ଗୃହପାଳିତ, ପୋଷା *domesticated animals*

dominate /ˈdɒmɪneɪt/ *verb* (**dominates, dominating, dominated**) control somebody or something because you are stronger or more important ଆଧିପତ୍ୟ ବିସ୍ତାର କରିବା, ନିୟନ୍ତ୍ରଣରେ ରଖିବା *He dominates his younger brother.*

donate /dəʊˈneɪt/ *verb* (**donates, donating, donated**) give something to people who need it ଦାନ ଦେବା *They donated Rs 10,000 to the hospital.*

donation /dəʊˈneɪʃn/ *noun* something that you give to people who need it ଦାନ, ଚାନ୍ଦା *a donation of money*

done ଶବ୍ଦ **do** ର ଏକ ଧାତୁରୂପ

donkey /ˈdɒŋki/ *noun* (*plural* **donkeys**) an animal like a small horse with long ears ଗଧ, ଗର୍ଦ୍ଦଭ

don't = **do not**

doom /du:m/ *noun* (*no plural*) a terrible thing that happens suddenly and causes a lot of destruction ଦୁର୍ଭାଗ୍ୟ, ସର୍ବନାଶ

doomed *adjective* ବିଫଳତା ବା ବିଧ୍ୱଂସ ପାଇଁ ପୂର୍ବନିର୍ଦ୍ଧାରିତ *The project was doomed from the start.*

door /dɔ:(r)/ *noun* the way into a building or room; a piece of wood, glass or metal that you use to open and close the way in to a building, room, cupboard, car, etc. ଦରଜା, ଦୁଆର, କବାଟ, ଦ୍ୱାର *Can you close the door, please?* ➪ ଚିତ୍ର ପାଇଁ **house** ଦେଖନ୍ତୁ ।

answer the door go to open the door when somebody knocks or rings the bell ଦୁଆର ଖୋଲିବା
out of doors outside; not in a building ଘର ବାହାର *Farmers spend a lot of time out of doors.*

doorbell /ˈdɔːbel/ *noun* a bell outside a house that you ring to tell people inside that you are there ବାଣ୍ଡ ଦୁଆର ପାଖରେ ଲଗାଯାଇଥିବା ଡାକିବା ଘଣ୍ଟି ବା ବେଲ୍

dormitory /ˈdɔːmətri/ *noun* (*plural* **dormitories**) a big bedroom for a lot of people, usually in a school ସ୍କୁଲ୍ ହଷ୍ଟେଲ ଇତ୍ୟାଦିରେ ଥିବା ବହୁ ଲୋକଙ୍କ ଶୋଇବା ପାଇଁ ବଡ଼ ପ୍ରକୋଷ୍ଠ ବା କୋଠରି

dose /dəʊs/ *noun* an amount of medicine that you take at one time ଥରକେ ଦିଆଯାଉଥିବା ଔଷଧର ପରିମାଣ; ପାନ, ମାତ୍ରା *The dose is one spoonful twice a day.*

dot /dɒt/ *noun* a small round mark ଛୋଟ ବିନ୍ଦୁ *The letter 'i' has a dot over it.*

double /ˈdʌbl/ *adjective* **1** two times as much or as many; with two parts that are the same ଦୁଇଗୁଣ, ଦ୍ୱିଗୁଣ, ଏକାପରି ଦୁଇଟି ଜିନିଷଥିବା *double doors* **2** for two people ଦୁଇଜଣଙ୍କ ପାଇଁ *a double room* **3** you use 'double' before a letter or a number to show that it comes twice ଏକା ଅକ୍ଷର ବା ସଂଖ୍ୟା ଦୁଇଥର ଥିବା *My phone number is two double four nine five one seven nine (24495179).* ✪ ବିପରୀତ **single**
double *verb* (**doubles, doubling, doubled**) make something twice as much or as many; become twice as much or as many ଦ୍ୱିଗୁଣ କରିବା ବା ହେବା *The price has doubled: last year it was Rs 100 and this year it's Rs 200.*

double-decker *noun* a bus with places to sit upstairs and downstairs ଦୁଇମହଲା ବିଶିଷ୍ଟ ବସ୍

doubt¹ /daʊt/ *noun* a feeling that you are not sure about something କୌଣସି ବିଷୟରେ ସଂଶୟ ବା ଅନିଶ୍ଚିତ ଭାବ, ଅବିଶ୍ୱାସ, ଦ୍ୱିଧା *She says the story is true but I have my doubts about it.*

doubt² /daʊt/ *verb* (**doubts, doubting, doubted**) not feel sure about something; think that something is probably not true or probably will not happen ବିଶ୍ୱାସ କରିବାକୁ ଦ୍ୱିଧାକରିବା *I doubt if he will come.*

doubtful /ˈdaʊtfl/ *adjective* not certain or not likely ଅନିଶ୍ଚିତ, ସନ୍ଦେହଜନକ *It is doubtful whether he will return next month.*

dough /dəʊ/ *noun* (*no plural*) flour, water and other things mixed together, for making bread, roti, etc. ପାଉଁରୁଟି, ରୁଟି ଇତ୍ୟାଦି କରିବା ପାଇଁ ଚକଟା ଅଟା ଇତ୍ୟାଦି।

dove /dʌv/ *noun* a bird that is like a pigeon. The white dove is often used as a sign of peace କପୋତ ପକ୍ଷୀ, କାପ୍ତା

down /daʊn/ *preposition, adverb* **1** in or to a lower place; not up ତଳକୁ ତଳେ, ତଳ ଆଡ଼କୁ ବା ନିମ୍ନ ସ୍ଥାନକୁ *The sun goes down in the evening.* ○ *We ran down the hill.* **2** from standing to sitting or lying ଠିଆ ଅବସ୍ଥାରୁ ଶୋଇବା ବା ବସିବା ଅବସ୍ଥାକୁ *Sit down.* ○ *Lie down on the bed.* **3** in a way that is smaller, less strong, lower, etc. ନ୍ୟୁନ, ଦୁର୍ବଳ, ଶସ୍ତା, କମ୍ *Prices are going down.*

downhill /ˌdaʊnˈhɪl/ *adverb* down, towards the bottom of a hill; ପାହାଡ଼ ତଳକୁ, ତଳ ଆଡ଼କୁ *My bicycle can go fast downhill.* ✪ ବିପରୀତ **uphill**

downstairs /ˌdaʊnˈsteəz/ *adverb* to or on a lower floor of a building ତଳ ମହଲାକୁ, ତଳ ମହଲାରେ *I went downstairs to open the door.* ✪ ବିପରୀତ **upstairs**

downstairs *adjective* ତଳ ମହଲାରେ *She lives in the downstairs flat.* ✪ ବିପରୀତ **upstairs**

downtrodden /ˈdaʊntrɒdn/ *adjective* not having any of the important things in life like food, shelter or work ଦଳିତ, ନିଷ୍ପୀଡ଼ିତ, ନିଷ୍ପେସିତ

downwards /ˈdaʊnwədz/, **downward** /ˈdaʊnwəd/ *adverb* down; towards a lower place or towards the ground ତଳ ଆଡ଼କୁ, ନିମ୍ନଗାମୀ ଭାବରେ *She was lying face downwards on the grass.* ✪ ବିପରୀତ **upwards, upward**

dowry /ˈdaʊri/ *noun* (*plural* **dowries**) the money or things that a bride brings to her husband's home at the time of marriage. Laws in many countries do not allow this ଯୌତୁକ, କନ୍ୟାସୁନା

doze /dəʊz/ *verb* (**dozes, dozing, dozed**) sleep lightly for a short time ଢୁଳେଇବା, ଘୁମେଇବା, ତନ୍ଦ୍ରାବିଷ୍ଟ ହେବା *My grandfather was dozing in his armchair.*

dozen /ˈdʌzn/ *noun* (*plural* **dozen**) a group of twelve people or things ବାର, ଦ୍ୱାଦଶ, ଡଜନ *a dozen red roses* ○ *two dozen boxes*

Dr ଶବ୍ଦ **doctor** ର ସଂକ୍ଷିପ୍ତ ରୂପ

drag /dræg/ *verb* (**drags, dragging, dragged**) **1** pull something along the ground slowly, often because it is heavy ଟାଣିବା, ଘୋଷାରି ନେବା *He couldn't lift the sack, so he dragged it out of the shop.* **2** if something drags, it seems to go slowly because it is not interesting ଚିତ୍ତାକର୍ଷକ ହୋଇ ନଥିବାରୁ ସମୟ ନଗଡ଼ିଲା ପରି ଲାଗିବା

dragon /ˈdrægən/ *noun* a big dangerous animal with wings, a long tail and fire in its mouth, that you find in stories କିଂବଦନ୍ତୀରେ ବର୍ଣ୍ଣିତ ଡେଣାଥିବା ଗୋଧି ପରି ବୃହତ୍ ଜୀବ ଯାହାର ନିଃଶ୍ୱାସରେ ନିଆଁ ବାହାରେ

dragon

dragonfly /ˈdrægənflaɪ/ *noun* (*plural* **dragonflies**) an insect with two pairs of transparent wings and a long thin body that is often brightly coloured କଙ୍କି ➪ ଚିତ୍ର ପାଇଁ **invertebrate** ଦେଖନ୍ତୁ ।

drain[1] /dreɪn/ *noun* a pipe that carries away dirty water from a building ପାଣି ମଇଳା ଇତ୍ୟାଦି ଯାଉଥିବା ନାଳ, ପାଇପ୍‌ନାଳ *The drain is blocked.*

drain² /dreɪn/ *verb* (**drains, draining, drained**) flow away ପାଣି ପ୍ରଭୃତି ତରଳ ପଦାର୍ଥ ନିଷ୍କାସନ ପ୍ରଭୃତି କରିବା ବା ନିଷ୍କାସିତ ହେବା *The water drained away slowly.*

drake /dreɪk/ *noun* a male duck ଅଣ୍ଡିରା ବତକ

drama /ˈdrɑːmə/ *noun* **1** a story that you watch in the theatre or on television, or listen to on the radio ନାଟକ *a TV drama* **2** an exciting thing that happens ନାଟକୀୟ ଘଟଣା

dramatic /drəˈmætɪk/ *adjective* **1** sudden, great or exciting ଆକସ୍ମିକ ବା ଚମକପ୍ରଦ, ନାଟକୀୟ *The finish of the race was very dramatic.* **2** of plays or the theatre ନାଟକ ବା ଥିଏଟର୍ ସମ୍ବନ୍ଧୀୟ *a dramatic society*

dramatist /ˈdræmətɪst/ *noun* a person who writes plays ନାଟ୍ୟକାର, ନାଟକର ଲେଖକ

drank ଶବ୍ଦ **drink¹** ର ଏକ ଧାତୁରୂପ

drastic /ˈdræstɪk/ *adjective* sudden, extreme and severe ପ୍ରବଳ, ଅତିବେଶୀ, ଖୁବ୍‌ଶୀଘ୍ର, ପ୍ରଖର *a drastic rise in property prices*

draw¹ /drɔː/ *verb* (**draws, drawing, drew** /druː/, **has drawn** /drɔːn/) **1** make a picture with a pencil, pen, chalk, etc. ଆଙ୍କିବା, ଚିତ୍ର କରିବା *She drew a picture of a horse.* **2** pull or take something from a place କାଢ଼ିବା, ଟାଣି ଆଣିବା *He drew a knife from his pocket.* **3** pull something to make it move ଟାଣିନେବା, ଭିଡ଼ିନେବା *The carriage was drawn by two horses.* **4** open or close curtains ପରଦା ଖୋଲିବା ବା ବନ୍ଦ କରିବା *I switched on the light and drew the curtains.*

draw² /drɔː/ *noun* the result of a game when both players or teams have the same number of points ଖେଳର ଅମୀମାଂସିତ ଅବସ୍ଥା, ଡ୍ର *The football match ended in a one-all draw.*

drawer /drɔː(r)/ *noun* a thing like a box that you can pull out from a cupboard or desk, for example ଢ଼ାଙ୍କୁଣୀ ନଥିବା ଟଣା ଡାଲା (ଟେବୁଲ୍ ଇତ୍ୟାଦିରେ)

drawing /ˈdrɔːɪŋ/ *noun* **1** (*plural* **drawings**) a picture made with a pencil, pen, chalk, etc. ରେଖାଚିତ୍ର *The children's drawings were put up on the noticeboard by the teacher.* **2** (*no plural*) the art of making pictures with a pencil, pen, chalk, etc. ରେଖାଙ୍କନ *Kaif is very good at drawing.*

drawing pin *noun* a short pin with a flat round top, that you use for attaching paper to a wall or board ଚିତ୍ର; ଲେଖା କାଗଜ ଇତ୍ୟାଦି କାଠ ପଟାରେ ଲଗାଇବା ପାଇଁ ବ୍ୟବହୃତ ଚଟକା ମୁଣ୍ଡ ଥିବା ସାନ କଣ୍ଟା *I put the poster up with drawing pins.* ➪ ଚିତ୍ର ପାଇଁ **notice** ଦେଖନ୍ତୁ ।

drawn ଶବ୍ଦ **draw¹** ର ଏକ ଧାତୁରୂପ

drawstring /ˈdrɔːstrɪŋ/ *noun* a string that is put inside the seams of the top of a bag or a piece of clothing and can be pulled tight or loose ବଟୁଆ; ବ୍ୟାଗ୍ ଇତ୍ୟାଦିର ମୁହଁରେ ଗଳା ଯାଇଥିବା ଫିତା ଯାହାକୁ ଟାଣିଲେ ତା'ର ମୁହଁ ବନ୍ଦ ହୁଏ ଓ ଖୋଲେ

dreaded /ˈdredɪd/ *adjective* making you feel scared ଭୟଙ୍କର, ଶଙ୍କିତ କଲାପରି

dreadful /ˈdredfl/ *adjective* very bad ଖୁବ୍ ଖରାପ, କଷ୍ଟକର *I had a dreadful journey—my train was two hours late!*

dream /dri:m/ *verb* (**dreams, dreaming, dreamt** /ˈdremt/ **dreamed, has dreamt** ବା **has dreamed**) **1** have a picture or idea in your mind when you are asleep ସ୍ୱପ୍ନ ଦେଖିବା *I dreamt about you last night.* **2** hope for something nice in the future ଭବିଷ୍ୟତ ସୁଖର କଳ୍ପନା କରିବା, ଭାବିବା *She dreams of becoming a famous actress.*
dream *noun* pictures or ideas in your mind when you are asleep ସ୍ୱପ୍ନ *I had a dream about school last night.* ✪ ଭୟାବହ ସ୍ୱପ୍ନକୁ **nightmare** କହନ୍ତି।

drench /drentʃ/ *verb* (**drenches, drenching, drenched**) get completely wet ପୂରା ଓଦାହୋଇଯିବା; ଭିଜିଯିବା *We forgot to carry our umbrellas and got drenched in the rain.*

dress[1] /dres/ *noun* **1** (*plural* **dresses**) a piece of clothing that is made in one piece and covers the body, sometimes till the ankles or the knees and which is worn by a woman or a girl ଝିଅମାନଙ୍କର ଆଣ୍ଠୁଲମ୍ବା ବା ପାଦଲମ୍ବ ଫ୍ରକ୍ ପରି ପୋଷାକ **2** (*no plural*) clothes ବସ୍ତ୍ର, ପୋଷାକ *The group of dancers wore their national dress.*

dress

dress[2] /dres/ *verb* (**dresses, dressing, dressed**) put clothes on yourself or another person ଲୁଗାପଟା ପିନ୍ଧିବା ବା ପିନ୍ଧାଇବା *She dressed quickly and went out.* ✪ ବିପରୀତ **undress**

dressing /ˈdresɪŋ/ *noun* a thing for covering a part of your body that is hurt ଆଘାତପ୍ରାପ୍ତ ଅଙ୍ଗରେ ବନ୍ଧାଯାଉଥିବା ବ୍ୟାଣ୍ଡେଜ; ପଟି ଇତ୍ୟାଦି *You should put a dressing on that cut.*

drew ଶବ୍ଦ **draw**[1] ର ଏକ ଧାତୁରୂପ

dried ଶବ୍ଦ **dry**[2] ର ଏକ ଧାତୁରୂପ

drier ଶବ୍ଦ **dry**[1] ର ଏକ ଧାତୁରୂପ

dries ଶବ୍ଦ **dry**[2] ର ଏକ ଧାତୁରୂପ

driest ଶବ୍ଦ **dry**[1] ର ଏକ ଧାତୁରୂପ

drift /drɪft/ *verb* (**drifts, drifting, drifted**) move slowly in the air or on water ପାଣି ବା ପବନ ସ୍ରୋତରେ ଧୀରେ ଧୀରେ ଭାସିଯିବା *The balloon drifted away.*

balloon **drifting** into the sky

drill /drɪl/ *noun* a tool that you use for making holes କଣା କରିବା ଯନ୍ତ୍ର, ବିନ୍ଧା, ଭଅଁର, ବିନ୍ଧଣୀ, ଡ୍ରିଲ୍ *an electric drill*
drill *verb* (**drills, drilling, drilled**) make a hole using a drill ଡ୍ରିଲ୍ ବା ବିନ୍ଧ ସାହାଯ୍ୟରେ କଣା କରିବା

drink[1] /drɪŋk/ *verb* (**drinks, drinking, drank** /dræŋk/, **has drunk** /drʌŋk/) take in liquid, for example water, milk or coffee, through your mouth ପିଇବା, ପାନ କରିବା *She was drinking a cup of tea.*

drink[2] /drɪŋk/ *noun* a liquid, for example water, milk or coffee, that you take in through your mouth ପିଇବା ପଦାର୍ଥ, ପାନୀୟ *Can I have a cold drink?*

drip /drɪp/ *verb* (**drips, dripping, dripped**) fall slowly in small drops ଟୋପା ଟୋପା ହୋଇ ପଡ଼ିବା *The tap is dripping.*

drive[1] /draɪv/ *verb* (**drives, driving, drove** /drəʊv/**, has driven** /ˈdrɪvn/) control a car, bus, etc. and make it go where you want to go କାର୍, ବସ୍ ଇତ୍ୟାଦି ଚଳାଇବା *Can you drive?*

drive[2] /draɪv/ *noun* a journey in a car କାର୍‌ରେ ଭ୍ରମଣ *It's a long drive from Delhi to Shimla.*

driver /ˈdraɪvə(r)/ *noun* a person who controls a car, bus, train, etc. କାର୍, ବସ୍, ରେଳଗାଡ଼ି ଇତ୍ୟାଦିର ଚାଳକ, ଡ୍ରାଇଭର

driving /ˈdraɪvɪŋ/ *noun* (*no plural*) controlling a car, bus, etc. ମଟର ଗାଡ଼ି ଇତ୍ୟାଦିର ଚାଳନ

driving licence *noun* (*plural* **driving licences**) a piece of paper that shows that you are allowed to drive a car, etc. ମଟର ଗାଡ଼ି ଚଳାଇବା ପାଇଁ ଅଧିକାର ପତ୍ର, ଡ୍ରାଇଭିଂ ଲାଇସେନ୍ସ୍

droop /dru:p/ *verb* (**droops, drooping, drooped**) bend or hang down ନଇଁ ପଡ଼ିବା ବା ଝୁଲି ପଡ଼ିବା *The flowers will droop if you don't put them in water.*

drop[1] /drɒp/ *verb* (**drops, dropping, dropped**) **1** fall or let something fall by accident ଆକସ୍ମିକ ଭାବେ ପଡ଼ିଯିବା ବା ପକାଇ ଦେବା *I dropped my watch and it broke.* **2** fall or make something fall ପଡ଼ିଯିବା ବା ପକାଇ ଦେବା *Food packets are being dropped in the drought-affected areas.*

drop[2] /drɒp/ *noun* **1** a very small amount of liquid ତରଳ ପଦାର୍ଥର ବିନ୍ଦୁ ବା ଟୋପା *a drop of blood* **2** a fall; going down ପତନ, ପଡ଼ିବା ପ୍ରକ୍ରିୟା; ଦରଦାମ, ଉତ୍ତାପ ଇତ୍ୟାଦିର ନିମ୍ନଗତି, କମିବା *a drop in temperature* ○ *a drop in prices*

droppings /ˈdrɒpɪŋz/ *noun* (*no singular*) solid waste matter from birds and small animals ପଶୁପକ୍ଷୀମାନଙ୍କର ମଳ ବା ବିଷ୍ଠା *Seeds travel to far-off places through bird droppings.*

drought /draʊt/ *noun* a long period of time when there is not enough rain ଅନାବୃଷ୍ଟି, ମରୁଡ଼ି *the worst drought in forty years*

drove ଶବ୍ଦ **drive**[1] ର ଏକ ଧାତୁରୂପ

drown /draʊn/ *verb* (**drowns, drowning, drowned**) die under water because it is not possible to breathe ପାଣିରେ ବୁଡ଼ିଯାଇ ମରିଯିବା

drowsy /ˈdraʊzi/ *adjective* sleepy ନିଦ ମାଡ଼ି ଆସୁଥିବା ତନ୍ଦ୍ରା ଲାଗି ଆସୁଥିବା; ତନ୍ଦ୍ରାଚ୍ଛନ୍ନ *I felt drowsy after the heavy meal.*

drug /drʌg/ *noun* **1** something that makes you better when you are ill ଔଷଧ, ଡାକ୍ତରି ଔଷଧ **2** a very dangerous substance that some people eat, smoke or inject because it makes them feel happy or excited. It is against the law to use drugs ଆନନ୍ଦ ବା ଉଦ୍ଦୀପନା ପାଇଁ କିଛି ଲୋକ ଖାଉଥିବା, ସିଗାରେଟ୍‌ରେ ଟାଣୁଥିବା ବା ଇଞ୍ଜେକ୍‌ସନରେ ନେଉଥିବା ମାରାତ୍ମକ ଦ୍ରବ୍ୟ। ଏସବୁ ଆଇନ୍ ଦ୍ୱାରା ନିଷିଦ୍ଧ

drum[1] /drʌm/ *noun* **1** a musical instrument that you hit with sticks or with your hands ଢୋଲ, ଢୋଲ ପରି ବାଜା, ମାଦଳ, ମୃଦଙ୍ଗ, ଡ୍ରମ୍ *He plays the drums in a band.* ➪ ଚିତ୍ର ପାଇଁ **musical instruments** ଦେଖନ୍ତୁ। **2** a big round container for water, oil, etc. ପିମ୍ପା

drum[2] /drʌm/ *verb* (**drums, drumming, drummed**) play a drum ଢୋଲ, ମାଦଳ, ମୃଦଙ୍ଗ, ଡ୍ରମ୍ ଇତ୍ୟାଦି ବଜାଇବା

drummer /ˈdrʌmə(r)/ *noun* a person who plays a drum ଡ୍ରମ୍ ବାଦକ, ବାଦ୍ୟକାର, ବାଜାବାଲା

drunk[1] ଶବ୍ଦ **drink**[1] ର ଏକ ଧାତୁରୂପ

drunk[2] /drʌŋk/ *adjective* if someone is drunk, they have had too much alcohol ମାତାଲ୍

dry[1] /draɪ/ *adjective* (**drier, driest**) **1** with no liquid in it or on it; not wet ଶୁଖିଲା, ଶୁଷ୍କ *The clothes aren't dry yet.* ✪ ବିପରୀତ **wet 2** with no rain ଶୁଖିଲା, ବର୍ଷା ହେଉନଥିବା *dry weather*

dry[2] /draɪ/ *verb* (**dries, drying, dried, has dried**) **1** become dry ଶୁଖିଲା *Our clothes were drying in the sun.* **2** make something dry ଶୁଖିବା ବା ଶୁଖାଇବା। *Dry your hands on this towel.*

dry up become completely dry ପୁରାଶୁଖିଯିବା *There was no rain for several months and all the rivers dried up.*

dry-clean *verb* (**dry-cleans, dry-cleaning, dry-cleaned**) make clothes clean by using chemicals, not water ବିନା ପାଣିରେ ପେଟ୍ରୋଲ୍ ଇତ୍ୟାଦି ଦ୍ରାବକ ଦ୍ୱାରା ଲୁଗାପଟା ସଫା କରିବା, ଡ୍ରାଇକ୍ଲିନ୍ *I had my suit dry-cleaned.*

dry-cleaner's *noun* a shop where clothes and other things are dry-cleaned ଡ୍ରାଇକ୍ଲିନ୍ ଦୋକାନ

duchess /ˈdʌtʃəs/ *noun* (*plural* **duchesses**) **1** a woman who has a special title ଡଚେସ୍ ଉପାଧିଧାରୀ ମହିଳା **2** the wife of a **duke** ଡ୍ୟୁକ୍‌ଙ୍କର ପତ୍ନୀ

duck[1] /dʌk/ *noun* a bird that lives on and near water ବତକ

> ✪ ଅଣ୍ଡିରା ବତକକୁ **drake** ଓ ବତକର ଛୁଆକୁ **duckling** କୁହାଯାଏ।

duck[2] /dʌk/ *verb* (**ducks, ducking, ducked**) move your head or body down quickly, so that something does not hit you or so that somebody does not see you ଲୁଚିବା ପାଇଁ ବା ଆଘାତରୁ ରକ୍ଷା ପାଇବା ପାଇଁ ମୁଣ୍ଡ ଓ ଦେହ ହଠାତ୍ ନୁଆଇଁ ଦେବା; ନଇଁ ପଡ଼ିବା *He saw the ball coming towards him and ducked.*

duckling /ˈdʌklɪŋ/ *noun* a young duck ବତକ ଛୁଆ, ବତକ ଚିଆଁ

due /dju:/ *adjective* **1** because of something କାରଣରୁ, ଯୋଗୁଁ *The accident happened due to bad driving.* **2** if something is due at a certain time, you expect it to happen or come then ଆଗରୁ ସ୍ଥିର କରାଯାଇଥିବା, ସ୍ଥିରୀକୃତ, ପ୍ରତ୍ୟାଶିତ *The new highway is due to open in April.* **3** if an amount of money is due, you must pay it ବାଧ୍ୟତାମୂଳକ ଦେୟ *My rent is due at the beginning of the month.*

duet /dju'et/ *noun* music for two people to sing or play on musical instruments ଦୁଇଜଣ ଗାଇଥିବା ଗୀତ, ଦ୍ୱୈତ ସଂଗୀତ, ଯୁଗଳବନ୍ଦୀ *Alka and Abhay sang a duet.*

dug ଶବ୍ଦ **dig** ର ଏକ ଧାତୁରୂପ

duke /dju:k/ *noun* a man who has a special title ଡ୍ୟୁକ୍ ଉପାଧିଧାରୀ ବ୍ୟକ୍ତି ➪ **duchess** ଦେଖନ୍ତୁ।

dull /dʌl/ *adjective* (**duller, dullest**) **1** not bright (ଆଲୁଅ, ରଙ୍ଗଇତ୍ୟାଦି) ଅନୁଜ୍ଜ୍ୱଳ, ଫିକା, ମେଘୁଆ *It was a dull, cloudy day.* **2** not interesting or exciting ଅନାକର୍ଷକ, ମାନ୍ଦା *Life is never dull in a big city.*

dumb /dʌm/ *adjective* not able to speak ମୂକ, ଜଡ଼ା

dump /dʌmp/ *verb* (**dumps, dumping, dumped**) **1** take something to a place and leave it there because you do not want it ଅଳିଆ ଗଦାରେ ଅଦରକାରୀ ଜିନିଷ ଫିଙ୍ଗି ଦେବା *They dumped their rubbish by the side of the road.* **2** put something down without being careful ଅଯତ୍ନଶୀଳ ଭାବରେ ଏଠିସେଠି ପକାଇବା *Don't dump your clothes on the floor!*

dump *noun* a place where you can take and leave things that you do not want ଅଳିଆଗଦା

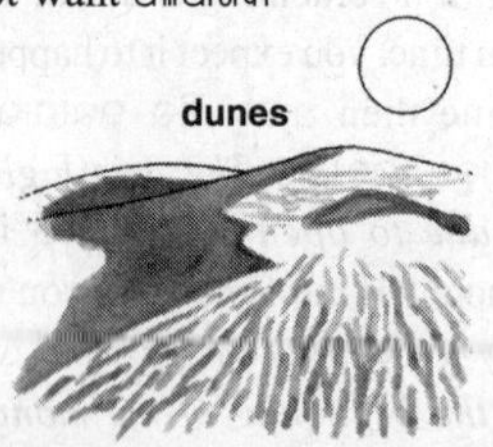
dunes

dune /dju:n/ (**sand dune** ମଧ୍ୟ) *noun* a small hill of sand near the sea or in a desert ପବନ ଦ୍ୱାରା ହୋଇଥିବା ବାଲି ସ୍ତୁପ; ବାଲିପାହାଡ଼, ବାଲିକୁଦ

dung /dʌŋ/ *noun* (*no plural*) solid waste from big animals ପଶୁମଳ *cow dung*

dungeon /'dʌndʒən/ *noun* a prison under the ground, for example in a castle ଭୂଗର୍ଭସ୍ଥ ବନ୍ଦୀଶାଳା, ଅନ୍ଧକୂପ

duplicate[1] /'dju:plɪkət/ *noun* a thing that is exactly like another thing ଏକାପରି ଦୁଇ ପଦାର୍ଥରୁ ଗୋଟିଏ *I have found the original key but can't find the duplicate.*

duplicate[2] /'dju:plɪkeɪt/ *verb* (**duplicates, duplicating, duplicated**) make something exactly like another thing କୌଣସି ପଦାର୍ଥର ଠିକ୍ ଏକାପରି ନକଲ କରିବା *duplicating somebody else's music*

durable /'djʊərəbl/ *adjective* something that is durable is strong and likely to last for a long time without breaking or tearing ବହୁକାଳ ସ୍ଥାୟୀ, ଦୀର୍ଘକାଳ ପାଇଁ ଉପଯୋଗୀ *durable shoes*

durability /ˌdjʊərə'bɪləti/ *noun* (*no plural*) the period for which something will work or last without causing trouble କ୍ଷୟଡ଼ତି ନ ହୋଇ, ଦୀର୍ଘକାଳ ବ୍ୟବହାର କରି ହେଉଥିବା ଗୁଣ; ଏହି ବ୍ୟବହାରର କାଳ; ବହୁକାଳ ସ୍ଥାୟିତ୍ୱ *the durability of the wire*

during /'djʊərɪŋ/ *preposition* **1** all the time that something is happening କୌଣସି ସମୟ ମଧ୍ୟରେ, ବେଳରେ, ବେଳେ

The sun gives us light during the day. **2** at some time while something else is happening ଠିକ୍ ସେତିକି ବେଳେ, ଆଉ କିଛି ଘଟୁଥିବା ସମୟରେ, ବେଳରେ, ବେଳେ *I fell asleep during the film.* ○ *She went shopping during the lunch break.*

dusk /dʌsk/ *noun* (*no plural*) the time in the evening when it is nearly dark ସନ୍ଧ୍ୟା ବେଳର ଝାପ୍‌ସା ସମୟ, ପ୍ରଦୋଷ, ଗୋଧୂଳି ➪ **dawn** ଦେଖନ୍ତୁ ।

Dussehra *noun* an autumn festival of the Hindus that celebrates the victory of good over evil ଦଶହରା, ଦୁର୍ଗାପୂଜା

dust /dʌst/ *noun* (*no plural*) dry dirt that is like powder ଧୂଳି, ଗୁଣ୍ଡ, ରେଣୁ *The old table was covered in dust.*

dust *verb* (**dusts, dusting, dusted**) take dust off something with a cloth ଧୂଳି ପୋଛି ସଫା କରିବା *I dusted the furniture.*

dustbin /ˈdʌstbɪn/ *noun* a container that you use to put rubbish in ଘରର ଅଳିଆ ରଖିବା ପାତ୍ର ବା ବଡ଼ ଡବା

duster /ˈdʌstə(r)/ *noun* a cloth that you use for taking the dust off furniture ଧୂଳି ଝଡ଼ାପୋଛା କରିବା କନା

dusty /ˈdʌsti/ *adjective* (**dustier, dustiest**) covered with dust ଧୂଳିଆ, ଧୂଳି ପରିପୂର୍ଣ୍ଣ, ଧୂଳିମୟ *The furniture was very dusty.*

duty /ˈdju:ti/ *noun* (*plural* **duties**) something that you must do because it is part of your job or because you think it is right କର୍ତ୍ତବ୍ୟ *It's your duty to look after your parents when they get older.*

DVD /ˌdi: vi: ˈdi:/ *noun* a disk on which information including pictures and sounds can be stored. This is played on a computer or a DVD player ଚିତ୍ର, ଧ୍ୱନି, ତଥ୍ୟ ଇତ୍ୟାଦି ଗଚ୍ଛିତ ରଖାଯାଉଥିବା ଚକତି ଯାହା କମ୍ପ୍ୟୁଟର୍ ବା ଡିଭିଡ଼ି ଯନ୍ତ୍ରରେ ଲଗାଇ ଦେଖା ବା ଶୁଣାଯାଇପାରେ ✪ DVD ର ବିସ୍ତୃତ ରୂପ **digital videodisc** ବା **digital versatile disk** ।

dwarf /dwɔ:f/ *noun* (*plural* **dwarfs** ବା **dwarves** /dwɔ:vz/) a person, animal or plant of a much smaller size than is the usual ବାଙ୍ଗର, ବାମନ, ଖର୍ବକାୟ ମଣିଷ, ପଶୁ ବା ଉଦ୍ଭିଦ

dwarf planet *noun* a nearly round thing in space that moves around the sun and is smaller than a planet ଏକ ଛୋଟ ଗ୍ରହ ମହାକାଶରେ ପ୍ରାୟ ଗୋଲାକୃତି ବିଶିଷ୍ଟ ଏକ ବସ୍ତୁ ଯିଏ ସୂର୍ଯ୍ୟ ଚାରିପଟେ ବୁଲୁଛି ଓ ଆକାରରେ ଗ୍ରହଠାରୁ ସାନ ଅଛି ➪ **Pluto** ଦେଖନ୍ତୁ ।

dwell /dwel/ *verb* (**dwells, dwelling, dwelt** /dwelt/ ବା **dwelled, has dwelt** ବା **has dwelled**) stay at a place ବାସ କରିବା, ବସବାସ କରି ରହିବା *The old farmer dwelt in a small hut.*

dwelling /ˈdwelɪŋ/ *noun* the house in which one lives ଘର, ଗୃହ, ବାସସ୍ଥାନ *a humble dwelling*

dye /daɪ/ *noun* a substance that you use to change the colour of something, for example cloth or hair ରଙ୍ଗ

dye *verb* (**dyes, dyeing, dyed**) change the colour of something ରଙ୍ଗ କରିବା, ରଙ୍ଗେଇବା *She dyed her hair red!*

dying ଶବ୍ଦ **die** ର ଏକ ଧାତୁରୂପ

dynamite /ˈdaɪnəmaɪt / *noun* a powerful explosive that is used for bringing down old buildings or making tunnels through mountains ଏକ ଉଚ୍ଚ ଶକ୍ତି ବିଶିଷ୍ଟ ବିସ୍ଫୋରକ ପଦାର୍ଥ, ଡାଇନାମାଇଟ୍ (ଯାହା ଘର ଇତ୍ୟାଦି ଭାଙ୍ଗିବାରେ ବା ପଥର, ପାହାଡ଼ ଭାଙ୍ଗିବାରେ ବ୍ୟବହାର କରାଯାଏ)

dynasty /ˈdɪnəsti/ *noun* (*plural* **dynasties**) a line of rulers belonging to the same family ରାଜବଂଶ *the Mughal dynasty*

E e

each /iːtʃ/ *adjective, pronoun* every person or thing in a group ପ୍ରତ୍ୟେକ *Each student has to buy a book and a cassette.*

each other words that show that somebody does the same thing as another person ପରସ୍ପର *Geet and Sarita looked at each other.*

eager /ˈiːɡə(r)/ *adjective* if you are eager to do something, you want to do it very much ବ୍ୟଗ୍ର, ଇଚ୍ଛୁକ, ଉତ୍ସୁକ *She's eager to help with the party.*

eagerly *adverb* ବ୍ୟଗ୍ର ଭାବରେ *The children were waiting eagerly for the film to begin.*

eagle /ˈiːɡl/ *noun* a large bird that catches and eats small birds and animals ଏକ ବଡ଼ ଶୀକାରୀ ପକ୍ଷୀ, ଇଗଲ୍ ➪ **kite**[2] ଦେଖନ୍ତୁ ।

ear /ɪə(r)/ *noun* one of the parts of a person or an animal that is used for hearing କାନ, କର୍ଣ୍ଣ ➪ ଚିତ୍ର ପାଇଁ **face** ଦେଖନ୍ତୁ ।

eardrum /ˈɪədrʌm/ *noun* a thin tightly stretched skin inside the ear that allows you to hear କାନର ପରଦା, କର୍ଣ୍ଣପଟହ

early /ˈɜːli/ *adjective, adverb* (**earlier, earliest**) **1** before the usual or right time ନିର୍ଦ୍ଦିଷ୍ଟ ସମୟ ପୂର୍ବରୁ (ଘଟିତ) ବା ଆଗତୁରା (ହୋଇଥିବା) *The train arrived ten minutes early.* **2** near the beginning of a time ଆରମ୍ଭ ସମୟରେ *early afternoon* ✪ ବିପରୀତ **late**

earn /ɜːn/ *verb* (**earns, earning, earned**) get money by working ରୋଜଗାର କରିବା, ଅର୍ଜନ କରିବା *How much do teachers earn in your country?*

earnest /ˈɜːnɪst/ *adjective* very serious and keen; hardworking ଆନ୍ତରିକତା ପୂର୍ଣ୍ଣ; ପରିଶ୍ରମୀ

in earnest if you do something in earnest, you are serious about doing it and put in a lot of effort to complete it ଆନ୍ତରିକ ଭାବରେ, ଦୃଢ଼ମନରେ *The children are preparing for their exams in earnest.*

earring /ˈɪərɪŋ/ *noun* a pretty thing that you wear on your ear କାନଫୁଲ *a pair of earrings*

earth[1] /ɜːθ/ *noun* (*no plural*) **1** (**Earth** ମଧ୍ୟ) this world; the planet that we live on ପୃଥିବୀ, ବସୁମତି, ଧରା *The moon travels round the earth.* ➪ ଚିତ୍ର ପାଇଁ **solar system** ଦେଖନ୍ତୁ । **2** what you grow plants in; soil ମାଟି, ଭୂମି, ମୃତ୍ତିକା *Cover the seeds with earth.*

earth[2] /ɜːθ/ *verb* make electronic machines safe by connecting them to the ground with a wire ବିଦ୍ୟୁତ୍ ପରିପଥର ଭୂ-ସଂଯୋଗ କରିବା (ବିଦ୍ୟୁତ୍‌ଚାଳିତ ଯନ୍ତ୍ରପାତିର ସୁରକ୍ଷା ପାଇଁ) *Earthing makes the supply of electricity safe.*

earthquake /ˈɜːθkweɪk/ *noun* a sudden strong shaking of the ground ଭୂକମ୍ପ, ଭୂମିକମ୍ପ

earthworm /ˈɜːθwɜːm/ *noun* a long thin worm that lives in the soil ଜିଆ, କେଞ୍ଚୁଆ ➪ ଚିତ୍ର ପାଇଁ **invertebrate** ଦେଖନ୍ତୁ ।

ease /iːz/ *noun* (*no plural*)
with ease with no difficulty ସହଜରେ, ସୁବିଧାରେ *She answered the questions with ease.*

easily /ˈiːzəli/ *adverb* with no difficulty ସହଜରେ, ସୁବିଧାରେ *The cinema was almost empty, so we easily found a seat.*

east /iːst/ *noun* (*no plural*) where the sun comes up in the morning ପୂର୍ବଦିଗ, ସୂର୍ଯ୍ୟ ଉଦୟ ହେବା ଦିଗ *Which way is east?* ➪ **west** ଦେଖନ୍ତୁ। ➪ ଚିତ୍ର ପାଇଁ **north** କିଂବା ପୃଷ୍ଠା ଦେଖନ୍ତୁ।
east *adjective*, *adverb* ପୂର୍ବ ପଟର; ପୂର୍ବ ଦିଗକୁ *They live on the east coast of Scotland.* ○ *We travelled east from Ahmedabad to Kolkata.*
eastern *adjective* in or of the east part of a place ପୂର୍ବଦିଗବର୍ତ୍ତୀ, ପୂର୍ବ *eastern India*

Easter /ˈiːstə(r)/ *noun* (*no plural*) a Sunday in March or April, and the days around it, when Christians remember Christ's death and His coming back to life ମାର୍ଚ୍ଚ ବା ଏପ୍ରିଲ୍ ମାସରେ ପଡୁଥିବା ଗୁଡ୍‌ଫ୍ରାଇଡେ ପର ରବିବାର ଯେଉଁଦିନ ଯୀଶୁଖ୍ରୀଷ୍ଟ ମୃତ୍ୟୁପରେ ପୁନରୁତ୍ଥାନ ଲାଭ କଲେ; ଏହି ଦିନର ଉତ୍ସବ

easy /ˈiːzi/ *adjective* (**easier, easiest**) if something is easy, you can do or understand it without any difficulty ସହଜ *The homework was very easy to do.* ✪ ବିପରୀତ **difficult** ବା **hard**[1]**2**
take it easy, take things easy not worry or work too much ଧୀରେ ସୁସ୍ଥେ କରିବା, ବ୍ୟସ୍ତ ନହେବା, ଆରାମ କରିବା *After my exams, I'm going to take it easy for a few days.*

eat /iːt/ *verb* (**eats, eating, ate** /et/, **has eaten** /ˈiːtn/) take in food through your mouth ଖାଇବା *Have you eaten all the chocolates?*

echo /ˈekəʊ/ *noun* (*plural* **echoes**) a sound that a wall sends back so that you hear it again ପ୍ରତିଧ୍ୱନି, ପ୍ରତିଦାନ
echo *verb* (**echoes, echoing, echoed**) ପ୍ରତିଧ୍ୱନିତ ହେବା *His footsteps echoed in the empty hall.*

eclipse /ɪˈklɪps/ *noun* **1** a time when the moon comes between the earth and the sun so that we cannot see the sun's light. This is called a **solar eclipse** ପରାଗ। ଚନ୍ଦ୍ର ପୃଥିବୀ ଓ ସୂର୍ଯ୍ୟଙ୍କ ମଝିରେ ଏକ ରେଖାରେ ରହିଲେ ପୃଥିବୀରୁ ସୂର୍ଯ୍ୟ ପୂରା ବା ଆଂଶିକ ଭାବେ ଦିଶିବେ ନାହିଁ; ଏହି ଘଟଣାକୁ ସୂର୍ଯ୍ୟପରାଗ କହନ୍ତି **2** a time when the earth comes between the sun and the moon so that we cannot see the moon's light. This is called a **lunar eclipse** ଗ୍ରହଣ। ପୃଥିବୀ ଚନ୍ଦ୍ର ଓ ସୂର୍ଯ୍ୟଙ୍କ ମଝିରେ ଏକ ରେଖାରେ ରହିଲେ ପୃଥିବୀର ଛାଇ ଚନ୍ଦ୍ର ଉପରେ

solar eclipse

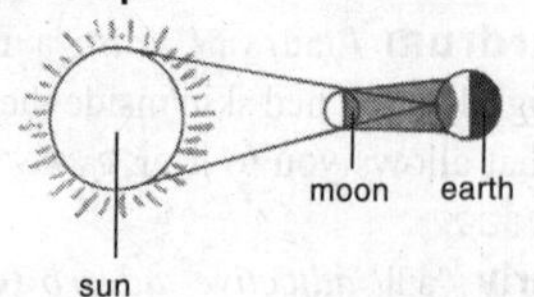

lunar eclipse

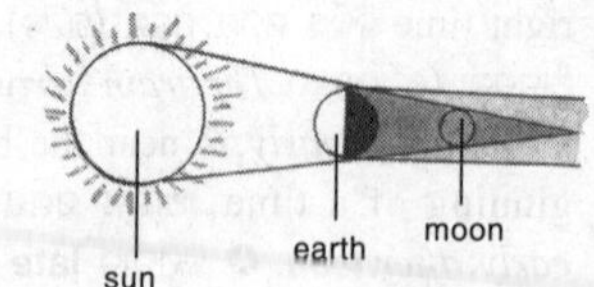

ପଢ଼ିବାରୁ ଚନ୍ଦ୍ର ପୂରା ବା ଆଂଶିକ ଭାବେ ଦିଶିବେ ନାହିଁ; ଏହାକୁ ଚନ୍ଦ୍ରଗ୍ରହଣ କହନ୍ତି

ecology /ɪˈkɒlədʒi/ *noun* (*no plural*) the study of the relation between living things and everything around them ପରିବେଶ ବିଜ୍ଞାନ; ପ୍ରାଣୀ ଓ ପରିବେଶ ମଧ୍ୟରେ ଥିବା ସୁସମ୍ପର୍କ ବିଷୟର ବିଜ୍ଞାନ

economic /ˌiːkəˈnɒmɪk/ *adjective* connected with managing money, business, industry, etc of a country, state or an area ଅର୍ଥନୈତିକ, ଅର୍ଥଶାସ୍ତ୍ର ସମ୍ବନ୍ଧୀୟ *economic problems of the state*

economy /ɪˈkɒnəmi/ *noun* (*plural* **economies**) the way that a country spends its money and makes, buys and sells things (ଦେଶର) ଅର୍ଥବ୍ୟବସ୍ଥା, ଦେଶର ସମ୍ପଦର ଅବସ୍ଥା ଓ ତାର ପରିଚାଳନା *the economies of India and Korea*

ecosystem /ˈiːkəʊsɪstəm/ *noun* all the plants and animals living in a particular area considered in relation to their surroundings ପରସ୍ପର ସହ ସଂଶ୍ଳିଷ୍ଟ ଜୈବ ସମାଜ ଓ ଏହାର ପରିବେଶ

edge /edʒ/ *noun* the part along the end or side of something ଧାର, ପ୍ରାନ୍ତ, କଡ଼ *Don't sit on the edge of your chair—you might fall!*

edible /ˈedəbl/ *adjective* safe to be eaten; not poisonous ଖାଇବା ଯୋଗ୍ୟ *edible mushrooms* ✪ ବିପରୀତ **inedible**

edition /ɪˈdɪʃn/ *noun* all the copies of a newspaper, book, etc. printed in the same form at the same time ଏକ ସମୟରେ ମୁଦ୍ରିତ ଗୋଟିଏ ବହି ବା ଖବରକାଗଜର ସବୁ ଖଣ୍ଡ ବା କପି, ସଂସ୍କରଣ *this month's edition of the magazine* ○ *the seventh edition of the dictionary*

editor /ˈedɪtə(r)/ *noun* a person whose job is to prepare or control a magazine, newspaper, book or film ସମ୍ପାଦକ

educate /ˈedʒukeɪt/ *verb* (**educates, educating, educated**) teach somebody about things like reading, writing and mathematics at school or college ଶିକ୍ଷାଦେବା *Where was she educated?*

education /ˌedʒuˈkeɪʃn/ *noun* (*no plural*) teaching somebody about things like reading, writing and mathematics at school or college ନିୟମିତ ଓ ବିଧିବଦ୍ଧ ଶିକ୍ଷା *He had a good education.*

educational *adjective* ଶିକ୍ଷା ସମ୍ବନ୍ଧୀୟ, ଶିକ୍ଷା ବିଷୟକ *an educational video*

eerie /ˈɪəri/ *adjective* unusual and frightening ଅନ୍ଧାରୁଆ, ଅଦ୍ଭୁତ ଓ ଡରମାଡ଼ିଲା ପରି *We heard an eerie sound from inside the house.*

effect /ɪˈfekt/ *noun* a change that happens because of something (କୌଣସି କାର୍ଯ୍ୟର) ପରିଣାମ, ଫଳାଫଳ *We are studying the effects of heat on different metals.*

have an effect on something make something change ପ୍ରଭାବ ପକାଇବା *His change of job had a good effect on him.*

effective /ɪˈfektɪv/ *adjective* something that is effective works well ଫଳପ୍ରଦ, କାର୍ଯ୍ୟକାରୀ *Cycling is an* *effective way of keeping fit.* ✪ ବିପରୀତ **ineffective**

efficient /ɪˈfɪʃnt/ *adjective* a person or thing that is efficient works well and in the best way ଦକ୍ଷ, ସୁଦକ୍ଷ *an efficient manager* ✪ ବିପରୀତ **inefficient**

effigy /ˈefɪdʒi/ *noun* (*plural* **effigies**) an ugly model of someone which is made in order to make fun of them କୌଣସି ବ୍ୟକ୍ତିଙ୍କର ବେଢ଼ଙ୍ଗିଆ ପ୍ରତିମୂର୍ତ୍ତି *On Dussehra, the effigies of Ravana, Kumbhakarna and Meghnada are set on fire.*

effort /ˈefət/ *noun* trying hard to do something; hard work ଉଦ୍ୟମ, ଚେଷ୍ଟା, ପ୍ରୟାସ *Thank you for all your efforts.*

make an effort try hard to do something ଚେଷ୍ଟା କରିବା, ପ୍ରୟାସ କରିବା

e.g. *abbreviation* for example ଉଦାହରଣ ସ୍ୱରୂପ, ଯଥା *She travels to a lot of European countries, e.g. Spain, Greece and Italy.*

egg /eg/ *noun* **1** a round or oval thing that has a baby bird, fish, insect or reptile inside it ପକ୍ଷୀ, ମାଛ, ପୋକ ବା ସରୀସୃପର ଅଣ୍ଡା, ଡିମ୍ବ *The duck has laid an egg.* **2** an egg from a hen that we eat କୁକୁଡ଼ା ଅଣ୍ଡା *Do you want eggs and toast for breakfast?*

eight /eɪt/ *number* 8 ୮ (8) ସଂଖ୍ୟା, ଆଠ

eighth /eɪtθ/ *adjective, adverb, noun* **1** 8th ଅଷ୍ଟମ **2** one of eight equal parts of something; $\frac{1}{8}$ ଆଠ ଭାଗରୁ ଏକ ଭାଗ; $\frac{୧}{୮}$

eighteen /ˌeɪˈtiːn/ *number* 18 ୧୮ ସଂଖ୍ୟା, ଅଠର

eighteenth /ˌeɪˈtiːnθ/ *adjective, adverb, noun* 18th ଅଠରତମ, ଅଷ୍ଟଦଶାଂଶ

eighty /ˈeɪti/ *number* **1** 80 ୮୦ ସଂଖ୍ୟା, ଅଶି **2 the eighties** (*plural*) the numbers, years or temperatures between 80 and 89, 80 ଠାରୁ 89 ପର୍ଯ୍ୟନ୍ତ ସଂଖ୍ୟା ବା ବର୍ଷ

eightieth /ˈeɪtiəθ/ *adjective, adverb, noun* 80th ଅଶିତମ

either[1] /ˈaɪðə(r), ˈiːðə(r)/ *adjective, pronoun* **1** one of two things or people ଦୁଇଟି ପଦାର୍ଥ ବା ବ୍ୟକ୍ତି ମଧ୍ୟରୁ ଗୋଟିଏ *There is cake and ice cream—you can have either.* **2** each ଉଭୟ *There are trees along either side of the street.*

either[2] /ˈaɪðə(r), ˈiːðə(r)/ *adverb* (used in sentences with 'not') also (ବାକ୍ୟରେ 'not' ସହିତ ବ୍ୟବହୃତ ହୁଏ) ମଧ୍ୟ, ବି *Lopa can't swim and I can't (swim) either.*

either ... or words that show two different things or people that you can choose ଏକ ସମ୍ଭାବନା ଭାବେ, କିମ୍ବା, ନହେଲେ *You can have either tea or coffee.*

elaborate /ɪˈlæbərət/ *adjective* not simple; with a lot of different parts ବହୁ ଅଂଶ ବିଶିଷ୍ଟ, ପୁଙ୍ଖାନୁପୁଙ୍ଖ, ସବିଶେଷ *an elaborate meal*

elastic /ɪˈlæstɪk/ *noun* (*no plural*) material that becomes longer when you pull it and then goes back to its usual size ଯାହା ଟଣା ବା ବଙ୍କା ହୋଇ ପାରୁଥିଲେ ମଧ୍ୟ ପୂର୍ବାବସ୍ଥାକୁ ଫେରିଆସେ। ସ୍ଥିତି ସ୍ଥାପକ *His trousers have elastic at the top.*

elbow /ˈelbəʊ/ *noun* the part in the middle of your arm where it bends କହୁଣି ➪ ଚିତ୍ର ପାଇଁ **body** ଦେଖନ୍ତୁ।

elder /ˈeldə(r)/ *adjective* older of two people of the same family ଦୁଇ ଜଣଙ୍କ ମଧ୍ୟରୁ ବୟସରେ ବଡ଼ *My elder brother lives in Hyderabad and the younger one lives in Jaipur.*

elder or **older** ?

ଦୁଇ ବ୍ୟକ୍ତି ବା ପଦାର୍ଥ ଆୟୁ ବିଷୟରେ ତୁଳନା କଲାବେଳେ ଆମେ ସାଧାରଣତଃ **older** ବ୍ୟବହାର କରୁ —
My sister is older than me. ○ *That building is older than this one.*
Elder ଶବ୍ଦଟା ଗୋଟିଏ ପରିବାରର ଦୁଇ ବ୍ୟକ୍ତିଙ୍କ ବୟସ ତୁଳନା କଲାବେଳେ ବ୍ୟବହୃତ ହୁଏ। ଯିଏ **elder** ସେ ବୟସରେ ବଡ଼ — *my elder sister* (କିନ୍ତୁ *My sister is elder than me.* ଭୁଲ୍ ହେବ)

elderly /ˈeldəli/ *adjective* quite old ବୁଢ଼ା, ବୃଦ୍ଧ, ପ୍ରୌଢ଼, ବୟସ୍କ *She is elderly and can't hear very well.*

eldest /ˈeldɪst/ *adjective* oldest of three or more people of the same family ପରିବାରର ତିନି ବା ତାଠାରୁ ଅଧିକ ଲୋକଙ୍କ ମଧ୍ୟରେ ବୟସରେ ସବୁଠାରୁ ବଡ଼ *Their eldest son is at university but the other two are at school.*

elect /ɪˈlekt/ *verb* (**elects, electing, elected**) choose somebody to be a leader (by **voting**) ନିର୍ବାଚନ କରିବା *The new president was elected in 2005.*

election /ɪˈlekʃn/ *noun* a time when people choose somebody to be a leader by voting ନିର୍ବାଚନ *The election will be held on Wednesday.*

electric /ɪˈlektrɪk/ *adjective* using or producing electricity ବୈଦ୍ୟୁତିକ, ବିଦ୍ୟୁତ୍ ଚାଳିତ *an electric guitar* ○ *an electric switch*

electrical /ɪˈlektrɪkl/ *adjective* using or relating to electricity ବୈଦ୍ୟୁତିକ, ସମ୍ବନ୍ଧୀୟ *electrical appliances*

electrician /ɪˌlekˈtrɪʃn/ *noun* a person whose job is to work with electricity ବିଦ୍ୟୁତ୍ ମିସ୍ତ୍ରୀ *This light isn't working—we need an electrician to mend it.*

electrician

electricity /ɪˌlekˈtrɪsəti/ *noun* (*no plural*) power that comes through wires. Electricity can make heat and light, and can make machines work ବିଦ୍ୟୁତ୍‌ଶକ୍ତି, ବିଦ୍ୟୁତ୍ ଏହା ତାପ ଓ ଆଲୋକ ଦେଇପାରେ ଓ ଯନ୍ତ୍ର ଚଳାଇପାରେ

electronic /ɪˌlekˈtrɒnɪk/ *adjective* Things like computers, calculators and radios are electronic. They use **microchips** or **transistors** to make them work ଇଲେକ୍‌ଟ୍ରୋନିକ୍ ଉପକରଣ ସମ୍ବନ୍ଧୀୟ। କମ୍ପ୍ୟୁଟର୍, କାଲକୁଲେଟର୍। ରେଡ଼ିଓ ଇତ୍ୟାଦି ଇଲେକ୍‌ଟ୍ରୋନିକ୍ ଯନ୍ତ୍ର। ଯାକୁ ଚଳାଇବାକୁ ମାଇକ୍ରୋଚିପ୍ ବା ଟ୍ରାନ୍‌ଜିଷ୍ଟର୍‌ଏଥିରେ ଲଗା ଯାଇଥାଏ *an electronic calculator*

electronics /ɪˌlekˈtrɒnɪks/ *noun* (*no plural*) using **microchips** or **transistors** to make things like computers, calculators and radios

ମାଇକ୍ରୋଚିପ୍, ଟ୍ରାନ୍‌ଜିଷ୍ଟର୍ ଇତ୍ୟାଦିର ପ୍ରସ୍ତୁତି ଓ ପ୍ରୟୋଗ ବିଦ୍ୟା *the electronics industry*

elegant /ˈelɪgənt/ *adjective* with a beautiful style or shape; showing or having good taste ରୂପ ଓ ଆକାରରେ ସୁନ୍ଦର; ଆଚରଣରେ ସୁନ୍ଦର ବା ମନୋହର *an elegant black dress*

element /ˈelɪmənt/ *noun* a simple chemical substance, for example oxygen or gold ଏକ ସରଳ ମୂଳବସ୍ତୁ ବା ଉପାଦାନ, ଯଥା: ଅମ୍ଳଜାନ ବା ସ୍ୱର୍ଣ୍ଣ *Water is made of the elements hydrogen and oxygen.*

elementary /ˌelɪˈmentri/ *adjective* for beginners; not difficult to do or understand ପ୍ରାଥମିକ, ପ୍ରାରମ୍ଭିକ; ସରଳ *an elementary dictionary*

elephant /ˈelɪfənt/ *noun* a very big wild animal from Asia or Africa, with a long nose (called a **trunk**) ହାତୀ, ହସ୍ତୀ ➪ ଚିତ୍ର ପାଇଁ **mammal** ଦେଖନ୍ତୁ।

eleven /ɪˈlevn/ *number* 11 ୧୧ ସଂଖ୍ୟା, ଏଗାର

eleventh /ɪˈlevnθ/ *adjective, adverb, noun* 11th ଏକାଦଶତମ

eligible /ˈelɪdʒəbl/ *adjective* suitable for something or to do something ଯୋଗ୍ୟ, ଚୟନଯୋଗ୍ୟ *The eligible age for admission to nursery is four years.*

eligibility *noun* (*no plural*) ଯୋଗ୍ୟତା, ଚୟନଯୋଗ୍ୟତା *the eligibility to vote*

eliminate /ɪˈlɪmɪneɪt/ *verb* (**eliminates, eliminating, eliminated**) **1** throw away something or get rid of something that you no longer require ବାହାର କରିଦେବା, ବାଦ୍‌ଦେବା, କାଢ଼ିଦେବା *eliminate harmful wastes from the body* **2** defeat a person or a team in a sport or competition so that they cannot participate further in that event ଖେଳରେ ବ୍ୟକ୍ତି ବା ଦଳକୁ ହରାଇ ପ୍ରତିଯୋଗିତାରୁ ବାଦ୍ ଦେବା *Their team was eliminated in the very first round of the quiz competition.*

else /els/ *adverb* **1** more; extra ଅଧିକ *What else would you like?* **2** different; other ଭିନ୍ନ, ଅନ୍ୟ *The Grand Hotel was full, so we stayed somewhere else.*

> ✪ ଆମେ **else** ବ୍ୟବହାର କରିବା **anybody, nothing** ଓ **somewhere** ପରେ ଏବଂ **where** ଓ **who** ପରି ପ୍ରଶ୍ନବାଚକ ଶବ୍ଦ ପରେ ।

elsewhere /ˌelsˈweə(r)/ *adverb* in or to another place ଅନ୍ୟତ୍ର, ଅନ୍ୟସ୍ଥାନକୁ, ଅନ୍ୟସ୍ଥାନରେ *He can't find a job in Bhopal so he's looking elsewhere for work.*

email /ˈiːmeɪl/ *noun* **1** (*no plural*) a way of sending messages to people through computers ପରସ୍ପର ସହ ଯୋଗାଯୋଗ ଥିବା କମ୍ପ୍ୟୁଟର ପଦ୍ଧତି (ଇଣ୍ଟରନେଟ୍) ସାହାଯ୍ୟରେ ଖବର, ଚିଠି ଇତ୍ୟାଦି ପଠାଇବା, ଇ-ମେଲ୍ ✪ Email ହେଲା **electronic mail** ର ସଂକ୍ଷିପ୍ତ ରୂପ। **2** (*plural* **emails**) a message sent by email ଇ-ମେଲ୍ ଦ୍ୱାରା ପଠାଯାଇଥିବା ବାର୍ତ୍ତା

embarrass /ɪmˈbærəs/ *verb* (**embarrasses, embarrassing, embarrassed**) make somebody feel shy or worried about what other people think of them (କୌଣସି ବ୍ୟକ୍ତିଙ୍କୁ) ଅସୁବିଧାରେ

ପକାଇବା, ଲଜ୍ଜିତ କରିବା, ଅପ୍ରତିଭ କରିବା *Mani embarrassed his friends by singing very loudly on the bus.*

embarrassing *adjective* something that is embarrassing makes you feel embarrassed ଅସୁବିଧାରେ ପକାଇଲା ପରି, ଲଜ୍ଜିତ କଲାପରି *I couldn't remember her name—it was so embarrassing!*

embarrassment *noun* (*no plural*) the feeling that you have when you are embarrassed; a person or thing that embarrasses you ଅସୁବିଧା, ଲଜ୍ୟା *His face was red with embarrassment.*

embassy /ˈembəsi/ *noun* (*plural* **embassies**) a group of people led by an **ambassador**, whose job is to speak and act for their government in another country ରାଜଦୂତ ଓ ତାଙ୍କ ସହକର୍ମୀବୃନ୍ଦ ଯେଉଁମାନେ ଅନ୍ୟ ଦେଶରେ ନିଜ ଦେଶର ପ୍ରତିନିଧିତ୍ୱ କରନ୍ତି; ରାଜଦୂତଙ୍କ କାର୍ଯ୍ୟାଳୟ, ଦୂତାବାସ *To get a visa to travel in America, you should apply to the American embassy.*

embroidery /ɪmˈbrɔɪdəri/ *noun* (*no plural*) the skill of sewing patterns on cloth with thread ଛୁଞ୍ଚସୂତାରେ କନାଉପରେ କାରୁକାର୍ଯ୍ୟ ଏମ୍ବ୍ରୟଡରୀ

embroidered *adjective* with embroidery on it ଏମ୍ବ୍ରୟଡରୀ କରାଯାଇଥିବା *embroidered jacket*

embryo /ˈembriəʊ/ *noun* an animal or a plant in its very early stages of development before birth ପଶୁର ଗର୍ଭ ଭିତରେ ଥିବା ଭ୍ରୁଣ, ଗର୍ଭାଙ୍କୁର; ଉଦ୍ଭିଦର ମଞ୍ଜିଭିତରେ ଥିବା ଅଙ୍କୁର

emergency /iˈmɜːdʒənsi/ *noun* (*plural* **emergencies**) sudden dangerous situation, when people must help quickly ଜରୁରୀ ଅବସ୍ଥା (ବିପଦ, ଦୁର୍ଘଟଣା, ଦ୍ୱନ୍ଦ ଇତ୍ୟାଦି ଯୋଗୁଁ) *Come quickly, doctor! It's an emergency!*

emotion /ɪˈməʊʃn/ *noun* a strong feeling, for example love or anger ପ୍ରବଳ ଆବେଗ (ପ୍ରେମ, କ୍ରୋଧ, ଉତ୍କଣ୍ଠା ଇତ୍ୟାଦି)

emotional *adjective* if you are emotional, you have strong feelings and you show them ଆବେଗପୂର୍ଣ୍ଣ *He got very emotional when we said goodbye.*

emperor /ˈempərə(r)/ *noun* a man who rules a group of countries (called an **empire**) ସମ୍ରାଟ, ଚକ୍ରବର୍ତ୍ତୀ, ସାର୍ବଭୌମ ଶାସକ ➪ **empress** ଦେଖନ୍ତୁ।

emphasis /ˈemfəsɪs/ *noun* (*plural* **emphases** /ˈemfəsiːz/) special importance given to something କୌଣସି ବିଷୟକୁ ଦିଆଯାଇଥିବା ପ୍ରାଧାନ୍ୟ, ଗୁରୁତ୍ୱ *There is a lot of emphasis on sports in our school.*

emphasize /ˈemfəsaɪz/ *verb* (**emphasizes, emphasizing, emphasized**) say something strongly to show that it is important ଗୁରୁତ୍ୱ ଆରୋପ କରିବା, ଜୋର୍ ଦେବା *She emphasized the importance of hard work.*

empire /ˈempaɪə(r)/ *noun* a group of states or countries that are controlled by one ruler or one country ସାମ୍ରାଜ୍ୟ, ଏକାଧିପତ୍ୟ ଭାବରେ ଶାସିତ ଅଞ୍ଚଳ *the Mughal Empire*

employ /ɪmˈplɔɪ/ *verb* (**employs, employing, employed**) pay somebody to do work for you (ବ୍ୟକ୍ତିଙ୍କୁ) କାମରେ ନିଯୁକ୍ତ କରିବା, ଚାକିରି ଦେବା *The factory employs 800 workers.*

employee /ɪmˈplɔɪiː/ *noun* a person who is paid to work କର୍ମଚାରୀ *This company treats its employees very well.*

employer /ɪmˈplɔɪə(r)/ *noun* a person or company that pays other people to do work ଚାକିରୀ ଦେଇଥିବା ବ୍ୟକ୍ତି ବା ସଂସ୍ଥା, ମାଲିକ

employment /ɪmˈplɔɪmənt/ *noun* (*no plural*) having a job that you are paid to do ନିଯୁକ୍ତି, ଚାକିରି *He went to Mumbai and found employment as a taxi driver.* ➪ **unemployment** ଦେଖନ୍ତୁ ।

empress /ˈemprəs/ *noun* (*plural* **empresses**) a woman who rules a group of countries (called an **empire**), or the wife of an emperor ମହାରାଣୀ, ସାମ୍ରାଜ୍ଞୀ ➪ **emperor** ଦେଖନ୍ତୁ ।

empty[1] /ˈempti/ *adjective* (**emptier, emptiest**) with nothing in it or nobody inside it ଖାଲି, ଶୂନ୍ୟ; ରିକ୍ତ *My glass is empty.* ○ *The cinema was almost empty.* ✪ ବିପରୀତ **full 1**

empty[2] /ˈempti/ *verb* (**empties, emptying, emptied, has emptied**) take everything out of something; become empty ଖାଲି କରିବା, ସବୁକାଢ଼ି ଦେବା

emu /ˈiːmjuː/ *noun* a tall heavy Australian bird that cannot fly. It has long legs which help it to run very fast ଉଡ଼ି ପାରୁନଥିବା ଏକ ଡେଙ୍ଗା ଅଷ୍ଟ୍ରେଲିଆର ପକ୍ଷୀ, ଏମ୍ୟୁ

enable /ɪˈneɪbl/ *verb* (**enables, enabling, enabled**) make it possible for somebody to do something (ବ୍ୟକ୍ତିଙ୍କୁ) କାମ କରିବା ପାଇଁ ସାମର୍ଥ୍ୟ ବା ଅଧିକାର ଦେବା, କର୍ମକ୍ଷମ କରିବା *Your help enabled me to finish the job.*

enamel /ɪˈnæml/ *noun* **1** the hard white outer layer of a tooth ଦାନ୍ତର କଠିଣ ଧଳା ବହିରାବଣ, ଏନାମେଲ୍ **2** a substance that is melted and put on a metal object or a clay pot to give it a hard shiny surface to protect or decorate it ଧାତୁ ବା ମାଟି ପାତ୍ରରେ ପ୍ରଲେପ ପାଇଁ ବ୍ୟବହୃତ ଏକ କାଚ ପରି ପଦାର୍ଥ

enchanted /ɪnˈtʃɑːntɪd/ *adjective* under the power of magic ବିମୁଗ୍ଧ, ବିମୋହିତ, କୁହୁକଭରା *an enchanted castle*

enclose /ɪnˈkləʊz/ *verb* (**encloses, enclosing, enclosed**) **1** put something inside a letter or parcel କୌଣସି ଆଧାରରେ ରଖିବା, ଯଥା: ଲଫାପାରେ ଚିଠି ଭର୍ତ୍ତି କରିବା *I am enclosing a cheque for Rs 5,000.* **2** put something, for example a wall or fence, around a place on all sides (କାନ୍ଥ ବା ବାଡ଼ ଦ୍ୱାରା) ଘେରାଇବା, ବେଷ୍ଟନ କରିବା *The house is enclosed by a high wall.*

enclosure /ɪnˈkləʊʒə(r)/ *noun* a piece of land with a fence around it, often for keeping animals ଘେର, ଘେରା ଯାଇଥିବା ଜାଗା (ଯଥା: ଜନ୍ତୁଜାନ୍ତାଙ୍କୁ ସୁରକ୍ଷିତ ରଖିବା ପାଇଁ ଘେର)

encounter[1] /ɪnˈkaʊntə(r)/ *verb* (**encounters, encountering, encountered**) meet someone by chance or come across an unpleasant or a difficult situation ଆକସ୍ମିକ ବା ଅପ୍ରତ୍ୟାଶିତ ଭାବରେ କାହା ସହ ସାକ୍ଷାତ ହେବା ବା କୌଣସି ଅସୁବିଧାଜନକ ପରିସ୍ଥିତିର ସମ୍ମୁଖୀନ ହେବା *He encountered many hardships in life.*

encounter[2] /ɪnˈkaʊntə(r)/ *noun* an unexpected meeting with somebody or an unpleasant situation ଅପ୍ରତ୍ୟାଶିତ ସାକ୍ଷାତ ବା ଅସୁବିଧା ଜନକ ପରିସ୍ଥିତିର ସମ୍ମୁଖୀନତା *The divers had an encounter with sharks.*

encourage /ɪnˈkʌrɪdʒ/ *verb* (**encourages, encouraging, encouraged**) give somebody hope or help so that they do something or continue doing something ଉତ୍ସାହିତ କରିବା, ସାହାସ ଦେବା *We encouraged him to write a book about his adventures.* ✪ ବିପରୀତ **discourage**

encouragement *noun* (*no plural*) giving somebody hope or help so that they do something or continue doing something ଉତ୍ସାହ, ଉତ୍ସାହନ, ପ୍ରୋତ୍ସାହନ *Keya's parents gave her a lot of encouragement when she was taking her exams.*

encouraging *adjective* something that is encouraging gives encouragement ଉତ୍ସାହଜନକ *Anu's school report is very encouraging.*

encyclopedia /ɪnˌsaɪkləˈpiːdiə/ *noun* (*plural* **encyclopedias**) a book or set of books that gives information about a lot of different things, usually arranged from A to Z ବିଶ୍ୱକୋଷ, ଜ୍ଞାନକୋଷ, ଜ୍ଞାନର ସବୁବିଭାଗ ଉପରେ କିଛି କିଛି ତଥ୍ୟ ଥିବା ଅକ୍ଷରକ୍ରମରେ ସଜ୍ଜିତ ବହି ବିଦ୍ୟାକଳ୍ପଦ୍ରୁମ; *an encyclopedia of world history*

end[1] /end/ *noun* the furthest or last part of something ଶେଷ, ପରିଶେଷ, ସମାପ୍ତି *Turn right at the end of the street.*

come to an end stop ଶେଷହେବା, ସମାପ୍ତ ହେବା *The holiday was coming to an end and we started to think about going back to work.*

end[2] /end/ *verb* (**ends, ending, ended**) **1** stop ଶେଷହେବା, ସମାପ୍ତ ହେବା *What time does the film end?* **2** finish something ସମାପ୍ତ କରିବା, ଶେଷ କରିବା *We ended our holiday in Karnataka with a trip to Mysore.*

endangered /ɪnˈdeɪndʒəd/ *adjective* if a plant or an animal is becoming endangered, it needs to be protected because it is becoming rare ବିପନ୍ନ, ବିପଦଗ୍ରସ୍ତ, ଲୋପପାଇ ଯାଉଥିବା *The Bengal tiger is an endangered species.*

endearing /ɪnˈdɪərɪŋ/ *adjective* making someone liked by somebody ଆଦରପୂର୍ଣ୍ଣ, ଅନୁରାଗ ଜାତ କରାଉଥିବା *an endearing look*

ending /ˈendɪŋ/ *noun* the last part of something, for example a word, story or film ସମାପ୍ତି, ପରିସମାପ୍ତି *The film has a happy ending.*

endless /ˈendləs/ *adjective* never stopping or finishing; very long ଅସୀମ, ଅନନ୍ତ, ଅବିରତ; ଖୁବ୍ ଦୀର୍ଘ *The journey seemed endless.*

endure /ɪnˈdjʊə(r)/ *verb* (**endures, enduring, endured**) suffer something patiently and without complaining; bear ଦୁଃଖ, କଷ୍ଟ ବା ଅସୁବିଧା ଭୋଗିବା; ସହିବା, ସହନ କରିବା *She endured her illness very bravely.*

enemy /ˈenəmi/ *noun* (*plural* **enemies**) **1** a person who hates you ଶତ୍ରୁ, ବୈରୀ, ରିପୁ *He has many enemies.* **2 the enemy** (*no plural*) the army or country that your country is fighting against in a war ବିରୋଧି ଦେଶ ବା ତାହାର ସୈନ୍ୟବାହିନୀ, ଶତ୍ରୁପକ୍ଷ *The enemy is attacking from the north.*

energetic /ˌenəˈdʒetɪk/ *adjective* full of energy so that you can do a lot of things ଶକ୍ତିସମ୍ପନ୍ନ, ତେଜସ୍ୱୀ

energy /ˈenədʒi/ *noun* (*no plural*) **1** the power that your body has to do things କର୍ମଶକ୍ତି, ବଳ, ତେଜ, କାୟିକ ଶକ୍ତି, ଶକ୍ତି *You need a lot of energy to work with young children.* **2** the power from electricity, gas, coal, etc. that is used to make machines work and to make heat and light ଶକ୍ତି; ବିଦ୍ୟୁତ୍, କୋଇଲା, ବାଷ୍ପ ଇତ୍ୟାଦିରୁ ଉତ୍ପନ୍ନ ଶକ୍ତି *atomic energy*

engage /ɪnˈɡeɪdʒ/ *verb* (**engages, engaging, engaged**) **1** interest somebody and keep them busy ଅଭିନିବେଶ କରାଇବା, ମନୋଯୋଗ କରାଇବା ବ୍ୟସ୍ତ ରଖିବା *The crossword engaged her attention completely.* **2** hire someone to do some work ନିଯୁକ୍ତ କରିବା, କାମରେ ଲଗାଇବା *engage a lawyer for preparing a will*

engaged /ɪnˈɡeɪdʒd/ *adjective* **1** if two people are engaged, they have agreed to get married ବିବାହ ପାଇଁ ସ୍ୱୀକୃତ, ଅଙ୍ଗୀକୃତ, ପ୍ରତିଶ୍ରୁତି **2** (used about a telephone) being used ସେହି ମୁହୂର୍ତ୍ତରେ ବ୍ୟବହୃତ ହେଉଥିବା (ଟେଲିଫୋନ୍) *I tried to phone him but his number was engaged.*

engagement /ɪnˈɡeɪdʒmənt/ *noun* an agreement to marry somebody ବିବାହ ନିର୍ବନ୍ଧ

engine /ˈendʒɪn/ *noun* **1** a machine that makes things move ଇଞ୍ଜିନ୍, ଚଳନଶୀଳ ବା ଚାଳନକ୍ଷମ ଯନ୍ତ୍ର *a car engine* **2** the front part of a train which pulls the rest ରେଳଗାଡ଼ିର ସାମନାରେ ଲାଗିଥିବା ଇଞ୍ଜିନ୍‌ଡବା

a steam **engine**

engineer /ˌendʒɪˈnɪə(r)/ *noun* a person whose job is to plan, make or repair things like machines, roads or bridges ଯନ୍ତ୍ରୀ, ଇଞ୍ଜିନିୟର୍

engineering /ˌendʒɪˈnɪərɪŋ/ *noun* (*no plural*) planning and making things like machines, roads or bridges ଯନ୍ତ୍ର, ରାସ୍ତା, ପୋଲ ଇତ୍ୟାଦି ତିଆରି

କରିବା ବିଦ୍ୟା, ଇଞ୍ଜିନିୟରିଂ *She's studying engineering at college.*

engrave /ɪnˈgreɪv/ *verb* (**engraves, engraving, engraved**) cut or carve words or designs on wood, metal or stone କାଠ, ଧାତୁ ବା ପଥର ଉପରେ ଖୋଦନ କରି ଲେଖିବା ବା ଆଙ୍କିବା *His name was engraved on the pen.*

engraving /ɪnˈgreɪvɪŋ/ *noun* a picture made from a design cut or carved into a wood, metal or stone; a design cut or carved into a piece of wood, metal or stone ଖୋଦିତ ଫଳକରୁ ମୁଦ୍ରିତ ଚିତ୍ର ଇତ୍ୟାଦି; ଏହି ଖୋଦିତ ଫଳକ *The engraving on the stone is beautiful.*

enjoy /ɪnˈdʒɔɪ/ *verb* (**enjoys, enjoying, enjoyed**) like something very much; have fun ଉପଭୋଗ କରିବା, ଆନନ୍ଦ ପାଇବା *I enjoy playing football.*

enjoyable *adjective* something that is enjoyable makes you feel happy ଉପଭୋଗ୍ୟ, ଆନନ୍ଦଦାୟକ, ସୁଖକର *an enjoyable film*

enjoyment /ɪnˈdʒɔɪmənt/ *noun* (*no plural*) a feeling of enjoying something; pleasure ଉପଭୋଗ, ଆନନ୍ଦ, ସୁଖ *I get a lot of enjoyment from travelling.*

enlarge /ɪnˈlɑːdʒ/ *verb* (**enlarges, enlarging, enlarged**) make something bigger ବଡ଼ କରିବା, ବଢ଼ାଇବା, ପ୍ରଶସ୍ତ କରିବା *Can you enlarge this photograph for me?*

enlightenment /ɪnˈlaɪtnmənt/ *noun* (*no plural*) the process of gaining knowledge or understanding of something ଜ୍ଞାନାଲୋକ ପ୍ରାପ୍ତି, ବିଜ୍ଞତା–ପ୍ରାପ୍ତି, ଜ୍ଞାନପ୍ରାପ୍ତି, ଜ୍ଞାନପ୍ରାପ୍ତ ଅବସ୍ଥା, ବିଜ୍ଞାବସ୍ଥା *Gautama Buddha gained enlightenment under the Bodhi tree.*

enormous /ɪˈnɔːməs/ *adjective* very big ପ୍ରକାଣ୍ଡ, ଖୁବ୍ ବଡ଼, ବିଶାଳ *an enormous dog*

enormously /ɪˈnɔːməsli/ *adverb* very or very much ଖୁବ୍ ବେଶୀ, ଅତିଶୟ *Kolkata has changed enormously since my grandmother was a child.*

enough /ɪˈnʌf/ *adjective, adverb, pronoun* as much or as many as you need ଯଥେଷ୍ଟ *There is enough food at home for ten people.*

enquire /ɪnˈkwaɪə(r)/ *verb* (**enquires, enquiring, enquired**) ask ପଚାରିବା, ଖବର ଅନ୍ବେଷଣ କରିବା *I enquired about trains to Lucknow.*

enquiry /ɪnˈkwaɪəri/ *noun* (*plural* **enquiries**) a question that you ask about something ପ୍ରଶ୍ନ ପଚାରିବା ବା ପ୍ରଶ୍ନ ପଚାରି ଖବର ସଂଗ୍ରହ କରିବା ପ୍ରକ୍ରିୟା *There is a counter in every college to answer students' enquiries about admission.*

> ✪ ମନେରଖନ୍ତୁ ! **Enquire** ବଦଳରେ **inquire** ବ୍ୟବହାର କରିବା ଓ **enquiry** ବଦଳରେ **inquiry** ର ବ୍ୟବହାର କରାଯାଇପାରେ ।

enrol /ɪnˈrəʊl/ *verb* (**enrols, enrolling, enrolled**) join a group, for example a school, college, course or club. You usually pay money (a **fee**) when you enrol ବ୍ୟକ୍ତିଙ୍କ ନାମ ତାଲିକାଭୁକ୍ତ

କରିବା, ନାମ ଲେଖାଇବା, ସଭ୍ୟ ଭାବେ, ଗୃହୀତ ହେବା (ସ୍କୁଲ୍, କଲେଜ୍, କ୍ଲବ ବା ଅନ୍ୟ ସଂସ୍ଥାରେ) *I've enrolled for English classes at the college.*

ensure /ɪnˈʃʊə(r)/ *verb* (**ensures, ensuring, ensured**) make certain ସୁନିଶ୍ଚିତ କରିବା *Please ensure that all the lights are switched off before you leave.*

entangled /ɪnˈtæŋgld/ *adjective* caught in something ଛନ୍ଦି ହୋଇଯିବା *The rope was entangled in the bush.*

enter /ˈentə(r)/ *verb* (**enters, entering, entered**) **1** come or go into a place ପ୍ରବେଶ କରିବା, ଭିତରକୁ ଆସିବା ବା ଯିବା *They stood up when she entered the room.* **2** write a name or other information ନାମ ତାଲିକାଭୁକ୍ତ କରିବା, ତାଲିକାରେ ନାଁ ଚଢ଼ାଇବା। *Please enter your name, address and date of birth at the bottom of the form.* **3** give your name to somebody because you want to do something like take an examination or run in a race ପରୀକ୍ଷା, ପ୍ରତିଯୋଗିତା ଇତ୍ୟାଦି ପାଇଁ ନାମ ଦେବା *I entered a competition last month and won a prize.*

entertain /ˌentəˈteɪn/ *verb* (**entertains, entertaining, entertained**) make somebody have a good time ଚିତ୍ତବିନୋଦନ କରିବା, ମନୋରଞ୍ଜନ କରିବା *She entertained us all with her funny stories.*

entertaining /ˌentəˈteɪnɪŋ/ *adjective* funny or interesting ଆନନ୍ଦଦାୟକ

entertainment /ˌentəˈteɪnmənt/ *noun* anything that entertains people, for example films, plays or concerts ମନୋରଞ୍ଜନ, ଆନନ୍ଦଦାୟକ କାର୍ଯ୍ୟକ୍ରମ (ଯଥା: ସିନେମା, ନାଟକ ଇତ୍ୟାଦି) *They watch TV for entertainment.*

enthusiasm /ɪnˈθjuːziæzəm/ *noun* (*no plural*) a strong feeling of liking something or of wanting to do something ପ୍ରବଳ ଆଗ୍ରହ ବା ଉତ୍ସାହ *Her friends share her enthusiasm for music.*

enthusiastic /ɪnˌθjuːziˈæstɪk/ *adjective* full of enthusiasm ଉତ୍ସାହୀ; ଆଗ୍ରହୀ *She's starting a new job next week and she's very enthusiastic about it.*

entire /ɪnˈtaɪə(r)/ *adjective* whole or complete; with no parts missing ସମୁଦାୟ, ପୂରା *We spent the entire day on the beach.*

entirely /ɪnˈtaɪəli/ *adverb* completely ସଂପୂର୍ଣ୍ଣରୂପେ, ପୂରାପୂରି *I entirely agree with you.*

entrance /ˈentrəns/ *noun* a door, gate, etc. to go into a place ପ୍ରବେଶଦ୍ୱାର *I'll meet you at the entrance to the museum.* ⇨ **exit** ଦେଖନ୍ତୁ।

entry /ˈentri/ *noun* (*plural* **entries**) **1** a door, gate or passage where you enter a building ପ୍ରବେଶ, ପ୍ରବେଶ ପଥ ⇨ **entrance** ଦେଖନ୍ତୁ। **2** something that you do to take part in a competition ନାମ ଲେଖା, ତାଲିକାଭୁକ୍ତ ହେବା ପ୍ରକ୍ରିୟା *The last date for sending entries to the painting competition is 30th June.*

envelope /ˈenvələʊp/ *noun* a paper cover for a letter ଲଫାପା *Have you written his address on the envelope?*

environment /ɪnˈvaɪrənmənt/ *noun* **1 the environment** (*no plural*) the air, water, land, animals and plants around us ପରିବେଶ *We must do more to protect the environment.* **2** everything around you ଆମ ଚାରିପଟେ ଥିବା ସବୁକିଛି *Children need a happy home environment.*

environmental *adjective* ପରିବେଶ ସମ୍ବନ୍ଧୀୟ *We talked about pollution and other environmental problems.*

envy /ˈenvi/ *noun* (*no plural*) the feeling of wanting what another person has ଈର୍ଷା, ପରଶ୍ରୀକାତରତା *He was filled with envy when he saw his friend's new bike.*

epic /ˈepɪk/ *noun* a long and exciting poem that tells about the actions and adventures of great men and women ମହାକାବ୍ୟ; କୌଣସି ବ୍ୟକ୍ତି ବା ଦେଶର ବୀରତ୍ୱପୂର୍ଣ୍ଣ ଘଟଣା ଥିବା କାବ୍ୟ The Mahabharata *is one of the longest epics in the world.*

epidemic /ˌepɪˈdemɪk/ *noun* a disease that many people in a place have at the same time ମଡକ, ମହାମାରୀ, ଜନପଦ ପ୍ରସାରକ ରୋଗ *a flu epidemic*

episode /ˈepɪsəʊd/ *noun* a programme on radio or television that is part of a longer story ଧାରାବାହିକ ଲମ୍ବା ନାଟକ ବା ଗପର ଏକ ଭାଗ ବା ଅଂଶ (ଟିଭି ସିରିଆଲ୍ ପରି) *You can see the final episode of the series on Monday.*

epitaph /ˈepɪtɑːf/ *noun* words said or written about a dead person, specially words written on a tomb or gravestone ସମାଧିଲିପି, ମୃତବ୍ୟକ୍ତିଙ୍କ ବିଷୟରେ ସ୍ମୃତିଲେଖ (ବିଶେଷତଃ କବର ପଥର ଉପରେ) *Her epitaph read, 'Kind and Gentle Lady.'*

equal[1] /ˈiːkwəl/ *adjective* the same; as big, as much or as good as another ସମାନ, ସମ ପରିମାଣ, ସଂଖ୍ୟା, ଆକାର ବା ଗୁଣଥିବା *I gave the two children an equal number of sweets.*

equal[2] /ˈiːkwəl/ *verb* (**equals, equalling, equalled**) **1** be exactly the same amount as something ସମାନ ହେବା *Two plus two equals four* (2 + 2 = 4). **2** be as good as somebody or something ସମ ମାନ ବା ଗୁଣର ହେବା, ସମୋତ୍ତମ ହେବା, ସମକକ୍ଷ ହେବା *He ran the race in 21.2 seconds, equalling the world record.*

equality /iˈkwɒləti/ *noun* (*no plural*) being the same or having the same rights ସମାନତା, ସମତା, ସାମ୍ୟ *In some countries black people are still fighting for equality.* ✪ ବିପରୀତ **inequality**

equally /ˈiːkwəli/ *adverb* in equal parts; in the same way ସମାନ ଭାବରେ *Don't eat all the chocolates yourself—share them out equally!*

equation /iˈkweɪʒn/ *noun* (in mathematics) a statement which shows that two quantities are equal ସମୀକରଣ *$2x + 3y = 15$ is an equation.*

equator /iˈkweɪtə(r)/ *noun* (*no plural*) an imaginary line drawn on maps that runs round the middle of the earth. Countries near the equator are very hot ଭୂମଣ୍ଡଳର ଚାରିପଟେ ଉତ୍ତର ଓ ଦକ୍ଷିଣ ମେରୁ ଠାରୁ ସମାନ ଦୂରରେ ଥିବା ଏକ କଳ୍ପିତ ରେଖା; ବିଷୁବ ରେଖା, ନିରକ୍ଷ ବୃତ୍ତ, ମୂମଧ୍ୟରେଖା। ଏହି ରେଖା ପାଖ ଅଞ୍ଚଳ ଖୁବ୍ ଗରମ ➪ **globe** ଦେଖନ୍ତୁ।

equidistant /ˌiːkwɪˈdɪstənt/ *adjective* equally far from two or more things or places ସମଦୂରବର୍ତ୍ତୀ, ସମଦୂରସ୍ଥ *My house is equidistant from the market as well as the school.*

equilateral /ˌiːkwɪˈlætərəl/ *adjective* a triangle that is equilateral has all its three sides of equal length ସମବାହୁ, ସମଭୂଜ (ତ୍ରିଭୁଜ) *an equilateral triangle*

equinox /ˈiːkwɪnɒks/ *noun* (*plural* **equinoxes**) one of the two days (20 March and 22 September) in a year when the rays of the sun fall directly over the **equator**. As a result of this, day and night are of equal length ବର୍ଷର ଯେଉଁ ଦୁଇ ଦିନ ସୂର୍ଯ୍ୟ ବିଷୁବ ରେଖାର ଠିକ୍ ଉପରେ ଥିବା ହେତୁ ସମ ଦିବାରାତ୍ରି ହୁଏ, କ୍ରାନ୍ତିପାତ, ସମଦିବାରାତ୍ରି

equipment /iˈkwɪpmənt/ *noun* (*no plural*) a set of things that is required for a particular purpose (କୌଣସି କାର୍ଯ୍ୟପାଇଁ) ସରଞ୍ଜାମ, ଉପକରଣ, ଯନ୍ତ୍ରପାତି *sports equipment*

equivalent /ɪˈkwɪvələnt/ *adjective* equal to something in quantity, value, importance or meaning ସମତୁଲ୍ୟ, ସମାନ ପରିମାଣ, ଗୁଣ, ମାନ ଇତ୍ୟାଦି ଥିବା *Can you give me the equivalent of ten dollars in rupees?*

eradicate /ɪˈrædɪkeɪt/ *verb* (**eradicates, eradicating, eradicated**) get rid of something (that is bad) completely (କୌଣସି ଖରାପ ଜିନିଷ) ମୂଳୋତ୍ପାଟନ କରିବା *We are trying to eradicate polio from our country.*

erase /ɪˈreɪz/ *verb* (**erases, erasing, erased**) remove something completely (କୌଣସି ଚିହ୍ନ, ଲେଖା ଇତ୍ୟାଦି) ଲିଭାଇ ଦେବା, ନିଶ୍ଚିହ୍ନ କରିବା *erase some information from the computer*

eraser /ɪˈreɪze(r)/ *noun* ➪ **rubber 2** ଦେଖନ୍ତୁ।

erect[1] /ɪˈrekt/ *adjective* in an upright position ଉଭା, ଲମ୍ବଭାବରେ ଅବସ୍ଥିତ, ସାହସୀ, ଅବିଚଳିତ

erect[2] /ɪˈrekt/ *verb* (**erects, erecting, erected**) build something or put something in an upright position ଠିଆ କରାଇବା, ଉଠାଇବା, ଭୂଲମ୍ବ ଭାବେ ଗଠନ ବା ନିର୍ମାଣ କରିବା *erect a wall*

erode /ɪˈrəʊd/ *verb* (**erodes, eroding, eroded**) if something erodes, it is being slowly destroyed by wind, water or the heat of the sun (ପବନ, ପାଣି, ସୂର୍ଯ୍ୟତାପ ଦ୍ୱାରା) କ୍ରମଶଃ କ୍ଷୟପ୍ରାପ୍ତ ହେବା ବା କରିବା *Many of the mountains in our country have got eroded because of the cutting down of trees.*

erosion /ɪˈrəʊʒn/ *noun* (*no plural*) the process of getting eroded କ୍ରମକ୍ଷୟ, କ୍ଷୟ, କ୍ଷୟପ୍ରାପ୍ତି *soil erosion*

error /ˈerə(r)/ *noun* a thing that is done wrongly; a mistake ତ୍ରୁଟି, ଭୁଲ୍, *Exam results could not be declared today because of a computer error.*

erupt /ɪˈrʌpt/ *verb* (**erupts, erupting, erupted**) when a **volcano** erupts, very hot liquid rock (called **lava**) suddenly comes out ହଠାତ୍ ପ୍ରବଳ ଭାବରେ ଉଦ୍‌ଗତ ହେବା, ନିର୍ଗତ ହେବା; (ଆଗ୍ନେୟଗିରିରୁ) ଲାଭା ଉଦ୍‌ଗିରଣ ହେବା। *When Mount Vesuvius erupted, it buried the town of Pompeii.*

eruption /ɪˈrʌpʃn/ *noun* ଉଦ୍‌ଗିରଣ, ନିର୍ଗମନ *a volcanic eruption*

escalator /ˈeskəleɪtə(r)/ *noun* stairs that move and carry people up and down ଚଳନଶୀଳ ସିଢ଼ି ବା ପାହାଚ

escape[1] /ɪˈskeɪp/ *verb* (**escapes, escaping, escaped**) **1** get free from somebody or something ବନ୍ଧନ ବା ନିୟନ୍ତ୍ରଣରୁ ନିଜକୁ ମୁକ୍ତ କରିବା, ଖସିଯିବା, ପଳେଇଯିବା। *The prisoner escaped, but he was caught.* **2** if a liquid or gas escapes, it comes out of a place ବାଷ୍ପ, ତରଳ ପଦାର୍ଥ ଇତ୍ୟାଦି ଝରିବା, ନିର୍ଗତ ହେବା, ବାହାରିଯିବା।

escape[2] /ɪˈskeɪp/ *noun*

make your escape get free; get away from a place ପଳାୟନ *They jumped out of a window and made their escape.*

escort[1] /ɪsˈkɔːt/ *noun* a person or a group of people or vehicles that go along with somebody to protect them or to honour them ସମ୍ମାନ ବା ସୁରକ୍ଷା ପାଇଁ ସାଙ୍ଗରେ ଯାଉଥିବା ବ୍ୟକ୍ତି, ଦଳ ବା ଗାଡ଼ି *police escort*

escort[2] /ɪsˈkɔːt/ *verb* (**escorts, escorting, escorted**) go with somebody, for example to make sure that they arrive somewhere ସୁରକ୍ଷା ଓ ସୁବିଧା ପାଇଁ ବାଟ କଢ଼େଇ ନେବା। *The President was escorted by his bodyguards.*

especially /ɪˈspeʃəli/ *adverb* very; more than usual or more than others ବିଶେଷତଃ *I hate getting up early, especially in winter.*

essay /ˈeseɪ/ *noun* a short piece of writing about a subject ପ୍ରବନ୍ଧ *Our teacher asked us to write an essay on our favourite author.* ➪ **composition 2** ଦେଖନ୍ତୁ।

essence /ˈesns/ *noun* **1** the basic or most important feature of something ମୂଳତଥ୍ୟ *the essence of Indian philosophy of life* **2** a liquid from a plant having a strong smell or taste of that plant ଉଦ୍ଭିଦରୁ ସଂଗୃହିତ ସୁଗନ୍ଧ ଦ୍ରବ୍ୟ, ଅତର *vanilla essence*

essential /ɪˈsenʃl/ *adjective* if something is essential, you must have or do it ଆବଶ୍ୟକ, ପ୍ରୟୋଜନୀୟ, ଅତି ଦରକାରୀ *It is essential that you work hard for this exam.*

establish /ɪˈstæblɪʃ/ *verb* (**establishes, establishing, established**) start something new ସ୍ଥାପନ କରିବା, ସ୍ଥାପିତ ହେବା, ପ୍ରତିଷ୍ଠା କରିବା *This company was established in 1852.*

establishment *noun* **1** a large organization or institution ସଂସ୍ଥା, ପ୍ରତିଷ୍ଠାନ **2** the act of starting or creating something new, an organization for example ସଂସ୍ଥା ଇତ୍ୟାଦିର ସ୍ଥାପନା ବା ପ୍ରତିଷ୍ଠା

Since the establishment of the party ten years ago, the membership has grown to over two thousand.

estate /ɪˈsteɪt/ *noun* **1** land with a lot of houses or factories on it ଭୂସମ୍ପତ୍ତି; ଘର, ବାଡ଼ି, କାରଖାନା ଇତ୍ୟାଦି ଥିବା ଭୂଖଣ୍ଡ ବା ଭୂସମ୍ପତ୍ତି *We live on a housing estate.* ○ *an industrial estate* **2** a large piece of land in the countryside that one person or family owns କୌଣସି ବ୍ୟକ୍ତି ବା ପରିବାରର ଗ୍ରାମାଞ୍ଚଳରେ ଥିବା ବଡ଼ ଭୂସମ୍ପତ୍ତି

estimate /ˈestɪmət/ *verb* (**estimates, estimating, estimated**) say how much you think something will cost, how big something is, how long it will take to do something, etc. (କୌଣସି କାମରେ କେତେ ଖର୍ଚ୍ଚ ହେବ, କେତେ ସମୟ ଲାଗିବ ଇତ୍ୟାଦିର) ପ୍ରାକ୍‌କଳନ, ପୂର୍ବାନୁମାନ ବା ଅଟକଳ କରିବା। *The builders estimated that it would take a week to repair the roof.*

estimate /ˈestɪmət/ *noun* ପ୍ରାକ୍‌କଳନ, ପୂର୍ବାନୁମାନ, ଅଟକଳ *The estimate for repairing the roof was Rs 20,000.*

etc. /ˌetˈsetərə/ *abbreviation* etc. is short for 'et cetera'. You use 'etc.' at the end of a list to show that there are other things but you are not going to name them all ଇତ୍ୟାଦି, ପ୍ରଭୃତି *We bought coffee, milk, bread, etc. at the shop.*

eucalyptus /ˌjuːkəˈlɪptəs/ *noun* (*plural* **eucalyptuses**) a tall straight tree that grows in Asia and Australia. The leaves produce an oil with a strong smell. This oil is used in many medicines (ଏସିଆ ଓ ଅଷ୍ଟ୍ରେଲିଆରେ ମିଳୁଥିବା) ଲମ୍ବା ସଦାସବୁଜ ଗଛ, ଇଉକାଲିପଟାସ୍ ଗଛ। ଏହାର ପତ୍ରରୁ ପ୍ରାପ୍ତ କଡ଼ା ବାସ୍ନାଯୁକ୍ତ ତେଲ ବହୁତ ଔଷଧରେ ବ୍ୟବହୃତ ହୁଏ

evacuate /ɪˈvækjueɪt/ *verb* (**evacuates, evacuating, evacuated**) take people away from a dangerous place to a safer place ବିପଜ୍ଜନକ ସ୍ଥାନରୁ ଲୋକଙ୍କୁ ନେଇଯିବା। *The area near the factory was evacuated after the explosion.*

evaporate /ɪˈvæpəreɪt/ *verb* (**evaporates, evaporating, evaporated**) if a liquid evaporates, it changes into a gas ବାଷ୍ପରେ ପରିଣତ ହେବା ବା କରିବା *Water evaporates if you heat it.*

eve /iːv/ *noun* the evening or the day before a special day ସଂଧ୍ୟା; କୌଣସି ବିଶେଷ ଦିନର ପୂର୍ବ ସଂଧ୍ୟା *I went to a party on New Year's Eve.*

even[1] /ˈiːvn/ *adjective* **1** flat and smooth ସମତଳ, ଚିକ୍କଣ *an even surface* ✪ ବିପରୀତ **uneven** **2** even numbers can be divided exactly by 2 ୨ରେ ସଂପୂର୍ଣ୍ଣ ରୂପେ ବିଭାଜିତ ହୋଇ ପାରୁଥିବା ସଂଖ୍ୟା ସବୁ *4, 6 and 8 are even numbers.* ✪ ବିପରୀତ **odd 2**

even[2] /ˈiːvn/ *adverb* **1** a word that you use to say that something is surprising ଯେ, ମଧ୍ୟ, ବି; ଆଶ୍ଚର୍ଯ୍ୟର କଥା ଯେ *This game is so easy that even a child can play it.* **2** a word that you use when comparing things to make one stronger than the other ଆହୁରି, ତା'ଠାରୁ ବି *That car is big, but this one is even bigger.*

even if it does not change anything if ଯଦିଓ, ଯଦିଚ *Even if you run, you won't be able to catch the bus.*

even though although ଯଦିଓ, ସତ୍ତ୍ୱେ *I went to the party, even though I was tired.*

evening /ˈiːvnɪŋ/ *noun* the part of the day between the afternoon and when you go to bed ସଂଧ୍ୟା *What are you doing this evening?*

event /ɪˈvent/ *noun* something important that happens ଘଟଣା, ବିଶେଷତଃ ଗୁରୁତ୍ୱପୂର୍ଣ୍ଣ ଘଟଣା *My sister's wedding was a big event for our family.*

eventually /ɪˈventʃuəli/ *adverb* after a long time ପରିଶେଷରେ *I waited for him for three hours, and eventually he came.*

ever /ˈevə(r)/ *adverb* at any time କୌଣସି ସମୟରେ, କେବେ ବି *'Have you ever been to Africa?' 'No, I haven't.'*

ever since in all the time since (କୌଣସି ଘଟଣାର ବା ଅବସ୍ଥାର) ପରଠାରୁ, ସେଇ ଦିନୁ, ସେତିକି ବେଳୁ *I have known Leena ever since we were children.*

evergreen /ˈevəgriːn/ *noun* a tree that has green leaves all the year ଚିର ସବୁଜ, ଚିର ଶ୍ୟାମଳ ➪ **deciduous** ଦେଖନ୍ତୁ।

every /ˈevri/ *adjective* all of the people or things in a group ପ୍ରତ୍ୟେକ *She knows every student in the school.*

everybody /ˈevribɒdi/, **everyone** /ˈevriwʌn/ *pronoun* each person; all people ପ୍ରତ୍ୟେକ ବ୍ୟକ୍ତି *Everybody at school likes my coat.*

everyday /ˈevrideɪ/ *adjective* normal; not special ନିତିଦିନିଆ, ସାଧାରଣ *Computers are now part of everyday life.*

everything /ˈevriθɪŋ/ *pronoun* each thing; all things ପ୍ରତ୍ୟେକ ବସ୍ତୁ, ସବୁ ଜିନିଷ *Everything in that shop is very expensive.*

everywhere /ˈevriweə(r)/ *adverb* in all places or to all places ସବୁ ଜାଗାରେ, ଚାରିଆଡ଼େ *I've looked everywhere for my pen, but I can't find it.*

evidence /ˈevɪdəns/ *noun* (*no plural*) a thing that makes you believe that something is true or that helps you know who did something କୌଣସି ବିଷୟ ପ୍ରମାଣ କରୁଥିବା ତଥ୍ୟ, ପ୍ରମାଣ *a piece of evidence*

give evidence tell what you know about somebody or something in a court of law ସାକ୍ଷୀ ଦେବା (ଅଦାଲତରେ)

evident /ˈevɪdənt/ *adjective* easy to see or understand ସୁସ୍ପଷ୍ଟ

evidently *adverb* clearly ସ୍ପଷ୍ଟ ଭାବରେ

evil /ˈiːvl/ *adjective* very bad ମନ୍ଦ, ଖଳ, ଅତି ଖରାପ *an evil person*

ewe /juː/ *noun* (*plural* **ewes**) a female sheep ମେଣ୍ଢୀ ➪ ଚିତ୍ର ପାଇଁ **sheep** ଦେଖନ୍ତୁ।

exact /ɪgˈzækt/ *adjective* completely correct; without any mistakes ନିର୍ଭୁଲ, ସଠିକ୍ *Do you know the exact time that the train arrives?*

exactly /ɪgˈzæktli/ *adverb* **1** you use 'exactly' when you are asking for or giving information that is completely correct ସଠିକ୍ ଭାବରେ, ନିର୍ଭୁଲ ଭାବରେ *Can you tell me exactly what happened?* **2** just ଠିକ୍ *This shirt is exactly what I wanted.*

exaggerate /ɪgˈzædʒəreɪt/ *verb* (**exaggerates, exaggerating, exaggerated**) say that something is bigger, better, worse, etc. than it really is ଅତି ରଞ୍ଜିତ କରିବା, ବନେଇ ଚୁନେଇ କହିବା *Don't exaggerate! I was only two minutes late, not twenty.*

exaggeration /ɪgˌzædʒəˈreɪʃn/ *noun* ଅତିରଞ୍ଜନ, ଅତ୍ୟୁକ୍ତି *It's an exaggeration to say you don't know any English!*

examination /ɪgˌzæmɪˈneɪʃn/ *noun* **1** (**exam** ମଧ୍ୟ) a test of what you know or can do ପରୀକ୍ଷା, ଜ୍ଞାନ ବା ପାରଦର୍ଶିତାର ପରୀକ୍ଷା *We've got an exam in English next week.*

> ✪ **Examination** ଶବ୍ଦ ସହିତ **sit** ବା **take** କ୍ରିୟାର ପ୍ରୟୋଗ କରାଯାଏ । ପରୀକ୍ଷାରେ ସଫଳ ବ୍ୟକ୍ତି **pass** ଓ ଅସଫଳ ବ୍ୟକ୍ତି **fail** ହୁଏ ।

2 looking carefully at somebody or something ପରୀକ୍ଷା ନିରୀକ୍ଷା *She went into hospital for an examination.*

examine /ɪgˈzæmɪn/ *verb* (**examines, examining, examined**) **1** ask questions to find out what somebody knows or what they can do ପ୍ରଶ୍ନ ପଚାରି ଜ୍ଞାନ ବା ପାରଦର୍ଶିତାର ପରୀକ୍ଷା କରିବା *You will be examined on everything you have learnt this year.* **2** look carefully at something or somebody ପର୍ଯ୍ୟବେକ୍ଷଣ କରିବା, ନିରୀକ୍ଷଣ କରିବା *I examined the car before I bought it.*

example /ɪgˈzɑ:mpl/ *noun* something that shows what other things of the same kind are like ଉଦାହରଣ *This dictionary gives many examples of how words are used in sentences.*

for example let me give you an example ଉଦାହରଣ ସ୍ୱରୂପ *Do you speak any other languages, for example Gujarati or Marathi?*

excavate /ˈekskəveɪt/ *verb* (**excavates, excavating, excavated**) dig up the ground to find very old objects or buildings ମାଟି ଖୋଳି ପୋତି ହୋଇଯାଇଥିବା ଜିନିଷ ବାହାର କରିବା *The ancient cities of Harappa and Mohenjodaro were first excavated in 1921.*

excavating old objects

excavation /ˌekskəˈveɪʃn/ *noun* the process of excavating ଖନନ, ଖୋଳିବା କାମ

exceed /ɪkˈsi:d/ *verb* (**exceeds, exceeding, exceeded**) do or be more than something ଅଧିକ ହେବା, ଅତିକ୍ରମ କରିବା *The price of the watch will not exceed Rs 350.*

excellent /ˈeksələnt/ *adjective* very good ଅତିଭଲ, ଉତ୍କୃଷ୍ଟ *She speaks excellent Japanese.*

except /ɪkˈsept/ *preposition* but not ଛଡ଼ା, ବାଦ୍ ଦେଇ *The restaurant is open every day except Monday.*

exception /ɪkˈsepʃn/ *noun* a person or thing that is not the same as the others ବ୍ୟତିକ୍ରମ *Most of his films are good but this one is an exception.*

excerpt /ˈeksɜːpt/ *noun* a part of a story, article, poem or music ଉଦ୍ଧୃତ ଅଂଶ (ଗପ, ପ୍ରବନ୍ଧ, କବିତା, ସଙ୍ଗୀତ ଇତ୍ୟାଦିରୁ ଉଦ୍ଧୃତ ବା ନିର୍ବାଚିତ ଅଂଶ) *This is an excerpt from the book* Discovery of India *by Jawaharlal Nehru.*

exchange /ɪksˈtʃeɪndʒ/ *verb* (**exchanges, exchanging, exchanged**) give one thing and get another thing for it ଅଦଳବଦଳ ବା ବିନିମୟ କରିବା *My new radio didn't work so I exchanged it for another one.*

exchange *noun* ଅଦଳ ବଦଳ, ବିନିମୟ *a new TV in exchange for your old one*

excite /ɪkˈsaɪt/ *verb* (**excites, exciting, excited**) make somebody have strong feelings of happiness or interest so that they are not calm ଉତ୍ତେଜିତ କରିବା, ଆଗ୍ରହାନ୍ୱିତ କରିବା, ଖୁସି କରିବା

excited *adjective* not calm, for example because you are happy about something that is going to happen ଉତ୍ତେଜିତ, ଆଗ୍ରହାନ୍ୱିତ ଆନନ୍ଦିତ *He's getting very excited about his holiday.*

excitement *noun* (*no plural*) a feeling of being excited ଉତ୍ତେଜନା। *There was great excitement in the stadium before the match began.*

exciting *adjective* something that is exciting makes you have strong feelings of happiness or interest ଆନନ୍ଦ ବା ଆଗ୍ରହ ଜନ୍ମାଉଥିବା *an exciting film*

exclaim /ɪkˈskleɪm/ *verb* (**exclaims, exclaiming, exclaimed**) say something suddenly and loudly because you are surprised, angry, etc. (କ୍ରୋଧ, ବିସ୍ମୟ ଆଦି ହେବାର କାରଣ) ହଠାତ୍ ପାଟି କରିବା ବା ବଡ଼ ପାଟିରେ କହିବା *'I don't believe it!' she exclaimed.*

exclamation /ˌekskləˈmeɪʃn/ *noun* a word or a phrase that you say suddenly to express surprise, anger, etc. ବିସ୍ମୟ ବୋଧକ ଶବ୍ଦ ବା ଅଭିବ୍ୟକ୍ତି। *Oh!, Ouch!* ଏବଂ *Look here!* ବିସ୍ମୟ ବୋଧକ ଶବ୍ଦ ଅଟେ।

exclamation mark *noun* a mark (!) that you use in writing to show loud or strong words or surprise ବିସ୍ମୟସୂଚକ ଚିହ୍ନ (!)

exclude /ɪkˈskluːd/ *verb* (**excludes, excluding, excluded**) shut or keep a person or thing out ବର୍ଜିତ କରିବା, ବାଦ୍ ଦେବା *We cannot exclude the students from the meeting. Their ideas are important.* ✪ ବିପରୀତ **include**

excluding *preposition* without; if you do not count ଛାଡ଼ି, ବାଦ୍ ଦେଇ *The meal cost Rs 600, excluding ice creams.* ✪ ବିପରୀତ **including**

excrete /ɪkˈskriːt/ *verb* (**excretes, excreting, excreted**) get rid of solid or liquid wastes from the body ମଳମୂତ୍ର ନିଷ୍କାସନ କରିବା

excursion /ɪkˈskɜ:ʃn/ *noun* a short journey to see something interesting or to enjoy yourself ଅଳ୍ପଦୂରର ପ୍ରମୋଦ ଭ୍ରମଣ *We're going on an excursion to Agra on Sunday.*

excuse[1] /ɪkˈskju:z/ *noun* words you say or write to explain why you have done something wrong କୈଫିୟତ୍, କ୍ଷମା ପ୍ରାର୍ଥନା *You're late! What's your excuse this time?*

excuse[2] /ɪkˈskju:z/ *verb* (**excuses, excusing, excused**) say that it is not important that a person has made a mistake କ୍ଷମା ଦେବା, ମାଫ୍ କରିବା *Please excuse us for being late.*

excuse me you use 'excuse me' when you want to stop somebody who is speaking, or when you want to speak to somebody you don't know. You can also use 'excuse me' to say that you are sorry ଅନ୍ୟ ଲୋକ କିଛି କହୁଥିଲା ବେଳେ ବାଧା ଦେଇ ନିଜ କଥା କହିବା ପାଇଁ 'excuse me' କୁହାଯାଏ। ଅଜଣା ଲୋକକୁ କିଛି କହିଲା ପୂର୍ବରୁ ମଧ୍ୟ 'excuse me' କୁହାଯାଏ। ନିଜର ଭୁଲ୍ କ୍ଷମା କରିବା ପାଇଁ ମଧ୍ୟ 'excuse me' କୁହାଯାଏ *Excuse me, could you tell me the time, please?* ○ *Excuse me ma'am. Could you please explain the sum again?*

exercise[1] /ˈeksəsaɪz/ *noun* **1** a piece of work that you do to learn something ଶିଖିବା ପାଇଁ ଅଭ୍ୟାସ ଲେଖା *The teacher asked us to do exercises 1 and 2 for homework.* **2** a special movement that you do to keep your body strong and well ବ୍ୟାୟମ *Touch your toes and stand up 20 times. This exercise is good for your legs, stomach and back.*

exercise book *noun* a book with clean pages that you use at school for writing in ପାଠ ଲେଖିବା ଖାତା

exercise[2] /ˈeksəsaɪz/ *verb* (**exercises, exercising, exercised**) move your body to keep it strong and well ବ୍ୟାୟାମ କରିବା, ଚଲାବୁଲା, ଦୌଡ଼ାଦୌଡ଼ି କରିବା *They exercise in the park every morning.*

exert /ɪgˈzɜ:t/ *verb* (**exerts, exerting, exerted**) apply a force on something or make a great deal of effort to do something ବଳ ପ୍ରୟୋଗ କରିବା, ପରିଶ୍ରମ କରିବା *Don't exert yourself so much that you can't go out in the evening.*

exertion /ɪgˈzɜ:ʃn/ *noun* the use of one's body or mind to carry out a job; the state of being tired after heavy work ଦେହ ଓ ମସ୍ତିଷ୍କର ପ୍ରୟୋଗ, ହାଲିଆ ହେଲାପରି ପରିଶ୍ରମ *mental/physical exertion*

exhale /eksˈheɪl/ *verb* (**exhales, exhaling, exhaled**) breathe out the air present in your lungs ନିଃଶ୍ୱାସ ଛାଡ଼ିବା *Lift your arms above your head and exhale.* ✪ ବିପରୀତ **inhale**

exhaust[1] /ɪgˈzɔ:st/ *verb* (**exhausts, exhausting, exhausted**) make somebody very tired ହାଲିଆ କରିବା *The long journey exhausted us.*

exhausted *adjective* very tired ହାଲିଆ, କ୍ଳାନ୍ତ *I'm exhausted—I think I'll go to bed.*

exhaust[2] /ɪɡˈzɔːst/ *noun* a pipe that lets waste gases out from an engine, for example in a car ଇଞ୍ଜିନ୍ ଇତ୍ୟାଦିରୁ ବାହାରିଥିବା ବାଷ୍ପ ନିଷ୍କାସନ ନଳ

exhibition /ˌeksɪˈbɪʃn/ *noun* a group of things shown in a place for people to come and look at them ପ୍ରଦର୍ଶନୀ *an exhibition of paintings by Husain*

exile /ˈeksaɪl/ *noun* (*no plural*) having to live away from your own country, for example as a punishment; ନିର୍ବାସନ; ନିର୍ବାସିତ ବ୍ୟକ୍ତି *He spent the last years of his life in exile.*

exist /ɪɡˈzɪst/ *verb* (**exists, existing, existed**) be real; live ବାସ୍ତବ ଜଗତରେ ରହିବା, ଅବସ୍ଥିତ ରହିବା, ବଞ୍ଚିରହିବା, ବିଦ୍ୟମାନ ରହିବା। *Does life exist on other planets?*

existence *noun* (*no plural*) being real; existing ବିଦ୍ୟମାନତା; ବଞ୍ଚିରହିବା ସ୍ଥିତି *This is one of the oldest books in existence.*

exit /ˈeksɪt/ *noun* a way out of a building ପ୍ରସ୍ଥାନ ପଥ ➪ **entrance** ଦେଖନ୍ତୁ।

expand /ɪkˈspænd/ *verb* (**expands, expanding, expanded**) become bigger or make something bigger ଆକାର ବଡ଼ ହେବା ବା ବଡ଼ କରିବା; ପ୍ରସାରିତ ହେବା ବା କରିବା *Metals expand when they are heated.*

expansion /ɪkˈspænʃn/ *noun* (*no plural*) the act of getting bigger ପ୍ରସାରଣ *The company needs bigger offices because of the expansion.*

expect /ɪkˈspekt/ *verb* (**expects, expecting, expected**) think that somebody or something will come or that something will happen ଆଶା କରିବା, ପ୍ରତ୍ୟାଶା କରିବା, ସମ୍ଭବ ବୋଲି ଭାବିବା *We expected it to be hot in Chandigarh, but it was quite cold.* ○ *She's expecting a baby in June.*

expectation /ˌekspekˈteɪʃn/ *noun* the belief that someone or something will come or something will happen ଆଶା, ପ୍ରତ୍ୟାଶା

expedition /ˌekspəˈdɪʃn/ *noun* a journey to find or do something special କୌଣସି ନିର୍ଦ୍ଦିଷ୍ଟ ଉଦ୍ଦେଶ୍ୟରେ ଯାତ୍ରା, ଅଭିଯାନ *Scott's expedition to the South Pole*

expel /ɪkˈspel/ *verb* (**expels, expelling, expelled**) send somebody away from a school or club ବହିଷ୍କାର କରିବା, ତଡ଼ିଦେବା *The boys were expelled from school for smoking.*

expenditure /ɪkˈspendɪtʃə(r)/ *noun* the amount of money you spend ଖର୍ଚ୍ଚ, ବ୍ୟୟ *the monthly expenditure of a family*

expense /ɪkˈspens/ *noun* the cost of something ଦାମ୍, ବ୍ୟୟ, ଖର୍ଚ୍ଚ *Having a car is a big expense.*

expensive /ɪkˈspensɪv/ *adjective* something that is expensive costs a lot of money ଉଚ୍ଚ ଦାମ୍‌ର, ବ୍ୟୟସାପେକ୍ଷ, ଦାମିକା *expensive clothes* ✪ ବିପରୀତ **cheap** ବା **inexpensive**

experience[1] /ɪkˈspɪəriəns/ *noun* **1** (*no plural*) knowing about something because you have seen it or done it ଅଭିଜ୍ଞତା *She has four* *years of teaching experience.* **2** (*plural* **experiences**) something that has happened to you ନିଜକୁ ପ୍ରଭାବିତ କଲାପରି ଘଟଣା, ଅନୁଭୂତି *He wrote a book about his experiences in Africa.*

experienced /ɪkˈspɪəriənst/ *adjective* if you are experienced, you know about something because you have done it many times before ଅଭିଜ୍ଞ, ଅନୁଭୂତି ସମ୍ପନ୍ନ, ଅନୁଭବୀ *She's an experienced driver.* ✪ ବିପରୀତ **inexperienced**

experience² /ɪkˈspɪəriəns/ *verb* (**experiences, experiencing, experienced**) when you experience something, it happens to you or you feel something ଅନୁଭବ କରିବା *We experienced problems with the water supply when we first came to this house.*

experiment /ɪkˈsperɪmənt/ *noun* you do an experiment to find out what will happen or to see if something is true ପରୀକ୍ଷା, ପରୀକ୍ଷଣ *They are doing experiments to find out if the drug is safe for humans.*

expert /ˈekspɜːt/ *noun* a person who knows a lot about something ବିଶେଷଜ୍ଞ *a computer expert*

explain /ɪkˈspleɪn/ *verb* (**explains, explaining, explained**) **1** tell somebody about something so that they understand it ବୁଝାଇବା, ବୋଧଗମ୍ୟ କରିବା, ସ୍ପଷ୍ଟ କରିବା *He explained how to use the machine.* **2** give a reason for something କାରଣ ଦର୍ଶାଇବା *I explained why we needed the money.*

explanation /ˌekspləˈneɪʃn/ *noun* telling somebody about something so that they understand it, or giving a reason for something ବ୍ୟାଖ୍ୟା, ଅର୍ଥପ୍ରକାଶ; କୈଫିୟତ *What explanation did they give for being late?*

explode /ɪkˈspləʊd/ *verb* (**explodes, exploding, exploded**) burst suddenly with a very loud noise ବିସ୍ଫୋରିତ ହେବା, (ବୋମା ଇତ୍ୟାଦି) ଫାଟିବା *A bomb exploded in the middle of the city, killing two people.* ✪ **Explode** ଶବ୍ଦର ସଂଜ୍ଞା ରୂପ **explosion** ଅଟେ।

exploit /ɪkˈsplɔɪt/ *verb* (**exploits, exploiting, exploited**) treat somebody badly to get what you want ଅନ୍ୟର କ୍ଷତି କରି ନିଜର ଫାଇଦା ଉଠାଇବା, ଶୋଷଣ କରିବା *People who work in homes are often exploited—they work long hours for very little money.*

exploitation /ˌeksplɔɪˈteɪʃn/ *noun* (*no plural*) ଶୋଷଣ *exploitation of workers*

explore /ɪkˈsplɔː(r)/ *verb* (**explores, exploring, explored**) travel around a new place to learn about it ଶିକ୍ଷା ପାଇଁ ବା ଆବିଷ୍କାର ପାଇଁ ନୂଆ ଜାଗାକୁ ଯିବା

exploration /ˌeksplеˈreɪʃn/ *noun* ଆବିଷ୍କାର ଉଦ୍ଦେଶ୍ୟରେ ପର୍ଯ୍ୟଟନ କରୁଥିବା ବ୍ୟକ୍ତି *the exploration of space*

explorer /ɪkˈsplɔːrə(r)/ *noun* a person who travels to look for new places and to learn about them ଅଜ୍ଞାତ ଅଞ୍ଚଳ ଅନୁସନ୍ଧାନ କରୁଥିବା ବ୍ୟକ୍ତି *Vasco da*

Gama, the Portuguese explorer, discovered a sea route to India via the Cape of Good Hope.

explosion /ɪk'spləʊʒn/ *noun* bursting suddenly with a very loud noise ବିସ୍ଫୋରଣ, ଧମାକା *There was an explosion and pieces of glass flew everywhere.* ✪ **Explosion** ଶବ୍ଦର କ୍ରିୟା ରୂପ **explode** ଅଟେ ।

explosive /ɪk'spləʊsɪv/ *adjective* something that is explosive can cause an explosion ବିସ୍ଫୋରକ, ବିସ୍ଫୋରଣଶୀଳ *an explosive gas*

explosive *noun* a substance that can make things explode ବିସ୍ଫୋରଣଶୀଳ ପଦାର୍ଥ, ବିସ୍ଫୋରକ *Dynamite is an explosive.*

export /ɪk'spɔːt/ *verb* (**exports, exporting, exported**) sell things to another country ରପ୍ତାନି କରିବା *India exports tea to Britain.* ✪ ବିପରୀତ **import**

export /ɪk'spɔːt/ *noun* **1** (*no plural*) selling things to another country *These cars are made for export.* **2** (*plural* **exports**) something that you sell to another country ରପ୍ତାନି ହେଉଥିବା ପଦାର୍ଥ *The counntry's biggest exports are tea and cotton.* ✪ ବିପରୀତ **import**

expose /ɪk'spəʊz/ *verb* (**exposes, exposing, exposed**) show something that is usually covered or hidden ଖୋଲିଦେବା, ଅନାବୃତ୍ତ କରିବା *A baby's skin should not be exposed to the sun for too long.*

express[1] /ɪk'spres/ *verb* (**expresses, expressing, expressed**) say or show how you think or feel କହିବା ବା ଭାବଭଙ୍ଗୀ ଦ୍ୱାରା ମନୋଭାବ ପ୍ରକାଶ କରିବା, ବ୍ୟକ୍ତ କରିବା *She expressed her ideas well.*

express[2] /ɪk'spres/ (*plural* **expresses**), **express train** *noun* a fast train that does not stop at all stations ଦ୍ରୁତଗାମୀ ରେଳଗାଡ଼ି, ଏକ୍ସପ୍ରେସ୍

expression /ɪk'spreʃn/ *noun* the look on your face that shows how you feel ମନୋଭାବ ବ୍ୟକ୍ତ କରୁଥିବା ମୁଖଭଙ୍ଗୀ, ମୁହଁରୁ ଜାଣିହେଉଥିବା ମନୋଭାବ *an expression of surprise*

extend /ɪk'stend/ *verb* (**extends, extending, extended**) make something longer or bigger ପ୍ରସାରଣ କରିବା, ବଢ଼ାଇବା, ସଂପ୍ରସାରଣ କରିବା *I'm extending my holiday for another week.*

extension /ɪk'stenʃn/ *noun* **1** a part that you add to something to make it bigger ପ୍ରସାରଣ, ସଂପ୍ରସାରଣ; ସଂପ୍ରସାରିତ ଅଂଶ *They've built an extension on the back of the house.* **2** one of the telephones in a building that is connected to the main telephone ଗୋଟିଏ ମୂଳ ଟେଲିଫୋନ୍ ସହ ସଂଯୁକ୍ତ ଅନ୍ୟ ଟେଲିଫୋନ୍ *Can I have extension 4110 please?*

extensive /ɪk'stensɪv/ *adjective* covering a large area or including a lot of things ବ୍ୟାପକ, ବହୁ ବିଷୟ ଥିବା *an extensive survey*

extent /ɪk'stent/ *noun* (*no plural*) how big something is ପରିସର, ଆୟତନ, ବିସ୍ତୃତ, ପରିମାଣ *I didn't know the full* *extent of the problem until he explained it to me.*

> ✪ କୌଣସି ବିଷୟରେ ପୂର୍ଣ୍ଣମାତ୍ରାରେ ନିଶ୍ଚିତ ନ ହେବାର ସ୍ଥିତିକୁ **to a certain extent** ଏବଂ **to some extent** ବାକ୍ୟାଂଶ ଦ୍ଵାରା ଦର୍ଶାଯାଏ —
> *I agree with you to a certain extent.*

exterior /ɪkˈstɪəriə(r)/ *noun* the outside part ବାହାରପଟ *We painted the exterior of the house white.* ✪ ବିପରୀତ **interior**

external /ɪkˈstɜːnl/ *adjective* on, of or from the outside ବାହାର ପଟର, ବାହ୍ୟ *external walls* ✪ ବିପରୀତ **internal**

extinct /ɪkˈstɪŋkt/ *adjective* if a type of animal or plant is extinct, it does not exist now ବିଲୁପ୍ତ, ଲୋପପ୍ରାପ୍ତ, ଲୋପ ପାଇ ଯାଇଥିବା *Dinosaurs became extinct millions of years ago*.

extinguish /ɪkˈstɪŋgwɪʃ/ *verb* (**extinguishes, extinguishing, extinguished**) put out a fire ଲିଭାଇବା, ନିର୍ବାପିତ କରିବା

extinguisher *noun* (**fire extinguisher** ମଧ୍ୟ) a device that is used to put out a fire ନିଆଁଲିଭା ଯନ୍ତ୍ର, ଅଗ୍ନିନିର୍ବାପକ ଯନ୍ତ୍ର

fire extinguisher

extra /ˈekstrə/ *adjective, adverb* more than what is usual ଅଧିକା, ଅତିରିକ୍ତ *I have put an extra blanket on your bed because it's cold tonight.*

extract /ɪkˈstrækt/ *verb* (**extracts, extracting, extracted**) **1** take out something using a lot of force or effort ଭିଡ଼ି କାଢ଼ିବା, ଓପାଡ଼ିବା; ଚିପୁଡ଼ି (ରସ) ବାହାର କରିବା *extract a tooth* **2** use a chemical process to get something from another thing ରାସାୟନିକ ପ୍ରକ୍ରିୟାରେ ଗୋଟିଏ ପଦାର୍ଥରୁ ଅନ୍ୟ ପଦାର୍ଥ କାଢ଼ିବା *extract metal from its ore*

extraordinary /ɪkˈstrɔːdnri/ *adjective* very unusual or strange ଅସାଧାରଣ *I had an extraordinary dream last night—I dreamt that I could fly.*

extravagant /ɪkˈstrævəgənt/ *adjective* if you are extravagant, you spend too much money ଅପବ୍ୟୟୀ, ଖର୍ଚ୍ଚୀ

extreme /ɪkˈstriːm/ *adjective* **1** very great or strong ଖୁବ୍ ବେଶୀ, ଅତିଶୟ *the extreme cold of the Arctic* **2** if you say that a person is extreme, you mean that his/her ideas are too strong ଅତି କଠୋର ମତ ପୋଷଣ କରୁଥିବା, ଚରମପନ୍ଥୀ

extremely *adverb* very ଖୁବ୍, ଅତି, ଅତ୍ୟନ୍ତ *He's extremely good looking.*

eye[1] /aɪ/ *noun* one of the two parts on your face that you see with ଆଖି, ଚକ୍ଷୁ, ନେତ୍ର *She's got blue eyes.* ➪ ଚିତ୍ର ପାଇଁ **face** ଦେଖନ୍ତୁ।

in somebody's eyes as somebody thinks ଅନ୍ୟର ଦୃଷ୍ଟିରେ *Rohit is 42, but in his mother's eyes, he's still a little boy!*

see eye to eye with somebody agree with somebody କାହାରି ସହ ସହମତ ହେବା *Mr Handa doesn't always see eye to eye with his neighbours.*

eye² /aɪ/ *noun* a loop or a hole in something ଛୁଞ୍ଚ ଇତ୍ୟାଦିର କଣା, ଛେଦ *the eye of a needle* ➪ **needle** ଦେଖନ୍ତୁ ।

eyebrow /ˈaɪbraʊ/ *noun* one of the two lines of hair above your eyes ଭ୍ରୂ, ଭ୍ରୂଲତା, ଭୂରୁ ➪ ଚିତ୍ର ପାଇଁ **face** ଦେଖନ୍ତୁ ।

eyelash /ˈaɪlæʃ/ *noun* (*plural* **eyelashes**) one of the hairs that grow along the edge of your eyelid ଆଖି ପତାର ବାଳ, ନେତ୍ରପକ୍ଷ୍ମ *She's got beautiful long eyelashes.* ➪ ଚିତ୍ର ପାଇଁ **face** ଦେଖନ୍ତୁ ।

eyelid /ˈaɪlɪd/ *noun* the piece of skin that can move to close your eye ଆଖିପତା, ଚକ୍ଷୁପଟ, ନେତ୍ରଛଦ, ନେତ୍ରପଲକ

eyesight /ˈaɪsaɪt/ *noun* (*no plural*) the power to see ଦୃଷ୍ଟିଶକ୍ତି *Your eyesight is very good.*

F f

F *abbreviation* ଶବ୍ଦ **Fahrenheit** ର ସଂକ୍ଷିପ୍ତ ରୂପ

fable /ˈfeɪbl/ *noun* a short story, usually about animals, that teaches something ପଶୁ ଚରିତ୍ର ଥିବା ଗପ

fabulous /ˈfæbjələs/ *adjective* very good; wonderful ଚମତ୍କାର *The food smells fabulous!*

face[1] /feɪs/ *noun* **1** the front part of your head ମୁହଁ, ମୁଖ **2** the front or one side of something ସାମନା ପଟ *He put the cards face down on the table.*

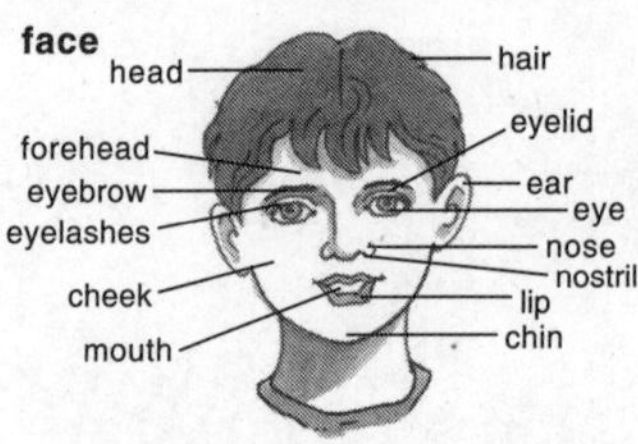

face to face if two people are face to face, they are looking straight at each other ସାମନା ସାମନି, ମୁହାଁମୁହିଁ

face[2] /feɪs/ *verb* (**faces, facing, faced**) **1** have the face or the front towards something (କୌଣସି ନିର୍ଦ୍ଦିଷ୍ଟ ଦିଗକୁ) ମୁହଁ କରିବା *My bedroom faces the garden.* **2** deal with someone unfriendly or a difficult situation (ଅସହଯୋଗୀ ବ୍ୟକ୍ତି ବା କଷ୍ଟକର ପରିସ୍ଥିତିର) ସାମନା କରିବା, ସମ୍ମୁଖୀନ ହେବା *The sailors faced a lot of difficulties during their voyage.*

facilities /fəˈsɪlətiz/ *noun* (*plural*) things in a place for you to use ବ୍ୟବସ୍ଥା, ସୁବିଧା, ଉପକରଣ *Our school has very good sports facilities.*

facility /fəˈsɪləti/ *noun* (*plural* **facilities**) if some machine has a facility, it has some extra feature that helps you to do something easily ବ୍ୟବସ୍ଥା, ସୁବିଧା *The new model of the fridge comes with the facility of making ice faster.*

fact /fækt/ *noun* something that you know has happened or is true ସତକଥା, ପ୍ରକୃତ ଘଟଣା, ଠିକ୍ ତଥ୍ୟ *It's a fact that the earth travels around the sun.*

factor /ˈfæktə(r)/ *noun* **1** one of the things that is an important cause of something else ଫଳଲାଭ ପାଇଁ ସହାୟକ ଉପାଦାନ ବା ପରିସ୍ଥିତି *What are the factors that led to the Second World War?* **2** a factor is a number that divides another number exactly, without leaving a **remainder** ଗୁଣକ; ଛଡ଼ା ଅନ୍ୟ ଯେ କୌଣସି ସଂଖ୍ୟା ଯାହା ଦ୍ୱାରା ଆଉ ଗୋଟିଏ ସଂଖ୍ୟା ପୂର୍ଣ୍ଣ ଭାବରେ ବିଭାଜିତ ହୋଇ ପାରିବ *2 and 5 are factors of 10.*

factory /ˈfæktri/ *noun* (*plural* **factories**) a place where people make things, usually with machines କାରଖାନା, ଶିଳ୍ପଶାଳା *He works at the car factory.*

fade /feɪd/ *verb* (**fades, fading, faded**) become less bright and colourful ଫିକା ପଡ଼ିବା *Will this shirt fade when I wash it?*

faeces /ˈfiːsiːz/ *noun* (*no singular*) the solid waste material that leaves the body ବିଷ୍ଠା, ମଳ

Fahrenheit /ˈfærənhaɪt/ *noun* (*no plural*) a way of measuring temperature. Water freezes at 32° Fahrenheit and boils at 212° Fahrenheit ଫାରେନ୍‌ହାଇଟ, ଉତ୍ତାପର ମାପକ୍ରମ ଯହିଁରେ ହିମାଙ୍କ (ପାଣି ବରଫ ହେବା ତାପମାତ୍ରା) ୩୨° ଓ ସ୍ଫୁଟନାଙ୍କ 0° (ପାଣି ଫୁଟିବା ତାପମାତ୍ରା) ୨୧୨° ✪ Fahrenheit ର ସଂକ୍ଷିପ୍ତ ରୂପ ହେଲା **F** *110°F*

fail /feɪl/ *verb* (**fails, failing, failed**) **1** try to do something but not be able to do it ବିଫଳ ହେବା, ଫେଲ୍ ମାରିବା, ଅକୃତକାର୍ଯ୍ୟ ହେବା *He played quite well but failed to win the match.* ✪ ବିପରୀତ **succeed 2** not pass an exam or test ପରୀକ୍ଷାରେ ଅସଫଳ ହେବା, ଫେଲ୍ ହେବା *How many students failed last term?*

failure /ˈfeɪljə(r)/ *noun* a person or thing that does not do well ଅସିଦ୍ଧି, ଅକୃତକାର୍ଯ୍ୟତା, ଅକୃତକାର୍ଯ୍ୟ ବ୍ୟକ୍ତି, ପଦାର୍ଥ ବା ଚେଷ୍ଟା *I felt that I was a failure because I didn't have a job.* ✪ ବିପରୀତ **success**

faint[1] /feɪnt/ *adjective* (**fainter, faintest**) **1** not clear or strong ଅସ୍ପଷ୍ଟ, ସ୍ୱଳ୍ପ, ଅଳ୍ପଟିକିଏ *We could hear the faint sound of music in the distance.* **2** if you feel faint, you feel that you are going to fall, for example because you are ill or tired ମୁଣ୍ଡ ବୁଲେଇଲାପରି, ଅଚେତ ହେଲାପରି

faint[2] /feɪnt/ *verb* (**faints, fainting, fainted**) fall down suddenly, for example because you are weak, ill or shocked ଅଚେତ ହେବା, ମୂର୍ଚ୍ଛା ହେବା

fair[1] /feə(r)/ *adjective* (**fairer, fairest**) **1** somebody or something that is fair treats people equally or in the right way ନ୍ୟାୟବାନ୍ (ବ୍ୟକ୍ତି) ନ୍ୟାୟସଙ୍ଗତ (ବିଷୟ), ନିରପେକ୍ଷ *a fair judge* ✪ ବିପରୀତ **unfair 2** of a light colour ହାଲୁକା ରଙ୍ଗର (କଳା ନୁହେଁ) *He's got fair hair.* ✪ ବିପରୀତ **dark**[1] **3 3** average, not very good ସାଧାରଣ, ଖୁବ୍ ଭଲ ହୋଇ ନଥିବା *She's good at English but only fair in Hindi.*

fair[2] /feə(r)/ *noun* a place outdoors where you can ride on big machines and play games to win prizes ମେଳା

fairly /ˈfeəli/ *adverb* **1** in a way that is right and honest ନିରପେକ୍ଷ ଭାବରେ, ନ୍ୟାୟୋଚିତ ଭାବରେ *This company treats its workers fairly.* ✪ ବିପରୀତ **unfairly 2** quite ବେଶ୍ *She speaks English fairly well.*

fairy /ˈfeəri/ *noun* (*plural* **fairies**) a very small person in stories. Fairies have wings and can do magic ପରୀ, ଅପ୍ସରା

fairy tale *noun* a story for children that is about magic or fairies ଅଦ୍ଭୁତ ଘଟଣା ଘଟୁଥିବା ବା ଅପସରା ଥିବା ପିଲାଙ୍କ ଗପ

faith /feɪθ/ *noun* **1** (*no plural*) feeling sure that somebody or something is good, right, honest, etc. ବିଶ୍ୱାସ, ଆସ୍ଥା, ପ୍ରତ୍ୟୟ *I've got great faith in your ability to do the job.* **2** (*plural* **faiths**) a religion ଧର୍ମ *the Muslim faith*

faithful /ˈfeɪθfl/ *adjective* always ready to help your friends and to do what you have promised to do ବିଶ୍ୱସ୍ତ, ପ୍ରଭୁଭକ୍ତ *a faithful friend* ✪ ବିପରୀତ **unfaithful**

faithfully /ˈfeɪθfəli/ *adverb* in a way you can rely on ବିଶ୍ୱସ୍ତ ଭାବରେ

Yours faithfully words that you write at the end of a letter, before your name, when you have addressed somebody as 'Dear Sir/Dear Madam' and not by their name ଯେଉଁ ଚିଠି 'Dear Sir/Dear Madam' (ମହାଶୟ/ମହାଶୟା) ସଂବୋଧନରେ ଆରମ୍ଭ ହୋଇଥାଏ, ତା'ର ଶେଷରେ Yours faithfully (ଆପଣଙ୍କ ବିଶ୍ୱସ୍ତ) ଲେଖାଯାଏ

fake /feɪk/ *noun* a copy of something made to trick people ନକଲି ପଦାର୍ଥ *This painting is not really by Picasso—it's a fake.*

fake *adjective* ନକଲି *a fake ten-rupee note*

fall[1] /fɔːl/ *verb* (**falls, falling, fell** /fel/, **has fallen** /ˈfɔːlən/) **1** go down quickly; drop ପଡ଼ିଯିବା, ଖସି ପଡ଼ିବା *The book fell off the table.* ○ *She fell down the stairs and broke her arm.* **2** become lower or less ହ୍ରାସ ହେବା, ନିମ୍ନତର ହେବା, ପତନ *Prices have fallen again.* ✪ ବିପରୀତ **rise**

fall apart break into pieces ପଡ଼ି ଖଣ୍ଡ ଖଣ୍ଡ ହୋଇଯିବା *The old chair fell apart when I sat down on it.*

fall asleep start sleeping ଶୋଇ ପଡ଼ିବା *She was so tired that she fell asleep in the armchair.*

fall[2] /fɔːl/ *noun* **1** a sudden drop from a higher place to a lower place ପତନ *He had a fall from his horse.* **2** becoming lower or less ପତନ, ହ୍ରାସ *a fall in the price of oil* ✪ ବିପରୀତ **rise** **3 falls** (*plural*) a place where a stream or river falls from a high place to a low place ଜଳପ୍ରପାତ *the Jog Falls* ➪ ଚିତ୍ରପାଇଁ ଦେଖନ୍ତୁ *waterfall*

false /fɔːls/ *adjective* **1** not correct; wrong ଭୁଲ୍, ମିଛ, ମିଥ୍ୟା, ଅସତ୍ୟ *A spider has eight legs—true or false?* ✪ ବିପରୀତ **true** **2** not real or not natural ଅପ୍ରାକୃତିକ, କୃତ୍ରିମ *People who have lost their teeth wear false teeth.* ✪ ବିପରୀତ **real 2** ବା **natural**

fame /feɪm/ *noun* (*no plural*) the state of being known by many people ଯଶ, ସୁଖ୍ୟାତି ✪ **Fame** ର ବିଶେଷଣ ହେଉଛି **famous** ।

familiar /fəˈmɪliə(r)/ *adjective* **1** that you know well ସୁପରିଚିତ, ଜଣାଶୁଣା *I heard a familiar voice in the next room.* **2** having a good knowledge of something କୌଣସି ବିଷୟ ଭଲ ଭାବେ ଜାଣିଥିବା, ସୁବିଦିତ ଥିବା *familiar with the laws of the state* ✪ ବିପରୀତ **unfamiliar**

familiarity /fəˌmɪliˈærəti/ *noun* (*no plural*) the state of knowing somebody or something well ଘନିଷ୍ଠ ପରିଚୟ, ସୌହାର୍ଦ୍ୟ, ଅଭ୍ୟସ୍ତତା *His familiarity with French helped him get the job.*

family /ˈfæməli/ *noun* (*plural* **families**) **1** parents and children ପରିବାର *How many people are there in your family?*

> ✪ କେତେକ କ୍ଷେତ୍ରରେ 'family' କେବଳ ବାପା, ମା ଓ ପିଲାଙ୍କ ଛଡ଼ା ଜେଜେ ବାପା, ଜେଜେମା, ଅଜା, ଆଇ, କକେଇ, ବଡ଼ବାପା, ପିଉସୀ, ମାମୁଁ, ମାଉସୀ ଓ ସେମାନଙ୍କ ପିଲାମାନଙ୍କୁ ମଧ୍ୟ ବୁଝାଏ।

2 a group of plants or animals ଉଦ୍ଭିଦ ବା ପ୍ରାଣୀର ଏକ ନିର୍ଦ୍ଦିଷ୍ଟ ବର୍ଗ *Lions belong to the cat family.*

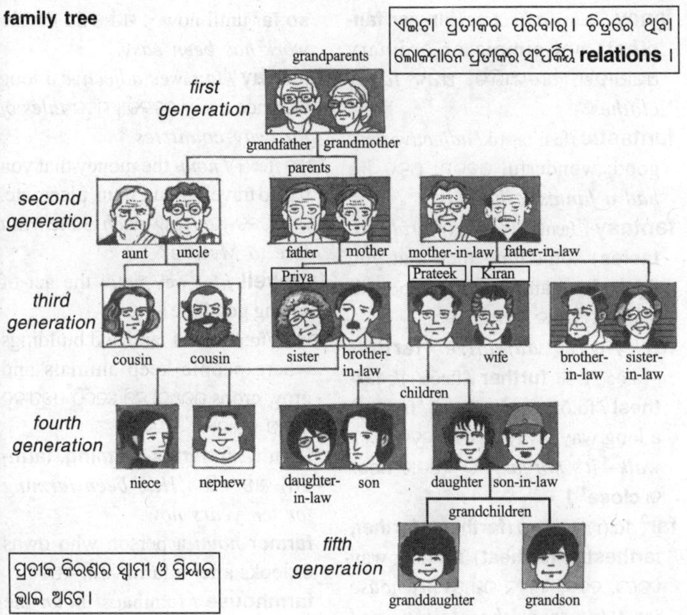

family tree *noun* a diagram that shows the relationship between members of a family over a long period of time ବଂଶବୃକ୍ଷ, ବଂଶାବଳୀ, ବଂଶାନୁକ୍ରମ ଚିତ୍ର

famine /ˈfæmɪn/ *noun* a famine happens when there is not enough food in a country ଦୁର୍ଭିକ୍ଷ

famous /ˈfeɪməs/ *adjective* known by many people ପ୍ରସିଦ୍ଧ, ବିଖ୍ୟାତ *Oxford is famous for its university.*
✪ **Famous** ଏହାର ବିଶେଷ୍ୟ ହେଲା **fame**।

fan[1] /fæn/ *noun* a machine with parts that go round and move the air to make you cooler ପଙ୍ଖା, ବିଞ୍ଚଣା, ଫ୍ୟାନ୍

fan *verb* (**fans, fanning, fanned**) make somebody or something cooler by moving the air ପଙ୍ଖା ବୁଲାଇ ପବନ କରିବା, ବିଞ୍ଚିବା *I fanned my face with a newspaper.*

fan[2] /fæn/ *noun* a person who likes somebody or something, for example a singer or a sport, very much ଆଗ୍ରହୀ ସମର୍ଥକ (ଗାୟକ, ଅଭିନେତା, ଖେଳ ଇତ୍ୟାଦିର) *She is a football fan.*

fanatic /fəˈnætɪk/ *noun* a person who is seriously interested in something but has extreme or dangerous opinions about it (especially on religion or politics) ଉଗ୍ର ଭାବରେ ଆଗ୍ରହୀ ବା ଉତ୍ସାହୀ ବ୍ୟକ୍ତି *He is a religious fanatic.*

fancy /ˈfænsi/ *adjective* (**fancier, fanciest**) not simple or ordinary ଅସାଧାରଣ, ଆଳଙ୍କାରିକ, ଅପୂର୍ବ *fancy clothes*

fantastic /fænˈtæstɪk/ *adjective* very good; wonderful ଖୁବ୍‌ଭଲ; ଅଦ୍ଭୁତ *We had a fantastic holiday.*

fantasy /ˈfæntəsi/ *noun* (*plural* **fantasies**) something nice that you think about and that you hope will happen ଅବାସ୍ତବ କଳ୍ପନା

far[1] /fɑː(r)/ *adjective* (**farther** /ˈfɑːðə(r)/ ବା **further** /ˈfɜːðə(r)/, **farthest** /ˈfɑːðɪst/ ବା **furthest** /ˈfɜːðɪst/) a long way away ଦୂରବର୍ତ୍ତୀ, ସୁଦୂର *Let's walk—it's not far.* ✪ ବିପରୀତ **near** ବା **close**[1] **1**

far[2] /fɑː(r)/ *adverb* (**farther** ବା **further, farthest** ବା **furthest**) **1** a long way ଦୂରରେ, ଦୂରକୁ, ବହୁଦୂର ପର୍ଯ୍ୟନ୍ତ। *My house isn't far from the station.* ○ *I walked much farther than you.* ✪ ବିପରୀତ **near** ବା **close**[1] **2** you use 'far' to ask about the distance from one place to another place ଦୂର, ଦୂରରେ *How far is it to Dehradun from here?* ✪ ନକାରାତ୍ମକ ବାକ୍ୟରେ ଓ ପ୍ରଶ୍ନ ପଚାରିଲା ବେଳେ ଆମେ **far** ବ୍ୟବହାର କରୁ। ଅନ୍ୟ ସମୟରେ ଆମେ କହୁ **a long way** *It's a long way to walk—let's take the bus.*

as far as I know words that you use when you think something is true but you are not certain ମୁଁ ଯେତିକି ଜାଣେ, ମୋ ଜାଣିବାରେ *As far as I know, she's well, but I haven't seen her for a long time.*

so far until now ଏ ପର୍ଯ୍ୟନ୍ତ *So far the work has been easy.*

faraway /ˈfɑːrəweɪ/ *adjective* a long distance away ଦୂରବର୍ତ୍ତୀ, ସୁଦୂର *tales of faraway countries*

fare /feə(r)/ *noun* the money that you pay to travel by bus, train, plane, etc. ଭଡ଼ା, ଟିକଟମୂଲ୍ୟ *How much is the train fare to Mysore?*

farewell /ˌfeəˈwel/ *noun* the act of saying goodbye ବିଦାୟ

farm /fɑːm/ *noun* land and buildings where people keep animals and grow crops ଘରଥିବା ଜମି ଯେଉଁଠି ପଶୁପାଳନ ଓ ଚାଷ କରାଯାଏ

farm *verb* (**farms, farming, farmed**) ଚାଷ କରିବା। *He's been farming for ten years now.*

farmer *noun* a person who owns or looks after a farm ଚାଷୀ, କୃଷକ

farmhouse /ˈfɑːmhaʊs/ *noun* the house on a farm where the farmer lives କୃଷିକ୍ଷେତ୍ରରେ ଥିବା ଘର

farming /ˈfɑːmɪŋ/ *noun* (*no plural*) the act of working on or managing a farm ଚାଷବାସ

farther, farthest ଶବ୍ଦ **far** ର ଧାତୁରୂପ

fascinating /ˈfæsɪneɪtɪŋ/ *adjective* very interesting ଆକର୍ଷଣୀୟ, ମନୋହର *She told us fascinating stories about her journey through Africa.*

fashion /ˈfæʃn/ *noun* a way of dressing or doing something that people like and try to copy for a short time (ପୋଷାକ ଇତ୍ୟାଦିର) ପ୍ରଚଳିତ ଜନପ୍ରିୟ ଢଙ୍ଗ, ଫେସନ *Long hair is in fashion again.*

fashionable *adjective* in the newest fashion ପ୍ରଚଳିତ ରୁଚିସମ୍ମତ *She was wearing a fashionable black skirt.* ✪ ବିପରୀତ **unfashionable** ବା **old-fashioned**

fashion designer *noun* a person whose job is to design clothes ନୂଆ ଢଙ୍ଗର ଲୁଗାପଟା ପରିକଳ୍ପନା କରିଥିବା ବ୍ୟକ୍ତି

fast[1] /fɑːst/ *adjective* (**faster, fastest**) **1** a person or thing that is fast can move quickly ଦ୍ରୁତଗାମୀ, କ୍ଷିପ୍ର *a fast car* **2** if a clock or watch is fast, it shows a time that is later than the real time ଆଗୁଆ ଚାଲୁଥିବା (ଘଣ୍ଟା) *My watch is five minutes fast.* ✪ ବିପରୀତ **slow**[1]

fast food *noun* (*no plural*) food like burgers and chips that can be cooked and eaten quickly ଚଞ୍ଚଳ ପ୍ରସ୍ତୁତ ଓ ପରିବେଷଣ କରାଯାଇ ପାରୁଥିବା ଖାଦ୍ୟ

fast[2] /fɑːst/ *adverb* (**faster, fastest**) quickly ଶିଘ୍ର, ଜୋର୍‌ରେ, ଜଲ୍‌ଦି *Don't talk so fast—I can't understand what you're saying.* ✪ ବିପରୀତ **slowly**

fast asleep sleeping very well ଗଭୀର ନିଦ

fast[3] /fɑːst/ *verb* (**fasts, fasting, fasted**) not eat food for a certain time ଓପାସ ରହିବା, ଉପବାସ କରିବା *Muslims fast during Ramzan.*

fasten /ˈfɑːsn/ *verb* (**fastens, fastening, fastened**) close something so that it will not come open; join one thing to another ଦୃଢ଼ ଭାବରେ ବନ୍ଧନ କରିବା, ଲଗାଇବା *He fastened the buttons on his shirt quickly.* ✪ ବିପରୀତ **unfasten**

fat[1] /fæt/ *adjective* (**fatter, fattest**) with a large round body ମୋଟା, ସ୍ଥୂଳକାୟ ✪ ବିପରୀତ **thin 2**

fat[2] /fæt/ *noun* (*no plural*) the oily substance under the skins of animals and people ଚର୍ବି *Cut the fat off the meat.*

fatal /ˈfeɪtl/ *adjective* something that is fatal causes death ମାରାତ୍ମକ, ସାଂଘାତିକ *a fatal car accident*

fate /feɪt/ *noun* (*no plural*) the power that some people believe controls everything that happens ଭାଗ୍ୟ, ନିୟତି, ଅଦୃଷ୍ଟ, ବିଧିବିଧାନ

father /ˈfɑːðə(r)/ *noun* a man who has a child ବାପା, ନନା, ପିତା *Where do your mother and father live?* ➪ **dad** ଓ **daddy** ଦେଖନ୍ତୁ। ➪ ଚିତ୍ର ପାଇଁ **family** ଦେଖନ୍ତୁ।

father-in-law *noun* (*plural* **fathers-in-law**) the father of your husband or wife ଶଶୁର ➪ ଚିତ୍ର ପାଇଁ **family** ଦେଖନ୍ତୁ।

fatigue /fəˈtiːg/ *noun* (*no plural*) the state of being tired କ୍ଳାନ୍ତି, ଅବସନ୍ନତା, ହାଲିଆ *mental fatigue*

fault /fɔːlt/ *noun* **1** (*no plural*) if something bad happens because of you, it is your fault ଭୁଲ, ତ୍ରୁଟି *It's Smita's fault that we are late.* **2** (*plural* **faults**) something that is wrong or bad in a person or thing ତ୍ରୁଟି *There is a serious fault in the machine.*

favour /ˈfeɪvə(r)/ *noun* something that you do to help somebody ସାହାଯ୍ୟ, ଉପକାର *Would you do me a favour and open the door?*

be in favour of something like or agree with something କୌଣସି ପକ୍ଷର ସମର୍ଥନ କରିବା *Are you in favour of the new plan?*

favourite /ˈfeɪvərɪt/ *adjective* your favourite person or thing is the one that you like more than any other ଅଧିକ ଆଦରଣୀୟ, ସବୁଠାରୁ ପ୍ରିୟ *What's your favourite colour?*

favourite *noun* a person or thing that you like more than any other ସବୁଠାରୁ ପ୍ରିୟ ବ୍ୟକ୍ତି ବା ପଦାର୍ଥ *I like all chocolates but this one is my favourite.*

fawn /fɔːn/ *noun* the young one of a deer ହରିଣ ଛୁଆ ➪ ଚିତ୍ର ପାଇଁ **deer** ଦେଖନ୍ତୁ ।

fax /fæks/ *verb* (**faxes, faxing, faxed**) send a copy of something like a letter or picture using telephone lines and a machine called a **fax machine** ଇଲେକ୍ଟ୍ରନିକ୍ ଫ୍ୟାକ୍ସ ଯନ୍ତ୍ର ସାହାଯ୍ୟରେ ଚିଠି, ଦଲିଲ ଇତ୍ୟାଦିର ପ୍ରତିଲିପି ବା ନକଲ ଦୂରଦୂରାନ୍ତକୁ ତତକ୍ଷଣାତ ପଠାଇବା *The drawings were faxed from New Delhi.*

fax *noun* (*plural* **faxes**) a copy of something that is sent by a fax machine ଫ୍ୟାକ୍ସ ଦ୍ୱାରା ପଠାଯାଇଥିବା ପ୍ରତିଲିପି

fear /fɪə(r)/ *noun* the feeling that you have when you think that something bad might happen ଭୟ, ଡର, ଶଙ୍କା

fear *verb* (**fears, fearing, feared**) be afraid of somebody or something ଭୟ କରିବା, ଡର ଲାଗିବା *We all fear illness and death.* ✪ ସାଧାରଣତଃ ଆମେ **be afraid (of)** ବା **be frightened (of)** ବ୍ୟବହାର କରୁ।

fearless /ˈfɪələs/ *adjective* a person who is fearless is not afraid of dangerous people or things ନିର୍ଭିକ, ସାହସୀ *a fearless warrior*

fearlessly *adverb* ନିର୍ଭିକ ଭାବରେ *The soldier fought fearlessly.*

fearlessness *noun* (*no plural*) ନିର୍ଭୀକତା *a sense of fearlessness*

feast /fiːst/ *noun* a large special meal for a lot of people ଭୋଜି *a wedding feast*

feat /fiːt/ *noun* something you do that is clever, difficult or dangerous ଉଲ୍ଲେଖଯୋଗ୍ୟ କାମ, କୃତିତ୍ୱ *Climbing Mount Everest was an amazing feat.*

feather /ˈfeðə(r)/ *noun* one of the soft, light things on the body of a bird that keeps it warm and helps it to fly ପକ୍ଷୀର ପର

feature /ˈfiːtʃə(r)/ *noun* **1** an important part of something ବୈଶିଷ୍ଟ୍ୟ, ବିଶେଷ ଗୁଣ *Pictures are a feature of this dictionary.* **2** a part of the face, for example the eyes, nose or mouth ମୁହଁର ବିଭିନ୍ନ ଅଂଶ (ଯଥା ଆଖି, ନାକ, କାନ ଇତ୍ୟାଦି) *His long nose is his most striking feature.*

February /ˈfebruəri/ *noun* the second month of the year ପାଶ୍ଚାତ୍ୟ ବର୍ଷର ଦ୍ୱିତୀୟ ମାସ, ଫେବ୍ରୁଆରୀ

fed ଶବ୍ଦ **feed** ର ଏକ ଧାତୁରୂପ

fee /fiː/ *noun* **1** money that you pay to somebody for special work ପାଉଣା, ଫି *The lawyer's fee was Rs 2,000.* **2 fees** (*plural*) the money that you pay for lessons at school, college or university ସ୍କୁଲ୍ କଲେଜରେ ଦିଆଯାଉଥିବା ପାଉଣା, ଫି *Who pays your college fees?*

feeble /ˈfi:bl/ *adjective* (**feebler, feeblest**) not strong; weak ଶକ୍ତିହୀନ, ଦୁର୍ବଳ *a feeble old man*

feed /fi:d/ *verb* (**feeds, feeding, fed** /fed/, **has fed**) **1** give food to a person or an animal ଖାଇବାକୁ ଦେବା *The baby's crying—I'll go and feed her.* **2** eat food ଖାଇବା *Cattle feed on grass.*

feel /fi:l/ *verb* (**feels, feeling, felt** /felt/, **has felt**) **1** know something because your body tells you ଅନୁଭବ କରିବା, ସ୍ପର୍ଶ କରି ଜାଣିବା *I'm feeling tired.* **2** be rough, smooth, wet, dry, etc. when you touch it ସ୍ପର୍ଶ ଦ୍ୱାରା ଅନୁଭୂତ ହେବା *The water felt cold.* **3** think; believe ଭାବିବା; ବିଶ୍ୱାସ କରିବା *I feel that we should talk about this.*

feel like want something ଇଚ୍ଛା କରିବା, ଆଗ୍ରହ କରିବା *Do you feel like a cup of tea?*

feeling /ˈfi:lɪŋ/ *noun* **1** (*plural* **feelings**) something that you feel inside yourself, like happiness or anger ଅନୁଭବ, ଆବେଗ *a feeling of sadness* **2** (*no plural*) the ability to feel in your body ସ୍ପର୍ଶ ଶକ୍ତି *I was so cold that I had no feeling in my feet.*

feet ଶବ୍ଦ **foot** ର ଏକ ଧାତୁରୂପ

fell ଶବ୍ଦ **fall** ର ଏକ ଧାତୁରୂପ

fellow /ˈfeləʊ/ *noun* a man ବ୍ୟକ୍ତି, ପୁରୁଷ ବା ବାଳକ *What is that fellow doing?*

felt ଶବ୍ଦ **feel** ର ଏକ ଧାତୁରୂପ

felt-pen *noun* a pen with a soft point ନରମ ମୁନ ଥିବା କଲମ

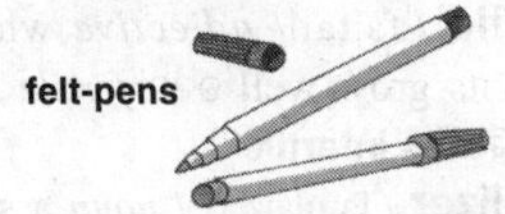

felt-pens

female /ˈfi:meɪl/ *noun* a person or animal that belongs to the sex that can have babies ସ୍ତ୍ରୀଲୋକ, ମାଈ ପଶୁ ବା ସ୍ତ୍ରୀ ବୃକ୍ଷ *My cat is a female.* ➪ **male** ଦେଖନ୍ତୁ ।

female *adjective* ସ୍ତ୍ରୀଜାତୀୟ *a female artist*

feminine /ˈfemənɪn/ *adjective* of or like a woman; right for a woman ନାରୀ ସମ୍ବନ୍ଧୀୟ ବା ନାରୀ ପରି; ନାରୀ ସୁଲଭ *feminine clothes* ➪ **masculine** ଦେଖନ୍ତୁ ।

fence /fens/ *noun* a thing like a wall that is made of pieces of wood or metal. Fences are put round gardens and fields (ଘର, ବଗିଚା, ପଡ଼ିଆ ଇତ୍ୟାଦିର) ବାଡ଼ ➪ ଚିତ୍ର ପାଇଁ **house** ଦେଖନ୍ତୁ ।

ferment /fəˈment/ *verb* (**ferments, fermenting, fermented**) bring about a chemical change in something, often by using **yeast** or **bacteria** ଖମୀର (ୟିଷ୍ଟ) ବା ଜୀବାଣୁ ଦ୍ୱାରା ପଚାଇବା ଅମ୍ଳିଭବନ କରିବା କିଣ୍ୱନ କରିବା *Fruit juices ferment if they are kept a long time.*

ferocious /fəˈrəʊʃəs/ *adjective* very fierce and wild ଭୟଙ୍କର, ଭୀଷଣ *A tiger is a ferocious animal.*

ferry /feri/ *noun* (*plural* **ferries**) a boat that takes people or things on short journeys across a river or a narrow part of the sea ଲୋକମାନେ ବା

ଜିନିଷପତ୍ର ନଦୀ ଇତ୍ୟାଦି ପାର କରାଇବା ପାଇଁ ନୌକା *We crossed the river by ferry.*

fertile /ˈfɜːtaɪl/ *adjective* where plants grow well ଉର୍ବର *fertile soil* ✪ ବିପରୀତ **infertile**

fertilizer /ˈfɜːtɪlaɪzə(r)/ *noun* a substance that is added to soil to help plants grow well ସାର, ଖତ

festival /ˈfestɪvl/ *noun* a time when people do special things to celebrate an event ପର୍ବ, ଉତ୍ସବ

fetch /fetʃ/ *verb* (**fetches, fetching, fetched**) go and bring back somebody or something ଯାଇ ଆଣିବା *Can you fetch me the books from the cupboard?*

fête /feɪt/ *noun* a party outside where you can buy things and play games to win prizes. Schools often have fêtes to collect money for a good cause କୌଣସି ବିଶେଷ ଉଦ୍ଦେଶ୍ୟରେ ବା ଦାନ ପାଇଁ ପାଣ୍ଠି ସଂଗ୍ରହ କରିବାକୁ ଖୋଲା ଜାଗାରେ କରାଯାଇଥିବା ମେଳା

fête

fever /ˈfiːvə(r)/ *noun* if you have a fever, your body is hotter than normal because you are ill ଜର, ଜ୍ୱର

few /fjuː/ *adjective* (**fewer, fewest**), *pronoun* not many ଅଳ୍ପ, ଅଳ୍ପସଂଖ୍ୟକ *There are fewer buses in the evenings.*

a few some but not many କେତେକ *Only a few people came to the meeting.*

fibre /ˈfaɪbə(r)/ *noun* a material that is made of threads ତନ୍ତୁ, ସୂତ୍ରତନ୍ତୁ, ସୂତା *cotton fibre*

fiddle /ˈfɪdl/ *verb* (**fiddles, fiddling, fiddled**) keep touching something a lot with your fingers ଆଙ୍ଗୁଠିରେ ବାରମ୍ବାର ଏପଟ ସେପଟ କରିବା *Stop fiddling with your pen and do some work!*

field /fiːld/ *noun* **1** a piece of land that usually has a fence or hedge around it. Fields are used for growing crops or keeping animals in ପଡ଼ିଆ, ପ୍ରାନ୍ତର, ଚାଷଜମି (ବେଳେ ବେଳେ ବାଡ଼ଘେରା) **2** a piece of land used for something special ବିଶେଷ କାମରେ ବ୍ୟବହୃତ ପଡ଼ିଆ *a sports field* ○ *an airfield* **3** a place where people find oil, coal, gold, etc. ଭୂତଳ ତେଲ, କୋଇଲା, ସୁନା ଇତ୍ୟାଦି ମିଳୁଥିବା ଜାଗା *a coalfield* ○ *oilfields*

fierce /fɪəs/ *adjective* (**fiercer, fiercest**) angry and wild ଭୟଙ୍କର, ହିଂସ୍ର, ଦୁର୍ଦ୍ଦାନ୍ତ *a fierce dog*

fiery /ˈfaɪəri/ *adjective* **1** bright red; like fire ନିଆଁ ପରି ଉଜ୍ଜ୍ୱଳ, ଜଳିଲା ପରି *fiery eyes* **2** becoming angry very quickly କ୍ଷଣକୋପୀ *a fiery temper*

fifteen /ˌfɪfˈtiːn/ *number* 15 ପନ୍ଦର (୧୫); ଅଙ୍କ

fifteenth /ˌfɪfˈtiːnθ/ *adjective, adverb, noun* 15th ପଞ୍ଚଦଶ, ପନ୍ଦରତମ

fifth /fɪfθ/ *adjective, adverb, noun* **1** 5th ୫ମ **2** one of five equal parts of something; $\frac{1}{5}$ ପାଞ୍ଚ ଭାଗରୁ ଭାଗେ $\frac{୧}{୫}$

fifty /ˈfɪfti/ *number* **1** 50 ପଚାଶ **2 the fifties** (*plural*) the numbers, years or temperatures between 50 and 59 ପଚାଶ ଦଶକ, ୫୦ ଠାରୁ ୫୯ ପର୍ଯ୍ୟନ୍ତ ସଂଖ୍ୟା, ବର୍ଷ ବା ଉତ୍ତାପମାତ୍ରା *He was born in the fifties.*

fiftieth /ˈfɪftiəθ/ *adjective*, *adverb*, *noun* 50th ପଚାଶତମ ୫୦ ତମ; ଅଂଶ

fig /fɪg/ *noun* a soft sweet fruit that is full of small seeds ଡିମ୍ବିରି ଫଳ ବା ଗଛ

fight[1] /faɪt/ *verb* (**fights, fighting, fought** /fɔ:t/, **has fought**) **1** when people fight, they try to hurt or kill each other using their hands, or using weapons like knives or guns ଲଢ଼େଇ କରିବା, ଯୁଦ୍ଧ କରିବା **2** talk in an angry way; argue କଳିକଜିଆ କରିବା; ଯୁକ୍ତିତର୍କ କରିବା

fight for something try very hard to do or get something କିଛି ପାଇବା ପାଇଁ ଲଢ଼ିବା *The workers are fighting for better pay.*

fight[2] /faɪt/ *noun* an act of fighting ଲଢ଼େଇ, ଯୁଦ୍ଧ *There was a fight outside the restaurant last night.*

figure /ˈfɪgə(r)/ *noun* **1** one of the symbols (0–9) that we use to show numbers ସଂଖ୍ୟା ଚିହ୍ନ (ବିଶେଷତଃ 0–୯) *Shall I write the numbers in words or figures?* **2** the shape of a person's body ଶାରୀରିକ ଆକୃତି, ଚେହେରା, ଗଠଣ *She's got a good figure.*

filament /ˈfɪləmənt/ *noun* **1** a thin wire in a light bulb that glows when electricity is passed through it (ବିଦ୍ୟୁତ୍ ପ୍ରବାହ ଦ୍ୱାରା ତାତି ଆଲୋକ ଦେଉଥିବା) ବଲ୍ବର ସରୁ ତାର। *The filament in the bulb has broken into two.* **2** a long and thin piece of something ସୂତାପରି ସରୁ ଓ ଲମ୍ବା ଖିଅ *gold filaments*

file[1] /faɪl/ *noun* **1** a box or cover for keeping papers in ନଥି, ଏକାଠି ଗୁନ୍ଥା କାଗଜପତ୍ରର ଧାରକ, ଫାଇଲ୍ **2** a collection of information on a computer କମ୍ପୁଟର୍‌ରେ ଗଚ୍ଛିତ ତଥ୍ୟ

file *verb* (**files, filing, filed**) put papers into a file ନଥି ବା ଫାଇଲ୍‌ରେ ରଖିବା *Can you file these letters, please?*

file[2] /faɪl/ *noun* a tool with rough sides that you use for making things smooth ଉହା *a nail file*

file[3] /faɪl/ *verb* (**files, filing, filed**) walk in a line, one behind the other ଗୋଟିଏ ଧାଡ଼ିରେ ଚାଲିବା *The students filed into the classroom.*

fill /fɪl/ *verb* (**fills, filling, filled**) make something full; become full ପୂର୍ଣ୍ଣ କରିବା; ପୂର୍ଣ୍ଣ ହେବା *Can you fill this glass with water, please?*

fill in write facts or answers in the spaces that have been left for them ଖାଲି ସ୍ଥାନରେ ତଥ୍ୟ ଲେଖି ଦରଖାସ୍ତ। ପ୍ରଶ୍ନପତ୍ର ଇତ୍ୟାଦି ପୂରା କରିବା *She gave me a form and told me to fill it in.*

fill up become or make something completely full ସମ୍ପୂର୍ଣ୍ଣ ଭାବରେ ପୂରଣ କରିବା, ପୂରା ଭର୍ତ୍ତି ହେବା *He filled up the tank with petrol.*

filling /ˈfɪlɪŋ/ *noun* something that you put into a space or hole ଦାନ୍ତ କଣା ବନ୍ଦ କରିବା ପାଇଁ ଦିଆଯାଉଥିବା ପଦାର୍ଥ; ସ୍ୟାଣ୍ଡୱିଚ କରିବା ପାଇଁ ବା ପିଠା, ସିଙ୍ଗଡ଼ା ଇତ୍ୟାଦି କରିବା ପାଇଁ ଦିଆଯାଉଥିବା ପୂର *I've got three fillings in my teeth.*

film[1] /fɪlm/ *noun* **1** moving pictures that you see at a cinema or on television ଚଳଚ୍ଚିତ୍ର, ଫିଲ୍ମ, ସିନେମା *There's a good film on at the cinema this week.* **2** the special thin plastic that you use in a camera for taking photographs କ୍ୟାମେରାରେ ଫଟ ଉଠାଇବା ପାଇଁ ଲଗାଯାଉଥିବା ପତଳା ପ୍ଲାଷ୍ଟିକ ଫିଲ୍ମ ବା ଆଲୋକ ଅନୁଭବୀ ପଦାର୍ଥ *I bought a roll of black and white film.*

film[2] /fɪlm/ *verb* (**films, filming, filmed**) use a camera to make moving pictures of a story, news, etc. ଚଳଚ୍ଚିତ୍ର ଉତ୍ତୋଳନ କରିବା (କ୍ୟାମେରା ଦ୍ୱାରା) *A TV company is filming outside my house.*

filter /ˈfɪltə(r)/ *noun* a thing used for holding back the solid parts in a liquid or gas ତରଳ ପଦାର୍ଥ ବା ବାଷ୍ପର ଛାଙ୍କୁଣି ବା ସୋଧକ ଯନ୍ତ୍ର *a coffee filter*

filter *verb* (**filters, filtering, filtered**) ଛାଣିବା, ସୋଧନ କରିବା *You should filter the water before you drink it.*

filthy /ˈfɪlθi/ *adjective* (**filthier, filthiest**) very dirty ଦୂଷିତ, ମଇଳା, ଅପରିଷ୍କୃତ *Go and wash your hands. They're filthy!*

filtration /fɪlˈtreɪʃn/ *noun* (*no plural*) the process of filtering a liquid or gas in order to remove materials that are not wanted ତରଳ ପଦାର୍ଥ ବା ବାଷ୍ପ ଛାଙ୍କି ବା ସୋଧନ କରି ପରିଷ୍କାର କରିବା *Filtration helps in removing the impurities present in water.*

fin /fɪn/ *noun* one of the thin flat parts on a fish that help it to swim ମାଛର ଡେଣା ➪ ଚିତ୍ର ପାଇଁ **fish** ଦେଖନ୍ତୁ।

final[1] /ˈfaɪnl/ *adjective* **1** last; at the end ଶେଷ, ଅନ୍ତିମ *The work is in its final stages.* **2** that will not be changed ଚୂଡ଼ାନ୍ତ *The referee's ruling is final.*

final[2] /ˈfaɪnl/ *noun* the last game in a competition to decide who wins ଖେଳ ପ୍ରତିଯୋଗିତାର ଶେଷ ଖେଳ ବା ମ୍ୟାଚ୍

finally /ˈfaɪnəli/ *adverb* after a long time; in the end ପରିଶେଷରେ *After a long wait the bus finally arrived.*

finance /ˈfaɪnæns/ *noun* money; planning how to get, save and use money for a business, country, etc. ଅର୍ଥ, ଟଙ୍କା ପଇସା; ଅର୍ଥ ନିୟନ୍ତ୍ରଣ, ବିତ୍ତ ବ୍ୟବସ୍ଥା *the Minister of Finance*

finance *verb* (**finances, financing, financed**) give money to pay for something ଅର୍ଥ ଯୋଗାଇବା *The building was financed by the government.*

financial /faɪˈnænʃl/ *adjective* of or about money ଆର୍ଥିକ, ଅର୍ଥ ସମ୍ବନ୍ଧୀୟ *financial problems*

find /faɪnd/ *verb* (**finds, finding, found** /faʊnd/, **has found**) **1** see or get something after looking or trying ଖୋଜି ପାଇବା *I can't find my glasses.* **2** see or get something that you did not expect ଆକସ୍ମିକ ଭାବେ ପାଇବା *I found some money in the street.* **3** think or have an idea about something because you have felt, tried, seen it, etc. (ପଢ଼ି, ଦେଖି, ବିଚାର କରି) ଜାଣିବା *I didn't find that book very interesting.*

find out discover something, for example by asking or studying

ଆବିଷ୍କାର କରିବା; ଖବର ଆଣିବା *Can you find out what time the train leaves?*

fine[1] /faɪn/ *adjective* (**finer, finest**) **1** well or happy ଭଲ, ସନ୍ତୋଷଜନକ, ସୁସ୍ଥ *'How are you?' 'Fine, thanks. And you?'* **2** good enough; okay ଠିକ୍ ଅଛି *'Let's meet on Monday.' 'Fine.'* **3** beautiful or of good quality ସୁନ୍ଦର; ଉତ୍କୃଷ୍ଟ *There's a fine view from the top of the hill.* **4** very thin ସୂକ୍ଷ୍ମ, ଅତି ପତଳା *I've got very fine hair.* ✪ ବିପରୀତ **thick 5** in very small pieces କ୍ଷୁଦ୍ର କଣାରେ ଗଠିତ *Salt is finer than sugar.* ✪ ବିପରୀତ **coarse**

finely *adverb* **1** beautifully or elegantly ସୁନ୍ଦର ଭାବରେ, ସୂକ୍ଷ୍ମ ଭାବରେ *finely embroidered cloth* **2** into very small pieces ଖୁବ୍ ଛୋଟ ଛୋଟ କରି *finely chopped carrots*

fine[2] /faɪn/ *noun* money that you must pay because you have done something wrong ଜୋରିମାନା, ଅର୍ଥଦଣ୍ଡ *He had to pay a fine for parking his car in the wrong place.*

fine *verb* (**fines, fining, fined**) make somebody pay a fine ଜୋରିମାନା ଲଗାଇବା, ଅର୍ଥଦଣ୍ଡ ଦେବା *I was fined Rs 500 for speeding.*

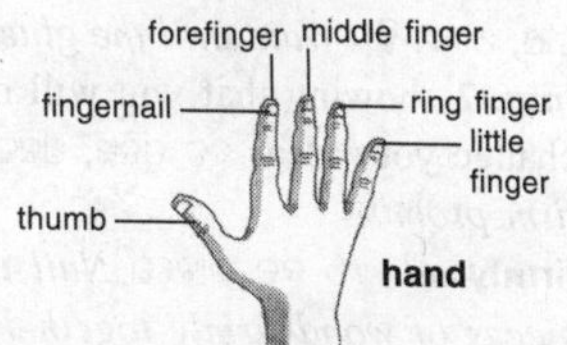

finger /ˈfɪŋɡə(r)/ *noun* one of the five parts at the end of each hand ଆଙ୍ଗୁଠି, ଆଙ୍ଗୁଳି *She wears a ring on her little finger.*

keep your fingers crossed hope that somebody or something will be successful ମଝି ଆଙ୍ଗୁଠି ବିଶି ଆଙ୍ଗୁଠି ଉପରେ ରଖି ଶୁଭକାମନା କରିବା

fingernail /ˈfɪŋɡəneɪl/ *noun* the hard part at the end of your finger ନଖ

fingerprint /ˈfɪŋɡəprɪnt/ *noun* the mark that a finger makes when it touches something ଟିପ ଚିହ୍ନ

finish[1] /ˈfɪnɪʃ/ *verb* (**finishes, finishing, finished**) stop doing something; come to the end of something ବନ୍ଦ କରିବା; ସମାପ୍ତ କରିବା, ଶେଷ କରିବା *I finish work at half past five.* ○ *Have you finished cleaning your room?* ✪ ବିପରୀତ **start[1]**

finish off do or eat the last part of something (ଖାଦ୍ୟ ଇତ୍ୟାଦି) ଶେଷ କରିବା, ସାରିଦେବା *He finished off all the milk.*

finish[2] /ˈfɪnɪʃ/ *noun* the last part of something; the end ଶେଷ, ସମାପ୍ତି *the finish of a race* ✪ ବିପରୀତ **start[2]**

finite /ˈfaɪnaɪt/ *adjective* having a limit or an end ସୀମିତ, ସୀମାବଦ୍ଧ, ପରିମିତି ✪ ବିପରୀତ **infinite**

fir /fɜː(r)/, **fir tree** *noun* a tree with thin sharp leaves (called **needles**) that do not fall off in winter. Fir trees are similar to **pine** trees ମୁନିଆ ପତ୍ର ଥିବା ଝାଉଁ ବା ପାଇନ୍ ଗଛପରି ସଦାସବୁଜ ଗଛ

fire[1] /ˈfaɪə(r)/ *noun* **1** the heat and bright light that comes from burning things ନିଆଁ, ଅଗ୍ନି *Many animals are afraid of fire.* **2** burning wood or coal that you use for keeping a place warm or for cooking ରାନ୍ଧିବା ବା ଘର ଉଷୁମ୍ ରଖିବା ପାଇଁ କାଠ ବା କୋଇଲାର ରଡ ନିଆଁ *They lit a fire to keep warm.*

catch fire start to burn ନିଆଁ ଲାଗିବା, ନିଆଁ ଧରିବା *He dropped his cigarette and the carpet caught fire.*

put out a fire stop something from burning ନିଆଁ ଲିଭାଇବା *We put out the fire with buckets of water.*

set fire to something, set something on fire make something start to burn ନିଆଁ ଲଗାଇବା, ନିଆଁ ଧରାଇବା *Somebody set the house on fire.*

fire² /ˈfaɪə(r)/ *verb* (**fires, firing, fired**) **1** shoot with a gun ବନ୍ଧୁକରୁ ଗୁଳି ଫୁଟାଇବା *The soldiers fired at the enemy.* **2** remove an employee from a job, company, etc. ଚାକିରିରୁ କାଢ଼ିଦେବା, ବରଖାସ୍ତ କରିବା।

fire alarm *noun* a bell that rings to tell people that there is a fire ନିଆଁ ଲାଗିବାର ସଙ୍କେତ ଘଣ୍ଟି

fire brigade *noun* a group of people whose job is to stop fires ନିଆଁ ଲିଭାଳି ଦଳ, ଅଗ୍ନି ନିର୍ବାପକ ଦଳ

firecracker /ˈfaɪəkrækə(r)/ *noun* a small device made of paper and containing powder that explodes with a loud noise when you burn it ବାଣ ⇨ **firework** ଦେଖନ୍ତୁ।

fire engine *noun* a vehicle that takes people and equipment to stop fires ନିଆଁ ଲିଭାଇବା ପାଇଁ ଯନ୍ତ୍ର ଥିବା ଗାଡ଼ି

fire escape *noun* stairs on the outside of a building from where people can leave quickly when there is a fire inside ନିଆଁ ଲାଗିଥିବା କୋଠାରୁ ବିପନ୍ନ ଲୋକ ବାହାରି ଆସିବା ପାଇଁ କୋଠା ବାହାର ପଟରେ ଥିବା ସିଡ଼ି

fireman

fireman /ˈfaɪəmən/ (*plural* **firemen), firefighter** /ˈfaɪəfaɪtə(r)/ *noun* a person whose job is to stop fires ନିଆଁ ଲିଭାଳି ଦଳର ବ୍ୟକ୍ତି

fireplace /ˈfaɪəpleɪs/ *noun* the place in a room where you can have a fire to make the room warm ଘରକୁ ଗରମ ରଖିବା ପାଇଁ ଘର ଭିତରେ ଥିବା ଅଗ୍ନିକୁଣ୍ଡ

fire station *noun* a building where fire engines are kept ନିଆଁ ଲିଭାଳି ଦଳର କାର୍ଯ୍ୟାଳୟ

firewood /ˈfaɪəwʊd/ *noun* (*no plural*) wood that has been cut into pieces to be used in fires ଜାଳେଣି କାଠ *The woodcutter went to the forest every day to collect firewood.*

firework /ˈfaɪəwɜːk/ *noun* a container with special powder in it that sends out coloured lights and smoke or makes a loud noise when you burn it ବାଣ, ଆତସବାଜି *We watched a firework display in the park.*

firm¹ /fɜːm/ *adjective* (**firmer, firmest**) **1** something that is firm is quite hard or does not move easily ଶକ୍ତ, ଟାଣ, ଅଟଳ, ସ୍ଥିର *Wait until the glue is firm.* **2** showing that you will not change your ideas ଦୃଢ଼ ପ୍ରତିଜ୍ଞ, ଅଟଳ *a firm promise*

firmly *adverb* ଦୃଢ଼ ଭାବରେ *Nail the pieces of wood firmly together.*

firm² /fɜːm/ *noun* a group of people working together in a business; a company ব্যবসায়িক প্রতিষ্ঠান; অংশীদারী বা যৌথ ব্যবসায় সংস্থা, কম্পানী *My father works for a building firm.*

first[1] /fɜ:st/ *adjective* before all the others ପ୍ରଥମ *January is the first month of the year.* ✪ ବିପରୀତ **last**[1]

firstly *adverb* a word that you use when you are giving the first thing in a list ପ୍ରଥମତଃ *We were angry firstly because he didn't come, and secondly because he didn't telephone.*

first[2] /fɜ:st/ *adverb* **1** before all the others ପ୍ରଥମେ, ପ୍ରଥମରେ *I arrived at the house first.* **2** for the first time *I first met Priti in 1986.* **3** before doing anything else ପ୍ରଥମେ, ଆରମ୍ଭରେ *First fry the onions, then add the potatoes.*

at first at the beginning ପ୍ରଥମରେ, ପ୍ରଥମେ *At first she was afraid of the water, but she soon learnt to swim.*

first[3] /fɜ:st/ *noun* (*no plural*) a person or thing that comes earliest or before all others ପ୍ରଥମ ବ୍ୟକ୍ତି ବା ପଦାର୍ଥ *I was the first to arrive at the party.*

first aid *noun* (*no plural*) the simple medical help that you give to an injured person before you can take them to a hospital or call a doctor ପ୍ରାଥମିକ ଚିକିତ୍ସା

first class *noun* (*no plural*) the part of a train, plane, etc. that it is more expensive to travel in ରେଳଗାଡ଼ି, ବିମାନ ଇତ୍ୟାଦିର ପ୍ରଥମ ଶ୍ରେଣୀ *I got a seat in first class.*

first name *noun* the name that your parents choose for you when you are born ବ୍ୟକ୍ତିଗତ ନାମ (ସାଙ୍ଗିଆ ନୁହେଁ) *'What is Mr Mohanty's first name?' 'Ajay.'* ➪ **name** ଠାରେ ଟିପ୍ପଣୀ ଦେଖନ୍ତୁ ।

fish[1] /fɪʃ/ *noun* (*plural* **fish** ବା **fishes**) an animal that lives and breathes in water and uses its fins and tail for swimming ମାଛ, ମତ୍ସ୍ୟ *I caught a big fish.*

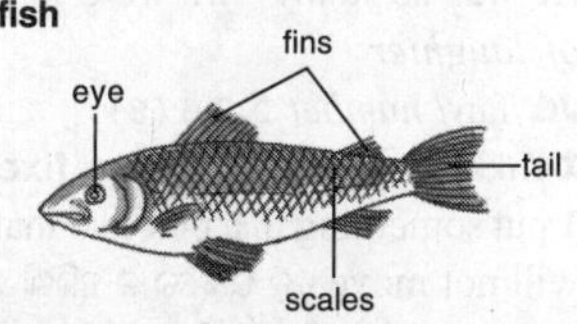

fish[2] /fɪʃ/ *verb* (**fishes, fishing, fished**) try to catch fish ମାଛ ଧରିବା

fisherman /ˈfɪʃəmən/ *noun* (*plural* **fishermen**) a person who catches fish as a job or sport କେଉଟ, କୈବର୍ତ୍ତ, ଧୀବର

fist /fɪst/ *noun* a hand with the fingers closed tightly ହାତ ମୁଠା, ମୁଷ୍ଟି *She banged on the door with her fist.*

fit[1] /fɪt/ *adjective* (**fitter, fittest**) **1** healthy and strong ସୁସ୍ଥ ଓ ସବଳ *I keep fit by going swimming every morning.* **2** good enough; right ଉପଯୁକ୍ତ, ଯୋଗ୍ୟ *Do you think she's fit for the job?* ✪ ବିପରୀତ **unfit**

fitness *noun* (*no plural*) the state of being healthy and strong ଔଚିତ୍ୟ, ଉପଯୁକ୍ତତା, ସୁସ୍ଥତା, ସବଳତା; ଯୋଗ୍ୟତା

fit[2] /fɪt/ *verb* (**fits, fitting, fitted**) **1** be the right size and shape for somebody or something ଉପଯୁକ୍ତ ଆକାର ଓ ଆକୃତିର ହେବା *This key doesn't fit the lock.* **2** put something in the right place ଠିକ୍ ଜାଗାରେ ଲଗାଇବା *Can you fit these pieces of the puzzle together?*

fit³ /fɪt/ *noun* **1** a sudden illness in which somebody becomes unconcious ଅପସ୍ମାର ବା ମୂର୍ଚ୍ଛାରୋଗ **2** doing something suddenly that you cannot stop ହସ, କାନ୍ଦ, କ୍ରୋଧ ଇତ୍ୟାଦିର ତୁହା *He was so funny—we were in fits of laughter.*

five /faɪv/ *number* 5 ପାଞ୍ଚ (୫)

fix /fɪks/ *verb* (**fixes, fixing, fixed**) **1** put something in a place so that it will not move ଦୃଢ଼ ଭାବରେ ନ ହଲିଲା ପରି ଲଗାଇ ଦେବା *We fixed the shelf to the wall.* **2** repair something ମରାମତି କରିବା *The light isn't working—can you fix it?* **3** decide something; make a plan for something ନିଷ୍ପତ୍ତି ନେବା, ସ୍ଥିର କରିବା; ଯୋଜନା କରିବା *They've fixed a date for the wedding.*

fixed /fɪkst/ *adjective* something that is fixed does not change or move ସ୍ଥିର, ଅପରିବର୍ତ୍ତନୀୟ *a fixed price*

fizzy /ˈfɪzi/ *adjective* (**fizzier, fizziest**) with a lot of small bubbles of gas ଫେନିଳ, ବୁଦ୍‌ବୁଦ୍‌ଯୁକ୍ତ *Do you like fizzy drinks?*

flag /flæg/ *noun* a piece of cloth with a special pattern on it which is sometimes joined to a stick (called a **flagpole**). Every country has its own flag ପତାକା, ଧ୍ୱଜା (ପତାକା ଉଡ଼ାଇବା ଲାଠିକୁ ପତାକା ଖମ୍ବ କହନ୍ତି। ପ୍ରତ୍ୟେକ ଦେଶର ନିଜସ୍ୱ ପତାକା ଅଛି)

flake /fleɪk/ *noun* a small thin piece of something କୌଣସି ପଦାର୍ଥର ଛୋଟ ପତଳା ପତ୍ରପରି ଖଣ୍ଡ *snowflakes*

flame /fleɪm/ *noun* a hot bright pointed piece of fire ଅଗ୍ନିଶିଖା

in flames burning ଜଳିବା *The house was in flames.*

flap¹ /flæp/ *noun* a flat piece of something that hangs down, for example to cover an opening. A flap is joined to something on one side ଲଫାଫାର ବନ୍ଦ କରିବା ଅଂଶପରି ବାହାରିଥିବା କାଗଜ ବା କନା *the flap of an envelope*

flap² /flæp/ *verb* (**flaps, flapping, flapped**) move quickly up and down or from side to side ଦୋହଲିବା, ତଳକୁ ଉପରକୁ ବା ଏ କଡୁ ସେକଡ଼କୁ ହଲିବା *Birds flap their wings when they fly.*

flare /fleə(r)/ *verb* (**flares, flaring, flared**)

flare up if a fire flares up, it suddenly burns more brightly or strongly ଉଜ୍ଜ୍ୱଳ ଭାବେ ଜଳିଉଠିବା

flash¹ /flæʃ/ *verb* (**flashes, flashing, flashed**) send out a bright light that comes and goes quickly (ଆଲୋକ) ଝଟକିବା ବା ଧପ ଧପ ହେବା *The disco lights flashed on and off.*

flash² /flæʃ/ *noun* (*plural* **flashes**) **1** a bright light that comes and goes quickly ଧପ ଧପ ହେଉଥିବା ଆଲୋକ *a flash of lightning* **2** a bright light that you use with a camera for taking photographs ଫଟ ଉଠେଇବା ପାଇଁ ବ୍ୟବହୃତ କ୍ଷଣିକ ଉଜ୍ଜ୍ୱଳ ଆଲୋକ, ଫ୍ଲାସ୍

flash flood *noun* a sudden flood that is caused by heavy rains ଖୁବ୍ ବର୍ଷା ଯୋଗୁ ହେଉଥିବା ଆକସ୍ମିକ ବନ୍ୟା

flask /flɑ:sk/ *noun* a container that is used to keep hot liquids hot and cold liquids cold for a long time ଗରମ ପାନୀୟ ଗରମ ରଖିପାରୁଥିବା ଓ ଥଣ୍ଡା ପାନୀୟ ଥଣ୍ଡା ରଖିପାରୁଥିବା ନିର୍ବାତ କାଚକୁମ୍ପୀ ଲଗା ଡବା, ଫ୍ଲାସ୍କ

flat[1] /flæt/ *noun* a group of rooms for living in. A flat is usually on one floor of a house or big building ଆବାସ ଭାବରେ ବ୍ୟବହୃତ କେତେକ ଲଗାଲଗି ପ୍ରକୋଷ୍ଠ ଥିବା ଘର (ସାଧାରଣତଃ ଗୋଟିଏ ମହଲାରେ), ଫ୍ଲାଟ୍ ✪ ବହୁ ଫ୍ଲାଟ୍ ଥିବା ଉଚ୍ଚ କୋଠାକୁ **a block of flats** କହନ୍ତି ।

flat[2] /flæt/ *adjective* (**flatter, flattest**) **1** smooth, with no parts that are higher or lower than the rest ସମତଳ, ଆନୁଭୂମିକ *A table has a flat top*. **2** a tyre that is flat does not have enough air inside it ପବନ ବାହାରି ଯାଇଥିବା (ଗାଡ଼ି ଚକ ବା ଟାୟାର୍)

flat *adverb* with no parts that are higher or lower than the rest ସମତଳ ଭାବେ, ଆନୁଭୂମିକ ଭାବେ *He lay flat on his back on the floor*.

flatten /ˈflætn/ *verb* (**flattens, flattening, flattened**) make something flat ସମତଳ ବା ସିଧା କରିବା *I sat on the box and flattened it*.

flatter /ˈflætə(r)/ *verb* (**flatters, flattering, flattered**) try to please somebody by saying too many nice things about them that are not completely true ତୋଷାମଦ ବା ଖୋସାମତ କରିବା, ଚାଟୁବଚନ କରିବା

flavour /ˈfleɪvə(r)/ *noun* the taste of food ବିଶେଷ ପ୍ରକାରର ସ୍ୱାଦ ଓ ବାସେନା *They sell twenty different flavours of ice cream*.

flaw /flɔ:/ *noun* a defect in something ତ୍ରୁଟି, ଦୋଷ *There were serious flaws in her argument*.

flea /fli:/ *noun* a very small insect without wings that can jump. Fleas live on the blood of animals and people ଡାଉଁଶ, ରକ୍ତପାୟୀ ଡେଣା ନଥିବା ଡେଉଁଥିବା ମାଛିପରି କୀଟ *Our cat has got fleas*.

fledgling /ˈfledʒlɪŋ/ *noun* a young bird that has just learnt to fly ନୂଆ କରି ଉଡ଼ି ଶିଖୁଥିବା ଚଢ଼େଇ ଛୁଆ

fledgling

flee /fli:/ *verb* (**flees, fleeing, fled** /fled/, **has fled**) run away from something bad or dangerous ଦୌଡ଼ି ପଳାଇବା, ପଳାୟନ କରିବା (ବିପଦ ଆପଦରୁ) *During the war, thousands of people fled the country*.

fleet /fli:t/ *noun* a big group of ships ବହୁ ଜାହାଜର ଏକ ଦଳ

flesh /fleʃ/ *noun* (*no plural*) **1** the soft part of your body under your skin ମାଂସ, ମାଂଶପେଶୀ ✪ ଖାଦ୍ୟ ଭାବରେ ବ୍ୟବହୃତ ମାଂସକୁ **meat** କହନ୍ତି । **2** the soft part of a fruit or vegetable that can be eaten ଫଳ ବା ପରିବାର ନରମ ମାଂସଳ ଅଂଶ

flew ଶବ୍ଦ **fly**[2] ର ଏକ ଧାତୁରୂପ

flexible /ˈfleksɪbl/ *adjective* **1** that can bend easily without breaking ନମନୀୟ, ସହଜରେ ବଙ୍କେଇ ହେଉଥିବା **2** that can change easily ସହଜରେ ପରିବର୍ତ୍ତନ କରି ହେଉଥିବା, ପରିବର୍ତ୍ତନକ୍ଷମ

flicker /ˈflɪkə(r)/ *verb* (**flickers, flickering, flickered**) burn unsteadily

ଅସ୍ଥିର ଭାବେ ଜଳିବା, ଧପ ଧପ ହୋଇ ଜଳିବା *The candle flickered because of the breeze.*

flies ଶବ୍ଦ **1 fly**[1] ର ବହୁବଚନ **2** ଶବ୍ଦ **fly**[2] ର ଏକ ଧାତୁରୂପ

flight /flaɪt/ *noun* a journey in an aeroplane ଉଡ଼ାଣ *a direct flight from Chennai to New Delhi*

flight of stairs *noun* a group of steps ସୋପାନ ଶ୍ରେଣୀ, ଶିଡ଼ି

fling /flɪŋ/ *verb* (**flings, flinging, flung** /flʌŋ/, **has flung**) throw something strongly or without care ଫୋପାଡ଼ିବା, ଫିଙ୍ଗିବା *She flung a book and it hit me.*

flip /flɪp/ *verb* (**flips, flipping, flipped**) when you flip something, you turn it over quickly ଶୀଘ୍ର ଓଲଟାଇବା *When one side of the omelette is done, flip it over to cook the other side.*

float /fləʊt/ *verb* (**floats, floating, floated**) **1** stay on top of a liquid ଭାସିବା, ଭାସମାନ ହୋଇ ରହିବା *Wood floats on water.* ✪ ବିପରୀତ **sink**[2] **2** move slowly in the air ପବନରେ ଧୀରେ ଭାସିବା *Clouds were floating across the sky.*

flock /flɒk/ *noun* a group of birds, sheep or goats ପଶୁ ବା ପକ୍ଷୀଙ୍କ ପଲ *a flock of seagulls*

flood /flʌd/ *noun* when there is a flood, a lot of water covers the land ବନ୍ୟା, ବଢ଼ି *Many homes were destroyed in the flood.*

flood *verb* (**floods, flooding, flooded**) ଜଳପୂର୍ଣ୍ଣ ହେବା, ବନ୍ୟା ଆସିବା *A pipe burst and flooded the kitchen.*

floor /flɔ:(r)/ *noun* **1** the part of a room that you walk on ଚଟାଣ, ତଳ *There weren't any chairs so we sat on the floor.* **2** all the rooms at the same height in a building ମହଲା *Our hotel room was on the sixth floor.* ✪ ଭୂମି ସମତଳରେ ଥିବା ତଳ ମହଲାକୁ **ground floor** କହନ୍ତି।

floppy disk *noun* a small flat piece of plastic that stores information for a computer (କମ୍ପ୍ୟୁଟର୍‌ରେ ବ୍ୟବହୃତ) ତଥ୍ୟ ସଞ୍ଚିତ କରି ରଖିବା ପାଇଁ ଏକ ଛୋଟ ଚଟକା ଫଳକ, ଫ୍ଲପିଡିସ୍କ ➪ ଚିତ୍ର ପାଇଁ **computer** ଦେଖନ୍ତୁ।

florist /ˈflɒrɪst/ *noun* a person who sells flowers ଫୁଲ ବ୍ୟବସାୟୀ, ଫୁଲ ବିକାଳି ✪ ଫୁଲ ଦୋକାନକୁ **florist's** କହନ୍ତି।

flour /ˈflaʊə(r)/ *noun* (*no plural*) a soft white or brown powder made from grains like wheat. We use flour to make bread, cakes, rotis, etc. ଅଟା, ମଇଦା, ଚୂନା ଇତ୍ୟାଦି

flourish /ˈflʌrɪʃ/ *verb* (**flourishes, flourishing, flourished**) **1** grow well ଭଲ ଭାବରେ ବଢ଼ିବା *The garden flourished after all the rain.* **2** become strong or successful ଶକ୍ତିଶାଳୀ ଓ ସଫଳ ହେବା *Their business is flourishing.*

flow /fləʊ/ *verb* (**flows, flowing, flowed**) move along like a river ପ୍ରବାହିତ ହେବା, ବହିଯିବା, ଗଡ଼ିଯିବା *This river flows into the Bay of Bengal.*

flow *noun* (*no plural*) ପ୍ରବାହ, ସ୍ରୋତ *I used a handkerchief to stop the flow of blood.*

flower /ˈflaʊə(r)/ *noun* the brightly coloured part of a plant that comes before the seeds or fruit ଫୁଲ, ପୁଷ୍ପ *She gave me a bunch of flowers.* ➪ ଚିତ୍ର ପାଇଁ **plant** ଦେଖନ୍ତୁ।

flown ଶବ୍ଦ **fly²** ର ଏକ ଧାତୁରୂପ

flu /flu:/ *noun* (*no plural*) an illness like a bad cold that makes you ache and gives you a fever ଜର, ସର୍ଦ୍ଦି, କାଶ, କଫ ଓ ଦେହପୀଡ଼ା କରାଉଥିବା ରୋଗ, ଫ୍ଲୁ *I think I've got flu.* ✪ ଏ ରୋଗକୁ **influenza** (ଇନ୍‌ଫ୍ଲୁଏଞ୍ଜା) ମଧ୍ୟ କହନ୍ତି।

fluent /ˈflu:ənt/ *adjective* able to speak easily and correctly ଅନର୍ଗଳ ଭାବରେ କହିପାରୁଥିବା *Raman is fluent in English and Hindi.*

fluently *adverb* ଅନର୍ଗଳ ଭାବରେ, ପ୍ରାଞ୍ଜଳ ଭାବରେ *She speaks five languages fluently.*

fluffy /ˈflʌfi/ *adjective* (**fluffier, fluffiest**) soft and light ନରମ ଓ ହାଲ୍‌କା, ତୁଳା ବା ପର ପରି *fluffy white clouds*

fluid /ˈflu:ɪd/ *noun* anything that can flow; a liquid ତରଳ ପଦାର୍ଥ *Water is a fluid.*

flung ଶବ୍ଦ **fling** ର ଏକ ଧାତୁରୂପ

flush /flʌʃ/ *verb* (**flushes, flushing, flushed**) **1** clean something by sending water through it ଜଳ ପ୍ରବାହ ଦ୍ୱାରା ସଫା କରିବା, ପାଣି ଅଜାଡ଼ି ସଫାକରିବା *Please flush the toilet.* **2** if you flush, your face becomes red ମୁହଁ ଲାଲ ହେବା *He flushed with anger.*

flute /flu:t/ *noun* a musical instrument like a pipe with holes, that you blow into ବଂଶୀ, ବେଣୁ, ମୁରଲୀ

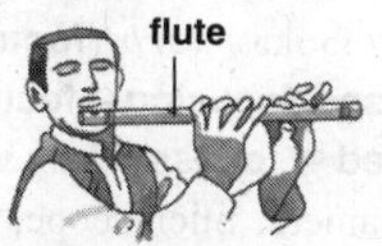

flutter /ˈflʌtə(r)/ *verb* (**flutters, fluttering, fluttered**) move something lightly and quickly in the air ପବନ (ପକ୍ଷୀ ଡେଣାପରି) ହଲିବା; (ପତାକା ଇତ୍ୟାଦି) ପବନରେ ଫର୍‌ଫର୍ ହେଇ ଉଡ଼ିବା *flags fluttering in the wind*

fly¹ /flaɪ/ *noun* (*plural* **flies**) a small insect with two wings ମାଛି, ମକ୍ଷିକା ➪ ଚିତ୍ର ପାଇଁ **insect** ଦେଖନ୍ତୁ।

fly² /flaɪ/ *verb* (**flies, flying, flew** /flu:/, **has flown** /fləʊn/) **1** move through the air ଉଡ଼ିବା *In autumn some birds fly to warmer countries.* **2** make an aircraft move through the air ଉଡ଼ାଜାହାଜ ଉଡ଼ାଇବା *A pilot is a person who flies an aircraft.* **3** travel in an aeroplane ଉଡ଼ାଜାହାଜରେ ଯିବା *I'm flying to Mumbai tomorrow.*

flying /ˈflaɪɪŋ/ *adjective* able to fly ଉଡ଼ୁଥିବା, ଉଡ଼ିପାରୁଥିବା, ଉଡ଼ା *flying insects*

flyover /ˈflaɪəʊvə(r)/ *noun* a bridge that carries a road over other roads ଗୋଟିଏ ରାସ୍ତା ବା ରେଳପଥ ଆଉ ଗୋଟିଏ ରାସ୍ତା ଯିବାପାଇଁ ଥିବା ସେତୁ ବା ପୋଲ

foal /fəʊl/ *noun* a young horse or donkey ଘୋଡ଼ା ବା ଗଧ ଛୁଆ

foam /fəʊm/ *noun* (*no plural*) **1** a lot of very small white bubbles that you see on some liquids ଫେଣ **2** a spongy kind of rubber ତୁଳାପରି ନରମ ରବର, ପ୍ଲାଷ୍ଟିକ ଇତ୍ୟାଦି *a foam mattress*

focus /ˈfəʊkəs/ *verb* (**focuses** ବା **focusses, focusing** ବା **focussing, focused** ବା **focussed**) move parts of a camera, microscope, etc. so that you can see things through it clearly କ୍ୟାମେରା, ଅଣୁବୀକ୍ଷଣ ଯନ୍ତ୍ର ଇତ୍ୟାଦିର ଯନ୍ତ୍ରାଂଶ ଘୂରାଇ ଦେଖୁଥିବା ବସ୍ତୁକୁ ସ୍ପଷ୍ଟ ଦୃଷ୍ଟିକୁ ଆଣିବା

fodder /ˈfɒdə(r)/ *noun* (*no plural*) food given to animals on a farm ପଶୁ ଖାଦ୍ୟ

foe /fəʊ/ *noun* (*plural* **foes**) an enemy ଶତ୍ରୁ

fog /fɒg/ *noun* (*no plural*) thick cloudy air near the ground, that is difficult to see through କୁହୁଡ଼ି, କୁଜ୍ଝଟିକା, କୁହେଳିକା

foggy *adjective* (**foggier, foggiest**) କୁହୁଡ଼ିଆ, କୁହୁଡ଼ିପୂର୍ଣ୍ଣ *a foggy day*

fold[1] /fəʊld/ *verb* (**folds, folding, folded**) bend something so that one part is on top of another part ଚଉତିବା, ଭାଙ୍ଗ କରିବା *I folded the letter and put it in the envelope.* ✪ ବିପରୀତ **unfold**

folding *adjective* (used to describe a bed, chair, etc.) that which can be folded or bent when not in use or be carried easily from one place to another ଚଉତି ହୋଇପାରୁଥିବା (ଖଟ, ଚଉକି ଇତ୍ୟାଦି), ଚଉତା (ଚଉକି, ଖଟ ଇତ୍ୟାଦି) *a folding bed*

fold[2] /fəʊld/ *noun* a line that is made when you bend cloth or paper; crease ଭାଙ୍ଗ, ପ୍ରସ୍ଥ, ମେଣ୍ଢା ଖୁଆଡ଼

folder /ˈfəʊldə(r)/ *noun* ✪ a cover made of cardboard or plastic for keeping papers in ପ୍ଲାଷ୍ଟିକ ବା କାର୍ଡ଼ବୋର୍ଡରେ ତିଆରି ଏକ ଜିନିଷ ଯେଉଁଥିରେ କାଗଜ ରଖାଯାଇ ପାରିବ

foliage /ˈfəʊliɪdʒ/ *noun* the leaves of a tree or plant ଗଛର ପତ୍ରସମୂହ *It was difficult to spot the bird through the dense foliage of the tree.*

folk /fəʊk/ *noun* (*plural*) people ଜନସାଧାରଣ, ଲୋକମାନେ *There are a lot of old folk living in this village.*

folk dance *noun* an old dance of the people of a particular place ଲୋକନୃତ୍ୟ *the folk dances of Rajasthan*

folk song *noun* an old song of the people of a particular place ଲୋକସଙ୍ଗୀତ

follow /ˈfɒləʊ/ *verb* (**follows, following, followed**) **1** come or go after somebody or something କାହାରି ପଛରେ ଯିବା ବା ଆସିବା, ଅନୁସରଣ କରିବା, ଅନୁଧାବନ କରିବା *Follow me and I'll show you the way.* **2** do what somebody says you should do ଆଦେଶ ପାଳନ କରିବା *Did you follow my advice?* **3** understand something ବୁଝିପାରିବା *Has everyone followed the lesson so far?*

follower /ˈfɒləʊə(r)/ *noun* a person who follows and supports another person or the teachings of a religion ସମର୍ଥକ, ଅନୁଗାମୀ, ଭକ୍ତ *followers of Islam*

following /ˈfɒləʊɪŋ/ *adjective* next ତା'ପର; ନିମ୍ନଲିଖିତ *I came back from holiday on Sunday and went to work on the following day.* ○ *Answer the following questions.*

fond /fɒnd/ *adjective* (**fonder, fondest**)

be fond of somebody or **something** like somebody or something a lot ଆସକ୍ତ, ଅନୁରକ୍ତ *They are very fond of their uncle.*

food /fu:d/ *noun* (*no plural*) things that people and animals eat so that they can live and grow ଖାଦ୍ୟ

food chain *noun* a series of animals and plants each of which feeds on the ones below them in the chain ଖାଦ୍ୟ ପାଇଁ ପରସ୍ପର ନିର୍ଭରଶୀଳ ଜୀବସମୂହ *A food chain always starts with plants.*

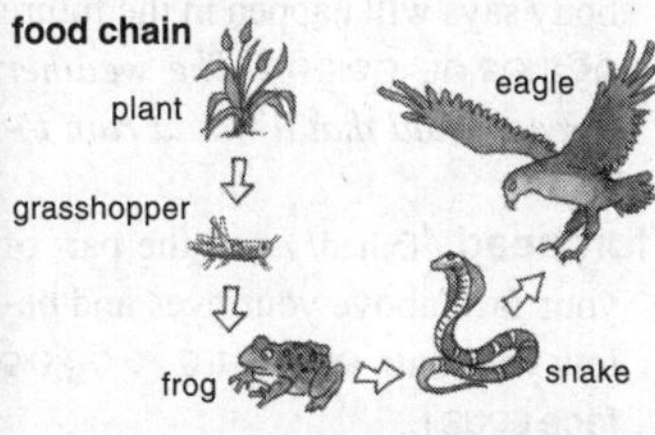

fool[1] /fu:l/ *noun* a person who is silly or who does something silly ବୋକା, ନିର୍ବୋଧ ବ୍ୟକ୍ତି

make a fool of yourself do something that makes you look silly ନିଜକୁ ବୋକା ବନେଇବା *He always makes a fool of himself at parties.*

fool[2] /fu:l/ *verb* (**fools, fooling, fooled**) make somebody think something that is not true; trick somebody କୌଣସି ବ୍ୟକ୍ତିଙ୍କୁ ଠକିବା, ପ୍ରତାରଣା କରିବା *You can't fool me! I know you're lying!*

foolish /ˈfu:lɪʃ/ *adjective* stupid; silly ନିର୍ବୋଧ, ବୋକା *a foolish mistake*

foot /ˈfʊt/ *noun* **1** (*plural* **feet** /fi:t/) the part of your leg that you stand on ପାଦ *I've been walking all day and my feet hurt.* ➪ ଚିତ୍ର ପାଇଁ **body** ଦେଖନ୍ତୁ । **2** (*plural* **foot** ବା **feet**) a measure of length (=30.48 centimetres). There are twelve **inches** in a foot ବାର ଇଞ୍ଚର ମାପ (=୩.୪୮ ସେଣ୍ଟିମିଟର୍), ଫୁଟ୍, ୧୨ ଇଞ୍ଚ *'How tall are you?' 'Five foot six.'* ✪ **Foot** ର ସଂକ୍ଷିପ୍ତ ରୂପ ହେଲା **ft** *90 ft*

put your foot down say strongly that something must or must not happen ଦୃଢ଼ ହେବା, ଦୃଢ଼ ଭାବରେ କହିବା

football /ˈfʊtbɔ:l/ *noun* (*no plural*) a game for two teams of eleven players who try to kick a ball into a **goal** on a field called a **pitch** ଫୁଟବଲ୍ ଖେଳ; ପ୍ରତ୍ୟେକ ଟିମ୍‌ରେ ଏଗାର ଜଣ ଖେଳାଳୀ ଥିବା ଦୁଇଟି ଟିମ୍ ମଧ୍ୟରେ ଖେଳା ଯାଉଥିବା ଖେଳ ଯେଉଁଥିରେ ବଲକୁ ଗୋଲ ଭିତରକୁ ମାରିବାକୁ ହୁଏ *I'm going to a football match on Saturday.*

footballer *noun* a person who plays football ଫୁଟବଲ ଖେଳାଳି

foothills /ˈfʊthɪlz/ *noun* the low hills at the base of a high mountain range ପର୍ବତ ପାଦଦେଶରେ ଥିବା ଛୋଟ ପାହାଡ଼ସମୂହ *the foothills of the Himalayas*

footpath /ˈfʊtpɑ:θ/ *noun* a path made specially for people to walk on ପଦଚାରୀଙ୍କ ରାସ୍ତା, ଚଲାବାଟ

footprint /ˈfʊtprɪnt/ *noun* a mark that your foot or shoe makes on the ground ପାଦଚିହ୍ନ ।

footstep /ˈfʊtstep/ *noun* the mark of your feet that is made on the ground or the sound that is produced when you walk or run ପାଦଚିହ୍ନ, ପାଦଶବ୍ଦ *I could hear footsteps behind me, but when I turned around there was no one!*

footwear /ˈfʊtweə(r)/ *noun* (*no plural*) the things, like shoes and slippers, that you wear on your feet ଜୋତା, ମୋଜା, ଚଟି ଇତ୍ୟାଦି

for[1] /fɔ:(r)/ *preposition* **1** a word that shows who will get or have something ପାଇଁ, ନିମନ୍ତେ *These flowers are for you.* **2** a word that shows how something is used or why something is done ପାଇଁ, ହିତ ବା ଉପକାର ପାଇଁ *Take this medicine for your cold.* **3** a word that shows how long ସମୟ, କାଳ *She has lived here for twenty years.* ➪ **since** ଠାରେ ଟିପ୍ପଣୀ ଦେଖନ୍ତୁ। **4** a word that shows how far ଦୂର *We walked for miles.* **5** a word that shows how much something is ରେ, ଦାମ୍‌ରେ *I bought that book for Rs 50.*

for[2] /fɔ:(r)/ *conjunction* because କାରଣ *She was crying, for she knew they could never meet again.* ✪ ଆମେ ସାଧାରଣତଃ **because** ଓ **as** ବ୍ୟବହାର କରୁ।

forbid /fəˈbɪd/ *verb* (**forbids, forbidding, forbade** /fəˈbeɪd/, **has forbidden** /fəˈbɪdn/) say that somebody must not do something ନିଷେଧ କରିବା, ବାରଣ କରିବା, ମନା କରିବା *Smoking is forbidden inside the building.*

force[1] /fɔ:s/ *noun* **1** (*no plural*) power or strength ବଳ, ଶକ୍ତି *The roof of the hut was blown away by the force of the wind.* **2** (*plural* **forces**) a group of people, for example police or soldiers, who do a special job ସଙ୍ଗଠିତ ଦଳ ବା ଗୋଷ୍ଠୀ (ଯଥା: ପୁଲିସ୍ ବା ସେନାର) *the police force*

force[2] /fɔ:s/ *verb* (**forces, forcing, forced**) **1** make somebody do something that they do not want to do ବାଧ୍ୟ କରିବା, ଜବରଦସ୍ତି (କୌଣସି କାମ) କରାଇବା *They forced him to give them the money.* **2** do something by using a lot of strength ବଳ ପ୍ରୟୋଗ କରି କୌଣସି କାମ କରିବା *The rescuers forced the window open.*

forecast /ˈfɔ:kɑ:st/ *noun* what somebody says will happen in the future ଭବିଷ୍ୟତବାଣୀ, ପୂର୍ବାନୁମାନ *The weather forecast said that it would rain today.*

forehead /ˈfɔ:hed/ *noun* the part of your face above your eyes and below your hair କପାଳ, ଲଲାଟ ➪ ଚିତ୍ର ପାଇଁ **face** ଦେଖନ୍ତୁ।

foreign /ˈfɒrən/ *adjective* of or from another country ବିଦେଶୀ, ବୈଦେଶିକ *a foreign language*

foreigner *noun* a person from another country ବିଦେଶୀ ଲୋକ ➪ **stranger** ଦେଖନ୍ତୁ।

foremost /ˈfɔ:məʊst/ *adjective* the most important ମୁଖ୍ୟତମ, ପ୍ରଥମ, ସର୍ବାଗ୍ରବର୍ତ୍ତୀ

forest /ˈfɒrɪst/ *noun* a big piece of land with a lot of trees ଜଙ୍ଗଲ, ବଣ, ଅରଣ୍ୟ *We went for a walk in the forest.*

✪ Forest ହେଉଛି **wood** ଠାରୁ ବଡ଼ **jungle** ହେଉଛି ଗ୍ରୀଷ୍ମପ୍ରଧାନ ଦେଶର ବଣ।

foretell /fɔːˈtel/ *verb* (**foretells, foretelling, foretold** /fɔːˈtəʊld/, **has foretold**) tell about all the things that will happen in future ଭବିଷ୍ୟତ କଥା କହିବା

forever /fərˈevə(r)/ *adverb* for all time; always ଅନବରତ; ସବୁବେଳେ

forgave ଶବ୍ଦ **forgive** ର ଏକ ଧାତୁରୂପ

forge /fɔːdʒ/ *verb* (**forges, forging, forged**) make a copy of something because you want to trick people and make them think it is real ଜାଲ୍ କରିବା, ନକଲ କରିବା *He was put in prison for forging money.*

forgery /ˈfɔːdʒəri/ *noun* (*no plural*) the crime of making a copy of something to trick people ଜାଲ; ନକଲ; ଜାଲ୍ କରାଯାଇଥିବା କାଗଜପତ୍ର

forget /fəˈget/ *verb* (**forgets, forgetting, forgot** /fəˈgɒt/, **has forgotten** /fəˈgɒtn/) not remember something; not have something in your mind any more ଭୁଲିଯିବା। *I've forgotten her name.* ○ *Don't forget to feed the cat.*

forgive /fəˈgɪv/ *verb* (**forgives, forgiving, forgave** /fəˈgeɪv/, **has forgiven** /fəˈgɪvn/) stop being angry with somebody for a bad thing that they did କ୍ଷମା କରିବା *He never forgave me for forgetting his birthday.*

fork /fɔːk/ *noun* **1** a thing with long points at one end, that you use for putting food in your mouth ଖାଇବା ପାଇଁ ବ୍ୟବହୃତ କଣ୍ଟାଚାମୁଚ ⇨ ଚିତ୍ର ପାଇଁ **cutlery** ଦେଖନ୍ତୁ। **2** a large tool with points at one end, that you use for digging the ground ମାଟି ଖୋଳିବା ପାଇଁ କଣ୍ଟା ମୁନପରି ଶାଖା ଥିବା ଉପକରଣ **3** a place where a road or river divides into two parts ନଦୀ ବା ରାସ୍ତାର ଦୁଇ କେନା *When you get to the fork in the road, go left.*

form[1] /fɔːm/ *noun* **1** a type of something ପ୍ରକାର *Cars, trains and buses are all forms of transport.* **2** a piece of paper with questions and spaces for you to answer these questions ତଥ୍ୟ ଯୋଗାଇବା ପାଇଁ ଏକ ମୁଦ୍ରିତ ଶୂନ୍ୟସ୍ଥାନ ଥିବା କାଗଜ, ଫର୍ମ *You need to fill in this form to get a new passport.* **3** the shape of a person or thing ଆକୃତି, ଗଠନ *For her birthday I made her a cake in the form of a cat.*

form[2] /fɔːm/ *verb* (**forms, forming, formed**) **1** make something or give a shape to something ନିର୍ଦ୍ଦିଷ୍ଟ ଆକୃତିରେ ଗଢ଼ିବା *We formed a line outside the cinema.* **2** grow; take shape ବଢ଼ିବା; ଗଠିତ ହେବା *Ice forms when water freezes.* **3** start a group, etc. ଗଠନ କରିବା। *They formed a club for Bengalis living in Delhi.*

formal /ˈfɔːml/ *adjective* you use formal language or behave in a formal way at important or serious times and with people you do not know very well ପ୍ରଚଳିତ ପ୍ରଥାରେ କରାଯାଇଥିବା, ପ୍ରଥା ସମର୍ଥିତ *'Yours faithfully' is a formal way of ending a letter.* ✪ ବିପରୀତ **informal**

formally *adverb* ପ୍ରଥା ସମର୍ଥିତ ଭାବରେ *They dressed formally for the meeting.*

format[1] /ˈfɔːmæt/ *noun* the way something is arranged ଗଠନ, ରୂପ, ଢାଞ୍ଚା *The same article in a different format looks new.*

format[2] /ˈfɔːmæt/ *verb* (**formats, formatting, formatted**) **1** arrange matter in a particular way on a page or computer screen ଏକ ପ୍ରକାର ଢାଞ୍ଚାରେ ଗଠନ କରିବା *He formatted the book in a more attractive way.* **2** prepare a computer disk to record data on it କମ୍ପ୍ୟୁଟର ଡିସ୍କ ବା ଚକତିକୁ ତଥ୍ୟ ରଖିବା ପାଇଁ ପ୍ରସ୍ତୁତ କରିବା

former /ˈfɔːmə(r)/ *adjective* of a time before now ପୂର୍ବକାଳୀନ *the former Prime Minister*

formerly /ˈfɔːməli/ *adverb* before this time ପୂର୍ବ କାଳରେ, ପୂର୍ବରେ, ଅତୀତରେ *Sri Lanka was formerly called Ceylon.*

formula /ˈfɔːmjələ/ *noun* (*plural* **formulae** /ˈfɔːmjəliː/ ବା **formulas**) a list of the substances that you need to make something କୌଣସି ପଦାର୍ଥ ତିଆରି କରିବା ପାଇଁ ଉପାଦାନ ତାଲିକା ଓ ପଦ୍ଧତି *a formula for a new drug*

fort /fɔːt/ *noun* a strong building or a group of buildings that were made to protect a place against its enemies ଦୁର୍ଗ, ଗଡ଼, ସେନାର ସୁରକ୍ଷିତ ଗଠନ

forthcoming /ˌfɔːθˈkʌmɪŋ/ *adjective* if something is forthcoming, it is going to happen soon ଆଗାମୀ, ଆସନ୍ତା *forthcoming exams*

fortnight /ˈfɔːtnaɪt/ *noun* two weeks ଦୁଇ ସପ୍ତାହ କାଳ, ପକ୍ଷ *I'm going on holiday for a fortnight.*

fortress /ˈfɔːtrəs/ *noun* (*plural* **fortresses**) a large strong building that was made to protect a place against its enemies ସୁରକ୍ଷିତ ଦୁର୍ଗ, ଗଡ଼ ବା ସହର

fortunate /ˈfɔːtʃənət/ *adjective* lucky ଭାଗ୍ୟବାନ୍, ସୌଭାଗ୍ୟଶାଳୀ *I was very fortunate to get the job.* ✪ ବିପରୀତ **unfortunate**

fortunately *adverb* ଭାଗ୍ୟକୁ, ସୌଭାଗ୍ୟକ୍ରମେ *There was an accident but fortunately nobody was hurt.* ✪ ବିପରୀତ **unfortunately**

fortune /ˈfɔːtʃuːn/ *noun* **1** (*no plural*) things that happen that you cannot control; luck ଭାଗ୍ୟ *I had the good fortune to get the job.* **2** (*plural* **fortunes**) a lot of money ବହୁ ଧନ ସମ୍ପତ୍ତି *He made a fortune selling old cars.*

forty /ˈfɔːti/ *number* **1** 40 ଚାଳିଶି (୪୦) **2 the forties** (*plural*) the numbers, years or temperatures between 40 and 49 ✪ ୪୦ରୁ ୪୯ ପର୍ଯ୍ୟନ୍ତ (ବର୍ଷ ତାପମାତ୍ରା ଇତ୍ୟାଦି); ଶତାବ୍ଦୀର ଏହି ଦଶନ୍ଧି।

fortieth /ˈfɔːtiəθ/ *adjective*, *adverb*, *noun* 40th ଚାଳିଶତମ

forward[1] /ˈfɔːwəd/ *adverb* **1** (**forwards**) in the direction that is in front of you ଆଗକୁ, ସମ୍ମୁଖକୁ *Move forwards to the front of the train.* ✪ ବିପରୀତ **back** ବା **backwards** **2** to a later time ଭବିଷ୍ୟତ ଆଡ଼କୁ *When you travel from Dubai to Delhi, you need to put your watch forward.*

look forward to something wait for something with pleasure ଆନନ୍ଦରେ ଅପେକ୍ଷା କରିବା *We're looking forward to seeing you again*

forward² /ˈfɔːwəd/ *verb* (**forwards, forwarding, forwarded**) send a letter to somebody at their new address ଆସିଥିବା ଚିଠିକୁ ପ୍ରାପ୍ତକାରୀଙ୍କ ନୂଆ ଠିକଣାକୁ ପଠାଇବା *Could you forward all my post to me while I'm in Lucknow?*

fossil /ˈfɒsl/ *noun* a part of a dead plant or an animal that has been in the ground for a very long time and has become hard ବହୁ କାଳ ମାଟି ତଳେ ପୋତି ହୋଇ ରହିବା ଫଳରେ ପ୍ରସ୍ତରୀଭୂତ ପଶୁ ବା ଉଦ୍ଭିଦ, ଜୀବାଶ୍ମ, ଫସିଲ୍

fossil of a fish

foster /ˈfɒstə(r)/ *adjective* receiving or taking care in a family not connected by blood or legal adoption ନିଜ ପରିବାର ନ ହୋଇ ମଧ୍ୟ ଲାଳନପାଳନ କରୁଥିବା (ବ୍ୟକ୍ତି) ବା ଲାଳିତ ପାଳିତ ହେଉଥିବା (ପିଲା) *foster child* ○ *foster parents*

fought ଶବ୍ଦ **fight¹** ର ଏକ ଧାତୁରୂପ

foul¹ /faʊl/ *adjective* (**fouler, foulest**) dirty, or with a bad smell or taste ଅପରିଷ୍କାର ଓ ଦୁର୍ଗନ୍ଧ ବାହାରୁଥିବା ବା ଖରାପ ସ୍ୱାଦ ଥିବା *What a foul smell!*

foul² /faʊl/ *noun* something you do that is against the rules of a game ଖେଳରେ ବେନିୟମ କାମ

found¹ ଶବ୍ଦ **find** ର ଏକ ଧାତୁରୂପ

found² /faʊnd/ *verb* (**founds, founding, founded**) start something, for example a school or business ସ୍ଥାପନ କରିବା, ପ୍ରତିଷ୍ଠା କରିବା *This school was founded in 1865.*

founder *noun* a person who founds something ପ୍ରତିଷ୍ଠାତା, ସଂସ୍ଥାପକ

foundations /faʊnˈdeɪʃnz/ *noun* (*plural*) the strong parts of a building which you build first under the ground ଘର ଇତ୍ୟାଦିର ମୂଳଦୁଆ।

fountain /ˈfaʊntən/ *noun* water that shoots up into the air and then falls down again. You often see fountains in gardens and parks ଝରଣା, ନିର୍ଝର, ପ୍ରସ୍ରବଣ; ପାର୍କ, ବଗିଚା ଇତ୍ୟାଦିରେ ଥିବା ଉପରକୁ ପ୍ରକ୍ଷିପ୍ତ ହେଉଥିବା ପାଣି ଝର

fountain-pen *noun* a pen that you fill with ink କାଳି ଭରା ଯାଉଥିବା କଲମ

four /fɔː(r)/ *number* 4 ଚାରି ସଂଖ୍ୟା (୪)

on all fours with your hands and knees on the ground ହାତ ଓ ଆଣ୍ଠୁରେ ଭରାଦେଇ ଗୁରୁଣ୍ଡିବା *We went through the tunnel on all fours.*

fourteen /ˌfɔːˈtiːn/ *number* 14 ଚଉଦ ସଂଖ୍ୟା (୧୪)

fourteenth /ˌfɔːˈtiːnθ/ *adjective, adverb, noun* 14th ୧୪ତମ, ଚତୁର୍ଦ୍ଦଶତମ

fourth /fɔːθ/ *adjective, adverb, noun* **1** 4th ଚତୁର୍ଥ, ୪ର୍ଥ **2** one of four equal parts of something; $\frac{1}{4}$ ଏକ ଚୁତର୍ଥାଂଶ, ଚାରି ଭାଗରୁ ଭାଗେ

fox /fɒks/ *noun* (*plural* **foxes**) a wild animal that looks like a dog and has a long thick tail and red fur କୋକିଶିଆଳି ➪ **jackal** ଦେଖନ୍ତୁ।

fraction /ˈfrækʃn/ *noun* **1** an exact part of a number ପୂର୍ଣ୍ଣ ସଂଖ୍ୟାର ଏକ ଅଂଶ, ଭଗ୍ନାଂଶ (ଯଥା $\frac{୧}{୨}$, $\frac{୧}{୩}$ ଇତ୍ୟାଦି) *$\frac{1}{4}$ (= a quarter) and $\frac{1}{3}$ (= a third) are fractions.* **2** a very small part of something କ୍ଷୁଦ୍ର ଖଣ୍ଡ, ଟୁକୁରା (ପଦାର୍ଥର), ଅତି କ୍ଷୁଦ୍ର ଭାଗ (ସମୟର) *For a fraction of a second I thought you were my sister.*

fracture /ˈfræktʃə(r)/ *verb* (**fractures, fracturing, fractured**) break a bone in your body ହାଡ଼ ଭାଙ୍ଗିଯିବା *She fell and fractured her leg.*

fracture *noun* ଅସ୍ଥିଭଙ୍ଗ, ହାଡ଼ ଭାଙ୍ଗିଥିବା ଅବସ୍ଥା *a fracture of the arm*

fragile /ˈfrædʒaɪl/ *adjective* a thing that is fragile can break easily ଭଙ୍ଗୁର, ସହଜରେ ଭାଙ୍ଗିଯାଉଥିବା *Be careful with those glasses. They're very fragile.*

fragment /frægˈmənt/ *noun* a very small piece that has broken off from something larger ଭଙ୍ଗା ଖଣ୍ଡ, ଟୁକୁରା *The window broke and fragments of glass went everywhere.*

fragrance /ˈfreɪgrəns/ *noun* a pleasant smell ସୁଗନ୍ଧ, ସୁବାସ

fragrant /ˈfreɪgrənt/ *adjective* if something is fragrant, it has a pleasant smell ସୁବାସିତ, ଭଲ ବାସେନା ଥିବା *fragrant flowers*

frame[1] /freɪm/ *noun* **1** a thin piece of wood or metal round the edge of a picture, window, mirror, etc. ଫଟ, ଦର୍ପଣ ଇତ୍ୟାଦି ଚାରିପଟେ ଲଗାଯାଉଥିବା କାଠ ବା ଧାତୁର ବନ୍ଧେଇ; କବାଟ, ଝରକା ଇତ୍ୟାଦିର ଚାରିପଟେ ଲଗାଯାଇଥିବା ଧାରକ ଢାଞ୍ଚା ବା ଫ୍ରେମ୍ **2** the basic structure that gives something its shape ମୂଳ ଆଧାର ବା ଢାଞ୍ଚା *the frame of a sports car* **3** the part of a pair of glasses that holds the two lenses ଚଷମା କାଚ ଲଗାଯାଉଥିବା ଢାଞ୍ଚା ବା ଫ୍ରେମ୍

frame[2] /freɪm/ *verb* (**frames, framing, framed**) put a picture in a frame ଫଟ ବନ୍ଧେଇ କରିବା *She had her daughter's photograph framed.*

framework /ˈfreɪmwɜ:k/ *noun* the strong part of something that gives it shape ମୂଳ ଆଧାର *The bridge has a steel framework.*

frank /fræŋk/ *adjective* (**franker, frankest**) if you are frank, you say exactly what you think ସ୍ପଷ୍ଟବାଦୀ, ସ୍ପଷ୍ଟଭାଗୀ,

frankly *adverb* କପଟ ନକରି, ସ୍ପଷ୍ଟ ଭାବରେ *Tell me frankly what you think of my work.*

fraud /frɔ:d/ *noun* **1** (*no plural*) doing things that are not honest to get money ଠକାମି, ପ୍ରତାରଣା, ପ୍ରବଞ୍ଚନା (ଟଙ୍କା ପାଇଁ) *Two of the company's directors were sent to prison for fraud.* **2** (*plural* **frauds**) a person or thing that is not what he/she/it seems to be ଛଦ୍ମବେଶୀ ପ୍ରତାରକ ବା ଠକ; ନକଲି ବା ଠକାମି ଜିନିଷ *He said he was a police officer but I knew he was a fraud.*

free[1] /fri:/ *adjective, adverb* (**freer, freest**) **1** if you are free, you can go where you want and do what you want ମୁକ୍ତ, ସ୍ୱାଧୀନ **2** if something is free, you do not have to pay for it ମଗଣା *We've got some free tickets for the concert.* **3** not busy ମୁକ୍ତ, ଜଞ୍ଜାଳଶୂନ୍ୟ *Are you free this afternoon?*

set free let a person or animal go out of a prison or cage ମୁକ୍ତ କରିବା, ଛାଡ଼ିଦେବା *We set the bird free and it flew away.*

freely *adverb* ମୁକ୍ତ ଭାବରେ, ମାଗଣାରେ *This medicine is freely available.*

free² /friː/ *verb* (**frees, freeing, freed**) make somebody or something free ମୁକ୍ତ କରିବା, ଛାଡ଼ିଦେବା, ଖଲାସ କରିବା *He was freed after ten years in prison.*

freedom /ˈfriːdəm/ *noun* (*no plural*) being free ମୁକ୍ତି, ସ୍ୱାଧୀନତା

freedom fighter *noun* a person who fights for the freedom of his country ସ୍ୱାଧୀନତା ସଂଗ୍ରାମୀ *Amongst all the Indian freedom fighters, she admires Bhagat Singh the most.*

freeze /friːz/ *verb* (**freezes, freezing, froze** /frəʊz/, **has frozen** /ˈfrəʊzn/) become hard because it is so cold. When water freezes, it becomes ice ବରଫ ପାଲଟି ଯିବା

freezing /ˈfriːzɪŋ/ *adjective* very cold ଅତି ଥଣ୍ଡା *Can you close the window? I'm freezing!*

freezing point *noun* (*no plural*) the temperature at which a liquid becomes a solid ହିମାଙ୍କ (ଯେଉଁ ତାପମାତ୍ରାରେ ପାଣି ବରଫ ହୁଏ : *0°* ସେଣ୍ଟିଗ୍ରେଡ୍) *The freezing point of water is 0°C.* ➪ ଦେଖନ୍ତୁ **boiling point**।

French fries *noun* ➪ **chip¹ 1** ଦେଖନ୍ତୁ।

French fries

frequency /ˈfriːkwənsi/ *noun* the number of times something happens କୌଣସି ଘଟଣାର ବାରମ୍ବାରତା ବା ପୌନଃପୁନ୍ୟ *The frequency of buses to the railway station has increased.*

frequent /ˈfriːkwənt/ *adjective* something that is frequent happens often ବହୁଥର ବା ବାରମ୍ବାର ଘଟୁଥିବା *There is a frequent bus service to the airport.*

frequently *adverb* often ବାରମ୍ବାର, ଥରକୁ ଥର

fresh /freʃ/ *adjective* (**fresher, freshest**) **1** made or picked not long ago; not old ତଟକା, ସଦ୍ୟ, ସଜ *I love the smell of fresh bread.* **2** clean and cool ସଫା ଓ ଥଣ୍ଡା *Open the window and let some fresh air in.*

freshly *adverb* ନୂଆ, ତଟକା, ସଜ *freshly baked bread*

freshen /ˈfreʃn/ *verb* (**freshens, freshening, freshened**)

freshen up wash your hands and face in order to feel clean and cool ମୁହଁ ହାତ ଧୋଇ ସଫାସୁତୁରା ହେବା

friction /ˈfrɪkʃn/ *noun* **1** the action of one surface or thing rubbing against another ଘର୍ଷଣ **2** the force that reduces the motion of objects that come into contact with each other ଘର୍ଷଣଜନିତ ପ୍ରତିରୋଧ *Put oil to reduce friction.* **3** a disagreement amongst a group of people ବ୍ୟକ୍ତି ବା ଗୋଷ୍ଠୀ ମଧ୍ୟରେ ମତଭେଦ *friction between the management and the union*

Friday /ˈfraɪdeɪ/ *noun* the fifth day of the week, next after Thursday ସପ୍ତାହର ପଞ୍ଚମ ଦିନ, ଶୁକ୍ରବାର

fridge /frɪdʒ/ *noun* a big metal box for keeping food and drink cold and fresh ପ୍ରଶୀତନ ଯନ୍ତ୍ର, ଫ୍ରିଜ୍, ରେଫ୍ରିଜରେଟର୍ *Is there any milk in the fridge?* ✪ ଫ୍ରିଜ୍‌କୁ **refrigerator** ମଧ୍ୟ କୁହାଯାଏ।

fried ଶବ୍ଦ **fry** ର ଏକ ଧାତୁରୂପ

friend /frend/ *noun* a person whom you like and know very well ସାଙ୍ଗ, ବନ୍ଧୁ, ସହଚର *Dipti is my best friend.* **make friends with somebody** become a friend of somebody କାହା ସାଙ୍ଗେ ସାଙ୍ଗ ବସ, ବନ୍ଧୁତ୍ୱ କର

friendly /ˈfrendli/ *adjective* (**friendlier, friendliest**) a person who is friendly is kind and helpful ବନ୍ଧୁତ୍ୱପୂର୍ଣ୍ଣ, ବନ୍ଧୁଭାବାପନ୍ନ *My neighbours are very friendly.* ✪ ବିପରୀତ **unfriendly**

friendship /ˈfrendʃɪp/ *noun* being friends with somebody ବନ୍ଧୁତା, ବନ୍ଧୁତ୍ୱ

fries ଶବ୍ଦ **fry** ର ଏକ ଧାତୁରୂପ

fright /fraɪt/ *noun* a sudden feeling of fear ଭୟ, ଆତଙ୍କ *Why didn't you knock on the door before you came in? You gave me a fright!*

frighten /ˈfraɪtn/ *verb* (**frightens, frightening, frightened**) make somebody feel afraid ଡରାଇବା, ଭୟଭୀତ କରିବା *Sorry, did I frighten you?*
frightened *adjective* if you are frightened, you are afraid of something ଭୟଭୀତ, ଭୀତତ୍ରସ୍ତ *He's frightened of spiders.*
frightening *adjective* something that is frightening makes you feel afraid ଭୟଙ୍କର, ଡରାଇ ଦେଲାପରି *That was the most frightening film I have ever seen.*

frigid /ˈfrɪdʒɪd/ *adjective* **1** very cold ଅତି ଥଣ୍ଡା **2** not showing any emotion; unfriendly ଆଦରହୀନ *a frigid expression*

frisky /ˈfrɪski/ *adjective* full of energy and life, and wanting to play ସତେଜ, ଖୁସିବାସିଆ *a frisky dog*

fro /frəʊ/ *adverb*
to and fro first one way and then backwards, many times ଇଆଡ଼କୁ ସିଆଡ଼କୁ *She travels to and fro between Agra and Delhi.*

frog /frɒg/ *noun* a small animal that lives in and near water. Frogs have long back legs and they can jump ବେଙ୍ଗ, ମଣ୍ଡୁକ ➪ **toad** ଦେଖନ୍ତୁ। ➪ ଚିତ୍ର ପାଇଁ **food chain** ଦେଖନ୍ତୁ।

from /frəm; frɒm/ *preposition* **1** a word that shows where something starts (ଆସୁଥିବା ସ୍ଥାନ) ଠାରୁ, ରୁ *We travelled from Kolkata to Guwahati.* **2** a word that shows where somebody lives or was born (ଜନ୍ମସ୍ଥାନ, ବାସସ୍ଥାନ, ଦେଶ ଠାରୁ, ରୁ) *I come from India.* **3** a word that shows when somebody or something starts (ଦୋକାନ ଇତ୍ୟାଦି ଖୋଲୁଥିବା ସମୟ) ଠାରୁ, ରୁ *The shop is open from 9.30 a.m. to 5.30 p.m. every day.* **4** a word that shows who gave or sent something (ବ୍ୟକ୍ତିଙ୍କ) ଠାରୁ *I borrowed a dress from my sister.* **5** a word that shows the place where you find something (ପ୍ରାପ୍ତିସ୍ଥାନ) ରୁ *He took the money from my bag.*

front /frʌnt/ *noun* the side or part of something that faces forwards and that you usually see first ଆଗପଟ, ସାମନାପଟ *The book has a picture of a lion on the front.* ✪ ବିପରୀତ **back**[1] **1**

in front of somebody or **something 1** further forward than another person or thing ଆଗରେ, ସାମନାରେ *Aparna was sitting in the car that was in front of me.* **2** when other people are there (ଅନ୍ୟମାନଙ୍କ) ଉପସ୍ଥିତିରେ, ଆଗରେ *Please don't talk about it in front of my brother.*

front *adjective* ଆଗ, ସାମନା *the front door*

frost /frɒst/ *noun* a thin white layer of ice that covers the ground when the weather is very cold ନୀହାର, ବରଫ ହୋଇଯାଇଥିବା ଶିଶିର ବା କାକର *There was a frost last night.*

frosty *adjective* (**frostier, frostiest**) ଖୁବ୍ ଥଣ୍ଡା *a frosty morning*

frown /fraʊn/ *verb* (**frowns, frowning, frowned**) move your eyebrows together so that lines appear on your forehead. You frown when you are worried, angry or thinking hard ଅସନ୍ତୋଷ ବା ଗଭୀର ଚିନ୍ତା ଯୋଗୁ ଭ୍ରୂକୁଞ୍ଚନ କରିବା

frown *noun* ଭ୍ରୂକୁଞ୍ଚନ *Why is there a frown on your face?*

froze, frozen ଶବ୍ଦ **freeze** ର ଏକ ଧାତୁରୂପ

fruit /fru:t/ *noun* the part of a plant or tree that holds the seeds and that you can eat. Bananas, oranges and apples are kinds of fruit ଫଳ (ଗଛର)

> ✪ ମନେରଖନ୍ତୁ ! ଆମେ 'a fruit' କହିବାନି; କହିବା 'a piece of fruit' ବା 'some fruit'—
>
> *Would you like a piece of fruit?* ○ *'Would you like some fruit?' 'Yes please — I'll have a pear.'*

fruitful /ˈfru:tfl/ *adjective* something that is fruitful brings good results ଫଳପ୍ରଦ, ସଫଳ *The talks between the two countries were fruitful.*

frustrating /frʌˈstreɪtɪŋ/ *adjective* if something is frustrating, it makes

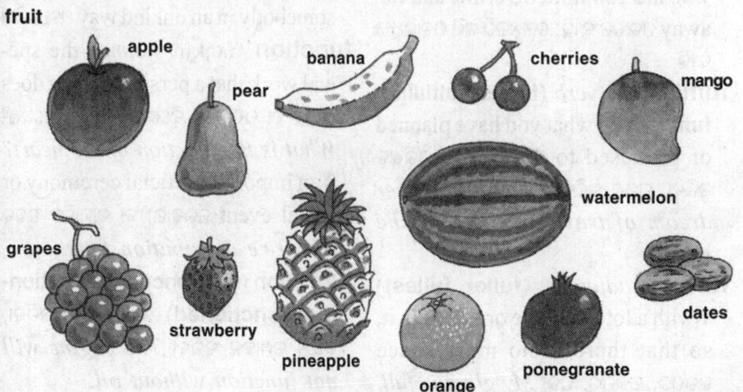

you angry because you cannot do what you want to do (ଉଦ୍ଦେଶ୍ୟ ସିଦ୍ଧିରେ ବ୍ୟର୍ଥ ହେବା ଯୋଗୁ) ବିରକ୍ତିକର

frustration /frʌˈstreɪʃn/ *noun* **1** something that makes you feel frustrated ଅସନ୍ତୋଷ, ନୈରାଶ୍ୟ **2** a feeling of anger because something is blocking the way to success କାର୍ଯ୍ୟସିଦ୍ଧି ନ ହେବା ଯୋଗୁ ବିରକ୍ତି ଓ କ୍ରୋଧ

fry /fraɪ/ *verb* (**fries, frying, fried, has fried**) cook something or be cooked in hot oil ଭାଜିବା *Fry the onions in butter.*

frying pan *noun* a flat metal container with a long handle that you use for frying food ଭାଜିବା ପାଇଁ ମଙ୍ଗ ଓ ବେଣ୍ଟଥିବା ଚଟକା ପାତ୍ର

ft *abbreviation* ଶବ୍ଦ **foot 2** ର ସଂକ୍ଷିପ୍ତ ରୂପ

fuel /ˈfjuːəl/ *noun* (*no plural*) anything that you burn to make heat or power. Wood, coal and oil are kinds of fuel ଜାଳ, ଜାଳେଣି, ଇନ୍ଧନ; ଉତ୍ତାପ ଓ ଶକ୍ତିର ଉତ୍ସ (କାଠ, କୋଇଲା, ତେଲ ଇତ୍ୟାଦି)

fugitive /ˈfjuːdʒətɪv/ *noun* a person who has committed a crime and run away ପଳାତକ ବ୍ୟକ୍ତି; ଦୋଷକରି ଖସି ପଳାଇଥିବା ବ୍ୟକ୍ତି

fulfil /fʊlˈfɪl/ *verb* (**fulfils, fulfilling, fulfilled**) do what you have planned or promised to do କାର୍ଯ୍ୟରେ ପରିଣତ କରିବା, ପୂରଣ କରିବା *Zeba fulfilled her dream of travelling around the world.*

full /fʊl/ *adjective* (**fuller, fullest**) **1** with a lot of people or things in it, so that there is no more space ଭରପୂର, ପରିପୂର୍ଣ୍ଣ, ପୂରା *My glass is full.* ○ *The bus was full so we waited for the next one.* ✪ ବିପରୀତ **empty**[1] **2** as much, big, etc. as possible ପୂରା, ସମ୍ପୂର୍ଣ୍ଣ *The train was travelling at full speed.*

in full completely; with nothing missing ପୂରା, ସମ୍ପୂର୍ଣ୍ଣଭାବରେ *Please write your name in full.*

full stop *noun* a mark (·) that you use in writing to show the end of a sentence, or after the short forms of some words (·); ପୂର୍ଣ୍ଣଚ୍ଛେଦ (।) ବିନ୍ଦୁ

fully /ˈfʊli/ *adverb* completely; totally ପୂର୍ଣ୍ଣଭାବରେ

fumble /ˈfʌmbl/ *verb* (**fumbles, fumbling, fumbled**) search for something with your hands in a messy way ଦରାଣ୍ଡିବା, ଅଣ୍ଡାଳିବା *He fumbled for the papers in the drawer.*

fun /fʌn/ *noun* (*no plural*) something that you enjoy; pleasure କୌତୁକ, ଆମୋଦ *We had great fun at the New Year's party.*

make fun of somebody laugh about somebody in an unkind way ଥଟ୍ଟା କରିବା

function /ˈfʌŋkʃn/ *noun* **1** the special work that a person or thing does (ବ୍ୟକ୍ତି ବା ପଦାର୍ଥର) ବିଶେଷ କାମ ବା ଉଦ୍ଦେଶ୍ୟ *What is the function of the heart?* **2** an important official ceremony or social event ସରକାରୀ ବା ସାମାଜିକ ଉତ୍ସବ *the prize distribution function*

function *verb* (**functions, functioning, functioned**) work କାମ କରିବା, କାର୍ଯ୍ୟ ସମ୍ପାଦନ କରିବା *The engine will not function without oil.*

fund /fʌnd/ *noun* money that will be used for something special ବିଶେଷ କାମପାଇଁ ରହିଥିବା ପାଣ୍ଠି ବା ସଂଗୃହୀତ ଅର୍ଥ *The money from the concert will go into a fund to help homeless people.*

fundamental /ˌfʌndəˈmentl/ *adjective* most important; basic ଅତ୍ୟାବଶ୍ୟକ; ମୌଳିକ *You are making a fundamental mistake.*

funeral /ˈfju:nərəl/ *noun* the time when a dead person is buried or burned ଶବ ସତ୍କାର, ଅନ୍ତ୍ୟେଷ୍ଟି କ୍ରିୟା

fungus /ˈfʌŋgəs/ *noun* (*plural* **fungi** /ˈfʌŋgi; ˈfʌŋgaɪ/) a type of plant that does not have leaves or flowers and grows on dead plants and animals or food that has gone bad. Mushrooms and moulds are types of fungi ଓଦା ସ୍ଥାନରେ, ପଚରା ଗଛ ଇତ୍ୟାଦି ଉପରେ ଉଠୁଥିବା ପତ୍ର ଫୁଲ ନଥିବା ଛତୁ, ଶିଉଳି ଇତ୍ୟାଦି ଉଦ୍ଭିଦ

funnel /ˈfʌnl/ *noun* **1** a tube that is wide at the top to help you pour things into bottles କାହାଳୀ, ତୁଙ୍ଗା **2** a large pipe on a ship or railway engine through which smoke comes out ଜାହାଜ ବା ରେଳଇଞ୍ଜିନ୍ ଉପରେ ଧୂଆଁ ଯିବାପାଇଁ ଥିବା ଧୂମନଳୀ ➪ **engine** ଦେଖନ୍ତୁ।

funny /ˈfʌni/ *adjective* (**funnier, funniest**) **1** a person or thing that is funny makes you laugh or smile କୌତୁକଜନକ, ହସାଇଲା ପରି *a funny story* **2** strange or surprising ରହସ୍ୟମୟ, ଅଦ୍ଭୁତ *There's a funny smell in this room.*

fur /fɜ:(r)/ *noun* (*no plural*) the soft thick hair on animals. Cats and rabbits have fur ପଶୁଲୋମ, ରୁମ

furry *adjective* (**furrier, furriest**) ଲୋମଶ, ରୁମରୁମିଆ *a furry animal*

furious /ˈfjʊəriəs/ *adjective* very angry କ୍ରୋଧାନ୍ଧ, ଅତି କ୍ରୁଦ୍ଧ

furnace /ˈfɜ:nɪs/ *noun* a very hot fire in a closed place, used for heating metals, making glass, etc. ଅଗ୍ନିକୁଣ୍ଡ, ଚୁଲି, ଭାଟି

furnish /ˈfɜ:nɪʃ/ *verb* (**furnishes, furnishing, furnished**) put furniture in a room, house, etc. (ପ୍ରକୋଷ୍ଠ, ଘର ଇତ୍ୟାଦିରେ) ଚଉକି, ଟେବୁଲ, ଖଟ ଇତ୍ୟାଦି ଆସବାସ ପତ୍ର ସଜାଇବା

furnished *adjective* with furniture already in it ଆସବାସ ପତ୍ର ଥିବା *I want to buy a furnished flat.*

furniture /ˈfɜ:nɪtʃə(r)/ *noun* (*no plural*) tables, chairs, beds, etc. ଟେବୁଲ, ଚଉକି, ଖଟ ଇତ୍ୟାଦି ଆସବାସ ପତ୍ର *They've bought some furniture for their new house.*

furrow /ˈfʌrəʊ/ *noun* a long narrow cut that is made in the soil with a plough for planting seeds ମାଟିରେ ହଳ ଇତ୍ୟାଦି ଦ୍ୱାରା ଖୋଳାଯାଇଥିବା ଧାର, ଶିଆର, ସିରା, ଶୀତା

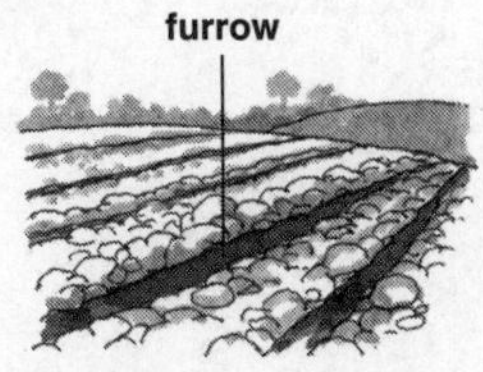

further /ˈfɜ:ðə(r)/ *adjective, adverb* more far ଅଧିକ ଦୂରରେ *Which is further—Delhi or Chandigarh?*

furthest ଶବ୍ଦ **far** ର ଏକ ଧାତୁରୂପ

fury /ˈfjʊəri/ *noun* (*no plural*) a state of being very angry and sometimes violent ପ୍ରଚଣ୍ଡ କ୍ରୋଧ, କୋପ *red with fury*

fuse /fju:z/ *noun* a small piece of wire that stops too much electricity from going through an electrical device. Plugs usually have fuses in them ବିଦ୍ୟୁତ୍ ପରିପଥରେ ଖଞ୍ଜା ଯାଇଥିବା ତାର ଯାହା ଅତ୍ୟଧିକ ବିଦ୍ୟୁତ ପ୍ରବାହ କରାଇ ଦିଏ ନାହିଁ

fuss /fʌs/ *noun* (*no plural*) a lot of excitement or worry about small things that are not important ଅନାବଶ୍ୟକ ଉତ୍ତେଜନା ବା ଚିନ୍ତା *He makes a fuss even when I'm five minutes late.*

fussy *adjective* (**fussier, fussiest**) A person who is fussy cares a lot about small things that are not important, and is difficult to please ଛୋଟ ଛୋଟ କଥା ବା ଅନାବଶ୍ୟକ ବିଷୟରେ ଉଦ୍‌ବିଗ୍ନ; ତୁଷ୍ଟୋଷ୍ୟ

future /ˈfju:tʃə(r)/ *noun* **1** the time that will come ଭବିଷ୍ୟତ *Nobody knows what will happen in the future.* **2 the future** (*no plural*) the form of a verb that shows what will happen after now ଭବିଷ୍ୟତ ଘଟଣାବଳୀ ➪ **past**[1] 2 ଏବଂ **present**[2] 2 ଦେଖନ୍ତୁ ।

G g

g *abbreviation* ଶବ୍ଦ **gram** ର ସଂକ୍ଷିପ୍ତ ରୂପ

gadget /ˈgædʒɪt/ *noun* a small machine or tool ଛୋଟ ଯାନ୍ତ୍ରିକ ଉପକରଣ ବା ଯନ୍ତ୍ରପାତି *Their kitchen is full of electrical gadgets.*

gain /geɪn/ *verb* (**gains, gaining, gained**) **1** get something that you want or need which you did not have before ଲାଭକରିବା, ପାଇବା **2** get more of something ଅଧିକ ଭାବରେ ପାଇବା, ଲାଭ, ଉପାର୍ଜନ କରିବା *He has gained a lot of weight.*

galaxy /ˈgæləksi/ *noun* (*plural* **galaxies**) a very large group of stars and planets ତାରାପୁଞ୍ଜ, ନକ୍ଷତ୍ରପୁଞ୍ଜ

galaxy

gale /geɪl/ *noun* a very strong wind ପ୍ରବଳ ବାୟୁ ବା ବାତ୍ୟା *The trees were blown down in the gale.*

gallant /ˈgælənt/ *adjective* a person who is gallant is brave and fearless ସାହସୀ, ନିର୍ଭୀକ *The gallant knight saved the princess from the one-eyed monster.*

gallantry /ˈgæləntri/ *noun* (*no plural*) the courage of a soldier in the battlefield ଯୁଦ୍ଧରେ ସୈନ୍ୟର ସାହସିକତା, ବୀରତ୍ୱ *The President rewarded the soldier for his gallantry.*

gallery /ˈgæləri/ *noun* (*plural* **galleries**) a building or room where people can go to look at works of art ଚାରୁକଳା ପ୍ରଦର୍ଶନ ପ୍ରକୋଷ୍ଠ ବା ଗୃହ *We visited the art galleries in Delhi.*

galley /ˈgæli/ *noun* (*plural* **galleys**) a flat long ship with sails which used to be rowed by slaves or prisoners in former times ଏକ ଲମ୍ୱା ଚଟକା ପାଲଟଣା ଜାହାଜ ଯାହାର ଆହୁଲା ପୂର୍ବ କାଳରେ କ୍ରୀତଦାସ ବା ଅପରାଧୀମାନେ ଚାଳନ କରୁଥିଲେ

gallop /ˈgæləp/ *verb* (**gallops, galloping, galloped**) when a horse gallops, it runs very fast while taking all its feet off the ground at the same time ଘୋଡ଼ା ଲମ୍ଫ ପ୍ରଦାନକରି ଦ୍ରୁତ ଗତିରେ ଦୌଡ଼ିବା *The horses galloped round the field.*

gallows /ˈgæləʊz/ *noun* (*plural* **gallows**) a wooden frame used in the past to hang criminals to death ଫାଶୀଖୁଣ୍ଟ

send somebody to the gallows kill a person by hanging କାହାରିକୁ ଫାଶୀଦଣ୍ଡ ଦେବା

gamble /ˈgæmbl/ *verb* (**gambles, gambling, gambled**) **1** try to win money by playing games that need luck ଜୁଆ ଖେଳିବା, ଦ୍ୟୂତକ୍ରୀଡ଼ା କରିବା *He gambled a lot of money on the last race.* **2** do something, although there is a chance that you might lose ହାରିବାର ସମ୍ଭାବନ ସତ୍ତ୍ୱେ କୌଣସି କାମ କରିବା

gambler *noun* a person who tries to win money by playing games that need luck ଟଙ୍କା ପାଇବା ପାଇଁ ଜୁଆ ଖେଳୁଥିବା ବ୍ୟକ୍ତି; ଜୁଆଡ଼ି

game /geɪm/ *noun* **1** (*plural* **games**) something you play that has rules ବିଧିବଦ୍ଧ ନିୟମ ଥିବା ଖେଳ ବା କ୍ରୀଡ଼ା *Shall we have a game of football?* **2 games** (*plural*) sports that you play at school or in a competition ସ୍କୁଲରେ ବା ପ୍ରତିଯୋଗିତାରେ ହେଉଥିବା ଖେଳ *the Olympic Games*

gander /ˈgændə(r)/ *noun* (*plural* **geese** /gi:s/) a male goose ଅଣ୍ଡିରା ବତକ ➪ ଚିତ୍ର ପାଇଁ **goose** ଦେଖନ୍ତୁ ।

gang /gæŋ/ *noun* a group of people who do things together ଏକାଠି କାମ କରୁଥିବା ଦଳ ବା ଗୋଷ୍ଠୀ *a gang of pick-pockets*

gangster /ˈgæŋstə(r)/ *noun* one of a group of dangerous criminals ଦୁର୍ଦ୍ଦାନ୍ତ ଅପରାଧୀ ଦଳର ସଭ୍ୟ

gap /gæp/ *noun* a space in something or between two things; a space where something should be ଫାଙ୍କ, ଫାଟ *The sheep escaped through a gap in the fence.*

gape /geɪp/ *verb* (**gapes, gaping, gaped**) look at somebody or something with your mouth open because you are surprised ଆଶ୍ଚର୍ଯ୍ୟ ହୋଇ ପାଟି ମେଲାକରି ଚାହିଁବା, ଆଁ କରି ଚାହିଁବା *She gaped at me when I said I was getting married.*

gaping *adjective* wide open ଖୁବ୍ ବଡ଼ ଆଁ କଲାପରି *There was a gaping hole in the ground.*

garage /ˈgærɑ:ʒ/ *noun* **1** a building where you keep your car ମଟରଗାଡ଼ି ରଖିବା ସ୍ଥାନ, ଗ୍ୟାରେଜ୍ **2** a place where cars are repaired ମଟରଗାଡ଼ି ମରାମତ କରିବା ସ୍ଥାନ **3** a place where you can buy petrol ପେଟ୍ରୋଲ ପମ୍ପ

garbage /ˈgɑ:bɪdʒ/ *noun* **rubbish 1** ର ଏକ ପ୍ରତିଶବ୍ଦ

garden /ˈgɑ:dn/ *noun* a piece of land next to a house or in a public place where flowers, fruit and vegetables are grown ବଗିଚା, ଉଦ୍ୟାନ

gardener *noun* a person who works in a garden as a job or someone who enjoys gardening ମାଳି, ଉଦ୍ୟାନ ରକ୍ଷକ, ବଗିଚା ରକ୍ଷକ ।

gardening *noun* (*no plural*) ବଗିଚା କାମ *My father enjoys gardening.*

garlic /ˈgɑ:lɪk/ *noun* (*no plural*) a plant like a small onion with a strong taste and smell, that is used in cooking ରସୁଣ ଗଛ, ରସୁଣ ➪ ଚିତ୍ର ପାଇଁ **clove** ଦେଖନ୍ତୁ ।

garment /ˈgɑ:mənt/ *noun* a piece of clothing ପୋଷାକ

garnish /ˈgɑ:nɪʃ/ *verb* (**garnishes, garnishing, garnished**) decorate a dish of food with a small quantity of another food ରନ୍ଧା ଖାଦ୍ୟ ସଜାଇବା ସଯନ୍ ପରିବେଷଣ କରିବା (ତା ଉପରେ ଧନିଆ ପତ୍ର ଇତ୍ୟାଦି ଦେଇ) *a bowl of mushroom soup garnished with cream*

garrison /ˈgærɪsn/ *noun* a group of soldiers who are living in a town or fort so that they can defend it ଦୁର୍ଗ, ସହର ଇତ୍ୟାଦିର ରକ୍ଷକ ସୈନ୍ୟଦଳ, ସଂଗୃହୀତ ସୈନ୍ୟଦଳ

gas /gæs/ *noun* **1** (*plural* **gases**) anything that is like air ବାଷ୍ପ, ଗ୍ୟାସ୍ *Hydrogen and oxygen are gases.* **2** (*no plural*) a gas with a strong smell, that is used for heating or cooking ରାନ୍ଧିବା ବା ଉତ୍ତାପ ଦେବାପାଇଁ ବ୍ୟବହୃତ ଜାଳେଣି ବାଷ୍ପ ବା ଗ୍ୟାସ୍ *a gas stove*

gaseous /ˈgæsiəs/ *adjective* in the form of a gas ବାଷ୍ପୀୟ, ବାଷ୍ପ ପରି *Water vapour is the gaseous state of water.*

gasp /gɑːsp/ *verb* (**gasps, gasping, gasped**) when you gasp, you take deep breaths, usually through the mouth because you have difficulty in breathing, you are surprised or you are in pain ଧଇଁସଇଁ ହେବା, ଖର ନିଶ୍ୱାସ ନେବା, କଷ୍ଟରେ ନିଶ୍ୱାସ ନେବା *The runners were all gasping for breath at the end of the race.*

gate /geɪt/ *noun* a kind of door in a fence or wall outside a building ଫାଟକ, ଗେଟ୍ *We closed the gate to stop the cows from entering the garden.* ➪ ଚିତ୍ର ପାଇଁ **house** ଦେଖନ୍ତୁ ।

gather /ˈgæðə(r)/ *verb* (**gathers, gathering, gathered**) **1** come together in a group; meet ଏକାଠି ହେବା; ଏକତ୍ର କରିବା *A crowd gathered to watch the fight.* **2** take things that are in different places and bring them together ବିଭିନ୍ନ ଜିନିଷ ଆଣି ଏକାଠି କରିବା *I gathered up all the books and papers and put them in my bag.*

gathering *noun* a time when people come together ଜନସଭା, ଜନସମାବେଶ, ଲୋକସମାଗମ *There was a large gathering outside the palace.*

gaudy /ˈgɔːdi/ *adjective* (**gaudier, gaudiest**) something that is gaudy is too brightly coloured or over-decorated and so looks unpleasant ରୁଚିହୀନ ଭାବେ ଆଡ଼ମ୍ବରପୂର୍ଣ୍ଣ *a gaudy necklace*

gauge /geɪdʒ/ *noun* an instrument that measures how much of something there is ଚାପ, ଲମ୍ବ, ପ୍ରସ୍ଥ, ଘନତ୍ୱ ଇତ୍ୟାଦିର ମାପକ ଯନ୍ତ୍ର, ଗେଜ୍ *Where is the petrol gauge in this car?*

petrol gauge

gave ଶବ୍ଦ **give** ର ଏକ ଧାତୁରୂପ

gaze /geɪz/ *verb* (**gazes, gazing, gazed**) look at somebody or something for a long time ସ୍ଥିର ଦୃଷ୍ଟିରେ ଚାହିଁବା, ଏକଲୟରେ ଚାହିଁବା *She sat and gazed out of the window.*

gear /gɪə(r)/ *noun* **1** (*plural* **gears**) a set of wheels that work together in a machine to pass power from one part to another. The gears of a car or bicycle help to control it when it goes up and down hills and help it to go faster or slower ଗିଅର୍; ଘୂର୍ଣ୍ଣାୟମାନ ଗତିକୁ ପ୍ରେରିତ କରିବା ପାଇଁ ଥିବା ଦନ୍ତଚକ୍ର ସମୂହ (ଯଥା : ମଟରଗାଡ଼ି ଇଞ୍ଜିନର ଘୂର୍ଣ୍ଣନକୁ ସ୍ଥାନାନ୍ତର କରି ଚକକୁ ଗତିଶୀଳ କରୁଥିବା ଗିଅର୍) *You need to change gear to go round the corner.* **2** (*no plural*) special clothes or things that you need for a job or sport ବିଶେଷ କାମ, ଖେଳ ଇତ୍ୟାଦିରେ ବ୍ୟବହୃତ ପୋଷାକ ଓ ଉପକରଣ *camping gear*

geese ଶବ୍ଦ **goose** ର ବହୁବଚନ

gel /dʒel/ *noun* a thick jelly-like substance ଅଠାଳିଆ ପଦାର୍ଥ *hair gel*

gem /dʒem/ *noun* a beautiful stone that is very valuable; a jewel ବହୁମୂଲ୍ୟ ସୁନ୍ଦର ପଥର, ମଣି, ରତ୍ନ

Gemini /ˈdʒemɪnaɪ/ *noun* the third sign of the **zodiac** ରାଶିଚକ୍ରର ତୃତୀୟ ରାଶି, ମିଥୁନ ରାଶି

gender /ˈdʒendə(r)/ *noun* the gender of a person tells you if that person is male or female ବ୍ୟକ୍ତିର ଲିଙ୍ଗଗତ ସଂଜ୍ଞା

gene /dʒiːn/ *noun* the part of a plant or animal cell which passes on certain features of the parent to the children ଉଦ୍ଭିଦ ବା ପ୍ରାଣୀ କୋଷରେ ଥିବା କୌଳିକ ଗୁଣ ନିୟନ୍ତ୍ରକ ଉପାଦାନ ଯାହା ବାପା ମାଙ୍କ ଠାରୁ ପିଲାଙ୍କ ପାଖକୁ ପ୍ରଦତ୍ତ ହୁଏ; ଜିନ୍ *Good looks are in his genes.*

general[1] /ˈdʒenrəl/ *adjective* **1** of, by or for most people or things ସାଧାରଣ, ସାର୍ବଜନୀନ *Is this car park for general use?* **2** not in detail ପୁଙ୍ଖାନୁପୁଙ୍ଖ ବା ସବିଶେଷ ବିବରଣ ନଥିବା, ସାଧାରଣ *The back cover gives you a general idea of what the book is about.*

general election *noun* a time when people choose a new government ସାରା ଦେଶରୁ ସଂସଦକୁ ପ୍ରତିନିଧି ପଠାଇବା ପାଇଁ ହେଉଥିବା ନିର୍ବାଚନ, ସାଧାରଣ ନିର୍ବାଚନ *Did you vote in the last general election?*

general knowledge *noun* (*no plural*) what you know about a lot of different things ସାଧାରଣ ଜ୍ଞାନ, ସବୁ ବିଷୟରେ ସମ୍ୟକ୍ ଜ୍ଞାନ

general[2] /ˈdʒenrəl/ *noun* a very important officer in the army ସେନା ନାୟକ, ସେନାଧିପତି

generally /ˈdʒenrəli/ *adverb* usually; mostly ସାଧାରଣତଃ *I generally get up at about seven o'clock.*

generate /ˈdʒenəreɪt/ *verb* (**generates, generating, generated**) make heat, electricity, etc. ଉତ୍ତାପ, ବିଦ୍ୟୁତ୍ ଇତ୍ୟାଦି ଉତ୍ପାଦନ କରିବା *Power stations generate electricity.*

generation /ˌdʒenəˈreɪʃn/ *noun* all the people who were born around the same time ଏକା ସମୟ ଅବଧିରେ ଜନ୍ମ ହୋଇଥିବା ସବୁ ଲୋକ, ପିଢ଼ୀ *This photo shows three generations of my family.* ➪ **family** ଦେଖନ୍ତୁ।

generator /ˈdʒenəreɪtə(r)/ *noun* a machine that produces electricity ବିଦ୍ୟୁତ୍ ଉତ୍ପାଦନ ଯନ୍ତ୍ର, ଜେନେରେଟର୍

generosity /ˌdʒenəˈrɒsəti/ *noun* (*no plural*) liking to give things to other people ବଦାନ୍ୟତା

generous /ˈdʒenərəs/ *adjective* always ready to give things or to spend money ଯିଏ ସଦାବେଳେ ଜିନିଷ ବା ପଇସା ଦିଏ, ଦାତା; ବଦାନ୍ୟ ସଦାଶୟ *She is very generous—she often buys me presents.* ✪ ବିପରୀତ **mean**[2] **1**

generously *adverb* ବଦାନ୍ୟ ଭାବରେ *Please donate generously.*

genius /ˈdʒiːniəs/ *noun* (*plural* **geniuses**) a person with an extraordinary ability ଅସାଧାରଣ ବୁଦ୍ଧିଶକ୍ତି ଥିବା ବ୍ୟକ୍ତି *Einstein was a genius.*

gentle /ˈdʒentl/ *adjective* (**gentler, gentlest**) quiet and kind, not rough

ଧୀରସ୍ଥିର; କୋମଳ *Be gentle with the baby.* ○ *a gentle voice*

gently *adverb* କୋମଳ ଭାବରେ, ଧୀରେ *Close the door gently or you'll wake the children up.*

gentleman /ˈdʒentlmən/ *noun* (*plural* **gentlemen**) **1** a polite way of saying 'man' ଭଦ୍ରଲୋକ, ବ୍ୟକ୍ତି *There is a gentleman here to see you.* **2** a man who is polite and kind to other people ଭଦ୍ର ଓ ଦୟାଶୀଳ ବ୍ୟକ୍ତି ➪ **lady** ଦେଖନ୍ତୁ।

genuine /ˈdʒenjuɪn/ *adjective* real and true ପ୍ରକୃତ, ଅସଲି *Those aren't genuine diamonds—they're pieces of glass!*

genuinely *adverb* really ପ୍ରକୃତରେ, ଅସଲରେ *Do you think he's genuinely sorry?*

geography /dʒiˈɒgrəfi/ *noun* (*no plural*) the study of the earth and its countries, mountains, rivers, weather, etc. ଭୂଗୋଳ

geometry /dʒiˈɒmətri/ *noun* (*no plural*) the study of things like lines, angles and shapes ଜ୍ୟାମିତି

germ /dʒɜ:m/ *noun* a very small living thing that can make you ill (ରୋଗଜନକ) ଜୀବାଣୁ ବା କୀଟାଣୁ *It is important to keep the kitchen clean and free of germs.*

germinate /ˈdʒɜ:mɪneɪt/ *verb* (**germinates, germinating, germinated**) when a seed germinates, it starts to grow (ମଞ୍ଜିରୁ) ଗଜା ବାହରିବା, ଅଙ୍କୁରିତ ହେବା

germination /ˌdʒɜ:mɪˈneɪʃn/ *noun* (*no plural*) the growth of a seed ଅଙ୍କୁରଣ, ଅଙ୍କୁରୋଦ୍‌ଗମ

gesture /ˈdʒestʃə(r)/ *noun* a movement of your head or hand to show how you feel or what you want ଅଙ୍ଗଭଙ୍ଗୀ, ଇଙ୍ଗିତ, ଠାର

get /get/ *verb* (**gets, getting, got** /gɒt/, **has got**) **1** receive something ପାଇବା, ପ୍ରାପ୍ତହେବା *I got a lot of presents for my birthday.* **2** buy or take something କିଣିବା, ଆଣିବା *Will you get some bread when you go shopping?* **3** become ହେବା *It's getting cold.* **4** start to have an illness ରୋଗ ଧରିବା *I think I'm getting a cold.* **5** a word that you use with part of another verb to show that something happens to somebody or something (ଅନ୍ୟ କ୍ରିୟା ସହ ବ୍ୟବହୃତ) ହେବା *Sarita got angry with Manu.*

get back return ଫେରିବା *When did you get back from your holiday?*

get in, get into something climb into a car ଚଢ଼ିବା, ଭିତରକୁ ଯିବା *Sunil got into the car.*

get off leave a train, bus, bicycle, etc. ଓହ୍ଲାଇବା *Where did you get off the bus?*

get on, get onto something climb onto a bus, train or bicycle (ବସ୍, ଟ୍ରେନ୍, ସାଇକେଲ୍‌ରେ) ଚଢ଼ିବା *I got on the train at Delhi.*

get on with somebody live or work in a friendly way with somebody ଖୁସିବାସିରେ ଚଳିବା, ମିଳିମିଶି ଖୁସିହସିରେ *We get on well with our neighbours.*

get out leave a car, etc. ଓହ୍ଲାଇବା (କାର୍ ଇତ୍ୟାଦିରୁ); ବାହାରକୁ ଯିବା *I opened the door and got out.*

get something out take something from the place where it was କିଛି ଜିନିଷ ତା ସ୍ଥାନରୁ କାଢ଼ିବା *She opened her bag and got out a pen.*

get together meet; come together in a group ଏକାଠି ହେବା, ଏକଜୁଟ ହେବା *The whole family got together for the wedding.*

get up stand up; get out of bed ଠିଆ ହେବା; ନିଦରୁ ବା ଶେଯରୁ ଉଠିବା *What time do you usually get up?*

have got have something ଥିବା, ଅଛି *She has got brown eyes.* ○ *Have you got any money?*

have got to if you have got to do something, you must do it ନିଶ୍ଚିତ ଭାବେ କରିବାକୁ ହେବ *I have got to leave soon.*

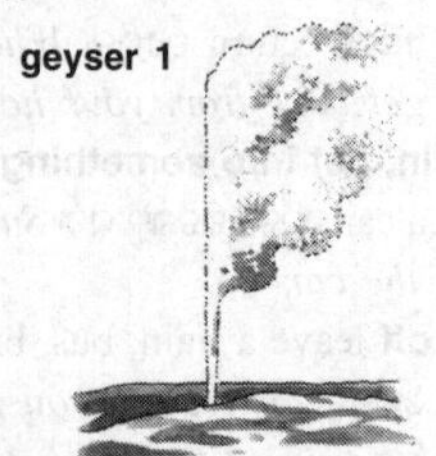

geyser /ˈgi:zə(r)/ *noun* **1** a place through which hot water comes out from below the ground ଜଳୋଦ୍‌କ୍ଷେପୀ ଉଷ୍ଣ ପ୍ରସ୍ରବଣ **2** an electrical appliance that you have in the kitchen or bathroom to heat water ପାଣି ଗରମ କରି ନଳ ବାଟେ ଛାଡ଼ିବା ଇଲେକ୍‌ଟ୍ରି ଉପକରଣ (ଗାଧୁଆ ଘର ଇତ୍ୟାଦିରେ ଲଗାଯାଏ)

ghost /gəʊst/ *noun* the form of a dead person that a living person thinks he/she sees ଭୂତ, ପ୍ରେତାତ୍ମା *Do you believe in ghosts?*

giant /ˈdʒaɪənt/ *noun* a very big tall person in stories ଗଳ୍ପରେ ବର୍ଣ୍ଣିତ ବିରାଟକାୟ ମନୁଷ୍ୟ, ଦାନବ *Bhim was a giant.*

giant *adjective* very big ଅତିବଡ଼, ବୃହତ *a giant insect*

gift /gɪft/ *noun* something that you give to or get from somebody, for example on birthdays; a present ଉପହାର *wedding gifts*

gigantic /dʒaɪˈgæntɪk/ *adjective* very big ବିରାଟକାୟ, ଅତି ବଡ଼

giggle /ˈgɪgl/ *verb* (**giggles, giggling, giggled**) laugh in a silly way ନିର୍ବୋଧ ଭାବେ ହସିବା *The children couldn't stop giggling.*

giggle *noun* ନିର୍ବୋଧ ହସ *There was a giggle from the back of the class.*

gill /gɪl/ *noun* the part on each side of a fish's head that it breathes through ମାଛର ଗାଲି (ଯାହା ସାହାଯ୍ୟରେ ମାଛ ନିଶ୍ୱାସପ୍ରଶ୍ୱାସ ନିଏ)

ginger /ˈdʒɪndʒə(r)/ *noun* (*no plural*) a plant whose root has a very hot strong taste, that is used in cooking ଅଦା

gipsy = **gypsy**

giraffe /dʒəˈrɑ:f/ *noun* (*plural* **giraffe** ବା **giraffes**) a big animal from Africa with a very long neck and long legs ଆଫ୍ରିକାର ଲମ୍ବାବେକ ଓ ଲମ୍ବାଗୋଡ଼ ଥିବା ପଶୁ, ଜିରାଫ୍

girl /gɜ:l/ *noun* a female child; a young woman ଝିଅ, ବାଳିକା; ଯୁବତୀ, ତରୁଣୀ

Girl Guide *noun* a member of a special club for girls ଝିଅମାନଙ୍କ ଗାଇଡ୍ ସଂସ୍ଥାର ସଭ୍ୟା ⇨ **boy scout** ଦେଖନ୍ତୁ।

give /gɪv/ *verb* (**gives, giving, gave** /geɪv/, **has given** /ˈgɪvn/) **1** let somebody have something ଦେବା, ଦାନ କରିବା *She gave me a watch for my birthday.* **2** make somebody have or feel something ଉକ୍ତ ଭାବରେ ଅନୁଭବ କରାଇବା *That noise is giving me a headache.*

give somebody back something, give something back to somebody return something to somebody ଫେରାଇବା *Can you give me back the cassette I lent you last week?*

give something out give something to many people ବହୁ ଲୋକଙ୍କୁ ଦେବା *Could you give out these books to the class, please?*

give up stop trying to do something, because you know that you cannot do it ଆଶା ଛାଡ଼ି ଦେବା; କୌଣସି କାମ ବନ୍ଦକରି ଦେବା; ସମର୍ପଣ କରିବା *I give up—what's the answer?*

give something up stop doing or having something କୌଣସି ଅଭ୍ୟାସ ଛାଡ଼ିଦେବା *He's trying to give up smoking.*

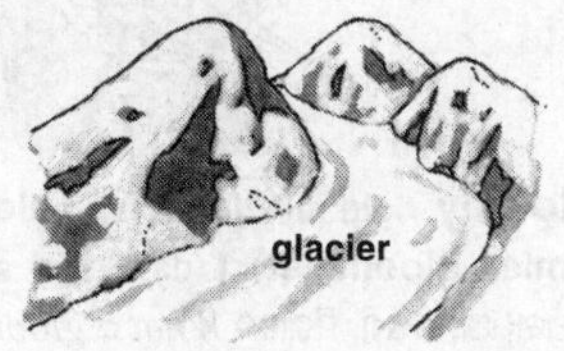
glacier

glacier /ˈglæsiə(r)/ *noun* a large river of ice that moves slowly down a mountain valley ଧୀର ପ୍ରବାହୀ ବରଫାବୃତ ନଦୀ, ହିମସ୍ରୋତ

glad /glæd/ *adjective* happy; pleased ଖୁସି, ଆନନ୍ଦିତ *He was glad to see us.*

gladly *adverb* if you do something gladly, you are happy to do it ଆନନ୍ଦରେ, ଖୁସିରେ *I'll gladly help you.*

glance /glɑːns/ *verb* (**glances, glancing, glanced**) look quickly at somebody or something ଦୃଷ୍ଟି ନିକ୍ଷେପ କରିବା, ଆଖିବୁଲାଇ ଆଣିବା *Soni glanced at her watch.*

glance *noun* ଦୃଷ୍ଟି ନିକ୍ଷେପ *a glance at the newspaper*

at a glance with one look ଏକ ଦୃଷ୍ଟି ନିକ୍ଷେପରେ, ଥରେ ଚାହିଁଦେଇ

glare /gleə(r)/ *verb* (**glares, glaring, glared**) **1** look angrily at somebody ରାଗି ଚାହିଁବା, ତୀକ୍ଷ୍ଣ ଦୃଷ୍ଟିରେ ଭୀଷଣ ଦୃଷ୍ଟିରେ, କଟମଟକରି ଅନାଇବା *He glared at her.* **2** shine with a strong light that hurts your eyes ଚାହିଁ ନହେଲା ପରି ତୀବ୍ରୋଜ୍ଜ୍ୱଳ ଆଲୋକ ଦେବା, ଆଖି ଝଲସେଇ ଦେବା *The sun glared down.*

glare *noun* **1** (*plural* **glares**) a long angry look ରାଗ ଗରଗର ଚାହାଣୀ **2** (*no plural*) strong light that hurts your eyes ଆଖି ଝଲସେଇ ବେଶି ଉଜ୍ଜ୍ୱଳ ଆଲୋକ *the glare of the car's headlights*

glass /glɑːs/ *noun* **1** (*no plural*) a hard substance that you can see through. It is used to make windows and bottles for example କାଚ **2** (*plural* **glasses**) a thing made of glass that you drink from କାଚରେ ତିଆରି, ପ୍ରଭୃତି ଗିଲାସ *Could I have a glass of milk, please?* **3 glasses** (*plural*) two pieces of special glass (called **lenses**) in a frame that people wear over their eyes to help them see better ଚଷମା *Does she wear glasses?* ➪ **sunglasses** ମଧ୍ୟ ଦେଖନ୍ତୁ ।

> ✪ ମନେରଖନ୍ତୁ ! ଆପଣ 'a glasses' କହିବା ଭୁଲ୍ ହେବ । କହିବେ **a pair of glasses**– *I need a new pair of glasses.* [କିମ୍ବା *I need (some) new glasses.*]

gleam /gliːm/ *verb* (**gleams, gleaming, gleamed**) shine with a soft light ଦୀପ୍ତି ପ୍ରକାଶ କରିବା, ଝଲସିବା *The lake gleamed in the moonlight.*

glide /glaɪd/ *verb* (**glides, gliding, glided**) move smoothly and silently ଅନାୟାସରେ ଶବ୍ଦ ନକରି ଗତି କରିବା *The bird glided through the air.*

glider /ˈglaɪdə(r)/ *noun* a very light aeroplane without an engine ଇଞ୍ଜିନ୍ ନଥିବା ଏକ ହାଲ୍କା ଉଡ଼ାଜାହାଜ, ଗ୍ଲାଇଡର୍
gliding *noun* (*no plural*) flying in a glider as a sport ଗ୍ଲାଇଡର, ଉଡ଼ାଇବା ଖେଳ

glimmer /ˈglɪmə(r)/ *verb* (**glimmers, glimmering, glimmered**) shine with a small, weak light କ୍ଷୀଣ ଆଲୋକ, ଭୁଲୁଭୁଲୁ ହେଉଥିବା ଆଲୋକ

glimpse /glɪmps/ *noun*
catch a glimpse of somebody or **something** see somebody or something quickly, but not clearly କ୍ଷଣିକ ଦର୍ଶନ ପାଇବା *I caught a glimpse of myself in the mirror as I walked past.*

glisten /ˈglɪsn/ *verb* (**glistens, glistening, glistened**) shine because it is wet or smooth ଝଲସିବା, ଚକ୍‌ଚକ୍ ହେବା *His eyes glistened with tears.*

glitter /ˈglɪtə(r)/ *verb* (**glitters, glittering, glittered**) shine brightly with a lot of small flashes of light ଚକମକ ହେବା, ଝଲସିବା *The piece of glass glittered in the sun.*

global /ˈgləʊbl/ *adjective* of or about the whole world ପୃଥିବୀ ସମ୍ବନ୍ଧୀୟ, ପୃଥିବୀବ୍ୟାପୀ, ବିଶ୍ୱବ୍ୟାପୀ *Pollution is a global problem.*

global warming *noun* (*no plural*) the increase in the temperature of the earth's atmosphere that is caused by harmful gases that are given out by vehicles and industries ଗାଡ଼ିମଟର, କାରଖାନା ଇତ୍ୟାଦିର ଦୂଷିତ ବାଷ୍ପ ଉପରକୁ ଉଡ଼ିଯିବା ଦ୍ୱାରା ବାୟୁମଣ୍ଡଳର ତଳ ଭାଗରେ ସୂର୍ଯ୍ୟଙ୍କ ଉତ୍ତାପ ଆବଦ୍ଧ ରହି ବାୟୁମଣ୍ଡଳର ଉତ୍ତାପ ବୃଦ୍ଧି

globe /gləʊb/ *noun* **1** a ball with a map of the world on it ପୃଥିବୀ ଗୋଲକର ଗୋଲାକାର ମାନଚିତ୍ର **2 the globe** (*no plural*) the earth ପୃଥିବୀ *He's travelled all over the globe.*

globe

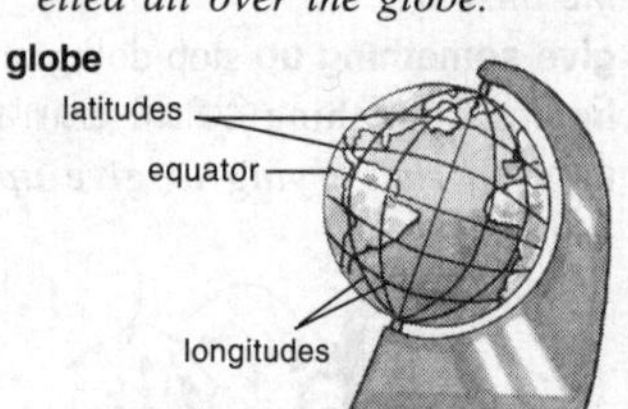

gloomy /ˈgluːmi/ *adjective* (**gloomier, gloomiest**) **1** dark and sad ଅନ୍ଧାରୁଆ; ବିଷର୍ଣ୍ଣ, ନିରାନନ୍ଦ *What a gloomy day!* **2** sad and without hope ବିଷାଦପୂର୍ଣ୍ଣ, ନିରାନନ୍ଦ, ଆଶାହୀନ *He's feel* *ing very gloomy because he can't get a job.*

glorious /ˈglɔ:riəs/ *adjective* **1** wonderful or beautiful ଚମତ୍କାର, ସୁନ୍ଦର, ଉପଭୋଗ୍ୟ *The weather was glorious.* **2** famous and full of glory ପ୍ରସିଦ୍ଧ, ମହାନ *a glorious history*

glory /ˈglɔ:ri/ *noun* (*no plural*) **1** fame and respect that you get when you do great things ଯଶ, ସୁନାମ *the glory of winning at the Olympics* **2** great beauty ସୌନ୍ଦର୍ଯ୍ୟ, ଶୋଭା, ଉଜ୍ଜ୍ୱଳ ମହିମା *Autumn is the best time to see the forest in all its glory.*

glossy /ˈglɒsi/ *adjective* (**glossier, glossiest**) smooth and shiny ଉଜ୍ଜ୍ୱଳ, ଚକଚକିଆ *glossy hair*

glove /glʌv/ *noun* a thing that you wear to keep your hand warm or safe ହାତମୋଜା, ଦସ୍ତାନା, ଗ୍ଲୋଭ୍ *rubber gloves*

glow /gləʊ/ *verb* (**glows, glowing, glowed**) **1** send out soft light or heat without flames or smoke ତାପ ଉତ୍ପନ୍ନ କରି ଅଗ୍ନିଶିଖା ନଥାଇ ଆଲୋକ ଦେବା *The hot coals glowed in the dark.* **2** look very happy ଆନନ୍ଦିତ ଦିଶିବା, ମୁହଁ ଉଜ୍ଜ୍ୱଳ ଦିଶିବା

glow *noun* ଶିଖାବିହୀନ ଆଲୋକ, ଦୀପ୍ତି, ଉଜ୍ଜ୍ୱଳତା *the glow of the sky at sunset*

glucose /ˈglu:kəʊs/ *noun* (*no plural*) a type of sugar that is found in fruit and gives you energy ଫଳରସରେ ଥିବା ଶର୍କରା ବା ଚିନି ଜାତୀୟ ପଦାର୍ଥ

glue /glu:/ *noun* (*no plural*) a thick liquid that you use for sticking things together ଅଠା

glutton /ˈglʌtn/ *noun* someone who eats too much ପେଟୁ ଲୋକ, ଉଦରମ୍ଭରି ଲୋକ, ଲୋଭୀ

gnaw /nɔ:/ *verb* (**gnaws, gnawing, gnawed**) keep biting something ଦାନ୍ତରେ କାମୁଡ଼ିବା, ଚୋବାଇବା *The dog was gnawing a bone.*

go /gəʊ/ *verb* (**goes, going, went** /went/, **has gone** /gɒn/) **1** move from one place to another ଯିବା *I went to Pune by train.* **2** travel to a place to do something କୌଣସି କାମରେ ଅନ୍ୟ ସ୍ଥାନକୁ ଯିବା *I'll go and make some coffee.* **3** leave a place ଯିବା, ସ୍ଥାନ ଛାଡ଼ିବା *I must go now—it's four o'clock.* **4** lead to a place ଯିବା, କୌଣସି ସ୍ଥାନ ଆଡ଼କୁ ଯିବା *Does this road go to the station?* **5** happen in a certain way ଅତିବାହିତ ହେବା *The week went very quickly.* **6** disappear ଚାଲିଯିବା, ଛାଡ଼ିଯିବା *My headache has gone.*

go back go again to a place where you were before; return ଫେରିଯିବା *We're going back to school tomorrow.*

go off 1 explode ବିସ୍ଫୋରଣ ଘଟିବା *A bomb went off at the station today.* **2** when food or drink goes off, it becomes too old to eat or drink ଖାଦ୍ୟ ବା ପାନୀୟ ଖରାପ ହୋଇଯିବା *This milk has gone off—it smells horrible.*

go on 1 happen ଘଟିବା *What's going on?* **2** continue; not stop ହେଇଚାଲିବା, କରିଚାଲିବା *I went on working.*

go out 1 leave the place where you live or work ବାହାରକୁ ଯିବା *I went out* *for a walk.* **2** stop shining or burning ଲିଭିଯିବା, ନ ଜଳିବା *The fire has gone out.*

go through something 1 look at or explain something carefully from the beginning to the end ତନ୍ନତନ୍ନ କରି ଦେଖିବା; ଆରମ୍ଭରୁ ଶେଷ ପର୍ଯ୍ୟନ୍ତ ବୁଝାଇବା *The teacher went through our homework.* **2** suffer something ସହିବା *She went through a difficult time when her husband was ill.*

go up become higher or more (ଦର ଇତ୍ୟାଦି) ବଢ଼ିବା *The price of petrol has gone up again.*

> **been** or **gone**?
>
> ଯଦି କୌଣସି ବ୍ୟକ୍ତି ଗୋଟେ ସ୍ଥାନକୁ ଯାଇ ସେଠାରୁ ଫେରି ଆସିଅଛି ତେବେ **been** ହୁଏ — *I've* ***been*** *to Manali three times.* ଯଦି କେହି ଗୋଟେ ସ୍ଥାନକୁ ଯାଇ ଅଛି ଏବଂ ବର୍ତ୍ତମାନ ସେଠାରେ ଅଛି, ତେବେ **gone** ହୁଏ, —
> *Jassi isn't here. She has* ***gone*** *to Manali.*

goal /ɡəʊl/ *noun* **1** the place where the ball must go to win a point in a game like football ଫୁଟବଲ୍‌ର ଗୋଲ୍‌ପୋଷ୍ଟ ଯାହା ଭିତରକୁ ବଲ୍ ମାରିଲେ ପଏଣ୍ଟ୍ ମିଳେ **2** a point that a team wins in a game like football when the ball goes into the goal ଗୋଲ୍‌ପୋଷ୍ଟ ଭିତରକୁ ବଲ୍ ମାରି ଗୋଲ୍ କରିବା ପ୍ରକ୍ରିୟା *Jai has scored another goal.* **3** the purpose or aim of something ଲକ୍ଷ, ଉଦ୍ଦେଶ୍ୟ *the goal of completing the work in a month's time*

goalkeeper /ˈɡəʊlkiːpə(r)/ *noun* a player in a game like football who must stop the ball from going into the goal (ଫୁଟବଲ୍ ଖେଳରେ) ଗୋଲ୍‌ରକ୍ଷକ

goat /ɡəʊt/ *noun* an animal with horns. People keep goats for their milk ଛେଳି, ଛାଗ, ଛାଗଳ ✪ ଛେଳି ଛୁଆକୁ **kid** କହନ୍ତି।

gobble /ˈɡɒbl/ *verb* (**gobbles, gobbling, gobbled**) eat quickly and hungrily ଖାଦ୍ୟକୁ ଚଞ୍ଚଳ ଗିଳିପକାଇବା *He gobbled up the food meant for three people, but he still felt hungry.*

god /ɡɒd/ *noun* **1** (*plural* **gods**) a being that people believe controls them and nature ଈଶ୍ୱର, ଭଗବାନ, ଦେବତା **2 God** (*no plural*) the one great being that Christians, Jews and Muslims believe made the world and controls everything ଖ୍ରୀଷ୍ଟିଆନ୍, ଇହୁଦୀ ଓ ମୁସଲମାନ ଧର୍ମରେ ବିଶ୍ୱର ସୃଷ୍ଟିକର୍ତ୍ତା ଓ ରକ୍ଷକ

goddess /ˈɡɒdes/ *noun* (*plural* **goddesses**) a female god ଦେବୀ

goes ଶବ୍ଦ **go** ର ଏକ ଧାତୁରୂପ

goggles /ˈɡɒɡlz/ *noun* (*plural*) big glasses that you wear so that water, dust, wind, etc cannot get in your eyes. ପହଁରାଳି, ବରଫରେ ସ୍କି କରୁଥିବା ବ୍ୟକ୍ତି, ମଟର୍‌ସାଇକେଲ୍ ଚଢ଼ାଳି ପିନ୍ଧୁଥିବା ପାଣି ପବନ ଧୂଳିରୁ ରକ୍ଷା କରୁଥିବା ବଡ଼ ଚଷମା *a pair of goggles* ➪ **sunglasses** ଦେଖନ୍ତୁ।

going ଶବ୍ଦ **go** ର ଏକ ଧାତୁରୂପ

be going to 1 words that show what you plan to do in the future ଭବିଷ୍ୟତ କାମ ସୂଚାଉଥିବା ବାକ୍ୟାଂଶ; କରିବ *Ajay's going to cook the dinner tonight.* **2** words that you use when you are sure that something will happen ନିଶ୍ଚିତ ଘଟିବାକୁ ଥିବା ଘଟଣା ସୂଚାଉଥିବା ବାକ୍ୟାଂଶ; ହେବ, ଘଟିବ *It's going to rain.*

gold /gəʊld/ *noun* (*no plural*) a yellow metal that is very valuable ସୁନା, ସ୍ୱର୍ଣ୍ଣ *Is your ring made of gold?*

golden /ˈgəʊldən/ *adjective* **1** made of gold ସୁନାରେ ତିଆରି *a golden crown* **2** having the colour of gold ସୁନେଲି ରଙ୍ଗର *golden hair*

golf /gɒlf/ *noun* (*no plural*) a game that you play by hitting a small ball into holes with a long stick (called a **golf club**) ଗଲ୍ଫ୍‌ କ୍ଲବ୍‌ ବା ଗଲ୍ଫ୍‌ ବାଡ଼ିଦ୍ୱାରା ବଲ ମାରି ଗାତରେ ପକାଇବା ଖେଳ

gone ଶବ୍ଦ **go** ର ଏକ ଧାତୁରୂପ

good[1] /gʊd/ *adjective* (**better, best**) **1** that does what you want; done or made very well ଭଲ, ଉତ୍ତମ *It's a good knife—it cuts very well.* ○ *The film was really good.* **2** that you enjoy; nice ଆନନ୍ଦଦାୟକ, ସନ୍ତୋଷଜନକ, ଉପଭୋଗ୍ୟ *The weather was very good.* **3** able to do something well ଭଲ, ନିପୁଣ *She's a good driver.* **4** kind, or doing the right thing ଦୟାଶୀଳ, ନୀତିନିଷ୍ଠ *It's good of you to help.* **5** right or suitable ଠିକ୍‌ ବା ଉପଯୁକ୍ତ *This is a good place for a picnic.*

good at something able to do something well (କିଛି କାମ) ଠିକ୍‌ ଭାବରେ କରିପାରୁଥିବା *James is very good at tennis.*

good[2] /gʊd/ *noun* (*no plural*) something that is right or helpful ନୈତିକ ଭାବରେ ଠିକ୍‌ ବା ସାହାଯ୍ୟକାରୀ କାମ

do somebody good make somebody well or happy କାହାରି ଭଲ କରିବା *It will do you good to go to bed early tonight.*

for good for all time; for ever ସ୍ଥାୟୀ ଭାବରେ; ସବୁ ଦିନ ପାଇଁ *She has gone to Australia for good.*

good afternoon *interjection* words that you say when you see or speak to somebody in the afternoon ଅପରାହ୍ଣ ସମୟର ସମ୍ଭାଷଣ, ଶୁଭ ଅପରାହ୍ଣ ✪ ଅନେକ ସମୟରେ ଆମେ ଖାଲି **Afternoon** କହୁ *'Good afternoon, Leena.' 'Afternoon, Mihir.'*

goodbye /ˌgʊdˈbaɪ/ *interjection* a word that you say when somebody goes away, or when you go away ବିଦାୟ ସମ୍ଭାଷଣ; ଶୁଭ ବିଦାୟ *'Goodbye! See you tomorrow.'*

good evening *interjection* words that you say when you see or speak to somebody in the evening ସନ୍ଧ୍ୟା କାଳର ସମ୍ଭାଷଣ; ଶୁଭ ସନ୍ଧ୍ୟା ✪ ଅନେକ ସମୟରେ ଆମେ କେବଳ **Evening** କହୁ *'Good evening, Mr Sundar.' 'Evening, Mrs Pandit.'*

good-looking *adjective* nice to look at; handsome ସୁନ୍ଦର ➪ **beautiful** ର ଟିପ୍ପଣୀ ଦେଖନ୍ତୁ ।

good morning *interjection* words that you say when you see or speak to somebody in the morning ସକାଳର

ଅଭିବାଦନ ଶବ୍ଦ ସମ୍ଭାଷଣ; ସୁପ୍ରଭାତ ✪ ଅନେକ ସମୟରେ ଆମେ ଖାଲି **Morning** କୁହାଯାଇଥାଏ। *'Good morning, Mohit.' 'Morning.'*

goodness /ˈgʊdnəs/ *noun* (*no plural*) **1** being good or kind ସଦ୍‌ଗୁଣ **2** something in food that is good for your health (ଖାଦ୍ୟର) ଉତ୍କୃଷ୍ଟତା *Fresh vegetables have a lot of goodness in them.*

for goodness' sake words that show anger କ୍ରୋଧସୂଚକ ବାକ୍ୟାଂଶ; ହେ ଭଗବାନ୍ *For goodness' sake, hurry up!*

thank goodness words that show you are happy because a problem or danger has gone away ବିପଦ ଚଳିଗଲା ପରେ ବ୍ୟକ୍ତ ବାକ୍ୟାଂଶ; ରକ୍ଷା ମିଳିଗଲା *Thank goodness it's stopped raining.*

good night *interjection* words that you say when you leave somebody in the evening ରାତିର ବିଦାୟ ସମ୍ଭାଷଣ, ଶୁଭରାତ୍ରି

goods /gʊdz/ *noun* (*plural*) **1** things that you buy or sell କିଣାବିକା ହେଉଥିବା ଜିନିଷପତ୍ର *That shop sells electrical goods.* **2** things that a train or lorry carries ରେଳଗାଡ଼ି, ଟ୍ରକ ଇତ୍ୟାଦି ନେଉଥିବା ମାଲ

good-tempered *adjective* not often angry ଭଦ୍ର, ସହଜରେ ବିଚଳିତ ହେଉନଥିବା *My dad is very good-tempered.*

goose /gu:s/ *noun* (*plural* **geese** /gi:s/) a bird like a large duck that has a long neck ଲମ୍ବା ବେକ ଥିବା ବଡ଼ ବତକ ପରି ପକ୍ଷୀ, ଗୁଜ୍

gorgeous /ˈgɔ:dʒəs/ *adjective* very good; wonderful ଅତି ସୁନ୍ଦର; ଚମତ୍କାର *The weather was gorgeous!*

gorilla /gəˈrɪlə/ *noun* an African animal like a very big black monkey, but with no tail ଆଫ୍ରିକାର ବିରାଟ ଓ ଶକ୍ତିଶାଳୀ ଲାଞ୍ଜବିହୀନ ବାନର; ଗରିଲା

gosling /ˈgɒzlɪŋ/ *noun* a young goose ଗୁଜ୍ ଛୁଆ

gossip /ˈgɒsɪp/ *noun* (*no plural*) talk about other people that is often unkind ପର ବିଷୟରେ ଚର୍ଚ୍ଚା, ଚୁଗୁଲି *Don't believe all the gossip you hear.*

gossip *verb* (**gossips, gossiping, gossiped**) ଚୁଗୁଲି କରିବା, ପର ବିଷୟରେ ଇଆଡୁସିଆଡୁ କହିବା *They were gossiping about Maya's sister.*

got ଶବ୍ଦ **get** ର ଏକ ଧାତୁରୂପ

gourd /gʊəd/ *noun* a long fruit with a hard skin and soft flesh that is cooked and eaten as a vegetable ଲାଉ, ଛଚିନ୍ଦ୍ରା ଇତ୍ୟାଦି ପରିବା ➪ ଚିତ୍ର ପାଇଁ **vegetable** ଦେଖନ୍ତୁ।

govern /ˈgʌvn/ *verb* (**governs, governing, governed**) control a country or part of a country ଶାସନ କରିବା *India is governed by a parliament.*

government /ˈgʌvənmənt/ *noun* a group of people who control a country ସରକାର, ଶାସକ ଗୋଷ୍ଠୀ *A new government was formed last month*

governor /ˈɡʌvənə(r)/ *noun* the head of government of some regions such as the states in India ରାଜ୍ୟପାଳ

gown /ɡaʊn/ *noun* **1** a long dress that a woman wears at a special time ସ୍ତ୍ରୀଲୋକମାନଙ୍କର ଲମ୍ବା ବାହ୍ୟ ପୋଷାକ, ଗାଉନ୍ **2** a long loose piece of clothing that people wear to do a special job. Judges sometimes wear gowns ବିଚାରପତି, ଧର୍ମଯାଜକମାନଙ୍କର ନିର୍ଦ୍ଦିଷ୍ଟ ପୋଷାକ, ଗାଉନ୍

grab /ɡræb/ *verb* (**grabs, grabbing, grabbed**) take something quickly and roughly ହଠାତ୍ ଧରିପକାଇବା, ଝିଙ୍କି-ନେବା, ଝାମ୍ପିନେବା *The thief grabbed her bag and ran away.*

grace /ɡreɪs/ *noun* (*no plural*) a beautiful way of moving ସୁନ୍ଦର ସାବଲୀଳ ଆଚରଣ, ଚାଲି ଇତ୍ୟାଦି *She dances with grace.*

graceful /ˈɡreɪsfl/ *adjective* a person or thing that is graceful moves in a beautiful way ସୁନ୍ଦର ଓ ସାବଲୀଳ *a graceful dancer*

gracefully *adverb* ସୁନ୍ଦର ଓ ସାବଲୀଳ ଭାବରେ *She danced gracefully.*

gracious /ˈɡreɪʃəs/ *adjective* if you are gracious, you are kind and polite and have pleasing manners ଦୟାଶୀଳ, କ୍ଷମାଶୀଳ ଓ ଭଲ ବ୍ୟବହାର କରୁଥିବା *a gracious lady*

graciously *adverb* ସଦୟ ଭାବରେ *She greeted us graciously.*

grade[1] /ɡreɪd/ *noun* **1** a number or letter that a teacher gives for your work to show how good it is ପରୀକ୍ଷାରେ ପାଇଥିବା ନମ୍ବର ଅନୁସାରେ ଛାତ୍ରର ଯୋଗ୍ୟତାର ସ୍ତର, ଗ୍ରେଡ୍ *She got very good grades in all her exams.* **2** how good something is; the level or quality of something ଉତ୍ତମତାର ସ୍ତର; ଗୁଣ ଓ ମାନର ସ୍ତର *Which grade of petrol does your car use?*

grade[2] /ɡreɪd/ *verb* (**grades, grading, graded**) sort things or people into sizes, kinds, etc. ଶ୍ରେଣୀରେ ବିଭକ୍ତ କରିବା; କ୍ରମ ଅନୁସାରେ ରଖିବା *The eggs are graded by size.*

gradual /ˈɡrædʒuəl/ *adjective* something that is gradual happens slowly ଧୀରେ ଧୀରେ ବା କ୍ରମେ କ୍ରମେ ଘଟୁଥିବା

gradually *adverb* ଧୀରେ ଧୀରେ, କ୍ରମଶଃ *Her health gradually improved.*

graduate[1] /ˈɡrædʒuət/ *noun* a person who has finished studying at a university or college and who has passed his/her last exams ବିଶ୍ୱବିଦ୍ୟାଳୟର ସ୍ନାତକ ଉପାଧି ପାଇଥିବା ବ୍ୟକ୍ତି, ଗ୍ରାଜୁଏଟ୍

graduate[2] /ˈɡrædʒueɪt/ *verb* (**graduates, graduating, graduated**) finish your studies at a university or college and pass your last exams ସ୍ନାତକ ପରୀକ୍ଷାରେ ଉତ୍ତୀର୍ଣ୍ଣ ହେବା *I graduated from Delhi University in 1994.*

grains

barley
oats
wheat
maize

grain /ɡreɪn/ *noun* **1** (*no plural*) the seeds of a plant like wheat or rice that we eat ଚାଉଳ, ଗହମ ଇତ୍ୟାଦି ଶସ୍ୟ, ଏହିପରି ଶସ୍ୟ ବା ବୀଜ *grain exports* **2** (*plural* **grains**) a small hard piece of something ଦାନା, କଣିକା, କ୍ଷୁଦ୍ର ଶକ୍ତ ଖଣ୍ଡ *grains of rice* ○ *a grain of sand*

gram, gramme /græm/ *noun* a measure of weight. There are 1000 grams in a **kilogram** ଓଜନ ମାପର ଏକ ଏକକ ଗ୍ରାମ୍। ୧୦୦୦ ଗ୍ରାମ୍‌ରେ ଏକ କିଲୋଗ୍ରାମ ହୁଏ। ✪ **Gram** ର ସଂକ୍ଷିପ୍ତ ରୂପ **g** *400 g*

grammar /ˈgræmə(r)/ *noun* (*no plural*) the rules of a language that tell you how to put words together when you speak or write ବ୍ୟାକରଣ

grammatical /grəˈmætɪkl/ *adjective* **1** of or about grammar ବ୍ୟାକରଣ ନିୟମ ଅନୁଯାୟୀ, ବ୍ୟାକରଣ ବିଷୟକ *What is the grammatical rule for making plurals in English?* **2** correct because it follows the rules of grammar ବ୍ୟାକରଣସିଦ୍ଧ, ଶୁଦ୍ଧ *The sentence 'They is happy.' is not grammatical.* ✪ ବିପରୀତ **ungrammatical**

grammatically *adverb* ବ୍ୟାକରଣ ଅନୁଯାୟୀ *The sentence is grammatically not correct.*

granary /ˈgrænəri/ *noun* (*plural* **granaries**) a building used for storing grain ଖମାର, ଶସ୍ୟଭଣ୍ଡାର, ଶସ୍ୟାଗାର *Most farms have their own granaries.*

grand /grænd/ *adjective* (**grander, grandest**) very big, important, rich, etc. ଉତ୍କୃଷ୍ଟ, ଖୁବ୍ ଜାକଜମକିଆ, ଚମତ୍କାର, ଖୁବ ବଡ଼ *They live in a grand house in the centre of the town.*

grandad /ˈgrændæd/ *noun* grandfather ଜେଜେ ବାପା; ଅଜା

grandchild /ˈgræntʃaɪld/ *noun* (*plural* **grandchildren**) the child of your child ନାତି, ନାତୁଣୀ ➪ ଚିତ୍ର ପାଇଁ **family** ଦେଖନ୍ତୁ।

granddaughter /ˈgrændɔːte(r)/ *noun* the daughter of your child ନାତୁଣୀ ➪ ଚିତ୍ର ପାଇଁ **family** ଦେଖନ୍ତୁ।

grandfather /ˈgrænfɑːðə(r)/ *noun* the father of your mother or father ଅଜା, ଜେଜେ ବାପା ➪ ଚିତ୍ର ପାଇଁ **family** ଦେଖନ୍ତୁ।

grandma /ˈgrænmɑː/ *noun* grandmother ଜେଜେ ମା, ଆଈ

grandmother /ˈgrænmʌðə(r)/ *noun* the mother of your mother or father ଆଈ, ଜେଜେ ମା ➪ ଚିତ୍ର ପାଇଁ **family** ଦେଖନ୍ତୁ।

grandpa /ˈgrænpɑː/ *noun* grandfather ଜେଜେ ବାପା, ଅଜା

grandparents /ˈgrænpeərənts/ *noun* (*plural*) the mother and father of your mother or father ଜେଜେ ବାପା, ଜେଜେମା, ଅଜା, ଆଈ ➪ ଚିତ୍ର ପାଇଁ **family** ଦେଖନ୍ତୁ।

grandson /ˈgrænsʌn/ *noun* the son of your child ନାତି ➪ ଚିତ୍ର ପାଇଁ **family** ଦେଖନ୍ତୁ।

grandstand /ˈgrænstænd/ *noun* rows of seats, with a roof over them, where you sit to watch a sport ଖେଳପଡ଼ିଆରେ ଦର୍ଶକ ବସିବା ପାଇଁ ଥିବା ଛାତଯୁକ୍ତ ମୁଖ୍ୟ ବସିବା ସ୍ଥାନ

granny /ˈgræni/ *noun* (*plural* **grannies**) grandmother ଜେଜେମା, ଆଈ

grant /grɑːnt/ *verb* (**grants, granting, granted**) give somebody what they have asked for ମାଗିଥିବା ପଦାର୍ଥ ଦେବାକୁ

ମଞ୍ଜୁର କରିବା *They granted him more time to complete the course.*

grant *noun* money that is given for a special reason ବିଶେଷ କାମ ପାଇଁ ଦିଆଯାଇଥିବା ଅର୍ଥ ବା ଟଙ୍କା *special grant for higher education*

grape /greɪp/ *noun* a small round green or purple fruit that grows in bunches on a climbing plant (called a **vine**). Grapes are used for making wine ଅଙ୍ଗୁର (ଅଙ୍ଗୁର ଲତାକୁ vine କହନ୍ତି) *a bunch of grapes* ➪ ଚିତ୍ର ପାଇଁ **fruit** ଦେଖନ୍ତୁ।

graph /græf/ *noun* a picture that shows how two or more numbers, amounts, etc. are related to each other ଦୁଇଟି ଅକ୍ଷରେଖା ମାଧ୍ୟମରେ ଦୁଇଟି ବିଷୟରେ ପରିବର୍ତ୍ତନଶୀଳ ସମ୍ପର୍କ ଦେଖାଉଥିବା ଚିତ୍ର; ଗ୍ରାଫ୍

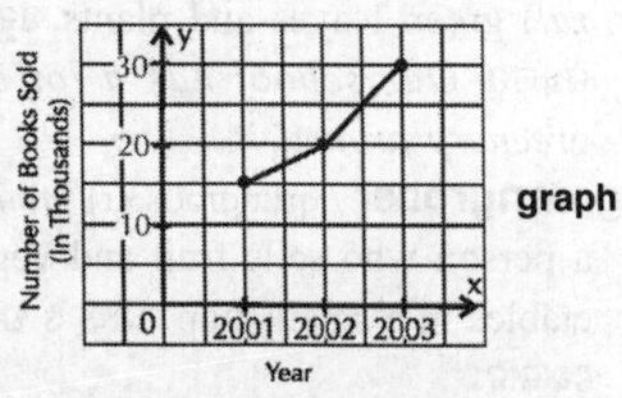

graph

grasp /grɑːsp/ *verb* (**grasps, grasping, grasped**) **1** hold something tightly ଜାବୁଡ଼ି ଧରିବା, ମୁଠେଇ ଧରିବା *Madhu grasped my arm to stop herself from falling.* **2** understand something ବୁଝିବା, ଜାଣିବା *He could not grasp what I was saying.*

grasp *noun* ଜାବୁଡ଼ *The ball fell from my grasp.*

grass /grɑːs/ *noun* (*no plural*) a plant with thin green leaves that covers fields and gardens. Cows and sheep eat grass ଘାସ

grassy *adjective* covered with grass ଘାସ ଆଚ୍ଛାଦିତ

grasshopper /ˈgrɑːshɒpə(r)/ *noun* an insect that has long back legs that help it to jump high into the air ଝିଣ୍ଟିକା ➪ ଚିତ୍ର ପାଇଁ **insect** ଦେଖନ୍ତୁ।

grasslands /ˈgrɑːslænds/ *noun* (*plural*) a very large piece of land that is covered with wild grass and has very few trees ବିସ୍ତୃତ ଘାସପଡ଼ିଆ, ତୃଣଭୂମି (ବିଶେଷତଃ ଗୋଚର)

grate /greɪt/ *verb* (**grates, grating, grated**) if you grate food, you rub it over a metal or plastic tool (called a **grater**) so that it comes out in very small pieces କୋରଣା ପଟା (ଗ୍ରେଟର୍) ବା କୋରଣା ପନିକିରେ ଘଷି କ୍ଷୁଦ୍ର ଖଣ୍ଡ କରିବା *Can you grate some cheese?*

grateful /ˈgreɪtfl/ *adjective* if you are grateful, you feel thankful for what somebody has done for you କୃତଜ୍ଞ *We are grateful to you for the help you have given us.* ✪ ବିପରୀତ **ungrateful**

grave[1] /greɪv/ *adjective* (**graver, gravest**) very bad or serious ଗମ୍ଭୀର; ଗୁରୁତ୍ୱପୂର୍ଣ୍ଣ ✪ ଆମେ ସାଧାରଣତଃ **serious** ଶବ୍ଦ ହିଁ ବ୍ୟବହାର କରୁଁ।

grave[2] /greɪv/ *noun* a place in the ground where a dead person's body is put କବର *We put flowers on the grave.*

gravity /ˈgrævəti/ *noun* (*no plural*) the force that pulls everything towards the earth. This is the reason when you drop something, it falls down to the ground ମାଧ୍ୟାକର୍ଷଣ ଶକ୍ତି; ସବୁ ପଦାର୍ଥକୁ ପୃଥିବୀ ଆଡ଼କୁ ଟାଣି ରଖୁଥିବା ଶକ୍ତି

gravy /ˈgreɪvi/ *noun* (*no plural*) a spicy brown liquid that meat or vegetables are cooked in ଝୋଳ (ତରକାରିର), ରସା

graze¹ /greɪz/ *verb* (**grazes, grazing, grazed**) eat grass ଘାସ ଚରିବା *The sheep were grazing in the fields.*

graze² /greɪz/ *verb* (**grazes, grazing, grazed**) hurt your skin by rubbing it against something rough ରାଞ୍ଜୁଡ଼ି ବା ଆଞ୍ଜୁଡ଼ି ହୋଇଯିବା *He fell and grazed his arm.*

grease /gri:s/ *noun* (*no plural*) any thick stuff that is like oil or fat from animals ବହଳିଆ ତେଲିଆ ପଦାର୍ଥ, ଗ୍ରୀଜ୍ *You will need very hot water to get the grease off these plates.*

greasy /ˈgri:si/ *adjective* (**greasier, greasiest**) with a lot of grease on or in it ତେଲ ଚିକିଟା ଲାଗିଥିବା *Greasy food is not good for you.* ○ *greasy hair*

great /greɪt/ *adjective* (**greater, greatest**) **1** very large or very much ଖୁବ୍ ବେଶୀ; ବଡ଼ *It's a great pleasure to meet you.* **2** important or special ପ୍ରଧାନ, ପ୍ରସିଦ୍ଧ *Einstein was a great scientist.* **3** very; very good ଖୁବ୍; ଖୁବ୍ ଭଲ *They are great friends.*

> **great-** *prefix*
>
> କୌଣସି ଶବ୍ଦ ପୂର୍ବରୁ **great-** ଲଗାଇଲେ ପୂର୍ବପୀଢ଼ୀ (**generation**)କୁ ବୁଝାଇଥାଏ । ଯେମିତି **great-grandmother** ହେଲେ ପଣି–ଜେଜିମା ବା **great-grandfather** ହେଲେ ପଣି ଜେଜିବାପା ବା **great-grandson** ହେଲେ ପଣନାତି ହୋଇଥାଏ ।

greatly /ˈgreɪtli/ *adverb* very much ଖୁବ୍ ବେଶୀ *I wasn't greatly surprised to see her.*

greed /gri:d/ *noun* (*no plural*) the feeling that you want more of something than you need ଲୋଭ

greedy *adjective* (**greedier, greediest**) a person who is greedy wants or takes more of something than he/she needs ଲୋଭୀ *She's so greedy—she's eaten all the chocolates!*

green /gri:n/ *adjective* (**greener, greenest**) with the colour of leaves and grass ସବୁଜ (ବର୍ଣ୍ଣ), ଶାଗୁଆ (ବର୍ଣ୍ଣ) *dark green cloth*

green *noun* the colour of leaves and grass ସବୁଜ ବା ଶାଗୁଆ ରଙ୍ଗ *Riya was dressed in green.*

greenery /ˈgri:nəri/ *noun* (*no plural*) green leaves and plants ସବୁଜ ଗଛପତ୍ର *Our school has a lot of greenery around it.*

greengrocer /ˈgri:ngrəʊsə(r)/ *noun* a person who sells fruit and vegetables in a small shop ପରିବା ଓ ଫଳ ଦୋକାନୀ

greenhouse

greenhouse /ˈgri:nhaʊs/ *noun* a building made of glass, where plants are grown ବୃକ୍ଷପାଳନ ପାଇଁ ବ୍ୟବହୃତ କାଚଘର

greet /gri:t/ *verb* (**greets, greeting, greeted**) say or do something when you meet somebody (ଆଗନ୍ତୁକ ବ୍ୟକ୍ତିଙ୍କୁ) ଅଭିବାଦନ କରିବା, ନମସ୍କାର କରିବା *He greeted me with a smile.*

greeting /ˈgri:tɪŋ/ *noun* **1** words that you say when you meet somebody ଅଭିବାଦନ, ନମସ୍କାର, ସାଦର ସମ୍ଭାଷଣ; ଅଭ୍ୟର୍ଥନା *'Hello' and 'Good morning' are greetings.* **2 greetings** (*plural*) words that you write to somebody at a special time ଅଭିନନ୍ଦନ ପତ୍ରରେ ଲେଖାଯାଉଥିବା ଶୁଭେଚ୍ଛା *My sister sends birthday greetings to you.*

grenade /grəˈneɪd/ *noun* a small bomb that is thrown by hand or fired from a gun ହାତବୋମା ବା ବନ୍ଧୁକଦ୍ୱାରା ନିକ୍ଷିପ୍ତ ଛୋଟ ବୋମା, ଗ୍ରେନେଡ୍ ➪ ଚିତ୍ର ପାଇଁ **ammunition** ଦେଖନ୍ତୁ।

grew ଶବ୍ଦ **grow** ର ଏକ ଧାତୁରୂପ

grey /greɪ/ *adjective* (**greyer, greyest**) with a colour like black and white mixed together ଧୂସର ବା ପାଉଁଶିଆ ବର୍ଣ୍ଣ *My grandmother has grey hair.*

grey *noun* ଧୂସର ବା ପାଉଁଶିଆ ବର୍ଣ୍ଣ *He was dressed in grey.*

grief /gri:f/ *noun* (*no plural*) great sadness ଗଭୀର ଦୁଃଖ

grievance /ˈgri:vəns/ *noun* something that you think is not right and feel that you should complain against it ଅଭିଯୋଗର ପ୍ରକୃତ ଓ କଳ୍ପିତ କାରଣ *The students decided to take their grievances to the principal.*

grieve /gri:v/ *verb* (**grieves, grieving, grieved**) when a person grieves, he/she is very sad because someone whom he/she loved dearly has died ପ୍ରିୟ ଲୋକଙ୍କ ମୃତ୍ୟୁରେ ଦୁଃଖ କରିବା

grill /grɪl/ *verb* (**grills, grilling, grilled**) cook meat, fish, etc. on metal bars under or over heat ତଳୁ ବା ଉପରୁ ନିଆଁ ଧାସ ଦେଇ ଏକ ଲୁହା ଜାଲି ଉପରେ ମାଛ, ମାଂସ ଇତ୍ୟାଦି ପୋଡ଼ି ରାନ୍ଧିବା *Grill the fish for ten minutes.*

grill *noun* the part of an oven, or a special metal tray, where you grill food ପୋଡ଼ି ରାନ୍ଧିବା ପାଇଁ ଉପରପଟୁ ଉତ୍ତାପ ଦେଉଥିବା ଅଭେନ୍ (ବନ୍ଦ ଚୁଲି) ରେ ଥିବା ଉପକରଣ ବା ତଳୁ ଉତ୍ତାପ ଦେଉଥିବା ଉପକରଣ

grime /graɪm/ *noun* (*no plural*) a layer of dirt (ଚର୍ମ, ଚଟାଣ, କାନ୍ଥ ଇତ୍ୟାଦିରେ ବସିଥିବା) ଧୂଳିର ପ୍ରସ୍ଥ; କୋଚଟ

grin /grɪn/ *verb* (**grins, grinning, grinned**) have a big smile on your face ଦାନ୍ତ ଦେଖାଇ ହସିବା *She grinned at me.*

grin *noun* ଦାନ୍ତ ଦିଶୁଥିବା ଈଷତ ହସ *He had a big grin on his face.*

grind /graɪnd/ *verb* (**grinds, grinding, ground** /graʊnd/, **has ground**) make something into very small pieces or powder by crushing it ଚୂରିବା, ଚୂନା କରିବା, ରଗଡ଼ିବା *They ground the wheat into flour.*

grip /grɪp/ *verb* (**grips, gripping, gripped**) hold something tightly ଦୃଢ଼ ମୁଠାରେ ଧରିବା *Salima gripped my hand as we crossed the road.*

groan /grəʊn/ *verb* (**groans, groaning, groaned**) when you groan, you make a deep heavy sound because you are unhappy or in pain ଯନ୍ତ୍ରଣା ବା ଦୁଃଖରେ ମୃଦୁ ଗର୍ଜନ କରିବା *The rider fell off the horse and groaned in pain.*

grocer /ˈgrəʊsə(r)/ *noun* a person who sells food and other things that we need at home ଖାଦ୍ୟସାମଗ୍ରୀ ବିକୁଥିବା ଦୋକାନୀ

groceries /ˈgrəʊsəriz/ *noun* (*plural*) things that are sold by a **grocer** ଖାଦ୍ୟସାମଗ୍ରୀ ବିକ୍ରି ହେଉଥିବା ଦୋକାନର ଦ୍ରବ୍ୟସମୂହ

groom /gru:m/ *noun* **1** a man on the day of his wedding; a bridegroom ବର, ବରପାତ୍ର **2** a person whose job is to look after horses ଅଶ୍ୱପାଳ, ଅଶ୍ୱରକ୍ଷକ

ground[1] ଶବ୍ଦ **grind** ର ଏକ ଧାତୁରୂପ

ground[2] /graʊnd/ *noun* **1** (*no plural*) the top solid part of the earth ଭୂପୃଷ୍ଠ, ଭୂମି *We sat down on the ground to eat our sandwiches.* **2** (*plural* **grounds**) a piece of land that is used for something special ବିଶେଷ କାମରେ ବ୍ୟବହୃତ ଭୂମି ବା ପଡ଼ିଆ *a playground*

groundnut /ˈgraʊndnʌt/ *noun* a nut that grows under the ground in a thin shell ଚିନାବାଦାମ୍, ବାଦାମ୍ ➪ ଚିତ୍ର ପାଇଁ **nut** ଦେଖନ୍ତୁ।

groundwater /ˈgraʊndwɔ:tə(r)/ *noun* (*no plural*) water that is found under the ground ଭୂମି ତଳେ ଥିବା ପାଣି, ଭୂତଳ ଜଳ

group /gru:p/ *noun* **1** a number of people or things together ଦଳ, ଗୋଷ୍ଠୀ *A group of people were standing outside the shop.* **2** people who play pop music together ଜନପ୍ରିୟ ସଙ୍ଗୀତ ଗାଉଥିବା ଦଳ ବା ଗୋଷ୍ଠୀ

grow /grəʊ/ *verb* (**grows, growing, grew** /gru:/, **has grown** /grəʊn/) **1** become bigger ବଢ଼ିବା, ଆକାର ଇତ୍ୟାଦିରେ ବଡ଼ ହେବା *Children grow very quickly.* **2** when a plant grows somewhere, it lives there (ଗଛପତ୍ର ଉପଯୁକ୍ତ ସ୍ଥାନରେ) ବଢ଼ିବା *Oranges grow in warm countries.* **3** plant something in the ground and look after it ଚାଷକରି ଉତ୍ପାଦନ କରିବା *We grow potatoes and carrots in our garden.* **4** let something grow (ଦାଢ଼ି ଇତ୍ୟାଦି) ବଢ଼ାଇବା, ଛାଡ଼ିବା *Mark has grown a beard.*

grow into something get bigger and become something ବଢ଼ି ପୂର୍ଣ୍ଣାକାର ପାଇବା *Kittens grow into cats.*

grow up become an adult; change from a child to a man or woman ପରିଣତ ବୟସ ବା ଅବସ୍ଥାକୁ ଆସିବା *I want to be a doctor when I grow up.*

growl /graʊl/ *verb* (**growls, growling, growled**) if an animal growls, it makes a low angry sound ଚାପା ଗର୍ଜନ କରିବା, ଗାଁଉ ଗାଁଉ କରିବା *The dog growled at the stranger.*

growl *noun* ଚାପା ଗର୍ଜନ *The dog gave a fierce growl.*

grown-up *noun* (*plural* **grown-ups**) a man or woman, not a child; an adult ବୟସ୍କ ବ୍ୟକ୍ତି

growth /grəʊθ/ *noun* (*no plural*) the process of getting bigger or growing ବୃଦ୍ଧି ହେବା ପ୍ରକ୍ରିୟା; ବୃଦ୍ଧି *the growth of a baby*

grub /grʌb/ *noun* the young one of an insect that has just hatched out of its egg and looks like a small worm ପୋକ, ମାଛି ଇତ୍ୟାଦିଙ୍କ ଶୂକ

grumble /ˈgrʌmbl/ *verb* (**grumbles, grumbling, grumbled**) say many times that you do not like something ବାରମ୍ବାର ଅସନ୍ତୋଷ ପ୍ରକାଶ କରିବା *The children often grumble about the food at the school canteen.*

grunt /grʌnt/ *verb* (**grunts, grunting, grunted**) make a short rough sound, like a pig makes ଘୁଷୁରି ବୋବାଳି ପରି କର୍କଶ ଶବ୍ଦ

guarantee /ˌgærənˈtiː/ *noun* **1** a special promise on paper that a company will repair a thing you have bought, or give you a new one, if it breaks or goes wrong before a certain time କିଣୁଥିବା ଜିନିଷର ଗୁଣ ଓ ସ୍ଥାୟିତ୍ୱ ସମ୍ପର୍କରେ ଦିଆଯାଉଥିବା ଲିଖିତ ସମୟବଦ୍ଧ ପ୍ରତିଶ୍ରୁତି (ଯାହାର ଖିଲାପ ହେଲେ ସେ ଜିନିଷ ମରାମତି ବା ବଦଳି କରିଦେବା ପାଇଁ) *This watch has a two-year guarantee.* **2** a promise that something will happen ନିର୍ଭରୋକ୍ତି *I want a guarantee that you will do the work today.*

guarantee *verb* (**guarantees, guaranteeing, guaranteed**) **1** say that you will repair a thing that somebody buys, or give them a new one, if it breaks or goes wrong within a certain time କିଣାଯାଉଥିବା ଜିନିଷ ଠିକ୍ ନ ପଡ଼ିଲେ ମରାମତି କରିବା ବା ବଦଳାଇ ଦେବାପାଇଁ ଲିଖିତ ପ୍ରତିଶ୍ରୁତି ଦେବା *The television is guaranteed for three years.* **2** promise something ପ୍ରତିଶ୍ରୁତି ଦେବା *I can't guarantee that I will be able to help you, but I'll try.*

guard[1] /gɑːd/ *verb* (**guards, guarding, guarded**) keep somebody or something safe from other people, or stop somebody from escaping ଜଗିବା, ରକ୍ଷା କରିବା *The house was guarded by two large dogs.*

guard[2] /gɑːd/ *noun* **1** a person who keeps somebody or something safe from other people, or who stops somebody from escaping ରକ୍ଷକ, ପ୍ରହରୀ, ଜଗାଳି, ଜଗୁଆଳି *There are guards outside the palace.* **2** a person whose job is to look after people and things on a train ରେଳଗାଡ଼ିର ଦାୟିତ୍ୱରେ ଥିବା ଅଧିକାରୀ, ଗାର୍ଡ

guava /ˈgwɑːvə/ *noun* a round fruit with a thin yellow skin, sweet white or pink flesh and lots of seeds, that grows in hot countries ପିଜୁଳି, ଜାମୁ, ଚାଉଳିଆ

guerrilla /gəˈrɪlə/ *noun* a person who is not in an army but who fights secretly against a government or an army ସରକାର ବା ସେନା ବିରୁଦ୍ଧରେ ଲୁଚିଛପି ଛୋଟ ଛୋଟ ଦଳରେ ଆକ୍ରମଣ କରୁଥିବା ବ୍ୟକ୍ତି

guess /ges/ *verb* (**guesses, guessing, guessed**) give an answer when you do not know if it is right ଅନୁମାନ କରିବା, ଅନ୍ଦାଜ କରିବା *Can you guess how old he is?*

guess *noun* (*plural* **guesses**) ଅନୁମାନ, ଅନ୍ଦାଜ *If you don't know the answer, take a guess!*

guest /gest/ *noun* **1** a person who you invite to your home, to a party, etc. ଅତିଥି, ନିମନ୍ତ୍ରିତ ବ୍ୟକ୍ତି *There were two hundred guests at the wedding.* **2** a person who is staying in a hotel ହୋଟେଲ୍‌ରେ ରହୁଥିବା ବ୍ୟକ୍ତି, ହୋଟେଲ୍‌ର ଅତିଥି

guest house *noun* (*plural* **guest houses**) a small hotel ଛୋଟ ହୋଟେଲ୍

guidance /ˈgaɪdns/ *noun* (*no plural*) help and advice ପରାମର୍ଶ, ଉପଦେଶ, ସାହାଯ୍ୟ *I want some guidance on how to find a job.*

guide[1] /gaɪd/ *noun* **1** a person who shows other people where to go and tells them interesting things about a place ପଥପ୍ରଦର୍ଶକ ବ୍ୟକ୍ତି, ପର୍ଯ୍ୟଟକଙ୍କୁ ଦ୍ରଷ୍ଟବ୍ୟ ସ୍ଥାନ ଦେଖାଉଥିବା ବ୍ୟକ୍ତି, ଗାଇଡ୍ **2** (**guidebook** ମଧ୍ୟ) a book that tells you about a town, country, etc. (ଯାତ୍ରୀ ବା ପର୍ଯ୍ୟଟକମାନଙ୍କ ପାଇଁ ଉଦ୍ଦିଷ୍ଟ) ଏକ ସ୍ଥାନରେ ବିଭିନ୍ନ ତଥ୍ୟ ସମ୍ବଳିତ ବହି **3 Guide** = **girl guide**

guide[2] /gaɪd/ *verb* (**guides, guiding, guided**) show somebody where to go or how to do something ପଥପ୍ରଦର୍ଶନ କରିବା, ବାଟ କଢ଼େଇ ନେବା, ବତାଇବା *He guided us through the busy streets to our hotel.*

guilt /gɪlt/ *noun* (*no plural*) **1** the fact that someone has done something wrong ଅପରାଧ, ଦୋଷ *The police could not prove his guilt.* ✪ ବିପରୀତ **innocence** **2** the feeling that you have when you know that you have done something wrong ଦୋଷୀ ମନୋଭାବ *She felt a terrible guilt after stealing the money.*

guilty /ˈgɪlti/ *adjective* (**guiltier, guiltiest**) **1** if you are guilty, you have done something wrong ଦୋଷୀ, ଅପରାଧୀ, ଅପରାଧ ପାଇଁ ଦାୟୀ *He is guilty of fraud.* ✪ ବିପରୀତ **innocent** **2** if you feel guilty, you feel that you have done something wrong ଦୋଷୀ *He felt guilty about lying to his friend.*

guitar /gɪˈtɑ:(r)/ *noun* a musical instrument with strings ଆଙ୍ଗୁଠିରେ ବଜାଯାଉଥିବା ତାରଯୁକ୍ତ ବାଦ୍ୟଯନ୍ତ୍ର, ଗିଟାର୍ *I play the guitar in a band.*

guitar

strings

guitarist *noun* a person who plays the guitar ଗିଟାର୍ ବାଦକ

gulf /gʌlf/ *noun* a large part of the sea that is partly surrounded by land ଉପସାଗର *the Gulf of Mannar*

gulp /gʌlp/ *verb* (**gulps, gulping, gulped**) eat or drink something quickly ଚଞ୍ଚଳ ଖାଇ ବା ପିଇଦେବା, ଗିଳିଦେବା; ଢୋକିଦେବା *He gulped down a cup of tea and left.*

gulp *noun* ଢୋକ *She took a gulp of coffee.*

gum /gʌm/ *noun* **1** (*plural* **gums**) your gums are the hard pink parts of your mouth that hold your teeth (ଦାନ୍ତ) ମାଢ଼ି **2** (*no plural*) a thick liquid that you use for sticking pieces of paper together ଅଠା

gun /gʌn/ *noun* a thing that shoots out pieces of metal (called **bullets**) ବନ୍ଧୁକ (ଏହାର ଗୁଳିକୁ ବୁଲେଟ କୁହାଯାଏ ।)

gush /gʌʃ/ *verb* (**gushes, gushing, gushed**) flow out suddenly and strongly ହଠାତ୍ ନିର୍ଗତ ହେବା, ଭସଭସ କରି ବହିଆସିବା *Water was gushing out from a leak in the pipe.*

gust /gʌst/ *noun* a sudden strong wind ଆକସ୍ମିକ ପ୍ରବଳ ବାୟୁପ୍ରବାହ, ପ୍ରଚଣ୍ଡ ପବନ ଝଲକା *A gust of wind blew his hat off.*

gutter /ˈgʌtə(r)/ *noun* **1** a pipe under the edge of a roof to carry away rainwater ଓଳିତଳେ ଥିବା ଅଗଭୀର ନାଳୀ (ବର୍ଷାପାଣି ପାଇପ୍ ବାଟେ ତଳକୁ ଛାଡ଼ିବା ପାଇଁ) **2** a channel along the edge of a road which carries away water ରାସ୍ତା କଡ଼ରେ ଥିବା ନର୍ଦ୍ଦମା ବା ନାଳ

guy /gaɪ/ *noun* a man ପୁରୁଷଲୋକ, ପୁରୁଷ ସାଥୀ *He's a nice guy!*

gymnasium /dʒɪmˈneɪziəm/ *noun* (*plural* **gymnasiums** ବା **gymnasia** /dʒɪmˈneɪziə/) a room with equipment where you do exercises for your body ବ୍ୟାୟାମ ଉପକରଣ ରହିଥିବା ବ୍ୟାୟାମଶାଳା, ଆଖଡ଼ାଘର ✪ **Gymnasium** ର ସଂକ୍ଷିପ୍ତ ରୂପ ହେଲା **gym**।

gymnastics /dʒɪmˈnæstɪks/ *noun* (*no plural*) exercises for your body that show your body's strength and ability to bend easily. This is often done as a sport ମାଂସପେଶୀର ବିକାଶ ବା କ୍ଷିପ୍ରତାର ପଦର୍ଶନ ପାଇଁ ବ୍ୟାୟାମ ବା କସରତ; ଏହା ବିଭିନ୍ନ ଖେଳ ଭାବରେ ମଧ୍ୟ ପ୍ରଦର୍ଶନ କରାଯାଏ

gypsy /ˈdʒɪpsi/ *noun* (*plural* **gypsies**) gypsies are people who live in **caravans** and travel from one place to another ଯାଯାବର ଜାତୀୟ ଲୋକ (ଯେଉଁମାନେ କାରଭାନ ରେ ରହନ୍ତି ଓ ବିଭିନ୍ନ ସ୍ଥାନକୁ ଯାଆନ୍ତି)

H h

habit /ˈhæbɪt/ *noun* something that you do so often that you do it almost without thinking ଅଭ୍ୟାସ, ପ୍ରବୃତ୍ତି *It's my habit to have two cups of tea every morning.*

habitat /ˈhæbɪtæt/ *noun* the natural living place of a plant or an animal ଉଦ୍ଭିଦ ବା ପଶୁର ପ୍ରାକୃତିକ ଆବାସ ବା ପରିବେଶ *I have seen tigers in zoos but not in their natural habitat.*

hack /hæk/ *verb* (**hacks, hacking, hacked**) **1** secretly look at, change and use the information stored in somebody else's computer କମ୍ପ୍ୟୁଟର୍ ଓ ଇଣ୍ଟରନେଟ୍‌ର୍ ସାହାଯ୍ୟରେ ଅନ୍ୟ ସଂସ୍ଥାର କମ୍ପ୍ୟୁଟର୍ ତଥ୍ୟ ଭଣ୍ଡାର (ଡାଟାବେଶ୍) ରେ ପ୍ରବେଶ କରି ତଥ୍ୟ ଅବଗତ କରିବା ବା ବଦଳାଇ ଦେବା **2** cut something with heavy blows ହାଣିବା *She was so angry that she hacked the vegetables into small pieces.*

hacker /ˈhækə(r)/ *noun* someone who spends a lot of time looking at and changing computer data without permission ପ୍ରବେଶାନୁମତି ବିନା ଅନ୍ୟର କମ୍ପ୍ୟୁଟର୍ ନେଟ୍‌ୱର୍କରେ ପ୍ରବେଶ କରୁଥିବା ବ୍ୟକ୍ତି

had ଶବ୍ଦ **have** ର ଏକ ଧାତୁରୂପ

hadn't = **had not**

haggle /ˈhægl/ *verb* (**haggles, haggling, haggled**) argue about the price of something ଦର କଷାକଷି କରିବା, ମୂଲ କରିବା *She haggled over the price of the sari for almost half an hour.*

hail /heɪl/ *noun* (*no plural*) small hard balls of icc that fall as rain କୁଆପଥର, କରକା

hair /heə(r)/ *noun* **1** (*plural* **hairs**) one of the thin things that grow on the skin of people and some animals ଲୋମ, ରୁମ *There's a hair in my soup.* **2** (*no plural*) all the hairs on a person's head ମୁଣ୍ଡର ବାଳ, କେଶ, ଚୁଟି, ଚୁଳ *She's got long black hair.* ➪ ଚିତ୍ର ପାଇଁ **body** ଦେଖନ୍ତୁ। ✪ ମୁଣ୍ଡର ବାଳକୁ **shampoo** ରେ ଧୋଇ ସଫା କରାଯାଏ ଓ **hairbrush** ବା **comb** ରେ କୁଣ୍ଡାଯାଏ। ବାଳ **straight, curly** ବା **wavy** ହୋଇପାରେ।

hairbrush /ˈheəbrʌʃ/ *noun* (*plural* **hairbrushes**) a brush that you use to make your hair tidy ମୁଣ୍ଡ ବା ବାଳ କୁଣ୍ଡେଇବା ବ୍ରସ୍ ➪ ଚିତ୍ର ପାଇଁ **brush** ଦେଖନ୍ତୁ।

haircut /ˈheəkʌt/ *noun* the act of somebody cutting your hair ବାଳ କଟେଇବା କାମ, ବାଳକଟା, ଚୁଟିକଟା, ଚୁଳକଟା *I need a haircut.*

hairdresser /ˈheədresə(r)/ *noun* a person whose job is to wash, cut and arrange hair ବାଳ କାଟି ସଜେଇବା ଲୋକ, ଭଣ୍ଡାରି, ନାପିତ, ବାରିକ ✪ ବାଳକାଟିବା ଲୋକର କାର୍ଯ୍ୟସ୍ଥଳୀକୁ **'hairdresser's** କୁହାଯାଏ।

hairstyle /ˈheəstaɪl/ *noun* the way that your hair is cut and arranged କେଶ ବିନ୍ୟାସ, ବାଳ କାଟି ସଜାଇବା ପଦ୍ଧତି ବା ଢାଞ୍ଚା

hairy /ˈheəri/ *adjective* (**hairier, hairiest**) covered with a lot of hair ଲୋମଶ; କେଶବହୁଳ

hale /heɪl/ *adjective*

hale and hearty a person who is hale and hearty is in very good health ସୁସ୍ଥସବଳ *a hale and hearty old man*

half /hɑːf/ *noun* (*plural* **halves** /hɑːvz/), *adjective, pronoun* one of two equal parts of something; $\frac{1}{2}$

ଅଧା; $\frac{୧}{୨}$ *Half of six is three.* ○ *The cup is half full.* ○ *She gave me half of her apple.*

half past thirty minutes after an hour on the clock କୌଣସି ସମୟ (ଯଥା: ଦଶଟା, ଏଗାରଟା ଇତ୍ୟାଦି) ର ତିରିଶ୍ ମିନିଟ୍ ପରେ, ସାଢ଼େ ଦି'ଟା, ସାଢ଼େ ଚାରିଟା ଇତ୍ୟାଦି) *It's half past nine.*

half-heartedly *adverb* if you do something half-heartedly, you do not have much interest in doing it ଉତ୍ସାହହୀନ ଭାବରେ

halfway /ˌhɑːfˈweɪ/ *adverb* in the middle ଅଧାବାଟରେ; ମଝିରେ *They live halfway between Delhi and Agra.*

hall /hɔːl/ *noun* **1** a big room or building where a lot of people meet ବଡ଼ ଓ ପ୍ରଶସ୍ତ ପ୍ରକୋଷ୍ଠ, ହଲ୍ *We did our exams in the school hall.* **2** the room in a house that is near the front door and has doors to other rooms ବାଟଘର, ଦାଣ୍ଡଘର, ପ୍ରବେଶ ପ୍ରକୋଷ୍ଠ

hallo = **hello, hullo**

halt /hɔːlt/ *noun* (*no plural*)

come to a halt stop ରହିଯିବା *The car came to a halt.*

halve /hɑːv/ *verb* (**halves, halving, halved**) divide something into two equal parts ଅଧା କରିବା, ଫାଳ କରିବା *There were two of us, so I halved the orange.*

halves ଶବ୍ଦ **half** ର ବହୁବଚନ

hammer /ˈhæmə(r)/ *noun* a tool with a handle and a heavy metal part, that you use for driving **nails** into things ହାତୁଡ଼ି ➪ ଚିତ୍ର ପାଇଁ **tools** ଦେଖନ୍ତୁ।

hamper /ˈhæmpə(r)/ *verb* (**hampers, hampering, hampered**) make something difficult for someone ବାଧା ଦେବା, କାମରେ ପ୍ରତିବନ୍ଧ ସୃଷ୍ଟି କରିବା *Rains hampered relief efforts.*

hand[1] /hænd/ *noun* **1** the part of the body at the end of your arm that you use for holding things ହାତ, କଚଟି ବା ମଣିବନ୍ଧରୁ ଆଙ୍ଗୁଠି ପର୍ଯ୍ୟନ୍ତ ହାତର ଭାଗ *She held the letter in her hand.* ➪ ଚିତ୍ର ପାଇଁ **body** ଦେଖନ୍ତୁ। **2** one of the parts of a clock or watch that move to show the time ଘଣ୍ଟାର କଣ୍ଟା ➪ ଚିତ୍ର ପାଇଁ **dial** ଦେଖନ୍ତୁ।

in good hands well looked after ସୁରକ୍ଷିତ ଅବସ୍ଥାରେ, ଭଲରେ *Don't worry —your son is in good hands.*

on the one hand ... on the other hand words that show the good and bad things about an idea ଏକ ଦୃଷ୍ଟିକୋଣରୁ... ଅନ୍ୟ ଦୃଷ୍ଟିକୋଣରୁ; ଏପଟୁ ଦେଖିଲେ... ସେପଟୁ ଦେଖିଲେ *On the one hand the hotel has a lovely view, but on the other hand it doesn't have a restaurant.*

hand[2] /hænd/ *verb* (**hands, handing, handed**) put something into somebody's hand କାହାରି ହାତରେ ଦେବା *Can you hand me the scissors, please?*

hand over give something to somebody ଦେବା, ବଢ଼େଇବା *'Hand over that knife!' said the police officer.*

handbag /ˈhændbæg/ *noun* a small bag for money, keys, etc. carried by women ଟଙ୍କା ଇତ୍ୟାଦି ରଖିବା ପାଇଁ ଛୋଟ ଥଳି, ହାତମୁଣା, ହ୍ୟାଣ୍ଡବ୍ୟାଗ୍ ➪ ଚିତ୍ର ପାଇଁ **bag** ଦେଖନ୍ତୁ।

handcuffs /ˈhændkʌfs/ *noun* (*no singular*) two metal rings with a chain that are put around a prisoner's wrists so that he or she cannot escape ହାତକଡ଼ି

handicapped /ˈhændikæpt/ *adjective* not able to use a part of your body well ମାନସିକ ବା ଶାରୀରିକ ଅସାମର୍ଥ୍ୟ ଥିବା, ବିକଳାଙ୍ଗ *He had become handicapped because of his illness.*

handicraft /ˈhændikrɑːft/ *noun* **1** a skill, like weaving and sewing, that some people have which helps them to make things with their hands ହସ୍ତଶିଳ୍ପ **2** things made by hand using a skill like weaving and sewing ହସ୍ତଶିଳ୍ପ ଦ୍ୱାରା ତିଆରି ପଦାର୍ଥ *traditional handicrafts*

handkerchief /ˈhæŋkətʃɪf/ *noun* (*plural*) **handkerchiefs handkerchieves** /ˈhæŋkətʃiːvz/) a square piece of cloth or paper that you use for clearing your nose ରୁମାଲ

handle[1] /ˈhændl/ *noun* the part of a thing that you use to hold or open it ବେଣ୍ଟ, କୌଣସି ଜିନିଷର ଯେଉଁ ଅଂଶ ହାତରେ ଧରାଯାଏ *I turned the handle and opened the door.* ○ *Hold that cup by the handle.*

handle[2] /ˈhændl/ *verb* (**handles, handling, handled**) **1** touch something with your hands ହାତରେ ଛୁଇଁବା, ହାତରେ ବ୍ୟବହାର କରିବା, ପରିଚାଳିତ କରିବା, ଧରିବା ବା ଘୁଞ୍ଚାଇବା *Please wash your hands before you handle the food.* **2** control somebody or something ଅଧିକାରରେ ରଖିବା, ଆୟତ୍ତ କରିବା *That dog is too big for a small child to handle.*

handsome /ˈhænsəm/ *adjective* good-looking ସୁନ୍ଦର, ସୁଶ୍ରୀ *a handsome man* ⇨ **beautiful** ପାଖରେ ଟିପ୍ପଣୀ ଦେଖନ୍ତୁ ।

handwriting /ˈhændraɪtɪŋ/ *noun* (*no plural*) the way you write ହସ୍ତାକ୍ଷର *Her handwriting is difficult to read.*

handy /ˈhændi/ *adjective* (**handier, handiest**) **1** useful ଦରକାରୀ, ବ୍ୟବହାର-ଯୋଗ୍ୟ, ସୁବିଧାଜନକ *This bag will be handy for carrying my books.* **2** near and easy to find or reach ପାଖରେ ଥିବା, ହାତ ପହଞ୍ଚରେ ଥିବା *Always keep your pen handy.*

hang /hæŋ/ *verb* **1** (**hangs, hanging, hung** /hʌŋ/, **has hung**) fix something, or be fixed at the top so that the lower part is free ଟାଙ୍ଗିବା, ଝୁଲେଇବା *Hang your coat (up) on the hook.* **2** (**hangs, hanging, hanged, has hanged**) kill somebody by holding them above the ground by a rope around the neck ଫାସିଦେବା, ଦଉଡ଼ିରେ ବେକକୁ ବାନ୍ଧି ଓ ଝୁଲାଇ ମୃତ୍ୟୁଦଣ୍ଡ ଦେବା ବା ମାରିଦେବା

hangar /ˈhæŋə(r)/ *noun* a large building where aeroplanes are kept ଉଡ଼ାଜାହାଜ ରଖିବା ଘର, ବିମାନଶାଳା

hanger /ˈhæŋə(r)/ *noun* a piece of metal, wood or plastic with a hook.

You use it for hanging clothes on ଲୁଗାପଟା ଟାଙ୍ଗିବା ପାଇଁ ଉପକରଣ, ହ୍ୟାଙ୍ଗର୍

hanky /ˈhæŋki/ *noun* (*plural* **hankies**) a handkerchief ରୁମାଲ

haphazard /hæpˈhæzəd/ *adjective* in no particular order; not properly planned or organized କୌଣସି ପଦ୍ଧତି ଅନୁସାରେ କରାଯାଇ ନଥିବା; ଆବୁରୁଜାବୁରୁ *The book has been written in a haphazard manner.*

happen /ˈhæpən/ *verb* (**happens, happening, happened**) take place ଘଟିବା। *Did you hear what happened to me yesterday?*

happen to do something by chance ଆକସ୍ମିକ ଭାବେ କରିବା ବା ହେବା *I happened to meet Tony yesterday.*

happy /ˈhæpi/ *adjective* (**happier, happiest**) **1** if you are happy, you feel very pleased. People often laugh or smile when they are happy ଖୁସି, ସୁଖୀ, ସନ୍ତୁଷ୍ଟ *She looks very happy.* ✪ ବିପରୀତ **unhappy** ବା **sad** **2** a word that you use to say that you hope somebody will enjoy a special time ସୁଖ ଅଭିନନ୍ଦନ ସୂଚାଉଥିବା ଶବ୍ଦ *Happy New Year!* ○ *Happy Birthday!* ✪ **Many Happy Returns (of the day)** ଏବଂ **Happy Birthday** ର ଅର୍ଥ ସମାନ।

happily *adverb* **1** in a happy way ଆନନ୍ଦରେ, ଖୁସିରେ, ଖୁସିମନରେ *She happily announced that she had won the contest.* ✪ ବିପରୀତ **unhappily** **2** it is lucky that ଭାଗ୍ୟକୁ *Happily, the damage was not serious.*

happiness *noun* (*no plural*) being happy ଆନନ୍ଦ, ସୁଖ ✪ ବିପରୀତ **unhappiness**

harbour /ˈhɑ:bə(r)/ *noun* a place on the coast where ships can shelter or unload ପୋତାଶ୍ରୟ, ବନ୍ଦର

hard[1] /hɑ:d/ *adjective* (**harder, hardest**) **1** not soft; firm ଶକ୍ତ, ଟାଣ, କଠିନ *These apples are very hard.* ✪ ବିପରୀତ **soft** **2** difficult to do or understand କଷ୍ଟକର, କଠିନ (କରିବାକୁ) ଦୁର୍ବୋଧ *The exam was very hard.* ○ *hard work* ✪ ବିପରୀତ **easy** **3** full of problems ସମସ୍ୟାପୂର୍ଣ୍ଣ *He's had a hard life.* **4** not kind or gentle କଠୋର (ବ୍ୟବହାର ବା ପ୍ରକୃତି) *She is very hard on her children.* ✪ ବିପରୀତ **soft**

hard[2] /hɑ:d/ *adverb* **1** a lot ଖୁବ୍‌ବେଶୀ, ବହୁତ *She works very hard.* **2** strongly ଖୁବ୍ ଜୋର୍‌ରେ, ପ୍ରବଳ *It's raining hard.*

hard disk *noun* a plastic part inside a computer that stores information କମ୍ପ୍ୟୁଟର୍‌ରେ ତଥ୍ୟ ଗଚ୍ଛିତ ରଖିବା ପାଇଁ ଥିବା ଚୁମ୍ବକୀୟ ଫଳକ, ହାର୍ଡ୍‌ଡିସ୍କ ⇨ ଚିତ୍ର ପାଇଁ **computer** ଦେଖନ୍ତୁ।

harden /ˈhɑ:dn/ *verb* (**hardens, hardening, hardened**) become hard କଠିନ ହୋଇଯିବା, ଟାଣ ଧରିଯିବା, ବାନ୍ଧିଯିବା *Wait for the cement to harden.*

hardly /ˈhɑ:dli/ *adverb* almost not; only just କ୍ୱଚିତ୍, ଅତି ଅଳ୍ପ *She spoke so quietly that I could hardly hear her.*

hardware /ˈhɑ:dweə(r)/ *noun* (*no plural*) **1** the physical machinery of a computer କମ୍ପ୍ୟୁଟର୍‌ରେ ଖଞ୍ଜା ଯାଇଥିବା

ଯାନ୍ତ୍ରିକ ବା ଇଲେକ୍ଟ୍ରୋନିକ୍ ଉପକରଣ ➪ **software** ମଧ ଦେଖନ୍ତୁ । **2** all the metal tools and articles used in the house, garden, etc. ଘର, ବଗିଚା ଇତ୍ୟାଦିରେ ବ୍ୟବହୃତ ଧାତୁ ନିର୍ମିତ ଉପକରଣ

hard-working *adjective* if you are hard-working, you work very hard to do something well ପରିଶ୍ରମୀ *hard-working students*

hardy /ˈhɑ:di/ *adjective* (**hardier, hardiest**) something that is hardy is firm and can survive even in difficult conditions ଟାଣୁଆ, ସହଜରେ ନଷ୍ଟ ହେଉ ନଥିବା *a hardy tree*

hare /heə(r)/ *noun* an animal like a big rabbit. Hares have long ears and can run very fast ବଡ଼ ଆକାରର, ଲମ୍ବା କାନ ଥିବା ଓ କ୍ଷିପ୍ର ଗତିରେ ଦୌଡ଼ି ପାରୁଥିବା ଏକ ପ୍ରକାର ଠେକୁଆ

harm[1] /hɑ:m/ *noun* (*no plural*) damage or injury କ୍ଷତି, ହାନି; କ୍ଷତ

harm[2] /hɑ:m/ *verb* (**harms, harming, harmed**) hurt somebody or damage something ଅନିଷ୍ଟ କରିବା, କ୍ଷତି କରିବା *The dog won't harm you.*

harmful /ˈhɑ:mfl/ *adjective* something that is harmful can hurt or damage people or things କ୍ଷତିକାରକ *Strong sunlight can be harmful to young babies.*

harmless /ˈhɑ:mləs/ *adjective* not dangerous କ୍ଷତିକାରକ ହୋଇ ନଥିବା; ନିରୀହ

harmony /ˈhɑ:məni/ *noun* (*no plural*) a state of living together peacefully ମେଳ ଖାଉଥିବା ଅବସ୍ଥା; ମିଳିମିଶି ରହିପାରୁଥିବା ଅବସ୍ଥା; ସୁମଙ୍ଗତ ସ୍ଥିତି *people from different cultures living in harmony*

harness /ˈhɑ:nɪs/ *verb* (**harnesses, harnessing, harnessed**) **1** tie a horse to a cart with a set of long leather straps so that it can pull the cart along ଚମଡ଼ା ଫିତା ଦ୍ୱାରା ଘୋଡ଼ାକୁ ଗାଡ଼ିରେ ବାନ୍ଧିବା **2** use the energy and power of something for our benefit ବିଦ୍ୟୁତ୍‌ଶକ୍ତି ଇତ୍ୟାଦି ଉତ୍ପାଦନ ପାଇଁ (ନଦୀ ଇତ୍ୟାଦିକୁ) ଉପଯୋଗ କରିବା *The heat and light of the sun are harnessed to produce solar energy.*

harsh /hɑ:ʃ/ *adjective* (**harsher, harshest**) not kind; cruel କଠୋର, କର୍କଶ *a harsh punishment*

harvest /ˈhɑ:vɪst/ *noun* **1** the time when fruit, crops or vegetables are ready to cut or pick ଶସ୍ୟ, ଫଳ ଇତ୍ୟାଦି ଗଛରୁ କାଟି ସଂଗ୍ରହ କରିବା ପ୍ରକ୍ରିୟା, ଅମଳ *It is harvest time now.* **2** all the fruit, crops or vegetables that are cut or picked ସଂଗୃହୀତ ଫଳ, ଶସ୍ୟ, ପରିବା ଇତ୍ୟାଦି *We had a good harvest this year.*

harvest *verb* (**harvests, harvesting, harvested**) cut or pick fruit, crops or vegetables ଅମଳ କରିବା; ଫଳ, ଶସ୍ୟ, ପରିବା ଇତ୍ୟାଦି ଗଛରୁ ତୋଳି ବା କାଟି ସଂଗ୍ରହ କରିବା *When does the farmer harvest his wheat?*

has ଶବ୍ଦ **have** ର ଏକ ଧାତୁରୂପ

hasn't = **has not**

haste /heɪst/ *noun* (*no plural*) doing things too quickly କ୍ଷିପ୍ରତା, ଚଞ୍ଚଳତା, ବେଗ *In his haste to get up, he knocked the chair over.*

hasten /ˈheɪsn/ *verb* (**hastens, hastening, hastened**) move or do something in a hurry ତ୍ୱରାନ୍ୱିତ ହେବା ବା

କରିବା, ତତ୍ପର ହେବା ବା ତତ୍ପର ଭାବରେ କରିବା *Seeing the look of worry on his face, she hastened to give an explanation.*

hasty /ˈheɪsti/ *adjective* (**hastier, hastiest**) if you are hasty, you do something too quickly ଦ୍ରୁତ, ସତ୍ୱର *Don't make a hasty decision.*

hat /hæt/ *noun* a covering that you wear on your head ଟୋପି *She's wearing a hat.*

hatch /hætʃ/ *verb* (**hatches, hatching, hatched**) when baby birds, insects, fish, etc. hatch, they come out of an egg (ଚଢ଼େଇ ଛୁଆ, କୀଟ, ମାଛ ଇତ୍ୟାଦି) ଅଣ୍ଡାରୁ ବାହାରିବା

hate /heɪt/ *verb* (**hates, hating, hated**) have a very strong feeling of not liking somebody or something ଘୃଣା କରିବା *Most cats hate water.*

hate, hatred *noun* (*no plural*) a very strong feeling of not liking somebody or something ଘୃଣା

haul /hɔ:l/ *verb* (**hauls, hauling, hauled**) pull something heavy with a lot of effort ଖୁବ୍ ଜୋର୍ ଲଗେଇ ଭାରି ପଦାର୍ଥକୁ ଟାଣି ନେବା *They hauled the boat out of the river.*

haunt /hɔ:nt/ *verb* (**haunts, haunting, haunted**) if a ghost haunts a place, it visits it often କୌଣସି ସ୍ଥାନରେ ଭୂତପ୍ରେତ ନିୟମିତ ଭାବେ ଦିଶିବା

haunted *adjective* often visited by ghosts ଭୂତପ୍ରେତ ଗ୍ରସ୍ତ *a haunted house*

haunting *adjective* something that is haunting stays in your mind because it is very frightening or beautiful ମନରେ ଲାଖି ରହିଥିବା ବା ବାରମ୍ବାର ମନେ ପଡୁଥିବା (ଗୀତ, କଥା, ଡର ଇତ୍ୟାଦି) *a haunting melody*

have[1] /həv/ *verb* a word that you use with parts of other verbs to show that something happened or started in the past ଅତୀତରେ ଘଟିଥିବା ବା ଆରମ୍ଭ ହୋଇଥିବା କଥା ସୂଚାଉଥିବା ଶବ୍ଦ *I have seen that film.* ○ *We have been in Chennai for six months.* ➪ 252 ପୃଷ୍ଠାରେ ଟେବୁଲ ଦେଖନ୍ତୁ।

have[2] /həv/ *verb* (**has** /həz/, **having, had** /həd/, **has had**) **1** (**have got**) own or keep something ଥିବା। (ଅଧିକାରରେ ଥିବା ବା ନିଜ ପାଖରେ ଥିବା) *She has brown eyes.* ○ *Do you have any brothers and sisters?* **2** be ill with something; feel something ରୋଗଗ୍ରସ୍ତ ହେବା; ଅନୁଭବ କରିବା *She has got a headache.* **3** eat or drink something ଖାଇବା ବା ପିଇବା *What time do you have breakfast?* **4** a word that shows that something happens to somebody or something ଘଟିବା *I had a shower.* **5** (**have got** ମଧ୍ୟ) a word that you use with some nouns ଅଛି *I have an idea.*

have to, have got to must ନିଶ୍ଚୟ *I have to/have got to go to school tomorrow.*

haven't = **have not**

hawk /hɔ:k/ *noun* a big bird that catches and eats other birds and small animals ଛଞ୍ଚାଣ, ବାଜପକ୍ଷୀ

hawker /hɔ:kə(r)/ *noun* a person who sells things on a footpath or by going from place to place ଫେରିବାଲା, ବୁଲା ବିକାଳି

have[1] ର ଧାତୁରୂପ

present tense		*short forms*	*negative short forms*	
I	**have**	I'**ve**	I	**haven't**
you	**have**	you'**ve**	you	**haven't**
he/she/it	**has**	he'**s**/she'**s**/it'**s**	he/she/it	**hasn't**
we	**have**	we'**ve**	we	**haven't**
you	**have**	you'**ve**	you	**haven't**
they	**have**	they'**ve**	they	**haven't**

past tense **had**
present participle **having**
past participle **had**

past tense short forms
I'**d**
you'**d**
he'**d**/she'**d**/it'**d**
we'**d**
you'**d**
they'**d**

hay /heɪ/ *noun* (*no plural*) dry grass that is used as food for farm animals ଶୁଖିଲା ଘାସ; ନଡ଼ା

haystack /ˈheɪstæk/ *noun* a large bundle of dried grass that is stored for later use ନଡ଼ାଗଦା

haystack

hazard /ˈhæzəd/ *noun* a danger ବିପଦ *Pollution is causing a serious health hazard in cities.*

hazy /ˈheɪzi/ *adjective* (**hazier, haziest**) not clear ଅସ୍ପଷ୍ଟ, ଧୂଆଁଳିଆ *Even early in the mornings, the mountains appeared hazy.*

he /hiː/ *pronoun* (*plural* **they**) the man or boy that the sentence is about ସେ (ପୁରୁଷ) *I saw Jayant when he arrived at the party.* ○ *'Where is Manas?' 'He's at home.'*

head[1] /hed/ *noun* **1** the part of your body above your neck, that has your eyes, ears, nose and mouth in it ମୁଣ୍ଡ, ମସ୍ତକ *She turned her head to look at me.* ➪ ଚିତ୍ର ପାଇଁ **body** ଦେଖନ୍ତୁ । **2** what you use for thinking ମସ୍ତିଷ୍କ *A strange thought came into his head.* **3** the top, front or most important part of something ଅଗ୍ରଭାଗ, ସାମନାପଟ ବା ସବୁଠାରୁ ଗୁରୁତ୍ୱପୂର୍ଣ୍ଣ ସ୍ଥାନ *She sat at the head of the table.* **4** the most important person ମୁଖ୍ୟ ବ୍ୟକ୍ତି, ମୁଖିଆ, ପ୍ରମୁଖ **5 heads** (*plural*) the side of a coin that has the head of a person on it ଧାତୁ ମୁଦ୍ରାର ମୁଣ୍ଡ ଚିତ୍ର ଥିବା ପଟ ✪ ଖେଳ କିଏ ଆରମ୍ଭ କରିବ ସେ କଥା ନିର୍ଣ୍ଣୟ କରିବା ପାଇଁ ଆମେ ଯେତେ ବେଳେ ଧାତୁ ମୁଦ୍ରାଟିଏ ଉପରକୁ ଫିଙ୍ଗୁ (ଟସ୍ କରୁ) ଆମେ କହୁଁ **heads or tails**।

a head, per head for one person ଜଣପିଛା, ଜଣକୁ, ମୁଣ୍ଡପିଛା *The meal cost Rs 200 per head.*

head first with your head before the rest of your body ମୁଣ୍ଡଆଗକୁ କରି

✪ 'ହଁ' କହିବା ପାଇଁ ଆମେ ମୁଣ୍ଡ (head) କୁ ଉପରତଳ କରି ହଲାଉ ବା **'nod'** କହୁଁ। 'ନା' କହିବାକୁ ହେଲେ ଆମେ ମୁଣ୍ଡ (head)କୁ ଏକଡ଼ ସେକଡ଼ ହଲାଉ ବା **'shake'** କହୁଁ।

head² /hed/ *verb* (**heads, heading, headed**) **1** be at the front or top of a group ଅଗ୍ରଣୀ ହେବା, ଆଗରେ ରହିବା *Suparna's name heads the list.* **2** hit a ball with your head ମୁଣ୍ଡରେ ବଲ୍ ମାରିବା

headache /ˈhedeɪk/ *noun* a pain in your head ମୁଣ୍ଡବ୍ୟଥା, ମୁଣ୍ଡବିନ୍ଧା *He's got a headache.*

heading /ˈhedɪŋ/ *noun* the words at the top of a piece of writing to show what it is about; a title ଶିରୋନାମା; ଲେଖାର ଶୀର୍ଷରେ ଦିଆଯାଇଥିବା ବିଷୟ ନାମ, ଶୀର୍ଷକ।

headlight /ˈhedlaɪt/, **headlamp** /ˈhedlæmp/ *noun* one of the two big strong lights on the front of a car ମଟରଗାଡ଼ି ଆଗରେ ଥିବା ବଡ଼ ଆଲୁଅ, ହେଡ୍‌ଲାଇଟ୍ ➪ ଚିତ୍ର ପାଇଁ **car** ଦେଖନ୍ତୁ।

headline /ˈhedlaɪn/ *noun* **1** words in big letters at the top of a newspaper story ଖବର କାଗଜର ପ୍ରତ୍ୟେକ ଖବର ଶୀର୍ଷରେ ବଡ଼ ଅକ୍ଷରରେ ଲେଖାଯାଇଥିବା ଶିରୋନାମା **2 the headlines** (*plural*) the most important news on radio or television ରେଡ଼ିଓ ବା ଟେଲିଭିଜନ୍‌ରେ ଦିଆଯାଉଥିବା ମୁଖ୍ୟ ଖବର *Here are the news headlines.*

headmaster /ˌhedˈmɑːstə(r)/ *noun* a man who is in charge of a school ସ୍କୁଲ୍ ବା ବିଦ୍ୟାଳୟର ପ୍ରଧାନଶିକ୍ଷକ, ହେଡ୍‌ମାଷ୍ଟର୍

headmistress /ˌhedˈmɪstrəs/ *noun* (*plural* **headmistresses**) a woman who is in charge of a school ସ୍କୁଲ୍ ବା ବିଦ୍ୟାଳୟର ପ୍ରଧାନ ଶିକ୍ଷୟିତ୍ରୀ, ହେଡ୍‌ମିଷ୍ଟ୍ରେସ୍

headphones /ˈhedfəʊnz/ *noun* (*plural*) things that you put over your ears for listening to a radio, cassette player, etc. without other people hearing it ମୁଣ୍ଡପଟି ଦ୍ୱାରା କାନରେ ଲଗାଯାଉଥିବା ରେଡ଼ିଓ, କ୍ୟାସେଟ୍ ପ୍ଲେୟାର୍ ଇତ୍ୟାଦି ଶୁଣିବା ଯନ୍ତ୍ର, ଶିରଭାଷ

headquarters /ˌhedˈkwɔːtəz/ *noun* (*plural* **headquarters**) the main offices from where an organization is controlled କୌଣସି ସଂସ୍ଥାର ମୁଖ୍ୟ କାର୍ଯ୍ୟାଳୟ *The company's headquarters are in Delhi.* ✪ Headquarters ର ସଂକ୍ଷିପ୍ତ ରୂପ ହେଲା **HQ**।

headway /ˈhedweɪ/ *noun* (*no plural*) if you make headway, you make progress in some difficult task ଅଗ୍ରଗତି, ଉନ୍ନତି *The clue helped the police make headway in the case of the missing boy.*

heal /hiːl/ *verb* (**heals, healing, healed**) become well again; make something well again ଭଲ ହୋଇଯିବା, ଆରୋଗ୍ୟ ଲାଭ କରିବା *The cut on his leg has healed.*

health /helθ/ *noun* (*no plural*) how well your body is; how you are ସ୍ୱାସ୍ଥ୍ୟ, ସୁସ୍ଥତା *Fresh fruits and vegetables are good for your health.*

healthy /ˈhelθi/ *adjective* (**healthier, healthiest**) **1** well; not ill ସୁସ୍ଥ, ନିରୋଗ *healthy children* **2** that helps to make or keep you well ସ୍ୱାସ୍ଥ୍ୟକର *healthy food* ✪ ବିପରୀତ **unhealthy**

heap /hi:p/ *noun* a lot of things on top of one another in an untidy way; a large amount of something ଗଦା, ସ୍ତୁପ *She left her clothes in a heap on the floor.*

heap *verb* (**heaps, heaping, heaped**) put a lot of things on top of one another ଗଦା କରିବା *She heaped food onto my plate.*

hear /hɪə(r)/ *verb* (**hears, hearing, heard** /hɜ:d/, **has heard**) **1** take in sounds through your ears ଶୁଣିବା *Can you hear that noise?*

hear or **listen**?

Hear ବା **listen** ର ପ୍ରୟୋଗ ଭିନ୍ନ ଭିନ୍ନ ଭାବରେ ବ୍ୟବହୃତ ହୁଏ ଯେତେବେଳେ ଆମେ **hear** କରୁ ଶବ୍ଦ ଆମ କାନକୁ ଆସେ — *I **heard** the door close.*

ଯେତେବେଳେ କୌଣସି ଧ୍ୱନିର ପ୍ରୟାସ ଦ୍ୱାରା ଶୁଣାଯାଏ, ତେବେ **listen** ଶବ୍ଦର ପ୍ରୟୋଗ କରାଯାଏ —

*I **listen to** the radio every morning.*

2 learn about something with your ears ଜାଣିବା ପାଇଁ ଶୁଣିବା *Have you heard the news?*

hear of somebody or **something** know about somebody or something କାହାରି ବା କୌଣସି ବିଷୟରେ ଜାଣିବା

hearing /ˈhɪərɪŋ/ *noun* (*no plural*) the power to hear ଶୁଣିବା ଶକ୍ତି, ଶ୍ରବଣଶକ୍ତି *Speak louder—her hearing isn't very good.*

heart /hɑ:t/ *noun* **1** the part of a person's or animal's body that makes the blood go round inside ହୃତ୍ପିଣ୍ଡ *Your heart beats faster when you run.* **2** your feelings ହୃଦୟ, ମନୋଭାବ *She has a kind heart.* **3** the centre; the middle part କେନ୍ଦ୍ରସ୍ଥଳ, ମଝିଭାଗ, ମଧ୍ୟସ୍ଥଳ *They live in the heart of the city.* **4** the shape ପାନ ପତ୍ର ପରି ଚିହ୍ନ **5 hearts** (*plural*) the playing cards that have red shapes like hearts on them ତାସ୍‌ର ନାଲିପାନ ଘର *the six of hearts*

by heart so that you remember every word ମୁଖସ୍ଥ କରିବା *I have learnt the poem by heart.*

lose heart stop hoping ଆଶା ଛାଡ଼ିଦେବା *Don't lose heart—you can still win if you try.*

heart attack *noun* a sudden dangerous illness when a person's heart stops working properly ହୃତ୍ପିଣ୍ଡର ଆକସ୍ମିକ ଅକ୍ଷମତା

heartbeat /ˈhɑ:tbi:t/ *noun* the movement or sound of your heart as it pushes blood around your body ହୃତ୍ପିଣ୍ଡର ସ୍ପନ୍ଦନ

heartbroken /ˈhɑ:tbrəʊkən/ *adjective* someone who is heartbroken is very sad because something very bad has happened to them ଦୁଃଖାଭିଭୂତ, ଦୁଃଖାର୍ତ୍ତ

heartless /ˈhɑ:tləs/ *adjective* not kind; cruel ନିର୍ଦ୍ଦୟ; ନିଷ୍ଠୁର

hearty /ˈhɑ:ti/ *adjective* (**heartier, heartiest**) **1** warm and friendly ବନ୍ଧୁତ୍ୱପୂର୍ଣ୍ଣ **2** strong and enthusiastic ସବଳ ଓ ଉତ୍ସାହପୂର୍ଣ୍ଣ

heartily *adverb* with a lot of enthusiasm ବନ୍ଧୁତ୍ୱ ପୂର୍ଣ୍ଣ ଭାବରେ, ଉତ୍ସାହପୂର୍ଣ୍ଣ ଭାବରେ

heat /hi:t/ *noun* (*no plural*) the feeling of something hot ଉତ୍ତାପ, ଉଷ୍ଣତା, ଗରମ, ତାପ *the heat of the sun*

heat *verb* (**heats, heating, heated**) make something hot; become hot ଗରମ କରିବା, ଉତ୍ତପ୍ତ କରିବା; ଉତ୍ତପ୍ତ ହେବା *I heated some milk in a saucepan.*

heater *noun* a thing that makes a place warm or heats water କୌଣସି ସ୍ଥାନକୁ ବା ପାଣିକୁ ଗରମ କରିବା ଉପକରଣ *Switch on the heater if you feel cold.*

heave /hi:v/ *verb* (**heaves, heaving, heaved**) lift or pull something heavy ଭାରି ଜିନିଷକୁ ଟେକିବା ବା ଟାଣିବା *We heaved the suitcase up the stairs.*

heaven /ˈhevn/ *noun* (*no plural*) many people believe that God lives in heaven and that good people go to heaven when they die ସ୍ୱର୍ଗ, ଦେବଲୋକ, ଆକାଶ ➪ **hell** ଦେଖନ୍ତୁ।

Good Heavens! words that you use to show surprise ଆଶ୍ଚର୍ଯ୍ୟ ସୂଚକ ବାକ୍ୟାଂଶ; ହେ ଭଗବାନ୍! ଆରେ ବାପ୍‌ରେ! *Good Heavens! I've won Rs 1,000!*

heavy /ˈhevi/ *adjective* (**heavier, heaviest**) **1** with a lot of weight, so it is difficult to lift or move ଭାରି, ଗୁରୁ, ଓଜନିଆ *I can't carry this bag—it's too heavy.* **2** larger, stronger or more than usual ପ୍ରବଳ *heavy rain* ✪ ବିପରୀତ **light² 2**

heavily *adverb* ପ୍ରବଳ ଭାବରେ *It was raining heavily.*

hectic /ˈhektɪk/ *adjective* very busy ଅତ୍ୟନ୍ତ କାର୍ଯ୍ୟ ବ୍ୟସ୍ତ *I had a hectic day at work.*

he'd 1 = he had 2 = he would

hedge /hedʒ/ *noun* a row of bushes that makes a kind of wall around a garden or field ବାଡ଼

hedgehog /ˈhedʒhɒg/ *noun* a small animal covered with hairs that are like sharp needles ଝିଙ୍କ

heel /hi:l/ *noun* **1** the back part of your foot ଗୋଇଠି ➪ ଚିତ୍ର ପାଇଁ **body** ଦେଖନ୍ତୁ। **2** the back part of a shoe or a sock under the heel of your foot ଯୋତା ବା ମୋଜାର ଗୋଇଠି ତଳ ଅଂଶ

height /haɪt/ *noun* how far it is from the bottom to the top of somebody or something ଉଚ୍ଚତା। *What is the height of this mountain?* ○ *She asked me my height, weight and age.*

heir /eə(r)/ *noun* a person who receives money, goods, etc. when another person dies ଉତ୍ତରାଧିକାରୀ, ଦାୟାଦ

heiress /ˈeəres/ *noun* (*plural* **heiresses**) an heir who is a woman ଉତ୍ତରାଧିକାରିଣୀ

held ଶବ୍ଦ **hold**[1] ର ଏକ ଧାତୁରୂପ

helicopter /ˈhelɪkɒptə(r)/ *noun* a kind of small aircraft without wings, that can go straight up in the air. It has long metal parts on top that turn to help it fly ଉପରସ୍ଥ ପଙ୍ଖା ସାହାଯ୍ୟରେ ଉଡ଼ି ପାରୁଥିବା ଡେଣା ନ ଥିବା ବିମାନ ➪ ଚିତ୍ର ପାଇଁ **aircraft** ଦେଖନ୍ତୁ ।

hell /hel/ *noun* (*no plural*) some people believe that bad people go to hell when they die ନର୍କ; ପରଲୋକରେ ପାପୀ ମାନେ ରହୁଥିବା ସ୍ଥାନ ➪ **heaven** ଦେଖନ୍ତୁ ।

he'll = **he will**

hello /həˈləʊ/ *interjection* a word that you say when you meet somebody or when you answer the telephone କାହାରି ସାଙ୍ଗେ ଦେଖାହେଲେ ବା ଟେଲିଫୋନ୍ ସଂଯୋଗ ହେଲେ କୁହାଯାଉଥିବା ସଂଭାଷଣ, ହ୍ୟାଲୋ।

helm /helm/ *noun* a wheel or handle used to steer a boat or ship ଜାହାଜର ମଙ୍ଗ ଚାଳକ ଚକ, ଜାହାଜର ମଙ୍ଗ ବା କର୍ଣ୍ଣ

at the helm in charge of something କୌଣସି ସଂସ୍ଥା ବା କାମର ମୁଖ୍ୟକର୍ତ୍ତାଙ୍କ ସ୍ଥାନରେ

helmet /ˈhelmɪt/ *noun* a hard hat that keeps your head safe ମୁଣ୍ଡ ସୁରକ୍ଷିତ ରଖିବା ପାଇଁ ପିନ୍ଧା ଯାଉଥିବା ଟାଣ ପଦାର୍ଥରେ ପ୍ରସ୍ତୁତ ଶିରସ୍ତ୍ରାଣ ବା ଟୋପି, ହେଲ୍‌ମେଟ୍ *Motorcyclists in Delhi must wear helmets.*

help /help/ *verb* (**helps, helping, helped**) **1** do something useful for somebody; make somebody's work easier ସାହାଯ୍ୟ, ସହଯୋଗ, ସହାୟତା *She helped me to carry the box.* **2** a word that you shout when you are in danger ବିପଦ ବେଳେ କୁହା ଯାଉଥିବା ଶବ୍ଦ; ରକ୍ଷା କର, ବଞ୍ଚାଅ *Help! I can't swim!*

help yourself take what you want ଯାହା ଦରକାର ନେଇଯିବା *Help yourself to a sandwich.*

help *noun* (*no plural*) **1** the act of helping somebody ସାହାଯ୍ୟ, ସହାୟତା *Do you need any help?* **2** a person or thing that helps ସାହାଯ୍ୟକାରୀ ବ୍ୟକ୍ତି ବା ପଦାର୍ଥ *He was a great help to me when I was ill.*

helpful /ˈhelpfl/ *adjective* a person or thing that is helpful gives help ସାହାଯ୍ୟକାରୀ *helpful advice* ✪ ବିପରୀତ **unhelpful**

helpless /ˈhelpləs/ *adjective* not able to do things without help ଅସହାୟ

hem /hem/ *noun* the bottom edge of something like a shirt or trousers, that is folded and sewn ମୋଡ଼ି ସିଲେଇ କରାଯାଇଥିବା ଲୁଗାପଟାର ପ୍ରାନ୍ତଭାଗ

hemisphere /ˈhemɪsfɪə(r)/ *noun* one half of the earth ପୃଥିବୀର ଗୋଲାର୍ଦ୍ଧ; ଅର୍ଦ୍ଧଗୋଲକ *the northern/southern hemisphere*

hen /hen/ *noun* **1** a female bird that people keep on farms for its eggs କୁକୁଡ଼ା, କୁକ୍କୁଟୀ ➪ **chicken** ଦେଖନ୍ତୁ । **2** any female bird ଯେକୌଣସି ମାଇ ପକ୍ଷୀ ✪ ଅଣ୍ଡିରା ପକ୍ଷୀକୁ **cock** କହନ୍ତି ।

hence /hens/ *adverb* **1** for this reason; therefore ତେଣୁ, ସେଥିପାଇଁ *The* *government has rejected the workers' demand, hence the strike.* **2** from this time ଏହି ସମୟରୁ, ପରେ *Property prices would go up several times five years hence.*

henceforth /ˌhensˈfɔːθ/ *adverb* from now on ଏଣିକି, ବର୍ତ୍ତମାନ ଠାରୁ *The company will henceforth be known as Surya Lights Limited.*

her[1] /hɜː(r)/ *pronoun* (*plural* **them**) a word that shows a woman or girl ସେ (ସ୍ତ୍ରୀଲୋକ ବା ବାଳିକା) *I wrote to her yesterday.*

her[2] /hɜː(r)/ *adjective* of the woman or girl that you have just talked about ତା'ର (ସ୍ତ୍ରୀଲୋକ ବା ବାଳିକାର) *That's her book.*

herald /ˈherəld/ *verb* (**heralds, heralding, heralded**) announce or be the sign that something is going to happen soon (ଭବିଷ୍ୟତ ଘଟଣାର) ପୂର୍ବାଭାଷ ଦେବା *The president's speech heralded a new era of peace.*

herb /hɜːb/ *noun* a plant that people use to make food taste good, or in medicine ଖାଦ୍ୟକୁ ସୁବାସିତ କରିବା ବା ଔଷଧରେ ବ୍ୟବହୃତ ଗଛର ପତ୍ର, ମଞ୍ଜି ଇତ୍ୟାଦି

herbivore /ˈhɜːbɪvɔː(r)/ *noun* an animal which eats only grass and plants ତୃଣଭୋଜୀ ବା ତୃଣଜୀବୀ ପଶୁ, ମୃଗ, ଛାଗ *Cows and buffaloes are herbivores.* ➪ **carnivore, insectivore** ଏବଂ **omnivore** ଦେଖନ୍ତୁ।

herbivorous *adjective* ତୃଣଭୋଜୀ, ତୃଣଜୀବୀ

herd /hɜːd/ *noun* a big group of animals of the same kind that feed together ଗୋଠ, ଯୁଥ, ପଶୁପଲ *a herd of cows* ○ *a herd of elephants*

here /hɪə(r)/ *adverb* in, at or to this place ଏଠାରେ, ଏଇଠି *Your glasses are here.* ○ *Come here, please.*

here and there in different places ଏଠି ସେଠି *There were groups of people here and there along the beach.*

hereditary /həˈredɪtri/ *adjective* that which passes or can pass from parent to child ବଂଶାନୁକ୍ରମିକ, ବଂଶଗତ *a hereditary disease* ○ *a hereditary title*

heritage /ˈherɪtɪdʒ/ *noun* (*no plural*) the tradition and culture of a country or society that is valued because it has been its part for many years and has been passed from one generation to the next ପରମ୍ପରା, ଐତିହ୍ୟ *the cultural heritage of India*

hero /ˈhɪərəʊ/ *noun* (*plural* **heroes**) **1** a person who has done something brave or good ବୀର, ଯୋଦ୍ଧା, ସାହସିକ କାମ କରିଥିବା ବ୍ୟକ୍ତି *a war hero* **2** the most important man or boy in a book, play or film ବହି, ନାଟକ, ସିନେମା ଇତ୍ୟାଦିର ମୁଖ୍ୟ ନାୟକ

heroine /ˈherəʊɪn/ *noun* **1** a woman who has done something brave or good ବୀରାଙ୍ଗନା, ନାୟିକା **2** the most important woman or girl in a book, play or film ବହି, ନାଟକ ବା ସିନେମାର ନାୟିକା

hers /hɜːz/ *pronoun* something that belongs to her ତା'ର (ସେ ସ୍ତ୍ରୀଲୋକର ବା ବାଳିକାର) *Mita says this book is hers.*

herself /hɜːˈself/ *pronoun* (*plural* **themselves**) **1** a word that shows the same woman or girl that you have just talked about ସେ (ସ୍ତ୍ରୀଲୋକ ବା ବାଳିକା) ନିଜକୁ *She kept herself busy while he worked.* **2** a word that makes 'she' stronger ସେ (ସ୍ତ୍ରୀଲୋକ ବା ବାଳିକା) ନିଜେ *'Who told you Priya was married?' 'She told me herself.'*

by herself 1 alone; without other people ସେ (ସ୍ତ୍ରୀଲୋକ ବା ବାଳିକା) ନିଜେ ହିଁ, ଏକାକୀ *She lives by herself.* **2** without help ଏକା, ଅନ୍ୟର ସାହାଯ୍ୟ ବିନା *She can carry the box by herself.*

he's 1 = he is 2 = he has

hesitate /ˈhezɪteɪt/ *verb* (**hesitates, hesitating, hesitated**) stop for a moment before you do or say something because you are not sure about it ଦ୍ୱିଧା କରିବା, ସନ୍ଦିଗ୍ଧ ହେବା, ଇତସ୍ତତଃ ହେବା *He hesitated before answering the question.*

hesitation /ˌhezɪˈteɪʃn/ *noun* (*no plural*) ଦ୍ୱିଧା, ଇତସ୍ତତଃ ଭାବ *They agreed without hesitation.*

hey /heɪ/ *interjection* a word that you shout to make somebody listen to you, or when you are surprised ଅନ୍ୟକୁ ଡାକିବା ପାଇଁ ବ୍ୟବହୃତ ଶବ୍ଦ: ହେ; ଆହେ; ଆଶ୍ଚର୍ଯ୍ୟ ସୂଚକ ଶବ୍ଦ: ହେ *Hey! Where are you going?*

hi /haɪ/ *interjection* a word that you say when you meet somebody; hello ଅନ୍ୟ ସହିତ ଦେଖା ହେଲା ବେଳର ସମ୍ବୋଧନ, ହାଇ *Hi Tony! How are you?*

hibernate /ˈhaɪbəneɪt/ *verb* (**hibernates, hibernating, hibernated**) when (some) animals hibernate, they spend the winter in a state of deep sleep (କେତେକ ପଶୁଙ୍କର) ଶୀତକାଳରେ ଲମ୍ବା ଶୟନ କରିବା, ହିମଶୟନ କରିବା *Most cold-blooded animals hibernate.*

hibernation /ˌhaɪbəˈneɪʃn/ *noun* (*no plural*) (କେତେକ ପଶୁଙ୍କର) ହିମଶୟନ, ଶୀତକାଳର ଲମ୍ବା ନିଦ୍ରା

hiccup /ˈhɪkʌp/ *noun* a sudden noise that you make in your throat. You sometimes get hiccups when you have eaten or drunk too quickly ହେକୁଟି, ହାକୁଟି

hide /haɪd/ *verb* (**hides, hiding, hid** /hɪd/, **has hidden** /ˈhɪdn/) **1** put something where people cannot find it ଲୁଚାଇ ଦେବା *I hid the box under the bed.* **2** be or get in a place where people cannot see or find you ଲୁଚିଯିବା *Somebody was hiding behind the door.* **3** not tell or show something to somebody କୌଣସି କଥା ବା ଜିନିଷ ଗୁପ୍ତ ରଖିବା, ଲୁଚାଇବା *She tried to hide her feelings.*

hide-and-seek *noun* (*no plural*) a game that children play. Some children hide and one child tries to find them ପିଲାଙ୍କ ଲୁଚକାଳି ଖେଳ

hiding /ˈhaɪdɪŋ/ *noun* (*no plural*) the state of being in or going into a place where people will not find you ଲୁଚି ରହିବା ଅବସ୍ଥା, ଲୁଚି ରହିବା ସ୍ଥାନ

hi-fi /ˈhaɪ faɪ/ *noun* an electronic system that produces sound of very high quality ଉଚ୍ଚକୋଟିର ଧ୍ୱନି ଉତ୍ପନ୍ନ କରୁଥିବା ବୈଦ୍ୟୁତିକ ଯନ୍ତ୍ର ✪ Hi-fi ହେଲା **high fidelity** ର ସଂକ୍ଷିପ୍ତ ରୂପ।

high /haɪ/ *adjective* (**higher, highest**) **1** something that is high goes up a long way ଉଚ୍ଚ *a high wall* ○ *Mount Everest is the highest mountain in the world.* ✪ ବିପରୀତ **low 1 2** you use 'high' to say or ask how far something is from the bottom to the top ଉଚ୍ଚ, ଉଚ୍ଚା *The table is 80 cm high.* ✪ ମଣିଷମାନଙ୍କ ବିଷୟରେ ଆମେ **tall** କହୁଁ, **high** ର ପ୍ରୟୋଗ କରାଯାଏ ନାହିଁ *How tall are you?* ○ *He's 1.72 metres tall.* **3** more than usual ଉଚ୍ଚ, ଦ୍ରୁତ, ଖୁବ୍ *The car was travelling at high speed.* ○ *high temperatures*

high *adverb* a long way above the ground ଖୁବ୍ ଉପରେ, ଉଚ୍ଚତାରେ *The plane flew high above the clouds.*

high jump *noun* (*no plural*) a sport where people jump over a high bar କୁଦମାରି ଉଚ୍ଚକୁ ଡେଇଁବା ଖେଳ

highlight /ˈhaɪlaɪt/ *noun* the best or most exciting part of something ମୁଖ୍ୟାଂଶ, ପ୍ରଧାନ ବିଷୟ *highlights of the game*

highly /ˈhaɪli/ *adverb* **1** very or very much ବେଶ୍, ଖୁବ୍ *Their children are highly intelligent.* **2** very well ଅନୁକୂଳ ଭାବରେ, ଖୁବ୍ ଭଲ ବୋଲି *I think very highly of your work.*

Highness /ˈhaɪnəs/ *noun* (*plural* **Highnesses**) a word that you use when speaking to or about a royal person (ରାଜା ମହାରାଜାଙ୍କ ବିଷୟରେ କହିଲା ବେଳର) ସମ୍ବୋଧନ, ମଣିମା *His Highness the Prince of Wales*

highway /ˈhaɪweɪ/ *noun* a main road between towns ରାଜପଥ, (ବିଭିନ୍ନ ସହରମାନଙ୍କୁ ସଂଯୋଗ କରୁଥିବା) ମୁଖ୍ୟରାସ୍ତା

hijack /ˈhaɪdʒæk/ *verb* (**hijacks, hijacking, hijacked**) take control of an aeroplane or a car by force and make the pilot or driver take you somewhere ବିମାନ, ମଟରଗାଡ଼ି ଇତ୍ୟାଦିକୁ ଜବରଦସ୍ତ ଅପହରଣ କରିବା

hijacker *noun* a person who hijacks a plane or car ଅପହରଣକାରୀ ବ୍ୟକ୍ତି

hill /hɪl/ *noun* a high piece of land that is not as high as a mountain ପାହାଡ଼ *I pushed my bike up the hill.* ➪ **uphill** ଓ **downhill** ମଧ୍ୟ ଦେଖନ୍ତୁ।

hilly *adjective* (**hillier, hilliest**) with a lot of hills ପାହାଡ଼ିଆ, ପାହାଡ଼ମୟ *The countryside where I live is very hilly.*

him /hɪm/ *pronoun* (*plural* **them**) a word that shows a man or boy ତାକୁ, ତାଙ୍କୁ (ପୁରୁଷ ବା ବାଳକ) *I spoke to him yesterday.*

himself /hɪmˈself/ *pronoun* (*plural* **themselves**) **1** a word that shows the same man or boy that you have just talked about ସେ (ପୁରୁଷ ବା ବାଳକ) ନିଜକୁ *Rohit looked at himself in the mirror.* **2** a word that makes 'he' stronger ସେ (ପୁରୁଷ ବା ବାଳକ) ନିଜେ *Did he make this cake himself?*

by himself 1 alone; without other people (ପୁରୁଷ ବା ବାଳକ) ନିଜେ, ଏକା *Dad went shopping by himself.* **2** without help ଏକା, ବିନା ସାହାଯ୍ୟରେ *He did it by himself.*

hind legs *noun* (*plural*) the hind legs of an animal with four legs are the two legs placed at the back ପଛ ଗୋଡ଼

Hindu *noun* a person who follows **hinduism** ହିନ୍ଦୁ, ହିନ୍ଦୁଧର୍ମର ବ୍ୟକ୍ତି

Hinduism *noun* (*no plural*) the major religion of India that includes the worship of several gods and goddesses ହିନ୍ଦୁତ୍ୱ, ହିନ୍ଦୁଧର୍ମ

hint /hɪnt/ *verb* (**hints, hinting, hinted**) say something, but not in a direct way ସୂଚନା ଦେବା, ଆଭାସ ଦେବା *Sujata looked at her watch, hinting that she wanted to go home.*

hint *noun* something that you say, but not in a direct way ସୂଚନା, ଆଭାସ *When he said he had no money, it was a hint that he wanted you to pay for his dinner.*

hip /hɪp/ *noun* the place where your leg joins the side of your body ନିତମ୍ବ, ପିଚା, ଅଣ୍ଟା ଓ ଜଙ୍ଘ ମଧ୍ୟସ୍ଥ ଅଂଶ ➪ ଚିତ୍ର ପାଇଁ **body** ଦେଖନ୍ତୁ।

hippopotamus /ˌhɪpəˈpɒtəməs/ *noun* (*plural* **hippopotamuses** ଅଥବା **hippopotami** /ˌhɪpəˈpɒtəmaɪ/) a large African animal with thick skin and short legs, that lives in or near water ମୋଟା ଚମଡ଼ା, ବିଶାଳ ଶରୀର ଅନୁପାତରେ ଛୋଟ ଗୋଡ଼ ଥିବା ପଶୁ ଉଭୟ ଜଳ ଓ ସ୍ଥଳରେ ଆଫ୍ରିକା ଅଞ୍ଚଳରେ ଦେଖାଯାଇଥାଏ। ଜଳହସ୍ତୀ, ହିପୋପୋଟାମସ୍ ✪ Hippopotamus ର ସଂକ୍ଷିପ୍ତ ରୂପ ହେଲା **hippo**।

hippopotamus

hire /ˈhaɪə(r)/ *verb* (**hires, hiring, hired**) **1** pay to use something for a short time ଭଡ଼ାରେ ଆଣିବା *We hired a car when we were on holiday.* **2** pay somebody to do a job for you ମଜୁରି ଦେଇ ଲୋକଙ୍କୁ ନିଯୁକ୍ତ କରିବା *We hired somebody to mend the roof.*

hire *noun* (*no plural*) ଭଡ଼ା *Have you got any boats for hire?*

his /hɪz/ *adjective* of him ତା'ର (ପୁରୁଷ ବା ବାଳକର) *Ravi came with his sister.*

his *pronoun* something that belongs to him ତା'ର (ପୁରୁଷ ବା ବାଳକର) *Are these books yours or his?*

hiss /hɪs/ *verb* (**hisses, hissing, hissed**) make a noise like a very long 's' ସୁ-ସୁ ଶବ୍ଦ *The snake hissed at him.*

historical /hɪˈstɒrɪkl/ *adjective* of or about past times ଐତିହାସିକ, ଇତିହାସ ସମ୍ବନ୍ଧୀୟ *She writes historical novels.*

history /ˈhɪstri/ *noun* (*no plural*) the study of things that happened in the past ଇତିହାସ *History is my favourite subject at school.*

hit[1] /hɪt/ *verb* (**hits, hitting, hit, has hit**) touch somebody or something hard ପିଟିବା; ବାଡ଼େଇବା; ଆଘାତ କରିବା *The car hit a wall.*

hit[2] /hɪt/ *noun* **1** the act of hitting something ପ୍ରହାର, ଆଘାତ *That was a good hit!* **2** a person or a thing that a lot of people like ବହୁଲୋକ ଭଲ ପାଉଥିବା ବ୍ୟକ୍ତି ବା ପଦାର୍ଥ *This song was a hit last year.*

hive /haɪv/ *noun* a box-like structure where bees live ମହୁଫେଣା, ମହୁମାଛି ବାକ୍ସ

hoard /hɔːd/ *noun* a secret store of something, for example food or money ଖାଦ୍ୟ ବା ଟଙ୍କାର ଗୁପ୍ତ ଭଣ୍ଡାର

hoarse /hɔːs/ *adjective* if your voice is hoarse, it is rough and quiet, for example because you have a cold କର୍କଶ (ସ୍ୱର)

hoax /həʊks/ *noun* (*plural* **hoaxes**) a trick that makes somebody believe something that is not true ପରିହାସରେ କରାଯାଇଥିବା ଠକାମି *There wasn't really a bomb at the station—it was a hoax.*

hobby /ˈhɒbi/ *noun* (*plural* **hobbies**) something that you like doing when you are not working ଆନନ୍ଦ ପାଇଁ କରାଯାଉଥିବା କାମ (ବୃତ୍ତିପାଇଁ ନୁହେଁ) *My hobbies are reading and swimming.*

hockey /ˈhɒki/ *noun* (*no plural*) a game for two teams of eleven players who try to hit a small ball into the other team's goal with long curved sticks on a field ହକି ଖେଳ (ଏଗାରଜଣିଆ ଦୁଇଦଳ ମଧ୍ୟରେ ଖେଳାଯାଉଥିବା ହକିଷ୍ଟିକ୍ ଦ୍ୱାରା ବଲ୍‌ମାରି ଗୋଲ୍ ଦେବା ଖେଳ)

hoist /hɔɪst/ *verb* (**hoists, hoisting, hoisted**) pull something up to a higher level, usually with ropes (ଦଉଡ଼ି ଇତ୍ୟାଦି ଦ୍ୱାରା) ଉତ୍ତୋଳନ କରିବା, ଉପରକୁ ଉଠାଇବା *The Prime Minister of India hoists the national flag at Red Fort every year on Independence Day.*

hold[1] /həʊld/ *verb* (**holds, holding, held** /held/, **has held**) **1** have something in your hand or arms ହାତରେ ଧରିବା *He held the baby in his arms.* **2** keep something in a certain way କୌଣସି ଜିନିଷ ନିର୍ଦ୍ଦିଷ୍ଟ ଭାବେ ରଖିବା *Hold your hand up.* **3** have space for a certain number or amount ଧାରଣ କରିବା *The car holds five people.* **4** make something happen ଘଟିବା, ହେବା *The meeting was held in the town hall.*

hold on 1 wait ଅପେକ୍ଷାକର, ରୁହ *Hold on, I'm coming.* **2** not stop holding something tightly ଧରି ରଖିବା *The child held on to her mother's hand.*

hold up make somebody or something late ବିଳମ୍ବ ହେବା ବା କରିବା *The plane was held up for forty minutes.*

hold[2] /həʊld/ *noun* (*no plural*) the action of having something in your hand ଧାରଣ, ଧରିବା କାମ *Can you get hold of the other end of the table and help me move it?*

hold[3] /həʊld/ *noun* the part of a ship or an aeroplane where you keep the goods ଜାହାଜ ବା ବିମାନର ଜିନିଷପତ୍ର ରଖିବା ସ୍ଥାନ

hole /həʊl/ *noun* an empty space or opening in something ଗାତ, କଣା *I'm going to dig a hole in the garden.*

holiday /ˈhɒlədeɪ/ *noun* a day or days when you do not go to work or school, or when you go away somewhere to enjoy yourself ଛୁଟି ଦିନ, ଅବକାଶ, ଅବସର *The school holidays start next week.*

hollow /ˈhɒləʊ/ *adjective* with an empty space inside ପୋଲା, ଫମ୍ପା, ଭିତରଟା ଖାଲିଥିବା *A drum is hollow.*

holy /ˈhəʊli/ *adjective* (**holier, holiest**) **1** very special because it is about God ପବିତ୍ର, ଈଶ୍ୱରଙ୍କ ସମ୍ବନ୍ଧୀୟ *The* Guru Granth Sahib *is the holy book of the Sikhs*. **2** a holy person lives a good and religious life ନୈତିକ ଓ ଧାର୍ମିକ ଜୀବନ ଯାପନ କରୁଥିବା

homage /ˈhɒmɪdʒ/ *noun* (*no plural*) the act of showing your respect for somebody ଭକ୍ତି, ସମ୍ମାନ, ଶ୍ରଦ୍ଧାଞ୍ଜଳି *Many people go to Rajghat to pay homage to Mahatma Gandhi*.

home /həʊm/ *noun* the place where you live ବାସସ୍ଥାନ, ଘର, ନିବାସ *Satish left home at the age of 18*.

at home in your house or flat ଘରେ, ନିବାସରେ *Is Shashi at home?*

homeless /ˈhəʊmləs/ *adjective* if you are homeless, you have nowhere to live ବାସଶୂନ୍ୟ *The floods made many people homeless*.

home-made *adjective* made at home, not bought from a shop ଘରେ ତିଆରି *home-made jam*

homesick /ˈhəʊmsɪk/ *adjective* sad because you are away from home ଦୂର ଜାଗାରେ ଘର କଥା ମନେ ପକାଇ ଦୁଃଖ କରୁଥିବା

homework /ˈhəʊmwɜːk/ *noun* (*no plural*) work that a teacher gives to you to do at home ଘରେ ପଢ଼ିବା ବା ଲେଖିବା ପାଇଁ ଶିକ୍ଷକଙ୍କ ଦ୍ୱାରା ଦିଆଯାଇଥିବା ପାଠ

homonym /ˈhɒmənɪm/ *noun* one of two or more words that are pronounced and spelt the same way but are different in meaning and origin, for example *kite* (the bird) and *kite* (the toy) ସମାନ ବନାନ ଓ ଉଚ୍ଚାରଣ କିନ୍ତୁ ଭିନ୍ନ ଅର୍ଥ ଥିବା ଶବ୍ଦ

homophone /ˈhɒməfəʊn/ *noun* one of two or more words that are pronounced the same way but are different in spelling and meaning, for example *know* and *no* ର ଉଚ୍ଚାରଣ ଏକ କିନ୍ତୁ ଭିନ୍ନ ବନାନ ଓ ଅର୍ଥ ଥିବା ଶବ୍ଦ

honest /ˈɒnɪst/ *adjective* a person who is honest says what is true and does not steal or cheat ସଚ୍ଚୋଟ, ନିଷ୍ପାପର, ଅକପଟ *She's a very honest person*. ✪ ବିପରୀତ **dishonest**

honestly *adverb* ସଚ୍ଚୋଟ ବା ବିଶ୍ୱାସଯୋଗ୍ୟ ଭାବରେ *Try to answer the question honestly*.

honesty *noun* (*no plural*) the quality of being honest ସାଧୁତା, ସଚ୍ଚୋଟତା

honey /ˈhʌni/ *noun* (*no plural*) the sweet sticky food that bees make ମହୁ, ମଧୁ

honeycomb /ˈhʌnikəʊm/ *noun* a structure with several six-sided cells made by bees in which they store honey ମହୁଫେଣା, ମହୁଘରା, ମହୁ ରଖିବା ପାଇଁ ଷଡ଼ଭୁଜ ଆକାରର ମହୁମାଛି ଲାଖରେ ଗଠିତ ଘରାସମୂହ

honour /ˈɒnə(r)/ *noun* (*no plural*) the respect from other people that a person or country gets because of something very good that they have done ସମ୍ମାନ, ଶ୍ରଦ୍ଧା, ଭକ୍ତି, ସମାଦର *They are fighting for the honour of their country*.

honourable /ˈɒnərəbl/ *adjective* an honourable act gets you a lot of respect ସମ୍ମାନଯୋଗ୍ୟ, ସମ୍ମାନପ୍ରଦ

hood /hʊd/ *noun* the part of a coat or jacket that covers your head and neck (କୋଟ୍ ବା ଜ୍ୟାକେଟ୍‌ରେ ଲାଗିଥିବା) ମୁଣ୍ଡ ଓ ବେକର ଆବରଣ

hoof /hu:f/ *noun* (*plural* **hoofs** **hooves** /hu:vz/) the hard part of the foot of horses and some other animals (ଘୋଡ଼ା, ଗାଇ ଇତ୍ୟାଦିଙ୍କ) ଖୁରା

hook /hʊk/ *noun* a curved piece of metal or plastic for hanging things on, or for catching something ଟାଣିଆଣିବା ପାଇଁ ଆଙ୍କୁଡ଼ି; ଲଟକାଇବା ପାଇଁ ବଙ୍କା ମୁଣ୍ଡଥିବା ହୁକ *Hang your coat on that hook.*

hoot /hu:t/ *noun* the sound that an owl or a car's horn makes ପେଚାର ରାବ; ମଟରଗାଡ଼ି ଇତ୍ୟାଦିର ହର୍ଣ୍ଣର ଶବ୍ଦ

hoot *verb* (**hoots, hooting, hooted**) make this sound ପେଚା ଡାକିବା; ମଟରଗାଡ଼ିର ହର୍ଣ୍ଣ ବଜାଇବା *The driver hooted at the dog.*

hooves ଶବ୍ଦ **hoof** ର ବହୁବଚନ

hop /hɒp/ *verb* (**hops, hopping, hopped**) **1** jump on one foot ଏକ ଗୋଡ଼ିଆ ହେଇ ଡେଇଁବା **2** jump with two or all feet together ଦୁଇ ବା ସବୁ ଗୋଡ଼ ଉଠାଇ ଡେଇଁବା *The frog hopped onto the stone.*

hope[1] /həʊp/ *noun* a feeling of wanting something to happen and thinking that it will ଆଶା, ଇଚ୍ଛା, ପ୍ରତ୍ୟାଶା *He has worked very hard, so there is hope that he will pass the exam this time.*

hope[2] /həʊp/ *verb* (**hopes, hoping, hoped**) want something to happen or come true ଆଶା କରିବା *I hope to see you tomorrow.*

hopeful /ˈhəʊpfl/ *adjective* if you are hopeful, you think that something that you want will happen ଆଶାୟୀ, ଆଶାନ୍ୱିତ *I'm hopeful about getting a job.*

hopefully *adverb* **1** in a hopeful way ଆଶାପ୍ରଦ ଭାବରେ *The cat looked hopefully at our plates.* **2** I hope ମୁଁ ଆଶା କରୁଛି *Hopefully he won't be late.*

hopeless /ˈhəʊpləs/ *adjective* **1** very bad ଆଶାହୀନ, ନିରାଶ, ଅତିଖରାପ *I'm hopeless at tennis.* **2** useless ହତାଶ, ଆଶାଶୂନ୍ୟ, କଷ୍ଟକର, ଅସମ୍ଭବ *It's hopeless trying to work when my brother is here—he's so noisy!*

horizon /həˈraɪzn/ *noun* the line where the land or sea seems to meet the sky ଦିଗ୍‌ବଳୟ, ଚକ୍ରବାଳ *We could see a ship on the horizon.*

horizontal /ˌhɒrɪˈzɒntl/ *adjective* something that is horizontal goes from side to side, not up and down ଭୂସମାନ୍ତର, ଆନୁଭୂମିକ *a horizontal line* ⇨ **vertical** ଦେଖନ୍ତୁ।

horn /hɔ:n/ *noun* **1** one of the hard pointed things that some animals have on their heads (କିଛି ପଶୁଙ୍କ ମୁଣ୍ଡରେ ଥିବା) ଶିଙ୍ଗ, ଶୃଙ୍ଗ **2** a thing in a car, ship, etc. that makes a loud sound to warn people ମଟରଗାଡ଼ି, ଜାହାଜ ଇତ୍ୟାଦିର ହର୍ଣ୍ଣ, ପୁଙ୍ଗା, ଶିଙ୍ଗା

horrible /ˈhɒrəbl/ *adjective* **1** something that is horrible makes you feel afraid or shocked ଭୀଷଣ, ଭୟଙ୍କର *When mother came home, she found the kitchen in a horrible mess!* **2** very bad ଅତି ଖରାପ *What horrible weather!*

horrid /ˈhɒrɪd/ *adjective* very bad or unkind ଅତି ଖରାପ ବା ନିର୍ଦ୍ଦୟ; ବିଭତ୍ସ *Don't be so horrid!*

horrify /ˈhɒrɪfaɪ/ *verb* (**horrifies, horrifying, horrified**) shock and frighten somebody ଭୀତତ୍ରସ୍ତ କରିବା, ଆତଙ୍କିତ କରିବା *We were horrified to learn about the number of killings in the war.*

horror /ˈhɒrə(r)/ *noun* (*no plural*) a feeling of great fear or shock ଆତଙ୍କ, ଭୟ, ଶଙ୍କା *They watched in horror as the plane came crashing down.*

horse /hɔːs/ *noun* a big animal that can carry people and pull heavy things ଘୋଡ଼ା, ଅଶ୍ୱ *Can you ride a horse?* ✪ ଘୋଡ଼ା ଛୁଆକୁ **foal** କହନ୍ତି।

horseshoe /ˈhɔːsʃuː/ *noun* a piece of metal like a U that is nailed to a horse's hoof ଘୋଡ଼ା ଖୁରାର ନାଲ

hose /həʊz/, **hosepipe** /ˈhəʊzpaɪp/ *noun* a long soft tube that you use to bring water, for example in the garden or when there is a fire (ବଗିଚାରେ ପାଣିଦେବା ପାଇଁ ବା ନିଆଁ ଲିଭାଇବା ପାଇଁ ବ୍ୟବହୃତ) ଜଳବାହୀ ନମନୀୟ ନଳୀ

hospitable /hɒˈspɪtəbl/ *adjective* friendly, kind and caring towards guests ଅତିଥିସେବା ପରାୟଣ, ସୌହାର୍ଦ୍ଦ୍ୟପୂର୍ଣ୍ଣ, ସଦୟ

hospital /ˈhɒspɪtl/ *noun* a place where doctors and nurses look after people who are ill or hurt ଡାକ୍ତରଖାନା, ହସପିଟାଲ୍ *My brother is in hospital—he's broken his leg.*

✪ ହସ୍‌ପିଟାଲ୍‌ରେ ରହୁଥିବା ରୋଗୀକୁ **patient** କୁହାଯାଏ। ବହୁ ରୋଗୀ ରହିବା ପାଇଁ ହସ୍‌ପିଟାଲ୍‌ରେ ଥିବା ବଡ଼ ପ୍ରକୋଷ୍ଠକୁ **ward** କୁହାଯାଏ।

host /həʊst/ *noun* a person who invites guests, for example to a party ଅତିଥିଙ୍କୁ ଆମନ୍ତ୍ରିତ କରୁଥିବା ଓ ତାଙ୍କ ଭଲମନ୍ଦ ବୁଝୁଥିବା ବ୍ୟକ୍ତି

hostage /ˈhɒstɪdʒ/ *noun* somebody who is kept as a prisoner by a person or group until the person or the group is given what they are asking for ଦାବିର ପୂରଣ ପାଇଁ ବନ୍ଧକ ସ୍ୱରୂପ ରଖାଯାଇଥିବା ବ୍ୟକ୍ତି *The hijackers have freed all the hostages.*

take somebody hostage capture somebody and keep them as a hostage କାହାରିକୁ ଧରି ନେଇ ବନ୍ଧକ ଭାବରେ ରଖିବା

hostel /ˈhɒstl/ *noun* a place like a cheap hotel where students can stay ଛାତ୍ରାବାସ *a youth hostel*

hostess /ˈhəʊstəs/ *noun* (*plural* **hostesses**) a woman who invites guests, for example to a party ନାରୀ ଆମନ୍ତ୍ରକ, ଅତିଥିଙ୍କ ଭଲମନ୍ଦ ବୁଝିଥିବା ମହିଳା, ବ୍ୟବସ୍ଥାପିକା ➪ **air-hostess** ମଧ ଦେଖନ୍ତୁ।

hostile /ˈhɒstaɪl/ *adjective* very unfriendly ବନ୍ଧୁତ୍ୱହୀନ, ଶତ୍ରୁଭାବାପନ୍ନ *a hostile army*

hot /hɒt/ *adjective* (**hotter, hottest**)
1 not cold. A fire is hot ଗରମ, ଉତ୍ତପ୍ତ *It's hot today, isn't it?* ○ *hot water*
2 food that is hot has a strong, burning taste (ଲଙ୍କାମରିଚ ପରି) ରାଗ *a hot curry*

hotel /həʊˈtel/ *noun* a place where you pay to sleep and eat when you

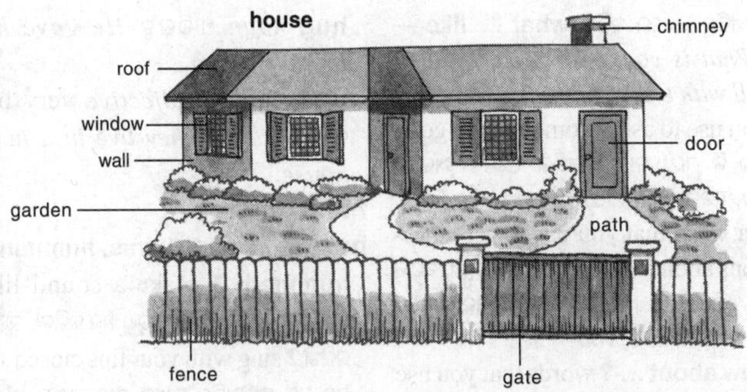

are on a holiday or travelling ପଇସା ନେଇ ରହିବା ଓ ଖାଇବା ଯୋଗାଉଥିବା ସଂସ୍ଥା, ହୋଟେଲ୍ *I stayed at a hotel near the airport.*

hour /ˈaʊə(r)/ *noun* a measure of time. There are sixty **minutes** in an hour ଏକ ଘଣ୍ଟା ବା ଷାଠିଏ ମିନିଟ୍, ଘଣ୍ଟାଏ *The journey took two hours.*

hourglass /ˈaʊəglɑːs/ *noun* (*plural* **hourglasses**) a glass container in which a quantity of sand takes exactly an hour to pass through the small opening between the upper and lower parts ବାଲି ଭରା ଡମ୍ବରୁ ଆକାରର କାଚ ଉପକରଣ ଯେଉଁଥିରେ ଉପର ବାଲି ତଳ ଘରାକୁ ଆସିବାକୁ ଘଣ୍ଟାଏ ସମୟ ଲାଗେ

house /haʊs/ *noun* a building where a person or a family lives ଘର, ଗୃହ, ଭବନ, ସଦନ *We're having dinner at Jyoti's house tonight.* ➪ **bungalow, cottage** ଓ **flat**[1] ଦେଖନ୍ତୁ।

household /ˈhaʊshəʊld/ *noun* all the people living together in a house ଗୋଟିଏ ଘରେ ରହୁଥିବା ସବୁଲୋକ ବା ପରିବାର ବର୍ଗ *a survey of high-income households*

household *adjective* of or related to looking after a house and all the people living together in it ଘର ଓ ପରିବାରବର୍ଗ ସମ୍ବନ୍ଧୀୟ *household expenses* ○ *household goods*

housewife /ˈhaʊswaɪf/ *noun* (*plural* **housewives** /ˈhaʊswaɪvz/) a woman who takes care of her family while her husband is away at work ଗୃହିଣୀ, ଘର ଚଳାଉଥିବା ପତ୍ନୀ

housing /ˈhaʊzɪŋ/ *noun* (*no plural*) flats and houses for people to live in ବାସଗୃହ ସମୂହ, ଆବାସ *We need more housing for young people.*

hover /ˈhɒvə(r)/ *verb* (**hovers, hovering, hovered**) stay in the air in one place ଆକାଶରେ ଗୋଟିଏ ସ୍ଥାନରେ ସ୍ଥିର ହୋଇ ଉଡ଼ିରହିବା *A helicopter hovered above the building.*

how /haʊ/ *adverb* **1** in what way କିପରି, କିମିତି, କେମିତି, କିପ୍ରକାର *How does this machine work?* **2** a word that you use to ask if somebody is well *How is your sister?* ✪ ଆମେ how ବ୍ୟବହାର କରିବା କାହାରି ସ୍ୱାସ୍ଥ୍ୟ ବିଷୟରେ ପଚାରିବାବେଳେ। ଅନ୍ୟ ଲୋକକୁ ବର୍ଣ୍ଣନା କରିବାକୁ

କାହାରିକୁ କହିଲେ କହିବା **what ... like** — *'What is your sister like?' 'She's tall with brown hair.'* **3** a word that you use to ask if something is good ଭଲ କି ମନ୍ଦ ବୋଲି ପଚାରିଲା ବେଳେ ବ୍ୟବହୃତ ଶବ୍ଦ, କେମିତି ଲାଗିଲା *How was the film?* **4** a word that you use to ask questions about amount, etc. ପରିମାଣ, ବୟସ ଇତ୍ୟାଦି ପଚାରିଲା ବେଳେ ବ୍ୟବହୃତ ଶବ୍ଦ; କେତେ *How old are you?*

how about ... ? words that you use when you suggest something (ଏଇଟା କେମିତି) ହେବ ? *How about going for a walk?*

how do you do? polite words that you say when you meet somebody for the first time କାହାରି ସାଙ୍ଗେ କୌଣସି ଦିନ ପ୍ରଥମ ଦେଖାର ସମ୍ଭାଷଣ; କେମିତି ଅଛନ୍ତି ✪ ଯଦି କେହି ତୁମକୁ ପଚାରେ, ତୁମେ କହିବ 'How do you do?'

however /haʊˈevə(r)/ *adverb* in whatever way ଯେତେ, ଯେତେ ପାର ସେତେ, ଯଥାସାଧ୍ୟ *You won't catch the train, however hard you try.*

howl /haʊl/ *noun* a long loud sound, like a dog or wolf makes କୁକୁରର ଆର୍ତ୍ତନାଦ; ହେଟା, ବିଲୁଆ ଇତ୍ୟାଦିଙ୍କ ବୋବାଳି

howl *verb* (**howls, howling, howled**) make this sound ଚିତ୍କାର କରିବା *The dogs howled all night.*

HQ *abbreviation* **headquarters** ର ସଂକ୍ଷିପ୍ତ ରୂପ

hug /hʌg/ *verb* (**hugs, hugging, hugged**) put your arms around somebody to show that you love them ସ୍ନେହରେ କୁଣ୍ଢେଇ ପକେଇବା, ଆଲିଙ୍ଗନ *She hugged her parents and said goodbye.*

hug *noun* ଆଲିଙ୍ଗନ *He gave his brother a hug.*

huge /hjuːdʒ/ *adjective* very big ଖୁବ୍ ବଡ଼, ବିରାଟ *They live in a huge house.*

hullo = **hello**

hum /hʌm/ *verb* (**hums, humming, hummed**) **1** make a sound like bees (ମହୁମାଛି ପରି) ଗୁଣୁଗୁଣୁ ଶବ୍ଦ କରିବା, ଗୁଞ୍ଜନ କରିବା **2** sing with your lips closed ଓଠ ବନ୍ଦ କରି ଅନୁନାସିକ ଭାବେ ଗୀତ ଗୁଞ୍ଜନ କରିବା *If you don't know the words of the song, hum it.*

human /ˈhjuːmən/ *adjective* of or like people, not animals or machines ମଣିଷ ସମ୍ବନ୍ଧୀୟ; ମଣିଷ ପରି, ମାନୁଷିକ, ମାନବୀୟ *the human body*

human, human being *noun* a person ମଣିଷ, ମନୁଷ୍ୟ *Human beings have lived on earth for thousands of years.*

humble /ˈhʌmbl/ *adjective* (**humbler, humblest**) **1** a humble person does not think he/she is better or more important than other people ନମ୍ର, ବିନୀତ, ବିନମ୍ର *Becoming rich and famous has not changed her—she is still very humble.* **2** simple or poor ସାଧାସିଧା; ଗରିବ, ଦରିଦ୍ର *a humble cottage*

humid /ˈhjuːmɪd/ *adjective* used to describe a condition of the weather when it is hot and the air is so damp that your sweat does not evaporate quickly, making you feel uneasy ଆର୍ଦ୍ର (ଜଳବାଷ୍ପ)

humidity /hju:ˈmɪdəti/ *noun* (*no plural*) the amount of **water vapour** in the air ଆର୍ଦ୍ରତା

humiliate /hju:ˈmɪlieɪt/ *verb* (**humiliates, humiliating, humiliated**) make someone feel ashamed or embarrassed before other people ଲଜ୍ଜିତ କରିବା, ଅପମାନ ଦେବା

humorous /ˈhju:mərəs/ *adjective* a person or thing that is humorous makes you smile or laugh କୌତୁକିଆ, ହସେଇ ପାରୁଥିବା, ହାସ୍ୟଜନକ *a humorous story*

humour /ˈhju:mə(r)/ *noun* (*no plural*) being funny କୌତୁକ, ଆନନ୍ଦଦାୟକ ଗୁଣ *a story full of humour*

have a sense of humour be able to laugh and make other people laugh at funny things ହସ କୌତୁକର ଅନୁଭବ ଓ ଉପଭୋଗ ଶକ୍ତିଥିବା *Ria has a good sense of humour.*

hump /hʌmp/ *noun* a round lump (ମଣିଷ ବା ଓଟ ପିଠିର) କୁଜ *A camel has a hump on its back.* ➪ **camel** ଦେଖନ୍ତୁ।

humus /ˈhju:məs/ *noun* (*no plural*) dark-coloured substance made of dead leaves and plants which makes the soil very fertile ସଢ଼ା ପତ୍ର ଇତ୍ୟାଦିରେ ହେଉଥିବା ଜୈବସାର, ଖତ

hundred /ˈhʌndrəd/ *number* 100 ଏକଶହ, ଏକ ଶତ *We invited a hundred people to the party.* ○ *hundreds of people*

hundredth /ˈhʌndrədθ/ *adjective, adverb, noun* 100th; one of the hundred equal parts of something ଏକ ଶତାଂଶ, ଶହେ ଭାଗରୁ ଭାଗେ

hung ଶବ୍ଦ **hang 1** ର ଏକ ଧାତୁରୂପ

hunger /ˈhʌŋgə(r)/ *noun* (*no plural*) the feeling that you want or need to eat କ୍ଷୁଧା, ଭୋକ ✪ ମନେରଖନ୍ତୁ ! ଇଂରାଜୀରେ 'I have hunger' କହିବା ଠିକ୍ ହେବନାହିଁ। 'I am hungry' କହିବା ଠିକ୍ ହେବ।

hungry /ˈhʌŋgri/ *adjective* (**hungrier, hungriest**) if you are hungry, you want to eat ଭୋକିଲା, କ୍ଷୁଧାର୍ତ୍ତ

hunt /hʌnt/ *verb* (**hunts, hunting, hunted**) **1** chase animals to kill them for food or as a sport ଶିକାର କରିବା *Young lions have to learn to hunt.* **2** search for something ଖୋଜିବା, ଅନୁସନ୍ଧାନ କରିବା

hunt for something try to find something କୌଣସି ପଦାର୍ଥକୁ ଖୋଜି ପାଇବାକୁ ଚେଷ୍ଟା କରିବା *I've hunted everywhere for my watch but I can't find it.*

hunter *noun* a person who chases and kills animals ଶିକାରୀ, ବାଣୁଆ, ବ୍ୟାଧ

hunting *noun* (*no plural*) ଶିକାର *Hunting is banned in many countries.*

hurdle /ˈhɜ:dl/ *noun* a problem or difficulty in something that you do ପ୍ରତିବନ୍ଧ, ଅସୁବିଧା *One of the major hurdles of laying the railway lines to connect the village to the town was a huge mountain.*

hurl /hɜ:l/ *verb* (**hurls, hurling, hurled**) throw something with great force ଖୁବ୍ ଜୋର୍‌ରେ ଫୋପାଡ଼ିବା ବା ଫିଙ୍ଗିବା *She hurled the book across the room.*

hurray /həˈreɪ/, **hooray** /huˈreɪ/, **hurrah** /həˈrɑ:/ *interjection* a word that you say aloud when you are very pleased about something ଖୁସି ବ୍ୟକ୍ତ କରିବା ପାଇଁ କୁହାଯାଉଥିବା ଶବ୍ଦ; ହୁରରେ *Hurray! She's won!*

hurricane /ˈhʌrɪken/ *noun* a violent storm over the Atlantic Ocean with very strong winds ପ୍ରବଳ ତୋଫାନ (ବିଶେଷତଃ ଆଟ୍‌ଲାଣ୍ଟିକ୍ ମହାସାଗରର ୱେଷ୍ଟଇଣ୍ଡିଜ୍ ଅଞ୍ଚଳର)

hurry[1] /ˈhʌri/ *noun* (*no plural*) **in a hurry** if you are in a hurry, you need to do something quickly ଶିଘ୍ରତାର ସହିତ, ତରବର ହୋଇ *I can't talk to you now—I'm in a hurry.*

hurry[2] /ˈhʌri/ *verb* (**hurries, hurrying, hurried, has hurried**) move or do something quickly ତରବରରେ ଯିବା ବା କରିବା *We hurried home after school.*

hurry up move or do something more quickly ଶିଘ୍ର ଆସ, ଶିଘ୍ର କାମ ସାର *Hurry up or we'll be late!*

hurt /hɜːt/ *verb* (**hurts, hurting, hurt, has hurt**) make somebody or something feel pain ଯନ୍ତ୍ରଣା ଦେବା ବା ଆଘାତ କରିବା *Did you hurt yourself?* ○ *You hurt her feelings when you said she was fat.*

husband /ˈhʌzbənd/ *noun* the man that a woman is married to ସ୍ୱାମୀ, ପତି ➪ ଚିତ୍ର ପାଇଁ **family** ଦେଖନ୍ତୁ ।

husk /hʌsk/ *noun* the dry outer covering of grains and seeds ଚଷ୍ଣୁ, ଚୋପା

hut /hʌt/ *noun* a small building with one room. Huts are usually made of mud or wood କୁଡ଼ିଆ, କୁଟୀର, ଛୋଟ ଝାଟିମାଟି ଘର

hydroelectricity /ˌhaɪdrəʊɪˌlekˈtrɪsəti/ *noun* (*no plural*) electricity produced from the power of water ଜଳ ବିଦ୍ୟୁତ, ଜଳ ଶକ୍ତିରୁ ଉତ୍ପନ୍ନ ବିଦ୍ୟୁତ୍‌ଶକ୍ତି

hydrogen /ˈhaɪdrədʒən/ *noun* (*no plural*) a light gas that you cannot see or smell ଉଦ୍‌ଜାନ, ଗନ୍ଧହୀନ, ସ୍ୱାଦହୀନ ଏକ ଅତିହାଲ୍‌କା ବାଷ୍ପ *Water is made of hydrogen and oxygen.*

hygiene /ˈhaɪdʒiːn/ *noun* (*no plural*) the practice of keeping yourself and things around you clean ସ୍ୱାସ୍ଥ୍ୟ ରକ୍ଷା ନିୟମ *Good hygiene is very important when you are preparing food.*

hygienic *adjective* clean and free from germs that cause diseases ସଫାସୁତୁରା, ରୋଗ ଜୀବାଣୁ ନ ଥିବା, ସ୍ୱାସ୍ଥ୍ୟକର *hygienic conditions* ✪ ବିପରୀତ **unhygienic**

hyphen /ˈhaɪfn/ *noun* a mark (-) that you use in writing. It joins two words together to make a new one (for example **cold-blooded**) or shows that a word continues on the next line ଦୁଇଟି ଶବ୍ଦକୁ ସଂଯୋଗ କରିବା ପାଇଁ ଦିଆଯାଉଥିବା ଯୋଗରେଖା (–)

hypotenuse /haɪˈpɒtənjuːz/ *noun* the side opposite the right-angle of a right-angled triangle ସମକୋଣୀ ତ୍ରିଭୁଜର ସମକୋଣର ବିପରୀତ ବାହୁ, କର୍ଣ୍ଣ

I i

I[1] /aɪ/ *pronoun* (*plural* **we**) the person who is speaking ମୁଁ *I am an Indian.* ○ *I'll see you tomorrow.*

I[2] /aɪ/ *symbol* the number 1 in Roman numerals ରୋମୀୟ ସଂଖ୍ୟାର ୧ ସଂଖ୍ୟା

ice /aɪs/ *noun* (*no plural*) water that has become hard because it is very cold ବରଫ, ଘନୀଭୂତ ଜଳ

iceberg

iceberg /ˈaɪsbɜːɡ/ *noun* a very big piece of ice floating in the sea ସମୁଦ୍ରରେ ଭାସୁଥିବା ପ୍ରକାଣ୍ଡ ବରଫ ଖଣ୍ଡ

ice cream *noun* a very cold sweet food made from milk ଆଇସକ୍ରିମ୍, ମଲାଇ ବରଫ *Two chocolate ice creams, please.*

ice rink *noun* a special place where you can ice-skate ବରଫ ଚଟାଣ ଯାହା ଉପରେ ଏକ ବିଶେଷ ପ୍ରକାର ଯୋତା ପିନ୍ଧି ଖସି ଚାଲିବା ଖେଳ ଖେଳାଯାଏ

icicle /ˈaɪsɪkl/ *noun* a pointed piece of ice formed by water that freezes as it falls or runs down from something ଲମ୍ବା ହୋଇ ଓହଳିଥିବା ମୁନିଆ ବରଫ ଖଣ୍ଡ

icing /ˈaɪsɪŋ/ *noun* (*no plural*) a sweet substance that you use for covering or decorating cakes କେକ୍ ଉପରେ ବୋଳା ଯାଉଥିବା ଓ ଚିତ୍ର କରାଯାଉଥିବା ମିଠା ପଦାର୍ଥ *a cake with pink icing*

icon /ˈaɪkɒn/ *noun* a small symbol or picture on a computer screen that represents a program or a file କମ୍ପ୍ୟୁଟର ଚାଳନା ପାଇଁ ପରଦା ଉପରେ ଆସୁଥିବା ସଂକେତ *To print, click on the printer icon.*

ID *abbreviation* ଶବ୍ଦ **identification** ର ସଂକ୍ଷିପ୍ତ ରୂପ

Id *noun* the name given to some of the important Muslim festivals. Id-ul-Fitr is celebrated at the end of a month of fasting called Ramzan. Id-ul-Zuha and Id-i-Milad are the other important Ids ମୁସଲମାନ ମାନଙ୍କର (କେତେକ ପର୍ବର ନାମ ଯଥା:ଇଦ୍-ଉଲ୍-ଫିତର୍, ଇଦ୍-ଉଲ୍-ଜୁହା, ଓ ଇଦ୍-ଇ-ମିଲାଦ୍), ଇଦ୍

I'd 1 = **I had 2** = **I would**

idea /aɪˈdɪə/ *noun* **1** a plan or new thought ଏକ ନୂଆ ଧାରଣା, କଳ୍ପନା ବା ଭାବନା *I've got an idea. Let's have a party!* **2** a picture in your mind ଧାରଣା *The film gives you a good idea of what Iceland is like.*

ideal /aɪˈdiːəl/ *adjective* the best or exactly right ଆଦର୍ଶ, ସବୁ ଠାରୁ ଭଲ, ଠିକ୍ *This is an ideal place for picnics.*

ideal *noun* **1** someone or something that is the best or perfect ଆଦର୍ଶ ବ୍ୟକ୍ତି ବା ପଦାର୍ଥ *She considered her teacher her ideal.* **2** an idea or a standard that seems best to you and that you want to achieve ଆଦର୍ଶ

identical /aɪˈdentɪkl/ *adjective* exactly the same ଏକାପରି, ସମାନ, ସର୍ବସମ *These two cameras are identical.*

identify /aɪˈdentɪfaɪ/ *verb* (**identifies, identifying, identified, has identified**) say or know who somebody is or what something is ଚିହ୍ନଟ କରିବା, ଚିହ୍ନି ପାରିବା *Rima was able to identify the animals at the zoo.*

identification /aɪˌdentɪfɪˈkeɪʃn/ *noun* (*no plural*) **1** the process of identifying somebody or something, ଚିହ୍ନଟ କରିବା ପ୍ରକ୍ରିୟା, ଚିହ୍ନିବା, ପରିଚୟ ପାଇବା, ଜାଣିପକାଇବା *The identification of luggage is compulsory before boarding a plane.* **2** something that shows who you are, for example a passport ଚିହ୍ନଟ କରିବାର ପଦାର୍ଥ ବା ଚିହ୍ନ, ପରିଚୟ ପତ୍ର *Do you have any identification?* ✪ **ID** ହେଲା **identification** ର ସଂକ୍ଷିପ୍ତ ରୂପ।

identity /aɪˈdentəti/ *noun* (*plural* **identities**) who or what a person or thing is ନିଜତ୍ୱ; ଆତ୍ମପରିଚୟ, ପରିଚୟ *The identity of the killer is not known.*

identity card *noun* (*plural* **identity cards**) a small card that has your name, photograph and address to show who you are ପରିଚୟ ପତ୍ର

idiom /ˈɪdiəm/ *noun* a group of words with a special meaning ରୂଢ଼ି, ବକ୍ରୋକ୍ତି, ବାକ୍ୟାଂଶ ଯାହାର ପ୍ରକୃତ ଅର୍ଥ ଶବ୍ଦାର୍ଥ ଠାରୁ ଭିନ୍ନ (ଢ଼ଗ, ଢ଼ମାଳି ଇତ୍ୟାଦି) *The idiom 'break somebody's heart' means 'make somebody very unhappy'.*

idiot /ˈɪdiət/ *noun* a person who is stupid or does something silly ବୋକା, ନିର୍ବୋଧ

idle /ˈaɪdl/ *adjective* **1** lazy; not wanting to work hard ଅଳସୁଆ *an idle boy* **2** not being used; not doing any work ବ୍ୟବହାର ହେଉ ନଥିବା; କାମ କରୁ ନଥିବା, ଅଚଳ *idle equipment*

idol /ˈaɪdl/ *noun* **1** something that people worship as a god ଦେବତାଙ୍କ ମୂର୍ତ୍ତି, ବିଗ୍ରହ **2** a famous person that people love ଲୋକେ ଭଲ ପାଉଥିବା ପ୍ରସିଦ୍ଧ ବ୍ୟକ୍ତି *She is the idol of millions of teenagers.*

i.e. *abbreviation* this is what I mean ଅର୍ଥାତ୍ *You can buy hot drinks, i.e. tea and coffee, on the train.* ✪ i.e. ର ପ୍ରୟୋଗ କେବଳ ଲେଖିବାରେ ବ୍ୟବହାର କରାଯାଏ, କହିବାରେ ନୁହେଁ।

if /ɪf/ *conjunction* **1** a word that you use to say what is possible or true when another thing happens or is true ଯଦି *If you press this button, the machine starts.* ○ *If you see him, give him this letter.* **2** a word that shows a question; whether ହୁଏତ *Do you know if Priti is at home?*

as if in a way that makes you think something ସତେ ଯେମିତି *She looks as if she has been on holiday.*

ignite /ɪgˈnaɪt/ *verb* (**ignites, igniting, ignited**) make something start to burn ନିଆଁ ଲଗାଇବା, ଅଗ୍ନି ସଂଯୋଗ କରିବା *A spark from the bonfire ignited the fire crackers.*

ignorance /ˈɪgnərəns/ *noun* (*no plural*) the state of not knowing about something ଅଜ୍ଞତା, ଜ୍ଞାନାଭାବ, ଅଜ୍ଞ

ignorant /ˈɪgnərənt/ *adjective* if you are ignorant, you do not know about something ଅଜ୍ଞ, ଜ୍ଞାନହୀନ, ମୁର୍ଖ *He's completely ignorant about computers.*

ignore /ɪɡˈnɔː(r)/ *verb* (**ignores, ignoring, ignored**) not pay attention to somebody or something ଉପେକ୍ଷା କରିବା, ଅବହେଳା କରିବା *I said hello to her, but she ignored me!*

il- *prefix*
କୌଣସି କୌଣସି ଶବ୍ଦର ଆରମ୍ଭରେ **il-** ସଂଯୋଗ କଲେ ବିପରୀତ ଅର୍ଥ ସୂଚାଏ, ଯଥା — **illegal** = ଅନ୍ୟାୟ

ill /ɪl/ *adjective* **1** not well; not in good health ରୋଗାକ୍ରାନ୍ତ, ଅସୁସ୍ଥ, ରୋଗଗ୍ରସ୍ତ *Mohit is in bed because he is ill.* ✪ **Illness** ହେଲା **ill** ର ବିଶେଷ୍ୟ ପଦ । **2** bad ଖରାପ *ill-health* ○ *ill-effects*
be taken ill become ill ରୋଗଗ୍ରସ୍ତ ହେବା, ରୋଗରେ ପଡ଼ିବା *Shikha was taken ill yesterday.*

I'll = **I shall, I will**

illegal /ɪˈliːɡl/ *adjective* not allowed by the law; not legal ବେଆଇନ୍, ବେନିୟମ *It is illegal to drive a car if you are under the age of 18.* ✪ ବିପରୀତ **legal 1**
illegally *adverb* ବେଆଇନ୍ ଭାବେ *She came into the country illegally.*

illiterate /ɪˈlɪtərət/ *adjective* unable to read or write ଅପାଠୁଆ, ଲେଖିପଢ଼ି ପାରୁନଥିବା, ନିରକ୍ଷର ✪ ବିପରୀତ **literate**
illiteracy /ɪˈlɪtərəsi/ *noun* (*no plural*) ନିରକ୍ଷରତା ✪ ବିପରୀତ **literacy**

illness /ˈɪlnəs/ *noun* (*plural* **illnesses**) the state of being ill ରୋଗ, ଅସୁସ୍ଥ *He could not come to the meeting because of illness.*

illogical /ɪˈlɒdʒɪkl/ *adjective* if something is illogical, it does not make any sense ଅଯୌକ୍ତିକ, ଯୁକ୍ତିହୀନ ✪ ବିପରୀତ **logical**

ill-treat *verb* (**ill-treats, ill-treating, ill-treated**) do unkind things to a person or an animal ନିଷ୍ଠୁର ବ୍ୟବହାର କରିବା

illuminate /ɪˈluːmɪneɪt/ *verb* (**illuminates, illuminating, illuminated**) put lights on something so that it can be seen well or to decorate it ଆଲୋକିତ କରିବା, ଆଲୋକରେ ସଜାଇବା *Rashtrapati Bhavan is illuminated on Republic Day.*

illusion /ɪˈluːʒn/ *noun* **1** an idea, opinion or a belief that is false ଭ୍ରାନ୍ତି ଧାରଣା, ମିଥ୍ୟା ବିଶ୍ୱାସ, ଭ୍ରମ *She was under the illusion that she would be promoted very soon.* **2** something that appears to be true but is not so in reality ବିଭ୍ରାନ୍ତିକର ରୂପ ବା ଆକୃତି *an optical illusion*

illustration /ˌɪləˈstreɪʃn/ *noun* a picture ଚିତ୍ର; ଚିତ୍ରାଙ୍କନ *This dictionary has a lot of illustrations.*

im- *prefix*
କିଛି ଶବ୍ଦର ଆରମ୍ଭରେ **im-** ଲଗାଇଲେ ବିପରୀତ ଅର୍ଥ ସୂଚାଏ, ଯଥା — **impatient** = ଅଧୈର୍ଯ୍ୟ, ଧୈର୍ଯ୍ୟହୀନତା

I'm = **I am**

image /ˈɪmɪdʒ/ *noun* a picture on paper, in a mirror or in people's minds of somebody or something କାଗଜ ଇତ୍ୟାଦିରେ ଚିତ୍ର; ଛବି; ଦର୍ପଣରେ ଦେଖାଯାଉଥିବା ପ୍ରତିଛବି; ମନଭିତରେ ଦେଖାଯାଉଥିବା ପ୍ରତିମୂର୍ତ୍ତି

imaginary /ɪˈmædʒɪnəri/ *adjective* not real; only in your mind କାଳ୍ପନିକ, ଭାବନାମୂଳକ *The film is about an imaginary country.*

imagination /ɪˌmædʒɪˈneɪʃn/ *noun* the ability to think of new ideas or make pictures in your mind କଳ୍ପନା ଶକ୍ତି *You need a lot of imagination to write stories for children.*

imagine /ɪˈmædʒɪn/ *verb* (**imagines, imagining, imagined**) **1** make a picture of something in your mind କଳ୍ପନା କରିବା *Can you imagine life without electricity?* **2** think that something will happen or that something is true କୌଣସି ଘଟଣା ଘଟିବ ବୋଲି ବା କୌଣସି ବିଷୟ ସତ ବୋଲି ଭାବିବା *I imagine Mr Sharma will come by car.*

imitate /ˈɪmɪteɪt/ *verb* (**imitates, imitating, imitated**) try to do the same as somebody or something; copy somebody or something ଅନୁକରଣ କରିବା *He imitated his teacher's voice.*

imitation /ˌɪmɪˈteɪʃn/ *noun* something that you make to look like another thing; a copy ନକଲ, କୃତ୍ରିମ *It's not a diamond, it's only a glass imitation.*

immature /ˌɪməˈtjʊə(r)/ *adjective* **1** not fully developed ଅପରିପକ୍ୱ, ଅପରିଣତ *immature seeds* **2** not behaving in a sensible manner ଉଚିତ୍ ଆଚରଣ କରି ପାରୁନଥିବା *Don't be immature. Grow up!* ✪ ବିପରୀତ **mature**

immediate /ɪˈmiːdiət/ *adjective* happening at once ତତ୍କ୍ଷଣାତ୍, ସଙ୍ଗେ ସଙ୍ଗେ *I can't wait—I need an immediate answer.*

immediately *adverb* now; at once ବର୍ତ୍ତମାନ, ତତ୍କ୍ଷଣାତ୍

immense /ɪˈmens/ *adjective* very big ଖୁବ୍ ବଡ଼, ଖୁବ୍ କଷ୍ଟକର *immense problem.*

immensely /ɪˈmensli/ *adverb* very or very much ଖୁବ୍ ଭଲ ଭାବରେ, ବହୁତ୍ *We enjoyed the party immensely.*

immerse /ɪˈmɜːs/ *verb* (**immerses, immersing, immersed**) put something into a liquid so that it is completely covered by it ତରଳ ପଦାର୍ଥରେ ବୁଡ଼ାଇବା ବା ଡୁବାଇବା *They immersed the idols in the river.*

immortal /ɪˈmɔːtl/ *adjective* something that is immortal lives or lasts forever ଅମର; ଚିରସ୍ଥାୟୀ

immune /ɪˈmjuːn/ *adjective* safe, so that you cannot get a disease ରୋଗରୁ ସୁରକ୍ଷିତ *You're immune to measles if you've had it before.*

immunity /ɪˈmjuːnəti/ *noun* (*no plural*) the ability of the body to fight against disease ରୋଗପ୍ରତିରୋଧକ ଶକ୍ତି *immunity against chickenpox*

immunize /ˈɪmjʊnaɪz/ *verb* (**immunizes, immunizing, immunized**) make a person or an animal immune from a disease by injecting a substance (called a **vaccine**) inside their body (ଟିକା, ଭ୍ୟାକ୍ସିନ୍ ଇଞ୍ଜେକ୍ସନ୍ ଦ୍ୱାରା) ରୋଗରୁ ସୁରକ୍ଷିତ ରଖିବା, ରୋଗ ନିରୋଧ କରିବା, ରୋଗ ପ୍ରତିଷେଧ କରିବା *All children should be immunized against polio.*

immunization /ˌɪmjʊnaɪˈzeɪʃn/ *noun* the act of making a person or an animal immune against a disease by injecting a **vaccine** inside their body (ରୋଗ) ପ୍ରତିଷେଧନ, ପ୍ରତିରୋଧ ବ୍ୟବସ୍ଥା

impact /ˈɪmpækt/ *noun* **1** the effect of something ପ୍ରଭାବ, ପ୍ରତିଫଳ *The windowpanes were shattered because of the impact of the explosion.* **2** the act of one thing hitting against another ପିଟି ହେବା ବା ବାଡ଼େଇ ହେବା ପ୍ରକ୍ରିୟା, ସଂଘାତ, ଧକ୍କା *The front of the car was smashed due to the impact of the collision.*

impatient /ɪmˈpeɪʃnt/ *adjective* if you are impatient, you are annoyed because you have had to wait for something ଧୈର୍ଯ୍ୟହୀନ, ଅଧୈର୍ଯ୍ୟ, ବ୍ୟାକୁଳ *Don't be so impatient! The bus will be here soon.* ✪ ବିପରୀତ **patient**[1]

impatience /ɪmˈpeɪʃns/ *noun* (*no plural*) ଧୈର୍ଯ୍ୟହୀନତା, ବ୍ୟାକୁଳତା, ଅଧୈର୍ଯ୍ୟ *He showed his impatience by looking at his watch five or six times.* ✪ ବିପରୀତ **patience**

impatiently *adverb* ଅଧୈର୍ଯ୍ୟ ଭାବରେ *'Hurry up!' she said impatiently.*

impeach /ɪmˈpiːtʃ/ *verb* charge a person in a high public office with a serious crime ଉଚ୍ଚ ସରକାରୀ ଅଧିକାରୀ ବା ରାଜନୀତିରେ ନିଯୁକ୍ତ ବ୍ୟକ୍ତିଙ୍କୁ ଘୋର ଅପରାଧ ପାଇଁ ମହାଭିଯୋଗ ବିଚାର ପ୍ରକ୍ରିୟାକୁ ଆଣିବା *No president has ever been impeached in this country.*

imperative /ɪmˈperətɪv/ *noun* the form of a verb that you use for giving orders ଅତ୍ୟାବଶ୍ୟକ, ଅତି ଜରୁରୀ, (ବ୍ୟାକରଣ) ଅନୁଜ୍ଞାସୂଚକ କ୍ରିୟା *'Listen!' and 'Go away!' are in the imperative.*

implement[1] /ˈɪmplɪmənt/ *noun* a tool used for doing something ହତିଆର, ଉପକରଣ, ଯନ୍ତ୍ରପାତି *garden implements*

implement[2] /ˈɪmplɪment/ *verb* (**implements, implementing, implemented**) start an official plan କାର୍ଯ୍ୟରେ ପରିଣତ କରିବା *A new method of collecting garbage will be implemented from next month.*

imply /ɪmˈplaɪ/ *verb* (**implies, implying, implied**) suggest something without actually saying it ସୂଚାଇବା, ଆଭାସ ଦେବା *He asked if I had any work to do. He was implying that I was lazy.*

impolite /ˌɪmpəˈlaɪt/ *adjective* rude ଅଭଦ୍ର, ଅମାର୍ଜିତ, ଅଶିଷ୍ଟ *It's impolite to stare at people.* ✪ ବିପରୀତ **polite**

import /ɪmˈpɔːt/ *verb* (**imports, importing, imported**) buy things from another country and bring them into your country ଅନ୍ୟ ଦେଶରୁ ଜିନିଷପତ୍ର ଆମଦାନି କରିବା *a car imported from Germany* ✪ ବିପରୀତ **export**

import /ˈɪmpɔːt/ *noun* a thing that is imported ଆମଦାନି ହେଉଥିବା ଦ୍ରବ୍ୟ ✪ ବିପରୀତ **export**

important /ɪmˈpɔːtnt/ *adjective* **1** if something is important, you must do, have or think about it ଗୁରୁତ୍ୱପୂର୍ଣ୍ଣ *It is important to sleep well the night before an exam.* **2** powerful or special ଶକ୍ତିଶାଳୀ; ବିଶେଷତ୍ୱ ଥିବା; ବିଶିଷ୍ଟ, ପ୍ରଧାନ *The Prime Minister is a very important person.* ✪ ବିପରୀତ **unimportant**

importance /ɪmˈpɔːtns/ *noun* (*no plural*) the quality of being important or of great value ପ୍ରାଧାନ୍ୟ, ଗୁରୁତ୍ୱ *Oil is of great importance to industry.*

impossible /ɪmˈpɒsəbl/ *adjective* if something is impossible, you cannot do it, or it cannot happen ଅସମ୍ଭବ *It is impossible to finish this work by five o'clock.* ✪ ବିପରୀତ **possible**

impress /ɪmˈpres/ *verb* (**impresses, impressing, impressed**) make somebody have good feelings or thoughts about you or about something that is yours କାହାରି ମନରେ ସୁପ୍ରଭାବ ପକାଇବା। *He was so impressed by Chandra's singing that he asked her to sing on the radio.*

impressive *adjective* if something is impressive, it impresses people, for example because it is very good or very big ହୃଦୟଗ୍ରାହୀ, ଚିତ୍ତାକର୍ଷକ *an impressive building*

impression /ɪmˈpreʃn/ *noun* **1** feelings or thoughts you have about somebody or something ମନରେ ପଡ଼ିଥିବା ପ୍ରଭାବ ବା ଧାରଣା। *My first impressions of London were not very good.* **2** a mark or design that is left by pressing something on a surface କୌଣସି ପଦାର୍ଥ ଉପରେ ଅନ୍ୟ ଜିନିଷ ଚାପିବା ଫଳରେ ହୋଇଥିବା ଚିହ୍ନ

make an impression give somebody a certain idea of yourself ଅନ୍ୟ ମନରେ ନିଜ ବିଷୟରେ ନିର୍ଦ୍ଦିଷ୍ଟ ଧାରଣା ସୃଷ୍ଟି କରିବା, ପ୍ରଭାବ ପକାଇବା। *He made a good impression on his first day at work.*

imprison /ɪmˈprɪzn/ *verb* (**imprisons, imprisoning, imprisoned**) put somebody in prison କାରାରୁଦ୍ଧ କରିବା, ବନ୍ଦୀ କରିବା। *He was imprisoned for five years.*

imprisonment *noun* (*no plural*) the state of being in prison ଜେଲ୍ ଦଣ୍ଡ, କାରାଦଣ୍ଡ *two years' imprisonment*

improper /ɪmˈprɒpə(r)/ *adjective* if something is improper, it is not right in that particular situation ଅନୁଚିତ, ଅଶିଷ୍ଟ, ଅସମୀଚୀନ, ଅସଂଗତ, ଅନୁପଯୁକ୍ତ *improper conduct* ✪ ବିପରୀତ **proper**

improve /ɪmˈpruːv/ *verb* (**improves, improving, improved**) become better or make something better ଉନ୍ନତି କରିବା। *Your English has improved a lot this year.*

improvement *noun* a change that makes something better than it was before ଉନ୍ନତି, ଉତ୍କର୍ଷ ସାଧନ *There has been a big improvement in Alka's work.*

impulse /ˈɪmpʌls/ *noun* a sudden strong wish to do something ହଠାତ୍ ଜାତ ହୋଇଥିବା ଇଚ୍ଛା, ମନର ତାଡ଼ନା। *She bought the shoes on impulse.*

impure /ɪmˈpjʊə(r)/ *adjective* not clean, dirty ଅଶୁଦ୍ଧ, ଦୂଷିତ, କଳୁଷିତ, ଅପରିଷ୍କାର *impure water* ✪ ବିପରୀତ **pure**

impurity /ɪmˈpjʊərəti/ *noun* (*plural* **impurities**) if something contains impurities, it has some substances in it that make it dirty ଅଶୁଦ୍ଧ ପଦାର୍ଥ, ମଇଳା *Impurities in water should be filtered out before drinking.*

in[1] /ɪn/ *adverb* to a place, from outside ଭିତରକୁ *I opened the door and went in.* ✪ ବିପରୀତ **out 1**

in[2] /ɪn/ *preposition* **1** a word that shows where ରେ, ଭିତରେ (ସ୍ଥାନସୂଚକ)

He put his hand in the water. **2** a word that shows when ରେ (ସମୟସୂଚକ) *My birthday is in May*. **3** a word that shows how long after ରେ, ମଧ୍ୟରେ, ଭିତରେ (ସମୟାନ୍ତର ସୂଚକ) *I'll be ready in ten minutes*. **4** a word that shows how somebody or something is ଅବସ୍ଥାରେ *This room is in a mess*. **5** a word that shows somebody's job ରେ *He's in the army*.

in- *prefix*
କିଛି ଶବ୍ଦର ଆରମ୍ଭରେ **in-** ଯୋଗ କଲେ ବିପରୀତ ଅର୍ଥ ବୁଝାଏ, ଯଥା — **incomplete** = ଅସମ୍ପୂର୍ଣ୍ଣ

inability /ˌɪnəˈbɪləti/ *noun* (*no plural*) not being able to do something ଅସାମର୍ଥ୍ୟ, ଅକ୍ଷମତା, ଅପାରଗତା *inability to concentrate for long*

inaccessible /ˌɪnækˈsesəbl/ *adjective* if something is inaccessible, you cannot reach it ଅଗମ୍ୟ, ଦୁର୍ଗମ୍ୟ, ପହଞ୍ଚି ହେଉ ନଥିବା; ଦୁଷ୍ପ୍ରାପ୍ୟ, ସହଜେ ପାଇ ହେଉ ନଥିବା *The village is inaccessible during the rains*. ✪ ବିପରୀତ **accessible**

inaccurate /ɪnˈækjərət/ *adjective* not correct; with mistakes in it ଭୁଲ୍, ତ୍ରୁଟିପୂର୍ଣ୍ଣ ✪ ବିପରୀତ **accurate**

inadequate /ɪnˈædɪkwət/ *adjective* not as much as you need, or not good enough ଅଳ୍ପ, ଅପ୍ରଚୁର, ଅଯଥେଷ୍ଟ, ନିଅଣ୍ଟ *inadequate food* ✪ ବିପରୀତ **adequate**

inauguration /ɪˌnɔːgjəˈreɪʃn/ *noun* the formal ceremony of opening or starting something new ଉଦ୍‌ଘାଟନ *the inauguration of the showroom*

incapable /ɪnˈkeɪpəbl/ *adjective* not having the skill, ability or knowledge to do something ଅସମର୍ଥ, ଅକ୍ଷମ, ଅପାରଗ, ଅଯୋଗ୍ୟ *The students were incapable of taking care of themselves, so two teachers accompanied them on the trip*. ✪ ବିପରୀତ **capable**

inch /ɪntʃ/ *noun* (*plural* **inches**) a measure of length (= 2.54 centimetres). There are twelve inches in a **foot** ଲମ୍ବର ମାପ ଯାହା ଏକ ଫୁଟର ୧୨ ଭାଗରୁ ଭାଗେ; ୨.୫୪ ସେଣ୍ଟିମିଟର୍ *I am five foot six inches tall*.

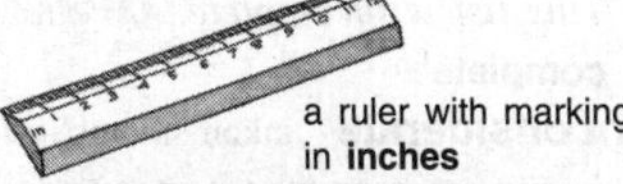
a ruler with markings in **inches**

incident /ˈɪnsɪdənt/ *noun* something that happens ଘଟଣା *a funny incident at school*

incisor /ɪnˈsaɪzə(r)/ *noun* one of the eight sharp teeth at the front of the mouth. Incisors are used for biting ଉପର ବା ତଳ ପାଟିର ସାମନାର ଆଠଟି ଦାନ୍ତୁଆ ଦାନ୍ତ, କର୍ତ୍ତନ ଦାନ୍ତ ➪ **canine, molar** ଓ **premolar** ମଧ୍ୟ ଦେଖନ୍ତୁ। ➪ ଚିତ୍ର ପାଇଁ **tooth** ଦେଖନ୍ତୁ।

include /ɪnˈkluːd/ *verb* (**includes, including, included**) **1** have somebody or something as one part of the whole ସମଷ୍ଟିରେ ଅନ୍ତର୍ଭୁକ୍ତ କରିବା *The price of the room includes breakfast*. **2** make somebody or something part of a group ଶ୍ରେଣୀ ବା ବିଭାଗରେ ଅନ୍ତର୍ଭୁକ୍ତ କରିବା *Have you included tea on the list of things to buy?* ✪ ବିପରୀତ **exclude**

including *preposition* with; if you count ଅନ୍ତର୍ଭୁକ୍ତ କରି, ମିଶାଇ *There were five people in the car, including the driver.* ✪ ବିପରୀତ **excluding**

income /ˈɪnkʌm/ *noun* all the money that you receive for your work ମୋଟ ଆୟ ବା ଅର୍ଜିତ ଧନ (କାମ ପାଇଁ), ଦରମା

incoming /ˈɪnkʌmɪŋ/ *adjective* arriving at a place, or being received ଆସୁଥିବା, ଆଗତପ୍ରାୟ *incoming flights* ○ *free incoming calls* ✪ ବିପରୀତ **outgoing**

incomplete /ˌɪnkəmˈpliːt/ *adjective* not finished; with parts missing ଅସମ୍ପୂର୍ଣ୍ଣ *This list is incomplete.* ✪ ବିପରୀତ **complete**[1]

inconsiderate /ˌɪnkənˈsɪdərət/ *adjective* a person who is inconsiderate does not think or care about other people and their feelings ଅନ୍ୟର ସୁବିଧା ଅସୁବିଧା ବିଷୟ ଭାବୁ ନଥିବା (ବ୍ୟକ୍ତି) *It's inconsiderate of you to make so much noise when people are asleep.* ✪ ବିପରୀତ **considerate**

inconvenient /ˌɪnkənˈviːniənt/ *adjective* if something is inconvenient, it gives you problems or difficulty ଅସୁବିଧାଜନକ, ଅବ୍ୟବସ୍ଥିତ *She came at an inconvenient time—I was on the telephone.* ✪ ବିପରୀତ **convenient**

incorrect /ˌɪnkəˈrekt/ *adjective* not correct; not right or true ଭୁଲ୍, ବେଠିକ୍, ଅଶୁଦ୍ଧ, ଅସତ୍ୟ *It is incorrect to say that two plus two equals five.* ✪ ବିପରୀତ **correct**[1]

increase /ɪnˈkriːs/ *verb* (**increases, increasing, increased**) become bigger or more; make something bigger or more ବଢ଼ିବା; ବର୍ଦ୍ଧିତ କରିବା ବା ହେବା *The number of working women has increased over the years.* ✪ ବିପରୀତ **decrease**

increase /ˈɪnkriːs/ *noun* ବୃଦ୍ଧି *a price increase* ✪ ବିପରୀତ **decrease**

incredible /ɪnˈkredəbl/ *adjective* surprising and very difficult to believe ଅବିଶ୍ୱାସ୍ୟ, ବିଶ୍ୱାସଯୋଗ୍ୟ ହୋଇନଥିବା, ଅତୁଲ୍ୟ *Deepak told us an incredible story about his grandmother catching a thief.*

indeed /ɪnˈdiːd/ *adverb* really; certainly ସତରେ, ବାସ୍ତବରେ, ପ୍ରକୃତରେ *'Did you have a good holiday?' 'I did indeed.'*

indefinite /ɪnˈdefɪnət/ *adjective* not definite; not clear or certain ଅନିର୍ଦ୍ଦିଷ୍ଟ *They are staying for an indefinite length of time.* ✪ ବିପରୀତ **definite**

indefinitely *adverb* for a long time, perhaps for ever ଅନିର୍ଦ୍ଦିଷ୍ଟ କାଳ ପାଇଁ; ସବୁଦିନ ପାଇଁ *I can't wait indefinitely.*

independence /ˌɪndɪˈpendəns/ *noun* (*no plural*) the state of being free from another person, thing or country ସ୍ୱାଧୀନତା, ସ୍ୱାତନ୍ତ୍ର୍ୟ *America declared its independence from Britain in 1776.*

independent /ˌɪndɪˈpendənt/ *adjective* **1** not controlled by another person, thing or country ସ୍ୱାଧୀନ, ମୁକ୍ତ, ସ୍ୱାୟତ୍ତ *India has been independent since 1947.* **2** a person who is independent does not need help ସ୍ୱାବଲମ୍ବୀ *She lives alone now and *she is very independent.* ✪ ବିପରୀତ **dependent**

independently *adverb* ସ୍ୱାଧୀନ ଭାବରେ *She has been working independently ever since she left the company.*

index /ˈɪndeks/ *noun* (*plural* **indexes**) a list of words from A to Z at the end of a book. It tells you what things are in the book and where you can find them ବହି ଶେଷରେ ଦିଆଯାଇଥିବା ବର୍ଣ୍ଣାନୁକ୍ରମିକ ବିଷୟ ଓ ପୃଷ୍ଠା, ତାଲିକା

indicate /ˈɪndɪkeɪt/ *verb* (**indicates, indicating, indicated**) **1** show something, usually by pointing with your finger ଦେଖାଇ ଦେବା (ବିଶେଷତଃ ଆଙ୍ଗୁଠି ଦେଖାଇ) *Can you indicate your school on the map?* **2** give a sign about something ସଂକେତ ଦେବା, ସୂଚାଇବା *Black clouds indicate that it's going to rain.* **3** show that your car is going to turn by using a light ସଂକେତ ଆଲୁଅ ବା ଇଣ୍ଡିକେଟର୍ ଲାଇଟ୍ ଦ୍ୱାରା ଗାଡ଼ି ବୁଲାଇବା ସଂକେତ ଦେବା *You should indicate left now.*

indication /ˌɪndɪˈkeɪʃn/ *noun* something that shows something; a sign ସୂଚନା, ଆଭାସ, ଇଙ୍ଗିତ, ଚିହ୍ନ *He gave no indication that he was going to leave his job.*

indigestion /ˌɪndɪˈdʒestʃən/ *noun* (*no plural*) a feeling of discomfort caused by difficulty in digestion of food ବଦହଜମ, ଅଜୀର୍ଣ୍ଣ

indignant /ɪnˈdɪgnənt/ *adjective* angry because somebody has done or said something that you do not like or agree with କ୍ରୁଦ୍ଧ, ରାଗୀ, କ୍ଷୁବ୍ଧ *She was indignant when I said she was lazy.*

indigo /ˈɪndɪgəʊ/ *adjective* with a colour of very dark blue ଘନ ନୀଳ (ରଙ୍ଗ) *She has an indigo skirt.*

indigo *noun* very dark blue in colour ଘନନୀଳ ରଙ୍ଗ, ନୀଳ *I love indigo.*

indirect /ˌɪndəˈrekt/ *adjective* not straight or direct ଅପ୍ରତ୍ୟକ୍ଷ, ପରୋକ୍ଷ *We took an indirect route to avoid the traffic.* ✪ ବିପରୀତ **direct**[1]

indirectly *adverb* in an indirect way ପରୋକ୍ଷ ଭାବରେ ✪ ବିପରୀତ **directly**

individual[1] /ˌɪndɪˈvɪdʒuəl/ *noun* one person ଏକ ବ୍ୟକ୍ତି *Teachers must treat each child as an individual.*

individual[2] /ˌɪndɪˈvɪdʒuəl/ *adjective* **1** for only one person or thing ଅଲଗା, ପୃଥକ୍ *receive individual attention* **2** single and different ଏକକ ଓ ଭିନ୍ନ *Each individual country has its own flag.*

individually *adverb* separately; alone; not together ପୃଥକ୍ ଭାବରେ, ଅଲଗା ଅଲଗା ଭାବରେ *The teacher spoke to each student individually.*

indoor /ˈɪndɔː(r)/ *adjective* done or used inside a building ଘର ଭିତରର; ଘର ଭିତରେ କରାଯାଉଥିବା *an indoor swimming pool* ✪ ବିପରୀତ **outdoor**

indoors /ˌɪnˈdɔːz/ *adverb* in or into a building ଘର ଭିତରକୁ *Let's go indoors. I'm cold.* ✪ ବିପରୀତ **outdoors**

industrial /ɪnˈdʌstriəl/ *adjective* for or about industry ଶିଳ୍ପରେ ବ୍ୟବହୃତ, ଶିଳ୍ପ ସମ୍ବନ୍ଧୀୟ, ଶିଳ୍ପରେ ନିଯୁକ୍ତ *industrial machines*

industry /ˈɪndəstri/ *noun* **1** (*no plural*) the work of making things in factories କଳକାରଖାନାରେ ଜିନିଷ ତିଆରି କରିବା ପ୍ରକ୍ରିୟା; ଶିଳ୍ପ କାର୍ଯ୍ୟ *Is there much industry in your country?* **2** (*plural* **industries**) all the companies that make the same thing ଏକା ପ୍ରକାର ପଦାର୍ଥ ତିଆରି କରୁଥିବା ସବୁ ଶିଳ୍ପ ସଂସ୍ଥା *the car industry*

inedible /ɪnˈedəbl/ *adjective* that you cannot eat; not fit for eating ଅଖାଦ୍ୟ, ଖାଇବା ପାଇଁ ଅନୁପଯୁକ୍ତ *inedible wild berries* ✪ ବିପରୀତ **edible**

ineffective /ˌɪnɪˈfektɪv/ *adjective* something that is ineffective does not work well ନିଷ୍ଫଳ, ବ୍ୟର୍ଥ, ଅଫଳପ୍ରଦ *We found the new medicine ineffective.* ✪ ବିପରୀତ **effective**

inefficient /ˌɪnɪˈfɪʃnt/ *adjective* a person or thing that is inefficient does not work well or in the best way ଅଦକ୍ଷ, ଅପାରଗ, ଅସମର୍ଥ *This machine is very old and inefficient.* ✪ ବିପରୀତ **efficient**

inequality /ˌɪnɪˈkwɒləti/ *noun* (*plural* **inequalities**) the difference between groups of people because some have more money or power than others ଅସମାନତା, ଅସମତା ✪ ବିପରୀତ **equality**

inevitable /ɪnˈevɪtəbl/ *adjective* if something is inevitable, it will certainly happen ଅବଶ୍ୟମ୍ଭାବୀ, ଅପରିହାର୍ଯ୍ୟ, ନିଶ୍ଚିତ ଭାବେ ଘଟିବାକୁ ଥିବା *inevitable consequences of the war*

inevitably *adverb* ନିଶ୍ଚିତ ଭାବରେ, ଅପରିହାର୍ଯ୍ୟ ଭାବରେ *Building the new hospital will inevitably cost a lot of money.*

inexpensive /ˌɪnɪkˈspensɪv/ *adjective* something that is inexpensive does not cost a lot of money କମ୍ ଦାମ୍‌ର, ଶସ୍ତା ✪ ବିପରୀତ **expensive**

inexperienced /ˌɪnɪkˈspɪəriənst/ *adjective* if you are inexperienced, you do not know about something because you have not done it many times before ଅନଭିଜ୍ଞ, ନିର୍ଦ୍ଦିଷ୍ଟ କାମରେ ଅଭିଜ୍ଞତା ନଥିବା *an inexperienced driver* ✪ ବିପରୀତ **experienced**

infant /ˈɪnfənt/ *noun* a very young child ନବଜାତ ଶିଶୁ

infantry /ˈɪnfəntri/ *noun* (*no plural*) the part of the army that fights on foot ସେନାର ପଦାତିକ ବାହିନୀ *He serves in the infantry.*

infect /ɪnˈfekt/ *verb* (**infects, infecting, infected**) give a disease to somebody ଅନ୍ୟକୁ ରୋଗ ଦେବା, ରୋଗ ସଞ୍ଚାର କରିବା, ରୋଗ ବ୍ୟାପିବା

infected *adjective* full of germs that can make you ill ଜୀବାଣୁ ବା ଭୂତାଣୁ ପରିପୂର୍ଣ୍ଣ *Clean that cut or it could become infected.*

infection /ɪnˈfekʃn/ *noun* a disease; the spread of a disease ରୋଗ; ରୋଗର ସଂକ୍ରମଣ ବା ସଂଚାର *Murli has an ear infection.*

infectious /ɪnˈfekʃəs/ *adjective* something that is infectious goes easily from one person to another ସଂକ୍ରାମକ, ସଂକ୍ରମଣ ଦ୍ୱାରା ବ୍ୟାପ୍ତ *This disease is infectious.*

nferior /ɪnˈfɪəriə(r)/ *adjective* not as good or important as another person or thing (ଅନ୍ୟ ଠାରୁ) ନିକୃଷ୍ଟ, ଅପକୃଷ୍ଟ ✪ ବିପରୀତ **superior**

infertile /ɪnˈfɜːtaɪl/ *adjective* not good for growing crops ଅନୁର୍ବର ✪ ବିପରୀତ **fertile**

infinite /ˈɪnfɪnət/ *adjective* with no end; too much or too many to count or measure ସୀମାହୀନ, ଅସୀମ; ଅସଂଖ୍ୟ; ଅନନ୍ତ, ଅଶେଷ *There are an infinite number of stars in the sky.* ✪ ବିପରୀତ **finite**

infinitive /ɪnˈfɪnətɪv/ *noun* the simple form of a verb କର୍ତ୍ତା ନିରପେକ୍ଷ କ୍ରିୟା; ତୁମର୍ଥକ *'Eat', 'go' and 'play' are infinitives.*

infinity /ɪnˈfɪnəti/ *noun* the state of having no beginning and no end ଆଦି ଓ ଅନ୍ତ ନଥିବା ଅବସ୍ଥା; ଅକଳନୀୟ ସଂଖ୍ୟା, ଦୂରତା ବା ସମୟ; ଅସୀମତା *Space extends into infinity.*

inflammable /ɪnˈflæməbl/ *adjective* if something is inflammable, it can catch fire easily ସହଜରେ ଜଳି ପାରୁଥିବା, ଦହନଶୀଳ *Petrol is a highly inflammable liquid.*

inflammation /ˌɪnfləˈmeɪʃn/ *noun* a condition in which a part of your body becomes red, swollen and painful because of an infection or injury ଦେହର ଅଙ୍ଗରେ ଲାଲ୍ ପଡ଼ିଯିବା, ଫୁଲିଯିବା ଓ ଦରଜ ହେବା ଅବସ୍ଥା; ପ୍ରଦାହ *Pollution often causes inflammation of the eyes.*

inflate /ɪnˈfleɪt/ *verb* (**inflates, inflating, inflated**) fill something with air or gas to make it bigger ପବନ ବା ବାଷ୍ପ ଦ୍ୱାରା ଫୁଲାଇବା *He inflated the tyre.* ✪ ବିପରୀତ **deflate**

inflict /ɪnˈflɪkt/ *verb* (**inflicts, inflicting, inflicted**) force somebody to suffer something unpleasant ଆଘାତ କରିବା, କଷ୍ଟଦେବା *casualty inflicted on the enemy*

influence /ˈɪnfluəns/ *noun* (*no plural*) the power to change what somebody believes or does ପ୍ରଭାବ ପକାଇବା ଶକ୍ତି; ପ୍ରଭାବ *Television has a strong influence on people.*

influence *verb* (**influences, influencing, influenced**) change somebody or something; make somebody do what you want ପ୍ରଭାବ ପକାଇବା; ପ୍ରଭାବ ପକାଇ ପରିବର୍ତ୍ତନ ଆଣିବା; କିଛି କରିବା ପାଇଁ କାହାରି ଉପରେ ପ୍ରଭାବ ପକାଇବା *She is easily influenced by her friends.*

influenza /ˌɪnfluˈenzə/ *noun* ➪ **flu** ଦେଖନ୍ତୁ ।

inform /ɪnˈfɔːm/ *verb* (**informs, informing, informed**) tell something to somebody ଖବର ଦେବା, ଜଣାଇବା *She informed us that we would be going on a trip next week.*

informal /ɪnˈfɔːml/ *adjective* you use informal language or behave in an informal way in situations that are friendly and easy, not serious or important, and with people whom you know well ସାଦାସିଧା, ନୀତି ନିୟମ ଅନୁସାରେ ନ ହୋଇ ବନ୍ଧୁତ୍ୱପୂର୍ଣ୍ଣ ଭାବରେ ହୋଇଥିବା; ଅନୌପଚାରିକ ✪ ବିପରୀତ **formal**

information /ˌɪnfəˈmeɪʃn/ *noun* (*no plural*) what you tell somebody;

facts ଖବର, ବାର୍ତ୍ତା, ସଂବାଦ; ତଥ୍ୟ *Can you give me some information about trains to Goa?*

✪ ମନେ ରଖନ୍ତୁ ! ଆପଣ 'an information' କହିବା ଭୁଲ୍ ହେବ। ଆପଣ କହିବେ 'some information' ବା 'a piece of information'— *She gave me an interesting piece of information.*

informative /ɪnˈfɔːmətɪv/ *adjective* with a lot of information ବହୁ ଖବର ବା ତଥ୍ୟ ଥିବା। *an informative programme on television*

ingredient /ɪnˈgriːdiənt/ *noun* one of the things that you add when you are making something to eat ଉପାଦାନ *The ingredients for this cake are flour, butter, sugar and eggs.*

inhabitant /ɪnˈhæbɪtənt/ *noun* a person or an animal that lives in a place ଅଧିବାସୀ, ସ୍ଥାୟୀ ନିବାସୀ *The town has 30,000 inhabitants.*

inhale /ɪnˈheɪl/ *verb* (**inhales, inhaling, inhaled**) breathe in ପ୍ରଶ୍ୱାସ ନେବା ✪ ବିପରୀତ **exhale**

inherit /ɪnˈherɪt/ *verb* (**inherits, inheriting, inherited**) receive something from somebody who has died ଉତ୍ତରାଧିକାରୀ ଭାବରେ (ସମ୍ପତ୍ତି ବା ଉପାଧି) ପାଇବା *Shama has just inherited a house from her grandmother.*

inheritance *noun* something that you inherit ଉତ୍ତରାଧିକାରୀ ଭାବରେ ପାଇଥିବା ସମ୍ପତ୍ତି, ଉପାଧି ଇତ୍ୟାଦି

initial /ɪˈnɪʃl/ *adjective* first ପ୍ରାରମ୍ଭିକ, ପ୍ରାଥମିକ, ଆଦ୍ୟ *Our initial plan was to go to Ahmedabad, but then we decided to go to Mumbai.*

initially /ɪˈnɪʃəli/ *adverb* in the beginning; at first ଆରମ୍ଭରେ, ପ୍ରଥମରେ *Initially, she enjoyed the work.*

initials /ɪˈnɪʃlz/ *noun* (*plural*) the first letters of all your names ବ୍ୟକ୍ତି ନାମରେ ଥିବା ଶବ୍ଦମାନଙ୍କର ପ୍ରଥମ ଅକ୍ଷରର ସମ *Rajat Kumar Ray's initials are R.K.R.*

initiative /ɪˈnɪʃətɪv/ *noun* **1** (*no plural*) the ability to do something that is necessary without waiting for someone else to tell you to do it ସ୍ୱତଃ ପ୍ରବୃତ୍ତ ଉଦ୍ୟମ (କୌଣସି କାମ ଆରମ୍ଭ କରିବାକୁ) *She took the initiative to wash the dishes after dinner.* **2** (*plural* **initiatives**) a new step or action taken officially to achieve something (ସରକାରୀ ବା ଔପଚାରିକ ଭାବରେ ନିଆଯାଇଥିବା) ପ୍ରାଥମିକ ବା ନୂତନ ପଦକ୍ଷେପ *government initiatives to increase employment opportunities*

inject /ɪnˈdʒekt/ *verb* (**injects, injecting, injected**) use a special needle to put a drug into a person's body ଇଞ୍ଜେକ୍ସନ୍ ଦେବା, ଛୁଞ୍ଚିଲଗା ସିରିଞ୍ଜ୍ ବା ପିଚ୍‌କାରି ଦ୍ୱାରା ଔଷଧକୁ ଦେହ ଭିତରେ ପ୍ରବେଶ କରାଇବା

injection /ɪnˈdʒekʃn/ *noun* ଇଞ୍ଜେକ୍ସନ୍ ଦେବା *The doctor gave the baby an injection.*

injure /ˈɪndʒə(r)/ *verb* (**injures, injuring, injured**) hurt somebody or something ଆଘାତ ବା କ୍ଷତ କରିବା *She injured her arm when she was playing tennis.*

injured *adjective* ଆଘାତପ୍ରାପ୍ତ *The injured woman was taken to the hospital.*

injury /ˈɪndʒəri/ *noun* (*plural* **injuries**) harm done to the body of a person or an animal ଶାରୀରିକ କ୍ଷତି, କ୍ଷତ *He had serious head injuries.*

injustice /ɪnˈdʒʌstɪs/ *noun* the act of not being treated fairly ଅନ୍ୟାୟ, ଅବିଚାର *She always fought against poverty and injustice.* ✪ ବିପରୀତ **justice**

ink /ɪŋk/ *noun* a coloured liquid for writing and printing କାଳି, ସ୍ୟାହି

inland /ˈɪnlænd/ *adjective* in the middle of a country, not near the sea ଦେଶର ଅଭ୍ୟନ୍ତରରେ ଥିବା, ଅଭ୍ୟନ୍ତରୀଣ *an inland lake*

in-laws *noun* (*no singular*) the relatives by marriage; the parents or other relations of your husband or wife ବୈବାହିକ ସମ୍ପର୍କ ଫଳରେ ହୋଇଥିବା ବନ୍ଧୁବାନ୍ଧବ *Her in-laws live in Bangalore.*

inn /ɪn/ *noun* (in the West) a house or small hotel, usually in the country, where you can buy drinks and food and stay the night (ପାଶ୍ଚାତ୍ୟ ଦେଶର ଗାଁ ଗହଳିରେ ଥିବା) ଖାଇବା ଓ ରହିବା ଯୋଗାଉଥିବା ଛୋଟ ହୋଟେଲ ବା ପାନ୍ଥଶାଳା ✪ **Inn** ସାଧାରଣତଃ ହୋଟେଲ, ପାନ୍ଥଶାଳା ଇତ୍ୟାଦିକୁ ବୁଝାଏ । *Holiday Inn*

inner /ˈɪnə(r)/ *adjective* of the inside; near the centre ଆଭ୍ୟନ୍ତରୀଣ; କେନ୍ଦ୍ର ପାଖର *the inner walls* ✪ ବିପରୀତ **outer**

innermost /ˈɪnəməʊst/ *adjective* nearest to the centre ଅନ୍ତରତମ, କେନ୍ଦ୍ରୀୟ *Mercury is the innermost planet of the solar system.* ✪ ବିପରୀତ **outermost**

innocent /ˈɪnəsnt/ *adjective* if you are innocent, you have not done wrong ନିର୍ଦ୍ଦୋଷ, ନିରୀହ *The police say the servant stole the money, but I think he's innocent.* ✪ ବିପରୀତ **guilty 1**

innocence /ˈɪnəsns/ *noun* (*no plural*) ନିର୍ଦ୍ଦୋଷତା, ନିରୀହତା *The prisoner's family are sure of his innocence.* ✪ ବିପରୀତ **guilt 1**

inoculate /ɪˈnɒkjuleɪt/ *verb* (**inoculates, inoculating, inoculated**) protect a person or animal against a disease by giving an injection of a small amount of germs of that disease ଟୀକା ଦେବା; ଟୀକା ବା ଇଞ୍ଜେକ୍ସନ୍ ଦ୍ୱାରା ରୋଗର ପ୍ରତିଷେଧନ ବା ନିରୋଧ କରିବା *Has she been inoculated against chicken pox?*

inoculation /ɪˌnɒkjuˈleɪʃn/ *noun* the process of protecting a person or an animal from a disease by injecting a small amount of germs of the same disease ଟୀକାଦାନ; ଟୀକାଦାନ ଦ୍ୱାରା ରୋଗନିରୋଧ

inquire, inquiry = **enquire, enquiry**

insane /ɪnˈseɪn/ *adjective* mad ପାଗଳ, ଉନ୍ମତ୍ତ

inscription /ɪnˈskrɪpʃn/ *noun* words that are written or cut on something ଲିଖନ, ଖୋଦନ; ଶିଳାଲିପି, ମୁଦ୍ରାଲିପି ଇତ୍ୟାଦି *Ashokan inscriptions*

insect /ˈɪnsekt/ *noun* a very small animal that has six legs and a body divided into three parts ପୋକ, କୀଟ, ପତଙ୍ଗ (ଏମାନେ ସାଧାରଣତଃ ଛ' ଗୋଡ଼ିଆ ଓ ଏମାନଙ୍କ ଦେହ ତିନି ଭାଗରେ ବିଭକ୍ତ) *Ants,*

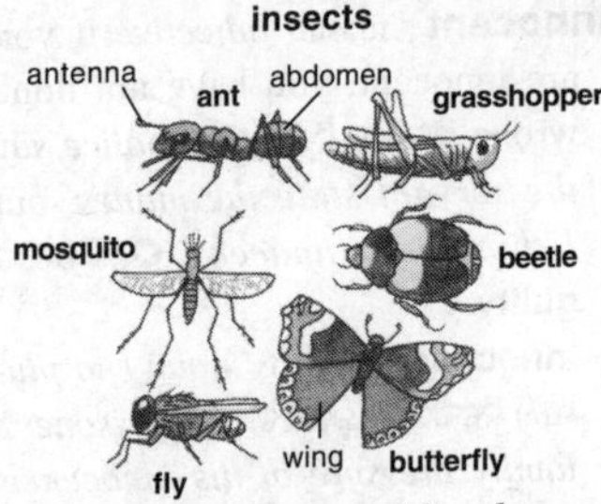

flies, butterflies and beetles are all insects.

insecticide /ɪnˈsektɪsaɪd/ *noun* a substance that is used to kill insects that are harmful to crops and plants କୀଟମରା ଔଷଧ, ପୋକମରା ଔଷଧ

insectivore /ɪnˈsektɪvɔː(r)/ *noun* an animal that eats insects କୀଟଭୋଜୀ ପଶୁ *Lizards and spiders are insectivores.* ➪ **carnivore, herbivore** ଓ **omnivore** ମଧ୍ୟ ଦେଖନ୍ତୁ ।

insectivorous *adjective* କୀଟଭୋଜୀ, କୀଟପତଙ୍ଗ ଖାଉଥିବା *insectivorous animals*

insecure /ˌɪnsɪˈkjʊə(r)/ *adjective* not safe or firm ଅସୁରକ୍ଷିତ, ବିପଦପୂର୍ଣ୍ଣ, ନିରାପତ୍ତାହୀନ *He was insecure about his job.* ✪ ବିପରୀତ **secure**

insert /ɪnˈsɜːt/ *verb* (**inserts, inserting, inserted**) put something into something or between two things ପୂରାଇବା, ଗଳାଇବା, ଭର୍ତ୍ତି କରିବା *Insert the key in the lock.*

inside[1] /ˌɪnˈsaɪd/ *noun* the part near the middle of something ଭିତରପଟ, ଭିତର ଭାଗ *The inside of a pear is white and the outside is green or yellow.* ✪ ବିପରୀତ **outside**[1]

inside out with the wrong side on the outside ଭିତରପଟ ବାହାରକୁ ଟାଣି ଆଣିବା (ପକେଟ୍, ଜାମା ଇତ୍ୟାଦିର) *You've got your sweater on inside out.*

inside[2] /ˌɪnˈsaɪd/ *adjective* in or near the middle ଭିତରପଟେ ଥିବା, ମଧ୍ୟସ୍ଥ *the inside pages of a newspaper.* ✪ ବିପରୀତ **outside**[2]

inside[3] /ˌɪnˈsaɪd/ *preposition, adverb* in or to the inside of something ଭିତରେ, ଭିତରକୁ *What's inside the box?* ○ *It's raining—let's go inside.* ✪ ବିପରୀତ **outside**[3]

insignificant /ˌɪnsɪgˈnɪfɪkənt/ *adjective* of no importance or value ନଗନ୍ୟ, ଗୁରୁତ୍ୱହୀନ, ମୂଲ୍ୟହୀନ ✪ ବିପରୀତ **significant**

insist /ɪnˈsɪst/ *verb* (**insists, insisting, insisted**) say very strongly that you must do or have something or that something must happen ଦାବି କରିବା, ଜିଦ୍ କରିବା, ଜିଗର କରିବା *I said I would walk to the station, but Rahul insisted on driving me there.*

insoluble /ɪnˈsɒljəbl/ *adjective* that cannot be dissolved in a liquid (ତରଳ ପଦାର୍ଥରେ) ଅଦ୍ରବଣୀୟ, ମିଳେଇ ଯାଉ ନଥିବା *Sand is insoluble in water.* ✪ ବିପରୀତ **soluble**

inspect /ɪnˈspekt/ *verb* (**inspects, inspecting, inspected**) look at something carefully ଭଲଭାବେ ପରୀକ୍ଷା କରି ଦେଖିବା, ପରିଦର୍ଶନ କରିବା, ତଦାରଖ କରିବା, ଯାଞ୍ଚ କରିବା *I inspected the car before I bought it.*

inspection /ɪn'spekʃn/ *noun* the act of looking at something carefully ତନ୍ନତନ୍ନ ପରୀକ୍ଷା, ପରିଦର୍ଶନ, ତଦାରଖ, ଯାଞ୍ଚ *The police made an inspection of the house.*

inspector /ɪn'spektə(r)/ *noun* **1** a person whose job is to see that things are done correctly ପରିଦର୍ଶକ, ନିରୀକ୍ଷକ *On the train, the inspector asked to see my ticket.* **2** a police officer (ଡି.ଏସ୍.ପି.ଙ୍କ ତଳ ପାହ୍ୟାର) ପୁଲିସ୍ ଅଧିକାରୀ ବା ଅଫିସର, ଇନ୍ସପେକ୍ଟର୍

inspiration /ˌɪnspə'reɪʃn/ *noun* a person or thing that gives you ideas which help you do something good, for example write or paint; (ଲେଖିବା, ଚିତ୍ରାଙ୍କନ କରିବା ଇତ୍ୟାଦି ପାଇଁ) ପ୍ରେରଣା ଦେଉଥିବା ବ୍ୟକ୍ତି ବା ପଦାର୍ଥ, ହଠାତ୍ ମନକୁ ଆସିଥିବା ସୃଜନଶୀଳ ଭାବନା; ପ୍ରେରଣା *The beauty of the mountains is a great inspiration to many artists.*

install /ɪn'stɔːl/ *verb* (**installs, installing, installed**) put a new thing in its place so it is ready to use ବ୍ୟବହାର ପାଇଁ (ଯନ୍ତ୍ର ଇତ୍ୟାଦି) ସ୍ଥାପନ କରିବା ବା ଲଗାଇବା *She installed a new washing machine.*

installation /ˌɪnstə'leɪʃn/ *noun* the act of fixing something in a place so that it can be used ସ୍ଥାପନା, ନିବେଶନ *charges for installation of the water cooler*

instalment /ɪn'stɔːlmənt/ *noun* **1** one part of a long story on radio or television, or in a magazine ରେଡିଓ, ଟେଲିଭିଜନ ବା ପତ୍ରିକାରେ ପ୍ରକାଶିତ ଲମ୍ବା ଗପର ଏକ ଭାଗ ବା କିସ୍ତି **2** a part of the cost of something that you pay each week or month, for example ସାପ୍ତାହିକ ବା ମାସିକ ଭାବେ ଦିଆଯାଉଥିବା କୌଣସି ପଦାର୍ଥର ଦାମର କିସ୍ତି *She's paying for her new television in twelve monthly instalments.*

instance /'ɪnstəns/ *noun*

for instance as an example ଉଦାହରଣ, ବିଶେଷ ଦୃଷ୍ଟାନ୍ତ *There are many things to see in Delhi—for instance, the Qutub Minar and the Red Fort.*

instant /'ɪnstənt/ *adjective* that happens very quickly; immediate ତତ୍‌କ୍ଷଣାତ୍, ତୁରନ୍ତ, ସାଙ୍ଗେ ସାଙ୍ଗେ *The film was an instant success.*

instant coffee *noun* (*no plural*) coffee that you can make quickly with coffee powder and hot water କଫି ପାଉଡର୍ ପକାଇ କରାଯାଉଥିବା ଯାହା ତତ୍‌କ୍ଷଣାତ୍ ପ୍ରସ୍ତୁତ ହୋଇଯାଏ

instantly *adverb* immediately; at once ତତ୍‌କ୍ଷଣାତ୍, ସାଙ୍ଗେ ସାଙ୍ଗେ *I asked him a question and he replied instantly.*

instead /ɪn'sted/ *adverb* in the place of somebody or something ବଦଳରେ, ପରିବର୍ତ୍ତେ *Shalini can't go to the meeting so I will go instead.*

instead of *preposition* in the place of ପରିବର୍ତ୍ତେ *Can you come at 7.30 p.m. instead of 8.00 p.m.?*

instinct /'ɪnstɪŋkt/ *noun* something that makes people and animals do certain things without thinking or learning about them (ଜନ୍ମଗତ ବା ସହଜାତ) ପ୍ରବୃତ୍ତି, ପ୍ରତିକ୍ରିୟା ବା ଆଚରଣ *Birds build their nests by instinct.*

institute /ˈɪnstɪtjuːt/ *noun* an organization that has a special purpose; the building that is used by this organization ବିଶେଷ କାମ ପାଇଁ ଗଠିତ ସଂସ୍ଥା; ଏହି ସଂସ୍ଥାର କାର୍ଯ୍ୟାଳୟ *the Institute of Science*

institution /ˌɪnstɪˈtjuːʃn/ *noun* an important organization like a bank, school or university ବ୍ୟାଙ୍କ, ସ୍କୁଲ୍ ବା ୟୁନିଭର୍ସିଟି ପରି ଏକ ବିଶିଷ୍ଟ ସଂସ୍ଥା *There are many educational institutions in our town.*

instruct /ɪnˈstrʌkt/ *verb* (**instructs, instructing, instructed**) **1** tell somebody what they must do ନିର୍ଦ୍ଦେଶ ଦେବା *He instructed the driver to take him to the hotel.* **2** teach somebody ପାଠ ପଢ଼ାଇବା, ଶିକ୍ଷାଦାନ କରିବା, ବତାଇବା *She instructed me in the use of computers.*

instruction /ɪnˈstrʌkʃn/ *noun* words that tell you what you must do or how to do something ନିର୍ଦ୍ଦେଶ; ଶିକ୍ଷାଦାନ *Read the instructions on the box before you make the cake.*

instructor /ɪnˈstrʌktə(r)/ *noun* a person who teaches you how to do something ଶିକ୍ଷକ, ଉପଦେଷ୍ଟା *a driving instructor*

instrument /ˈɪnstrəmənt/ *noun* **1** a thing that you use for doing a special job ଯନ୍ତ୍ର, ହତିଆର, ଉପକରଣ *medical instruments* **2** a thing that you use for playing music ବାଦ୍ୟଯନ୍ତ୍ର *Violins and sitars are musical instruments.* ◦ *What instrument do you play?*

insufficient /ˌɪnsəˈfɪʃnt/ *adjective* not enough ଅପ୍ରଚୁର, କମ୍, ଅଳ୍ପ *The food was insufficient for ten people.* ✪ ବିପରୀତ **sufficient**

insulate /ˈɪnsjuleɪt/ *verb* (of a substance) not allow heat or electricity to pass through ଉତ୍ତାପ, ବିଦ୍ୟୁତ୍, ଧ୍ୱନି ଇତ୍ୟାଦିରୁ ସୁରକ୍ଷିତ ରଖିବା ପାଇଁ ନିରୋଧକ ପଦାର୍ଥ ଆଚ୍ଛାଦନ କରିବା।

insult /ɪnˈsʌlt/ *verb* (**insults, insulting, insulted**) be rude to somebody ଅପମାନ ଦେବା, ଅବମାନନା କରିବା, ଗାଳିଦେବା *She insulted my brother by calling him fat.*

insurance /ɪnˈʃɔːrəns/ *noun* (*no plural*) an agreement where you pay some amount of money to a company regularly so that it will give you a lot of money if something bad happens ବୀମା; ନିର୍ଦ୍ଧାରିତ ଧନ ଦେଲାପରେ କ୍ଷତି, ନଷ୍ଟ ବା ଆଘାତ ଜନିତ କ୍ଷତିପୂରଣ ପାଇବା ପାଇଁ ବୀମା କମ୍ପାନୀ ସହ ଚୁକ୍ତି

intact /ɪnˈtækt/ *adjective* if something is intact, it is not harmed ଅକ୍ଷତ, ଅକ୍ଷୁର୍ଣ୍ଣ *The Iron Pillar near the Qutub Minar remains intact to this day.*

integer /ˈɪntɪdʒə(r)/ *noun* a whole number, such as 1, 2 and 3 (and not a fraction) ୧, ୨, ୩ ପରି ପୂର୍ଣ୍ଣସଂଖ୍ୟା (ଭଗ୍ନାଂଶ ନୁହେଁ) ➪ **fraction** ଦେଖନ୍ତୁ।

integrate /ˈɪntɪgreɪt/ *verb* (**integrates, integrating, integrated**) bring together many people or things as a whole or to work together as a group ଏକାଠି କରିବା, ଏକୀଭୂତ କରିବା, ମିଳିମିଶି ଏକ ଗୋଷ୍ଠୀ ଭାବେ କାମ କରିବା ପାଇଁ ଏକତ୍ରିତ କରିବା

integration /ˌɪntɪˈgreɪʃn/ *noun* ଏକତା, ଏକତ୍ରିକରଣ *national integration*

intelligence /ɪnˈtelɪdʒəns/ *noun* (*no plural*) the ability to think, learn and understand quickly and well ଜ୍ଞାନ; ବୁଦ୍ଧି, ଧୀଶକ୍ତି, ଚାତୁର୍ଯ୍ୟ *He is a man of great intelligence.*

intelligent /ɪnˈtelɪdʒənt/ *adjective* able to think, learn and understand quickly and well ବୁଦ୍ଧିମାନ୍, ଚତୁର *Their daughter is very intelligent.*

intend /ɪnˈtend/ *verb* (**intends, intending, intended**) plan to do something ଉଦ୍ଦେଶ୍ୟ ରଖିବା, ଇଚ୍ଛାପୋଷଣ କରିବା, ଅଭିପ୍ରାୟ କରିବା *When do you intend to go to Kolkata?*

intense /ɪnˈtens/ *adjective* very great or strong ପ୍ରବଳ, ତୀବ୍ର *intense pain*

intensity /ɪnˈtensəti/ *noun* (*plural* **intensities**) the strength or power of something ଶକ୍ତିର ପରିମାଣ; ତୀବ୍ରତା, ପ୍ରାବଲ୍ୟ *Such was the intensity of the earthquake that all the houses collapsed.*

intensive /ɪnˈtensɪv/ *adjective* **1** involving a lot of work that is done in a short period of time ଅଳ୍ପ ସମୟରେ ବହୁ କାମଯାଉଥିବା *an intensive training programme* **2** thorough and with a lot of care ବହୁତ ଯତ୍ନ ନିଆ ଯାଉଥିବା, ତନ୍ନତନ୍ନ ଭାବେ କରାଯାଉଥିବା *an intensive search for the missing boy*

intention /ɪnˈtenʃn/ *noun* what you plan to do ଉଦ୍ଦେଶ୍ୟ, ଅଭିପ୍ରାୟ *Their intention is to win the contest.*

interactive /ˌɪntərˈæktɪv/ *adjective* if something is interactive, it involves two or more people who work together and have an influence on each other ପରସ୍ପର ସହ ଆଦାନପ୍ରଦାନ ଉପରେ ଆଧାରିତ *interactive teaching methods*

interconnect /ˌɪntəˈkʌnekt/ *verb* (**interconnects, interconnecting, interconnected**) connect with or to things of the same kind ପରସ୍ପର ସଂଯୋଗ କରିବା

interest[1] /ˈɪntrəst/ *noun* **1** (*no plural*) wanting to know or learn about somebody or something କୌଣସି ବିଷୟ ଜାଣିବା ପାଇଁ କୌତୂହଳ ବା ଉଦ୍‌ବେଗ, ଇଚ୍ଛା *He read the story with interest.* **2** (*plural* **interests**) something that you like doing or learning about ଆସକ୍ତି ଥିବା କାମ ବା ଶିକ୍ଷା *His interests are computers and rock music.* **3** (*no plural*) the extra money that you pay back if you borrow money or that you receive if you put money in a bank ସୁଧ, କଳନ୍ତର

interest[2] /ˈɪntrəst/ *verb* (**interests, interesting, interested**) make somebody want to know more ଆଗ୍ରହ ଜାତ କରାଇବା, ଆଗ୍ରହାନ୍ୱିତ ହେବା *History doesn't interest her.*

interested *adjective* if you are interested in somebody or something, you want to know more about them ଆଗ୍ରହାନ୍ୱିତ, କୌତୂହଳୀ *Are you interested in cars?*

interesting *adjective* a person or thing that is interesting makes you want to know more about him /her/it କୌତୂହଳଜନକ, ଦୃଷ୍ଟି ଆକର୍ଷକ, ଆଗ୍ରହ ଯାତକାର *This book is very interesting.* ○ *That's an interesting idea!* ✪ ବିପରୀତ **uninteresting, dull 2** ବା **boring**

interfere /ˌɪntəˈfɪə(r)/ *verb* (**interferes, interfering, interfered**) try to do something with or for somebody, when they do not want your help ହସ୍ତକ୍ଷେପ କରିବା, ବାଧାଦେବା *Don't interfere! Let Neeraj decide what he wants to do.*

interior /ɪnˈtɪəriə(r)/ *noun* the inside part ଭିତର ଭାଗ, ଅଭ୍ୟନ୍ତର *We painted the interior of the house white.* ✪ ବିପରୀତ **exterior**

interjection /ˌɪntəˈdʒekʃn/ *noun* a word or phrase that expresses happiness, surprise or pain ଉତ୍ତେଜିତ ମନୋଭାବ (ଖୁସି, ଆଶ୍ଚର୍ଯ୍ୟ ବା କଷ୍ଟ) ପ୍ରକାଶକ ଅବ୍ୟୟ ପଦ *'Hurray!', 'Oh!' and 'Alas!' are interjections.*

internal /ɪnˈtɜːnl/ *adjective* of or on the inside ଆଭ୍ୟନ୍ତରୀଣ, ଅଭ୍ୟନ୍ତରରେ ଥିବା ବା ହୋଇଥିବା *He has internal injuries* ✪ ବିପରୀତ **external**

internally *adverb* on the inside ଅଭ୍ୟନ୍ତରୀଣ ଭାବରେ, ଭିତରିଆ ଭାବରେ, ଭିତରୁ

international /ˌɪntəˈnæʃnəl/ *adjective* of or between different countries ଆନ୍ତର୍ଜାତିକ, ଆନ୍ତଃରାଷ୍ଟ୍ରୀୟ *an international flight* ➪ **domestic 2** ଦେଖନ୍ତୁ।

Internet /ˈɪntənet/ *noun* (*no plural*) a very large network of computers that are interconnected. It helps you to find information from around the world on your computer and to send messages to other computers ବହୁ କମ୍ପ୍ୟୁଟର୍ ସଂଯୋଗରେ ଗଚ୍ଛିତ ବହୁ ବିଷୟର ତଥ୍ୟ ଥିବା ତଥ୍ୟାଗାର ଯେଉଁଥିରୁ ତଥ୍ୟ ଆହରଣ କର ଯାଇପାରେ ଓ ଯେଉଁ ସଂଯୋଗ ଦ୍ୱାରା ଅନ୍ୟ ପାଖକୁ ଚିଠିପତ୍ର ପଠା ଯାଇପାରେ ✪ **Internet** କୁ ସଂକ୍ଷେପରେ **the Net** କୁହାଯାଏ।

interpret /ɪnˈtɜːprɪt/ *verb* (**interprets, interpreting, interpreted**) **1** say in one language what somebody has said in another language ମୌଖିକ ଭାବେ ଗୋଟିଏ ଭାଷାରୁ ଅନ୍ୟ ଭାଷାକୁ ଅନୁବାଦ ବା ଭାଷାନ୍ତର କରିବା *I can't understand Marathi—can you interpret it for me?* **2** understand, explain or view something in a particular way ଅର୍ଥ ବୁଝାଇବା, ବ୍ୟାଖ୍ୟା କରିବା *interpret Wordsworth's poems*

interpreter *noun* a person who translates what somebody has said in one language into another ମୌଖିକ ଅନୁବାଦକ *The president was accompanied by an interpreter when he went to Japan.*

interpretation /ɪnˌtɜːprɪˈteɪʃn/ *noun* the way in which something is interpreted ବ୍ୟାଖ୍ୟା, ସମାଲୋଚନା

interrogation /ɪnˌterəˈɡeɪʃn/ *noun* the act of asking somebody a lot of questions, often as part of an enquiry and usually in a strict and harsh way ପ୍ରଶ୍ନ କରିବା ବା ପଚରାଉଚୁରା କରିବା ପ୍ରକ୍ରିୟା

interrupt /ˌɪntəˈrʌpt/ *verb* (**interrupts, interrupting, interrupted**) **1** stop somebody from speaking or doing something by saying or doing something yourself କିଛି କହି ବା କରି ଅନ୍ୟର କଥା ବା କାମରେ ବାଧା ଦେବା, ଅନ୍ତରାୟ ସୃଷ୍ଟି କରିବା *Please don't interrupt me when I'm speaking.* **2** stop something for a time କିଛି କାମ ଅଳ୍ପ ସମୟ ପାଇଁ ବନ୍ଦ କରିବା ବା କରାଇବା *The game was interrupted by rain for two hours.*

interruption /ˌɪntəˈrʌpʃn/ *noun* ବାଧା, ପ୍ରତିବନ୍ଧକ, ବ୍ୟାଘାତ, ଅନ୍ତରାୟ *He worked for six hours without interruption.*

intersect /ˌɪntəˈsekt/ *verb* (**intersects, intersecting, intersected**) when two lines or roads intersect, they meet or cross each other at a point (ରେଖା, ରାସ୍ତା ଇତ୍ୟାଦି) ପରସ୍ପରକୁ ଛେଦ କରିବା *All the diameters of a circle intersect at the centre.*

interval /ˈɪntəvl/ *noun* **1** a short time between two events ବିରତି, ବିରାମ *She has worked for 25 years, except for a brief interval of two months.* **2** a short break between parts of a movie or play (ସିନେମା ବା ନାଟକର ମଝିରେ ଦିଆଯାଉଥିବା) ବିରତି ବା ମଧ୍ୟାନ୍ତର *have snacks during the interval*

intervene /ˌɪntəˈviːn/ *verb* (**intervenes, intervening, intervened**) **1** interrupt somebody when they are speaking or doing something କେହି କିଛି କହିବା ବା କରିବା ବେଳେ ବାଧା ଦେବା ବା ମଝିରେ ପଶି କହିବା *'He always intervenes when I am speaking,' she protested loudly.* **2** get involved in something to prevent a bad situation from getting worse ହସ୍ତକ୍ଷେପ କରିବା; କୌଣସି ବିଗିଡୁଥିବା କାମରେ ହସ୍ତକ୍ଷେପ କରି ତାର ଉନ୍ନତି ସାଧନ କରିବା *The principal intervened personally to end the dispute between the two teachers.*

interview /ˈɪntəvjuː/ *noun* **1** a meeting when somebody asks you questions to decide if you are right for a job or for admission to a school or college (ଚାକିରି ବା ସ୍କୁଲ୍ କଲେଜ୍‌ରେ ପ୍ରବେଶ ପାଇଁ) ମୌଖିକ ପରୀକ୍ଷା **2** a meeting when somebody answers questions for a newspaper or for a television or radio programme ଖବରକାଗଜ, ରେଡ଼ିଓ ବା ଟେଲିଭିଜନରେ ପ୍ରକାଶ ପାଇଁ କାହାରି ସହ କଥାବାର୍ତ୍ତା, ସାକ୍ଷାତ୍‌କାର *There was an interview with the Prime Minister on TV last night.*

interview *verb* (**interviews, interviewing, interviewed**) ask somebody questions in an interview ସାକ୍ଷାତ୍‌କାରରେ ପ୍ରଶ୍ନ ପଚାରିବା

intestine /ɪnˈtestɪn/ *noun* a long tube in the body that carries food from the stomach to the place where it leaves the body ଖାଦ୍ୟ ନଳୀର ନିମ୍ନ ଭାଗ, ଅନ୍ତ୍ର, ଅନ୍ତ ବୁଜୁଳା, ଅନ୍ତ୍ରନାଡ *large/small intestine*

into /ˈɪntə; ˈɪntu; ˈɪntuː/ *preposition* **1** to the middle or the inside of something ଭିତରକୁ *Come into the house.* ✪ ବିପରୀତ **out of 1** **2** a word that shows how somebody or something changes ରେ, କୁ (ବଦଳି ଯିବା, ପାଲଟି ଯିବା) *When it is very cold, water changes into ice.* **3** against something ରେ, ଦେହରେ (ବାଡ଼େଇ ହେବା ଇତ୍ୟାଦି) *The car crashed into a tree.*

intransitive /ɪnˈtrænsətɪv/ *adjective* an intransitive verb is one that is used without a direct object. For example, in the sentence 'He died suddenly', the verb 'die' is intransitive ଅକର୍ମକ (କ୍ରିୟା) ➪ **transitive** ଦେଖନ୍ତୁ।

intricate /ˈɪntrɪkət/ *adjective* having many small details or parts put together in a complicated way ଜଟିଳ *This novel has an intricate plot.*

introduce /ˌɪntrəˈdjuːs/ *verb* (**introduces, introducing, introduced**) **1** bring people together for the first time and tell each of them the name of the other ନାମ ଇତ୍ୟାଦି କହି ପରିଚୟ କରାଇବା ବା ଦେବା *She introduced me to her brother.* **2** bring in something new ନୂଆ ଜିନିଷ ପ୍ରଚଳିତ କରିବା *This law was introduced in 1990.*

introduce yourself tell somebody your name ନିଜର ପରିଚୟ ଦେବା *He introduced himself to me.*

introduction /ˌɪntrəˈdʌkʃn/ *noun* **1** (*plural* **introductions**) the act of bringing people together to meet each other ପରିଚୟ ପ୍ରଦାନ **2** (*no plural*) the act of bringing in something new ନୂଆ ଜିନିଷର ପ୍ରଚଳନ *the introduction of computers in schools* **3** (*plural* **introductions**) a piece of writing at the beginning of a book that tells you about the book (ବହିର) ମୁଖବନ୍ଧ, ଭୂମିକା

invade /ɪnˈveɪd/ *verb* (**invades, invading, invaded**) go into another country to attack it (ଅନ୍ୟ ଦେଶକୁ) ଆକ୍ରମଣ କରିବା

invader *noun* a person who invades ଆକ୍ରମଣକାରୀ

invalid[1] /ɪnˈvælɪd/ *adjective* something that is invalid is not officially acceptable ଅଚଳ, ଅକାମୀ *an invalid contract*

invalid[2] /ˈɪnvəlɪd/ *noun* a person who is very ill and needs another person to look after him/her ଅସୁସ୍ଥତା ଯୋଗୁଁ ଦୁର୍ବଳ ବା ଅଚଳ ହୋଇଥିବା ବ୍ୟକ୍ତି

invaluable /ɪnˈvæljuəbl/ *adjective* very useful ଅମୂଲ୍ୟ *Your help was invaluable.*

invasion /ɪnˈveɪʒn/ *noun* a time when an army from one country goes into another country to attack it ଗୋଟିଏ ଦେଶର ଅନ୍ୟ ଦେଶ ଉପରେ ଆକ୍ରମଣ ବା ଯୁଦ୍ଧ ଅଭିଯାନ *Germany's invasion of Poland in 1939*

invent /ɪnˈvent/ *verb* (**invents, inventing, invented**) **1** make or think of something for the first time ଉଦ୍ଭାବନ କରିବା, ନୂଆ ପଦାର୍ଥ ସୃଷ୍ଟି କରିବା *Who invented the bicycle?* **2** tell something that is not true (ମିଛ କଥା) ସୃଷ୍ଟି କରିବା *She invented a story about where she lost her purse last night.*

inventor *noun* a person who makes or thinks of something new ଉଦ୍ଭାବକ, ନୂଆ କଥା ସୃଷ୍ଟି କରିଥିବା ବ୍ୟକ୍ତି

invention /ɪnˈvenʃn/ *noun* **1** (*plural* **inventions**) a thing that somebody has made for the first time ଉଦ୍ଭାବନ କରିଥିବା ପଦାର୍ଥ **2** (*no plural*) inventing something ଉଦ୍ଭାବନ *The invention of the telephone changed the world.*

inverse /ˌɪnˈvɜːs/ *adjective* opposite to something in amount or position; in a reverse way ବିପରୀତ, ପ୍ରତୀପ *inverse relation*

invertebrate /ɪnˈvɜːtɪbrət/ *noun* an animal with a soft body that is not supported by a backbone ଅମେରୁଦଣ୍ଡୀ, ମେରୁଦଣ୍ଡବିହୀନ (ପ୍ରାଣୀ) *Worms and insects are invertebrates.* ✪ ବିପରୀତ **vertebrate**

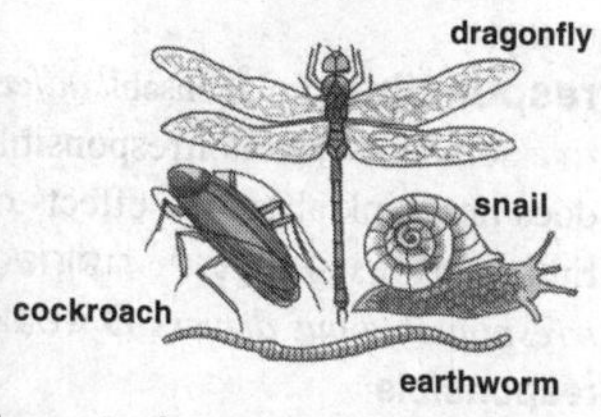

inverted commas *noun* (*no singular*) the sign (" ") or (' ') that you use in writing before and after words that somebody said ଓଲଟା କମା ବା ଉଦ୍ଧୃତ ଚିହ୍ନ (" ") ବା (' ') ➪ **quotation marks** ଦେଖନ୍ତୁ ।

invest /ɪnˈvest/ *verb* (**invests, investing, invested**) give money to a business or bank so that you will get back more money ଲାଭ ପାଇଁ ବ୍ୟବସାୟ, ବ୍ୟାଙ୍କ ଇତ୍ୟାଦିରେ ଟଙ୍କା ବିନିଯୋଗ କରିବା

investment *noun* **1** (*no plural*) the act of investing money ଅର୍ଥ ବିନିଯୋଗ **2** (*plural* **investments**) money that you invest ବିନିଯୋଗ କରାଯାଇଥିବା ଟଙ୍କା ବା ସମ୍ପତ୍ତି *an investment of Rs 10,000*

investigate /ɪnˈvestɪgeɪt/ *verb* (**investigates, investigating, investigated**) try to find out about something ଅନୁସନ୍ଧାନ କରିବା *The police are investigating the robbery.*

investigation /ɪnˌvestɪˈgeɪʃn/ *noun* ଅନୁସନ୍ଧାନ *There will be an investigation into the cause of the fire.*

invisible /ɪnˈvɪzəbl/ *adjective* if something is invisible, you cannot see it ଅଦୃଶ୍ୟ, ଦେଖାଯାଉ ନଥିବା ✪ ବିପରୀତ **visible**

invitation /ˌɪnvɪˈteɪʃn/ *noun* if you have an invitation to go somewhere, somebody has requested you to do something or to go somewhere ନିମନ୍ତ୍ରଣ, ଆମନ୍ତ୍ରଣ *Leena sent me an invitation to her party.*

invite /ɪnˈvaɪt/ *verb* (**invites, inviting, invited**) ask somebody to come to a party or a meeting, for example ନିମନ୍ତ୍ରଣ କରିବା *Let's invite them for dinner.*

involuntary /ɪnˈvɒləntri/ *adjective* an involuntary action is something that happens suddenly and you cannot control ସ୍ୱତଃଜାତ, ଅନଭିପ୍ରେତ, ସ୍ୱୟଂଜାତ ✪ ବିପରୀତ **voluntary**

involve /ɪnˈvɒlv/ *verb* (**involves, involving, involved**) have something as a part ଜଡ଼ିତ କରିବା, ସମ୍ପୃକ୍ତ କରିବା *The job involves using a computer.*

inward /ˈɪnwəd/, **inwards** /ˈɪnwədz/ *adverb* towards the inside or centre ଭିତରପଟୁ *The doors open inwards.* ✪ ବିପରୀତ **outward** ବା **outwards**

iodine /ˈaɪədiːn/ *noun* (*no plural*) a chemical substance that is blue-black in colour. An iodine solution is sometimes used as an antiseptic ନୀଳ-କଳା ରଙ୍ଗର ଏକ ରାସାୟନିକ ପଦାର୍ଥ ଯାହା ଜୀବାଣୁନାଶକ ପଦାର୍ଥ ଯାହା ଜୀବାଣୁନାଶକ ଭାବରେ ବ୍ୟବହୃତ ହୁଏ (ଘା, ଖଣ୍ଡିଆ ଇତ୍ୟାଦିରେ)

ir- *prefix*
କିଛି ଶବ୍ଦର ଆରମ୍ଭରେ **ir-** ଲଗାଇଲେ ବିପରୀତ ଅର୍ଥ ସୂଚାଏ ଯଥା — **irregular** = ଅନିୟମିତ

iris /ˈaɪrɪs/ *noun* the coloured part of your eye ଆଖିର ସ୍ୱଚ୍ଛପଟଳ ପଛପଟେ ଥିବା ରଞ୍ଜିତ ପରଦା ଯାହା ମଝିରେ ଛିଦ୍ର ଥାଏ; ଶବଳକ

iron /ˈaɪən/ *noun* **1** (*no plural*) a strong hard metal ଲୁହା, ଲୌହ *The gates are made of iron.* ✪ **Iron** ଲୌହତତ୍ତ୍ୱ ରକ୍ତରେ ଓ ଅନ୍ୟ କିଛି ଖାଦ୍ୟ ପଦାର୍ଥରେ ଅଳ୍ପ ପରିମାଣରେ ମିଳିଥାଏ। **2** (*plural* **irons**) an electrical tool that gets hot and that you use for making clothes smooth ଲୁଗା ଇସ୍ତ୍ରୀ କରିବା ଯନ୍ତ୍ର, ଇସ୍ତ୍ରୀ

iron *verb* (**irons, ironing, ironed**) make clothes smooth with an iron ଲୁଗା ଇସ୍ତ୍ରୀ କରିବା *Can you iron this shirt for me?*

irony /ˈaɪrəni/ *noun* (*no plural*) **1** the use of words in such a way that you mean the opposite of what you say, often as a joke or to express anger (କ୍ରୋଧରେ ବା ବ୍ୟଙ୍ଗ ପାଇଁ) ଶବ୍ଦାର୍ଥର ବିପରୀତ ଭାବ ବ୍ୟକ୍ତ କରୁଥିବା ଶବ୍ଦ ବ୍ୟବହାର, ବକ୍ରୋକ୍ତି *'You should become an artist,' she said with irony when she saw my clumsy drawings.* **2** a situation or an idea that is amusing or the opposite of what was expected or hoped for ଆଶା ବା ପ୍ରତ୍ୟାଶା କରିଥିବା ଘଟଣାର ଓଲଟା ଘଟଣା ଘଟିବା ପ୍ରକ୍ରିୟା *The little child was eagerly looking forward to putting on his new raincoat but the irony was that there were no rains that season.*

irregular /ɪˈregjələ(r)/ *adjective* **1** that happens again and again, but with different periods of time in between ଅସମାନ ସମୟାନ୍ତରରେ ଘଟୁଥିବା *Their visits were irregular.* **2** not having a regular shape or pattern ଅସମାନ ରୂପ ବା ଢାଞ୍ଚା ଥିବା ➪ **regular** ଦେଖନ୍ତୁ।

irresponsible /ˌɪrɪˈspɒnsəbl/ *adjective* someone who is irresponsible does not think about the effects of their actions ଦାୟିତ୍ୱହୀନ, ଲଗାମଛଡ଼ା *irresponsible bus drivers* ✪ ବିପରୀତ **responsible**

irreversible /ˌɪrɪˈvɜːsəbl/ *adjective* that cannot be stopped and changed back to its earlier position ଅପରିବର୍ତ୍ତନୀୟ; ବିପରୀତ ଦିଗରେ ଯିବାପାଇଁ ଅକ୍ଷମ, ଫେରି ବା ଓଲଟି ପାରୁନଥିବା *an irreversible change* ✪ ବିପରୀତ **reversible**

irrigate /ˈɪrɪgeɪt/ *verb* (**irrigates, irrigating, irrigated**) supply water to farms through rivers, dams, canals and channels so that crops can grow well (ଚାଷ ପାଇଁ ନଦୀ, ବନ୍ଧ, କେନାଲ୍ ଇତ୍ୟାଦି ଦ୍ୱାରା) ଜଳସେଚନ କରିବା

irrigation /ˌɪrɪˈgeɪʃn/ *noun* the process of irrigating a farm ଜଳସେଚନ ବ୍ୟବସ୍ଥା

irritate /ˈɪrɪteɪt/ *verb* (**irritates, irritating, irritated**) **1** make somebody quite angry ବିରକ୍ତ କରିବା, ରଗାଇବା, ଚିଡ଼ାଇବା *He irritates me when he* *asks so many questions.* **2** make a part of your body hurt or itch a little ଶରୀରର କୌଣସି ଅଂଶରେ କ୍ଷତ, କୁଣ୍ଡିଆ, ଜ୍ୱଳନ ଇତ୍ୟାଦି ଦ୍ୱାରା କଷ୍ଟ ଦେବା ବା ପାଇବା *Cigarette smoke irritates my eyes.*

irritation /ˌɪrɪˈteɪʃn/ *noun* କ୍ରୋଧ, ଉତ୍ତେଜନା, ବିରକ୍ତି, କଷ୍ଟ *Something is causing an irritation in my eye.*

is ଶବ୍ଦ **be** ର ଏକ ଧାତୁରୂପ

Islam /ˈɪzlɑːm/ *noun* (*no plural*) the religion of the Muslim people. Islam teaches that there is only one God and that Muhammad is His messenger ଇସ୍‌ଲାମ୍ (ମୁସଲ୍‌ମାନ ଲୋକଙ୍କ ଧର୍ମ ଯେଉଁଥିରେ ଈଶ୍ୱର ଏକ ଓ ମହମ୍ମଦ୍ ତାଙ୍କ ବାର୍ତ୍ତାବହ ବୋଲି ଗ୍ରହଣ କରାଯାଏ)

Islamic *adjective* ଇସ୍‌ଲାମ ସମ୍ବନ୍ଧୀୟ, ଇସ୍‌ଲାମୀୟ *Islamic law*

island /ˈaɪlənd/ *noun* a piece of land with water all around it ଦ୍ୱୀପ, ଟାପୁ

isn't = **is not**

isolated /ˈaɪsəleɪtɪd/ *adjective* far from other people or things ଅଲଗା, ପୃଥକ୍, ବିଚ୍ଛିନ୍ନ; ଏକୁଟିଆ; ଜନସମାଜରୁ ଦୂରରେ ଥିବା *an isolated house in the mountains*

issue[1] /ˈɪʃuː/ *noun* **1** an important subject or problem that people talk about ଆଲୋଚନାର ଏକ ଗୁରୁତ୍ୱପୂର୍ଣ୍ଣ ବିଷୟ *Pollution is a serious issue.* **2** a magazine or newspaper of a particular day, week or month (ପତ୍ର ପତ୍ରିକାର) ଏକ ସଂସ୍କରଣ (ଦୈନିକ, ସାପ୍ତାହିକ ବା ମାସିକ) *Have you read this week's issue of the magazine?*

issue[2] /ˈɪʃuː/ *verb* (**issues, issuing, issued**) give something to people (ବ୍ୟବହାର ପାଇଁ ଲୋକଙ୍କୁ) ଯୋଗାଣ ବା ବଣ୍ଟନ କରିବା *The soldiers were issued new uniforms.*

it /ɪt/ *pronoun* (*plural* **they, them**) **1** a word that shows a thing or an animal that you have just talked about ଏହା, ଏଇଟା (କ୍ଲୀବଲିଙ୍ଗ ବିଶେଷଣ) *I've got a new shirt. It's blue.* ○ *Where is the coffee? I can't find it.* **2** a word that points to an idea that follows କ୍ରିୟାର କର୍ତ୍ତୃପଦ ବା କର୍ମପଦ ରୂପେ ବ୍ୟବହୃତ ଶବ୍ଦ; ଏହା *It is difficult to learn Japanese.* **3** a word that shows who somebody is ଉଦ୍ଦିଷ୍ଟ ବ୍ୟକ୍ତି ସୂଚକ ଶବ୍ଦ *'Who's on the telephone?' 'It's Priya.'* **4** a word at the beginning of a sentence about time, the weather, distance, etc. ନିର୍ବ୍ୟକ୍ତିକ କ୍ରିୟାର ବିଶେଷ୍ୟ ପଦ; ଏହା *It's six o'clock.* ○ *It's hot today.*

italics /ɪˈtælɪks/ *noun* (*plural*) letters that lean to the side ତୀର୍ଯ୍ୟକ, ବକ୍ର, ଡାହାଣ ପଟକୁ ଢ଼ଳିଥିବା (ମୁଦ୍ରିତ ବା ଛପା ଅକ୍ଷର) *This sentence is in italics.*

itch /ɪtʃ/ *verb* (**itches, itching, itched**) have a feeling on your skin that makes you want to rub or scratch it କୁଣ୍ଡେଇ ହେବା, କଣ୍ଡୁ ଜାତ ହେବା

itchy *adjective* if something is itchy, it itches or it makes you itch କୁଣ୍ଡେଇ ହେଉଥିବା *itchy skin*

it'd **1** = **it had** **2** = **it would**

item /ˈaɪtəm/ *noun* one thing in a list or group of things ତାଲିକାରେ ଥିବା ପଦାର୍ଥ ମଧ୍ୟରୁ ଗୋଟିଏ *She had the most expensive item on the menu.*

it'll = **it will**

its /ɪts/ *adjective* of the thing or animal that you have just talked about ଏହାର (ପଦାର୍ଥ ବା ପଶୁର)

> **its** or **it's**?
>
> **It's** ର ଅର୍ଥ କିନ୍ତୁ ସମ୍ପୂର୍ଣ୍ଣ ଭିନ୍ନ। ଏହା **it is** ବା **it has** ର ଏକ ସଂକ୍ଷିପ୍ତ ରୂପ ଯେଉଁଥିରେ ଉଦ୍ଧୃତ ଚିହ୍ନ (') **it** ଓ **s** ମଝିର କିଛି ଅକ୍ଷରର ବିଲୋପ ସୂଚାଏ। ତେଣୁ 'The dog has hurt it's tail' ଲେଖିବା ଭୁଲ୍ ହେବ। **It's** ର ଠିକ୍ ବ୍ୟବହାର ହେଲା 'It's five o'clock in the evening'. ଏଠାରେ **it's** ହେଲା **it is** ର ସଂକ୍ଷିପ୍ତ ରୂପ। ଅର୍ଥାତ୍ 'It is five o'clock in the evening'.

it's 1 = **it is 2** = **it has**

itself /ɪtˈself/ *pronoun* (*plural* **themselves**) a word that shows the same thing or animal that you have just talked about ନିଜକୁ *The cat was licking itself.*

by itself 1 alone ନିଜେ, ଏକୁଟିଆ ଭାବରେ *The house stands by itself in the forest.* **2** without being controlled by a person ନିଜେ, ଆପେ *The machine will start by itself.*

I've = **I have**

ivory /ˈaɪvəri/ *noun* (*no plural*) the hard white substance that an elephant's **tusks** are made of ହାତୀଦାନ୍ତ, ଗଜଦନ୍ତ, ହସ୍ତୀଦନ୍ତ

ivy

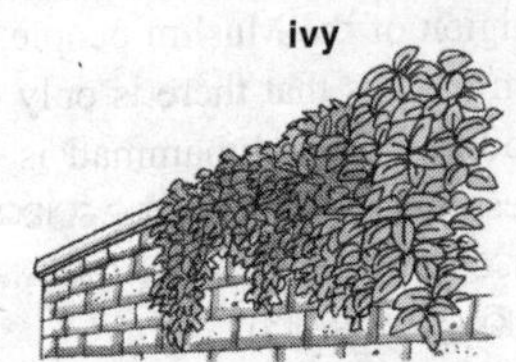

ivy /ˈaɪvi/ *noun* (*no plural*) a plant with dark-green leaves, that climbs up walls or trees କାନ୍ଥ, ଗଛ ଇତ୍ୟାଦିରେ ମାଡ଼ୁଥିବା ଗାଢ଼ ସବୁଜ ପତ୍ର ଥିବା ଏକ ଲତା, ଆଇଭି

J j

jackal /ˈdʒækl/ *noun* a wild animal like a fox, that is found in Asia and Africa (ଏସିଆ ଓ ଆଫ୍ରିକାର) ବିଲୁଆ, ଶୃଗାଳ ➪ ଚିତ୍ର ପାଇଁ **fox** ଦେଖନ୍ତୁ।

jacket /ˈdʒækɪt/ *noun* a short coat with sleeves ପୂରା ହାତଥିବା ଛୋଟ କୋଟ୍ ➪ ଚିତ୍ର ପାଇଁ **suit** ଦେଖନ୍ତୁ।

jagged /ˈdʒægɪd/ *adjective* rough, with a lot of sharp points ଦନ୍ତୁରିତ, ଦାନ୍ତପରି ବହୁତ ମୁନ ବାହାରିଥିବା ଦାନ୍ତୁଆ *jagged rocks*

jail /dʒeɪl/ *noun* a prison ଜେଲ୍, କାରାଗାର *He was sent to jail for two years.*

jail *verb* (**jails, jailing, jailed**) put somebody in prison ଜେଲରେ ରଖିବା

jam¹ /dʒæm/ *noun* (*no plural*) food made from fruit and sugar. You eat jam on bread ଫଳ ଓ ଚିନିରେ ପ୍ରସ୍ତୁତ ଏକ ପ୍ରକାର ମେଞ୍ଚାଳିଆ ଖାଦ୍ୟ (ଯାହା ପାଉଁରୁଟିରେ ଲଗାଇ ଖିଆଯାଏ) ମୁରବା *a jar of strawberry jam*

jam² /dʒæm/ *noun* a lot of people or things stuck in a place, making it difficult to move ଭିଡ଼ ଯୋଗୁ ଚଳାଚଳ ବନ୍ଦ ହୋଇଯିବା ଅବସ୍ଥା *a traffic jam*

jam³ /dʒæm/ *verb* (**jams, jamming, jammed**) fix something or become fixed so that you cannot move it ଖୁନ୍ଦି ବା ଖିଲ ମାରି ଦୃଢ଼ଭାବେ ବନ୍ଦ ହୋଇଯିବା; ଲାଖିଯିବା *I can't open the window—it's jammed.*

January /ˈdʒænjuəri/ *noun* the first month of the year ପାଶ୍ଚାତ୍ୟ ବର୍ଷର ପ୍ରଥମ ମାସ, ଜାନୁଆରୀ

jar /dʒɑ:(r)/ *noun* a glass container with a wide mouth for keeping food ବଡ଼ ମୁହଁ ଥିବା ଚଉଡ଼ା କାଚ ବୋତଲ, ଜାର୍ *a jar for keeping coffee* ➪ ଚିତ୍ର ପାଇଁ **container** ଦେଖନ୍ତୁ।

javelin /ˈdʒævlɪn/ *noun* a long pointed stick that people throw as a sport ଖେଳ ପ୍ରତିଯୋଗିତାରେ ବ୍ୟବହୃତ ବର୍ଚ୍ଛା, ଯାଭେଲିନ୍

jaw /dʒɔ:/ *noun* one of the two bones around your mouth that hold your teeth ଉପର ପାଟିର ହନୁହାଡ଼ ବା ତଳ ପାଟିର ହାଡ଼

jealous /ˈdʒeləs/ *adjective* angry or sad because you want what another person has ଈର୍ଷ୍ୟାପରାୟଣ, ଈର୍ଷ୍ୟାନ୍ୱିତ *Kanan was jealous of his brother's new car.*

jealousy *noun* (*no plural*) being jealous ଈର୍ଷ୍ୟା; ଦ୍ୱେଷ; ପରଶ୍ରୀକାତରତା

jeans /dʒi:nz/ *noun* (*no singular*) trousers made of strong cotton material (called **denim**) ମୋଟା କନା (ଡେନିମ୍) ରେ ତିଆରି ପୂରାପ୍ୟାଣ୍ଟ *a pair of jeans*

Jeep /dʒi:p/ *noun* a strong car that can go well over rough land ଖରାପ ରାସ୍ତାରେ ଯାଇପାରୁଥିବା ଜିପଗାଡ଼ି ✪ **Jeep** ହେଲା ବ୍ୟାପାରିକ ସ୍ୱତ୍ୱ ଥିବା ନାମ।

jelly /ˈdʒeli/ *noun* (*plural* **jellies**) a soft sweet food made from fruit juice and sugar, that shakes when you move it ଜେଲାଟିନ୍ ସହ ପ୍ରସ୍ତୁତ ଥଲଥଲିଆ ମିଠା, ଜେଲୀ

jellyfish /ˈdʒelifɪʃ/ *noun* (*plural* **jellyfish** ବା **jellyfishes**) a sea animal like jelly, that you can see through ଜେଲୀପରି ନରମ ଓ ସ୍ୱଚ୍ଛ ଦେହଥିବା ତାରା ଚିହ୍ନପରି ଦଂଶନକ୍ଷମ ବାହୁଥିବା ସାମୁଦ୍ରିକ ଜୀବ *I saw a jellyfish on the beach.*

jerk /dʒɜ:k/ *noun* a sudden pull or other movement ଆକସ୍ମିକ ଟଣା ବା ଧକ୍କା, ଧକର କଚର *The bus started with a jerk.*

jersey /ˈdʒɜ:zi/ *noun* a woollen piece of clothing with long sleeves and no buttons that you wear over your shirt to keep you warm ପଶମ ସୂତା ବା ଉଲ୍‌ରେ ବୁଣା ପୂରାହାତ ଥିବା ମୁଣ୍ଡଗଳା ସ୍ୱେଟର୍

jester /ˈdʒestə(r)/ *noun* a person who worked in the courts of kings and queens in the past and amused them by telling jokes and funny stories ମଧ୍ୟଯୁଗୀୟ ରାଜାଙ୍କ ସଭାରେ ଥିବା ହସେଇବା ଲୋକ, ବିଦୂଷକ *a court jester*

jet /dʒet/ *noun* **1** an aeroplane that flies when its engines push out hot gas ପଛପଟକୁ ବାଷ୍ପ ପ୍ରକ୍ଷେପଣ କରୁଥିବା ଇଞ୍ଜିନ୍ ଲଗା ଉଡ଼ାଜାହାଜ **2** a liquid or gas that comes out very quickly from a small hole ଛୋଟ କଣା ବା ନଳୀ ବାଟେ ଜୋର୍‌ରେ ବାହାରୁଥିବା ତରଳ ପଦାର୍ଥ ବା ବାଷ୍ପ *jets of water*

Jew /dʒu:/ *noun* a person who follows the old religion of Israel, called **Judaism** ଇସ୍ରାଏଲ୍‌ର ଜୁଡାଇଜ୍ମ ଧର୍ମର ବ୍ୟକ୍ତି, ଜ୍ୟୁ

Jewish *adjective* ଜ୍ୟୁ ଧର୍ମର *She is Jewish.*

jewel /ˈdʒu:əl/ *noun* a beautiful stone, for example a diamond, that is very valuable ବହୁମୂଲ୍ୟ ପଥର, ରତ୍ନ (ହୀରା, ନୀଳା, ମାଣିକ୍ୟ ଇତ୍ୟାଦି)

jeweller *noun* a person who sells, makes or repairs jewellery ଅଳଙ୍କାର ବା ରତ୍ନ ବ୍ୟବସାୟୀ, ଜହୁରୀ, ବଣିଆ, କମିଳା

jewellery *noun* (*no plural*) things like rings, bracelets, bangles and necklaces ଅଳଙ୍କାର *She wears a lot of jewellery.*

jigsaw /ˈdʒɪgsɔ:/, **jigsaw puzzle** *noun* a picture in many pieces that you must put together ଖଣ୍ଡ ଖଣ୍ଡ ହୋଇ କଟାହୋଇଥିବା ଚିତ୍ର (ଯାହାକୁ ଯୋଡ଼ି ଚିତ୍ରଟିକୁ ପୁଣି ସମ୍ପୂର୍ଣ୍ଣ କରିବା ଗୋଟାଏ ବୁଦ୍ଧିଖେଳ), ଜିଗ୍‌ସ

jingle /ˈdʒɪŋgl/ *verb* (**jingles, jingling, jingled**) make a pleasant sound like the ringing of small bells ଘଣ୍ଟି ବାଜିଲାପରି ଝଣଝଣ ଶବ୍ଦ

job /dʒɒb/ *noun* **1** the work that you do to get money regularly ଚାକିରି, ଟଙ୍କା ଅର୍ଜନ କରୁଥିବା କାମ, ନିଯୁକ୍ତି *She's looking for a new job.* **2** a piece of work that you must do କାମ *I have a lot of jobs to do in the house.*

make a good job of something do something well ଭଲ ଭାବରେ କାର୍ଯ୍ୟ ସମ୍ପାଦନ କରିବା *You made a good job of the painting.*

jockey /ˈdʒɒki/ *noun* (*plural* **jockeys**) a person who rides horses in races ଘୋଡ଼ା ଦୌଡ଼ରେ ଭାଗ ନେଉଥିବା ଅଶ୍ୱାରୋହୀ

joey /ˈdʒəʊi/ *noun* (*plural* **joeys**) the young one of a kangaroo କଙ୍ଗାରୁ ଛୁଆ ➪ ଚିତ୍ର ପାଇଁ **kangaroo** ଦେଖନ୍ତୁ।

jog /dʒɒg/ *verb* (**jogs, jogging, jogged**) run slowly for exercise ବ୍ୟାୟାମ ପାଇଁ ଧୀର ଗତିରେ ଦୌଡ଼ିବା *I jogged round the park.* ✪ ଆମେ ଅନେକ ସମୟରେ କହୁ **go jogging** *I go jogging every morning.*

jog *noun* (*no plural*) a slow run for exercise ବ୍ୟାୟାମ ପାଇଁ ଧୀର ଦୌଡ଼ *I went for a jog.*

jogger *noun* a person who jogs ବ୍ୟାୟାମ ପାଇଁ ଧୀରେ ଦୌଡୁଥିବା ବ୍ୟକ୍ତି

jogging *noun* (*no plural*) the activity of running slowly for exercise ବ୍ୟାୟାମ ପାଇଁ ଧୀରେ ଦୌଡ଼ିବା ପ୍ରକ୍ରିୟା

join /dʒɔɪn/ *verb* (**joins, joining, joined**) **1** bring or fix one thing to another thing ଯୋଡ଼ିବା, ଦେଖିବା, ସଂଯୁକ୍ତ କରିବା, ସଂଲଗ୍ନ କରିବା *Join the two pieces of wood together.* **2** come together with somebody or something ଅନ୍ୟମାନଙ୍କ ସହ ଯୋଗଦେବା *Will you join us for dinner?* **3** become a member of a group କୌଣସି ସଂସ୍ଥା ବା ଗୋଷ୍ଠୀର ସଭ୍ୟ ହେବା। *He joined the army.*

joint[1] /dʒɔɪnt/ *noun* **1** a place where two parts of something join together ଯୋଡ଼େଇ ସ୍ଥଳ, ସଂଯୁକ୍ତ ହୋଇଥିବା ସ୍ଥାନ *the joints of a pipe* **2** a place where two bones fit together ହାଡ଼ର ଗଣ୍ଠି ବା ସନ୍ଧିସ୍ଥାନ *Elbows and knees are joints.*

joint[2] /dʒɔɪnt/ *adjective* that people do or have together ଏକାଠି ମିଶି କରାଯାଇଥିବା, ଯୁଗ୍ମ *Monica and Preeti gave a joint party.*

joke[1] /dʒəʊk/ *noun* something that you say or do to make people laugh ହସକଥା *She told us a joke.*

play a joke on somebody do something to somebody to make other people laugh; trick somebody ଥଟ୍ଟାରେ କାହାରିକୁ ବୁଦ୍ଧୁ ବନାଇବା

joke[2] /dʒəʊk/ *verb* (**jokes, joking, joked**) say things that are not serious; say funny things ହସକଥା କହିବା, ପରିହାସ କରିବା, ଥଟ୍ଟା ଟାପରା କରିବା *I didn't really mean what I said—I was only joking.*

joker /ˈdʒəʊkə(r)/ *noun* **1** a person in a **circus** who paints his face, wears funny clothes and does silly things to make people laugh ସର୍କସ୍‌ରେ ଅଦ୍ଭୁତ ପୋଷାକ ପିନ୍ଧି ବିଚିତ୍ର ମୁହଁ ରଙ୍ଗକରି ଲୋକଙ୍କୁ ହସାଉଥିବା ବ୍ୟକ୍ତି। ଜୋକର୍ **2** a person who says or does silly things to make people laugh ଓଲଟା ସିଧା ବା ମଉଜିଆ କଥା କହି ଲୋକଙ୍କୁ ହସାଉଥିବା ବ୍ୟକ୍ତି

jolly /ˈdʒɒli/ *adjective* (**jollier, jolliest**) happy and full of fun ଖୁସିବାସିଆ, ପ୍ରଫୁଲ୍ଲ, ଆନନ୍ଦଚିତ୍ତ, କୌତୁକିଆ

jolt /dʒəʊlt/ *noun* a sudden movement ହଠାତ୍ ଧକ୍କା; ଉଠପଡ଼୍, ଝଟ୍‌କା *The train stopped with a jolt.*

journalism /ˈdʒɜːnəlɪzəm/ *noun* (*no plural*) the work of collecting news and writing about it for newspapers, magazines, television or radio ସାମ୍ବାଦିକତା (ପେଶା ଭାବରେ)

journalist /ˈdʒɜːnəlɪst/ *noun* a person whose job is to collect and write about news for newspapers, magazines, television or radio ସାମ୍ବାଦିକ

journey /ˈdʒɜ:ni/ *noun* (*plural* **journeys**) the act of going from one place to another ଦୂର ସ୍ଥାନକୁ ଗମନ ବା ଯାତ୍ରା; ଭ୍ରମଣ *Did you have a good journey?*

joy /dʒɔɪ/ *noun* (*no plural*) a very happy feeling ଆନନ୍ଦ, ଉଲ୍ଲାସ *Their children give them so much joy.*

joyful *adjective* very happy ଆନନ୍ଦପୂର୍ଣ୍ଣ, ସୁଖୀ, ହୃଷ୍ଟ *She was in a joyful mood.*

joystick /ˈdʒɔɪstɪk/ *noun* a handle that you move to control something, for example a computer or an aeroplane ବିମାନର ନିୟନ୍ତ୍ରକ ଦଣ୍ଡ; କମ୍ପ୍ୟୁଟର ମନିଟର୍‌ରେ ଛବିର ଚାଳନ ପାଇଁ ଥିବା ଚାଳକ ବାଡ଼ି, ଜଏଷ୍ଟିକ୍

Judaism /ˈdʒu:deɪɪzəm/ *noun* (*no plural*) the religion of the Jewish people ଜ୍ୟୁମାନଙ୍କର ଧର୍ମ

judge[1] /dʒʌdʒ/ *noun* **1** the person in a court of law who decides if somebody is to be punished ଅଦାଲତର ବିଚାରକ, ବିଚାରପତି, ନ୍ୟାୟାଧୀଶ *The judge sent the man to prison for twenty years for killing his wife.* **2** a person who chooses the winner of a competition ପ୍ରତିଯୋଗିତାରେ ବିଜୟୀ ବାଛୁଥିବା ବିଚାରକ

judge[2] /dʒʌdʒ/ *verb* (**judges, judging, judged**) **1** decide if something is good or bad, right or wrong, for example ବିଚାର କରିବା **2** decide who or what wins a competition ପ୍ରତିଯୋଗିତାରେ ଜିତିବା ହାରିବା ବିଷୟ ବିଚାର କରିବା

judgement /ˈdʒʌdʒmənt/ *noun* **1** what a judge in a court of law decides ବିଚାରପତିଙ୍କ ନିଷ୍ପତ୍ତି **2** what you think about somebody or something ଦୋଷଗୁଣ ବିଚାର *In my judgement, she will do the job very well.*

judo /ˈdʒu:dəʊ/ *noun* (*no plural*) a Japanese sport where two people fight and try to throw each other onto the floor ଜାପାନ୍ ଦେଶର ଏକ ପ୍ରକାର କୁସ୍ତି

jug /dʒʌg/ *noun* a container with a handle that you use for holding or pouring water or milk, for example ପାଣି, ଦୁଧ ଇତ୍ୟାଦି ରଖିବା ପାଇଁ ଏକ ବେଣ୍ଟଥିବା ପାତ୍ର, ଜଗ୍

juggle /ˈdʒʌgl/ *verb* (**juggles, juggling, juggled**) keep two or more things in the air by throwing and catching them quickly ଏକକାଳୀନ ଅନେକ ବସ୍ତୁ ବାରଂବାର ଉପରକୁ ଫିଙ୍ଗି ହାତରେ ଧରିବା, ଜଗ୍ *The clown juggled with four oranges.*

juggle

juggler *noun* a person who juggles ଅନେକ ବସ୍ତୁ ଉପରକୁ ଫିଙ୍ଗି ହାତରେ ଧରିପାରୁଥିବା ବ୍ୟକ୍ତି, ଜଗାର୍

juice /dʒu:s/ *noun* the liquid from fruit and vegetables ଫଳ ବା ପରିବାର ରସ *a glass of orange juice*

juicy /ˈdʒuːsi/ *adjective* (**juicier, juiciest**) with a lot of juice ରସାଳ, ରସପୂର୍ଣ୍ଣ *big juicy tomatoes*

July /dʒuˈlaɪ/ *noun* the seventh month of the year ପାଶ୍ଚାତ୍ୟ ବର୍ଷର ସପ୍ତମ ମାସ, ଜୁଲାଇ

jumble /ˈdʒʌmbl/ *verb* (**jumbles, jumbling, jumbled**)

jumble up mix things so that they are untidy or in the wrong place ଗୋଳିଆ ଘଣ୍ଟା କରିବା *I couldn't find the photos I was looking for because they were all jumbled up in that box.*

jumble *noun* (*no plural*) a lot of things that are mixed together in an untidy way ବିଶୃଙ୍ଖଳ ଅବସ୍ଥାରେ ଥିବା ପଦାର୍ଥ ସମୂହର ଗଦା *a jumble of old clothes and books*

jump /dʒʌmp/ *verb* (**jumps, jumping, jumped**) **1** move quickly off the ground, using your legs to push you up ଉପରକୁ ଡେଇଁବା, ଲମ୍ଫ ଦେବା *The cat jumped onto the table.* **2** move suddenly because you are surprised or frightened ଆଶ୍ଚର୍ଯ୍ୟ ବା ଭୟରେ ଚମକି ଘୁଞ୍ଚିଯିବା ବା ଡେଇଁ ପଡ଼ିବା *A loud noise made me jump.*

jump *noun* ଲମ୍ଫ, ଉଲ୍ଲମ୍ଫନ, ଡିଆଁ *With one jump, the horse was over the fence.*

junction /ˈdʒʌŋkʃn/ *noun* a place where roads or railway lines meet ବିଭିନ୍ନ ରାସ୍ତା ବା ରେଳଲାଇନ୍‌ର ସଂଗମସ୍ଥଳ *Turn right at the next junction.*

June /dʒuːn/ *noun* the sixth month of the year ପାଶ୍ଚାତ୍ୟ ବର୍ଷର ଷଷ୍ଠ ମାସ, ଜୁନ୍

jungle /ˈdʒʌŋgl/ *noun* a thick forest in a hot part of the world ଜଙ୍ଗଲ, ବଣ, ଅରଣ୍ୟ, ବନ ➪ **forest** ଦେଖନ୍ତୁ।

junior /ˈdʒuːniə(r)/ *adjective* **1** less important ସ୍ତର ବା ଅଧିକାରରେ କନିଷ୍ଠ *He's a junior officer in the army.* **2** younger (ବୟସରେ) ସାନ, କନିଷ୍ଠ *a junior pupil* ✪ ବିପରୀତ **senior**

junk /dʒʌŋk/ *noun* (*no plural*) things that are old or useless ପୁରୁଣା ଓ ଅଦରକାରୀ ଜିନିଷପତ୍ର *The cupboard is full of junk.*

junk food *noun* food that is not very good for you, but that is quick and easy to prepare ପୁଷ୍ଟିକାରକ ହୋଇନଥିବା ଖାଦ୍ୟ (ଯାହା ଶିଘ୍ର ତିଆରି କରି ହୁଏ)

Jupiter /ˈdʒuːpɪtə(r)/ *noun* (*no plural*) the fifth planet from the sun. Jupiter is the largest planet in the solar system ସୌରମଣ୍ଡଳର ପଞ୍ଚମ ଓ ବୃହତ୍ତମ ଗ୍ରହ, ବୃହସ୍ପତି ➪ ଚିତ୍ର ପାଇଁ **solar system** ଦେଖନ୍ତୁ।

jury /ˈdʒʊəri/ *noun* (*plural* **juries**) a group of people in a court of law who decide if somebody has done something wrong or not ବିଚାରାଳୟରେ ମକଦ୍ଦମାର ଦୋଷାଦୋଷର ସିଦ୍ଧାନ୍ତ ଦେବାପାଇଁ ସ୍ଥାନୀୟ ବାସିନ୍ଦାଙ୍କ ମଧ୍ୟରୁ ବଛାଯାଇଥିବା ସିଦ୍ଧାନ୍ତ ଗ୍ରହଣକାରୀ ବ୍ୟକ୍ତିବୃନ୍ଦ, ଜ୍ୟୁରୀ

just[1] /dʒʌst/ *adverb* **1** a very short time before ଅଳ୍ପ ସମୟ ପୂର୍ବରୁ *Akshay isn't here—he's just gone out.* **2** at this or that moment; now or very soon ଏହିକ୍ଷଣି, ବର୍ତ୍ତମାନ; ଅଳ୍ପ ସମୟରେ *I'm just going to make some coffee.* **3** only କେବଳ *It's just a small present.*

just a minute, just a moment wait for a short time ଟିକିଏ ଅପେକ୍ଷା କରନ୍ତୁ *Just a minute—there's someone at the door.*

just[2] /dʒʌst/ *adjective* fair and right *a just decision* ✪ ବିପରୀତ **unjust**

justice /ˈdʒʌstɪs/ *noun* (*no plural*) the act of being fair and right ନ୍ୟାୟସଙ୍ଗତ, ଠିକ୍, ଯଥାର୍ଥ *Justice for all!* ✪ ବିପରୀତ **injustice**

justify /ˈdʒʌstɪfaɪ/ *verb* (**justifies, justifying, justified, has justified**) be or give a good reason for something ଠିକ୍ ବା ଉଚିତ୍ ବୋଲି ଦେଖାଇବା ବା ପ୍ରମାଣ କରିବା *Can you justify what you did?*

jute /dʒuːt/ *noun* (*no plural*) the fibre of a plant of the same name. It is used to make ropes and sacks ଝୋଟ, ଲଳିତା, ନଳିତା

K k

kaleidoscope /kə'laɪdəskəʊp/ *noun* a toy that consists of a tube with mirrors and pieces of coloured glass at one end. When you look through the other end of the tube and turn it, the pieces of glass move and form different patterns ଏକ ନଳାକାର ଖେଳନା ଯାହା ଭିତରେ ଦର୍ପଣ କାଚ ଲାଗିଥାଏ ଓ ଛୋଟ ଛୋଟ ରଙ୍ଗିନ୍ କାଚ ଖଣ୍ଡ ଥାଏ ଓ ଯାହାକୁ ଗୋଟିଏ ପଟୁ ଦେଖି ବୁଲାଇଲେ କାଚଖଣ୍ଡଗୁଡ଼ିକ ବିଭିନ୍ନ ଆକାରରେ ଭିତର ଦର୍ପଣରେ ପ୍ରତିଫଳିତ ହୋଇ ଦିଶନ୍ତି । କେଲିଡୋସ୍କୋପ୍

kangaroo /ˌkæŋgə'ru:/ *noun* (*plural* **kangaroos**) a large animal found in Australia that moves by jumping on its strong back legs. A female kangaroo has a pocket of skin (called a **pouch**) on the front of its body in which it carries its young ଅଷ୍ଟ୍ରେଲିଆର ଦେଖାଯାଉଥିବା ଏକ ବଡ଼ ଜନ୍ତୁ ଓ ଶକ୍ତ ପଛ ଗୋଡ଼ ଦ୍ୱାରା ଡିଆଁ ମାରି ଚାଲୁଥିବା ପଶୁ (ମାଈ କଙ୍ଗାରୁ ପେଟରେ ପିଲାଙ୍କୁ ରଖିବା ପାଇଁ ମୁଣା ଥାଏ) କଙ୍ଗାରୁ ✪ କଙ୍ଗାରୁ ଛୁଆକୁ **joey** କହନ୍ତି ।

karate /kə'rɑ:ti/ *noun* (*no plural*) a Japanese sport where you fight with your hands and feet କେବଳ ହାତ ଓ ଗୋଡ଼ ପାହାର ମାରି ଜାପାନୀ କୁସ୍ତି ଖେଳ, କରାଟେ

keen /ki:n/ *adjective* (**keener, keenest**) **1** if you are keen, you want to do something and are interested in it ବ୍ୟଗ୍ର, ଉତ୍ସାହପୂର୍ଣ୍ଣ *Ravi was keen to go out but I wanted to stay at home.* **2** very good or strong ଖୁବ୍ ଭଲ ବା ଶକ୍ତିଶାଳୀ; (ତୀକ୍ଷ୍ଣ ଦୃଷ୍ଟି) । ତୀକ୍ଷ୍ଣ ବୁଦ୍ଧି ସମ୍ପନ୍ନ *keen eyesight* ○ *a keen mind*

keep /ki:p/ *verb* (**keeps, keeping, kept** /kept/, **has kept**) **1** have something and not give it to another person ନିଜ ପାଖରେ ରଖିବା *You can keep that book—I don't need it.* **2** make somebody or something stay the same and not change ଅପରିବର୍ତ୍ତିତ ଅବସ୍ଥାରେ ରଖିବା *Keep this door closed.* **3** have something in a special place ରଖିବା *Where do you keep the coffee?* **4** not stop doing something; do something many times କରି ଚାଲିବା; ବାରଂବାର କରିବା *She keeps forgetting my name.* **5** look after and buy food and other things for a person or an animal ରଖି ଲାଳନ ପାଳନ କରିବା *They keep sheep and pigs on their farm.*

keep away from somebody or **something** not go near somebody or something ଦୂରେଇ ରହିବା, ପାଖକୁ ନଯିବା; ଦୂରେଇ ରହ । ପାଖକୁ ଯାଅ ନାହିଁ *Keep away from the river, please.*

keep off something not go on something (କୌଣସି ପଦାର୍ଥ ଉପରେ) ନଚାଲିବା; (କୌଣସି ଖାଦ୍ୟ, ପାନୀୟ ଇତ୍ୟାଦି) ବର୍ଜନ କରିବା, ବର୍ଜନକର *Keep off the grass!*

keep on not stop doing something; do something many times କରି ଚାଲିବା;

ବାରଂବାର କରିବା; କରି ଚାଲ; ବାରଂବାର କର *We kept on driving all night!*
keep out stay outside ବାହାରେ ରହିବା; ବାହାରେ ରୁହ *The sign on the door said: 'Danger. Keep out!'*

keeper /ˈki:pə(r)/ *noun* a person who looks after something ରକ୍ଷକ, ପାଳକ *He's a keeper at the zoo—he looks after the lions.* ⇨ **goal-keeper** ମଧ୍ୟ ଦେଖନ୍ତୁ ।

kennel /ˈkenl/ *noun* a small house where a dog sleeps କୁକୁର ରହିବା ପାଇଁ ଛୋଟ ଘର

kept ଶବ୍ଦ **keep** ର ଏକ ଧାତୁରୂପ

kerosene /ˈkerəsi:n/ *noun* (*no plural*) a type of oil that is obtained from **petroleum** and is used to light lamps and stoves କିରୋସିନି, ମାଟିତେଲ

ketchup /ˈketʃəp/ *noun* (*no plural*) a cold sauce made from tomatoes ଟମାଟୋ ବା ବିଲାତି ବାଇଗଣରୁ ତିଆରି ବହଳିଆ ସସ୍ (ଚଟଣି ପରି), କେଚପ୍ *Do you want any ketchup with your chips?*

kettle /ˈketl/ *noun* a metal or plastic pot with a lid and a **spout** that you use for making water hot ପାଣି ଫୁଟାଇବା ପାଇଁ ବ୍ୟବହୃତ ନଳପରି ମୁହଁ ଥିବା ଓ ଧରିବା ପାଇଁ ବେଣ୍ଟଥିବା ଧାତୁ ପାତ୍ର, କେଟ୍ଲ, କେଟିଲି

key[1] /ki:/ *noun* **1** a piece of metal that opens or closes a lock ଚାବି, ଚାବିକାଠି, କୁଞ୍ଚି *He turned the key and opened the door.* **2** one of the parts of a typewriter, computer, piano, etc. that you press with your fingers ଟାଇପ୍ ମେସିନ୍, ବାଦ୍ୟଯନ୍ତ୍ର ଇତ୍ୟାଦିର ଆଙ୍ଗୁଠିରେ ଚିପିବା ଚାବି ବା ପଟି **3** a set of answers to questions (ବହିରେ ଥିବା ପ୍ରଶ୍ନଗୁଡ଼ିକର ବହି ପଛରେ ଥିବା) ଉତ୍ତର, ପ୍ରଶ୍ନୋତ୍ତର *Check your answers with the key at the back of the book.*

key[2] /ki:/ *verb* (**keys, keying, keyed**)
key in put words or numbers into a computer by pressing the keys କମ୍ପ୍ୟୁଟର୍ କି'ବୋର୍ଡର କି' ଚିପି ଅକ୍ଷର ବା ସଂଖ୍ୟା ଲେଖିବା *Key in your name.*

keyboard /ˈki:bɔ:d/ *noun* **1** all the keys on a piano, computer or type-writer, for example ପିଆନୋ, କମ୍ପ୍ୟୁଟର୍ ବା ଟାଇପ୍ ମେସିନ୍‌ର ଆଙ୍ଗୁଠିରେ ଚିପିବା ପାଇଁଥିବା ଚାବିପଟା ବା କି'ବୋର୍ଡ୍ ⇨ ଚିତ୍ର ପାଇଁ **computer** ଦେଖନ୍ତୁ । **2** an electronic musical instrument like a small piano ପିଆନୋ ପରି ଏକ ଇଲେକ୍‌ଟ୍ରୋନିକ୍ ବାଦ୍ୟଯନ୍ତ୍ର *a keyboard player* ⇨ **musical** ଚିତ୍ର ଦେଖନ୍ତୁ । ⇨ **synthesizer** ମଧ୍ୟ ଦେଖନ୍ତୁ ।

keyhole /ˈki:həʊl/ *noun* the hole in a lock where you put a key ତାଲାର ଚାବିକଣା

kg *abbreviation* ଶବ୍ଦ **kilogram** ର ସଂକ୍ଷିପ୍ତ ରୂପ

khadi *noun* (*no plural*) a cloth that is made from a kind of cotton thread made on a spinning wheel ଖଦି, ଅରଟକଟା ସୂତାରୁ ତିଆରି ଲୁଗା

khaki *adjective* a pale brownish-yellow colour ଖାକି, ମାଟିଆ–ହଳଦିଆ ମିଶ୍ରିତ ବର୍ଣ୍ଣ ବା ରଙ୍ଗଥିବା *a khaki uniform*

kick[1] /kɪk/ *verb* (**kicks**, **kicking**, **kicked**) **1** hit somebody or something with your foot ଗୋଡ଼ରେ ମାରିବା, ଗୋଇଠା ମାରିବା, ପଦାଘାତ କରିବ, ନାଡ ମାରିବା *I kicked the ball to Rohan.* **2** move your legs quickly ଗୋଡ଼ ଛାଟିବା

The child was kicking and screaming.

kick² /kɪk/ *noun* the act of hitting something or somebody with your foot, or moving your foot or feet up quickly ପଦାଘାତ, ନାତ, ଗୋଇଠା *give a kick*

kid /kɪd/ *noun* **1** a child ଶିଶୁ, ଛୁଆ *How old are your kids?* ✪ ଏଇଟା ଏକ କଥାବାର୍ତ୍ତାରେ ବ୍ୟବହୃତ ଶବ୍ଦ। **2** a young goat ଛେଳିଛୁଆ ➪ ଚିତ୍ର ପାଇଁ **goat** ଦେଖନ୍ତୁ।

kidnap /ˈkɪdnæp/ *verb* (**kidnaps, kidnapping, kidnapped**) take somebody away and hide them, so that their family or friends will pay money to get them back କାହାରିକୁ ଅପହରଣ କରିବା (ପରିବାରବର୍ଗଙ୍କ ଠାରୁ ପଇସା ଆଦାୟ କରିବା ପାଇଁ) *The son of a rich businessman was kidnapped today.*

kidnapper *noun* a person who kidnaps somebody ଅପହରଣକାରୀ ବ୍ୟକ୍ତି, ଅପହରଣକର୍ତ୍ତା

kidney /ˈkɪdni/ *noun* (*plural* **kidneys**) one of two organs inside your body that remove waste products from your blood ବୃକକ୍, ପେଟର ଦୁଇ ପାଖରେ ଥିବା ଗ୍ରନ୍ଥି ଯାହା ଶରୀରରୁ ନିଷ୍କାସିତ ହେବାକୁ ଥିବା ଅଦରକାରୀ ପଦାର୍ଥକୁ ମୂତ୍ର ଦ୍ୱାରା ବାହାର କରିଦିଏ।

kill /kɪl/ *verb* (**kills, killing, killed**) make somebody or something die ହତ୍ୟା କରିବା, ବଧ କରିବା, ମାରିଦେବା *Three people were killed in the accident.*

killer *noun* a person, animal or thing that kills ହତ୍ୟାକାରୀ

kilogram, kilogramme /ˈkɪləgræm/, **kilo** /ˈkiːləʊ/ *noun* a measure of weight. There are 1,000 **grams** in a kilogram ଓଜନ ମାପର ଏକ ଏକକ, କିଲୋଗ୍ରାମ, ଏକ କିଲୋଗ୍ରାମ ସମାନ ୧,୦୦୦ ଗ୍ରାମ୍ *I bought two kilos of potatoes.* ✪ ଶବ୍ଦ **kilogram** ର ସଂକ୍ଷିପ୍ତ ରୂପ ହେଲା **kg** ଯେଭଳି *20 kg*

kilometre /ˈkɪləmiːtə(r)/ *noun* a measure of distance. There are 1,000 **metres** in a kilometre ୧,୦୦୦ ମିଟର୍‌ର ଦୂରତ୍ୱ ✪ Kilometre ଶବ୍ଦର ସଂକ୍ଷିପ୍ତ ରୂପ ହେଲା **km** *100 km*

kind¹ /kaɪnd/ *adjective* (**kinder, kindest**) friendly and good to other people ଦୟାଶୀଳ, ଦୟାଳୁ *'Can I carry your bag?' 'Thanks. That's very kind of you.'* ○ *Be kind to animals.* ✪ ବିପରୀତ **unkind** ବା **cruel**

kind-hearted *adjective* a person who is kind-hearted is kind and gentle to other people ଦୟାଳୁ, ଦୟାଶୀଳ

kindness *noun* (*no plural*) being kind ଦୟା, ଅନୁକମ୍ପା *Thank you for your kindness.*

kind² /kaɪnd/ *noun* a group of things or people that are the same in some way; a sort or type ପଦାର୍ଥ, ପଶୁ ବା ମଣିଷଙ୍କର ପ୍ରାକୃତିକ ଶ୍ରେଣୀ, ପ୍ରକାର ବା ଜାତି *What kind of dog do you have?*

kindly /ˈkaɪndli/ *adverb* in a kind way ଦୟାଶୀଳ ଭାବରେ, ଦୟାକରି *She kindly drove me to the station.*

king /kɪŋ/ *noun* a man who rules a country and who is from a royal family ରାଜା, ନରପତି *King Juan Carlos of Spain* ➪ **queen** ଦେଖନ୍ତୁ।

kingdom /ˈkɪŋdəm/ *noun* a country where a king or queen rules ରାଜ୍ୟ; ରାଜା ବା ରାଣୀଙ୍କ ଦ୍ୱାରା ଶାସିତ ଦେଶ *the United Kingdom*

kingfisher /ˈkɪŋfɪʃə(r)/ *noun* a small colourful bird with a long beak, that lives near water and catches fish ଭଦଭଦଳିଆ ପକ୍ଷୀ, ମାଛରଙ୍କା ପକ୍ଷୀ ➪ ଚିତ୍ର ପାଇଁ **bird** ଦେଖନ୍ତୁ।

kiosk /ˈkiːɒsk/ *noun* a small shop in a street where you can buy things like cold drinks or newspapers through an open window or make telephone calls ରାସ୍ତା କଡ଼ରେ ଥିବା ଗୁମୁଟି ବା ବୁଥ, ଯେଉଁଥିରେ କିଛି ଜିନିଷ କିଣିବା ପାଇଁ, ଥଣ୍ଡାପାନୀୟ ବା ଖବର କାଗଜ ମିଳିଥାଏ ଓ ଟେଲିଫୋନ୍ କରିବାର ସୁବିଧା ଥାଏ

kiss /kɪs/ *verb* (**kisses, kissing, kissed**) touch somebody with your lips to show love or to say hello or goodbye ଚୁମା ଦେବା, ଚୁମ୍ବନ କରିବା (ଦେଖା ହେବା ବା ବିଦାୟ ସମୟରେ କିଂବା ଭଲପାଇବାର ନିଦର୍ଶନ ଭାବେ) *She kissed me on the cheek.*

kiss *noun* (*plural* **kisses**) ଚୁମା, ଚୁମ୍ବନ *She gave the baby a kiss on the cheek.*

kit /kɪt/ *noun* **1** all the clothes or other things that you need to do something or to play a sport ନିର୍ଦ୍ଦିଷ୍ଟ କାମପାଇଁ ଆବଶ୍ୟକ ହେଉଥିବା ପୋଷାକ ଓ ଉପକରଣ *Where is my football kit?* **2** a set of small pieces that you put together to make something କୌଣସି ଉପକରଣ ନିଜେ ଯୋଖି ତିଆରି କରିବା ପାଇଁ ମିଳୁଥିବା ଏହାର ସବୁ ଖଣ୍ଡବଖଣ୍ଡା *a kit for making a model aeroplane*

kitchen /ˈkɪtʃɪn/ *noun* a room where food is cooked ରୋଷେଇଘର, ରନ୍ଧନଶାଳା

kite¹ /kaɪt/ *noun* a light toy made of paper or cloth on a long string. You can make a kite fly in the wind ଗୁଡ଼ି

kite² /kaɪt/ *noun* a large powerful bird with strong wings, that kills other birds and small animals for food ଚିଲପକ୍ଷୀ ➪ ଚିତ୍ର ପାଇଁ **bird** ଦେଖନ୍ତୁ।

kitten /ˈkɪtn/ *noun* a young cat ବିଲେଇ ଛୁଆ

km *abbreviation* ଶବ୍ଦ **kilometre** ର ସଂକ୍ଷିପ୍ତ ରୂପ

knee /niː/ *noun* the part in the middle of your leg where it bends ଆଣ୍ଠୁ *I fell and cut my knee.* ➪ ଚିତ୍ର ପାଇଁ **body** ଦେଖନ୍ତୁ।

kneel /niːl/ *verb* (**kneels, kneeling, knelt** /nelt/ **kneeled, has knelt** ବା **has kneeled**) go down or stay with your knees on the ground ଆଣ୍ଠେଇବା, ଆଣ୍ଠୁମାଡ଼ି ବସିବା *Kneel on the floor.*

knew ଶବ୍ଦ **know** ର ଏକ ଧାତୁରୂପ

knife /naɪf/ *noun* (*plural* **knives** /naɪvz/) a sharp metal thing with a handle, that you use to cut things or to fight ଛୁରୀ, ଛୁରା, ଛୁରିକା

knight /naɪt/ *noun* **1** (in Britain) a man who has been given a special title by the king or queen and who can use 'Sir' in front of his name (ବ୍ରିଟେନ୍‌ରେ) ରାଜା ବା ରାଣୀଙ୍କ ଦ୍ୱାରା 'ସାର୍' ଉପାଧି ଦିଆଯାଉଥିବା ବ୍ୟକ୍ତି **2** a soldier from a long time ago who rode a horse and fought for his king (ମଧ୍ୟଯୁଗର) ରାଜାଙ୍କ ପାଇଁ ଲଢୁଥିବା ଏକ ସମ୍ମାନପ୍ରାପ୍ତ ଅଶ୍ୱାରୋହୀ ଯୋଦ୍ଧା

knit /nɪt/ *verb* (**knits, knitting, knitted**) use long sticks of metal or plastic (called **knitting needles**) to make clothes from wool (ଉଲ୍ ବା ପଶମ ସୂତାରେ କଣ୍ଟା ସାହାଯ୍ୟରେ ସ୍ୱେଟର୍ ଇତ୍ୟାଦି) ବୁଣିବା

knitting *noun* (*no plural*) the activity of making clothes from wool ବୁଣିବା କାମ *She likes knitting.*

knob /nɒb/ *noun* **1** a round handle on a door or drawer କବାଟ ବା ଟେବୁଲ୍ ଦରଜା ଖୋଲିବା ବା ବନ୍ଦ କରିବାପାଇଁ ଲଗା ଯାଇଥିବା ଗୋବ **2** a round thing that you turn to control part of a machine ରେଡିଓ ବା ଯନ୍ତ୍ରପାତି ଚାଳନ ପାଇଁଥିବା ଗୋବପରି ସ୍ୱିଚ୍

knock[1] /nɒk/ *verb* (**knocks, knocking, knocked**) **1** hit something to make a noise ସଶବ୍ଦେ ବାଡ଼େଇବା *I knocked on the door, but nobody answered.* **2** hit something hard ଜୋର୍‌ରେ ବାଡ଼େଇବା *She knocked a glass off the table.*

knock somebody down, knock somebody over hit somebody so that they fall onto the ground (କାହାରିକୁ) ବାଡ଼େଇ ତଳେ ପକାଇଦେବା

knock something over hit something so that it falls (କିଛି ପଦାର୍ଥ) ପିଟି ବା ଠେଲି ତଳେ ପକାଇଦେବା *He knocked over a vase of flowers.*

knock[2] /nɒk/ *noun* the act of hitting something hard or the sound that this makes ସଶବ୍ଦ ବାଡ଼ିଆ ବା ଆଘାତ *I heard a knock at the door.*

knot /nɒt/ *noun* a place where you have tied two ends of rope, string, etc. tightly together (ସୂତା ବା ଦଉଡ଼ିର) ଗଣ୍ଠି *I tied a knot in the rope.*

knot *verb* (**knots, knotting, knotted**) tie a knot in something ଗଣ୍ଠି ପକାଇବା *He knotted the ends of the rope together.*

know /nəʊ/ *verb* (**knows, knowing, knew** /ju:/, **has known** /nəʊn/) **1** have information or knowledge about something because you have learnt it ଜାଣିବା, ଶିଖିବା, ମନେରଖିବା *He knows a lot about cars.* ○ *Do you know how to use this machine?* **2** have met or seen somebody or something before, perhaps many times ଜାଣିପାରିବା, ଚିହ୍ନିପାରିବା (ଆଗରୁ ଦେଖିଥିବା ହେତୁ) *I have known Mary for six years.*

get to know somebody start to know somebody well ପରିଚୟ ଦ୍ୱାରା କାହା ବିଷୟରେ ଜାଣିବା

let somebody know tell somebody (କାହାରିକୁ) ଜଣାଇବା *Let me know if you need any help.*

knowingly /ˈnəʊɪŋli/ *adverb* when you do something knowingly, you do it on purpose ଜାଣିଶୁଣି *He can never hurt anyone knowingly.*

knowledge /ˈnɒlɪdʒ/ *noun* (*no plural*) what you know and understand about something ଜ୍ଞାନ, ଯାହାକିଛି ଜଣା ଅଛି *He has a good knowledge of Indian history.*

known ଶବ୍ଦ **know** ର ଏକ ଧାତୁରୂପ

knuckle /ˈnʌkl/ *noun* the bones where your fingers join your hand and where your hands bend ଆଙ୍ଗୁଠିର ଗଣ୍ଠିହାଡ଼

koala /kəʊˈɑːlə/ *noun* a wild animal, like a small bear, that lives in Australia ଅଷ୍ଟ୍ରେଲିଆର ଥିବା ଛୋଟ ଭାଲୁ ପରି ବୃକ୍ଷାରୋହୀ ବନ୍ୟଜନ୍ତୁ

koala

Koran *noun* the holy book of the Muslims ମୁସଲମାନ୍‌ମାନଙ୍କର ଧର୍ମଗ୍ରନ୍ଥ, କୋରାନ୍

kung fu /ˌkʌŋˈfuː/ *noun* (*no plural*) a Chinese form of fighting using arms and feet. This is similar to **karate** କେବଳ ହାତ ଓ ଗୋଡ଼ ପ୍ରହାର ଦ୍ୱାରା କରାଯାଉଥିବା ଚୀନଦେଶୀୟ ମୁହାଁମୁହିଁ ଲଢ଼େଇ

L l

L /el/ *symbol* the number 50 in Roman numerals ରୋମୀୟ ସଂଖ୍ୟାରେ ୫୦

l *abbreviation* ଶବ୍ଦ **litre** ର ସଂକ୍ଷିପ୍ତ ରୂପ

lab *abbreviation* ଶବ୍ଦ **laboratory** ର ସଂକ୍ଷିପ୍ତ ରୂପ

label /ˈleɪbl/ *noun* a piece of paper or plastic on something that tells you about it ଦ୍ରବ୍ୟ ବିଷୟରେ କେତେକ କଥା ଲେଖା ହୋଇଥିବା କାଗଜ ବା ପ୍ଲାଷ୍ଟିକ୍ ପଟି, ଲେବଲ୍ *The label on the bottle says 'Made in Mexico'.*

label *verb* (**labels, labelling, labelled**) put a label on something ଲେବଲ୍ ଲଗାଇବା *I labelled all the boxes with my name and address.*

laboratory /ləˈbɒrətri/ *noun* (*plural* **laboratories**) a special room where scientists work ବୈଜ୍ଞାନିକ ପରୀକ୍ଷାଗାର, ଗବେଷଣାଗାର ✪ Laboratory ର ସଂକ୍ଷିପ୍ତ ରୂପ **lab**।

labour /ˈleɪbə(r)/ *noun* (*no plural*) hard work that you do with your hands and body ପରିଶ୍ରମ, ଦୈହିକ ଶ୍ରମ

labourer /ˈleɪbərə(r)/ *noun* a person who does hard work with his/her hands and body ଶ୍ରମିକ, ଶ୍ରମଜୀବୀ *a farm labourer*

lace /leɪs/ *noun* **1** (*plural* **laces**) a string that you use to tie up your shoe ଯୋତାର ଫିତା, ଲେସ୍ **2** (*no plural*) a thin pretty material with a pattern of very small holes in it କଣାକଣା ହୋଇ କାରୁକାର୍ଯ୍ୟ ହୋଇଥିବା ପତଳା ସୁନ୍ଦର କନା, ଝାଲର୍ *lace curtains*

lack /læk/ *verb* (**lacks, lacking, lacked**) not have something, or not have enough of something ଅଭାବରେ ରହିବା, ଅଭାବ ଅନୁଭବ କରିବା *The children lacked the food they needed.*

lack *noun* (*no plural*) ଅଭାବ, ନିଅଣ୍ଟ *There is a lack of good teachers.*

lad /læd/ *noun* a boy or young man ବାଳକ ବା ଯୁବକ, ଟୋକା

ladder /ˈlædə(r)/ *noun* two tall pieces of metal or wood with shorter pieces (called **rungs**) between them. You use a ladder for climbing up something ଶିଢ଼ି, ନିଶୁଣି

laden /ˈleɪdn/ *adjective* heavily loaded or carrying a lot of things ବୋଝେଇ ହୋଇଥିବା, ବୋଝଦ୍ୱାରା ଭାରାକ୍ରାନ୍ତ *The donkeys were laden with apples.*

lady /ˈleɪdi/ *noun* (*plural* **ladies**) a polite way of saying 'woman' ଭଦ୍ରମହିଳା *an old lady* ⇨ **gentleman** ଦେଖନ୍ତୁ।

ladybird /ˈleɪdibɜːd/ *noun* a small round flying insect that is usually red or yellow with black spots ଈଷତ୍ ଲାଲ୍–ବାଦାମୀ ବା ହଳଦିଆ ରଙ୍ଗ ଓ କଳା ଦାଗ ଥିବା ଛୋଟ ଗୋଲିଆ ଉଡ଼ାପୋକ

lag /læg/ *verb* (**lags, lagging, lagged**) move or grow more slowly than others ଅନ୍ୟମାନଙ୍କ ପଛରେ ରହିଯିବା *Pradeep lagged behind the other runners.*

lagoon /ləˈguːn/ *noun* a salt water lake that is separated from the sea by an area of rock or sand ସମୁଦ୍ରଠାରୁ ବାଲିଚର କିଂବା ପ୍ରବାଳ ପ୍ରାଚୀର ଦ୍ୱାରା ବିଚ୍ଛିନ୍ନ

ହୋଇଥିବା ଲବଣାକ୍ତ ହ୍ରଦ, ଲୁଣା ହ୍ରଦ *Lagoons are usually found in coastal regions.*

laid ଶବ୍ଦ **lay²** ର ଏକ ଧାତୁରୂପ

lain ଶବ୍ଦ **lie²** ର ଏକ ଧାତୁରୂପ

lake /leɪk/ *noun* a big area of water with land all around it ହ୍ରଦ *the Dal Lake* ➪ **pond** ଦେଖନ୍ତୁ।

lamb /læm/ *noun* a young sheep ମେଣ୍ଢାଛୁଆ, ମେଷ ଶାବକ ➪ ଚିତ୍ର ପାଇଁ **sheep** ଦେଖନ୍ତୁ।

lame /leɪm/ *adjective* if an animal is lame, it cannot walk well because it has hurt its leg or foot ଛୋଟା, ପଙ୍ଗୁ *My horse is lame, so I can't ride her.*

lamp /læmp/ *noun* a thing that gives light ପ୍ରଦୀପ, ଦୀପ, ବତି *It was dark, so I switched on the lamp.*

lamp post *noun* (*plural* **lamp posts**) a tall thing in the street with a light on the top ବତିଖୁଣ୍ଟ

lampshade /ˈlæmpʃeɪd/ *noun* a cover for a lamp ଉଜ୍ଜ୍ୱଳ ଆଲୁଅକୁ ଅଳ୍ପ ଢ଼ାଙ୍କିବା ପାଇଁ ଥିବା ଟୋପିପରି ଆବରଣ

land¹ /lænd/ *noun* **1** (*no plural*) the part of the earth that is not the sea ଭୂପୃଷ୍ଠ, ଭୂମି, ଭୂଖଣ୍ଡ *After two weeks in a boat, we were happy to see land.* **2** (*no plural*) a piece of ground ପଡ଼ିଆ, ଜମି *farming land* **3** (*plural* **lands**) a country ଦେଶ *She returned to the land where she was born.* ✪ ଏ ଅର୍ଥରେ ଆମେ ସାଧାରଣତଃ **country** ଶବ୍ଦ ବ୍ୟବହାର କରିଥାଉଁ।

land² /lænd/ *verb* (**lands, landing, landed**) come onto the ground from the air (ବିମାନ, ବିମାନଯାତ୍ରୀ ପ୍ରଭୃତି) ଆକାଶରୁ ଭୂମି ଉପରକୁ ଓହ୍ଲାଇବା *The plane landed at 5 a.m.* ✪ ବିପରୀତ **take off**

landing /ˈlændɪŋ/ *noun* the act of coming down onto the ground ଅବତରଣ *The plane made a safe landing in a field.* ✪ ବିପରୀତ **take-off**

landlady /ˈlændleɪdi/ *noun* (*plural* **landladies**) a woman who has a house and lets you live there if you pay her money ଘର, ବଖରା ଇତ୍ୟାଦି ଭଡ଼ା ଦେଉଥିବା ସ୍ତ୍ରୀଲୋକ, ଘର ମାଲିକାଣୀ ➪ **landlord** ଦେଖନ୍ତୁ।

landlord /ˈlændlɔːd/ *noun* a man who has a house and lets you live there if you pay him money ଘର, ବଖରା ଇତ୍ୟାଦି ଭଡ଼ା ଦେଉଥିବା ପୁରୁଷ; ଜମିଦାର, ଘର ମାଲିକ ➪ **landlady** ଦେଖନ୍ତୁ।

landmark /ˈlændmɑːk/ *noun* a big building or another thing that you can see easily from far away ଦୂରରୁ ଦେଖି ସ୍ପଷ୍ଟ ଭାବେ ଚିହ୍ନି ହେଉଥିବା କୋଠା, ମନ୍ଦିର, ପାହାଡ଼ ଇତ୍ୟାଦି ସଂକେତିକ ସ୍ଥାନ *India Gate is one of Delhi's most famous landmarks.*

landscape /ˈlændskeɪp/ *noun* everything you can see in an area of land ଭୂଭାଗର ଦୃଶ୍ୟ, ପ୍ରାକୃତିକ ଦୃଶ୍ୟ, ଆଞ୍ଚଳିକ ଦୃଶ୍ୟ *The hilly landscape around Ooty is very beautiful.*

landslide /ˈlændslaɪd/ *noun* a mass of earth and rocks that slides suddenly down the side of a mountain, usually during heavy rains ଅତଡ଼ା ଖସିବା ବା ପାହାଡ଼ କଡ଼ ଖସିବା ପ୍ରକ୍ରିୟା

lane /leɪn/ *noun* **1** a narrow road in the countryside or in towns ସଂକୀର୍ଣ୍ଣ ରାସ୍ତା, ଗଳି **2** one part of a wide road

ଏକ ଧାଡ଼ିରେ ଯାତାୟତ କରିବାପାଇଁ ରାସ୍ତାର ଗୋଟିଏ ଧାର *We were driving in the middle lane of the highway.*

language /ˈlæŋgwɪdʒ/ *noun* **1** (*no plural*) words that people use to speak or write to each other ଭାଷା **2** (*plural* **languages**) words that a certain group of people say and write କୌଣସି ଏକ ଭାଷା *Do you speak any foreign languages?*

langur *noun* a large monkey usually with white hair on its body, a black face and a long tail. Langurs live in groups ହନୁମାଙ୍କଡ଼

lantern /ˈlæntən/ *noun* a lamp with a metal frame and usually glass sides, that can be carried ଲଣ୍ଠନ, ହାରିକେନ୍

lap¹ /læp/ *noun* the flat part formed by the top of your legs when you are sitting କୋଡ଼, କ୍ରୋଡ଼ *The child was sitting on his mother's lap.*

lap² /læp/ *noun* going once round the track in a race ଦୌଡ଼ ପ୍ରତିଯୋଗିତାର ଦୀର୍ଘବୃତ୍ତାକାର ପଥର ଥରେ ବୁଲିଆସିବା ପ୍ରକ୍ରିୟା *The runner fell on the last lap.*

laptop /ˈlæptɒp/ *noun* a small computer that you can easily carry to work and that can work with batteries ସାଙ୍ଗରେ ନେଇ ହେଉଥିବା ବ୍ୟାଟେରି ଚାଳିତ ଛୋଟ କମ୍ପ୍ୟୁଟର୍

large /lɑːdʒ/ *adjective* (**larger**, **largest**) big ବଡ଼, ବୃହତ, ବିଶାଳ, ବିରାଟ *She has a large family.* ○ *Have you got this shirt in a large size?* ✪ ବିପରୀତ **small**

larva /ˈlɑːvə/ *noun* (*plural* **larvae** /ˈlɑːviː/) a young insect that has just come out of an egg and looks like a worm ପୋକ ଅଣ୍ଡାରୁ ବାହାରିବା ପରର ପ୍ରଥମାବସ୍ଥା, ଶୂକ

laser /ˈleɪzə(r)/ *noun* an instrument that sends out a very strong line of light (called a **laser beam**). Some lasers are used to cut metal and others are used by doctors in operations ତୀବ୍ର ଓ ଅତିମାତ୍ରାରେ ଘନୀଭୂତ ଆଲୋକ ରଶ୍ମି ଉତ୍ପାଦକ ଓ ବିକିରଣକାରୀ ଯନ୍ତ୍ର (ଯାହା ଧାତୁ କାଟିବାରେ ବା ଅସ୍ତ୍ର ଚିକିତ୍ସାରେ ବ୍ୟବହୃତ ହୁଏ); ଲେଜର୍

last¹ /lɑːst/ *adjective* **1** after all the others ସମସ୍ତଙ୍କ ପଛରେ, ଶେଷରେ *December is the last month of the year.* ✪ ବିପରୀତ **first¹** **2** just before now ଗତ, ବିଗତ, ଅଳ୍ପ ଦିନ ବା ସମୟ ତଳର *I was at school last week, but this week I'm on holiday.* **3** only one left ଶେଷ, ସର୍ବଶେଷ *Who wants the last piece of cake?*

lastly *adverb* finally, as the last thing ଶେଷରେ, ସର୍ବଶେଷରେ *Lastly, I want to thank my parents for all their help.*

last² /lɑːst/ *adverb* **1** after all the others ସମସ୍ତଙ୍କ ପରେ, ଶେଷରେ *He finished last in the race.* **2** at a time that is nearest to now ଅଳ୍ପ ସମୟ ପୂର୍ବରୁ; କିଛି ଦିନ ପୂର୍ବରୁ *I last saw Parul in 1993.*

last[3] /lɑːst/ *noun* (*no plural*) a person or thing that comes after all the others; what comes at the end ଶେଷ ବ୍ୟକ୍ତି ବା ପଦାର୍ଥ *I was the last to arrive at the party.*

at last in the end; after some time ପରିଶେଷରେ *She waited all week, and at last the letter arrived.*

last[4] /lɑːst/ *verb* (**lasts, lasting, lasted**) **1** continue for a time ଦୀର୍ଘକାଳ ପାଇଁ ଚାଲିବା, ନିର୍ଦ୍ଦିଷ୍ଟ ସମୟ ପାଇଁ ଚାଲିବା *The film lasted for three hours.* **2** be enough for a certain time ନିର୍ଦ୍ଦିଷ୍ଟ କାଳପାଇଁ ପର୍ଯ୍ୟାପ୍ତ ହେବା *We have enough food to last us till next week.*

latch /lætʃ/ *noun* (*plural* **latches**) a small metal object that you use to fasten a door or a gate କିଳିଣୀ, ଦୁଆର ଶିକୁଳି ଇତ୍ୟାଦି

late /leɪt/ *adjective*, *adverb* (**later, latest**) **1** after the usual or right time ବିଳମ୍ବରେ, ଡେରିରେ; ବିଳମ୍ବିତ *I went to bed late last night.* ○ *My train was late.* **2** near the end of a time କୌଣସି ସମୟ ସୀମାର ଶେଷଭାଗରେ *She's in her late twenties.* ✪ ବିପରୀତ **early**

at the latest not later than ନିର୍ଦ୍ଦିଷ୍ଟ ସମୟ ଭିତରେ, ତା' ପରେ ନୁହେଁ *Please be here by twelve o'clock at the latest.*

lately /ˈleɪtli/ *adverb* not long ago; recently ସାଂପ୍ରତିକ ସମୟରେ; ଅଳ୍ପଦିନ ପୂର୍ବେ *Have you seen Vikas lately?*

latest /ˈleɪtɪst/ *adjective* newest ନୂଆ, ଏବକାର, ସର୍ବାଧୁନିକ *the latest fashions*

lather /ˈlɑːðə(r)/ *noun* (*no plural*) the soft mass of white bubbles that you get when you mix soap with water ସାବୁନ୍ ଫେଣ

latitude /ˈlætɪtjuːd/ *noun* the distance of a place to the north or south of the **equator** ଅକ୍ଷରେଖା, ଅକ୍ଷାଂଶ, ବିଷୁବରେଖା ଠାରୁ ଉତ୍ତର ବା ଦକ୍ଷିଣ ଆଡ଼କୁ କୌଣସି ସ୍ଥାନର କୌଣିକ ଦୂରତ୍ୱ ➪ **globe** ଏବଂ **longitude** ମଧ୍ୟ ଦେଖନ୍ତୁ ।

laugh /lɑːf/ *verb* (**laughs, laughing, laughed**) make sounds that show you are happy or that you think something is funny ହସିବା, ବଡ଼ ପାଟିରେ, କୌତୁକରେ ହସିବା *His jokes always make me laugh.*

laugh at somebody or **something** laugh to show that you think somebody or something is funny or silly ପରିହାସ କରିବା, ଥଟ୍ଟା କରିବା, ଅନ୍ୟର ଦୁର୍ବଳତାରେ ହସିବା *The children laughed at the clown.* ○ *They all laughed at me when I said I was frightened of dogs.*

laugh *noun* ହସ *My brother has a loud laugh.*

laughter *noun* (*no plural*) the sound of laughing ହସ ଶବ୍ଦ, ହସି ହସି ବେଦମ, ହସରେ ଫାଟି ପଡ଼ିବା *I could hear laughter in the next room.*

launch /lɔːntʃ/ *verb* (**launches, launching, launched**) put a newly built ship into the water or a spacecraft into the sky ନୂଆ ଜାହାଜକୁ ପ୍ରଥମ ଥର ପାଇଁ ପାଣିରେ ଭସାଇବା; କ୍ଷେପଣାସ୍ତ୍ର ବା ମହାକାଶଯାନ ଇତ୍ୟାଦି ନିକ୍ଷେପ କରିବା, ଆରମ୍ଭ କରିବା *This rocket is being launched tomorrow.*

laundry /ˈlɔːndri/ *noun* (*plural* **laundries**) a place where you send things like sheets and clothes so that somebody can wash them for you ଲୁଗାସଫା କରିବା ଓ ଇସ୍ତ୍ରୀ କରିବା ସ୍ଥାନ ବା ଦୋକାନ

lava /ˈlɑːvə/ *noun* (*no plural*) hot liquid rock that comes out of a **volcano** ଆଗ୍ନେୟଗିରିରୁ ବାହାରୁଥିବା ଉତ୍ତପ୍ତ ତରଳ ପଦାର୍ଥ, ଲାଭା ➪ ଚିତ୍ର ପାଇଁ **volcano** ଦେଖନ୍ତୁ ।

law /ˈlɔː/ *noun* a rule of a country that says what people may and may not do ଆଇନ୍, ବିଧି, ନିୟମ *There is a law against stealing.* ➪ **legal** ଦେଖନ୍ତୁ ।

against the law not allowed by the rules of a country ଆଇନ୍ ବିରୁଦ୍ଧ

break the law do something that the laws of a country say you must not do ଆଇନ୍ ଭଙ୍ଗ କରିବା, ଆଇନ୍ ଅମାନ୍ୟ କରିବା

law court *noun* a place where people (a **judge** or **jury**) decide if somebody has done something wrong, and what the punishment will be ବିଚାରାଳୟ, ଅଦାଲତ

lawn /lɔːn/ *noun* a piece of land covered with short grass in a garden or park ବଗିଚା, ପାର୍କର ଛୋଟ ଛୋଟ କରି କଟାଯାଇଥିବା ସୂକ୍ଷ୍ମ ଘାସ ଆଚ୍ଛାଦିତ ସମତଳ ଭୂମି *They were sitting on the lawn.*

lawnmower /ˈlɔːnməʊə(r)/ *noun* a machine that cuts grass ଘାସ କାଟିବା ଯନ୍ତ୍ର

lawyer /ˈlɔːjə(r)/ *noun* a person who has studied the law and who helps people or talks for them in a court of law ଓକିଲ, ଆଇନ୍‌ଜୀବୀ

lay[1] ଶବ୍ଦ **lie[2]** ର ଏକ ଧାତୁରୂପ

lay[2] /leɪ/ *verb* (**lays, laying, laid** /leɪd/, **has laid**) **1** put something carefully on another thing କିଛି ଜିନିଷ ଅନ୍ୟ ଜିନିଷ ଉପରେ ଯତ୍ନରେ ରଖିବା ବା ଥୋଇବା; ସ୍ଥାପନ କରିବା *I laid the papers on the desk.* **2** produce an egg (ପକ୍ଷୀ) ଅଣ୍ଡା ଦେବା *Birds and insects lay eggs.*

layer /ˈleɪə(r)/ *noun* a thing of the same thickness that lies on another thing or that is between two things ପରସ୍ତ, ସ୍ତର *The table was covered with a thin layer of dust.* ○ *The cake has a layer of jam in the middle.*

lazy /ˈleɪzi/ *adjective* (**lazier, laziest**) a person who is lazy does not want to work ଅଳସୁଆ, ଆଳସ୍ୟ ପରାୟଣ *His teacher said that he was lazy.*

laziness *noun* (*no plural*) being lazy ଅଳସୁଆମି, ଆଳସ୍ୟ

lead[1] /liːd/ *verb* (**leads, leading, led** /led/, **has led**) **1** take a person or an animal somewhere by going in front ଲୋକଙ୍କୁ ବା ପଶୁଙ୍କୁ ବାଟ କଢ଼ାଇବା, ନେତୃତ୍ୱ ନେବା *He led me to my room.* **2** control a group of people କୌଣସି ଗୋଷ୍ଠୀର ଦାୟିତ୍ୱରେ ରହିବା, ଅଗ୍ରଣୀ ବା ପରିଚାଳକ ଭାବରେ ରହିବା *The team was led by Abha Gupta.*

lead to something make something happen ଘଟାଇବା, ଫଳାଫଳ ଭାବେ ଘଟିବା *Smoking can lead to heart disease.*

lead[2] /liːd/ *noun* (*no plural*) the position in front or the act of doing something before other people ଅଗ୍ରଣୀ ସ୍ଥାନ; ନେତୃତ୍ୱ

be in the lead be in the first place ଆଗରେ ରହି, ଅଗ୍ରଣୀ ସ୍ଥାନରେ ରହିବା *At the start of the race, her horse was in the lead.*

lead[3] /led/ *noun* **1** (*no plural*) a soft grey metal that is very heavy. Lead is used for making things like water pipes and roofs ସୀସା, ସୀସକ **2** (*plural* **leads**) the grey part inside a pencil that you use to write with ପେନ୍‌ସିଲ୍‌ର କଳା ସୀସା ବା ଗ୍ରାଫାଇଟ୍ ଯାହାଦ୍ୱାରା ଲେଖିହୁଏ

leader /ˈliːdə(r)/ *noun* a person who leads a group of people ଅଗ୍ରଣୀ, ନେତା *They chose a new leader.*

leadership /ˈliːdəʃɪp/ *noun* (*no plural*) the state or position of leading a group of people ନେତୃତ୍ୱ *The leadership of the party changed last year.*

leaf /liːf/ *noun* (*plural* **leaves** /liːvz/) one of the flat green parts that grow on a plant or tree ଗଛର ପତ୍ର, ପର୍ଣ୍ଣ ➪ ଚିତ୍ର ପାଇଁ **plant** ଦେଖନ୍ତୁ ।

leafy /ˈliːfi/ *adjective* (**leafier, leafiest**) that which has many leaves ବହୁ ପତ୍ରଥିବା, ପତ୍ର ଆଚ୍ଛାଦିତ *leafy green vegetables*

leak /liːk/ *verb* (**leaks, leaking, leaked**) have a hole or crack that liquid or gas can go through କଣା ବା ଫାଟ ବାଟେ ତରଳ ପଦାର୍ଥ ବୋହିଯିବା *The boat is leaking.*

leak *noun* ଛିଦ୍ର, କଣା ବା ଫାଟ *There's a leak in the pipe.*

lean[1] /liːn/ *adjective* (**leaner, leanest**) thin but strong ପତଳା, ସରୁ (କିନ୍ତୁ ଟାଣୁଆ) *He is tall and lean.*

lean[2] /liːn/ *verb* (**leans, leaning, leant** /ˈlent/ ବା **leaned, has leant** ବା **has leaned**) put your body or a thing against another thing ଆଉଜିବା; ଗୋଟିଏ ପଟକୁ ଢଳିବା; ଭରା ଦେବା *Lean your bike against the wall.*

leap /liːp/ *verb* (**leaps, leaping, leapt** /lept/ ବା **leaped, has leapt** ବା **has leaped**) make a big jump ଡେଇଁବା, ଲମ୍ଫ ଦେବା, ଉଲ୍ଲମ୍ଫନ କରିବା *The cat leapt onto the table.*

leap *noun* a big jump ଡିଆଁ, ଲମ୍ଫ, ଉଲ୍ଲମ୍ଫନ *With one leap, he was over the wall.*

leap year *noun* a year when February has 29 days. Leap years happen every four years ପ୍ରତି ଚାରି ବର୍ଷରେ ଆସୁଥିବା ୩୬୬ ଦିନ ଥିବା ବର୍ଷ ଯେଉଁଥିରେ ଫେବୃଆରୀର ୨୯ ଦିନ ଥାଏ; ଅଧିବର୍ଷ

learn /lɜːn/ *verb* (**learns, learning, learnt** /ˈlɜːnt/ ବା **learned, has learnt** ବା **has learned**) find out something, or how to do something, by studying or by doing it often ଶିଖିବା, ଜାଣିବା, କୌଣସି ବିଷୟରେ ଜ୍ଞାନ ଆହରଣ କରିବା *Uma is learning to swim.* ➪ **teach** ଦେଖନ୍ତୁ ।

learned /ˈlɜːnɪd/ *adjective* having a lot of knowledge because one has studied very much ଜ୍ଞାନୀ, ବିଦ୍ୱାନ୍, ସୁଶିକ୍ଷିତ *a learned man*

learner /ˈlɜːnə(r)/ *noun* a person who is learning ଶିଖୁଥିବା ବ୍ୟକ୍ତି, ଶିକ୍ଷାନବିସ୍ *This dictionary is for learners of English.*

lease[1] /li:s/ *noun* an agreement that allows you to use a building or a piece of land for a fixed period of time for a certain amount of rent ଚୁକ୍ତି, ପଟ୍ଟା ବା ଇଜରା ଯାହାଦ୍ୱାରା ଜମିମାଲିକ ନିର୍ଦ୍ଦିଷ୍ଟ ସମୟ ପାଇଁ ଅନ୍ୟ ଜଣଙ୍କୁ ଭଡ଼ା ନେଇ ଜମି ଇତ୍ୟାଦି ବ୍ୟବହାର ପାଇଁ ଦିଅନ୍ତି; ଲିଜ୍ *We have to renew the lease on our flat.*

lease[2] /li:s/ *verb* (**leases, leasing, leased**) use or allow someone else to use a building or a piece of land for a fixed period in exchange for a regular payment (ଜମି, ଘର ଇତ୍ୟାଦି) ଚୁକ୍ତି କରି ନିର୍ଦ୍ଦିଷ୍ଟ ସମୟ ପାଇଁ ଭଡ଼ାରେ ଦେବା *I have leased the flat to tenants.*

leash /li:ʃ/ *noun* a long piece of leather or a chain that you tie to a dog's neck so that it walks with you କୁକୁର ବେକରେ ଲଗାଯାଇଥିବା ଲମ୍ବା ଚମଡ଼ା ପଟି ବା ଶିକୁଳି

least[1] /li:st/ *adjective, pronoun* the smallest amount of something ସବୁଠାରୁ କମ୍; ଅତି ଅଳ୍ପ *Charu has a lot of money. Jaya has less, and Kiran has the least.* ➪ **less** ଦେଖନ୍ତୁ।

least[2] /li:st/ *adverb* less than all others ନୂନତମ, ସବୁଠାରୁ କମ୍ *This is the least expensive camera in the shop.* ✪ ବିପରୀତ **most**[2]

at least 1 not less than ଅତି କମ୍‌ରେ *It will cost at least Rs 250.* **2** although other things are bad ଅନ୍ତତ କମ୍‌ରେ, ଯାହା ହେଲେବି *We're not rich, but at least we're happy.*

leather /ˈleðə(r)/ *noun* (*no plural*) the skin of an animal that is used for making things like shoes, jackets or bags (କଷାଯାଇ ପ୍ରସ୍ତୁତ କରାଯାଇଥିବା) ଚମଡ଼ା *a leather jacket*

leave[1] /ˈli:v/ *verb* (**leaves, leaving, left** /left/, **has left**) **1** go away from somebody or something ଚାଲିଯିବା, ପ୍ରସ୍ଥାନ କରିବା *The train leaves at 8.40 a.m.* ○ *She left home when she was twenty-one.* **2** let somebody or something stay in the same place or in the same way କାହାରିକୁ ବା କୌଣସି ପଦାର୍ଥକୁ କୌଣସି ଏକ ସ୍ଥାନରେ ରଖିଯିବା *I left my books at home.*

leave somebody or **something behind** not take somebody or something with you କାହାରିକୁ ବା କୌଣସି ପଦାର୍ଥକୁ ଛାଡ଼ିଯିବା *She went shopping and left the children behind.*

leave out not put in or do something; not include somebody or something ବାଦ୍ ଦେବା, ଛାଡ଼ିଦେବା *I left out question 3 in the exam because it was too difficult.*

leave[2] /ˈli:v/ *noun* (*no plural*) a time when you do not go to work ଛୁଟି *I have twenty-five days' leave each year.*

on leave having a holiday from your job କାର୍ଯ୍ୟରୁ ଛୁଟି ନେବା *He's on leave for a month.*

leaves ଶବ୍ଦ **leaf** ର ବହୁବଚନ

lecture /ˈlektʃə(r)/ *noun* a talk given to a group of people to teach them about something ବକ୍ତୃତା, ଭାଷଣ *She gave an interesting lecture on the wildlife of the area.*

lecturer /ˈlektʃərə(r)/ *noun* a person who teaches at a university or college ମହାବିଦ୍ୟାଳୟ ବା ବିଶ୍ୱବିଦ୍ୟାଳୟର ଅଧ୍ୟାପକ *He is a university lecturer.*

led ଶବ୍ଦ **lead**[2] ର ଏକ ଧାତୁରୂପ

ledge /ledʒ/ *noun* a long narrow flat place, for example under a window or on the side of a cliff ଝରକା ତଳପଟର ସମତଳ ଥାକ ପରିଧାର; ପାହାଡ଼ ଇତ୍ୟାଦିର ତିଖା ପଟର ଉପର ଭାଗରେ ଥିବା ସରୁ ଓ ଲମ୍ବା ସମତଳ ଚଟାଣ *a window ledge*

leech /liːtʃ/ *noun* (*plural* **leeches**) a small worm that attaches itself to large animals and sucks their blood ଜୋକ, ଟିଙ୍କ, କେଣ୍ଟି

left[1] ଶବ୍ଦ **leave**[1] ର ଏକ ଧାତୁରୂପ

be left be there after the rest have gone ବଳିପଡ଼ିବା, ଶେଷକୁ ରହିଯିବା *There is only a small piece of cake left.*

left[2] /left/ *adjective*, *adverb* opposite of right ବାଁ ପଟର, ବାମ *My left leg hurts.* ✪ ବିପରୀତ **right**[1]

left *noun* (*no plural*) ବାଁ ପଟ, ବାମ ପାର୍ଶ୍ୱ *The house is on your left.* ✪ ବିପରୀତ **right**[1]

left-hand *adjective* of or on the left ବାଁ ପଟର, ବାମ ପାର୍ଶ୍ୱସ୍ଥ *Your heart is on the left-hand side of your body.* ✪ ବିପରୀତ **right-hand**

leg /leg/ *noun* **1** one of the long parts of the body of a person or an animal that is used for walking and standing ଗୋଡ଼, ଚରଣ, ପଦ ➪ ଚିତ୍ର ପାଇଁ **body** ଦେଖନ୍ତୁ । **2** one of the long parts that a table or chair stands on ଟେବୁଲ୍, ଚଉକି ଇତ୍ୟାଦିର ଗୋଡ଼

legal /ˈliːgl/ *adjective* **1** allowed by the law ଆଇନ୍‌ସମ୍ମତ, ଆଇନ୍ ଉପରେ ଆଧାରିତ ✪ ବିପରୀତ **illegal** **2** of or about the law ଆଇନ୍ ସମ୍ବନ୍ଧୀୟ *legal advice*

legend /ˈledʒənd/ *noun* an old story that is perhaps not true କିଂବଦନ୍ତୀ ଆଧାରିତ କାହାଣୀ *the legend of Robin Hood*

leisure /ˈleʒə(r)/ *noun* (*no plural*) the time when you are not working and can do what you want ଅବକାଶ, ଅବସର, କାମ ନଥିବା ସମୟ

lemon /ˈlemən/ *noun* a yellow fruit with a sour taste ଲେମ୍ବୁ

lend /lend/ *verb* (**lends, lending, lent** /lent/, **has lent**) give something to somebody for a short time ଧାର ଦେବା, ଉଧାରରେ ଦେବା, ଅଳ୍ପ ସମୟ ପରେ ଫେରି ପାଇବା ସର୍ତ୍ତରେ ଦେବା *Ruby lent me her car for an hour.*

length /leŋθ/ *noun* (*no plural*) how long something is ଲମ୍ବ *The table is two metres in length.*

lengthen /ˈleŋθən/ *verb* (**lengthens, lengthening, lengthened**) become longer or make something longer ଅଧିକ ଲମ୍ବା ହେବା ବା କରିବା

lengthy /ˈleŋθi/ *adjective* (**lengthier, lengthiest**) very long ଅତି ଲମ୍ବା, ଦୀର୍ଘ ସମୟର *a lengthy meeting*

lens /lenz/ *noun* (*plural* **lenses**) a special piece of glass in things like cameras, microscopes or glasses

ଯବକାଚ, ବୀକ୍ଷଣ କାଚ, ଲେନ୍ସ୍, ➪ **contact lens** ଦେଖନ୍ତୁ ।

lent ଶବ୍ଦ **lend** ର ଏକ ଧାତୁରୂପ

lentil /ˈlentl/ *noun* a small round green, orange, yellow or brown dried seed that Indians call dal. You cook lentils in water before you eat them ଡାଲି ବା ଛୁଇଁ ଜାତୀୟ ପରିବାର ମଞ୍ଜି; ମସୁର

lentils

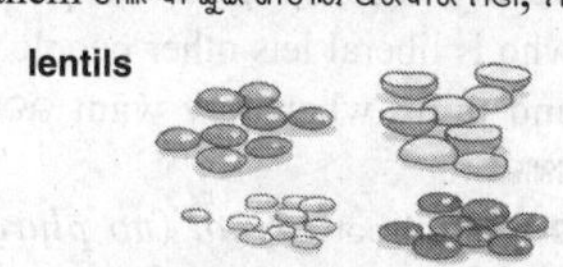

Leo /ˈliːəʊ/ *noun* the fifth sign of the **zodiac** ରାଶିଚକ୍ରର ପଞ୍ଚମ ରାଶି, ସିଂହରାଶି

leopard /ˈlepəd/ *noun* a wild animal like a big cat with yellow fur and black spots. Leopards are found in Africa and southern Asia ଆଫ୍ରିକା ଓ ଏସିଆର ହଳଦିଆ ଲୁମ ଓ କଳା ଦାଗ ଥିବା ଚିତା ବାଘ ବା କଲରାପତ୍ରିଆ ବାଘ; ଚିତାବାଘ

leopard

less¹ /les/ *adjective*, *pronoun* a smaller amount of something; not so much କମ୍, ଊଣା; ବେଶି ନହୋଇଥିବା ➪ **least** ଦେଖନ୍ତୁ । ✪ ବିପରୀତ **more¹**

less² /les/ *adverb* not so much କମ୍ ପରିମାଣରେ, କମ୍ ମାତ୍ରାରେ *Here it rains less in winter*. ➪ **least** ଦେଖନ୍ତୁ । ✪ ବିପରୀତ **more²**

lessen /ˈlesn/ *verb* (**lessens**, **lessening**, **lessened**) make something become smaller or weaker କମେଇବା, କମ୍ କରିବା; କମିଯିବା, କମ୍‌ହେବା *The noise lessened as soon as the principal entered the school auditorium.*

lesson /ˈlesn/ *noun* **1** a time when you learn something with a teacher ଶିକ୍ଷାଦାନର କାଳ ବା ଅବଧି *We have a history lesson after recess*. **2** something learnt or to be learnt ପାଠ, ଶିକ୍ଷାର ବିଷୟ *We have covered only four lessons so far.* **3** an experience, often an unpleasant one, that teaches you to be careful about something in future ଅନୁଭୂତି ଦ୍ୱାରା ପ୍ରାପ୍ତ ଶିକ୍ଷା; ଭୁଲ୍ କାମକରି ପାଇଥିବା ଶିକ୍ଷା, ଠିକ୍ ଶିଖିଥିବା ବିଷୟ

let /let/ *verb* (**lets, letting, let, has let**) allow somebody or something to do something ଅନୁମତି ଦେବା *Let me carry your bag.*

let's you use **let's** to ask somebody to do something with you ନିଜ ସଙ୍ଗେ ମିଶି କାମ କରିବାକୁ କହିବା *Let's go to the theatre this evening.*

letter /ˈletə(r)/ *noun* **1** a sign in writing ଅକ୍ଷର, ବର୍ଣ୍ଣ, ଲିପି *Z is the last letter in the English alphabet.*

> ✪ A, B ଓ C ହେଲେ **capital letters** (ବଡ଼ ଅକ୍ଷର) ଏବଂ a, b ଓ c ହେଲେ **small letters** (ସାନ ଅକ୍ଷର)

2 a message written on paper that one person sends to or receives from another person ଚିଠି, ପତ୍ର *Did you post my letter?*

letter box *noun* (*plural* **letter boxes**) **1** a box for letters outside a house ପୋଷ୍ଟମ୍ୟାନ୍ ଚିଠି ରଖିଦେଇ ଯିବା ପାଇଁ

ଘର ବାହାରେ ଥିବା ବାକ୍ସ, ଚିଠିବାକ୍ସ **2** a box in the street where you put letters that you want to send ରାସ୍ତା କଡ଼ରେ ଡାକବିଭାଗ ଦ୍ୱାରା ସ୍ଥାପିତ ଚିଠି ପକାଇବା ବାକ୍ସ, ଡାକବାକ୍ସ

level¹ /ˈlevl/ *adjective* **1** with no part higher than another part; flat ସମତଳ, ଅନୁଭୂମିକ, ଅନୁପ୍ରସ୍ଥ ଖାଲଢ଼ିପ ନଥିବା, ଅବନ୍ଧୁର *We need level ground to play football on.* **2** with the same points, heights, positions, for example ସଂଖ୍ୟା, ଉଚ୍ଚତା, ସ୍ଥିରେ ସମାନ ହୋଇଥିବା *The two teams are level with 40 points each.*

level² /ˈlevl/ *noun* **1** how high something is ଉଚ୍ଚତା, ପତ୍ତନ *The town is 500 metres above sea level.* **2** the amount, size, number or standard of something that exists at a particular time or in a particular place (ଏକ ସମୟରେ, ଏକା ସ୍ଥାନରେ ଥିବା ପରିମାଣ, ଆକାର, ସଂଖ୍ୟା ବା ମାନର) ସ୍ତର *strive to bring down pollution levels* ○ *talks at the highest level*

level crossing *noun* a place where a road crosses a railway line ସମସ୍ତରରେ ଥିବା ରାସ୍ତା ଓ ରେଳପଥ ପରସ୍ପରକୁ ଅତିକ୍ରମ କରୁଥିବା ସ୍ଥାନ, ଲେଭଲ୍‌କ୍ରସିଂ

lever /ˈliːvə(r)/ *noun* **1** a bar for lifting something heavy or opening something. You put one end of the lever under the thing you want to lift or open, and push the other end down ଭାରୀ ଜିନିଷକୁ ତାଡ଼ି ଟେକିବା ପାଇଁ ବ୍ୟବହୃତ ଶାବଳ ପରି ଶକ୍ତ ଦଣ୍ଡ (ଯାହାର ଗୋଟିଏ ପଟ ଜିନିଷ ତଳେ ପୂରାଇ ଅନ୍ୟ ପଟଟି ତଳକୁ ମାଡ଼ି ଜିନିଷଟକୁ ଉଠାଯାଏ; ଉତ୍ତୋଳନ ଦଣ୍ଡ **2** a thing that you pull or push to make a machine work ଯନ୍ତ୍ର ଚାଳନ ପାଇଁ ଥିବା ଦଣ୍ଡ, ଯନ୍ତ୍ରଚାଳନ ଦଣ୍ଡ *Pull this lever to reduce the speed.*

liar /ˈlaɪə(r)/ *noun* a person who says or writes things that are not true ମିଥ୍ୟାବାଦୀ ବ୍ୟକ୍ତି, ମିଛୁଆ ଲୋକ *I don't believe him—he's a liar.*

liberal /ˈlɪbərəl/ *adjective* a person who is liberal lets other people do and think what they want ଉଦାର, ଖୋଲା ମନ

liberty /ˈlɪbəti/ *noun* (*no plural*) being free to go where you want and do what you want ସ୍ୱାଧୀନତା, ନିଜ ଇଚ୍ଛା ଅନୁସାରେ ଚଳିବାର ଅଧିକାର

Libra /ˈliːbrə/ *noun* the seventh sign of the **zodiac** ରାଶିଚକ୍ରର ସପ୍ତମ ରାଶି, ତୁଳାରାଶି; ତୁଳା ନକ୍ଷତ୍ରପୁଞ୍ଜି

library /ˈlaɪbrəri/ *noun* (*plural* **libraries**) a room or building where you go to borrow or read books ପାଠାଗାର, ପୁସ୍ତକାଗାର ✪ ମନେରଖନ୍ତୁ, ଏଠାରୁ ବହି କିଣାଯାଏ ନାହିଁ। ବହି କିଣିବା ସ୍ଥାନ ହେଲା **bookshop** ।

librarian /laɪˈbreəriən/ *noun* a person who works in a library ପାଠାଗାରର ପରିଚାଳକ ବା ତତ୍ତ୍ୱାବଧାୟକ; ପାଠାଗାରର ସହାୟକ ବ୍ୟକ୍ତି; ଲାଇବ୍ରେରିଆନ୍

licence /ˈlaɪsns/ *noun* a piece of paper that shows you are allowed to do or have something (କୌଣସି କାମ କରିବା ପାଇଁ) ଅନୁମତି ପତ୍ର, ଲାଇସେନ୍ସ୍ *Do you have a driving licence?*

license /ˈlaɪsns/ *verb* (**licenses, licensing, licensed**) give somebody a licence ଅନୁମତି ପତ୍ର ଦେବା *This shop is licensed to sell guns.*

lick /lɪk/ *verb* (**licks, licking, licked**) move your tongue over something ଚାଟିବା, ଲେହନ କରିବା *The cat was licking its paws.*

lid /lɪd/ *noun* the top part of a box, pot or other container that covers it and that you can take off ଢାଙ୍କୁଣୀ, ଘୋଡ଼ଣୀ ➪ **eyelid** ମଧ୍ୟ ଦେଖନ୍ତୁ।

lie[1] /laɪ/ *verb* (**lies, lying, lied, has lied**) say something that you know is not true ମିଛ କହିବା *He lied about his age. He said he was twenty-one but actually he's eighteen.*

lie *noun* something you say that you know is not true ମିଛ କଥା, ମିଥ୍ୟା କଥା *She told me a lie.* ✪ ଯିଏ ମିଛ କହେ ତାକୁ **liar** କହନ୍ତି।

lie[2] /laɪ/ *verb* (**lies, lying, lay** /leɪ/, **has lain** /leɪn/) **1** put your body flat on something so that you are not sitting or standing ଶୋଇଯିବା, ଶାୟିତ ହେବା *He lay on the bed and went to sleep.* **2** be or stay on something (କୌଣସି ଜାଗାରେ) ପଡ଼ି ରହିବା *Snow lay on the ground.*

lie down put or have your body flat on something ଶୋଇଯିବା, ଶାୟିତ ହେବା *She lay down on the bed.*

lieutenant /lef'tenənt/ *noun* an officer in the army or navy ସେନାବାହିନୀର କ୍ୟାପ୍‌ଟେନ୍ ତଳ ପାହ୍ୟାର ଅଫିସର୍

life /laɪf/ *noun* **1** (*no plural*) people, animals and plants have life, but things like stone, metal and water do not ଜୀବନ, ଜୀବିତ ଅବସ୍ଥା; ଜୀବନ୍ତ ବସ୍ତୁ *Is there life on the moon?* **2** (*plural* **lives** /laɪvz/) the state of being alive ଜୀବିତ ଅବସ୍ଥା, ଜୀବନ *The doctor saved her life.* **3** (*plural* **lives**) the time that you have been alive ଜୀବନ କାଳ, ଜୀବକାଳ *He has lived here all his life.* **4** (*no plural*) the way that you live ଜୀବନ ଢଙ୍ଗ, ଜୀବନର ଅବସ୍ଥା *a happy life* **5** (*no plural*) energy; being busy and interested ସଜୀବତା, ପ୍ରସନ୍ନତା, ଶକ୍ତି *Young children are full of life.*

lead a life live in a certain way (ନିର୍ଦ୍ଦିଷ୍ଟ ଭାବେ) ଜୀବନଯାପନ କରିବା *She leads a busy life.*

lifebelt /'laɪfbelt/ *noun* a big ring that floats and which you hold on to if you fall into water to stop you from drowning ପାଣିରେ ନ ବୁଡ଼ି ଭାସି ରହିବା ପାଇଁ ପବନ ଫୁଙ୍କା ଚକପରି ରବର ଉପକରଣ (ଯାହା ଦେହରେ ଲଗାଯାଏ)

lifebelt

lifeboat /'laɪfbəʊt/ *noun* a boat that is used to help people who are in danger at sea ସମୁଦ୍ରରେ ବିପଦଗ୍ରସ୍ତ ଲୋକଙ୍କୁ ରକ୍ଷା କରିବା ପାଇଁ ବ୍ୟବହୃତ ଡଙ୍ଗା ବା ବୋଟ୍

life cycle *noun* (*plural* **life cycles**) a series of changes goes through as it grows up ଜୀବର କ୍ରମବିକାଶର ପଦ୍ଧତି, ଜୀବନଚକ୍ର *the life cycle of a butterfly* ➪ ଚିତ୍ର ପାଇଁ **caterpillar** ଦେଖନ୍ତୁ।

life jacket *noun* a special jacket that you wear to stop you from drowning if you fall into water ବ୍ୟକ୍ତିଙ୍କୁ ପାଣିରେ ଭସାଇ ରଖିବା ପାଇଁ ତିଆରି ହୋଇଥିବା ଜାମା।

lifespan /ˈlaɪfspæn/ *noun* the period for which someone lives or something works or lasts ଜୀବନର ଅବଧି, ଜୀବନକାଳ *The lifespan of a mosquito is just a few days.*

lifestyle /ˈlaɪfstaɪl/ *noun* the way that you live ବ୍ୟକ୍ତିଙ୍କ ଦୈନନ୍ଦିନ ଜୀବନ ପ୍ରଣାଳୀ, ଜୀବନ ଶୈଳୀ *They have a healthy lifestyle.*

lifetime /ˈlaɪftaɪm/ *noun* all the time that you are alive ଜୀବନକାଳ, ଜୀବକାଳ *There has been a lot of change in my grandmother's lifetime.*

lift[1] /lɪft/ *verb* (**lifts, lifting, lifted**) move somebody or something up ଉପରକୁ ଉଠାଇବା, ଉତ୍ତୋଳନ କରିବା *I can't lift this box. It's too heavy.*

lift[2] /lɪft/ *noun* **1** a machine that takes people and things up and down in a high building ଉଚ୍ଚ କୋଠାରେ ଗୋଟିଏ ମହଲାରୁ ଉପର ବା ତଳ ମହଲାକୁ ଯିବାପାଇଁ ଏକ ଯାନ୍ତ୍ରିକ ଉପକରଣ, ଲିଫ୍ଟ *Shall we use the stairs or take the lift?* **2** a free journey in another person's car ଅନ୍ୟର ଗାଡ଼ିରେ ମାଗଣା ଯାତ୍ରା *Can you give me a lift to the station?*

lift-off *noun* the act of a rocket leaving the ground and rising into the air ମହାକାଶ ଯାନ ବା କ୍ଷେପଣାସ୍ତ୍ର ଆକାଶମାର୍ଗକୁ ଉଠିବା ପ୍ରକ୍ରିୟା

light[1] /laɪt/ *noun* **1** (*no plural*) light comes from the sun, fire and lamps. It helps us to see things ଆଲୋକ, ଆଲୁଅ, ଆଲୋକ ରଶ୍ମି *sunlight* **2** (*plural* **lights**) a thing that gives light, for example an electric lamp ଆଲୁଅ (ବତି, ଇଲେକ୍ଟ୍ରିକ ବଲବ୍ ଇତ୍ୟାଦି) ଲାଇଟ୍ ➪ **traffic lights** ଦେଖନ୍ତୁ।

> ✪ ଲାଇଟ୍ **on** ବା **off** କରାଯାଇପାରେ ଆମେ ଲାଇଟ୍ ଜଳାଇବାକୁ **put on, turn on** ବା **switch on** କହିପାରିବା କିଂବା ଲିଭାଇବାକୁ **put off, turn off** ବା **switch off (out)** କହିପାରିବା —
> *Turn the lights off before you go to bed.* ○ *It's getting dark. Shall I switch the light on?*

light[2] /laɪt/ *adjective* (**lighter, lightest**) **1** with a pale colour; not dark ହାଲ୍କା ରଙ୍ଗର; ଗାଢ଼ ହୋଇ ନଥିବା *a light-blue shirt* ✪ ବିପରୀତ **dark**[1] **2** ବା **deep 2** **2** easy to lift or move; not heavy ହାଲ୍କା, ଭାରୀ ହୋଇ ନଥିବା *Will you carry this bag for me? It's very light.* ✪ ବିପରୀତ **heavy** **3** not very much or not very strong ଖୁବ୍ ବେଶି ହୋଇ ନଥିବା, ଖୁବ୍ ଜୋର୍‌ରେ ହେଉ ନଥିବା, ସାମାନ୍ୟ *light rain*

lightly *adverb* ସାମାନ୍ୟ ଭାବରେ *She touched me lightly on the arm.*

light[3] /laɪt/ *verb* (**lights, lighting, lit** /lɪt/ ବା **lighted, has lit** ବା **has lighted**) **1** make something start to burn ନିଆଁ ଲଗାଇବା, ନିଆଁ ଧରାଇବା, ଅଗ୍ନି ସଂଯୋଗ କରିବା, ଜଳାଇବା। *Will you light the fire?* **2** give light to something ଆଲୋକିତ କରିବା, ଆଲୋକିତ ହେବା *The room is lit by two big lamps.*

lighthouse /ˈlaɪthaʊs/ *noun* (*plural* **lighthouses**) a tall building by or in the sea, with a strong light to warn ships that there are rocks ସମୁଦ୍ରରେ

ଯାଉଥିବା ଜାହାଜ ପାଇଁ ପଥ ପଦର୍ଶକ ବତିଘର, ଲାଇଟ୍‌ହାଉସ୍

lightning /ˈlaɪtnɪŋ/ *noun* (*no plural*) a sudden bright light in the sky when there is a storm ବିଜୁଳି, ମେଘମାନଙ୍କ ମଧ୍ୟରେ ବିଚ୍ଛୁରିତ ବିଦ୍ୟୁତ୍ *The tower on the hill was struck by lightning.* ⇨ **thunder** ଦେଖନ୍ତୁ।

like[1] /laɪk/ *verb* (**likes, liking, liked**) feel that somebody or something is good or nice; enjoy something ଭଲପାଇବା, ପସନ୍ଦ କରିବା; ଉପଭୋଗ କରିବା *I like carrots a lot.* ○ *I like playing cricket.* ✪ ବିପରୀତ **dislike**

> ✪ **Want** କହିବା ଅପେକ୍ଷା **would like** କହିବା ଭଲ — *Would you like some coffee?*

like[2] /laɪk/ *preposition, conjunction* **1** the same as somebody or something ସଦୃଶ, ଅନୁରୂପ, ପରି *Rajiv looks like his father.* ✪ ବିପରୀତ **unlike** **2** for example ଯଥା *I bought a lot of things, like books and clothes.* **what is ... like?** words that you say when you want to know more about somebody or something କେମିତି, କେମିତିକା *'What's that book like?' 'It's very interesting.'*

likely /ˈlaɪkli/ *adjective* (**likelier, likeliest**) if something is likely, it will probably happen ସମ୍ଭବ, ସମ୍ଭବପର *It's likely that she will agree.* ✪ ବିପରୀତ **unlikely**

lily /ˈlɪli/ *noun* (*plural* **lilies**) a plant with big flowers କଇଁ ବା କମଳ ଗଛ; କଇଁ ବା କମଳ ଫୁଲ

limb /lɪm/ *noun* an arm or a leg or a wing ଶରୀରର ଅଙ୍ଗ (ଯଥା ହାତ, ଗୋଡ଼, ଡେଣା ଇତ୍ୟାଦି)

lime /laɪm/ *noun* a small green fruit like a lemon ଲେମ୍ବୁ ପରି ଏକ ଖଟା ସବୁଜ ଫଳ; ଜମ୍ବୀରଲେମ୍ବୁ, କାଗେଜିଲେମ୍ବୁ

limit /ˈlɪmɪt/ *noun* the most that is possible or allowed ସୀମା, ପ୍ରାନ୍ତ; ପରିସୀମା *What is the speed limit within the city?*

limp /lɪmp/ *verb* (**limps, limping, limped**) walk with difficulty because you have hurt your foot or leg ଛୋଟେଇ ଛୋଟେଇ ଚାଲିବା, ଛୋଟେଇବା

limp *noun* (*no plural*) ଛୋଟା ଚାଲି, ଖଞ୍ଜ ଗତି *He walks with a limp.*

line /laɪn/ *noun* **1** a long thin mark like his ଗାର, ରେଖା **2** people or things beside each other or one after the other (ଲୋକମାନଙ୍କର ବା ଜିନିଷର) ଧାଡ଼ି *Stand in a line.* **3** all the words in one row on a page ବହି ପୃଷ୍ଠାରେ ଧାଡ଼ି *How many lines are there on this page?* **4** what a train moves on ରେଳମାର୍ଗର ଲୁହା ରେଳ, ରେଳ ଲାଇନ୍

linear /ˈlɪniə(r)/ *adjective* **1** of or using lines ରୈଖିକ, ରେଖାପରି, ରେଖାଙ୍କନ ଦ୍ୱାରା କରାଯାଇଥିବା *linear diagrams* **2** going from one stage to another in a straight sequence ସିଧାସଳଖ ଗୋଟିଏ ସ୍ତରରୁ ଅନ୍ୟ ସ୍ତରକୁ ଯାଉଥିବା, ରୈଖିକ *linear motion* **3** of length ଦୈର୍ଘ୍ୟ ସମ୍ବନ୍ଧୀୟ

linen /ˈlɪnɪn/ *noun* (*no plural*) things like tablecloths and sheets that are made of cotton or a strong cloth called linen ତୁଳା ବା ସୂତାରୁ ତିଆରି ଚାଦର, ଟେବୁଲ୍ କ୍ଲଥ୍ ଇତ୍ୟାଦି

lining /ˈlaɪnɪŋ/ *noun* material that covers the inside of something କୌଣସି ଜିନିଷର ଭିତରପଟ ଲଗାଯାଇଥିବା ଆଚ୍ଛାଦନ, ଅନ୍ତରାଚ୍ଛାଦନ, ଅସ୍ତର *My coat has a thick lining so it's very warm.*

link /lɪŋk/ *noun* something that joins things or people together ସଂଯୋଗ କରୁଥିବା ଅଂଶ, ସଂଯୋଜକ ବ୍ୟକ୍ତି, ପଦାର୍ଥ ବା ବିଷୟ *trade links between India and France*

link *verb* (**links, linking, linked**) join two people or things (ଦୁଇ ବ୍ୟକ୍ତି ବା ପଦାର୍ଥକୁ) ସଂଯୁକ୍ତ କରିବା, ସଂଯୋଗ କରିବା *The new highway links the two towns.*

lion /ˈlaɪən/ *noun* a wild animal like a big cat with yellow fur. Lions live in Africa and parts of Asia. In India, lions are now found only in the Gir Forest in Gujarat ସିଂହ; ପଶୁରାଜ ➪ ଚିତ୍ର ପାଇଁ **mammal** ଦେଖନ୍ତୁ।

> ✪ ମାଈ ସିଂହ ବା ସିଂହୀକୁ **lioness** କୁହାଯାଏ ଓ ସିଂହ ଛୁଆକୁ **cub** କୁହାଯାଏ

lip /lɪp/ *noun* one of the two soft edges of the mouth ଓଠ, ଓଷ୍ଠ, ଅଧର ➪ ଚିତ୍ର ପାଇଁ **face** ଦେଖନ୍ତୁ।

lipstick /ˈlɪpstɪk/ *noun* a thing like a small stick that is used for colouring the lips ଓଠ ରଙ୍ଗ କରିବାପାଇଁ ବ୍ୟବହୃତ ରଙ୍ଗକାଠି, ଲିପ୍‌ଷ୍ଟିକ୍, ଓଧର ଓଷ୍ଠ ରଙ୍ଗେଇବା ପଦାର୍ଥ

liquid /ˈlɪkwɪd/ *noun* anything that is not a solid or a gas. Water, oil and milk are liquids ତରଳ ପଦାର୍ଥ

list /lɪst/ *noun* a lot of names or things that you write, one after another ତାଲିକା *a shopping list*

list *verb* (**lists, listing, listed**) make a list ତାଲିକା କରିବା, ତାଲିକାଭୁକ୍ତ କରିବା *The teacher listed all our names.*

listen /ˈlɪsn/ *verb* (**listens, listening, listened**) hear something carefully ଯତ୍ନସହକାରେ ଶୁଣିବା *I was listening to the radio.* ➪ **hear** ଠାରେ ଟିପ୍ପଣୀ ଦେଖନ୍ତୁ।

lit ଶବ୍ଦ **light**[3] ର ଏକ ଧାତୁରୂପ

literacy /ˈlɪtərəsi/ *noun* (*no plural*) the ability to read and write ସାକ୍ଷରତା, ପଢ଼ିବା ଓ ଲେଖିବାର ସାମର୍ଥ୍ୟ *an adult literacy campaign* ✪ ବିପରୀତ **illiteracy**

literary /ˈlɪtərəri/ *adjective* connected with or related to literature ସାହିତ୍ୟିକ, ସାହିତ୍ୟ ସମ୍ବନ୍ଧୀୟ, ସାହିତ୍ୟ ବିଦ୍ୟା ସମ୍ବନ୍ଧୀୟ *a literary approach*

literate /ˈlɪtərət/ *adjective* able to read and write ସାକ୍ଷର, ପଢ଼ିଲେଖି ପାରୁଥିବା ବ୍ୟକ୍ତି ✪ ବିପରୀତ **illiterate**

literature /ˈlɪtrətʃə(r)/ *noun* (*no plural*) books, plays and poetry ସାହିତ୍ୟ *He is studying English literature.*

litre /ˈliːtə(r)/ *noun* a measure of liquid ତରଳ ପଦାର୍ଥର ଏକ ମାପ କରିବାର ଏକକ ✪ **litre** ର ସଂକ୍ଷିପ୍ତ ରୂପ ହେଲା **l** *30 l*

litter[1] /ˈlɪtə(r)/ *noun* **1** (*no plural*) pieces of paper like rubbish that people leave on the ground ଅଳିଆରେ

ଫୋପଡ଼ା ଯାଇଥିବା କାଗଜ ଇତ୍ୟାଦିର ଅଳିଆ *The park was full of litter after the concert.* **2** (*plural* **litters**) all the baby animals that are born to the same mother at the same time ନବଜାତ ପଶୁଛୁଆ ସମୂହ, ଏକା ଥୋକରେ ଜନ୍ମ ହୋଇଥିବା ସବୁ ପଶୁଛୁଆ, ଛୁଆପଲ *a litter of six puppies*

litter[2] /ˈlɪtə(r)/ *verb* (**litters**, **littering**, **littered**) be or make something untidy with litter ଅଳିଆ କରିବା *My desk was littered with papers.*

little[1] /ˈlɪtl/ *adjective* **1** not big; small ଛୋଟ, ଛୋଟିଆ *a little village* **2** young ଅଳ୍ପ ବୟସର, ସାନ, ଟିକି *a little girl* **3** not much ଅଳ୍ପ *We have very little money.*

little[2] /ˈlɪtl/ *adverb* not much ଅଳ୍ପ *I'm tired—I slept very little last night.*

a little quite; rather ଅଳ୍ପ ଟିକିଏ, ଟିକିଏ *This skirt is a little too short for me.*

little by little slowly ଧୀରେ ଧୀରେ *Little by little she started to feel better.*

little[3] /ˈlɪtl/ *pronoun* a small amount; not much ଅଳ୍ପ ପରିମାଣ, ଟିକିଏ *I've got some ice cream. Would you like a little?*

live[1] /lɪv/ *verb* (**lives, living, lived**) **1** be or stay alive ବଞ୍ଚିବା, ବଞ୍ଚିରହିବା, ଜୀବତ ରହିବା *He lived to the age of 93.* **2** have your home somewhere ବାସ କରିବା, ରହିବା *Where do you live?*

live on something 1 stay alive by eating something (କିଛି ଖାଇ) ବଞ୍ଚିରହିବା, ଜୀବନ ଧାରଣ କରିବା, ଖାଇବା *Cows live on grass.* **2** have a certain amount of money (କିଛି ଟଙ୍କାରେ) ଜୀବିକା ନିର୍ବାହ କରିବା, ଚଳିବା

live[2] /laɪv/ *adjective* **1** not dead ଜୀଅନ୍ତା, ଜୀବନ୍ତ *The snake ate a live mouse.* **2** if a radio or television programme is live, you see or hear it at the same time as it happens କୌଣସି ଘଟଣା ଘଟୁଥିବା ବା ନାଟକ ଇତ୍ୟାଦି ଅଭିନୀତ ହେଉଥିବା ସମୟରେ ପ୍ରେରିତ ରେଡିଓ ବା ଟେଲିଭିଜନ କାର୍ଯ୍ୟକ୍ରମ *a live concert*

livelihood /ˈlaɪvlihʊd/ *noun* (*no plural*) a means of earning money so that one can live ଜୀବିକା, ଜୀବନଯାପନର ପନ୍ଥା, ଜୀବିକା ଅର୍ଜନ

lively /ˈlaɪvli/ *adjective* (**livelier**, **liveliest**) full of life; always moving or doing things ଉତ୍‌ଫୁଲ୍ଲ, ସତେଜ, କର୍ମତତ୍ପର, ଚଳଚଞ୍ଚଳ, ପ୍ରାଣବନ୍ତ *The children are very lively.*

liver /ˈlɪvə(r)/ *noun* the part inside the body of a person or an animal that cleans the blood ଯକୃତ, କଳିଜା, ଲିଭର୍

lives ଶବ୍ଦ **life 2** ଓ **life 3** ର ବହୁବଚନ

livestock /ˈlaɪvstɒk/ *noun* (*no singular*) animals that are kept on a farm, for example cows or sheep ପଶୁସମ୍ପଦ, ସମ୍ପତ୍ତି ଭାବରେ ପାଳିଥିବା ଗାଈ, ଗୋରୁ, ଛେଳି ଇତ୍ୟାଦି ଗୃହପାଳିତ ପଶୁ ସମୂହ

living[1] /ˈlɪvɪŋ/ *adjective* alive; not dead ଜୀବନ୍ତ, ଜୀଅନ୍ତା, ଜୀବିତ *Some people say he is the greatest living writer.*

the living *noun* (*plural*) the people who are alive ବଞ୍ଚିଥିବା ଲୋକମାନେ ✪ ବିପରୀତ **the dead**

living² /ˈlɪvɪŋ/ *noun* the way that you earn money ଜୀବିକା, ଟଙ୍କା ଅର୍ଜନର ଉପାୟ, ବୃତ୍ତି *What do you do for a living?*

living room *noun* a room in a house where people sit and watch television or talk, for example ଘରେ ସମସ୍ତଙ୍କ ସାଧାରଣ ବ୍ୟବହାର ପାଇଁ ଥିବା ପ୍ରକୋଷ୍ଠ (ଯୋଉଠି ବସି ଗପସପ କରାଯାଏ, ଟେଲିଭିଜନ୍ ଦେଖାଯାଏ ଇତ୍ୟାଦି)

lizard /ˈlɪzəd/ *noun* a small reptile that has four legs, a long tail and rough skin ଝିଟିପିଟି, ଏଣ୍ଡୁଅ ଇତ୍ୟାଦି

load¹ /ləʊd/ *noun* something heavy that is being carried ଭାର, ବୋଝ *The lorry brought another load of wood.*

load² /ləʊd/ *verb* (**loads, loading, loaded**) **1** put things in or on something, for example a car or ship, that will carry them (ମଟର ଗାଡ଼ି, ଜାହାଜ ଇତ୍ୟାଦିରେ ମାଲପତ୍ର) ବୋଝେଇ କରିବା, ଲଦିବା *Two men loaded the furniture into the van.* **2** put bullets in a gun or film in a camera ବନ୍ଧୁକରେ ଗୁଳି ପୂରାଇବା; କ୍ୟାମେରାରେ ଫିଲ୍ମ ଲଗାଇବା ✪ ବିପରୀତ **unload**

loaf /ləʊf/ *noun* (*plural* **loaves** /ləʊvz/) a big piece of bread ପାଉଁରୁଟି ବା ଏହି ଆକାରର ଅନ୍ୟ ଖାଦ୍ୟ ଖଣ୍ଡ *a loaf of bread* ⇨ **bread** ଦେଖନ୍ତୁ।

loan /ləʊn/ *noun* money that somebody lends you ଧାର, ଉଧାର, କରଜ, ଋଣ *The bank gave me a loan to buy a car.*

lobby /ˈlɒbi/ *noun* (*plural* **lobbies**) a large hall inside the entrance of a building ଘର ବା କୋଠାର ପ୍ରବେଶ ଦ୍ୱାର ପରେ ଥିବା ବଡ଼ ପ୍ରକୋଷ୍ଠ

lobster /ˈlɒbstə(r)/ *noun* a sea animal with a hard shell, two big claws, eight legs and a long tail ବଡ଼ ଚୁଙ୍ଗୁଡ଼ି ମାଛ, ବୁଢ଼ା ଚୁଙ୍ଗୁଡ଼ି

lobster

local /ˈləʊkl/ *adjective* of a place near you ସ୍ଥାନୀୟ *local newspaper*

locality /ləʊkæləti/ *noun* (*plural* **localities**) the area around the place where you live ଜାଗା, ସ୍ଥାନ, ଅଞ୍ଚଳ *There is a school in our locality.*

locate /ləʊˈkeɪt/ *verb* (**locates, locating, located**) find and show the exact position of someone or something ସଠିକ୍ ସ୍ଥାନ ନିରୂପଣ କରିବା, ଅବସ୍ଥିତି ନିର୍ଣ୍ଣୟ କରିବା; (କାହାରିକୁ) ଠାବ କରିବା *Locate the world's largest country on the globe.*

located /ləʊˈkeɪtɪd/ *adjective* in a place ଅବସ୍ଥିତ *The factory is located near Rourkela.*

location /ləʊˈkeɪʃn/ *noun* the position or place of something ନିର୍ଦ୍ଦିଷ୍ଟ ଜାଗା *Finding the location of the house is difficult.*

lock¹ /lɒk/ *noun* a metal thing that keeps a door, gate, box, etc. closed so that you cannot open it without a key ତାଲା, କୋଲପ

lock² /lɒk/ *verb* (**locks, locking, locked**) close with a key ତାଲା ପକାଇବା *Don't forget to lock the door when you leave.* ✪ ବିପରୀତ **unlock**

lock in lock a door so that somebody cannot go out ଭିତରପଟୁ ଦୁଆରରେ ତାଲା ପକାଇଦେବା

lock up lock all the doors and windows of a building ଘରର ସବୁ ଦୁଆର ଝରକା କିଳି ଦେବା

lock[3] /lɒk/ *noun* **1** a bunch of hairs on the head ଝୁଲି ରହିଥିବା କେଶ **2 locks** (*plural*) all the hair on a person's head ମୁଣ୍ଡର ବାଳ, କେଶରାଶି, ଚୂର୍ଣ୍ଣକୁନ୍ତଳ ✪ ଏ ଅର୍ଥରେ ଏ ଶବ୍ଦଟି ସାହିତ୍ୟିକ ଲେଖାରେ ବ୍ୟବହୃତ ହୋଇଥାଏ ।

locomotion /ˌləʊkəˈməʊʃn/ *noun* (*no plural*) the act of moving or the ability to move ଚଳନ ଶକ୍ତି, ଗତି ଶକ୍ତି *The eight arms of the octopus help it in locomotion.*

locomotive /ˌləʊkəˈməʊtɪv/ *noun* a railway engine that pulls a train ରେଳ ଇଞ୍ଜିନ୍ *a diesel locomotive*

lodge /lɒdʒ/ *verb* (**lodges, lodging, lodged**) make a formal statement to an authority ଧ୍ୟାନାକର୍ଷଣ ପାଇଁ ଅଭିଯୋଗ ଦାଖଲ କରିବା *He lodged a complaint with the police.*

loft /lɒft/ *noun* the room or space under the roof of a house ଆଟୁ, ଚାଳ ବା ସେହିପରି ନୁଆଣିଆ ଛାତ ତଳର ଛୋଟ ବଖରା *My old books are in a box in the loft.*

lofty /ˈlɒfti/ *adjective* (**loftier, loftiest**) very high ଅତି ଉଚ୍ଚ *a lofty building*

log /lɒg/ *noun* a thick piece of wood from a tree କାଠଗଡ଼ *Put another log on the fire.*

logic /ˈlɒdʒɪk/ *noun* (*no plural*) a sensible reason for doing something ଯୁକ୍ତିଯୁକ୍ତ କାରଣ *There is no logic behind his arguments.*

logical /ˈlɒdʒɪkl/ *adjective* if something is logical, it makes sense ଯୁକ୍ତିଯୁକ୍ତ *I don't want excuses. Give me a logical reason for coming late.* ✪ ବିପରୀତ **illogical**

logo /ˈləʊgəʊ/ *noun* a special sign or symbol that a company or an organization uses to represent itself ପ୍ରତୀକ ଭାବରେ କୌଣସି ସଂସ୍ଥା ବ୍ୟବହାର କରୁଥିବା ଚିହ୍ନ

lollipop /ˈlɒlipɒp/, **lolly** /ˈlɒli/ (*plural* **lollies**) *noun* a big sweet on a stick କାଠିରେ ଲାଗିଥିବା ଏକ ପ୍ରକାର ମିଠା ଟେଲା, ଗୋଟଲା

lonely /ˈləʊnli/ *adjective* (**lonelier, loneliest**) **1** unhappy because you are not with other people ଏକୁଟିଆ, ବନ୍ଧୁହୀନ, ସଙ୍ଗହୀନ *I was very lonely when I first came to Delhi.* **2** far from other places ଜନଗମାଗମ ଶୂନ୍ୟ, ନିର୍ଜନ *a lonely house in the hills*

loneliness *noun* (*no plural*) the state of being lonely ନିଃସଙ୍ଗତା; ନିର୍ଜନତା

long[1] /lɒŋ/ *adjective* (**longer, longest**) **1** far from one end to the other ଲମ୍ବା, ବହୁ ଦୂର ବିସ୍ତୃତ *This is the longest road in Bhopal.* ○ *She has long black hair.* ✪ ବିପରୀତ **short 1** **2** you use 'long' to say or ask how far something is from one end to the other ଲମ୍ବା *The wall is 5 metres long.* **3** that continues for a lot of time ଦୀର୍ଘକାଳ ବ୍ୟାପି, ବହୁ ସମୟ ନେଉଥିବା *a long film* ✪ ବିପରୀତ **short 3**

long[2] /lɒŋ/ *adverb* for a lot of time ବହୁ ସମୟ ଧରି, ବହୁଦିନ ଧରି *I can't stay long.*

long ago many years in the past ବହୁ ଦିନ ପୂର୍ବେ, ପୂର୍ବ କାଳରେ *Long ago there were no cars.*

long before at a time much before ବହୁ ଦିନ ଆଗରୁ *My grandfather died long before I was born.*

no longer, not any longer not now; not as before ଆଉ ନୁହେଁ, ଏବେ ନୁହେଁ *She doesn't live here any longer.*

longitude /ˈlɒŋgɪtjuːd/ *noun* the distance of a place to the east or west of the Greenwich meridian ଦ୍ରାଘିମାରେଖା; ଗ୍ରୀନିଚ୍ ଠାରୁ ପୂର୍ବ ବା ପଶ୍ଚିମ ଦିଗରେ ଡିଗ୍ରୀରେ ମପାଯାଉଥିବା ଦୂରତା ➪ **globe** ଓ **latitude** ଦେଖନ୍ତୁ।

long jump *noun* (*no plural*) a sport where you try to jump as far as you can ସବୁଠୁ ଦୂରକୁ ଡେଇଁବା ପାଇଁ ଖେଳ ପ୍ରତିଯୋଗିତା

look[1] /lʊk/ *verb* (**looks, looking, looked**) **1** turn your eyes towards somebody or something and try to see them ଦେଖିବା, ଦୃଷ୍ଟି ନିକ୍ଷେପ କରିବା, ଚାହିଁବା *Look at this picture.* ○ *You should look both ways before you cross the road.* ➪ **see** ଠାରେ ଟିପ୍ପଣୀ ଦେଖନ୍ତୁ। **2** seem to be; appear ଦିଶିବା, ଲାଗିବା, ବୋଧ ହେବା, ମନେ ହେବା, ପ୍ରତୀୟମାନ ହେବା *You look tired!*

look after somebody or **something** take care of somebody or something ଅନ୍ୟର ଯତ୍ନ ନେବା *Can you look after my cat when I'm on holiday?*

look for somebody or **something** try to find somebody or something ଖୋଜିବା *I'm looking for my keys.*

look out be careful ସାବଧାନ ରୁହ *Look out! There's a car coming!*

look[2] /lʊk/ *noun* **1** the act of looking at somebody or something ଦୃଷ୍ଟି, ଚାହାଣି, ଦୃଷ୍ଟିପାତ *Take a look at these books.* **2 looks** (*no singular*) how a person's face and body is ମୁଖାକୃତି, ଚେହେରା *good looks*

have a look see something *Can I have a look at your photographs?*

loom /luːm/ *noun* a machine that is used for weaving cloth ଲୁଗାବୁଣା ତନ୍ତ

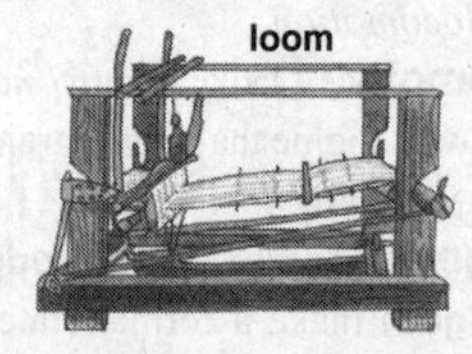

loop /luːp/ *noun* a round shape made by something like a string or rope ସୂତା ବା ଦଉଡ଼ିର ଫାସ

loose /luːs/ *adjective* (**looser, loosest**) **1** not tied or fixed ବନ୍ଧା ହୋଇ ନଥିବା, ବନ୍ଧନମୁକ୍ତ *One of his teeth is loose.* **2** not tight ଢିଲା, ଢୁଗୁଲା *a loose white dress* ✪ ବିପରୀତ **tight**

loosely *adverb* not tightly or firmly ଢିଲା ଭାବରେ ✪ ବିପରୀତ **tightly**

loosen /ˈluːsn/ *verb* (**loosens, loosening, loosened**) become looser or make something looser ଢିଲା କରିବା, ଢୁଗୁଲା କରିବା *Can you loosen this knot? It's too tight.* ✪ ବିପରୀତ **tighten**

lorry /ˈlɒri/ *noun* (*plural* **lorries**) a big vehicle for carrying heavy things

ଭାରି ଜିନିଷ ବା ବସ୍ତୁକୁ ବୋହିବା ପାଇଁ ମଟରଗାଡ଼ି, ଟ୍ରକ୍, ଲରୀ ✪ **lorry** ମଧ୍ୟ **truck** କୁ କୁହାଯାଏ ।

lose /lu:z/ *verb* (**loses, losing, lost** / lɒst/, **has lost**) **1** not be able to find something ହଜେଇବା, ହରାଇବା *I can't open the door because I've lost my key.* **2** not have somebody or something that you had before ହରାଇବା, ବଞ୍ଚିତ ହେବା *He lost his job when the factory closed.* **3** not win ହାରିବା, ପରାସ୍ତ ହେବା *Our team lost the match.* ✪ ବିପରୀତ **win**

loser /ˈlu:zə(r)/ *noun* a person who does not win a game, race or competition ହାରି ଯାଇଥିବା ବ୍ୟକ୍ତି, ପରାଜିତ ବ୍ୟକ୍ତି (ବିଶେଷତଃ ଖେଳ, ଦୌଡ଼ ବା ପ୍ରତିଯୋଗିତାରେ) ✪ ବିପରୀତ **winner**

loss /lɒs/ *noun* (*plural* **losses**) **1** the state of having lost something କ୍ଷତି; ହଜିବା ଅବସ୍ଥା *Has she told the police about the loss of her car?* **2** the amount of money a business loses (ବ୍ୟବସାୟରେ ଟଙ୍କାପଇସାର) କ୍ଷତି *The company made a loss of Rs 50,000.* ✪ ବିପରୀତ **profit**

lost[1] ଶବ୍ଦ **lose** ର ଏକ ଧାତୁରୂପ

lost[2] /lɒst/ *adjective* **1** if you are lost, you do not know where you are ହଜି ଯାଇଥିବା, ନିଜର ସ୍ଥିତି ଜାଣିପାରୁ ନଥିବା *Take this map so that you don't get lost!* **2** if something is lost, you cannot find it ହଜି ଯାଇଥିବା

lot[1] /lɒt/ *noun*

a lot very much; a big amount or number ବହୁତ *We ate a lot.*

a lot of, lots of a big number or amount of something ବହୁତ ସଂଖ୍ୟା ବା ପରିମାଣ, ଖୁବ୍ ଗୁଡ଼ାଏ, ବହୁତ *She's got a lot of friends.*

lot[2] /lɒt/ *adverb*

a lot very much or often ବହୁତ ଥର *I go to the cinema a lot.*

lotion /ˈləʊʃn/ *noun* a liquid that you put on your skin to clean it or protect it ଚର୍ମରେ ଲଗାଇବା ପାଇଁ ଏକ ତରଳ ଔଷଧ ବା ପ୍ରସାଧାନ ଦ୍ରବ୍ୟ, ପ୍ରସାଧନ ସାମଗ୍ରୀ

loud /laʊd/ *adjective, adverb* (**louder, loudest**) that makes a lot of noise; not quiet ବଡ଼ ପାଟିକ ଉଚ୍ଚ ସ୍ୱର କରୁଥିବା; ବଡ଼ପାଟି, ଉଚ୍ଚ ସ୍ୱର *I couldn't hear what he said because the music was too loud.* ○ *loud voices* ✪ ବିପରୀତ **low 3**

out loud so that other people can hear it ଅନ୍ୟମାନେ ଶୁଣି ପାରିଲାପରି ଉଚ୍ଚ ସ୍ୱର *I read the story out loud.*

loudly *adverb* ଉଚ୍ଚ ସ୍ୱରରେ, ବଡ଼ ପାଟିରେ *She laughed loudly.*

loudspeaker /ˌlaʊdˈspi:kə(r)/ *noun* an instrument for making sounds louder ସ୍ୱର ପରିବର୍ଦ୍ଧକ ଯନ୍ତ୍ର, ଧ୍ୱନି ବିସ୍ତାରକ ଉପକରଣ, ଲାଉଡ୍‌ସ୍ପିକର୍ *Music was coming from the loudspeakers.*

love[1] /lʌv/ *verb* (**loves, loving, loved**) **1** have a strong warm feeling for somebody କୌଣସି ବ୍ୟକ୍ତି ପ୍ରତି ଗଭୀର ଅନୁରାଗ କରିବା, ପ୍ରେମ କରିବା, ଭଲପାଇବା *She loves her parents.* **2** ମଧ୍ୟ like something very much (କୌଣସି ଜିନିଷ) ଖୁବ୍ ଭଲପାଇବା, ଖୁବ୍ ଭଲ ଲାଗିବା *I would love to go to America.*

love[2] /lʌv/ *noun* (*no plural*) **1** a strong warm feeling of liking somebody or something ଅନୁରାଗ, ପ୍ରେମ, ସ୍ନେହ, ଭଲପାଇବା, ଆସକ୍ତି *a love of cricket* **2** (**love from** ମଧ୍ୟ) a way of ending a letter to somebody that you know well ଚିଠି ଶେଷରେ ନିଜର ଭଲପାଇବା ସୂଚାଉଥିବା ଶବ୍ଦ *Lots of love from Amita.*

lovely /ˈlʌvli/ *adjective* (**lovelier, loveliest**) beautiful or very nice ସୁନ୍ଦର, ଆନନ୍ଦଦାୟକ *That's a lovely dress.* ○ *We had a lovely holiday.*

loving /ˈlʌvɪŋ/ *adjective* feeling or showing love ସ୍ନେହଶୀଳ, ସ୍ନେହୀ *loving parents*

low /ˈləʊ/ *adjective* (**lower**, **lowest**) **1** near the ground; not high ନିମ୍ନ, ଅନୁଚ୍ଚ, ତଳୁଆ *There was a low wall round the garden.* ✪ ବିପରୀତ **high1** **2** less than usual ସ୍ୱାଭାବିକ ପରିମାଣ ଠାରୁ କମ୍, ଅଳ୍ପ *low temperatures* ✪ ବିପରୀତ **high 3** **3** soft and quiet ମୃଦୁ, ନରମ, ଅନୁଚ୍ଚ *I heard low voices in the next room.* ✪ ବିପରୀତ **loud**

lower[1] /ˈləʊə(r)/ *verb* (**lowers, lowering, lowered**) **1** move somebody or something down ତଳକୁ ଆଣିବା *They lowered the flag.* **2** make something less ଊଣା କରିବା, କମାଇବା *Please lower your voice.* ✪ ବିପରୀତ **raise**

lower[2] /ˈləʊə(r)/ *adjective* that is under another; bottom ତଳ, ତଳପଟର *the lower lip* ✪ ବିପରୀତ **upper**

loyal /ˈlɔɪəl/ *adjective* a person who is loyal does not change his/her friends or beliefs ବିଶ୍ୱସ୍ତ, ଅନୁଗତ *a loyal friend.*

loyalty *noun* (*no plural*) being loyal ବିଶ୍ୱସ୍ତତା, ଆନୁଗତ୍ୟ

luck /lʌk/ *noun* (*no plural*) things that happen to you which you cannot control; chance ଭାଗ୍ୟ, ଅଦୃଷ୍ଟ **good luck** words that you say to somebody when you hope that they will do well ସୁଭାଗ୍ୟ, ଭଲ ଭାଗ୍ୟ (ବିଶେଷତଃ ଅନ୍ୟକୁ ଶୁଭେଚ୍ଛା ଜଣେଇବାକୁ କୁହାଯାଏ) *Good luck! I'm sure you'll get the job.*

lucky /ˈlʌki/ *adjective* (**luckier, luckiest**) **1** if you are lucky, you have good luck ଭାଗ୍ୟବାନ୍ **2** something that is lucky brings good luck ଶୁଭ, ଶୁଭଦାୟକ *My lucky number is 3.* ✪ ବିପରୀତ **unlucky**

luckily /ˈlʌkɪli/ *adverb* it is lucky that ଭାଗ୍ୟକୁ *I was late, but luckily I didn't miss the train.*

luggage /ˈlʌɡɪdʒ/ *noun* (*no plural*) bags and suitcases that you take with you when you travel ଦୂର ଜାଗାକୁ ଯାତ୍ରା କଲାବେଳେ ସାଙ୍ଗରେ ନେଉଥିବା ଜିନିଷପତ୍ର (ବ୍ୟାଗ୍, ବାକ୍ସ ଇତ୍ୟାଦି) *How much luggage have you got?*

lukewarm /ˌluːkˈwɔːm/ *adjective* a little warm but not hot ଉଷୁମ୍, ଅଳ୍ପ ଗରମ୍ *Wash the clothes in lukewarm water.*

lump /lʌmp/ *noun* **1** a hard piece of something ଖଣ୍ଡ, ଟେଳା; ମେଞ୍ଚା, ମେଦା *two lumps of sugar* **2** a place on your body which has become hard and bigger ଦେହରେ ହୋଇଥିବା ଫୁଲା, ଷ୍ଫୀତି *I've got a lump on my head where I hit it.*

lunar /ˈluːnə(r)/ *adjective* about the moon ଚନ୍ଦ୍ର ସମ୍ବନ୍ଧୀୟ, ଚନ୍ଦ୍ରର *a lunar eclipse*

lunch /lʌntʃ/ *noun* (*plural* **lunches**) a meal that you eat in the middle of the day ମଧ୍ୟାହ୍ନ ଭୋଜନ *What would you like for lunch?*

lunchtime /ˈlʌntʃtaɪm/ *noun* the time when you eat lunch ମଧ୍ୟାହ୍ନ ଭୋଜନ ସମୟ *I'll meet you at lunchtime.*

lung /lʌŋ/ *noun* one of the two parts inside your body that you use for breathing ଫୁସଫୁସ, ବାୟୁକୋଷ, କ୍ଲୋମ

lush /lʌʃ/ *adjective* growing thickly and abundantly in a way that looks attractive ଘଞ୍ଚ ଭାବରେ ବଢ଼ିଥିବା ଓ ସୁନ୍ଦର ଦିଶୁଥିବା *lush vegetation*

luxury /ˈlʌkʃəri/ *noun* (*plural* **luxuries**) something that is very nice and expensive that you do not really need ବିଳାସ ଓ ଆମୋଦପ୍ରମୋଦ ପାଇଁ ବ୍ୟୟବହୁଳ ବ୍ୟବସ୍ଥା *Eating in a restaurant is a luxury for most people.*

lychee (lichi ମଧ୍ୟ**)** *noun* a small round fruit with a thin rough red skin, white juicy flesh and a big seed inside ଲିଚୁ ଫଳ, ଲିଚୁକୋଳି

lying ଶବ୍ଦ **lie** ର ଏକ ଧାତୁରୂପ

lyrics /ˈlɪrɪks/ *noun* (*no singular*) the words of a song ଗୀତ ଭାବେ ଗାଇବା ପାଇଁ ଲେଖାଯାଇଥିବା କବିତା

M m

M /em/ *symbol* the number 1,000 in Roman numerals ରୋମୀୟ ଅକ୍ଷରରେ ୧୦୦୦ ସଂଖ୍ୟା

m *abbreviation* ଶବ୍ଦ **metre** ମିଟର୍‌ର ସଂକ୍ଷିପ୍ତ ରୂପ

machine /məˈʃiːn/ *noun* a thing with parts that move to do work or to make something. Machines often use electricity ଯନ୍ତ୍ର, କଳ, ମେସିନ୍ *a washing machine*

machinery /məˈʃiːnəri/ *noun* (*no plural*) the parts of a machine ଯନ୍ତ୍ରପାତି, କଳକବ୍‌ଜା *the machinery inside a clock*

mad /mæd/ *adjective* (**madder, maddest**) **1** having something wrong with the mind ପାଗଳ, ବାତୁଳ **2** very stupid; crazy ବୋକା *I think you're mad to go out in this snow!*

go mad 1 become ill in the mind ପାଗଳ ହୋଇଯିବା **2** become very angry ଖୁବ୍ ରାଗିଯିବା *Mother will go mad when she finds out what you did at school.*

madam /ˈmædəm/ *noun* (*no plural*) a polite way of speaking to a woman, instead of using her name ମହିଳାମାନଙ୍କର ଶିଷ୍ଟ ସମ୍ବୋଧନ ପଦ *'Can I help you, madam?' asked the shopkeeper.* ➪ **sir** ଦେଖନ୍ତୁ ।

made ଶବ୍ଦ **make**[1] ର ଏକ ଧାତୁରୂପ

made of something from this material ତିଆରି *This shirt is made of cotton.*

madness /ˈmædnəs/ *noun* (*no plural*) a state of having something wrong with the mind ପାଗଳାମି, ବାତୁଳତା

magazine /ˌmægəˈziːn/ *noun* a kind of thin book with a paper cover that you can buy every week or every month. It has a lot of different stories and pictures inside ବିବିଧ ଲେଖା ଓ ଚିତ୍ର ଥିବା ସାମୟିକ ପତ୍ରିକା, ମ୍ୟାଗାଜିନ୍

magic /ˈmædʒɪk/ *noun* (*no plural*) **1** clever tricks that somebody can do to surprise people ହସ୍ତକୌଶଳ ଦ୍ୱାରା ଇନ୍ଦ୍ରଜାଲ ସୃଷ୍ଟି, ଯାଦୁବିଦ୍ୟା, ମ୍ୟାଜିକ୍, ହଟଚମଟ **2** a special power that is supposed to make strange or impossible things happen ମନ୍ତ୍ରଯନ୍ତ୍ର, ଗୁଣିଗାରେଡ଼ି, କୁହୁକ *The witch changed the prince into a frog by magic.*

magic, magical /ˈmædʒɪkl/ *adjective* କୁହୁକୀ, ମାୟାବୀ, ଐନ୍ଦ୍ରିଜାଲିକ *The witch had magical powers.*

magician /məˈdʒɪʃn/ *noun* **1** a person who does clever tricks to surprise people ଯାଦୁକର **2** a man in stories who has strange, unusual powers (ଗପରେ ଥିବା) କୁହୁକ ଶକ୍ତି ଥିବା ବ୍ୟକ୍ତି

magistrate /ˈmædʒɪstreɪt/ *noun* a government official in charge of the law and order of a place କୌଣସି ସ୍ଥାନର ସୁରକ୍ଷା ଓ ସୁବ୍ୟବସ୍ଥା ବୁଝୁଥିବା ସରକାରୀ ଅଧିକାରୀ ବା ଅଫିସର୍

magnet /ˈmægnət/ *noun* a piece of **iron** that can make other things made of iron move towards it ଚୁମ୍ବକ

magnetic *adjective* with the power of a magnet ଚୁମ୍ବକୀୟ ଶକ୍ତିଥିବା, ଚୁମ୍ବକୀୟ *Is this metal magnetic?*

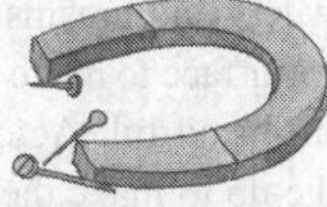
magnet

magnificent /mæg'nɪfɪsnt/ *adjective* very good or beautiful ଚମତ୍କାର, ଅତି ସୁନ୍ଦର *What a magnificent building!*

magnify /'mægnɪfaɪ/ *verb* (**magnifies, magnifying, magnified, has magnified**) make something look bigger than it really is (କୌଣସି ପଦାର୍ଥକୁ ତା' ଆକାର ଠାରୁ) ବଡ଼ କରି ଦେଖାଇବା ବା ବଡ଼ ଆକାରରେ ଦେଖାଇବା

magnifying glass *noun* (*plural* **magnifying glasses**) a special piece of glass that you hold in your hand and look through to make things look bigger than they really are ବଡ଼ କରି ଦେଖାଇବା ପାଇଁ ଉଦ୍ଦିଷ୍ଟ ଲେନସ୍, ଅଭିବର୍ଦ୍ଧକ ଲେନ୍ସ

maid /meɪd/ *noun* a woman who does work like cleaning in a house or hotel (ଘର ବା ହୋଟେଲ୍‌ର, ପରିଚାଳିକା, ସଫାସୁତୁରା ଝାଡୁପୋଛା କରୁଥିବା ସ୍ତ୍ରୀଲୋକ

maiden /'meɪdn/ *noun* an unmarried young girl or woman ଅବିବାହିତା ଯୁବତୀ, କୁମାରୀ

mail /meɪl/ *noun* (*no plural*) the way of sending and receiving letters, parcels, etc.; post ଚିଠିପତ୍ର, ପାର୍ସଲ୍ ଇତ୍ୟାଦି ଆଦାନପ୍ରଦାନ କରିବା ପ୍ରଥା, ଡାକ *airmail*

mail *verb* (**mails, mailing, mailed**) send something by post ଡାକରେ ପଠାଇବା *I'll mail the photograph to you.* ➪ **email** ମଧ୍ୟ ଦେଖନ୍ତୁ।

main /meɪn/ *adjective* most important ମୁଖ୍ୟ, ପ୍ରଧାନ *My main reason for learning English is to get a better job.*

main road *noun* a big important road ପ୍ରଧାନ ରାସ୍ତା, ମୁଖ୍ୟ ରାସ୍ତା

mainly *adverb* mostly ପ୍ରାୟତଃ, ପ୍ରଧାନତଃ *The students here are mainly from Japan.*

maintain /meɪn'teɪn/ *verb* (**maintains, maintaining, maintained**) **1** continue with something ଚାଲୁ ରଖିବା *If he can maintain this speed, he'll win the race.* **2** keep something working well (କୌଣସି ଜିନିଷ) ଠିକ୍ ଭାବରେ ରଖିବା ପାଇଁ ଯତ୍ନ ନେବା, ଠିକ୍‌ଠାକ୍ ରଖିବା *The roads are well maintained.*

maintenance /'meɪntənəns/ *noun* (*no plural*) things that you do to keep something working well ଠିକ୍ ଠିକ୍ ରଖିବା ପାଇଁ କରାଯାଉଥିବା କାମ *maintenance of a machine*

maize /meɪz/ *noun* (*no plural*) a tall plant with big yellow seeds that you can eat; corn ମକାଗଛ, ମକା ➪ ଚିତ୍ର ପାଇଁ **grain** ଦେଖନ୍ତୁ।

Majesty /'mædʒəsti/ *noun* (*plural* **Majesties**) a word that you use to talk to or about a king or queen ରାଜା ଓ ରାଣୀଙ୍କୁ ସଂବୋଧନ କଲାବେଳେ ବା ତାଙ୍କ ବିଷୟରେ କଥାବାର୍ତ୍ତା ହେଲା ବେଳେ ବ୍ୟବହୃତ ସମ୍ମାନସୂଚକ ଶବ୍ଦ *Her Majesty Queen Elizabeth II*

major[1] /'meɪdʒə(r)/ *adjective* very large, important or serious ବଡ଼, ମୁଖ୍ୟ ବା ଗୁରୁତ୍ୱପୂର୍ଣ୍ଣ *There are airports in all the major cities.* ○ *major problems* ✪ ବିପରୀତ **minor**

major[2] /ˈmeɪdʒə(r)/ *noun* an officer in the army (କ୍ୟାପ୍ଟେନ୍‌ଙ୍କ ଉପର ପାହ୍ୟାର) ସେନାବାହିନୀର ଅଧିକାରୀ ବା ଅଫିସର୍

majority /məˈdʒɒrəti/ *noun* (*no plural*) most things or people in a group ଗୋଷ୍ଠୀ ବା ଦଳର ଅଧିକାଂଶ ଲୋକ *The majority of families in Japan have a colour television.* ✪ ବିପରୀତ **minority**

make[1] /meɪk/ *verb* (**makes, making, made** /meɪd/, **has made**) **1** put things together so that you have a new thing ତିଆରି କରିବା, ଗଠନ କରିବା, ପ୍ରସ୍ତୁତ କରିବା *They make cars in that factory.* **2** cause something to be or to happen; produce something କରିବା, ସୃଷ୍ଟି କରିବା *I made a mistake.* ○ *The plane made a loud noise when it landed.* **3** force somebody to do something (କିଛି କରିବାକୁ) ବାଧ୍ୟ କରିବା *My father made me stay at home.* **4** give somebody a job କରାଇବା, କରିବା *They made him President.*

make up 1 tell something that is not true ମନଗଢ଼ା କଥା ସୃଷ୍ଟି କରିବା ବା ସତ କଥା ବୋଲି କହିବା *Nobody believes that story—he made it up!* **2** end a quarrel with somebody କଳହ ସମାପ୍ତ କରିବା *Rohit and Sunil had an argument last week, but they've made up now.*

make[2] /meɪk/ *noun* the name of the company that has made something ନିର୍ମାତାର ନାମ *'What make is your car?' 'It's a Maruti.'*

maker /ˈmeɪkə(r)/ *noun* a person or company that makes something ନିର୍ମାଣକାରୀ ବ୍ୟକ୍ତି ବା ସଂସ୍ଥା, ନିର୍ମାତା *a film maker*

make-up *noun* (*no plural*) special powders and creams that you put on your face to make yourself look more beautiful. Actors also wear make-up to make themselves look different ପାଉଡର୍, କ୍ରିମ୍ ଇତ୍ୟାଦି ପ୍ରସାଧାନ ଦ୍ରବ୍ୟ

malaria /məˈleəriə/ *noun* (*no plural*) a disease caused by the bite of a certain type of mosquito ମଶା କାମୁଡ଼ାରୁ ହେଉଥିବା ପୁନରାବର୍ତକ ଜ୍ୱର, ମ୍ୟାଲେରିଆ

male /meɪl/ *adjective* a male animal or person belongs to the sex that can become fathers ପୁରୁଷ ଜାତୀୟ *a male nurse*

male *noun* ପୁରୁଷ *If you look at these fish you can see that the males are bigger than the females.* ⇨ **female** ଦେଖନ୍ତୁ।

malice /ˈmælɪs/ *noun* (*no plural*) hating somebody so much that you wish to harm them ଅନ୍ୟମାନଙ୍କର ଅପକାର କରିବାର ଇଚ୍ଛା, ଦ୍ୱେଷ

malnourished /ˌmælˈnʌrɪʃt/ *adjective* having bad health because of not having enough food or not eating the right kind of food ଖାଦ୍ୟାଭାବରେ ପୀଡ଼ିତ *The children were malnourished.*

malnutrition /ˌmælnjuːˈtrɪʃn/ *noun* (*no plural*) a condition that is caused when a person does not take enough food or the right kind of food ଶରୀର ପାଇଁ ଆବଶ୍ୟକ ଖାଦ୍ୟର ଅଭାବ ଜନିତ ଦୁର୍ବଳତା

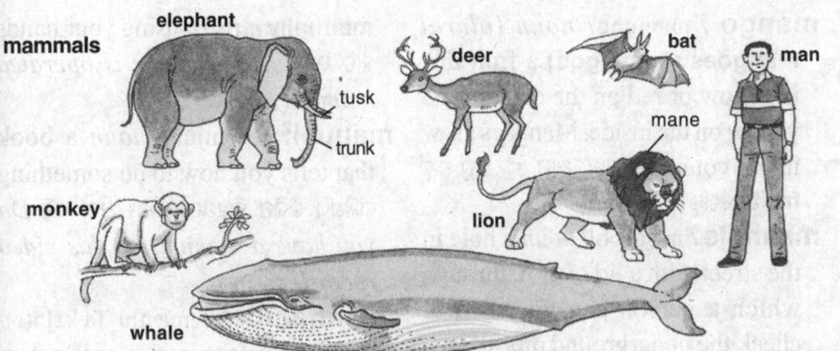

mammal /ˈmæml/ *noun* any animal that drinks milk from its mother's body when it is young ସ୍ତନ୍ୟପାୟୀ ଜନ୍ତୁ *Dogs, horses, whales and human beings are all mammals.*

man[1] /mæn/ *noun* **1** (*plural* **men** /men/) a grown-up male person ବୟସ୍କ ପୁରୁଷ *I saw a tall man with dark hair.* **2** (*plural* **men**) any person ମଣିଷ, ମନୁଷ୍ୟ, ମାନବ *All men need water to live.* **3** (*no plural*) all human beings taken as a group; people ମାନବଜାତି *How long has man lived on the earth?*

man[2] /mæn/ *verb* (**mans, manning, manned**) control or operate something କୌଣସି କାମର ପରିଚାଳନା କରିବା, କାର୍ଯ୍ୟରେ ନିୟୋଜିତ ହେବା *The spacecraft was manned by a crew of seven people.*

manage /ˈmænɪdʒ/ *verb* (**manages, managing, managed**) **1** be able to do something that is difficult କୌଣସି କଷ୍ଟ କାମ କରିବାକୁ ସକ୍ଷମ ହେବା, ସମ୍ଭାଳି ନେବା *The box was heavy but she managed to carry it to the car.* **2** control somebody or something ନିୟନ୍ତ୍ରଣ କରିବା, ପରିଚାଳନା କରିବା *She manages a department of thirty people.*

management /ˈmænɪdʒmənt/ *noun* **1** (*plural* **managements**) all the people who control a business ପରିଚାଳକ ଗୋଷ୍ଠୀ *The management have decided to close the factory.* **2** (*no plural*) control of something, for example a business, and the people who work in it ପରିଚାଳନା *He was awarded for good management.*

manager /ˈmænɪdʒə(r)/ *noun* a person who controls a business, bank or hotel, for example ପରିଚାଳନା, ନିର୍ବାହକ *a bank manager*

mane /meɪn/ *noun* the long hair on the neck of a horse or lion ଘୋଡ଼ା ବା ସିଂହ ବେକରେ ଥିବା କେଶର ବା ଲମ୍ବାବାଳ; ଲମ୍ବାବାଳ

man-eater *noun* (*plural* **man-eaters**) a wild animal that attacks and eats human beings ମଣିଷଖିଆ ହିଂସ୍ର ପଶୁ *the man-eater of Kumaon*

man-eating *adjective* ମଣିଷଖିଆ *a man-eating tiger*

mango /ˈmæŋgəʊ/ *noun* (*plural* **mangoes** ବା **mangos**) a fruit that is yellow or red on the outside and yellow on the inside. Mangoes grow in hot countries ଆମ୍ବ, ଆମ୍ର ➪ ଚିତ୍ର ପାଇଁ **fruit** ଦେଖନ୍ତୁ।

manhole /ˈmænhəʊl/ *noun* a hole in the street with a lid over it, through which a person can go down to check the underground pipes ଭୂଗର୍ଭସ୍ଥ ନର୍ଦ୍ଦମା, ପାଇପ୍ ଇତ୍ୟାଦି ନିରୀକ୍ଷଣ ବା ମରାମତି କରିବା ପାଇଁ ରାସ୍ତାରେ ଥିବା ଘୋଡ଼ଣୀ ଲଗା ପ୍ରବେଶ ପଥ, ମ୍ୟାନ୍‌ହୋଲ୍

mankind /mænˈkaɪnd/ *noun* (*no plural*) all the people in the world ମାନବଜାତି

man-made *adjective* made by people; not natural ମନୁଷ୍ୟକୃତ (ପ୍ରାକୃତିକ ନୁହେଁ) *man-made materials*

manner /ˈmænə(r)/ *noun* **1** the way that you do something or the way that something happens କାମ କରିବାର ଢଙ୍ଗ ବା ପଦ୍ଧତି; ଭାବ *Don't get angry. Let's try to talk about this in a calm manner.* **2 manners** (*no singular*) the way you behave when you are with other people ବ୍ୟବହାର, ଆଚରଣ *It's bad manners to talk with your mouth full.*

mansion /ˈmænʃn/ *noun* a very big house ଖୁବ୍ ବଡ଼ କୋଠା ବା ବାସଗୃହ

mantelpiece /ˈmæntlpi:s/ *noun* a shelf above a fireplace ଘର ଉଷ୍ଣତା ରଖିବା ପାଇଁ କାନ୍ଥରେ ଥିବା ଫାୟାର୍‌ପ୍ଲେସ୍ (ନିଆଁ ଜଳେଇବା ସ୍ଥାନ) ଉପରେ ଥିବା ଥାକ

manual[1] /ˈmænjuəl/ *adjective* that you do with your hands ହାତ ନିଆରି, ହସ୍ତକୃତ

manually *adverb* using your hands ହାତ ଦ୍ୱାରା *This machine is operated manually.*

manual[2] /ˈmænjuəl/ *noun* a book that tells you how to do something କୌଣସି ଜିନିଷ ବିଷୟରେ ତଥ୍ୟ ଥିବା ବହି *Do you have a manual for this video recorder?*

manufacture /ˌmænjuˈfæktʃə(r)/ *verb* (**manufactures, manufacturing, manufactured**) make things in a factory using machines ଯନ୍ତ୍ରପାତି ସାହାଯ୍ୟରେ ବା କଳକାରଖାନାରେ ବହୁଳ ଭାବରେ ଜିନିଷ ତିଆରି କରିବା, ବିନିର୍ମାଣ କରିବା *The company manufactures radios.*

manufacturer *noun* ବିନିର୍ମାଣ, ବିନିର୍ମାଣ କାରୀ ସଂସ୍ଥା *If it doesn't work, send it back to the manufacturers.*

manure /məˈnjʊə(r)/ *noun* (*no plural*) animal dung that is mixed with soil to help plants grow well ଖତ, ସାର

manuscript /ˈmænjuskrɪpt/ *noun* **1** handwritten or typed pages before they get printed in a book form ପାଣ୍ଡୁଲିପି, ହାତଲେଖା ବା ଟାଇପ୍‌କରା ବହି *The final book was very different from the original manuscript.* **2** an old book or document written by hand before printing was invented ଛପାକଳ ଉଦ୍ଭାବନ ପୂର୍ବର ହାତଲେଖା ପାଣ୍ଡୁଲିପି ବା ବହି

many /ˈmeni/ *adjective* (**many, more, most**), *pronoun* a large number of people or things ଅନେକ, ବହୁସଂଖ୍ୟକ *Many people in this country are very poor.* ○ *There aren't many students in my class.*

as many as the same number that ଯେତେଇଚ୍ଛା ସେତେ *Take as many cakes as you want.*

how many ...? words that you use to ask about the number of people or things କେତେ? *How many brothers and sisters have you got?*

⇨ **much** ଦେଖନ୍ତୁ।

map /mæp/ *noun* a drawing of a town, a country or the world. It shows things like mountains, rivers and roads ମାନଚିତ୍ର (ଦେଶ, ପୃଥିବୀ ଇତ୍ୟାଦିର) *Can you find Mysore on the map?* ○ *a street map of Delhi* ✪ କେବଳ ମାନଚିତ୍ର ଥିବା ବହିକୁ **atlas** କୁହାଯାଏ।

marble /ˈmɑːbl/ *noun* **1** (*no plural*) a very hard stone that is used in building and for making statues ମର୍ମର ବା ଶଂଖମଲ୍‌ମଲ୍ ପଥର, ମାର୍ବଲ୍ **2** (*plural* **marbles**) a small glass ball that children use in a game ପିଲାମାନେ ଖେଳୁଥିବା କାଚର ଗୁଳି *They are playing marbles.*

March /mɑːtʃ/ *noun* the third month of the year ପାଶ୍ଚାତ୍ୟ ବର୍ଷର ତୃତୀୟ ମାସ, ମାର୍ଚ୍ଚ (ମାସ)

march /mɑːtʃ/ *verb* (**marches, marching, marched**) **1** walk like a soldier ସୈନ୍ୟମାନଙ୍କ ପରି ନିୟମିତ ପାଦୁଣ୍ଡ ପକାଇ ଚାଲିବା *The soldiers marched along the road.* **2** walk with a large group of people to show that you have strong feelings about something ଉଦ୍ଦେଶ୍ୟ ସାଧନ ପାଇଁ ଦଳବଦ୍ଧ ପଦଯାତ୍ରା କରିବା *They marched through the town shouting 'Stop the war!'*

march *noun* (*plural* **marches**) **1** the action of marching ପଦଯାତ୍ରା **2** a long walk by a large group of people to show that they have strong feelings about something ଉଦ୍ଦେଶ୍ୟ ସାଧନ ପାଇଁ ଦଳବଦ୍ଧ ପଦଯାତ୍ରା *a peace march*

mare /meə(r)/ *noun* a female horse ମାଈ ଘୋଡ଼ା, ଘୋଡ଼ୀ, ଘୋଟକୀ

margin /ˈmɑːdʒɪn/ *noun* the space at the side of a page that has no writing or pictures in it ଲେଖା ବା ଛପା ପୃଷ୍ଠାର ଚାରିକଡ଼େ ଥିବା ଅଲେଖା ଅଂଶ, ମାର୍ଜିନ୍

marigold /ˈmærigəʊld/ *noun* a plant with yellow or orange flowers ଗେଣ୍ଡୁ ଗଛ; ଗେଣ୍ଡୁ ଫୁଲ

marine /məˈriːn/ *adjective* **1** of the sea and the creatures living in it ସାମୁଦ୍ରିକ *the study of the marine life* **2** of ships and shipping ଜାହାଜ ବା ନୌଚାଳନା ସମ୍ବନ୍ଧୀୟ *marine engineering*

mark[1] /mɑːk/ *noun* **1** a spot or line that makes something less clean than it was before ଦାଗ, ଚିହ୍ନ *There's a dirty mark on the front of your shirt.* **2** a shape or special sign on something ଚିହ୍ନଟକାରୀ ସଙ୍କେତ, ଚିହ୍ନ ବା ମୋହର *This mark shows that the ring is made of silver.* **3** a number or letter that a teacher gives for your work to show how good it is ନିଜ ଲେଖା ପାଇଁ ଶିକ୍ଷକ ଦେଉଥିବା ମାନସଂଖ୍ୟା, ମାର୍କ *She got very good marks in the exam.*

mark[2] /mɑːk/ *verb* (**marks, marking, marked**) **1** put a sign on something by writing or drawing on it ଲେଖି ବା ମୋହର ମାରି ଚିହ୍ନିତ କରିବା *The price is* *marked on the bottom of the box.* **2** put a tick (✓) or cross (×) on school work to show if it is right or wrong, or write a number or letter to show how good it is ପାଠପଢ଼ାରେ ଟିକ୍ (✓) ବା ଛକି (×) ଦ୍ୱାରା ଠିକ୍ ବା ଭୁଲ୍ ସୂଚାଇବା କିମ୍ବା ସଂଖ୍ୟା ଦ୍ୱାରା ମୂଲ୍ୟାଙ୍କନ କରିବା *The teacher marked all my answers right.*

market /ˈmɑːkɪt/ *noun* a place where people go to buy and sell things, usually outdoors ବଜାର, ହାଟ *There is a fruit and vegetable market close to where we live.*

marriage /ˈmærɪdʒ/ *noun* **1** the time when a man and woman become husband and wife; a wedding ବାହାଘର, ବିବାହ *The marriage will take place tomorrow.* **2** the time when two people are together as husband and wife ବିବାହିତ ଜୀବନ, ବିବାହିତ ଅବସ୍ଥା *They had a long and happy marriage.*

marry /ˈmæri/ *verb* (**marries, marrying, married, has married**) take somebody as your husband or wife ବାହା ହେବା, ବିବାହ କରିବା *Will you marry me?*

get married take somebody as your husband or wife ବାହା ହେବା । ବିବାହ କରିବା *Rajat and Sujata got married last year.*

Mars /mɑːz/ *noun* (*no plural*) the fourth planet from the sun, between the Earth and Jupiter ସୌରଜଗତର ସୂର୍ଯ୍ୟଙ୍କ ଠାରୁ ଚତୁର୍ଥ ଗ୍ରହ (ଯାହା ପୃଥିବୀ ଓ ବୃହସ୍ପତି ମଧ୍ୟରେ ଅବସ୍ଥିତ), ମଙ୍ଗଳଗ୍ରହ ➪ ଚିତ୍ର ପାଇଁ **solar system** ଦେଖନ୍ତୁ ।

marsupial /mɑːˈsuːpiəl/ *noun* a member of a group of animals that are found in Australia. The female has a pouch on the front of its body in which it carries its young ones ଅବିକଶିତ ଶିଶୁମାନଙ୍କୁ ରଖିବା ପାଇଁ ମାଈ ପଶୁର ପେଟରେ ଥଳି ଥିବା କଙ୍ଗାରୁ ଜାତୀୟ ଅଷ୍ଟ୍ରେଲୀୟ ପଶୁ *Kangaroos and koala bears are marsupials.*

martial /ˈmɑːʃl/ *adjective* of or for war ଯୁଦ୍ଧ ସମ୍ବନ୍ଧୀୟ, ଯୁଦ୍ଧ ପାଇଁ ଉଦ୍ଦିଷ୍ଟ *martial training*

martyr /ˈmɑːtə(r)/ *noun* someone who is punished or killed because of their beliefs ସହିଦ, ନିଜର ମତ ପାଇଁ ନିର୍ଯ୍ୟାତିତ ବ୍ୟକ୍ତି *a martyr to the cause of freedom*

marvel /ˈmɑːvl/ *noun* someone or something that is wonderful and that you admire very much ଆଶ୍ଚର୍ଯ୍ୟଜନକ ପଦାର୍ଥ; ଅତି ପ୍ରଶଂସନୀୟ ବ୍ୟକ୍ତି *marvels of nature*

marvellous /ˈmɑːvələs/ *adjective* very good; wonderful ଚମତ୍କାର *I had a marvellous holiday.*

mascot /ˈmæskət/ *noun* a person, an animal or a thing that people believe will bring good luck ଶୁଭବ୍ୟକ୍ତି, ଜନ୍ତୁ ବା ବସ୍ତୁ *Appu was the mascot of the 1982 Asian Games held in New Delhi.*

masculine /ˈmæskjəlɪn/ *adjective* of or like a man; right for a man ପୁରୁଷ ଗୁଣ ବା ଆକୃତି ବିଶିଷ୍ଟ, ପୁରୁଷୋଚିତ *a masculine voice* ➪ **feminine** ଦେଖନ୍ତୁ ।

mask /mɑːsk/ *noun* a thing that you wear over your face to hide or protect it ମୁଖା, କୃତ୍ରିମ ମୁଖାବରଣ *The doctor wore a mask.*

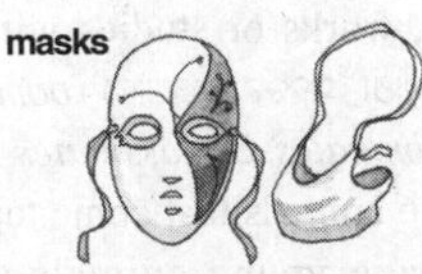

mason /ˈmeɪsn/ *noun* a person who works with stone and brick ରାଜମିସ୍ତ୍ରୀ

mass /mæs/ *noun* **1** (*plural* **masses**) a large amount of a substance without any particular shape or form ପଦାର୍ଥର ଏକୀଭୂତ କିନ୍ତୁ ନିର୍ଦ୍ଦିଷ୍ଟ ଆକାର ନଥିବା ଅବସ୍ଥା; ଗଦା, ମେଦା, ସ୍ତୂପ *a mass of clay* ○ *a mass of dried leaves* **2 the masses** (*no singular*) common people in society who are not leaders or who are not considered to be very well-educated ଜନସାଧାରଣ *the revolt by the masses* **3** (*plural* **masses**) the amount of material in something କୌଣସି ବସ୍ତୁରେ ଥିବା ପଦାର୍ଥର ପରିମାଣ ବା ଓଜନ *the mass of the planet*

massage /ˈmæsɑːʒ/ *noun* the action of rubbing and pressing somebody's body to relax their muscles or reduce pain ଶରୀରମର୍ଦ୍ଦନ, ଘଷାମୋଡ଼ା, ମାଲିସ୍

massage *verb* (**massages, massaging, massaged**) **1** rub something into the skin or hair ଦେହ ବା ମୁଣ୍ଡରେ କିଛି ଘଷିବା *Massage the oil into your skin.* **2** rub or press someone's body to reduce pain ଶରୀରମର୍ଦ୍ଦନ କରିବା, ଘଷାମୋଡ଼ା କରିବା, ମାଲିସ୍ କରିବା *The doctor advised her to massage the aching muscles.*

massive /ˈmæsɪv/ *adjective* very big ଖୁବ୍‌ବଡ଼, ବିରାଟ *The house is massive—it has sixteen bedrooms!*

mass media *noun* (*plural*) the means of spreading information to a large number of people in a very short time through newspapers, television and radio, for example ଖବର ଯୋଗାଯୋଗ ବ୍ୟବସ୍ଥା (ଖବରକାଗଜ, ଟି.ଭି. ରେଡ଼ିଓ ଇତ୍ୟାଦି)

mast /mɑːst/ *noun* **1** a tall piece of wood or metal that holds up a flag or the sails on a boat ଜାହାଜର ମାସ୍ତୁଲ; ରେଡ଼ିଓ, ଟି.ଭି. ଇତ୍ୟାଦିର ଏରିଆଲ୍ ବା ଆଣ୍ଟିନା ଲଗାଯାଇଥିବା ଖୁଣ୍ଟ **2** a very tall metal tower that sends out sounds or pictures for radio or television ରେଡ଼ିଓ ବା ଟି.ଭି. କାର୍ଯ୍ୟକ୍ରମ ସଞ୍ଚାର ପାଇଁ ତିଆରି ହୋଇଥିବା ଉଚ୍ଚ ଧାତବ ସ୍ତମ୍ଭ

master[1] /ˈmɑːstə(r)/ *noun* a man who has people or animals in his control ମାଲିକ, ପରିଚାଳକ *The dog ran to its master.*

master[2] /ˈmɑːstə(r)/ *verb* (**masters, mastering, mastered**) learn how to do something well କୌଣସି ବିଷୟ ଭଲ ଭାବରେ ଶିଖିଯିବା, ପୂର୍ଣ୍ଣ ଦକ୍ଷତା ବା ଜ୍ଞାନ ଲାଭ କରିବା *It takes a long time to master a foreign language.*

mastery /ˈmɑːstəri/ *noun* (*no plural*) **1** great skill and knowledge about something ସମ୍ପୂର୍ଣ୍ଣ ଜ୍ଞାନ ବା ଦକ୍ଷତା *She has mastery of several subjects.* **2** control of or over something ଆଧିପତ୍ୟ, ପ୍ରାଧାନ୍ୟ, ଦଖଲ

human mastery of the natural world

mat /mæt/ *noun* **1** a small thing that covers a part of the floor ଘର ଚଟାଣର କିଛି ଅଂଶରେ ପକା ଯାଉଥିବା ଆବରଣ; ଚଟେଇ, ପଟି, ମସିଣା; ପାପୋଛ *Wipe your feet on the doormat before you go in.* **2** a small thing that you put on a table under a hot dish or cup or a glass ଗରମ ଖାଦ୍ୟ ଟେବୁଲ୍ ଉପରେ ରଖିଲାବେଳେ ତା' ତଳେ ରଖାଯାଉଥିବା ଛୋଟ ପଟି, ମ୍ୟାଟ୍ *a table mat*

match[1] /mætʃ/ *noun* (*plural* **matches**) a short thin piece of wood with a special tip that makes fire when you rub it on something rough ଦିଆସିଲି କାଠି *a box of matches*

matchbox /ˈmætʃbɒks/ *noun* (*plural* **matchboxes**) a small box for matches ଦିଆସିଲି ପେଡ଼ି, ନିଆଁପେଡ଼ି

match[2] /mætʃ/ *noun* (*plural* **matches**) a game between two people or teams ପ୍ରତିଯୋଗିତା ମୂଳକ ଖେଳ *a cricket match*

match[3] /mætʃ/ *verb* (**matches, matching, matched**) **1** have the same colour, shape or pattern as something else, or look good with something else ଏକା ରଙ୍ଗ, ଆକାର ବା ଢାଞ୍ଚାର ହେବା, ଅନୁରୂପ ହେବା, ଏକା ଭଳି ହେବା *That scarf matches your dress very well.* **2** find something that is like another thing or that you can put with it ଏକା ପରି ଦ୍ରବ୍ୟ ଯୋଗାଡ଼ କରିବା, ମେଳ ଖୁଆଇବା *Match the word with the right picture.*

matching *adjective* ଏକାପରି, ମେଳ ଖାଇଲା ପରି *She was wearing a blue sari and matching earrings.*

mate /meɪt/ *noun* **1** a person who lives, works or studies with you ସାଙ୍ଗ, ସାଥୀ, ସହଚର, ସହପାଠୀ *room-mate* ○ *teammates* ○ *classmates* **2** one of two animals that come together to make young animals ପଶୁ ବା ପକ୍ଷୀମାନଙ୍କର ପ୍ରଜନନ ସାଥୀ *The bird is looking for a mate.*

mate *verb* (**mates, mating, mated**) when animals mate, they come together to make young animals ପଶୁ ବା ପକ୍ଷୀ ପ୍ରଜନନ ପାଇଁ ଏକାଠି ହେବା

material /məˈtɪəriəl/ *noun* **1** what you use for making or doing something ବସ୍ତୁ, ଦ୍ରବ୍ୟ ବା ପଦାର୍ଥ *Wood and stone are building materials.* **2** cloth made of wool, cotton, etc. and that you use for making clothes and other things କନା, ଲୁଗା ବା ବସ୍ତ୍ର *I don't have enough material to make a dress.*

mathematics /ˌmæθəˈmætɪks/, **maths** /mæθs/ *noun* (*no plural*) the study of numbers, measurements and shapes ଅଙ୍କଶାସ୍ତ୍ର, ଗଣିତ ଶାସ୍ତ୍ର *Maths is my favourite subject.*

matter[1] /ˈmætə(r)/ *noun* something that you must talk about or do ବିଷୟ, ବିଷୟବସ୍ତୁ *There is a matter I would like to discuss with you.*

as a matter of fact words that you use when you say something true, important or interesting ବାସ୍ତବରେ,

ପ୍ରକୃତରେ *I'm going home early today. As a matter of fact, it's my birthday.*

no matter how, what, when, who, etc. however, whatever, whenever, whoever, etc. ଯେମିତି ବି ହେଉ; ଯାହା ବି ହେଉ; ଯେବେ ବି ହେଉ; ଯିଏ ବି ହେଉ *No matter how hard I try, I can't open the door.*

matter[2] /ˈmætə(r)/ *verb* (**matters, mattering, mattered**) be important ଗୁରୁତ୍ୱପୂର୍ଣ୍ଣ ହେବା, ଦରକାରୀ ହେବା *It doesn't matter if you're late—we'll wait for you.*

matter[3] /ˈmætə(r)/ *noun* (*no plural*) what you and everything around you is made up of ଭୌତିକ ପଦାର୍ଥ *Matter is of three kinds—solid, liquid and gas.*

mattress /ˈmætrəs/ *noun* (*plural* **mattresses**) the thick soft part of a bed that you lie on ଗଦି, ଶେଯ

mature /məˈtʃʊə(r)/ *adjective* like an adult; fully grown ପୂର୍ଣ୍ଣ ବିକଶିତ; ପରିଣତ ବୟସର ✪ ବିପରୀତ **immature**

maximize /ˈmæksɪmaɪz/ *verb* (**maximizes, maximizing, maximized**) increase the size or value of something as much as possible ସର୍ବାଧିକ ଆକାର ବା ପରିମାଣ ପର୍ଯ୍ୟନ୍ତ ବୃଦ୍ଧି କରିବା ✪ ବିପରୀତ **minimize**

maximum /ˈmæksɪməm/ *noun* (*no plural*) the most; the biggest possible size, amount or number ସର୍ବୋଚ୍ଚ ଆକାର, ପରିମାଣ ବା ସଂଖ୍ୟା *This plane can carry a maximum of 150 people.*

maximum *adjective* ସର୍ବାଧିକ, ସର୍ବୋଚ୍ଚ *Today's maximum temperature was 32°C.* ✪ ବିପରୀତ **minimum**

May /meɪ/ *noun* the fifth month of the year ପାଶ୍ଚାତ୍ୟ ବର୍ଷର ପଞ୍ଚମ ମାସ, ମେଁ

may /meɪ/ *modal verb* **1** a word that shows what will perhaps happen or what is possible ସମ୍ଭାବନାସୂଚକ କ୍ରିୟାପଦ *I may go to Spain next year.* **2** be allowed to do something ଅନୁମତି ପ୍ରାପ୍ତ ବା ପ୍ରଦାନ ସୂଚାଉଥିବା ଶବ୍ଦ *May I open the window?* **3** I hope that this will happen ଇଚ୍ଛା ପ୍ରକାଶକ ଶବ୍ଦ *May God be with you.* ➪ **modal verb** ପାଇଁ ଟିପ୍ପଣୀ ଦେଖନ୍ତୁ।

maybe /ˈmeɪbi/ *adverb* perhaps; possibly ବୋଧହୁଏ, ସମ୍ଭବତଃ, ହୁଏତ *Maybe you should phone him.*

mayor /meə(r)/ *noun* the elected leader of a council that manages the affairs of a town or city ନଗରପାଳ

me /mi:/ *pronoun* (*plural* **us** /əs/) the person who is speaking ମୁଁ; ମୋତେ *When he saw me, he told me about the accident.* ○ *'Who rang the bell?' 'It was me.'*

meadow /ˈmedəʊ/ *noun* a field of grass ଘାସପଡ଼ିଆ

meal /mi:l/ *noun* food that you eat at a certain time of the day ଭୋଜନ, ଖାଦ୍ୟ *Breakfast is the first meal of the day.*

mean[1] /mi:n/ *verb* (**means, meaning, meant** /ment/, **has meant**) **1** say or show something in a different way; have as a meaning କହି ବା ଦେଖାଇ ଭିନ୍ନ ଭାବ ବା ଅର୍ଥ ବ୍ୟକ୍ତ କରିବା;

ମାନେ ହେଲା *What does 'medicine' mean?* **2** plan or want to do something ଅଭିପ୍ରାୟ କରିବା, ଉଦ୍ଦେଶ୍ୟ କରିବା *I meant to phone you, but I forgot.*

mean something to somebody be important to somebody କାହାରି ପାଇଁ ଗୁରୁତ୍ୱପୂର୍ଣ୍ଣ ହେବା *My family means a lot to me.*

mean[2] /miːn/ *adjective* (**meaner, meanest**) **1** a person who is mean does not like to give things or to spend money ଅନୁଦାର; କୃପଣ; ନୀଚମନା *Pradeep is very mean—he never buys anybody a present.* ✪ ବିପରୀତ **generous 2** unkind ନିର୍ଦ୍ଦୟ *It was mean of you to say that Rahul was fat.*

meaning /ˈmiːnɪŋ/ *noun* what something means or shows ଅର୍ଥ, ମାନେ ତାତ୍ପର୍ଯ୍ୟ *The word 'bark' has two different meanings.*

means /miːnz/ *noun* (*plural* **means**) a way of doing something; a way of going somewhere (କିଛି କରିବାର) ଉପାୟ, ସାଧନ ବା ସମ୍ବଳ *means of livelihood* ○ *means of transport*

by means of something by using something ଦ୍ୱାରା, ସାହାଯ୍ୟରେ *We crossed the river by means of a small bridge.*

meant ଶବ୍ଦ **mean**[1] ର ଏକ ଧାତୁରୂପ

meantime /ˈmiːntaɪm/ *noun* (*no plural*)

in the meantime in the time between two things happening ଇତି ମଧ୍ୟରେ, ଯା ଭିତରେ *The doctor will be here soon—in the meantime you should stay calm.*

meanwhile /ˈmiːnwaɪl/ *adverb* at the same time as another thing is happening ସେହି ସମୟରେ ଇତି ମଧ୍ୟରେ *Sumit cooked the dinner. Meanwhile, Neha cleaned the house.*

measles /ˈmiːzlz/ *noun* (*no plural*) an illness because of which small red spots appear on your skin ମିଳିମିଳା ରୋଗ

measure[1] /ˈmeʒə(r)/ *verb* (**measures, measuring, measured**) find the size or weight of somebody or the amount of something ଆକାର, ଓଜନ ବା ପରିମାଣ ମାପିବା *I measured the box with a ruler.*

measure[2] /ˈmeʒə(r)/ *noun* **1** a unit for finding out the size, weight or amount of something ମାପ, ମାପର ଏକକ *A metre is a measure of length.* **2** an action that is done in order to deal with something ଉଦ୍ଦେଶ୍ୟ ସାଧନ ପାଇଁ ଉପଯୁକ୍ତ ଉପାୟ ବା ପଦକ୍ଷେପ *safety measures*

measurement /ˈmeʒəmənt/ *noun* the act of finding out how long, wide, high, etc. something is ମାପ, ମାପର ପ୍ରକ୍ରିୟା *What are the measurements of the kitchen?*

meat /miːt/ *noun* (*no plural*) the flesh of an animal's body that people can eat ମାଂସ

mechanic /məˈkænɪk/ *noun* a person whose job is to repair or work with machines ଯନ୍ତ୍ରପାତି ବ୍ୟବହାର ଓ ମରାମତିରେ ନିପୁଣ କାରିଗର *a car mechanic*

medal /ˈmedl/ *noun* a piece of metal with words and pictures on it that is given to somebody who has done something very good ପଦକ *She won a gold medal in the Olympic Games.*

meddle /ˈmedl/ *verb* (**meddles, meddling, meddled**) take too much interest in other people's work and things when they do not want you to (ଅନ୍ୟର କାମରେ) ଅଯଥା ହସ୍ତକ୍ଷେପ କରିବା *Don't meddle in my affairs.*

media /ˈmi:diə/ *noun* (*plural*) **the media** television, radio and newspapers ଟି.ଭି., ରେଡ଼ିଓ, ଖବରକାଗଜ ଇତ୍ୟାଦି ବାର୍ତ୍ତାବାହକ ସଂସ୍ଥାସମୂହ *The media is always interested in the lives of film stars.*

medical /ˈmedɪkl/ *adjective* of or about medicine, hospitals or doctors ସ୍ୱାସ୍ଥ୍ୟ ସମ୍ବନ୍ଧୀୟ ଡାକ୍ତରୀ *a medical student* ○ *medical treatment*

medicine /ˈmedsn/ *noun* **1** (*no plural*) the science of understanding illnesses and making sick people well again ଚିକିତ୍ସା ଶାସ୍ତ୍ର, ଡାକ୍ତରୀ ବିଦ୍ୟା *He studied medicine for five years before becoming a doctor.* **2** (*plural* **medicines**) pills or special liquids that help you to get better when you are ill ଔଷଧ *Take this medicine every morning.*

meditation /ˌmedɪˈteɪʃn/ *noun* (*no plural*) the act of thinking deeply to make your mind calm ଧ୍ୟାନ, ଗଭୀର ଚିନ୍ତା

medium /ˈmi:diəm/ *adjective* not big and not small; middle ମଝିମଝିଆ, ମଧ୍ୟମ ଆକାରର *Would you like a small, medium or large Coke?*

meek /mi:k/ *adjective* quiet, gentle and always ready to obey others without asking any questions; timid ଧୀର, ଶାନ୍ତ, ଅଜ୍ଞାନୁବର୍ତ୍ତୀ, ଡରୁଆ *a meek child*

meet /mi:t/ *verb* (**meets, meeting, met** /met/, **has met**) **1** come together at a certain time and place when you have planned it (ପୂର୍ବନିର୍ଦ୍ଧାରିତ ଯୋଜନା ଅନୁସାରେ) ଦେଖା କରିବା, ସାକ୍ଷାତ କରିବା *Let's meet outside the cinema at eight o'clock.* **2** see and say hello to somebody ଦେଖା ହେବା *I met Kapil in the library today.* **3** see and speak to somebody for the first time ପରିଚୟ କରିବା, ପରିଚୟ ହେବା *When did you first meet your wife?*

meeting /ˈmi:tɪŋ/ *noun* a time when a group of people come together for a special reason ସଭା, ସମ୍ମିଳନୀ, ମିଳନ, ସାକ୍ଷାତ *We had a meeting to talk about the plans for the new swimming pool.*

melody /ˈmelədi/ *noun* (*plural* **melodies**) a group of musical notes that make a nice sound when you play or sing them together; a tune ଗୋଟିଏ ପରେ ଗୋଟିଏ ସ୍ୱର ବା ଧ୍ୱନି ସଜାଇ ଗଢ଼ାଯାଇଥିବା ଗୀତ ବା ସ୍ୱର *This song has a lovely melody.*

melodious /məˈləʊdiəs/ *adjective* ସୁମଧୁର, ସୁଶ୍ରାବ୍ୟ (ସ୍ୱର) *She has a melodious voice.*

melon /ˈmelən/ *noun* a big round yellow or green fruit with a lot of seeds inside ତରଭୁଜ, ଖରଭୁଜ

melt /melt/ *verb* (**melts, melting, melted**) warm something so that it becomes liquid; get warmer so that it becomes liquid ତରଳାଇବା; ତରଳିବା *Melt the butter in a saucepan.*

member /ˈmembə(r)/ *noun* a person who belongs to a group କୌଣସି ସମାଜ ବା ଗୋଷ୍ଠୀର ସଭ୍ୟ *I'm a member of the school hockey team.*

Member of Parliament *noun* (*plural* **Members of Parliament**) a person whom the people of a town or city choose to speak for them in Parliament ସାଂସଦ, ପାର୍ଲିଆମେଣ୍ଟର ସଭ୍ୟ ବା ସଦସ୍ୟ ✪ Member of Parliament ର ସଂକ୍ଷିପ୍ତ ରୂପ ହେଲା **MP**।

membership *noun* (*no plural*) being in a group ସଭ୍ୟପଦ ସଦସ୍ୟତା *Membership of the club costs Rs 1,500 a year.*

membrane /ˈmembreɪn/ *noun* a thin layer of skin that covers certain parts of the body ଝିଲ୍ଲୀ, କୋଷାବରଣ; ପଶୁ ବା ଉଦ୍ଭିଦର ଆଭ୍ୟନ୍ତରୀଣ ଅଙ୍ଗକୁ ଆଚ୍ଛାଦନ କରୁଥିବା ନମନୀୟ ସୂକ୍ଷ୍ମ ଚର୍ମପରି ପରଦା

memento /məˈmentəʊ/ *noun* (*plural* **mementos** ବା **mementoes**) something that you keep to remind you of somebody or something ସ୍ମରଣଚିହ୍ନ, ସ୍ମାରକ ବସ୍ତୁ

memorable /ˈmemərəbl/ *adjective* easy to remember because it is special in some way ସ୍ମରଣୀୟ, ସ୍ମରଣଯୋଗ୍ୟ

memorial /məˈmɔːriəl/ *noun* something that people build or do to help us remember somebody, or something that happened କୌଣସି ବ୍ୟକ୍ତି ବା ଘଟଣାର ସ୍ମୃତିଚିହ୍ନ *The statue is a memorial to all the soldiers who died in the war.*

memorize /ˈmeməraɪz/ *verb* (**memorizes, memorizing, memorized**) learn something so that you can remember it exactly ମୁଖସ୍ଥ କରିବା, ଘୋଷିବା, କଣ୍ଠସ୍ଥ କରିବା *We have to memorize a poem for homework.*

memory /ˈmeməri/ *noun* (*plural* **memories**) **1** the power to remember things ସ୍ମରଣ ଶକ୍ତି, ସ୍ମୃତି ଶକ୍ତି, ମନେ ରଖିବା ଶକ୍ତି *She's got a very good memory—she never forgets people's names.* **2** something that you remember ମନେ ରଖିବା ବିଷୟ *I have very happy memories of that holiday.* **3** the part of a computer that holds information କମ୍ପ୍ୟୁଟରର ତଥ୍ୟ ସଂଚୟ ଶକ୍ତି ⇨ **RAM** ଓ **ROM** ମଧ୍ୟ ଦେଖନ୍ତୁ।

men ଶବ୍ଦ **man**[1] ର ବହୁବଚନ

menace /ˈmenəs/ *noun* if someone or something is a menace, they create a lot of trouble ବିପଜ୍ଜନକ ବ୍ୟକ୍ତି ବା ପଦାର୍ଥ *the tiger menace*

mend /mend/ *verb* (**mends, mending, mended**) repair something so that it can be used again ମରାମତି କରିବା *Can you mend this chair?*

mental /ˈmentl/ *adjective* of or in someone's mind ମାନସିକ *mental health*

mentally *adverb* ମାନସିକ ସ୍ତରରେ, ମନେମନେ, ମନଭିତରେ *He solved the sum mentally.*

mention /ˈmenʃn/ *verb* (**mentions, mentioning, mentioned**) speak or write a little about something ଉଲ୍ଲେଖ କରିବା, କହିବା *When Sheeba telephoned, she mentioned that she was going to buy a new car.*

menu /ˈmenju:/ *noun* (*plural* **menus**) **1** a list of the food that you can choose in a restaurant ଭୋଜନାଳୟର ଖାଦ୍ୟତାଲିକା, ମେନ୍ୟୁ *Can I have the menu, please?* **2** a list on the screen of a computer that shows what all you can do କମ୍ପ୍ୟୁଟର୍ ପରଦାରେ ପ୍ରଦର୍ଶିତ କାର୍ଯ୍ୟକ୍ରମର ତାଲିକା

computer menu

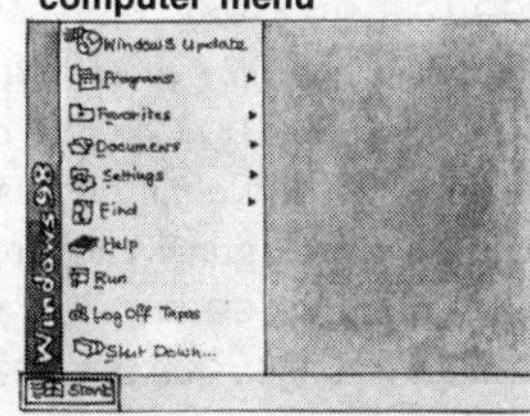

merchant /ˈmɜ:tʃənt/ *noun* a person who buys and sells things, usually of one type, in large quantities ବ୍ୟବସାୟୀ, ବେପାରୀ

Mercury /ˈmɜ:kjəri/ *noun* (*no plural*) the planet that is nearest to the sun ସୌର ମଣ୍ଡଳର ସୂର୍ଯ୍ୟଙ୍କ ନିକଟତମ ଗ୍ରହ, ବୁଧଗ୍ରହ ➪ ଚିତ୍ର ପାଇଁ **solar system** ଦେଖନ୍ତୁ।

mercury /ˈmɜ:kjəri/ *noun* (*no plural*) a thick silver-coloured metal that is liquid. It is used in thermometers to measure temperature ପାରଦ, ପାରା

mercy /ˈmɜ:si/ *noun* (*no plural*) being kind and not hurting somebody who has done wrong ଦୟା, ଅନୁକମ୍ପା, କ୍ଷମା *The prisoners asked the king for mercy.*

mere /mɪə(r)/ *adjective* only; not more than କେବଳ, ମାତ୍ର; ଅଧିକ ନହେଇଥିବା *She was a mere child when they migrated to the US.*

merely *adverb* only କେବଳ *I don't want to buy the watch—I am merely asking its price.*

meridian /məˈrɪdiən/ *noun* an imaginary line on the surface of the earth that joins the North Pole to the South Pole and passes through a particular place ଦ୍ରାଘିମାବୃତ୍ତ; ଯେଉଁ କଳ୍ପିତ ରେଖା କୌଣସି ସ୍ଥାନକୁ ଉତ୍ତରମେରୁ ଓ ଦକ୍ଷିଣମେରୁ ସହ ସଂଯୋଗ କରି ଭୂ-ଗୋଲକକୁ ଆବର୍ତ୍ତନ କରିଥାଏ *the Greenwich meridian*

merit /ˈmerɪt/ *noun* what is good about somebody or something ଗୁଣ, ସଦ୍‌ଗୁଣ *What are the merits of this plan?*

mermaid /ˈmɜ:meɪd/ *noun* a woman in stories who has a fish's tail instead of legs and lives in the sea ନାରୀ ପରି ମୁହଁ ଓ ଦେହ ଏବଂ ମାଛ ପରି ତଳ ଶରୀର ଥିବା କିଂବଦନ୍ତୀ ବର୍ଣ୍ଣିତ ସାମୁଦ୍ରିକ ଜୀବ; ପୁରାତ୍ତୋକ୍ତ ମତ୍ସକନ୍ୟା

merry /ˈmeri/ *adjective* (**merrier, merriest**) happy and full of fun ପ୍ରଫୁଲ୍ଲ, ଆନନ୍ଦିତ, ଆହ୍ଲାଦିତ, ଖୁସି *Merry Christmas!*

mess /mes/ *noun* (*no plural*) a lot of untidy or dirty things all in the wrong place ଅପରିଷ୍କାର ଅବସ୍ଥା, ବିଶୃଙ୍ଖଳ ଅବସ୍ଥା *There was a terrible mess after the party.*

be in a mess 1 be untidy ବିଶୃଙ୍ଖଳ ଅବସ୍ଥାରେ ରହିବା *My bedroom is in a mess.* **2** have problems ଅସୁବିଧା ଅବସ୍ଥାରେ ରହିବା *She's in a mess—she's* *got no money and nowhere to live.*

message /ˈmesɪdʒ/ *noun* words, information, etc. that one person sends to another ଖବର, ସଂବାଦ, ବାର୍ତ୍ତା *Could you give a message to Jyoti, please? Please tell her I will be late.*

messenger /ˈmesɪndʒə(r)/ *noun* a person who brings a message ବାର୍ତ୍ତାବାହକ

messy /ˈmesi/ *adjective* (**messier, messiest**) **1** untidy or dirty ଅପରିଷ୍କାର; ବିଶୃଙ୍ଖଳ *a messy kitchen* **2** that makes you untidy or dirty ଅପରିଷ୍କାର କରୁଥିବା *Painting is a messy job.*

met ଶବ୍ଦ **meet** ର ଏକ ଧାତୁରୂପ

metal /ˈmetl/ *noun* a substance that is usually hard and shiny. Iron, lead, tin and gold are all metals ଧାତୁ (ଯଥା: ଲୁହା, ଟିଣ, ସୁନା ଇତ୍ୟାଦି)

meteor /ˈmiːtiə(r)/ *noun* a small piece of rock from space that enters the earth's atmosphere and burns up making a bright line in the night sky. Meteors are also called shooting stars ଉଲ୍କା (ମହାକାଶରୁ ଆସୁଥିବା ଛୋଟ ପଦାର୍ଥ ଖଣ୍ଡ ଯାହା ପୃଥିବୀର ବାୟୁ ମଣ୍ଡଳରେ ପ୍ରବେଶ କଲାବେଳେ ଜଳି ଉଠେ)

meteorite /ˈmiːtiəraɪt/ *noun* a piece of rock from outer space that has hit the earth's surface ପୃଥିବୀ ପୃଷ୍ଠରେ ପଡୁଥିବା ଉଲ୍କା; ଉଲ୍କାପିଣ୍ଡ

meteorological /ˌmiːtiərəˈlɒdʒɪkl/ *adjective* related to the study of weather or climate ପାଣିପାଗ ସମ୍ବନ୍ଧୀୟ *the meteorological department*

meter /ˈmiːtə(r)/ *noun* a machine that measures or counts something ପରିମାପକ ଯନ୍ତ୍ର *An electricity meter shows how much electricity you have used.*

method /ˈmeθəd/ *noun* a way of doing something ପଦ୍ଧତି, କାର୍ଯ୍ୟପ୍ରଣାଳୀ *What is the best method of cooking vegetables?*

metre /ˈmiːtə(r)/ *noun* a measure of length. There are 100 **centimetres** in a metre ଦଶାଂଶ ପଦ୍ଧତିରେ ଲମ୍ବ ପରିମାପର ଏକକ (ପ୍ରାୟ ୩୯.୪ ଇଞ୍ଚ), ୧୦୦ସେଣ୍ଟିମିଟର୍ *The wall is eight metres long.* ✪ Metre ର ସଂକ୍ଷିପ୍ତ ରୂପ ହେଲା **m** *2 m*

metric system *noun* the system of using metres, grams and litres to measure things ଦଶମିକ ପରିମାପ ପଦ୍ଧତି (ଯେଉଁଥିରେ ମିଟର୍, ଗ୍ରାମ୍, ଲିଟର୍ ଇତ୍ୟାଦି ପରିମାପ ବ୍ୟବହୃତ ହୁଏ)।

metro /ˈmetrəʊ/ *noun* (*plural* **metros**) **1** an underground railway system in a large city ବଡ଼ ସହରରେ ଥିବା ଭୂତଳ ରେଳପଥ **2** a large and important city ବଡ଼ ସହର, ମହାନଗର

miaow /miˈaʊ/ *noun* a sound that a cat makes ବିଲେଇର ମିଆଁଉ ଡାକ

miaow *verb* (**miaows, miaowing, miaowed**) make a sound that a cat makes ମିଆଁଉ ଶବ୍ଦ କରିବା

mice ଶବ୍ଦ **mouse** ର ବହୁବଚନ

microbe /ˈmaɪkrəʊb/ *noun* a very small living thing that may cause diseases ରୋଗ କରାଉଥିବା ଅଣୁଜୀବ, ସୂକ୍ଷ୍ମଜୀବାଣୁ, ବୀଜାଣୁ, ଭୂତାଣୁ

microchip /ˈmaɪkrəʊtʃɪp/ *noun* a very small thing inside a computer etc., for example, that makes it work କମ୍ପ୍ୟୁଟର୍ ଇତ୍ୟାଦି ଭିତରେ ଥିବା ବିଦ୍ୟୁତ୍ ଅର୍ଦ୍ଧପରିବାହୀ କ୍ଷୁଦ୍ରଖଣ୍ଡ (ଯାହା ଇଲେକ୍ଟ୍ରନିକ୍ ଯନ୍ତ୍ରକୁ ଚାଳନ କରେ)

microorganism /ˌmaɪkrəʊˈɔɡənɪzəm/ *noun* (*plural* **microorganisms**) a very small living thing ଅଣୁଜୀବ, ସୂକ୍ଷ୍ମ ଜୀବାଣୁ

microphone /ˈmaɪkrəfəʊn/ *noun* an electrical thing that makes sounds louder or records them so you can listen to them later ଶବ୍ଦଗ୍ରହଣ ଯନ୍ତ୍ର (ଯେଉଁଥିରେ ଗୃହୀତ ଶବ୍ଦକୁ ଉଚ୍ଚସ୍ୱରର କରାଯାଇ ପାରେ ବା ରେକର୍ଡ଼ କରାଯାଇପାରେ)

microscope /ˈmaɪkrəskəʊp/ *noun* an instrument with special glass in it, that makes very small things look much bigger ଅଣୁବୀକ୍ଷଣ ଯନ୍ତ୍ର *The scientist looked at the insect under the microscope.*

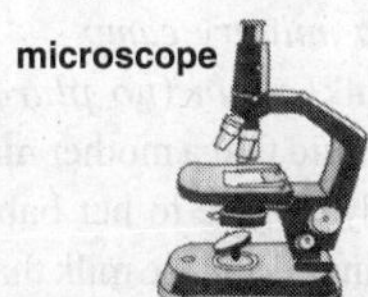

microwave /ˈmaɪkrəweɪv/ **microwave oven** *noun* a special oven that cooks food very quickly ଶୀଘ୍ର ରାନ୍ଧିବା ପାଇଁ ଏକ ବିଶେଷ ପ୍ରକାରର ଚୁଲି

mid- *prefix*
(in) the middle of ମଧ୍ୟବର୍ତ୍ତୀ, ମଧ୍ୟଭାଗରେ *I'm going on holiday in mid-July.*

midday /ˌmɪdˈdeɪ/ *noun* (*no plural*) twelve o'clock in the day ମଧ୍ୟାହ୍ନ *We met at midday.* ➪ **midnight** ଓ **noon** ମଧ୍ୟ ଦେଖନ୍ତୁ ।

middle /ˈmɪdl/ *noun* **1** the part that is at the same distance from the sides, edges or ends of something ମଧ୍ୟଭାଗ, ମଝି *A peach has a stone in the middle.* **2** the time after the beginning and before the end ମଧ୍ୟଭାଗ, ଅଧ *The phone rang in the middle of the night.*

middle-aged *adjective* not old and not young; between the ages of about 40 and 60 ମଧ୍ୟବୟସ୍କ *a middle-aged man*

midnight /ˈmɪdnaɪt/ *noun* (*no plural*) twelve o'clock at night ମଧ୍ୟରାତ୍ରି, ଅଧରାତ୍ରି *We left the party at midnight.* ➪ **midday** ଓ **noon** ମଧ୍ୟ ଦେଖନ୍ତୁ ।

midway /ˌmɪdˈweɪ/ *adverb* in the middle ମଝିରେ, ମଝିଆମଝି *The town is midway between Delhi and Jaipur.*

might¹ /ˈmaɪt/ *modal verb* **1** a word for 'may' in the past; may ର ଅତୀତ କାଳ ଧାତୁରୂପ *He said he might be late, but he was early.* **2** a word that shows what will perhaps happen or what is possible ସମ୍ଭାବ୍ୟତା ପ୍ରକାଶକ କ୍ରିୟା (ହୋଇପାରେ) *Don't run because you might fall.* **3** a word that you use to ask something in a very polite way ପ୍ରଶ୍ନ ପଚାରିବା ପାଇଁ ଅନୁମତି ମାଗିବା ଅର୍ଥରେ ବ୍ୟବହୃତ ଶବ୍ଦ *Might I say something?* ➪ **modal verb** ପାଇଁ ଟିପ୍ପଣୀ ଦେଖନ୍ତୁ ।

might² /ˈmaɪt/ *noun* great strength or power ପ୍ରବଳ ଶକ୍ତି, ବଳ

mighty /ˈmaɪti/ *adjective* (**mightier, mightiest**) very great, strong or powerful ଶକ୍ତିଶାଳୀ, ବଳବାନ, କ୍ଷମତାଶାଳୀ *a mighty giant*

migrate /maɪˈgreɪt/ *verb* (**migrates, migrating, migrated**) **1** when birds and animals migrate, they regularly move from one part of the world to another with the change in season ପଶୁ ପକ୍ଷୀମାନଙ୍କର ଋତୁ ଅନୁସାରେ ସାମୟିକ ସ୍ଥାନାନ୍ତର, ଭ୍ରମଣ କରିବା *Swallows migrate to warmer climates in winters*. **2** when people migrate, they go to another part of the world to settle there ଦେଶାନ୍ତର ଗମନ କରିବା; ବିଦେଶରେ ରହିବା

migration /maɪˈgreɪʃn/ *noun* the movement of large numbers of people, animals or birds from one part of the world to another ମଣିଷ, ପଶୁ ଓ ପକ୍ଷୀଙ୍କର ସମୂହ ସ୍ଥାନାନ୍ତର ଗମନ

migratory /ˈmaɪgreɪtri/ *adjective* moving from one part of the world to another ଭ୍ରମଣଶୀଳ, ଯାଯାବର *migratory birds*

mild /maɪld/ *adjective* (**milder, mildest**) **1** gentle; not strong or rough କୋମଳ, କୋହଳ, ମୃଦୁ **2** not too hot and not too cold ଖୁବ୍ ଥଣ୍ଡା ବା ଗରମ ହୋଇ ନଥିବା, ନାତିଶୀତୋଷ୍ଣ *a mild winter*

mile /maɪl/ *noun* a measure of distance that is used in Britain and the USA (1 mile = 1.6 kilometres) ଦୂରତାର ମାପ, ମାଇଲ୍ (୧୭୬୦ ଗଜ, ପ୍ରାୟ ୧.୬ କିଲୋମିଟର)

milestone /ˈmaɪlstəʊn/ *noun* **1** a stone by the side of the road to show how far it is to the next town ଦୂରତ୍ୱ ଲେଖାଥିବା ମାଇଲ୍ ଖୁଣ୍ଟ **2** an important development or event ଗୁରୁତ୍ୱପୂର୍ଣ୍ଣ ଘଟଣା

militant[1] /ˈmɪlɪtənt/ *adjective* using or ready to use strong or violent methods to bring about a political or social change କୌଣସି ଉଦ୍ଦେଶ୍ୟରେ ହିଂସାତ୍ମକ ପନ୍ଥା ଗ୍ରହଣ କରୁଥିବା *a demonstration by militant groups*

militancy /ˈmɪlɪtənsi/ *noun* ସଂଘର୍ଷ ପ୍ରବଣତା, ଯୁଦ୍ଧ ପ୍ରବଣତା

militant[2] /ˈmɪlɪtənt/ *noun* a person who uses or is ready to use strong or violent methods to bring about a political or social change କୌଣସି ଉଦ୍ଦେଶ୍ୟରେ ହିଂସାତ୍ମକ ପନ୍ଥା ଗ୍ରହଣ କରୁଥିବା ବ୍ୟକ୍ତି

military /ˈmɪlətri/ *adjective* of or for soldiers or the army ସୈନ୍ୟ ବା ସେନାବାହିନୀ ସମ୍ବନ୍ଧୀୟ, ସେନାପାଇଁ ଉଦ୍ଦିଷ୍ଟ, ସାମରିକ *a military camp*

milk /mɪlk/ *noun* (*no plural*) the white liquid that a mother makes in her body to give to her baby. Human beings drink the milk that cows and some other animals make ଦୁଧ, ଦୁଗ୍ଧ, କ୍ଷୀର

milk *verb* (**milks, milking, milked**) take milk from a cow or another animal ଦୁଧ ଦୁହିଁବା

milkman /ˈmɪlkmən/ *noun* (*plural* **milkmen**) a person who brings milk to your house ଦୁଧ ବିକାଳି, ଗଉଡ଼

Milky Way *noun* (*no plural*) the **galaxy** that contains our solar system ଏକ ବିରାଟ ତାରକା ଗୁଚ୍ଛ ବା ଗ୍ୟାଲାକ୍ସି ଯେଉଁଥିରେ ସୌରମଣ୍ଡଳ ଅବସ୍ଥିତ, ଛାୟାପଥ

mill /mɪl/ *noun* **1** a building where a machine makes wheat into flour ଅଟାକଳ ➪ **windmill** ମଧ୍ୟ ଦେଖନ୍ତୁ। **2** a factory for making things like steel or paper କାରଖାନା *a paper mill*

millennium /mɪˈleniəm/ *noun* (*plural* **millennia** /mɪˈlenɪə/ **millenniums**) a period of 1,000 years ୧,୦୦୦ ବର୍ଷ, ସହସ୍ରବର୍ଷ

millimetre /ˈmɪlimi:tə(r)/ *noun* a measure of length. There are 10 millimetres in a **centimetre** ଲମ୍ବର ମାପକ, ମିଲିମିଟର, (୧୦ ମିଲିମିଟରକୁ ନେଇ ୧ ସେଣ୍ଟିମିଟର ହୁଏ) ✪ Millimetre ର ସଂକ୍ଷିପ୍ତ ରୂପ ହେଲା **mm** *60 mm*

million /ˈmɪljən/ *number* 1,000,000; one thousand thousand ଦଶ ଲକ୍ଷ, ଏକ ନିୟୁତ *millions of dollars* ○ *six million pounds*

millionth /ˈmɪljənθ/ *adjective*, *adverb*, *noun* 1,000,000th ଏକ ନିୟୁତ ଭାଗରୁ ଭାଗେ, ନିୟୁତତମ

millionaire /ˌmɪljəˈneə(r)/ *noun* a very rich person who has more than a million dollars, rupees, etc. ଏକ ନିୟୁତ ଟଙ୍କା, ଡଲାର ଇତ୍ୟାଦିର ଅଧିପତି

mimic /ˈmɪmɪk/ *verb* (**mimics, mimicking, mimicked**) copy the manners or actions, often to make fun of them or make others laugh (ହାସ୍ୟ ବା ବିଦ୍ରୁପ ପାଇଁ) କାହାରି ଚେହେରା, ଭାବଭଙ୍ଗୀ ବା କଥାବାର୍ତ୍ତାର ଅନୁକରଣ କରିବା *She mimics her boss very well.*

minaret /ˌmɪnəˈret/ *noun* a tall narrow tower that is usually a part of a mosque ସାଧାରଣତଃ ମସଜିଦ୍‌ରେ ଥିବା ଉଚ୍ଚ ଗମ୍ବୁଜ।

mind[1] /maɪnd/ *noun* the part of you that thinks and remembers ମନ, ଚୈତନ୍ୟ, ଭାବନା, ଇଚ୍ଛା ଓ ଆବେଗର ସ୍ଥଳ *He has a very quick mind.*

change your mind have an idea, then decide to do something different ମତ ବଦଳାଇବା, ମତ ପରିବର୍ତ୍ତନ କରିବା

make up your mind decide something ନିର୍ଣ୍ଣୟ କରିବା *Should I buy the blue shirt or the red one? I can't make up my mind.*

mind[2] /maɪnd/ *verb* (**minds, minding, minded**) **1** feel unhappy or angry about something ଆପତ୍ତି କରିବା, ରାଗିବା *'Do you mind if I leave now?' 'No, I don't mind.'* **2** be careful of somebody or something ସାବଧାନ ହେବା *Mind the step!* ○ *Mind! There's a dog on the road.* **3** take care of or watch something or somebody for a short while ଅଳ୍ପ ସମୟ ପାଇଁ କାହାରି ଯତ୍ନ ନେବା, ଦେଖାଶୁଣା କରିବା

never mind don't worry; there is no problem; it doesn't matter ବ୍ୟସ୍ତ ହୁଅନି *'I forgot your book.' 'Never mind, I don't need it today.'*

miner working in a coal **mine**

mine[1] /maɪn/ *noun* a very big hole below the ground where people work to dig out things like coal, gold or diamonds ଖଣି *a coal mine*

mine *verb* (**mines, mining, mined**) dig in the ground for things like coal or gold ଖଣି ଖୋଳି ଭୂଗର୍ଭରୁ କୋଇଲା, ସୁନା ଇତ୍ୟାଦି ବାହାର କରିବା

miner *noun* a person who works in a mine ଖଣିଶ୍ରମିକ *His father was a miner.*

mine[2] /maɪn/ *pronoun* something that belongs to me ମୋର *Those books are mine.*

mineral /ˈmɪnərəl/ *noun* minerals are things like coal, gold, salt or oil that are found in the ground and that people use ଅଜୈବ ଖଣିଜ ପଦାର୍ଥ (ଯଥା: କୋଇଲା, ସୁନା, ପଥର ଲୁଣ, ଭୂଗର୍ଭସ୍ଥ ତେଲ ଇତ୍ୟାଦି)

mingle /ˈmɪŋgl/ *verb* (**mingles, mingling, mingled**) mix with other things or people ମିଶିବା, ମିଶ୍ରିତ ହେବା

mini- *prefix*

କିଛି ବସ୍ତୁକୁ ଛୋଟ ଆକାର ବିଷୟରେ କହିବା ପାଇଁ ସେହି ବସ୍ତୁ ନାମ ଆରମ୍ଭରେ **mini-** ଯୋଡ଼ା ଯାଇପାରିବ —
The school has a minibus that can carry twelve people.

minimize /ˈmɪnɪmaɪz/ *verb* (**minimizes, minimizing, minimized**) reduce something in amount or value ସର୍ବନିମ୍ନ ସ୍ତର ବା ପରିମାଣ ପର୍ଯ୍ୟନ୍ତ ହ୍ରାସ କରିବା *minimize the expenditure* ✪ ବିପରୀତ **maximize**

minimum /ˈmɪnɪməm/ *noun* (*no plural*) the smallest size, amount or number that is possible ସର୍ବନିମ୍ନ ଆକାର, ପରିମାଣ ବା ସଂଖ୍ୟା *We need a minimum of six people to play this game.* ✪ ବିପରୀତ **maximum**

minimum *adjective* ସର୍ବନିମ୍ନ *What is the minimum age for joining the army in your country?* ✪ ବିପରୀତ **maximum**

minister /ˈmɪnɪstə(r)/ *noun* one of the most important people in a government ମନ୍ତ୍ରୀ *the Minister of Railways*

ministry /ˈmɪnɪstri/ *noun* (*plural* **ministries**) a government department ମନ୍ତ୍ରୀଙ୍କ ଅଧିନରେ ଥିବା ସରକାରୀ ବିଭାଗ *the Ministry of Defence*

minor /ˈmaɪnə(r)/ *adjective* not very big or important ଗୌଣ, ଅଳ୍ପ ଗୁରୁତ୍ୱଥିବା; ଛୋଟମୋଟ *Don't worry—it's only a minor problem.* ✪ ବିପରୀତ **major**[1]

minority /maɪˈnɒrəti/ *noun* (*no plural*) the smaller part of a group ସଂଖ୍ୟାଲଘୁ ଗୋଷ୍ଠୀ *Only a minority of the students speak English.* ➪ **majority** ଦେଖନ୍ତୁ।

mint /mɪnt/ *noun* (*no plural*) a small plant with a strong fresh smell and taste, that you put in food and drinks ପୋଦନା *mint chewing gum*

minus /ˈmaɪnəs/ *preposition* **1** less; when you take away ବିଯୁକ୍ତ *Six minus two is four* (6 – 2 = 4). ➪ **plus** ଦେଖନ୍ତୁ। **2** below zero ଶୂନ୍ୟଠାରୁ କମ୍ *The temperature falls to minus ten degrees at night.*

minute[1] /ˈmɪnɪt/ *noun* a measure of time. There are 60 **seconds** in a minute and 60 minutes in an **hour** ସମୟର ମାପ, ମିନିଟ୍ (୬୦ ସେକେଣ୍ଡରେ ଏକ ମିନିଟ୍, ୬୦ମିନିଟ୍‌ରେ ଏକ ଘଣ୍ଟା) *It's nine minutes past six.*

minute² /maɪˈnjuːt/ *adjective* very small ଅତି କ୍ଷୁଦ୍ର *I can't read his writing—it's minute.*

miracle /ˈmɪrəkl/ *noun* a wonderful and surprising thing that happens and that you cannot explain ଅଲୌକିକ ଘଟଣା, ଅଦ୍ଭୁତ କାଣ୍ଡ

mirror /ˈmɪrə(r)/ *noun* a piece of special glass where you can see yourself ଦର୍ପଣ, ଆଇନା, ଆରସି *Look in the mirror.*

mis- *prefix*
କିଛି ଶବ୍ଦ ପୂର୍ବରେ **mis-** ଲଗାଇଲେ ଭୁଲ୍ ବା ଖରାପ କାମ ବୁଝାଏ । ଯଥା — **misbehave** = ଦୁର୍ବ୍ୟବହାର କରିବା **misunderstand** = ଭୁଲ୍ ବୁଝାମଣା

misbehave /ˌmɪsbɪˈheɪv/ *verb* (**misbehaves, misbehaving, misbehaved**) when you misbehave, you do not behave well ଦୁର୍ବ୍ୟବହାର କରିବା, ଖରାପ ବ୍ୟବହାର କରିବା ✪ ବିପରୀତ **behave**

mischief /ˈmɪstʃɪf/ *noun* (*no plural*) bad behaviour of children which is not very serious and does not cause much damage ବିରକ୍ତିକର ଆଚରଣ (ବିଶେଷତଃ ପିଲାମାନଙ୍କର), ଚଗଲାମି *My brother's always getting into mischief.*

mischievous /ˈmɪstʃɪvəs/ *adjective* making trouble in a playful way ଚଗଲା *a mischievous child*

miserable /ˈmɪzrəbl/ *adjective* **1** very unhappy ଖୁବ୍ ଦୁଃଖିତ *What's wrong? You look miserable!* **2** very bad, unpleasant and uncomfortable ଖୁବ୍ ଖରାପ, ଅପ୍ରୀତିକର, ବାଜେ *What a miserable day!*

miserably *adverb* ଦୁଃଖିତ ଭାବରେ, ଦୁଃଖ କଷ୍ଟରେ

misery /ˈmɪzəri/ *noun* (*no plural*) great unhappiness ଅତ୍ୟଧିକ ଦୁଃଖ ବା ଅଶାନ୍ତି

misfortune /ˌmɪsˈfɔːtʃuːn/ *noun* something bad that happens; bad luck ଦୁର୍ଭାଗ୍ୟ, ମନ୍ଦଭାଗ୍ୟ

mishap /ˈmɪshæp/ *noun* a small accident ଦୁର୍ଭାଗ୍ୟପୂର୍ଣ୍ଣ ଘଟଣା, ଦୁର୍ଘଟଣା *Nobody was hurt in the mishap.*

Miss /mɪs/ *noun* a word that you use before the name of a girl or woman who is not married ବାଳିକା ବା ଅବିବାହିତା ନାରୀର ସମ୍ବୋଧନରେ ବ୍ୟବହୃତ ଉପାଧି *Dear Miss Gupta …* ➪ **Mrs** ଓ **Ms** ଦେଖନ୍ତୁ ।

miss /mɪs/ *verb* (**misses, missing, missed**) **1** not hit or not catch something ପ୍ରହାର କରିବା ବା ଧରିବାରେ ଅସଫଳ ହେବା *I tried to hit the ball but I missed.* **2** feel sad about somebody or something that has gone ମନେ ପକାଇ ଦୁଃଖ ଅନୁଭବ କରିବା, ଝୁରିବା *I'll miss you when you go to Canada.* **3** be too late for a train, bus, plane or boat ରେଳଗାଡ଼ି, ବସ୍, ଜାହାଜ ବା ଉଡ଼ାଜାହାଜ ଧରି ନପାରିବା *I just missed my bus.* ✪ ବିପରୀତ **catch 3** **4** not see, hear, etc. something ଦେଖିବା, ଶୁଣିବା ବା ବୁଝିବାରେ ବିଫଳ ହେବା *You missed a good programme on TV last night.*

missile /ˈmɪsaɪl/ *noun* a thing that you throw or send through the air to hurt somebody କ୍ଷେପଣାସ୍ତ୍ର; କାହାକୁ ଆଘାତ କରିବା ପାଇଁ ଫୋପଡ଼ା ଯାଉଥିବା ପଦାର୍ଥ *The boys were throwing stones, bottles and other missiles.* ○ *nuclear missiles* ➪ ଚିତ୍ର ପାଇଁ **ammunition** ଦେଖନ୍ତୁ।

missing /ˈmɪsɪŋ/ *adjective* lost; or not in the usual place ହଜିଯାଇଥିବା; ନିର୍ଦ୍ଦିଷ୍ଟ ସ୍ଥାନରେ ନଥିବା *My keys have gone missing.*

mission /ˈmɪʃn/ *noun* a journey to do a special job ବିଶେଷ କାମ ପାଇଁ କରୁଥିବା ଯାତ୍ରା *They were sent on a mission to the moon.*

mist /mɪst/ *noun* a thin cloud near the ground, that is difficult to see through କୁହୁଡ଼ି, କଇଁଝଟିକା *Early in the morning, the fields were covered in mist.*

misty *adjective* (**mistier, mistiest**) କୁହୁଡ଼ିଆ *a misty morning*

mistake[1] /mɪˈsteɪk/ *noun* something that you think or do that is wrong ଭୁଲ୍ *It was a mistake to go by bus the journey took two hours!*

by mistake when you did not plan to do it ଭୁଲରେ *I took your book by mistake—I thought it was mine.*

mistake[2] /mɪˈsteɪk/ *verb* (**mistakes, mistaking, mistook** /mɪˈstʊk/, **has mistaken** /mɪˈsteɪkən/) think that somebody or something is a different person or thing ଭୁଲ୍ ବୁଝିବା, ଭୁଲ୍ ଧାରଣା କରିବା

misunderstand /ˌmɪsʌndəˈstænd/ *verb* (**misunderstands, misunderstanding, misunderstood** /ˌmɪsʌndəˈstʊd/, **has misunderstood**) not understand something correctly ଭୁଲ୍ ବୁଝିବା, ଠିକ୍ ଭାବରେ ବୁଝି ନପାରିବା *I'm sorry. I misunderstood what you said.*

misunderstanding *noun* a situation of not understanding something correctly ଭୁଲ୍ ବୁଝାମଣା *I think there's been a misunderstanding—I ordered two tickets, not four.*

mitten /ˈmɪtn/ *noun* a thing that you wear to keep your hand warm. It has one part for your thumb and another part for your other fingers ହାତ ପିନ୍ଧା ମୋଜା

mix /mɪks/ *verb* (**mixes, mixing, mixed**) **1** put different things together to make something new ବିଭିନ୍ନ ଜିନିଷ ମିଶାଇ ନୂଆ ଜିନିଷ କରିବା *Mix yellow and blue paint together to make green.* **2** be with and talk to different people ଲୋକଙ୍କ ସହ ମିଳାମିଶା କରିବା *In my job, I have to mix with a lot of young people.*

mix up 1 think that one person or thing is a different person or thing ବିଭ୍ରାନ୍ତ ହେବା, ଗୋଟିଏ ବ୍ୟକ୍ତି ବା ପଦାର୍ଥକୁ ଅନ୍ୟ ବ୍ୟକ୍ତି ବା ପଦାର୍ଥ ବୋଲି ଭାବିବା *People often mix up Asha with her sister.* **2** make things untidy ଗୋଳିଆଘଣ୍ଟା କରିବା *Don't mix up my papers!*

mixed /mɪkst/ *adjective* made of different kinds of the same thing ମିଶାମିଶି, ମିଶ୍ରିତ, ବିଭିନ୍ନ ଜିନିଷ ମିଶା ଯାଇଥିବା *a mixed salad*

mixer /ˈmɪksə(r)/ *noun* a machine that mixes things ମିଶ୍ରଣ କରିବା (ବାଟିବା, ପିଠୋଉ କରିବା, ଗୋଲାଇବା) ପାଇଁ ଉପକରଣ *a food mixer*

mixture /ˈmɪkstʃə(r)/ *noun* something that you make by mixing different things together ମିଶ୍ରିତ ପଦାର୍ଥ ମିଶ୍ରଣ ଦ୍ୱାରା ପ୍ରସ୍ତୁତ ପଦାର୍ଥ *Air is a mixture of gases.* ○ *a cake mixture*

mm *abbreviation* ଶବ୍ଦ **millimetre** ର ସଂକ୍ଷିପ୍ତ ରୂପ

moan /məʊn/ *verb* (**moans, moaning, moaned**) **1** make a long sad sound when you are hurt or very unhappy ଅନୁଚ୍ଚ ବିଲମ୍ବିତ ବିଳାପ ବା ଆର୍ତ୍ତନାଦ କରିବା *He was moaning with pain.* **2** talk a lot about something that you do not like ଅସନ୍ତୋଷ ପ୍ରକାଶ କରି କହିବା *He's always moaning about the weather in winters.*

moan *noun* ଅନୁଚ୍ଚ ବିଲମ୍ବିତ ବିଳାପ ବା ଆର୍ତ୍ତନାଦ *I heard a loud moan.*

moat /məʊt/ *noun* a deep channel that was dug around a fort and filled with water to make it difficult for enemies to attack ଗଡ଼ଖାଇ, ପରିଖା

mob /mɒb/ *noun* a big noisy group of people who are shouting or fighting ବିଶୃଙ୍ଖଳ ଜନତା

mobile /ˈməʊbaɪl/ *adjective* able to move easily from place to place ଚଳନଶୀଳ *A mobile library visits the village every week.*

mobile phone *noun* (*plural* **mobile phones**) a phone that works by radio and that you can carry around ସାଙ୍ଗରେ ନେଇ ହେଉଥିବା ଛୋଟ ବେତାର ପରିଚାଳିତ ଟେଲିଫୋନ୍; ପକେଟ୍ ଫୋନ୍

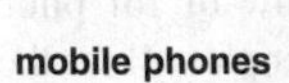

mobile phones

modal verb *noun* a verb, for example 'might', 'can' or 'must', that you use with another verb (ବ୍ୟାକରଣ) ଉକ୍ତି ବା ଆଦେଶ ପ୍ରକାଶକ କ୍ରିୟାପଦ; ଆସ୍ଥାବାଚକ କ୍ରିୟାପଦ

Modal verbs

Can, could, may, might, should, must, will, shall, would, used to ଓ **ought to** ହେଲେ modal verbs. Modal verbs ମାନଙ୍କର 'he/she' ପାଇଁ '**s**' ଲାଗେ ନାହିଁ —

She can drive. (*She cans drive.* ବ୍ୟବହାର କରାଯାଏ ନାହିଁ)

(**ought to** ବ୍ୟତିତ), **verb** ପରେ ଆପଣ **to** ନ ଲଗାଇ 'infinitive' (କର୍ତ୍ତା ନିରପେକ୍ଷ କ୍ରିୟା ବା ତୁମର୍ଥକ କ୍ରିୟା) ବ୍ୟବହାର କରିବେ —

I must go now. (*I must to go now.* ଠିକ୍ ନୁହେଁ) ଏଥିରେ ଆପଣ 'do' or 'did' ନ ଲଗାଇ ପ୍ରଶ୍ନବାକ୍ୟ ଓ ନାସ୍ତିବାଚକ ବାକ୍ୟ ଗଢ଼ି ପାରିବେ —

Will you come me? (*Do you will come with me?* ଠିକ୍ ନୁହେଁ)

They might not know. (*They don't might know.* ଠିକ୍ ନୁହେଁ)

model /ˈmɒdl/ *noun* **1** a small copy of something କୌଣସି ପଦାର୍ଥର ଏକ ଛୋଟ ଆକାରର ପ୍ରତିକୃତି *a model of the Taj Mahal* **2** one of the cars, machines, etc. that a certain company makes କୌଣସି କମ୍ପାନୀ ତିଆରି କରିଥିବା ଏକ ନିର୍ଦ୍ଦିଷ୍ଟ ପ୍ରକାର

ବା ଢ଼ଙ୍ଗର କାର୍, ଯନ୍ତ୍ର ଇତ୍ୟାଦି, ମଡେଲ୍ *Have you seen the latest model of that car?* **3** a person who wears clothes at a special show or for photographs, so that people will see them and buy them ଫଟୋ ଉଠାଇବା ପାଇଁ ବା ଲୋକମାନଙ୍କ ଆଗରେ ଦେଖାଇବା ପାଇଁ ନୂଆ ଧରଣର ବା ଷ୍ଟାଇଲ୍‌ର ଲୁଗାପଟା ପିନ୍ଧି ପ୍ରଦର୍ଶନ କରୁଥିବା ବ୍ୟକ୍ତି, ମଡେଲ୍

moderate /ˈmɒdərɪt/ *adjective* in the middle; not too much and not too little; not too big and not too small ମଧ୍ୟମ ଧରଣର; ବେଶୀ ନୁହଁ କି ଅଳ୍ପ ନୁହଁ; ବେଶୀ ବଡ଼ ନୁହଁ କି ବେଶୀ ଛୋଟ ନୁହଁ *Cook the vegetables over a moderate heat.*

modern /ˈmɒdn/ *adjective* of the present time; of the kind that is usual now ଆଧୁନିକ, ଅଧୁନାତନ, ସାଂପ୍ରତିକ *modern art* ○ *The airport is very modern.*

modest /ˈmɒdɪst/ *adjective* a person who is modest does not talk much about good things that they have done or about things that they can do well ବିନୀତ; ନିଜ ଗୁଣଗାନ କରୁନଥିବା *You didn't tell me you could sing so well—you're very modest!*

modestly *adverb* ବିନୀତ ଭାବରେ, ନମ୍ରଭାବରେ *He spoke quietly and modestly about his success.*

modesty *noun* (*no plural*) the quality of being modest ନିର୍ମଦ, ଶାଳୀନତା

moist /mɔɪst/ *adjective* a little wet ଓଦାଳିଆ, ଅଳ୍ପ ଆର୍ଦ୍ର *Keep the soil moist or the plant will die.*

moisture /ˈmɔɪstʃə(r)/ *noun* (*no plural*) very small drops of water on something or in the air ଆର୍ଦ୍ରତା

molar /ˈməʊlə(r)/ *noun* one of the large flat-topped teeth at the back of your mouth for grinding and crushing food କଳଦାନ୍ତ, ଚର୍ବଣଦାନ୍ତ ➪ **canine, incisor** ଓ **premolar** ଦେଖନ୍ତୁ। ➪ ଚିତ୍ର ପାଇଁ **tooth** ଦେଖନ୍ତୁ।

mole /məʊl/ *noun* a small dark spot on a person's skin ଜାଇ, କଳାଜାଇ, ନାଲିଜାଇ

molecule /ˈmɒlɪkju:l/ *noun* the smallest unit of a substance that has the same chemical properties of that substance ଅଣୁ, କୌଣସି ପଦାର୍ଥର କ୍ଷୁଦ୍ରତମ ଅଂଶ ଯାହା ନିଜ ଗୁଣ ରଖିଥାଏ

molten /ˈməʊltən/ *adjective* melted by heat (ତାପ ଦ୍ୱାର) ତରଳିବା *molten lava*

moment /ˈməʊmənt/ *noun* a very short time ମୁହୂର୍ତ୍ତ, ନିମିଷ, କ୍ଷଣ *He thought for a moment before he answered.*

at the moment now ଏହିକ୍ଷଣି, ବର୍ତ୍ତମାନ *She's on holiday at the moment, but she'll be back next week.*

monastery /ˈmɒnəstri/ *noun* (*plural* **monasteries**) a place where religious men, called **monks,** live, work and pray ସନ୍ୟାସୀ ବା ମଙ୍କମାନଙ୍କର ଆଶ୍ରମ ବା ମଠ ➪ **convent** ମଧ୍ୟ ଦେଖନ୍ତୁ।

Monday /ˈmʌndeɪ/ *noun* the first day of the week, next after Sunday ସୋମବାର।

money /ˈmʌni/ *noun* (*no plural*) small round metal things (called **coins**) and pieces of paper (called **notes**) that you use when you buy or sell something ଧାତୁମୁଦ୍ରା, କାଗଜମୁଦ୍ରା

ଇତ୍ୟାଦି ଟଙ୍କା ପଇସା *How much money did you spend?*

make money get or earn money ଅର୍ଥ ଅର୍ଜନ କରିବା

mongoose /ˈmɒŋguːs/ *noun* (*plural* **mongooses**) a small furry animal that lives in hot countries and kills snakes, rats, etc. ନେଉଳ

monitor /ˈmɒnɪtə(r)/ *noun* **1** a screen that shows information from a computer କମ୍ପ୍ୟୁଟର୍‌ର ତଥ୍ୟ ଦେଖାଇବାକୁ ପରଦା ଥିବା ଟି.ଭି. ପରି ଯନ୍ତ୍ର ⇨ ଚିତ୍ର ପାଇଁ **computer** ଦେଖନ୍ତୁ । **2** a student in school who helps in maintaining discipline in the class when the teacher is absent ସ୍କୁଲର ଶ୍ରେଣୀରେ ପିଲାଙ୍କୁ ନିୟନ୍ତ୍ରଣ କରୁଥିବା ଛାତ୍ର ବା ଛାତ୍ରୀ

monk /mʌŋk/ *noun* a member of a group of religious men who live in a **monastery** away from other people ସଂସ୍ଥାଗତ ଭାବେ ଦୀକ୍ଷା ନେଇଥିବା ଓ ମୋନାଷ୍ଟରୀରେ ରହୁଥିବା

monkey /ˈmʌŋki/ *noun* (*plural* **monkeys**) an animal with a long tail, that can climb trees ମାଙ୍କଡ଼, ମର୍କଟ ⇨ ଚିତ୍ର ପାଇଁ **mammal** ଦେଖନ୍ତୁ ।

monopolize /məˈnɒpəlaɪz/ *verb* (**monopolizes, monopolizing, monopolized**) have complete control over something so that no one else can use or share it ଏକାୟତ୍ତ କରିବା, ଏକାଧିକାଭୁକ୍ତ କରିବା, ଏକଚାଟିଆ, କାରବାର କରିବା *My brother monopolizes the television every evening.*

monopoly /məˈnɒpəli/ *noun* (*plural* **monopolies**) the complete control of something by only one person or group ଏକାଧିକାର, ଏକାଧିପତ୍ୟ, ଏକଚାଟିଆ କାରବାର *In the past, higher education was the monopoly of the rich.*

monsoon /ˌmɒnˈsuːn/ *noun* a season that brings a lot of rain to India and its neighbouring countries ଭାରତ ଓ ଦକ୍ଷିଣ ଏସିଆରେ ନିର୍ଦ୍ଦିଷ୍ଟ ଋତୁରେ ବହୁଥିବା ମୌସୁମୀ ବାୟୁ

monster /ˈmɒnstə(r)/ *noun* an animal in stories that is big, ugly and frightening କିଂବଦନ୍ତୀରେ ବର୍ଣ୍ଣିତ ଭୟଙ୍କର ଜୀବ; ଅସୁର, ଦାନବ *a prehistoric monster*

month /mʌnθ/ *noun* one of the twelve parts into which a year is divided ମାସ *December is the last month of the year.*

monthly /ˈmʌnθli/ *adjective*, *adverb* that happens or comes every month or once a month ମାସିକ *a monthly magazine*

monument /ˈmɒnjumənt/ *noun* a thing that is built to help people remember a person or something that happened ସ୍ମୃତିଚିହ୍ନ, ସ୍ମାରକ ସ୍ତମ୍ଭ, ସ୍ମାରକ ଗୃହ *This is a monument to war heroes.*

moo /muː/ *noun* the sound that a cow makes ଗାଈର ହମ୍ବା ବୋବାଳି

moo *verb* (**moos, mooing, mooed**) make a sound that a cow makes ଗାଈ ହମ୍ବା ବୋବାଳି କରିବା

mood /mu:d/ *noun* how you feel at a particular time ମନର ସାମୟିକ ଅବସ୍ଥା, ମିଜାଜ୍, ମନ *Our teacher is in a very good mood today.*

moon /mu:n/ *noun*

the moon (*no plural*) the big round thing that moves around the earth and shines in the sky at night ଚନ୍ଦ୍ର, ଚନ୍ଦ୍ରମା (ପୃଥିବୀର ପ୍ରାକୃତିକ ଉପଗ୍ରହ)

full moon *noun* the time when you can see all of the moon ପୂର୍ଣ୍ଣ ଚନ୍ଦ୍ର, ପୂର୍ଣ୍ଣିମାର ଚନ୍ଦ୍ର

new moon *noun* the time when you can see only the first thin part of the moon ଅମାବାସ୍ୟାର ଚନ୍ଦ୍ର

moonlight /ˈmu:nlaɪt/ *noun* (*no plural*) the light from the moon ଚନ୍ଦ୍ରାଲୋକ

moor /mɔ:(r)/ *verb* (**moors, mooring, moored**) tie a boat or ship to something so that it will stay in one place ନୌକା ବା ଜାହାଜକୁ ଦଉଡ଼ି ବା ଶିକୁଳି ଦ୍ୱାରା ବାନ୍ଧି ରଖିବା

mop /mɒp/ *noun* a thing with a long handle that you use for cleaning floors ଘର ଧୁଆ ପୋଛା କରିବା ପାଇଁ ବାଡ଼ି ଅଗରେ କନା, ଫିତା ଇତ୍ୟାଦିର ଗୋଛା ବନ୍ଧାହୋଇଥିବା ଉପକରଣ; ପୋଛା, ମପ୍

mop *verb* (**mops, mopping, mopped**) clean something with a cloth or mop ପୋଛା ବା ମପ୍ ଦ୍ୱାରା ସଫା କରିବା *I mopped the floor.*

moral[1] /ˈmɒrəl/ *adjective* about what you think is right or wrong ନୈତିକ *a moral problem*

moral[2] /ˈmɒrəl/ *noun* a lesson about what is right and wrong, that you can learn from a story or from something that happens ଗପ ଇତ୍ୟାଦିରେ ଥିବା ନୈତିକ ସିଦ୍ଧାନ୍ତ, ନୀତି ବାକ୍ୟ *The moral of the story is that we should be kind to animals.*

more[1] /mɔ:(r)/ *adjective, pronoun* a bigger amount or number of something ଅଧିକ *Can I have some more sugar in my tea?* ➪ **most**[1] ଦେଖନ୍ତୁ। ✪ ବିପରୀତ **less**[1]

more[2] /mɔ:(r)/ *adverb* a word that makes an adjective or adverb stronger ଅଧିକ, ବେଶୀ *Your book was more expensive than mine.* ➪ **most**[2] ଦେଖନ୍ତୁ। ✪ ବିପରୀତ **less**[2]

more or less almost, but not exactly ଊଣାଅଧିକ, ପ୍ରାୟ *We are more or less the same age.*

morning /ˈmɔ:nɪŋ/ *noun* the first part of the day, between the time when the sun comes up and midday ସକାଳ, ପ୍ରଭାତ, ପ୍ରାତଃକାଳ *I went swimming this morning.* ○ *The letter arrived on Tuesday morning.*

mosque /mɒsk/ *noun* a building where Muslims go to pray ମସଜିଦ୍

mosquito /məˈski:təʊ/ *noun* (*plural* **mosquitoes**) a small flying insect that bites people and animals and sucks their blood ମଶା ➪ ଚିତ୍ର ପାଇଁ **insects** ଦେଖନ୍ତୁ।

moss /mɒs/ *noun* a soft green plant that grows like a carpet on damp things like trees, walls and stones ଶିଉଳି, ଶୈବାଳ

most[1] /məʊst/ *adjective, pronoun* the biggest amount or number of something ସବୁଠାରୁ ବେଶୀ, ସର୍ବାଧିକ,

ଅଧିକାଂଶ *Medha did a lot of work, but I did the most.* ➪ **more¹** ଦେଖନ୍ତୁ।

at most, at the most not more than; but not more ଖୁବ୍ ବେଶୀ ହେଲେ *We can stay for two days at the most.*

most² /məʊst/ *adverb* more than all others ସବୁଠୁ ବେଶୀ, ସମସ୍ତଙ୍କଠାରୁ ବେଶୀ *Which part of your holiday did you most enjoy?* ➪ **more²** ଦେଖନ୍ତୁ। ✪ ବିପରୀତ **least²**

mostly /ˈməʊstli/ *adverb* almost all ପ୍ରାୟତଃ, ମୁଖ୍ୟତଃ *The students in my class are mostly older.*

moth /mɒθ/ *noun* an insect with big wings that flies at night ପ୍ରଜାପତି ପରି ଏକ ଛୋଟ ପୋକ ବା କୀଟ ଲୁଗାପଟା କର୍ତ୍ତନକାରୀ ପକ୍ଷଯୁକ୍ତ

mother /ˈmʌðə(r)/ *noun* a woman who has a child ମା, ବୋଉ *My mother is a doctor.* ➪ **mum** ଓ **mummy** ଦେଖନ୍ତୁ। ➪ ଚିତ୍ର ପାଇଁ **family** ଦେଖନ୍ତୁ।

mother-in-law *noun* (*plural* **mothers-in-law**) the mother of your husband or wife ଶାଶୁ ➪ ଚିତ୍ର ପାଇଁ **family** ଦେଖନ୍ତୁ।

motion /ˈməʊʃn/ *noun* (*no plural*)

in motion moving ଗତିଶୀଳ *Don't put your head out of the window while the train is in motion.*

motor /ˈməʊtə(r)/ *noun* the part inside a machine that makes it move or work ଯନ୍ତ୍ରରେ ଥିବା ଗତି ସଂଚାଳକ ଉପକରଣ, ମୋଟର *an electric motor*

motorbike /ˈməʊtəbaɪk/, **motorcycle** /ˈməʊtəsaɪkl/ *noun* a large bicycle with an engine ମଟର ସାଇକେଲ୍

motorcyclist /ˈməʊtəsaɪklɪst/ *noun* a person who rides a motorcycle ମଟର ସାଇକେଲ୍ ଚାଳକ

motorboat /ˈməʊtəbəʊt/ *noun* a small fast boat that has an engine ମୋଟର୍ ଇଞ୍ଜିନ୍ ଲଗା ଡଙ୍ଗା

motorist /ˈməʊtərɪst/ *noun* a person who drives a car ମଟରଗାଡ଼ି ଚାଳକ

motto /ˈmɒtəʊ/ *noun* (*plural* **mottoes** ବା **mottos**) a short sentence or phrase that tells what a person or an organization believes in ବ୍ୟକ୍ତି ବା ସଂସ୍ଥାର ଆଦର୍ଶବାକ୍ୟ ବା ସଂକ୍ଷିପ୍ତ ନୀତିବାକ୍ୟ *Live and let live—that is his motto of life.*

mould¹ /məʊld/ *noun* a soft green, grey or blue substance that is a type of **fungus**. It usually grows on old food ଫିମ୍ପି

mouldy *adjective* covered with mould ଫିମ୍ପି ଲାଗିଥିବା, ଫିମ୍ପି ମରା *mouldy cheese*

mould² /məʊld/ *verb* (**moulds, moulding, moulded**) make something soft into a certain shape ନରମ ପଦାର୍ଥକୁ ନିର୍ଦ୍ଦିଷ୍ଟ ଆକାରରେ ଗଢ଼ିବା *The children moulded animals out of clay.*

moult /məʊlt/ *verb* (**moults, moulting, moulted**) (of birds, insects and snakes) lose feathers, hair or a layer of skin before new ones grow (ପଶୁ, ପକ୍ଷୀ ବା କୀଟ) ପର, ଲୋମ, କାତି, ଚର୍ମ ଇତ୍ୟାଦି ତ୍ୟାଗ କରିବା

mound /maʊnd/ *noun* a large pile of something; a small hill ଗଦା, ସ୍ତୁପ; ସାନ ପାହାଡ଼, ମୁଣ୍ଡିଆ

Mount /maʊnt/ *noun* you use 'Mount' before the name of a mountain ('Mount' ପର୍ବତର ନାମ ପୂର୍ବରୁ ବ୍ୟବହୃତ) *Mount Everest* ✪ Mount ର ସଂକ୍ଷିପ୍ତ ରୂପ ହେଲା **mt** ।

mount /maʊnt/ *verb* (**mounts, mounting, mounted**) get onto a bicycle or a horse to ride it ସାଇକେଲ୍, ଘୋଡ଼ା ଇତ୍ୟାଦି ଚଢ଼ିବା

mountain /ˈmaʊntən/ *noun* a very high hill ପର୍ବତ, ଉଚ୍ଚପର୍ବତ *Mt Everest is the highest mountain in the world.*

mountaineer /ˌmaʊntəˈnɪə(r)/ *noun* a person who climbs mountains ପର୍ବତାରୋହୀ, ପାହାଡ଼ ଚଢୁଥିବା ବ୍ୟକ୍ତି

mountaineering *noun* (*no plural*) the sport of climbing mountains ପର୍ବତାରୋହଣ

mountainous /ˈmaʊntənəs/ *adjective* having many mountains ପର୍ବତମୟ, ପାର୍ବତୀୟ, ପାର୍ବତ୍ୟ *mountainous regions*

mourn /mɔːn/ *verb* (**mourns, mourning, mourned**) feel very sad, usually because somebody has died (କାହାରି ମୃତ୍ୟୁରେ ଶୋକ କରିବା) *She is still mourning for her son.*

mouse /maʊs/ *noun* (*plural* **mice** /maɪs/) **1** a small animal with a long tail ମୂଷା, ମୂଷିକ *Our cat caught a mouse.* **2** a thing that you move with your hand to tell a computer what to do କମ୍ପ୍ୟୁଟର୍, ସଂଚାଳନ ପାଇଁ ଥିବା ଏକ ହସ୍ତଚାଳିତ ଯନ୍ତ୍ର ➪ ଚିତ୍ର ପାଇଁ **computer** ଦେଖନ୍ତୁ ।

moustache /məˈstɑːʃ/ *noun* the hair between a man's nose and mouth ନିଶ, ମୁଛ

mouth /maʊθ/ *noun* (*plural* **mouths** /maʊðz/) **1** the part of your face below your nose that you use for eating and speaking ପାଟି, ତୁଣ୍ଡ, ମୁହଁ, ମୁଖଗୋହର *Open your mouth, please!* ➪ ଚିତ୍ର ପାଇଁ **face** ଦେଖନ୍ତୁ । **2** the place where a river goes into the sea ନଦୀର ମୁହାଁଣ

movable /ˈmuːvəbl/ *adjective* that which can be moved ଗୋଟିଏ ଜାଗାରୁ ଅନ୍ୟଜାଗାକୁ ନେଇ ହେଉଥିବା, ଅପସାରଣୀୟ

move[1] /muːv/ *verb* (**moves, moving, moved**) **1** go from one place to another; change the way you are standing or sitting ଘୁଞ୍ଚିବା, ସ୍ଥାନାନ୍ତରିତ ହେବା; ଘୁଞ୍ଚାଇବା *We moved to the front of the cinema.* **2** put something in another place or in another way (କୌଣସି ଜିନିଷ) ଘୁଞ୍ଚାଇ ଅନ୍ୟ ସ୍ଥାନରେ ରଖିବା *Can you move your car, please?* **3** go to live in another place ଅନ୍ୟ ସ୍ଥାନରେ ବସବାସ କରିବାକୁ ଯିବା, ବାସସ୍ଥାନ ପରିବର୍ତ୍ତନ କରିବା *They sold their house in Delhi and moved to Chennai.* ○ *We are moving house soon.*

move[2] /muːv/ *noun* the action of going from one place to another; the action of changing the way you are standing or sitting ସ୍ଥାନ ପରିବର୍ତ୍ତନ; ଘୁଞ୍ଚିବା *The police are watching every move she makes.*

movement /ˈmuːvmənt/ *noun* **1** the action of moving or being moved ଚଳନ, ସ୍ଥାନ ପରିବର୍ତ୍ତନ, ଚଲାବୁଲା *The old man's movements were slow and painful.* **2** a group of people who have the same ideas or beliefs ଆନ୍ଦୋଳନ *a political movement*

movie /ˈmu:vi/ *noun* **1** a film that you see at the cinema ଚଳଚ୍ଚିତ୍ର, ସିନେମା *Would you like to see a movie?* **2 the movies** (*plural*) films in general ଚଳଚ୍ଚିତ୍ର, ସିନେମା *We went to the movies last night.*

mow /məʊ/ *verb* (**mows, mowing, mowed, has mown** /məʊn/) cut grass ଘାସ କାଟିବା *Sanjana is mowing the grass.*

mower *noun* a machine that cuts grass; a lawnmower ଘାସ କାଟିବା ଯନ୍ତ୍ର

MP /ˌem ˈpi:/ *noun* **Member of Parliament** ର ସଂକ୍ଷିପ୍ତ ରୂପ

Mr /ˈmɪstə(r)/ *abbreviation* a word that you use before the name of a man ବ୍ୟକ୍ତିଙ୍କ ନାମ ପୂର୍ବରୁ ବ୍ୟବହୃତ ଶବ୍ଦ ବା ଉପାଧି *Mr Ajay Gupta* ○ *Mr Kumar*

Mrs /ˈmɪsɪz/ *abbreviation* a word that you use before the name of a woman who is married ବିବାହିତା ନାରୀଙ୍କ ନାମ ପୂର୍ବରୁ ବ୍ୟବହୃତ ଶବ୍ଦ ବା ଉପାଧି *Mrs Anita Rao* ○ *Mrs Kapoor* ➪ **Miss** ବା **Ms** ଦେଖନ୍ତୁ ।

Ms /mɪz/ *abbreviation* a word that you use before the name of any woman, instead of **Mrs** or **Miss** ଉଭୟ ବିବାହିତା ଓ ଅବିବାହିତା ନାରୀଙ୍କ ନାମ ପୂର୍ବରୁ ବ୍ୟବହୃତ ଉପାଧି *Ms Fatima Khan*

Mt *abbreviation* ଶବ୍ଦ **mount** ର ସଂକ୍ଷିପ୍ତ ରୂପ

much[1] /mʌtʃ/ *adjective* (**much, more, most**), *pronoun* a big amount of something; a lot of something ବହୁତ, ପ୍ରଚୁର *There was so much food that we couldn't eat it all.*

✪ କେବଳ ନାସ୍ତିବାଚକ ବାକ୍ୟରେ, ପ୍ରଶ୍ନବାକ୍ୟରେ ଏବଂ 'too', 'so', 'as' ଓ 'how' ପରେ 'much' ବ୍ୟବହୃତ ହୁଏ, ଅନ୍ୟାନ୍ୟ ବାକ୍ୟରେ **a lot (of)** ବ୍ୟବହାର କରାଯାଏ *She's got a lot of money.* ➪ **many** ଦେଖନ୍ତୁ ।

as much as the same amount that ଯେତେ ପାରିବ *Eat as much as you can.*

how much ... ? 1 what amount? କେତେ.. ? *How much paper do you want?* **2** what price? କେତେ ଦାମ୍ ? *How much is this shirt?*

much[2] /mʌtʃ/ *adverb* a lot ବହୁତ, ପ୍ରଚୁର *I like him very much.*

mud /mʌd/ *noun* (*no plural*) soft wet earth କାଦୁଅ *Akhil came home from the football match covered in mud.*

muddle /ˈmʌdl/ *noun*

in a muddle untidy; not able to think clearly ଅପରିଷ୍କାର ଅବସ୍ଥାରେ; ବିଶୃଙ୍ଖଳ ଅବସ୍ଥାରେ *Your room is in a terrible muddle.*

muddy /mʌdi/ *adjective* (**muddier, muddiest**) covered with mud କାଦୁଆ, ପଙ୍କିଳ *When it rains, the roads get very muddy.*

muffler /ˈmʌflə(r)/ *noun* a thick piece of material worn around the neck for warmth (ଉଷ୍ମତା ପାଇଁ) ଗଳାର ଆବରଣ, ମଫଲର୍ ➪ **scarf** ମଧ୍ୟ ଦେଖନ୍ତୁ ।

mug /mʌg/ *noun* a big cup with straight sides and a handle ବେଣ୍ଟଥିବା ବଡ଼ କପ୍ ବା ପାନୀୟ ପାତ୍ର, ମଗ୍ *a mug of tea*

mule /mju:l/ *noun* an animal whose parents were a horse and a donkey. Mules are used for carrying loads ଖଚର; ଘୋଡ଼ା ଓ ଗଧର ସଂଯୋଗରୁ ଜାତ ପଶୁ

multimedia /ˌmʌltiˈmiːdiə/ *adjective* using words, pictures and sound ଶବ୍ଦ, ଚିତ୍ର ଓ ଧ୍ୱନି ବ୍ୟବହାର କରୁଥିବା *multimedia games*

multiple¹ /ˈmʌltɪpl/ *adjective* involving many things or people ବହୁ, ବହୁବିଧ *multiple injuries*

multiple² /ˈmʌltɪpl/ *noun* a number that contains a smaller number an exact number of times ଗୁଣିତକ *10, 15, 20, 25, etc. are multiples of 5.*

multiplication /ˌmʌltɪplɪˈkeɪʃn/ *noun* (*no plural*) the process of multiplying a number ଗୁଣନ

multiply /ˈmʌltɪplaɪ/ *verb* (**multiplies, multiplying, multiplied, has multiplied**) make a number bigger by a certain number of times ଗୁଣନ କରିବା *Two multiplied by three is six* (2×3 = 6). ○ *Multiply 3 and 7 together.*

multi-purpose *adjective* that can be used for different purposes ବହୁ କାମ କରି ପାରୁଥିବା *The food processor is a multi-purpose machine.*

multi-storeyed *adjective* with many floors ବହୁ ମହଲା ଥିବା, ବହୁତଳ *a multi-storeyed building*

mum /mʌm/ *noun* mother ମାଁ, ବୋଉ *This is my mum.*

mumble /ˈmʌmbl/ *verb* (**mumbles, mumbling, mumbled**) speak quietly in a way that is not clear and people cannot hear you well ଅସ୍ପଷ୍ଟ ଭାବରେ ଅନ୍ୟକୁ ନଶୁଭିଲା ପରି କହିବା *She mumbled something about a party, but I couldn't hear what she said.*

mummy /ˈmʌmi/ *noun* (*plural* **mummies**) a word for 'mother' that children use ପିଲାମାନଙ୍କର ମାଁ'କୁ ଡାକିବା ଶବ୍ଦ, ମାଁ, ମମି

munch /mʌntʃ/ *verb* (**munches, munching, munched**) bite and eat something noisily ସଶବ୍ଦେ ଚୋବାଇବା *He munched on a bar of chocolate.*

municipal /mjuːˈnɪsɪpl/ *adjective* related to a town, city or district that has its own local government ସହରର ମ୍ୟୁନିସିପାଲିଟି ବା ପୌରସଂସ୍ଥା ସମ୍ବନ୍ଧୀୟ *municipal workers*

murder /ˈmɜːdə(r)/ *verb* (**murders, murdering, murdered**) kill somebody ନରହତ୍ୟା କରିବା

murder *noun* the act of killing somebody ନରହତ୍ୟା

murmur /ˈmɜːmə(r)/ *verb* (**murmurs, murmuring, murmured**) speak in a low quiet voice or make a low sound that is not very clear ଗୁଣୁଗୁଣୁ ହୋଇ କହିବା, ମର୍ମର ଶବ୍ଦ କରିବା, ଗୁଞ୍ଜନ କରିବା

murmur *noun* ଗୁଣୁଗୁଣୁ ଶବ୍ଦ ମର୍ମର, ଗୁଞ୍ଜନ *I heard a murmur of voices from the next room.*

muscle /ˈmʌsl/ *noun* one of the parts inside your body that becomes tight or loose to help you move ମାଂସପେଶୀ, ପେଶୀ, ମସ୍ଲ୍

muscular /ˈmʌskjələ(r)/ *adjective* **1** of or about muscles ପେଶୀ ସମ୍ବନ୍ଧୀୟ, ପେଶୀର *muscular tissue* **2** having strong muscles ସୁ ବିକଶିତ ପେଶୀଥିବା *a muscular body*

museum /mjuˈziːəm/ *noun* a building where people can look at old or interesting things ପୁରାତନ ପଦାର୍ଥର ସଂଗ୍ରାହଳୟ, ଯାଦୁଘର, ମ୍ୟୁଜିଅମ୍ *Have you ever been to the National Museum?*

mushroom /ˈmʌʃruːm/ *noun* a **fungus** with a flat top and no leaves. Some mushrooms can be eaten ଛତୁ (କିଛି ଛତୁ ଖାଇବା ଯୋଗ୍ୟ)

music /ˈmjuːzɪk/ *noun* (*no plural*) the sounds that you make by singing, or by playing instruments ସଙ୍ଗୀତ *What sort of music do you like?*

musical /ˈmjuːzɪkl/ *adjective* **1** of music ସମ୍ବନ୍ଧୀୟ *musical instruments* **2** good at making music ସଙ୍ଗୀତରେ ଦକ୍ଷ *She's a very musical child—she plays the piano and the violin.*

musician /mjuˈzɪʃn/ *noun* a person who writes music or plays a musical instrument ସଙ୍ଗୀତଜ୍ଞ, ସଙ୍ଗୀତ ବିଶାରଦ

Muslim /ˈmʊzlɪm/ *noun* a person who follows the religion of **Islam** ମୁସଲ୍‌ମାନ୍ ବ୍ୟକ୍ତି

Muslim *adjective* ମୁସଲ୍‌ମାନ୍ ଧର୍ମର, ଇସ୍‌ଲାମୀୟ *the Muslim way of life*

must /mʌst/ *modal verb* **1** a word that you use to tell somebody what to do or what is necessary ଆବଶ୍ୟକତା ବା ବାଧ୍ୟତା ସୂଚକ କ୍ରିୟା *You must look before you cross the road.*

> ✪ କୌଣସି ବ୍ୟକ୍ତିଙ୍କୁ କିଛି କରିବା ପାଇଁ ମନା କରିବା ହେତୁ **must not** ର ପ୍ରୟୋଗ କରଯାଏ । **must not** ର ସଂକ୍ଷିପ୍ତ ରୂପ **mustn't** ଅଟେ —
>
> *You mustn't be late.*
>
> ଯଦି ଆପଣ କହିବାକୁ ଚାହୁଁଛନ୍ତି ଯେ ଏକ ବ୍ୟକ୍ତି କୌଣସି କାର୍ଯ୍ୟ କରିବାକୁ ଚାହୁଁଛି ତା'ହେଲେ କରିପାରନ୍ତି ମାତ୍ର ସେହି କାମ କରିବାର କୌଣସି ଜରୁରୀ ଆବଶ୍ୟକତା ନାହିଁ, ସେଭଳି କ୍ଷେତ୍ରରେ ଆପଣ **don't have to** ବ୍ୟବହାର କରି ପାରିବେ ।
>
> *You don't have to do your home work today.*

2 a word that shows that you are sure something is true କୌଣସି ବିଷୟରେ ନିଶ୍ଚୟ ସୂଚାଉଥିବା ଶବ୍ଦ; ନିଶ୍ଚୟ *You must be tired after your long journey.* ⇨ **modal verb** ପାଇଁ ଟିପ୍ପଣୀ ଦେଖନ୍ତୁ ।

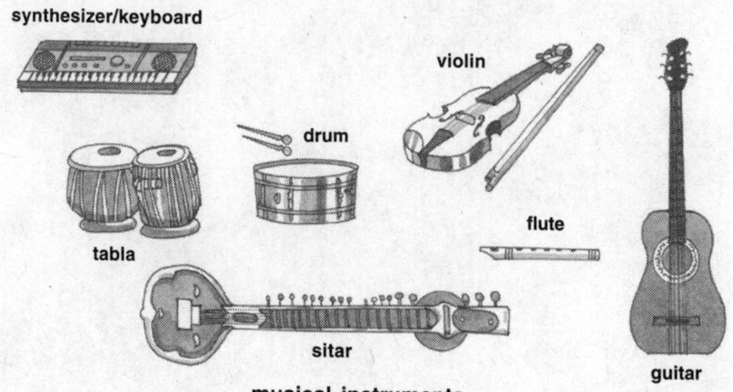

musical instruments

mustard /ˈmʌstəd/ *noun* (*no plural*) a plant with black or brown seeds. The seeds are used as a spice or ground to get a thick yellow sauce with a strong taste ସୋରିଷ ଗଛ, ସୋରିଷ

mustn't = **must not**

mutiny /ˈmju:təni/ *noun* (*plural* **mutinies**) an act of a group of people, especially soldiers, who refuse to obey the orders of their leader ବିଦ୍ରୋହ (ବିଶେଷତଃ ସୈନ୍ୟମାନଙ୍କର ସେନାପତିଙ୍କ ବିରୋଧରେ ବିଦ୍ରୋହ) *the Sepoy Mutiny of 1857*

my /maɪ/ *adjective* of me ମୋ, ମୋର *Where is my watch?*

myself /maɪˈself/ *pronoun* (*plural* **ourselves**) **1** a word that shows the same person as the one who is speaking ମୁଁ, ମୁଁ ନିଜେ, ନିଜକୁ *I bought myself a new shirt.* **2** a word that makes 'I' stronger 'ମୁଁ' ଶବ୍ଦକୁ ବିଶେଷତ୍ୱ ଦେଉଥିବା ଶବ୍ଦ, ମୁଁ ନିଜେ *'Did you buy this cake?' 'No, I made it myself.'*

by myself 1 alone; without other people ଏକା, ଏକାକୀ *I live by myself.* **2** without help ମୁଁ ଏକାକୀ *I made dinner by myself.*

mysterious /mɪˈstɪəriəs/ *adjective* something that is mysterious is strange and you do not understand it or know why it happens ରହସ୍ୟପୂର୍ଣ୍ଣ, ଅଦ୍ଭୁତ *The house is empty but some people say they have seen mysterious lights there in the night.*

mysteriously *adverb* ରହସ୍ୟମୟ ଭାବରେ, ଅଦ୍ଭୁତ ଭାବରେ *The plane disappeared mysteriously.*

mystery /ˈmɪstri/ *noun* (*plural* **mysteries**) something strange that you cannot understand or explain ରହସ୍ୟ, ବୁଝି ହେଉନଥିବା ବିଷୟ ବା ଘଟଣା

myth /mɪθ/ *noun* **1** a very old story କିଂବଦନ୍ତୀ, ପୌରାଣିକ ଗପ **2** a story or belief that is not true କାଳ୍ପନିକ ଗପ; ଭୁଲ ଧାରଣା

mythology /mɪˈθɒlədʒi/ *noun* (*plural* **mythologies**) very old stories and the beliefs and values expressed in them ପୁରୁଣା କଥା, କିମ୍ବଦନ୍ତୀ *Greek mythology*

N n

nail /neɪl/ *noun* **1** the hard part at the end of a finger or toe ନଖ *fingernails* ○ *toenails* ➪ ଚିତ୍ର ପାଇଁ **finger** ଦେଖନ୍ତୁ । **2** a small thin piece of metal with one sharp end which you hit into wood (with a **hammer**) to fix things together ଧାତୁ ନିର୍ମିତ କଣ୍ଟା; କଣ୍ଟା, ନଖ

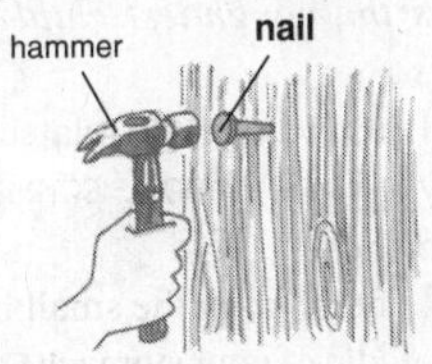

naked /ˈneɪkɪd/ *adjective* if someone is naked, they are not wearing any clothes ଲଙ୍ଗଳା, ନଗ୍ନ, ଉଲଗ୍ନ

name[1] /neɪm/ *noun* a word or words that you use to call a person, place, animal or thing ନାମ, ନାଁ *What's your name?* ○ *Do you know the name of this flower?*

call somebody names say bad or unkind words about somebody ଗାଳିଦେବା, ଅସଭ୍ୟ ସଂବୋଧନ କରିବା

> ✪ ତମର **first name** ହେଲା ତମର ପ୍ରଦତ୍ତ ନାମ ଯାହା ନାମକରଣ ଦିନ ଦିଆଯାଏ । ତମର **surname** ହେଲା ତମର କୁଳ ନାମ । ତମର **nickname** ହେଲା ତମର ଡାକନାମ ।

name[2] /neɪm/ *verb* (**names, naming, named**) **1** give a name to somebody or something ନାମ ଦେବା *They named their baby Shivani.* **2** know and say the name of somebody or something ନାମ ଡାକିବା, ନାମ କହିବା *The principal could name every one of his 600 pupils.* ○ *Name two countries that export oil.*

nap /næp/ *noun* a short sleep that you have during the day ଦିନ ବେଳର ଅଳ୍ପ କାଳର ନିଦ *I had a nap after lunch.*

napkin /ˈnæpkɪn/ *noun* a piece of cloth or paper that you use when you are eating, to clean your mouth and hands and to keep your clothes clean ଖାଇଲା ବେଳେ ପୋଷାକକୁ ରକ୍ଷା କରିବା ପାଇଁ ଓ ଆଙ୍ଗୁଠି, ଓଠ ଇତ୍ୟାଦି ପୋଛିବା ପାଇଁ ବ୍ୟବହୃତ ଏକ ପ୍ରକାର ରୁମାଲ୍; ଗାମୁଛା

nappy /ˈnæpi/ *noun* (*plural* **nappies**) a piece of cloth or strong paper that a baby wears around its bottom and between its legs ଶିଶୁର ଗୁହ ମୁତ ଧରି ରଖିବା ପାଇଁ ପିନ୍ଧା ଯାଉଥିବା କଟିବସ୍ତ୍ର; କଟିବସ୍ତ୍ର

narrow /ˈnærəʊ/ *adjective* (**narrower, narrowest**) not far from one side to the other ସଂକୀର୍ଣ୍ଣ, କମ୍ ଓସାରିଆ, ଅପ୍ରଶସ୍ତ *The road was too narrow for two cars to pass.* ✪ ବିପରୀତ **wide 1** ବା **broad 1**

have a narrow escape if you have a narrow escape, you have just got away from something bad almost happening to you ଅଳ୍ପକେ ବଞ୍ଚିଯିବା

narrowly *adverb* only just ଅଳ୍ପକେ *The car narrowly missed hitting a tree.*

nasty /ˈnɑːsti/ *adjective* (**nastier, nastiest**) bad; not nice ଅତ୍ୟନ୍ତ ଅପ୍ରୀତିକର *There's a nasty smell in this room.* ○ *Don't be so nasty!*

nation /ˈneɪʃn/ *noun* a country and all the people who live in it ରାଷ୍ଟ୍ର, ଦେଶ, ଜାତି

national /ˈnæʃnəl/ *adjective* of or for all of a country ଜାତୀୟ, ରାଷ୍ଟ୍ରୀୟ *She carried the national flag of Greece.*

national anthem *noun* the official song of a country that is sung on special days ଜାତୀୟ ସଂଗୀତ

nationality /ˌnæʃəˈnæləti/ *noun* (*plural* **nationalities**) belonging to a certain country ଜାତୀୟତା, ଜାତି *'What nationality are you?' 'I'm Indian.'*

nationwide /ˌneɪʃnˈwaɪd/ *adjective, adverb* happening all over a country ଦେଶବ୍ୟାପୀ, ରାଷ୍ଟ୍ରବ୍ୟାପୀ *a nationwide campaign against polio*

native /ˈneɪtɪv/ *adjective* of the place where you were born ଦେଶୀୟ, ସ୍ଥାନୀୟ, ଜନ୍ମସ୍ଥାନର *I returned to my native country.*

natural /ˈnætʃrəl/ *adjective* **1** made or caused by nature, not by people ପ୍ରାକୃତିକ *Earthquakes and floods are natural disasters.* **2** normal or usual ସାଧାରଣ, ସ୍ୱାଭାବିକ *It's natural for parents to feel sad when their children leave home.* ✪ ବିପରୀତ **unnatural**

naturally /ˈnætʃrəli/ *adverb* in a way that is not made or caused by people ପ୍ରାକୃତିକ ଭାବରେ, ପ୍ରାକୃତିକ ପ୍ରକ୍ରିୟାରେ, ସ୍ୱାଭାବିକ ଭାବେ *Is your hair naturally curly?*

nature /ˈneɪtʃə(r)/ *noun* **1** (*no plural*) everything in the world that has not been made by people ପ୍ରକୃତି, ପ୍ରାକୃତିକ ଜଗତ *the beauty of nature* **2** (*plural* **natures**) the way a person or thing is ଗୁଣ, ବୈଶିଷ୍ଟ୍ୟ, ପ୍ରକୃତି *Our cat has a very friendly nature.*

naughty /ˈnɔːti/ *adjective* (**naughtier, naughtiest**) you say that a child is naughty when he/she does bad things or does not do what you ask him/her to do ଦୁଷ୍ଟ, ମନ୍ଦ ଆଚରଣ କରୁଥିବା *She's the naughtiest child in the class.*

naval /ˈneɪvl/ *adjective* related to the navy ନୌବାହିନୀ ବିଷୟକ, ନୌବାହିନୀର *a naval base*

navel /ˈneɪvl/ *noun* the small hole in the middle of your stomach ନାଭି, ନାହି, ଲାହି

navigate /ˈnævɪgeɪt/ *verb* (**navigates, navigating, navigated**) use a map, etc. to find which way a ship, an aeroplane or a car should go ମାନଚିତ୍ର ଇତ୍ୟାଦି ସାହାଯ୍ୟରେ ଜାହାଜ, ବିମାନ ଇତ୍ୟାଦି ଠିକ୍ ଦିଗରେ ଚଳାଇବା *Long ago, explorers used to navigate by the stars.*

navy /ˈneɪvi/ *noun* (*plural* **navies**) the ships that a country uses when there is a war, and the people who work on them ନୌସେନା

near /nɪə(r)/ *adjective, adverb* (**nearer, nearest**) not far; close ପାଖରେ ଥିବା; ପାଖରେ; ନିକଟରେ; ପାଖକୁ, ନିକଟକୁ *My parents live quite near.*

near *preposition* close to somebody or something ପାଖରେ *I don't need a car because I live near the town centre.*

nearby /ˌnɪəˈbaɪ/ *adjective* not far away; close ପାଖ, ପାଖରେ ଥିବା *He goes to a nearby school.*

nearby *adverb* ପାଖରେ, ନିକଟରେ; ପାଖକୁ, ନିକଟକୁ *Let's go and see Aziz—he lives nearby.*

nearly /ˈnɪəli/ *adverb* almost; not quite ପ୍ରାୟ *I'm nearly sixteen—it's my birthday next week.*

neat /niːt/ *adjective* (**neater, neatest**) with everything in the right place; tidy ପରିଚ୍ଛନ୍ନ, ସୁସଜ୍ଜିତ *Keep your room neat and tidy.*

neatly *adverb* ପରିଷ୍କାର ଭାବରେ *Write your name neatly.*

necessarily /ˈnesəsərəli/ *adverb*

not necessarily not always ସବୁବେଳେ ନୁହଁ *Big men aren't necessarily strong.*

necessary /ˈnesəsəri/ *adjective* if something is necessary, you must have or do it ଦରକାରୀ *Warm clothes are necessary in winter.* ✪ ବିପରୀତ **unnecessary**

necessity /nəˈsesəti/ *noun* (*plural* **necessities**) something that you must have ଦରକାରୀ ପଦାର୍ଥ *Food and clothes are necessities of life.*

neck /nek/ *noun* **1** the part of your body between your shoulders and your head ବେକ *Sheela wore a thick scarf round her neck.* ➪ ଚିତ୍ର ପାଇଁ **body** ଦେଖନ୍ତୁ। **2** the thin part at the top of a bottle ବୋତଲର ସରୁ ଉପରଭାଗ ବା ବେକ

necklace /ˈnekləs/ *noun* a piece of jewellery that is worn round the neck ହାର *a diamond necklace*

need¹ /niːd/ *verb* (**needs, needing, needed**) have to do something; want something important and necessary that is not there ଦରକାର ହେବା, ଦରକାର କରିବା *You need to fill in this form to apply for a telephone connection.* ○ *Does she need help?*

need² /niːd/ *noun*

be in need of something want something important and necessary that is not there ଦରକାର କରିବା *She's in need of rest.*

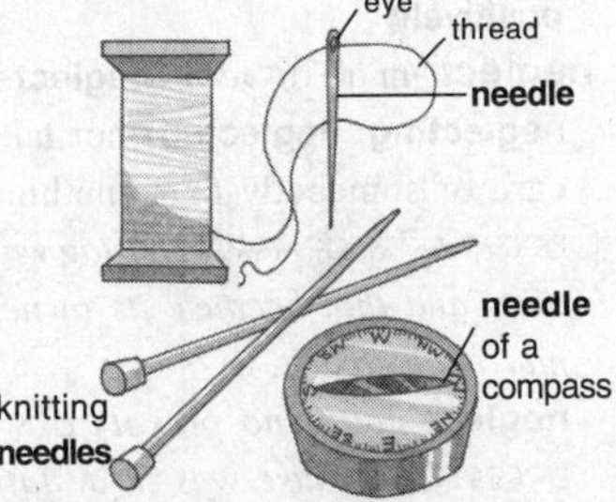

needle /ˈniːdl/ *noun* **1** a small thin piece of metal with a hole (called **eye**) for thread at one end and a sharp point at the other. You use a needle for sewing ଛୁଞ୍ଚ, ସୂଚି ➪ **knitting needle** ମଧ୍ୟ ଦେଖନ୍ତୁ। **2** something that is like a needle ଛୁଞ୍ଚପରି ପଦାର୍ଥ *the needle of a compass* **3** the long, thin leaf of a **conifer** tree ଦେବଦାରୁ ଗଛର ସରୁ ପତ୍ର *pine needles* ➪ ଚିତ୍ର ପାଇଁ **pine** ଦେଖନ୍ତୁ।

needn't = **need not**

negative /ˈnegətɪv/ *adjective* **1** bad or harmful ଖରାପ, ଅନିଷ୍ଟକାରୀ *the nega-*

tive effects of watching television **2** that which does not give any hope ନିରାଶ କରୁଥିବା, ନାସ୍ତିସୂଚକ *a negative attitude* **3** used for saying 'no' ନାସ୍ତିସୂଚକ *He gave a negative reply.* ✪ ବିପରୀତ **positive 4** using words like 'no', 'not' and 'never' 'ନାଁ', 'ନାହିଁ', 'ନୁହେଁ', 'କେବେ ନୁହେଁ', ଅର୍ଥ ସୂଚାଉଥିବା *'I don't like going out in the afternoon' is a negative sentence.*

negatively *adverb* in a bad way ନାସ୍ତିସୂଚକ ଭାବରେ *He reacted negatively to my question.* ✪ ବିପରୀତ **positively**

neglect /nɪˈglekt/ *verb* (**neglects, neglecting, neglected**) not take care of somebody or something ଅବହେଳା କରିବା, ଯତ୍ନ ନନେବା *The dog was dirty and thin because its owner had neglected it.*

neglect *noun* (*no plural*) ଅଯତ୍ନ, ଅବହେଳା *The house was in a state of neglect.*

negligence /ˈneglɪdʒəns/ *noun* (*no plural*) the act of being careless and not paying enough attention ଅବହେଳା, ଅସାବଧାନତା, ଅମନୋଯୋଗ *The accident occurred because of the driver's negligence.*

negligent /ˈneglɪdʒənt/ *adjective* not taking enough care of somebody or something ଅବହେଳା କରୁଥିବା, ଯତ୍ନ ନେଉ ନଥିବା, ଅଯତ୍ନଶୀଳ *negligent parents/students*

negotiate /nɪˈgəʊʃieɪt/ *verb* (**negotiates, negotiating, negotiated**) talk with someone and try to come to an agreement about something ବୁଝାମଣା ପାଇଁ ଆଲୋଚନା କରିବା *The leaders of the two countries have been negotiating to reach a settlement on the border dispute.*

negotiation /nɪˌgəʊʃiˈeɪʃn/ *noun* ସମାଧାନମୂଳକ ଆଲୋଚନା *Trade negotiations between the two countries are continuing.*

neigh /neɪ/ *noun* the sound that a horse makes ଅଶ୍ୱରଡ଼ି, ହ୍ରେଷାରବ

neigh *verb* (**neighs, neighing, neighed**) make the sound that a horse makes ହ୍ରେଷାରବ କରିବା, ଅଶ୍ୱରଡ଼ି ଛାଡ଼ିବା

neighbour /ˈneɪbə(r)/ *noun* a person who lives near you ପଡ଼ିଶା, ପଡ଼ୋଶୀ, ପ୍ରତିବେଶୀ *Don't make so much noise or you'll wake the neighbours up.*

neighbouring *adjective* that is near ନିକଟବର୍ତ୍ତୀ, ପାଖରେ ଥିବା *We played football against a team from a neighbouring town.*

neighbourhood /ˈneɪbəhʊd/ *noun* a part of a town ସହରର ଏକ ଅଞ୍ଚଳ *They live in a friendly neighbourhood.*

neither[1] /ˈnaɪðə(r); ˈni:ðə(r)/ *adjective, pronoun* not one and not the other of two things or people ଏହା ନୁହେଁ କି ତାହା ନୁହେଁ; ଯେ ନୁହେଁ କି ସେ ନୁହେଁ *Neither book was very interesting.*

neither[2] /ˈnaɪðə(r); ˈni:ðə(r)/ *adverb* (used in sentences with 'not') also not ଦୁଇଟି ମଧ୍ୟରୁ କେଉଁଟି ବି ନୁହେଁ *Lydia can't swim and neither can I*

neither ... nor ... not ... and not... ଯେ ନୁହେଁ କି ସେ ନୁହେଁ *Neither Rajeev nor I went to the party.*

nephew /ˈnefjuː/ *noun* the son of your brother or sister ପୁତୁରା; ଭଣଜା ➪ ଚିତ୍ର ପାଇଁ **family** ଦେଖନ୍ତୁ।

Neptune /ˈneptjuːn/ *noun* (*no plural*) the eighth planet from the sun ସୌର ମଣ୍ଡଳର ଅଷ୍ଟମଗ୍ରହ ➪ ଚିତ୍ର ପାଇଁ **solar system** ଦେଖନ୍ତୁ।

nerve /nɜːv/ *noun* **1** (*plural* **nerves**) one of the long thin things inside your body that carry messages to and from your brain, so that you can feel and move ସ୍ନାୟୁ; ସୂକ୍ଷ୍ମ ଶିରା ବା ତନ୍ତୁ ଯାହା ଦ୍ୱାରା ମସ୍ତିଷ୍କ, ମେରୁଦଣ୍ଡ ଓ ଶରୀରର ବିଭିନ୍ନ ଅଙ୍ଗ ମଧ୍ୟରେ ସ୍ନାୟବିକ ବାର୍ତ୍ତାପ୍ରବାହ ହୁଏ **2** (*no plural*) being brave or calm when there is danger ସାହସ *You need a lot of nerve to be a racing driver.*

get on somebody's nerves annoy somebody କାହାରିକୁ ବିରକ୍ତ ବା ବିବ୍ରତ କରିବା *Stop making that noise—you're getting on my nerves!*

nervous /ˈnɜːvəs/ *adjective* **1** worried or afraid ଉଦ୍‌ବିଗ୍ନ ବା ଭୟଭୀତ *I'm quite nervous about starting my new job.* **2** of the nerves in your body ଶରୀରର ସ୍ନାୟୁ ସମ୍ବନ୍ଧୀୟ, ସ୍ନାୟୁବିକ *the nervous system*

nervously *adverb* ଉଦ୍‌ବିଗ୍ନ ଭାବରେ *He laughed nervously because he didn't know what to say.*

nervousness *noun* (*no plural*) being nervous ଉଦ୍‌ବିଗ୍ନତା, ଶଙ୍କା

nervous system *noun* the network of nerves that connects your body with your brain ମସ୍ତିଷ୍କକୁ ଶରୀର ସହ ସଂଯୁକ୍ତ କରୁଥିବା ସ୍ନାୟୁବିକ ବ୍ୟବସ୍ଥା

nest /nest/ *noun* a home which a bird makes or finds, where it lays its eggs and where its babies grow up. Some insects and reptiles also build nests ପକ୍ଷୀର ବସା, ନୀଡ଼ (କିଛି ପୋକ ଓ ସରୀସୃପ ଜାତୀୟ ପ୍ରାଣୀ ମଧ୍ୟ ବସା କରନ୍ତି)।

net /net/ *noun* material that is made of long pieces of string, etc. with small spaces between them ଜାଲ, ଫାଶ *a fishing net*

network /ˈnetwɜːk/ *noun* a system of things like roads, lines, computers, etc. that are connected to one another ଜାଲ ପରି ପରସ୍ପର ସହ ସଂଯୁକ୍ତ ଗଠନ ବା ବ୍ୟବସ୍ଥା *the railway network*

never /ˈnevə(r)/ *adverb* not at any time; not ever କେବେ ନୁହେଁ *She never works on Saturdays.* ○ *I will never forget you.*

nevertheless /ˌnevəðəˈles/ *adverb* but; however; although that is true ତଥାପି, ଏହା ସତ୍ତ୍ୱେ *They played very well. Nevertheless, they didn't win.*

new /njuː/ *adjective* (**newer**, **newest**) **1** something that is new has just been made or bought ନୂଆ, ନୂତନ *I bought a new pair of shoes yesterday.* ✪ ବିପରୀତ **old 2** **2** that you have not seen, had, learnt, etc. before ସଦ୍ୟ ଆବିଷ୍କୃତ, ଆଗରୁ ଦେଖି ନଥିବା ବା ଜାଣିନଥିବା *The teacher usually explains the new words to us.*

new year the beginning of the year; the time around 1 January ନୂଆବର୍ଷ *Happy New Year!* ✪ ଜାନୁଆରୀ ୧ କୁ **New Year's Day** କୁହାଯାଏ ଏବଂ ଡିସେମ୍ବର 31 କୁ **New Year's Eve** କୁହାଯାଏ।

newly /ˈnju:li/ *adverb* not long ago; recently ନୂଆକରି *Our school is newly built.*

news /nju:z/ *noun* (*no plural*) **1** words that tell people about things that have just happened ଖବର, ବାର୍ତ୍ତା *I've got some good news for you.*

> ✪ ମନେରଖନ୍ତୁ ! ଆପଣ 'a news' କହିବା ଭୁଲ୍ ହେବ ଆପଣ 'some news' ବା 'a piece of news' କହିପାରିବେ — *Julie told us an interesting piece of news.*

2 the news (*no plural*) a programme on television or radio that tells people about important things that have just happened ଟେଲିଭିଜନ୍ ବା ରେଡ଼ିଓର ଖବର କାର୍ଯ୍ୟକ୍ରମ *We heard about the result of the match on the news.*

newspaper /ˈnju:zpeɪpə(r)/ *noun* a set of large pieces of paper with news, advertisements and other things printed on them, that you can buy every day or every week ଖବରକାଗଜ

next[1] /nekst/ *adjective* **1** that comes after this one ଠିକ୍ ପରବର୍ତ୍ତୀ, ଏହାପର *I'm going on leave next week.* **2** nearest to this one ଠିକ୍ ପରବର୍ତ୍ତୀ, ପାଖ (ଘର ଇତ୍ୟାଦି) *My friend stays in the next house.*

next to at the side of somebody or something; beside ପାଖରେ, ପାଖକୁ ଲାଗି *The bank is next to the post office.*

next[2] /nekst/ *adverb* after this; then ଏହା ପରେ, ତା' ପରେ *I've finished this work. What shall I do next?*

next door *adjective, adverb* in or to the nearest house ସବୁଠୁଁ ପାଖରେ ଥିବା ଘର *next-door neighbours* ○ *Who lives next door?*

nibble /ˈnɪbl/ *verb* (**nibbles, nibbling, nibbled**) eat something in very small bites ଅଳ୍ପ ଅଳ୍ପ କରି କାମୁଡ଼ି ଖାଇବା *The rabbit was nibbling the carrot.*

nice /naɪs/ *adjective* (**nicer, nicest**) pleasant, good or kind ଆନନ୍ଦଦାୟକ, ସୁଖକର, ଭଲ *Did you have a nice holiday?* ○ *It's nice to see you.*

nicely *adverb* ଭଲଭାବରେ , ଶିଷ୍ଟଭାବରେ *You can go to the cinema if you ask nicely.*

nickname /ˈnɪkneɪm/ *noun* a name that your friends or family sometimes use to call you by instead of your real name ଡାକନାମ ➪ ଟିପ୍ପଣୀ ପାଇଁ **name** ଦେଖନ୍ତୁ।

niece /ni:s/ *noun* the daughter of your brother or sister ଝିଆରୀ, ଭାଣିଜୀ ➪ ଚିତ୍ର ପାଇଁ **family** ଦେଖନ୍ତୁ।

night /naɪt/ *noun* the time when it is dark because there is no light from the sun ରାତି, ରାତ୍ରି, ନିଶି, ନିଶା *Most people sleep at night.* ○ *She stayed at my house last night.* ✪ ଆଜିର ସନ୍ଧ୍ୟା ବା ରାତିକୁ **tonight** କୁହାଯାଏ।

nightdress /ˈnaɪtdres/ *noun* (*plural* **nightdresses**) a loose dress that a woman or girl wears in bed ସ୍ତ୍ରୀ ଓ ପିଲାମାନଙ୍କର ଲମ୍ବା ଢ଼ୁଗୁଲା ଶୋଇବା ଜାମା

nightingale /ˈnaɪtɪŋgeɪl/ *noun* a small brown bird that sings beautifully ବୁଲ୍‌ବୁଲ୍ ଜାତୀୟ ମଧୁର କଣ୍ଠବିଶିଷ୍ଟ ରାତିରେ ଗୀତ ଗାଉଥିବା ଏକ ପ୍ରକାର ଛୋଟ ପକ୍ଷୀ, ନାଇଟିଙ୍ଗେଲ୍ ।

nightmare /ˈnaɪtmeə(r)/ *noun* a dream that frightens you ଦୁଃସ୍ୱପ୍ନ, ଭୟପ୍ରଦ ସ୍ୱପ୍ନ *I had a nightmare last night.*

nil /nɪl/ *noun* (*no plural*) nothing କିଛି ନାହିଁ *Our team won the match by two goals to nil.*

nine /naɪn/ *number* 9 ୯ ସଂଖ୍ୟା

ninth /naɪnθ/ *adjective, adverb, noun* **1** 9th ନବମ, ୯ମ **2** one of nine equal parts of something; $\frac{1}{9}$ ନଅ ଭାଗରୁ ଭାଗେ; ୧/୯

nineteen /ˌnaɪnˈtiːn/ *number* 19 ଉଣେଇଶି ୧୯

nineteenth /ˌnaɪnˈtiːnθ/ *adjective, adverb, noun* 19th ଉଣେଇଶିତମ, ଊନବିଂଶତମ, ୧୯ତମ

ninety /ˈnaɪnti/ *number* **1** 90 ନବେ ୯୦ **2 the nineties** (*plural*) the numbers, years or temperatures between 90 and 99, ୯୦ ଓ ୯୯ ମଧ୍ୟରେ ଥିବା ସଂଖ୍ୟା, ବର୍ଷ ବା ଉତ୍ତାପର ମାତ୍ରା

ninetieth /ˈnaɪntiəθ/ *adjective, adverb, noun* 90th ନବେତମ, ୯୦ତମ

nitrogen /ˈnaɪtrədʒən/ *noun* (*no plural*) a gas that has no colour, smell or taste. It forms about eighty per cent of the air ଯବକ୍ଷାରଜାନ (ଏକ ରଙ୍ଗ, ଗନ୍ଧ, ସ୍ୱାଦ ବିହୀନ ବାଷ୍ପ ଯାହା ବାୟୁମଣ୍ଡଳର ଅଶୀପ୍ରତିଶତ ପରିମାଣରେ ଥାଏ)

No., no. *abbreviation* ଶବ୍ଦ **number** ର ସଂକ୍ଷିପ୍ତ ରୂପ

no¹ /nəʊ/ *adjective* **1** not one; not any କିଛି ନାହିଁ *I have no money.* **2** a word that shows you are not allowed to do something କିଛି କାର୍ଯ୍ୟ କରିବା ପାଇଁ ଅନୁମତି ନଦେବା *The sign said 'No smoking'.*

no² /nəʊ/ *interjection* a word that you use to show that something is not right or true, or that you do not want something; not yes ଯାହାକି ଠିକ୍ ନୁହେଁ ବା ସତ୍ୟ ନୁହେଁ, ଯେଉଁଟାକି ତୁମର ଇଚ୍ଛା ନୁହେଁ *'Do you want a sandwich?' 'No, thank you.'*

Oh no! words that you say when something bad happens ଯେତେବେଳେ କିଛି ବିସ୍ମୟଭାବକ ବା ଖରାପ ଘଟଣା ଘଟେ *Oh no! I've broken my watch!*

noble /ˈnəʊbl/ *adjective* (**nobler, noblest**) **1** of a rich important family ଧନୀ ବା ଉଚ୍ଚ ବଂଶୀୟ *a noble prince* **2** good, honest and not selfish ଭଲ, ସଚ୍ଚୋଟ, ନିଃସ୍ୱାର୍ଥପର *noble thoughts*

nobleman /ˈnəʊblmən/ *noun* (*plural* **noblemen**) in olden times, a person from a family of high social rank ଉଚ୍ଚ ବା ସଂଭ୍ରାନ୍ତ ବଂଶୀୟ ପରିବାରର ଲୋକ

nobody /ˈnəʊbədi/ *pronoun* no person; not anybody କେହି ନୁହେଁ *There was nobody at home.*

nod /nɒd/ *verb* (**nods, nodding, nodded**) move your head down and up again quickly as a way of saying 'yes' or 'hello' to somebody ହଁ କହିବା ପାଇଁ ବା ସ୍ୱାଗତ କରିବା ପାଇଁ ମୁଣ୍ଡ ତଳକୁ ଓ ଉପରକୁ ହଲାଇବା। *'Do you understand?' asked the teacher, and everybody nodded.*

noise /nɔɪz/ *noun* **1** something that you hear; a sound ଶବ୍ଦ, ଧ୍ୱନି *I heard a noise upstairs.* **2** a loud sound that you do not like ଉଚ୍ଚ ଶବ୍ଦ ବା ଧ୍ୱନି, କୋଳାହଳ *Don't make so much noise!*

noisy /ˈnɔɪzi/ *adjective* (**noisier, noisiest**) **1** full of loud noise କୋଳାହଳ ପୂର୍ଣ୍ଣ *The restaurant was too noisy.* **2** if a person or thing is noisy, he/she/it makes a lot of noise ପାଟିତୁଣ୍ଡ ବା କୋଳାହଳ କରୁଥିବା, ଉଚ୍ଚଶବ୍ଦ କରୁଥିବା *The children were very noisy yesterday.* ✪ ବିପରୀତ **quiet**

noisily *adverb* କୋଳାହଳ କରି *He ate his dinner noisily.*

nomad /ˈnəʊmæd/ *noun* a member of a group of people who do not stay in one place for very long but move from one place to another in search of food and land for grazing their animals ଯାଯାବର, ଚାରଣଭୂମି ଅନ୍ୱେଷଣରେ ବିଭିନ୍ନ ଜାଗାକୁ ଯାଉଥିବା ଗୋଷ୍ଠୀର ବ୍ୟକ୍ତି

nomadic *adjective* of nomads ଯାଯାବର (ଜାତି, ବୃତ୍ତି ଇତ୍ୟାଦି), ଯାଯାବର ସମ୍ବନ୍ଧୀୟ *nomadic life*

nominate /ˈnɒmɪneɪt/ *verb* (**nominates, nominating, nominated**) formally suggest that somebody or something should be given a job, role, prize, etc. ନିର୍ବାଚନ ପାଇଁ ବ୍ୟକ୍ତିଙ୍କ ନାମ ପ୍ରସ୍ତାବ କରିବା

> **non-** *prefix*
>
> କିଛି ଶବ୍ଦର ପୂର୍ବରେ **non-** ଲଗାଇଲେ ବିପରୀତ ଅର୍ଥ ବୁଝାଏ, ଯଥା —
>
> a **non-smoker** = ଧୂମ୍ରପାନ କରୁ ନଥିବା ବ୍ୟକ୍ତି
>
> a **non-stop** train = ବାଟରେ ରହୁ ନଥିବା ରେଳଗାଡ଼ି

none /nʌn/ *pronoun* not any; not one କେହି ନାହିଁ; କିଛି ନାହିଁ; କେହି ବା କିଛି ନୁହେଁ *She has eaten all the chocolates—there are none in the box.* ○ *I went to every bookshop, but none of them had the book I wanted.*

non-renewable *adjective* something that is non-renewable cannot be replaced after it has been used ଯାହା ପୁନର୍ବ୍ୟବହାର କରାଯାଇ ପାରିବନାହିଁ; ଯାହା ସରିଗଲେ ଆଉ ମିଳିବ ନାହିଁ *non-renewable sources of energy* ✪ ବିପରୀତ **renewable**

nonsense /ˈnɒnsns/ *noun* (*no plural*) words or ideas that have no meaning or that are not true ଅସଙ୍ଗତ, ଅବାନ୍ତର ବା ଅଯୌକ୍ତିକ କଥା; ଅର୍ଥହୀନ କଥା; ମିଛ କଥା *What nonsense! Jassi is not lazy.*

non-stop *adjective, adverb* without any stops or breaks ବିରତିହୀନ; ବାଟରେ ରହୁନଥିବା *a non-stop flight to London*

non-violence *noun* (*no plural*) the policy of fighting for change without the use of violence ଅହିଂସା *Mahatma Gandhi's policy of non-violence*

non-violent *adjective* ହିଂସା ବ୍ୟବହାର କରୁନଥିବା, ଅହିଂସା *non-violent protests*

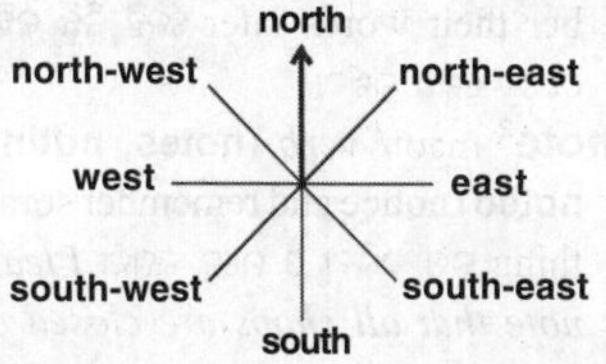

noodles /ˈnuːdlz/ *noun* (*plural*) long thin pieces of food made from flour, eggs and water ଅଟା, ଅଣ୍ଡା, ମଇଦା ଇତ୍ୟାଦିରେ ଗଢ଼ା ସିମେଇଁ ପରି ଖଣ୍ଡ ଯାହା ଖାଦ୍ୟ ଭାବରେ ବ୍ୟବହୃତ ହୁଏ

noon /nuːn/ *noun* (*no plural*) twelve o'clock in the middle of the day; midday ମଧ୍ୟାହ୍ନ, ଦ୍ୱିପ୍ରହର *I met Parul at noon.* ➪ **midnight** ମଧ୍ୟ ଦେଖନ୍ତୁ।

no one *pronoun* no person; not anybody କେହି ନୁହେଁ; କେହିନାହୁଁ *There was no one in the classroom.*

nor /nɔː(r)/ *conjunction* (used after 'neither' and 'not') also not ନୁହେଁ (ଯେ ନୁହେଁ କି ସେ ନୁହେଁ) *Neither Priya nor I eat meat.* ○ *I did not go to the party. Nor did Preeti.*

normal /ˈnɔːml/ *adjective* usual and ordinary; not different or special ସାଧାରଣ, ସ୍ୱାଭାବିକ *I will be home at the normal time.*

normally *adverb* **1** usually ସାଧାରଣତଃ *I normally go to bed at about eleven o'clock.* **2** in a normal way ସ୍ୱାଭାବିକ ଭାବରେ *He isn't behaving normally.*

north /nɔːθ/ *noun* (*no plural*) the direction that is on your left when you watch the sun come up in the morning ଉତ୍ତର ଦିଗ

north *adjective*, *adverb* ଉତ୍ତର; ଉତ୍ତର ଦିଗରୁ *a north wind*

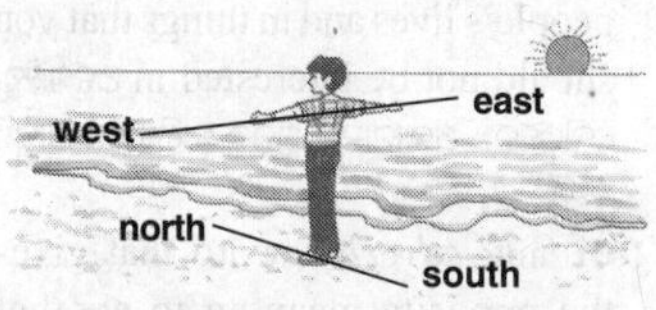

northern /ˈnɔːðən/ *adjective* in or of the north part of a place ଉତ୍ତର ଦିଗସ୍ଥ, ଉତ୍ତର ଦିଗର *Chandigarh is in northern India.*

north-east *noun* (*no plural*) the direction that is halfway between north and east ଉତ୍ତର-ପୂର୍ବ ଦିଗ

the North-East *noun* (*no plural*) the region situated in the north-eastern part of India which includes the states Assam, Arunachal Pradesh, Manipur, Meghalaya, Mizoram, Nagaland and Tripura ଭାରତର ଉତ୍ତର-ପୂର୍ବ ଅଞ୍ଚଳ (ଆସାମ୍, ଅରୁଣାଚଳ ପ୍ରଦେଶ, ମଣିପୁର, ମେଘାଳୟ, ମିଜୋରାମ୍, ନାଗାଲାଣ୍ଡ୍ ଓ ତ୍ରିପୁରା

north-west *noun* (*no plural*) the direction that is halfway between north and west ଉତ୍ତର-ପଶ୍ଚିମ ଦିଗ

nose /nəʊz/ *noun* the part of your face, above your mouth, that you use for breathing and smelling ନାକ, ନାଶା, ନାଶିକା ➪ ଚିତ୍ର ପାଇଁ **face** ଦେଖନ୍ତୁ।

blow your nose blow air out through your nose to clear it, into a piece of cloth or paper (a **handkerchief** or a **tissue**) ନାକ ସୁଁ ସୁଁ କରି ସଫା କରିବା

nostril /ˈnɒstrəl/ *noun* one of the two holes in your nose ନାକପୁଡ଼ା ➪ ଚିତ୍ର ପାଇଁ **face** ଦେଖନ୍ତୁ।

nosy /ˈnəʊzi/ *adjective* (**nosier, nosiest**) too interested in other people's lives and in things that you should not be interested in ଅନୁସନ୍ଧିତ୍ସୁ, କୌତୁହଳୀ; ଅନ୍ୟମାନଙ୍କ ଗୁମର ଜାଣିବାରେ ଆଗ୍ରହି ବ୍ୟକ୍ତି

not /nɒt/ *adverb* a word that gives the opposite meaning to another word or a sentence ନା, ନାହିଁ, ନୁହେଁ *I'm not hungry.* ✪ ଆମେ ଅନେକ ସମୟରେ not ଜାଗାରେ **n't** ଲେଖୁ *Vivek isn't here.* ○ *I haven't got any sisters.*

not at all 1 no; not a little bit ନା, ଆଦୌ ନୁହେଁ *'Are you tired?' 'Not at all.'* 2 polite words that you say when somebody has said 'Thank you' 'ଧନ୍ୟବାଦ'ର ଏକ ଭଦ୍ର ପ୍ରତ୍ୟୁତ୍ତର; ଯେ କିଛି ନୁହେଁ *'Thanks for your help.' 'Oh, not at all.'*

notation /nəʊˈteɪʃn/ *noun* a system of symbols used to represent something, especially in mathematics, science and music ଗଣିତ, ବିଜ୍ଞାନ ଓ ସଙ୍ଗୀତରେ ବ୍ୟବହୃତ ଚିହ୍ନ ବା ସଙ୍କେତର ପଦ୍ଧତି *musical notation*

note[1] /nəʊt/ *noun* 1 some words that you write quickly to help you remember something ମନେ ରଖିବା ପାଇଁ ଲେଖି ରଖୁଥିବା ଟିପ୍ପଣୀ *I made a note of her address.* 2 a short letter ଛୋଟ ଚିଠି *Sunny sent me a note to thank me for the present.* 3 a piece of paper money କାଗଜ ମୁଦ୍ରା, ନୋଟ୍ *He gave me a fifty-rupee note.* 4 a short piece of extra information about something in a book ବହିର ଏକ ଶବ୍ଦ ବା କ୍ଷୁଦ୍ର ଅଂଶ ଉପରେ ଦିଆଯାଇଥିବା ବ୍ୟାଖ୍ୟା; ଟିପ୍ପଣୀ *See the note on page 39.*

take notes write when somebody is speaking so that you can remember their words later କେହି କିଛି କହିବା ବେଳେ ଲେଖି ରଖିବା

note[2] /nəʊt/ *verb* (**notes, noting, noted**) notice and remember something ଲକ୍ଷ କରିବା ଓ ମନେ ରଖିବା *Please note that all shops are closed on Mondays.*

notebook /ˈnəʊtbʊk/ *noun* a small book where you write things that you want to remember ଖାତା

notepad /ˈnəʊtpæd/ *noun* some pieces of paper that are joined together at one edge, where you write things that you want to remember ଟିପାଖାତା

nothing /ˈnʌθɪŋ/ *pronoun* not anything; no thing କିଛି ନାହିଁ *There's nothing in this bottle—it's empty.*

nothing but only କେବଳ *He eats nothing but salad.*

notice[1] /ˈnəʊtɪs/ *noun* 1 (*plural* **notices**) a piece of writing that tells people something ବିଜ୍ଞପ୍ତି, ବିଜ୍ଞାପନ; କୌଣସି ବିଷୟରେ ସୂଚନା ଦେଉଥିବା ଲେଖା *The notice on the wall says 'No Smoking'.* 2 (*no plural*) a warning that something is going to happen କୌଣସି

ଭବିଷ୍ୟତ ଘଟଣା ପାଇଁ ସତର୍କ ରହିବା ପାଇଁ ସୂଚନା *Our teacher gave us two weeks' notice of the history exam.*

at short notice with not much time to get ready ଅଳ୍ପ ସମୟରେ, ହଠାତ୍ *We left for Shimla at very short notice and I forgot to take my coat.*

take notice of somebody or **something** listen to or look at somebody or something; pay attention to somebody or something ଆଗ୍ରହ ଦେଖାଇବା, ଧ୍ୟାନ ଦେବା (କୌଣସି ବ୍ୟକ୍ତି ବା ପଦାର୍ଥ ପାଇଁ) *Take no notice of what she said—she's not feeling well today.*

notice² /ˈnəʊtɪs/ *verb* (**notices, noticing, noticed**) see somebody or something ଦେଖିବା, ଧ୍ୟାନ ଦେବା *I noticed that he was driving a new car.*

noticeable /ˈnəʊtɪsəbl/ *adjective* easy to see ସହଜରେ ଦିଶୁଥିବା *I've got a mark on my shirt. Is it noticeable?*

noticeboard /ˈnəʊtɪsbɔːd/ *noun* a flat piece of wood on a wall. You put notices on a noticeboard so that everybody can read them ବିଜ୍ଞପ୍ତି ଫଳକ; ନୋଟିସ୍ ବା ବିଜ୍ଞପ୍ତି ଲଗାଯାଉଥିବା ପଟା, ନୋଟିସ୍‌ବୋର୍ଡ଼ *The teacher put the exam results on the noticeboard.*

notion /ˈnəʊʃn/ *noun* an idea or something that you have in your mind ଧାରଣା, ମନୋଭାବ *She had a vague notion that she had met Rahul before.*

noun /naʊn/ *noun* a word that is the name of a person, place, thing or idea (ବ୍ୟାକରଣ) ବିଶେଷ୍ୟ ପଦ *'Shruti', 'Delhi', 'cat' and 'happiness' are all nouns.*

nourish /ˈnʌrɪʃ/ *verb* (**nourishes, nourishing, nourished**) give a person, an animal or a plant the right food so that they grow up to be strong and healthy (ବ୍ୟକ୍ତି, ପଶୁ ବା ଉଦ୍ଭିଦକୁ) ଭଲ ଭାବରେ ଖାଦ୍ୟ ଯୋଗାଇ ପୋଷଣ କରିବା

nourishment *noun* (*no plural*) ପୋଷଣ; ଖାଦ୍ୟ *Are the plants getting enough nourishment?*

novel /ˈnɒvl/ *noun* a book that tells a story about people and things that are not real ଉପନ୍ୟାସ David Copperfield *is a novel by Charles Dickens.*

novelist *noun* a person who writes novels ଔପନ୍ୟାସିକ, ଉପନ୍ୟାସର ଲେଖକ

November /nəʊˈvembə(r)/ *noun* the eleventh month of the year ପାଶ୍ଚାତ୍ୟ ବର୍ଷର ୧୧ତମ ମାସ, ନଭେମ୍ବର୍

now /naʊ/ *adverb* at this time ବର୍ତ୍ତମାନ *I can't see you now—can you come back later?*

from now on after this time; in the future ଆଜିଠାରୁ, ବର୍ତ୍ତମାନ ଠାରୁ *From now on Mr John will be your teacher.*

now and again, now and then sometimes, but not often କେବେ କେବେ *We go to the cinema now and again.*

nowadays /ˈnaʊədeɪz/ *adverb* at this time ଆଜିକାଲି *A lot of people work with computers nowadays.*

nowhere /ˈnəʊweə(r)/ *adverb* not anywhere; at, in or to no place କୁଆଡ଼େ

ବି ନୁହେଁ *There's nowhere to stay in this village.*

nuclear /ˈnju:kliə(r)/ *adjective* using or relating to the great power that is made by breaking or joining parts of atoms ପରମାଣୁ ବିଖଣ୍ଡନ ଦ୍ୱାରା ମିଳୁଥିବା ଶକ୍ତି ସମ୍ବନ୍ଧୀୟ, ନାଭିକୀୟ, ନ୍ୟୁକ୍ଲୀୟ *nuclear energy* ○ *nuclear weapons*

nudge /nʌdʒ/ *verb* (**nudges, nudging, nudged**) touch or push somebody or something gently with your elbow ଦୃଷ୍ଟି ଆକର୍ଷଣ ପାଇଁ କହୁଣୀରେ ଆସ୍ତେ ଖେଞ୍ଚିବା *Nudge me if I fall asleep.*

nuisance /ˈnju:sns/ *noun* a person or thing that causes you trouble ବିରକ୍ତିକର ବ୍ୟକ୍ତି ବା ପଦାର୍ଥ *I've lost my keys. What a nuisance!*

numb /nʌmb/ *adjective* not able to feel anything ବଧିର, ଅନୁଭୂତି ଶୂନ୍ୟ, ସ୍ତବ୍ଧ *My fingers were numb with cold.*

number /ˈnʌmbə(r)/ *noun* **1** a word like 'two' or 'fifteen', or a symbol or group of symbols like 7 or 130 ସଂଖ୍ୟା *Choose a number between ten and one hundred.* ✪ ଆମେ ପ୍ରାୟ 'number' ସ୍ଥାନରେ **No.** ବା **no.** ଲେଖୁ। **2** a group of more than one person or thing ଲୋକମାନଙ୍କର ବା ପଦାର୍ଥଗୁଡ଼ିକର ସମଷ୍ଟି *A large number of our students come from Kerala.*

number *verb* (**numbers, numbering, numbered**) give a number to something ସଂଖ୍ୟା ଦ୍ୱାରା ଚିହ୍ନିତ କରିବା *Number the pages from one to ten.*

number plate *noun* a flat piece of metal or plastic on the front and back of a car that has numbers and letters on it (called the **registration number**) ମଟର ଗାଡ଼ିରେ ଲଗାଯାଉଥିବା ସଂଖ୍ୟା ଓ ଅକ୍ଷର ଲେଖା ଚିହ୍ନଟ ଫଳକ (ଏହାକୁ ରେଜିଷ୍ଟ୍ରେସନ୍ ନମ୍ବର କୁହାଯାଏ) ➪ ଚିତ୍ର ପାଇଁ **car** ଦେଖନ୍ତୁ।

numeral /ˈnju:mərəl/ *noun* a sign or symbol that stands for a quantity or number ସଂଖ୍ୟାବାଚକ ଚିହ୍ନ, ସଂଖ୍ୟା ଚିହ୍ନ *Roman numerals*

numerical /nju:ˈmerɪkl/ *adjective* of or about numbers ସଂଖ୍ୟା ବିଷୟକ, ସଂଖ୍ୟାର

numerator /ˈnju:məreɪtə(r)/ *noun* the number written above the line in a fraction, for example 1 in $\frac{1}{4}$ ଭଗ୍ନାଂଶର ଗୁଣନାଶଂ ବା ଲବ ($\frac{୧}{୪}$ ରେ ୧ ହେଲା ଲବ ବା ଗୁଣନାଂଶ) ➪ **denominator** ଦେଖନ୍ତୁ।

numerous /ˈnju:mərəs/ *adjective* very, many ବହୁ, ବହୁତ, ଅସଂଖ୍ୟ *He writes a lot of letters because he has numerous friends.*

nun /nʌn/ *noun* a member of a religious group of women who live together in a **convent** away from other people ଅନ୍ୟଙ୍କ ଠାରୁ ଦୂରରେ ଏକ କନ୍‌ଭେଣ୍ଟ ବା ମଠରେ ରହୁଥିବା ସନ୍ୟାସିନୀ ଗୋଷ୍ଠୀର ସଭ୍ୟା

nurse[1] /nɜ:s/ *noun* a person whose job is to look after people who are sick or hurt ରୋଗୀର ସେବା କରିବା *My sister works as a nurse in a hospital.*

nurse[2] /nɜ:s/ *verb* (**nurses, nursing, nursed**) look after somebody who is sick or hurt ରୋଗୀର ସେବକ ବା ସେବିକା

I nursed my father when he was ill.

nursery /ˈnɜːsəri/ *noun* (*plural* **nurseries**) **1** a class in a school for children between the ages of three and five ତିନିରୁ ପାଞ୍ଚ ବର୍ଷର ପିଲାଙ୍କ ପାଇଁ ଥିବା ସ୍କୁଲର ଶ୍ରେଣୀ **2** a place where people grow and sell plants ଚାରା ଉଦ୍ୟାନ୍, ତଳିଜମି ।

nursery rhyme *noun* (*plural* **nursery rhymes**) a song or poem for young children ଶିଶୁଗୀତ

nursery school *noun* (*plural* **nursery schools**) a school for children between the ages of three and five ତିନିରୁ ପାଞ୍ଚ ବର୍ଷର ପିଲାମାନଙ୍କର ସ୍କୁଲ୍ ବା ବିଦ୍ୟାଳୟ ।

nursing /ˈnɜːsɪŋ/ *noun* (*no plural*) the job of being a nurse ରୋଗୀସେବା କାମ *He has decided to go into nursing when he leaves school.*

nut /nʌt/ *noun* **1** the hard fruit of a tree or bush. Almonds, cashew nuts, walnuts and groundnuts are different kinds of nuts ବାଦାମ (ଯଥା: ଚିନାବାଦାମ, କାଜୁବାଦାମ, ବାଦାମ, ପିସ୍ତା, ଅଖରୋଟ୍ ଇତ୍ୟାଦି)
2 a small piece of metal with a hole in the middle that you put on the end of a long piece of metal (called a **bolt**). You use nuts and bolts for fixing things together ପେଚକୁ ଘୂରାଇ ପଶାଇବା ପାଇଁ କଣା ଓ ଘରଥିବା ଚଟକା ଧାତୁ ଖଣ୍ଡ

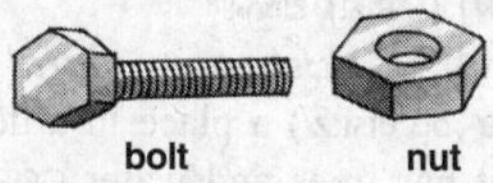

nutrient /ˈnjuːtriənt/ *noun* a substance that you need to grow healthy and strong ପୁଷ୍ଟିକାରକ ଦ୍ରବ୍ୟ

nutrition /njuˈtrɪʃn/ *noun* (*no plural*) the process by which living things take in the food that helps them grow and be healthy ପୁଷ୍ଟି, ପୁଷ୍ଟିସାଧନ *Plants get their nutrition from the soil.*

nutritious /njuˈtrɪʃəs/ *adjective* food that is nutritious has substances that help you grow and be healthy ପୁଷ୍ଟିକର

nylon /ˈnaɪlɒn/ *noun* (*no plural*) a very strong material made by machines. Nylon is used for making clothes and other things ଅତି ହାଲୁକା ଓ ଶକ୍ତ କୃତ୍ରିମ ତନ୍ତୁ *a nylon brush*

O o

O = **Oh**

oak /əʊk/ *noun* a kind of large tree କଠିନ କାଠ ଥିବା ଏକ ବଡ଼ ଗଛ, ଓକ୍ ➪ ଚିତ୍ର ପାଇଁ **acorn** ଦେଖନ୍ତୁ ।

oar /ɔ:(r)/ *noun* a long piece of wood with one flat end. You use oars to move a small boat through water (to **row**) (ଡଙ୍ଗାର) ଆହୁଲା

oasis /əʊˈeɪsɪs/ *noun* (*plural* **oases** /əʊˈeɪsi:z/) a place in a desert that has trees and water ମରୁଦ୍ୟାନ; ମରୁଭୂମି ମଧ୍ୟରେ ପାଣି ଓ ଗଛପତ୍ର ଥିବା ସ୍ଥାନ

oath /əʊθ/ *noun* a formal and serious promise ଶପଥ *I took an oath in front of a lawyer.*

oats /əʊts/ *noun* (*plural*) a plant with seeds that we use as food for people and animals ମଣିଷ ଓ ପଶୁଙ୍କ ଖାଦ୍ୟ ଭାବେ ବ୍ୟବହୃତ, ଏକ ପ୍ରକାର ଯବ ପରି ଶସ୍ୟ ଓ ତାହାର ଗଛ ➪ ଚିତ୍ର ପାଇଁ **grain** ଦେଖନ୍ତୁ ।

obedient /əˈbi:diənt/ *adjective* an obedient person does what somebody tells him/her to do ଆଜ୍ଞାଧୀନ, କଥା ମାନୁଥିବା *He was an obedient child.* ✪ ବିପରୀତ **disobedient**

obedience /əˈbi:diəns/ *noun* (*no plural*) the act of being obedient ଆଜ୍ଞାଧିନତା, ଆଜ୍ଞା ମାନୁଥିବା ସ୍ୱଭାବ ବା ବ୍ୟବହାର ✪ ବିପରୀତ **disobedience**

obediently *adverb* ଆଜ୍ଞାଧିନ ଭାବରେ କଥାମାନି *I called the dog and it followed me obediently.*

obey /əˈbeɪ/ *verb* (**obeys, obeying, obeyed**) do what somebody or something tells you to do ଆଦେଶପାଳନ କରିବା । *You must obey the law.* ✪ ବିପରୀତ **disobey**

object¹ /ˈɒbdʒɪekt/ *noun* **1** a thing that you can see and touch ଭୌତିକ ପଦାର୍ଥ, ବସ୍ତୁ, ଦ୍ରବ୍ୟ *There was a small round object on the table.* **2** what you plan to do ଉଦ୍ଦେଶ୍ୟ *His object in life is to become as rich as possible.* **3** in the sentence 'Jane painted the door', the object of the sentence is 'the door' (ବ୍ୟାକରଣ) ବାକ୍ୟର କର୍ମ ➪ **subject 3** ଦେଖନ୍ତୁ ।

object² /əbˈdʒeɪkt/ *verb* (**objects, objecting, objected**) not like something or not agree with something ଆପତ୍ତି କରିବା, ଏକମତ ନହେବା *I object to the plan.*

objection /əbˈdʒekʃn/ *noun* saying or feeling that you do not like something or that you do not agree with something ଆପତ୍ତି *I have no objections to the plan.*

objective¹ /əbˈdʒektɪv/ *noun* something that you are trying to achieve or reach; an aim ଅଭିପ୍ରାୟ, ଲକ୍ଷ *His objective at the moment is to buy a car.*

objective² /əbˈdʒektɪv/ *adjective* based on facts alone, and not influenced by your personal feelings ବାସ୍ତବ ଘଟଣା ବା ବସ୍ତୁ ଜଗତ ଉପରେ ଆଧାରିତ, ବସ୍ତୁନିଷ୍ଠ; ନିରପେକ୍ଷ *an objective review of the film* ✪ ବିପରୀତ **subjective**

oblong /ˈɒblɒŋ/ *noun* a shape like a **rectangle**, with two long sides, two short sides and four angles of 90 degrees ସମଚତୁଷ୍କୋଣ ଆୟତାକାର କ୍ଷେତ୍ର ➪ ଚିତ୍ର ପାଇଁ **shape** ଦେଖନ୍ତୁ ।

observant /əbˈzɜːvənt/ *adjective* someone who is observant is good at noticing things around them ଚାରିଆଡ଼ର ଜିନିଷ ବା ଅବସ୍ଥା ଭଲଭାବେ ଲକ୍ଷ କରି ପାରୁଥିବା ବ୍ୟକ୍ତି *She is very observant about the surroundings.*

observation /ˌɒbzəˈveɪʃn/ *noun* (*no plural*) the act of watching something or someone carefully for a long time to learn about them ପର୍ଯ୍ୟବେକ୍ଷଣ

be under observation be watched carefully ପର୍ଯ୍ୟବେକ୍ଷଣରେ ରହିବା *The doctors kept the patient under observation.*

observatory /əbˈzɜːvətri/ *noun* (*plural* **observatories**) a large building with telescopes and other scientific instruments to help scientists study stars, planets and other objects in space ଗ୍ରହ ନକ୍ଷତ୍ର ଇତ୍ୟାଦି ମହାଶୂନ୍ୟର ବସ୍ତୁ ଦେଖିବା ପାଇଁ ଦୂରବୀକ୍ଷଣ ଇତ୍ୟାଦି ଯନ୍ତ୍ରଥିବା ପର୍ଯ୍ୟବେକ୍ଷଣାଗାର

observe /əbˈsɜːv/ *verb* (**observes, observing, observed**) watch somebody or something carefully; see somebody or something ପର୍ଯ୍ୟବେକ୍ଷଣ କରିବା; ଦେଖିବା ବା ନିଘାରଖିବା

obsession /əbˈseʃn/ *noun* a person or thing that you think about all the time କୌଣସି ବ୍ୟକ୍ତି ବା ପଦାର୍ଥ ବିଷୟରେ ସବୁବେଳେ ଭାବିବା ଅବସ୍ଥା; ଘାରିହେବା ଅବସ୍ଥା *Cars are his obsession.*

obstacle /ˈɒbstəkl/ *noun* something that is in front of you, that you must go over or round before you can go on ପ୍ରତିବନ୍ଧ, ବାଡ଼ *The horse jumped over the obstacle.*

obstinate /ˈɒbstɪnət/ *adjective* not changing your ideas or not doing what other people want you to do ଅମାନିଆ, ଅବାଧ, ଜିଦ୍‌ଖୋର୍, ଜିଦିଆ।

obstruct /əbˈstrʌkt/ *verb* (**obstructs, obstructing, obstructed**) be in the way so that somebody or something cannot go past ବାଧାଦେବା, ଆଗୋଳିବା *Please move your car—you're obstructing the traffic.*

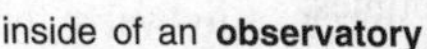
inside of an **observatory**

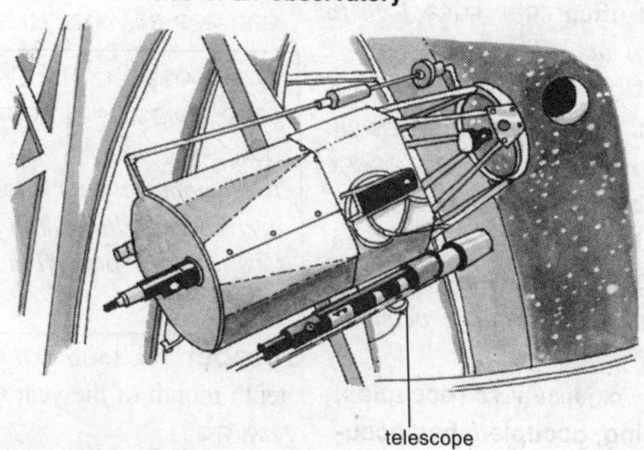

obtain /əbˈteɪn/ *verb* (**obtains, obtaining, obtained**) get something ପାଇବା, ହସ୍ତଗତ କରିବା *Where can I obtain tickets for the play?* ✪ ଏ ସ୍ଥାନରେ ଆମେ ସାଧାରଣତଃ **get** ବ୍ୟବହାର କରୁ ।

obvious /ˈɒbviəs/ *adjective* very clear and easy to see or understand ସ୍ପଷ୍ଟ, ସୁସ୍ପଷ୍ଟ, ସ୍ପଷ୍ଟ ଭାବରେ ଜାଣି ହେଲା ପରି *It's obvious that she's not happy.*

obviously *adverb* used to say that something is easy to see or understand; clearly ସୁସ୍ପଷ୍ଟ ଭାବରେ; ସ୍ପଷ୍ଟ ଭାବରେ ଜାଣି ହେଉଛି ଯେ *He obviously learnt English at school—he speaks it very well.*

occasion /əˈkeɪʒn/ *noun* **1** a time when something happens ଘଟଣାର ସମୟ, ଥର *I've been to Jaipur on three or four occasions.* **2** a special time ସ୍ୱତନ୍ତ୍ର ସମୟ– *A wedding is a big family occasion.*

occasional /əˈkeɪʒənl/ *adjective* that happens sometimes, but not very often କେବେ କେବେ ଘଟୁଥିବ

occasionally *adverb* sometimes, but not often କେବେ କେବେ *I go to Chennai occasionally.*

occupation /ˌɒkjuˈpeɪʃn/ *noun* **1** a job କାମ, ବୃତ୍ତି, ଚାକିରି *What is your mother's occupation?* ✪ ସାଧାରଣତଃ ଆମେ **job** ଶବ୍ଦ ବ୍ୟବହାର କରୁ । **2** something that you do in your free time ଅବସର ସମୟରେ କରାଯାଉଥିବା କାମ *Fishing is his favourite occupation.*

occupy /ˈɒkjupaɪ/ *verb* (**occupies, occupying, occupied, has occupied**) **1** live or be in a place ବାସ କରିବା, ଦଖଲ କରିବା; *Who occupies the house next door?* **2** make somebody busy; take somebody's time ବ୍ୟସ୍ତ ରଖିବା, କାର୍ଯ୍ୟରତ ରଖିବା; ସମୟ ବିତାଇବା *The children occupy most of her free time.*

occupied *adjective* **1** busy ବ୍ୟସ୍ତ *This work will keep me occupied all week.* **2** being used ବ୍ୟବହାର ହେଉଥିବା *Excuse me—is this seat occupied?*

occur /əˈkɜː(r)/ *verb* (**occurs, occurring, occurred**) happen ଘଟିବା *The accident occurred this morning.*

occur to somebody come into somebody's mind କୌଣସି କଥା ମନକୁ ଆସିବା *It occurred to me much later that she didn't know our new address.*

ocean /ˈəʊʃn/ *noun* a very big sea ସମୁଦ୍ର, ମହାସାଗର *the Atlantic Ocean*

o'clock /əˈklɒk/ *adverb* a word that you use after the numbers one to twelve for saying what time it is ସମୟ ସୂଚକ ଶବ୍ଦ, ଘଟିକା, (ଯଥା: ୧୨:୧୦)

> ✪ ମନେ ରଖନ୍ତୁ! 'O'clock' ର ପ୍ରୟୋଗ କେବଳ, ପୂରାଘଣ୍ଟା ସମୟ ପରେ ବ୍ୟବହୃତ ହୁଏ; ଯଥା । —
> *I left home at four o'clock and arrived in Delhi at half past five* (କିନ୍ତୁ *at half past five o'clock* କୁହାଯାଏ ନାହିଁ ।).

October /ɒkˈtəʊbə(r)/ *noun* the tenth month of the year ପାଶ୍ଚାତ୍ୟ ବର୍ଷର ଦଶମ ମାସ

octopus /ˈɒktəpəs/ *noun* (*plural* **octopuses**) a sea animal with eight arms ଏକ ଅଷ୍ଟବାହୁଥିବା ସାମୁଦ୍ରିକ ଜୀବ, ଅକ୍ଟୋପସ୍

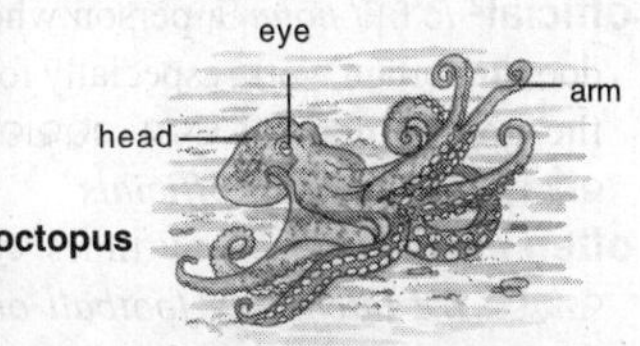

octopus

ଆପଣ ଜାଣନ୍ତି କି ?

Octopus ଶବ୍ଦଟା ଏକ ଗ୍ରୀସୀୟ ଶବ୍ଦରୁ ଉଦ୍ଭବ ହୋଇଚି, ଯାହାର ଅର୍ଥ ହେଉଛି 'ଆଠ ପାଦ ବିଶିଷ୍ଟ'।

odd /ɒd/ *adjective* (**odder, oddest**) **1** strange or unusual ଅଦ୍ଭୁତ, ଅସାଧାରଣ; ଅଖାଡୁଆ, ଅସଙ୍ଗତ *It's odd that he left without telling anybody.* **2** odd numbers cannot be divided exactly by two ଦୁଇ ସଂଖ୍ୟା ଦ୍ୱାରା ପୂର୍ଣ୍ଣ ରୂପେ ବିଭକ୍ତ ହୋଇ ନପାରୁଥିବା ସଂଖ୍ୟା *1, 3, 5 and 7 are all odd numbers.* ✪ ବିପରୀତ **even[1] 2 3** part of a pair when the other one is not there ହଳକରୁ ଦୁଇପଟ ଭିନ୍ନ ଭିନ୍ନ ପ୍ରକାରର ହୋଇଥିବା *You're wearing odd socks! One is black and the other is green!*

the odd one out one that is different from all the others ଗୋଷ୍ଠୀ ଠାରୁ ଭିନ୍ନପ୍ରକାରର *'Apple', 'orange', 'cabbage'—which is the odd one out?*

oddly *adverb* strangely ଅଦ୍ଭୁତ ଭାବରେ, ଅକାନୁଆ ଭାବରେ *She behaved very oddly.*

of /əv; ɒv/ *preposition* **1** a word that shows who or what has or owns something ର (ଯଥା: ଚଉକିର; ପାହାଡ଼ର) *the back of the chair* ○ *What's the name of this mountain?* **2** a word that you use after an amount, etc. କୌଣସି ପଦାର୍ଥର ପରିମାଣ ପରେ ବ୍ୟବହୃତ ଶବ୍ଦ *a litre of water* **3** a word that shows what something is, what is in something or what something is made of ର, ରୁ, ରେ, (ଯଥା: କାଠର ଖଣ୍ଡ; ଚା'ରୁ କପେ; ସୂତାର ଜାମା) *a piece of wood* ○ *a cup of tea* ○ *a shirt made of cotton* **4** a word that shows that somebody or something is part of a group ରୁ, ମଧ୍ୟରୁ; ଗୋଷ୍ଠି ମଧ୍ୟରୁ ଜଣେ (ଯଥା: ତାଙ୍କ ସାଙ୍ଗ ମଧ୍ୟରୁ ଜଣେ ହେଲା ଡାକ୍ତର) *One of her friends is a doctor.*

off /ɒf/ *preposition, adverb* **1** down or away from something ରୁ (ଯଥା: ଛାତରୁ; ବସ୍‌ରୁ) *He fell off the roof.* ○ *We got off the bus.* **2** away from the place where it was ଦୂରକୁ ନେବା, କାଢ଼ି ଦେବା ବା ଅବସାରଣ କରିବା *If you're feeling hot, take your coat off.* **3** not working; not being used ବ୍ୟବହାର ହେଉ ନଥିବା; ଲିଭା ଯାଇଥିବା ବନ୍ଦ କରାଯାଇଥିବା *All the lights are off.* ✪ ବିପରୀତ **on 4**

offence /əˈfens/ *noun* an action that is against the law ବେଆଇନ୍ କାମ *It is an offence to drive at night without lights.*

offend /əˈfend/ *verb* (**offends, offending, offended**) make somebody feel angry or unhappy; hurt somebody's feelings ଅପମାନ ଦେବା *She was offended when you said she was fat.*

offensive /ə'fensɪv/ *adjective* **1** rude, insulting and hurting somebody's feelings ଅପମାନଜନକ, ମନରେ କଷ୍ଟ ଦେଲା ପରି *offensive remarks about her personal appearance* **2** related to making an attack ଆକ୍ରମଣାତ୍ମକ *an offensive player.*

offer /'ɒfə(r)/ *verb* (**offers, offering, offered**) say or show that you will do or give something if another person wants it ଯାଚିବା *I offered to help her.* ○ *She offered me some tea.*

offer *noun* କିଛି ଦେବା ବା କରିଦେବା ପାଇଁ ପ୍ରସ୍ତାବ *Thanks for the offer, but I don't need any help.*

office /'ɒfɪs/ *noun* **1** a room or building with desks and telephones, where people work କାର୍ଯ୍ୟାଳୟ, ଅଫିସ୍ **2** a room or building where you can buy something or get information କିଛି ଜିନିଷ କିଣିବା ବା ଖବର ପାଇବା ପାଇଁ ଥିବା ଗୃହ *the post office*

officer /'ɒfɪsə(r)/ *noun* **1** a person in the army, navy or air force who gives orders to other people ସେନା ବାହିନୀର ଉଚ୍ଚ ପଦସ୍ଥ କର୍ମଚାରୀ, ଅଫିସର୍ *a naval officer* **2** a person who does important work, especially for the government ଉଚ୍ଚ ପଦସ୍ଥ ସରକାରୀ କର୍ମଚାରୀ *police officers*

official[1] /ə'fɪʃl/ *adjective* of or from the government or somebody who is important ସରକାରୀ; ବିଧିବଦ୍ଧ ଭାବେ ଅନୁମୋଦିତ *an official report*
✪ ବିପରୀତ **unofficial**

officially *adverb* ବିଧିବଦ୍ଧ ଭାବେ *I think I've got the job, but they will tell me officially on Friday.*

official[2] /ə'fɪʃl/ *noun* a person who does important work, especially for the government ଉଚ୍ଚପଦସ୍ଥ ସରକାରୀ କର୍ମଚାରୀ *government officials*

often /'ɒfn/ *adverb* many times ବହୁ ସମୟରେ *We often play football on Sundays.* ○ *How often do you visit her?*

Oh /əʊ/ *interjection* a word that shows a strong feeling, like surprise or fear ଆଶ୍ଚର୍ଯ୍ୟ, ଭୟ ଇତ୍ୟାଦି ସୂଚାଉଥିବା ଶବ୍ଦ; ଓହ୍ *Oh no! I've lost my keys!*

oil /ɔɪl/ *noun* (*no plural*) **1** a thick liquid that comes from plants or animals and that is used in cooking ତେଲ, ତୈଳ *Fry the onions in oil.* **2** a thick liquid that comes from under the ground or the sea. We burn oil or use it in machines ମାଟିତଳୁ ମିଳୁଥିବା ଇନ୍ଧନ ତେଲ (ଯଥା: ପେଟ୍ରୋଲ୍)

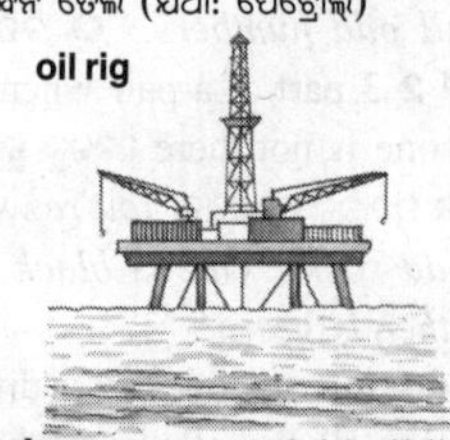
oil rig

oil rig *noun* a special building with machines that dig for oil under the sea or on land ସମୁଦ୍ର ତଳ ଖୋଳିବା ପାଇଁ ସମୁଦ୍ର ଉପରେ ସ୍ଥାପିତ ଯନ୍ତ୍ର ଖଚିତ କୋଠା ପରି ଗଠନ।

oily /'ɔɪli/ *adjective* (**oilier, oiliest**) like oil or covered with oil ତେଲିଆ *I don't like oily food.*

OK, okay /əʊˈkeɪ/ *interjection* yes; all right ହଁ; ଠିକ୍ ଅଛି *'Do you want to go to a party?' 'OK.'*

OK, okay *adjective, adverb* all right; good or well enough ଠିକ୍ ଅଛି *Is it okay to sit here?*

old /əʊld/ *adjective* (**older, oldest**) **1** if you are old, you have lived for a long time ବୁଢ଼ା, ବୃଦ୍ଧ *My grandfather is very old.* ○ *My sister is older than me.* ✪ ବିପରୀତ **young[1]** ➪ **elder** ଟିପ୍ପଣୀ ଦେଖନ୍ତୁ। **2** made or bought a long time ago ପୁରୁଣା, ପୁରାତନ *an old house* ✪ ବିପରୀତ **new 1** **3** you use 'old' to show the age of somebody or something ବୟସ ସୂଚକ ଶବ୍ଦ; ବର୍ଷର *He's nine years old.* ○ *How old are you?* **4** that you have known for a long time ବହୁ ଦିନରୁ ଜାଣିଥିବା *Shahnaz is an old friend—we were at school together.*

the old *noun* (*plural*) old people ବୁଢ଼ାଲୋକମାନେ

old age *noun* (*no plural*) the part of your life when you are old ବୁଢ଼ାବୟସ

old-fashioned *adjective* not modern; that people do not often use or wear now ପୁରୁଣାକାଳିଆ *Clothes from the 1960s look old-fashioned now.* ✪ ବିପରୀତ **fashionable**

omelette

omelette /ˈɒmlət/ *noun* a food that is made by mixing eggs together and frying in oil ଅଣ୍ଡାପିଠା, ଅମ୍ଲେଟ୍ *a cheese omelette*

omit /əˈmɪt/ *verb* (**omits, omitting, omitted**) not include something; leave something out ବାଦ୍‌ଦେବା, *Omit question 2 and do question 3.* ✪ ଏହା ବଦଳରେ ଆମେ ସାଧାରଣତଃ **leave out** କହୁ।

omnivore /ˈɒmnɪvɔː(r)/ *noun* an animal that eats both plants and animals ଉଭୟ ଉଦ୍ଭିଦ ଓ ପଶୁ ଖାଉଥିବା ଜୀବ ➪ **carnivore, herbivore** ଏବଂ **insectivore** ଦେଖନ୍ତୁ।

omnivorous /ɒmˈnɪvərəs/ *adjective* ଉଭୟ ପଶୁ ଓ ଉଦ୍ଭିଦ ଖାଉଥିବା *omnivorous animals*

on /ɒn/ *preposition, adverb* **1** a word that shows where ସ୍ଥାନ ସୂଚକ ଶବ୍ଦ; ଠାରେ, ଉପରେ, ରେ *Your book is on the table.* **2** a word that shows when ସମୟ ସୂଚକ ଶବ୍ଦ; ରେ, ଦିନ *My birthday is on 6 May.* ○ *I'll see you on Monday.* **3** about ବିଷୟକ, ସମ୍ବନ୍ଧୀୟ *a book on cars* **4** working; being used କାର୍ଯ୍ୟକାରୀ ରହିବା *Is the light on or off?* ✪ ବିପରୀତ **off 5** using something ରେ ଦ୍ୱାରା *I spoke to Malati on the telephone.* **6** covering your body ପିନ୍ଧିବା *Put your coat on.*

on and on without stopping ଅବିରତ ଭାବେ

once /wʌns/ *adverb* **1** one time ଥରେମାତ୍ର *I've only been to Shimla once.* **2** at some time in the past ଏକଦା, ଅତୀତର ଏକ ସମୟରେ *This house was once a school.*

at once 1 immediately; now ବର୍ତ୍ତମାନ *Come here at once!* **2** at the same time ଏକା ସମୟରେ, ଏକାବେଳେ *I can't do two things at once!*

once again, once more again, as before ଆହୁରି ଥରେ ଆଉଥରେ *Can you explain it to me once more?*

once or twice a few times; not often ଥରେ ଦି'ଥର *I've only met them once or twice.*

once *conjunction* as soon as କ୍ଷଣି *Once you've finished your homework, you can go out.*

one¹ /wʌn/ *noun, adjective* **1** the number 1 ୧ ସଂଖ୍ୟା, ଏକ; ଜଣେ *One and one make two.* ○ *Only one person spoke.* **2** a ଏକ *I saw her one day last week.*

one by one first one, then the next, etc.; one at a time ଜଣକ ପରେ ଜଣେ, ଗୋଟାକ ପରେ ଆଉ ଗୋଟିଏ *Please come in one by one.*

one² /wʌn/ *pronoun* a word that you say instead of repeating the name of a person or thing you have just said ଗୋଟାଏ, ଗୋଟେ *I've got some bananas. Do you want one?*

one another words that show that somebody does the same thing as another person ପରସ୍ପର *Prateek and Tarun looked at one another.*

one³ /wʌn/ *pronoun* any person; a person ଯେକେହି, କୌଣସି ବ୍ୟକ୍ତି *One can take a train to Agra.* ✪ ଏ ଜାଗାରେ 'one' ର ବ୍ୟବହାର ସାହିତ୍ୟିକ। ଆମେ ସାଧାରଣତଃ **you** ବ୍ୟବହାର କରୁ।

oneself /wʌnˈself/ *pronoun* **1** a word that shows the same person as 'one' in a sentence ସ୍ୱୟଂ, ନିଜେ *to hurt oneself* **2** a word that makes 'one' stronger ଶବ୍ଦକୁ ଗୁରୁତ୍ୱ ଦେବା ପାଇଁ ବ୍ୟବହୃତ ଶବ୍ଦ 'one'

by oneself 1 alone; without other people ଏକା ନିଜେ ନିଜେ **2** without help ଅନ୍ୟର ସାହାଯ୍ୟ ବିନା

onion /ˈʌnjən/ *noun* a round vegetable with a strong taste and smell ପିଆଜ ⇨ ଚିତ୍ର ପାଇଁ **vegetable** ଦେଖନ୍ତୁ।

onlooker /ˈɒnlʊkə(r)/ *noun* a person who watches something happen but does not take part in it ଦେଖଣାହାରୀ, ଦର୍ଶକ *None of the onlookers offered to help the accident victim.*

only¹ /ˈəʊnli/ *adjective* with no others of the same kind ଏକମାତ୍ର *She's the only girl in her class—all the other students are boys.*

only² /ˈəʊnli/ *adverb* nobody or nothing else; no more than କେବଳ, ମାତ୍ର, ମୋଟେ *I invited twenty people to the party, but only five came.*

onto, on to /ˈɒntə; ˈɒntu/ *preposition* a word that is used with verbs to express movement on or to a particular place or position ସ୍ଥାନକୁ, ଉପରକୁ *The cat jumped onto the table.*

onwards /ˈɒnwədz/, **onward** /ˈɒnwəd/ *adverb* **1** continuing from a particular time ନିର୍ଦ୍ଦିଷ୍ଟ ସମୟଠାରୁ ଚାଲୁରଖିବା, କୌଣସି ସମୟଠାରୁ, ପରେ *I shall be at home from eight o'clock onwards.* **2** forward ଆଗକୁ *Inspite* *of the heavy rain we drove onwards towards the hill.*

ooze /uːz/ *verb* (**oozes, oozing, oozed**) flow out slowly ଧୀରେ ଧୀରେ ଝରିବା *Blood oozed out from the wound.*

opaque /əʊˈpeɪk/ *adjective* that you cannot see through ଅସ୍ୱଚ୍ଛ, ଯାହା ମଧ୍ୟ ଦେଇ ଅନ୍ୟ ପଟ ଦିଶେ ନାହିଁ *opaque glass* ➪ **transparent** ଦେଖନ୍ତୁ।

open¹ /ˈəʊpən/ *adjective* **1** not closed, so that people or things can go in or out ଖୋଲା, ଉନ୍ମୁକ୍ତ, ମେଲା *Leave the windows open.* **2** not closed or covered, so that you can see inside ଖୋଲା, ଅନାବୃତ *an open box* **3** ready for people to go in (କାମ ପାଇଁ) ଖୋଲା, ଉନ୍ମୁକ୍ତ *The bank is open from 9 a.m. to 5 p.m.* **4** with not many buildings, trees, etc. ଖୋଲାମେଲା *open fields*

in the open air outside ଘର ବାହାରେ ଖୋଲାଜାଗାରେ *We had our lunch in the open air.*

open² /ˈəʊpən/ *verb* (**opens, opening, opened**) **1** move so that people or things can go in, out or through ଖୋଲି ଦେବା, ମେଲାକରି ଦେବା *It was hot, so I opened a window.* **2** move so that something is not closed or covered ଖୋଲିବା *Open your eyes!* **3** be ready for people to use; start ଖୋଲିବା; ଆରମ୍ଭ ହେବା *Banks don't open on Sundays.* ✪ ବିପରୀତ **close²** ବା **shut¹**

open-air *adjective* outside ଖୋଲା–ଜାଗାରେ ହେଉଥିବା *an open-air concert*

opener /ˈəʊpnə(r)/ *noun* a tool that you use for opening tins or bottles ବୋତଲ ବା ଠିପି ଖୋଲିବା ଉପକରଣ ଖୋଲିବା, ଠିପି ଖୋଲା *a bottle-opener*

bottle-opener

opening /ˈəʊpnɪŋ/ *noun* **1** a hole or space in something where people or things can go in and out; a hole ଫାଙ୍କ କଣା *The sheep got out of the field through an opening in the fence.* **2** the beginning or the start of something ଆରମ୍ଭ, ଉନ୍ମୋଚନ *the opening of the new theatre*

openly /ˈəʊpənli/ *adverb* not secretly; without trying to hide anything ଖୋଲାଖୋଲି ଭାବରେ, କିଛି ନ ଲୁଚାଇ

operate /ˈɒpəreɪt/ *verb* (**operates, operating, operated**) **1** work or make something work କାର୍ଯ୍ୟକାରୀ କରିବା *How do you operate this machine?* **2** cut a person's body to take out or mend a part inside ଦେହରେ ଅସ୍ତ୍ରୋପଚାର କରିବା *The doctor will operate on her leg tomorrow.*

operation /ˌɒpəˈreɪʃn/ *noun* **1** the process of cutting a person's body to take out or mend a part inside ଅସ୍ତ୍ରୋପଚାର **2** something that happens, which needs a lot of people or careful planning ବହୁ ଲୋକଙ୍କର ମିଳିତ କାର୍ଯ୍ୟାନୁଷ୍ଠାନ *a military operation*

operator /ˈɒpəreɪtə(r)/ *noun* **1** a person who makes a machine work ଯନ୍ତ୍ରଚାଳକ *She's a computer operator.* **2** a person who helps people to make and receive telephone calls ଟେଲିଫୋନ୍‌ରେ କଥାବାର୍ତ୍ତା ପାଇଁ ସଂଯୋଗ କରୁଥିବା ବ୍ୟକ୍ତି, ଟେଲିଫୋନ୍ ସଂଯୋଜକ

opinion /əˈpɪnjən/ *noun* what you think about something or someone ମତ, ମତାମତ *In my opinion, she's wrong.*

opponent /əˈpəʊnənt/ *noun* a person that you fight or argue with, or play a game against ପ୍ରତିଦ୍ୱନ୍ଦୀ, ପ୍ରତିପକ୍ଷ *The team beat their opponents easily.*

opportunity /ˌɒpəˈtjuːnəti/ *noun* (*plural* **opportunities**) a time when you can do something that you want to do; a chance ସୁଯୋଗ, ମୌକା

oppose /əˈpəʊz/ *verb* (**opposes, opposing, opposed**) try to stop or change something because you do not like it ବିରୋଧ କରିବା *A lot of people opposed the new law.*

opposite[1] /ˈɒpəzɪt/ *adjective, adverb, preposition* **1** across from where somebody or something is; on the other side ଆରପଟର, ଆର ପଟେ ଥିବା, ଅପର ପକ୍ଷରେ ଥିବା *The bank is opposite the post office.* **2** as different as possible ବିପରୀତ *North is the opposite direction to south.*

opposite[2] /ˈɒpəzɪt/ *noun* a word or thing that is as different as possible from another word or thing ବିପରୀତ *'Big' is the opposite of 'small'.*

opposition /ˌɒpəˈzɪʃn/ *noun* (*no plural*) the act of disagreeing with something and trying to stop it ବିରୁଦ୍ଧାଚରଣ, ବିରୋଧ *There was a lot of opposition to the plan.*

oppress /əˈpres/ *verb* (**oppresses, oppressing, oppressed**) treat a group of people in a cruel and unjust way and not give them the same freedom and rights as others ନିର୍ଯ୍ୟାତନା ଦେବା *The tribals were oppressed by the government for years.*

oppression /əˈpreʃn/ *noun* (*no plural*) ନିର୍ଯ୍ୟାଦନା *victims of oppression*

optimistic /ˌɒptɪˈmɪstɪk/ *adjective* if you are optimistic, you think that good things will happen ଶୁଭଦର୍ଶୀ, ଆଶାବାନ୍ *I'm optimistic about winning.* ✪ ବିପରୀତ **pessimistic**

option /ˈɒpʃn/ *noun* a thing that you can choose ଯାହା ବଛାଯାଇପାରେ, ଉପାୟ, ପନ୍ଥା *If you're going to Indore, there are two options—you can go by train or by plane.*

or /ɔː(r)/ *conjunction* **1** a word that tells you that you can choose one from among different things ବା, କିଂବା, ନା *Is it blue or green?* ○ *You can have soup, salad or sandwiches.* **2** if not, then ନହେଲେ *Go now, or you'll be late.*

oral /ˈɔːrəl/ *adjective* spoken, not written କଥିତ *an oral test in English*

orange[1] /ˈɔːrɪndʒ/ *noun* a round fruit with a colour between red and yellow, and a thick skin କମଳା (ଲେମ୍ବୁ) *orange juice* ➪ ଚିତ୍ର ପାଇଁ **fruit** ଦେଖନ୍ତୁ।

orange² /ˈɔːrɪndʒ/ *adjective* with a colour that is between red and yellow କମଳା ରଙ୍ଗର *orange paint*

orange *noun* କମଳା ରଙ୍ଗ *Orange is my favourite colour.*

orbit /ˈɔːbɪt/ *noun* the path of one thing that is moving round another thing in space ଗ୍ରହକକ୍ଷ, ଉପଗ୍ରହ ଇତ୍ୟାଦିର ପରିଭ୍ରମଣ ପଥ

orbit *verb* (**orbits, orbiting, orbited**) move round something in space ପ୍ରଦକ୍ଷିଣ କରିବା, ଚାରିପଟେ ଘୂରିବୁଲିବା *The spacecraft is orbiting the moon.*

orchard /ˈɔːtʃəd/ *noun* a place where a lot of fruit trees are grown ବଗିଚା, ଉଦ୍ୟାନ

orchestra /ˈɔːkɪstrə/ *noun* a big group of people who play different musical instruments together ବାଦକଦଳ, ବାଦ୍ୟବୃନ୍ଦ

order¹ /ˈɔːdə(r)/ *noun* **1** (*no plural*) the way that you place people or things together (ଲୋକ, ପଦାର୍ଥ, ବିଷୟ ଇତ୍ୟାଦିର) କ୍ରମ *The names are in alphabetical order.* **2** (*no plural*) when everything is in the right place or everybody is doing the right thing ଶୃଙ୍ଖଳିତ ଅବସ୍ଥା *Our teacher likes order in the classroom.* **3** (*plural* **orders**) words that tell somebody to do something ଆଦେଶ *Soldiers must always obey orders.* **4** (*plural* **orders**) asking somebody to make, send or bring you something କୌଣସି ପଦାର୍ଥ ଯୋଗାଇବା ପାଇଁ ନିର୍ଦ୍ଦେଶ ବା ବରାଦ *The waiter came and took our order.*

in order to so that you can do something ପାଇଁ, ଉଦ୍ଦେଶ୍ୟରେ *We arrived early in order to buy our tickets.*

out of order not working ଅକାମୀ, ଖରାପ *I couldn't ring you—the phone was out of order.*

order² /ˈɔːdə(r)/ *verb* (**orders, ordering, ordered**) **1** tell somebody that they must do something ଆଦେଶ ଦେବା *The doctor ordered me to stay in bed.* **2** say that you want something to be made, sent, brought, etc. କିଛି ଯୋଗାଇବା ପାଇଁ ବରାଦ ଦେବା *When the waiter came, I ordered an omelette.*

ordinal number *noun* a number that tells you the order or position of something in a series, for example first, second, third, etc. ସଂଖ୍ୟାର କ୍ରମିକ ସ୍ଥାନ (ପ୍ରଥମ, ଦ୍ୱିତୀୟ, ତୃତୀୟ ଇତ୍ୟାଦି) ⇨ **cardinal number** ଦେଖନ୍ତୁ।

ordinance /ˈɔːdɪnəns/ *noun* a special order given by the government or ruler କର୍ତ୍ତୃପକ୍ଷଙ୍କ ଆଦେଶ, ଅଧ୍ୟାଦେଶ

ordinary /ˈɔːdnri/ *adjective* normal; not special or unusual ସାଧାରଣ

ordnance /ˈɔːdnəns/ *noun* (*no plural*) military supplies and materials କମାଣ ଓ ସାମରିକ ଦ୍ରବ୍ୟ, ଯୁଦ୍ଧ ସରଞ୍ଜାମ *an ordnance depot*

ore /ɔː(r)/ *noun* rock or earth from which you get metal ଖଣିଜ ପଥର (ଯେଉଁଥିରୁ ଧାତୁ ବାହାର କରାଯାଏ) *iron ore*

organ /ˈɔːgən/ *noun* **1** a part of the body that has a special purpose, for example the heart or the liver ନିର୍ଦ୍ଦିଷ୍ଟ କାମ କରିବା ପାଇଁ ଥିବା ଶରୀରର ଅଙ୍ଗପ୍ରତ୍ୟଙ୍ଗ

2 (ମଧ୍ୟ **pipe organ**) a big musical instrument like a piano. Sounds are produced by air forced through pipes ହର୍ମୋନିଅମ୍ ଠାରୁ ବଡ଼ ବାଦ୍ୟ ଯନ୍ତ୍ର ଯେଉଁଥିରେ ବଂଶୀପରି ନଳୀମାନଙ୍କ ପେଡାଲ ଚାଳନ ଦ୍ୱାରା ପବନ ପ୍ରବେଶ କରାଇ ବିଭିନ୍ନ ସ୍ୱର ବାହାର କରାଯାଏ *She plays the organ in church.*

organic /ɔːˈgænɪk/ *adjective* grown in a natural way, without using **fertilizers** or **pesticides** କୃତ୍ରିମ ସାର ବା ପୋକ ମରା ଔଷଧ ନ ଦେଇ ପ୍ରାକୃତିକ ଭାବେ ଉତ୍ପାଦିତ (ଖାଦ୍ୟପଦାର୍ଥ) *organic vegetables*

organism /ˈɔːgənɪzm/ *noun* a tiny living thing that you can see only with the help of a **microscope** ଅତିସୂକ୍ଷ୍ମ ଜୀବ, ଅଣୁଜୀବ, (ଯାହା ଅଣୁବୀକ୍ଷଣ ଯନ୍ତ୍ର ସାହାଯ୍ୟରେ ଦେଖିହୁଏ)

organization /ˌɔːgənaɪˈzeɪʃn/ *noun* a group of people who work together for a special purpose ସଂଗଠିତ ସଂସ୍ଥା *He works for an organization that helps old people.*

organize /ˈɔːgənaɪz/ *verb* (**organizes, organizing, organized**) plan or arrange something ସଙ୍ଗଠିତ କରିବା, ଯୋଗାଡ଼ କରିବା *Our teacher has organized a visit to the museum.*

origin /ˈɒrɪdʒɪn/ *noun* the beginning; the start of something ପ୍ରାରମ୍ଭ *origin of the universe*

original /əˈrɪdʒənl/ *adjective* **1** first; earliest ପ୍ରଥମରୁ ବିଦ୍ୟମାନ ଥିବା; ସର୍ବପ୍ରଥମ *I have the car now, but my sister was the original owner.* **2** new and different ନୂତନ ଧରଣର *His poems are very original.* **3** real, not copied ମୂଳସ୍ରଷ୍ଟା ସୃଷ୍ଟି କରିଥିବା *original paintings*

originally /əˈrɪdʒənəli/ *adverb* in the beginning; at first ପ୍ରାରମ୍ଭରେ, ପ୍ରଥମେ *This building was originally the home of a rich family, but now it's a hotel.*

ornament /ˈɔːnəmənt/ *noun* a thing that we have because it is beautiful, not because it is useful ଗହଣା

orphan /ˈɔːfn/ *noun* a child whose mother and father are dead ବାପା ମା ଛେଉଣ୍ଡ ପିଲା, ଅନାଥ ପିଲା

orphanage /ˈɔːfənɪdʒ/ *noun* a home for children whose parents are dead ଅନାଥାଶ୍ରମ

orthodox /ˈɔːθədɒks/ *adjective* **1** followed or accepted by most people; usual ସାଧାରଣ ଭାବେ ପ୍ରଚଳିତ ବା ଅନୁମୋଦିତ *orthodox theories on education* **2** firmly believing in and practising old and traditional customs, ceremonies, etc. ପରମ୍ପରାଗତ, ପୁରାତନ ନିତି ନିୟମ ମାନୁଥିବା *orthodox Hindus*

ostrich

ostrich /ˈɒstrɪtʃ/ *noun* (*plural* **ostriches**) a very big bird from Africa. Ostriches have very long legs and can run fast, but they cannot fly ଓଟପକ୍ଷୀ

other /ˈʌðə(r)/ *adjective, pronoun* as well as or different from the one or ones you have just talked about ଅନ୍ୟ, ଅପର *I can only find one shoe. Have you seen the other one?* ○ *Ruchi and Prachi arrived at nine o'clock, but the others were late.*

other than except; apart from ଛଡ଼ା, ବ୍ୟତୀତ *I haven't told anybody other than you.*

the other day not many days ago ଅଳ୍ପ ଦିନ ତଳେ *I saw your brother the other day.*

otherwise /ˈʌðəwaɪz/ *adverb* in all other ways ଅନ୍ୟ ସବୁ ବିଷୟରେ *The house is a bit small, but otherwise it's very nice.*

otherwise *conjunction* if not ନ ହେଲେ *Hurry up, otherwise you'll be late.*

otter /ˈɒtə(r)/ *noun* a small furry animal with webbed feet that lives in rivers and eats fish ଓଧ

ouch /aʊtʃ/ *interjection* you say 'ouch' when you suddenly feel pain ହଠାତ୍ ଯନ୍ତ୍ରଣା ଅନୁଭବ କଲେ କୁହାଯାଉଥିବା ଶବ୍ଦ *Ouch! That hurts!*

ought to /ˈɔːt tə ; ˈɔːt tu/ *modal verb* **1** words that you use to tell or ask somebody what is the right thing to do ଉଚିତ୍ *It's late—you ought to go home.* **2** words that you use to say what you think will happen or what you think is true ଉଚିତ୍; ଆଶା କରାଯାଏ *That film ought to be good.* ➪ **modal verb** ପାଇଁ ଟିପ୍ପଣୀ ଦେଖନ୍ତୁ ।

our /ɑː(r) ; ˈaʊə(r)/ *adjective* of us ଆମ, ଆମ୍ଭର *This is our house.*

ours /ɑːz ; ˈaʊəz/ *pronoun* something that belongs to us ଆମ *Your car is the same as ours.*

ourselves /ɑːˈselvz ; aʊəˈselvz/ *pronoun (plural)* **1** a word that shows the same people that you have just talked about ନିଜ ପାଇଁ *We made ourselves some coffee.* **2** a word that makes 'we' stronger, 'we' ଶବ୍ଦକୁ ପ୍ରାଧାନ୍ୟ ଦେବା ପାଇଁ କୁହାଯାଉଥିବା ଶବ୍ଦ *We built the house ourselves.*

by ourselves **1** alone; without other people ଆମେ ନିଜେ; ଅନ୍ୟର ସାହାଯ୍ୟ, ନେଇ, ଅନ୍ୟଙ୍କୁ ନ ନେଇ *We went on holiday by ourselves.* **2** without help ନିଜେ, କାହାରି ସାହାଯ୍ୟ ବିନା *We finished the work all by ourselves.*

out /aʊt/ *adverb, preposition* **1** away from the inside of a place ବାହାରକୁ *When you go out, please close the door.* ✪ ବିପରୀତ **in**[1] **2** not at home or not in the place where you work ବାହାରକୁ *I phoned Shashi but he was out.* **3** not burning or shining ନିର୍ବାପିତ ବା ଲିଭିବା ଅବସ୍ଥାରେ *The fire went out.* **4** in a loud voice ଉଚ୍ଚସ୍ୱରରେ *She cried out in pain.* **5** if you are out of a game, you can no longer play (ଖେଳରୁ) ବାହାରି ଯାଉଥିବା *The batsman got out after scoring 225 runs.*

outdoor /ˈaʊtdɔː(r)/ *adjective* done or used outside a building ଘର ବାହାରେ ଖୋଲାଜାଗାରେ ସଂଘଟିତ *Football and cricket are outdoor games.* ✪ ବିପରୀତ **indoor**

outdoors /ˌaʊtˈdɔːz/ *adverb* outside a building ଘର ବାହାରେ *In summer, we sometimes eat outdoors.* ✪ ବିପରୀତ **indoors**

outer /ˈaʊtə(r)/ *adjective* on the outside; far from the centre ବାହାର ପଟର, ବାହ୍ୟ *The outer walls of the house have small windows.* ✪ ବିପରୀତ **inner**

outermost /ˈaʊtəməʊst/ *adjective* furthest from the centre କେନ୍ଦ୍ର ଠାରୁ ସବୁଠୁଁ ଦୂରବର୍ତ୍ତୀ *the outermost planet of the solar system* ✪ ବିପରୀତ **innermost**

outgoing /ˈaʊtgəʊɪŋ/ *adjective* going away from a place କୌଣସି ସ୍ଥାନରୁ ଅନ୍ୟଆଡ଼କୁ ଯାଉଥିବା *outgoing flights* ○ *outgoing calls* ✪ ବିପରୀତ **incoming**

outing /ˈaʊtɪŋ/ *noun* a short journey to enjoy yourself ପ୍ରମୋଦ ଭ୍ରମଣ *We went on an outing to the zoo last Saturday.*

outline /ˈaʊtlaɪn/ *noun* a line that shows the shape or edge of something କେବଳ ସୀମାରେଖାର ନକ୍ସା, ବାହ୍ୟ ସୀମାରେଖା *It was dark, but we could see the outline of the castle on the hill.*

out of *preposition* **1** words that show where from ରୁ, ଠାରୁ, ଭିତରୁ *She took a cake out of the box.* ✪ ବିପରୀତ **into 1** **2** not in ବାହାର *Fish can't live out of water.* **3** by using something; from ଦ୍ୱାରା, ବ୍ୟବହାର କରି *He made a table out of some old pieces of wood.*

output /ˈaʊtpʊt/ *noun* (*no plural*) **1** the number or amount of things produced by a machine, factory, person, etc. ଯନ୍ତ୍ର, କାରଖାନା, ବ୍ୟକ୍ତି ଇତ୍ୟାଦି ଦ୍ୱାରା ପ୍ରସ୍ତୁତ ସାମଗ୍ରୀସମୂହ **2** the information produced by a computer କମ୍ପ୍ୟୁଟର ଦ୍ୱାରା ପ୍ରଦତ୍ତ ବୃତ୍ତାନ୍ତ *data output*

outrageous /aʊtˈreɪdʒəs/ *adjective* very shocking and unacceptable ହତବାକ୍ କଲା ପରି ଅସମୀଚୀନ *Sita says the most outrageous things sometimes.*

outside¹ /ˌaʊtˈsaɪd/ *noun* the part of something that is away from the middle ବାହାର ପଟ *The outside of a pear is green or yellow and the inside is white.* ✪ ବିପରୀତ **inside¹**

outside² /ˌaʊtˈsaɪd/ *adjective* away from the middle of something ବାହାର, ବାହାର ପଟର *the outside walls of a house* ✪ ବିପରୀତ **inside²**

outside³ /ˌaʊtˈsaɪd/ *preposition, adverb* not in; in or to a place that is not inside a building ବାହାର, ବାହାର ପଟେ *I left my bicycle outside the shop.* ✪ ବିପରୀତ **inside³**

outsider /ˌaʊtˈsaɪdə(r)/ *noun* someone who does not belong to your home, group or country ବାହାର ଲୋକ, ଅପର ବ୍ୟକ୍ତି *Although she has been living in Pune for four years, she feels like an outsider.*

outskirts /ˈaʊtskɜːts/ *noun* (*no singular*) the parts of a town or city that are far from the centre ପ୍ରାନ୍ତ, ଉପାନ୍ତ *The airport is on the outskirts of the city.*

outstanding /aʊtˈstændɪŋ/ *adjective* very good; much better than others ଖୁବ୍ ଭଲ, ଅତି ଉତ୍ତମ, ଅନ୍ୟ ମାନଙ୍କ ଠାରୁ ଭଲ *Her work is outstanding.*

outward /ˈaʊtwəd/, **outwards** /ˈaʊtwədz/ *adverb* towards the outside ବାହାରପଟକୁ *The windows open outwards.* ✪ ବିପରୀତ **inward** ବା **inwards**

oval /ˈəʊvl/ *noun* a shape like an egg ଅଣ୍ଡା ପରି ଆକାର ➪ ଚିତ୍ର ପାଇଁ **shape** ଦେଖନ୍ତୁ ।

oval *adjective* with a shape like an egg ଅଣ୍ଡା ଆକାରର *an oval mirror*

oven /ˈʌvn/ *noun* a machine shaped like a metal box with a door, inside which you can cook food ଦ୍ୱାର ଥିବା ଧାତୁ ବାକ୍ସ, ଯାହା ଭିତରେ ଖାଦ୍ୟ ରନ୍ଧା ଯାଇପାରେ ➪ **microwave** ମଧ୍ୟ ଦେଖନ୍ତୁ ।

over /əʊvə(r)/ *adverb*, *preposition* **1** above something; higher than something ଉପରେ, ଉର୍ଦ୍ଧ୍ୱରେ *A plane flew over our heads.* **2** on somebody or something so that it covers them ଉପରେ *She put a blanket over the sleeping child.* **3** across; to the other side of something ଆରପଟକୁ *The dog jumped over the wall.* **4** so that the other side is on top ଓଲଟାଇ *Turn the cassette over.* **5** more than a number, price, etc. ଅଧିକ, ବେଶି *She lived in Patna for over twenty years.* **6** a word that shows that you repeat something ଥରକୁ ଥର ବାରମ୍ବାର *He said the same thing over and over again.* **7** finished ଶେଷ, ସମାପ୍ତ *My exams are over.*

all over in every part ଚାରିଆଡ଼େ *She travels all over the world.*

over here here ଏଇଠି, ଏଠିକି *Come over here!*

over there there ସେଠି, ସେଠିକି *Go over there and see if you can help.*

over- *prefix*
over- ବହୁ ଶବ୍ଦର ପୂର୍ବରୁ ଲଗାଇଲେ 'ଅତି ବେଶି' ଅର୍ଥ ବୁଝାଇବ, ଯଥା — **overeat** = ଅତି ବେଶି ଖାଇବା **oversleep** = ଅତିବେଶି ଶୋଇବା

overall /ˌəʊvərˈɔ:l/ *adjective* of everything; total ସମୁଦାୟ, ମୋଟ *The overall cost of the repairs will be about Rs 4,500.*

overall *adverb* ମୋଟରେ, ସବୁ ମିଶାଇ *How much will it cost overall?*

overalls /ˈəʊvərɔ:lz/ *noun* (*plural*) a piece of clothing that covers your legs, body and arms. You wear it over your other clothes to keep them clean when you are working ଦେହ, ହାତ ଓ ଗୋଡ଼ ଘୋଡ଼ାଇ ପାରୁଥିବା ବସ୍ତ୍ର (ଜାମା ପଟା ଉପରେ ଏହାକୁ ପିନ୍ଧିଲେ ଜାମା ପଟା ସଫା ରହେ)

overboard /ˈəʊvəbɔ:d/ *adverb* over the side of a boat and into the water ଜାହାଜରୁ ପାଣିକୁ *She fell overboard.*

overcoat /ˈəʊvəkəʊt/ *noun* a long thick coat that you wear in cold weather ଶୀତ ଦିନେ ପିନ୍ଧା ଯାଉଥିବା ଲମ୍ବା କୋଟ୍

overcome /ˌəʊvəˈkʌm/ *verb* (**overcomes, overcoming, overcame, has overcome**) find an answer to a difficult thing in your life; control something ସମ୍ପୂର୍ଣ୍ଣ ଭାବେ ଆୟତ୍ତ କରିବା, ଜୟଲାଭ କରିବା *He overcame his fear of flying.*

overcrowded /ˌəʊvəˈkraʊdɪd/ *adjective* too full of people or things ଅତି ଭିଡ଼ ହୋଇଥିବା *The trains are overcrowded during the summer months.*

overdue /ˌəʊvəˈdjuː/ *adjective* late ଯଥା ସମୟରୁ ବିଳମ୍ବ ହୋଇଥିବା *Our landlady is angry because the rent is overdue.*

overflow /ˌəʊvəˈfləʊ/ *verb* (**overflows, overflowing, overflowed**) come over the edge of something because there is too much in it ପ୍ରାନ୍ତରୁଉଛୁଳି ପଡ଼ିବା *After the rain, the river overflowed its banks.*

overhead /ˈəʊvəhed/ *adjective* above your head ମୁଣ୍ଡଠାରୁ ଊର୍ଦ୍ଧ୍ୱରେ ଥିବା *an overhead light*

overjoyed /ˌəʊvəˈdʒɔɪd/ *adjective* very happy ଅତି ଆନନ୍ଦିତ *She was overjoyed to hear that her son had won the competition.*

overlap /ˌəʊvəˈlæp/ *verb* (**overlaps, overlapping, overlapped**) when two things overlap, part of one thing covers part of the other thing ଗୋଟିଏ ଜିନିଷର ପ୍ରାନ୍ତ ପାଖ ଜିନିଷର ପ୍ରାନ୍ତ ଉପରେ ମାଡ଼ି ହୋଇ ରହିବା *The tiles on the roof overlap.*

overlook /ˌəʊvəˈlʊk/ *verb* (**overlooks, overlooking, overlooked**) not see or notice something ଠିକ୍ ଭାବେ ଦେଖି ନ ପାରିବା *He overlooked a spelling mistake.*

overnight /ˌəʊvəˈnaɪt/ *adjective, adverb* for or during the night ରାତ୍ରି କାଳୀନ, ରାତାରାତି *an overnight journey*

overpower /ˌəʊvəˈpaʊə(r)/ *verb* (**overpowers, overpowering, overpowered**) defeat someone using your strength ବଳ ପ୍ରୟୋଗ ଦ୍ୱାରା ଆୟତ୍ତ କରିବା, ପରାସ୍ତ କରିବା *The wrestler overpowered his opponent in just a couple of minutes.*

overripe /ˌəʊvəˈraɪp/ *adjective* too ripe ଅତିବେଶି ପାଚିଲା

oversleep /ˌəʊvəˈsliːp/ *verb* (**oversleeps, oversleeping, overslept** /ˌəʊvəˈslept/, **has overslept**) sleep too long and not wake up at the right time ନିର୍ଦ୍ଦିଷ୍ଟ ସମୟ ଅପେକ୍ଷା ବେଶି ସମୟ ଶୋଇବା *I overslept and was late for work.*

overtake /ˌəʊvəˈteɪk/ *verb* (**overtakes, overtaking, overtook** /ˌəʊvəˈtʊk/, **has overtaken** /ˌəʊvəˈteɪkən/) go past somebody or something that is going more slowly ପଛରୁ ଆସି ବ୍ୟକ୍ତି ବା ଗାଡ଼ିକୁ ଟପିଯିବା *The car overtook a bus.*

overtime /ˈəʊvətaɪm/ *noun* (*no plural*) extra time that you spend at work ନିର୍ଦ୍ଦିଷ୍ଟ ସମୟରୁ ଅଧିକ କାମ *I have done a lot of overtime this week.*

overweight /ˌəʊvəˈweɪt/ *adjective* too heavy or fat ଅତିଭାରୀ ବା ମୋଟା *The doctor said I was overweight and that I should eat less.* ✪ ବିପରୀତ **underweight**

overwhelm /ˌəʊvəˈwelm/ *verb* (**overwhelms, overwhelming, overwhelmed**) **1** if you are overwhelmed by something, you feel such strong emotions about it that you do not know how to react to or deal with it ଭାରାକ୍ରାନ୍ତ କରିବା, ଅଭିଭୂତ କରିବା *I felt completely overwhelmed by their kindness.* **2** defeat an enemy completely ଶତ୍ରୁକୁ ସମ୍ପୂର୍ଣ୍ଣ ରୂପେରେ ପରାସ୍ତ କରିବା

overwhelming /ˌəʊvəˈwelmɪŋ/ *adjective* so strong in effect that you do not know how to react to or deal with it ବହୁଳ, ବହୁସଂଖ୍ୟକ ଲୋକଙ୍କର, ଅତିବେଶି, ସମ୍ଭାଳି ନହେଲା ପରି *an overwhelming feeling of loneliness*

ow /aʊ/ *interjection* you say 'ow' when you suddenly feel pain ହଠାତ୍ ଯନ୍ତ୍ରଣା ପାଇଲେ କୁହାଯାଉଥିବା ଶବ୍ଦ *Ow! You're standing on my foot.*

owe /əʊ/ *verb* (**owes, owing, owed**) **1** have to pay money to somebody because they have given you something ଉଧାରଗ୍ରସ୍ତ ରହିବା, ଋଣଗ୍ରସ୍ତ ରହିବା, ଋଣି ରହିବା *I lent you Rs 50 last week and Rs 50 the week before, so you owe me Rs 100.* **2** feel that you have something because of what another person has done for you କୌଣସି ବ୍ୟକ୍ତିଙ୍କ ପ୍ରତି କୃତଜ୍ଞ ରହିବା *She owes her life to the man who pulled her out of the river.*

owl /aʊl/ *noun* a bird that flies at night and eats small animals ପେଚା ➪ ଚିତ୍ର ପାଇଁ **birds** ଦେଖନ୍ତୁ।

own¹ /əʊn/ *adjective, pronoun* you use 'own' to say that something belongs to a person or thing ନିଜର *Is that your own camera or did you borrow it?*

> ✪ ମନେ ରଖନ୍ତୁ! 'own' ଶବ୍ଦର ପ୍ରୟୋଗ 'a' ବା 'an' ପରେ କରାଯାଏ ନାହିଁ। କହିବା ଭୁଲ ହେବ। *'I would like an own room'* ଆପଣ କହିବେ *'I would like my own room'* ବା *I would like a room of my own'.*

of your own that belongs to you and not to anybody else ନିଜର, ନିଜସ୍ୱ *I want a house of my own.*

on your own 1 alone ଏକା, ଏକାକୀ, ଏକୁଟିଆ *She lives on her own.* **2** without help ଅନ୍ୟର ସାହାଯ୍ୟ ନ ନେଇ *I can't move this box on my own—can you help me?*

own² /əʊn/ *verb* (**owns, owning, owned**) have something that is yours ନିଜ ସମ୍ପତ୍ତି ଭାବରେ ରଖିବା *We don't own this flat—it's rented.*

owner /ˈəʊnə(r)/ *noun* a person who has something ମାଲିକ *Who is the owner of that red car?*

ox /ɒks/ *noun* (*plural* **oxen** /ˈɒksn/) a male cow. Oxen are sometimes used to pull or carry heavy things on farms ବଳଦ

oxygen /ˈɒksɪdʒən/ *noun* (*no plural*) a gas in the air. Plants and animals need oxygen to live ରଙ୍ଗ, ଗନ୍ଧ ଓ ସ୍ୱାଦ ବିହୀନ ଜୀବନ ସହାୟକ ଅମ୍ଳଜାନ ବାଷ୍ପ

oyster /ˈɔɪstə(r)/ *noun* a sea creature with a soft body and a hard shell that is divided in two parts.

Some oysters produce **pearls** inside their shells ଶୁକ୍ତି, ଶାମୁକା (ଯାହା ଭିତରେ ବେଳେ ବେଳେ ମୁକ୍ତା ମିଳେ)

ozone layer *noun* (*no plural*) a layer of ozone gas that is present in the earth's **atmosphere**. It protects us from the harmful rays of the sun ବାୟୁ ମଣ୍ଡଳ ଉପର ଭାଗରେ ଥିବା ଓଜୋନ୍ ବାଷ୍ପର ପରସ୍ତ (ଯାହା ପୃଥିବୀକୁ ହାନିକାରକ ରଶ୍ମିରୁ ରକ୍ଷା କରେ)

P p

pace /peɪs/ *noun* **1** a step ପାହୁଣ୍ଡ, ପଦକ୍ଷେପ *Take two paces forward!* **2** how fast you do something or how fast something happens କାମ କରିବାର ବା ଘଟଣାର ବେଗ *The race began at a fast pace.*

keep pace with somebody or **something** go as fast as somebody or something ଅନ୍ୟ ସହ ପାଦକୁ ପାଦ ମିଳାଇ ଚାଲିବା ବା ଏକା ବେଗରେ ଯିବା *She couldn't keep pace with the other runners.*

pack¹ /pæk/ *noun* **1** a group of things that you buy together ଗୋଛା, ପ୍ୟାକେଟ୍ *I bought a pack of five exercise books.* **2** a group of animals that hunt together ଏକାଠି ଶିକାର କରୁଥିବା ପଶୁଦଳ *a pack of wolves*

pack² /pæk/ *verb* (**packs, packing, packed**) **1** put things into a bag or suitcase before you go somewhere ଜିନିଷ ପତ୍ର ଏକାଠି କରି ବ୍ୟାଗ୍ ବା ସୁଟ୍‌କେସ୍‌ରେ ଭର୍ତ୍ତି କରିବା *Have you packed your suitcase?* **2** put things into a box, bag, etc. ବାକ୍ସ ଇତ୍ୟାଦିରେ ଜିନିଷ ଭର୍ତ୍ତି କରି ରଖିବା *Pack all these books into boxes.* ✪ ବିପରୀତ **unpack**

package /ˈpækɪdʒ/ *noun* something that is wrapped in paper ପୁଟୁଳି, ପୁଟୁଳା କାଗଜ, କନା ଇତ୍ୟାଦିରେ ଗୁଡ଼ାଯାଇଥିବା ପୁଟୁଳା

packed /ˈpækt/ *adjective* full ପୂର୍ଣ୍ଣ, ଭରପୂର *The train was packed.*

packet /ˈpækɪt/ *noun* a small box or bag that you buy things in କିଣା ଯାଉଥିବା ଜିନିଷର ପୁଟୁଳା, ପ୍ୟାକେଟ୍ *a packet of biscuits* ➪ ଚିତ୍ର ପାଇଁ **container** ଦେଖନ୍ତୁ।

pad /pæd/ *noun* **1** some pieces of paper for writing or drawing, that are joined together at one end ଗୋଟେ ପଟେ ଆବଦ୍ଧ ହୋଇଥିବା ଅଲେଖା କାଗଜ ତାଡ଼ା, ପ୍ୟାଡ୍ *a writing pad* **2** a thick flat piece of soft material ସୁରକ୍ଷା କାରୀ ମୋଟା ନରମ ପଦାର୍ଥ *Cricketers wear pads on their legs to protect them.*

paddle¹ /ˈpædl/ *noun* a piece of wood with a flat end, that you use for moving a small boat through water ଆହୁଲା

paddle *verb* (**paddles, paddling, paddled**) move a small boat through water with a paddle ଆହୁଲା ମାରି ଡଙ୍ଗା ଚଳାଇବା *We paddled up the river.*

paddle² /ˈpædl/ *verb* (**paddles, paddling, paddled**) walk in water that is not deep, with no shoes on your feet ଖାଲି ଗୋଡ଼ରେ ଅଳ୍ପ ପାଣିରେ ଚାଲିବା *The children were paddling in the pool.*

paddy /ˈpædi/ *noun* the rice plant ଧାନଗଛ

page /peɪdʒ/ *noun* one side of a piece of paper in a book, magazine or newspaper ପୃଷ୍ଠା, ଫର୍ଦ୍ଦ *Please turn to page 120.*

paid ଶବ୍ଦ **pay¹** ର ଏକ ଧାତୁରୂପ

pail /peɪl/ *noun* a bucket ବାଲ୍ଟି

pain /peɪn/ *noun* **1** (*plural* **pains**) the feeling that you have in your body when you are hurt or ill ଯନ୍ତ୍ରଣା, ବଥା *He's in pain.* ○ *back pain* **2** (*no plural*) unhappiness ଅସୁଖୀ

painful /ˈpeɪnfl/ *adjective* something that is painful gives pain ଯନ୍ତ୍ରଣା ଦାୟକ *I've cut my leg—it is very painful.* ✪ ବିପରୀତ **painless**

painless /ˈpeɪnləs/ *adjective* something that is painless does not cause any pain ଯନ୍ତ୍ରଣା ବିହୀନ ✪ ବିପରୀତ **painful**

paint[1] /peɪnt/ *noun* a coloured liquid that you put on things with a brush, to change the colour or to make a picture ତରଳ ରଙ୍ଗ *red paint* ○ *Is the paint dry yet?*

paint[2] /peɪnt/ *verb* (**paints, painting, painted**) **1** put paint on something to change the colour ରଙ୍ଗ ଲଗାଇବା *We painted the walls blue.* **2** make a picture of somebody or something with paints ରଙ୍ଗ ଦେଇ ଚିତ୍ର ଆଙ୍କିବା *I'm painting some flowers.* ○ *My brother paints very well.*

paintbrush /ˈpeɪntbrʌʃ/ *noun* (*plural* **paintbrushes**) a brush that you use for painting ରଙ୍ଗ ଲଗାଇବା ପାଇଁ ତୂଳି ବା ବ୍ରସ୍ ⇨ ଚିତ୍ର ପାଇଁ **brush** ଦେଖନ୍ତୁ।

painter /ˈpeɪntə(r)/ *noun* **1** a person whose job is to paint things like walls or houses ଘର, କାନ୍ଥ ଇତ୍ୟାଦିରେ ରଙ୍ଗ ଲଗାଇବା କାରିଗର, ରଙ୍ଗ ମିସ୍ତ୍ରୀ **2** a person who paints pictures ଚିତ୍ରକର *M. F. Husain is a famous painter.*

painting /ˈpeɪntɪŋ/ *noun* a picture that somebody makes with paint ରଙ୍ଗଦିଆ ଚିତ୍ର

pair /peə(r)/ *noun* **1** two things of the same kind that you use together ହଳ, ଯୁଗଳ, ଏକାଯୋଡ଼ିର ଦୁଇ ପଟ ପଦାର୍ଥ *a pair of shoes* ○ *a pair of earrings* **2** a thing with two parts that are joined together ପାଖାପାଖି ଖଞ୍ଜା ଯାଇଥିବା ଏକା ପରି ଦୁଇଟି ପଦାର୍ଥ *a pair of glasses* ○ *a pair of scissors* **3** two people or animals together ଏକାଠି ଥିବା ଦୁଇଟି ମଣିଷ ବା ପଶୁ *a pair of ducks*

in pairs with two things or people together ହଳ ହଳ ହୋଇ *Shoes are sold only in pairs.*

paisa *noun* (*plural* **paise**) a unit of money that is used in India, Pakistan and Nepal. There are 100 paise in one **rupee** ଭାରତ, ପାକିସ୍ଥାନ ଓ ନେପାଳରେ ପ୍ରଚଳିତ ସର୍ବନିମ୍ନ ମୂଲ୍ୟ ମୁଦ୍ରା, ପଇସା

palace /ˈpæləs/ *noun* a very large house where a king or queen lives ପ୍ରାସାଦ, ମହଲ

palanquin /ˌpælənˈkiːn/ *noun* a big covered box usually containing a seat for one person. It is attached to poles and is carried on the shoulders by four or six men ପାଲିଙ୍କି, ଶବାରି

pale /peɪl/ *adjective* (**paler, palest**) **1** with not much colour in your face; white (ମୁହଁ ଇତ୍ୟାଦିର ରଙ୍ଗ) ଈଶତ୍ ଧଳା, ଶେତା, ପାଉଁଶିଆ। *Are you ill? You look pale.* **2** with a light colour; not strong or dark ଫିକା, ଗାଢ଼ ହୋଇ ନଥିବା ରଙ୍ଗ *a pale blue dress* ✪ ବିପରୀତ **dark**[1] **2** ବା **deep 2**

palette /ˈpælət/ *noun* a thin board with a curved edge and a hole for the thumb to go through, on which an artist mixes colours ଚିତ୍ରକରଙ୍କର ରଙ୍ଗଗୋଳାଇବା ପଟା

palm /pɑːm/ *noun* **1** the flat inner part of your hand between your wrist and fingers ପାପୁଲି **2** (**palm tree** ମଧ୍ୟ) a tree that grows in hot countries, with no branches and a lot of big leaves at the top ନଡ଼ିଆ, ଖଜୁରି, ତାଳ ଇତ୍ୟାଦି ଗଛ *a coconut palm* ⇨ ଚିତ୍ର ପାଇଁ **tree** ଦେଖନ୍ତୁ ।

pamper /ˈpæmpə(r)/ *verb* (**pampers, pampering, pampered**) give a lot of attention to somebody and look after them well; sometimes give more attention than is required ଗେହ୍ଲା କରିବା, ଅଧିକ ପ୍ରଶ୍ରୟ ଦେବା *a pampered child*

pan /pæn/ *noun* a metal pot with a handle or handles that you use for cooking ମଙ୍ଗ ଓ ବେଣ୍ଟ ଥିବା ରନ୍ଧା ବାସନ *a frying pan* ○ *a saucepan*

pancake /ˈpænkeɪk/ *noun* a very thin flat round cake that is made by mixing flour, eggs and milk together, and cooking it in a frying pan ଚକୁଳି ପିଠା

panchayat *noun* a village council in India responsible for managing the local affairs of the village ପଞ୍ଚାୟତ

giant panda

panda /ˈpændə/ *noun* a large black and white animal like a bear, that lives in China ଚୀନ ଦେଶର କଳାଧଳା ରୁମ ଥିବା ଭାଲୁ ପରି ପଶୁ, ପାଣ୍ଡା

pane /peɪn/ *noun* a piece of glass in a window ଝରକାରେ ଲଗାଯାଉଥିବା କାଚ ଫଳକ

panel /ˈpænl/ *noun* **1** a flat piece of wood, metal or glass that is part of a door, wall or ceiling କବାଟ, କାନ୍ଥ, ଛାତ ଇତ୍ୟାଦିରେ ଲଗାଯାଉଥିବା କାଠ, ଧାତୁ, କାଚ ଇତ୍ୟାଦିର ପଟାପରି ଫଳକ **2** a flat part on a machine, where there are things to help you control it ଯନ୍ତ୍ରଚାଳନ ପାଇଁ ସ୍ୱିଚ୍ ଇତ୍ୟାଦି ଥିବା ଫଳକ *the control panel of a TV* **3** a group of persons who give their expert opinion on something ଆଲୋଚନା ବା ପରାମର୍ଶ ପାଇଁ ସମବେତ ହୋଇଥିବା ବିଶେଷଜ୍ଞ ଦଳ

panic /ˈpænɪk/ *noun* a sudden feeling of fear that you cannot control and that makes you do things without thinking carefully ଆକସ୍ମିକ ଭୟ, ଆତଙ୍କ *There was panic in the shop when the fire started.*

panic *verb* (**panics, panicking, panicked**) ଆତଙ୍କିତ ହେବା *Don't panic!*

pant /pænt/ *verb* (**pants, panting, panted**) take in and let out air quickly through your mouth, for example after running or because you are very hot ଧଇଁ ସଇଁ ହେବା *The dog was panting.*

panther /ˈpænθə(r)/ *noun* a wild animal like a big cat. Panthers are usually black କଳା ଚିତାବାଘ

pants /pænts/ *noun* (*no singular*) **trousers** ପ୍ୟାଣ୍ଟ୍

papaya /pəˈpaɪə/ *noun* a large fruit with yellow and green skin, orange flesh and small black seeds.

Papayas grow in hot countries ଗ୍ରୀଷ୍ମପ୍ରଧାନ ଦେଶଗୁଡ଼ିକରେ ଉତ୍ପନ୍ନ ହୁଏ ଅମୃତଭଣ୍ଡା

paper /ˈpeɪpə(r)/ *noun* **1** (*no plural*) a thin material for writing or drawing on or for wrapping things in କାଗଜ *a sheet of paper* ○ *a paper bag* **2** (*plural* **papers**) a newspaper ଖବର କାଗଜ *Have you seen today's paper?* **3** (*plural* **papers**) a set of questions in an examination ପରୀକ୍ଷାର ପ୍ରଶ୍ନ ପତ୍ର *The English paper was easy.*

paper clip *noun* a small metal thing that you use for holding pieces of paper together ଅଳ୍ପ କାଗଜ ଫର୍ଦ୍ଦକୁ ଚିପି ଧରି ରଖିବା ପାଇଁ ତାର ବା ପ୍ଲାଷ୍ଟିକ୍ ଧାରକ ବଙ୍କା ପେପର କ୍ଲିପ୍

parachute /ˈpærəʃu:t/ *noun* a thing like a big umbrella that helps people to slowly fall to the ground when they jump from a plane ଆକାଶ ଛତା, ପ୍ୟାରାଚୁଟ୍

parade /pəˈreɪd/ *noun* a line of people who march together for a special reason, while other people watch them ପ୍ରଦର୍ଶନ ପାଇଁ ଧାଡ଼ିଧାଡ଼ି ଲୋକଙ୍କର ସମୂହ ଚଳନ *a military parade*

paradise /ˈpærədaɪs/ *noun* (*no plural*) the place where some people think good people go after they die; heaven ସ୍ୱର୍ଗ

paragraph /ˈpærəgrɑ:f/ *noun* a group of lines of writing on a single subject. A paragraph always begins on a new line ଲେଖାର ଏକ ଅନୁଚ୍ଛେଦ, ପାରାଗ୍ରାଫ୍ ଅଂଶ।

parallel /ˈpærəlel/ *adjective* parallel lines are straight lines that are always the same distance from each other ସମାନ୍ତରାଳ

paralyse /ˈpærəlaɪz/ *verb* to make somebody unable to feel or move all or part of their body ଅଚଳ ଓ ଅକ୍ଷମ *The shock paralysed him.*

paralysed /ˈpærəlaɪzd/ *adjective* if someone is paralysed, they cannot move their body or a part of it ଅଚଳ ଓ ଅକ୍ଷମ *Rama's paralysed legs made life difficult for her.*

parasite /ˈpærəsaɪt/ *noun* a plant or an animal that lives in or on another plant or animal to get food from it. Parasites can cause diseases ପରଜୀବୀ, ପରାଙ୍ଗଜୀବ, ପରାଙ୍ଗପୁଷ୍ଟ, ଜୀବ ବା ଉଦ୍ଭିଦ; ପାରାସାଇଟ୍ (ପାରାସାଇଟ୍ ଅଣୁଜୀବ ରୋଗ କରାଇ ପାରେ)

parcel /ˈpɑ:sl/ *noun* something wrapped in paper, cloth, etc., so that you may send it or carry it ନେବାପାଇଁ ବା ଡାକରେ ପଠାଇବା ପାଇଁ ପୁଟୁଳି ବା ପ୍ୟାକେଟ୍; ପାର୍ଶଲ *She sent a parcel of books to her aunt.*

pardon /ˈpɑ:dn/ *verb* (**pardons, pardoning, pardoned**) forgive somebody for something bad that they have done କ୍ଷମା କରିବା ✪ ଆମେ ସାଧାରଣତଃ **forgive** ବ୍ୟବହାର କରୁ।

pardon? What did you say? କ'ଣ କହିଲେ ? (ଶୁଣି ପାରିଲି ନାହିଁ)

pardon me **1** What did you say? କ'ଣ କହିଲେ ? (ଶୁଣି ପାରିଲି ନାହିଁ) **2** I am sorry କ୍ଷମା କରିବେ

parent /ˈpeərənt/ *noun* a mother or father ବାପା-ମାଆ, ପିତା-ମାତା *Her parents live in Jodhpur.* ➪ ଚିତ୍ର ପାଇଁ **family tree** ଦେଖନ୍ତୁ।

park[1] /pɑ:k/ *noun* a large place in a city or town with grass and trees, where anybody can go to walk, play games, etc. ସହରରେ ଥିବା ପ୍ରମୋଦ ଉଦ୍ୟାନ, ପାର୍କ *We had a picnic in the park.*

park[2] /pɑ:k/ *verb* (**parks, parking, parked**) stop and leave a car, lorry, etc. somewhere for some time ମଟର ଗାଡ଼ି ଇତ୍ୟାଦି କୌଣସି ସ୍ଥାନରେ ଅଳ୍ପ ସମୟ ପାଇଁ ରଖିବା *I have parked my car opposite the bank.*

parking *noun* (*no plural*) ରଖିବା କାମ, ଗାଡ଼ି ରଖିବା ସ୍ଥାନ *The sign says 'No Parking'.* ○ *There is no parking here between 8 a.m. and 8 p.m.*

parliament /ˈpɑ:ləmənt/ *noun* the people who make the laws in a country କୌଣସି ଦେଶର ବ୍ୟବସ୍ଥାପକ ସଭା ସଂସଦ *the Indian parliament*

> ✪ ଭାରତରେ ସଂସଦ ସଦସ୍ୟ (ଯାହାଙ୍କୁ ଇଂରାଜୀରେ **Members of Parliament** କୁହାଯାଏ)। ସଂସଦଭବନର ବୈଠକ **Parliament House** ରେ ହୁଏ। ଭାରତୀୟ ସଂସଦର ଦୁଇଟି ଭାଗ ହେଲା—**Lok Sabha** (ଲୋକସଭା) ଏବଂ **Rajya Sabha** (ରାଜ୍ୟସଭା)।

parrot /ˈpærət/ *noun* a bird with very bright feathers. Parrots can be taught to copy what people say ଶୁଆ, ଶୁକପକ୍ଷୀ ➪ ଚିତ୍ର ପାଇଁ **birds** ଦେଖନ୍ତୁ।

part[1] /pɑ:t/ *noun* **1** some, but not all of something; one of the pieces of something ଅଂଶ, ଭାଗ *We spent part of the day on the beach.* **2** a piece of a machine କୌଣସି ଯନ୍ତ୍ରର ଲାଗୁଥିବା ଅଂଶ ବା ଉପକରଣ; ଯନ୍ତ୍ରାଂଶ *Is there a shop nearby that sells bicycle parts?* **3** the person you are in a play or film ନାଟକ, ଫିଲ୍ମ, ଇତ୍ୟାଦିର ଭୂମିକା ବା ଚରିତ୍ର *He played the part of Devdas.*

take part in something do something together with other people ଅନ୍ୟଙ୍କ ସହ ମିଶି କୌଣସି କାର୍ଯ୍ୟକ୍ରମ କରିବା; କୌଣସି କାର୍ଯ୍ୟକ୍ରମରେ ଭାଗନେବା *All the students took part in the concert.*

part[2] /pɑ:t/ *verb* (**parts, parting, parted**) go away from each other ବିଦାୟ ନେବା *We parted at the station.*

partial /ˈpɑ:ʃl/ *adjective* **1** not complete ଆଂଶିକ *a partial solar eclipse* **2** liking someone or something very much ପକ୍ଷପାତୀ; ଅତିଭଲ ଲାଗୁଥିବା *I am partial to chocolates.* **3** supporting a person, group, idea, etc. in an unfair way ✪ ବିପରୀତ **impartial**

participate /pɑ:ˈtɪsɪpeɪt/ *verb* (**participates, participating, participated**) do something together with other people ଅନ୍ୟମାନଙ୍କ ସହ ଏକାଠି ହୋଇ କୋଣସି କାର୍ଯ୍ୟକ୍ରମରେ ଯୋଗ ଦେବା, ଭାଗ ନେବା; ଅଂଶଗ୍ରହଣ କରିବା *Ten countries participated in the conference.*

participant /pɑ:ˈtɪsɪpənt/ *noun* a person who does something together with other people ଯୋଗଦାନ କାରୀ, ବ୍ୟକ୍ତି

participation /pɑ:ˌtɪsɪˈpeɪʃn/ *noun* (*no plural*) the act of taking part in something with other people ଯୋଗଦାନ, ଅଂଶଗ୍ରହଣ

participle /ˈpɑ:tɪsɪpl/ *noun* a form of a verb (ବ୍ୟାକରଣ) କ୍ରିୟାର ଏକ ଧାତୁରୂପ *The present participle of 'eat' is 'eating' and the past participle is 'eaten'.*

particle /ˈpɑːtɪkl/ *noun* a very small piece or part of something ଦ୍ରବ୍ୟର କ୍ଷୁଦ୍ରତମ ଅଂଶ; କଣା *dust particles*

particular /pəˈtɪkjələ(r)/ *adjective* **1** one only, and not any other ନିର୍ଦ୍ଦିଷ୍ଟ *You need a particular kind of flour to make bread.* **2** if you are particular, you want something to be exactly right ଠିକ ନିଖୁଣ ଭାବେ ଦେଖୁଥିବା *He's very particular about the food he eats.*

particularly *adverb* more than others; especially ବିଶେଷ ଭାବେ, ବିଶେଷତଃ *I don't particularly like fish.*

parties ଶବ୍ଦ **party** ର ବହୁବଚନ

parting /ˈpɑːtɪŋ/ *noun* **1** when people leave each other ବିଦାୟ *It was a sad parting for Shashi and Tara.* **2** a line that you make on your head by combing your hair in different directions ମୁଣ୍ଡ ବାଳର ସୁନ୍ଥା

partition /pɑːˈtɪʃn/ *noun* **1** (*plural* **partitions**) a structure or a thin wall that divides a room into two ପ୍ରକୋଷ୍ଠକୁ ଭାଗ ଭାଗ କରିବା ପାଇଁ ଲଗା ଯାଉଥିବା ସରୁ ପଟା, କାଚ ଇତ୍ୟାଦିର କାନ୍ଥେଣି ବା ବିଭାଜକ **2** (*no plural*) the division of a country into two or more parts ବିଭାଜନ *the partition of India*

partly /ˈpɑːtli/ *adverb* not completely but in some way ଆଂଶିକ ଭାବରେ *The window was partly open.*

partner /ˈpɑːtnə(r)/ *noun* **1** the person you sit next to in your class in school ଶ୍ରେଣୀରେ ପାଖରେ ବସୁଥିବା ସହପାଠୀ **2** a person you are playing a game with or dancing with ଯୁଗ୍ମ ଭାବେ ଏକାଠି ଖେଳୁଥିବା ବା ନାଚୁଥିବା ସହଭାଗୀ **3** one of the people who owns a business ବ୍ୟବସାୟର ମାଲିକାନାରେ ସହଭାଗୀ **4** your husband or wife ପତି ବା ପତ୍ନୀ

partnership *noun* being partners ଭାଗୀଦାରିତା *The two friends went into partnership and opened a restaurant.*

part of speech *noun* (*plural* **parts of speech**) one of the groups into which you can divide the words of a language based on grammar. 'Noun', 'verb', 'adjective' and 'adverb' are parts of speech (ବ୍ୟାକରଣ) ପଦ (ଯଥା–ବିଶେଷ୍ୟ, ବିଶେଷଣ, ସର୍ବନାମ, କ୍ରିୟା, ଅବ୍ୟୟ ଇତ୍ୟାଦି)

party /ˈpɑːti/ *noun* (*plural* **parties**) **1** a meeting of friends, often in somebody's house, to eat, drink and perhaps dance ଖିଆ ପିଆ ବା ନାଚ ପାଇଁ ଆୟୋଜିତ ବନ୍ଧୁ ମିଳନ; ଭୋଜି *We're having a party this Saturday. Can you come?* ○ *a birthday party* **2** a group of people who have the same ideas about politics ରାଜନୈତିକ ଦଳ *the Congress Party*

pass¹ /pɑːs/ *noun* (*plural* **passes**) **1** a special piece of paper or card that says you can go somewhere or do something ଅବାଧ ପ୍ରବେଶ ବା ଯାତ୍ରା ପାଇଁ ଅନୁମତି ପତ୍ର *You need a pass to get into the factory.* **2** the act of kicking, throwing or hitting a ball to somebody in your team in a game ବଲ୍‌କୁ ସାଥି ଖେଳାଳିଙ୍କ ପାଖକୁ ଦେବା ପ୍ରକ୍ରିୟା **3** a road or way through mountains ଗିରିପଥ, ଗିରିସଙ୍କଟ *the Khyber Pass*

pass² /pɑːs/ *verb* (**passes, passing, passed**) **1** go by somebody or something ପାଖ ଦେଇ ଯିବା *Do you pass any shops on your way to the station?* **2** give something to somebody ବଢ଼ାଇଦେବା *Could you pass me the salt, please?* **3** do well enough in an examination or test ପରୀକ୍ଷାରେ ଉତ୍ତୀର୍ଣ୍ଣ ହେବା *Did you pass your driving test?* ✪ ବିପରୀତ **fail 4** spend time ସମୟ କାଟିବା *How did you pass the time in hospital?*

pass away die ମରିଯିବା *Her grandfather passed away when she was two.*

pass on give or tell something to another person ଅନ୍ୟକୁ ଦେବା ବା କହିବା *Will you pass on a message to Mohit for me?*

pass through go through a place କୌଣସି ସ୍ଥାନ ହୋଇଯିବା *The train passes through Kanpur on its way to Lucknow.*

passage /ˈpæsɪdʒ/ *noun* **1** a short part of a book or speech ବହିର ଏକ ଅଂଶ ବା ବାକ୍ୟ, ପଂକ୍ତି *We studied a passage from the story for homework.* **2** a narrow way, usually with walls on either side, that connects two places ଦୁଇପଟର କାନ୍ଥ ମଧ୍ୟର ସରୁବାଟ

passenger /ˈpæsɪndʒə(r)/ *noun* a person who is travelling in a car, bus, train, plane, etc. but is not driving it ମଟରଗାଡ଼ି, ବସ, ରେଳ, ବିମାନ ଇତ୍ୟାଦିର ଯାତ୍ରୀ

passion /ˈpæʃn/ *noun* a very strong feeling, usually of love, but sometimes of anger or hate (ଭଲପାଇବାର) ଆବେଗ; (କ୍ରୋଧର) ଆବେଶ, ଭାବପ୍ରବଣତା

passionate /ˈpæʃənət/ *adjective* with very strong feelings ଭାବପ୍ରବଣ *She's passionate about helping the poor.*

passive voice *noun* (*no plural*) the form of a verb that shows that the action is done by a person or thing to another person or thing (ବ୍ୟାକରଣ କର୍ମବାଚ୍ୟର କ୍ରିୟା) ➪ **active voice** ଦେଖନ୍ତୁ ।

passport

passport /ˈpɑːspɔːt/ *noun* a small book with your name and photograph in it and that tells that you are the **citizen** of a particular country. You must take it with you when you travel to other countries ବିଦେଶ ଯାତ୍ରା ପାଇଁ ପ୍ରଦତ୍ତ ସରକାରୀ ଅନୁମତି ପୁସ୍ତିକା; ପାସ୍‌ପୋର୍ଟ

password /ˈpɑːswɜːd/ *noun* a secret word that you must say to enter a place or type in to open a file on a computer, for example ପୂର୍ବନିର୍ଦ୍ଧାରିତ ଗୁପ୍ତ ଶବ୍ଦ ବା ବାକ୍ୟାଂଶ ଯାହା ବ୍ୟବହାର କରି ବିଶେଷ ସ୍ଥାନରେ ପ୍ରବେଶ କରାଯାଏ ବା କମ୍ପ୍ୟୁଟର୍ ଚାଳନ କରାଯାଏ

past¹ /pɑːst/ *noun* (*no plural*) **1** the time before now, and the things that happened then ଅତୀତ କାଳ, ଅତୀତ ସମୟ *In the past, many people had large families.* **2** (**past tense** ମଧ୍ୟ) the form of a verb that you use to talk about the time before now ଅତୀତ କାଳର କ୍ରିୟା ରୂପ *The past tense of the* *verb 'go' is 'went'.* ⇨ **present² 2** ଓ **future** ଦେଖନ୍ତୁ ।

past *adjective* of the time that has gone ଅତୀତ ବିଗତ *We will forget your past mistakes.*

past² /pɑːst/ *preposition, adverb* **1** a word that shows how many minutes after the hour ଘଣ୍ଟା ପରେ ବିଗତ ମିନିଟ୍, ସୂଚାଉଥିବା ଶବ୍ଦ, ପରେ, ବାଜି *It's two minutes past four.* ○ *It's half past seven.* **2** from one side of somebody or something to the other; by; on the other side of somebody or something (କୌଣସି ବ୍ୟକ୍ତି, ସ୍ଥାନ ଇତ୍ୟାଦି) ଅତିକ୍ରମ କରିବା *The bus went past without stopping.*

pasta /ˈpæstə/ *noun (no plural)* a food made from flour, eggs and water and formed into different shapes. Uncooked pasta is hard but cooked pasta is soft ଦଳା ଅଟାକୁ ବିଭିନ୍ନ ଭାବରେ ଗଢ଼ି ଶୁଖାଇ କରାଯାଉଥିବା ରନ୍ଧନ ଯୋଗ୍ୟ ଖାଦ୍ୟ ପଦାର୍ଥ

paste¹ /peɪst/ *noun* a soft wet substance, that can be spread over something; glue ମେଞ୍ଚାଳିଆ ଦଳା ବା ଚକଟା ପଦାର୍ଥ, ଅଠା *Mix the powder with water to make a paste.*

paste² /peɪst/ *verb* (**pastes, pasting, pasted**) stick something on a surface using **glue** ଅଠା ଲଗାଇ ଯୋଖିବା

pasteurize /ˈpɑːstʃəraɪz/ *verb* (**pasteurizes, pasteurizing, pasteurized**) make a liquid free from bacteria by first heating it up to a certain temperature and then cooling it ତାପ ଦ୍ୱାରା ଦୁଧ ଇତ୍ୟାଦିର କ୍ଷୁଦ୍ର ଜୀବାଣୁ ନଷ୍ଟ କରିବା *pasteurized milk*

pasteurization /ˌpɑːstʃəraɪˈzeɪʃn/ *noun (no plural)* ଉତ୍ତାପ ଦ୍ୱାରା ଜୀବାଣୁ ନାଶନ

pastry /ˈpeɪstri/ *noun* (*plural* **pastries**) a small cake ଛୋଟ କେକ୍

pasture /ˈpɑːstʃə(r)/ *noun* a large piece of land covered with grass on which animals can feed ପଶୁ ଚାରଣ ଭୂମି

pat /pæt/ *verb* (**pats, patting, patted**) touch somebody or something lightly with your hand flat ଥାପୁଡ଼େଇବା *She patted the dog on the head.*

pat *noun* ମୃଦୁ ଥାପୁଡ଼ା *He gave me a pat on the shoulder.*

patch /pætʃ/ *noun* (*plural* **patches**) **1** a piece of cloth that you use to cover a hole in things like clothes ଲୁଗା ମରାମତି ପାଇଁ ବ୍ୟବହୃତ ଟୁକୁରା କନା, ତାଳି, ପଟି *I sewed a patch on my jeans.* **2** a small area of something that is not the same as the other parts ଭିନ୍ନ ପ୍ରକାର ବା ରଙ୍ଗର ଛୋଟ ଖଣ୍ଡ *a black cat with a white patch on its back*

path /pɑːθ/ *noun* (*plural* **paths** /pɑːðz/) a way across a piece of land, on which people can walk ଚଲାବାଟ *a path through the woods*

patience /ˈpeɪʃns/ *noun (no plural)* the ability of staying calm and not getting angry when you are waiting for something or when you have problems ଧୈର୍ଯ୍ୟ, ସହିଷ୍ଣୁତା ✪ ବିପରୀତ **impatience**

patient[1] /ˈpeɪʃnt/ *adjective* able to stay calm and not get angry when you are waiting for something or when you have problems ଧୈର୍ଯ୍ୟଶୀଳ, ସହିଷ୍ଣୁ *Just sit there and be patient. Your mother will be here soon.* ✪ ବିପରୀତ **impatient**

patiently *adverb* ଧୈର୍ଯ୍ୟ ସହକାରେ *She waited patiently for the bus.*

patient[2] /ˈpeɪʃnt/ *noun* a sick person who is being looked after by a doctor ଡାକ୍ତରଙ୍କର ଚିକିତ୍ସାଧୀନ ବ୍ୟକ୍ତି, ରୋଗୀ

patriot /ˈpeɪtriət/ *noun* a person who loves his country very much and is ready to protect it from enemies ଦେଶଭକ୍ତ

patriotic /ˌpeɪtriˈɒtɪk/ *adjective* ଦେଶହିତୈଷୀ *patriotic songs*

patrol /pəˈtrəʊl/ *noun* **1** a group of people, ships, aircraft, etc. that go round a place to see that everything is all right ପହରା ଦେବା ପାଇଁ ଥିବା ବ୍ୟକ୍ତିବୃନ୍ଦ, ଜାହାଜ, ବିମାନ ଇତ୍ୟାଦି *an army patrol* **2** the act of going around an area, building, etc. at regular intervals to make sure there is no trouble ପହରା ଦେବା କାମ *an army car on patrol*

patrol *verb* (**patrols, patrolling, patrolled**) ପହରା ଦେବା *A guard patrols the gate at night.*

patron /ˈpeɪtrən/ *noun* **1** someone who gives money and support to a person, group or institution ବ୍ୟକ୍ତି, ଗୋଷ୍ଠୀ ବା ସଂସ୍ଥାର ପୃଷ୍ଠପୋଷକ ବା ସହାୟକ ବ୍ୟକ୍ତି *He is a patron of many writers.* **2** someone who regularly goes to a particular shop, hotel, theatre, etc. ନିର୍ଦ୍ଦିଷ୍ଟ ଦୋକାନ, ହୋଟେଲ, ଥିଏଟର୍ ଇତ୍ୟାଦିର ନିୟମିତ ଗ୍ରାହକ *The special discount is only for our patrons.*

patter /ˈpætə(r)/ *verb* (**patters, pattering, pattered**) make quick light sounds ଟପର ଟପର ଶବ୍ଦ କରିବା *Rain pattered against the window.*

pattern /ˈpætn/ *noun* shapes and colours on something ନିର୍ଦ୍ଦିଷ୍ଟ ଆକାର ବା ରଙ୍ଗର ଢାଞ୍ଚା *The curtains had a pattern of flowers and leaves.*

pauper /ˈpɔːpə(r)/ *noun* a very poor person ଅତି ଦରିଦ୍ର ବ୍ୟକ୍ତି

pause /pɔːz/ *noun* a short stop ବିରତି *She played for 30 minutes without a pause.*

pause *verb* (**pauses, pausing, paused**) stop for a short time ବିରତି ନେବା, ରହିଯିବା *He paused before answering my question.*

pavement /ˈpeɪvmənt/ *noun* a raised flat part at the side of a road for people to walk on (ପଦଚାରୀଙ୍କ ପାଇଁ) ରାସ୍ତା କଡ଼ରେ ଥିବା ପକ୍କା ପଥ

paw /pɔː/ *noun* the foot of an animal that has claws, for example a dog, cat or bear ପଶୁର ନଖ ଯୁକ୍ତ ପାଦ, ପଂଝା

pay[1] /peɪ/ *verb* (**pays, paying, paid** /ˈpeɪd/, **has paid**) **1** give money to get something ପଇସା ଦେବା (କିଛି ଜିନିଷ ପାଇବା ବା କିଣିବା ପାଇଁ) *She paid Rs 90,000 for her car.* ○ *Are you paying in cash or by cheque?* **2** give money for work that somebody does (କାମ ପାଇଁ) ପାଉଣା ଦେବା

I paid the builder for mending the roof.

pay back give back the money that somebody has lent to you ଋଣ ପରିଶୋଧ କରିବା *Can you lend me fifty rupees? I'll pay you back next week.*

pay for something give money for what you buy କିଛି କିଣିବା ପାଇଁ ପଇସା ଦେବା

pay² /peɪ/ *noun* (*no plural*) the money that you get for work ଦରମା, ମଜୁରି

payment /ˈpeɪmənt/ *noun* **1** (*no plural*) the act of paying somebody or being paid ଅର୍ଥପ୍ରଦାନ *You can make the payment by cheque or cash.* **2** (*plural* **payments**) an amount of money that you pay ପ୍ରଦତ୍ତ ଅର୍ଥର ପରିମାଣ *I make monthly payments of Rs 500.*

PC /ˌpiːˈsiː/ *abbreviation* a small computer ଛୋଟ କମ୍ପ୍ୟୁଟର୍ ✪ PC ର ବିସ୍ତୃତ ରୂପ **personal computer** ।

pea /piː/ *noun* a very small round green vegetable. Peas grow in **pods** ମଟର ଛୁଇଁ, ମଟର ମଞ୍ଜି ➪ ଚିତ୍ର ପାଇଁ **vegetable** ଦେଖନ୍ତୁ ।

peace /piːs/ *noun* (*no plural*) a time when there is no war, fighting or trouble between people or countries ଶାନ୍ତି

make peace agree to end a war or fight ଯୁଦ୍ଧ ବନ୍ଦ କରି ଶାନ୍ତି ସ୍ଥାପନ କରିବା *The two countries made peace.*

peaceful /ˈpiːsfl/ *adjective* **1** with no fighting ଶାନ୍ତିପୂର୍ଣ୍ଣ *a peaceful demonstration* **2** quiet and calm ସ୍ଥିର ଓ ନିଃଶବ୍ଦ *a peaceful evening*

peacefully *adverb* ଶାନ୍ତିରେ *She's sleeping peacefully.*

peach /piːtʃ/ *noun* (*plural* **peaches**) a soft round fruit with a yellow and red skin and a large stone in the centre ହଳଦିଆ ଓ ଲାଲ୍ ଚୋପା ଥିବା ଓ ଭିତରେ ବଡ଼ ମଞ୍ଜି ଥିବା ଏକ ପ୍ରକାର ଫଳ

peacock /ˈpiːkɒk/ *noun* a large bird with beautiful long blue and green feathers in its tail ମୟୂର ➪ ଚିତ୍ର ପାଇଁ **bird** ଦେଖନ୍ତୁ ।

peak /piːk/ *noun* **1** the pointed top of a mountain (ପର୍ବତ, ପାହାଡ଼ ଇତ୍ୟାଦିର) ଶୃଙ୍ଗ, ଶିଖର, ଚୂଡ଼ା **2** the time when something is highest, biggest, etc. ସବୁଠାରୁ କାର୍ଯ୍ୟରତ ଅବସ୍ଥା *The traffic is at its peak between five and six in the evening.*

peal /piːl/ *noun* a sound like the loud ringing of a bell or a number of bells ଘଣ୍ଟା ବାଜିଲା ପରି ଶବ୍ଦ, ଘଡ଼ ଘଡ଼ିର ଶବ୍ଦ, ହସର ରୋଳ ।

peanut /ˈpiːnʌt/ *noun* ➪ **groundnut** ଦେଖନ୍ତୁ ।

pear /peə(r)/ *noun* a fruit that is green or yellow on the outside and white on the inside ସାମାନ୍ୟ ହଳଦିଆ ସବୁଜ ମାଂସଳ ନାସପାତି ଜାତୀୟ ଫଳ ➪ ଚିତ୍ର ପାଇଁ **fruit** ଦେଖନ୍ତୁ ।

pearl /pɜːl/ *noun* a small round white thing that comes from an **oyster**. Pearls are used for making things like necklaces and earrings ମୁକ୍ତା *a pearl necklace* ➪ ଚିତ୍ର ପାଇଁ **oyster** ଦେଖନ୍ତୁ ।

pebble /ˈpebl/ *noun* a small round stone found in or near water ଛୋଟ ମସୃଣ ବାଲିଗିରିଡ଼ା ବା ବାଲିଗରଡ଼ା ପଥର

peck /pek/ *verb* (**pecks, pecking, pecked**) when a bird pecks at something, it eats or bites that thing with its beak ପକ୍ଷୀ ଥଣ୍ଟରେ ଖୁମ୍ପିବା ବା ଖୁମ୍ପି ଖାଇବା *The hens were pecking at the corn.*

peculiar /pɪˈkju:liə(r)/ *adjective* strange; not usual ଅଦ୍ଭୁତ, ବିଚିତ୍ର; ଅନ୍ୟଠାରୁ ଭିନ୍ନ *What's that peculiar smell?*

pedal /ˈpedl/ *noun* a part of a bicycle or other machine that you move with your feet ସାଇକେଲ୍ ଇତ୍ୟାଦିର ଗୋଡ଼ରେ ଠେଲି ଚଳାଇବା ଯନ୍ତ୍ର, ପେଡାଲ୍

pedestrian /pəˈdestriən/ *noun* a person who is walking in the street ରାସ୍ତାର ଯାଉଥିବା ପଦଚାରୀ ବ୍ୟକ୍ତି

peel /pi:l/ *noun* (*no plural*) the skin of some fruit and vegetables ଫଳ, ପରିବା ଇତ୍ୟାଦିର ଚୋପା *orange peel*

peel *verb* (**peels, peeling, peeled**) take the skin off a fruit or vegetable ଫଳ, ପରିବା ଇତ୍ୟାଦିର ଚୋପା ଛଡ଼ାଇବା *Can you peel the potatoes?*

peep /pi:p/ *verb* (**peeps, peeping, peeped**) **1** look at something quickly or secretly ଉଙ୍କି ମାରିବା, ଉଣ୍ଡିବା, ସତର୍କ ଭାବରେ ଚାହିଁବା *I peeped through the window and saw her.* **2** come out for a short time ଅଳ୍ପକ୍ଷଣ ପାଇଁ ବାହାରି ଆସିବା ବା ଦିଶିବା *The moon peeped out from behind the clouds.*

peer /pɪə(r)/ *verb* (**peers, peering, peered**) look closely at something because you cannot see well ଭଲଭାବେ ଦିଶୁ ନ ଥିବା ଜିନିଷକୁ ଆଖି କୁଞ୍ଚି ଚାହିଁବା *I peered outside but I couldn't see anything because it was dark.*

peg /peg/ *noun* **1** a small thing on a wall or door where you can hang clothes ଲୁଗାପଟା ଝୁଲାଇବା ପାଇଁ କାନ୍ଥ ବା କବାଟରେ ଲଗାଯାଇଥିବା ଧାତୁ ବା କାଠର କିଲା ବା ଖିଲ *Your coat is on the peg.* **2** a small wooden or plastic thing that holds wet clothes on a line when they are drying ଓଦା ଲୁଗା ତାର ବା ଦଉଡ଼ିରେ ଶୁଖାଇବା ପାଇଁ ବ୍ୟବହୃତ କାଠ, ପ୍ଲାଷ୍ଟିକ୍ ଇତ୍ୟାଦିର ଚୁମୁଟା ପରି ଉପକରଣ *a clothes peg*

pen¹ /pen/ *noun* a thing that you use for writing with a coloured liquid (called **ink**) କଲମ

pen² /pen/ *noun* a small place with a fence around it for keeping farm animals in ପଶୁମାନଙ୍କୁ ରଖିବା ପାଇଁ ବଡ଼ ଘେରା ସ୍ଥାନ, ଖୁଆଡ଼, ଅଟେଇ

penalty /ˈpenəlti/ *noun* (*plural* **penalties**) a punishment ନିୟମଭଙ୍ଗ ଯୋଗୁଁ ଦିଆଯାଉଥିବା ଦଣ୍ଡ *The penalty for travelling without a ticket is Rs 100.*

penance /ˈpenəns/ *noun* a punishment that you give yourself to show that you are sorry for something ପାପମୋଚନ ପାଇଁ ସ୍ୱୟଂକୃତ ପ୍ରାୟଶ୍ଚିତ; ବ୍ରତ, ଉପାସ ଇତ୍ୟାଦି

pencil /ˈpensl/ *noun* a thin piece of wood with grey or coloured substance (called **lead**) inside it. Pencils are used for writing or drawing ପେନ୍‌ସିଲ୍

penguin /ˈpeŋgwɪn/ *noun* a black and white bird that lives in very cold places. Penguins can swim but they cannot fly କୁମେରୁ ଅଞ୍ଚଳରେ ଉଡ଼ି ପାରୁ ନ ଥିବା କଳାଧଳା ସାମୁଦ୍ରିକ ପକ୍ଷୀ, ପେଙ୍ଗୁଇନ୍

penguin

peninsula /pəˈnɪnsjələ(r)/ *noun* an area of land which is almost surrounded by water but is joined to a large piece of land ଉପଦ୍ୱୀପ *the Indian peninsula*

penknife /ˈpennaɪf/ *noun* (*plural* **penknives** /ˈpennaɪvz/) a small knife with one or more parts that can be folded ଛୋଟ ବନ୍ଦହୋଇ ପାରୁଥିବା ଛୁରି, ପକେଟ୍ ଛୁରି

penniless /ˈpeniləs/ *adjective* having no money; very poor ନିଃସ୍ୱ, ଅତି ଗରିବ *The penniless old lady was taken to the old-age home.*

penny /ˈpeni/ *noun* (*plural* **pence** /pens/ ବା **pennies**) a small coin that people use in Britain. There are 100 pence in a **pound** ବ୍ରିଟେନ୍‌ରେ ପଇସା (୧୦୦ ପେନି ୧ ପାଉଣ୍ଡ)

pension /ˈpenʃn/ *noun* money that you get regularly from a government or a company when you are old and do not work any more (when you are **retired**) ଅବସର କାଳୀନ ଭତ୍ତା

people /ˈpi:pl/ *noun* (*no singular*) more than one person ଲୋକମାନେ, ଲୋକ *How many people came to the meeting? ○ People often arrive late at parties.*

pepper /ˈpepə(r)/ *noun* (*no plural*) a grey or black powder with a hot taste that you put on food ଗୋଲମରିଚ *salt and pepper*

per /pə(r)/ *preposition* for each; in each ମୁଣ୍ଡପିଛା, ଜଣପିଛା *These apples cost Rs 20 per kg. ○ I was driving at 60 kilometres per hour.*

per cent /pəˈsent/ *noun* (*plural* **per cent**) in each hundred ଶତକଡ଼ା, ପ୍ରତିଶତ, ଶତାଂଶ *Ninety per cent of the people who work here are men.* ✪ ପ୍ରତିଶତର ଚିହ୍ନ ହେଲା % (ପ୍ରତି ୧୦୦ ବ୍ୟକ୍ତି ମଧ୍ୟରୁ ୯୦ ଜଣ ପୁରୁଷ ଅଟନ୍ତି)।

percentage /pəˈsentɪdʒ/ *noun* ଶତକଡ଼ା ହାର *What percentage of students passed the exam?' 'Oh, about eighty per cent.'*

perch /pɜ:tʃ/ *noun* (*plural* **perches**) a place where a bird sits ଚଢ଼େଇ ବସିବା ଡାଳ, ବାଡ଼ି ଇତ୍ୟାଦି।

perennial /pəˈreniəl/ *adjective* something that is perennial continues for a very long time ଦୀର୍ଘସ୍ଥାୟୀ, ଚିରସ୍ଥାୟୀ *the perennial problem of water shortage*

perfect /ˈpɜ:fɪkt/ *adjective* **1** so good that it cannot be better; with nothing wrong ଏକ୍‌ଦମ୍ ଠିକ୍, ଦୋଷ ଶୂନ୍ୟ *Her English is perfect.* **2** made from 'has', 'have' or 'had' and the **past participle** of a verb (ବ୍ୟାକରଣରେ) କ୍ରିୟା ସମାପ୍ତିବାଚକ କାଳ 'has', 'have' ବା 'had' *perfect tenses*

perfectly /ˈpɜːfɪktli/ *adverb* **1** completely; very ସମ୍ପୂର୍ଣ୍ଣଭାବେ, ଏକ୍‌ଦମ୍, ଏକବାରେ *I'm perfectly all right.* **2** in a perfect way ଦୋଷ ଶୂନ୍ୟ ଭାବରେ, ନିର୍ଭୁଲ୍ ଭାବରେ *She played the piece of music perfectly.*

perform /pəˈfɔːm/ *verb* (**performs, performing, performed**) **1** do a piece of work କାର୍ଯ୍ୟସମ୍ପାଦନ କରିବା *She has been performing well right through school.* **2** be in a play, concert, etc. ନାଟକ, ଫିଲ୍ମ ଇତ୍ୟାଦିରେ ଅଭିନୟ କରିବା; ସଙ୍ଗୀତ କାର୍ଯ୍ୟକ୍ରମ ଇତ୍ୟାଦିରେ ଭାଗ ନେବା *The band is performing at the stadium tonight.*

performer *noun* a person who is in a play, concert, etc. କାମ କରୁଥିବା ବ୍ୟକ୍ତି; ଅଭିନେତା, ଗାୟକ, ବାଦକ ଇତ୍ୟାଦି

performance /pəˈfɔːməns/ *noun* **1** (*plural* **performances**) a time when a play, etc. is shown or music is played in front of a lot of people ନାଟକ ଇତ୍ୟାଦିରେ ଅଭିନୟ; ସଙ୍ଗୀତ କାର୍ଯ୍ୟକ୍ରମ *We went to the evening performance of the play.* **2** (*no plural*) how well you do something କାର୍ଯ୍ୟ ସମ୍ପାଦନର ଢଙ୍ଗ, ଅଭିନୟର ମାନ *My parents were pleased with my performance in the exam.*

perfume /ˈpɜːfjuːm/ *noun* **1** a nice smell ସୁଗନ୍ଧ, ସୁବାସ **2** a liquid with a nice smell that you put on your body ଅତର *a bottle of perfume*

perhaps /pəˈhæps/ *adverb* a word that you use when you are not sure about something ବୋଧହୁଏ *There were three men, or perhaps four.*

period /ˈpɪəriəd/ *noun* **1** an amount of time ସମୟକାଳ *a period of three years* **2** a lesson ବିଦ୍ୟାଳୟରେ ପାଠ ପଢ଼ା ଯିବାର ନିର୍ଦ୍ଦିଷ୍ଟ ସମୟ, ପିରିୟଡ୍ *We have five periods of German a week.* **3** a certain time in the life of a person or the history of a country ବ୍ୟକ୍ତିଙ୍କ ଜୀବନର ବା ଦେଶର ଇତିହାସର ଏକ ବିଶେଷ ଅଂଶ ବା କାଳ *What period of history are you studying?*

periodic /ˌpɪəriˈɒdɪk/ *adjective* happening at regular intervals ନିର୍ଦ୍ଦିଷ୍ଟ ସମୟାନ୍ତରେ ଘଟୁଥିବା ପର୍ଯ୍ୟାୟବୃତ୍ତ *a periodic pollution control test*

periodically *adverb* ସମୟ ସମୟରେ, ନିର୍ଦ୍ଦିଷ୍ଟ ସମୟାନ୍ତରେ, ପର୍ଯ୍ୟାୟବୃତ୍ତ ଭାବେ

perish /ˈperɪʃ/ *verb* (**perishes, perishing, perished**) die or get destroyed ମରିଯିବା, ବିନାଶ ହେବା *Hundreds perished in the fire.*

permanent /ˈpɜːmənənt/ *adjective* something that is permanent continues for ever or for a very long time and does not change ସ୍ଥାୟୀ, ଚୀରସ୍ଥାୟୀ *I'm looking for a permanent job.* ✪ ବିପରୀତ **temporary**

permanently *adverb* ସ୍ଥାୟୀଭାବରେ *Has he left permanently or is he going to come back?* ✪ ବିପରୀତ **temporarily**

permission /pəˈmɪʃn/ *noun* (*no plural*) the act of allowing somebody to do something ଅନୁମତି *She gave me permission to leave early.*

permit[1] /pəˈmɪt/ *verb* (**permits, permitting, permitted**) allow somebody to do something ଅନୁମତି ଦେବା *You are not permitted to smoke in the hospital.* ✪ ଆମେ ସାଧାରଣତଃ **allow** ର ବ୍ୟବହାର କରିଥାଉଁ।

permit² /ˈpɜːmɪt/ *noun* a piece of paper that says you can do something or go somewhere ଅନୁମତି ପତ୍ର *Have you got a permit for fishing in this river?*

persecute /ˈpɜːsɪkjuːt/ *verb* (**persecutes, persecuting, persecuted**) treat someone cruelly or unfairly, especially because of their race, religion or political beliefs ଉତ୍ପୀଡ଼ନ କରିବା, ନିର୍ଯ୍ୟାତନା ଦେବା *He fled the city to escape being persecuted.*

persecution /ˌpɜːsɪˈkjuːʃn/ *noun* the act of being cruel and unfair to someone, especially because of their race, religion or political beliefs ନିର୍ଯ୍ୟାତନା, ଉତ୍ପିଡ଼ନ, ଅତ୍ୟାଚାର

persist /pəˈsɪst/ *verb* (**persists, persisting, persisted**) if someone persists, they carry on doing something in spite of difficulties ଦୃଢ଼ ଓ ଅବିଚଳିତ ଭାବେ କାମ କରିଚାଲିବା

person /ˈpɜːsn/ *noun* (*plural* **people** ବା **persons**) a man or woman ବ୍ୟକ୍ତି *I think she's the best person for the job.*

personal /ˈpɜːsənl/ *adjective* of or for one person; private ବ୍ୟକ୍ତିଗତ *This letter is personal, so I don't want anyone else to read it.*

personality /ˌpɜːsəˈnæləti/ *noun* (*plural* **personalities**) **1** what sort of person you are; your character ବ୍ୟକ୍ତିତ୍ୱ; ଚରିତ୍ର *Vivek has a great personality.* **2** a famous person ଖ୍ୟାତିସମ୍ପନ୍ନ ବ୍ୟକ୍ତି, ଖ୍ୟାତନାମା ବ୍ୟକ୍ତି *a TV personality*

personally /ˈpɜːsənəli/ *adverb* you say 'personally' when you are saying what you think about something ବ୍ୟକ୍ତିଗତ ଭାବେ, ନିଜ ଭାବନା ଅନୁସାରେ *Personally, I like her, but a lot of people don't.*

perspiration /ˌpɜːspəˈreɪʃn/ *noun* drops of liquid that form on your skin to cool it down in hot weather ଝାଳ, ଘର୍ମ ✪ ଆମେ ସାଧାରଣତଃ **sweat** ଶବ୍ଦର ବ୍ୟବହାର କରିଥାଉଁ।

persuade /pəˈsweɪd/ *verb* (**persuades, persuading, persuaded**) make somebody think or do something by talking to them ମନାଇବା, ପ୍ରବର୍ତ୍ତାଇବା, ପ୍ରରୋଚିତ କରିବା *The man in the shop persuaded me to buy the most expensive pen.*

persuasion /pəˈsweɪʒn/ *noun* (*no plural*) the act of persuading somebody or being persuaded ପ୍ରବର୍ତ୍ତନା, ମନାଇବା *After a lot of persuasion she agreed to come.*

pessimistic /ˌpesɪˈmɪstɪk/ *adjective* if you are pessimistic, you think that bad things will happen ନିରାଶାବାଦୀ, ନୈରାଶ୍ୟବାଦୀ, ନିରାଶାତ୍ମକ*Don't be so pessimistic!* ✪ ବିପରୀତ **optimistic**

pest /pest/ *noun* **1** an insect or animal that damages plants or food ଗଛ ପତ୍ର ବା ଖାଦ୍ୟ ପଦାର୍ଥ ନଷ୍ଟ କରୁଥିବା କୀଟ ବା ପଶୁ **2** a person or thing that makes you a little angry ବିରକ୍ତିକର ଲୋକ *My* *sister won't leave me alone when I'm working—she's a real pest!*

pesticide /ˈpestɪsaɪd/ *noun* a substance that is used to kill insects that harm crops କୀଟନାଶକ ପଦାର୍ଥ

pet /pet/ *noun* an animal that you keep in your home ପୋଷାଜନ୍ତୁ *I've got two pets—a cat and a dog.*

petal /ˈpetl/ *noun* one of the coloured parts of a flower (ଫୁଲର) ପାଖୁଡ଼ା ➪ ଚିତ୍ର ପାଇଁ **plant** ଦେଖନ୍ତୁ ।

petition /pəˈtɪʃn/ *noun* a special letter, from a group of people, that asks for something ବହୁଲୋକଙ୍କ ସ୍ୱାକ୍ଷର ଥିବା ଆବେଦନ ପତ୍ର *Hundreds of people signed the petition for a new bridge across the river.*

petrol /ˈpetrəl/ *noun* (*no plural*) a liquid that you put in a car to make the engine work ପେଟ୍ରୋଲ୍

petrol station *noun* (*plural* **petrol stations**) a place where you can buy petrol for your car ପେଟ୍ରୋଲ ବିକା ଯାଉଥିବା ସ୍ଥାନ, ପେଟ୍ରୋଲ୍ ପମ୍ପ, ପେଟ୍ରୋଲ୍ ଷ୍ଟେସନ୍

petroleum /pəˈtrəʊliəm/ *noun* (*no plural*) a kind of oil that is found under the ground or sea and is used to produce petrol, diesel, etc. ପେଟ୍ରୋଲ୍, ଡିଜେଲ୍ ଇତ୍ୟାଦି ତିଆରି ପାଇଁ ଭୂତଳରୁ ମିଳୁଥିବା ତେଲ, ପେଟ୍ରୋଲିୟମ୍

phase /feɪz/ *noun* a time when something is changing or growing ବିକାଶ ବା ବର୍ଦ୍ଧନର ପର୍ଯ୍ୟାୟ *My first year at university was a very exciting phase of my life.*

phenomenon /fəˈnɒmɪnən/ *noun* (*plural* **phenomena** /fəˈnɒmɪnə/) an unusual or remarkable happening ଉଲ୍ଲେଖଯୋଗ୍ୟ ବା ଅସାଧାରଣ ଘଟଣା *natural phenomena*

philosophy /fəˈlɒsəfi/ *noun* **1** (*no plural*) the study of ideas about the meaning of life ଦର୍ଶନ ଶାସ୍ତ୍ର, ଜ୍ଞାନଶାସ୍ତ୍ର, ତତ୍ତ୍ୱ ଶାସ୍ତ୍ର **2** (*plural* **philosophies**) what one person thinks about life ଜୀବନ ଦର୍ଶନ *Enjoy yourself today and don't worry about tomorrow—that's my philosophy!*

philosopher /fəˈlɒsəfə(r)/ *noun* a person who studies philosophy ଦାର୍ଶନିକ

phone /fəʊn/ *noun* a telephone; an instrument that you use for talking to somebody who is in another place ଫୋନ୍, ଟେଲିଫୋନ୍, ଦୂରଭାଷ *The phone's ringing—can you answer it?* ○ *What's your phone number?* ○ *I need to make a phone call.*

phone *verb* (**phones, phoning, phoned**) use a telephone ଫୋନ୍ କରିବା, ଟେଲିଫୋନ୍‌ରେ କଥାବାର୍ତ୍ତା କରିବା *I phoned Tina last night.*

phone booth *noun* (*plural* **phone booths**) a small covered place in the street with a public telephone ସର୍ବସାଧାରଣଙ୍କ ବ୍ୟବହାର ପାଇଁ ଟେଲିଫୋନ୍ ଥିବା ଛୋଟ ପ୍ରକୋଷ୍ଠ

photocopy /ˈfəʊtəʊkɒpi/ *noun* (*plural* **photocopies**) a copy of something on paper that you make with a special machine (called a **photocopier**) ଦଲିଲ୍ ଇତ୍ୟାଦିର୍ ଫଟୋ ଚିତ୍ର

photocopy *verb* (**photocopies, photocopying, photocopied, has photocopied**) ଦଲିଲ୍ ଇତ୍ୟାଦିର ଫଟୋ ଚିତ୍ର

କରିବା *Can you photocopy this letter for me?*

photograph /ˈfəʊtəgrɑːf/, **photo** /ˈfəʊtəʊ/ *noun* (*plural* **photographs, photos**) a picture that you take with a camera ଆଲୋକ ଚିତ୍ର, ଫଟୋ, ଫଟୋଗ୍ରାଫ୍ *I took a photo of the bridge.*

photographer /fəˈtɒgrəfə(r)/ *noun* a person who takes photographs ଫଟୋ ଉଠାଇଲା ବାଲା, ଫଟୋଗ୍ରାଫର୍

photographic /ˌfəʊtəˈgræfɪk/ *adjective* about photographs or photography ଆଲୋକ ଚିତ୍ର ବା ଫଟୋଗ୍ରାଫ ସମ୍ବନ୍ଧୀୟ *photographic equipment*

photography /fəˈtɒgrəfi/ *noun* (*no plural*) the skill or process of taking photographs ଆଲୋକ ଚିତ୍ର ବା ଫଟୋ ଉଠାଇବା ଦକ୍ଷତା ବା ପଦ୍ଧତି

photosynthesis /ˌfəʊtəʊˈsɪnθəsɪs/ *noun* (*no plural*) the process by which green plants make their food using carbon dioxide, water and sunlight ସବୁଜ ଉଦ୍ଭିଦର ଅଙ୍ଗାରକାମ୍ଳ, ପାଣି ଓ ସୂର୍ଯ୍ୟାଲୋକରୁ ଖାଦ୍ୟ ପ୍ରସ୍ତୁତ କରିବା ପଦ୍ଧତି; ଆଲୋକସଂଶ୍ଳେଷଣ ପଦ୍ଧତି

phrase /freɪz/ *noun* a group of words that you use together as part of a sentence ଭାବ ପ୍ରକାଶକ ବାକ୍ୟାଂଶ ବା ଖଣ୍ଡ ବାକ୍ୟ *'First of all' and 'a bar of chocolate' are phrases.*

physical /ˈfɪzɪkl/ *adjective* **1** related to things that you feel or do with your body ଶାରୀରିକ, ଦେହ ସମ୍ବନ୍ଧୀୟ *physical exercise* **2** related to things that you can touch or about the natural features of the earth ବସ୍ତୁ ସମ୍ବନ୍ଧୀୟ, ଭୌତିକ *the physical world* ○ *the physical map of the town* **3** related to the study of natural forces like heat, light and sound ପଦାର୍ଥବିଦ୍ୟା ସମ୍ବନ୍ଧୀୟ

physically *adverb* ଶାରୀରିକ ଭାବରେ *I'm physically very fit.*

physics /ˈfɪzɪks/ *noun* (*no plural*) the study of things like heat, light and sound ପଦାର୍ଥ ବିଜ୍ଞାନ

piano /piˈænəʊ/ *noun* (*plural* **pianos**) a big musical instrument that you play by pressing black and white bars (called **keys**) କି'ବୋର୍ଡ଼ ଥିବା ବଡ଼ ବାଦ୍ୟଯନ୍ତ୍ର ଯାହାର କି' ଚିପିଲେ ଶବ୍ଦ ବାହାରେ, ପିଆନୋ

pianist /ˈpɪənɪst/ *noun* a person who plays the piano ପିଆନୋ ବାଦକ

pick /pɪk/ *verb* (**picks, picking, picked**) **1** take the person or thing you like best; choose ବାଛିବା, ଚୟନ କରିବା *They picked Sushil as their captain.* **2** take a flower, fruit or vegetable from the place where it grows ଫୁଲ, ଫଳ, ପରିବା ଇତ୍ୟାଦି ତୋଳିବା *I've picked some flowers for you.*

pick out be able to see somebody or something in a lot of others (ବ୍ୟକ୍ତି ବା ପଦାର୍ଥ ମଧ୍ୟରୁ) ବାଛିବା ବା ଚୟନ କରିବା *Can* *you pick out my father in this photo?*

pick up 1 take and lift somebody or something ଉଠାଇ ନେବା *She picked up the bags and put them on the table.* **2** come to take somebody or something away କାହାରିକୁ ବା କିଛି ପଦାର୍ଥକୁ ଆସି ନେଇଯିବା *My father picks me up from school.*

pickle /ˈpɪkl/ *noun* a food made from vegetables, fruits and spices that have been preserved in **oil** or **vinegar** ତେଲରେ ପକାଇ କରାଯାଇଥିବା ଆଚାର ଆଚାର; ଭିନେଗାର୍, ଲୁଣପାଣି *a jar of mango pickle*

pickpocket /ˈpɪkpɒkɪt/ *noun* a person who steals things from people's pockets ପକେଟ୍‌ମାର୍

picnic /pɪknɪk/ *noun* a meal that you eat outside, away from home ପିକ୍‌ନିକ୍ ବା ବଣଭୋଜି *We had a picnic by the river.*

picture /ˈpɪktʃə(r)/ *noun* **1** a drawing, painting or photograph ଛବି *Julie drew a picture of her dog.* ○ *They showed us some pictures of their wedding.* **2 the pictures** (*plural*) the cinema ସିନେମା, ଚଳଚ୍ଚିତ୍ର *We're going to the pictures this evening.*

take a picture photograph something ଫଟୋ ଉଠାଇବା *I took a picture of the house.*

pie /paɪ/ *noun* a food made by baking meat, fruit, vegetables, etc. inside a covering of dough. The dough is usually made from flour, oil, etc. ଦଳା ଅଟା ଭିତରେ ମାଂସ, ଫଳ ବା ପରିବା ପୁର ଦେଇ ନିଆଁ ଧାସରେ ବନ୍ଦ ଚୁଲିରେ ସେକାଯାଇଥିବା ଖାଦ୍ୟପଦାର୍ଥ; *an apple pie*

piece /piːs/ *noun* **1** a part of something ଅଂଶ, ଭାଗ, ଖଣ୍ଡ *Would you like another piece of cake?* **2** one single thing ଗୋଟିଏ ଖଣ୍ଡ *Have you got a piece of paper?*

in pieces broken ଭଙ୍ଗା ଅବସ୍ଥାରେ, ଖଣ୍ଡ ବିଖଣ୍ଡିତ ଅବସ୍ଥାରେ *The teapot lay in pieces on the floor.*

pierce /pɪəs/ *verb* (**pierces, piercing, pierced**) make a hole in something with a sharp point କଣାକରିବା, ଫୋଡ଼ିବା *The nail pierced her skin.*

piercing /ˈpɪəsɪŋ/ *adjective* a piercing sound is very loud and sharp ତୀବ୍ର (ସ୍ୱର) *a piercing cry*

piety /ˈpaɪəti/ *noun* (*no plural*) a behaviour that shows great respect for God and religion ଈଶ୍ୱରଭକ୍ତି, ଧର୍ମପରାୟଣତା ➪ **piety** ର ବିଶେଷଣ ରୂପ **pious** ।

pig /pɪg/ *noun* a fat animal that people keep on farms ଘୁଷୁରି, ଶୂକର ✪ **Boar**, ଅଣ୍ଡିରା ଘୁଷୁରିକୁ କୁହାଯାଏ, ମାଈ ଘୁଷୁରିକୁ **sow** କୁହାଯାଏ ଏବଂ ଘୁଷୁରି ଛୁଆକୁ **piglet** କୁହାଯାଏ ।

pigeon /ˈpɪdʒɪn/ *noun* a grey bird that you often see in towns ପାରା ➪ ଚିତ୍ର ପାଇଁ **bird** ଦେଖନ୍ତୁ ।

piglet /ˈpɪglət/ *noun* a young pig ଘୁଷୁରି ଛୁଆ

pigsty /ˈpɪgstaɪ/ *noun* (*plural* **pigsties**) a small building in a farm where pigs are kept ଘୁଷୁରି ଶାଳ

pile /paɪl/ *noun* a lot of things on top of one another; a large amount of something ଗଦା, ସ୍ତୂପ *There's a pile of clothes on the floor.* ○ *a pile of sand*

pile *verb* (**piles, piling, piled**) put a lot of things on top of one another ଗଦାଇବା

pilgrim /ˈpɪlgrɪm/ *noun* a person who travels a long way to a place because it has a special religious meaning ତୀର୍ଥଯାତ୍ରୀ

pilgrimage /ˈpɪlgrɪmɪdʒ/ *noun* a journey that a pilgrim makes ତୀର୍ଥଯାତ୍ରା

pill /pɪl/ *noun* a small round hard piece of medicine that you swallow ବଟିକା, ପିଲ୍

pillar /ˈpɪlə(r)/ *noun* a tall strong piece of stone, wood or metal that holds up part of a building ଖମ୍ବ

pillow /pɪləʊ/ *noun* a soft thing that you put your head on when you are in bed ତକିଆ

pilot /ˈpaɪlət/ *noun* a person who flies an aircraft ବିମାନ ଚାଳକ, ପାଇଲଟ୍

pin¹ /pɪn/ *noun* a small thin piece of metal with a flat part at one end and a sharp point at the other. You use a pin for holding pieces of cloth or paper together ଧାତୁ କଣ୍ଟା, ପିନ୍‌କଣ୍ଟା ➪ **drawing pin** ଓ **safety pin** ମଧ୍ୟ ଦେଖନ୍ତୁ ।

pins and needles *noun* (*no singular*) the feeling that you sometimes get in a part of your body when you have not moved it for a long time ଦେହର ଅଙ୍ଗରେ ଝିମା ମାରିବା ଅନୁଭୂତି

pin² /pɪn/ *verb* (**pins, pinning, pinned**) **1** fix things together with a pin or pins ପିନ୍ ମାରି ଯୋଖିବା *Pin the pieces of material together before you sew them.* ○ *Could you pin this notice to the board?* **2** hold somebody or something down or against something so that they cannot move ଧରି ପକାଇବା, ମାଡ଼ିବସି କାବୁକରିବା

pinch /pɪntʃ/ *verb* (**pinches, pinching, pinched**) press somebody's skin tightly between your thumb and finger ଚିମୁଟିବା, ଚୁମୁଟିବା

pinch *noun* (*plural* **pinches**) **1** the act of pinching something ଚିମୁଟା, ଚୁମୁଟା *He gave my leg a pinch.* **2** the amount of something that you can hold between your thumb and finger ଚିମୁଟାଏ ପଦାର୍ଥ *Add a pinch of salt to the soup.*

pine /paɪn /, **pine tree** *noun* a tall tree with thin sharp leaves (called **needles**) that do not fall off in winter ଛୁଞ୍ଚିପରି ଥିବା ଲମ୍ବା ଦେବଦାରୁ ଜାତୀୟ ସରୁପତ୍ର, ଝାଉଁଗଛ, ପାଇନ୍

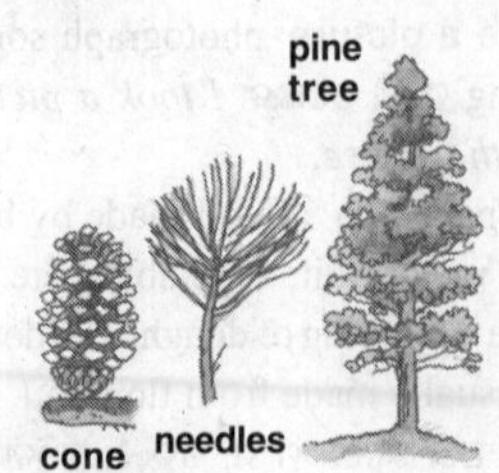

pineapple /ˈpaɪnæpl/ *noun* a big fruit that has a rough brown skin and a yellow inside part ସପୁରି ➪ ଚିତ୍ର ପାଇଁ **fruit** ଦେଖନ୍ତୁ ।

ping-pong *noun* (*no plural*) a game where players use a round **bat** to hit a small light ball over a net on a big table; table tennis ପିଙ୍ଗ ପଙ୍ଗ ବା ଟେବୁଲ୍ ଟେନିସ୍ ଖେଳ (ହାଲୁକା ବଲ୍ ଓ ଛୋଟ ବ୍ୟାଟ ଧରି ଟେବୁଲ୍ ଉପରେ ଖେଳାଯାଉଥିବା ଖେଳ)

pink /pɪŋk/ *adjective* with a light red colour ଗୋଲାପି, ପାଟଳ *a pink dress*

pink *noun* ଗୋଲାପି ରଙ୍ଗ, ପଟଳ ବର୍ଣ୍ଣ *She was dressed in pink.*

pioneer /ˌpaɪəˈnɪə(r)/ *noun* a person who goes somewhere or does something before other people କୌଣସି ସ୍ଥାନକୁ ଯିବାରେ ବା କୌଣସି କାମ କରିବାରେ ପ୍ରଥମ ବ୍ୟକ୍ତି; ଅଗ୍ରଣୀ ପଥ ପ୍ରଦର୍ଶକ *the pioneers of aircraft design*

pious /ˈpaɪəs/ *adjective* behaving in a manner that shows strong belief in God and religion ଧାର୍ମିକ, ଧର୍ମନିଷ୍ଠ *a pious lady* ➪ Pious ଶବ୍ଦର ବିଶେଷ୍ୟ ଶବ୍ଦ ହେଲା **piety** ।

pip /pɪp/ *noun* the small seed of some fruits. Lemons, oranges and apples have pips ଛୋଟ ମଞ୍ଜି (ଲେମ୍ବୁ, କମଳା, ସେଓ ଇତ୍ୟାଦିର)

pipe /paɪp/ *noun* **1** a long tube that takes water, oil, gas, etc. from one place to another ପାଣି, ତେଲ, ବାଷ୍ପ ଇତ୍ୟାଦି ବହନ କରିବା ପାଇଁ ଥିବା ନଳ, ପାଇପ୍ **2** a thing that you put tobacco in to smoke it ଧୂଆଁପତ୍ର ଖୁନ୍ଦି ଧୂମ୍ରପାନ କରିବାକୁ ଥିବା ଉପକରଣ, ପାଇପ୍

pipeline /ˈpaɪplaɪn/ *noun* a big pipe that carries oil or gas a long way ତେଲ, ବାଷ୍ପବହନ କରୁଥିବା ବଡ଼ ଆକାରର ନଳ ବା ପାଇପ୍

piracy /ˈpaɪrəsi/ *noun* (*no plural*) **1** the act of attacking ships at sea in order to rob them ଜଳଦସ୍ୟୁତା **2** the act of making copies of video tapes, music cassettes, computer programs, books, DVDs, etc. without permission, in order to sell them ଭିଡ଼ିଓ, ଟେପ୍, ଗୀତ କ୍ୟାସେଟ୍, କମ୍ପ୍ୟୁଟର୍ କାର୍ଯ୍ୟକ୍ରମ ବହି ଇତ୍ୟାଦିରେ ଚୋରାରେ ନକଲ କରି ବିକିବା ବ୍ୟବସାୟ *The government should make stricter laws to curb video piracy.*

pirate¹ /ˈpaɪrət/ *noun* a person on a ship who robs other ships ଜଳଦସ୍ୟୁ

pirate² /ˈpaɪrət/ *verb* (**pirates, pirating, pirated**) copy, use or sell someone's work without their permission ଚୋରାରେ ନକଲ କରି ବିକିବା

Pisces /ˈpaɪsiːz/ *noun* the twelfth sign of the **zodiac** ମୀନ ରାଶି

pistol /ˈpɪstl/ *noun* a small hand-held gun ପିସ୍ତଲ୍

pit /pɪt/ *noun* **1** a deep hole in the ground ଖାତ, ଗାତ; ଭୂଗର୍ଭରେ ଖୋଳା ଯାଇଥିବା ଗଭୀର ଖାତ **2** a coal mine କୋଇଲା ଖଣି ➪ **mine** ଦେଖନ୍ତୁ ।

pitch¹ /pɪtʃ/ *noun* **1** (*plural* **pitches**) a piece of ground where you play games like football, cricket or hockey ଫୁଟ୍‌ବଲ୍, କ୍ରିକେଟ୍ ଖେଳିବା ପାଇଁ ପ୍ରସ୍ତୁତ କରାଯାଇଥିବା ପଡ଼ିଆ **2** (*no plural*) a measure of how high or low a sound is ସ୍ୱରର ଉଚ୍ଚତା ବା ନିମ୍ନତାର ମାତ୍ରା

pitch² /pɪtʃ/ *verb* (**pitches, pitching, pitched**) put up a tent ତମ୍ବୁ ବାନ୍ଧିବା *We pitched our tent under a big tree.*

pity¹ /ˈpɪti/ *noun* (*no plural*) the sad feeling you have for a person or an animal who is in pain or who has problems କରୁଣା, ଦୟା *I felt pity for the old dog, so I gave it some food.*

it's a pity, what a pity it is sad ବଡ଼ ଦୁଃଖର କଥା *It's a pity you can't come to the party.*

take pity on somebody help somebody because you feel sad for them କାହାରି ପ୍ରତି କରୁଣା କରିବା, ଦୟା ଦେଖାଇବା *I took pity on her and gave her some money.*

pity² /ˈpɪti/ *verb* (**pities, pitying, pitied, has pitied**) feel sad for somebody who is in pain or who has problems କରୁଣା କରିବା, ଦୟା କରିବା *I really pity people who haven't got anywhere to live.*

pizza /ˈpiːtsə/ *noun* (*plural* **pizzas**) a flat round piece of bread with tomatoes, cheese, vegetables, meat, etc. on top, that is cooked in an oven ଗୋଲିଆ ମୋଟା ରୁଟି ଉପରେ ଚିଜ୍, ପରିବା, ଟମାଟୋ ମାଂସ ଇତ୍ୟାଦି ରଖି ବନ୍ଦ ଚୁଲି ଉପରେ ବା ଓଭନରେ ସେକା ଯାଇଥିବା ଖାଦ୍ୟ ପଦାର୍ଥ, ପିଜ୍ଜା

place¹ /pleɪs/ *noun* **1** where somebody or something is ସ୍ଥାନ, ଜାଗା *Put the book back in the right place.* **2** a building, town, country, etc. ଘର, ସହର, ଦେଶ ଇତ୍ୟାଦି *Mysore is a very interesting place.* **3** a seat or space for one person ବସିବା ସ୍ଥାନ *An old man was sitting in my place.*

in place where it should be; in the right place ଠିକ୍ ସ୍ଥାନରେ *She tied her hair with a ribbon to keep it in place.*

in place of somebody or **something** instead of somebody or something କୌଣସି ବ୍ୟକ୍ତି ବା ପଦାର୍ଥର ସ୍ଥାନରେ ବା ବଦଳରେ *Amit became goalkeeper in place of Mohit, who had broken his leg.*

take place happen ଘଟିବା, ସଂଘଠିତ ହେବା *The wedding of Rajiv and Priya will take place on 24 April.*

place² /pleɪs/ *verb* (**places, placing, placed**) put something somewhere କୌଣସି ପଦାର୍ଥ ନିର୍ଦ୍ଦିଷ୍ଟ ସ୍ଥାନରେ ରଖିବା *The waiter placed the dish in front of me.*

plain¹ /pleɪn/ *adjective* (**plainer, plainest**) **1** with no pattern; all in one colour ସାଦା; ଏକ ରଙ୍ଗର *She wore a plain blue dress.* **2** simple and ordinary ସାଧାରଣ *plain food* **3** easy to see, hear or understand; clear ସହଜରେ ଦେଖି ହେଉଥିବା, ଶୁଣି ହେଉଥିବା ବା ବୁଝିହେଉଥିବା *It's plain that he's unhappy.*

plainly *adverb* clearly ସ୍ପଷ୍ଟ ଭାବରେ *They were plainly very angry.*

plain² /pleɪn/ *noun* a large piece of flat land ବିସ୍ତୀର୍ଣ୍ଣ ସମତଳ ଭୂମି

plait /plæt/ *verb* (**plaits, plaiting, plaited**) put long pieces of hair, rope, etc. over and under each other to make one thick piece ବେଣୀ କରିବା

plait *noun* a long piece of hair that somebody has plaited କେଶର ବେଣୀ *She wears her hair in plaits.*

plan¹ /plæn/ *noun* **1** something that you have decided to do, and how you are going to do it କାର୍ଯ୍ୟର ଯୋଜନା; କାର୍ଯ୍ୟ ସମ୍ପାଦନର ପଦ୍ଧତି *They have plans to build a new school.* **2** a map ନକ୍ସା *a street plan of Delhi* **3** a drawing for a new building, machine, etc. ପରିକଳ୍ପିତ ଘର, ଯନ୍ତ୍ର ଇତ୍ୟାଦିର ନକ୍ସା ବା ଚିତ୍ର *Have you seen the plans for the new shopping centre?*

plan² /plæn/ *verb* (**plans, planning, planned**) decide what you are going to do and how you are going to do it ଯୋଜନା କରିବା *They're planning a holiday in Goa next summer.*

plane /pleɪn/ *noun* an aeroplane ବିମାନ, ଉଡ଼ାଜାହାଜ *What time does your plane land?* ➪ ଚିତ୍ର ପାଇଁ **aircraft** ଦେଖନ୍ତୁ।

planet /ˈplænɪt/ *noun* a large round thing in space that moves around the sun ସୂର୍ଯ୍ୟକୁ ପ୍ରଦକ୍ଷିଣ କରୁଥିବା ଗ୍ରହ *Earth, Mars and Venus are planets.*

planetarium /ˌplænɪˈteəriəm/ *noun* a building with a curved ceiling on the inside of which the position and movement of stars and planets are projected ଚିତ୍ରବିକ୍ଷେପ ଯନ୍ତ୍ର ଥିବା ଗମ୍ବୁଜାକାର ଛାତରେ ତାରା, ନକ୍ଷତ୍ର ଇତ୍ୟାଦିର ଚଳନ ଚିତ୍ର ପ୍ରଦର୍ଶିତ ହୁଏ *a special show at the Nehru planetarium in Delhi*

plank /plæŋk/ *noun* a long flat piece of wood ଲମ୍ବା କାଠ ପଟା

plant¹ /plɑːnt/ *noun* anything that grows from the ground ଉଦ୍ଭିଦ; ଗଛ, ଗୁଳ୍ମ ଇତ୍ୟାଦି *Don't forget to water the plants.*

plant² /plɑːnt/ *verb* (**plants, planting, planted**) put plants or seeds in the ground to grow ଗଛର ମଞ୍ଜି ବା ଡାଳି ପୋତିବା ବା ରୋଇବା *We planted some roses in the garden.*

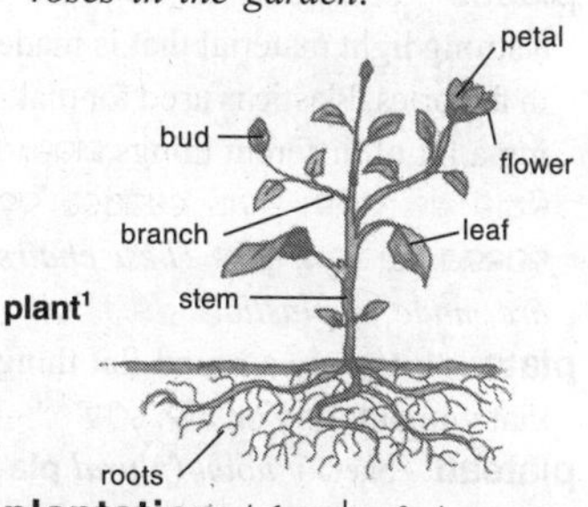

plantation /plɑːnˈteɪʃn/ *noun* a piece of land where tea, cotton, tobacco, etc. are grown ବହୁ ରୋପିତ ଗଛର ବଡ଼ ବଗିଚା ବା ଉଦ୍ୟାନ *a sugarcane plantation*

plaque /plɑːk/ *noun* (*no plural*) a soft white layer that forms on your teeth and can cause tooth decay ଦାନ୍ତ ଉପରେ ଜମିଯାଉଥିବା ଅନିଷ୍ଟକାରୀ ପରସ୍ତ, ପ୍ଲାକ୍

plaster /plɑːstə(r)/ *noun* **1** (*no plural*) a soft substance that becomes hard and smooth when it is dry. Plaster is used for covering walls ପଲସ୍ତରା ପାଇଁ ବାଲି ବା ସିମେଣ୍ଟର ମିଶ୍ରିତ ପଦାର୍ଥ **2** (*plural* **plasters**) a small piece of sticky material that you put over a cut on your body to keep it clean ଘା' ଉପରେ ଲଗାଯାଉଥିବା ସୁରକ୍ଷାକାରୀ ଅଠାପଟି **3** (*no plural*) a white substance that you put round a broken arm or leg. It becomes hard and keeps the arm or leg safe until it is better ଦେହର ହାଡ଼ ଭାଙ୍ଗି ଯାଇଥିଲେ ତାକୁ ଠିକ୍ ଭାବରେ ଯୋଡ଼ି ସୁରକ୍ଷିତ

ରଖିବା ପାଇଁ ଲଗା ଯାଉଥିବା ଏକ ଧଳା ଚିକିଟା ପଦାର୍ଥ ଯାହା ଅଳ୍ପସମୟରେ କଠିନ ହୋଇଯାଏ *When I broke my leg it was in plaster for two months.*

plastic /ˈplæstɪk/ *noun* (*no plural*) a strong light material that is made in factories. Plastic is used for making a lot of different things କାରଖାନା ତିଆରି ଶକ୍ତ ହାଲୁକା ପଦାର୍ଥ ଯେଉଁଥିରେ ବହୁ ଉପକରଣ ତିଆରି ହୁଏ, ପ୍ଲାଷ୍ଟିକ୍ *These chairs are made of plastic.*

plate /pleɪt/ *noun* a round flat thing that you put food on ଥାଳି, ପ୍ଲେଟ୍

plateau /ˈplætəʊ/ *noun* (*plural* **plateaux** ବା **plateaus** /ˈplætəʊz/) a large area of flat land that is higher than the land around it ମାଳଭୂମି, ଉପତ୍ୟକା *the Deccan plateau*

platform /ˈplætfɔːm/ *noun* **1** the raised flat part of a railway station where you get on or off a train ରେଳ ଷ୍ଟେସନ୍‌ରେ ଗାଡ଼ିରୁ ଓହ୍ଲାଇବା ଜାଗା, ପ୍ଲାଟ୍‌ଫର୍ମ୍ *The train to Chennai leaves from platform 5.* **2** a place that is higher than the floor, where people stand so that other people can see and hear them ମଞ୍ଚ, ବେଦି *The headmaster went up to the platform to make his speech.*

play¹ /pleɪ/ *verb* (**plays, playing, played**) **1** have fun; do something to enjoy yourself ଆମୋଦ ପ୍ରମୋଦରେ ଭାଗନେବା, ମଉଜ କରିବା *The children were playing with their toys.* **2** take part in a game ଖେଳିବା *I like playing tennis.* **3** make music with a musical instrument ବାଦ୍ୟଯନ୍ତ୍ର ବଜାଇବା *My sister plays the sitar very well.* ✪ ବାଦ୍ୟଯନ୍ତ୍ରର ନାମ ପୂର୍ବରୁ ସବୁବେଳ **the** ର ବ୍ୟବହାର କରିବା ଉଚିତ *I'm learning to play the violin.* **4** put a record, tape or compact disc in a machine and listen to it ରେକର୍ଡ୍, ଟେପ୍, ସିଡି ଇତ୍ୟାଦି ଯନ୍ତ୍ରରେ ଲଗାଇ ଶୁଣିବା *Shall I play the tape again?*

playful /ˈpleɪfl/ *adjective* fond of playing ଖେଳିବାକୁ ଉତ୍ସୁକ *playful kittens*

play² /pleɪ/ *noun* **1** (*plural* **plays**) a story that you watch in the theatre or on television, or listen to on the radio ଥିଏଟର, ଟେଲିଭିଜନ୍ ବା ରେଡ଼ିଓରେ ପ୍ରସାରିତ ନାଟକ **2** (*no plural*) games; what children do for fun ଖେଳ; ପିଲାଙ୍କ ଖେଳାଧୂଳା *work and play*

player /ˈpleɪə(r)/ *noun* **1** a person who plays a game ଖେଳାଳି *football players* **2** a person who plays a musical instrument ବାଦ୍ୟଯନ୍ତ୍ର ବାଦକ *a tabla player*

playground /ˈpleɪgraʊnd/ *noun* a piece of land where children can play ଖେଳ ପଡ଼ିଆ

plea /pliː/ *noun* the act of asking for something with strong feeling ଅନୁରୋଧ, ପ୍ରାର୍ଥନା *He made a plea for help.*

plead /pliːd/ *verb* (**pleads, pleading, pleaded**) ask for something in a very strong way ନିବେଦନ କରିବା, ଅନୁନୟ କରିବା, ପ୍ରାର୍ଥନା କରିବା *He pleaded with his parents to buy him a guitar.*

pleasant /ˈpleznt/ *adjective* nice, enjoyable or friendly ପ୍ରୀତିକର, ଆନନ୍ଦ ଦାୟକ *The weather here is very* *pleasant.* ○ *He's a very pleasant person.* ✪ ବିପରୀତ **unpleasant**

pleasantly *adverb* ଆନନ୍ଦରେ *She smiled pleasantly.*

please /pli:z/ *interjection* a word that you use when you ask someone for something politely ଭଦ୍ର ଭାବରେ ବ୍ୟବହୃତ ଅନୁରୋଧ ସୂଚକ ଶବ୍ଦ *What's the time, please?* ○ *Two cups of coffee, please.* ✪ କୌଣସି ପ୍ରସ୍ତାବ ଅନୁରୋଧ ସ୍ୱୀକାର କରିବା ପାଇଁ **yes, please** ପ୍ରୟୋଗ କରାଯାଏ *'Would you like a toast?' 'Yes, please.'*

please *verb* (**pleases, pleasing, pleased**) make somebody happy କାହାରିକୁ ଖୁସି କରିବା *I wore my best clothes to please my mother.*

pleased /pli:zd/ *adjective* happy ଖୁସି, ସନ୍ତୁଷ୍ଟ *Are you pleased with your new watch?*

pleasing /ˈpli:zɪŋ/ *adjective* something that is pleasing gives you pleasure and satisfaction; pleasant ଆନନ୍ଦଦାୟକ; ଉପଭୋଗ୍ୟ *a pleasing face*

pleasure /ˈpleʒə(r)/ *noun* **1** (*no plural*) the feeling of being happy or enjoying something ଆନନ୍ଦ, ତୃପ୍ତି *She likes to read for pleasure.* **2** (*plural* **pleasures**) something that makes you happy ଆନନ୍ଦର ଉତ୍ସ, ଖୁସି କଲାପରି ପଦାର୍ଥ *It was a pleasure to meet you.*

it's a pleasure you say 'it's a pleasure' as a polite way of replying to somebody who thanks you କେହି ଧନ୍ୟବାଦ ଦେଲେ ତାଙ୍କୁ ଦିଆଯାଉଥିବା ଭଦ୍ର ପ୍ରତ୍ୟୁତ୍ତର *'Thank you for your help.' 'It's a pleasure.'*

pleat /pli:t/ *noun* a fold in a piece of cloth ଲୁଗାର ପରସ୍ତ, ଭାଙ୍ଗ

pledge[1] /pledʒ/ *noun* a formal and serious promise or agreement ଶପଥ *a pledge of loyalty*

pledge[2] /pledʒ/ *verb* (**pledges, pledging, pledged**) make a formal or serious promise ଶପଥ କରିବା *He pledged his support for the plan.*

plenty /ˈplenti/ *pronoun* as much or as many as you need; a lot ପ୍ରଚୁର *Do you want to stay for dinner? There's plenty of food.*

pliers /ˈplaɪəz/ *noun* (*no singular*) a tool for holding things tightly or for cutting wire ସଣ୍ଢୁଆଶି, ଚିମୁଟା, ପ୍ଲାସ୍ *Have you got a pair of pliers?*

pliers

plod /plɒd/ *verb* (**plods, plodding, plodded**) walk slowly in a heavy tired way କଷ୍ଟେ ମଷ୍ଟେ ଚାଲିବା *We plodded up the hill in the rain.*

plot /plɒt/ *noun* **1** a secret plan to do something that is wrong ଗୁପ୍ତ ଯୋଜନା, ଷଡ଼ଯନ୍ତ୍ର *a plot to kill the president* **2** what happens in a story, play or film ନାଟକ, ସିନେମା, ଗପ ଇତ୍ୟାଦିର କଥାବସ୍ତୁ *This book has a very exciting plot.* **3** a piece of land, often for building a house ଘର ଇତ୍ୟାଦି କରିବା ପାଇଁ ଖଣ୍ଡେ ଜମି

plot *verb* (**plots, plotting, plotted**) make a secret plan to do something that is wrong ଷଡ଼ଯନ୍ତ୍ର କରିବା, ଗୁପ୍ତ ଯୋଜନା କରିବା ବା ଗୁପ୍ତ ମନ୍ତ୍ରଣା କରିବା *They plotted to rob the bank.*

plough /plaʊ/ *noun* a tool used on farms for digging and turning over the soil before seeds are sown. Ploughs are usually pulled by animals or tractors ହଳ ଲଙ୍ଗଳ
plough *verb* (**ploughs, ploughing, ploughed**) use a plough to dig and turn over the soil ହଳଚଲେଇ ଜମି ଚଷିବା *The farmer ploughed his fields.*

pluck /plʌk/ *verb* (**plucks, plucking, plucked**) pull something out from where it is growing (ଫୁଲ, ଫଳ ଇତ୍ୟାଦି) ତୋଳିବା *Do not pluck flowers from this garden.*

plug /plʌg/ *noun* a thing that joins a lamp, machine, etc. to a place in the wall (called a **socket**) where there is electricity ଦୁଇ ବା ତିନି କଣ୍ଟା ଥିବା ଉପକରଣ ଯାହାକୁ ସକେଟ୍‌ରେ ଲଗାଇ ବିଦ୍ୟୁତ୍ ସଂଚାର କରାଯାଏ, ପ୍ଲଗ୍
plug *verb* (**plugs, plugging, plugged**) fill a hole with something ଛିଦ୍ର ବନ୍ଦ କରିବା *I plugged the hole in the pipe with a rag.*
plug in put an electric plug into a place in the wall where there is electricity ଇଲେକ୍‌ଟ୍ରିକ୍ ପ୍ଲଗ୍ ସଂଯୋଗ କରିବା *Can you plug the radio in, please?* ✪ ବିପରୀତ **unplug**

plum /plʌm/ *noun* a soft round fruit with a hard round seed in the middle ଏକ ପ୍ରକାର ରସାଳ ଫଳ, ଆଳୁବଖରା ପ୍ଲମ୍

plumber /ˈplʌmə(r)/ *noun* a person whose job is to put in and repair things like water pipes and taps ପାଣିପାଇପ୍ ମିସ୍ତ୍ରୀ

plump /plʌmp/ *adjective* (**plumper, plumpest**) having a soft, round body; slightly fat ମୋଟା ସୋଟା, ହୃଷ୍ଟପୁଷ୍ଟ *a plump baby*

plunge /plʌndʒ/ *verb* (**plunges, plunging, plunged**) fall or push something suddenly down ହଠାତ୍ ତଳକୁ ତଳକୁ ଖସିବା; ଭୁଷିବା; ପୂରାଇବା *She plunged into the pool.* ○ *I plunged my hand into the water.*

plural /ˈplʊərəl/ *noun* the form of a word that shows there is more than one ଏକାଧିକ ସୂଚନା ଶବ୍ଦ; (ବ୍ୟାକରଣ) ବହୁବଚନ; ଏକାଧିକ ସଂଖ୍ୟା *The plural of 'child' is 'children'.*
plural *adjective* ଏକାଧିକ; ବହୁବଚନ *Most plural nouns in English end in 's'.* ➪ **singular** ଦେଖନ୍ତୁ।

plus /plʌs/ *preposition* added to; and ଯୁକ୍ତ; ଏବଂ *Two plus three is five* (2 + 3 = 5). ➪ **minus** ଦେଖନ୍ତୁ।

Pluto /ˈpluːtəʊ/ *noun* (*no plural*) a **dwarf planet** that moves round the sun and comes after the eight planet Neptune ଛୋଟ ଗ୍ରହ ଯାହାକି ସୂର୍ଯ୍ୟ ଚତୁଃପାର୍ଶ୍ୱରେ ଘୂରେ ଏବଂ ଏହା ଅଷ୍ଟମ ଗ୍ରହ ନେପଚ୍ୟୁନ୍ ପରେ ଆସେ ➪ ଚିତ୍ର ପାଇଁ **solar system** ଦେଖନ୍ତୁ।

p.m. /ˌpiːˈem/ *abbreviation* you use 'p.m.' after a time to show that it is between midday and midnight ଦିନ ୧୨ଟାରୁ ରାତି ୧୨ଟା ମଧ୍ୟସ୍ଥ ସମୟ *The plane leaves at 3 p.m.* ➪ **a.m.** ଦେଖନ୍ତୁ।

poach /pəʊtʃ/ *verb* (**poaches, poaching, poached**) cook food, especially egg or fish gently in a small amount of liquid ଅଣ୍ଡାକୁ ଭାଙ୍ଗି ଫୁଟୁଥିବା ପାଣିରେ ପକାଇ ରାନ୍ଧିବା; ମାଛ ଇତ୍ୟାଦି

ଅଳ୍ପ ପାଣି ଇତ୍ୟାଦିରେ ଅଳ୍ପ ନିଆଁରେ ରାନ୍ଧିବା *a poached egg*

pocket /ˈpɒkɪt/ *noun* a small bag in your clothes for carrying things ଜାମାପଟାରେ ଥିବା ମୁଣା, ପକେଟ୍ *I put the key in my pocket.*

pocket money *noun* (*no plural*) money that parents give to their child each week or month to buy things ହାତ ଖର୍ଚ୍ଚ *How much pocket money do you get?*

pod /pɒd/ *noun* the long green part of some plants, that has seeds inside it. Peas grow in pods ମଟର, ବିନ୍ ଇତ୍ୟାଦିର ଚୋପା ବା ଖୋଳ ➪ ଚିତ୍ର ପାଇଁ **vegetable** ଦେଖନ୍ତୁ।

poem /ˈpəʊɪm/ *noun* a piece of writing, usually with short lines that may rhyme. Poems try to show feelings or ideas କବିତା *I have written a poem.*

poet /ˈpəʊɪt/ *noun* a person who writes poems କବି *William Wordsworth was a famous English poet.*

poetry /ˈpəʊətri/ *noun* (*no plural*) a set of poems କାବ୍ୟ; କବିତାଗୁଚ୍ଛ *William Wordsworth wrote beautiful poetry.*

point[1] /pɔɪnt/ *noun* **1** a small round mark (.) that separates a whole number from a number that is less than one ଦଶମିକ ଚିହ୍ନ (.) *2.5* (= ଦୁଇ ଦଶମିକ ପାଞ୍ଚ) ➪ **decimal** ଦେଖନ୍ତୁ। **2** a certain time or place ନିର୍ଦ୍ଦିଷ୍ଟ ସମୟ ବା ସ୍ଥାନ *It started to rain and at that point we decided to go home.* **3** (*no plural*) the most important idea; the purpose or reason ତାତ୍ପର୍ଯ୍ୟପୂର୍ଣ୍ଣ ବା ଅତ୍ୟାବଶ୍ୟକ ବିଷୟ; ଉଦ୍ଦେଶ୍ୟ ବା କାରଣ *The point of going to school is to learn.* **4** the sharp end of something କୌଣସି ପଦାର୍ଥର ତୀକ୍ଷ୍ଣ ମୁନ *the point of a needle* **5** a mark that you win in a game or sport ଖେଳରେ ମିଳୁଥିବା ମାନସୂଚକ ସଂଖ୍ୟା *Our team scored six points.*

point of view your way of thinking about something ଦୃଷ୍ଟିକୋଣ, ମତ *I understand your point of view.*

point[2] /pɔɪnt/ *verb* (**points, pointing, pointed**) show where something is, using your finger, a stick, etc. ଆଙ୍ଗୁଠି, ବାଡ଼ି, ଇତ୍ୟାଦି ଦେଖାଇ ନିର୍ଦ୍ଦିଷ୍ଟ ପଦାର୍ଥ ସୂଚାଇବା ବା ଦେଖାଇବା। *I asked him where the bank was and he pointed across the road.*

point out tell or show something ସୂଚିତ କରିବା *Esha pointed out that my bag was open.*

pointed /ˈpɔɪntɪd/ *adjective* with a sharp end ମୁନିଆ, ତୀକ୍ଷ୍ଣ *a pointed nose*

pointless /ˈpɔɪntləs/ *adjective* with no use or purpose ନିରର୍ଥକ, ଅର୍ଥହୀନ *It's pointless telling Lalit anything —he never listens.*

poison /ˈpɔɪzn/ *noun* a substance that can harm or kill someone if they eat, drink or breathe it ବିଷ, ଗରଳ, ହଳାହଳ *rat poison*

poison *verb* (**poisons, poisoning, poisoned**) use poison to kill or hurt somebody or something ମାରିବା ବା କଷ୍ଟଦେବା ପାଇଁ ବିଷ ଦେବା

poisonous /ˈpɔɪzənəs/ *adjective* something that is poisonous can kill someone or make them very ill if they eat, drink or breathe it ବିଷାକ୍ତ *Some berries are poisonous.*

poke /pəʊk/ *verb* (**pokes, poking, poked**) push somebody or something hard with your finger or another long thin thing ଆଙ୍ଗୁଠି, ବାଡ଼ି ଇତ୍ୟାଦିରେ କାହାରିକୁ ବା କୌଣସି ପଦାର୍ଥକୁ ଠେଲିବା ବା କେଞ୍ଚିବା

poke *noun* ଠେଲା ବା କେଞ୍ଚା *I gave her a poke to wake her up.*

polar /ˈpəʊlə(r)/ *adjective* of the North or South Pole ଉତ୍ତର ବା ଦକ୍ଷିଣ ମେରୁ ସମ୍ବନ୍ଧୀୟ, ଏହିସ୍ଥାନର

polar bear *noun* (*plural* **polar bears**) a white bear that lives near the North Pole ଉତ୍ତର ମେରୁ ଅଂଚଳର ଧଳା ଭାଲୁ

pole¹ /pəʊl/ *noun* a long thin piece of wood or metal. Poles are often used to hold something up କାଠ ବା ଧାତୁର ଲମ୍ବା ବାଡ଼ି ବା ଖୁଣ୍ଟ *a flagpole*

pole² /pəʊl/ *noun* one of two places at the northernmost or southernmost end of the earth ଉତ୍ତର ବା ଦକ୍ଷିଣ ମେରୁ *the North Pole* ○ *the South Pole*

police /pəˈliːs/ *noun* (*no singular*) a group of people whose job is to make sure that people do not break the laws of a country ଦେଶର ଶାନ୍ତିଶୃଙ୍ଖଳା ରକ୍ଷା କରୁଥିବା ବେସାମରିକ ଅଧିକାରି, ପୁଲିସ୍ *Have the police found the burglar?*

policeman /pəˈliːsmən/ *noun* (*plural* **policemen**) a man who works in the police ପୋଲିସ୍ ବାଲା, ସିପାହୀ

police station *noun* (*plural* **police stations**) an office where police officers work ଥାନା, ଫାଣ୍ଡି

policewoman /pəˈliːswʊmən/ *noun* (*plural* **policewomen**) a woman who works in the police ମହିଳା ପୋଲିସ୍

policy /ˈpɒləsi/ *noun* (*plural* **policies**) the plans of a group of people ଦେଶ ବା କୌଣସି ଗୋଷ୍ଠିର ନୀତି *What is the government's policy on education?*

polio /ˈpəʊliəʊ/ *noun* (*no plural*) a disease that affects the nervous system and sometimes results in a part of the body becoming paralysed ସୂକ୍ଷ୍ମାଣୁ (ଭାଇରସ୍) ଜନିତ ସ୍ନାୟୁବିକ ରୋଗ ଯାହା ପେଶିର କ୍ଷୟ କରି ଅଙ୍ଗକୁ ବିକଳାଙ୍ଗ ବା ଅଚଳ କରିଦିଏ

polish /ˈpɒlɪʃ/ *verb* (**polishes, polishing, polished**) rub something so that it shines ପାଲିସ୍ କରିବା *Have you polished your shoes?*

polish *noun* (*no plural*) a substance that you rub over something to make it shine ପାଲିସ୍ କରିବା ପାଇଁ ବ୍ୟବହୃତ ପଦାର୍ଥ *shoe polish*

polite /pəˈlaɪt/ *adjective* if you are polite, you are helpful and kind to other people and you do not do or say things that make them sad or angry ଶିଷ୍ଟ, ଭଦ୍ର, ସୌଜନ୍ୟପୂର୍ଣ୍ଣ *It is polite to say 'please' when you ask for something.* ✪ ବିପରୀତ **impolite** ବା **rude**

politely *adverb* ଶିଷ୍ଟଭାବରେ, ଭଦ୍ର ଭାବରେ *He asked politely for a glass of water.* ✪ ବିପରୀତ **rudely**

politeness *noun* (*no plural*) being polite ଶିଷ୍ଟତା, ଭଦ୍ରତା

political /pəˈlɪtɪkl/ *adjective* of or about the work of government ରାଜନୀତି ସମ୍ବନ୍ଧୀୟ, ରାଜନୈତିକ *A political party is a group of people who have the same ideas about how to control their country.*

politically *adverb* ରାଜନୈତିକ ଭାବରେ *a politically powerful country*

politician /ˌpɒləˈtɪʃn/ *noun* a person who works in the government or who wants to work in the government ରାଜନୀତିରେ ବୃତ୍ତିଗତ ଭାବେ ନିୟୋଜିତ ବ୍ୟକ୍ତି, ରାଜନୈତିକ ବ୍ୟକ୍ତି *Members of Parliament are politicians.*

politics /ˈpɒlətɪks/ *noun* (*no plural*) the ideas and activities relating to the work of a government in a country or a state ରାଜନୀତି, ରାଜନୈତିକ ବ୍ୟାପାର *Are you interested in politics?*

poll /pəʊl/ *noun* the process of voting in an election ଭୋଟଦାନ ପ୍ରକ୍ରିୟା *The country goes to the polls next month.*

pollen /ˈpɒlən/ *noun* (*no plural*) the fine powder found in flowers ପରାଗ, ପୁଷ୍ପରେଣୁ

pollinate /ˈpɒləneɪt/ *verb* (**pollinates, pollinating, pollinated**) make a plant or flower produce seeds by putting **pollen** into it ପରାଗ ସଂଯୋଗ ଦ୍ୱାରା ଗଛକୁ ଫଳପ୍ରଦ କରିବା

pollination /ˌpɒləˈneɪʃn/ *noun* (*no plural*) ପରାଗ ସଙ୍ଗମ, ପରାଗଯୋଗ, ପରାଗଣ

pollutant /pəˈluːtənt/ *noun* a substance that pollutes, the air and water, for example ଦୂଷିତ କରିବା ପଦାର୍ଥ *harmful pollutants in the atmosphere*

pollute /pəˈluːt/ *verb* (**pollutes, polluting, polluted**) make air, rivers, etc. dirty and dangerous ଦୂଷିତ କରିବା, ପ୍ରଦୂଷିତ କରିବା *Many rivers are polluted by chemicals from factories.*

pollution /pəˈluːʃn/ *noun* (*no plural*) **1** the process of polluting air, rivers, etc. ପ୍ରଦୂଷଣ *environmental pollution* **2** dirty and dangerous substances from cars, factories, etc. that pollute (ଗାଡ଼ି, ମଟର କାରଖାନା, ଇତ୍ୟାଦିରୁ ବାହାରୁ ଥିବା ପ୍ରଦୂଷକ ପଦାର୍ଥ)

polyandry /ˌpɒliˈændri/ *noun* (*no plural*) the practice of having more than one husband at one time ଏକ ସମୟରେ ବହୁ ସ୍ୱାମୀ ଗ୍ରହଣ ପ୍ରଥା, ବହୁ ପତିତ୍ୱ ପ୍ରଥା

polygamy /pəˈlɪgəmi/ *noun* (*no plural*) the practice of having more than one wife at one time ଏକ ସମୟ କାଳରେ ବହୁ ପତ୍ନୀ ଗ୍ରହଣ କରିବା ପ୍ରଥା

pomegranate /ˈpɒmɪgrænɪt/ *noun* a round fruit with thick red skin and sweet juicy flesh with many seeds ଡାଳିମ୍ବ, ବେଦାନା ➪ ଚିତ୍ର ପାଇଁ **fruit** ଦେଖନ୍ତୁ।

pond /pɒnd/ *noun* a small area of water which is usually quite still

ପୋଖରୀ, ପୁଷ୍କରିଣୀ *We have a fish pond in our garden.* ➪ **lake** ଦେଖନ୍ତୁ।

pony /ˈpəʊni/ *noun* (*plural* **ponies**) a small horse ଛୋଟ ଘୋଡ଼ା, ଟଟ୍ଟୁ ଘୋଡ଼ା

ponytail /ˈpəʊniteɪl/ *noun* long hair that is tied at the back of the head so that it hangs down ମୁଣ୍ଡ ପଛ ପଟେ ବନ୍ଧାଯାଇ ଝୁଲୁଥିବା କେଶ (ଘୋଡ଼ା ଲାଞ୍ଜ ପରି)

pool /puːl/ *noun* **1** a small area of still water, especially one that has formed naturally freshwater pools ସ୍ଥିର ପାଣିର ଏକ ଛୋଟ ସ୍ଥାନ, ବିଶେଷରୂପେ ପ୍ରାକୃତିକ ରୂପେ ସୃଷ୍ଟି ସ୍ଥିର ଜଳାଶୟ **2** a small amount of liquid or light on the ground ତଳେ ପଡ଼ିଥିବା ସ୍ୱଳ୍ପ ପରିମାଣର ତରଳ ପଦାର୍ଥ *After the rain there were pools of water on the road.* ○ *a pool of blood/water* **3** a place for swimming ପହଁରିବା ପାଇଁ ବିଶେଷଭାବେ ପ୍ରସ୍ତୁତ ଜଳଧାର, ସୁଇମିଂପୁଲ୍ *Kareena dived into the pool.*

poor /pɔː(r)/ *adjective* (**poorer, poorest**) **1** with very little money ଗରିବ, ଦରିଦ୍ର, ନିର୍ଦ୍ଧନ, *She was too poor to buy clothes for her children.* ✪ ବିପରୀତ **rich 1** ✪ Poor ର ବିଶେଷ୍ୟ ହେଲା **poverty**। **2** not good ଖରାପ *My grandfather is in very poor health.*

the poor *noun* (*no singular*) people who do not have much money ଗରିବ ଲୋକମାନେ, ନିର୍ଦ୍ଧନ ବ୍ୟକ୍ତି ସମୂହ

pop¹ /pɒp/ *noun* (*no plural*) modern music that a lot of young people like ବହୁ ଯୁବକ, ଯୁବତୀ ଭଲ ପାଉଥିବା ଆଧୁନିକ ସଙ୍ଗୀତ *What's your favourite pop group?* ○ *pop music*

pop² /pɒp/ *verb* (**pops, popping, popped**) **1** make a short sharp sound; make something make a short sharp sound ଆକସ୍ମିକ ତୀବ୍ର ଶବ୍ଦ କରିବା ବା କରାଇବା, 'ପପ୍' ଶବ୍ଦ କରିବା *The balloon will pop if you put a pin in it.* **2** put or take something somewhere quickly ଝଟ୍‌କରି କିଛି ପଦାର୍ଥ ଦେବା ବା ନେଇଯିବା *Feroza popped a sweet into her mouth.*

pop up appear suddenly ହଠାତ୍ ଆବିର୍ଭାବ ହେବା ବା ତିଆରି ହୋଇଯିବା *Fast food restaurants are popping up everywhere.*

popcorn /ˈpɒpkɔːn/ *noun* (*no plural*) dried seeds of maize which are heated until they burst to form light white balls ମକାମଞ୍ଜି ଭଜା, ମକା ଖଇ

popular /ˈpɒpjələ(r)/ *adjective* liked by a lot of people ଲୋକପ୍ରିୟ *Cricket is a popular sport in India.* ✪ ବିପରୀତ **unpopular**

popularity /ˌpɒpjuˈlærəti/ *noun* (*no plural*) the state of being liked by a lot of people ଲୋକପ୍ରିୟତା

population /ˌpɒpjuˈleɪʃn/ *noun* the number of people who live in a place ଜନସଂଖ୍ୟା *What is the population of your country?*

porcupine /ˈpɔːkjupaɪn/ *noun* a small animal with long sharp needle-like parts (called **quills**). A porcupine uses its quills to protect itself when attacked ଝିଙ୍କ

porridge /ˈpɒrɪdʒ/ *noun* (*no plural*) a soft food made from oats cooked with milk or water, that people eat for breakfast ଯବ ଜାତୀୟ ଶସ୍ୟର ଚୂନାକୁ ଦୁଧ ବା ପାଣିରେ ସିଝାଇ ପ୍ରସ୍ତୁତ କରାଯାଇଥିବା କ୍ଷୀର

port /pɔ:t/ *noun* a town or city by the sea, where ships arrive and leave ବନ୍ଦର, ପୋତାଶ୍ରୟ

portable /ˈpɔ:təbl/ *adjective* that you can move or carry easily ଛୋଟ, ସହଜରେ ବହନୀୟ *a portable television*

porter /ˈpɔ:tə(r)/ *noun* a person whose job is to carry people's bags in places like railway stations and hotels ବାହକ, କୁଲି

portion /ˈpɔ:ʃn/ *noun* a part of something that one person gets ଅଂଶ, ଭାଗ *He gave a portion of the money to each of his children.* ○ *a large portion of chips*

portrait /pɔ:treɪt/ *noun* a painting or picture of a person ବ୍ୟକ୍ତିଙ୍କର ଅଙ୍କିତ ଛବି

pose /pəʊz/ *verb* (**poses, posing, posed**) **1** sit or stand in a particular way so that you can be painted or photographed ଚିତ୍ରାଙ୍କନ ବା ଫଟୋ ଉଠାଇବା ପାଇଁ ପୋଜ୍ ଦେବା ବା ଏକ ଭଙ୍ଗୀରେ ରହିବା **2** pretend to be someone to cheat people ଠକିବା ପାଇଁ ନିଜକୁ ଭିନ୍ନ ବ୍ୟକ୍ତି ବୋଲି କହିବା *The stranger posed as Aladdin's uncle.* **3** ask a question or present a difficult situation ପ୍ରଶ୍ନ ପଚାରିବା ବା ସମସ୍ୟା ଉତ୍ପାଦନ କରିବା *Pollution is posing a major threat to the environment.*

pose *noun* the particular way in which someone sits or stands, so that they can be photographed, etc. ବସିବା ବା ଠିଆ ହେବାର ଭଙ୍ଗୀ

position /pəˈzɪʃn/ *noun* **1** the place where somebody or something is ସ୍ଥାନ, ନିର୍ଦ୍ଦିଷ୍ଟ ଜାଗା, ଅବସ୍ଥିତି *Can you show me the position of your town on the map?* **2** the way a person is sitting or lying, or the way a thing is standing ବ୍ୟକ୍ତିଙ୍କର ବସିବା ବା ଶୋଇବାର ଭଙ୍ଗୀ, କୌଣସି ପଦାର୍ଥର ସ୍ଥିତି ବା ଅବସ୍ଥା *She was still sitting in the same position when I came back.* **3** how things are at a certain time ଅବସ୍ଥା, ପରିସ୍ଥିତି *He's in a difficult position—he hasn't got enough money to finish his studies.*

positive /ˈpɒzətɪv/ *adjective* **1** completely certain; sure ସୁନିଶ୍ଚିତ, ନିଃସନ୍ଦେହ *Are you positive that you closed the door?* **2** that helps you or gives you hope ଆଶାପୂର୍ଣ୍ଣ *The teacher was very positive about my work.* **3** used for saying 'yes' or that you agree or support something ହଁ ଅର୍ଥ ସୂଚାଉଥିବା, ସ୍ୱୀକାରାତ୍ମକ *We got a positive response to our appeal for help.* ✪ ବିପରୀତ **negative**

positively *adverb* really; certainly ନିଶ୍ଚିତଭାବେ *The idea is positively stupid.*

possess /pəˈzes/ *verb* (**possesses, possessing, possessed**) have or own something ଅଧିକାର କରିବା, ଦଖଲରେ ରଖିବା *He lost everything that he possessed in the fire.* ✪ ଆମେ ସାଧାରଣତଃ **have** ଓ **own** ଶବ୍ଦ ବ୍ୟବହାର କରୁ।

possessions /pəˈzeʃn/ *noun* (*plural*) the things that you have or own ନିଜସ୍ୱ ସମ୍ପତ୍ତିବାଡ଼ି

possibility /ˌpɒsəˈbɪləti/ *noun* (*plural* **possibilities**) something that might happen ସମ୍ଭାବ୍ୟତା, ସମ୍ଭବପରତା *There's a possibility that it will rain, so take your umbrella.*

possible /ˈpɒsəbl/ *adjective* if something is possible, it can happen or you can do it ସମ୍ଭବ *Is it possible to go shopping today?* ✪ ବିପରୀତ **impossible**

possibly /ˈpɒsəbli/ *adverb* in a way that can be done ସମ୍ଭବ, ସମ୍ଭବତଃ, ସମ୍ଭବପରଭାବେ *I'll come as soon as I possibly can.*

post[1] /pəʊst/ *noun* **1** a tall piece of wood or metal that stands in the ground to hold something or to show where something is ଧାତୁ ବା କାଠର ଖମ୍ବ, ଖୁଣ୍ଟ, ଖୁଣ୍ଟି, ସ୍ତମ୍ଭ *Can you see a signpost anywhere?* **2** a job; a position in an organization ଚାକିରି, ପଦ ବା ନିଯୁକ୍ତିର *He has held the post of manager in that company for twenty-five years!*

post[2] /pəʊst/ *noun* (*no plural*) **1** the way of sending and receiving letters, parcels, etc. ପଠାଇବା ବା ପାଇବା ପଦ୍ଧତି ବା ପ୍ରକ୍ରିୟା, ଡାକ *I sent your photographs by post.* **2** letters and parcels that you send or receive ଚିଠପତ୍ର *Did you get any post this morning?*

postage /ˈpəʊstɪdʒ/ *noun* (*no plural*) money that you must pay to send a letter or parcel by post ଡାକ ଖର୍ଚ୍ଚ

postal /ˈpəʊstl/ *adjective* of the post ଡାକ ସମ୍ବନ୍ଧୀୟ *postal collections*

postbox /ˈpəʊstbɒks/ *noun* (*plural* **postboxes**) a box in the street where you put letters that you want to send ଡାକବାକ୍ସ

postcard /ˈpəʊstkɑːd/ *noun* a card without an envelope, especially one with a picture on one side, that you write on and send by post ପୋଷ୍ଟକାର୍ଡ଼

postcode /ˈpəʊstkəʊd/, **pincode** /ˈpɪnkəʊd/ *noun* a group of numbers and, in some countries, letters that you write at the end of an address ଠିକଣା ଶେଷରେ ଲେଖାଯାଉଥିବା ସ୍ଥାନର ଚିହ୍ନଟ ସଂଖ୍ୟା

postman /ˈpəʊstmən/ *noun* (*plural* **postmen**) a man who takes (**delivers**) letters and parcels to people ଡାକବାଲା ପୋଷ୍ଟମ୍ୟାନ୍

post office *noun* (*plural* **post offices**) a building where you go to send letters and parcels and to buy stamps ଡାକଘର

post[3] /pəʊst/ *verb* (**posts, posting, posted**) **1** send a letter or parcel ଚିଠିପତ୍ର ଡାକରେ ପଠାଇବା *Could you post this letter for me?* **2** send somebody to a place to do a job କୌଣସି ବ୍ୟକ୍ତିକୁ ନିର୍ଦ୍ଦିଷ୍ଟ କାମ ପାଇଁ କୌଣସି ସ୍ଥାନକୁ ପଠାଇବା ବା ସେଠାରେ ଅବସ୍ଥାପନ କରିବା *Gauri's company has posted her to Japan for two years.*

poster /ˈpəʊstə(r)/ *noun* a big piece of paper on a wall, with pictures or words on it କାନ୍ଥରେ ଲଗାଯାଉଥିବା ଛବି ବା ଲେଖାଥିବା ବଡ଼ କାଗଜ, ପୋଷ୍ଟର

postpone /pəˈspəʊn/ *verb* (**postpones, postponing, postponed**) say that something will happen at a later time, not now କୌଣସି କାର୍ଯ୍ୟକୁ ନିର୍ଦ୍ଧାରିତ ସମୟରୁ ପର ସମୟକୁ ଘୁଞ୍ଚାଇବା *It's raining, so we will postpone the game until tomorrow.*

pot /pɒt/ *noun* **1** a deep round container for cooking ରାନ୍ଧିବା ପାଇଁ ଗୋଲିଆ ଗଭୀର ପାତ୍ର (ହାଣ୍ଡି, ଡେକଚି ଇତ୍ୟାଦି) *a big pot of soup* **2** a container that you use for a special thing ବିଶେଷ କାମରେ ବ୍ୟବହୃତ ପାତ୍ର *a teapot* ○ *a flower pot*

potato /pəˈteɪtəʊ/ *noun* (*plural* **potatoes**) a round vegetable that grows under the ground, that is white on the inside and brown or yellow on the outside. You cook it before eating it ଆଳୁ ➪ ଚିତ୍ର ପାଇଁ **vegetable** ଦେଖନ୍ତୁ ।

potter /ˈpɒtə(r)/ *noun* a person who makes pots and other containers from **clay** କୁମ୍ଭାର

pottery /ˈpɒtəri/ *noun* (*no plural*) **1** cups, plates and other things made from **clay** (heavy earth that becomes hard when it dries) ମାଟିରେ ତିଆରି ପାତ୍ରସମୂହ *This shop sells beautiful pottery.* **2** the skill of making cups, plates and other things from clay ମାଟିପାତ୍ର ଗଢ଼ିବାର ଦକ୍ଷତା *Her hobby is pottery.*

pouch /paʊtʃ/ *noun* (*plural* **pouches**) **1** a small bag ଛୋଟଥଳି **2** a bag of skin on the stomach of some female animals, like kangaroos, in which they carry their young ଛୁଆଙ୍କୁ ବହନ କରିବା ପାଇଁ କଙ୍ଗାରୁ ଇତ୍ୟାଦି ଦ୍ୱିଗର୍ଭ ପ୍ରାଣୀଙ୍କ ପେଟରେ ପକେଟ୍ ସଦୃଶ ଆଧାର

poultry /pəʊltri/ *noun* (*no singular*) birds like chickens that people keep for their eggs or their meat ଖାଦ୍ୟ ପାଇଁ ବ୍ୟବହୃତ କୁକୁଡ଼ା, ବତକ ଇତ୍ୟାଦି ଗୃହପାଳିତ ପକ୍ଷୀ

pounce /paʊns/ *verb* (**pounces, pouncing, pounced**) jump on somebody or something suddenly ହଠାତ୍ ଡେଇଁ, ମାଡ଼ି ବସିବା ପଡ଼ି ଝାମ୍ପ ମାରିବା *The cat pounced on the bird.*

pound /paʊnd/ *noun* money that people use in Britain. There are 100 **pence** in a pound ବ୍ରିଟେନ୍‌ର ମୁଦ୍ରା (୧୦୦ ପେନ୍ସରେ ଏକପାଉଣ୍ଡ) *The computer cost six hundred pounds.*

pour /pɔː(r)/ *verb* (**pours, pouring, poured**) make liquid flow out of or into something ତରଳ ପଦାର୍ଥ ଅଜାଡ଼ିବା *She poured some water into my glass.*
it's pouring it is raining very hard ପ୍ରବଳ ବର୍ଷା ହେଉଛି

poverty /ˈpɒvəti/ *noun* (*no plural*) the state of being poor ଦରିଦ୍ର ଅବସ୍ଥା *There are many people living in poverty in this city.*

powder /ˈpaʊdə(r)/ *noun* a dry substance that is made of a lot of very small pieces ଚୂର୍ଣ୍ଣ ସୂକ୍ଷ୍ମ ଗୁଣ୍ଡ *washing powder*

power /ˈpaʊə(r)/ *noun* **1** (*no plural*) the ability to make people do what you want ଶକ୍ତି, ସାମର୍ଥ୍ୟ, ଆଦେଶ ଦେବାର କ୍ଷମତା ବା ଅଧିକାର *The president has a lot of power.* **2** (*no plural*) strength or ability to do something ଶକ୍ତି, ସାମର୍ଥ୍ୟ, ଦକ୍ଷତା *I did everything in my power to help her.* **3** (*no *plural*) what makes things work; energy ଶକ୍ତି; ଯନ୍ତ୍ର, କଳ ଇତ୍ୟାଦିର ଚାଳନରେ ବ୍ୟବହୃତ ଇନ୍ଧନ *nuclear power* **4** (*plural* **powers**) the right to do something ଅଧିକାର, କ୍ଷମତା *Police officers have the power to arrest people.*

power station *noun* (*plural* **power stations**) a place where electricity is made ବିଦ୍ୟୁତ୍ ଉତ୍ପାଦନ କେନ୍ଦ୍ର

power station

powerful /ˈpaʊəfl/ *adjective* **1** very strong; with a lot of power ଶକ୍ତିଶାଳୀ *The car has a very powerful engine.* **2** that you can smell or hear clearly, or feel strongly ପ୍ରଭାବଶାଳୀ (ଅନୁଭୂତି, ମତ, ବକ୍ତୃତା ଇତ୍ୟାଦି) ତୀବ୍ର (ଶବ୍ଦ, ଗନ୍ଧ ଇତ୍ୟାଦି) *a powerful speech*

practical /ˈpræktɪkl/ *adjective* **1** that is about doing or making things, not just about ideas ବ୍ୟବହାରିକ, ପ୍ରାୟୋଗିକ, ପ୍ରକୃତରେ କରା ଯାଉଥିବା (ଖାଲି ଭାବନା ନୁହେଁ) *Have you got any practical experience of teaching?* **2** possible to do easily ସହଜସାଧ୍ୟ *Your plan isn't practical.*

practically /ˈpræktɪkli/ *adverb* almost; nearly ପ୍ରାୟ *It rained practically all day.*

practice /ˈpræktɪs/ *noun* (*no plural*) the act of doing something many times so that you will do it well ଅଭ୍ୟାସ, ବାରମ୍ବାର ଚେଷ୍ଟା *You need lots of practice when you're learning to play a musical instrument.*

out of practice not good at something, because you have not done it for a long time ଅଭ୍ୟାସ ଛାଡ଼ିଯାଇଥିବାବସ୍ଥା

practise /ˈpræktɪs/ *verb* (**practises, practising, practised**) do something many times so that you will do it well ଅଭ୍ୟାସ କରିବା, ବାରମ୍ବାର କରିବା *If you want to play the piano well, you must practise every day.*

praise /preɪz/ *verb* (**praises, praising, praised**) say that somebody or something is good ପ୍ରଶଂସା କରିବା *She was praised for her hard work.*

praise *noun* (*no plural*) ପ୍ରଶଂସା *The book has received a lot of praise.*

pram /præm/ *noun* a thing for a baby to go out in. It has wheels so you can push it as you walk along ଛୋଟ ପିଲାଙ୍କୁ ନେବା ପାଇଁ ଠେଲାଗାଡ଼ି

prawn /prɔːn/ *noun* a small sea animal with ten legs and a long tail, that can be eaten ଚିଙ୍ଗୁଡ଼ି

pray /preɪ/ *verb* (**prays, praying, prayed**) speak to God or a god ପ୍ରାର୍ଥନା କରିବା *They prayed for help.*

prayer /preə(r)/ *noun* words that you say when you speak to God ପ୍ରାର୍ଥନା। *They said a prayer for peace.*

preach /priːtʃ/ *verb* (**preaches, preaching, preached**) talk about God to a group of people ଧର୍ମସମ୍ବନ୍ଧରେ ବକ୍ତୃତା ଦେବା

precaution /prɪˈkɔːʃn/ *noun* something that you do so that bad things will not happen ପୂର୍ବ ସତର୍କତା, ସତର୍କତା ମୂଳକ ପଦକ୍ଷେପ *I took the precaution of locking all the windows when I went out.*

precede /prɪˈsiːd/ *verb* (**precedes, preceding, preceded**) come or happen before something ପୂର୍ବରୁ ଆସିବା ବା ଯିବା, ପୂର୍ବଗାମୀ ହେବା; ପୂର୍ବରୁ ଘଟିବା *Lightning precedes thunder during a storm.*

precious /ˈpreʃəs/ *adjective* **1** very valuable ମୂଲ୍ୟବାନ୍, ବହୁମୂଲ୍ୟ *Diamonds are precious stones*. **2** that you love very much ଅତି ଆଦରଣୀୟ *My family is very precious to me.*

precise /prɪˈsaɪs/ *adjective* exactly right ଠିକ୍, ସଠିକ୍ *I gave him precise instructions on how to get to my house.*

precisely *adverb* exactly ସଠିକ୍ ଭାବରେ

predator /ˈpredətə(r)/ *noun* an animal that hunts and kills other animals for food ଖାଇବା ପାଇଁ ଅନ୍ୟ ଜୀବ ଜନ୍ତୁ ଶିକାର କରୁଥିବା ପଶୁ ➪ **prey** ଦେଖନ୍ତୁ।

predicate /ˈpredɪkeɪt/ *noun* a part of a sentence with a verb that tells what the subject is or does. In the sentence 'He went cycling after returning from school' the predicate is 'went cycling after returning from school' (ବ୍ୟାକରଣ) କର୍ତ୍ତା ବା ଉଦ୍ଦେଶ୍ୟ ଭାବେ କୁହାଯାଉଥିବା ବାକ୍ୟାଂଶ; ବିଧେୟ

predict /prɪˈdɪkt/ *verb* (**predicts, predicting, predicted**) say what you think will happen ଭବିଷ୍ୟତ କଥା କହିବା, ଭବିଷ୍ୟତ ବାଣୀ କହିବା *She predicted that it would rain, and she was right.*

prefer /prɪˈfɜː(r)/ *verb* (**prefers, preferring, preferred**) like one thing or person better than another ଅଧିକ ପସନ୍ଦ କରିବା ବା ବାଛିବା *Would you prefer tea or coffee?*

preference /ˈprefrəns/ *noun* liking one thing or person better than another ପସନ୍ଦ

prefix /priːfɪks/ *noun* (*plural* **prefixes**) a group of letters that you add to the beginning of a word to make another word ଉପପଦ, ଉପସର୍ଗ, ପୂର୍ବପଦ *The prefix 'im-' means 'not', so 'impossible' means 'not possible'.* ➪ **suffix** ଦେଖନ୍ତୁ।

pregnant /ˈpregnənt/ *adjective* if a woman or female animal is pregnant, she has a baby growing in her body ଗର୍ଭବତୀ, ଗର୍ଭିଣୀ

prehistoric /ˌpriːhɪˈstɒrɪk/ *adjective* about or of a period very long ago when people had not started keeping records about things as they happened ପ୍ରାଗୈତିହାସିକ, ପ୍ରାଗ୍ ଐତିହାସିକ *The mammoth is a prehistoric animal.*

prejudice /ˈpredʒudɪs/ *noun* a feeling of not liking somebody or something, before you know much about them ପୂର୍ବଧାରଣାଗତ ମତ; ପକ୍ଷପାତ *She has a prejudice against foreigners.*

premolar /priːˈməʊlə(r)/ *noun* one of the wide and flat grinding teeth between **canines** and **molars**

କଳଦାନ୍ତ ଓ ଶ୍ୱାନଦାନ୍ତ ମଝିରେ ଥିବା ଦାନ୍ତ, ଅଗ୍ରପେଷକ ଦାନ୍ତ ➪ **canine, incisor** ଓ **molar** ଦେଖନ୍ତୁ। ➪ ଚିତ୍ର ପାଇଁ **tooth** ଦେଖନ୍ତୁ।

preparation /ˌprepəˈreɪʃn/ *noun* **1** (*no plural*) the act of making something ready ପ୍ରସ୍ତୁତି *the preparation of food* **2 preparations** (*plural*) what you do to get ready for something ଆୟୋଜନ *wedding preparations*

in preparation for something to get ready for something କିଛି କାମର ପ୍ରସ୍ତୁତି ପାଇଁ *I packed my bags in preparation for the journey.*

prepare /prɪˈpeə(r)/ *verb* (**prepares, preparing, prepared**) make somebody or something ready; make yourself ready ପ୍ରସ୍ତୁତ କରିବା, ତିଆରି କରିବା; ପ୍ରସ୍ତୁତ ହେବା *I prepared well for the exam.*

prepared to happy to do something (କିଛି କରିବାକୁ) ଆଗ୍ରହରେ ପ୍ରସ୍ତୁତ ରହିବା *I'm not prepared to give you any money.*

preposition /ˌprepəˈzɪʃn/ *noun* a word that you use before a noun or pronoun to show where, when, how, etc. (ବ୍ୟାକରଣ) ସମ୍ବନ୍ଧସୂଚକ ଅବ୍ୟୟପଦ *'In', 'for', 'after' and 'above' are all prepositions.*

prescribe /prɪˈskraɪb/ *verb* (**prescribes, prescribing, prescribed**) say that somebody must take a medicine ବ୍ୟବହାର ପାଇଁ ଔଷଧ ନିର୍ଦ୍ଧାରଣ କରିବା *The doctor prescribed some tablets for her cough.*

prescription /prɪˈskrɪpʃn/ *noun* a piece of paper where a doctor writes what medicine you need. You take it to a **chemist's** and get the medicine there ଔଷଧ ବ୍ୟବହାର ପାଇଁ ଡାକ୍ତରଙ୍କ ଲିଖିତ ଉପଦେଶ

presence /ˈprezns/ *noun* (*no plural*) the act of being in a place ଉପସ୍ଥିତି *She was so quiet that I didn't notice her presence.* ✪ ବିପରୀତ **absence**

present¹ /ˈpreznt/ *adjective* **1** in a place ଉପସ୍ଥିତ *There were 200 people present at the meeting.* ✪ ବିପରୀତ **absent 2** being or happening now ବର୍ତ୍ତମାନର *What is your present job?*

present² /ˈpreznt/ *noun* (*no plural*) **1** the time now ବର୍ତ୍ତମାନ ସମୟ *She's in the office at present.* **2** (**present tense** ମଧ୍ୟ) the form of a verb that you use to talk about now (ବ୍ୟାକରଣ) ବର୍ତ୍ତମାନ କାଳ ➪ **past¹ 2** ଏବଂ **future** ଦେଖନ୍ତୁ।

present³ /ˈpreznt/ *noun* something that you give to or get from somebody, on birthdays for example ଉପହାର *a birthday present*

present⁴ /prɪˈznt/ *verb* (**presents, presenting, presented**) give something to somebody at a special ceremony ଉପହାର ଦେବା *Who presented the prizes to the winners?*

presentation /ˌpreznˈteɪʃn/ *noun* the act of presenting something ଉପହାର ପ୍ରଦାନ *The presentation of the prizes will take place at 7.30 p.m.*

preservation /ˌprezəˈveɪʃn/ *noun* (*no plural*) the act of keeping something safe or in good condition; making something stay the same ସଂରକ୍ଷଣ, ସଯତ୍ନ ରକ୍ଷଣ, ନିରାପଦ, ଅକ୍ଷତ ଓ ପଚନ ମୁକ୍ତ ଭାବରେ ରକ୍ଷଣ *the preservation of rare books*

preserve /prɪˈzɜːv/ *verb* (**preserves, preserving, preserved**) keep something safe or in good condition; make something stay the same ସଂରକ୍ଷଣ କରିବା, ଯତ୍ନରେ ରଖିବା; ସାଇତି ରଖିବା *Parts of the town are new, but they have preserved many of the old buildings.*

president /ˈprezɪdənt/ *noun* **1** the head of government in many countries ରାଷ୍ଟ୍ରପତି, ପ୍ରେସିଡେଣ୍ଟ *the President of the United States of America* **2** the most important person in a big company, club, etc. କୌଣସି ବଡ଼ ସଂସ୍ଥାର ମୁଖ୍ୟ ବା ଅଧ୍ୟକ୍ଷ, ପ୍ରେସିଡେଣ୍ଟ; (ସଭା, ସମିତିର) ସଭାପତି

presidential /ˌprezɪˈdenʃl/ *adjective* of a president or his/her work ରାଷ୍ଟ୍ରପତି, ଅଧ୍ୟକ୍ଷ ବା ସଭାପତି ସମ୍ବନ୍ଧୀୟ *the presidential elections*

press¹ /pres/ *verb* (**presses, pressing, pressed**) **1** push something strongly ଚାପିବା, ମାଡ଼ିବା, ଚିପିବା *If you press this button, the door will open.* **2** make clothes flat and smooth using an iron ଲୁଗାପଟା ଇସ୍ତ୍ରୀକରିବା *This shirt needs to be pressed.*

press² /pres/ *noun* **1** (*plural* **presses**) a machine for printing things like books and newspapers ଛାପାକଳ, ମୁଦ୍ରାଣାଳୟ, ପ୍ରେସ୍ **2 the press** (*no plural*) newspapers and magazines and the people who write them ସମୂହଭାବେ ସମ୍ବାଦପତ୍ର, ପତ୍ରିକା ଇତ୍ୟାଦି ଓ ସେଥିରେ ଲେଖୁଥିବା ସାମ୍ବାଦିକ ମଣ୍ଡଳୀ *She told her story to the press.*

printing press

pressure /ˈpreʃə(r)/ *noun* **1** (*no plural*) the force that presses on something ଚାପ *the air pressure in a car tyre* **2** (*plural* **pressures**) a feeling of worry or unhappiness, for example because you have too many things to do ଚିନ୍ତା, ଦୁଃଖ, କାମ, ପାଠପଢ଼ା ଇତ୍ୟାଦିର ଚାପ ବା ତାଡ଼ନା *the pressures of city life*

pretend /prɪˈtend/ *verb* (**pretends, pretending, pretended**) try to make somebody believe something that is not true ଛଳନା କରିବା, ବାହାନା କରିବା *He didn't want to talk, so he pretended to be asleep.*

pretty /ˈprɪti/ *adjective* (**prettier, prettiest**) nice to look at ସୁନ୍ଦର, କମନୀୟ *a pretty little girl* ○ *These flowers are very pretty.* ➪ ଟିପ୍ପଣୀ ଦେଖନ୍ତୁ ।

prevalent /ˈprevələnt/ *adjective* something that is prevalent is very common at a particular time or in a particular place ସାଧାରଣରେ ପ୍ରଚଳିତ, ସାଧାରଣ ଭାବେ ଘଟୁଥିବା *the prevalent view among young people*

prevent /prɪˈvent/ *verb* (**prevents, preventing, prevented**) stop somebody from doing something or stop something from happening କିଛି କାମ କରିବାରେ ବାଧା ଦେବା, ନିବାରଣ କରିବା (କୌଣସି ଘଟଣାକୁ) ପ୍ରତିରୋଧ କରିବା; ବିରୋଧ କରିବା *He tried to prevent the fire from spreading.*

prevention /prɪˈvenʃn/ *noun* (*no plural*) the act of preventing something ପ୍ରତିରୋଧ, ନିବାରଣ, ନିରୋଧ *People say that prevention is better than cure.*

previous /ˈpriːviəs/ *adjective* that happened or came before or earlier ପୂର୍ବବର୍ତ୍ତୀ, ପୂର୍ବର, ଆଗରୁ *Who was the previous owner of the car?*

previously *adverb* ପୂର୍ବରେ, ଆଗେ *I work as a teacher now, but previously I was a secretary.*

prey /preɪ/ *noun* (*no plural*) an animal or a bird that another animal or bird kills for food ଖାଦ୍ୟ ପାଇଁ ଅନ୍ୱେଷିତ ପଶୁପକ୍ଷୀ, ଶିକାର *Zebras are prey for lions.* ➪ **predator** ଦେଖନ୍ତୁ।

price /praɪs/ *noun* the amount of money you pay to buy something ମୂଲ୍ୟ, ଦର, ଦାମ୍ *The price of that book is Rs 45.*

priceless /praɪsləs/ *adjective* extremely valuable ଅତିମୂଲ୍ୟବାନ, ବହୁମୂଲ୍ୟ, ଦୁର୍ମୂଲ୍ୟ *the priceless jewels of the Nizam*

prick /prɪk/ *verb* (**pricks, pricking, pricked**) make a very small hole in something, or in the skin, with a sharp point ଫୋପାଡ଼ି, ଛିଦ୍ର କରିବା *I pricked my finger on a needle.*

prickle /ˈprɪkl/ *noun* a sharp point on a plant or an animal ଉଦ୍ଭିଦର କଣ୍ଟା; ଝିଙ୍କ କାଠି *A hedgehog has prickles.*

prickly *adjective* covered with prickles କଣ୍ଟକିତ, କଣ୍ଟାଯୁକ୍ତ *a prickly bush*

pride /praɪd/ *noun* (*no plural*) **1** the feeling of being pleased about something that you or others have done or about something that you have; the feeling of being proud ଗର୍ବ, ଆତ୍ମାଭିମାନ *She showed us her painting with great pride.* **2** the feeling that you are better than other people ଅହମିକା, ଗର୍ବ **3** a group of lions ସିଂହଦଳ

priest /priːst/ *noun* a person who leads people in their religion ଧର୍ମଯାଜକ, ପୁରୋହିତ

primary /ˈpraɪməri/ *adjective* first; most important ପ୍ରାଥମିକ; ମୌଳିକ, ମୁଖ୍ୟ *What is the primary cause of the illness?*

prime /praɪm/ *adjective* main, important or the best ମୁଖ୍ୟ, ଗୁରୁତ୍ୱପୂର୍ଣ୍ଣ, ସର୍ବଶ୍ରେଷ୍ଠ

prime minister *noun* (*plural* **prime ministers**) the leader of the government in some countries, for example in India ପ୍ରଧାନମନ୍ତ୍ରୀ

primitive /ˈprɪmətɪv/ *adjective* **1** about a time very long ago ପ୍ରାଚୀନ, ଆଦିମ *Primitive man lived in caves.* **2** simple; not modern or comfortable ସରଳ; ପୁରୁଣାକାଳିଆ ଓ ଅସୁବିଧାଜନକ *a primitive washing machine*

prince /prɪns/ *noun* **1** a man in a royal family, especially the son of a king or queen ରାଜାଙ୍କ ଛଡ଼ା ରାଜପରିବାରର

ପୁରୁଷ ଲୋକ, ଯୁବରାଜ **2** a man who is the ruler of a small country ସାମନ୍ତ ରାଜା

princess /ˌprɪnˈses/ *noun* (*plural* **princesses**) a woman in a royal family, especially the daughter of a king or queen or the wife of a prince ରାଜପରିବାରର ସ୍ତ୍ରୀଲୋକ; ରାଜକୁମାରୀ; ଯୁବରାଜଙ୍କ ପତ୍ନୀ

principal[1] /ˈprɪnsəpl/ *adjective* most important ମୁଖ୍ୟ *My principal reason for going to Rome was to learn Italian.*

principal[2] /ˈprɪnsəpl/ *noun* a person who is in charge of a school or college ସ୍କୁଲ ବା କଲେଜର ଅଧକ୍ଷ, ପ୍ରିନ୍ସିପାଲ୍

principle /ˈprɪnsəpl/ *noun* **1** a rule that you believe in because you think it is right ବିଶ୍ୱାସ କରୁଥିବା ସିଦ୍ଧାନ୍ତ, ନୀତି, ନିୟମ; ବ୍ୟକ୍ତିଗତ ଭାବଧାରା ବା ଆଚରଣ *He has very strong principles.* **2** a rule or fact about how something happens (କୌଣସି ବିଷୟର) ମୂଳ ସିଦ୍ଧାନ୍ତ, ନିୟମ ବା ପଦ୍ଧତି *scientific principles*

> **principal** or **principle**?
>
> ମନେ ରଖନ୍ତୁ ! **Principal** ଓ **principle** ଶବ୍ଦର ଉଚ୍ଚାରଣ ଏକାପରି, କିନ୍ତୁ ବନାନ ଓ ଅର୍ଥ ଭିନ୍ନ।

print /prɪnt/ *verb* (**prints, printing, printed**) put words or pictures onto paper using a machine. Books, newspapers and magazines are printed ଛାପିବା, ମୁଦ୍ରଣ କରିବା

print *noun* **1** (*no plural*) letters or pictures that a machine makes on paper ମୁଦ୍ରିତ ଲେଖା ବା ଛବି *The print is too small to read.* **2** (*plural* **prints**) a mark on a surface that something has made by pressing ଚାପ ପ୍ରୟୋଗ ଦ୍ୱାରା ହୋଇଥିବା ଚିହ୍ନ *footprints in the snow* **3** (*plural* **prints**) a copy on paper of a painting or photograph ଚିତ୍ର ବା ଫଟୋର ନକଲ ବା କପି

printer /ˈprɪntə(r)/ *noun* **1** a person or company that prints things like books or newspapers ମୁଦ୍ରଣ ବା ଛପାଇବା କାର୍ଯ୍ୟ କରୁଥିବା ବ୍ୟକ୍ତି ବା ସଂସ୍ଥା, ମୁଦ୍ରାକର **2** a machine that prints words from a computer କମ୍ପ୍ୟୁଟରର ମୁଦ୍ରଣ ଯନ୍ତ୍ର

printout /ˈprɪntaʊt/ *noun* a page with printed information produced by a computer କମ୍ପ୍ୟୁଟର୍ ମୁଦ୍ରଣ ଯନ୍ତ୍ର ଛାପୁଥିବା ପୃଷ୍ଠା

priority /praɪˈɒrəti/ *noun* **1** (*plural* **priorities**) something that is most important and which you must do before anything else ଅନ୍ୟ ବିଷୟଠାରୁ ଅଧିକ ଗୁରୁତ୍ୱପୂର୍ଣ୍ଣ ବିଷୟ ବା କାମ *Her priority is to buy a house in a good locality.* **2** (*no plural*) the state of being more important or coming before something or someone else ଅଗ୍ରାଧିକାର, ପ୍ରାଧାନ୍ୟ *In emergency cases, priority is given to children and old people.*

prism /ˈprɪzəm/ *noun* a transparent glass or plastic object which separates light that passes through it into seven different colours ସ୍ୱଚ୍ଛ କାଚ ବା ପ୍ଲାଷ୍ଟିକର ତ୍ରିପାର୍ଶ୍ୱ ସମାନ୍ତରାଳ ଘନକ୍ଷେତ୍ର ଯାହା ଆଲୋକକୁ ଏହାର ସାତ ରଙ୍ଗରେ ବିଭାଜିତ କରେ ପ୍ରିଜ୍ମ

prison /ˈprɪzn/ *noun* a place where people are kept as a punishment because they have done something that is against the law, jail କାରାଗାର, ଜେଲ୍, କଇଦୀଖାନା, ବନ୍ଦୀଶାଳ, *He was sent to prison for robbing a bank.*

prisoner /ˈprɪznə(r)/ *noun* a person who is in prison or any person who is not free ବନ୍ଦୀ, କଇଦୀ, କାରାରୁଦ୍ଧ ବ୍ୟକ୍ତି

private /ˈpraɪvət/ *adjective* **1** for one person or a small group of people only, and not for anybody else ନିଜସ୍ୱ, ବ୍ୟକ୍ତିଗତ, ଗୁପ୍ତ *You shouldn't read his letters—they're private.* **2** not controlled by the government ବ୍ୟକ୍ତିଗତ ଭାବରେ ପରିଚାଳିତ *a private hospital*

in private alone; without other people there ଏକାନ୍ତରେ, ଏକୁଟିଆରେ *Can I speak to you in private?*

privately *adverb* ଏକାନ୍ତରେ ଘରୋଇ ଭାବରେ *Let's go into my office—we can talk more privately there.*

privilege /ˈprɪvəlɪdʒ/ *noun* something special that only one person or a few people may do or have (ଜଣଙ୍କ ବା କିଛି ଲୋକଙ୍କ ପାଇଁ) ବିଶେଷ ଅଧିକାର ବା ସୁବିଧା

prize /praɪz/ *noun* something that you give to the person who wins a game, race, etc. ପୁରସ୍କାର

probable /ˈprɒbəbl/ *adjective* if something is probable, it is likely to happen or is likely to be true ସମ୍ଭବ *It is probable that he will win the elections.* ✪ ବିପରୀତ **improbable**

probably /ˈprɒbəbli/ *adverb* used for something that is likely to happen ସମ୍ଭବତଃ, ହୁଏତ

probe¹ /prəʊb/ *verb* (**probes, probing, probed** ମଧ୍ୟ) search for something or check something very carefully ଅନୁସନ୍ଧାନ କରିବା *He didn't like people probing about his past jobs.*

probe² /prəʊb/ *noun* **1** the act of searching for something very carefully ଅନୁସନ୍ଧାନ **2** (**space probe** ମଧ୍ୟ) a spacecraft with no people on it, that sends back information about planets, their moons and other objects in space ମଣିଷ ବିହିନ ମହାକାଶଯାନ ଯାହା ଗ୍ରହ ନକ୍ଷତ୍ରମାନଙ୍କ ବିଷୟରେ ତଥ୍ୟ ପଠାଏ ।

problem /ˈprɒbləm/ *noun* something that is difficult; something that makes you worry ଜଟିଳ ସମସ୍ୟା *There is a problem with my telephone—it doesn't work.*

procedure /prəˈsiːdʒə(r)/ *noun* a correct way of doing something କାର୍ଯ୍ୟପଦ୍ଧତି, ସଠିକ୍ ପଦ୍ଧତି ବା ପ୍ରଣାଳୀ *the standard procedures for admission to a school*

proceed /prəˈsiːd/ *verb* (**proceeds, proceeding, proceeded**) continue; go on ଅଗ୍ରସର ହେବା, ଆଗେଇ ଯିବା *If everyone is here, then we can proceed with the meeting.* ✪ ଆମେ ସାଧାରଣତଃ **continue** ଓ **go on** ବ୍ୟବହାର କରୁଁ ।

process¹ /ˈprəʊses/ *noun* (*plural* **processes**) a number of actions, one after the other, for doing or making something କାର୍ଯ୍ୟପ୍ରକ୍ରିୟା, କାର୍ଯ୍ୟଧାରା, କୌଣସି କାମର କ୍ରମ *Learning a language is usually a slow process.*

process² /ˈprəʊses/ *verb* (**processes, processing, processed**) **1** treat something to give it colour, make it safe, etc. ରଙ୍ଗିନ୍ କରିବା ପାଇଁ ବା ସୁରକ୍ଷିତ ରଖିବା ପାଇଁ ବ୍ୟବସ୍ଥା କରିବା *processed cheese* **2** deal with information, for example on a computer ତଥ୍ୟ ଇତ୍ୟାଦି (ଯଥା–କମ୍ପ୍ୟୁଟର୍‌ରେ) ସଜାଇ ରଖିବା *process data*

procession /prəˈseʃn/ *noun* a line of people or cars that are moving slowly along, as a part of a ceremony ଶୋଭାଯାତ୍ରା, ପଟୁଆର *We watched the carnival procession.*

produce¹ /prəˈdju:s/ *verb* (**produces, producing, produced**) **1** make or grow something to be sold ଉତ୍ପାଦନ କରିବା, ତିଆରି କରିବା *This factory produces cars.* ○ *What does the farm produce?* **2** make or grow something naturally ପ୍ରାକୃତିକ ପ୍ରକ୍ରିୟାରେ ଉତ୍ପନ୍ନ କରାଇବା ବା ଉତ୍ପନ୍ନ ହେବା; ଜାତକରିବା *These trees produce flowers in winter.* **3** make something happen ଘଟାଇବା, କରାଇବା *His hard work produced good results.* **4** organize something like a play or film ଫିଲ୍ମ ଇତ୍ୟାଦି ନିର୍ମାଣ କରିବା ବା ପ୍ରଯୋଜନ କରିବା *The play was produced by Umesh Patel.*

produce² /ˈprɑdju:s/ *noun* (*no plural*) food that you grow on a farm or in a garden to sell ଉତ୍ପାଦିତ ଚାଷ ଦ୍ରବ୍ୟ *fresh farm produce*

producer /prəˈdju:sə(r)/ *noun* **1** a person who organizes something like a play or film ଫିଲ୍ମ ଇତ୍ୟାଦିର ନିର୍ମାତା ବା ପ୍ରଯୋଜକ *a television producer* **2** a company or country that makes or grows something ଉତ୍ପାଦନକାରୀ ବା ଉତ୍ପାଦକ ସଂସ୍ଥା ବା ଦେଶ *Brazil is an important producer of coffee.*

product /ˈprɒdʌkt/ *noun* something that people make or grow to sell ଉତ୍ପନ୍ନ ଦ୍ରବ୍ୟ; ଉତ୍ପାଦିତ ସାମଗ୍ରୀ *Coffee is Brazil's main product.*

production /prəˈdʌkʃn/ *noun* (*no plural*) the process of making or growing something ଉତ୍ପାଦନ ପ୍ରକ୍ରିୟା, ପ୍ରଯୋଜନ *the production of oil*

profession /prəˈfeʃn/ *noun* a job that needs a lot of studying and special training ବୃତ୍ତି; ପେସା *She's a doctor by profession.*

professional /prəˈfeʃənl/ *adjective* **1** of or about somebody who has a profession ବୃତ୍ତିଗତ, ପେସାଗତ; ବୃତ୍ତି ବା ପେସା ସମ୍ବନ୍ଧୀୟ *I got professional advice from a lawyer.* **2** who does something for money as a job ପେସାଦାର ବୃତ୍ତି କରୁଥିବା ➪ **amateur** ଦେଖନ୍ତୁ।

professor /prəˈfesə(r)/ *noun* an important teacher at a university ବିଶ୍ୱବିଦ୍ୟାଳୟର ଉଚ୍ଚ ସ୍ତରର ଶିକ୍ଷକ, ଅଧ୍ୟାପକ *a maths professor*

profit /ˈprɒfɪt/ *noun* money that you get when you sell something for more than it cost to buy or make it ଆର୍ଥିକ ଲାଭ *If you buy a cycle for Rs 700 and sell it for Rs 800, you make a profit of Rs 100.* ✪ ବିପରୀତ **loss**

profitable /ˈprɒfɪtəbl/ *adjective* if something is profitable, it brings you money ଲାଭଜନକ, ଲାଭଦାୟକ

program /ˈprəʊgræm/ *noun* a list of instructions that you give to a computer କମ୍ପ୍ୟୁଟର୍ କାର୍ଯ୍ୟନିୟନ୍ତ୍ରଣ ପାଇଁ ଦିଆଯାଇଥିବା ନିର୍ଦ୍ଦେଶାବଳୀ

program *verb* (**programs, programming, programmed**) give instructions to a computer କମ୍ପ୍ୟୁଟର୍ କର୍ଯ୍ୟକ୍ରମ ପ୍ରସ୍ତୁତ କରିବା

programmer *noun* a person whose job is to write programs for a computer କମ୍ପ୍ୟୁଟର୍ କର୍ଯ୍ୟକ୍ରମ ପ୍ରସ୍ତୁତ କରୁଥିବା ବ୍ୟକ୍ତି, ପ୍ରୋଗ୍ରାମର

programme /ˈprəʊgræm/ *noun* **1** something on television or radio ଟେଲିଭିଜନ୍ ବା ରେଡ଼ିଓ କାର୍ଯ୍ୟକ୍ରମ *Did you watch that programme about Nepal on TV last night?* **2** a plan of things to do କାର୍ଯ୍ୟକ୍ରମ *What is your programme for tomorrow?*

progress /ˈprəʊgres/ *noun* (*no plural*) the act or process of moving forward or becoming better ଅଗ୍ରଗତି *Jyoti has made good progress in maths this year.*

prohibit /prəˈhɪbɪt/ *verb* (**prohibits, prohibiting, prohibited**) say that people must not do or use something ମନାକରିବା, ନିଷେଧ କରିବା, ନିବାରଣ କରିବା *Smoking is prohibited in the theatre.*

project /ˈprɒdʒekt/ *noun* **1** a big plan to do something ପରିକଳ୍ପନା, ଯୋଜନା *a project to build a new airport* **2** a piece of work that you do at school. You find out a lot about something and write about it କୌଣସି ବିଷୟରେ ଛାତ୍ରଛାତ୍ରୀ କରୁଥିବା ଗବେଷଣା ଓ ତା'ର ଲେଖା *We did a project on Africa.*

projector /prəˈdʒektə(r)/ *noun* a machine that shows films or pictures on a wall or screen (ଚିତ୍ର, ସ୍ଲାଇଡ୍, ଚଳଚ୍ଚିତ୍ର ଇତ୍ୟାଦିର) ପ୍ରକ୍ଷେପଣ ଯନ୍ତ୍ର

prominent /ˈprɒmɪnənt/ *adjective* **1** easy to see, for example because it is bigger than usual ସହଜରେ ଦେଖି ବା ଜାଣି ହେଉଥିବା ସୁବିଦିତ *prominent teeth* **2** important and famous ସୁପ୍ରସିଦ୍ଧ *a prominent writer*

promise[1] /ˈprɒmɪs/ *verb* (**promises, promising, promised**) say that you will certainly do or not do something ପ୍ରତିଶ୍ରୁତି ଦେବା, ପ୍ରତିଜ୍ଞା କରିବା *I promise I'll come.*

promise[2] /ˈprɒmɪs/ *noun* a written or spoken statement that you will certainly do or not do something ପ୍ରତିଶ୍ରୁତି, ପ୍ରତିଜ୍ଞା

break a promise not do what you promised ପ୍ରତିଶ୍ରୁତି ଭାଙ୍ଗିବା

keep a promise do what you promised ପ୍ରତିଶ୍ରୁତି ପାଳନ କରିବା

make a promise say that you will certainly do or not do something ପ୍ରତିଶ୍ରୁତି ଦେବା, ପ୍ରତିଜ୍ଞା କରିବା

promote /prəˈməʊt/ *verb* (**promotes, promoting, promoted**) give somebody a more important job ପଦୋନ୍ନତି *She worked hard, and after a year she was promoted to manager.*

promotion /prəˈməʊʃn/ *noun* ପଦୋନ୍ନତି *The new job is a promotion for me.*

prompt /prɒmpt/ *adjective* quick ତୁରନ୍ତ, ତତ୍ପର, ଅବିଳମ୍ବେ *She gave me a prompt answer.*

promptly *adverb* quickly; not late ଶୀଘ୍ର, ଅବିଳମ୍ବେ

pronoun /ˈprəʊnaʊn/ *noun* a word that you use in place of a noun (ବ୍ୟାକରଣ) ସର୍ବନାମ *'He', 'it', 'me' and 'them' are all pronouns.*

pronounce /prəˈnaʊns/ *verb* (**pronounces, pronouncing, pronounced**) make the sound of a letter or word ଉଚ୍ଚାରଣ କରିବା *You don't pronounce the 'b' at the end of 'comb'.*

pronunciation /prəˌnʌnsiˈeɪʃn/ *noun* the way you say a word ଉଚ୍ଚାରଣ, ଉଚ୍ଚାରଣ ପ୍ରଣାଳୀ *There are two different pronunciations for the word 'either'.* ○ *His pronunciation is very good.*

proof /pru:f/ *noun* (*no plural*) something that shows that an idea or information is true ପ୍ରମାଣ, ପ୍ରମାଣପତ୍ର *Do you have any proof that you are the owner of this car?* ✪ Proof ର କ୍ରିୟାପଦ ହେଲା **prove** ।

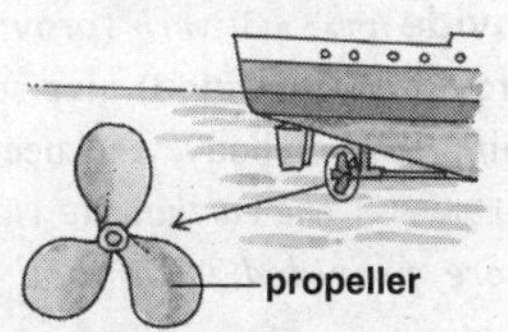

propeller /prəˈpelə(r)/ *noun* a thing that is joined to the engine on a ship or an aeroplane. It turns round fast to make the ship or aeroplane move forward ଜାହାଜ ବା ବିମାନକୁ ଚାଳନ କରୁଥିବା ପଙ୍ଖାଟପରି ଘୂର୍ଣ୍ଣଚକ୍ର, ନୋଦକ

proper /ˈprɒpə(r)/ *adjective* right or correct ଉଚିତ୍, ନିର୍ଭୁଲ, ଠିକ୍ *I haven't got the proper tools to mend the car.*

properly *adverb* well or correctly ଉପଯୁକ୍ତ ଭାବରେ, ଉଚିତ-ରୂପେ, ଠିକ୍ ଭାବେ *Close the door properly.*

property /ˈprɒpəti/ *noun* **1** something that you have or own ସମ୍ପତ୍ତି *This book is the property of Rohit Sharma.* **2** land and buildings ଘରଦ୍ୱାର, ଜମିବାଡ଼ି

prophet /ˈprɒfɪt/ *noun* a person who, it is believed, God chooses to give His message to people ଈଶ୍ୱରଙ୍କର ଇଚ୍ଛା ବୁଝିପାରୁଥିବା ଓ ପ୍ରଚାର କରିପାରୁଥିବା ବ୍ୟକ୍ତି, ଧର୍ମପ୍ରବର୍ତ୍ତକ

proportion /prəˈpɔ:ʃn/ *noun* **1** a part of something ଅଂଶ, ଭାଗ *A large proportion of children leave school when they are 16.* **2** the amount or size of one thing compared to another thing ଆପେକ୍ଷିକ ଅଂଶ, ଅନୁପାତ *What is the proportion of boys to girls in this school?*

proposal /prəˈpəʊzl/ *noun* **1** a plan or idea about how to do something କାର୍ଯ୍ୟକ୍ରମର ପ୍ରସ୍ତାବ *a proposal to build a new railway station* **2** asking somebody to marry you ବିବାହ ପ୍ରସ୍ତାବ

propose /prəˈpəʊz/ *verb* (**proposes, proposing, proposed**) **1** say what you think should happen or be done ପ୍ରସ୍ତାବ ଦେବା *I propose that we meet again on Monday.* **2** ask somebody to marry you ବିବାହ ପ୍ରସ୍ତାବ ଦେବା

prosper /ˈprɒspə(r)/ *verb* (**prospers, prospering, prospered**) be successful; do or grow well ସଫଳ ହେବା; ଉନ୍ନତି କରିବା; ବୃଦ୍ଧି ହେବା *His business prospered in just a few years.*

prosperous /prɒspərəs/ *adjective* rich and successful ସଫଳ ଓ ଧନବାନ *Wish you a happy and prosperous New Year!*

protect /prəˈtekt/ *verb* (**protects, protecting, protected**) keep somebody or something safe ରକ୍ଷା କରିବା, ସୁରକ୍ଷିତ ଭାବେ ରଖିବା *Wear a hat to protect your head against the sun.*

protection /prəˈtekʃn/ *noun* (*no plural*) the act or process of keeping somebody or something safe ସୁରକ୍ଷା, ଆଶ୍ରୟ *protection against disease*

protective *adjective* for protection ସୁରକ୍ଷା ପାଇଁ ଥିବା ବା କରାଯାଇଥିବା *a protective cream against the sun's rays*

protein /ˈprəʊtiːn/ *noun* an important **nutrient** found in food like meat, fish, eggs, beans, dals, etc. It helps people and animals to grow and be healthy ମାଛ, ମାଂସ, ଅଣ୍ଡା, ଡାଲି ଇତ୍ୟାଦିରେ ଥିବା ଶରୀର ବର୍ଦ୍ଧକ ପଦାର୍ଥ; ପୁଷ୍ଟିସାର

protest /prəˈtest/ *verb* (**protests, protesting, protested**) say or show strongly that you do not like something ପ୍ରତିବାଦ, ଆପତ୍ତି ବା ବିରୋଧ କରିବା *They protested against the government's plans.*

protest /prəʊtest/ *noun* ପ୍ରତିବାଦ, ଆପତ୍ତି ବା ବିରୋଧ କରିବା *They made a protest against the new tax.*

proud /praʊd/ *adjective* (**prouder, proudest**) **1** if you feel proud, you are pleased about something that you or others have done or about something that you have ଗର୍ବ, ଗୌରବାନ୍ୱିତ *They are very proud of their new house.* **2** a person who is proud thinks that he or she is better than other people ଗର୍ବ, ଉଦ୍ଧତ, ଅହଂକାରୀ *She was too proud to say she was sorry.* ✪ Proud ର ବିଶେଷ୍ୟ ରୂପ ହେଲା **pride** ।

proudly *adverb* ଗର୍ବକରି, ଗର୍ବିତ ଭାବରେ *'I made this myself,' he said proudly.*

prove /pruːv/ *verb* (**proves, proving, proved, has proved** ବା **has proven** /ˈpruːvn/) show that something is true ସତ ବୋଲି ପ୍ରମାଣ କରିବା *He proved that he wasn't lying.* ✪ Prove ର ବିଶେଷ୍ୟ ପଦ ହେଲା **proof** ।

proverb /ˈprɒvɜːb/ *noun* a short sentence that people often say, that gives help or advice ପ୍ରବାଦ, ଢ଼ଗ *The early bird catches the worm' is an English proverb.*

provide /prəˈvaɪd/ *verb* (**provides, providing, provided**) give something to somebody who needs it ଯୋଗାଇଦେବା *The earthquake victims were provided with food and medicines.*

provided /prəˈvaɪdɪd/, **providing** /prəˈvaɪdɪŋ/ *conjunction* only if ଯଦି *I'll go provided that the children can come with me.*

province /ˈprɒvɪns/ *noun* a part of a country ପ୍ରଦେଶ *Canada has ten provinces.*

prowl /praʊl/ *verb* (**prowls, prowling, prowled**) move silently and carefully so that nobody hears you ଚୁପ୍‌ଚାପ୍, ଛପି ଛପି ଯିବା *Last night, the tiger was seen prowling through the jungle.*

PS /ˌpiː ˈes/ *abbreviation* you write 'PS' at the end of a letter, after your name, when you want to add something that you have forgotten ଚିଠିରେ ଲେଖିବାକୁ ଭୁଲିଯାଇଥିବା କଥାକୁ ଚିଠିଶେଷରେ PS ଲେଖି ଉଲ୍ଲେଖ କରିବା ✪ PS ର ବିସ୍ତୃତ ରୂପ ହେଲା **postscript** ... *Love from Paul. PS I'll bring the car.*

psychiatrist /saɪˈkaɪətrɪst/ *noun* a doctor who helps people who are ill in the mind ମାନସିକ ରୋଗର ବିଶେଷଜ୍ଞ ବା ଡାକ୍ତର

psychology /saɪˈkɒlədʒi/ *noun* (*no plural*) the study of the mind and how it works ମନୋବିଜ୍ଞାନ, ମନସ୍ତତ୍ତ୍ୱ

psychologist /saɪˈkɒlədʒɪst/ *noun* a person who studies or knows a lot about psychology ମନସ୍ତତ୍ତ୍ୱବିତ୍

PTO /ˌpiː tiː ˈəʊ/ *abbreviation* please turn over (words at the bottom of a page that tell you to turn to the next page) 'ଦୟାକରି ପୃଷ୍ଠା ଓଲଟାନ୍ତୁ'

pub /pʌb/ *noun* a place where people go to drink and meet their friends ମଦ୍ୟଶାଳା, ମଦପିଇବା ଓ ବନ୍ଧୁମିଳନ ସ୍ଥାନ

public¹ /ˈpʌblɪk/ *adjective* of or for everybody ସର୍ବସାଧାରଣଙ୍କ ପାଇଁ ଉଦ୍ଦିଷ୍ଟ *a public telephone*

public transport *noun* (*no plural*) buses and trains that everybody can use ସର୍ବସାଧାରଣଙ୍କ ପାଇଁ ଥିବା ଯାତାୟତ ବ୍ୟବସ୍ଥା (ଟ୍ରେନ୍, ବସ୍ ଇତ୍ୟାଦି) *I usually travel by public transport.*

publicly *adverb* to everybody; not secretly ସମସ୍ତଙ୍କ ପାଇଁ, ସାର୍ବଜନୀନ ଭାବରେ *She spoke publicly about her friendship with the Prince.*

public² /ˈpʌblɪk/ *noun*

in public when other people are there ସର୍ବସାଧାରଣରେ, ସମସ୍ତଙ୍କ ଆଗରେ *I don't want to talk about it in public.*

the public (*no plural*) people in general ଜନସାଧାରଣ *The museum is open to the public between 10 a.m. and 4 p.m.*

publicity /pʌbˈlɪsəti/ *noun* (*no plural*) the information that you give about something so that people know about it ପ୍ରଚାର *There was a lot of publicity for the new film.*

publish /ˈpʌblɪʃ/ *verb* (**publishes, publishing, published**) prepare and print a book, magazine or newspaper for selling ବହି, ସମ୍ବାଦ ପତ୍ର ଇତ୍ୟାଦି ଛାପି ପ୍ରକାଶ କରିବା *This dictionary has been published by Oxford University Press.*

publisher *noun* a person or company that publishes books, magazines or newspapers ପ୍ରକାଶକ

pudding /ˈpʊdɪŋ/ *noun* a type of sweet food that is made from bread, flour or rice with eggs, milk, etc. ଭୋଜନ ଶେଷରେ ଖିଆଯାଉଥିବା ଏକପ୍ରକାର

ମିଷ୍ଟାନ୍ନ *I have made some pudding for dinner today.*

puddle /ˈpʌdl/ *noun* a small pool of water on the ground ରାସ୍ତା ଇତ୍ୟାଦିର ଖାଲରେ ପାଣି ଜମିଥିବା ଜାଗା

puff /pʌf/ *noun* a small amount of air, wind, smoke, etc that blows ଧୂଆଁ, ନିଃଶ୍ୱାସ, ବାୟୁ ଇତ୍ୟାଦିର ଝଲକ *a puff of smoke*

puff *verb* (**puffs, puffing, puffed**) **1** come out in puffs ଝଲକା ଝଲକା ହୋଇ ଆସିବା ବା ବାହାରିବା *Smoke was puffing out of the chimney.* **2** breathe quickly ଖର ନିଃଶ୍ୱାସ ନେବା *She was puffing as she ran up the hill.*

pull¹ /pʊl/ *verb* (**pulls, pulling, pulled**) **1** move somebody or something strongly towards you ଟାଣିବା, ଝିଙ୍କିବା, ଘୋଷାରିବା *She pulled the drawer open.* **2** go forward, moving something behind you ଟାଣି ଆଣିବା, ଘୋଷାରି ଆଣିବା *The cart was pulled by two horses.* **3** move something somewhere ଟାଣି ଘୁଞ୍ଚାଇବା *He pulled up his trousers.*

pull² /pʊl/ *noun* the act of pulling something ଟାଣିବା କାର୍ଯ୍ୟ *Give the rope a pull.*

pulley /ˈpʊli/ *noun* (*plural* **pulleys**) a machine consisting of a wheel and a rope that goes over the wheel. A pulley helps to lift or move heavy things କପିକଳ, ଓଜନିଆ ଜିନିଷ ଟାଣି ଉଠାଇବା ପାଇଁ ଚକରେ ଦଉଡ଼ି ଲାଗିଥିବା ଯନ୍ତ୍ର।

pullover /ˈpʊləʊvə(r)/ *noun* a warm piece of clothing with sleeves, that you wear on the top part of your body. Pullovers are often made of wool ମୁଣ୍ଡଗଳା ପୁରାହାତ ପଶମ ବୁଣା ଜାମା ବା ସ୍ୱେଟର୍

pulp /pʌlp/ *noun* (*no plural*) a soft and wet mass of something ନରମ ମେଞ୍ଚାଳିଆ ପଦାର୍ଥ, ମଣ୍ଡ *mango pulp*

pulse /pʌls/ *noun* the constant movement of blood as the heart pumps it around your body. The pulse can be felt in your wrists ନାଡ଼ୀରେ ରକ୍ତ ପ୍ରବାହର ସ୍ପନ୍ଦନ *The nurse felt his pulse.*

pulses /pʌlsɪz/ *noun* (*plural*) the seeds of plants such as peas and beans which are cooked and eaten as food. In India, we usually use the word **dal** for pulses ଡାଲିଜାତୀୟ ପଦାର୍ଥ

pump /pʌmp/ *noun* a machine that moves a liquid or gas into or out of something ତରଳ ବା ବାଷ୍ପୀୟ ପଦାର୍ଥ ଉତ୍ତୋଳନ ବା ବିସ୍ଥାପନ କରିବା ଯନ୍ତ୍ର; ପାଣି ଉଠାଇବା କଳ, ପମ୍ପ *a bicycle pump* ○ *a petrol pump*

pump *verb* (**pumps, pumping, pumped**) move a liquid or gas with a pump ପମ୍ପ ସାହାଯ୍ୟରେ ତରଳ ପଦାର୍ଥ ବା ବାଷ୍ପ ଉଠାଇବା ବା ସ୍ଥାନାନ୍ତରିତ କରିବା *Your heart pumps blood around your body.*

pumpkin /ˈpʌmpkɪn/ *noun* a very large round vegetable with a thick orange skin କଖାରୁ ⇨ ଚିତ୍ର ପାଇଁ **vegetable** ଦେଖନ୍ତୁ।

punch /pʌntʃ/ *verb* (**punches, punching, punched**) **1** hit somebody or something hard with your closed hand (your **fist**) ବିଧା ମାରିବା, ମୁଥା ମାରିବା *She punched me in the stomach.* **2** make a hole in something with a special tool ବିଶେଷ ଉପକରଣ ଦ୍ୱାରା କଣା କରିବା *He punched my ticket.*

punch *noun* (*plural* **punches**) ବିଧା, ମୁଥା *a punch on the chin*

punctual /ˈpʌŋktʃuəl/ *adjective* if you are punctual, you come or do something at the right time ସମୟାନୁବର୍ତ୍ତୀ, ସମୟନିଷ୍ଠ *Please try to be punctual for your classes.*

punctuation /ˌpʌŋktʃuˈeɪʃn/ *noun* (*no plural*) the marks that you use in writing that divide sentences and phrases (ଲେଖାରେ) ବିରାମ ଚିହ୍ନ

punctuation mark *noun* (*plural* **punctuation marks**) one of the signs that you use when you are writing. Commas (,), full stops (.) and colons (:) are all punctuation marks ଲେଖିବାରେ ବ୍ୟବହୃତ ବିରାମ ଚିହ୍ନ, ଯଥା: କମା, (,) ଫୁଲଷ୍ଟପ୍ (.) ଓ କଲୋନ୍ (:)

puncture /ˈpʌŋktʃə(r)/ *noun* a hole in a tyre, that lets the air go out ଚକର ଟାୟାର ଟ୍ୟୁବ୍‌ର କଣା ବା ଛିଦ୍ର (ଯାହା ଦ୍ୱାରା ପବନ ବାହାରିଯାଏ) *My bike has got a puncture.*

puncture *verb* (**punctures, puncturing, punctured**) make a puncture in something କଣା ଫୁଟେଇବା *A piece of glass punctured the tyre.*

punish /ˈpʌnɪʃ/ *verb* (**punishes, punishing, punished**) make somebody suffer because they have done something wrong ଶାସ୍ତି ବା ଦଣ୍ଡ ଦେବା *He was punished for telling lies.*

punishment /ˈpʌnɪʃmənt/ *noun* ଶାସ୍ତି, ଦଣ୍ଡ *She was sent out of the room as a punishment for being naughty.*

pup /pʌp/ *noun* **puppy** ର ସଂକ୍ଷିପ୍ତ ରୂପ

pupa /ˈpjuːpə/ *noun* (*plural* **pupae** /ˈpjuːpiː/) କୀଟର ଉପ୍ତତ୍ତି ଓ ପୂର୍ଣ୍ଣ ପ୍ରାପ୍ତିର ମଧ୍ୟବର୍ତ୍ତୀ ଅବସ୍ଥା, କୋଷା, ପ୍ୟୁପା) one of the stages of growth in the life of an insect just before it becomes an adult ➪ **caterpillar** ଦେଖନ୍ତୁ।

pupil /ˈpjuːpl/ *noun* **1** a person who is learning at school ଛାତ୍ର, ବିଦ୍ୟାର୍ଥୀ *There are 30 pupils in the class.* **2** the small round black part at the centre of your eye through which light enters ଆଖିର କେନ୍ଦ୍ରରେ ଥିବା କଳା ଉନ୍ମୁକ୍ତାଂଶ, ପୂତଳୀ, ପୁଅ

puppet /ˈpʌpɪt/ *noun* a doll that you move by pulling strings or by putting your hand inside it and moving your fingers ସୂତା ବା ହାତ ଦ୍ୱାରା ଚାଳିତ କଣ୍ଢେଇ, ସଖୀ କଣ୍ଢେଇ

puppy /ˈpʌpi/ *noun* (*plural* **puppies**) a young dog କୁକୁର ଛୁଆ

purchase /ˈpɜːtʃəs/ *verb* (**purchases, purchasing, purchased**) buy something କିଣିବା, କ୍ରୟକରିବା ପଦାର୍ଥ *The company has purchased three new buildings.* ✪ ଆମେ ସାଧାରଣତଃ **buy** ର ବ୍ୟବହାର କରୁଁ।

purchase *noun* buying something; something that you have bought କ୍ରୟ, କିଣି; କିଣା ଯାଇଥିବା ପଦାର୍ଥ *She made several purchases and then left.*

pure /pjʊə(r)/ *adjective* (**purer, purest**) not mixed with anything else; clean ଶୁଦ୍ଧ, ବିଶୁଦ୍ଧ, ଖାଣ୍ଟି; ପରିଷ୍କାର *This shirt is pure cotton.* ○ *pure mountain air* ✪ ବିପରୀତ **impure**

purely *adverb* completely or only ବିଶୁଦ୍ଧ ଭାବରେ; କେବଳ *He doesn't like his job—he does it purely for money.*

purify /ˈpjʊərɪfaɪ/ *verb* (**purifies, purifying, purified, has purified**) remove dirty and harmful substances from something ବିଶୁଦ୍ଧତା

purity /ˈpjʊərəti/ *noun* (*no plural*) the quality of being pure ବିଶୁଦ୍ଧତା *the purity of water*

purple /ˈpɜːpl/ *adjective* having the colour of red and blue mixed together ନୀଳଲୋହିତ ବା ବାଇଗଣୀ ବର୍ଣ୍ଣର

purple *noun* ନୀଳଲୋହିତ ବା ବାଇଗଣୀ ରଙ୍ଗ;ଏହି ରଙ୍ଗର ପୋଷାକ *She often wears purple.*

purpose /ˈpɜːpəs/ *noun* the reason for doing something ଉଦ୍ଦେଶ୍ୟ, ଅଭିପ୍ରାୟ, କାରଣ *What is the purpose of your visit?*

on purpose because you want to; not by accident ଜାଣିଶୁଣି, ଇଚ୍ଛାପୂର୍ବକ *'You've broken my pen!' 'I'm sorry. I didn't do it on purpose.'*

purr /pɜː(r)/ *verb* (**purrs, purring, purred**) when a cat purrs, it makes a low sound that shows that it is happy ବିଲେଇର ସୁଖ ସୂଚକ ଘୁଡୁଘୁଡୁ ଶବ୍ଦ

purse /pɜːs/ *noun* a small bag that you keep money in ଟଙ୍କା ପଇସା ରଖିବା ପାଇଁ ଛୋଟ ମୁଣା, ପର୍ସ, ମନିବ୍ୟାଗ୍

pursue /pəˈsjuː/ *verb* (**pursues, pursuing, pursued**) follow somebody or something because you want to catch them (ଧରିବା ପାଇଁ) ଗୋଡ଼ାଇବା, ଅନୁଧାବନ କରିବା *The police pursued the stolen car for several kilometres.* ✪ ଆମେ ସାଧାରଣତଃ **chase** ବ୍ୟବହାର କରୁଁ।

push /pʊʃ/ *verb* (**pushes, pushing, pushed**) **1** move somebody or something strongly away from you ଠେଲିବା, ପେଲିବା *The car broke down so we had to push it to a garage.* **2** press something with your finger ଆଙ୍ଗୁଠିରେ ପେଲିବା ବା ଚିପିବା *Push the red button to stop the lift.*

push *noun* (*plural* **pushes**) ଠେଲା, ପେଲା *She gave him a push and he fell.*

pussy /ˈpʊsi/ *noun* (*plural* **pussies**) a word for 'cat' that children use ବିଲେଇ ପାଇଁ ପିଲାମାନେ ବ୍ୟବହାର କରୁଥିବା ଶବ୍ଦ

put /pʊt/ *verb* (**puts, putting, put, has put**) move something to a place ନିର୍ଦ୍ଦିଷ୍ଟ ସ୍ଥାନରେ ରଖିବା, ଥୋଇବା *She put the book on the table.* ○ *He put his hand in his pocket.*

put away put something in its usual place ଯଥା ସ୍ଥାନରେ ରଖିବା *She put the box away in the cupboard.*

put down put something on another thing, for example on the floor or a table ତଳେ, ଟେବୁଲ୍ ଇତ୍ୟାଦି ଉପରେ ରଖିବା

put on 1 wear clothes ଲୁଗାପଟା ପିନ୍ଧିବା *Put on your coat.* ✪ ବିପରିତ

take off 2 press or turn something to make an electrical thing start working ସ୍ୱିଚ୍ ଚିପି ବା ଘୁରାଇ ଲାଇଟ୍, ଫ୍ୟାନ୍ ଇତ୍ୟାଦି ଚାଳନ କରିବା *I put on the TV.* ○ *Put the lights on.* **3** make a record, cassette or compact disc start to play ରେକର୍ଡ଼ କ୍ୟାସେଟ୍, କମ୍ପ୍ୟାକ୍ଟ ଡିସ୍କ ଇତ୍ୟାଦି ଲଗାଇ ଚାଳନ କରିବା *Let's put my new cassette on.*

put out stop a fire or stop a light from shining ନିଆଁ ବା ଆଲୋକ ଲିଭାଇବା *She put out the fire with a bucket of water.*

put somebody through connect somebody on the telephone to the person they want to speak to ଟେଲିଫୋନ୍‌ରେ କଥାବାର୍ତ୍ତା ପାଇଁ ଜଣକୁ ଆଉଜଣଙ୍କ ସାଙ୍ଗରେ ସଂଯୋଗ କରିବା *Can you put me through to the manager, please?*

put somebody up let somebody stay in your home କାହାରିକୁ ଘରେ ରଖିବା *Can you put me up for the night?*

put up with somebody or **something** have pain or problems without complaining ସହ୍ୟ କରିବା, ସହିଯିବା *We can't change the bad weather, so we have to put up with it.*

puzzle[1] /ˈpʌzl/ *noun* **1** something that is difficult to understand or explain ପ୍ରହେଳିକା, ଗୋଲକଧନ୍ଦା *Rakhi's reason for leaving her job is a puzzle to me.* **2** a game that is difficult and makes you think a lot ବହୁତ ଭାବିବାକୁ ପଡୁଥିବା ଖେଳ *a crossword puzzle* ⇨ **jigsaw puzzle** ଦେଖନ୍ତୁ

puzzle[2] /ˈpʌzl/ *verb* (**puzzles, puzzling, puzzled**) make you think a lot because you cannot understand or explain it ବିଭ୍ରାନ୍ତ କରିବା, ହତବୁଦ୍ଧି କରିବା *Anand's illness puzzled his doctors.*

puzzling *adjective* if something is puzzling, you cannot understand or explain it ବିଭ୍ରାନ୍ତିକାରି

pyjamas /pəˈdʒɑːməz/ *noun* (*plural*) a loose night suit that you wear in bed ଶୋଇଲା ବେଳର ଢିଲା ପାଇଜାମା ଓ ଜାମା

> ✪ **Pyjamas** ଭାରତରେ ଶବ୍ଦ କେବଳ ଅଣ୍ଟାରୁ ତଳଅଂଶ ପାଇଁ ବ୍ୟବହୃତ ପାଇଜାମାକୁ ବୁଝାଇଥାଏ, ପାଇଜାମା ଓ କୁର୍ତ୍ତା ସେଟ୍ ପାଇଁ ବ୍ୟବହାର କରାଯାଇ ନଥାଏ।

pyramid /ˈpɪrəmɪd/ *noun* a shape with a flat bottom and three or four sides that meet at a point at the top (ଇଜିପ୍ଟ ଦେଶର) ପଥର ତିଆରି ବର୍ଗାକାର ମୂଳଦୁଆ ଓ ତ୍ରିକୋଣ ପାର୍ଶ୍ୱ ଥିବା ସୂକ୍ଷ୍ମାଗ୍ର ସ୍ମୃତିମନ୍ଦିର, ପିରାମିଡ଼ *the pyramids of Egypt*

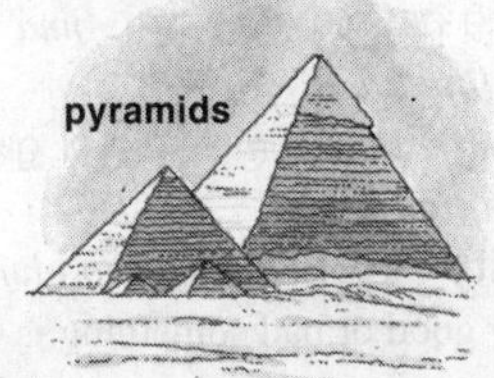

python /ˈpaɪθən/ *noun* a large snake that coils its long body around its prey and crushes them to death before swallowing them ଅଜଗର ସାପ

Q q

quack /kwæk/ *noun* the sound that a duck makes ବତକର ଧ୍ୱନି

quack *verb* (**quacks, quacking, quacked**) make this sound ବତକ ଧ୍ୱନି କରିବା

quake /kweɪk/ *verb* (**quakes, quaking, quaked**) shake because of fear or cold ଥରିବା, କମ୍ପିବା

qualification /ˌkwɒlɪfɪˈkeɪʃn/ *noun* an examination that you have passed, or a skill or knowledge that you need to do a special job ଯୋଗ୍ୟତା, ଉପଯୁକ୍ତତା *Do you have the qualifications to apply for this job?*

qualify /ˈkwɒlɪfaɪ/ *verb* (**qualifies, qualifying, qualified, has qualified**) get the right knowledge and training or pass an examination so that you can do a certain job ଯୋଗ୍ୟ ବିବେଚିତ ହେବା; ଉପଯୁକ୍ତ ଜ୍ଞାନ ଓ ତାଲିମ୍ ପାଇବା; କୌଣସି ପରୀକ୍ଷାରେ ଉତ୍ତୀର୍ଣ୍ଣ ହେବା *Anna has qualified as a doctor.*

qualified *adjective* ଯୋଗ୍ୟତା ପ୍ରାପ୍ତ *a qualified nurse*

quality /ˈkwɒləti/ *noun* (*no plural*) how good or bad something is ଗୁଣ, ଶ୍ରେଣୀ ବା ପ୍ରକାର; ଉତ୍କର୍ଷର ମାତ୍ରା ବା ସ୍ତର *The tea we bought was of the best quality.*

quantity /ˈkwɒntəti/ *noun* (*plural* **quantities**) how much of something there is; amount ପରିମାଣ *I only bought a small quantity of cheese.*

quarrel /ˈkwɒrəl/ *verb* (**quarrels, quarrelling, quarrelled**) talk angrily with somebody because you do not agree କଳି କରିବା, ଝଗଡ଼ା କରିବା; ମତ ପ୍ରଭେଦ ଯୋଗୁଁ ଉଚ୍ଚବାଚ କରିବା *They quarrelled because they both wanted to use the car.*

quarrel *noun* a fight using words; an argument କଳି, ଝଗଡ଼ା; ଯୁକ୍ତିତର୍କ *He had a quarrel with his wife about who should do the housework.*

quarrelsome /ˈkwɒrəlsəm/ *adjective* someone who is quarrelsome likes to quarrel କଳହପ୍ରିୟ, କଳିହୁଡ଼ା *a quarrelsome person*

quarry /ˈkwɒri/ *noun* (*plural* **quarries**) a place where people dig stone, chalk, slate, etc. out of the ground to make things like buildings or roads (ପଥର, ଚକ୍, ସ୍ଲେଟ୍ ଇତ୍ୟାଦିର) ଖୋଲା ଖଣି ⇨ **mine**[1] ଦେଖନ୍ତୁ।

quarter /ˈkwɔːtə(r)/ *noun* one of four equal parts of something; $\frac{1}{4}$ ଏକ ଚତୁର୍ଥାଂଶ, ଚାରି ଭାଗରୁ ଭାଗେ; $\frac{1}{9}$ *a mile and a quarter* ○ *The film starts in three quarters of an hour.*

(a) quarter past fifteen minutes after the hour ଘଣ୍ଟା ଆରମ୍ଭର ପନ୍ଦର ମିନିଟ୍ ପରେ *It's quarter past two.*

(a) quarter to fifteen minutes before the hour ଘଣ୍ଟା ଆରମ୍ଭର ପନ୍ଦର ମିନିଟ୍ ପୂର୍ବରୁ *quarter to nine*

quarter-final *noun* in a competition, a quarter-final is one of the four games that are played to choose who will play in the **semi finals** ଖେଳ ପ୍ରତିଯୋଗିତାର ସେମି ଫାଇନାଲର ପୂର୍ବବର୍ତ୍ତୀ

ଖେଳ

quay /kiː/ *noun* (*plural* **quays**) a place in a harbour where ships go so that people can move things on and off them ଜାହାଜ ଲାଗିବା ଘାଟ ଯେଉଁଠାରେ ମାଲ ବୋଝେଇ ହୁଏ ବା ଲଦାଯାଏ

queen /kwiːn/ *noun* **1** a woman who rules a country and who is from a royal family ରାଣୀ, ରାଜ୍ଞୀ *Queen Elizabeth II, the Queen of England* **2** the wife of a king ରାଜପତ୍ନୀ, ରାଣୀ

queer /kwɪə(r)/ *adjective* (**queerer, queerest**) strange or unusual ବିଚିତ୍ର; ଅସାଧାରଣ; ଅଦ୍ଭୁତ, ଅପରୂପ, ଅବାଗିଆ *She wore a queer dress.*

quench /kwentʃ/ *verb* (**quenches, quenching, quenched**) drink water or any other liquid so that you are no longer thirsty ପାଣି ଇତ୍ୟାଦି ପିଇ ଶୋଷ ଉପଶମ କରିବା ବା ତୃଷା ମେଣ୍ଟାଇବା

query /ˈkwɪəri/ *noun* (*plural* **queries**) a question ପ୍ରଶ୍ନ *Phone me if you have any queries.*

question[1] /ˈkwestʃən/ *noun* **1** something that you ask ପ୍ରଶ୍ନ *They asked me a lot of questions.* ○ *She didn't answer my question.* **2** a problem that needs an answer ଉତ୍ତର ଦେବା ପାଇଁ ଦିଆ ଯାଇଥିବା ପ୍ରଶ୍ନ; ସମାଧାନ ପାଇଁ ଥିବା ସମସ୍ୟା *We need more money. The question is, where are we going to get it from?*

out of the question not possible ଅସମ୍ଭବ *No, I won't give you any more money. It's out of the question!*

question mark *noun* the sign (?) that you write at the end of a question ପ୍ରଶ୍ନବାଚକ ଚିହ୍ନ (?)

question[2] /ˈkwestʃən/ *verb* (**questions, questioning, questioned**) ask somebody questions about something ପ୍ରଶ୍ନ ପଚାରିବା *The police questioned him about the stolen car.*

questionnaire /ˌkwestʃəˈneə(r)/ *noun* a list of questions about a particular subject for people to answer କୌଣସି ବିଷୟରେ ଲୋକଙ୍କ ମତାମତ ଜାଣିବା ପାଇଁ କରାଯାଇଥିବା ପ୍ରଶ୍ନାବଳୀ *Please fill the questionnaire.*

queue /kjuː/ *noun* a line of people who are waiting for something or to do something ଧାଡ଼ିରେ ଅପେକ୍ଷା କରୁଥିବା ଲୋକ ବା ଯାନବାହନ *There's a long queue outside the cinema.*

queue, queue up *verb* (**queues, queuing, queued**) stand in a queue ଧାଡ଼ିବାନ୍ଧି ଅପେକ୍ଷା କରିବା *We queued up for a bus.*

quick /kwɪk/ *adjective, adverb* (**quicker, quickest**) fast; that takes little time କ୍ଷିପ୍ର, ତତ୍ପର, ଶୀଘ୍ର; ଚଞ୍ଚଳ, ସତ୍ୱର, ଅଳ୍ପ ସମୟର *It's quicker to travel by plane than by train.* ○ *Can I make a quick telephone call?* ➪ **slow**[1] ଦେଖନ୍ତୁ।

quickly *adverb* ଚଞ୍ଚଳ, ଶୀଘ୍ର *Come as quickly as you can!*

quiet /ˈkwaɪət/ *adjective* (**quieter, quietest**) with little sound or no sound ନୀରବ, ଚୁପ୍ *Be quiet—the baby's asleep.* ○ *a quiet voice* ✪ ବିପରୀତ **loud** ବା **noisy**

quietly *adverb* ଚୁପ୍‌ଚାପ୍, ନୀରବ ଭାବରେ, ଶବ୍ଦ ନ କରି *Please close the door quietly.*

quill /kwɪl/ *noun* **1** a feather from the wing or tail of a bird ଚଢ଼େଇର ଡେଣା ବା ଲାଞ୍ଜର ପର **2** a pen made from a bird's feather ଚଢ଼େଇ ପରରେ ତିଆରି କଲମ, ପରକଲମ **3** a long sharp thing on the body of a **porcupine** ଝିଙ୍କ କାଠି

quilt /kwɪlt/ *noun* a cover for a bed that has a soft, thick warm material inside it ରେଜେଇ

quit /kwɪt/ *verb* ⇨ **leave[1] 1** ଦେଖନ୍ତୁ ।

quite /kwaɪt/ *adverb* not very; rather; fairly କେତେକ ପରିମାଣରେ; ପ୍ରାୟ; ବେଶ୍ *It's quite warm today, but it's not hot.* ○ *He plays the guitar quite well.*

quite a few or **quite a lot** a lot of something ବେଶ୍ କିଛି, ବହୁତ *There were quite a few people at the party.* ○ *They drank quite a lot of juice.*

quiver[1] /ˈkwɪvə(r)/ *verb* (**quivers, quivering, quivered**) shake because of cold, fear or anger ଥରିବା, କମ୍ପିବା *Her voice quivered when she began to speak.*

quiver[2] /ˈkwɪvə(r)/ *noun* a container for carrying arrows ଶର ରଖିବା ଆଧାର, ତୂଣୀର, ତୂଣୀ, ତୂଣ

quiz /kwɪz/ *noun* (*plural* **quizzes**) a game where you try to answer questions ପ୍ରଶ୍ନୋତ୍ତର ଖେଳ *a quiz on television*

quotation /kwəʊˈteɪʃn/, **quote** /kwəʊt/ *noun* words that you say or write, that another person said or wrote before ଉଦ୍ଧୃତି; ଉଦ୍ଧୃତାଂଶ *That's a quotation from a poem by Keats.*

quotation marks or **quotes** /kwəʊts/*noun* (*plural*) the signs (“ ”) or (‘ ’) that you use in writing before and after words that somebody said ଉଦ୍ଧୃତି ଚିହ୍ନ, ଉଦ୍ଧାରଣ ଚିହ୍ନ (ଉଦ୍ଧୃତାଂଶ ସୂଚାଇବା ପାଇଁ) (“ ”) (‘ ’)

quote /kwəʊt/ *verb* (**quotes, quoting, quoted**) say or write the exact words that another person said or wrote before ଅନ୍ୟ କେହି କହିଥିବା ବା ଲେଖିଥିବା ଶବ୍ଦାବଳୀର ଅବିକଳ ଉଦ୍ଧାରଣ ବା ଉଦ୍ଧୃତି କରିବା *She quoted from the Bible.*

quotient /ˈkwəʊʃnt/ *noun* a number that you get when you divide one number by another ଭାଗଫଳ, ଲବ୍ଧି *When you divide 20 by 5, the quotient is 4.*

R r

rabbit /ˈræbɪt/ *noun* a small furry animal with long ears. Rabbits live in holes under the ground (called **burrows**) ଠେକୁଆ, ଶଶକ, ଶଶା

race[1] /reɪs/ *noun* a competition to see who can run, drive, ride, etc. fastest ଦୌଡ଼ ପ୍ରତିଯୋଗିତା, ବେଗ ପ୍ରତିଯୋଗିତା *Who won the race?* ○ *a horse race*

race[2] /reɪs/ *verb* (**races, racing, raced**) run, drive, ride, etc. in a competition to see who is the fastest ଦୌଡ଼ ପ୍ରତିଯୋଗିତା ବା ବେଗ ପ୍ରତିଯୋଗିତାରେ ଦୌଡ଼ିବା, ଗାଡ଼ି ଚଲାଇବା, ଘୋଡ଼ା ଦୌଡ଼ାଇବା ଇତ୍ୟାଦି *The cars raced round the track.*

race[3] /reɪs/ *noun* a group of people of the same kind, for example with the same colour of skin ଜନ୍ମଗତ ଭିନ୍ନତା ଉପରେ ଆଧାରିତ ମାନବଜାତିର ଶ୍ରେଣୀ; ଜାତି, ପ୍ରଜାତି *People of many different races live together in this country.*

racial /ˈreɪʃl/ *adjective* to do with people's races ଜାତୀୟ, ଜାତିଗତ *racial differences*

racism /ˈreɪsɪzəm/ *noun* (*no plural*) the belief that some groups (**races**) of people are better than others ଜାତିଗତ ଉତ୍କର୍ଷତା ଉପରେ ଆଧାରିତ ତତ୍ତ୍ୱ; କିଛି ଜାତି ଅନ୍ୟଜାତି ଠାରୁ ଶ୍ରେଷ୍ଠତର ବୋଲି ବିଶ୍ୱାସ, ଜାତିଆଣଭାବ, ଅସ୍ପୃଶ୍ୟ, ଛୁଆଁଣ

racist /ˈreɪsɪst/ *noun* a person who believes that some races of people are better than others କିଛି ଜାତି ଅନ୍ୟ ଜାତିଠାରୁ ଶ୍ରେଷ୍ଠତର ବୋଲି ବିଶ୍ୱାସ କରୁଥିବା ବ୍ୟକ୍ତି; ବଡ଼ପଣ୍ଡା

rack /ræk/ *noun* a kind of shelf, made of bars, that you put things in or on ଥାକ *Put your bag in the luggage rack.*

racket[1] /ˈrækɪt/ *noun* a thing that you use for hitting the ball in games like tennis and badminton ଟେନିସ୍ ଓ ବ୍ୟାଡ୍‌ମିଣ୍ଟନ୍ ଖେଳରେ ବ୍ୟବହୃତ ର୍ୟାକେଟ୍

racket[2] /ˈrækɪt/ *noun* a loud noise ଗଣ୍ଡଗୋଳ, ପାଟିତୁଣ୍ଡ, ହୋହାଲ୍ଲା *Stop making such a terrible racket.*

radar /ˈreɪdɑː(r)/ *noun* (*no plural*) a way of finding where a ship or an aircraft is and how fast it is travelling by using radio waves ରେଡ଼ିଓ ସଙ୍କେତ ପ୍ରତିଧ୍ୱନିରୁ କୌଣସି ଜାହାଜ, ଉଡ଼ାଜାହାଜ ଇତ୍ୟାଦିର ସ୍ଥିତି, ବେଗ, ଉଚ୍ଚତା ଇତ୍ୟାଦି ଜାଣିବା ପାଇଁ ଯନ୍ତ୍ର; ରାଡ଼ାର୍

radiation /ˌreɪdiˈeɪʃn/ *noun* (*no plural*) very dangerous energy that some **radioactive** substances send out ବିକିରଣଶୀଳ ପଦାର୍ଥରୁ ବାହାରୁଥିବା ହାନୀକାରକ ବିକିରଣ ବା ଶକ୍ତି *ultraviolet radiation*

radio /ˈreɪdiəʊ/ *noun* **1** (*no plural*) the process of sending or receiving sounds and messages through the air by special waves ବେତାର; ବେତାର ବାର୍ତ୍ତା ଗ୍ରହଣ ବା ପ୍ରେରଣ କରିବା ପ୍ରକ୍ରିୟା *The captain of the ship sent a message by radio.* **2** (*plural* **radios**) an instrument that brings programmes or music from far away so that you can hear them ବେତାର କାର୍ଯ୍ୟକ୍ରମ ବା ବାର୍ତ୍ତା ଶୁଣିବା ଯନ୍ତ୍ର, ରେଡ଼ିଓ *We* *listened to an interesting programme on the radio.*

radioactive /ˌreɪdiəʊˈæktɪv/ *adjective* if an element is radioactive, it gives out powerful rays that you cannot see but which can cause harmful diseases ବିକିରଣଶୀଳ; ବିକିରଣ ଦ୍ୱାରା ହାନୀକାରକ ରୋଗ କରାଉଥିବା

radish /rædɪʃ/ *noun* (*plural* **radishes**) a long white or small red vegetable that grows under the soil and is often eaten raw in salads ମୂଳା ➪ ଚିତ୍ର ପାଇଁ **vegetable** ଦେଖନ୍ତୁ ।

radius /ˈreɪdiəs/ *noun* (*plural* **radii** /ˈreɪdii/) a straight line that joins the centre of a circle to any point on the circle ବୃତ୍ତର ପରିଧି ଠାରୁ କେନ୍ଦ୍ର ପର୍ଯ୍ୟନ୍ତ ସରଳରେଖା, ବ୍ୟାସାର୍ଦ୍ଧ ➪ ଚିତ୍ର ପାଇଁ **circle** ଦେଖନ୍ତୁ ।

raft /rɑːft/ *noun* a flat thing that is made by tying together pieces of wood and used as a boat କାଠ, ବାଉଁଶ ଇତ୍ୟାଦି ବାନ୍ଧି ତିଆରି କରାଯାଉଥିବା ଭାସମାନ ଭେଳ ।

rag /ræg/ *noun* **1** a small piece of old cloth that you use for cleaning ଝାଡୁପୋଛା ପାଇଁ ବ୍ୟବହୃତ ଛିଣ୍ଡା କନା **2 rags** (*plural*) clothes that are very old and torn ପୁରୁଣା, ଘଷରା ଜାମାପଟା *She was dressed in rags.*

rage /reɪdʒ/ *noun* a feeling of strong anger ପ୍ରବଳ କ୍ରୋଧ, କୋପ

raid /reɪd/ *noun* **1** a sudden attack on a place ଅତର୍କିତ ଆକ୍ରମଣ, ଚଢ଼ାଉ *an air raid* **2** a surprise visit by the police in search of something illegal ପୋଲିସ୍‌ର ଅତର୍କିତ ତଲାସ

raid *verb* (**raids, raiding, raided**) ଅତର୍କିତ ଆକ୍ରମଣ କରିବା; (ପୋଲିସ୍) ଅତର୍କିତ ତଲାସ କରିବା *Police raided the house looking for stolen goods.*

rail /reɪl/ *noun* **1** (*plural* **rails**) a long piece of wood or metal that is fixed to a wall, for hanging things on ଜିନିଷପତ୍ର ଝୁଲାଇବା ପାଇଁ କାନ୍ଥରେ ଲଗାଯାଇଥିବା କାଠ ବା ଧାତୁର ବାଡ଼ି *There's a rail in the bathroom for hanging your towel on.* **2 rails** (*plural*) the two long pieces of metal that trains move on ରେଳଗାଡ଼ି ଯିବା ପାଇଁ ଲୁହା ଧାରଣା, ରେଳଲାଇନ୍; ରେଳପଥ

railings /ˈreɪlɪŋz/ *noun* (*plural*) a fence made of metal bars ଧାତୁ ବାଡ଼ି, ଛଡ଼ ବା ପଟିର ବାଡ଼

railway /ˈreɪlweɪ/ *noun* **1** (**railway line**) the metal lines that trains move on from one place to another ରେଳଲାଇନ୍, ରେଳପଥ **2** a train service that carries people and things ଯାତାୟାତ ଓ ପରିବହନ ପାଇଁ ରେଳସେବା *a railway timetable*

railway station *noun* a place where trains stop so that people can get on and off ରେଳ ଷ୍ଟେସନ୍

rain /reɪn/ *noun* (*no plural*) the water that falls from the sky ବର୍ଷା, ବୃଷ୍ଟି, ବୃଷ୍ଟିପାତ

rain *verb* (**rains, raining, rained**) when it rains, water falls from the sky ବର୍ଷା ହେବା ବା ପଡ଼ିବା, ବୃଷ୍ଟିପାତ ହେବା *It's raining.* ○ *It rained all day.*

rainbow /ˈreɪnbəʊ/ *noun* a half circle of bright colours that you sometimes see in the sky when the sun shines through rain ଇନ୍ଦ୍ରଧନୁ

raincoat /ˈreɪnkəʊt/ *noun* a long light coat that you wear when it rains to keep you dry ବର୍ଷାତି, ଜଳରୋଧି ଲମ୍ବା କୋଟ୍

rainfall /ˈreɪnfɔːl/ *noun* (*no plural*) the amount of rain that falls over a region in a particular season ବୃଷ୍ଟିପାତ, ବର୍ଷାର ପରିମାଣ ବା ମାତ୍ରା *an average rainfall of 25 cm*

rainforest /ˈreɪnfɒrɪst/ *noun* a thick forest in a hot part of the world where there is a lot of rain ଗ୍ରୀଷ୍ମମଣ୍ଡଳୀୟ ବୃଷ୍ଟିବନ, ବର୍ଷାରଣ୍ୟ

rainy /ˈreɪni/ *adjective* (**rainier, rainiest**) with a lot of rain ବୃଷ୍ଟିବହୁଳ *a rainy day*

raise /reɪz/ *verb* (**raises, raising, raised**) **1** move something or somebody up ଉପରକୁ ଉଠାଇବା, ଉତ୍ତୋଳନ କରିବା *Raise your hand if you want to ask a question.* **2** make something bigger, higher, stronger, etc. ବଢ଼ାଇବା, ଉଠାଇବା *They've raised the price of petrol.* ○ *She raised her voice.* ✪ ବିପରୀତ **lower**[1]

raisin /ˈreɪzn/ *noun* a dried grape କିସ୍‌ମିସ୍, ଶୁଖିଲା ଅଙ୍ଗୁର

rake /reɪk/ *noun* a tool with a long handle and a row of metal teeth at one end, that you use in a garden for collecting leaves or for making the soil flat ଶୁଖିଲା ଘାସପତ୍ର ଏକାଠି କରିବା ବା ଉପର ମାଟି ରାମ୍ପି ସମାନ କରିବା ପାଇଁ ବ୍ୟବହୃତ ଦାନ୍ତି କୋଦାଳ

rally /ˈræli/ *noun* (*plural* **rallies**) **1** a group of people who march together or hold a meeting to show that they feel strongly about something ଦୃଢ଼ ମତ ବ୍ୟକ୍ତ କରିବା ପାଇଁ କୌଣସି ବ୍ୟକ୍ତି ବା ବିଷୟରେ ଏକମତ ଥିବା ଲୋକମାନଙ୍କର ପଦଯାତ୍ରା ବା ସଭା *a peace rally* **2** a race for cars or motorcycles କାର୍ ବା ମଟର ସାଇକେଲ୍ ଦୌଡ଼ ପ୍ରତିଯୋଗିତା

RAM /ræm/ *abbreviation* the part of a computer's memory that you can change or remove କମ୍ପ୍ୟୁଟର୍, ମେମୋରି ବା ସ୍ମୃତି ଯେଉଁଥିରୁ ତଥ୍ୟ କାଢ଼ି ଓ ବଦଳାଇ ହୁଏ ✪ **RAM** ଶବ୍ଦର ବିସ୍ତୃତ ରୂପ **Random Access Memory**। ➪ **ROM** ଦେଖନ୍ତୁ।

ram[1] /ræm/ *noun* a male sheep ମେଣ୍ଢା, ମେଷ ➪ ଚିତ୍ର ପାଇଁ **sheep** ଦେଖନ୍ତୁ।

ram[2] /ræm/ *verb* (**rams, ramming, rammed**) crash into something with great force ଖୁବ୍ ଜୋର୍ ଧକ୍କା ହେବା *The car rammed into a tree.*

ramp /ræmp/ *noun* a sloping path that you can take instead of stairs to go to a higher or lower place ଉଚ୍ଚ ଓ ନିଚ୍ଚ ଜାଗାକୁ ସଂଯୋଗ କରୁଥିବା ଗଡ଼ାଣିଆ ଚଟାଣ (ସିଢ଼ି ବଦଳରେ), ର୍‍ୟାମ୍ପ୍ *I pushed the wheelchair up the ramp.*

ran ଶବ୍ଦ **run**[1] ର ଏକ ଧାତୁରୂପ

random /ˈrændəm/ *adjective*
at random without any special plan ଲକ୍ଷହୀନ ବା ଉଦ୍ଦେଶ୍ୟହୀନ ଭାବରେ *She chose a few books at random.*

rang ଶବ୍ଦ **ring**[2] ର ଏକ ଧାତୁରୂପ

range[1] /reɪndʒ/ *noun* **1** a number of different things of the same kind କୌଣସି ଜିନିଷର ବିଭିନ୍ନ ପ୍ରକାରର ସମଷ୍ଟି *This shop sells a range of bicycles.* **2** the amount between the highest and the lowest ପରିସର, ଉଚ୍ଚତମ ଓ ନିମ୍ନତମ ମଧ୍ୟସ୍ଥ ପରିମାଣ *Most children in this group are in the 8–10 age range.* **3** the distance over which you can see, hear, shoot, travel, etc. ଦେଖିପାରିବା, ଶୁଣିପାରିବା, ବନ୍ଧୁକ ଗୁଳିଯିବା, ଯାନବାହାନ ଯାଇପାରିବାର ଦୂରତ୍ୱ ବା ସୀମା *This gun has a range of 700 metres.* **4** a line of mountains or hills ପର୍ବତମାଳା *the Himalayan range*

range[2] /reɪndʒ/ *verb* (**ranges, ranging, ranged**) be at different points between two things ଦୁଇ ସୀମା ମଧ୍ୟରେ ବିଭିନ୍ନ ବିନ୍ଦୁରେ ରହିବା *The ages of the students in the class range from 18 to 30.*

rank /ræŋk/ *noun* the position that somebody has in a group of people, for example in the army (ସେନା, ଚାକିରି ଇତ୍ୟାଦିରେ) ଶ୍ରେଣୀ, ସ୍ତର, ପଦବୀ *General is one of the highest ranks in the army.*

rank *verb* (**ranks, ranking, ranked**) give a position or grade to somebody or something in a group ଶ୍ରେଣୀବଦ୍ଧ କରିବା *She was ranked the best artist in her class.*

ransom /ˈrænsəm/ *noun* money that you must pay so that a criminal will free a person whom he or she has captured ବନ୍ଦୀମୁକ୍ତିର ମୂଲ୍ୟ *The kidnappers have demanded a ransom of twenty lakh rupees.*

rapid /ˈræpɪd/ *adjective* quick; fast କ୍ଷିପ୍ର; ଦ୍ରୁତ *rapid changes*

rapidly *adverb* କ୍ଷିପ୍ରଭାବରେ; ଦ୍ରୁତ ଭାବରେ *The ice melted rapidly.*

rare /reə(r)/ *adjective* (**rarer, rarest**) if something is rare, you do not find or see it often ବିରଳ, ଦୁର୍ଲଭ *Pandas are rare animals.*

rarely *adverb* not often କଦବା, କ୍ୱଚିତ୍ *I rarely go to my village.*

rash[1] /ræʃ/ *noun* (*plural* **rashes**) a lot of small red spots on your skin ଚର୍ମରେ ଲାଲି ଲାଲି ହୋଇ ଫଳି ଯାଉଥିବା ରୋଗ, କୁଣ୍ଡିଆ

rash[2] /ræʃ/ *adjective* (**rasher, rashest**) if you are rash, you do things too quickly, without thinking ଅସାବଧାନ, ତରବରିଆ *You were rash to leave your job before you had found a new one.*

rat /ræt/ *noun* an animal like a big mouse ବଡ଼ମୂଷା

rate /reɪt/ *noun* **1** the speed of something or how often something happens ଗତିର ହାର; କୌଣସି ଘଟଣା ଘଟିବାର ହାର; କୌଣସି ଜିନିଷର ପ୍ରତି ଏକକର ଦର ବା ହାର **2** the value, cost or price per unit of a thing କୌଣସି ଜିନିଷର ପ୍ରତି ଏକକର ଦର ବା ହାରର ମୂଲ୍ୟ *The rate of population growth was lower in 1950 than in 2001.*

rather /ˈrɑːðə(r)/ *adverb* more than a little but not very; quite କିଛି ପରିମାଣରେ; ଅନେକାଂଶରେ *We were rather tired after our long journey.*

rather than in place of; instead of ବଦଳରେ; ପରିବର୍ତ୍ତେ *Could I have tea rather than juice?*

would rather would prefer to ବରଂ *I would rather go by train than by bus.*

ratio /ˈreɪʃiəʊ/ *noun* the relationship between two numbers which show how much bigger one number is than the other ଦୁଇଟି ପରିମାଣ ଭିତରେ ଥିବା ସମ୍ପର୍କ (ଗୋଟିଏ ଅନ୍ୟଟିର କେତେଭାଗ), ଅନୁପାତ *Mix flour and water in the ratio three to one.* ✪ ଗଣିତରେ ଅନୁପାତର ପ୍ରତୀକ (:)

ration /ˈræʃn/ *noun* a small amount of something that you are allowed to have when there is not enough for everybody to have what they want ଅଭାବ ସମୟରେ ଜଣ ପିଛା ଦିଆଯାଉଥିବା ଅଳ୍ପ ସାମଗ୍ରୀ; ପଡ଼ି, ଭାଗ *food rations*

rattle /ˈrætl/ *verb* (**rattles, rattling, rattled**) **1** make a lot of short sounds because it is shaking ଖଡ଼ ଖଡ଼ ଶବ୍ଦ କରିବା (କୌଣସି ପଦାର୍ଥ ହଲିବା ଫଳରେ) *The windows were rattling all night in the wind.* **2** shake something so that it makes a lot of small sounds କୌଣସି ଜିନିଷ ହଲାଇ ଖଡ଼ ଖଡ଼ ଶବ୍ଦ କରିବା *She rattled the money in the tin.*

rattle *noun* **1** the noise of things hitting each other ଖଡ଼ ଖଡ଼ ଶବ୍ଦ *the rattle of empty bottles* **2** a toy for a baby that makes a sound when shaken ଝୁମୁକା, ପିଲାଙ୍କ ଖେଳନା (ଯାହାକୁ ହଲାଇଲେ ଖଡ଼ ଖଡ଼ ଶବ୍ଦ ହୁଏ)

raw /rɔː/ *adjective* **1** not cooked କଞ୍ଚା, ଅରନ୍ଧା *raw vegetables* **2** natural; as it comes from the soil, from plants, etc. ପ୍ରାକୃତିକ ଅବସ୍ଥାରେ ଥିବା *raw cotton*

ray /reɪ/ *noun* (*plural* **rays**) a straight line of light or heat ଆଲୋକ ବା ଉତ୍ତାପର ରଶ୍ମି ଧାରା *the rays of the sun*

razor /ˈreɪzə(r)/ *noun* a sharp thing that people use to cut hair off their skin, especially the face (to **shave**) (ଖିଅର ହେବା ପାଇଁ) କ୍ଷୁର, ଖୁର *an electric razor*

re- *prefix*	
Re- କିଛି ଶବ୍ଦର ଆରମ୍ଭରେ ଲଗାଇଲେ 'ଆଉଥରେ' ବା 'ପୁନର୍ବାର' ଅର୍ଥ ବୁଝାଯାଏ ଯଥା—	
rebuild =	ଆଉଥରେ ଗଢ଼ିବା *We rebuilt the fence after the storm.*
redo =	ଆଉଥରେ କରିବା *We are redoing our homework. None of us got it right.*

reach /riːtʃ/ *verb* (**reaches, reaching, reached**) **1** arrive somewhere ପହଞ୍ଚିବା। *It was dark when we reached Agra.* ○ *Have you reached the end of the book yet?* **2** put out your hand to do or get something; be able to touch something କିଛି କରିବା ବା ଆଣିବା ପାଇଁ ହାତ ବଢ଼ାଇବା (ହାତ, ଗୋଡ଼ ଇତ୍ୟାଦି) ବଢ଼ାଇ ଛୁଇଁପାରିବା *I reached for the telephone.*

reach *noun* (*no plural*)

beyond reach, out of reach too far away to touch ଛୁଇଁ ନ ପାରିଲା ପରି *Keep this medicine out of the reach of children.*

react /ri'ækt/ *verb* (**reacts, reacting, reacted**) say or do something when another thing happens ପ୍ରତିକ୍ରିୟା କରିବା *How did Akhil react to the news?*

reaction /ri'ækʃn/ *noun* what you say or do because of something that has happened ପ୍ରତିକ୍ରିୟା *What was her reaction when you told her about your exam results?*

read /ri:d/ *verb* (**reads, reading, read** /red/, **has read**) **1** look at words and understand them ପଢ଼ିବା; ପଢ଼ି ବୁଝିପାରିବା *Have you read this book? It's very interesting.* **2** say words aloud ବଡ଼ ପାଟିରେ ପଢ଼ିବା, ପଢ଼ି ଶୁଣାଇବା *I read a story to the children.*

read out read something aloud so that other people can hear ଅନ୍ୟମାନେ ଶୁଣିପାରିଲା ପରି ବଡ଼ ପାଟିରେ ପଢ଼ିବା *The teacher read out the list of names.*

reading *noun* (*no plural*) ପଢ଼ିବା *My interests are reading and football.*

reader /'ri:də(r)/ *noun* **1** a person who reads something ପାଠକ **2** a book for reading at school which helps you to learn to read your own or a foreign language ପଢ଼ିବା ଅଭ୍ୟାସ ପାଇଁ ଉଦ୍ଦିଷ୍ଟ ପାଠ ବହି *an English reader*

ready /'redi/ *adjective* **1** prepared so that you can do something ପ୍ରସ୍ତୁତ (କିଛି କରିବା ପାଇଁ) *I'll be ready to leave in five minutes.* **2** prepared so that you can use it (ବ୍ୟବହାର ପାଇଁ) ପ୍ରସ୍ତୁତ, ଉପଯୁକ୍ତ ଅବସ୍ଥାରେ *Dinner will be ready soon.* **3** happy to do something ଇଚ୍ଛୁକ, ଉଦ୍ୟତ *He's always ready to help.*

get ready make yourself ready for something (ବ୍ୟକ୍ତି ନିଜକୁ) ପ୍ରସ୍ତୁତ କରିବା *I'm getting ready to go out.*

ready-made *adjective* prepared and ready to use (କିଣି ସାଙ୍ଗେ ସାଙ୍ଗେ ପିନ୍ଧିବା ପାଇଁ) ପ୍ରସ୍ତୁତ (ପୋଷାକ) *ready-made clothes*

real /'ri:əl/ *adjective* **1** not just in the mind; that which really exists ବାସ୍ତବ, ପ୍ରକୃତ *The film is about something that happened in real life.* **2** true ସତ୍ୟ, ପ୍ରକୃତ, ଠିକ୍ *The name he gave to the police wasn't his real name.* ✪ ବିପରୀତ **false 2** **3** natural; not a copy ଅକୃତ୍ରିମ; ଅସଲ (ନକଲ ନୁହେଁ), ଖାଣ୍ଟି *This ring is real gold.*

reality /ri'æləti/ *noun* (*plural* **realities**) the way that something really is ବାସ୍ତବତା, ବାସ୍ତବିକତା *He refuses to face reality.*

realize /'rɪəlaɪz/ *verb* (**realizes, realizing, realized**) understand or know that something is true or that something has happened ଠିକ୍ ଭାବେ ବୁଝିପାରିବା; ହୃଦୟଙ୍ଗମ କରିବା, ଉପଲବ୍ଧି କରିବା *When I got home, I realized that I had lost my key.*

realization /ˌrɪəlaɪ'zeɪʃn/ *noun* (*no plural*) the process of understanding or knowing that something is true or has happened ହୃଦୟଙ୍ଗମ କରିବା ପ୍ରକ୍ରିୟା, ଠିକ୍ ଭାବେ ବୁଝିପାରିବା ପ୍ରକ୍ରିୟା

really /'rɪəli/ *adverb* **1** in fact; truly ପ୍ରକୃତ ପକ୍ଷେ; ପ୍ରକୃତରେ *Do you really like him?* **2** very or very much ପ୍ରକୃତରେ, ଖୁବ୍ *I'm really hungry.*

reap /riːp/ *verb* (**reaps, reaping, reaped**) cut and collect crop ଶସ୍ୟ କାଟି ସଂଗ୍ରହ କରିବା

rear[1] /rɪə(r)/ *noun* (*no plural*) the back part of something ପଛପଟ *The kitchen is at the rear of the house.*

rear[2] /rɪə(r)/ *verb* (**rears, rearing, reared**) **1** keep animals on a farm and look after them (ପଶୁପକ୍ଷୀ) ପାଳନ କରିବା **2** bring up children ପିଲାଙ୍କୁ ଲାଳନପାଳନ କରି ବଡ଼ କରିବା

rearrange /ˌriːəˈreɪndʒ/ *verb* (**rearranges, rearranging, rearranged**) change the way something is to make it look better ଆଉଥରେ ଭିନ୍ନ ପ୍ରକାର ବା ଢ଼ାଞ୍ଚାରେ ସଜାଇବା *Let's rearrange the furniture in the room.*

reason /ˈriːzn/ *noun* a cause for something you do or for something that happens କାରଣ, ଉଦ୍ଦେଶ୍ୟ, ଯଥାର୍ଥତା *The reason I didn't come to the party was that I was ill.*

reasonable /ˈriːznəbl/ *adjective* **1** fair, practical and willing to listen to what other people say ବିଚାରବନ୍ତ, ବୁଦ୍ଧିମାନ ଓ ସମସ୍ତଙ୍କ ମତାମତ ଶୁଣୁଥିବା *Her request was perfectly reasonable.* **2** fair or right ଯଥାର୍ଥ, ଠିକ୍, ଉଚିତ *I think Rs 100 is a reasonable price for this bag.* ✪ ବିପରୀତ **unreasonable**

reasonably *adverb* **1** quite, but not very ଠିକ୍ଠାକ୍, ଭଲ କିନ୍ତୁ ଖୁବ୍ ଭଲ ନୁହେଁ *The food was reasonably good.* **2** in a reasonable way ଯୁକ୍ତିଯୁକ୍ତ ଭାବେ, ଯଥାର୍ଥ ଭାବରେ *Don't get angry—let's talk about this reasonably.*

reassure /ˌriːəˈʃɔː(r)/ *verb* (**reassures, reassuring, reassured**) say or do something to make somebody feel safer or happier ଆଶ୍ୱସ୍ତ କରିବା, ଆଶ୍ୱାସନା ଦେବା, ଉତ୍ସାହିତ କରିବା *The doctor reassured her that she was not seriously ill.*

rebel[1] /ˈrebl/ *noun* a person who fights against the people in control ବିଦ୍ରୋହୀ; ପରିଚାଳକ ଗୋଷ୍ଠୀକୁ ବିରୋଧ କରୁଥିବା ବ୍ୟକ୍ତି

rebel[2] /rɪˈbel/ *verb* (**rebels, rebelling, rebelled**) fight against the people in control ବିଦ୍ରୋହ କରିବା *She rebelled against her parents by refusing to have her dinner.*

rebellion /rɪˈbeljən/ *noun* a time when a lot of people fight against the people in control ବିଦ୍ରୋହ *Many people took part in the rebellion last year.*

rebuild /ˌriːˈbɪld/ *verb* (**rebuilds, rebuilding, rebuilt** /ˌriːˈbɪlt/, **has rebuilt**) build something again ପୁନଃନିର୍ମାଣ କରିବା *The houses that were destroyed in the earthquake are being rebuilt.*

recall /rɪˈkɔːl/ *verb* (**recalls, recalling, recalled**) remember something ମନେ ପକାଇବା, ମନେ ପଡ଼ିଯିବା *I can't recall the name of the hotel.* ✪ ସାଧାରଣତଃ **remember** ଶବ୍ଦ ବ୍ୟବହାର କରାଯାଇଥାଏ ।

receipt /rɪˈsiːt/ *noun* a piece of paper that shows you have paid for something ରସିଦ୍ *Can I have a receipt?*

receive /rɪˈsiːv/ *verb* (**receives, receiving, received**) get something that somebody has given or sent to you ଅନ୍ୟ କାହାଦ୍ୱାରା ପଠାଯାଇଥିବା ଜିନିଷ ପାଇବା, ପ୍ରାପ୍ତ କରିବା; ଗ୍ରହଣ କରିବା *Did you receive my letter?* ✪ ସାଧାରଣତଃ **get** ଶବ୍ଦ ବ୍ୟବହାର କରାଯାଇଥାଏ।

receiver /rɪˈsiːvə(r)/ *noun* the part of a telephone that you use for listening and speaking ଟେଲିଫୋନ୍‌ର କହିବା ଶୁଣିବା ଯନ୍ତ୍ର

recent /ˈriːsnt/ *adjective* that happened a short time ago ଅଳ୍ପ ଦିନ ତଳର, ଏବେକାର *Is this a recent photo of your son?*

recently *adverb* not long ago ଏବେ, ଅଳ୍ପ ଦିନ ତଳେ *She's been on holiday recently—that's why she has no leave left.*

reception /rɪˈsepʃn/ *noun* **1** (*no plural*) the place where you go first when you arrive at a hotel, office, etc. ହୋଟେଲ୍, ଅଫିସ୍ ଇତ୍ୟାଦିର ସ୍ୱାଗତ କକ୍ଷ ବା ଟେବୁଲ୍ *Leave your key at the reception if you go out.* **2** (*plural* **receptions**) a big important party ଅଭ୍ୟର୍ଥନା ସଭା, ଅତିଥିମାନଙ୍କ ପାଇଁ ବଡ଼ ଧରଣର ଭୋଜି (ବିଶେଷତଃ ବାହାଘରରେ) *a wedding reception*

receptionist /rɪˈsepʃənɪst/ *noun* a person in a hotel, office, etc. who helps you when you arrive there and who may also answer the telephone ହୋଟେଲ୍, ଅଫିସ୍ ଇତ୍ୟାଦିରେ ନିୟୋଜିତ ସ୍ୱାଗତ ଅଧିକାରୀ

recess /rɪˈses/ *noun* (*no plural*) **1** a short break that you get between classes (କ୍ଲାସ୍, ବ୍ୟବସ୍ଥାପକ ସଭା ଇତ୍ୟାଦିର) ସାମୟିକ ବିରତି **2** a certain time during the year when members of a committee, parliament, etc. do not meet ବର୍ଷର ଏକ ନିଶ୍ଚିତ ସମୟ ଯେତେବେଳେ ସଂଗଠନ, ସଂବିଧାନ ଇତ୍ୟାଦିର ସଭ୍ୟମାନେ ମିଳିତ ହୋଇପାରନ୍ତି ନାହିଁ

recipe /ˈresəpi/ *noun* a piece of writing that tells you how to cook something ଖାଦ୍ୟ ପ୍ରସ୍ତୁତିର ଲିଖିତ ବିବରଣୀ

recipe

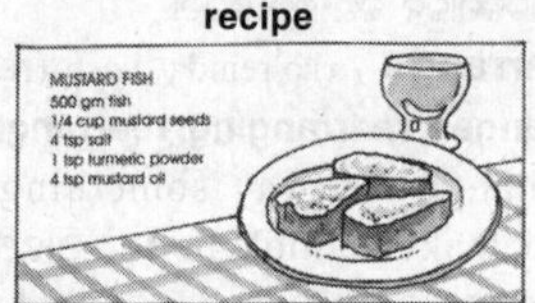

recite /rɪˈsaɪt/ *verb* (**recites, reciting, recited**) say aloud a poem or a passage that you have learnt by heart ଆବୃତ୍ତି କରିବା

recitation /ˌresɪˈteɪʃn/ *noun* ଆବୃତ୍ତି; ଆବୃତ୍ତିର ବିଷୟବସ୍ତୁ *We learnt many poems in school for recitation.*

reckless /ˈrekləs/ *adjective* showing a lack of care about danger and the possible results of this action ବିପଦ ବା ଫଳାଫଳକୁ ବେଖାତିର କରୁଥିବା; ଦୁଃସାହସୀ (ବ୍ୟକ୍ତି); ଦୁଃସାହସିକ (କାମ) *reckless driving*

reckon /ˈrekən/ *verb* (**reckons, reckoning, reckoned**) believe something because you have thought about it ଭାବିଚିନ୍ତି କୌଣସି ବିଷୟରେ ବିଶ୍ୱାସ କରିବା ବା ସିଦ୍ଧାନ୍ତରେ ପହଞ୍ଚିବା *I reckon the holiday will cost us Rs 10,000.*

reclaim /rɪˈkleɪm/ *verb* (**reclaims, reclaiming, reclaimed**) **1** get back something that has been lost or taken away ନିଜ ଜିନିଷ ଫେରସ୍ତ ଦାବି କରିବା ବା ଫେରସ୍ତ ପାଇବା *You will have to go to the police station to reclaim your mobile phone.* **2** get back useful products from waste materials ଅଳିଆର ଉପଯୋଗି ପଦାର୍ଥ କାଢ଼ି ନୂଆଜିନିଷ ତିଆରି କରିବା *metal reclaimed from old cars* **3** make an area of land suitable for farming ପତିତ ଜମି ଚାଷଯୋଗ୍ୟ କରିବା

recognize /ˈrekəgnaɪz/ *verb* (**recognizes, recognizing, recognized**) **1** remember somebody or something because you have seen or heard them before ଚିହ୍ନିବା, ପରିଚିତ ବୋଲି ଜାଣିବା *I didn't recognize you without your glasses.* **2** know or admit that something is true ବୁଝିପାରିବା; ପ୍ରକୃତ ସ୍ଥିତି ଉପଲବ୍ଧି କରିବା *They recognize that there is a problem.*

recognition /ˌrekəgˈnɪʃn/ *noun* (*no plural*) the act of recognizing somebody or something ଚିହ୍ନିବା ପ୍ରକ୍ରିୟା

recommend /ˌrekəˈmend/ *verb* (**recommends, recommending, recommended**) tell somebody that another person or thing is good or useful ସୁପାରିଶ କରିବା, ଭଲ ବୋଲି କହିବା *Can you recommend a hotel near the airport?*

recommendation /ˌrekəmenˈdeɪʃn/ *noun* ସୁପାରିଶ *We stayed at the Grand Hotel on Ali's recommendation.*

record[1] /ˈrekɔːd/ *noun* **1** notes about things that have happened ଲିଖିତ ଦଲିଲ୍, ପ୍ରମାଣ, ତଥ୍ୟ, ହିସାବ ଇତ୍ୟାଦି *Keep a record of all the money you spend.* **2** a round plastic thing that makes music when you play it on a **record player** ଗ୍ରାମଫୋନ୍, ରେକର୍ଡ଼ ପ୍ଲେୟାର ଇତ୍ୟାଦିରେ ବଜାଇବା ପାଇଁ ପ୍ଲାଷ୍ଟିକ୍ ଚକତି, ରେକର୍ଡ଼ *Put another record on.* **3** the best that has been done in a sport କ୍ରିଡ଼ାରେ ସବୁଠାରୁ ଭଲ ଯଶ ପ୍ରଦର୍ଶନ କରିବା *She holds the national record for long jump.*

break a record do better in a sport than anybody has done before କ୍ରୀଡ଼ା ପ୍ରତିଯୋଗିତାରେ ପୂର୍ବମାନ ଭାଙ୍ଗିବା

record[2] /rɪˈkɔːd/ *verb* (**records, recording, recorded**) **1** write notes about or make pictures of things that happen so you can remember them later ଲେଖି ରଖିବା·*In his diary, he recorded everything that he did.* **2** put music or a film on a tape or record so that you can listen to or watch it later ଗୀତ ବା ଫିଲ୍ମ ଟେପ୍, ଡିସ୍କ ଇତ୍ୟାଦିରେ ଉତାରିବା (ଯେପରି ପରେ ତାକୁ ବଜାଇ ଶୁଣି ବା ଦେଖି ହେବ), ରେକର୍ଡ଼ କରିବା *I recorded a concert from the radio.*

record player *noun* a machine for playing records on ଗ୍ରାମୋଫୋନ୍, ରେକର୍ଡ଼ ପ୍ଲେୟାର୍

recover /rɪˈkʌvə(r)/ *verb* (**recovers, recovering, recovered**) **1** become well or happy again after you have been ill or sad ଆରୋଗ୍ୟ ହେବା, ସ୍ୱାସ୍ଥ୍ୟ ଲାଭ କରିବା *She is slowly recovering from her illness.* **2** get back something that you had lost ପୁନର୍ଲାଭ କରିବା, ଫେରି ପାଇବା; ପୁନରୁଦ୍ଧାର କରିବା *Police recovered the stolen car.*

recovery *noun* (*no plural*) ସ୍ୱାସ୍ଥ୍ୟ ଲାଭ; ଆରୋଗ୍ୟ ଲାଭ; ପୁନର୍ଲାଭ *He made a quick recovery after his illness.*

rectangle /ˈrektæŋgl/ *noun* a shape with two long sides, two short sides and four angles of 90 degrees ଆୟତକ୍ଷେତ୍ର, ସମକୋଣୀ ଚତୁର୍ଭୁଜ ➪ ଚିତ୍ର ପାଇଁ **shape** ଦେଖନ୍ତୁ ।

rectangular /ˈrekˈtæŋgjələ(r)/ *adjective* with the shape of a rectangle ଆୟତାକାର, ସମଚତୁଷ୍କୋଣ, ସମକୋଣିକ *This page is rectangular.*

recycle /ˌriːˈsaɪkl/ *verb* (**recycles, recycling, recycled**) do something to materials like paper and glass so that they can be used again (ଅଦରକାରି ପଦାର୍ଥର) ମୂଳବସ୍ତୁରେ ପରିବର୍ତ୍ତନ କରି ଆଉଥରେ ବ୍ୟବହାର ସାପେକ୍ଷ କରିବା *Old newspapers can be recycled.*

red /red/ *adjective* (**redder, reddest**) with the colour of blood ଲାଲ୍, ରକ୍ତ ବର୍ଣ୍ଣର *She's wearing a bright red dress.*

red *noun* ଲାଲ୍ ରଙ୍ଗ *Lucy was dressed in red.*

redo /ˌriːˈduː/ *verb* do something again ଆଉଥରେ କରିବା

reduce /rɪˈdjuːs/ *verb* (**reduces, reducing, reduced**) make something smaller or less କମାଇବା, ହ୍ରାସକରିବା, ସାନ କରିବା *I bought this shirt because the price had been reduced from Rs 250 to Rs 200.*

reduction /rɪˈdʌkʃn/ *noun* କମ୍ କରିବା ପ୍ରକ୍ରିୟା, ହ୍ରାସକରଣ *price reductions*

reel /riːl/ *noun* a thing with round sides that holds thread for sewing, film for cameras, etc. ସୂତା, ଫିଲ୍ମ ଇତ୍ୟାଦି ଗୁଡ଼ାଇ ରଖିବା ପାଇଁ ଥିବା ଛୋଟ ନଟେଇ ପରି ଧାରକ, ରିଲ୍ *a reel of film*

refer /rɪˈfɜː(r)/ *verb* (**refers, referring, referred**)

refer to somebody or **something** **1** look in a book or ask somebody for information ବହି ପଢ଼ି ବା ଅନ୍ୟକୁ ପଚାରି ବୁଝିବା *If you don't understand a word, you can refer to a dictionary.* **2** talk about somebody or something କୌଣସି ବ୍ୟକ୍ତି ବା ବିଷୟରେ କହିବା ବା ନଜିର ଦେବା, ମନ୍ତବ୍ୟ ଦେବା *She referred to her father in her speech.*

referee /ˌrefəˈriː/ *noun* a person in a sport like football or boxing who controls the match ଖେଳ ପରିଚାଳକ ବା ବିଚାରକ, ରେଫରି

reference /ˈrefrəns/ *noun* **1** (*plural* **references**) what somebody says or writes about somebody or something else ଲେଖା ବା ବକ୍ତୃତାରେ ଅନ୍ୟର ମନ୍ତବ୍ୟ ବା କିଛି ତଥ୍ୟର ଉଲ୍ଲେଖ *There are many references to Kashmir in this book.* **2** (*no plural*) the act of referring to a book, etc. for information ବହି ଇତ୍ୟାଦିରେ ତଥ୍ୟ ଖୋଜିବା କାମ *Use this encyclopedia for further reference.* **3** (*plural* **references**) a letter from somebody who knows you, giving infromation about your character, qualifications and abilities, usually written to a new employer; the person who provides such information ପ୍ରମାଣ ପତ୍ର; ପ୍ରଶଂସା ପତ୍ର *Did your boss give you a reference?*

reference book *noun* (*plural* **reference books**) a book where you look for information, for example a dictionary or an encyclopedia ତଥ୍ୟ ସମ୍ବଳିତ ଥିବା ବହି (ଅଭିଧାନ, ଜ୍ଞାନକୋଷ ଇତ୍ୟାଦି)

refine /rɪˈfaɪn/ *verb* (**refines, refining, refined**) **1** make a substance more pure by taking other substances out of it ବିଶୋଧନ କରିବା, ବିଶୁଦ୍ଧ କରିବା *refine oil* **2** make changes in something to improve it ଅଧିକ ମାର୍ଜିତ, ସୁନ୍ଦର ବା ସଭ୍ୟ କରିବା

refinery /rɪˈfaɪnəri/ *noun* (*plural* **refineries**) a factory where a substance is made pure by taking other substances out of it (ତେଲ ଇତ୍ୟାଦିର) ବିଶୋଧନାଗାର *an oil refinery*

reflect /rɪˈflekt/ *verb* (**reflects, reflecting, reflected**) send back light, heat or sound from a surface ପ୍ରତିଫଳିତ କରିବା, ପ୍ରତିବିମ୍ବିତ କରିବା *A mirror reflects a picture of you when you look in it.*

reflection /rɪˈflekʃn/ *noun* **1** (*plural* **reflections**) a picture that you see in a mirror or in water ପ୍ରତିବିମ୍ବ, ପ୍ରତିଫଳନ *He looked into the pool and saw a reflection of himself.* **2** (*no plural*) the process of sending back light, heat or sound from a surface ଆଲୋକ, ଉତ୍ତାପ, ଧ୍ୱନି ଇତ୍ୟାଦିର ପ୍ରତିଫଳନ

reform /rɪˈfɔːm/ *verb* (**reforms, reforming, reformed**) change something to make it better ତ୍ରୁଟି ସଂଶୋଧନ କରି ଉନ୍ନତ କରିବା, ସୁଧାରିବା, ସଂସ୍କାର କରିବା *The government wants to reform the education system in the country.*

reform *noun* a change to make something better ସଂସ୍କାର, ପରିମାର୍ଜନ *political reform*

reformer *noun* a person who works to improve a social or political system ସଂସ୍କାରକ

refresh /rɪˈfreʃ/ *verb* (**refreshes, refreshing, refreshed**) make somebody feel cooler, stronger or less tired ସତେଜ, ସଜୀବ ବା ସବଳ କରିବା ବା ହେବା *Sleep will refresh you after your long journey.*

refreshing *adjective* ଉତ୍ଫୁଲ୍ଲ କଲାଭଳି *a cool refreshing drink*

refreshments /rɪˈfreʃmənts/ *noun* (*no singular*) food and drinks that you can buy in a place like a cinema or theatre ସିନେମା ଘର, ଥିଏଟର ଇତ୍ୟାଦିରେ ମିଳୁଥିବା ଖାଦ୍ୟ ବା ପାନୀୟ *Refreshments will be sold during the interval.*

refrigerator /rɪˈfrɪdʒəreɪtə(r)/ *noun* a big metal box for keeping food and drink cold and fresh ଖାଦ୍ୟ, ପାନୀୟ ଇତ୍ୟାଦି ଥଣ୍ଡା ଓ ତଟକା ରଖିବା ପାଇଁ ଯନ୍ତ୍ରଥିବା ଧାତୁ ବାକ୍ସ ✪ ଆମେ ସାଧାରଣତଃ **fridge** ଶବ୍ଦ ବ୍ୟବହାର କରିଥାଉଁ।

refuge /ˈrefjuːdʒ/ *noun* a place where you are safe from somebody or something ସୁରକ୍ଷିତ ରହିବା ସ୍ଥାନ, ଆଶ୍ରୟସ୍ଥଳ, ସୁରକ୍ଷାଶ୍ରୟ

take refuge from something go to a safe place to get away from something bad or dangerous ବିପଦରୁ ବଞ୍ଚିବା ପାଇଁ ସୁରକ୍ଷିତ ସ୍ଥାନକୁ ଯିବା, ସୁରକ୍ଷିତ ସ୍ଥାନରେ ଆଶ୍ରୟ ନେବା *We took refuge from the hot sun under a tree.*

refugee /ˌrefjuˈdʒiː/ *noun* a person who must leave his or her country because of danger ବିପଦ ଯୋଗୁଁ ନିଜ ଦେଶ ଛାଡ଼ି ଅନ୍ୟ ଦେଶରେ ଆଶ୍ରୟ ନେବା ବ୍ୟକ୍ତି; ଶରଣାର୍ଥୀ

refund /ˈriːfʌnd/ *verb* (**refunds, refunding, refunded**) give somebody their money back because they had earlier paid extra or because they are not satisfied with what they bought ପୂର୍ବରୁ ନେଇଥିବା ବା ଭୁଲରେ ଦେଇଥିବା ଅଧିକା ଟଙ୍କା ଫେରସ୍ତ ଦେବା; କିଣିଥିବା ଜିନିଷ ଠିକ୍ ନଥିବା ହେତୁ ଟଙ୍କା ଫେରସ୍ତ ଦେବା *I took the camera back to the shop and they refunded my money.*

refuse /rɪˈfjuːz/ *verb* (**refuses, refusing, refused**) say 'no' when somebody asks you to do or have something ମନା କରିବା, ନାହିଁ କରିବା *I asked Matthew to help, but he refused.*

refusal /rɪˈfjuːzl/ *noun* saying 'no' when somebody asks you to do or have something ଅସମ୍ମତି, ମନା (କରିବା) *a refusal to pay the fine*

regard /rɪˈɡɑːd/ *noun* **1** (*no plural*) what you think about somebody or something ମତ, ଭାବନା *I have high regard for his work.* **2** (*no plural*) care ଯତ୍ନ, ସମ୍ମାନ, ଭ୍ରୂକ୍ଷେପ *She shows no regard for other people's feelings.* **3 regards** (*plural*) kind wishes ସଦିଚ୍ଛା *Please give my regards to your parents.*

regarding /rɪˈɡɑːdɪŋ/ *preposition* about or in connection with something ସମ୍ପର୍କରେ, ସମ୍ବନ୍ଧରେ *She said nothing regarding her health problems.*

regenerate /rɪˈdʒenəreɪt/ *verb* (**regenerates, regenerating, regenerated**) make something grow and develop again ପୁଣି ଜନ୍ମ ନେବା, ପୁନରୁତ୍ପତ୍ତି କରିବା *regenerate a plan* ○ *blood cells that regenerate rapidly*

regeneration /rɪˌdʒenəˈreɪʃn/ *noun* (*no plural*) the process of growing and developing something again ପୁନରୁତ୍ପତ୍ତି *regeneration of red blood cells*

regiment /ˈredʒɪmənt/ *noun* a group of soldiers in an army (କର୍ଣ୍ଣେଲଙ୍କ ଅଧିନରେ ଥିବା) ସୈନ୍ୟଗୋଷ୍ଠୀ

region /ˈriːdʒən/ *noun* a part of a country or of the world ଦେଶର ଏକ ପ୍ରାନ୍ତ ବା ଅଞ୍ଚଳ *There will be rain in the northern regions today.*

regional *adjective* of a certain region ଆଞ୍ଚଳିକ, ପ୍ରାନ୍ତୀୟ

register[1] /ˈredʒɪstə(r)/ *noun* a list of names or a book that contains such a list (ଜନ୍ମ, ମୃତ୍ୟୁ, ଭୋଟଦାତା ଇତ୍ୟାଦିଙ୍କ) ବିବରଣୀ ଖାତା, ନାମତାଲିକା *The teacher keeps a register of all the students in the class.*

register[2] /ˈredʒɪstə(r)/ *verb* (**registers, registering, registered**) put a name on a list ତାଲିକାଭୁକ୍ତ କରିବା ବା ହେବା *I would like to register for the English course.*

registration /ˌredʒɪˈstreɪʃn/ *noun* (*no plural*) the action of putting a name on a list ତାଲିକାଭୁକ୍ତ କରିବା ପ୍ରକ୍ରିୟା,

ପଞ୍ଜିକରଣ, ରେଜିଷ୍ଟ୍ରେଶନ୍ *registration of births, marriages and deaths*

regret /rɪˈgret/ *verb* (**regrets, regretting, regretted**) feel sorry about something that you did ପଶ୍ଚାତ୍ତାପ କରିବା, ଅନୁତାପ କରିବା, ଭୁଲ୍ କାମ ପାଇଁ ଦୁଃଖ କରିବା *She regrets selling her car.*

regret *noun* ପଶ୍ଚାତ୍ତାପ, ଅନୁତାପ, ଖେଦ *I don't have any regrets about leaving my job.*

regular /ˈregjələ(r)/ *adjective* **1** that happens again and again with the same amount of space or time in between ନିୟମିତ ଭାବେ ଘଟୁଥିବା, ସମ ଅନ୍ତରାଳରେ ଘଟୁଥିବା *We have regular meetings every week.* **2** having an even shape or pattern ସୁସମନ୍ୱିତ ଆକାର ବା ଢାଞ୍ଚାଥିବା ➪ **irregular** ଦେଖନ୍ତୁ।

regularly *adverb* ନିୟମିତ ଭାବରେ *We meet regularly every Friday.*

regulation /ˌregjuˈleɪʃn/ *noun* something that controls what people do; a rule or law ଧାର୍ଯ୍ୟ ନିୟମ; ଆଇନ୍ *You can't smoke here—it's against fire regulations.*

rehearse /rɪˈhɜːs/ *verb* (**rehearses, rehearsing, rehearsed**) practise a play, etc. before you do it in front of other people (ନାଟକ ଇତ୍ୟାଦିର) ପୂର୍ବାଭ୍ୟାସ କରିବା, ରିହର୍ସାଲ୍ କରିବା *We are rehearsing for the play.*

rehearsal /rɪˈhɜːsl/ *noun* a time when you rehearse (ନାଟକ ଇତ୍ୟାଦିର) ପୂର୍ବାଭ୍ୟାସ, ରିହର୍ସାଲ୍ *There's a rehearsal for the play tonight.*

reign /reɪn/ *noun* a time when a king or queen rules a country ରାଜତ୍ୱକାଳ, ଶାସନକାଳ, ରାଜୁତି *The reign of Queen Elizabeth II began in 1952.*

reign *verb* (**reigns, reigning, reigned**) rule as king or queen of a country ରାଜତ୍ୱ କରିବା *Emperor Akbar reigned for a long time.*

rein /reɪn/ *noun* a long thin piece of leather that is used by a rider to control a horse, etc. ଲଗାମ୍

reindeer /ˈreɪndɪə(r)/ *noun* (*plural* **reindeer**) a big animal like a deer that lives in very cold countries ମେରୁ ବଳୟର ବଲ୍‌ଗା ହରିଣ

reject /rɪˈdʒekt/ *verb* (**rejects, rejecting, rejected**) say that you do not want somebody or something ପ୍ରତ୍ୟାଖ୍ୟାନ କରିବା, ଅଗ୍ରାହ୍ୟ କରିବା *He rejected my offer of help.* ✪ ବିପରୀତ **accept 1**

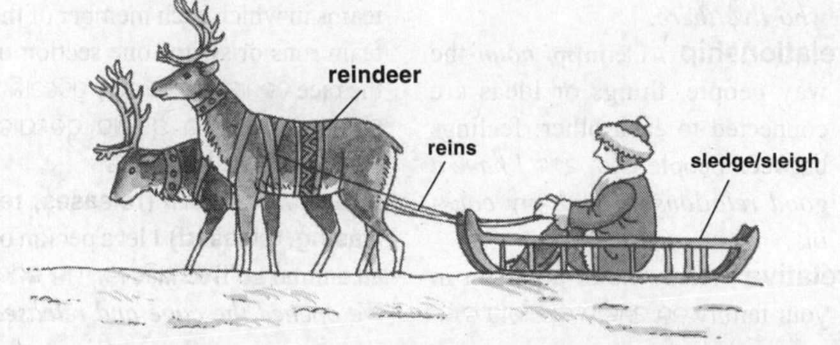

rejection /rɪˈdʒekʃn/ *noun* the act of refusing to accept something or someone ପ୍ରତ୍ୟାଖ୍ୟାନ, ବର୍ଜନ *a rejection letter*

rejoice /rɪˈdʒɔɪs/ *verb* (**rejoices, rejoicing, rejoiced**) express joy and happiness at something ଖୁସି ହେବା, ଆନନ୍ଦିତ ହେବା, ଉତ୍ଫୁଲ୍ଲିତ ହେବା

relate /rɪˈleɪt/ *verb* (**relates, relating, related**) **1** tell or narrate something ବର୍ଣ୍ଣନା କରିବା, ବିବରଣ ଦେବା *She related the story of how she lost her luggage.* **2** show the connection between two or more things ଭିନ୍ନ ଭିନ୍ନ ଜିନିଷ ମଧ୍ୟରେ ସମ୍ପର୍କ ଦେଖାଇବା *The report relates tension to heart diseases.*

related /rɪˈleɪtɪd/ *adjective* in the same family; connected ରକ୍ତ ସମ୍ପର୍କ ଥିବା, ଆତ୍ମୀୟ; ସମ୍ପୃକ୍ତ, ସମ୍ପର୍କ ଥିବା *'Are those two boys related?' 'Yes, they're brothers.'*

relation /rɪˈleɪʃn/ *noun* **1** a person in your family ଆତ୍ମୀୟ ବ୍ୟକ୍ତି *He met a close relation of his mother today.* **2** a connection between two things ସମ୍ପର୍କ, ସମ୍ବନ୍ଧ *There is no relation between the size of the countries and the number of people who live there.*

relationship /rɪˈleɪʃnʃɪp/ *noun* the way people, things or ideas are connected to each other; feelings between people ସମ୍ବନ୍ଧ, ସମ୍ପର୍କ *I have a good relationship with my cousins.*

relative /ˈrelətɪv/ *noun* a person in your family ରକ୍ତ ସମ୍ପର୍କୀୟ ବା ଆତ୍ମୀୟ ବ୍ୟକ୍ତି

relatively /ˈrelətɪvli/ *adverb* to a large degree, especially when compared to other similar things ଆପେକ୍ଷିକ ଭାବେ, ତୁଳନାତ୍ମକ ଭାବେ *This room is relatively small.*

relax /rɪˈlæks/ *verb* (**relaxes, relaxing, relaxed**) **1** rest and be calm; become less worried or angry ଆରାମ କରିବା, ବିଶ୍ରାମ ନେବା *After a hard day at work, I spent the evening relaxing in front of the television.* **2** become less tight or make something become less tight କଠିନତା କମାଇବା; କୋହଳ କରିବା *Let your body relax.*

relaxation /ˌriːlækˈseɪʃn/ *noun* (*no plural*) ବିଶ୍ରାମ, ଆରାମ *You need more rest and relaxation.*

relaxed /rɪˈlækst/ *adjective* ଶାନ୍ତ, ଶିଥିଳ, ଆରାମରେ ଥିବା *She felt relaxed after her holiday.*

relay /rɪˈleɪ/ *verb* (**relays, relaying, relayed**) **1** receive and then send on something like information or news to somebody ଖବର ଅନ୍ତର ଇତ୍ୟାଦି ପାଇଁ ଅନ୍ୟ ପାଖକୁ ପଠାଇବା **2** broadcast a programme କୌଣସି ଘଟଣାର ପ୍ରସାରଣ କରିବା

relay race *noun* a race between teams in which each member of the team runs or swims one section of the race ଦଳମାନଙ୍କ ମଧ୍ୟରେ ଦୌଡ଼ ପ୍ରତିଯୋଗିତା ଯେଉଁଥିରେ ପ୍ରତି ଦଳର ପ୍ରତ୍ୟେକ ପ୍ରତିଯୋଗୀ ଦୌଡ଼ର ଗୋଟିଏ ପର୍ଯ୍ୟାୟ ଦୌଡ଼ନ୍ତି

release /rɪˈliːs/ *verb* (**releases, releasing, released**) **1** let a person or an animal go free ଛାଡ଼ିଦେବା, ମୁକ୍ତ କରିବା *We opened the cage and released* *the bird.* ✪ ବିପରୀତ **capture** **2** make a film, book, etc. available so that people can watch or read it ସର୍ବସାଧାରଣରେ ପ୍ରଦର୍ଶନ ପାଇଁ ଫିଲ୍ମ, ବହି ଇତ୍ୟାଦିକୁ ଉନ୍ମୁକ୍ତ କରିବା, ରିଲିଜ୍ କରିବା, ଉନ୍ମୋଚନ କରିବା *The film was released on Friday.*

release *noun* **1** the act of freeing an animal or a person ମୁକ୍ତି, ନିବନ୍ଧନ *the release of prisoners* **2** the act of making a film, book, etc. available for people to watch or read it **3** a newly released CD, film, etc. (ଫିଲ୍ମ, ବହି ଇତ୍ୟାଦିର) ଉନ୍ମୋଚନ; ଉନ୍ମୋଚିତ ଫିଲ୍ମ, ବହି ଇତ୍ୟାଦି *the film release function*

relevant /ˈreləvənt/ *adjective* connected with what you are talking or writing about; important ପ୍ରଯୁଜ୍ୟ, ସଙ୍ଗତ, ପ୍ରାସଙ୍ଗିକ; ଦରକାରୀ, ଗୁରୁତ୍ୱପୂର୍ଣ୍ଣ *We need somebody who can do the job well—your age is not relevant.*

reliable /rɪˈlaɪəbl/ *adjective* that you can trust ବିଶ୍ୱାସଯୋଗ୍ୟ, ବିଶ୍ୱସ୍ତ *He is a reliable person.* ✪ ବିପରୀତ **unreliable** ✪ Reliable ର କ୍ରିୟା ରୂପ ହେଲା **rely**।

relied ଶବ୍ଦ **rely** ର ଏକ ଧାତୁରୂପ

relief /rɪˈliːf/ *noun* (*no plural*) **1** the feeling when pain or worry stops ଯନ୍ତ୍ରଣା ବା ଚିନ୍ତାରୁ ମୁକ୍ତ ହେବାର ଅନୁଭୂତି *It was a great relief to know she was safe.* **2** food or money for people who need it ଅଭାବଗ୍ରସ୍ତ ବା ବିପନ୍ନ ଲୋକଙ୍କୁ ଦିଆଯାଉଥିବା ଖାଦ୍ୟ, ଟଙ୍କା ଇତ୍ୟାଦି *Many countries sent relief to the people who had lost their homes in the floods.*

relies ଶବ୍ଦ **rely** ର ଏକ ଧାତୁରୂପ

relieved /rɪˈliːvd/ *adjective* pleased because a problem or danger has gone away ସମସ୍ୟା ବା ବିପଦରୁ ମୁକ୍ତ ହେବାର ଆଶ୍ୱସ୍ତି *I was relieved to hear that you weren't hurt in the accident.*

religion /rɪˈlɪdʒən/ *noun* **1** (*no plural*) the belief in God or gods and the worship of them ଧର୍ମ, ଈଶ୍ୱର ବିଶ୍ୱାସ **2** (*plural* **religions**) one of the ways of believing in God, for example Hinduism, Christianity, Islam or Sikhism ଧର୍ମ (ଯଥା: ହିନ୍ଦୁ, ଖ୍ରୀଷ୍ଟୀୟାନ୍, ଇସଲାମ୍, ଶିଖ, ବୌଦ୍ଧ, ଜୈନ ଇତ୍ୟାଦି ଧର୍ମ)

religious /rɪˈlɪdʒəs/ *adjective* **1** of religion ଧର୍ମ ସମ୍ବନ୍ଧୀୟ *a religious leader* **2** with a strong belief in a religion ଧାର୍ମିକ, ଧର୍ମବିଶ୍ୱାସୀ *My grandmother is very religious.*

reluctant /rɪˈlʌktənt/ *adjective* if you are reluctant to do something, you do not want to do it (କୌଣସି କାମ କରିବା ପାଇଁ) ଅନିଚ୍ଛୁକ, ବିମୁଖ, ବିତୃଷ୍ଣ, କୁଣ୍ଠିତ, କୁଛକୁଛ *Seema was reluctant to give me the money.*

reluctance /rɪˈlʌktəns/ *noun* (*no plural*) being reluctant କୁଣ୍ଠା, ଅନିଚ୍ଛା, ବିମୁଖତା *He agreed to come, but with great reluctance.*

rely /rɪˈlaɪ/ *verb* (**relies, relying, relied, has relied**)

rely on somebody or **something** feel sure that somebody or something will do what they should do କୌଣସି କାମ କରିଦେବା ପାଇଁ କାହାରି ଉପରେ ନିର୍ଭର ବା ଭରସା କରିବା *You can rely on him to help you.* ✪ Rely ର ବିଶେଷଣ ଶବ୍ଦ ରୂପ **reliable**।

remain /rɪˈmeɪn/ *verb* (**remains, remaining, remained**) **1** stay after other people or things have gone (ବ୍ୟକ୍ତି) ଅନ୍ୟମାନେ ଗଲା ପରେ ରହିବା; (ପଦାର୍ଥ) ବଳକା ରହିବା, ଅବଶିଷ୍ଟ ରହିବା *After the party, very little remained of the food we had cooked.* **2** stay in the same way; not change; stay in the same place ଯଥାପୂର୍ବ ରହିବା; ବଦଳି ନ ଯିବା; ଏକା ସ୍ଥାନରେ କ୍ରମାଗତ ରହିବା *I asked her a question but she remained silent.* ○ *They remained behind after the others had left.*

remainder /rɪˈmeɪndə(r)/ *noun* the number that you are left with when you divide one number by another or subtract one number from another ଭାଗଶେଷ; ହରଣ ଓ ଫେଡାଣ ପରେ ବାକି ରହିଥିବା ସଂଖ୍ୟା *When you divide 11 by 2, the quotient is 5 and the remainder is 1.*

remains /rɪˈmeɪnz/ *noun* (*plural*) what is left when most of something has gone ଅବଶେଷ, ଭଗ୍ନାବଶେଷ *the remains of an old fort*

remark /rɪˈmɑːk/ *verb* (**remarks, remarking, remarked**) say something ମନ୍ତବ୍ୟ ଦେବା, ଟିପ୍ପଣୀ ଭାବରେ କହିବା *'It's cold today,' he remarked.*

remark *noun* something that you say or write which expresses an opinion ଲିଖିତ ବା କଥିତ ମନ୍ତବ୍ୟ *He made a remark about the food.*

remarkable /rɪˈmɑːkəbl/ *adjective* unusual and surprising in a good way ଅସାଧାରଣ, ଚମତ୍କାର ଦେଖିଲା ପରି, ଉଲ୍ଲେଖଯୋଗ୍ୟ *a remarkable discovery*

remarkably *adverb* ଖୁବ୍ ଭଲ ଭାବରେ; ଅସାଧାରଣ ଭାବରେ *She speaks Marathi remarkably well.*

remedy /ˈremədi/ *noun* (*plural* **remedies**) a way of making something better; a medicine or treatment for a disease ପ୍ରତିକାର, ପ୍ରତିବିଧାନ; ରୋଗ ଉପଶମକାରୀ ଔଷଧ ବା ଚିକିତ୍ସା *a remedy for toothache*

remember /rɪˈmembə(r)/ *verb* (**remembers, remembering, remembered**) keep something in your mind or bring something back into your mind; not forget something ମନେ ରଖିବା; ଭୁଲି ନ ଯିବା; ସ୍ମରଣ କରିବା *Can you remember his name?* ○ *Did you remember to go to the bank?*

remembrance /rɪˈmembrəns/ *noun* (*no plural*) the act of remembering a past event or a person who is dead ସ୍ମରଣ, ସ୍ମୃତି, ସ୍ମୃତିଚାରଣ *A service was held in remembrance of those who were killed in the plane crash.*

remind /rɪˈmaɪnd/ *verb* (**reminds, reminding, reminded**) make somebody remember somebody or something ମନେ ପକେଇଦେବା, ଚେତାଇବା, ସ୍ମରଣ କରାଇଦେବା *This picture reminds me of my holiday in Jaipur.* ○ *I reminded her to buy some bread.*

reminder *noun* something that makes you remember somebody as something ସ୍ମାରକ, ସ୍ମୃତିଚିହ୍ନ; ସ୍ମାରକ ଚିଠି, ଦୋହରା ଚିଠି

remote /rɪˈməʊt/ *adjective* (**remoter, remotest**) far away from other places ଦୂର ଜାଗାରେ ଥିବା, ଦୂରସ୍ଥ,

ଦୂରବର୍ତ୍ତୀ *They live in a remote farmhouse in Karnal.*

remote control *noun* a piece of equipment that helps you to control a television, etc. from a distance ଦୂରରୁ ଯନ୍ତ୍ର ଇତ୍ୟାଦି ଚାଳନ କରି ପାରୁଥିବା ଉପକରଣ

remove /rɪˈmuːv/ *verb* (**removes, removing, removed**) take somebody or something away or off ସ୍ଥାନାନ୍ତର କରିବା; କାଢ଼ିଦେବା *The statue was removed from the museum.* ○ *Please remove your shoes.*

removal /rɪˈmuːvl/ *noun* (*no plural*) the act of removing something ସ୍ଥାନାନ୍ତର କରିବା ପ୍ରକ୍ରିୟା *arrange for the removal of garbage*

renew /rɪˈnjuː/ *verb* (**renews, renewing, renewed**) **1** start something again after a gap of some time ପୁନରାରମ୍ଭ କରିବା *renew peace talks* **2** get or give something new in place of something old ପୁରୁଣା ଜିନିଷ ପରିବର୍ତ୍ତେ ନୂଆ ଜିନିଷ ଆଣିବା ବା ଲଗାଇବା, ବଦଳାଇବା *renew window panes* **3** make something valid for a further period of time ଅନୁମତି ପତ୍ର ଇତ୍ୟାଦି ପୁନଃ ମଂଜୁର କରିବା *If you want to stay in America for another month, you must renew your visa.*

renewable /rɪˈnjuːəbl/ *adjective* **1** a source of energy that is renewable can be replaced naturally and therefore always exists (ଶକ୍ତିର ଉତ୍ସ) ପୁନରୁଦ୍ଧାରକ୍ଷମ, ନବୀକରଣକ୍ଷମ, ଦୋହରା ଯାଇ ପାରୁଥିବା *Solar power is a renewable source of energy.* **2** if something is renewable, it can be made valid or replaced for a further period of time ନବୀକରଣକ୍ଷମ (ଅନୁମତି ପତ୍ର ଇତ୍ୟାଦି); ସମୟସୀମା ବଢ଼ାଯାଇ ପାରୁଥିବା *a renewable work permit* ✪ ବିପରୀତ **non-renewable**

renounce /rɪˈnaʊns/ *verb* (**renounces, renouncing, renounced**) say formally that you do not want something or do not want to be connected with something ପରିତ୍ୟାଗ କରିବା, ଛାଡ଼ିଦେବା *Will they renounce their property rights?*

renunciation /rɪˌnʌnsiˈeɪʃn/ *noun* the act of stating that you give something up formally or that you do not want to be connected with it ପରିତ୍ୟାଗ, ବର୍ଜନ; ତ୍ୟାଗ *the renunciation of nuclear weapons*

renowned /rɪˈnaʊnd/ *adjective* famous ପ୍ରସିଦ୍ଧ, ପ୍ରଖ୍ୟାତ, ବିଖ୍ୟାତ *M.F. Husain is a renowned artist.*

rent /rent/ *verb* (**rents, renting, rented**) **1** pay to live in a place or to use something that belongs to another person (ଘର ଇତ୍ୟାଦି) ଭଡ଼ାରେ ନେବା; (ଜିନିଷପତ୍ର) ଭଡ଼ାରେ ଆଣିବା *I have rented a flat in the centre of town.* **2** let somebody live in a place or use something that belongs to you, if they pay you (ଘର, ଜିନିଷ ଇତ୍ୟାଦି) ଭଡ଼ାରେ ଦେବା *Mr Mirza rents out rooms to students.*

rent *noun* the money that you pay to live in a place or to use something that belongs to another person ଭଡ଼ା *My rent is Rs 5,000 a month.*

repair /rɪˈpeə(r)/ *verb* (**repairs, repairing, repaired**) make something that is broken good again; mend something ଭଙ୍ଗା ଜିନିଷ ସଜାଡ଼ିବା; ମରାମତି କରିବା *Can you repair my bicycle?*

repay /rɪˈpeɪ/ *verb* (**repays, repaying, repaid, has repaid**) **1** pay back money to somebody (ଟଙ୍କା) ଫେରାଇବା, (ଋଣ) ପରିଶୋଧ କରିବା **2** do something for somebody to show your thanks ସେବା ପାଇଁ ପ୍ରତିଦାନ ଦେବା *How can I repay you for all your help?*

repeat /rɪˈpi:t/ *verb* (**repeats, repeating, repeated**) **1** say or do something again ପୁଣିଥରେ କହିବା, କରିବା ବା ଦେବା *He didn't hear my question, so I repeated it.* **2** say what another person has said ପୁନରାବୃତ୍ତି କରିବା *Repeat this sentence after me.*

repetition /ˌrepəˈtɪʃn/ *noun* the act of saying or doing something again and again ପୁନରାବୃତ୍ତି *This book is boring—it's full of repetition.*

replace /rɪˈpleɪs/ *verb* (**replaces, replacing, replaced**) **1** put something back in the right place ପୂର୍ବ ସ୍ଥାନରେ ରଖିବା *Please replace the books on the shelf when you have finished reading them.* **2** take the place of somebody or something ଅନ୍ୟର ସ୍ଥାନ ନେବା **3** put a new or different person or thing in the place of another ବଦଳରେ ରଖିବା, ପ୍ରତିସ୍ଥାପନ କରିବା *The watch that I bought was broken, so the shop replaced it with a new one.*

replacement /rɪˈpleɪsmənt/ *noun* a new or different person or thing that takes the place of another କୌଣସି ବ୍ୟକ୍ତି ବା ପଦାର୍ଥ ବଦଳରେ ଅଣାଯାଇଥିବା ଅନ୍ୟ ବ୍ୟକ୍ତି ବା ପଦାର୍ଥ *Smriti is leaving the company next month, so we need to find a replacement.*

replay /riˈpleɪ/ *noun* **1** a game that is played again because neither of the teams won the first time ଅମିମାଂସିତ ଖେଳ ପୁଣି ଥରେ ଖେଳିବା ପ୍ରକ୍ରିୟା **2** the playing of a small part of a film, tape, etc. again because you want to see or hear it carefully ଫିଲ୍ମ, ଟେପ୍ ଇତ୍ୟାଦି ପୁଣିଥରେ ଚଳାଇ ଦେଖିବା ବା ଶୁଣିବା ପ୍ରକ୍ରିୟା *Here's the action replay of how the batsman got out.*

reply /rɪˈplaɪ/ *verb* (**replies, replying, replied, has replied**) answer ଉତ୍ତର ଦେବା, ପ୍ରତ୍ୟୁତ୍ତର ଦେବା *I have written to my aunt but she hasn't replied.*

reply *noun* (*plural* **replies**) an answer ଉତ୍ତର, ପ୍ରତ୍ୟୁତ୍ତର *Did you receive a reply to your letter?*

report[1] /rɪˈpɔ:t/ *verb* (**reports, reporting, reported**) tell or write about something that has happened ଘଟଣାର ବିବରଣୀ କହିବା ବା ଲେଖିବା, ବିବରଣୀ ଦେବା *We reported the theft to the police.*

report² /rɪˈpɔːt/ *noun* **1** something that somebody says or writes about something that has happened (ଘଟଣାର) ବିବରଣୀ ବା ବର୍ଣ୍ଣନା; (ଘଟଣା ସମ୍ପର୍କରେ) ମତାମତ *Did you read the newspaper reports about the film awards function?* **2** something that teachers write about a student's work ଛାତ୍ରଛାତ୍ରୀଙ୍କ ବିଷୟରେ ଶିକ୍ଷକଙ୍କ ସାମୟିକ ବିବରଣୀ ବା ଟିପ୍ପଣୀ

reporter /rɪˈpɔːtə(r)/ *noun* (ମଧ୍ୟ **news reporter**) a person who collects or reports news for a newspaper, radio or television programme (ଖବରକାଗଜ, ରେଡ଼ିଓ ବା ଟେଲିଭିଜନ୍‌ର) ସମ୍ବାଦଦାତା

represent /ˌreprɪˈzent/ *verb* (**represents, representing, represented**) **1** be a sign for something (କୌଣସି ପଦାର୍ଥ) ପ୍ରତୀକ ବା ଚିହ୍ନ ଦ୍ୱାରା ସୂଚିତ ହେବା *The yellow lines on the map represent roads.* **2** speak or do something for another person or other people ପ୍ରତିନିଧିତ୍ୱ କରିବା *Shweta will represent our school at the next inter-school quiz competition.*

representative /ˌreprɪˈzentətɪv/ *noun* a person who speaks or does something for a group of people ପ୍ରତିନିଧି *There were representatives from every state in India at the meeting.*

reproduce /ˌriːprəˈdjuːs/ *verb* (**reproduces, reproducing, reproduced**) when animals or plants reproduce, they have young ones ସନ୍ତାନ ସନ୍ତତି ପ୍ରଜନନ କରିବା, ଗଛ ମଞ୍ଜିରୁ ନୂଆ ଗଛ ଉଠିବା

reproduction /ˌriːprəˈdʌkʃn/ *noun* (*no plural*) ପ୍ରଜନନ *We are studying plant reproduction at school.*

reptile /ˈreptaɪl/ *noun* a cold-blooded animal that lays eggs. Snakes, lizards, crocodiles and tortoises are reptiles ସରିସୃପ ଜାତୀୟ ପ୍ରାଣୀ (ସାପ, ଝିଟିପିଟି, କୁମ୍ଭୀର, କଇଁଛ ଇତ୍ୟାଦି)

republic /rɪˈpʌblɪk/ *noun* a country whose head is the **president** and where people choose the government ଜନସାଧାରଣଙ୍କ ଦ୍ୱାରା ନିର୍ବାଚିତ ସଭ୍ୟଙ୍କ ଦ୍ୱାରା ଶାସିତ ରାଜ୍ୟ, ଗଣତନ୍ତ୍ର, ପ୍ରଜାତନ୍ତ୍ର *the Republic of Ireland*

reputation /ˌrepjuˈteɪʃn/ *noun* what people think or say about somebody or something କାହାରି ବିଷୟରେ ଲୋକଙ୍କ ମତାମତ *This restaurant has a good reputation.*

request /rɪˈkwest/ *verb* (**requests, requesting, requested**) politely ask for something or ask someone to do something ଅନୁରୋଧ କରିବା *I requested the teacher to explain the chapter again.* ✪ ଆମେ ସାଧାରଣତଃ **ask (for)** ବ୍ୟବହାର କରୁଁ।

request *noun* the act of asking for something politely ଅନୁରୋଧ *They made a request for money.*

require /rɪˈkwaɪə(r)/ *verb* (**requires, requiring, required**) need something ଦରକାର କରିବା *Do you require anything else?* ✪ ଆମେ ସାଧାରଣତଃ **need** ଶବ୍ଦ ବ୍ୟବହାର କରୁଁ।

requirement *noun* something that you need or something that you must do or have in order to get something ଚାହିଦା, ଆବଶ୍ୟକତା; ଆବଶ୍ୟକ ପଦାର୍ଥ *My* *basic requirements are few.* ○ *What are the requirements of the job?*

rescue /ˈreskjuː/ *verb* (**rescues, rescuing, rescued**) save somebody or something from danger (ବିପଦ ବା କ୍ଷତିରୁ) ରକ୍ଷା କରିବା, ଉଦ୍ଧାର କରିବା, ବଞ୍ଚାଇବା *She rescued the child when he fell into the river.*

rescue *noun* (*no plural*) ଉଦ୍ଧାର, ରକ୍ଷା *A fisherman came to the rescue of the drowning boy.*

research /rɪˈsɜːtʃ/ *noun* the act of studying something carefully to find out new things or more about it ଗବେଷଣା, ଅନୁସନ୍ଧାନ, ତତ୍ତ୍ୱର ପରୀକ୍ଷାନିରୀକ୍ଷା *scientific research*

resemble /rɪˈzembl/ *verb* (**resembles, resembling, resembled**) look like somebody or something ଏକା ପରି ଦେଖାଯିବା, ସଦୃଶ ହେବା *Rekha resembles her mother.*

resemblance /rɪˈzembləns/ *noun* the state of being or looking similar to something or somebody ସାଦୃଶ୍ୟ, ସାମ୍ୟ *strong family resemblance*

resent /rɪˈzent/ *verb* (**resents, resenting, resented**) feel angry about something because you feel it is not fair ଅନ୍ୟାୟ ଯୋଗୁଁ ରାଗିବା, କ୍ଷୋଭ କରିବା, ଅସନ୍ତୁଷ୍ଟ ହେବା *I resent Atul getting the job. He got it because he's the manager's son!*

resentment *noun* (*no plural*) a feeling of anger about something that you feel is not fair ଅସନ୍ତୋଷ, ରାଗ, କ୍ଷୋଭ

reserve[1] /rɪˈsɜːv/ *verb* (**reserves, reserving, reserved**) keep something for a special reason or to use later; ask somebody to keep something for you ଭବିଷ୍ୟତରେ ବ୍ୟବହାର କରିବା ପାଇଁ ସଞ୍ଚୟ କରିବା, ସାଇତି ରଖିବା; ନିଜ ପାଇଁ ଅନ୍ୟଦ୍ୱାରା କୌଣସି ଜିନିଷ ସଂରକ୍ଷିତ କରାଇବା, ଆରକ୍ଷିତ ରଖିବା *I would like to reserve two seats for the Friday afternoon show.*

reservation /ˌrezəˈveɪʃn/ *noun* a room, seat, etc. that you have reserved ଆରକ୍ଷଣ, ସଂରକ୍ଷଣ *I made a reservation for a table for two.*

reserve[2] /rɪˈzɜːv/ *noun* something that you keep to use later ପରେ ବ୍ୟବହାର କରିବା ପାଇଁ ସାଇତି ରଖିଥିବା ପଦାର୍ଥ *reserves of food*

reservoir /ˈrezəvwɑː(r)/ *noun* a big lake or tank where a town or city keeps water to use later ଜଳଭଣ୍ଡାର, ଜଳାଧାର, କୃତ୍ରିମ ହ୍ରଦ

residence /ˈrezɪdəns/ *noun* **1** (*plural* **residences**) the house where someone lives, especially a big one ବାସଗୃହ, ନିବାସ *the Prime Minister's residence* **2** (*no plural*) the state of living in a particular place ଗୋଟିଏ ସ୍ଥାନରେ ବସବାସ

resident /ˈrezɪdənt/ *noun* a person who lives in a place ଅଧିବାସୀ, ବସବାସ କରୁଥିବା ବ୍ୟକ୍ତି

residential /ˌrezɪˈdenʃl/ *adjective* (of a place or an area) having houses rather than offices or factories ଘରୋଇ ନିବାସ ପାଇଁ ଉପଯୁକ୍ତ, ବାସସ୍ଥାନ ପାଇଁ ବ୍ୟବହୃତ *a residential complex*

resign /rɪˈzaɪn/ *verb* (**resigns, resigning, resigned**) leave your job ପଦ, ଚାକିରି ଇତ୍ୟାଦି ପରିତ୍ୟାଗ କରିବା ବା ଛାଡ଼ିଦେବା *The director has resigned.*

resignation /ˌrezɪgˈneɪʃn/ *noun* the act of leaving your job ପଦତ୍ୟାଗ, ଚାକିରି ପରିତ୍ୟାଗ

resist /rɪˈzɪst/ *verb* (**resists, resisting, resisted**) fight against somebody or something ବାଧାଦେବା, ପ୍ରତିରୋଧ କରିବା, ବିରୋଧ କରିବା *He always resists changes at home and in the office.*

resistance /rɪˈzɪstəns/ *noun* (*no plural*) the act of resisting somebody or something ବାଧା, ବିରୋଧ, ପ୍ରତିରୋଧ *There was a lot of resistance to the plan to build a new highway.*

resolve /rɪˈzɒlv/ *verb* (**resolves, resolving, resolved**) **1** find a way to deal with a difficulty or problem; solve ସମସ୍ୟାର ସମାଧାନ କରିବା *a special session to resolve the dispute between the two groups* **2** firmly decide to do something ଦୃଢ଼ ନିଷ୍ପତ୍ତି ନେବା, ଦୃଢ଼ ସଂକଳ୍ପ କରିବା *He resolved to give up smoking.*

resolution /ˌrezəˈluːʃn/ *noun* **1** (*no plural*) the act of solving a difficulty or problem ସମସ୍ୟାର ସମାଧାନ *resolution of the dispute through negotiations* **2** something that you decide to do ଦୃଢ଼ ସଂକଳ୍ପ *He made a resolution to stop smoking.*

resort /rɪˈzɔːt/ *noun* a place where a lot of people go on holiday ଛୁଟିଦିନ ପାଇଁ ପର୍ଯ୍ୟଟନ ସ୍ଥଳ *Goa is a popular seaside resort.*

resources /rɪˈsɔːsɪz/ *noun* (*plural*) things that a person or a country has and can use ଚାହିଦା ପୂରଣ କରିବାର ଉତ୍ସ ବା ସମ୍ବଳ *Oil is one of our most important natural resources.*

respect[1] /rɪˈspekt/ *noun* (*no plural*) **1** the feeling that you have for somebody because of their good qualities or achievements ସମ୍ମାନ, ଭକ୍ତି, ଆଦର *I have a lot of respect for your father.* **2** the act of being polite to somebody ଶ୍ରଦ୍ଧା, ଆଦର, ସହୃଦୟତା *You should treat old people with respect.*

respect[2] /rɪˈspekt/ *verb* (**respects, respecting, respected**) admire somebody because of their good qualities or achievements ସମ୍ମାନ ଦେଖାଇବା, ମର୍ଯ୍ୟାଦା କରିବା *The students respect their teacher.*

respectable /rɪˈspektəbl/ *adjective* if a person or thing is respectable, people think he/she/it is good or correct ସମ୍ମାନନୀୟ, ମାନନୀୟ *She comes from a respectable family.*

respectively /rɪˈspektɪvli/ *adverb* in the same order as something or somebody that was mentioned କ୍ରମ-ଅନୁଯାୟୀ, ଯଥାକ୍ରମେ *Her two daughters Tina and Minu are nine and six respectively.*

respire /rɪˈspaɪə(r)/ *verb* (**respires, respiring, respired**) breathe ନିଶ୍ୱାସପ୍ରଶ୍ୱାସ ନେବା; ପ୍ରଶ୍ୱାସନେବା

respiration /ˌrespəˈreɪʃn/ *noun* (*no plural*) the act of breathing ନିଶ୍ୱାସପ୍ରଶ୍ୱାସ; ଶ୍ୱାସବାୟୁ

respond /rɪˈspɒnd/ *verb* (**responds, responding, responded**) do or say something to answer somebody or something ଉତ୍ତର ଦେବା, ପ୍ରତ୍ୟୁତ୍ତର ଦେବା; ଅନୁରୂପ ବ୍ୟବହାର ଦେଖାଇବା *I said hello and he responded by smiling.*

response /rɪˈspɒns/ *noun* **1** a spoken or written answer ଲିଖିତ ବା କଥିତ ଉତ୍ତର ବା ଜବାବ *There was an encouraging response to our ad.* **2** a reaction to something that has happened or been said ପ୍ରତିକ୍ରିୟା *The incident provoked an angry response.*

responsible /rɪˈspɒnsəbl/ *adjective* **1** if you are responsible for somebody or something, you must look after them or you will be blamed if something bad happens to them ଦାୟିତ୍ୱ ସମ୍ପନ୍ନ, ଦାୟିତ୍ୱ ନେଇଥିବା *The driver is responsible for the lives of the people on the bus.* **2** a responsible person is somebody whom you can trust ବିଶ୍ୱସ୍ତ *We need a responsible person to look after our baby.*
✪ ବିପରୀତ **irresponsible**

responsibility /rɪˌspɒnsəˈbɪləti/ *noun* **1** (*no plural*) the quality of being responsible for somebody or something; the duty to look after somebody or something ଦାୟିତ୍ୱ, ଭାର; କର୍ତ୍ତବ୍ୟ *It is her responsibility to look after all the students on the bus.* **2** (*plural* **responsibilities**) something that you must do; somebody or something that you must look after ଦାୟିତ୍ୱ, କର୍ତ୍ତବ୍ୟ *The dog is my brother's responsibility.*

rest¹ /rest/ *verb* (**rests, resting, rested**) **1** sleep, lie down or stop doing something for some time because you are tired or because you have completed your work ବିଶ୍ରାମ ନେବା *We worked all morning and then rested for an hour before starting work again.* **2** be on something; put something on or against another thing କୌଣସି ଜିନିଷ ଉପରେ ରହିବା, ଭରାଦେବା; କୌଣସି ଜନିଷ ଉପରେ ରଖିବା ବା ଡେରା ଦେଇ ରଖିବା; ନିର୍ଭର କରିବା *His arms were resting on the table.*

rest² /rest/ *noun* the time when you rest because you are tired or because you have completed your work ବିଶ୍ରାମ, ଆରାମ କରିବା ସମୟ *After walking for an hour, we stopped for a rest.*

rest³ /rest/ *noun* (*no plural*) **the rest 1** what is there when a part has gone ବଳକା ଅଂଶ ବା ପରିମାଣ *If you don't want the rest, I'll eat it.* **2** the other people or things ବାକି ଲୋକମାନେ ବା ଜିନିଷପତ୍ର *Jagat watched TV and the rest of us went for a walk.*

restaurant /ˈrestrɒnt/ *noun* a place where you buy a meal and eat it ସାଧାରଣ ଭୋଜନାଳୟ

restless /ˈrestləs/ *adjective* not able to be still ଅସ୍ଥିର, ଚଳଚଞ୍ଚଳ *The children always get restless on long journeys.*

restore /rɪˈstɔ:(r)/ *verb* (**restores, restoring, restored**) make something as good as it was before ମରାମତି ବା ନିର୍ମାଣ କରି ପୂର୍ବ ପରି କରିବା, ପୁନରୁଦ୍ଧାର କରିବା *The old palace was restored.*

restrain /rɪˈstreɪn/ *verb* (**restrains, restraining, restrained**) stop somebody or something from doing something; control somebody or something ନିରୋଧ କରିବା, ବାଧାଦେବା; ନିୟନ୍ତ୍ରଣ କରିବା *I couldn't restrain my anger.*

restrict /rɪˈstrɪkt/ *verb* (**restricts, restricting, restricted**) allow only a certain amount, size, sort, etc. ସୀମିତ ରଖିବା *Our house is very small, so we had to restrict the number of people we invited to the party.*

restriction /rɪˈstrɪkʃn/ *noun* a rule to control somebody or something କଟକଣା, ସୀମାବଦ୍ଧତା *There are a lot of parking restrictions in this part of the town.*

result[1] /rɪˈzʌlt/ *noun* **1** something that happens because something else has happened ପରିଣାମ, ଫଳାଫଳ *His success was the result of hard work.* **2** the score or mark at the end of a game, competition or exam ଖେଳ, ପ୍ରତିଯୋଗିତା ବା ପରୀକ୍ଷାର ଫଳାଫଳ *When will you know your exam results?*

as a result because of something ଫଳରେ, ପରିଣାମ ସ୍ୱରୂପ *I got up late, and as a result I missed the train.*

result[2] /rɪˈzʌlt/ *verb* (**results, resulting, resulted**)

result in something make something happen ପରିଣାମ ହେବା, ଘଟିବା *Rash driving can result in accidents.*

retire /rɪˈtaɪə(r)/ *verb* (**retires, retiring, retired**) stop working because you are of a certain age (ବୟସ ସୀମା ଯୋଗୁଁ ଚାକିରିରୁ) ଅବସର ଗ୍ରହଣ କରିବା *My grandfather retired when he was 60.*

retired *adjective* ଅବସରପ୍ରାପ୍ତ *a retired teacher*

retirement *noun* (*no plural*) the time when a person stops working because he or she is of a certain age ଅବସର ପ୍ରାପ୍ତି

retreat /rɪˈtri:t/ *verb* (**retreats, retreating, retreated**) move back or away from somebody or something, for example because you have lost a fight ପଛଘୁଞ୍ଚା ଦେବା *The enemy is retreating.* ✪ ବିପରୀତ **advance[2] 2**

retrieve /rɪˈtri:v/ *verb* (**retrieves, retrieving, retrieved**) **1** get something back from the place where it was left or lost ପୁନରୁଦ୍ଧାର କରିବା, ପୁନର୍ଲାଭ କରିବା *The dog retrieved the newspaper from the water.* **2** find data or information that has been stored in the computer କମ୍ପ୍ୟୁଟର୍‌ରେ ଗଚ୍ଛିତ ତଥ୍ୟ ଖୋଜି ପାଇବା *Retrieve the information from the database.*

return[1] /rɪˈtɜ:n/ *verb* (**returns, returning, returned**) **1** come or go back to a place ଫେରି ଆସିବା ବା ଫେରିଯିବା *They returned from Puri last week.* **2** bring, give, put or send something back ଫେରାଇ ଆଣିବା ବା ଫେରାଇ ଦେବା *Will you return this book to the library?*

return² /rɪˈtɜːn/ *noun* **1** (*no plural*) the act of coming or going back to a place ଫେରସ୍ତ, ଫେରିବା ପ୍ରକ୍ରିୟା *They met me at the airport on my return to Delhi.* **2** the act of bringing, giving, putting or sending something back ଫେରସ୍ତ, ଫେରାଇବା ପ୍ରକ୍ରିୟା *the return of the borrowed money*

returns /rɪˈtɜːns/ *noun* (*plural*)

many happy returns (**of the day**) words that you say to wish somebody on their birthday ଜନ୍ମ ଦିନର ଅଭିବାଦନ (ଆଜି ତୁମର ବହୁତ ଶୁଭ କଥା ଘଟୁ)

reveal /rɪˈviːl/ *verb* (**reveals, revealing, revealed**) tell something that was a secret or show something that was hidden (ଗୁପ୍ତ କଥା) କହିଦେବା; (ଲୁଚାଇଥିବା ଜିନିଷ) ଦେଖାଇଦେବା *She refused to reveal any names to the police.*

revenge /rɪˈvendʒ/ *noun* (*no plural*)

get, have or **take your revenge on somebody** do something bad to somebody who has done something bad to you ପ୍ରତିଶୋଧ ନେବା *He says he will take his revenge on the boy who pushed him down.*

reverse¹ /rɪˈvɜːs/ *verb* (**reverses, reversing, reversed**) **1** make a car, etc. go backwards (କାର୍ ଇତ୍ୟାଦି) ପଛକୁ ଚଲାଇବା, ପଛାଇ ଆଣିବା *I reversed the car into the garage.* **2** turn something the other way round ଓଲଟାଇବା, ବିପରୀତମୁଖ କରିନେବା *Writing gets reversed in a mirror.*

reverse² /rɪˈvɜːs/ *noun* (*no plural*) the opposite thing or way ଓଲଟା, ବିପରୀତ

in reverse in the opposite way; starting at the end and finishing at the beginning ଓଲଟା ବା ବିପରୀତ ଭାବରେ; ଶେଷରୁ ଆରମ୍ଭ ପର୍ଯ୍ୟନ୍ତ

reversible /rɪˈvɜːsəbl/ *adjective* **1** (clothes, etc.) that can be worn with either side on the outside ଭିତରପଟ ବାହାରକୁ କରି ପିନ୍ଧି ହେଉଥିବା ଜାମା *a reversible coat* **2** (of a process, reaction, etc.) that can be so changed that it returns to its original state or situation (କୌଣସି ପ୍ରକ୍ରିୟା ଇତ୍ୟାଦି) ପ୍ରଥମାବସ୍ଥାକୁ ଫେରାଇ ହୋଇ ପାରୁଥିବା, ପୂର୍ବାବସ୍ଥାକୁ ଫେରିପାରୁଥିବା *a reversible reaction* ✪ ବିପରୀତ **irreversible**

review /rɪˈvjuː/ *noun* **1** a piece of writing in a newspaper or magazine that says what somebody thinks about a book, film, play, etc. (ବହି, ସିନେମା, ନାଟକ ଇତ୍ୟାଦିର) ସାଧାରଣ ସର୍ବେକ୍ଷଣ ସମୀକ୍ଷା, ଚର୍ଚ୍ଚା ବା ଟିପ୍ପଣୀ *The film got very good reviews.* **2** the act of thinking again about something that happened before ପୁନର୍ବିଚାର, ପୁନର୍ଭାବନା *a review of all the important events of the year*

review *verb* (**reviews, reviewing, reviewed**) **1** write a review about a book, film, play, etc. (ବହି, ଫିଲ୍ମ, ନାଟକ ଇତ୍ୟାଦିର) ସମୀକ୍ଷା ଲେଖିବା **2** think again about something that happened before ପୁନର୍ବିଚାର କରିବା; ପୁଣିଥରେ ଭାବିବା

revise /rɪˈvaɪz/ *verb* (**revises, revising, revised**) **1** study again something that you have learnt, before an exam (ପରୀକ୍ଷା ପାଇଁ) ପୁଣିଥରେ ପଢ଼ିବା, ପାଠ ଦୋହରାଇବା, ପୁନର୍ପଠନ କରିବା, ରିଭାଇଜ୍ କରିବା *I'm revising for the Geography test.* **2** make changes in a book, plan, etc. to make it better or more correct (ବହି, ପ୍ରକଳ୍ପ, ମତ ଇତ୍ୟାଦି) ପୁନର୍ବିଚାର କରି ଠିକ୍ କରିବା, ସଂଶୋଧନ ବା ପରିମାର୍ଜନା *The book was revised.*

revision /rɪˈvɪʒn/ *noun* (*no plural*) **1** the process of studying again something that you have learnt, before an exam (ପରୀକ୍ଷା ପୂର୍ବରୁ) ପାଠର ପୁନର୍ପଠନ, ପାଠ ଦୋହରାଇବା କାମ *I haven't done any revision for the English exam.* **2** the process of changing something to make it better or more correct ସଂଶୋଧନ, ପରିମାର୍ଜନା

revive /rɪˈvaɪv/ *verb* (**revives, reviving, revived**) become or make somebody or something well or strong again ପୂର୍ବପରି ଭଲ ଓ ସବଳ କରିଦେବା ବା ହେବା; ଚେତା ଫେରାଇ ଆଣିବା ବା ଫେରି ଆସିବା

revolt /rɪˈvəʊlt/ *verb* (**revolts, revolting, revolted**) fight against the people in control ବିଦ୍ରୋହ କରିବା *The army revolted against the king.*

revolt *noun* when people fight against the people in control ବିଦ୍ରୋହ

revolution /ˌrevəˈluːʃn/ *noun* **1** a fight by people against their government, to put a new government in its place ବିଦ୍ରୋହ, ବିପ୍ଳବ, ସରକାରଙ୍କ ବିରୁଦ୍ଧରେ ଯୁଦ୍ଧ *The French Revolution took place in 1789.* **2** a big change in the way of doing things ଜୀବନ ଶୈଳୀରେ ବା ସାମାଜିକ ବ୍ୟବସ୍ଥାରେ ବଡ଼ ପରିବର୍ତ୍ତନ *the Industrial Revolution* **3** one complete circular movement around a point ଆବର୍ତ୍ତନ, ଘୂର୍ଣ୍ଣନ, ଘୂରିବା *the earth's revolution around the sun*

revolve /rɪˈvɒlv/ *verb* (**revolves, revolving, revolved**) move in a circle around something କାହାରି ଚାରିପଟରେ ଏକ କକ୍ଷରେ ପରିକ୍ରମଣ କରିବା *The earth revolves around the sun once in 365 $\frac{1}{4}$ days.*

revolver /rɪˈvɒlvə(r)/ *noun* a small gun with a container for bullets, that can fire one shot after another quickly ବାରମ୍ବାର ଫୁଟାଇବା ପାଇଁ ଗୁଳି ଘରା ବା ଧାରକ ଥିବା ପିସ୍ତଲ୍, ରିଭଲଭର୍

reward /rɪˈwɔːd/ *noun* something that you give to somebody for something good or useful that they have done ପୁରସ୍କାର *She is offering a reward of Rs 500 to anyone who finds her dog.*

reward *verb* (**rewards, rewarding, rewarded**) give a reward to somebody ପୁରସ୍କାର ଦେବା *Amit's parents bought him a computer to reward him for doing well in his exam.*

rewind /ˌriˈwaɪnd/ *verb* (**rewinds, rewinding, rewound** /ˌriˈwaʊnd/, **has rewound**) make a tape (in a **tape recorder** or **video recorder**) go backwards ପଛକୁ ଯିବା, ପଛପଟିଆ ଗୁଡ଼ାଇ ହେବା *Rewind the tape and play it again.*

rhinoceros /raɪˈnɒsərəs/ *noun* (*plural* **rhinoceros** ବା **rhinoceroses**) a big wild animal with thick skin and with one or two horns on its nose. Rhinoceroses live in Africa and Asia ଗଣ୍ଡାର ✪ Rhinoceros ର ସଂକ୍ଷିପ୍ତ ରୂପ ଶବ୍ଦ **rhino**।

rhinoceros

rhyme¹ /raɪm/ *noun* **1** a word that has the same sound as another word, for example 'bell' and 'well' ମିତ୍ରାକ୍ଷର ଧ୍ୱନିମେଳ *Her poetry is written in rhyme.* **2** a short poem where the lines end with the same sounds ମିତ୍ରାକ୍ଷର ଛନ୍ଦରେ ଲେଖା ଛୋଟ କବିତା *a collection of rhymes*

rhyme² /raɪm/ *verb* (**rhymes, rhyming, rhymed**) have the same sound as another word ଧ୍ୱନିମେଳ ହେବ। *'Moon' rhymes with 'spoon' and 'chair' rhymes with 'bear'.*

rhythm /ˈrɪðəm/ *noun* a regular pattern of sounds or movements that come again and again (ସଙ୍ଗୀତର) ଲୟ, ତାଳ, (କବିତାର) ଯମକ *This music has a good rhythm.*

rib /rɪb/ *noun* one of the curved bones around your chest ପଞ୍ଜରା ହାଡ଼ ➪ ଚିତ୍ର ପାଇଁ **skeleton** ଦେଖନ୍ତୁ।

ribbon /ˈrɪbən/ *noun* a long thin piece of material used for tying things or for decoration ରେଶମ ଫିତା, ରିବନ୍ *She wore a ribbon in her hair.*

rice /raɪs/ *noun* (*no plural*) white or brown seeds from a plant that grows in hot countries, that we use as food ଚାଉଳ; ଭାତ *Would you like to have rice for lunch?* ➪ ଚିତ୍ର ପାଇଁ **grain** ଦେଖନ୍ତୁ।

rich /rɪtʃ/ *adjective* (**richer, richest**) **1** with a lot of money ଧନୀ, ଧନବାନ୍. ବିତ୍ତଶାଳୀ *a rich family* ✪ ବିପରୀତ **poor** **2** with a lot of something ପ୍ରଚୁର, ପ୍ରାଚୁର୍ଯ୍ୟଥିବା *This country is rich in oil.*

the rich *noun* (*plural*) people who have a lot of money ଧନୀଲୋକ

rickshaw /ˈrɪkʃɔː/ *noun* a small light vehicle with two wheels that is used in some Asian countries to carry people over short distances ରିକ୍ସା

rid /rɪd/ *verb* (**rids, ridding, rid, has rid**)

get rid of somebody or **something** throw something away or become free of somebody or something (ବ୍ୟକ୍ତି ବା ପଦାର୍ଥକୁ) ଦୂରେଇ ଦେବା, ପରିତ୍ୟାଗ କରିବା, ଛାଡ଼ିଦେବା *I got rid of my old coat and bought a new one.* ○ *This dog is following me—I can't get rid of it.*

ridden ଶବ୍ଦ **ride** ର ଏକ ଧାତୁରୂପ

riddle /ˈrɪdl/ *noun* a question that has a clever or funny answer ରହସ୍ୟାବୃତ ପ୍ରଶ୍ନ ଯାହାର ଉତ୍ତର ଚତୁରତା ସହ ବାହାର କରିବାକୁ ହୁଏ *Here's a riddle—What has four legs but can't walk? The answer is a chair!*

ride /raɪd/ *verb* (**rides, riding, rode** /rəʊd/, **has ridden** /ˈrɪdn/) **1** sit on a horse or bicycle and control it as it moves ଘୋଡ଼ା ବା ସାଇକେଲ୍ ଚଢ଼ିବା ଓ ଚଳାଇବା *I'm learning to ride.* ○ *Don't ride your bicycle on the grass!* ✪ ଘୋଡ଼ାରେ ଚଢ଼ି ଯିବାକୁ **go riding** କହନ୍ତି *I went riding today.* **2** travel in a car, bus or train କାର୍, ବସ୍ ବା ରେଳଗାଡ଼ିରେ ଯାତ୍ରା *We rode in the back of the car.*

ride *noun* a journey on a horse or bicycle, or in a car, bus or train ଘୋଡ଼ା, ସାଇକେଲ୍, କାର୍ ଇତ୍ୟାଦିରେ ଯାତ୍ରା *I had a ride in his new car.*

rider *noun* a person who rides a horse or bicycle ଅଶ୍ୱାରୋହୀ ବା ସାଇକେଲ୍ ଚଢ଼ାଳି

riding *noun* (*no plural*) the sport of riding a horse ଅଶ୍ୱଚାଳନ ଖେଳ

ridiculous /rɪˈdɪkjələs/ *adjective* so silly that it makes people laugh ଉପହାସଯୋଗ୍ୟ, ଅବାନ୍ତର *You can't play tennis with a football—that's ridiculous!*

rifle /ˈraɪfl/ *noun* a long gun that you hold against your shoulder when you fire it କାନ୍ଧରେ ଲଗାଇ ଗୁଳି ଫୁଟାଇବା ପାଇଁ ଲମ୍ୱାନଳ ଥିବା ବନ୍ଧୁକ

right[1] /ˈraɪt/ *adjective, adverb* opposite of left. ବାମପଟର ବିପରୀତ *Turn right at the end of the street.* ○ *Most people write with their right hand.* ✪ ବିପରୀତ **left**[2]

right *noun* (*no plural*) ଡାହାଣପଟ *We live in the first house on the right.* ✪ ବିପରୀତ **left**[2]

right[2] /raɪt/ *adjective* **1** correct or true ଠିକ୍ *That's not the right answer.* ○ *'Are you Ravi?' 'Yes, that's right.'* **2** good; fair or what the law allows ଭଲ; ଉଚିତ, ଠିକ୍ *It's not right to drive a scooter without a helmet.* **3** best; suitable ସର୍ବଶ୍ରେଷ୍ଠ; ଉପଯୁକ୍ତ *Is she the right person for the job?* ✪ ବିପରୀତ **wrong**[1]

The flowerpot is on the **right** of the boy.
The watering can is on the **left** of the boy.

right[3] /raɪt/ *adverb* **1** correctly ଠିକ୍ ଭାବରେ *Have I spelt your name right?* ✪ ବିପରୀତ **wrong**[1] **2** exactly ଠିକ୍ *He was sitting right next to me.* **3** all the way ଏକେବାରେ, ପୂରାପୂରି *Go right to the end of the road.* **4** immediately ସାଙ୍ଗେସାଙ୍ଗେ *We left right after dinner.*

right away immediately; now ତତ୍କ୍ଷଣାତ୍, ସାଙ୍ଗେସାଙ୍ଗେ; ବର୍ତ୍ତମାନ *Phone the doctor right away.*

right[4] /raɪt/ *noun* **1** (*no plural*) something that is good or fair ଭଲ, ନ୍ୟାୟ, ଉଚିତ୍, ଠିକ୍ *Young children have to learn the difference between right and wrong.* ✪ ବିପରୀତ **wrong**[2] **2** (*plural* **rights**) something that you are allowed to do, especially by law ନ୍ୟାୟୋଚିତ ଅଧିକାର *In India, everyone gets the right to vote at 18.*

right angle *noun* (*plural* **right angles**) an angle of 90 degrees. A square has four right angles

୯୦° କୋଣ, ସମକୋଣ ➪ ଚିତ୍ର ପାଇଁ **shape** ଦେଖନ୍ତୁ ।

right-hand *adjective* of or on the right ଡାହାଣପଟର, ଡାହାଣ ପଟେ ଥିବା *The supermarket is on the right-hand side of the road.* ✪ ବିପରୀତ **left-hand**

rigid /ˈrɪdʒɪd/ *adjective* **1** hard and not easy to bend or move କଠିନ, ଶକ୍ତ; ଅନମନୀୟ (ଯାହା ବଙ୍କାକରି ହେବନାହିଁ) **2** not able to be changed; strict ଦୃଢ଼, କଠୋର *My school has very rigid rules.*

rim /rɪm/ *noun* the edge of something round ଫନ୍ଦ, ମଙ୍ଗ, ପ୍ରାନ୍ତ *the rim of a cup*

ring[1] /rɪŋ/ *noun* **1** a circle of metal that you wear on your finger ମୁଦି **2** a space with seats around it, for a circus or boxing match (ସର୍କସ ବା ବକ୍ସିଂ ଇତ୍ୟାଦିରେ) ଖେଳ ଦେଖାଇବା ପାଇଁ ଚଉକି ଘେରା ଗୋଲାକାର ବା ଚାରିକୋଣିଆ ସ୍ଥାନ

ring[2] /rɪŋ/ *verb* (**rings, ringing, rang** /ræŋ/, **has rung** /rʌŋ/) **1** make a sound like a bell ଘଣ୍ଟିବାଜିବା, ଘଣ୍ଟି ବାଜିଲାପରି ଶବ୍ଦ ହେବା *The telephone is ringing.* **2** press or move a bell so that it makes a sound ଘଣ୍ଟି ବଜାଇବା *We rang the doorbell again but nobody answered.* **3** telephone somebody ଟେଲିଫୋନ୍ କରିବା *I'll ring you up on Sunday.*

ring somebody back telephone somebody again ଆଉଥରେ ଟେଲିଫୋନ୍ କରିବା *I wasn't at home when Jaya called, so I rang her back later.*

rinse /rɪns/ *verb* (**rinses, rinsing, rinsed**) wash something with water to take away dirt or soap ମଇଳା ବା ସାବୁନ ଫେଣ ପାଣିରେ ଧୋଇ ସଫା କରିବା; (ବାସନପତ୍ର) ପିଛୁଳାଇବା *Shampoo your hair and rinse it well.*

riot /raɪət/ *noun* a time when a group of people fight and make a lot of noise and trouble ଦଙ୍ଗା, ବିଶୃଙ୍ଖଳା, ବାଡ଼ିଆପିଟା, ଗଣ୍ଡଗୋଳ *There were riots in the streets after the football match.*

rip /rɪp/ *verb* (**rips, ripping, ripped**) pull or tear something quickly and roughly ଟାଣିଭିଡ଼ି ଚିରିଦେବା *Parul ripped the letter open.*

ripe /raɪp/ *adjective* (**riper, ripest**) fruit that is ripe is ready to be picked or eaten ପାଚିଲା, ପକ୍ୱ *These bananas aren't ripe—they're still green.*

ripen /raɪpən/ *verb* (**ripens, ripening, ripened**) become or make something ripe ପାଚିବା, ପରିପକ୍ୱ ହେବା; ପରିପକ୍ୱ କରିବା, ପଚେଇବା

ripple /rɪpl/ *noun* a small wave that forms when you throw a stone into water that is still କ୍ଷୁଦ୍ର ତରଙ୍ଗ, ଛୋଟ ଢ଼େଉ

rise /raɪz/ *verb* (**rises, rising, rose** /rəʊz/, **has risen** /rɪzn/) **1** go up; become higher or more ଉପରକୁ ଯିବା; ଉପରକୁ ଉଠିବା; ବଢ଼ିବା *The sun rises in the east and sets in the west.* ○ *Prices are rising.* **2** get up from a chair, bed, etc. ଖଟ, ଚଉକି, ଇତ୍ୟାଦିରୁ ଉଠିବା

rise *noun* an increase in the number or amount of something (ସଂଖ୍ୟା ବା ପରିମାଣର) ବୃଦ୍ଧି, ବଢ଼ତି, ଉନ୍ନତି *a rise in the price of oil* ✪ ବିପରୀତ **fall**

risk /rɪsk/ *noun* the possibility that something bad may happen; danger କ୍ଷତି, ଅନିଷ୍ଟ ବା ବିପଦର ଆଶଙ୍କା; ବିପଦ *Do you think there's any risk of rain?*
at risk in danger ବିପଦରେ *Children are at risk from this disease.*
take a risk or **risks** do something when it is possible that something bad may happen because of it ବିପଦ ବା କଷ୍ଟର ସମ୍ଭାବନା ସତ୍ତ୍ୱେ କରିବା
risk *verb* (**risks, risking, risked**) put somebody or something in danger ବିପଦର ସମ୍ମୁଖୀନ ହେବା *He risked his life to save the child trapped in the burning house.*

risky /ˈrɪski/ *adjective* (**riskier, riskiest**) dangerous ବିପଦପୂର୍ଣ୍ଣ, ବିପଦ ବା କ୍ଷତିର ସମ୍ଭାବନା ଥିବା

rite /raɪt/ *noun* a ceremony that is performed in the same way on certain occasions, often as part of a religious practice ଧର୍ମବିଧି ବା ଅନ୍ୟାନ୍ୟ କ୍ରିୟାକର୍ମର ପଦ୍ଧତି

ritual /ˈrɪtʃuəl/ *noun* a series of actions that are always performed in the same way, often as part of a religious ceremony (ପୂଜା ଇତ୍ୟାଦିର) ବିଧି, କ୍ରିୟାପଦ୍ଧତି, କ୍ରିୟାକର୍ମ *the ritual of fasting*

rival /raɪvl/ *noun* a person who wants to do better than you or who is trying to take what you want ପ୍ରତିଦ୍ୱନ୍ଦୀ *John and Lucy are rivals for the job.*

river /ˈrɪvə(r)/ *noun* a long wide line of water that flows across land and into the sea ନଈ, ନଦୀ *the River Ganga* ➪ **delta** ମଧ୍ୟ ଦେଖନ୍ତୁ ।

road /rəʊd/ *noun* a long hard path that joins one place to another, on which cars, buses, etc. can travel ରାସ୍ତା, ପଥ *Is this the road to Agra?*
by road in a car, bus, etc. କାର୍‌, ବସ୍‌, ଇତ୍ୟାଦିରେ *It's a long journey by road—the train is faster.*

roam /rəʊm/ *verb* (**roams, roaming, roamed**) walk or travel with no special plan ଲକ୍ଷହୀନ ଭାବେ ବୁଲିବା *In our area, dogs roam the streets at night.*

roar /rɔː(r)/ *verb* (**roars, roaring, roared**) make a loud deep sound ଗର୍ଜନ କରିବା; ବଡ଼ପାଟିରେ ହସିବା *The lion roared.* ○ *Everybody roared with laughter.*
roar *noun* ଗର୍ଜନ; ଉଚ୍ଚହାସ୍ୟ *the roar of an aeroplane's engines*

roast /rəʊst/ *verb* (**roasts, roasting, roasted**) cook food in an oven or over a fire ଓଭନ୍‌ ଭିତରେ ବା ଖୋଲା ନିଆଁରେ (ମାଂସ, ରୁଟି ଇତ୍ୟାଦି) ସେକିବା ବା ପୋଡ଼ିବା *Roast the chicken in the oven for forty-five minutes.*

rob /rɒb/ *verb* (**robs, robbing, robbed**) take something that is not yours from a person or place ଚୋରାଇ ନେବା, ଚୋରି କରିବା *They robbed a bank.* ➪ ଚିତ୍ର ପାଇଁ **steal** ଦେଖନ୍ତୁ ।
robber /ˈrɒbə(r)/ *noun* a person who robs ଚୋର
robbery *noun* (*plural* **robberies**) the act of taking something that is not yours from a bank, etc. ଚୋରି *What time did the robbery take place?*

robe /rəʊb/ *noun* a piece of clothing that is long and loose ଲମ୍ବା ଓ ଢିଲା ପୋଷାକ

robin /rɒbɪn/ *noun* a small brown bird with a red front ଲାଲ୍ ଛାତିଥିବା ଛୋଟ ମାଟିଆ ରଙ୍ଗର ପକ୍ଷୀ

robot /ˈrəʊbɒt/ *noun* a machine that can work like a person ଯନ୍ତ୍ରମାନବ ବା ରୋବର୍ଟ୍ (ରୋବୋର୍ଟ) *This car was built by robots.*

rock[1] /rɒk/ *noun* 1 (*no plural*) the very hard substance that is found in the ground and in mountains ପଥର 2 (*plural* **rocks**) a big piece of this ବଡ଼ ପଥର ଖଣ୍ଡ *The ship hit the rocks.*

rock[2] /rɒk/, **rock music** *noun* (*no plural*) a type of modern music with a fast beat ଦ୍ରୁତ ତାଳର ଏକ ପ୍ରକାର ଆଧୁନିକ ଜନପ୍ରିୟ ସଙ୍ଗୀତ, ରକ୍ *a rock concert*

rock[3] /rɒk/ *verb* (**rocks, rocking, rocked**) move slowly backwards and forwards or from side to side; make somebody or something do this ଧୀରେ ଧୀରେ ଦୋହଲିବା ବା ଦୋହଲାଇବା *The boat was rocking gently on the lake.* ○ *I rocked the baby until she went to sleep.*

rocket /ˈrɒkɪt/ *noun* 1 an engine with long round sides that pushes a spacecraft up into space ପ୍ରକ୍ଷେପଣ ଯନ୍ତ୍ର; କ୍ଷେପଣାସ୍ତ୍ର; 2 a thing with long round sides that carries a bomb through the air ବୋମା ବହନକାରୀ କ୍ଷେପଣାସ୍ତ୍ର 3 a **firework** that goes up into the air and then explodes ହାଉଇ ବାଣ

rocket

rocky /rɒki/ *adjective* (**rockier, rockiest**) with a lot of rocks ପଥରମୟ, ପଥୁରିଆ *a rocky path*

rod /rɒd/ *noun* a thin straight piece of wood or metal ଧାତୁ ବା କାଠର ବାଡ଼ି, ଲାଠି, ଛଡ଼ *a fishing rod*

rode ଶବ୍ଦ **ride** ର ଏକ ଧାତୁରୂପ

rodent /ˈrəʊdnt/ *noun* a small animal like a rat or squirrel that has strong sharp front teeth କୃନ୍ତକ ବା କର୍ତ୍ତଦନ୍ତୀ ମୂଷାଜାତୀୟ ପ୍ରାଣୀ

role /rəʊl/ *noun* the person you are in a play or film ଅଭିନୟରେ ଭୂମିକା *The role of the king was played by Mukul.*

roll[1] /rəʊl/ *verb* (**rolls, rolling, rolled**) 1 move along, turning over and over; make something go over and over ଗଡ଼ିଗଡ଼ି ଯିବା *The pencil rolled off the table onto the floor.* ○ *We rolled the rock down the path.* 2 move on wheels (ଗାଡ଼ି ଇତ୍ୟାଦି) ଚକ ଉପରେ ଗଡ଼ି ଗଡ଼ି ଯିବା *The car rolled down the hill.* 3 make something flat by moving a heavy thing over it ଚାପି ଚଟକା କରିବା *Roll the dough into a large circle.*

roll up make something into a long round shape or the shape of a ball (ସେଜ ଇତ୍ୟାଦି) ଗୁଡ଼ାଇ ନଳାକାର କରିବା, (ସୂତା ଇତ୍ୟାଦି) ଗଡ଼ାଇ ଗୋଲାକାର କରିବା *Can you help me to roll up this carpet?*

roll[2] /rəʊl/ *noun* a long round shape that is made by rolling something around itself or a tube many times ନଳାକାରରେ ଗୁଡ଼ା ଯାଇଥିବା ବସ୍ତୁ *a roll of material* ○ *a roll of film*

roller skate *noun* a shoe with small wheels on the bottom, for moving quickly on smooth ground ଗଡ଼ାଇ ଚାଲିବା ପାଇଁ ଚକଲଗା ଜୋତା, ରୋଲର୍ ସ୍କେଟ୍

roller skating *noun* (*no plural*) the act of moving on roller skates ରୋଲ୍‌ର ସ୍କେଟ୍‌ରେ ଗାଡ଼ି ଚାଲିବା

ROM /rɒm/ *abbreviation* the part of a computer's memory that you cannot change or remove କମ୍ପ୍ୟୁଟରର କେବଳ ପଢ଼ିବା ପାଇଁ ଥିବା ତଥ୍ୟ (ଯାହା ବଦଳାଯାଇ ପାରିବ ନାହିଁ) ✪ ROM ର ବିସ୍ତୃତ ରୂପ **Read Only Memory**। ➪ ଚିତ୍ର ପାଇଁ **RAM** ଦେଖନ୍ତୁ।

romance /rəʊˈmæns/ *noun* **1** a time when two people are in love (ଦୁଇ ଜଣଙ୍କ ମଧ୍ୟରେ) ପ୍ରେମ, ଅନୁରାଗ **2** a story about love ପ୍ରେମକାହାଣୀ

romantic /rəʊˈmæntɪk/ *adjective* about love; full of feeling of love ପ୍ରେମ ବିଷୟକ; ପ୍ରେମଭାବ ପୂର୍ଣ୍ଣ *a romantic film*

roof /ruːf/ *noun* (*plural* **roofs**) the top of a building or car, that covers it ଛାତ ➪ ଚିତ୍ର ପାଇଁ **house** ଦେଖନ୍ତୁ।

room /ruːm/ *noun* **1** (*plural* **rooms**) a part of a house or building that has its own walls, ceiling, floor, doors and windows ଘରର ବଖରା, ପ୍ରକୋଷ୍ଠ *How many rooms does your flat have?* ○ *a classroom* **2** (*no plural*) space; enough space ସ୍ଥାନ; ଯଥେଷ୍ଟ ଜାଗା *There's no room for you in the car.*

root /ruːt/ *noun* the part of a plant that is under the ground ଗଛର ଚେର ➪ ଚିତ୍ର ପାଇଁ **plant** ଦେଖନ୍ତୁ।

rope /rəʊp/ *noun* a very thick strong string ଭାରି ଶକ୍ତ ଦଉଡ଼ି

rose[1] ଶବ୍ଦ **rise** ର ଏକ ଧାତୁରୂପ

rose[2] /rəʊz/ *noun* a flower with a sweet smell. It grows on a bush that has sharp points (called **thorns**) on it ଗୋଲାପ ଫୁଲ ➪ ଚିତ୍ର ପାଇଁ **thorn** ଦେଖନ୍ତୁ।

rosy /ˈrəʊzi/ *adjective* (**rosier, rosiest**) pink ଗୋଲାପି, ଲାଲିଆସିଆ *rosy cheeks*

rot /rɒt/ *verb* (**rots, rotting, rotted**) go bad and soft, as things do when they die ପଚିଯିବା, ସଢ଼ିଯିବା। *Nobody picked the apples from the tree so they rotted.*

rotate /rəʊˈteɪt/ *verb* (**rotates, rotating, rotated**) move around a central point ନିଜ କକ୍ଷରେ ଘୁରିବା, ଆବର୍ତ୍ତନ କରିବା; ଅକ୍ଷରେ ଘୂରିବା। *The earth rotates on its axis.*

rotation /rəʊˈteɪʃn/ *noun* the action of moving around a central point କକ୍ଷରେ ଘୂର୍ଣ୍ଣନ ବା ଆବର୍ତ୍ତନ; ଅକ୍ଷରେ ଘୂର୍ଣ୍ଣନ *The rotation of the earth on its axis causes day and night.*

rotten /rɒtn/ *adjective* old and not fresh; bad ପଚାସଢ଼ା; ଖରାପ *These eggs are rotten—they smell horrible!*

rough /rʌf/ *adjective* (**rougher, roughest**) **1** not smooth or flat ବନ୍ଧୁର, ଚିକ୍କଣ ବା ସମତଳ ହୋଇନଥିବା *It was difficult to walk on the rough ground.* ✪ ବିପରୀତ **smooth1** **2** not gentle or calm ଉଗ୍ର, କର୍କଶ, କୋଳାହଳକାରୀ *rough seas* **3** not exactly correct; made or done quickly ଆନୁମାନିକ, ହାରାହାରି *a rough drawing* ○ *a rough estimate*

roughly /ˈrʌfli/ *adverb* **1** not gently ରୁକ୍ଷ ଭାବରେ *He pushed me away roughly.* **2** about; not exactly ପ୍ରାୟ; ହାରାହାରି *The bicycle cost roughly Rs 3,000.*

round[1] /raʊnd/ *adjective* with the shape of a circle or a ball ବୃତ୍ତାକାର; ଗୋଲାକାର, ଗୋଲିଆ *a round dish*

round[2] /raʊnd/ *adverb, preposition* **1** on or to all sides of something, often in a circle ଚାରି ପାଖରେ, ଚାରିପଟେ *The earth moves round the sun.* ○ *We sat round the table.* ○ *He tied a scarf round his neck.* **2** in the opposite direction or in another direction ବିପରୀତ ବା ଅନ୍ୟଦିଗକୁ *Turn your chair round.* **3** in or to different parts of a place ଚାରିଆଡ଼େ *We travelled round Kerala last summer.*

round[3] /raʊnd/ *noun* **1** a lot of visits, one after another, for example as part of your job (ବିତରଣ ବା ତଦାରଖ ପାଇଁ) ବାରମ୍ବାର ଯିବାର ନିର୍ଦ୍ଦିଷ୍ଟ ପଥ; ବିତରଣ ପଥ; ତଦାରଖ ପଥ *The postman starts his round at ten o'clock in the morning.* **2** one part of a game or competition ଖେଳ ବା ପ୍ରତିଯୋଗିତାର ଏକ ପର୍ଯ୍ୟାୟ ବା ସ୍ତର *the third round of the boxing match*

roundabout /ˈraʊndəbaʊt/ *noun* a place where two or more roads meet, and where cars must drive round in a circle ରାସ୍ତା ଛକରେ ଥିବା ଗୋଲେଇ

route /ru:t/ *noun* a way that you take to go from one place to another ରାସ୍ତା, ପଥ, ବାଟ *Which is the quickest route from Jaipur to Amritsar?*

routine /ru:ˈti:n/ *noun* your usual way of doing things ନିତିଦିନିଆ କାର୍ଯ୍ୟକ୍ରମ; ନିତ୍ୟକର୍ମ *My morning routine is to get up at seven, bathe, have breakfast, then leave home at eight.*

row[1] /rəʊ/ *noun* a line of people or things ଧାଡ଼ି *We sat in the front row of the theatre.* ○ *a row of houses*

row[2] /rəʊ/ *verb* (**rows, rowing, rowed**) move a boat through water using long pieces of wood with flat ends (called **oars**) (ଡଙ୍ଗାର) ଆହୁଲା ମାରିବା *We rowed across the lake.*
✪ ଖେଳ ବା ଆମୋଦ ପ୍ରମୋଦ ପାଇଁ ଆହୁଲାମରା ଡଙ୍ଗା ଚଲାଇବାକୁ **go rowing** କହନ୍ତି *We went rowing on the river.*

row[3] /raʊ/ *noun* a noisy talk or quarrel between people who do not agree about something ଉଚ୍ଚବାଚ, କଳିକଜିଆ *She had a row with her friend.*

royal /ˈrɔɪəl/ *adjective* of or about a king or queen ରାଜା ବା ରାଣୀଙ୍କ ସମ୍ବନ୍ଧୀୟ; ରାଜକୀୟ *the royal family*

Rs *abbreviation* ହେଲା **rupees** ର ସଂକ୍ଷିପ୍ତ ରୂପ ⇨ **rupee** ଦେଖନ୍ତୁ ।

rub /rʌb/ *verb* (**rubs, rubbing, rubbed**) move something backwards and forwards on another thing ଘଷିବା *I rubbed my hands together to keep them warm.* ○ *The cat rubbed its head against my leg.*

rub out take writing or marks off something by using a rubber or a cloth ଘଷି ଲିଭାଇବା *I rubbed the word out and wrote it again.*

rubber /ˈrʌbə(r)/ *noun* **1** (*no plural*) a strong material that we use to make things like tyres, boots, etc. ଗାଡ଼ି ଚକ, ଜୋତା ଇତ୍ୟାଦିରେ ବ୍ୟବହାର ହେଉଥିବା ପଦାର୍ଥ, ରବର୍ **2** (*plural* **rubbers**) a small piece of rubber that you use for removing marks that you have made with a pencil ପେନ୍‌ସିଲ ଲେଖା ଇତ୍ୟାଦି ଲିଭାଇବା ପାଇଁ ଛୋଟ ପଦାର୍ଥ, ରବର୍

rubber band *noun* a thin circle of rubber that you use for holding things together ସରୁ ଓ ଗୋଲିଆ ରବର୍ ଫିତା, ରବର୍ ବ୍ୟାଣ୍ଡ୍

rubbish /ˈrʌbɪʃ/ *noun* (*no plural*) **1** things that you do not want or need any more ଅଳିଆ ଜିନିଷ, ଆବର୍ଜନା *old boxes, bottles and other rubbish* ○ *Throw this rubbish in the bin.* **2** something that is bad, stupid or wrong ଖରାପ, ଅର୍ଥହୀନ ବା ଭୁଲ୍ କଥା *You're talking rubbish.*

rucksack /ˈrʌksæk/ *noun* a large bag that you carry on your back, for example when you go walking or climbing ଚାଲିବା ବା ପାହାଡ଼ ଚଢ଼ିବା ବେଳେ ପିଠିରେ ବୋହି ନେଇ ହେଉଥିବା ବ୍ୟାଗ୍

rudder /ˈrʌdə(r)/ *noun* a flat piece of wood or metal at the back of a boat or an aeroplane. It moves to make the boat or aeroplane go left or right ଜାହାଜ ବା ଉଡ଼ାଜାହାଜର ପଛପଟେ ଥିବା ଗତିର ଦିଗନିୟନ୍ତ୍ରକ ଯନ୍ତ୍ର

rude /ru:d/ *adjective* (**ruder, rudest**) not polite ଅଶିଷ୍ଟ, ଅଭଦ୍ର ବା ରୁକ୍ଷ (ବ୍ୟବହାର) *It's rude to walk away when someone is talking to you.* ✪ ବିପରୀତ **polite**

rudely *adverb* ରୁକ୍ଷ ଭାବରେ, ଅଭଦ୍ର ଭାବରେ *'Shut up!' she said rudely.* ✪ ବିପରୀତ **politely**

rug /rʌg/ *noun* a small piece of thick material that you put on the floor ଛୋଟ ଗାଲିଚା

rugged /ˈrʌgɪd/ *adjective* rocky and rough ପଥୁରିଆ, ଖାଲଢ଼ିପ ଥିବା, ବନ୍ଧୁର *the rugged countryside*

ruin /ˈru:ɪn/ *verb* (**ruins, ruining, ruined**) damage something badly so that it is no longer good; destroy something completely ନଷ୍ଟ କରିଦେବା, ଧ୍ୱଂସ କରିବା, ଛାରଖାର କରିବା *I spilled coffee on my jacket and ruined it.*

ruins /ru:ɪnz/ *noun* (*plural*) the parts of an old building that remain after it has been badly damaged ଧ୍ୱଂସବିଶେଷ *the old ruins of the fort*

in ruins badly damaged or destroyed ଧ୍ୱଂସପ୍ରାପ୍ତ ଅବସ୍ଥା *The city was in ruins after the war.*

rule¹ /ru:l/ *noun* **1** (*plural* **rules**) something that tells you what you must or must not do ନିୟମ *It's against the office rules to smoke.* ○ *break the rules* **2** (*no plural*) the system of government of a country ଶାସନ *India was once under British rule.*

rule² /ru:l/ *verb* (**rules, ruling, ruled**) control a country ଦେଶ ଶାସନ କରିବା *King Ashoka ruled for many years.*

ruler /ˈruːlə(r)/ *noun* **1** a long straight piece of plastic, metal or wood that you use for drawing straight lines or for measuring things ରୁଲ୍‌ବାଡ଼ି ➪ ଚିତ୍ର ପାଇଁ **inch** ଦେଖନ୍ତୁ। **2** a person who rules a country ଦେଶର ଶାସକ, ଶାସନକର୍ତ୍ତା

rumble /ˈrʌmbl/ *verb* (**rumbles, rumbling, rumbled**) make a long deep sound ଘଡ଼ଘଡ଼ ଶବ୍ଦ କରିବା; (ପେଟ) ଗୁଘୁ କଳକଳ ହେବା *I'm so hungry that my stomach is rumbling.*

rumour /ruːmə(r)/ *noun* something that a lot of people are talking about, but is perhaps not true ଜନରବ, ଗୁଜବ, ଶୁଣାକଥା *There's a rumour that our teacher is leaving.*

run[1] /rʌn/ *verb* (**runs, running, ran** /ræn/, **has run**) **1** move very quickly on your legs ଦୌଡ଼ିବା, ଧାଇଁବା *I was late so I ran to the bus stop.* **2** go; make a journey ଯିବା, ଯାତାୟତ କରିବା *The buses don't run on Sundays.* **3** control something and make it work ପରିଚାଳନା କରିବା *Who runs the company?* **4** flow ପ୍ରବାହିତ ହେବା *The river runs into the Arabian Sea.* **5** work ଚାଲୁ ରହିବା, କାର୍ଯ୍ୟକାରୀ ଅବସ୍ଥାରେ ରହିବା *The car had stopped but the engine was still running.*

run after somebody or **something** try to catch a person or an animal ଗୋଡ଼ାଇବା। *The dog ran after a rabbit.*

run away go quickly away from a place; escape from someone or a place ଦୌଡ଼ି ପଳାଇଯିବା *She ran away from the playground when she saw the monkey.*

run[2] /rʌn/ *noun* the action of moving very quickly on your legs ଦୌଡ଼, ଧାବନ *I go for a run every morning.*

rung[1] ଶବ୍ଦ **ring**[2] ର ଏକ ଧାତୁରୂପ

rung[2] /rʌŋ/ *noun* one of the steps of a ladder ନିଶୁଣିର ଏକ ପାହାଚ ବା ଗୋଡ଼ ରଖିବା ବାଡ଼ି

runner /ˈrʌnə(r)/ *noun* a person who runs in a race ଦୌଡ଼ ପ୍ରତିଯୋଗିତାରେ ଭାଗ ନେଉଥିବା ବ୍ୟକ୍ତି

runner-up *noun* (*plural* **runners-up**) a person or team that comes second in a race or competition ଦୌଡ଼ ବା ପ୍ରତିଯୋଗିତାରେ ଦ୍ୱିତୀୟ ସ୍ଥାନ ପାଇଥିବା ବ୍ୟକ୍ତି ବା ଦଳ

runway /ˈrʌnweɪ/ *noun* (*plural* **runways**) a long piece of hard ground where aeroplanes take off from and land on ବିମାନ ଉଡ଼ିବା ଓ ଓହ୍ଲାଇବା ପାଇଁ ବିମାନ ବନ୍ଦରରେ ତିଆରି କରାଯାଇଥିବା ଲମ୍ବା ଓ ଶକ୍ତ ପଥ

rupee /ruˈpiː/ *noun* (*plural* **rupees**) the currency of India, Pakistan and Nepal ଭାରତ, ପାକିସ୍ଥାନ ଓ ନେପାଳର ମୁଦ୍ରା; ଟଙ୍କା ➪ **paisa** ଦେଖନ୍ତୁ।

rural /rʊərəl/ *adjective* to do with the countryside, not the town ଗ୍ରାମ୍ୟ, ଗ୍ରାମୀଣ, ଗ୍ରାମ ସମ୍ବନ୍ଧୀୟ *The book is about life in rural India.* ➪ **urban** ଦେଖନ୍ତୁ।

rush /rʌʃ/ *verb* (**rushes, rushing, rushed**) **1** go or come very quickly ଧାଇଁଯିବା ବା ଧାଇଁ ଆସିବା *The children rushed out of school.* **2** do something quickly or make somebody do something quickly ତରବରରେ କରିବା *We rushed to finish the work on time.* **3** take somebody or something quickly to a place ଦ୍ରୁତ ଗତିରେ ନେବା *She was rushed to hospital.*

rush /rʌʃ/ *noun* (*no plural*) **1** a sudden quick movement ହଠାତ୍ ମାଡ଼ିଆସିବା *At the end of the film there was a rush for the exits.* **2** a need to move or do something very quickly ତରବର ଅବସ୍ଥା *I can't stop now—I'm in a rush.* **3** a time when there is a great demand for something କିଛି ନେବା ପାଇଁ ତରବରରେ ଜମିଥିବା ଭିଡ଼ *There was a rush outside the cinema for tickets.*

the rush hour *noun* (*no plural*) the time when a lot of people are going to or coming from work (କାମକୁ ଯିବା ବା କାମରୁ ଫେରିବାର) ଭିଡ଼ ସମୟ

rust /rʌst/ *noun* (*no plural*) a reddish-brown substance that you sometimes see on iron or steel that has been wet କଳଙ୍କି

rust *verb* (**rusts, rusting, rusted**) become covered with rust କଳଙ୍କି ଲାଗିବା *My bike rusted because I left it out in the rain.*

rusty *adjective* (**rustier, rustiest**) covered with rust କଳଙ୍କି ଲଗା *a rusty nail*

rustle /ˈrʌsl/ *verb* (**rustles, rustling, rustled**) make a sound like dry leaves moving or rubbing together; make something make this sound ଶୁଖିଲା ପତ୍ରରେ ପବନ ଚାଲିବାର ଖସ୍‌ଖସ୍ ଶବ୍ଦ ହେବା; ସେହିପରି ଶବ୍ଦ କରିବା *We could hear the trees rustling in the breeze all night.*

rustle *noun* (*no plural*) ଖସ୍‌ଖସ୍ ଶବ୍ଦ *the rustle of leaves*

ruthless /ˈruːθləs/ *adjective* cruel and showing no mercy ନିଷ୍ଠୁର, ନିର୍ଦ୍ଦୟ, କ୍ରୁର *a ruthless warrior*

S s

sachet /ˈsæʃeɪ/ *noun* a small plastic or paper packet that contains a liquid or powder ଗୁଣ୍ଡ ବା ତରଳ ପଦାର୍ଥ ଥିବା ଛୋଟ ସିଲ୍‌କରା କାଗଜ ବା ପ୍ଲାଷ୍ଟିକ୍ ପୁଡ଼ିଆ *a sachet of shampoo*

sack[1] /sæk/ *noun* a big strong bag made of rough material for storing and carrying heavy things ଜିନିଷ ନେବା ପାଇଁ ବଡ଼ ମୁଣା; ଅଖା, ବସ୍ତା *a sack of potatoes*

sack[2] /sæk/ *verb* (**sacks, sacking, sacked**) say that somebody must leave their job ଚାକିରିରୁ ବରଖାସ୍ତ କରିବା ବା କାଢ଼ି ଦେବା *The manager sacked her because she was always late.*

sacred /ˈseɪkrɪd/ *adjective* with a special religious meaning ପବିତ୍ର *The peepul tree is considered sacred by many people in India.*

sacrifice /ˈsækrɪfaɪs/ *verb* (**sacrifices, sacrificing, sacrificed**) stop doing or having something important so that you can help somebody or get something else କିଛି ଶୁଭ ପାଇବା ପାଇଁ କୌଣସି ପଦାର୍ଥ ବା ଅଭ୍ୟାସ ଛାଡ଼ିଦେବା, ତ୍ୟାଗ କରିବା *During the war, many people sacrificed their lives for the country.*

sacrifice *noun* ତ୍ୟାଗ, ପରିତ୍ୟାଗ *They made a lot of sacrifices to pay for their son's education.*

sad /sæd/ *adjective* (**sadder, sad-dest**) **1** unhappy ଦୁଃଖୀ; ଦୁଃଖଜନକ *The children were very sad when their teacher left the school.* **2** that makes you feel unhappy ଦୁଃଖାତ୍ମକ, ଦୁଃଖଦାୟକ *a sad story*

sadly *adverb* ଦୁଃଖରେ, ଦୁଃଖିତ ଭାବରେ *She looked sadly at the empty house.*

sadness *noun* (*no plural*) the feeling of being sad ଦୁଃଖ

saddle /ˈsædl/ *noun* a seat on a horse or bicycle ଘୋଡ଼ା ଉପରେ ପକାଯାଉଥିବା ଆରୋହୀର ଆସନ; ସାଇକେଲ୍ ବା ମଟର ସାଇକେଲ୍‌ର ସିଟ୍

safari /səˈfɑːri/ *noun* (*plural* **safaris**) a journey to look at or hunt wild animals, usually in Africa ବନ୍ୟଜନ୍ତୁ ଦେଖିବା ବା ମାରିବା ପାଇଁ ଯାତ୍ରା (ବିଶେଷତଃ ଆଫ୍ରିକାରେ)

safe[1] /seɪf/ *adjective* (**safer, safest**) **1** not in danger; not hurt ନିରାପଦ, ବିପଦମୁକ୍ତ; ଅକ୍ଷତ *Don't go out alone at night—you won't be safe.* **2** not dangerous ନିରାପଦ, ବିପଦ ନ ଥିବା *Is it safe to swim in this river?* ○ *Always keep medicines in a safe place.* ✪ ବିପରୀତ **unsafe**

safe and sound not hurt or broken ଅକ୍ଷତ *The child was found safe and sound.*

safely *adverb* ନିରାପଦରେ; କିଛି ଅସୁବିଧା ନ ହୋଇ, ନିର୍ବିଘ୍ନରେ *Phone your parents to tell them you have arrived safely.*

safe[2] /seɪf/ *noun* a strong metal box with a lock where you keep money or things like jewellery ଲୁହା ସିନ୍ଧୁକ, ସେଫ୍

safety /ˈseɪfti/ *noun* (*no plural*) the state of being safe ନିର୍ବିଘ୍ନତା, ନିରାପତ୍ତା

He is worried about the safety of his children.

safety pin *noun* (*plural* **safety pins**) a pin that you use for joining things together. It has a cover over the point so that it is not dangerous ସେଫ୍ଟିପିନ୍

saffron /ˈsæfrən/ *noun* (*no plural*) a bright orange-yellow colour ଉଜ୍ଜ୍ୱଳ ନାରଙ୍ଗି ହଳଦିଆ ରଙ୍ଗ ବା ବର୍ଣ୍ଣ *The colours of our national flag are saffron, white and green.*

Sagittarius /ˈsædʒɪˈteəriəs/ *noun* the ninth sign of the **zodiac** ରାଶିଚକ୍ରର ନବମ ରାଶି, ଧନୁରାଶି; ଏକ ତାରାପୁଞ୍ଜ

said ଶବ୍ଦ **say** ର ଏକ ଧାତୁରୂପ

sail[1] /seɪl/ *noun* a big piece of cloth on a boat. The wind blows against the sail and moves the boat along ଡଙ୍ଗାର ବା ଜାହାଜର ପାଲ

yacht

sail[2] /seɪl/ *verb* (**sails, sailing, sailed**) **1** travel on water ଜଳଯାତ୍ରା କରିବା *The ship sailed along the coast.* **2** control a boat with sails ପାଲଦ୍ୱାରା ଡଙ୍ଗା ଚାଳନ କରିବା *We sailed the yacht down the river.* ✪ ନୌକା ବିହାର କରିବାର ଗତିବିଧିକୁ **go sailing** କହନ୍ତି *We often go sailing on the lake at weekends.*

sailing *noun* (*no plural*) the sport of controlling a boat with sails ପାଲ ନିୟନ୍ତ୍ରଣ କରି ଡଙ୍ଗା ଚାଳନ କରିବା ଖେଳ

sailor /ˈseɪlə(r)/ *noun* a person who works on a ship ନାବିକ

saint /seɪnt/ *noun* a very good and holy person ସନ୍ଥ, ପବିତ୍ରାତ୍ମା ✪ Saint ଲେଖିବା ପାଇଁ ସଂକ୍ଷିପ୍ତ ରୂପ **St** ର ପ୍ରୟୋଗ କରାଯାଏ *St George's School*

sake /seɪk/ *noun*

for the sake of somebody or **something, for somebody's** or **something's sake** to help somebody or something; because of somebody or something କାହାରି ପାଇଁ

salad /ˈsæləd/ *noun* a dish of cold, usually raw vegetables ସାଲାଡ୍, କଞ୍ଚା ପରିବା କାଟି କରାଯାଇଥିବା ଖାଦ୍ୟ *Do you want soup or salad with your dinner?*

salary /ˈsæləri/ *noun* (*plural* **salaries**) the money that people receive every month for the work that they do (ଚାକିରିରୁ ପାଉଥିବା) ଦରମା

sale /seɪl/ *noun* **1** (*no plural*) the action of selling something ବିକ୍ରି, ବିକ୍ରୟ **2** (*plural* **sales**) a time when a shop sells things for less money than usual ଦୋକାନର ଜିନିଷପତ୍ର କମ୍ ଦାମ୍‌ରେ ବିକ୍ରି, ରିହାତି ଦରରେ ବିକ୍ରି *In the sale, everything was half-price.*

for sale if something is for sale, its owner wants to sell it ବିକ୍ରି ପାଇଁ *Is this house for sale?*

on sale if something is on sale, you can buy it in shops ବିକ୍ରିପାଇଁ ଦୋକାନରେ

ରଖାଯାଇଥିବା *The book is on sale at most bookshops now.*

salesman /ˈseɪlzmən/ (*plural* **salesmen**), **saleswoman** /ˈseɪlzwʊmən/ (*plural* **saleswomen**), **salesperson** /ˈseɪlzpɜ:sn/ (*plural* **salespeople**) *noun* a person whose job is selling things ବିକ୍ରେତା, ବିକାଳି

saline /ˈseɪlaɪn/ *adjective* having salt ଲୁଣିଆ, ଲୁଣି, ଲୁଣଥିବା *He carefully washed the lenses in saline solution.*

saliva /səˈlaɪvə/ *noun* the liquid that is naturally produced in your mouth ଲାଳ, ଛେପ

salt /sɔ:lt/ *noun* (*no plural*) a white substance that comes from sea water and from the earth. We add it to food to make it taste better ଲୁଣ, ଲବଣ *Add a little more salt to the curry.*

salty *adjective* (**saltier, saltiest**) with salt in it ଲୁଣିଆ, ଲୁଣି *Sea water is salty.*

salute /səˈlu:t/ *verb* (**salutes, saluting, saluted**) lift your right hand to the side of your forehead to show respect ସାଲୁଟ୍ ମାରିବା *The soldiers saluted as the President walked past.*

salute *noun* ସାଲ୍ୟୁଟ୍ *The soldier gave a salute.*

salvation /sælˈveɪʃn/ *noun* (*no plural*) (used especially in religion) the act or condition of being saved from evil or death ଖଳତା ବା ମୃତ୍ୟୁରୁ ସୁରକ୍ଷା, ମୁକ୍ତି

same /seɪm/ *adjective*

the same not different; not another ଅଭିନ୍ନ; ସେହି; ଏକାପରି *Anita and I like the same kind of music.* ○ *I've lived in the same town all my life.* ○ *He went to the same school as me.*

same *pronoun*

same to you words that you use for saying to somebody what they have said to you ତମର ବି ସେଇଆ ହଉ, ତମେ ବି ସେମିତି ଥାଅ *'Have a good weekend.' 'Same to you.'*

sample /ˈsɑ:mpl/ *noun* a small amount of something that shows what the rest is like ନମୁନା *a free sample of perfume* ○ *a blood sample*

sanctuary /ˈsæŋktʃʊəri/ *noun* (*plural* **sanctuaries**) a large area where wild animals and birds are protected ପଶୁପକ୍ଷୀଙ୍କୁ ସୁରକ୍ଷିତ ରଖିବା ପାଇଁ ନିର୍ଦ୍ଧାରିତ ସ୍ଥାନ, ଅଭୟାରଣ୍ୟ

sand /sænd/ *noun* (*no plural*) a powder made of very small pieces of rock, that you find on beaches and in deserts ବାଲି, ବାଲୁକା

sandy *adjective* (**sandier, sandiest**) with sand ବାଲିଆ, ବାଲୁକାମୟ *a sandy beach*

sandal /ˈsændl/ *noun* a light open shoe that you wear in warm weather ଖୋଲା ଜୋତା, ସାଣ୍ଡାଲ୍

sand dune = **dune**

sandstorm /ˈsændstɔ:m/ *noun* a storm in a desert when strong winds carry sand into the air ବାଲିଝଡ଼; ଧୂଳିଝଡ଼

sandwich /ˈsænwɪdʒ/ *noun* (*plural* **sandwiches**) two slices of bread with other food between them ଦୁଇଖଣ୍ଡ ପାଉଁରୁଟି ମଝିରେ ଅନ୍ୟାନ୍ୟ ଜିନିଷଦେଇ ପ୍ରସ୍ତୁତ ଖାଦ୍ୟ, ସ୍ୟାଣ୍ଡୱିଚ୍ *a cheese sandwich*

sang ଶବ୍ଦ **sing** ର ଏକ ଧାତୁରୂପ

sanitation /ˌsænɪˈteɪʃn/ *noun* (*no plural*) a system for keeping places clean by removing human waste ଆବର୍ଜନା କାଢ଼ି ପରିବେଶ ସଫାସୁତୁରା ରଖିବା ପ୍ରକ୍ରିୟା ଓ ଏଥିରେ ଉନ୍ନତି ସାଧନ; ସ୍ୱାସ୍ଥ୍ୟରକ୍ଷା ବ୍ୟବସ୍ଥା *diseases caused by poor sanitation*

sank ଶବ୍ଦ **sink²** ର ଏକ ଧାତୁରୂପ

sapling /ˈsæplɪŋ/ *noun* a young tree ଛୋଟଗଛ, ଗଛର ଚାରା

sarcastic /sɑːˈkæstɪk/ *adjective* if you are sarcastic, you say the opposite of what you mean, in an unkind way ବିଦ୍ରୂପାତ୍ମକ, ଉପହାସ କଲାପରି

sari *noun* (*plural* **saris**) a long piece of material that Indian women wrap around their bodies as a dress ଶାଢ଼ୀ

sat ଶବ୍ଦ **sit** ର ଏକ ଧାତୁରୂପ

satchel /ˈsætʃəl/ *noun* a bag that children use for carrying books to and from school ସ୍କୁଲବ୍ୟାଗ୍

satellite /ˈsætəlaɪt/ *noun* **1** a thing in space that moves round a planet ପ୍ରାକୃତିକ ଉପଗ୍ରହ (ଯଥା:ଚନ୍ଦ୍ର ପୃଥିବୀର ଉପଗ୍ରହ) *The moon is a satellite of the earth.* **2** a thing that people have sent into space. Satellites travel round the earth and send back pictures or television and radio signals ମଣିଷ ମହାକାଶକୁ ପଠାଇଥିବା ଯାନ୍ତ୍ରିକ ଉପଗ୍ରହ (ଯାହା ମହାକାଶ ସନ୍ଧାନ ପଠାଏ, ଟେଲିଭିଜନ୍, ଟେଲିଫୋନ୍ ଇତ୍ୟାଦିର ସଞ୍ଚାର ଓ ସଂଯୋଗ କରେ) *satellite television*

satellite

satin /ˈsætɪn/ *noun* (*no plural*) a very shiny smooth cloth ଚିକ୍କଣ ଓ ଚକଚକିଆ ରେଶମ (ସିଲ୍କ) କନା

satisfaction /ˌsætɪsˈfækʃn/ *noun* (*no plural*) a state of being pleased with what you or other people have done ତୃପ୍ତି *She finished painting the picture and looked at it with satisfaction.*

satisfactory /ˌsætɪsˈfæktəri/ *adjective* good enough, but not very good ସନ୍ତୋଷଜନକ, ଠିକ୍‌ଠାକ୍ *Her work is not satisfactory.* ✪ ବିପରୀତ **unsatisfactory**

satisfy /ˈsætɪsfaɪ/ *verb* (**satisfies, satisfying, satisfied, has satisfied**) give somebody what they want or need; be good enough to make somebody pleased ବ୍ୟକ୍ତିଙ୍କୁ ତାଙ୍କର ଦରକାରୀ ପଦାର୍ଥ ଦେବା; ସନ୍ତୁଷ୍ଟ କରିବା *His exam results satisfied his father.*

satisfied *adjective* pleased because you have had or done what you wanted ସନ୍ତୁଷ୍ଟ *The teacher was not satisfied with my work.*

satisfying *adjective* something that is satisfying makes you pleased because it is what you want ତୃପ୍ତିକର, ସନ୍ତୋଷଜନକ

Saturday /ˈsætədeɪ/ *noun* the sixth day of the week, next after Friday ଶନିବାର

Saturn /ˈsætən/ *noun* (*no plural*) the sixth planet from the sun. Saturn has many rings around it ସୌରମଣ୍ଡଳର ଷଷ୍ଠ ଗ୍ରହ (ଏହାର ଚାରିପଟେ ଅନେକ ମୁଦିଘେର ଅଛି) ➪ ଚିତ୍ର ପାଇଁ **solar system** ଦେଖନ୍ତୁ ।

sauce /sɔːs/ *noun* a thick liquid that you eat on or with other food ଖାଦ୍ୟ ରୁଚିକର କରିବା ପାଇଁ ଏକ ପ୍ରକାର ବହଳିଆ ପଦାର୍ଥ *tomato sauce*

saucepan /ˈsɔːspən/ *noun* a round metal container with a lid and a handle which is used for cooking ଘୋଡ଼ଣୀ ଓ ବେଣ୍ଟଥିବା ଧାତୁ ନିର୍ମିତ ରୋଷେଇ ବାସନ

saucer /ˈsɔːsə(r)/ *noun* a small round plate that you put under a cup କପ୍ ରଖିବା ପାଇଁ ଥାଳିଆ, ସସର୍

sausage /ˈsɒsɪdʒ/ *noun* meat that is cut into very small pieces and made into a long, thin shape ମାଂସକୁ ବହୁତ ଛୋଟ ଖଣ୍ଡ କରି କାଟିଲାପରେ ଲମ୍ବା ଓ ପତଳା ଆକାରରେ ପ୍ରସ୍ତୁତ କରାଯାଇଥିବା ଖାଦ୍ୟ

savage /ˈsævɪdʒ/ *adjective* violent and fleice ହିଂସ୍ର ବା ଭୟଙ୍କର *a savage attack by a large dog*

save /seɪv/ *verb* (**saves, saving, saved**) **1** take somebody or something away from danger କ୍ଷତି ବା ବିପଦରୁ ରକ୍ଷା କରିବା *He saved me from the fire.* ○ *The doctor saved her life.* **2** keep something, especially money, to use later ଭବିଷ୍ୟତରେ ବ୍ୟବହାର ପାଇଁ ସଞ୍ଚୟ କରିବା (ବିଶେଷତଃ ଟଙ୍କା ପଇସା) *I've saved enough money to buy a car.* **3** use less of something ଅଳ୍ପଖର୍ଚ୍ଚ କରି ଅପବ୍ୟୟ ବନ୍ଦ କରିବା *She saves money by making her own clothes.* **4** when you save a file on a computer, you keep it for use later ପରେ ବ୍ୟବହାର କରିବା ପାଇଁ କମ୍ପ୍ୟୁଟର୍‌ରେ ଫାଇଲ୍ ସୁରକ୍ଷିତ ରଖିବା, ସେଭ୍ କରିବା

savings /ˈseɪvɪŋz/ *noun* (*plural*) money that you are keeping in a **bank** to use later ବ୍ୟାଙ୍କରେ ସଞ୍ଚିତ ଥିବା ଟଙ୍କା, ସଞ୍ଚୟ *I keep my savings in the bank.*

saw[1] ଶବ୍ଦ **see** ର ଏକ ଧାତୁରୂପ

saw[2] /sɔː/ *noun* a metal tool for cutting wood କରତ ➪ ଚିତ୍ର ପାଇଁ **tool** ଦେଖନ୍ତୁ ।

saw *verb* (**saws, sawing, sawed, has**)

sawn /sɔːn/ କରତରେ କାଟିବା *She sawed a branch off the tree.*

sawdust /ˈsɔːdʌst/ *noun* (*no plural*) powder that falls when you saw wood କରତ ଗୁଣ୍ଡ

say /seɪ/ *verb* (**says** /sez/, **saying, said** /sed/, **has said**) **1** make words with your mouth କହିବା *You say 'please' when you ask for something.* ○ *'This is my room,' he said.*

say or **tell**?

Say ও **tell** ଏକାପରି ବ୍ୟବହୃତ ହୁଏ ନାହିଁ। ନିମ୍ନଲିଖିତ ବାକ୍ୟଗୁଡ଼ିକ ମନଦେଇ ପଢ଼ନ୍ତୁ ଏବଂ ଏମାନଙ୍କ ଭିତରେ ପାର୍ଥକ୍ୟ ଦେଖନ୍ତୁ—
Jo ***said****, 'I'm ready.'*
Jo ***said*** *(that) she was ready.*
Jo ***said*** *to me that she was ready.*
Jo ***told*** *me (that) she was ready.*
Jo ***told*** *me to close the door.*

2 give information ସୂଚାଇବା, ଦେଖାଇବା *The notice on the door said 'Private'.* ○ *The clock says half past three.*

saying /ˈseɪɪŋ/ *noun* a sentence that people often say, that gives advice about something ପ୍ରବାଦ ବା ନୀତିବାକ୍ୟ *'Look before you leap' is an old saying.*

scab /skæb/ *noun* a hard covering that grows over your skin where it is cut or broken ଘା'ର ଖୋଳି

scale /skeɪl/ *noun* **1** a set of marks on something for measuring ମାପକାଠି, ସ୍କେଲ୍ *This ruler has one scale in centimetres and one scale in inches.* ➪ ଚିତ୍ର ପାଇଁ **inch** ଦେଖନ୍ତୁ। **2** how distances are shown on a map ମାନଚିତ୍ରରେ ଦୂରତାର ମାପଚିହ୍ନ ବା ପରିମାପ *This map has a scale of one centimetre to ten kilometres.* **3** one of the flat hard things that cover the body of animals like fish and reptiles ମାଛକାତି ➪ ଚିତ୍ର ପାଇଁ **fish** ଦେଖନ୍ତୁ। **4 scales** (*plural*) a machine for showing how heavy people or things are ତରାଜୁ; ଓଜନ ମାପିବା ଯନ୍ତ୍ର

scan /skæn/ *verb* (**scans, scanning, scanned**) look carefully because you are trying to find something କୌଣସି ବସ୍ତୁର ସବୁ ଅଂଶ ନିରୀକ୍ଷଣ କରିବା *They scanned the sea, looking for a boat.*

scandal /ˈskændl/ *noun* something that makes a lot of people talk about it because they think it is wrong or shocking ଖରାପ ବା ଅଚମ୍ଭିତ କଲାପରି ବିଷୟର ବହୁ ଲୋକଙ୍କର ଚର୍ଚ୍ଚା *There was a big scandal when the Prince decided to get married again.*

scanner /ˈskænə(r)/ *noun* **1** a machine that gives a picture of the inside of something. Doctors use one kind of scanner to look inside people's bodies କୌଣସି ପଦାର୍ଥ ବା ଶରୀର ଆଭ୍ୟନ୍ତରର ସମ୍ପୂର୍ଣ୍ଣ ଯାଞ୍ଚ କରୁଥିବା ଯନ୍ତ୍ର; କ୍ରମବୀକ୍ଷକ ଯନ୍ତ୍ର **2** a machine that is linked to a computer and that copies text and pictures onto the computer କମ୍ପ୍ୟୁଟର୍ ସହ ସଂଯୁକ୍ତ ଯନ୍ତ୍ର ଯାହା ଦ୍ୱାରା ଫଟୋ, ଲେଖା ଇତ୍ୟାଦି ନକଲ କରାଯାଇ କମ୍ପ୍ୟୁଟର୍‌ରେ ଗଚ୍ଛିତ ରଖାଯାଇପାରେ

scanty /ˈskænti/ *adjective* less than what is needed; not enough ଅଳ୍ପ, ନିଅଣ୍ଟିଆ; ଅପର୍ଯ୍ୟାପ୍ତ *scanty rainfall*

scar /skɑː(r)/ *noun* a mark on your skin, that an old cut has left କ୍ଷତଚିହ୍ନ, ଘା'ଦାଗ

scar *verb* (**scars, scarring, scarred**) leave a scar on skin କ୍ଷତଚିହ୍ନ ଛାଡ଼ିଯିବା (ଦେହରେ) *His face was badly scarred in the accident.*

scarce /skeəs/ *adjective* (**scarcer, scarcest**) difficult to find; not enough

ବିରଳ, ଦୁଷ୍ପ୍ରାପ୍ୟ; ଅପ୍ରଚୁର, ନିଅଣ୍ଟିଆ *Water is scarce in deserts.*

scarcity /ˈskeəsəti/ *noun* a situation in which something is very hard to get or find ଅଭାବ, ସ୍ୱଳ୍ପତା, ଅନାଟନ *scarcity of water in summers*

scare /skeə(r)/ *verb* (**scares, scaring, scared**) make somebody frightened ଡରାଇବା, ଭୟଦେଖାଇବା *That noise scared me!*

scare *noun* a feeling of being frightened ଆକସ୍ମିକ ଭୟ *You gave me a scare!*

scared *adjective* frightened ଭୟଭୀତ, ଡରିଯାଇଥିବା *Suman is scared of lizards.*

scarecrow /ˈskeəkrəʊ/ *noun* a figure that is made to look like a person and that farmers put in their fields to frighten away birds ପକ୍ଷୀ ହୁରୁଡାଇବା ପାଇଁ ଏକ ମଣିଷ ପରି ବିକଟ ମୂର୍ତ୍ତି, ପାଳଭୂତ

scarecrow

scarf /skɑːf/ *noun* (*plural* **scarves** /skɑːvz/) a piece of material worn around the neck or head ବେକ ବା ମୁଣ୍ଡ ଘୋଡ଼ାଇବା ବସ୍ତ୍ର

scatter /ˈskætə(r)/ *verb* (**scatters, scattering, scattered**) **1** move quickly in different directions ବିଭିନ୍ନ ଦିଗରେ ପଳାଇବା ବା ବିକ୍ଷିପ୍ତ ହେବା *The crowd scattered when it started to rain.* **2** throw things so that they fall in a lot of different places ବିଭିନ୍ନ ଦିଗରେ ବିକ୍ଷିପ୍ତ କରିବା, ଇଆଡ଼େ ସିଆଡ଼େ ଫୋପାଡ଼ିବା *She scattered the pieces of bread on the grass for the birds.*

scavenge /ˈskævɪndʒ/ *verb* (**scavenges, scavenging, scavenged**) **1** look for food or things, that can be used again, among waste products or rubbish ଅଳିଆଗଦାରୁ ଖାଦ୍ୟ ବା ଦରକାରୀ ପଦାର୍ଥ ଗୋଟାଇବା *The beggar scavenged through the trash for something to eat.* **2** (of animals and birds) eat dead animals that have been killed by another animal or something else (ପଶୁପକ୍ଷୀ) ମୃତ ଜନ୍ତୁଙ୍କ ମାଂସ ଖାଇବା

scene /siːn/ *noun* **1** a place where something happened ଘଟଣାସ୍ଥଳ *The ambulance arrived at the scene of the accident.* **2** what you see in a place; a view ଦୃଶ୍ୟ *a beautiful scene of the countryside* **3** a part of a play or film ନାଟକ ବା ଫିଲ୍ମର ଗୋଟିଏ ଦୃଶ୍ୟ ବା ସିନ୍ *Act 1, Scene 2 of* Hamlet

scenery /ˈsiːnəri/ *noun* (*no plural*) **1** things like mountains, rivers and forests that you see around you in the countryside ନଈ, ପାହାଡ଼, ଜଙ୍ଗଲ ବା ଗ୍ରାମ୍ୟାଞ୍ଚଳର ଦୃଶ୍ୟ *What a beautiful scenery!* **2** things on the stage of a theatre that make it look like a real place ରଙ୍ଗମଞ୍ଚର ଦୃଶ୍ୟାବଳୀ

scent /sent/ *noun* **1**(*plural* **scents**) a pleasant smell ସୁଗନ୍ଧ, ବାସ୍ନା *This flower has no scent.* **2** (*no plural*) a liquid with a nice smell, that you put on your body ଅତର *a bottle of scent*

schedule /ˈʃedjuːl/ *noun* a plan or list of times when things will happen or be done କାର୍ଯ୍ୟକ୍ରମର ସୂଚୀ ବା ତାଲିକା *I've got a busy schedule next week.*

scheme /skiːm/ *noun* a plan (କୌଣସି କାମର) ଯୋଜନା *a scheme to build more houses*

scholar /ˈskɒlə(r)/ *noun* a person who has learnt a lot about something କୌଣସି ବିଷୟରେ ବିଶେଷ ଜ୍ଞାନ ଥିବା ବ୍ୟକ୍ତି; ବିଦ୍ୱାନ, ପଣ୍ଡିତ *a famous history scholar*

scholarship /ˈskɒləʃɪp/ *noun* money that is given to a good student to help him or her to continue studying ଭଲ ଛାତ୍ରମାନେ ପାଉଥିବା ବୃତ୍ତି, ଛାତ୍ରବୃତ୍ତି

school /skuːl/ *noun* **1** a place where children go to learn ବିଦ୍ୟାଳୟ, ସ୍କୁଲ୍ *Hema is at school.* ○ *Which school do you go to?* **2** a place where you go to learn a special thing ନିର୍ଦ୍ଦିଷ୍ଟ ବିଷୟ ଶିଖିବା ପାଇଁ ଥିବା ବିଦ୍ୟାଳୟ ବା ସ୍କୁଲ୍ *a dance school*

schoolboy /ˈskuːlbɔɪ/, **school girl** /ˈskuːlɡɜːl/, **schoolchild** /ˈskuːlt-ʃaɪld/ (*plural* **schoolchildren** /ˈskuːltʃɪldrən/) *noun* a boy or girl who goes to school ସ୍କୁଲ୍ ବା ବିଦ୍ୟାଳୟରେ ପଢୁଥିବା ପିଲାମାନେ

schooldays /ˈskuːldeɪz/ *noun* (*plural*) the time in your life when you are at school ସ୍କୁଲ୍‌ରେ ପଢୁଥିବା ସମୟ

science /ˈsaɪəns/ *noun* the study of natural things ବିଜ୍ଞାନ *I'm interested in science.* ○ *Biology, chemistry and physics are all sciences.*

science fiction *noun* (*no plural*) stories about things like travel in space, life on other planets or life in the future ବିଜ୍ଞାନ ଉପରେ ଆଧାରିତ କାଳ୍ପନିକ ଗପ ବା ଉପନ୍ୟାସ ଯଥା ଅନ୍ୟ ଜଗତର ଜୀବ, ତାରା ନକ୍ଷତ୍ରକୁ ଯାତ୍ରା

scientific /ˌsaɪənˈtɪfɪk/ *adjective* of or about science ବିଜ୍ଞାନ ସମ୍ବନ୍ଧୀୟ, ବୈଜ୍ଞାନିକ *a scientific experiment*

scientist /ˈsaɪəntɪst/ *noun* a person who studies science or works with science ବୈଜ୍ଞାନିକ

scissors /ˈsɪzəz/ *noun* (*no singular*) a tool for cutting that has two sharp parts that are joined together କଇଁଚି *These scissors aren't very sharp.* ✪ ମନେ ରଖନ୍ତୁ! **a pair of scissors** କହିବା ଠିକ୍ ହେବ, 'a scissors' ଭୁଲ୍ ହେବ *I need a pair of scissors.*

scold /skəʊld/ *verb* (**scolds, scolding, scolded**) speak angrily to someone because they have done something wrong ଗାଳି ଦେବା, ଭର୍ତ୍ସନା କରିବା *The principal scolded the children for arriving late at the assembly.*

scolding *noun* ଗାଳି, ଭର୍ତ୍ସନା *He got a scolding from his father for breaking the windowpane.*

scooter /ˈskuːtə(r)/ *noun* a light motorcycle with a small engine ଅଳ୍ପ ଶକ୍ତିର ହାଲୁକା ମଟରସାଇକେଲ୍ ପରି ଯାନ, ସ୍କୁଟର୍

scope /skəʊp/ *noun* **1** the chance or ability to do or develop something କାମ କରିବାର ସୁଯୋଗ ବା ସାମର୍ଥ୍ୟ *scope for improvement* **2** the range of things that a person, idea, subject, etc.

deals with କର୍ମପରିଶର *The topic is beyond the scope of their investigation.*

scorch /skɔ:tʃ/ *verb* (**scorches, scorching, scorched**) burn and become slightly damaged ପୋଡ଼ିଦେବା *He scorched my dress while ironing it.*

scorching /ˈskɔ:tʃɪŋ/ *adjective* very hot ଅତି ଗରମ *scorching heat*

score /skɔ:(r)/ *noun* the number of points, goals, etc. that you win in a game or competition ଖେଳରେ ବା ପ୍ରତିଯୋଗିତାରେ ବ୍ୟକ୍ତି ବା ଦଳ ପାଇଥିବା ପଏଣ୍ଟ, ରନ୍ ବା ଗୋଲ୍ *The winner's score was 320 points.*

score *verb* (**scores, scoring, scored**) win a point in a game or competition ଖେଳ ବା ପ୍ରତିଯୋଗିତାରେ ପଏଣ୍ଟ ଜିତିବା, ରନ୍ କରିବା ବା ଗୋଲ୍ ଦେବା *Orissa scored three goals against Maharashtra.*

scoreboard /ˈskɔ:bɔ:d/ *noun* a large board that shows you the score during a game or a competition ଖେଳର ପଏଣ୍ଟ, ରନ୍, ଗୋଲ୍ ଇତ୍ୟାଦି ଲେଖା ହେଉଥିବା ବଡ଼ ପଟା

scorn /skɔ:n/ *noun* (*no plural*) the strong feeling you have when you think that somebody or something is not good enough ଘୃଣା, ନୀଚଭାବ *He was full of scorn for my idea.*

Scorpio /ˈskɔ:piəʊ/ *noun* the eighth sign of the **zodiac** ରାଶିଚକ୍ରର ଅଷ୍ଟମ ରାଶି, ବୃଶ୍ଚିକ ବା ବିଛା ରାଶି

scowl /skaʊl/ *noun* an angry expression on the face with wrinkles on the forehead ରୋଷପୂର୍ଣ୍ଣ ବା ବିରକ୍ତିପୂର୍ଣ୍ଣ ଚାହାଣି

scowl *verb* (**scowls, scowling, scowled**) ରୋଷ ବା ବିରକ୍ତିରେ ଚାହିଁବା

scrap /skræp/ *noun* a small piece of something ଛୋଟଖଣ୍ଡ, ଟୁକୁରା *a scrap of paper*

scrapbook /ˈskræpbʊk/ *noun* a large book with empty pages where you can stick pictures, newspaper cuttings, etc. ଏଠୁ ସେଠୁ ଅଣା ବା କଟାକାଗଜ, ଚିତ୍ର ଇତ୍ୟାଦି ରଖିବା ପାଇଁ ଥିବା ଅଲେଖା ଖାତା

scrape /skreɪp/ *verb* (**scrapes, scraping, scraped**) **1** move a rough or sharp thing across something to clean it ରାମ୍ପିବା, କୋରିବା, ରାଞ୍ଜୁଡ଼ିବା *I scraped the mud off my shoes with a knife.* **2** hurt or damage something by moving it against a rough or sharp thing ଘଷି ହୋଇଯିବା ଫଳରେ ଖରାପ କରିଦେବା *The paint has got scraped off the wall.*

scratch[1] /skrætʃ/ *verb* (**scratches, scratching, scratched**) **1** cut or make a mark on something with a sharp thing ରାମ୍ପିବା, ରାମ୍ପି ଖଣ୍ଡିଆ କରିବା *The cat scratched me!* **2** move your fingernails across your skin where it is itching କୁଣ୍ଡାଇବା *She scratched her head.*

scratch[2] /skrætʃ/ *noun* (*plural* **scratches**) a cut or mark that a sharp thing makes ଖଣ୍ଡିଆ; ରାମ୍ପୁଡ଼ା ଦାଗ, ରାଞ୍ଜୁଡ଼ା ଦାଗ *Her hands were covered in scratches from the rose bush.*

scrawl /skrɔ:l/ *verb* (**scrawls, scrawling, scrawled**) write quickly, untidily and carelessly, making it difficult for other people to read what you have written ତରତରରେ ଗେନ୍ଦରାମେନ୍ଦରା ବା ଅସୁନ୍ଦର ଭାବେ ଲେଖିବା

scrawl *noun* ଅସୁନ୍ଦର ଅକ୍ଷରର ଲେଖା

scream /skri:m/ *verb* (**screams, screaming, screamed**) make a loud high cry that shows you are afraid or hurt ଚିତ୍କାର କରିବା (ଭୟ ବା ବିପଦରେ) *She saw the snake and screamed.* ○ *He screamed for help.*

scream *noun* a loud high cry ଚିତ୍କାର *a scream of pain*

screech /skri:tʃ/ *verb* (**screeches, screeching, screeched**) make a harsh loud high sound କର୍କଶ ଓ ଉଚ୍ଚ ସ୍ୱରରେ ଚିତ୍କାର କରିବା, ଏହିପରି ଶବ୍ଦ କରିବା *The car's brakes screeched as it stopped suddenly.*

screen /skri:n/ *noun* **1** the flat square part of a television or computer monitor on which you see pictures or words ଟେଲିଭିଜନ୍, କମ୍ପ୍ୟୁଟରର ମନିଟର୍ ଇତ୍ୟାଦିର ଚିତ୍ର ପ୍ରତିଫଳିତ ହେଉଥିବା ପରଦା ➪ ଚିତ୍ର ପାଇଁ **computer** ଦେଖନ୍ତୁ । **2** the flat thing on the wall of a cinema, on which you see films ସିନେମାର ଚିତ୍ର ପ୍ରତିଫଳିତ ହେଉଥିବା ପରଦା **3** a kind of thin wall that you can move around. Screens are used to keep away cold, light, etc. or to stop people from seeing something ସରୁ କାନ୍ଥ ପରି ପରଦା ଯାହା ଘୁଞ୍ଚାଯାଇପାରେ; ଝରକା, କବାଟ ଇତ୍ୟାଦିର ପରଦା *The nurse put a screen around the bed.*

screw /skru:/ *noun* a metal thing like a nail that you use for fixing things together. It has a raised spiral edge and you push it into something by turning it with a **screwdriver** ପେଚ

screw *verb* (**screws, screwing, screwed**) turn something, usually in the **clockwise** direction, to fix it to another thing ପେଚ ଘୁରାଇ ଲଗାଇବା *Screw the lid on the jar.* ✪ ବିପରୀତ **unscrew**

screwdriver /ˈskru:draɪvə r/ *noun* a tool for turning screws ପେଚ ଲଗାଇବା ଉପକରଣ, ସ୍କ୍ରୁଡ୍ରାଇଭର

scribble /ˈskrɪbl/ *verb* (**scribbles, scribbling, scribbled**) write something or make marks on paper quickly and without care ତରତରରେ ଅପରିଚ୍ଛନ୍ନ ଭାବରେ ଲେଖିବା; ଗାରେଇବା *The children scribbled in my book.*

script /skrɪpt/ *noun* the written words for a play or film ନାଟକ ବା ଫିଲ୍ମର ଲେଖା, ସ୍କ୍ରିପ୍ଟ

scriptures /ˈskrɪptʃə(r)s/ *noun* (*plural*) the holy books of a particular religion ଧର୍ମଗ୍ରନ୍ଥ *Hindu scriptures*

scrub /skrʌb/ *verb* (**scrubs, scrubbing, scrubbed**) rub something hard to clean it, usually with a brush, soap and water ସାବୁନ୍, ପାଣି ଇତ୍ୟାଦି ପକାଇ ବ୍ରସ୍‌ରେ ଘଷି ସଫାକରିବା *He scrubbed the floor.*

sculptor /ˈskʌlptə(r)/ *noun* a person who makes solid figures or objects from things like stone, wood, clay or metal (ପଥର, କାଠ, ମାଟି ବା ଧାତୁରେ) ମୁର୍ତ୍ତି ତିଆରି କରୁଥିବା ଶିଳ୍ପୀ, ଭାସ୍କର

sculpture /ˈskʌlptʃə(r)/ *noun* solid figures or objects made from things like stone, wood, clay or metal ମୁର୍ତ୍ତି; ମୁର୍ତ୍ତି ଗଢ଼ିବା କଳା

sea /siː/ *noun* **1** (*no plural*) the salty water that covers most of the earth ସମୁଦ୍ର *We went for a swim in the sea.* ○ *The sea is very rough today.* **2** (*plural* **seas**) a big area of salty water smaller than an **ocean** ସାଗର *the Arabian Sea*

seagull /ˈsiːgʌl/ *noun* a big grey or white bird with a loud cry, that lives near the sea ଧଳା-ଧୂସର ବର୍ଣ୍ଣର ଉଚ୍ଚ ରାବ କରୁଥିବା ସାମୁଦ୍ରିକ ପକ୍ଷୀ, ଗଲ୍, ସିଗଲ୍

seal[1] /siːl/ *noun* an animal with short fur that lives in and near the sea, and that eats fish ଡେଣାଥିବା ମାଛଖିଆ ସ୍ତନ୍ୟପାୟୀ ସାମୁଦ୍ରିକ ଉଭୟଚର ପ୍ରାଣୀ, ସୀଲ୍, ସୀଲ୍‌ମାଛ

seal[2] /siːl/ *noun* an official design or mark that is stamped on something to show that it is genuine ମୋହର

seal[3] /siːl/ *verb* (**seals, sealing, sealed**) close something tightly by sticking two parts together ଅଠାଦ୍ୱାରା ଚିପ୍‌କାଇ ବନ୍ଦ କରିବା *She sealed the envelope.*

seam /siːm/ *noun* a line where two pieces of cloth are joined together ଜାମାପଟାରେ କନାର ଯୋଡ଼େଇ

search /sɜːtʃ/ *verb* (**searches, searching, searched**) look carefully because you are trying to find somebody or something ଖୋଜିବା *I searched everywhere for my pen.*

search *noun* (*plural* **searches**) ଖୋଜିବା *I found my key after a long search.*

in search of somebody or **something** looking for somebody or something କାହାରିକୁ ବା କିଛି ପଦାର୍ଥ ଖୋଜିବା ପାଇଁ *We drove round the town in search of a cheap hotel.*

seashell /ˈsiːʃel/ *noun* the hard outside part of a small animal that lives in the sea ସମୁଦ୍ର ଗେଣ୍ଡା ସାମୁକାର ଖୋଳ ➪ ଚିତ୍ର ପାଇଁ **sea** ଦେଖନ୍ତୁ ।

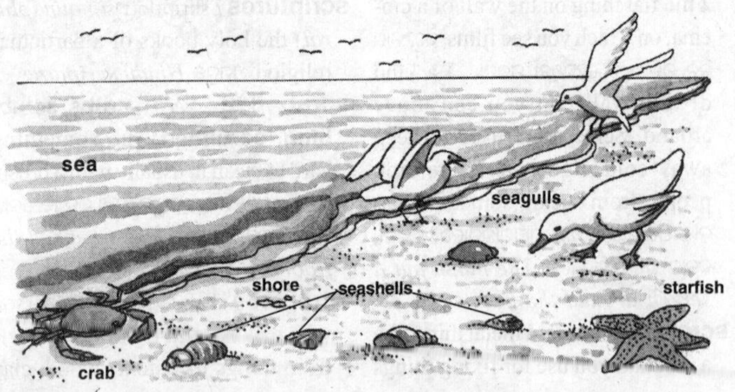

seashore /ˈsiːʃɔː(r)/ *noun* (*no plural*) the land next to the sea; the beach ସମୁଦ୍ରତଟ, ସମୁଦ୍ରର କୂଳ ବା ତୀର

seaside /ˈsiːsaɪd/ *noun* (*no plural*) a place by the sea where people go on holiday ସମୁଦ୍ରର ତଟରେ ଥିବା ସ୍ଥାନ *Let's go to the seaside.*

season /ˈsiːzn/ *noun* **1** one of the four parts of the year. The four seasons are **spring, summer, autumn** and **winter** (ବସନ୍ତ, ଗ୍ରୀଷ୍ମ, ଶରତ ଏବଂ ଶୀତ) ଋତୁ **2** a special time of the year for something ବର୍ଷର ନିର୍ଦ୍ଦିଷ୍ଟ ସମୟ ଯେତେବେଳେ ବିଶେଷ କାର୍ଯ୍ୟକ୍ରମ କରାଯାଏ *The cricket season starts in August.*

seasonal /ˈsiːzənəl/ *adjective* taking place or found at a particular time of the year ଋତୁଗତ, କୌଣସି ଏକ ଋତୁରେ ହେଉଥିବା *seasonal fruits*

seat /siːt/ *noun* a thing that you use to sit on ବସିବା ସ୍ଥାନ, ବସିବା ଜାଗା, ସିଟ୍ *the back seat of a car* ○ *We had seats at the front of the theatre.*

take a seat sit down ବସିବା; ବସନ୍ତୁ *Please take a seat.*

seat belt *noun* a belt that you put round your body in a car or an aeroplane to keep you safe if there is an accident ଯାତ୍ରୀମାନଙ୍କୁ ସୁରକ୍ଷିତ ରଖିବା ପାଇଁ କାର୍ ବା ଉଡ଼ାଜାହାଜର ସିଟ୍‌ରେ ଲାଗିଥିବା ସୁରକ୍ଷାପଟି

second[1] /ˈsekənd/ *adjective, adverb* next after first ଦ୍ଵିତୀୟ *February is the second month of the year.*

secondly *adverb* a word that you use when you are giving the second thing in a list ଦ୍ଵିତୀୟରେ; ଦ୍ଵିତୀୟତଃ *Firstly, it's too expensive and secondly, we don't really need it.*

second[2] /ˈsekənd/ *noun* (*no plural*) a person or thing that comes next after the first ଦ୍ଵିତୀୟ ସ୍ଥାନର ବ୍ୟକ୍ତି, ପଦାର୍ଥ, ଦିନ ଇତ୍ୟାଦି *Today is the second of April (April 2nd).* ○ *I was the first to arrive, and Ruby was the second.*

second[3] /ˈsekənd/ *noun* **1** a measure of time. There are 60 seconds in a **minute** ୧ ମିନିଟ୍‌ରେ ୬୦ ସେକେଣ୍ଡ **2** a very short time ଅତି ଅଳ୍ପ ସମୟ, କ୍ଷଣ, ମୁହୂର୍ତ୍ତ, ନିମିଷ *Wait a second!* ○ *I'll be ready in a second.*

secondary /ˈsekəndəri/ *adjective* if something is secondary, it is less important or urgent than something else ମୁଖ୍ୟ ବିଷୟର ପରବର୍ତ୍ତୀ, ଗୌଣ, ଅନ୍ୟତମ, ଦ୍ଵିତୀୟ *a secondary issue*

second class *noun* (*no plural*) the part of a train, etc. that is cheaper to travel in than the first class ଦ୍ଵିତୀୟ ଶ୍ରେଣୀ *We travelled in second class.*

second-class *adjective, adverb* ଦ୍ଵିତୀୟ ଶ୍ରେଣୀର, ଦ୍ଵିତୀୟ ଶ୍ରେଣୀରେ *a second-class ticket*

second-hand *adjective, adverb* not new; used by another person before ନୂଆ ହୋଇନଥିବା; ଆଗରୁ ଅନ୍ୟଦ୍ଵାରା ବ୍ୟବହୃତ *second-hand books* ○ *I bought this car second-hand.*

secrecy /ˈsiːkrəsi/ *noun* (*no plural*) the act of not telling other people a secret ଗୋପନୀୟତା *They worked in secrecy.*

secret¹ /ˈsiːkrət/ *adjective* if something is secret, other people do not or must not know about it ଗୋପନୀୟ, ଗୁପ୍ତ *a secret meeting*

secretly *adverb* without other people knowing ଗୋପନୀୟ ଭାବରେ, ଗୁପ୍ତରେ *We are secretly planning a big party for her.*

secret² /ˈsiːkrət/ *noun* something that you do not or must not tell other people ଗୋପନ ବା ଗୁପ୍ତ କଥା, କାହାରି ଆଗରେ ନ କହିଲା ପରି କଥା *I can't tell you where I'm going—it's a secret.*

keep a secret not tell other people a secret ଗୋପନ ରଖିବା, କାହାରିକୁ ନକହିବା *Can you keep a secret?*

secretariat /ˌsekrəˈteəriət/ *noun* the department of a large government or another similar organization that manages the way that organization is run ସଚିବାଳୟ; ଏହାର କୋଠା *the UN secretariat*

secretary /ˈsekrətri/ *noun* (*plural* **secretaries**) a person whose job is to type letters, answer the telephone and arrange other things in an office ଚିଠି ପତ୍ର ଟାଇପିଂ, ଟେଲିଫୋନ୍‌ର ଉତ୍ତର ଇତ୍ୟାଦି ଅଫିସ୍ କାମ ପାଇଁ ଥିବା କର୍ମଚାରୀ

secrete /sɪˈkriːt/ *verb* (**secretes, secreting, secreted**) (of a part of a plant, an animal or a person) produce a liquid substance ନିସୃତ କରିବା, କ୍ଷରଣ କରିବା, ଝରାଇବା *The pancreas secretes insulin.*

secretive /ˈsiːkrətɪv/ *adjective* if you are secretive, you do not like to tell other people about yourself or your plans (କୌଣସି ବିଷୟ) ଗୋପନ ରଖୁଥିବା ବା ଲୁଚାଉଥିବା *Mark is very secretive about his job.*

section /ˈsekʃn/ *noun* one of the parts of something ଏକ ନିର୍ଦ୍ଦିଷ୍ଟ ଅଂଶ, ଭାଗ, ଧାରା ବା ଦଳ *This section of the road is closed.*

sector /ˈsektər/ *noun* a part of a particular area or a group of people ଏକ ନିର୍ଦ୍ଦିଷ୍ଟ ସ୍ଥାନ ବା ଗୋଷ୍ଠୀ *We live in sector B of the area.*

secular /ˈsekjələr/ *adjective* if something is secular it is not related to religious or spiritual matters ଧର୍ମନିରପେକ୍ଷ, ଧର୍ମ ସହ ସମ୍ପୃକ୍ତ ନଥିବା *secular laws*

secure /sɪˈkjʊə(r)/ *adjective* **1** safe ନିରାପଦ, ସୁରକ୍ଷିତ *Don't climb that ladder—it's not very secure.* **2** if you are secure, you feel safe and you are not worried ସୁରକ୍ଷିତ, ବିପଦମୁକ୍ତ *Do you feel secure about the future?*
✪ ବିପରୀତ **insecure**

security /sɪˈkjʊərəti/ *noun* (*no plural*) **1** the feeling of being safe ସୁରକ୍ଷା, ସୁରକ୍ଷିତ ଅବସ୍ଥା, ନିରାପତ୍ତା *Children need love and security.* **2** things that you do to keep a place safe ସୁରକ୍ଷା ବ୍ୟବସ୍ଥା *We need better security at all the airports.*

sediment /ˈsedɪmənt/ *noun* the thick solid substance that settles at the bottom of a liquid ଖାଦ, କାଣ୍ଟି, ମଇଳା *A thick layer of black sediments was deposited at the bottom of the water tank.*

sedimentation /ˌsedɪmenˈteɪʃn/ *noun* (*no plural*) the process in which solid substances settle down at the bottom of a liquid ତରଳ ପଦାର୍ଥର ତଳଭାଗରେ ଖାଦ ବା ମଇଳା ଜମିବା ପ୍ରକ୍ରିୟା, ଅବକ୍ଷେପଣ *sedimentation of rocks at the bottom of the sea*

see /si:/ *verb* (**sees, seeing, saw** /sɔ:/, **has seen** /si:n/) **1** know something using your eyes ଦେଖିବା *Can you see that plane?* ○ *I'm going to see a film tonight.*

> **see** or **look**?
>
> **See** ଓ **look** ଶବ୍ଦର ବ୍ୟବହାର ଭିନ୍ନ। ବିନା ଚେଷ୍ଟାରେ ଯେତେବେଳେ ଆପଣ କୌଣସି ବସ୍ତୁକୁ ଦେଖନ୍ତି, **see** ଶବ୍ଦର ବ୍ୟବହାର କରାଯାଏ। ଯେତେବେଳେ ଆପଣ କୌଣସି ନିର୍ଦ୍ଦିଷ୍ଟ ଲକ୍ଷ୍ୟ ନେଇ କୌଣସି ବସ୍ତୁକୁ ଦେଖନ୍ତି, **look** ର ପ୍ରୟୋଗ କରାଯାଏ। ଯଥା —
> *Suddenly I **saw** a bird fly past the window.*
> ***Look** at this picture carefully. Can you **see** the bird?*

2 visit or meet somebody (କୌଣସି ବ୍ୟକ୍ତିଙ୍କ ସହ) ସାକ୍ଷାତ କରିବା, ଦେଖାକରିବା *I'll see you outside the station at ten o'clock.* **3** understand something ବୁଝିବା *'You have to turn the key this way.' 'I see.'* **4** find out about something ଦେଖି ବାହାର କରିବା ବା ଜାଣିବା *Look in the newspaper to see what time the film starts.* **5** make certain about something ସୁନିଶ୍ଚିତ କରିବା *Please see that everybody is here.*

see somebody off go to an airport or a station to say goodbye to somebody who is leaving ବିମାନ ବନ୍ଦର, ରେଳଷ୍ଟେସନ୍ ଇତ୍ୟାଦିକୁ ଯାଇ କାହାରିକୁ ବିଦାୟ ଦେବା

see you, see you later goodbye ବିଦାୟ, ପରେ ଦେଖା ହେବା

seed /si:d/ *noun* the small hard part of a plant from which a new plant grows (ଗଛର) ମଞ୍ଜି, ବୀଜ, ବିହନ

seedling /ˈsi:dlɪŋ/ *noun* a very young plant that has grown from a seed ଛୋଟ ଗଛ, ଚାରା, ତଳି

seek /si:k/ *verb* (**seeks, seeking, sought** /sɔ:t/, **has sought**) try to find or get something ଖୋଜିବା, ଖୋଜି ପାଇବା; ଲୋଡ଼ିବା, ପାଇବାକୁ ଇଚ୍ଛା କରିବା *You should seek help.*

seem /si:m/ *verb* (**seems, seeming, seemed**) make you think that something is true ମନେହେବା, ବୋଧହେବା, ଲାଗିବା *She seems tired.*

seen ଶବ୍ଦ **see** ର ଏକ ଧାତୁରୂପ

see-saw *noun* a special piece of wood, metal or plastic that can move up and down when a child sits on each end ଗୋଟିଏ ଦୁଇ ପଟେ ଦୁଇଟିପିଲା ବସି ଉପରତଳ ହୋଇପାରୁଥିବା ଖେଳ ଉପକରଣ, ଢ଼ିଙ୍କି ଖେଳ, ଉଠା-ପକା ଖେଳ

seize /si:z/ *verb* (**seizes, seizing, seized**) **1** arrest somebody, capture somebody or something ଗିରଫ କରିବା, କାହାରିକୁ ଧରିନେବା, କୌଣସି ପଦାର୍ଥକୁ ଜବତ କରିବା *The police seized a large quantity of drugs.* **2** take something quickly and strongly ହଠାତ୍ ବା ଜବରଦସ୍ତି ଧରିନେବା; ଅଧିକାର କରିବା *The thief seized my bag and ran away.* ○ *The army seized control of the town.*

seldom /ˈseldəm/ *adverb* not often କେବେ କେମିତି, କ୍ୱଚିତ୍ *It seldom rains in Jodhpur.*

select /sɪˈlekt/ *verb* (**selects, selecting, selected**) take the person or thing that you like from a group of people or things; choose ବାଛିବା, ଚୟନ କରିବା, ମନୋନୀତ କରିବା *The manager has selected two new players for the team.* ✪ ଆମେ ସାଧାରଣତଃ **choose** ବ୍ୟବହାର କରୁ ।

selection /sɪˈlekʃn/ *noun* **1** (*no plural*) the process of taking the person or thing you like from a group of people or things ମନୋନୟନ, ଚୟନ, ବାଛିବା ପ୍ରକ୍ରିୟା *the selection of the new school captain* **2** (*plural* **selections**) a group of people or things that somebody has chosen, or a group of things that you can choose from ମନୋନୀତ ବ୍ୟକ୍ତି ବା ପଦାର୍ଥ; ବାଛିବା ପାଇଁ ରଖାଯାଇଥିବା ପଦାର୍ଥ ସମୂହ *This shop has a good selection of books and cassettes.*

self /self/ *noun* a person's own character or behaviour ବ୍ୟକ୍ତିର ଚରିତ୍ର ଅଥବା ବ୍ୟବହାର ।

self- *prefix*
by yourself; for yourself ନିଜେ, ସ୍ୱତଃ–, ସ୍ୱ– *He is self-taught—he never went to university.*

self-confident *adjective* sure about yourself and what you can do ଆତ୍ମବିଶ୍ୱାସୀ

selfish /ˈselfɪʃ/ *adjective* if you are selfish, you think too much about what you want and not about what other people want ସ୍ୱାର୍ଥପର *It was selfish of you to go out when your mother was ill.* ✪ ବିପରୀତ **unselfish**

selfishly *adverb* ସ୍ୱାର୍ଥପର ଭାବେ *He behaved very selfishly.*

selfishness *noun* (*no plural*) ସ୍ୱାର୍ଥପରତା *Her selfishness made me very angry.*

sell /sel/ *verb* (**sells, selling, sold** /səʊld/, **has sold**) give something to somebody who pays you money for it ବିକିବା, ବିକ୍ରୟ କରିବା *I sold my bicycle for Rs 800.* ✪ ବିପରୀତ **buy**

Sellotape /ˈseləʊteɪp/ *noun* (*no plural*) a clear paper or plastic that you buy in a narrow roll. You use it for sticking things like paper and cardboard together ସ୍ୱଚ୍ଛ ଓ ପତଳା ଅଠାଫିତା, ସେଲୋଟେପ୍ ସ୍କଚ୍ ଟେପ୍ ✪ **Sellotape** ଟ୍ରେଡ୍‌ମାର୍କ ଅଟେ ।

semi- *prefix*
half ଅଧା, ଅର୍ଦ୍ଧ *A semicircle is a half circle.*

semicircle /ˈsemisɜːkl/ *noun* one half of a circle or something arranged in that shape ବୃତ୍ତାର୍ଦ୍ଧ ବା ଅର୍ଦ୍ଧବୃତ୍ତ

semicolon /ˌsemiˈkəʊlən/ *noun* a mark (;) that you use in writing to separate parts of a sentence ବାକ୍ୟ ଲେଖିବାରେ ବ୍ୟବହୃତ ଏକ ବିରାମ ଚିହ୍ନ (;)

semi-final *noun* in a competition, a semi-final is one of the two games that are played to find out who will play in the **final** ପ୍ରତିଯୋଗିତା ଶେଷ ଖେଳର ପୂର୍ବଖେଳ, ସେମିଫାଇନାଲ୍

send /send/ *verb* (**sends, sending, sent** /sent/, **has sent**) **1** make something go somewhere କିଛି ପଦାର୍ଥ ପଠାଇବା, ପ୍ରେରଣ କରିବା *I sent a letter to Maya.* **2** make somebody go somewhere (କାହାରିକୁ) ପଠାଇବା, ପ୍ରେରଣ କରିବା *My company is sending me to Chennai.*

send for somebody or **something** ask somebody to come to you or ask somebody to bring something for you କାହାରିକୁ ଡକାଇବା; କିଛି ଜିନିଷ ଆଣିବା ପାଇଁ କାହାରିକୁ ପଠାଇବା ବା କହିବା *Send for an ambulance!*

send something off post something ଚିଠିପତ୍ର ଡାକରେ ପଠାଇବା *I'll send the letter off today.*

senior /ˈsiːniə(r)/ *adjective* **1** more important ବରିଷ୍ଠ, ପଦମର୍ଯ୍ୟାଦାରେ ଉଚ୍ଚତର *a senior officer in the army* **2** older ବୟୋଜ୍ୟେଷ୍ଠ, ବୟସରେ ବଡ଼ *a senior pupil* ✪ ବିପରୀତ **junior**

sensation /senˈseɪʃn/ *noun* **1** a feeling ଇନ୍ଦ୍ରିୟାନୁଭୂତି, ଶାରୀରିକ ଅନୁଭୂତି *I felt a burning sensation on my skin.* **2** great excitement or interest; something that makes people very excited ବହୁଲୋକଙ୍କ ମଧ୍ୟରେ ସୃଷ୍ଟ ଆଚମ୍ବିତ ଭାବ, ବିସ୍ମୟ, ଉତ୍ତେଜନା, ଉତ୍ସାହ ଇତ୍ୟାଦି; ଚାଞ୍ଚଲ୍ୟ; ଏହିପରି ଚାଞ୍ଚଲ୍ୟ ସୃଷ୍ଟି କରୁଥିବା ବିଷୟ ବା ଘଟଣା *The new film caused a sensation in Delhi.*

sensational *adjective* very exciting or interesting ଚାଞ୍ଚଲ୍ୟକର *sensational news*

sense[1] /sens/ *noun* **1** (*plural* **senses**) the power to see, hear, smell, taste or touch ପଞ୍ଚ ଇନ୍ଦ୍ରିୟ (ଯାହାଦ୍ୱାରା ମଣିଷ ଦେଖେ, ଶୁଣେ, ସ୍ପର୍ଶ ଅନୁଭବ କରେ, ଶୁଙ୍ଘେ ବା ସ୍ୱାଦ ଜାଣିପାରେ); ଇନ୍ଦ୍ରିୟାନୁଭବ ଶକ୍ତି *Dogs have a good sense of smell.* **2** (*no plural*) the ability to feel or understand something ଅନୁଭବ କରିବା ବା ବୁଝିବା ଶକ୍ତି *Manpreet has a good sense of humour.* **3** (*no plural*) the ability to think carefully about something and to do the right thing ଭାବିଚିନ୍ତି ଠିକ୍ କାମ କରିବା ଶକ୍ତି ବା ସାମର୍ଥ୍ୟ *Did anybody have the sense to call the doctor?* **4** (*plural* **sen-ses**) a meaning (କୌଣସି କଥା, ଲେଖା ବା ବିଷୟର) ଅର୍ଥ ବା ତାତ୍ପର୍ଯ୍ୟ *This word has four senses.*

sense[2] /sens/ *verb* (**senses, sensing, sensed**) understand or feel something ବୁଝିବା ବା ଅନୁଭବ କରିବା *I sensed that he was worried.*

sensible /ˈsensəbl/ *adjective* able to think carefully about something and able to do the right thing କାଣ୍ଡଜ୍ଞାନ ଥିବା, ଭାବିଚିନ୍ତି ଠିକ୍ କାମ କରୁଥିବା *It was very sensible of you to call the doctor when your mother complained of stomach-ache.*

sensitive /ˈsensətɪv/ *adjective* **1** if you are sensitive about something, you easily become worried or unhappy about it କଥା କଥାକେ, ବ୍ୟସ୍ତ ବା ଦୁଃଖିତ ହେଉଥିବା; ଅଭିମାନୀ, ସ୍ପର୍ଶକାତର, ସୂକ୍ଷ୍ମାନୁଭବୀ *Don't say anything bad about her work—she's very sensitive about it.* **2** a person who is sensitive understands and is careful about other people's feelings ଅନ୍ୟଙ୍କ ଭାବନା ବୁଝୁଥିବା ଓ ସେଥିପ୍ରତି ଧ୍ୟାନ ଦେଉଥିବା *He's a very sensitive man.* **3** if something is sensitive, it gets hurt or damaged easily ସ୍ପର୍ଶକାତର *sensitive skin*

sensitivity /ˌsensəˈtɪvəti/ *noun* the ability to understand other people's feelings ଅନ୍ୟମାନଙ୍କ ଭାବନା ବୁଝିପାରିବା ଶକ୍ତି *lack of sensitivity to the needs of old people*

sensory /ˈsensəri/ *adjective* of or about the senses of sight, hearing, smell, taste or touch ଇନ୍ଦ୍ରିୟ ଦ୍ୱାରା ଅନୁଭୂତ, ଇନ୍ଦ୍ରିୟାନୁଭୂତ

sent ଶବ୍ଦ **send** ର ଏକ ଧାତୁରୂପ

sentence[1] /ˈsentəns/ *noun* a group of words that tells you something or asks a question. When a sentence is written, it always begins with a capital letter and usually ends with a full stop ବାକ୍ୟ

sentence[2] /ˈsentəns/ *noun* the punishment that a judge gives to somebody in a court of law ଅଦାଲତର ନିଷ୍ପତ୍ତି ବା ରାୟ

sentence *verb* (**sentences, sentencing, sentenced**) tell somebody in a court of law what their punishment will be (ଅପରାଧୀର) ଦଣ୍ଡାଦେଶ ଶୁଣାଇବା, ରାୟ ଦେବା *The judge sentenced the man to two years in prison.*

sentry /ˈsentri/ *noun* (*plural* **sentries**) a soldier who guards a building ଜଗୁଆଳୀ, ପ୍ରହରୀ, ଚୌକିଦାର

separate[1] /ˈseprət/ *adjective* **1** away from something; not together or not joined ଅଲଗା *Cut the cake into eight separate pieces.* **2** different; not the same ଅଲଗା, ଭିନ୍ନ *We stayed in separate rooms in the same hotel.*

separately *adverb* ଅଲଗା ଅଲଗା, ଭିନ୍ନ ଭାବରେ *Shall we pay separately or together?*

separate[2] /ˈsepəreɪt/ *verb* (**separates, separating, separated**) divide people or things; keep people or things away from each other ଅଲଗା କରିବା, ପୃଥକ କରିବା; ଅଲଗା ରଖିବା *The teacher separated the class into two groups.*

separation /ˌsepəˈreɪʃn/ *noun* ପୃଥକୀକରଣ, ବିଚ୍ଛେଦ *The separation from my family and friends made me very unhappy.*

September /sepˈtembə(r)/ *noun* the ninth month of the year ପାଶ୍ଚାତ୍ୟ ବର୍ଷର ନବମ ମାସ, ସେପ୍ଟେମ୍ବର୍

sequence /ˈsiːkwəns/ *noun* a set of things that happen or come one after the other ଅନୁକ୍ରମ, ପର୍ଯ୍ୟାୟକ୍ରମ *a sequence of events*

serene /səˈriːn/ *adjective* calm and peaceful ଶାନ୍ତ, ପ୍ରଶାନ୍ତ *the serene face of a child* ○ *the calm and serene lake*

sergeant /ˈsɑːdʒənt/ *noun* an officer in the army or police ସେନା ବା ପୁଲିସ୍‌ର ଏକ ସ୍ତରର ଅଧିକାରୀ ବା ଅଫିସର୍

serial /ˈsɪəriəl/ *noun* a story that is told in parts on television or radio, or in a magazine ଟେଲିଭିଜନ୍ ବା ପତ୍ରିକାରେ ଧାରାବାହିକ ଭାବେ ପ୍ରସାରିତ କାର୍ଯ୍ୟକ୍ରମ ବା ପ୍ରକାଶିତ ଉପନ୍ୟାସ ।

series /ˈsɪəriːz/ *noun* (*plural* **series**) **1** a number of things of the same kind that come one after another ଏକା ପରି ବହୁସଂଖ୍ୟକ ଗୋଟାଏ ପରେ ଗୋଟାଏ ଆସିବା *I heard a series of footsteps and then silence.* **2** a number of radio or television programmes, often on the same subject, that come one after another କ୍ରମ, ଅନୁକ୍ରମ, ପର୍ଯ୍ୟାୟ *a TV series on dinosaurs*

serious /ˈsɪəriəs/ *adjective* **1** very bad ଅତି ଖରାପ, ଗୁରୁତର *That was a serious mistake.* **2** not funny ଗମ୍ଭୀର, ହାସ୍ୟପୂର୍ଣ୍ଣ ହୋଇ ନଥିବା, ଗୁରୁଭାବାପନ୍ନ *a serious film* **3** if you are serious, you are not joking or playing ଗୁରୁତ୍ୱପୂର୍ଣ୍ଣ *Are you serious about going to live in a hostel?*

seriously *adverb* ଆନ୍ତରିକ ଭାବରେ, ଗାମ୍ଭୀର୍ଯ୍ୟପୂର୍ଣ୍ଣ ଭାବରେ; ଗୁରୁତ୍ୱପୂର୍ଣ୍ଣ ଭାବରେ *She's seriously ill.*

serpent /ˈsɜːpənt/ *noun* a large snake ବଡ଼ସାପ

servant /ˈsɜːvənt/ *noun* a person who works in another person's house, doing work like cooking and cleaning ଭୃତ୍ୟ, ସେବକ, ଚାକରପୂଖାରୀ

serve /sɜːv/ *verb* (**serves, serving, served**) **1** do work for other people କାହାରି ପାଇଁ କାମ କରିବା; କର୍ତ୍ତବ୍ୟ କରିବା *During the war he served in the army.* **2** give food or drink to somebody during a meal ଖାଇବା ପିଇବା ପରିବେଷଣ କରିବା, ବାଢ଼ିବା *Breakfast is served from 7.30 to 9.00 a.m.*

service /ˈsɜːvɪs/ *noun* **1** (*plural* **services**) a business that does useful work for all the people in a country or an area ଜନସେବା ବ୍ୟବସ୍ଥା *This town has a good bus service.* ○ *the postal service* **2** (*no plural*) help or work that you do for somebody ଚାକିରି *She left the company after ten years of service.* **3** (*no plural*) the work that somebody does for customers in a shop, restaurant or hotel ଦୋକାନ, ହୋଟେଲ୍ ଇତ୍ୟାଦିରେ କରାଯାଉଥିବା ଗ୍ରାହକଙ୍କର ସେବା ବା କାମ *The food was good but the service was very slow.* **4** (*plural* **services**) the time when somebody looks at a car or machine to see that it is working well ମଟରଗାଡ଼ି, ଯନ୍ତ୍ର ଇତ୍ୟାଦି ସଜାଡ଼ିବା ବା ସଫାସୁତୁରା କରିବା କାମ *She takes her car to the garage for a service every six months.* **5 the services** (*plural*) the army, navy and air force ସେନାବାହିନୀ (ସ୍ଥଳସେନା, ଜଳସେନା ଓ ବାୟୁସେନା)

session /ˈseʃn/ *noun* **1** a meeting or series of meetings where important things are discussed, in parliament, for example ବିଧାନସଭା, ନ୍ୟାୟାଳୟ ଇତ୍ୟାଦିର କାର୍ଯ୍ୟକାରୀ ସମୟ, ଅଧିବେଶନ **2** a time when people do some activity କିଛି କାମ କରିବା ସମୟ, କାର୍ଯ୍ୟକାଳ, ପର୍ଯ୍ୟାୟ

The first swimming session is at nine o'clock.

set[1] /set/ *noun* a group of things of the same kind, or a group of things that you use together ଗୁଚ୍ଛ, ମଛା, ଦଳ; ନିର୍ଦ୍ଦିଷ୍ଟ କାମ ପାଇଁ ଉଦ୍ଦିଷ୍ଟ ଉପକରଣ ବା ଯନ୍ତ୍ରପାତିର ଗୁଚ୍ଛ *a set of six glasses* ○ *a set of tools*

set[2] /set/ *verb* (**sets, setting, set, has set**) **1** put something somewhere ରଖିବା, ଥୋଇବା *Dad set the plate of fruits in front of me.* **2** make something ready to use or to start working କିଛି ଜିନିଷକୁ କାର୍ଯ୍ୟକାରୀ ହେବା ପାଇଁ ପ୍ରସ୍ତୁତ ରଖିବା *I set my alarm clock for seven o'clock.* **3** when the sun sets, it goes down from the sky (ସୂର୍ଯ୍ୟ) ଅସ୍ତହେବା ✪ ବିପରୀତ **rise** **4** become hard or solid ଟାଣହେବା *Wait for the cement to set.*

set off, set out start a journey ଯାତ୍ରା ଆରମ୍ଭ କରିବା *We set off for Amritsar at two o'clock in the afternoon.*

set up start something (କିଛି କାମ) ଆରମ୍ଭ କରିବା *The school was set up in 1981.*

settee /se'ti:/ *noun* a long soft seat for more than one person ଏକାଧିକ ଲୋକଙ୍କ ବସିବା ପାଇଁ ହାତବାଲା ଲମ୍ବା ଚଉକି, ସୋଫା

setting /'setɪŋ/ *noun* the place where something is or where something happens ପଟ୍ଟଭୂମି, ପରିବେଶ; ଘଟଣାସ୍ଥଳ *The house is in a beautiful setting on top of a hill.*

settle /'setl/ *verb* (**settles, settling, settled**) **1** decide something after talking with somebody; end a discussion or argument ନିଷ୍ପତ୍ତି କରିବା, ସ୍ଥିର କରିବା; ସମାଧାନ କରିବା *Have you settled your differences with Ranjit?* **2** go to live in a new place and stay there କୌଣସି ସ୍ଥାନରେ ସ୍ଥାୟୀ ଭାବରେ ରହିବା *Mr Bhasin left India and went to settle in America.* **3** come down and rest somewhere (ପକ୍ଷୀ ଇତ୍ୟାଦି) ଆସି ବସିବା *The bird settled on a branch.*

settle down 1 sit down or lie down so that you are comfortable ଆରାମରେ ବସିବା ବା ଶୋଇବା; ସ୍ଥାୟୀଭାବେ ବସବାସ କରିବା *I settled down in front of the television.* **2** become calm and quiet ଶାନ୍ତ ହେବା *The children settled down and went to sleep.*

settlement /'setlmənt/ *noun* **1** an agreement about something after much talking or arguing ବହୁ ଆଲୋଚନା କିମ୍ବା ଯୁକ୍ତିତର୍କ ପରେ କୌଣସି ବିଷୟ ନେଇ ଏକମତ ହେବା *After long talks about the pay, the workers and their boss reached a settlement.* **2** a group of homes in a place where no people have lived before ବସତି ସ୍ଥାପନ, ବସ୍ତି *a settlement in the forest*

seven /'sevn/ *number* 7 ସାତ(୭)

seventh /'sevnθ/ *adjective, adverb, noun* **1** 7th ସପ୍ତମ **2** one of seven equal parts of something; $\frac{1}{7}$ ସାତ ଭାଗରୁ ଭାଗେ; $\frac{୧}{୭}$

seventeen /ˌsevn'ti:n/ *number* 17 ସତର (୧୭)

seventeenth /ˌsevn'ti:nθ/ *adjective, adverb, noun* 17th ସପ୍ତଦଶତମ, ଏକାଦଶପ୍ତଦଶାଂଶ

seventy /ˈsevnti/ *number* **1** 70 ସତୁରି (୭୦) **2 the seventies** (*plural*) the numbers, years or temperatures between 70 and 79 ୭୦ ଠାରୁ ୭୯ ପର୍ଯ୍ୟନ୍ତ ସଂଖ୍ୟା, ଉତ୍ତାପ, ଶତାବ୍ଦୀର ବର୍ଷ, ବ୍ୟକ୍ତିଙ୍କ ବୟସ

seventieth /ˈsevntiəθ/ *adjective*, *adverb*, *noun* 70th ସପ୍ତତିତମ, ସତୁରିତମ; ସତୁରି ଭାଗରୁ ଏକ ଭାଗ

several /ˈsevrəl/ *adjective*, *pronoun* more than two but not many ଦୁଇରୁ ଅଧିକ କିନ୍ତୁ ବେଶୀ ନୁହେଁ *I've read this book several times.* ○ *Several letters arrived this morning.*

severe /sɪˈvɪə(r)/ *adjective* (**severer, severest**) **1** not kind or gentle ତୀବ୍ର, ପ୍ରଖର, କଠୋର *a severe punishment* **2** very bad ଖୁବ୍ ଖରାପ, ତୀବ୍ର *a severe headache* ○ *a severe winter*

severely *adverb* ଗୁରୁତର ଭାବରେ; କଠୋର ଭାବରେ *She was severely injured in the accident.*

sew /səʊ/ *verb* (**sews, sewing, sewed, has sewed** ବା **has sewn** /səʊn/) use a needle and thread to join pieces of material together or to join something to material ସିଲେଇ କରିବା *He sewed a button on his shirt.*

sewing /ˈsəʊɪŋ/ *noun* (*no plural*) something that you sew ସିଲେଇ କାମ

sewing machine *noun* a machine that you use for sewing ସିଲେଇ ମେସିନ୍

sewage /ˈsuːɪdʒ/ *noun* (*no plural*) dirty water and waste substances produced by our bodies that are carried away from our homes by large underground pipes ମାଟିତଳ ନର୍ଦ୍ଦମା, ନାଳ; ମଇଳା ପାଣି

sex /seks/ *noun* (*plural* **sexes**) **1** the state of being a male or a female ସ୍ତ୍ରୀ ପୁରୁଷ ଭେଦ *What sex is your dog?* ○ *the male sex* **2** the physcial act in which the sexual organs of two people touch and which can result in a woman having a baby ସ୍ତ୍ରୀ ଓ ପୁରୁଷର ଯୌନ ବା ସଂଯୋଗ ଦ୍ୱାରା ଯାହାର ଫଳାଫଳ ସ୍ତ୍ରୀ ଗୋଟାଏ ଶିଶୁ ଜନ୍ମ ଦେଇଥାଏ।

sexual /ˈsekʃuəl/ *adjective* connected with sex ସ୍ତ୍ରୀ ପୁରୁଷ ସଙ୍ଗମ ସମ୍ବନ୍ଧୀୟ, ଯୌନ

sh! /ʃ/ *interjection* be quiet! ଚୁପ୍ ହୋଇଯାଅ *Sh! You'll wake the baby up!*

shabby /ˈʃæbi/ *adjective* (**shabbier, shabbiest**) old and untidy or dirty because you have used it a lot ପୁରୁଣା, ଲୋଚାକୋଚା ବା ମଇଳା, ଅପରିଚ୍ଛନ୍ନ *a shabby coat*

shabbily *adverb* ଅପରିଚ୍ଛନ୍ନ ଭାବରେ *She was shabbily dressed.*

shack /ʃæk/ *noun* a roughly built small hut or cabin କୁଡ଼ିଆ ଘର, କୁଟୀର *He built a tin shack by the river.*

shackles /ˈʃæklz/ *noun* a pair of metal rings connected with a chain put around a prisorer's wrists or ankles ହାତ ବା ଗୋଡ଼ର କଡ଼ି, ବେଡ଼ି

shade[1] /ʃeɪd/ *noun* **1** (*no plural*) a place where it is dark and cool because sunlight does not reach there directly ଛାଇ, ଛାୟା *We sat in the shade of a big tree.* **2** (*plural* **shades**) a thing that keeps strong light from your eyes ପ୍ରଖର ଆଲୋକରୁ ଆଖିକୁ ରକ୍ଷା କରିବା ପାଇଁ ଆଲୋକରେ ଲଗାଯାଉଥିବା ଆବରଣ; ଖରାପିନ୍ଧା ଚଷମା, ଗଗଲ୍ସ, ସନ୍‌ଗ୍ଲାସେସ୍ *I bought a new shade for the lamp.* **3** (*plural* **shades**) a particular form of colour that tells you how light or dark it is ରଙ୍ଗର ଗାଢ଼ତା *I'm looking for a shirt in a darker shade of green.*

shade[2] /ʃeɪd/ *verb* (**shades, shading, shaded**) **1** stop light from shining on something ପ୍ରଖର ଆଲୋକ ନିବାରଣ କରିବା *He shaded his eyes with his hand.* **2** make certain parts of a drawing darker than the rest ଚିତ୍ରର କିଛି ଅଂଶ ଗାଢ଼ ବା ଛାଇଛାଇଆ କରିବା

shadow /ˈʃædəʊ/ *noun* a dark shape that forms on a surface when you stand between that and a light ଛାଇ, ଛାୟା

shadow

shady /ˈʃeɪdi/ *adjective* (**shadier, shadiest**) not in bright sunshine ଛାଇଥିବା, ଛାଇଛାଇଆ *We sat in a shady part of the garden.*

shaggy /ˈʃægi/ *adjective* (**shaggier, shaggiest**) (of hair, fur, etc.) long and untidy (ବାଳ, ଲୋମ ଇତ୍ୟାଦି) ଲମ୍ବା ଓ ଅଡୁଆ ତଡୁଆ *shaggy hair*

shake /ʃeɪk/ *verb* (**shakes, shaking, shook** /ʃʊk/, **has shaken** /ˈʃeɪkən/) **1** move quickly from side to side or up and down ହଲିବା, ଦୋହଲିବା *The house shakes when trains go past.* **2** make something move quickly from side to side or up and down ହଲାଇବା, ଦୋହଲାଇବା *Shake the bottle well before opening it.*

shake hands hold somebody's hand and move it up and down as a greeting or to show that you agree with them ଅଭିନନ୍ଦନରେ ହାତ ମିଳାଇବା

shake your head move your head from side to side to say 'no' ନାହିଁ କରିବା ପାଇଁ ମୁଣ୍ଡ ହଲାଇବା

shaky /ˈʃeɪki/ *adjective* (**shakier, shakiest**) not firm; not strong ଅସ୍ଥିର, ଟଳମଳ ଅବସ୍ଥାରେ ଥିବା; ଦୁର୍ବଳ *Don't sit in that chair—it's a bit shaky.*

shall /ʃəl; ʃæl/ *modal verb* **1** a word that you use instead of 'will' with 'I' and 'we' to show the future; 'I' ଓ 'we' ସାଙ୍ଗରେ ବ୍ୟବହୃତ ଭବିଷ୍ୟତ କାଳ ସୂଚକ ସହାୟକ କ୍ରିୟା *I shall see you tomorrow.* **2** a word that you use when you ask what is the right thing to do ଠିକ୍ କାମ କି ନାହିଁ ପଚାରିବା ପାଇଁ ବ୍ୟବହୃତ ସହାୟକ କ୍ରିୟା *Shall I close the window?* ○ *What shall we do tomorrow?*

> ✪ **Shall** ର ନକାରାତ୍ମକ ରୂପ ହେଲା **shall not** ଏହାର ସଂକ୍ଷିପ୍ତ ରୂପ **shan't** —
> *I shan't be there.*
> **Shall** ର ସଂକ୍ଷିପ୍ତ ରୂପ ହେଲା **'ll** —
> *I'll* (= I shall) *see you tomorrow.*
> ➪ **modal verb** ପାଇଁ ଟିପ୍ପଣୀ ଦେଖନ୍ତୁ ।

shallow /ˈʃæləʊ/ *adjective* (**shallower, shallowest**) not deep; with not much water ଅଗଭୀର; ଅଳ୍ପ ପାଣିଥିବା *This part of the river is shallow—we can walk across.* ✪ ବିପରୀତ **deep 1**

shame /ʃeɪm/ *noun* (*no plural*) the unhappy feeling that you have when you have done something wrong or stupid ଲଜ୍ଜା, ଲାଜ, ସରମ *I was filled with shame after I lied to my parents.* ✪ ଏହାର ବିଶେଷଣ ହେଲା **ashamed**

shampoo /ʃæmˈpuː/ *noun* (*plural* **shampoos**) a special liquid for washing your hair ମୁଣ୍ଡର ବାଳ ସଫା କରିବା ପାଇଁ ଏକ ପ୍ରକାର ସାବୁନ୍ ପାଣି, ଶ୍ୟାମ୍ପୁ *a bottle of shampoo*

shampoo *verb* (**shampoos, shampooing, shampooed**) wash your hair with a shampoo ଶ୍ୟାମ୍ପୁଲଗାଇ ବାଳ ସଫା କରିବା

shan't = **shall not**

shape[1] /ʃeɪp/ *noun* **1** (*plural* **shapes**) the form that you get if you draw a line round the outer edges of something; the form of something ଆକାର, ବାହ୍ୟ ଆକୃତି *What shape is the table—round or square?* ○ *I bought a bowl in the shape of a fish.* ○ *Circles, squares and triangles are all different shapes.* **2** (*no plural*) the condition that tells you how good or bad something or somebody is ଅବସ୍ଥା, ସ୍ଥିତି *He was in bad shape after the accident.*

out of shape not in the right shape ବେଢ଼ଙ୍ଗ, ବିକୃତାକାର; ଦେହ ଠିକ୍ ଠାକ୍ ନଥିବା ଅବସ୍ଥା *My sweater went out of shape when I washed it.*

shape[2] /ʃeɪp/ *verb* (**shapes, shaping, shaped**) give a certain shape to something ଗଢ଼ିବା, ନିର୍ଦ୍ଦିଷ୍ଟ ଆକାର ଦେବା *She shaped the clay into a pot.*

shaped /ʃeɪpt/ *adjective* with a certain shape ନିର୍ଦ୍ଦିଷ୍ଟ ଆକାରରେ ଗଠିତ *He gave me a birthday card shaped like a cat.*

share[1] /ʃeə(r)/ *verb* (**shares, sharing, shared**) **1** give parts of something to different people (କୌଣସି ପଦାର୍ଥର) ଅଂଶ ପାଇବା, ନେବା ବା ଦେବା, ଭାଗ ବାଣ୍ଟିବା *Share these sweets with your friends.* **2** have or use something with another person ଭାଗୀଦାର ହେବା,

shapes

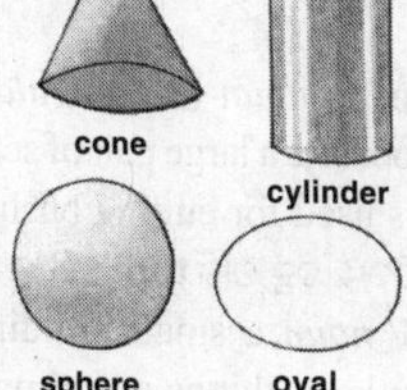

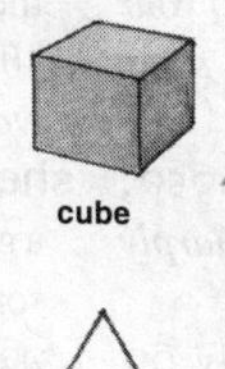

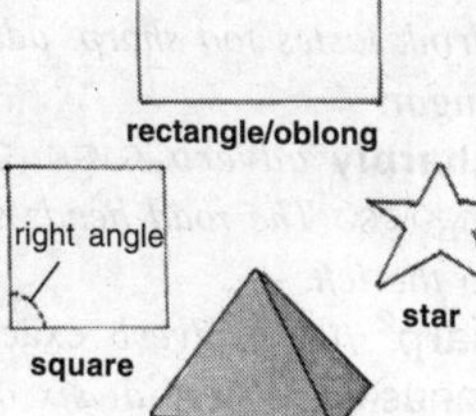

ଅନ୍ୟ ସହ ଏକାଠି ବ୍ୟବହାର କରିବା *I share my bedroom with my sister.*

share² /ʃeə(r)/ *noun* one part of something that has been divided between two or more people ଭାଗ, ଅଂଶ *Vikram got a larger share of the cake.* ○ *I did my share of the work.*

shark /ʃɑːk/ *noun* a big fish that lives in the sea. Some sharks have sharp teeth and are dangerous ସମୁଦ୍ରର ସାର୍କ୍ ମାଛ

sharp¹ /ʃɑːp/ *adjective* (**sharper, sharpest**) **1** with an edge or point that cuts or makes holes easily ଧାରୁଆ, ତୀକ୍ଷ୍ଣ, ମୁନିଆ *a sharp knife* ○ *a sharp needle* ✪ ବିପରୀତ **blunt 1** **2** strong and sudden ହଠାତ୍ ଓ ତୀବ୍ର ହୋଇଥିବା *I felt a sharp pain in my leg.* **3** clear and easy to see ସ୍ପଷ୍ଟ ଭାବରେ ଦେଖାଯାଉଥିବା *We could see the sharp outline of the mountains against the sky.* **4** able to see, hear or learn well ଭଲ ଭାବେ ଦେଖି, ଶୁଣି ଓ ଶିଖି ପାରୁଥିବା, ବୋଧଶକ୍ତି ସମ୍ପନ୍ନ *She's got a very sharp mind.* **5** sudden and angry ହଠାତ୍ ଓ କଟୁ, କ୍ରୁଦ୍ଧ, କଠୋର *sharp words* **6** with a strong and slightly bitter taste କଡୁଆ ଏବଂ ପିତା ସ୍ୱାଦ *If your drink tastes too sharp, add some sugar.*

sharply *adverb* ତୀକ୍ଷଣ ଭାବରେ; ତୀବ୍ରଭାବରେ *The road bends sharply to the left.*

sharp² /ʃɑːp/ *adverb* exactly ଠିକ୍ (ସମୟରେ) *Be here at six o'clock sharp.*

sharpen /ˈʃɑːpən/ *verb* (**sharpens, sharpening, sharpened**) make something sharp or sharper ଧାର୍ କରିବା *sharpen a knife*

sharpener *noun* a thing that you use for making something sharp ତୀକ୍ଷ୍ଣ କରିବା ଯନ୍ତ୍ର *a pencil sharpener*

shatter /ˈʃætə(r)/ *verb* (**shatters, shattering, shattered**) break into very small pieces; break something into very small pieces ଖଣ୍ଡ ଖଣ୍ଡ ହୋଇ ଭାଙ୍ଗିଯିବା ବା ଭାଙ୍ଗିଦେବା *The explosion shattered the windows.*

shave /ʃeɪv/ *verb* (**shaves, shaving, shaved**) cut hair off the face or body by cutting it very close with a **razor** ଖିଅର ହେବା ବା ଖିଅର କରିବା *He shaves every morning.*

shave *noun* ଖିଅର *I haven't had a shave today.*

shaver *noun* an electric tool for shaving ବୈଦ୍ୟୁତିକ ଖିଅର ଯନ୍ତ୍ର

shawl /ʃɔːl/ *noun* a large piece of warm cloth that is worn by a woman around her shoulders or head or that is put around a baby ଶାଲ୍

she /ʃiː/ *pronoun* (*plural* **they**) the woman or girl who has just been mentioned ନାରୀମାନଙ୍କର ସର୍ବନାମ ପଦ (ସେ) *'Where's your sister?' 'She's at work.'*

shears /ʃɪəz/ *noun* (*no singular*) a garden tool like a large pair of scissors that is used for cutting bushes ଗଛକଟା କଇଁଚି ➪ ଚିତ୍ର ପାଇଁ **tool** ଦେଖନ୍ତୁ।

shed¹ /ʃed/ *noun* a small building where you keep things or animals

ଜିନିଷ ପତ୍ର ବା ଜୀବଜନ୍ତୁ ରଖିବା ପାଇଁ ଛୋଟ ଘର; ଖୁଆଡ଼, ଗୁହାଳ ଇତ୍ୟାଦି *There's a shed in the garden where we keep our tools.*

shed[2] /ʃed/ *verb* (**sheds, shedding, shed, has shed**) let something fall off ଝାଡ଼ିବା, ଖସାଇବା, ଛାଡ଼ିବା *The snake shed its skin.*

she'd 1 = she had 2 = she would

sheep /ʃi:p/ *noun* (*plural* **sheep**) an animal that people keep on farms for its wool and its meat ମେଣ୍ଢା, ମେଷ

✪ ମେଣ୍ଢାକୁ **ram** କୁହାଯାଏ, ମେଣ୍ଢୀକୁ **ewe** କୁହାଯାଏ, ମେଣ୍ଢା ଛୁଆକୁ **lamb** କୁହାଯାଏ ।

sheep

sheet /ʃi:t/ *noun* **1** a big piece of thin cloth used on a bed to lie on or lie under *I put some clean sheets on the bed.* **2** a thin flat piece of something like paper, glass or metal କାଚ ବା ଧାତୁର ଫଳକ; କାଗଜର ଏକ ଖଣ୍ଡ ବା ଫର୍ଦ୍ଦ *a sheet of writing paper*

shelf /ʃelf/ *noun* (*plural* **shelves** /ʃelvz/) a long flat piece of wood, metal, etc. on a wall or in a cupboard, where things can stand ଥାକ *Put the plates on the shelf.* ○ *bookshelves*

shell /ʃel/ *noun* the hard outside part of birds' eggs and nuts and of some animals, for example snails and crabs ଅଣ୍ଡା, ମଞ୍ଜି, ବାଦାମ୍ ଇତ୍ୟାଦିର ଖୋଳ, ଖୋଳପା; ଗେଣ୍ଡା, ଚିଙ୍ଗୁଡ଼ି, କଙ୍କଡ଼ା ଇତ୍ୟାଦିଙ୍କ ଖୋଳ ବା ଖୋଳପା ➪ **seashell** ଦେଖନ୍ତୁ ।

she'll = she will

shelter[1] /ˈʃeltə(r)/ *noun* **1** (*no plural*) a state of being safe from bad weather or danger ଆଶ୍ରୟ *We took shelter from the rain under a tree.* **2** (*plural* **shelters**) a place where you are safe from bad weather or danger ଆଶ୍ରୟସ୍ଥଳ, ସୁରକ୍ଷିତ ରହିବା ସ୍ଥାନ *a bus shelter*

shelter[2] /ˈʃeltə(r)/ *verb* (**shelters, sheltering, sheltered**) make somebody or something safe from bad weather or danger ଆଶ୍ରୟ ଦେବା, ସୁରକ୍ଷିତ ରଖିବା *The trees shelter the house from the wind.*

shelves ଶବ୍ଦ **shelf** ର ବହୁବଚନ

shepherd /ˈʃepəd/ *noun* a person who looks after sheep ମେଣ୍ଢା ଜଗୁଆଳ, ମେଷପାଳକ

she's 1 = she is 2 = she has

shield[1] /ʃi:ld/ *noun* a big piece of metal, wood or leather that soldiers in the past carried to protect their bodies when they fought. Some police officers carry shields even now ଢାଲ, ରକ୍ଷା ଫଳକ

shield[2] /ʃi:ld/ *verb* (**shields, shielding, shielded**) keep somebody or something safe from danger or from being hurt (କାହାରିକୁ) ସୁରକ୍ଷିତ ରଖିବା *She shielded her eyes from the sun with her hand.*

shift /ʃɪft/ *verb* (**shifts, shifting, shifted**) move something to another place ଘୁଞ୍ଚିବା, ଘୁଞ୍ଚାଇବା, ସ୍ଥାନାନ୍ତରିତ କରିବା *Can you help me to shift the bed? I want to sweep the floor.*

shine /ʃaɪn/ *verb* (**shines, shining, shone** /ʃɑn/, **has shone**) **1** give out light ଆଲୋକ ଦେବା *The sun is shining.* **2** be bright ଉଜ୍ଜ୍ୱଳ ହେବା *I polished the silver until it shone.*

shine *noun* (*no plural*) brightness ଔଜ୍ଜ୍ୱଲ୍ୟ, ଉଜ୍ଜ୍ୱଳତା *This shampoo will give your hair a lovely shine.*

shiny *adjective* (**shinier, shiniest**) ଉଜ୍ଜ୍ୱଳ, ଚକଚକିଆ *a shiny new car*

ship /ʃɪp/ *noun* a big boat for long journeys on the sea ବଡ଼ ଜାହାଜ, ପୋତ *We went to the Andamans by ship.*

shipwreck /ˈʃɪprek/ *noun* an accident at sea when a ship breaks because of bad weather or because it hits rocks ତୋଫାନ ଇତ୍ୟାଦି ଦ୍ୱାରା ଜାହାଜର ଧ୍ୱଂସପ୍ରାପ୍ତି, ଜାହାଜଦୁର୍ଘଟଣା

shirt /ʃɜːt/ *noun* a thin piece of clothing with sleeves, a collar and buttons down the front that you wear on the top part of your body ଜାମା, କୁର୍ତ୍ତା ସାର୍ଟ୍ ➪ ଚିତ୍ର ପାଇଁ **suit** ଦେଖନ୍ତୁ।

shiver /ʃɪvə(r)/ *verb* (**shivers, shivering, shivered**) shake because you are cold, frightened or ill ଥରିବା, କମ୍ପିବା *We were shivering with cold.*

shoal /ʃəʊl/ *noun* a large group of fish that swims together ମାଛର ଦଳ ବା ପଲ

shock[1] /ʃɒk/ *noun* **1** a very bad surprise ବିସ୍ମୟକର ମାନସିକ ଆଘାତ *The news of his failure was a shock to all of us.* **2** a sudden pain when electricity goes through your body ବୈଦ୍ୟୁତିକ ପ୍ରଘାତ, ସକ୍ *Don't touch that wire—you'll get an electric shock.*

shock[2] /ʃɒk/ *verb* (**shocks, shocking, shocked**) give somebody a very bad surprise; upset somebody (କାହାରିକୁ) ବିସ୍ମିତ ବା ଆଚମ୍ବିତ କରିବା; ବିଚଳିତ କରିବା *She was shocked by his failure.*

shocking /ˈʃɒkɪŋ/ *adjective* if something is shocking, it makes you feel upset, angry, or surprised in a very bad way ଆଚମ୍ବିତ ବା ସ୍ତମ୍ଭିତ କଲାପରି; ବିଚଳିତ କଲାପରି *shocking behaviour*

shoe /ʃuː/ *noun* a covering made of leather or plastic that you wear on your feet ଜୋତା *a pair of shoes*

shoelace /ˈʃuːleɪs/ *noun* a string that you use to tie up your shoe with ଜୋତାଫିତା, ଜୋତାଲେସ୍ *Tie your shoelaces.*

shone ଶବ୍ଦ **shine** ର ଏକ ଧାତୁରୂପ

shook ଶବ୍ଦ **shake** ର ଏକ ଧାତୁରୂପ

shoot[1] /ʃuːt/ *verb* (**shoots, shooting, shot** /ʃɒt/, **has shot**) **1** send a bullet from a gun or an arrow from a bow; hurt or kill a person or an animal with a gun ବନ୍ଧୁକ ଇତ୍ୟାଦି ଫୁଟାଇବା ବା ଏଥିରୁ ଗୁଳି ମାରିବା; ଧନୁରୁ ତୀର ମାରିବା; ଗୁଳି ମାରି ଆହତ କରିବା ବା ମାରିଦେବା *She shot a bird.* ○ *The police officer was shot in the arm.* **2** move quickly or suddenly କ୍ଷିପ୍ର ଗତିରେ ଯିବା *The car shot past us.* **3** make a film ଚଳଚ୍ଚିତ୍ର ଉତ୍ତୋଳନ କରିବା, ଫିଲ୍ମ ଶୁଟିଂ କରିବା *They are shooting a film about the war.*

shoot² /ʃuːt/ *noun* a new part of a plant; the part of a plant that grows up from the ground when that plant starts to grow ଅଙ୍କୁର, ଗଜା, ମଞ୍ଜିରୁ ଗଜୁରିଥିବା ଅଂଶ *The first shoots appear in spring.*

shop¹ /ʃɒp/ *noun* a building where you buy things from ଦୋକାନ *a bookshop*

shopkeeper /ˈʃɒpkiːpə(r)/ *noun* a person who owns a small shop ଦୋକାନୀ

shop² /ʃɒp/ *verb* (**shops, shopping, shopped**) go to buy things from shops ଦୋକାନମାନଙ୍କରୁ କିଣିବା *I'm shopping for some new clothes.*

shopper *noun* a person who is buying things କିଣିଲା ବାଲା *The streets were full of shoppers.*

shopping /ˈʃɒpɪŋ/ *noun* (*no plural*) **1** the activity of buying things from shops ଦୋକାନରୁ ଜିନିଷପତ୍ର କିଣିବା *She does her shopping after work.* **2** the things that you have bought in a shop ଦୋକାନରୁ କିଣାଯାଇଥିବା ପଦାର୍ଥ *Will you carry my shopping for me?*

go shopping go to buy things from shops ବଜାର ଦୋକାନରୁ କିଣିବାକୁ ଯିବା

shopping centre *noun* (*plural* **shopping centres**) a place where there are a lot of shops together ବହୁ ଦୋକାନ ଥିବା ସ୍ଥାନ

shopping mall *noun* (*plural* **shopping malls**) a big building where there are a lot of shops together ବହୁ ଦୋକାନ ଥିବା ବଡ଼କୋଠା

shore /ʃɔː(r)/ *noun* the land along the edge of the sea or a lake ସମୁଦ୍ର ବା ହ୍ରଦରତଟ ➪ ଚିତ୍ର ପାଇଁ **sea** ଦେଖନ୍ତୁ।

short /ʃɔːt/ *adjective* (**shorter, shortest**) **1** very little from one end to the other ଲମ୍ବାରେ ଛୋଟ ହୋଇଥିବା, ସାନ *Her hair is very short.* ○ *We live a short distance from the beach.* ✪ ବିପରୀତ **long¹ 1** **2** very little from the bottom to the top ଉଚ୍ଚତାରେ ଛୋଟ, ଗେଡ଼ା *I'm too short to reach the top shelf.* ✪ ବିପରୀତ **tall 1** **3** that only lasts for a little time ଛୋଟ, ଅଳ୍ପକ୍ଷଣ ସ୍ଥାୟୀ *The film was very short.* ○ *a short holiday* ✪ ବିପରୀତ **long¹ 3**

be short of something not have enough of something ନିଅଣ୍ଟ ହେବା *I'm short of money this month.*

shortage /ˈʃɔːtɪdʒ/ *noun* a situation when there is not enough of something ସ୍ୱଳ୍ପତା, ଅଭାବ *a water shortage*

short cut *noun* (*plural* **short cuts**) a shorter or easier way to get somewhere or do something ଶୀଘ୍ର ପହଞ୍ଚିବାର ବାଟ; ସହଜ ପଦ୍ଧତି *We took a short cut to school across the field.*

shorten /ˈʃɔːtn/ *verb* (**shortens, shortening, shortened**) become shorter or make something shorter ଛୋଟ କରିବା *The trousers were too long, so I shortened them.*

shortly /ˈʃɔːtli/ *adverb* soon ଶୀଘ୍ର, ଅଳ୍ପ ସମୟରେ *The doctor will see you shortly, Mr Kapoor.* ○ *We left shortly after six o'clock.*

shorts /ʃɔ:ts/ *noun (no singular)* short trousers that end above your knees ଅଧା ପ୍ୟାଣ୍ଟ, ହାଫ୍ ପ୍ୟାଣ୍ଟ *a pair of shorts*

shot[1] ଶବ୍ଦ **shoot**[1] ର ଏକ ଧାତୁରୂପ

shot[2] /ʃɒt/ *noun* **1** the act of firing a gun, or the noise that this makes ବନ୍ଧୁକ ଚାଳନ, ଗୁଳି ନିକ୍ଷେପ *He fired a shot.* **2** a photograph ଆଲୋକଚିତ୍ର, ଫଟୋ *This is a good shot of you.* **3** the act of kicking or hitting a ball in a sport like football (ଫୁଟ୍‌ବଲ୍ ଇତ୍ୟାଦି ଖେଳରେ) ବଲ୍‌କୁ ଗୋଡ଼ରେ ମାରିବା

should /ʃʊd/ *modal verb* **1** a word that you use to tell or ask somebody what is the right thing to do କାହାରିକୁ ଠିକ୍ କାମ କରିବାକୁ କହିଲାବେଳେ ବ୍ୟବହୃତ ଶବ୍ଦ; ଉଚିତ୍ *If you feel ill, you should stay in bed.* ○ *Should I invite him to the party?* **2** a word that you use to say what you think will happen or what you think is true ଘଟିବାକୁ ଥିବା ବିଷୟ ସୂଚାଉଥିବା ଶବ୍ଦ; ଉଚିତ୍ *They should arrive soon.* **3** the word for 'shall' in the past; 'shall' ର ଭବିଷ୍ୟତ କାଳ *We asked if we should help her.*

> ✪ **Should** ର ନକାରାତ୍ମକ ଶବ୍ଦ ହେଲା **should not** ବା ଏହାର ସଂକ୍ଷିପ୍ତ ରୂପ **shouldn't**—*You shouldn't eat so much chocolate.*
> ➪ **modal verb** ପାଇଁ ଟିପ୍ପଣୀ ଦେଖନ୍ତୁ।

shoulder /ˈʃəʊldə(r)/ *noun* the part of your body between your neck and the top of your arm କାନ୍ଧ ➪ ଚିତ୍ର ପାଇଁ **body** ଦେଖନ୍ତୁ।

shouldn't = **should not**

shout /ʃaʊt/ *verb* (**shouts, shouting, shouted**) say or call very loudly ଚିତ୍କାର କରିବା, ପାଟିକରିବା *Don't shout at me!* ○ *'Go back!' she shouted.*

shout *noun* ଚିତ୍କାର, ବଡ଼ ପାଟିର ବା ଉଚ୍ଚ ସ୍ୱରର ଡାକ *We heard a shout for help.*

shovel /ˈʃʌvl/ *noun* a tool like a **spade** with a short handle, that you use for moving soil or sand, for example ମାଟି ଖୋଳା କୋଡ଼ି ➪ ଚିତ୍ର ପାଇଁ **tools** ଦେଖନ୍ତୁ।

shovel *verb* (**shovels, shovelling, shovelled**) move something with a shovel କୋଡ଼ିରେ ମାଟି ଇତ୍ୟାଦି ଖୋଳି କାଢ଼ିବା *We shovelled the snow off the path.*

show[1] /ʃəʊ/ *verb* (**shows, showing, showed, has shown** /ʃəʊn/ **has showed**) **1** let somebody see something ଦେଖାଇବା *She showed me her holiday photographs.* ○ *You have to show your ticket on the train.* **2** make something clear; explain something to somebody (କୌଣସି ବିଷୟ) ସ୍ପଷ୍ଟ କରିବା; ବୁଝାଇବା *Can you show me how to use the computer?*

show off talk loudly or do something silly to make people notice you ବଡ଼ ପାଟିରେ କଥାବାର୍ତ୍ତା ହେବା; ଦେଖେଇ ହେବା, ବାହାଦୁରୀ ମାରିବା *Rahul drove his new car very fast to show off.*

show up arrive ପହଞ୍ଚିଯିବା *What time did they show up?*

show² /ʃəʊ/ *noun* **1** a play or programme that you watch at the theatre or on television ନାଟକ ବା ଟେଲିଭିଜନ୍‌ର କାର୍ଯ୍ୟକ୍ରମ *a comedy show* ○ *Did you enjoy the show?* **2** a group of things in one place that people go to see ପ୍ରଦର୍ଶନୀ, ମେଳା *a flower show*

shower /ˈʃaʊə(r)/ *noun* **1** a place where you can wash yourself by standing under water that falls in a spray from above you ଝରଝର ପାଣି ପଡୁଥିବା ଶାୱାର (ଗାଧୋଇବା ପାଇଁ) *There's a shower in the bathroom.* **2** the act of washing yourself in a shower ଶାୱାର ତଳେ ଗାଧୁଆ *I had a shower after the football match.* **3** rain that falls for a short time ଅଳ୍ପ ସମୟର ବର୍ଷା

shown ଶବ୍ଦ **show¹** ର ଏକ ଧାତୁରୂପ

showroom /ˈʃəʊruːm/ *noun* a large shop where you can look at all the things that are kept on sale ଗ୍ରାହକ ମାନଙ୍କ ପାଇଁ ଜିନିଷପତ୍ର ସଜାହୋଇ ରଖାଯାଇଥିବା ଦୋକାନଘର; ଦୋକାନର ପ୍ରଦର୍ଶନୀ କୋଠରୀ *a car showroom*

shrank ଶବ୍ଦ **shrink** ର ଏକ ଧାତୁରୂପ

shred /ʃred/ *noun* a small thin piece torn or cut off from something ସରୁ ଟୁକୁରା *shreds of paper*

shrewd /ʃruːd/ *adjective* (**shrewder, shrewdest**) clever and having the ability to take good decisions ଚତୁର ଓ ନ୍ୟାୟବାନ୍ *a shrewd businessman*

shriek /ʃriːk/ *verb* (**shrieks, shrieking, shrieked**) make a loud high cry ଚିତ୍କାର କରିବା *She shrieked in fear.*

shriek *noun* ଚିତ୍କାର *He gave a shriek of pain.*

shrill /ʃrɪl/ *adjective* (**shriller, shrillest**) a shrill sound is high and loud ତୀବ୍ର ଓ ଉଚ୍ଚ ଧ୍ୱନି *a shrill whistle*

shrimp /ʃrɪmp/ *noun* a small sea animal like a small **prawn**, that you can eat ଛୋଟ ଚିଙ୍ଗୁଡ଼ି

shrine /ʃraɪn/ *noun* a special holy place ପ୍ରାର୍ଥନା ବା ଆରାଧନା ସ୍ଥାନ; ମନ୍ଦିର *the shrine at Badrinath*

shrink /ʃrɪŋk/ *verb* (**shrinks, shrinking, shrank** /ʃræŋk/ ବା **shrunk** /ʃrʌŋk/, **has shrunk**) become smaller or make something smaller ସଙ୍କୁଚିତ ହେବା ବା କରିବା *My jeans shrank when I washed them.*

shrub /ʃrʌb/ *noun* a plant like a small low tree ବୁଦା, ଗୁଳ୍ମ

shrug /ʃrʌg/ *verb* (**shrugs, shrugging, shrugged**) move your shoulders up slightly to show that you do not know or do not care about something (ସନ୍ଦେହ ବା ଔଦାସୀନ୍ୟ ସୂଚାଇବା ପାଇଁ) କାନ୍ଧକୁ ଟିକିଏ ଉପରକୁ ଉଠାଇବା *I asked her where Sanjay was but she just shrugged.*

shrug *noun* (*no plural*) (ସନ୍ଦେହ ବା ଔଦାସୀନ୍ୟ ସୂଚାଇବା ପାଇଁ) କାନ୍ଧହଲା *He answered my question with a shrug.*

shudder /ˈʃʌdə(r)/ *verb* (**shudders, shuddering, shuddered**) shake, for example because you are afraid ଥରିବା, କମ୍ପିବା (ଡର ବା ଥଣ୍ଡା ଯୋଗୁଁ) *He shuddered when he saw the snake.*

shut[1] /ʃʌt/ *verb* (**shuts, shutting, shut, has shut**) **1** move something to close an opening ବନ୍ଦ କରିବା *Could you shut the door, please?* **2** stop being open, so that people cannot go there ବନ୍ଦ ହେବା *The shops shut at 5.30 p.m.* ✪ ବିପରୀତ **open**[2]

shut down close and stop working; make something close and stop working ବନ୍ଦ କରିବା, ବନ୍ଦ ହେବା *The factory shut down last year.*

shut[2] /ʃʌt/ *adjective* closed; not open ବନ୍ଦ; ଖୋଲା ନଥିବା *The restaurant is shut today.* ○ *Is the door shut?*

shutter /ˈʃʌtə(r)/ *noun* a wooden or metal thing that covers the outside of a window ଝରକାର କବାଟ *Close the shutters.*

shuttle /ˈʃʌtl/ *noun* an aeroplane, a train or bus that goes regularly to a place and then back ନିୟମିତ ଭାବେ କୌଣସି ଜାଗାକୁ ଯାଇ ଫେରି ଆସୁଥିବା ରେଳଗାଡ଼ି, ବସ୍ ବା ଉଡ଼ାଜାହାଜ

shuttlecock /ˈʃʌtˌlkɒk/ *noun* a small light object that players hit with rackets over the net in a game of **badminton** ବ୍ୟାଡ୍‌ମିଣ୍ଟନ୍ ଖେଳରେ ବ୍ୟବହୃତ ପରଯୁକ୍ତ ସଟ୍ଲକକ୍

shy /ʃaɪ/ *adjective* (**shyer, shyest**) not able to talk easily to people you do not know ଲାଜକୁଳା *He was too shy to speak to her.*

shyness *noun* (*no plural*) the quality of being shy ଲାଜକୁଳା ସ୍ୱଭାବ

sick /sɪk/ *adjective* (**sicker, sickest**) not well; ill ପୀଡ଼ିତ, ଅସୁସ୍ଥ *She's looking after her sick mother.*

be sick when you are sick, food comes up from your stomach and out of your mouth ବାନ୍ତି କରିବା

feel sick feel that food is going to come up from your stomach ବାନ୍ତି ଲାଗିବା

sickness /ˈsɪknəs/ *noun* (*no plural*) illness ଅସୁସ୍ଥତା *He could not work for a long time because of sickness.*

side /saɪd/ *noun* **1** one of the flat surfaces of something କଡ଼, ପାର୍ଶ୍ୱ *A box has six sides.* **2** the part of something that is not the front, back, top or bottom କଡ଼, କଡ଼ପଟ, ପାର୍ଶ୍ୱ (ଆଗ, ପଛ, ଉପର ଓ ତଳକୁ ଛାଡ଼ି) *There is a door at the side of the house.* **3** the edge of something; the part that is away from the middle କଡ଼, ପ୍ରାନ୍ତ *I stood at the side of the road.* **4** the right or left part of something (କାହାରି) ଡାହାଣ ବା ବାଁ ପଟ *He lay on his side.* ○ *We drive on the left side of the road in India.* **5** one of two groups of people who fight or play a game against each other (ଲଢ଼େଇ ବା ଖେଳରେ) ପକ୍ଷ, ଦଳ *Which side won?*

be on somebody's side agree with or help somebody in a fight or an argument (କାହାରି) ପକ୍ଷରେ ରହିବା

side by side next to each other ପାଖକୁ ପାଖ, ଲଗାଲଗି *They walked side by side.*

sideways /ˈsaɪdweɪz/ *adjective, adverb* to or from the side କଡ଼ ପଟିଆ, କଡ଼କୁ *She looked sideways at the girl next to her.*

siege /si:dʒ/ *noun* a time when an army stays outside a town for a long time so that people and things cannot get in or out (ସହର, ଦୁର୍ଗ ଇତ୍ୟାଦିର ବିପକ୍ଷ ସୈନ୍ୟଙ୍କ ଦ୍ଵାରା) ଅବରୋଧ

sieve /sɪv/ *noun* a kitchen tool with a net, used for separating solids from liquid or smaller pieces of solids from larger ones ଚାଲୁଣୀ; ଛାଙ୍କୁଣୀ

sieve *verb* (**sieves, sieving, sieved**) ଚାଲୁଣୀରେ ଚଳାଇବା; ଛାଙ୍କିବା

sigh /saɪ/ *verb* (**sighs, sighing, sighed**) breathe once very deeply when you are sad, tired or pleased, for example ଦୀର୍ଘଶ୍ଵାସ ନେବା

sigh *noun* ଦୀର୍ଘଶ୍ଵାସ, ଲମ୍ବା ନିଶ୍ଵାସ *'I wish I had more money,' he said with a sigh.*

sight /saɪt/ *noun* **1** (*no plural*) the power to see ଦୃଷ୍ଟିଶକ୍ତି *She has poor sight.* **2** (*plural* **sights**) something that you see ଦୃଶ୍ୟ, ଦେଖାଯାଉଥିବା ବସ୍ତୁ ବା ଘଟଣା *The mountains were a beautiful sight.* **3** (*plural* **sights**) the interesting places to visit ସୁନ୍ଦର ବା ସୁଦୃଶ୍ୟ ସ୍ଥାନ *When you come to Agra, I'll show you the sights.*

at first sight the time when you see somebody or something for the first time ପ୍ରଥମ ଦେଖାରେ

come into sight come where you can see it ଦିଶିବା, ଦୃଷ୍ଟିଗୋଚର ହେବା *The train came into sight.*

out of sight where you cannot see it ଦୃଷ୍ଟି ପରିସର ବାହାରକୁ, ଦୃଷ୍ଟିଅଗୋଚର *We watched until the car was out of sight.*

sighting /ˈsaɪtɪŋ/ *noun* the act of spotting something ଦିଶିବା, ଦୃଷ୍ଟି ପରିସରକୁ ଆସିବା ପ୍ରକ୍ରିୟା, ଦୃଶ୍ୟମାନ ହେବା ପ୍ରକ୍ରିୟା *the sighting of a new comet*

sightseeing /ˈsaɪtsi:ɪŋ/ *noun* (*no plural*) the activity of visiting interesting places ବୁଲି ଦେଖିବା ପାଇଁ ପରିଭ୍ରମଣ *We did some sightseeing in Goa.*

sign[1] /saɪn/ *noun* **1** a mark, shape or movement that has a special meaning ଚିହ୍ନ, ସଙ୍କେତ *+ and – are signs that mean 'plus' and 'minus'.* ○ *I put up my hand as a sign for him to stop.* **2** a thing with writing or a picture on it that tells you something ଦିଗ, ରାସ୍ତା ଇତ୍ୟାଦି ଦେଖାଉଥିବା ଲେଖା, ଚିତ୍ର ବା ଚିହ୍ନଥିବା ଖୁଣ୍ଟ *The sign said: 'No Parking'* **3** something that tells you that another thing may happen ଭବିଷ୍ୟତ ଘଟଣାର ସଙ୍କେତ *Dark clouds are a sign of rain.*

sign[2] /saɪn/ *verb* (**signs, signing, signed**) write your name in your own way on something ଦସ୍ତଖତ କରିବା *Sign here, please.* ○ *I signed the cheque.* ✪ Sign ଶବ୍ଦର ବିଶେଷ୍ୟ ରୂପ ହେଲା **signature**।

signal /ˈsɪgnəl/ *noun* a light, sound or movement that tells you something ଆଲୋକ, ଧ୍ଵନି ବା ହାତ ଇତ୍ୟାଦିର ଚାଳନ

ଦ୍ୱାରା ଦିଆଯାଉଥିବା ସଙ୍କେତ *traffic signals* ○ *radio signals*

signal *verb* (**signals, signalling, signalled**) make a signal ସଙ୍କେତ ଦେବା *The policeman signalled to the children to cross the road.*

signature /ˈsɪgnətʃə(r)/ *noun* your name that you have written in your own way ଦସ୍ତଖତ, ସ୍ୱାକ୍ଷର

significance /sɪgˈnɪfɪkəns/ *noun* (*no plural*) the importance or meaning of something ତାତ୍ପର୍ଯ୍ୟ, ନିହିତାର୍ଥ, ପ୍ରକୃତ ଅର୍ଥ; ଗୁରୁତ୍ୱ *What is the significance of this discovery?*

significant /sɪgˈnɪfɪkənt/ *adjective* important; with a special meaning ଗୁରୁତ୍ୱପୂର୍ଣ୍ଣ; ଗୁଣ ଅର୍ଥ ଥିବା; ଉଲ୍ଲେଖଯୋଗ୍ୟ ✪ ବିପରୀତ **insignificant**

significantly *adverb* ବିଶେଷ ଭାବରେ, ଗୁରୁତ୍ୱପୂର୍ଣ୍ଣ ଭାବରେ *The new law is significantly different.*

signpost /ˈsaɪnpəʊst/ *noun* a sign beside a road, that shows the way to a place and how far it is ମାର୍ଗଦର୍ଶକ ସ୍ତମ୍ଭ ବା ଖୁଣ୍ଟ

signpost

Sikh *noun* a person who follows one of the religions of India, called **sikhism** ଶିଖ ଧର୍ମର ବ୍ୟକ୍ତି

Sikhism *noun* (*no plural*) a religion founded by Guru Nanak ଗୁରୁ ନାନକଙ୍କ ଦ୍ୱାରା ସ୍ଥାପିତ ଶିଖ ଧର୍ମ

silence /ˈsaɪləns/ *noun* when there is silence, there is no sound or nobody speaks ନୀରବତା, ନିସ୍ତବ୍ଧତା *I can work only in complete silence.*

silent /ˈsaɪlənt/ *adjective* **1** with no sound; completely quiet ନୀରବ, ନିସ୍ତବ୍ଧ *Everyone was asleep, and the house was silent.* **2** if you are silent, you are not speaking ନୀରବ *I asked him a question and he was silent for a moment before he answered.*

silently *adverb* ଚୁପଚାପ୍, ଶବ୍ଦନକରି *The cat moved silently towards the bird.*

silk /sɪlk/ *noun* (*no plural*) a thin smooth cloth that is made from the threads that an insect (called a silkworm) produces to make its **cocoon** ରେଶମ, ପାଟ, ସିଲ୍କ *This scarf is made of silk.*

silly /ˈsɪli/ *adjective* (**sillier, silliest**) stupid; not clever ବୋକା, ନିର୍ବୋଧ; ଅଚତୁର *It was silly of you to leave the door open when you went out.*

silver /ˈsɪlvə(r)/ *noun* (*no plural*) a shiny grey metal that is very valuable ରୁପା, ରଜତ, ରୌପ୍ୟ *a silver necklace*

silver *adjective* with the colour of silver ରୁପା ପରି, ରୁପା ରଙ୍ଗର *silver paper*

similar /ˈsɪmələ(r)/ *adjective* the same in some ways but not completely the same ଏକାପରି, ସମାନ, ସଦୃଶ *Rats are similar to mice, but they are bigger.* ✪ ବିପରୀତ **different**

similarity /ˌsɪməˈlærəti/ *noun* (*plural* **similarities**) a way that people or things are the same ସାଦୃଶ୍ୟ, ସମାନତା *There are a lot of similarities between the two countries.* ✪ ବିପରୀତ **difference**

similarly *adverb* ଏକାପରି *This door is similarly painted.*

simile /ˈsɪmɪli/ *noun* a word or phrase that compares something to something else by using words such as 'as' or 'like', for example 'as white as snow' or 'innocent like a child' ତୁଳନା, ଉପମା, ଯଥା କାଚକେନ୍ଦୁ ପରି ପାଣି

simple /ˈsɪmpl/ *adjective* (**simpler, simplest**) **1** easy to do or understand ସରଳ, ସହଜ *This dictionary is written in simple English.* **2** without a lot of different parts or extra things; plain ବହୁତଗୁଡ଼ାଏ ଜିନିଷ; ଯନ୍ତ୍ର ବା ଚିତ୍ର ନଥିବା; ସାଦାସିଧା *a simple design*

simplify /ˈsɪmplɪfaɪ/ *verb* (**simplifies, simplifying, simplified, has simplified**) make something easier to do or understand ସରଳ, ସୁଗମ ବା ସୁବୋଧ୍ୟ କରିବା *The story has been simplified so that children can understand it.*

simply /ˈsɪmpli/ *adverb* **1** in a simple way ସରଳ ଭାବରେ *Please explain it more simply.* **2** only କେବଳ *Don't get angry—I'm simply asking you to help.*

simultaneous /ˌsɪməlˈteɪniəs/ *adjective* happening or done at the same time as something else ଏକକାଳୀନ, ସମକାଳୀନ

sin /sɪn/ *noun* something that a religion says you should not do, because it is wrong ପାପ, ଅଧର୍ମ *Stealing is a sin.*

sin *verb* (**sins, sinning, sinned**) do something that a religion says is wrong ପାପ କରିବା, ଅଧର୍ମ କରିବା

since /sɪns/ *preposition* in all the time after ନିର୍ଦ୍ଦିଷ୍ଟ ସମୟ ବା ଘଟଣା ଠାରୁ *I haven't seen him since 1987.*

since *conjunction* **1** from the time when ସେହି ସମୟରୁ, ତା' ପରଠୁଁ *She has lived here since she was a child.* **2** because ଯେହେତୁ *Since it's your birthday, I'll buy you a gift.*

since *adverb* from then until now ଏହା ମଧ୍ୟରେ, ସେହି ସମୟଠାରୁ *Aman left three years ago and we haven't seen him since.*

for or **since**?

ଆମେ ଘଟଣାର ସମୟକାଳ ସୂଚାଇବା ପାଇଁ **for** ବ୍ୟବହାର କରୁ, ଯଥା— ସମୟ, ଦିନ ଗୁଡ଼ିକ ବା ବର୍ଷ

*She has been ill **for** three days.*
*I have lived in London **for** ten months.*
*We have been married **for** thirty years.*

ଆମେ ଅତୀତର ନିର୍ଦ୍ଦିଷ୍ଟ ତାରିଖ (date), ସମୟ (time) ବା ଘଟଣା (event) ସୂଚାଇବା ପାଇଁ **since** ବ୍ୟବହାର କରୁ ଯଥା—

*I have been here **since** six o'clock.*
*She has been alone **since** her son moved to Mumbai.*
*We have been married **since** 1965.*

sincere /sɪnˈsɪə(r)/ *adjective* if you are sincere, you are honest and you mean what you say ଆନ୍ତରିକତା ଥିବା, ଛଳନାମୁକ୍ତ; ସଚ୍ଚୋଟ, ଅକପଟ *a sincere student*

sincerely *adverb*

Yours sincerely words that you write at the end of a letter before your name, when you have addressed the person by their name like 'Dear Nandita' or 'Dear Vikram' ଚିଠି ଶେଷରେ ଲେଖାଯାଉଥିବା ସୂତ୍ର: ଆପଣଙ୍କର ବିଶ୍ୱସ୍ତ

sing /sɪŋ/ *verb* (**sings, singing, sang** /sæŋ/, **has sung** /sʌŋ) make music with your voice (ଗୀତ) ଗାଇବା, ଗାନ କରିବା *She sang a song.* ○ *The birds were singing.*

singer *noun* a person who sings ଗାୟକ, ଗାୟିକା

single /ˈsɪŋgl/ *adjective* **1** only one ଗୋଟିଏ ମାତ୍ର *There wasn't a single cloud in the sky.* **2** not married ଅବିବାହିତ ବା ଅବିବାହିତା *Are you married or single?* **3** for one person ଜଣଙ୍କ ପାଇଁ ଥିବା *I would like to book a single room, please.* ✪ ବିପରୀତ **double**

singular /ˈsɪŋgjələ(r)/ *noun* (*no plural*) (in grammar) the form of a word that you use for one person or thing (ବ୍ୟାକରଣରେ) ଏକବଚନ ଶବ୍ଦ *The singular of 'men' is 'man'.*

singular *adjective* ଏକବଚନ; ଅଦ୍ୱିତୀୟ; ଅସାଧାରଣ *'Table' is a singular noun.* ➪ **plural** ଦେଖନ୍ତୁ।

sink[1] /sɪŋk/ *noun* a large open container, especially in a kitchen that has taps to supply water and in which you wash dishes ବାସନକୁସନ ମଜାଧୁଆ ପାଇଁ ଥିବା କଳ ଓ ନିର୍ଗମ ନଳ ଥିବା କୁଣ୍ଡ ବା ବେସିନ୍; ସିଙ୍କ୍

sink[2] /sɪŋk/ *verb* (**sinks, sinking, sank** /sæŋk/, **has sunk** /sʌŋk/) go down under water towards the bottom ବୁଡ଼ିଯିବା, ଡୁବିଯିବା *If you throw a stone into water, it sinks.* ○ *The fishing boat sank to the bottom of the sea.* ✪ ବିପରୀତ **float 1**

sip /sɪp/ *verb* (**sips, sipping, sipped**) drink something slowly, taking only a little each time ଅଳ୍ପ ଅଳ୍ପ ବା ସୁଡୁକା ସୁଡୁକା କରି ପିଇବା *She sipped her coffee.*

sip *noun* ସିପ୍ ତରଳ ପଦାର୍ଥର ଅଳ୍ପ ଢ଼ୋକ, ସୁଡୁକା *Can I have a sip of your Coke?*

sir /sɜː(r)/ *noun* **1** (*no plural*) a polite way of speaking to a man, instead of using his name ବ୍ୟକ୍ତିଙ୍କ ପ୍ରତି ଭଦ୍ର ସମ୍ବୋଧନ, ମହାଶୟ, ସାର୍; ଶିକ୍ଷକଙ୍କ ପ୍ରତି ସମ୍ବୋଧନ ଶବ୍ଦ, ସାର୍ *'Can I help you, sir?' asked the salesman.* ➪ **madam** ଦେଖନ୍ତୁ। **2 Sir** (*no plural*) a word that you use at the beginning of a business letter to a man *Dear Sir...* ବ୍ୟବସାୟିକ ଚିଠିର ଆରମ୍ଭରେ ଲେଖାଯାଉଥିବା ସମ୍ବୋଧନ ଶବ୍ଦ ➪ **madam** ଦେଖନ୍ତୁ। **3 Sir** (*no plural*) the word that you use before the name of a **knight** ନାଇଟ୍ ବା ବ୍ୟାରନେଟ୍ ଉପାଧିଧାରୀ ବ୍ୟକ୍ତିଙ୍କ ପ୍ରତି ସମ୍ବୋଧନ ଶବ୍ଦ *Sir Winston Churchill*

siren /ˈsaɪrən/ *noun* a machine that makes a long loud sound to warn people about something. Police cars and fire engines have sirens ପ୍ରଲମ୍ବିତ ସତର୍କ ଘଣ୍ଟି ବା ଧ୍ୱନି କରୁଥିବା ଯନ୍ତ୍ର; ଏହାର ଧ୍ୱନି, ସାଇରେନ୍

sister /'sɪstə(r)/ *noun* **1** your sister is a girl or woman who has the same parents as you ଭଉଣୀ *I've got two sisters and one brother.* ➪ ଚିତ୍ର ପାଇଁ **family** ଦେଖନ୍ତୁ । **2** a nurse in a hospital ଡାକ୍ତରଖାନାର ନର୍ସ

sister-in-law *noun* (*plural* **sisters-in-law**) **1** the sister of your wife or husband ଶାଳୀ; ନଣନ୍ଦ **2** the wife of your brother ଭାଇବୋହୂ; ଭାଉଜ ➪ ଚିତ୍ର ପାଇଁ **family tree** ଦେଖନ୍ତୁ ।

sit /sɪt/ *verb* (**sits, sitting, sat** /sæt/, **has sat**) **1** rest on your bottom ବସିବା *We sat in the garden all afternoon.* ○ *She was sitting on the sofa.* **2** (**sit down** ମଧ୍ୟ) put yourself down on your bottom ବସିଯିବା *Come and sit next to me.* ○ *She came into the room and sat down.*

sit up sit when you have been lying ଶୋଇଥିବା ଅବସ୍ଥାରୁ ଉଠି ବସିବା *He sat up in bed and looked at the clock.*

sitting room /'sɪtɪŋ ru:m/ *noun* a room in a house where people sit and watch television or talk, for example ବସାଉଠା କରିବା କୋଠରି, ବୈଠକଖାନା, ଦାଣ୍ଡଘର

site /saɪt/ *noun* a place where something is, was, or will be (ଘର, ସହର ଇତ୍ୟାଦି ତିଆରି କରିବା) ସ୍ଥାନ ବା ଜାଗା *This house was built on the site of an old theatre.*

situated /'sɪtʃueɪtɪd/ *adjective* in a particular place ଅବସ୍ଥିତ *The hotel is situated close to the beach.*

situation /ˌsɪtʃu'eɪʃn/ *noun* the things that are happening in a certain place or at a certain time ପରିସ୍ଥିତି, ଅବସ୍ଥା *Seema is in a difficult situation—she can't decide what to do.*

six /sɪks/ *number* (*plural* **sixes**) 6 ସଂଖ୍ୟା ୬

sixth /sɪksθ/ *adjective, adverb, noun* **1** 6th ୬ଷ୍ଠ (ଷଷ୍ଠ) **2** one of six equal parts of something; $\frac{1}{6}$ ଛ' ଭାଗରୁ ଏକ ଭାଗ $\frac{୧}{୬}$

sixteen /ˌsɪks'ti:n/ *number* 16 ସଂଖ୍ୟା, ୧୬

sixteenth /ˌsɪks'ti:nθ/ *adjective, adverb, noun* 16th ୧୬ତମ

sixty /'sɪksti/ *number* **1** 60 ସଂଖ୍ୟା ୬୦ **2 the sixties** (*plural*) the numbers, years or temperatures between 60 and 69 ୬୦ ରୁ ୬୯ ପର୍ଯ୍ୟନ୍ତ ସଂଖ୍ୟା, ବୟସ, ଶତକର ବର୍ଷ ବା ଉତ୍ତାପ

sixtieth /'sɪkstiəθ/ *adjective, adverb, noun* 60th ୬୦ତମ

size /saɪz/ *noun* **1** (*no plural*) the amount or number that tells you how big or small something is ଆକାର, ଆୟତନ, ପରିମାଣ *My bedroom is the same size as yours.* **2** (*plural* **sizes**) an exact measurement ମାପ *Have you got these shoes in a bigger size?*

skate /skeɪt/ *noun* **1** an ice skate; a boot with a thin metal blade under it, that you wear for moving on ice ବରଫ ଉପରେ ଦ୍ରୁତ ଗତିରେ ଖସଡ଼ି ଯିବା ପାଇଁ ବ୍ୟବହୃତ ଲୁହାଧାରଯୁକ୍ତ ଜୋତା, ସ୍କେଟ୍ *a pair of skates* **2** a roller skate; a shoe with small wheels on the bottom, that you wear for moving quickly on smooth ground ଗଡ଼ି ଗଡ଼ି ଚାଲିବା ପାଇଁ ଚକଲଗା ଜୋତା, ରୋଲର୍ ସ୍କେଟ୍

skate *verb* (**skates, skating, skated**) move on skates ସ୍କେଟ୍ ପିନ୍ଧି ଖସଡ଼ି ବା ଗଡ଼ି ଗଡ଼ି ଚାଲିବା ✪ ସ୍କେଟିଂ କରିବାକୁ ଯିବାପାଇଁ **go skating** *We go skating every weekend.*

skating rink *noun* **1** ➪ **ice rink** ଦେଖନ୍ତୁ। **2** a special place for roller skating ରୋଲର୍ ସ୍କେଟ୍ ପିନ୍ଧି ଖେଳିବା ପାଇଁ ବିଶେଷ ସ୍ଥାନ, ସ୍କେଟିଂରିଙ୍କ୍

skeleton /ˈskelɪtn/ *noun* the bones of a whole animal or person କଙ୍କାଳ

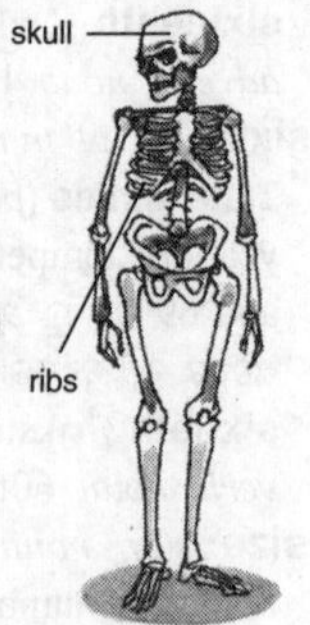

sketch /sketʃ/ *verb* (**sketches, sketching, sketched**) draw something quickly ଚଟାପଟ୍ ଅଙ୍କନ କରିବା। *I sketched the house.*

sketch *noun* (*plural* **sketches**) a picture that you draw quickly ଶୀଘ୍ର ଅଙ୍କା ଯାଇଥିବା ରେଖାଚିତ୍ର ବା ନକ୍ସା

ski /skiː/ *noun* (*plural* **skis**) a long flat piece of wood, metal or plastic that you fix to your boot so that you can move over snow ତୁଷାର ଉପରେ ଖସଡ଼ି ଯିବାପାଇଁ ବୁଟ ପାଦରେ ଲମ୍ବା ମାନ୍ଥିବା ପଟା, ସ୍କୀ *a pair of skis*

ski *verb* (**skis, skiing, skied, has skied**) move over snow on skis ସ୍କୀ ପିନ୍ଧି ତୁଷାର ଉପରେ ଖସଡ଼ି ଚାଲିବା *Can you ski?* ✪ ସ୍କୀ କରିବାକୁ ଯିବାପାଇଁ କହନ୍ତି **go skiing** *We went skiing in Gulmarg.*

skier *noun* a person who skis ସ୍କୀ କରୁଥିବା ବ୍ୟକ୍ତି

skiing *noun* (*no plural*) the sport of moving over snow on skis ସ୍କୀ କରି ଖେଳ

skid /skɪd/ *verb* (**skids, skidding, skidded**) if a car, lorry, etc. skids, it slides suddenly and dangerously to the side or to the front, for example because the road is wet (ଗାଡ଼ି ଇତ୍ୟାଦି) ଓଦା ବା ମସୃଣ ରାସ୍ତା ଉପରେ କଡ଼କୁ ବା ଆଗକୁ ଖସଡ଼ି ଯିବା *The lorry skidded on the icy road.*

skies ଶବ୍ଦ **sky** ର ବହୁବଚନ

skilful /ˈskɪlfl/ *adjective* very good at doing something ନିପୁଣ, ଦକ୍ଷ, କୁଶଳ *a skilful tennis player*

skilfully *adverb* ଦକ୍ଷତାର ସହ, ନିପୁଣ ଭାବରେ *The food was skilfully prepared.*

skill /skɪl/ *noun* **1** (*no plural*) the ability to do something well ଦକ୍ଷତା, ନିପୁଣତା *You need great skill to fly a plane.* **2** (*plural* **skills**) a special thing that you can do well ବିଶେଷ ଦକ୍ଷତା ଥିବା କାମ *What skills do you need for this job?*

skilled /skɪld/ *adjective* good at doing something because you have learnt about or done it for a long time ଦକ୍ଷ, ନିପୁଣ *skilled workers*

skimmed milk *noun* (*no plural*) milk from which cream has been removed ସରକଢ଼ା ଦୁଧ

skin /skɪn/ *noun* **1** (*no plural*) the outer covering of a person or an animal's body ଚମ, ଚର୍ମ, ତ୍ୱଚା *She has dark skin.* **2** (*plural* **skins**) the outside part of some fruit and vegetables (ଫଳ, ପରିବା ଇତ୍ୟାଦିର) ଚୋପା *a banana skin*

skinny /ˈskɪni/ *adjective* (**skinnier, skinniest**) too thin ପତଳା, ଶୀର୍ଣ୍ଣ, ଧେଡ଼ିଆ, ଅସ୍ଥିଚର୍ମସାର *He's very skinny—he doesn't eat enough.*

skip /skɪp/ *verb* (**skips, skipping, skipped**) **1** move along quickly with little jumps from one foot to the other foot ଡେଇଁବା, ଡେଇଁ, ଡେଇଁଚାଲିବା *The child skipped along the road.* **2** jump many times over a rope that is made to pass over your head and under your feet ଦଉଡ଼ି ଘୂରାଇ ତା' ଉପର ଦେଇ ଡେଇଁବା **3** not do or have something that you should do or have ଛାଡ଼ି ଦେବା, ବର୍ଜନ କରିବା *I skipped breakfast today because I was late.*

skip *noun* a little jump ଡିଆଁ

skipping rope *noun* a rope that you use for skipping ଦୁଇ ହାତରେ ଧରି ମୁଣ୍ଡ ଉପର ଓ ଗୋଡ଼ ତଳ ଦେଇ ବୁଲାଯାଉଥିବା ଦଉଡ଼ି (ଖେଳ ବା ବ୍ୟାୟମ ପାଇଁ) ସ୍କିପିଂ ରୋପ୍

skipper /ˈskɪpə(r)/ *noun* the captain of a sports team ଖେଳ ଦଳର ଅଧିନାୟକ ବା କ୍ୟାପ୍ଟେନ୍, ସ୍କିପର୍ *the skipper of the Indian cricket team*

skirt /skɜːt/ *noun* a piece of clothing for a woman or girl that is worn at the waist and hangs down to the knees or ankles (ଅଣ୍ଟାର ତଳକୁ ଝୁଲୁଥିବା) ବାଳିକା ବା ନାରୀମାନଙ୍କର ପୋଷାକ; ଘାଗରା; ସ୍କର୍ଟ୍

skit /skɪt/ *noun* a short funny performance or a piece of writing that copies something to show how silly it is ଛୋଟ ହାସ୍ୟାତ୍ମକ ବା ବ୍ୟଙ୍ଗାତ୍ମକ ନାଟକ *a skit on modern lifestyle*

skull /skʌl/ *noun* the bones in the head that protect the **brain** ଖପୁରି, ମୁଣ୍ଡର ହାଡ଼ ➪ ଚିତ୍ର ପାଇଁ **skeleton** ଦେଖନ୍ତୁ ।

sky /skaɪ/ *noun* (*plural* **skies**) the space above the earth where you can see the sun, moon and stars ଆକାଶ, ନଭୋମଣ୍ଡଳ, ବ୍ୟୋମ, ଗଗନ *a beautiful blue sky* ○ *There were no clouds in the sky.*

skyscraper /ˈskaɪskreɪpə(r)/ *noun* a very tall building ଅତିଉଚ୍ଚ କୋଠା, ଗଗନଚୁମ୍ବୀ ଅଟ୍ଟାଳିକା *He works on the 49th floor of a skyscraper.*

skyscrapers

slab /slæb/ *noun* a thick flat piece of something ଚଟକା ମୋଟା ଆୟତାକାର କଠିନ ପଦାର୍ଥ, ସ୍ଲାବ୍ *slabs of stone*

slam /slæm/ *verb* (**slams, slamming, slammed**) close something or put something down with a loud noise ଧଡ଼୍ କରି ବନ୍ଦ କରିବା ବା ତଳେ ରଖିବା *She slammed the door angrily.*

slant /slɑ:nt/ *verb* (**slants, slanting, slanted**) something that slants has one side higher than the other or does not stand straight up ଗଡ଼ାଣିଆ ହେବା, ତେରଛା ହୋଇ ରହିବା *My handwriting slants to the right.*

slap /slæp/ *verb* (**slaps, slapping, slapped**) hit somebody with the flat inside part of your hand ଚାପୁଡ଼ା ମାରିବା, ଚଟକଣା ମାରିବା *He slapped the thief in the face.*

slap *noun* ଚାପୁଡ଼ା, ଚଟକଣା *She gave him a slap across the face.*

slave /sleɪv/ *noun* a person who belongs to another person and must work for that person for no money ଦାସ, କ୍ରୀତଦାସ, ଗୋଲାମ୍

slavery /ˈsleɪvəri/ *noun* (*no plural*) **1** the state of being a slave ଦାସତ୍ୱ *They lived in slavery.* **2** the practice of keeping slaves ଦାସତ୍ୱପ୍ରଥା *When did slavery end in America?*

sledge /sledʒ/ *noun* a thing that you sit in to move over snow. A sledge has pieces of metal or wood instead of wheels. Large sledges are sometimes pulled by dogs ବରଫ ଓ ତୁଷାର ଉପରେ ଖସି ଚାଲିବା ପାଇଁ ଚକ ନଥିବା ଗାଡ଼ି ➪ ଚିତ୍ର ପାଇଁ **reindeer** ଦେଖନ୍ତୁ।

sleek /sli:k/ *adjective* **1** (hair or fur) smooth and shiny (ବାଳ ବା ଲୋମ) ଚିକ୍କଣ ଓ ଚକଚକିଆ **2** (a vehicle or another object) with an elegant and a smooth shape ସୁନ୍ଦର, ରୁଚିକର ଓ ମସୃଣ *a sleek car*

sleep /sli:p/ *verb* (**sleeps, sleeping, slept** /slept/, **has slept**) rest with your eyes closed, as you do at night ଶୋଇବା, ଶୟନ କରିବା *I sleep for eight hours every night.* ○ *Did you sleep well?*

> ✪ ମନେ ରଖନ୍ତୁ ! **Be asleep** କହିବା ଠିକ୍ ଅଟେ (**be sleeping** ର ପ୍ରୟୋଗ ଠିକ୍ ନୁହେଁ) —
> *I was asleep when you phoned.*
> ଶୋଇବାକୁ ଯିବା ପାଇଁ ଆମେ ସାଧାରଣତଃ **go to sleep** ବା **fall asleep** କହୁଁ ।

sleep *noun* (*no plural*) ନିଦ, ନିଦ୍ରା *I didn't get any sleep last night.*

go to sleep start to sleep ଶୋଇଯିବା, ଶୋଇପଡ଼ିବା *I got into bed and soon went to sleep.*

sleepless /ˈsli:pləs/ *adjective* without sleep ନିଦ ହୋଇନଥିବା, ନିଦ୍ରାବିହୀନ, ଅନିଦ୍ରା *I had a sleepless night.*

sleepy /ˈsli:pi/ *adjective* (**sleepier, sleepiest**) **1** tired and ready to sleep ନିଦୁଆ; ନିଦ୍ରାଳୁ *I felt sleepy after that big meal.* **2** quiet, with not many things happening ନିସ୍ତବ୍ଧ, ନିଶ୍ଚଳ *a sleepy little village*

sleet /sli:t/ *noun* (*no plural*) snow and rain together ଏକା ସାଙ୍ଗରେ ପଡୁଥିବା ବର୍ଷା ଓ ତୁଷାର

sleeve /sli:v/ *noun* the part of a coat, dress or shirt, for example, that covers your arm କମିଜ୍, କୋଟ୍ ଇତ୍ୟାଦିର ହାତ *a shirt with short sleeves*

sleigh /sleɪ/ *noun* a thing that you sit in to move over snow. A sleigh has pieces of metal or wood instead of wheels and is usually pulled by animals ବରଫ ଉପରେ ଟଣାଯାଉଥିବା ଚକ ବିହୀନ ଗାଡ଼ି ➪ ଚିତ୍ର ପାଇଁ **reindeer** ଦେଖନ୍ତୁ।

slender /ˈslendə(r)/ *adjective* thin, in a nice way ସୁନ୍ଦର ଭାବରେ, ପତଳା *She has long slender legs.*

slept ଶବ୍ଦ **sleep** ର ଏକ ଧାତୁରୂପ

slice /slaɪs/ *noun* a thin piece of bread, meat or other food that you cut off from a larger piece କଟା ହୋଇଥିବା ପାତଳ ଖଣ୍ଡ (ଯଥା: ପାଉଁରୁଟିର) *Would you like a slice of cake?* ○ *slices of bread* ➪ ଚିତ୍ର ପାଇଁ **bread** ଦେଖନ୍ତୁ।

slice *verb* (**slices, slicing, sliced**) cut something into slices ପାତଳ ଖଣ୍ଡ କରି କାଟିବା, ଚେନାଚେନା କରିବା *Slice the onions.*

slide[1] /slaɪd/ *verb* (**slides, sliding, slid** /slɪd/, **has slid**) move smoothly or make something move smoothly across something ଖସଡ଼ି ଚାଲିବା, ଖସଡ଼ିବା *The drawers slide in and out of the cupboard easily.*

slide[2] /slaɪd/ *noun* **1** a long metal thing that children play on. They climb up steps, sit down, and then slide down the other side ପିଲାମାନେ ଖସି ଖେଳିବା ପାଇଁ ଏକ ଗଡ଼ାଣିଆ ପୃଷ୍ଠ, ସ୍ଲାଇଡ୍ **2** a small photograph that you show on a **screen**, using a **projector** ପ୍ରୋଜେକ୍ଟର୍ ବା ପ୍ରକ୍ଷେପକରେ ଲଗାଇ ପରଦା ଉପରେ ପ୍ରକ୍ଷିପ୍ତ ଚିତ୍ର ଦେଖିବା ପାଇଁ ଥିବା ସ୍ୱଚ୍ଛ ଓ ପାରଗମ୍ୟ ଫିଲ୍ମ; ସ୍ଲାଇଡ୍ **3** a small piece of glass containing something that needs to be examined under a microscope ମାଇକ୍ରୋସ୍କୋପ୍ ବା ଅଣୁ-ବୀକ୍ଷଣରେ ଦେଖିବା ପଦାର୍ଥକୁ ଧାରଣ କରୁଥିବା ଛୋଟ ଆୟତାକାର କାଚଖଣ୍ଡ; ସ୍ଲାଇଡ୍

slight /slaɪt/ *adjective* (**slighter, slightest**) small; not important or serious ଛୋଟ; ସାମାନ୍ୟ; ଗୌଣ; ଗୁରୁତ୍ୱ ନଥିବା *I've got a slight problem.*

slightly /ˈslaɪtli/ *adverb* a little ଅଳ୍ପ, ସାମାନ୍ୟ *I'm feeling slightly better today.*

slim /slɪm/ *adjective* (**slimmer, slimmest**) thin, but not too thin ପତଳା (କିନ୍ତୁ ଅତି ପତଳା ନୁହଁ), ଛାଟିଦେଲା ପରି *a tall slim man*

sling /slɪŋ/ *noun* a piece of cloth that you wear to hold up an arm that is hurt ଆହତ ହାତକୁଟେକି ରଖିବା ପାଇଁ ବେକରୁ ଝୁଲା ଯାଉଥିବା ବ୍ୟାଣ୍ଡେଜ୍, ପଟି ବା ସ୍ଲିଙ୍ଗ୍

slip[1] /slɪp/ *verb* (**slips, slipping, slipped**) **1** move smoothly over something by mistake and fall or almost fall ଜାଣି ନ ପାରି ଗୋଡ଼ ଖସଡ଼ିଯିବା ବା ଖସଡ଼ି ପଡ଼ିଯିବା *He slipped on the ice and broke his leg.* **2** go quickly and quietly so that nobody sees you କେହି ନ ଜାଣିଲା ପରି ଚୁପ୍‌ଚାପ୍ ଖସି ପଳାଇବା ବା ଚାଲିଯିବା *Anshu slipped out of the room when the children were asleep.*

slip[2] /slɪp/ *noun* a small piece of paper ଛୋଟ କାଗଜ ଖଣ୍ଡ, ଚିରକୁଟ୍ *Write your address on this slip of paper.*

slipper /ˈslɪpə(r)/ *noun* a light soft shoe that you wear in the house ଚଟି *a pair of slippers*

slippery /ˈslɪpəri/ *adjective* so smooth or wet that you cannot move on it or hold it easily ଖସଡ଼ା, ପିଚ୍ଛିଳ *The road was wet and slippery.*

slit /slɪt/ *noun* a long thin hole or cut ଫାଟ, ଚିରା

slit *verb* (**slits, slitting, slit, has slit**) make a long thin cut in something ସିଧା ରେଖାରେ ଲମ୍ବା କରି କାଟିବା *I slit the envelope open with a knife.*

slogan /ˈsləʊgən/ *noun* a short sentence or group of words that is easy to remember. Slogans are used in **advertisements** to make people believe something or buy something ବିଜ୍ଞାପନ ପାଇଁ ଉଦ୍ଦିଷ୍ଟ ଛୋଟ ଓ ଆକର୍ଷଣୀୟ ବାକ୍ୟାଂଶ ବା କଥା, ସ୍ଲୋଗାନ୍ *'Faster than light' is the slogan for the new car.*

slope /sləʊp/ *noun* a piece of ground that has one end higher than the other, like the side of a hill ଉଠାଣି ବା ଗଡ଼ାଣି ଜାଗା *We walked down the mountain slope.*

slope *verb* (**slopes, sloping, sloped**) have one end higher than the other ଉଠାଣିଆ ବା ଗଡ଼ାଣିଆ ହେବା *The field slopes down to the river.*

slot /slɒt/ *noun* a long thin hole that you push something through କିଛି ଜିନିଷ ଗଳାଇବା ପାଇଁ ଖାପ ଖାଇଲା ପରି ଖୋପ ଇତ୍ୟାଦି *Put a coin in the slot and take your ticket.*

slow[1] /sləʊ/ *adjective* (**slower, slowest**) **1** a person or thing that is slow does not move or do something quickly ଧୀର, ମନ୍ଥର; ଧୀର ଗତିରେ ଯାଉଥିବା *a slow train* ○ *She hasn't finished her work yet—she's very slow.* **2** if a clock or watch is slow, it shows a time that is earlier than the real time ପ୍ରକୃତ ସମୟରୁ କମ୍ ସମୟ ଦେଖାଯାଉଥିବା ବା ଲେଟ୍ ଚାଲୁଥିବା (ଘଣ୍ଟା) *My watch is five minutes slow* ➪ **quick** ଓ **fast**[1] ଦେଖନ୍ତୁ।

slow *adverb* (**slower, slowest**) slowly ଧୀରେ ଧୀରେ, ଆସ୍ତେ ଆସ୍ତେ *Please drive slower.*

slowly *adverb* ଧୀରେ ଧୀରେ, ଆସ୍ତେ ଆସ୍ତେ *The old lady walked slowly up the hill.*

slow[2] /sləʊ/ *verb* (**slows, slowing, slowed**)

slow down start to go more slowly; make somebody or something start to go more slowly ଧୀରେ ଧୀରେ ଯିବା, ଧୀର ଗତିରେ ଯିବା *The train slowed down as it came into the station.*

slug /slʌg/ *noun* a small soft animal like a snail without a shell, that moves slowly and eats plants ଖୋଳ ନଥିବା ଛୋଟ ଗେଣ୍ଡା

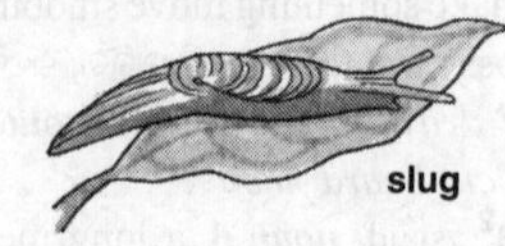
slug

slum /slʌm/ *noun* a part of a city where people live in poor conditions ବସ୍ତି; ଖୁଲାପେଲା ହୋଇ ବାସ କରୁଥିବା ଗରିବ ଲୋକଙ୍କ ବାସସ୍ଥାନ

sly /slaɪ/ *adjective* a person who is sly tricks people or does things secretly ଧୂର୍ତ୍ତ, ଶଠ, ଠକ

small /smɔːl/ *adjective* (**smaller, smallest**) **1** not big; little ଛୋଟ, ସାନ; ଅଳ୍ପ*This dress is too small for me.* ○ *My house is smaller than yours.* ✪ ବିପରୀତ **big** ବା **large** **2** young ଅଳ୍ପ ବୟସର *They have two small children.* ○ *When I was small, I wanted to be a pilot.* **3** not written or printed in **capital** letters ସାନ

ଅକ୍ଷରରେ (କ୍ୟାପିଟାଲରେ ନୁହେଁ) ଲେଖା ଯାଇଥିବା ➪ **capital 2** ଦେଖନ୍ତୁ।

smart /smɑ:t/ *adjective* (**smarter, smartest**) **1** right for a special or an important time; clean and tidy ସଫାସୁତୁରା ଓ ସମୟୋପଯୋଗୀ *She wore smart clothes for her job interview.* ○ *He looks very smart in his new jacket.* **2** clever ଚାଲାକ୍, ଚତୁର *a smart student*

smartly *adverb* ଚତୁର ଭାବରେ; ସୁନ୍ଦର ଭାବରେ *She was very smartly dressed.*

smash /smæʃ/ *verb* (**smashes, smashing, smashed**) break something into many pieces ଖଣ୍ଡ ବିଖଣ୍ଡିତ କରିବା, ଚୁରମାର କରିବା, ଖଣ୍ଡ ଖଣ୍ଡ କରି ଭାଙ୍ଗି ଦେବା *The boys smashed the window.*

smear /smɪə(r)/ *verb* (**smears, smearing, smeared**) spread a soft substance on something, making it dirty ବୋଳିବା, ଲେସିବା *The child smeared chocolate over his clothes.*

smear *noun* a dirty mark ମଇଳା ଦାଗ *She had smears of paint on her dress.*

smell /smel/ *verb* (**smells, smelling, smelt** /smelt/ ବା **smelled, has smelt** ବା **has smelled**) **1** notice something using your nose ଶୁଙ୍ଘିବା, ଆଘ୍ରାଣ କରିବା *Can you smell smoke?* **2** if something smells, you notice it with your nose ଶୁଙ୍ଘି ଗନ୍ଧ ଜାଣିପାରିବା *This fish smells bad.* ○ *The perfume smells of roses.* **3** have a bad smell ଦୁର୍ଗନ୍ଧ ହେବା, ଗନ୍ଧାଇବା *Your feet smell!*

smell *noun* **1** (*no plural*) the ability to notice something using your nose ଗନ୍ଧ ଶୁଙ୍ଘି ଜାଣି ପାରିବା ଶକ୍ତି, ଆଘ୍ରାଣ ଶକ୍ତି **2** (*plural* **smells**) something that you notice with your nose ଗନ୍ଧ *There's a smell of gas in this room.*

smelly /ˈsmeli/ *adjective* (**smellier, smelliest**) with a bad smell ଦୁର୍ଗନ୍ଧ ହେଉଥିବା *smelly socks*

smile /smaɪl/ *verb* (**smiles, smiling, smiled**) move your mouth to show that you are happy or because you think something is funny ସ୍ମିତ ହାସ୍ୟ କରିବା, ମୃଦୁହାସ କରିବା, ମୁରୁକି ହସାଦେବା *He smiled at me.*

smile *noun* ସ୍ମିତହାସ୍ୟ, ମୃଦୁହାସ୍ୟ, ମୁରୁକି ହସ *She had a big smile on her face.*

smith /smɪθ/ *noun* a person who works with metal, for example a **blacksmith** ଧାତୁଶିଳ୍ପୀ, ଧାତୁ କାରିଗର (ଯଥା: କମାର, ବଣିଆଁ)

smog /smɒg/ *noun* (*no plural*) a mixture of smoke and fog that hangs above large cities in the morning ଧୂଆଁମିଶା କୁହୁଡ଼ି

smoke[1] /sməʊk/ *noun* (*no plural*) the grey or black gas that is produced when something is burning ଧୂଆଁ *The room was full of smoke.*

smoke[2] /sməʊk/ *verb* (**smokes, smoking, smoked**) take in smoke from a cigarette, cigar or pipe into your mouth and then take it out ସିଗାରେଟ୍ ଇତ୍ୟାଦି ଟାଣିବା, ଧୂମ୍ରପାନ କରିବା

smoking *noun* (*no plural*) ଧୂମ୍ରପାନ *Smoking is not allowed inside the office.*

smoker /ˈsməʊkə(r)/ *noun* a person who smokes ଧୂମ୍ରପାନକାରୀ ବ୍ୟକ୍ତି

smooth /smu:ð/ *adjective* (**smoother, smoothest**) **1** flat; not rough ମସୃଣ, ଚିକ୍କଣ *Babies have smooth skin.* ✪ ବିପରୀତ **rough 1** **2** moving gently, without jerks ଧକରକର ସ୍ନିଗ୍ଧ ଆରାମଦାୟକ *The weather was good so we had a very smooth flight.*

smoothly *adverb* ସ୍ନିଗ୍ଧ ଓ ମସୃଣଭାବରେ, ଧକରକଚର ନହୋଇ *The plane landed smoothly.*

SMS /ˌes em ˈes/ *noun* a way of sending messages over mobile phones ମୋବାଇଲ୍ ଫୋନ୍‌ରେ ଖବର ଲେଖି ପଠାଇବା ବ୍ୟବସ୍ଥା ✪ SMS ର ବିସ୍ତୃତ ରୂପ **short message service**।

smug /smʌg/ *adjective* too pleased with yourself about something that you have done or achieved ଆତ୍ମତୁଷ୍ଟ *a smug smile*

smuggle /ˈsmʌgl/ *verb* (**smuggles, smuggling, smuggled**) take things secretly into or out of a country ବେଆଇନ୍ ଭାବେ ଜିନିଷ ଆମଦାନି ବା ରପ୍ତାନି କରି, ଜିନିଷପତ୍ର ଆମଦାନି ବା ରପ୍ତାନି କରି ଜିନିଷପତ୍ର ଏକ ଦେଶରୁ ଅନ୍ୟଦେଶକୁ ଚୋରାରେ ଆଣିବା ବା ନେବା *They were trying to smuggle gold into Nepal.*

smuggler *noun* a person who smuggles ଚୋରାରେ ଆମଦାନି ବା ରପ୍ତାନି କରୁଥିବା ବ୍ୟକ୍ତି, ସ୍ମଗ୍ଲର୍

snack /snæk/ *noun* a small quick meal ଅଳ୍ପ ଆହାର, ଜଳଖିଆ *We had a snack on the train.*

snail /sneɪl/ *noun* a small soft animal with a hard shell on its back. *Snails move very slowly* ଗେଣ୍ଡା। ➪ ଚିତ୍ର ପାଇଁ **invertebrates** ଦେଖନ୍ତୁ।

snake /sneɪk/ *noun* a reptile with a long thin body and no legs ସାପ *Do these snakes bite?* ➪ ଚିତ୍ର ପାଇଁ **mongoose** ଦେଖନ୍ତୁ।

snap[1] /snæp/ *verb* (**snaps, snapping, snapped**) **1** break suddenly with a sharp noise ହଠାତ୍ ସଶବ୍ଦେ ଭାଙ୍ଗିବା ବା ଛିଣ୍ଡିବା *He snapped the pencil in two.* **2** try to bite somebody or something ଖଟ୍ କରି ଦୁଇ ପାଟି ଦାନ୍ତ କାମୁଡ଼ିଲା ପରି ବନ୍ଦ କରିବା *The dog snapped at my leg.* **3** say something in a quick angry way ରାଗରେ ଶୀଘ୍ର କହିବା, ଖଙ୍କାରି ହେଲାପରି କହିବା *'Go away! I am busy!' she snapped.*

snap[2] /snæp/, **snapshot** /ˈsnæpʃɒt/ *noun* a photograph ଫଟୋ ବା ଛାୟାଚିତ୍ର *She showed us her holiday snaps.*

snare /sneər/ *noun* a trap used to catch small animals and birds ଯନ୍ତା, ଫାନ୍ଦ, ଫାଶ *The poor bird's foot was caught in a snare.*

snarl /snɑ:l/ *verb* (**snarls, snarling, snarled**) when an animal snarls, it shows its teeth and makes a low angry sound ଖଙ୍କାରି ହେବା *The dog snarled at the stranger.*

snatch /snætʃ/ *verb* (**snatches, snatching, snatched**) take something quickly and roughly ଝିଡ଼ି ନେଇଯିବା, ଛଡ଼ାଇ ନେବା *The thief snatched her handbag and ran away.*

sneak /sni:k/ *verb* (**sneaks, sneaking, sneaked**) go somewhere very quickly so that nobody sees or hears you ଚୁପ୍‌ଚାପ୍ କେହି ନଜାଣିଲା ପରି ଶୀଘ୍ର ଚାଲିଯିବା ବା ଆସିବା, ଚୁପ୍‌ଚାପ୍ ଖସି ଚାଲିଯିବା *He sneaked out of the classroom while the teacher was writing something on the blackboard.*

sneeze /sni:z/ *verb* (**sneezes, sneezing, sneezed**) send air out of your nose and mouth with a sudden loud noise, for example because you have a cold ଛିଙ୍କିବା *Dust may make you sneeze.*

sneeze *noun* ଛିଙ୍କ *She gave a loud sneeze.*

sniff /snɪf/ *verb* (**sniffs, sniffing, sniffed**) **1** make a noise by suddenly taking in air through your nose. People sometimes sniff when they have a cold or when they are crying ନାକ ସୁଁ ସୁଁ କରିବା **2** smell something ଶୁଙ୍ଘିବା *The dog was sniffing the meat.*

sniff *noun* ଆଘ୍ରାଣ ବା ଶୁଙ୍ଘିବା ଶବ୍ଦ *I heard a loud sniff.*

snore /snɔ:(r)/ *verb* (**snores, snoring, snored**) breathe very noisily through your nose and throat when you are asleep ଘୁଙ୍ଘୁଡ଼ି ମାରିବା *He was snoring loudly.*

snow /snəʊ/ *noun* (*no plural*) soft white frozen drops of water that fall from the sky when it is very cold ତୁଷାର, ଘନୀଭୂତ ଶିଶିର, ବରଫ

snow *verb* (**snows, snowing, snowed**) when it snows, snow falls from the sky ତୁଷାର ପଡ଼ିବା, ତୁଷାରପାତ ହେବା *It often snows in Srinagar during winter.*

snowflake /ˈsnəʊfleɪk/ *noun* one piece of falling snow ତୁଷାର କଣା

so[1] /səʊ/ *adverb* **1** a word that you use when you say how much, how big, etc. something is ଏତେ *This bag is so heavy that I can't carry it.* ➪ **such** ଦେଖନ୍ତୁ । **2** a word that makes another word stronger ଏତେ *Why are you so late?* **3** also ମଧ୍ୟ *Kiran is a teacher and so is her husband.* ✪ ନକରାତ୍ମକ ବାକ୍ୟରେ **neither** ବା **nor** ବ୍ୟବହାର କରାଯାଏ । **4** you use 'so' instead of saying words again ଗୋଟିଏ ଶବ୍ଦ ଆଉଥରେ; କହିବା ବଦଳରେ 'so' କୁହାଯାଏ *'Is Jeevan coming?' 'I think so.'*

and so on and other things like that ଇତ୍ୟାଦି *The shop sells pens, paper and so on.*

so[2] /səʊ/ *conjunction* **1** because of this or that ତେଣୁ, ସେଥିପାଇଁ *The shop is closed so I can't buy any bread.* **2** (**so that** ମଧ୍ୟ) in order that ଯାହା ଦ୍ୱାରା *Speak louder so that everybody can hear you.* ○ *I'll give you a map so you can find my house.*

soak /səʊk/ *verb* (**soaks, soaking, soaked**) **1** make somebody or something completely wet ଭିଜାଇବା, ଭିଜିଯିବା, ତିନ୍ତିବା *It was raining when I went out. I got soaked!* **2** be or let something stay in a liquid till it is completely wet ପୂରା ଭିଜିଯିବା ପର୍ଯ୍ୟନ୍ତ ପାଣିରେ ବୁଡ଼ାଇ ରଖିବା *Soak the rice for two hours.*

soak up take in a liquid ତରଳ ପଦାର୍ଥ ଅବଶୋଷଣ କରିବା; (କନା ଇତ୍ୟାଦିରେ) ଛାପି

ଶୁଖାଇ ଦେବା *Soak the water up with a cloth.*

soap /səʊp/ *noun* (*no plural*) a substance that you use with water for washing and cleaning ସାବୁନ୍ *a bar of soap*

soapy *adjective* with soap in it ସାବୁନ୍ ଫେଣ ଥିବା *soapy water*

soar /sɔ:(r)/ *verb* (**soars, soaring, soared**) **1** fly high in the sky ଆକାଶରେ ଉଚ୍ଚକୁ ଉଠିବା **2** go up very fast ଖୁବ୍ ବେଗରେ ଉପରକୁ ଉଠିବା *Prices are soaring.*

sob /sɒb/ *verb* (**sobs, sobbing, sobbed**) cry loudly, making short sounds କାନ୍ଦିବା, କୋହଛାଡ଼ି କାନ୍ଦିବା

sob *noun* କାନ୍ଦ, କୋହ *'She's broken my pen!' he said with a sob.*

social /ˈsəʊʃl/ *adjective* of people together; of being with other people ସାମାଜିକ; ସମାଜ ସମ୍ବନ୍ଧୀୟ *the social problems of big cities* ○ *Amita has a busy social life.*

social worker *noun* (*plural* **social workers**) a person whose job is to help people who have problems, for example because they are poor or ill ସମାଜ ସେବକ

society /səˈsaɪəti/ *noun* (*no plural*) a group of people living together, with the same ideas about how to live ସଙ୍ଗଠିତ ଓ ପରସ୍ପର ନିର୍ଭରଶୀଳ ସମ୍ପ୍ରଦାୟ, ସମାଜ

sock /sɒk/ *noun* a thing that covers your foot and the lower part of your leg. This is mostly worn inside a shoe ମୋଜା *a pair of socks*

socket /ˈsɒkɪt/ *noun* a place in a wall into which you can put an electric plug ଖୋପଥିବା ଧାରକ ବା ଗର୍ଭିକା ଯାହା ଭିତରେ ଅନ୍ୟକିଛି ଖଞ୍ଜାଯାଏ, ଯଥା: ବୈଦ୍ୟୁତିକ ପ୍ଲଗ୍‌ର ସକେଟ୍; ସକେଟ୍

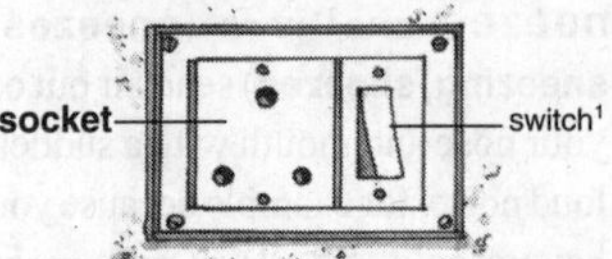

sofa /ˈsəʊfə/ *noun* a long soft seat for more than one person ସୋଫା, ଗଦିଲଗା ଲମ୍ବା ଚଉକି *Jane was sitting on the sofa.*

soft /sɒft/ *adjective* (**softer, softest**) **1** not hard or firm; that changes shape when you press it ନରମ, ନମନୀୟ *a soft bed* ✪ ବିପରୀତ **hard 1** **2** smooth and nice to touch; not rough ନରମ ଓ ମସୃଣ *soft skin* ○ *My cat's fur is very soft.* **3** quiet or gentle; not loud ଧୀର, କୋମଳ *soft music* ○ *He has a very soft voice.* **4** not bright or strong ଉଜ୍ଜ୍ୱଳ ହୋଇ ନଥିବା *the soft light of a candle* **5** kind and gentle; not strict ଦୟାଳୁ ଓ ନମ୍ର ସ୍ୱଭାବର *She's too soft with her class and they don't do any work.*

softly *adverb* gently or quietly ଧୀରେ; କୋମଳ ସ୍ୱରରେ; ଶବ୍ଦ ନକରି *She spoke very softly.*

software /ˈsɒftweə(r)/ *noun* (*no plural*) **programs** for a computer କମ୍ପ୍ୟୁଟର୍ କାର୍ଯ୍ୟକ୍ରମରେ ବ୍ୟବହୃତ ପ୍ରୋଗ୍ରାମ୍, ତଥ୍ୟ ଇତ୍ୟାଦି ➪ **hardware** ଦେଖନ୍ତୁ।

soil /sɔɪl/ *noun* the top layer of earth in which plants and trees grow ମାଟି, ମୃତ୍ତିକା

solar /ˈsəʊlə(r)/ *adjective* of or using the sun ସୂର୍ଯ୍ୟ ସଂକ୍ରାନ୍ତ; ସୂର୍ଯ୍ୟଙ୍କର; ସୂର୍ଯ୍ୟଙ୍କଠାରୁ ପ୍ରାପ୍ତ *solar energy*

the solar system *noun* (*no plural*) the sun and the planets that move around it ସୌରମଣ୍ଡଳ

sold ଶବ୍ଦ **sell** ର ଏକ ଧାତୁରୂପ

be sold out when things are sold out, there are no more to sell ବିକ୍ରିହୋଇ ଜିନିଷ ସରିଯିବା *I'm sorry—the bananas are sold out.*

soldier /ˈsəʊldʒə(r)/ *noun* a person in an army ସୈନିକ

sole[1] /səʊl/ *noun* the bottom part of your foot or of a shoe ପାଦ ବା ଜୋତାର ତଳ ଭାଗ, ସୋଲ୍ *These boots have leather soles.*

sole[2] /səʊl/ *adjective* only କେବଳ, ଏକମାତ୍ର *His sole interest is football.*

solemn /ˈsɒləm/ *adjective* serious ଗମ୍ଭୀର; ଗୁରୁତ୍ୱପୂର୍ଣ୍ଣ *slow solemn music*

solid /ˈsɒlɪd/ *adjective* **1** hard, not like a liquid or a gas କଠିନ, ଟାଣ, ଦୃଢ଼ (ତରଳ ପଦାର୍ଥ ବା ବାଷ୍ପ ନୁହେଁ) *Water becomes solid when it freezes.* **2** with no empty space inside; made of the same material inside and outside ନିବା (ଫମ୍ପା ନୁହେଁ) *a solid rubber ball*

solid *noun* not a liquid or gas ନିବା ଜିନିଷ, କଠିନ ଜିନିଷ *Milk is a liquid and cheese is a solid.*

solitary /ˈsɒlətri/ *adjective* without others; alone ଏକା, ଏକାକୀ *She went for a long solitary walk.*

solitude /ˈsɒlɪtjuːd/ *noun* (*no plural*) the state of being alone, especially when you like it ନିଃସଙ୍ଗତା; ନିର୍ଜନତା *She was enjoying the peace and solitude in the village.*

solo /ˈsəʊləʊ/ *adjective, adverb* alone; without other people ଏକକ (ସଙ୍ଗୀତ, ନୃତ୍ୟ ଇତ୍ୟାଦି); ଏକୁଟିଆ, ଏକାକୀ *a solo performance*

solution /səˈluːʃn/ *noun* **1** the answer to a question, problem or

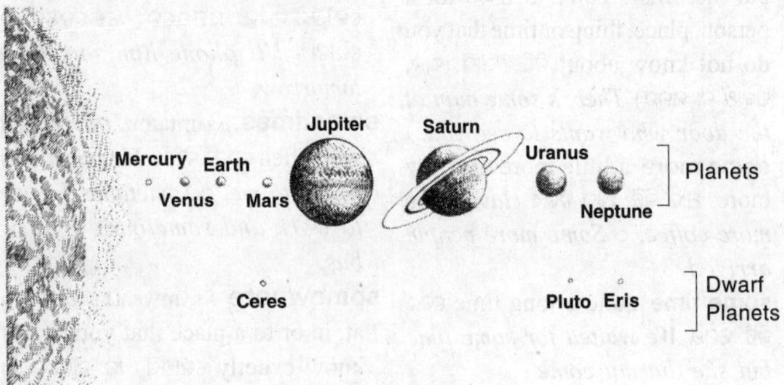

the solar system

puzzle ସମସ୍ୟାର ସମାଧାନ; ପ୍ରଶ୍ନର ଉତ୍ତର *I have not been able to find a solution to this problem.* **2** a liquid in which something has been **dissolved** ଦ୍ରବଣ, କିଛି ମିଳେଇ ଦିଆଯାଇଥିବା ତରଳ ପଦାର୍ଥ *salt solution*

solve /sɒlv/ *verb* (**solves, solving, solved**) find the answer to a question, problem or puzzle ପ୍ରଶ୍ନର ଉତ୍ତର କାଢ଼ିବା; ସମସ୍ୟାର ସମାଧାନ କରିବା *The students are trying to solve the sum.*

some /sʌm/ *adjective, pronoun* **1** a number or an amount of something କେତେକ, କିଛି, ଅଳ୍ପ *I bought some tomatoes and some butter.*

> ✪ ପ୍ରଶ୍ନାତ୍ମକ ଏବଂ ନକରାତ୍ମକ ବାକ୍ୟରେ **any** ର ପ୍ରୟୋଗ କରାଯାଏ । ଯଥା— *Did you buy any apples?* ○ *I didn't buy any meat.*

2 part of a number or an amount of something କିଛି ପରିମାଣର, କିଛି ସଂଖ୍ୟକ *Some of the children can swim, but the others can't.* **3** used for a person, place, thing or time that you do not know about କିଛି (ବ୍ୟକ୍ତି, ସ୍ଥାନ, ପଦାର୍ଥ ବା ସମୟ) *There's some man at the door who wants to see you.*

some more a little more or a few more ଆଉ କିଛି, ଆଉ ଟିକିଏ *Have some more coffee.* ○ *Some more people arrived.*

some time quite a long time ବେଶ୍ କିଛି ସମୟ *We waited for some time but she did not come.*

somebody /ˈsʌmbədi/, **someone** /ˈsʌmwʌn/ *pronoun* a person; a person whom you do not know କେହିଜଣେ; ଜଣେ କାହାରିକୁ *There's somebody at the door.* ○ *Someone has broken the window.* ○ *Ask somebody else to help you.*

somehow /ˈsʌmhaʊ/ *adverb* in some way that you do not know ଯେମିତି ବି ହେଉ, ଯେକୌଣସି ଉପାୟରେ *We must find her somehow.*

somersault /ˈsʌməsɔːlt/ *noun* a movement when you turn your body, with your feet going over your head ମାଙ୍କଡ଼ଚିତ୍; ଏହି ପ୍ରକାର ଡିଆଁ *The children were doing somersaults on the carpet.*

something /ˈsʌmθɪŋ/ *pronoun* a thing; a thing you cannot name କୌଣସି ପଦାର୍ଥ; କିଛି କଥା *There's something under the table. What is it?* ○ *I want to tell you something.* ○ *Would you like something else to eat?*

sometime /ˈsʌmtaɪm/ *adverb* at a time that you do not know exactly କୌଣସି ଏକ ସମୟରେ, କେତେବେଳେ ଗୋଟାଏ *I'll phone him sometime tomorrow.*

sometimes /ˈsʌmtaɪmz/ *adverb* not very often ବେଳେ ବେଳେ *He sometimes writes to me.* ○ *Sometimes I drive to work and sometimes I go by bus.*

somewhere /ˈsʌmweə(r)/ *adverb* at, in or to a place that you do not know exactly କୌଣସି ଏକ ସ୍ଥାନରେ ବା ସ୍ଥାନକୁ, କୋଉଠି ଗୋଟିଏ *They live somewhere near Chandigarh.* ○ *'Did she go to Sri Lanka last year?'*

'No, I think she went somewhere else.'

son /sʌn/ *noun* a boy or man who is somebody's child ପୁଅ, ପୁତ୍ର *They have a son and two daughters.* ➪ ଚିତ୍ର ପାଇଁ **family** ଦେଖନ୍ତୁ ।

song /sɒŋ/ *noun* a piece of music with words that you sing ଗୀତ *a pop song*

son-in-law *noun* (*plural* **sons-in-law**) the husband of your daughter ଜ୍ୱାଇଁ, ଜାମାତା ➪ ଚିତ୍ର ପାଇଁ **family** ଦେଖନ୍ତୁ ।

soon /su:n/ *adverb* not long after now, or not long after a certain time ଶୀଘ୍ର; ଅଳ୍ପ ସମୟରେ *Ratna will be home soon.* ○ *She arrived soon after two o'clock.*

as soon as at the same time that; when ସେହିକ୍ଷଣି, ଯେତେଶୀଘ୍ର ସମ୍ଭବ *Phone me as soon as you get home.*

soot /sʊt/ *noun* (*no plural*) black powder that comes from smoke ଧୂଆଁ, ଅଳନ୍ଧୁ, ଧୂଆଁର କଳାଗୁଣ୍ଡ

sophisticated /sə'fɪstɪkeɪtɪd/ *adjective* **1** having a lot of social experience and knowledge about life, and taste in things such as art, fashion, culture, etc. ସାଂସାରିକ ଜ୍ଞାନ ସମ୍ପନ୍ନ, ମାର୍ଜିତ ଓ ରୁଚି ସମ୍ପନ୍ନ *a sophisticated old lady* **2** able to understand difficult or complicated things ଜଟିଳ ବିଷୟ ବୁଝିପାରୁଥିବା *sophisticated voters* **3** (of machines) advanced and designed to perform complicated tasks (ଯନ୍ତ୍ରପାତି) ଉନ୍ନତ ଧରଣର ଓ ଜଟିଳ କାମ କରିପାରୁଥିବା

sore /sɔ:(r)/ *adjective* if a part of your body is sore, it gives you pain ଯନ୍ତ୍ରଣାପୂର୍ଣ୍ଣ *My feet were sore after the long walk.* ○ *I've got a sore throat.*

sorrow /'sɒrəʊ/ *noun* a feeling of great sadness ଦୁଃଖ, ବିଷାଦ

sorry /'sɒri/ *adjective* **1** a word that you use when you feel bad about something you have done ଦୁଃଖିତ ଯେ *I'm sorry I didn't phone you.* ○ *Sorry, I'm late!* **2** sad ଦୁଃଖିତ, ବିଷାଦପୂର୍ଣ୍ଣ *I'm sorry you can't come to the party.* **3** a word that you use to say 'no' politely ନାହିଁ କରିବାକୁ ଭଦ୍ରଭାବରେ କୁହାଯାଉଥିବା ଶବ୍ଦ: 'ସରି'; ଦୁଃଖିତ ଯେ *I'm sorry—I can't help you.* **4** a word that you use when you did not hear what somebody said and you want them to say it again କିଛି କଥା ଶୁଣି ପାରିନଥିଲେ ଆଉଥରେ କହିବାକୁ ଅନୁରୋଧ ସୂଚକ ଶବ୍ଦ: ସରି; ଆଜ୍ଞା *'My name is Latha Menon.' 'Sorry? Latha who?'*

feel sorry for somebody feel sad because somebody has problems କାହାରି ପାଇଁ ଦୁଃଖ କରିବା *I felt sorry for her and gave her some money.*

sort[1] /sɔ:t/ *noun* a group of things or people that are similar in some way; a type or kind (ଲୋକ, ପଦାର୍ଥ ଇତ୍ୟାଦିଙ୍କ) ପ୍ରକାର, ରକମ, ଶ୍ରେଣୀ *We found all sorts of shells on the beach.* ○ *What sort of music do you like best—pop or classical?*

sort[2] /sɔ:t/ *verb* (**sorts, sorting, sorted**) put things into groups ବିଭିନ୍ନ ପ୍ରକାରର ଜିନିଷ ବାଛି ଅଲଗା ଅଲଗା କରି ରଖିବା *The machine sorts the eggs into large ones and small ones.*

sort out **1** make something tidy ବାଛି ସଜାଇ ରଖିବା *I sorted out my clothes and put the old ones in a bag.* **2** find an answer to a problem ସମସ୍ୟାର ସମାଧାନ କାଢ଼ିବା

SOS /ˌes əʊ 'es/ *noun* a call for help from a ship or an aeroplane that is in danger ଉଡ଼ାଜାହାଜ, ଜାହାଜ ଇତ୍ୟାଦିରୁ ବିପଦବେଳେ ରକ୍ଷା କରିବା ପାଇଁ ସାଙ୍କେତିକ ଡାକରା : ଆମକୁ ବଞ୍ଚାଅ

sought ଶବ୍ଦ **seek** ର ଏକ ଧାତୁରୂପ

soul /səʊl/ *noun* the part of a person that some people believe does not die when the body dies ଆତ୍ମା

not a soul not one person କେହି ନାହିଁ *I looked everywhere, but there wasn't a soul in the building.*

sound[1] /saʊnd/ *noun* something that you hear ଶବ୍ଦ, ଧ୍ୱନି *I heard the sound of a baby crying.*

sound[2] /saʊnd/ *verb* (**sounds, sounding, sounded**) seem a certain way when you hear it (କାହାରି କଥା) ଶୁଣି (ତାଙ୍କର ଭାବନା) ଅନୁମାନ କରିବା; ପରି ଲାଗିବା *He sounded angry when I spoke to him on the phone.* ○ *That sounds like a good idea.*

soup /su:p/ *noun* (*no plural*) a liquid food that is made by cooking things like vegetables or meat in water ମାଂସ ବା ପରିବା ସିଝା ପାଣିରେ ପ୍ରସ୍ତୁତ ଖାଦ୍ୟ, ସରୁଆ, ସୁପ୍ *tomato soup*

sour /'saʊə(r)/ *adjective* **1** with a taste like lemon or vinegar ଖଟା, ଆମ୍ବିଳା *If it's too sour, put some sugar in it.* ✪ ବିପରୀତ **sweet[1] 1** **2** sour milk tastes bad because it is not fresh (ଦୁଧ ଇତ୍ୟାଦି) ଖରାପ, ଗନ୍ଧିଆ *This milk has gone sour.*

source /sɔ:s/ *noun* a place where something comes from ଉତ୍ପତ୍ତି ସ୍ଥଳ, ଉତ୍ସ, ମୂଳ *Our information comes from many sources.* ○ *The sun is a source of heat and light.*

south /saʊθ/ *noun* (*no plural*) the direction that is on your right when you watch the sun come up in the morning ଦକ୍ଷିଣ ଦିଗ ➪ ଚିତ୍ର ପାଇଁ **north** ଦେଖନ୍ତୁ।

south *adjective, adverb* ଦକ୍ଷିଣ; ଦକ୍ଷିଣ ଦିଗକୁ ବା ଦିଗରେ *Brazil is in South America.* ○ *Birds fly south in the winter.*

southern /'sʌðən/ *adjective* in or of the south part of a place ଦକ୍ଷିଣ; ଦକ୍ଷିଣ ସମ୍ବନ୍ଧୀୟ; ଦକ୍ଷିଣଦେଶୀୟ *Chennai is in southern India.*

south-east *noun* (*no plural*) the direction that is halfway between south and east ଦକ୍ଷିଣ ପୂର୍ବ (ଦିଗ) ➪ ଚିତ୍ର ପାଇଁ **north** ଦେଖନ୍ତୁ।

south-west *noun* (*no plural*) the direction that is halfway between south and west ଦକ୍ଷିଣ ପଶ୍ଚିମ (ଦିଗ) ➪ ଚିତ୍ର ପାଇଁ **north** ଦେଖନ୍ତୁ।

sovereign[1] /'sɒvrɪn/ *noun* a king or queen ରାଜା ବା ରାଣୀ, ଦେଶର ସର୍ବୋଚ୍ଚ ଶାସକ

sovereign[2] /'sɒvrɪn/ *adjective* **1** a sovereign country is independent and is free to govern itself ସ୍ୱୟଂଶାସିତ ଓ ସ୍ୱାଧୀନ (ଦେଶ) **2** something that is sovereign has the highest power in a country ସାର୍ବଭୌମ *a sovereign ruler*

sow[1] /səʊ/ *verb* (**sows, sowing, sowed, has sown** /səʊn/ ବା **has sowed**) put seeds in the ground ମଞ୍ଜି ପୋତିବା, ବୀଜ ରୋପଣ କରିବା *The farmer sowed the field with corn.*

sow[2] /saʊ/ *noun* (*plural* **sows**) a female pig ମାଈ ଘୁଷୁରି

soya /ˈsɔɪə/ *noun* (*no plural*) a plant which produces soya beans ଏକ ପ୍ରକାର ଶିମ୍ବଜାତିୟ ଉଦ୍ଭିଦ ବା ଏହାର ଖାଇବା ଯୋଗ୍ୟ ମଞ୍ଜି

space /speɪs/ *noun* **1** (*no plural*) the place far away outside the earth, where all the planets and stars are ମହାକାଶ, ମହାଶୂନ୍ୟ *space travel* **2** (*no plural*) an amount of an area or a place that is empty ଖାଲି ସ୍ଥାନ, ଜାଗା *Is there space for me in your car?* **3** (*plural* **spaces**) an empty place between two things ଦୁଇ ବସ୍ତୁ ଇତ୍ୟାଦି ମଝିରେ ଥିବା ଖାଲି ସ୍ଥାନ *There is a space here for you to write your name.*

spacecraft /ˈspeɪskrɑːft/ *noun* (*plural* **spacecraft**) a vehicle that travels in space ମହାକାଶଯାନ

spaceship /ˈspeɪsʃɪp/ *noun* a vehicle that travels in space and carries people ଯାତ୍ରୀ ନେଇଯାଇ ପାରୁଥିବା ମହାକାଶଯାନ

spacesuit /ˈspeɪssuit/ *noun* a special suit worn by **astronauts,** that covers the entire body and has a supply of air to help survive in space ମହାକାଶରେ କାମ କରିବା ପାଇଁ ପିନ୍ଧା ଯାଉଥିବା ଭିତରେ ବାୟୁଚାପ ଥିବା ନିବୁଜ ଭାବରେ ସିଲ୍‌ଯୁକ୍ତ ପୋଷାକ

spacious /ˈspeɪʃəs/ *adjective* with a lot of space inside ପ୍ରଶସ୍ତ, ବିସ୍ତୃତ, ଯଥେଷ୍ଟ ସ୍ଥାନଥିବା *a spacious kitchen*

spade /speɪd/ *noun* **1** a tool that you use for digging କୋଡ଼ି, କୋଦାଳ, ଫାଉଡ଼ା ➪ ଚିତ୍ର ପାଇଁ **tool** ଦେଖନ୍ତୁ। **2 spades** (*plural*) the playing cards that have the shape ♠ on them ତାସ୍‌ର କଳାପାନ ଘର *the queen of spades*

spaghetti /spəˈgeti/ *noun* (*no plural*) a kind of food made from flour and water, that looks like long pieces of string ଚକଟା ଅଟାରୁ ପ୍ରସ୍ତୁତ ଲମ୍ବା ଓ ସରୁ କାଠି ପରି ଖାଦ୍ୟ ପଦାର୍ଥ (ଯାହା ରାନ୍ଧିଲେ ନରମ ହୋଇଯାଏ)

spanner /ˈspænə(r)/ *noun* a tool that is used for turning **nuts** and **bolts** ନଟ୍ (ଏକ ପ୍ରକାର ପେଚ) ଲଗାଇ ମୋଡ଼ିବା ପାଇଁ ରେଞ୍ଚ୍ ➪ ଚିତ୍ର ପାଇଁ **tool** ଦେଖନ୍ତୁ।

spare[1] /speə(r)/ *adjective* extra; that you do not need now ଅତିରିକ୍ତ, ଅଧିକ; ବର୍ତ୍ତମାନ ଦରକାର ନଥିବା *Have you got a spare tyre in your car?*

spare[2] /speə(r)/ *verb* (**spares, sparing, spared**) be able to give something to somebody ଦେବାପାଇଁ ସମର୍ଥ ହେବା, ତ୍ୟାଗ କରିବା, ଦେଇ ପାରିବା *I can't spare the time to help you today.* ○ *Can you spare some money?*

spark /spɑːk/ *noun* a very small burning piece of something ଝଲକ, ଆଲୋକ କଣା

sparkle /ˈspɑːkl/ *verb* (**sparkles, sparkling, sparkled**) shine with a lot of very small points of light ଚକ୍ ଚକ୍ ହେବା, ଝଲସିବା *The sea sparkled in the sunlight.* ○ *Her eyes sparkled with excitement.*

sparkle *noun* (*no plural*) ଚକମକ, ଝଲସ; ପ୍ରଫୁଲ୍ଲତା *the sparkle of diamonds*

sparkling *adjective* that sparkles ଚକମକିଆ, ଝଲସୁଥିବା *sparkling blue eyes*

sparrow /ˈspærəʊ/ *noun* a small brown bird ଘରଚଟିଆ ଚଢ଼େଇ ➪ ଚିତ୍ର ପାଇଁ **bird** ଦେଖନ୍ତୁ।

sparse /spɑːs/ *adjective* very little ବିରଳ, ବେଶୀ ପରିମାଣରେ ମିଳୁନଥିବା, ସ୍ୱଳ୍ପ *the sparse population of a region*

spat ଶବ୍ଦ **spit** ର ଏକ ଧାତୁରୂପ

speak /spiːk/ *verb* (**speaks, speaking, spoke** /spəʊk/, **has spoken** /ˈspəʊkən/) **1** say words; talk to somebody କହିବା, କଥାବାର୍ତ୍ତା କରିବା *Please speak more slowly.* ○ *Can I speak to Ameena, please?* **2** know and use a language (କୌଣସି ଭାଷା) କହି ପାରିବା *I can speak French and Italian.*

speak up talk louder ଉଚ୍ଚ ସ୍ୱରରେ କହିବା; ବଡ଼ ପାଟିରେ କୁହ *Can you speak up? I can't hear you!*

speaker /ˈspiːkə(r)/ *noun* **1** a person who is talking to a group of people ବକ୍ତା, ବକ୍ତୃତା ଦେବା ବ୍ୟକ୍ତି **2** the part of a radio, cassette player, etc. from where the sound comes out ଲାଉଡ୍‌ସ୍ପିକର୍, ଶବ୍ଦବର୍ଦ୍ଧକ ଚୁଙ୍ଗା

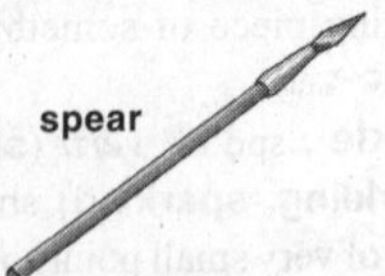

spear /spɪə(r)/ *noun* a long stick with a sharp point at one end, used for hunting or fighting ବର୍ଚ୍ଛା

special /ˈspeʃl/ *adjective* **1** not usual or ordinary; important for a reason ବିଶେଷ ପ୍ରକାରର (ସାଧାରଣ ନୁହେଁ) ସ୍ୱତନ୍ତ୍ର ପ୍ରକାରର; ବିଶେଷ କାମ ପାଇଁ ଉଦ୍ଦିଷ୍ଟ *It's my birthday today, so we are having a special dinner.* **2** for a particular person or thing ନିର୍ଦ୍ଦିଷ୍ଟ ବ୍ୟକ୍ତି ବା ଗୋଷ୍ଠୀ ପାଇଁ ଉଦ୍ଦିଷ୍ଟ *He goes to a special school for deaf children.*

specially *adverb* for a particular person or thing ସ୍ୱତନ୍ତ୍ର ଭାବରେ *I made this cake specially for you.*

specialist /ˈspeʃəlɪst/ *noun* a person who knows a lot about something ବିଶେଷଜ୍ଞ *She's a specialist in Indian history.*

specialize /ˈspeʃəlaɪz/ *verb* (**specializes, specializing, specialized**)

specialize in something study or know a lot about one special thing କୌଣସି ବୃତ୍ତି ବା ବିଷୟରେ ବିଶେଷଜ୍ଞ ହେବା *This doctor specializes in heart diseases.*

species /ˈspiːʃiːz/ *noun* (*plural* **species**) a group of animals or plants that are the same in some way ସମଜାତୀୟ ପଶୁ ବା ଉଦ୍ଭିଦ, ଜାତି *a rare species of plant*

specific /spəˈsɪfɪk/ *adjective* **1** particular ନିର୍ଦ୍ଦିଷ୍ଟ *Is there anything specific that you want to talk about?* **2** exact and clear ସଠିକ୍, ନିଶ୍ଚିତ ଓ ସ୍ପଷ୍ଟ *He gave us specific instructions on how to get there.*

specifically *adverb* ନିର୍ଦ୍ଦିଷ୍ଟଭାବରେ *I specifically asked you to buy butter, not cheese.*

specimen /ˈspesɪmən/ *noun* a small amount or part of something that shows what the rest is like; one example of a group of things (ବୈଜ୍ଞାନିକ ପରୀକ୍ଷା ପାଇଁ) ନମୁନା ରୂପେ ନିଆଯାଉଥିବା ପଦାର୍ଥ ବା ଏହାର ଅଂଶ *a specimen of rock* ○ *The doctor took a specimen of blood for testing.*

speck /spek/ *noun* a very small bit of something ପଦାର୍ଥର ଅତିକ୍ଷୁଦ୍ର ଅଂଶ, କଣା, କଣିକା *specks of dust*

spectacles /ˈspektəklz/ *noun* (*plural*) two pieces of special glass that people wear over their eyes to help them see better ଚଷମା, ପ୍ରଚକ୍ଷୁ *a pair of spectacles* ✪ ସାଧାରଣତଃ **glasses** ଶବ୍ଦର ପ୍ରୟୋଗ କରାଯାଏ ।

spectacular /spekˈtækjələ(r)/ *adjective* wonderful to see ଚିତ୍ତାକର୍ଷକ, ଦୃଷ୍ଟି ଆକର୍ଷଣକାରୀ *There was a spectacular view from the top of the mountain.*

spectator /spekˈteɪtə(r)/ *noun* a person who watches something that is happening ଦର୍ଶକ, ଦେଖଣାହାରୀ *There were 20,000 spectators at the football match.*

sped ଶବ୍ଦ **speed** ର ଏକ ଧାତୁରୂପ

speech /spiːtʃ/ *noun* **1** (*no plural*) the power to speak, or the way that you speak କଥନଶକ୍ତି; ବାକ୍‌ଶକ୍ତି **2** (*plural* **speeches**) a talk that you give to a group of people ବକ୍ତୃତା, ଭାଷଣ *The principal made a speech.*

speed¹ /spiːd/ *noun* how fast something moves ଗତି, ଗତିର କ୍ଷିପ୍ରତା, ବେଗ, ଦ୍ରୁତତା *The car was travelling at a speed of 50 kilometres per hour.*

speed² /spiːd/ *verb* (**speeds, speeding, sped** /sped/, **speeded, has sped** ବା **has speeded**) **1** go or move very quickly କ୍ଷିପ୍ର ଗତିରେ ଯିବା *He sped past me on his bike.* **2** drive too fast ଅତି ଦ୍ରୁତ ଗତିରେ ଗାଡ଼ି ଚଲାଇବା *The police stopped me because I was speeding.*

speed up go faster; make something go faster ବେଗ ବଢ଼ାଇବା; ଦ୍ରୁତ ଗତିରେ ଚଲାଇବା

spell¹ /spel/ *verb* (**spells, spelling, spelt** /spelt/ ବା **spelled, has spelt** ବା **has spelled**) use the right letters to make a word ବନାନ କରିବା ବା କହିବା *'How do you spell your name?' 'A-Z-I-Z.'* ○ *You have spelt this word wrong.*

spelling *noun* the right way of writing a word ବନାନ *Look in your dictionary to find the right spelling.*

spell² /spel/ *noun* magic words କୁହୁକ କରି ପାରୁଥିବା ମନ୍ତ୍ର

spend /spend/ *verb* (**spends, spending, spent** /spent/, **has spent**) **1** pay money for something ଖର୍ଚ୍ଚ କରିବା *Suman spends a lot of money on clothes.* **2** use time for something ସମୟ ବିତାଇବା *I spent the summer in Shimla.*

sphere /sfɪə(r)/ *noun* any round thing that is like a ball ଗୋଲକ, ଗୋଲାକାର ପଦାର୍ଥ *The earth is a sphere.* ➪ ଚିତ୍ର ପାଇଁ **shape** ଦେଖନ୍ତୁ ।

spice /spaɪs/ *noun* a powder or the seeds from a plant that you can put in food to give it a stronger taste.

Pepper and ginger are spices ରନ୍ଧାରେ ବ୍ୟବହୃତ ମସଲା

spicy *adjective* (**spicier, spiciest**) with spices in it ମସଲାପକା, ମସଲିଆ *He loves spicy food.*

spider /ˈspaɪdə(r)/ *noun* a small animal with eight legs, that catches and eats insects ବୁଢ଼ିଆଣି, ମାଙ୍କଡ଼ସା *Spiders spin webs to catch insects.* ➪ ଚିତ୍ର ପାଇଁ **web** ଦେଖନ୍ତୁ ।

spied ଶବ୍ଦ **spy** ର ଏକ ଧାତୁରୂପ

spies 1 ଶବ୍ଦ **spy** ର ବହୁବଚନ **2** ଶବ୍ଦ **spy** ର ଏକ ଧାତୁରୂପ

spike /spaɪk/ *noun* a piece of metal with a sharp point ମୁନିଆ ଧାତୁ କଣ୍ଟା *The fence has spikes along the top.*

spill /spɪl/ *verb* (**spills, spilling, spilt** /spɪlt/ ବା **spilled, has spilt** ବା **has spilled**) if you spill a liquid, it flows out of something by accident ତରଳ ପଦାର୍ଥ ଉଚ୍ଛୁଳି ପଡ଼ିବା, ଉଚ୍ଛୁଳାଇ ପକାଇ ଦେବା *I've spilt my milk!*

spin /spɪn/ *verb* (**spins, spinning, spun** /spʌn/, **has spun**) **1** turn round and round quickly; turn something round quickly ଘୂରିବା , ଘୂର୍ଣ୍ଣନ କରିବା, ଘୂରାଇବା; ଜୋର୍‌ରେ ଘୂରିବା *She spun a coin on the table.* **2** make thread from wool or cotton ଘୂରାଇ ଘୂରାଇ ତୁଳା ବା ପଶମରୁ ସୂତା କାଢ଼ିବା, ସୂତାଭିଣିବା **3** (of spider or silkworm) make a web (ବୁଢ଼ିଆଣୀ, ରେଶମପୋକ) ଜାଲ ବୁଣିବା *The spider spun a web.*

spinach /ˈspɪnɪtʃ/ *noun* (*no plural*) a vegetable with big green leaves ଏକ ପ୍ରକାର ଶାଗ

spinal cord *noun* the thick bundle of nerves inside the **spine** that connects all parts of the body to the brain ମେରୁ ହାଡ଼ର ମଜା ବା ସ୍ନାୟୁ, ମେରୁମଜ୍ଜା, ସୁଷୁମ୍ନାକାଣ୍ଡ

spine /spaɪn/ *noun* **1** the line of small bones in your back ମେରୁଦଣ୍ଡ **2** a thorn (ଗଛର) କଣ୍ଟା

spiral /ˈspaɪrəl/ *noun* a long shape that goes round and round as it goes up ପେଚଘରା ପରି ଘୂରି ଘୂରି ଯାଇଥିବା, କୁଣ୍ଡଳାକାର *A spring is a spiral.*

spiral *adjective* କୁଣ୍ଡଳାକାର *a spiral staircase*

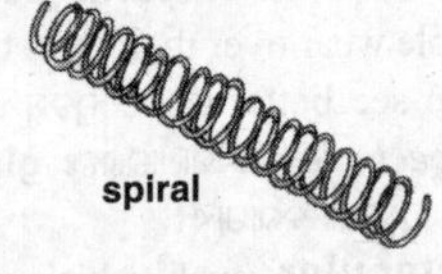
spiral

spirit /ˈspɪrɪt/ *noun* **1** the part of a person that is not the body. Some people believe that your spirit does not die when your body dies ଆତ୍ମା; ଭୂତ **2 spirits** (*plural*) the way you feel ମନୋଭାବ *She's in high spirits today.*

spiritual /ˈspɪrɪtʃuəl/ *adjective* **1** connected with the spirit rather than the body ଅଭୌତିକ, ଆଧାତ୍ମିକ *spiritual needs* **2** connected with religion ଧାର୍ମିକ *spiritual leaders*

spit /spɪt/ *verb* (**spits, spitting, spat** /spæt/, **has spat**) throw liquid or food out from your mouth ଛେପ ପକାଇବା *The baby spat her food out.*

spite /spaɪt/ *noun* (*no plural*) a feeling of wanting to hurt somebody ମନ୍ଦଇଚ୍ଛା, ଦ୍ୱେଷ *She broke my watch out of spite.*

in spite of something although something is true; not noticing or not caring about something ଯଦିଓ, ଏହାସତ୍ତ୍ୱେ *In spite of the bad weather, we went out.*

splash /splæʃ/ *verb* (**splashes, splashing, splashed**) **1** throw drops of liquid over somebody or something and make them wet ପାଣି ଇତ୍ୟାଦି ଛିଞ୍ଚାଡ଼ିବା ବା ଝିଟିକାଇବା *The car splashed us as it drove past.* **2** move through water so that drops of it fly in the air ପାଣି ଛିଟିକାଇବା *The children were splashing around in the pool.*

splash *noun* (*plural* **splashes**) **1** the sound that a person or thing makes when they fall into water ପାଣିରେ ଧସ୍‌କରି ପଡ଼ିବା ଶବ୍ଦ *Tina jumped into the pool with a big splash.* **2** a place where liquid has fallen ତରଳ ପଦାର୍ଥ ପଡ଼ିଥିବା ଜାଗା *There were splashes of paint on the floor.*

splendid /ˈsplendɪd/ *adjective* very beautiful or very good ଚମତ୍କାର, ଚାକଚମକପୂର୍ଣ୍ଣ *a splendid palace*

splendour /ˈsplendə(r)/ *noun* grand and very impressive beauty ଶୋଭା, ସୌନ୍ଦର୍ଯ୍ୟ *The fort was restored to its former splendour.*

split /splɪt/ *verb* (**splits, splitting, split, has split**) **1** break something into two parts ଦୁଇଭାଗ କରି ଲମ୍ବା ବାଗିଆ ଭାଙ୍ଗିଦେବା ବା କାଟିଦେବା *I split the wood with an axe.* **2** share something; give a part to each person ଭାଗ ଭାଗ କରି ବାଣ୍ଟିବା *We split the money between us.*

spoil /spɔɪl/ *verb* (**spoils, spoiling, spoilt** /spɔɪlt/ ବା **spoiled, has spoilt** ବା **has spoiled**) **1** make something less good than before ଖରାପ କରିଦେବା, ନଷ୍ଟ କରିଦେବା *Did the bad weather spoil your holiday?* **2** give a child too much so that they think they can have what they want ପିଲାମାନଙ୍କୁ ଅତି ଗେହ୍ଲାକରି ତାଙ୍କ ଆଚରଣ ଖରାପ କରିବା *She spoils her grandchildren.*

spoke[1] ଶବ୍ଦ **speak** ର ଏକ ଧାତୁରୂପ

spoke[2] /spəʊk/ *noun* one of the thin pieces of wire or bars that join the middle of a wheel to the outside, for example on a bicycle ଚକର କେନ୍ଦ୍ର ନାଭିରୁ ପହିଆକୁ ଲମ୍ବିଥିବା ଲୁହା ବା କାଠବାଡ଼ି, ସ୍ପୋକ୍

spoken ଶବ୍ଦ **speak** ର ଏକ ଧାତୁରୂପ

spokesperson /ˈspəʊksˌpɜːsn/ *noun* (*plural* **spokespersons**) a person who tells somebody what a group of people has decided ମୁଖପାତ୍ର ବା ମୁଖପାତ୍ରୀ

sponge /spʌndʒ/ *noun* a soft thing with a lot of small holes in it, that you use for washing yourself or cleaning things ଗାଧୋଇଲା ବେଳେ ଘସାଘସି ହେବା ପାଇଁ ବା ବାସନ ଇତ୍ୟାଦି ସଫା କରିବା ପାଇଁ ବ୍ୟବହୃତ ବହୁ କଣା ଥିବା ଏକ ନମନୀୟ ପଦାର୍ଥ, ସ୍ପଞ୍ଜ୍

spongy /ˈspʌndʒi/ *adjective* like a sponge; soft and able to absorb water ସ୍ପଞ୍ଜ୍ ପରି, ନରମ ଓ ପାଣି ଶୋଷି ପାରୁଥିବା

spontaneous /spɒnˈteɪniəs/ *adjective* that happens or is done suddenly without any planning ହଠାତ୍ ଯାହା ମନକୁ ଆସିଲା ତା ଅନୁସାରେ କରାଯାଉଥିବା; ସ୍ୱତଃ ସ୍ଫୁର୍ତ୍ତ, ସ୍ୱତଃପ୍ରବୃତ୍ତ *a spontaneous speech*

spoon /spu:n/ *noun* a thing with a round end that you use for putting food in your mouth or for mixing ଚାମୁଚି, ଚାମଚ *a wooden spoon* ○ *a teaspoon* ⇨ ଚିତ୍ର ପାଇଁ **cutlery** ଦେଖନ୍ତୁ।

spoonful /ˈspu:nfʊl/ *noun* the amount that you can put in one spoon ପୂରା ଚାମଚ *Two spoonfuls of sugar in my tea, please.*

sport /spɔ:t/ *noun* a game that you play to keep your body strong and well or because you enjoy it ଖେଳକୁଦ *Football, swimming and tennis are all sports.*

spot[1] /spɒt/ *noun* **1** a small round mark ଛୋଟ ଗୋଲ୍ ଦାଗ *a red dress with white spots* **2** a place ସ୍ଥାନ, ଜାଗା *This is a good spot for picnics.*

spotted *adjective* with small round marks on it ଗୋଲଗୋଲ ଦାଗ ଥିବା *a spotted shirt*

spot[2] /spɒt/ *verb* (**spots, spotting, spotted**) see somebody or something suddenly ହଠାତ୍ ଦେଖିଦେବା, ଠାବ କରିବା *She spotted her friend in the crowd.*

spout /spaʊt/ *noun* the part of a container that is like a short tube, through which liquid can be poured out. Teapots have spouts ନଳପରି ମୁହଁ, ନଳମୁହଁ

sprain /spreɪn/ *verb* (**sprains, spraining, sprained**) hurt a part of your body by twisting it suddenly ମକଚି ହେବା *Rajan fell and sprained his ankle.*

sprain *noun* a bad ankle sprain ମକଚି ଯିବା

sprang ଶବ୍ଦ **spring**[3] ର ଏକ ଧାତୁରୂପ

spray /spreɪ/ *noun* **1** (*no plural*) liquid in very small drops that flies through the air ଉଡ଼ିଆସୁଥିବା ଜଳକଣା ଇତ୍ୟାଦି *spray from the sea* **2** (*plural* **sprays**) a liquid in a can that comes out in very small drops when you press a button ଚାପ ଦ୍ୱାରା ବିଚ୍ଛୁରିତ ହେଉଥିବା ତରଳ ପଦାର୍ଥ (ଯଥା:ଅତର) *hairspray* ⇨ **aerosol** ଦେଖନ୍ତୁ।

spray *verb* (**sprays, spraying, sprayed**) make very small drops of liquid fall on something ବିଚ୍ଛୁରଣ କରିବା *Somebody has sprayed paint on my car.*

spread /spred/ *verb* (**spreads, spreading, spread, has spread**) **1** open something so that you can see all of it ଖୋଲିଦେବା; ବିଛାଇବା *Spread out the map on the table.* ○ *The bird spread its wings and flew away.* **2** put a soft substance all over something ବୋଳିବା, ଲଗାଇବା, ମାଖିବା *I spread butter on the bread.* **3** move to other places or to other people; make something do this ଖେଳେଇ ହୋଇଯିବା, ମାଡ଼ିଯିବା *Fire quickly spread to other parts of the building.*

spread *noun* (*no plural*) ବିସ୍ତାର; ସଂକ୍ରମଣ *Doctors are trying to stop the spread of the disease.*

spring[1] /sprɪŋ/ *noun* **1** a thin piece of metal that is bent round and round. A spring will go back to the same size and shape after you push or pull it ଚାପିଦେଲେ ପୁଣି ସମ୍ପ୍ରସାରିତ

ହୋଇଯାଉଥିବା ମଣ୍ଡଳାକାର ଧାତୁ ଉପକରଣ; କମାନି ଏକ ଜାଗା ଯେଉଁଠାରେ ଜଳକୁ ଭୂମିରୁ ନିର୍ଗତ ସ୍ପ୍ରିଙ୍ଗ କରାଯାଏ। **2** a place where water comes out of the ground ଝରଣା

spring² /sprɪŋ/ *noun* the season between winter and summer, and when plants start to grow ବସନ୍ତ ଋତୁ

spring³ /sprɪŋ/ *verb* (**springs, springing, sprang** /spræŋ/, **has sprung** /sprʌŋ/) jump or move suddenly ହଠାତ୍ ଡିଆଁ ମାରିବା *The cat sprang on the mouse.*

sprinkle /ˈsprɪŋkl/ *verb* (**sprinkles, sprinkling, sprinkled**) throw drops or small pieces of something on another thing ଛିଞ୍ଚିଲାପରି ପକାଇବା *Sprinkle some sugar on the fruit.*

sprout /spraʊt/ *verb* (**sprouts, sprouting, sprouted**) start to grow ଗଜୁରିବା, ଅଙ୍କୁରିତ ହେବା *New leaves are sprouting on the trees.*

sprung ଶବ୍ଦ **spring³** ର ଏକ ଧାତୁରୂପ

spun ଶବ୍ଦ **spin** ର ଏକ ଧାତୁରୂପ

spy /ˈspaɪ/ *noun* (*plural* **spies**) a person who tries to learn secret things about another country, person or company ଗୁପ୍ତଚର

spy *verb* (**spies, spying, spied, has spied**) try to learn secret things about somebody or something ଗୁପ୍ତ କଥା ଜାଣିବାକୁ ଚେଷ୍ଟା କରିବା

spy on somebody watch somebody or something secretly କାହାରି ଉପରେ ନଜର ରଖିବା

squad /skwɒd/ *noun* a small group of people who work together ନିର୍ଦ୍ଦିଷ୍ଟ କାମ ପାଇଁ ଗଠିତ ଦଳ *the Indian football squad* ○ *a squad of police officers*

square /skweə(r)/ *noun* **1** a shape with four straight sides that are the same length and have four right angles ବର୍ଗକ୍ଷେତ୍ର, ସମବାହୁ ଚତୁର୍ଭୁଜ ➪ ଚିତ୍ର ପାଇଁ **shape** ଦେଖନ୍ତୁ। **2** an open space in a town with buildings around it ଚାରି ପଟେ ଘରଥିବା (ଚାରିକୋଣିଆ) ଖୋଲା ଜାଗା *the market square*

square *adjective* with four straight sides that are of the same length and have four right angles ବର୍ଗାକାର *a square table*

squash¹ /skwɒʃ/ *verb* (**squashes, squashing, squashed**) press something hard and make it flat ଚାପିଦେଇ ଚଟକା କରିବା *She sat on my hat and squashed it.*

squash² /skwɒʃ/ *noun* a drink made from fruit juice and sugar. You add water before you drink it ଫଳ ରସରେ ଚିନି ଓ ପାଣି ମିଶାଇ କରାଯାଇଥିବା ପାନୀୟ *a glass of orange squash*

squash³ /skwɒʃ/ *noun* (*no plural*) a game where two players hit a small ball against a wall in a special room (called a **court**) ଏକ ନିବୁଜ ସ୍ଥାନ (କୋର୍ଟ) ରେ ର୍ୟାକେଟ୍ ଦ୍ୱାରା ଗୋଟିଏ ଛୋଟ ବଲ୍‌କୁ କାନ୍ଥକୁ ମାରିବା ଖେଳ *Have you ever played squash?*

squat /skwɒt/ *verb* (**squats, squatting, squatted**) sit with your feet on the ground, your legs bent and your bottom just above the ground ପାଦରେ ବସିବା, ଆଣ୍ଠୁଟେକି ବସିବା *I squatted down to light the fire.*

squeak /skwi:k/ *verb* (**squeaks, squeaking, squeaked**) make a short high sound like a mouse କ୍ଷଣିକ ତୀବ୍ରସ୍ୱରର ଚିତ୍କାର, ରାବ ବା ଶବ୍ଦ କରିବା, ଚିଁଚିଁ ବା କଁ କଁ ଶବ୍ଦ କରିବା *The door was squeaking, so I put some oil on it.*
squeak *noun* କ୍ଷଣିକ ତୀବ୍ର ଶବ୍ଦ, ଚିଁ ଚିଁ ବା କଁ କଁ ଶବ୍ଦ *the squeak of a mouse*

squeal /skwi:l/ *verb* (**squeals, squealing, squealed**) make a loud high sound ଉଚ୍ଚ ସ୍ୱରରେ ତୀବ୍ର ଶବ୍ଦ କରିବା *The children squealed with excitement.*
squeal *noun* ଉଚ୍ଚ ସ୍ୱରର ତୀବ୍ର ଶବ୍ଦ *the squeal of a pig*

squeeze /skwi:z/ *verb* (**squeezes, squeezing, squeezed**) press something hard between other things ଚିପିବା; ଚିପୁଡ଼ିରସ କାଢ଼ିବା *I squeezed an orange.*
squeeze *noun* ଚିପିବାକାମ, ଚିପା *She gave my arm a squeeze.*

squirrel /ˈskwɪrəl/ *noun* a small grey or brown animal with a big thick tail. Squirrels live in trees and eat nuts ଗୁଣ୍ଡୁଚିମୂଷା

squirrel

St ଶବ୍ଦ **saint** ର ସଂକ୍ଷିପ୍ତ ରୂପ

stab /stæb/ *verb* (**stabs, stabbing, stabbed**) push a knife or another sharp thing into somebody or something ଛୁରି ଇତ୍ୟାଦିରେ ଭୁସିଦେବା *He was stabbed in the back.*

stable[1] /ˈsteɪbl/ *noun* a building where horses are kept ଘୋଡ଼ାଶାଳ

stable[2] /ˈsteɪbl/ *adjective* something that is stable will not move, fall or change ସ୍ଥିର; ଦୃଢ଼ ଭାବରେ ସ୍ଥାପିତ; ସହଜରେ ବିଚଳିତ ହେଉନଥିବା *Don't stand on that table—it's not very stable.*
✪ ବିପରୀତ **unstable**

stack /stæk/ *noun* a lot of things on top of one another ତା ଉପରକୁ ତା ଉପର ରଖିବା ପଦାର୍ଥ; ଥାକ *a stack of books*
stack *verb* (**stacks, stacking, stacked**) put things on top of one another ତା ଉପରକୁ ତା'ଉପର ରଖିବା, ଥାକ କରି ରଖିବା *I stacked the chairs after the concert.*

stadium /ˈsteɪdiəm/ *noun* (*plural* **stadiums** ବା **stadia** /steɪdiə/) a place with seats around it where you can watch sports କ୍ରୀଡାଙ୍ଗନ ବା ଖେଳ ପଡ଼ିଆ ଓ ତାକୁ ଘେରି ରହୁଥିବା ଦର୍ଶକମଞ୍ଚ, ଷ୍ଟେଡିୟମ୍ *a football stadium*

staff /stɑ:f/ *noun* the group of people who work in a place କୌଣସି ସଂସ୍ଥାର କର୍ମଚାରୀବୃନ୍ଦ, ଷ୍ଟାଫ୍ *The hotel staff were very friendly.*
staffroom /ˈstɑ:fru:m/ *noun* a room in a school where teachers can work and rest ବିଦ୍ୟାଳୟରେ ଥିବା ଶିକ୍ଷକଙ୍କ ବସିବା ପ୍ରକୋଷ୍ଠ

stag /stæg/ *noun* a male deer ହରିଣ
➪ ଚିତ୍ର ପାଇଁ **deer** ଦେଖନ୍ତୁ ।

stage[1] /steɪdʒ/ *noun* the part of a theatre where actors, dancers, etc. stand and move ରଙ୍ଗମଞ୍ଚ

stage[2] /steɪdʒ/ *noun* ପ୍ରଗତି ବା ପ୍ରକ୍ରିୟାର ସ୍ତର ବା ପର୍ଯ୍ୟାୟ *The first stage of the course lasts for two weeks.*

at this stage now ବର୍ତ୍ତମାନ, ଏ ସ୍ଥିତିରେ *At this stage I don't know what I'll do when I leave school.*

stagger /ˈstægə(r)/ *verb* (**staggers, staggering, staggered**) walk as if you are going to fall ଟଳମଳ ହୋଇ ଚାଲିବା *He staggered across the room with the heavy box.*

stagnant /ˈstægnənt/ *adjective* if something is stagnant, it is not moving ନିଶ୍ଚଳ; ଗତିଶୂନ୍ୟ; ବହିଯାଉଥିବା *Mosquitoes breed in stagnant water.*

stain /steɪn/ *verb* (**stains, staining, stained**) make coloured or dirty marks on something ମଇଳା ଦାଗ କରାଇବା ବା ହେବା *The ink stained the carpet red.*

stain *noun* ମଇଳା ଦାଗ *She had soup stains on her shirt.*

stairs /steəz/ *noun* (*no plural*) steps that lead up and down in a building ପାହାଚ, ସୋପାନ *I ran up the stairs to the third floor.* ➪ **downstairs** ଓ **upstairs** ମଧ୍ୟ ଦେଖନ୍ତୁ।

staircase /ˈsteəkeɪs/, **stairway** /ˈsteəweɪ/ *noun* a set of stairs ପାହାଚ ମାର୍ଗ

stale /steɪl/ *adjective* (**staler, stalest**) not fresh ବାସି, ଶଢ଼ା, ଆମ୍ବିଲା *stale bread*

stalk /stɔːk/ *noun* one of the long thin parts of a plant that flowers, leaves or fruit grow on; a stem ଗଛର ପ୍ରଧାନ ଡେମ୍ଫ; ବୃନ୍ତ

stall /stɔːl/ *noun* a big table with things on it that somebody wants to sell, for example in a street or market (ବଜାରରେ) ବିକିବା ଜିନିଷ ସଜାଇ ରଖାଯାଇଥିବା ଟେବୁଲ୍; ଛୋଟ ଦୋକାନ *a fruit stall*

stammer /ˈstæmə(r)/ *verb* (**stammers, stammering, stammered**) say the same sound many times when you are trying to say a word ଖନେଇ ଖନେଇ କହିବା *'B-b-b-but wait for me,' he stammered.*

stamp[1] /stæmp/ *noun* **1** a small piece of paper that you put on a letter to show that you have paid to send it ଡାକ ଟିକଟ **2** a small piece of wood or metal that you press on paper to make marks or words ମୋହର; ମୋହର ଚିହ୍ନ *a date stamp*

stamp[1] 1

stamp[1] 2

stamp[2] /stæmp/ *verb* (**stamps, stamping, stamped**) **1** put your foot down quickly and hard ତଳେ ଗୋଡ଼ ବାଡ଼େଇବା, ଭୂମିକୁ ପଦାଘାତ କରିବା *She was stamping her feet to keep warm.* **2** walk by putting your feet down hard and loudly ଗୋଡ଼ ବାଡ଼େଇ ବାଡ଼େଇ ଚାଲିବା, ଧସ ଧସ କରି ଚାଲିବା *Maya stamped angrily out of the room.* **3** press a small piece of wood or metal on paper to make marks or words କାଗଜ ଉପରେ ମୋହର ମାରିବା *They stamped my passport at the airport.*

stand[1] /stænd/ *verb* (**stands, standing, stood** /stʊd/, **has stood**) **1** be on your feet ଠିଆ ହେବା *She was standing by the door.* **2** (**stand up** ମଧ୍ୟ) get up on your feet ଠିଆହେବା *The teacher asked us all to stand up.* **3** be in a place ଅବସ୍ଥିର ରହିବା, ଥିବା *The church stands on a hill.*

can't stand somebody or **something** hate somebody or something କାହାରିକୁ ବା କୌଣସି ପଦାର୍ଥକୁ ଘୃଣା କରିବା, ସହି ନପାରିବା *I can't stand this music.*

stand by somebody help somebody when they need it ବ୍ୟକ୍ତିଙ୍କୁ ଦରକାର ବେଳେ ସମର୍ଥନ କରିବା, ସାହାଯ୍ୟ କରିବା, ସହାୟକ ହେବା *Anita's parents stood by her when she was in trouble.*

stand for something be a short way of saying or writing something ସାଙ୍କେତିକ ବା ସଂକ୍ଷିପ୍ତ ରୂପ ହେବା; ପ୍ରତିନିଧିତ୍ୱ କରିବା ବା ପ୍ରତୀକ ହେବା *USA stands for 'the United States of America'.*

stand out be easy to see ସହଜରେ ଦିଶିବା, ଦୃଷ୍ଟିଗୋଚର ହେବା *Parthiv stands out in a crowd because he has got long hair.*

stand still not move ନିଶ୍ଚଳ ବା ସ୍ଥିର ହୋଇ ରହିବା *Stand still while I take your photograph.*

stand up for somebody or **something** say that somebody or something is right; support somebody or something କାହାର ସମର୍ଥନ କରିବା *Everyone else said I was wrong, but my sister stood up for me.*

stand[2] /stænd/ *noun* a piece of furniture that you can put things on ଜିନିଷ ପତ୍ର ରଖିବା ପାଇଁ ଆଧାର *an umbrella stand*

standard[1] /ˈstændəd/ *noun* how good somebody or something is ମାନ, ଆଦର୍ଶ *Her work is of a very high standard.*

standard[2] /ˈstændəd/ *adjective* normal; not special ସାଧାରଣ *Clothes are sold in standard sizes.*

stank ଶବ୍ଦ **stink** ର ଏକ ଧାତୁରୂପ

staple /ˈsteɪpl/ *noun* a small, very thin piece of metal that you push through pieces of paper to join them together, using a special tool (called a **stapler**) କାଗଜ ଗୁଛି ରଖିବା ପାଇଁ ଷ୍ଟେପ୍ଲର ସାହାଯ୍ୟରେ ଲଗାଯାଉଥିବା ଆକାରର ଧାତବକଣ୍ଟା, ଷ୍ଟେପ୍ଲ୍

staple *verb* (**staples, stapling, stapled**) ଷ୍ଟେପ୍ଲ୍ ଲଗାଇବା *Staple the sheets of paper together.*

stapler *noun* a small device that helps you put staples on paper ଷ୍ଟେପ୍ଲ୍ ଲଗାଇବା ଉପକରଣ

star[1] /stɑ:(r)/ *noun* **1** one of the small bright lights that you see in the sky at night ତାରା, ତାରକା, ନକ୍ଷତ୍ର **2** a shape with five or six points ପାଞ୍ଚମୁନିଆ ତାରକା ଚିହ୍ନ ➪ ଚିତ୍ର ପାଇଁ **shape** ଦେଖନ୍ତୁ।

star[2] /stɑ:(r)/ *noun* a famous person, for example an actor, a singer or a sportsperson ପ୍ରଖ୍ୟାତ ବ୍ୟକ୍ତି, ବିଶେଷତଃ ଚଳଚ୍ଚିତ୍ର ତାରକା, ଖେଳାଳି ବା ଗାୟକ *a film star* ○ *a pop star*

star *verb* (**stars, starring, starred**) be an important actor in a play or film ମୁଖ୍ୟ ଅଭିନେତା ବା ଅଭିନେତ୍ରୀ ଭାବରେ ଅଭିନୟ କରିବା *He has starred in many films.*

starch /stɑːtʃ/ *noun* **1** (*plural* **starches**) a white substance that is found in foods such as potatoes and rice ଖାଦ୍ୟ ପଦାର୍ଥରେ ଥିବା ଧଳା ପଦାର୍ଥ ବା ଶ୍ୱେତସାର **2** (*no plural*) a substance that is used for making your clothes stiff ଧୁଆ ଲୁଗାକୁ ଶକ୍ତ କରିବା ପାଇଁ ଏଥିରୁ ପ୍ରସ୍ତୁତ ମଣ୍ଡ

stare /steə(r)/ *verb* (**stares, staring, stared**) look at somebody or something for a long time ଏକ ଲୟରେ ଚାହିଁବା *Everybody stared at her bag.*

starfish /ˈstɑːfɪʃ/ *noun* (*plural* **starfish**) a sea creature with a flat body in the shape of a star with five arms ତାରକା ଚିହ୍ନ ଆକୃତିର ସମୁଦ୍ରଜୀବ ➪ ଚିତ୍ର ପାଇଁ **sea** ଦେଖନ୍ତୁ ।

start¹ /stɑːt/ *verb* (**starts, starting, started**) **1** begin to do something ଆରମ୍ଭ କରିବା *I start work at nine o'clock.* ○ *It started raining.* ✪ ବିପରୀତ **finish¹** ବା **stop¹** **2** begin to happen; make something begin to happen ଆରମ୍ଭ ହେବା, ଆରମ୍ଭ କରାଇବା *The film starts at 6.30 p.m.* ○ *The police do not know who started the fire.* ✪ ବିପରୀତ **finish¹** **3** begin to work or move; make something begin to work or move ଚାଳନ ଆରମ୍ଭ ହେବା; ଚାଳନ ଆରମ୍ଭ କରିବା *The engine won't start.* ○ *I can't start the car.*

start off begin ଆରମ୍ଭ କରିବା *The teacher started off by asking us our names.*

start² /stɑːt/ *noun* **1** the beginning or first part of something ଆରମ୍ଭ କରିବା ପ୍ରକ୍ରିୟା *She arrived after the start of the meeting.* **2** the act of starting something ଆରମ୍ଭ ସମୟ; ପ୍ରାରମ୍ଭ *We have got a lot of work to do, so let's make a start.* ✪ ବିପରୀତ **finish²**

startle /ˈstɑːtl/ *verb* (**startles, startling, startled**) make somebody suddenly surprised or frightened ହଠାତ୍ ଚମକାଇ ଦେବା *You startled me when you knocked on the window.*

starve /stɑːv/ *verb* (**starves, starving, starved**) suffer or die because there is not enough to eat ଅନାହାରରେ ଯନ୍ତ୍ରଣା ଭୋଗିବା ବା ମରିଯିବା *Millions of people are starving in some parts of the world.*

be starving be very hungry କ୍ଷୁଧିତ ବା ଭୋକିଲା ରହିବା *When will dinner be ready? I'm starving!*

starvation /stɑːˈveɪʃn/ *noun* (*no plural*) ଅନାହାର *Many people died of starvation last year.*

state¹ /steɪt/ *noun* **1** (*no plural*) the condition in which somebody or something is ଅବସ୍ଥା, ସ୍ଥିତି, ପରିସ୍ଥିତି *Your room is in a terrible state!* **2** (*plural* **states**) a country and its government ରାଜ୍ୟ, ରାଷ୍ଟ୍ର, ସରକାର *Many schools are run by the state.* **3** (*plural* **states**) a part of a country ପ୍ରଦେଶ, ରାଜ୍ୟର ଅଙ୍ଗ *Orissa is a state in India.*

state² /steɪt/ *verb* (**states, stating, stated**) say or write something clearly ସ୍ପଷ୍ଟ ଭାବରେ କହିବା ବା ଲେଖିବା, ବ୍ୟକ୍ତ କରିବା *I stated in my letter that I was looking for a job.*

statement *noun* something that you say or write formally ବକ୍ତବ୍ୟ *The driver made a statement to the police about the accident.*

statesman /ˈsteɪtsmən/ *noun* (*plural* **statesmen**) a respected and experienced political leader ସମ୍ମାନଯୋଗ୍ୟ ଓ ଅଭିଜ୍ଞ ରାଜନେତା *a party statesman*

station /ˈsteɪʃn/ *noun* **1** a place where trains stop so that people can get on and off; a railway station ରେଳଷ୍ଟେସନ୍ **2** a building for some special work ବିଶେଷ କାର୍ଯ୍ୟାଳୟ *a police station* ○ *a fire station* **3** a television or radio company (ଟେଲିଭିଜନ୍ ବା ରେଡ଼ିଓର) ସଞ୍ଚାର ସଂସ୍ଥାନ

stationary /ˈsteɪʃənri/ *adjective* if something is stationary, it is not moving ନିଶ୍ଚଳ; ଚଳନ ଶୂନ୍ୟ।

stationery /ˈsteɪʃənri/ *noun* (*no plural*) things that you use for writing, for example paper, pens, etc. କାଗଜ, କଲମ ଇତ୍ୟାଦି ଲେଖିବା ଜିନିଷ

statue /ˈstætʃuː/ *noun* the shape of a person or an animal that is made of stone or metal ମୂର୍ତ୍ତି, ପ୍ରତିମୂର୍ତ୍ତି ପ୍ରତିମା

statue

status /ˈsteɪtəs/ *noun* (*no plural*) **1** the legal position of a person, thing, country, etc. ବ୍ୟକ୍ତି, ଦେଶ ବା ପଦାର୍ଥର ନ୍ୟାୟସଙ୍ଗତ ସ୍ଥାନ *You have to state your marital status in the form.* **2** your position or rank in society as compared to others ପଦବୀ; ସାମାଜିକସ୍ଥାନ *Doctors have a high social status.*

stay[1] /steɪ/ *verb* (**stays, staying, stayed**) **1** be in the same place and not go away (କୌଣସି ସ୍ଥାନରେ) ରହିବା *Stay here until I come back.* **2** continue in the same way and not change (କୌଣସି ଅବସ୍ଥାରେ) ରହିବା *I tried to stay awake.* **3** live somewhere for a short time ଅଳ୍ପସମୟ ପାଇଁ ବସବାସ କରିବା *Which hotel are you staying at?*

stay behind be somewhere after other people have gone ପଛରେ ରହିଯିବା *The teacher asked me to stay behind after the class.*

stay up not go to bed ଚାହିଁ ରହିବା, ନ ଶୋଇବା *We stayed up until after midnight*

stay[2] /steɪ/ *noun* (*plural* **stays**) a short time when you live somewhere ଅଳ୍ପ ସମୟର ରହଣି, ରହିବା ସମୟ *Did you enjoy your stay in Puri?*

steady /ˈstedi/ *adjective* (**steadier, steadiest**) **1** if something is steady, it does not move or shake ଅଚଳ; ନିଶ୍ଚଳ, ନହଲିଲା ପରି *Hold the ladder steady while I stand on it.* ✪ ବିପରୀତ **unsteady** **2** if something is steady, it stays the same or it happens continuously ନିୟମିତ ବା ଅପରିବର୍ତ୍ତିତ ଭାବେ ଘଟୁଥିବା *We drove at a steady speed.* ○ *steady rain*

steadily *adverb* ନିୟମିତ ଭାବେ *Property prices are falling steadily.*

steal /sti:l/ *verb* (**steals, stealing, stole** /stəʊl/, **has stolen** /ˈstəʊlən/) secretly take something that is not yours ଚୋରିକରିବା; ଚୋରିହେବା *Her money has been stolen.*

> ✪ ଚୋରକୁ ଇଂରାଜୀରେ **thief** କହନ୍ତି । ଜିନିଷପତ୍ର ଚୋରାଇବାକୁ **steal** କହନ୍ତି, କିନ୍ତୁ ଲୋକମାନଙ୍କ ପାଖରୁ ବା କୌଣସି ସ୍ଥାନ ପରିପ୍ରେକ୍ଷୀରେ **rob** ଶବ୍ଦର ପ୍ରୟୋଗ ହୁଏ—
> *They* ***stole*** *my camera.*
> *I've been* ***robbed****.*
> *They* ***robbed*** *a bank.*

steam /sti:m/ *noun* (*no plural*) the hot gas that water becomes when it boils ବାଷ୍ପ, ଫୁଟା ପାଣିରୁ ବାହାରୁଥିବା ବାମ୍ପ *There was steam rising from my cup of coffee.*

steel /sti:l/ *noun* (*no plural*) a very strong metal that is used for making things like knives, tools or machines ଲୁହା ଓ ଅଙ୍ଗାରର ମିଶ୍ରଧାତୁ, ଇସ୍ପାତ୍

steep /sti:p/ *adjective* (**steeper, steepest**) a steep hill, mountain or road slopes up or down sharply ତୀକ୍ଷଣ୍ ଉଠାଣି ବା ଗଡ଼ାଣି, ଟିଖା *I can't cycle up the hill—it's too steep.*

steeply *adverb* ଟିଖା ହୋଇ, ଟିଖ ଭାବରେ *The path climbed steeply up the side of the mountain.*

steer /stɪə(r)/ *verb* (**steers, steering, steered**) make a car, boat, etc. go the way that you want by turning a wheel or handle (ଗାଡ଼ି ଇତ୍ୟାଦିର ଷ୍ଟିଅରିଂ ବା ଚାଳନ ଦଣ୍ଡ ଧରି) ଠିକ୍ ବାଟରେ ଚଲାଇବା

steering wheel *noun* the wheel in a vehicle that you turn to make it go in the direction you want (ଗାଡ଼ି ମଟରରେ ଥିବା) ଚାଳନଚକ୍ର, ଷ୍ଟିଅରିଂ ➪ ଚିତ୍ର ପାଇଁ **car** ଦେଖନ୍ତୁ ।

stem /stem/ *noun* the long thin part of a plant that the flowers and leaves grow on ଉଦ୍ଭିଦର ବୃନ୍ତ, କାଣ୍ଡ ➪ ଚିତ୍ର ପାଇଁ **plant** ଦେଖନ୍ତୁ ।

step[1] /step/ *noun* **1** a movement when you move your foot up and then put it down in another place to walk, run or dance ପଦକ୍ଷେପ *She took a step forward and then stopped.* ○ *a dance step* **2** a place to put your foot when you go up or down ସିଢ଼ି ବା ପାହାଚର ପାଦ ରଖିବା ଚଟାଣ ବା ବାଡ଼ି *These steps go down to the garden.* **3** one thing in a list of things that you must do to have or achieve something (କୌଣସି କାର୍ଯ୍ୟର) ପର୍ଯ୍ୟାୟ ବା କ୍ରମ *What is the first step in planning a holiday?*

step by step completing a process by doing one thing after another; slowly କ୍ରମ ଅନୁସାରେ; ଧିରେ ଧିରେ *This book shows you how to bake a cake, step by step.*

step[2] /step/ *verb* (**steps, stepping, stepped**) move your foot up and put it down in another place when you walk ପଦଚାଳନ କରିବା, ପାଦ ପକାଇବା *You stepped on my foot!*

stepfather /ˈstepfa:ðə(r)/ *noun* a man who has married your mother but who is not your father ସାବତ ବାପ

stepmother /ˈstepmʌðə(r)/ *noun* a woman who has married your father but who is not your mother ସାବତ ମା' ଆପଣଙ୍କ ✪ **Stepmother** ବା **stepfather** ଙ୍କ ପିଲାଙ୍କୁ **stepbrother** ବା **stepsister** କୁହାଯିବ।

stereo /ˈsteriəʊ/ *noun* (*plural* **stereos**) a machine for playing records, cassettes, compact discs or a radio, that has two boxes (called **speakers**) so that you hear separate sounds from each ଦୁଇ ସ୍ପିକର ଥିବା ଗୀତ ଶୁଣିବା ଯନ୍ତ୍ର; ଷ୍ଟେରିଓ

sterilization /ˌsterəlaɪˈzeɪʃn/ *noun* the process by which the germs present in something are killed ଜୀବାଣୁଲୋପ କରିବା ପ୍ରକ୍ରିୟା

sterilize /ˈsterəlaɪz/ *verb* (**sterilizes, sterilizing, sterilized**) **1** make something free of germs ଜୀବାଣୁ ଲୋପ କରିବା। **2** operate a person or an animal so that they cannot have babies ପିଲାଛୁଆ ନହେବା ପାଇଁ ଅସ୍ତ୍ରୋପଚାର କରିବା।

stern /stɜːn/ *adjective* (**sterner, sternest**) serious and strict with people; not smiling କଠୋର; ଗମ୍ଭୀର (ହସୁନଥିବା) *Our teacher is very stern.*

stethoscope /ˈsteθəskəʊp/ *noun* an instrument that doctors use to listen to your heartbeat and breathing ହୃତପିଣ୍ଡ, ଫୁସଫୁସ୍ ଇତ୍ୟାଦିର ଶବ୍ଦ ଶୁଣିବା ଯନ୍ତ୍ର

stew /stjuː/ *noun* food that you make by cooking meat or vegetables in liquid for a long time ଖାଦ୍ୟ ପଦାର୍ଥକୁ ପାଣିରେ ସିଝାଇ ରନ୍ଧା ଯାଉଥିବା ଖାଦ୍ୟ; ପାଣିସନ୍ତୁଳା, ଷ୍ଟ୍ର *vegetable stew*

stew *verb* (**stews, stewing, stewed**) cook something slowly in liquid ପାଣିରେ ସିଝାଇ ରାନ୍ଧିବା *We stewed some apples for dessert.*

steward /ˈstjuːəd/ *noun* a man whose job is to look after people on an aeroplane or a ship ଜାହାଜ ବା ବିମାନରେ ଯାତ୍ରୀଙ୍କର ସୁବିଧା ଅସୁବିଧା ବୁଝୁଥିବା କର୍ମଚାରୀ; ଷ୍ଟୁଆର୍ଡ

stewardess /ˌstjuːəˈdəs/ *noun* a woman whose job is to look after people on an aeroplane or a ship ଜାହାଜ ବା ବିମାନ ଯାତ୍ରୀଙ୍କ ସୁବିଧା ଅସୁବିଧା ବୁଝୁଥିବା ମହିଳା କର୍ମଚାରୀ

stick[1] /stɪk/ *noun* **1** a long thin piece of wood କାଠବାଡ଼ି *We found some sticks and made a fire.* ○ *The old man walked with a stick.* **2** a long thin piece of something (କୌଣସି ପଦାର୍ଥର) ସରୁ ଲମ୍ବାଖଣ୍ଡ *a stick of chalk*

stick[2] /stɪk/ *verb* (**sticks, sticking, stuck** /stʌk/, **has stuck**) **1** push a pointed thing into something ମୁନିଆ ଜିନିଷରେ ଖୋଞ୍ଚିବା ବା କେଞ୍ଚିବା *Stick a fork into the cake to see if it's cooked.* **2** join something to another thing with glue, for example; become joined in this way ଅଠାଦ୍ୱାରା ଯୋଡ଼ିବା; ଯୋଡ଼ି ହୋଇଯିବା *I stuck a stamp on the envelope.* **3** be fixed in one place so that it cannot move (ନ ଘୁଞ୍ଚିଲା ପରି) ଲାଖି ରହିବା *This door always sticks.* **stick out** come out of the side or top of something so that you can see it easily ଦେଖାଗଲା ପରି ବାହାରକୁ ବାହାରି ରହିବା

stick to something continue with something and not change it କୌଣସି କାମ ଇତ୍ୟାଦି ଦୃଢ଼ଭାବରେ କରିବା *We're sticking to our father's plan.*

sticker /ˈstɪkə(r)/ *noun* a small piece of paper with a picture or words on it, that you can stick onto things ଲଗାଯାଉଥିବା ଚିହ୍ନ ପତ୍ର ବା ଚିଠା, ଷ୍ଟିକର୍ *She has a sticker on the window of her car.*

sticky /ˈstɪki/ *adjective* (**stickier, stickiest**) something that is sticky can stick to things or is covered with something that can stick to things ଅଠାଳିଆ *Glue is sticky.* ○ *sticky fingers*

stiff /stɪf/ *adjective* (**stiffer, stiffest**) hard and not easy to bend or move ଶକ୍ତ, କଠିନ (ସହଜରେ ବଙ୍କାଇ ହେଉ ନଥିବା) *stiff cardboard*

still[1] /stɪl/ *adverb* **1** a word that you use to show that something has not changed or something is continuing until now ଅପରିବର୍ତ୍ତନୀୟ ଭାବରେ, ଏ ପର୍ଯ୍ୟନ୍ତ ବି *Do you still live in Lucknow?* ○ *Is it still raining?* **2** although that is true ତଥାପି *She felt ill, but she still went to the party.*

still[2] /stɪl/ *adjective, adverb* without moving ସ୍ଥିର; ସ୍ଥିର ହୋଇ *Please stand still while I take a photo.*

stimulus /ˈstɪmjələs/ *noun* (*plural* **stimuli** /ˈstɪmjəlaɪ/) something that produces a reaction in a human being, an animal or a plant ଜୀବ ଓ ଉଦ୍ଭିଦ ମଧ୍ୟରେ ପ୍ରତିକ୍ରିୟା ସୃଷ୍ଟି କରୁଥିବା ପଦାର୍ଥ, ଶକ୍ତି, ବ୍ୟବହାର ଇତ୍ୟାଦି

sting /stɪŋ/ *verb* (**stings, stinging, stung** /stʌŋ/, **has stung**) if an insect or a plant stings you, it hurts you by pushing a small sharp part into your skin ଦଂଶନ କରିବା, ନାହୁଡ଼ିରେ ଫୋଡ଼ିଦେବା, କାମୁଡ଼ିବା *I've been stung by a bee!*

sting *noun* **1** the sharp part of some insects that can hurt you କିଛି କୀଟଙ୍କର ନାହୁଡ଼ *A wasp's sting is in its tail.* **2** a place on your skin where an insect or plant has stung you ଶରୀରର ନାହୁଡ଼ମରା ସ୍ଥାନ *a bee sting*

stink /stɪŋk/ *verb* (**stinks, stinking, stank** /stæŋk/, **has stunk** /stʌŋk/) have a very bad smell ଗନ୍ଧେଇବା, ଦୁର୍ଗନ୍ଧ ହେବା *That fish stinks!*

stir /stɜː(r)/ *verb* (**stirs, stirring, stirred**) **1** move a spoon or another thing round and round to mix something well ଚାମଚ ଇତ୍ୟାଦିରେ ଗୋଳାଇବା ବା ଫେଣ୍ଟିବା *He put sugar in his coffee and stirred it.* **2** move a little or make something move a little ଅଳ୍ପ ଦୋହଲାଇବା ବା ହଲାଇବା *The wind stirred the leaves.*

stitch /stɪtʃ/ *noun* (*plural* **stitches**) **1** one movement in and out of a piece of material with a needle and thread when you are sewing ସିଲାଇର ଏକ ଘରା **2** one of the small circles of wool that you put round a knitting needle when you are knitting ଉଲ୍ କଣ୍ଟା ଦ୍ୱାରା ବୁଣୁଥିବା ଗୋଟିଏ ଘରା

stitch *verb* (**stitches, stitching, stitched**) make stitches in something; sew something ସିଲାଇ କରିବା *I stitched a button on my skirt.*

stock /stɒk/ *noun* things that a shop keeps ready to sell ବିକ୍ରିପାଇଁ ଦୋକାନରେ ଥିବା ଜିନିଷପତ୍ର; (କୌଣସି ଜିନିଷର) ଭଣ୍ଡାର, ଷ୍ଟକ୍ *That bookshop has a big stock of dictionaries.*

stocking /ˈstɒkɪŋ/ *noun* a long thin thing that a woman wears over her leg and foot ନାରୀମାନେ ପିନ୍ଧୁଥିବା ଲମ୍ବା ମୋଜା *a pair of stockings*

stole, stolen ଶବ୍ଦ **steal** ର ଏକ ଧାତୁରୂପ

stomach /ˈstʌmək/ *noun* **1** the part inside your body where food goes after you eat it ପାକସ୍ଥଳି, ପେଟ **2** the front part of your body below your chest and above your legs ପେଟ

stomach ache *noun* (*no plural*) a pain in your stomach ପେଟର ଯନ୍ତ୍ରଣା, ପେଟମୋଡ଼ା *I've got stomach ache.*

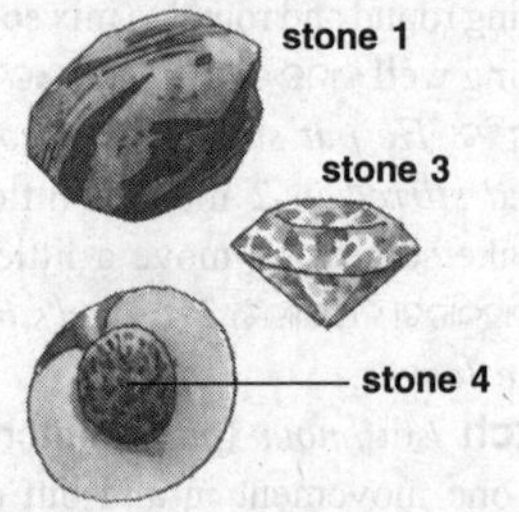

stone /stəʊn/ *noun* **1** (*no plural*) a hard substance that is found in the ground. Stone is sometimes used for building ପଥର, ପ୍ରସ୍ତର *a stone wall* **2** (*plural* **stones**) a small piece of rock ଛୋଟ ପଥର ଖଣ୍ଡ *The children were throwing stones into the river.* **3** (*plural* **stones**) a small piece of beautiful rock that is very valuable ହୀରା ଇତ୍ୟାଦି ମୂଲ୍ୟବାନ୍ ପଥର *A diamond is a precious stone.* **4** (*plural* **stones**) the hard part in the middle of some fruits, for example plums and peaches କିଛି ଫଳ ମଝିରେ ଥିବା ଟାକୁଆ ବା ଟାଣମଞ୍ଜି

stood ଶବ୍ଦ **stand**[1] ର ଏକ ଧାତୁରୂପ

stool /stu:l/ *noun* a small seat with no back ଜଣେଲୋକ ବସିବା ପାଇଁ ହାତ ଓ ହୃଷ୍ଟଭାଗ ନଥିବା ଚଉକି, ଷ୍ଟୁଲ

stoop /stu:p/ *verb* (**stoops, stooping, stooped**) if you stoop, you bend your body forward and down ଲଇଁ ପଡ଼ିବା, ଅବନତ ହେବା *She stooped to pick up the baby.*

stop[1] /stɒp/ *verb* (**stops, stopping, stopped**) **1** not move or work any longer; not be moving or working any more; become still ବନ୍ଦ କରିବା (କାମ ଇତ୍ୟାଦି) ରହିଯିବା, ଅଟକିଯିବା, ନିଶ୍ଚଳ ହେବା *The train stopped at every station.* ○ *The clock has stopped.* ○ *I stopped to post a letter.* **2** not do something any more; finish (କାମ ଇତ୍ୟାଦି); ବନ୍ଦ କରିବା, ଶେଷ କରିବା *Stop making that noise!* **3** make somebody or something finish moving or doing something ବନ୍ଦ କରାଇବା; ସମାପ୍ତ କରାଇବା *Ring the bell to stop the bus.*

stop somebody (from) doing something not let somebody do something ରୋକିବା *My dad stopped me from going out.*

stop[2] /stɒp/ *noun* **1** the moment when somebody or something finishes moving ବନ୍ଦ ଅବସ୍ଥା, ରୋକି ହୋଇଥିବା ଅବସ୍ଥା; ବିରତି *The train came to a* *stop*. **2** a place where buses or trains stop so that people can get on and off ବସ୍, ଟ୍ରେନ୍ ଇତ୍ୟାଦିର ରହିବା ସ୍ଥାନ *I'm getting off at the next stop.*

store¹ /stɔ:(r)/ *noun* **1** a big shop ବଡ଼ଦୋକାନ *Shoppers' Stop is a famous store.* **2** things that you are keeping to use later ଭଣ୍ଡାର; ଭବିଷ୍ୟତରେ ବ୍ୟବହାର ପାଇଁ ରଖାଯାଇଥିବା ଦ୍ରବ୍ୟ *a store of food*

store² /stɔ:(r)/ *verb* (**stores, storing, stored**) keep something to use later ଭବିଷ୍ୟତ ବ୍ୟବହାର ପାଇଁ ଗଚ୍ଛିତ ରଖିବା *The information is stored on a computer.*

storey /ˈstɔ:ri/ *noun* (*plural* **storeys**) one level in a building (ଘରର) ମହଲା *The building has four storeys.*

stork /stɔ:k/ *noun* a large white bird with a long beak, neck and legs. Storks live near water but often build their nests on the top of high buildings ବଗ, ବକ

storm¹ /stɔ:m/ *noun* very bad weather with strong winds and rain ଝଡ଼, ବତାସ, ତୋଫାନ *a thunderstorm*

storm² /stɔ:m/ *verb* (**storms, storming, stormed**) move in a way that shows you are angry କ୍ରୋଧାନ୍ୱିତ ଭାବରେ ଯିବା ବା ବ୍ୟବହାର କରିବା *He stormed out of the room.*

stormy /ˈstɔ:mi/ *adjective* (**stormier, stormiest**) if the weather is stormy, there is strong wind and rain ଝଡ଼ି ବା ତୋଫାନ (ପାଗ) *a stormy night*

story /ˈstɔ:ri/ *noun* (*plural* **stories**) **1** spoken or written words that tell you about people and things that are not real ଗପ, ଗଳ୍ପ *Ruskin Bond has written many stories for children.* **2** spoken or written words that tell you about things that really happened ପ୍ରକୃତ ଘଟଣାର ବର୍ଣ୍ଣନା *My grandmother told me stories about when she was a child.*

stove /stəʊv/ *noun* a thing that you use for cooking food on. A stove usually has one or more rings on top and uses gas or **kerosene** as fuel ଗ୍ୟାସ ବା କିରୋସିନି ବ୍ୟବହାର କରୁଥିବା ରାନ୍ଧିବା ଚୁଲି ➪ ଚିତ୍ର ପାଇଁ **kitchen** ଦେଖନ୍ତୁ।

straight¹ /streɪt/ *adjective* (**straighter, straightest**) **1** with no curve or bend ସିଧା, ସଳଖ, ବାଙ୍କ ବା ମୋଡ଼ ନଥିବା *Use a ruler to draw a straight line.* ○ *His hair is curly but mine is straight.* **2** with one side as high as the other ସମତଳ, ସିଧା, ସଳଖ *This picture isn't straight.*

straight² /streɪt/ *adverb* **1** in a straight line ସିଧା ଭାବରେ *Look straight in front of you.* **2** without stopping or doing anything else; directly ସିଧା (ଅନ୍ୟକିଛି ନକରି ବା ଅନ୍ୟ କୋଉଠି ନରହି) *Come straight home.*

straight away immediately; now ସାଙ୍ଗେସାଙ୍ଗେ, ବର୍ତ୍ତମାନ, ତତ୍‌କ୍ଷଣାତ୍ *I'll do it straight away.*

straighten /ˈstreɪtn/ *verb* (**straightens, straightening, straightened**) become or make something straight ସିଧା ହେବା; ସିଧା କରିବା; ସଳଖେଇବା

straightforward /ˌstreɪtˈfɔːwəd/ *adjective* **1** easy to understand or do ସହଜ, ସହଜବୋଧ୍ୟ, ସିଧା, ସରଳ *The question was straightforward.* **2** if someone is straightforward, they are honest and do not hide anything ସ୍ପଷ୍ଟବାଦୀ ଓ ସଙ୍କୋଚ (ବ୍ୟକ୍ତି)

strain /streɪn/ *verb* (**strains, straining, strained**) **1** pour a liquid through something with small holes in it, to take away any other things in the liquid ଛାଙ୍କୁଣିରେ ଛାଣିବା, ଛାଙ୍କିବା *You haven't strained the tea—there are tea leaves in it.* **2** hurt a part of your body by making it work too hard ବେଶୀ ପରିଶ୍ରମ କରିବା ଫଳରେ ଦେହର ଅଙ୍ଗ ପ୍ରତ୍ୟଙ୍ଗକୁ ଆଘାତ ଦେବା *Don't read in the dark. You'll strain your eyes.*

strain *noun* **1** the state of being pulled or being made to work too hard ଖୁବ୍ ଜୋର୍‌ରେ ଟାଣିବା; ଅତିବେଶୀ ବଳ ପ୍ରୟୋଗ କରିବା *The rope broke under the strain.* **2** an injury to a part of your body that is caused because you have made it work too hard ଖୁବ୍ ଜୋର୍‌ଲଗାଇବା ଫଳରେ ପେଶୀ ଇତ୍ୟାଦିର ଆଘାତ *back strain*

strait /streɪt/ *noun* a narrow strip of water that connects two seas ପ୍ରଣାଳୀ (ଦୁଇଟି ସମୁଦ୍ରକୁ ସଂଯୋଗ କରୁଥିବା ସଂକୀର୍ଣ୍ଣ ଜଳପଥ)

strand /strænd/ *noun* one piece of thread hair etc. ସୂତା, ବାଳ, ତାର ଇତ୍ୟାଦିର ଖିଅ

strange /streɪndʒ/ *adjective* (**stranger, strangest**) **1** unusual or surprising ଅସାଧାରଣ, ବିଚିତ୍ର, ଆଶ୍ଚର୍ଯ୍ୟ ଜନକ *Did you hear that strange noise?* **2** that you do not know ଅଜଣା, ଅଚିହ୍ନା *We were lost in a strange town.* ✪ ମନେ ରଖନ୍ତୁ! ବିଦେଶୀ ବ୍ୟକ୍ତି ବା ଜିନିଷ ପାଇଁ **foreign** ବ୍ୟବହାର କରାଯାଏ **strange** ନୁହେଁ।

strangely *adverb* in a surprising or unusual way ଆଶ୍ଚର୍ଯ୍ୟଜନକ ଭାବରେ *She usually talks a lot, but today she was strangely quiet.*

stranger /ˈstreɪndʒə(r)/ *noun* **1** a person who you do not know ଅଜଣା ବା ଅଚିହ୍ନା ଲୋକ **2** a person who is in a place that he or she does not know ଅଜଣା ସ୍ଥାନକୁ ଯାଇଥିବା ବ୍ୟକ୍ତି, ବାହାରର ଲୋକ *I'm a stranger to this city.* ✪ ମନେ ରଖନ୍ତୁ! ବିଦେଶୀ ଲୋକ ପାଇଁ **foreigner** ର ପ୍ରୟୋଗ କରାଯାଏ।

strangle /ˈstræŋgl/ *verb* (**strangles, strangling, strangled**) kill somebody by pressing their neck very tightly so that they cannot breathe ତଣ୍ଟି ଚିପି ମାରିଦେବା

strap /stræp/ *noun* a long flat piece of material that you use for carrying something or for keeping something in place ପତଳା ଲମ୍ବା ପଟି *a leather watch strap*

strap *verb* (**straps, strapping, strapped**) hold something in place with a strap ପଟିରେ ବାନ୍ଧିବା *I strapped the bag onto the back of my bike.*

strategy /ˈstrætədʒi/ *noun* **1** (*plural* **strategies**) a series of well-planned actions for achieving something କୌଶଳ, ଉପାୟ *strategy for ending unemployment in the* *country* **2** (*no plural*) the skill or action of planning how to achieve or do something କୁଶଳତା, କୌଶଳ ପ୍ରୟୋଗ କରିବାର ଦକ୍ଷତା

straw /strɔː/ *noun* **1** (*no plural*) the dry stems of plants like wheat କୁଟା, ନଡ଼ା **2** (*plural* **straws**) a thin paper or plastic tube that you can drink through ପାନୀୟ ପଦାର୍ଥ ପିଇବା ପାଇଁ ବ୍ୟବହୃତ ପ୍ଲାଷ୍ଟିକ୍ ବା କାଗଜର ସରୁନଳୀ

strawberry /ˈstrɔːbəri/ *noun* (*plural* **strawberries**) a small soft red fruit ଏକ ନରମ ରସାଳ ନାଲି ଫଳ *strawberry jam* ➪ ଚିତ୍ର ପାଇଁ **fruit** ଦେଖନ୍ତୁ।

stray /streɪ/ *adjective* having no home ଗୃହହୀନ *a stray dog*

stream /striːm/ *noun* **1** a small river ଛୋଟ ନଇ **2** moving liquid, or moving things or people ତରଳ ପଦାର୍ଥର ଧାର; ଲୋକଙ୍କର ବା ଗାଡ଼ିମଟରର ଧାର *a stream of blood* ○ *a stream of cars*

streamer /ˈstriːmə(r)/ *noun* a long narrow coloured strip of paper, used for decorating ସରୁ ଓ ଲମ୍ୱା ରଙ୍ଗିନ୍ କାଗଜ

street /striːt/ *noun* a road in a city, or a town with buildings along the sides ସହରର ରାସ୍ତା *I saw Ruby walking down the street.*

strength /streŋθ/ *noun* (*no plural*) the quality of being strong ବଳ, ଶାରୀରିକ ଶକ୍ତି *I don't have the strength to lift this box—it's too heavy.* ✪ ବିପରୀତ **weakness**

strengthen /streŋθn/ *verb* (**strengthens, strengthening, strengthened**) make something stronger ଶକ୍ତିଶାଳୀ କରିବା ✪ ବିପରୀତ **weaken**

stress /stres/ *noun* (*plural* **stresses**) **1** the act of saying one word or part of a word more strongly than another ଶବ୍ଦର କୌଣସି ଧ୍ୱନି ଉପରେ ଦିଆଯାଉଥିବା ଚାପ ବା ବଳାଘାତ *In the word 'dictionary', the stress is on the first part of the word.* **2** a feeling of worry because of problems in your life or because of too much work ମାନସିକ ଚାପ ବା ଉତ୍ତେଜନା *She's suffering from stress because she's got too much work to do.*

stress *verb* (**stresses, stressing, stressed**) say something strongly to show that it is important (ଗୁରୁତ୍ୱ ଦୃଷ୍ଟିରୁ କୌଣସି ବିଷୟ) ଜୋର୍ ଦେଇ କହିବା *I must stress how important this meeting is.*

stressful *adjective* ମାନସିକ ଚାପ ଦେଉଥିବା *a stressful job*

stretch[1] /stretʃ/ *verb* (**stretches, stretching, stretched**) **1** pull something to make it longer or wider; become longer or wider ଟାଣିବା, ଟାଣି ଲମ୍ୱା କରିବା; ଲମ୍ୱା ବା ଚଉଡ଼ା ହୋଇଯିବା *The T-shirt stretched when I washed it.* **2** push your arms and legs out as far as you can ହାତ ଗୋଡ଼ ପ୍ରସାରିତ କରି ମୋଡ଼ିଭିଡ଼ି ହେବା *Aarti got out of bed and stretched.* **3** continue ପ୍ରସାରଣ *The beach stretches for four kilometres.*

stretch out lie down with your whole body flat ହାତଗୋଡ଼ ପ୍ରସାରଣ କରି ଶୋଇବା *The cat stretched out in front of the fire and went to sleep.*

stretch² /stretʃ/ *noun* (*plural* **stretches**) a piece of land or water ବିସ୍ତୃତ ଜଳରାଶି ବା ଭୂମି *This is a beautiful stretch of countryside.*

stretcher /ˈstretʃə(r)/ *noun* a kind of bed for carrying somebody who is ill or hurt ରୋଗଗ୍ରସ୍ତ ବା ଆହତ ଲୋକଙ୍କୁ ନେବା ପାଇଁ ଖଟିଆପରି ଆଧାର, ଷ୍ଟ୍ରେଚର୍ *They carried him to the ambulance on a stretcher.*

strict /strɪkt/ *adjective* (**stricter, strictest**) if you are strict, you make people do what you want and do not allow them to behave badly କଠୋର, ସଂଯମୀ, କଡ଼ା *Her parents are very strict—she always has to be home before eight o'clock.*

strictly *adverb* definitely; in a strict way ନିଶ୍ଚିତ ଭାବରେ, କଡ଼ାକଡ଼ି ଭାବରେ *Smoking is strictly forbidden.*

stride /straɪd/ *verb* (**strides, striding, strode** /strəʊd/, **has stridden** /ˈstrɪdn/) walk with long steps ଲମ୍ବା ପଦକ୍ଷେପ ନେଇ ଚାଲିବା *The police officer strode across the road.*

strike¹ /straɪk/ *noun* a time when a group of people stop doing their work because they want more money or are angry about something ଧର୍ମଘଟ *There are no trains today because the drivers are on strike.*

strike² / straɪk / *verb* (**strikes, striking, struck** /strʌk/, **has struck**) **1** hit somebody or something or be hit by something ପ୍ରହାର କରିବା, ବାଡ଼େଇବା; ପଟି ଝୋଇଯିବା *A stone struck me on the back of the head.* ✪ ଏସବୁ କ୍ଷେତ୍ରରେ ସାଧାରଣତଃ **hit** ପ୍ରୟୋଗ କରାଯାଏ, କିନ୍ତୁ ଘଡ଼ଘଡ଼ି ଚଡ଼ଚଡ଼ି ପଡ଼ିବାକୁ **strike** କୁହାଯାଏ *The tree was struck by lightning.* **2** stop working because you want more money or are angry about something ଧର୍ମଘଟ କରିବା *The nurses are striking for better pay.* **3** ring a bell so that people know what time it is ଘଣ୍ଟା ବା ଘଣ୍ଟି ସମୟ ସୂଚାଇବା, ଘଣ୍ଟା ବାଜିବା *The clock struck nine.* **4** come suddenly into your mind ହଠାତ୍ ମନକୁ ଆସିବା *It suddenly struck me that she looked like my sister.*

strike a match make fire with a **match** ଦିଆସିଲି ମାରିବା

striking /ˈstraɪkɪŋ/ *adjective* if something is striking, you notice it because it is very unusual or interesting ଦୃଷ୍ଟି ଆକର୍ଷକ, ମୁଗ୍ଧକର *That's a very striking hat.*

string /ˈstrɪŋ/ *noun* **1** a very thin long rope that you use for tying things ସରୁ ଦଉଡ଼ି; ସୂତା *I tied up the parcel with string.* ○ *The little boy held a balloon on the end of a string.* **2** a line of similar things on a piece of thread ମାଳ, ମାଳା *She was wearing a string of blue beads.* **3** a piece of thin wire, etc. on a musical instrument ସିତାର୍, ଗିଟାର୍, ଇତ୍ୟାଦି ବାଦ୍ୟଯନ୍ତ୍ରର ତାର *guitar strings* ➪ **guitar** ଦେଖନ୍ତୁ।

strip¹ /strɪp/ *noun* a long thin piece of something ସରୁ ଲମ୍ବା ଖଣ୍ଡ ବା ପଟି *a strip of paper*

strip² /strɪp/ *verb* (**strips, stripping, stripped**) take off what is covering something ଆବରଣ କାଢ଼ି ଦେବା, ଲୁଗାପଟା କାଢ଼ିଦେବା *I stripped the paint off the walls.*

stripe /straɪp/ *noun* a long thin line of colour ରଙ୍ଗର ସରୁ ଲମ୍ବା ଚିହ୍ନ, ପଟା ପଟା ଚିହ୍ନ *Zebras have black and white stripes.*

striped /straɪv/ *adjective* with stripes ପଟାପଟା ଚିହ୍ନଥିବା *He wore a blue and white striped shirt.*

strode ଶବ୍ଦ **stride** ର ଏକ ଧାତୁରୂପ

stroke[1] /strəʊk/ *verb* (**strokes, stroking, stroked**) move your hand gently over somebody or something to show love କୋମଳ ଭାବରେ ହାତ ବୁଲାଇବା, ଆପୁଡାଇବା *She stroked her cat.*

stroke[2] /strəʊk/ *noun* a movement that you make with your arms when you are swimming, playing tennis, etc. ଟେନିସ୍, କ୍ରିକେଟ୍ ଇତ୍ୟାଦିରେ ବଲ୍‌କୁ ମାରିବା ପ୍ରକ୍ରିୟା, ପହଁରାରେ ହସ୍ତଚାଳନ ପ୍ରକ୍ରିୟା

stroll /strəʊl/ *verb* (**strolls, strolling, strolled**) walk slowly ଧୀରେ ଧୀରେ ଚାଲିବା, ବୁଲିବା *We strolled along the beach.*

stroll *noun* ଧୀର ଗତିର ବୁଲାଚଲା *We went for a stroll by the river.*

strong /strɒŋ/ *adjective* (**stronger, strongest**) **1** with a powerful body, so that you can carry heavy things ଶକ୍ତିଶାଳୀ, ବଳବାନ୍ ବଳୁଆ *I need somebody strong to help me move this bed.* ✪ ଏହାର ବିଶେଷ୍ୟ ପଦ ହେଲା **strength**। ✪ ବିପରୀତ **weak** **2** that you cannot break easily ସହଜରେ ଭାଙ୍ଗିବା *Don't stand on that chair—it's not very strong.* ○ *a strong belief* **3** that you can see, taste, smell, hear or feel very clearly ସ୍ପଷ୍ଟଭାବରେ ଅନୁଭୂତ କରିହେଉଥିବା ବା ଜାଣିହେଉଥିବା *a strong smell of oranges* ✪ ବିପରୀତ **weak**

strongly *adverb* ଦୃଢ଼ ଭାବରେ *I strongly believe that he is wrong.*

struck ଶବ୍ଦ **strike**[2] ର ଏକ ଧାତୁରୂପ

structure /ˈstrʌktʃə(r)/ *noun* **1** (*no plural*) the way that something is made ଗଠନ ପ୍ରଣାଳୀ, ଗଢ଼ଣ *We are studying the structure of the human body.* **2** (*plural* **structures**) a building or another thing that people have made with many parts ବହୁ ପ୍ରକାରର ପଦାର୍ଥ ଲାଗିଥିବା କୋଠା ଇତ୍ୟାଦି *The new post office is a tall glass and brick structure.*

struggle /ˈstrʌgl/ *verb* (**struggles, struggling, struggled**) **1** try very hard to do something that is not easy (କଷ୍ଟକର କାମ କରିବା ପାଇଁ) ପ୍ରବଳ ଚେଷ୍ଟା କରିବା *We struggled to lift the heavy box.* **2** move your arms and legs a lot when you are fighting or trying to get free or save yourself ମୁକ୍ତ ହେବା ପାଇଁ ପ୍ରବଳ ଚେଷ୍ଟା କରିବା, ଛାଟିପିଟି ହେବା *She struggled to get away from her attacker.*

struggle *noun* ସଂଘର୍ଷ *India's struggle for independence*

stubborn /ˈstʌbən/ *adjective* a person who is stubborn does not change his or her ideas easily or do what other people want him or her to do ଜିଦ୍‌ଖୋର୍, ଅବାଧ *She's too stubborn to say sorry.*

stuck[1] ଶବ୍ଦ **stick[2]** ର ଏକ ଧାତୁରୂପ

stuck[2] /stʌk/ *adjective* **1** not able to move ଲାଖି ବା ଅଟକି ଯାଇଥିବା *This drawer has got stuck—I can't open it.* **2** not able to do something because it is difficult (କିଛି କଷ୍ଟ କାମ) କରି ନପାରିବା ଅବସ୍ଥାରେ ଥିବା *If you get stuck, ask your teacher for help.*

student /ˈstju:dnt/ *noun* a person who is studying at a school, university or college ଛାତ୍ର ବା ଛାତ୍ରୀ *Tina is a student of history.*

studio /ˈstju:diəʊ/ *noun* (*plural* **studios**) **1** a room where an artist works ଚିତ୍ରକରର କାର୍ଯ୍ୟଶାଳା **2** a room where people make films, radio and television programmes, or records ଫଟୋ ବା ଚଳଚ୍ଚିତ୍ର ଉତ୍ତୋଳନର ସ୍ଥାନ, ଷ୍ଟୁଡ଼ିଓ *a television studio*

study[1] /ˈstʌdi/ *verb* (**studies, studying, studied, has studied**) **1** spend time learning about something ପାଠ ପଢ଼ିବା, ଅଧ୍ୟୟନ କରିବା *He studied English at university.* **2** look at something carefully ଭଲ କରି ଦେଖିବା, ଅନୁଧ୍ୟାନ କରିବା, ନିରୀକ୍ଷଣ କରିବା *We must study the map before we leave.*

study[2] /ˈstʌdi/ *noun* (*plural* **studies**) **1** the process of learning ପଠନ, ଅଧ୍ୟୟନ **2** a room in a house where you go to study, read or write ଘରର ଲେଖାପଢ଼ା କରିବା ପ୍ରକୋଷ୍ଠ, ପଢ଼ାଘର

stuff[1] /stʌf/ *noun* (*no plural*) any material, substance or group of things ପଦାର୍ଥ, ବସ୍ତୁ, ଜମାନାନ *What's this blue stuff on the carpet?*

stuff[2] /stʌf/ *verb* (**stuffs, stuffing, stuffed**) fill something with something else (କୌଣସି ପଦାର୍ଥ) ଭର୍ତ୍ତିକରିବା, ପୂରାଇବା *The pillow was stuffed with feathers.*

stuffy /ˈstʌfi/ *adjective* (**stuffier, stuffiest**) if a room is stuffy, it has no fresh air in it ରୁଦ୍ଧ (ପ୍ରକୋଷ୍ଠ), ଖୋଲା ପବନ ଆସୁନଥିବା *Open the window—it's very stuffy in here.*

stumble /ˈstʌmbl/ *verb* (**stumbles, stumbling, stumbled**) hit your foot against something when you are walking or running and almost fall ଝୁଣ୍ଟିପଡ଼ିବା *The old lady stumbled and fell as she was going upstairs.*

stump /stʌmp/ *noun* the small part that is left when something is cut off or broken (କଟାଯାଇଥିବା ବା ଭାଙ୍ଗିପଡ଼ିଥିବା) ଗଛର ଗୁଣ୍ଡି *a tree stump*

tree stump

stumps /stʌmps/ *noun* (*plural*) a set of three upright wooden sticks that form one of the two **wickets** in cricket କ୍ରିକେଟ୍ ଖେଳରେ ପିଚ୍‌ର ଦୁଇପଟେ ପୋତା ଯାଉଥିବା ବାଡ଼ି

stun /stʌn/ *verb* (**stuns, stunning, stunned**) **1** hit a person or animal on the head so hard that he/she/it cannot see, think or make a sound for a short time ସମ୍ମୋହିତ କରିବା, ସ୍ତବ୍ଧ କରିବା **2** make somebody very surprised ଆଶ୍ଚର୍ଯ୍ୟାନ୍ୱିତ କରିବା, ନିର୍ବାକ୍ କରିବା *His sud-*

den death stunned his family and friends.

stung ଶବ୍ଦ **sting** ର ଏକ ଧାତୁରୂପ

stunk ଶବ୍ଦ **stink** ର ଏକ ଧାତୁରୂପ

stunning /ˈstʌnɪŋ/ *adjective* very beautiful; wonderful ଅତି ସୁନ୍ଦର; ଚମତ୍କାର *a stunning dress*

stunt /stʌnt/ *noun* something dangerous or difficult done to entertain you ଆମୋଦ ପାଇଁ କରାଯାଉଥିବା ବିପଜ୍ଜନକ ଓ ଦୁଃସାହସିକ କାମ

stupid /ˈstju:pɪd/ *adjective* not intelligent; silly ନିର୍ବୁଦ୍ଧିଆ, ବୋକା; ବାଜେ *What a stupid question!*

stupidity /stju:ˈpɪdəti/ *noun* (*no plural*) behaviour that shows a lack of thought ବୋକାମି, ନିର୍ବୋଧତା

stupidly *adverb* ବୋକାଙ୍କ ପରି *I stupidly forgot to close the door.*

style /staɪl/ *noun* **1** a way of doing, making or saying something (କାମକରିବାର, କୌଣସି ପଦାର୍ଥ ବନାଇବାର, କଥା କହିବା ଇତ୍ୟାଦିର) ଶୈଳୀ, ଢଙ୍ଗ, ଷ୍ଟାଇଲ୍ *I don't like his style of writing.* **2** the shape or kind of something ପ୍ରକାର, ଢଙ୍ଗ, ଡିଜାଇନ୍; ବିନ୍ୟାସ *This shop sells children's clothes in lots of different colours and styles.* ○ *a hairstyle*

subcontinent /ˌsʌbˈkɒntɪnənt/ *noun* a large area of land that is a part of a continent. This word is often used to refer to the part of Asia that includes India, Pakistan and Bangladesh ମହାଦେଶର ଏକ ବଡ଼ ଭୂଭାଗ, ଉପମହାଦେଶ *the Indian subcontinent*

subject /ˈsʌbdʒɪkt/ *noun* **1** the person or thing that you are talking or writing about ବିଷୟ, ବିଷୟବସ୍ତୁ *What is the subject of the talk?* **2** something you study at school, university or college (ସ୍କୁଲ୍, କଲେଜ୍ ଇତ୍ୟାଦିର) ପାଠ୍ୟକ୍ରମର ବିଷୟ *I'm studying three subjects — Maths, Physics and Chemistry.* **3** the word in a sentence that does the action of the verb (ବ୍ୟାକରଣରେ) ବିଶେଷ୍ୟ ବା ଏହାର ସମସ୍ୱଦ *In the sentence 'Avi ate the cake', 'Avi' is the subject.* ⇨ **object**[1] ଦେଖନ୍ତୁ। **4** a person who belongs to a certain country (କୌଣସି ଦେଶର) ଅଧିବାସୀ ବା ନାଗରିକ

subjective /səbˈdʒektɪv/ *adjective* based on your personal tastes and opinions and not on facts ବ୍ୟକ୍ତିଗତ, ନିଜରୁଚୀ ଓ ମତ ଉପରେ ଆଧାରିତ (ତଥ୍ୟ ଉପରେ ନୁହେଁ) ✪ ବିପରୀତ **objective 2**

submarine /ˌsʌbməˈri:n/ *noun* a ship that can travel under the sea ବୁଡ଼ାଜାହାଜ, ସବ୍‌ମରିନ୍

submarine

submerge /səbˈmɜ:dʒ/ *verb* (**submerges, submerging, submerged**) go or make something go under water completely ପାଣିରେ ଡୁବିଯିବା ବା ଡୁବାଇବା, ଜଳମଗ୍ନ ହେବା ବା କରାଇବା *The whole village was submerged by the floods.*

subscriber /səbˈskraɪbə(r)/ *noun* someone who pays money to regularly receive copies of a magazine or newspaper (ଅଗ୍ରୀମ ଟଙ୍କା ଦେଇ ହୋଇଥିବା ପତ୍ରପତ୍ରିକା ଇତ୍ୟାଦିର) ଗ୍ରାହକ

subscription /səbˈskrɪpʃn/ *noun* money that you pay, for example to get the same magazine each month or to join a club ଗ୍ରାହକ ଦେଉଥିବା ଚାନ୍ଦା ବା ଅଭିଦାନ, ସବ୍ସକ୍ରିପସନ୍

substance /ˈsʌbstəns/ *noun* anything that you can see, touch or use for making things; a material ପଦାର୍ଥ, ବସ୍ତୁ, ଉପାଦାନ *Stone is a hard substance.* ○ *chemical substances*

substantial /səbˈstænʃl/ *adjective* large enough in amount, value or importance ଯଥେଷ୍ଟ ପରିମାଣର; ମୂଲ୍ୟବାନ୍ ଗୁରୁତ୍ୱପୂର୍ଣ୍ଣ *A substantial number of people were supporting the change.*

substitute /ˈsʌbstɪtju:t/ *noun* a person or thing that you put in the place of another ଅନ୍ୟ ବଦଳରେ ଅଣାଯାଉଥିବା ବ୍ୟକ୍ତି ବା ପଦାର୍ଥ; ପରିବର୍ତ୍ତେ *Our goalkeeper was ill, so we found a substitute.*

subtle /ˈsʌtl/ *adjective* **1** not easy to see or understand; delicate or fine ସହଜରେ ଦେଖି ବା ବୁଝିହେଉ ନଥିବା; ସୂକ୍ଷ୍ମ *the subtle taste of cardamom in the pudding* **2** very clever and using indirect ways to hide the real purpose behind something ପ୍ରକୃତ ଉଦ୍ଦେଶ୍ୟ ସହଜରେ ବୁଝି ନହେଲାପରି ଚତୁର ଭାବରେ କରାଯାଇଥିବା *a subtle plan*

subtract /səbˈtrækt/ *verb* (**subtracts, subtracting, subtracted**) take a number away from another number ଫେଡ଼ିବା, ବିୟୋଗ କରିବା *If you subtract 6 from 9, you get 3.* ✪ ବିପରୀତ **add**

subtraction /səbˈtrækʃn/ *noun* the act of taking a number away from another number ଫେଡ଼ାଣ, ବିୟୋଗ ➪ **addition1** ଦେଖନ୍ତୁ।

subway /ˈsʌbweɪ/ *noun* (*plural* **subways**) a path that goes under a busy road, so that people can cross safely ଗହଳି ରାସ୍ତା ତଳ ଦେଇ ଯାଇଥିବା ବାଟ, ଭୂତଳ ମାର୍ଗ (ରାସ୍ତା ପାର ହେବା ପାଇଁ); (ଆମେରିକାରେ) ଭୂତଳ ରେଳରାସ୍ତା

succeed /səkˈsi:d/ *verb* (**succeeds, succeeding, succeeded**) do or get what you wanted to do or get ସଫଳ ହେବା *She finally succeeded in getting a job.* ✪ ବିପରୀତ **fail 1**

success /səkˈses/ *noun* **1** (*no plural*) the fact that you have done or got what you wanted; the fact that you have done well ସଫଳତା *I wish you success with your studies.* **2** (*plural* **successes**) somebody or something that does well or that people like a lot ଲୋକେ ପସନ୍ଦ କରୁଥିବା ସଫଳ ବ୍ୟକ୍ତି ବା ଦ୍ରବ୍ୟ *The film Lagaan was a great success.* ✪ ବିପରୀତ **failure**

successful *adjective* ସଫଳ କୃତକାର୍ଯ୍ୟ *a successful actor* ○ *The party was very successful.* ✪ ବିପରୀତ **unsuccessful**

successfully *adverb* ସଫଳ ଭାବରେ, ସଫଳତା ସହ *He completed his studies successfully.*

successor /səkˈsesə(r)/ *noun* a person or thing that comes after another person or thing and takes their place ଉତ୍ତରାଧିକାରୀ ବ୍ୟକ୍ତି ବା ପଦାର୍ଥ *The party president's successor was chosen last week.*

such /sʌtʃ/ *adjective* **1** a word that you use when you say how much, how big, etc. something is ଏତେ, ଏଡ଼େ, ଏତେ ବେଶୀ *It was such a nice day that we decided to go to the beach.* ➪ **so** ଦେଖନ୍ତୁ। **2** a word that makes another word stronger ଏତେ *He wears such strange clothes.* **3** like this or that ଏମିତି ବା ସେମିତି *'Can I speak to Mrs Gupta?' 'I'm sorry. There's no such person here.'*

such as like something; for example ଯେମିତି; ଉଦାହରଣ ସ୍ୱରୂପ *Sweet foods such as chocolate contain a lot of calories.*

suck /sʌk/ *verb* (**sucks, sucking, sucked**) **1** pull something into your mouth, using your lips ଚୁଷିବା *The baby sucked milk from the bottle.* **2** hold something in your mouth and squeeze it using your tongue ଚୁଚୁମିବା *She was sucking a toffee.*

sudden /ˈsʌdn/ *adjective* if something is sudden, it happens quickly when you do not expect it ଆକସ୍ମିକ, ହଠାତ୍ ଘଟିଥିବା *His decision to leave was sudden.*

all of a sudden suddenly ହଠାତ୍, ଅକସ୍ମାତ୍ *We were watching TV when all of a sudden the door opened.*

suddenly *adverb* ହଠାତ୍, ଅକସ୍ମାତ୍ *He left very suddenly.*

suffer /ˈsʌfə(r)/ *verb* (**suffers, suffering, suffered**) feel pain, sadness or something else that is not pleasant କଷ୍ଟପାଇବା ବା ଭୋଗିବା, ଯନ୍ତ୍ରଣା ପାଇବା *I'm suffering from toothache.*

suffering /ˈsʌfərɪŋ/ *noun* (*no plural*) the feeling of pain and unhappiness that you have when you are hurt, sad, in difficulty, etc. ଯନ୍ତ୍ରଣା, କଷ୍ଟ, କ୍ଳେଶ

sufficient /səˈfɪʃnt/ *adjective* as much or as many as you need or want; enough ଯଥେଷ୍ଟ *There was sufficient food to last two weeks.* ✪ ଏହା ବଦଳରେ ଆମେ ସାଧାରଣତଃ **enough** ଶବ୍ଦର ବ୍ୟବହାର କରୁ। ✪ ବିପରୀତ **insufficient**

sufficiently *adverb* ଯଥେଷ୍ଟ ଭାବରେ *a sufficiently large room*

suffix /ˈsʌfɪks/ *noun* (*plural* **suffixes**) a letter or group of letters that you add to the end of a word to make another word ଗୋଟିଏ ଶବ୍ଦ ପଛରେ ଆଉ କିଛି ଅକ୍ଷର ଯୋଡ଼ି ଗଠିତ ଶବ୍ଦ; ଅନ୍ତ୍ୟପ୍ରତ୍ୟୟ, ବିଭକ୍ତି *If you add the suffix '-ly' to the adjective 'quick', you make the adverb 'quickly'.* ➪ **prefix** ଦେଖନ୍ତୁ।

suffocate /ˈsʌfəkeɪt/ *verb* (**suffocates, suffocating, suffocated**) **1** die because there is no air to breathe; kill someone by not letting them breathe ଶ୍ୱାସରୁଦ୍ଧ କରିବା; ଶ୍ୱାସରୁଦ୍ଧ କରି ମାରିଦେବା **2** feel uncomfortable because there is not enough fresh air ନିଶ୍ୱାସ ରୁନ୍ଧି ହୋଇଗଲା ପରି ଲାଗିବା (ଖୋଲା ପବନ

ଆସୁ ନଥିବାରୁ) *The smoke and fumes made them feel suffocated.*

suffocation /ˌsʌfəˈkeɪʃn/ *noun* (*no plural*) ଶ୍ୱାସରୋଧ *He thought he was going to die of suffocation.*

sugar /ˈʃʊgə(r)/ *noun* (*no plural*) a sweet substance that is made from the juices of some plants ଚିନି *Do you take sugar in your tea?*

sugar cane *noun* a tall tropical plant from which sugar is made ଆଖୁ

suggest /səˈdʒest/ *verb* (**suggests, suggesting, suggested**) say what you think somebody should do or what should happen ପ୍ରସ୍ତାବ ଦେବା *I suggest that you stay here tonight.* ○ *What do you suggest?*

suggestion /səˈdʒestʃən/ *noun* ପ୍ରସ୍ତାବ *I don't know what to buy for her birthday. Have you got any suggestions?*

suicide /ˈsuːɪsaɪd/ *noun* the act of killing oneself ଆତ୍ମହତ୍ୟା

commit suicide kill oneself ଆତ୍ମହତ୍ୟା କରିବା

suit[1] /suːt/ *noun* a jacket and trousers that you wear together and that are made from the same material ଏକା କନାର କୋଟ୍ ଓ ପୂରାପ୍ୟାଣ୍ଟର ଯୋଡ଼ା, ସୁଟ୍

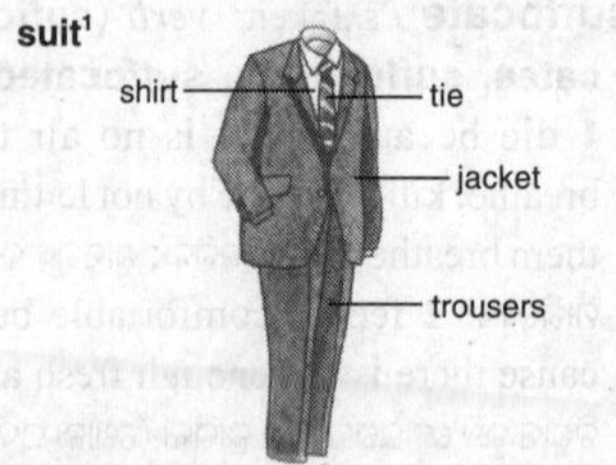

suit[2] /suːt/ *verb* (**suits, suiting, suited**) **1** if something suits you, it looks good on you (ଚେହେରାକୁ) ମାନିବା, ସୁନ୍ଦର ଲାଗିବା *Does this dress suit me?* **2** be right for you; be what you want or need ଠିକ୍ ହେବା, ସୁବିଧାଜନକ ହେବା; ସୁହାଇବା *Would it suit you if I came at five o'clock?*

suitable /ˈsuːtəbl/ *adjective* right for somebody or something ଉପଯୁକ୍ତ, ଉଚିତ୍ ପ୍ରକାରର *This film isn't suitable for children.* ✪ ବିପରୀତ **unsuitable**

suitably *adverb* ଉପଯୁକ୍ତ ଭାବରେ, ଠିକ୍ ଭାବରେ *Tony wasn't suitably dressed for a party.*

suitcase /ˈsuːtkeɪs/ *noun* a large bag with flat sides that you carry your clothes in when you travel ସୁଟ୍‌କେସ, ଦୂର ଜାଗାକୁ ଗଲାବେଳେ ସାଙ୍ଗରେ ନିଆଯାଉଥିବା ଲୁଗାପଟାର ବକ୍ସ

suitor /ˈsuːtər/ *noun* a man who wants to marry a particular woman ବିବାହପ୍ରାର୍ଥୀ

sulk /sʌlk/ *verb* (**sulks, sulking, sulked**) not speak because you are angry about something ରୁଷିବା *She's been sulking in her room all day because her mother wouldn't let her go to the party.*

sum /sʌm/ *noun* **1** a simple piece of work with numbers, for example adding or dividing ଗଣିତର ସହଜ ପ୍ରଶ୍ନ, ଅଙ୍କ (ମିଶାଣ, ଫେଡ଼ାଣ ଇତ୍ୟାଦି) *The children are learning how to do sums.* **2** an amount of money ଟଙ୍କାର ପରିମାଣ *Rs 20,000 is a large sum of money.* **3** the answer that you have when you add two or more numbers together ଯୋଗଫଳ *The sum of two and five is seven.*

summary /ˈsʌməri/ *noun* (*plural* **summaries**) a short way of telling something by giving only the most important facts ସଂକ୍ଷିପ୍ତ ବିବରଣୀ *Here is a summary of the news ...*

summer /ˈsʌmə(r)/ *noun* the warmest season of the year ଗ୍ରୀଷ୍ମଋତୁ *I am going to Dalhousie in the summer.*

summit /ˈsʌmɪt/ *noun* the top of a mountain ପାହାଡ଼ର ଶିଖର, ଚୂଡ଼ା, ଶୀର୍ଷସ୍ଥାନ

summon /ˈsʌmən/ *verb* (**summons, summoning, summoned**) **1** order someone to come to a particular place ଡକରା ପଠାଇବା, ନିର୍ଦ୍ଦିଷ୍ଟ ସ୍ଥାନକୁ ଆସିବା ପାଇଁ ଆଦେଶ ଦେବା *He was summoned to appear before the judge.* **2** make an effort to bring a particular quality in yourself, especially when you find it very difficult to do so (ନିଜର ସାହସ, ଶକ୍ତି ଇତ୍ୟାଦି) ଠୁଳ କରିବା; ନିଜର ନିହିତ ଶକ୍ତିକୁ ଜାଗରିତ କରିବା *She could not summon up her courage to tell him the truth.*

sun /sʌn/ *noun* (*no plural*) **1 the sun** the big round thing in the sky that gives us light in the day, and heat ସୂର୍ଯ୍ୟ, ତପନ *The sun is shining.* ➪ ଚିତ୍ର ପାଇଁ **solar system** ଦେଖନ୍ତୁ । **2** light and heat from the sun ସୂର୍ଯ୍ୟଙ୍କ ଠାରୁ ମିଳୁଥିବା ଆଲୋକ ଓ ଉତ୍ତାପ *We sat in the sun all morning.*

Sunday /ˈsʌndeɪ/ *noun* the last day of the week; next after Saturday ରବିବାର

sung ଶବ୍ଦ **sing** ର ଏକ ଧାତୁରୂପ

sunglasses /ˈsʌnglɑːsɪz/ *noun* (*no singular*) glasses with dark glass in them that you wear when you go out in the sun ସୂର୍ଯ୍ୟକିରଣରୁ ଆଖିକୁ ରକ୍ଷା କରିବା ପାଇଁ ପିନ୍ଧୁଥିବା ରଙ୍ଗିନ୍ ଚଷମା, ଗଗ୍‌ଲସ୍ *a pair of sunglasses*

sunk ଶବ୍ଦ **sink²** ର ଏକ ଧାତୁରୂପ

sunlight /ˈsʌnlaɪt/ *noun* (*no plural*) the light from the sun ସୂର୍ଯ୍ୟକିରଣ, ଖରା

sunny /ˈsʌni/ *adjective* (**sunnier, sunniest**) bright with light from the sun ସୂର୍ଯ୍ୟାଲୋକ ପରିପୂର୍ଣ୍ଣ *a sunny day*

sunrise /ˈsʌnraɪz/ *noun* (*no plural*) the time in the morning when the sun comes up ସୂର୍ଯ୍ୟୋଦୟ

sunset /ˈsʌnset/ *noun* (*no plural*) the time in the evening when the sun goes down ସୂର୍ଯ୍ୟାସ୍ତ *The park closes at sunset.*

sunshine /ˈsʌnʃaɪn/ *noun* (*no plural*) the light and heat from the sun ସୂର୍ଯ୍ୟାଲୋକ, ସୂର୍ଯ୍ୟକିରଣ *We sat outside in the sunshine.*

super /ˈsuːpə(r)/ *adjective* very good; wonderful ଖୁବ୍ ଭଲ, ଚମତ୍କାର *That was a super meal.*

superb /suːˈpɜːb/ *adjective* very good or beautiful ଅତି ଭଲ, ଅତି ସୁନ୍ଦର *a superb holiday* ○ *The view from the window is superb.*

superintendent /ˌsuːpərɪnˈtendənt/ *noun* **1** a police officer with a high position of a district ଜିଲ୍ଲା ପୁଲିସ୍ ପ୍ରଶାସକ *Superintendent Sen is in charge of the case.* **2** someone who manages or supervises an activity ପରିଚାଳକ

superior /suːˈpɪəriə(r)/ *adjective* better or more important than another person or thing ବରିଷ୍ଠ, ଉଚ୍ଚତର ପଦର *I think fresh coffee is superior to instant coffee.* ✪ ବିପରୀତ **inferior**

superlative /suˈpɜːlətɪv/ *noun* the form of an adjective or adverb that shows something (ବ୍ୟାକରଣରେ) ସର୍ବଶ୍ରେଷ୍ଠବାଚକ ଶବ୍ଦ *'Best', 'worst' and 'fastest' are all superlatives.*

superlative *adjective* ଅତି ଉତ୍କୃଷ୍ଟ *'Youngest' is the superlative form of 'young'.*

supermarket /ˈsuːpəmɑːkɪt/ *noun* a big shop where you can buy food and other things. You choose what you want and then pay for everything when you leave ଗ୍ରାହକ ନିଜ ଇଚ୍ଛା ଅନୁସାରେ ଦୋକାନରେ ବୁଲି ଜିନିଷପତ୍ର ବାଛି କିଣିବାର ସୁବିଧାଥିବା ବଡ଼ ଦୋକାନ

superstition /ˌsuːpəˈstɪʃn/ *noun* a belief in good and bad luck and other things that cannot be explained ଅନ୍ଧବିଶ୍ୱାସ *People say that walking under a ladder brings bad luck, but it's just a superstition.*

superstitious /ˌsuːpəˈstɪʃəs/ *adjective* if you are superstitious, you believe in good and bad luck and other things that cannot be explained ଅନ୍ଧବିଶ୍ୱାସୀ

supervise /ˈsuːpəvaɪz/ *verb* (**supervises, supervising, supervised**) watch to see that people are working or behaving correctly କାମ ତଦାରଖ କରିବା *I supervised the builders.*

supervision /ˌsuːpəˈvɪʒn/ *noun* (*no plural*) the act of supervising or being supervised ତଦାରଖ, ପର୍ଯ୍ୟବେକ୍ଷଣ, ତତ୍ତ୍ୱାବଧାନ *Children must not play here without the supervision of adults.*

supervisor /ˈsuːpə vaɪzə(r)/ *noun* a person who supervises ତଦାରଖ ବା ତତ୍ତ୍ୱାବଧାନ କରୁଥିବା ବ୍ୟକ୍ତି, ତତ୍ତ୍ୱାବଧାୟକ, ଅଧୀକ୍ଷକ

supper /ˈsʌpə(r)/ *noun* the last meal of the day, usually smaller than dinner ରାତିର ଶେଷ ହାଲୁକା ଭୋଜନ *We had supper and then went to bed.*

supplement[1] /ˈsʌplɪmənt/ *noun* a thing that is added to another thing to make it complete or better ପରିପୂରକ ବସ୍ତୁ *vitamin supplements* ○ *a supplement to the book*

supplement[2] /ˈsʌplɪment/ *verb* (**supplements, supplementing, supplemented**) add something to another thing to make it complete or better ପରିପୂରଣ କରିବା *supplement your diet with vitamin and calcium pills*

supplementary /ˌsʌplɪˈmentri/ *adjective* given in addition to something else in order to complete it or improve it ପରିପୂରକ, ଅଧିକା *a supplementary reading list*

supply /səˈplaɪ/ *verb* (**supplies, supplying, supplied, has supplied**) give or sell something that somebody needs ଯୋଗାଇଦେବା, ଆବଶ୍ୟକତା ପୂରଣକରିବା *The lake supplies water to thousands of* *homes.* ○ *The school supplies us with books.*

supply *noun* (*plural* **supplies**) an amount of something that you need ଯୋଗାଣ *supplies of food*

support /sə'pɔ:t/ *verb* (**supports, supporting, supported**) **1** hold somebody or something up, so that they do not fall ପଡ଼ିଯିବାରୁ ବା ଭାଙ୍ଗିପଡ଼ିବାରୁ ରକ୍ଷା କରିବା, ସମ୍ଭାଳିବା *The bridge isn't strong enough to support heavy lorries.* **2** help somebody to live by giving things like money, a home or food ସାହାଯ୍ୟ କରିବା *She has three children to support.* **3** say that you think that somebody or something is right or the best ସମର୍ଥନ କରିବା *Everybody else said I was wrong but Rekha supported me.*

support *noun* **1** (*no plural*) help ସାହାଯ୍ୟ, ସମର୍ଥନ *Thank you for all your support.* **2** (*plural* **supports**) something that holds up another thing ଢ଼ିରା, ଠେସ, ଭୁଷୁଡ଼ି ପଡ଼ିବାରୁ ରକ୍ଷା କରୁଥିବା ସହାୟକ ବସ୍ତୁ

supporter /sə'pɔ:tə(r)/ *noun* a person who helps somebody or something by giving money, or by showing interest, for example *football supporters*

suppose /sə'pəʊz/ *verb* (**supposes, supposing, supposed**) think that something is true or will happen but not be sure ଅନୁମାନ କରିବା, ଧରିନେବା *'Where's Bela?' 'I don't know—I suppose she's still at work.'*

supposing /sə'pəʊzɪŋ/ *conjunction* if ଯଦି *Supposing we miss the bus, how will we get to the airport?*

suppress /sə'pres/ *verb* (**suppresses, suppressing, suppressed**) **1** use force to stop something ଦମନ କରିବା, ଦବେଇ ଦେବା *The rebellion against the government was brutally suppressed.* **2** hide facts, information, etc. from people who should know them ତଥ୍ୟ ଇତ୍ୟାଦି ଲୁଚାଇ ଦେବା, ଗୁପ୍ତ ରଖିବା, ଛୁପେଇ ଦେବା *He tried his best to suppress the truth.*

supreme /su:'pri:m/ *adjective* highest or most important ସର୍ବୋଚ୍ଚ *the Supreme Court*

sure /ʃɔ:(r)/ *adjective* (**surer, surest**) *adverb* if you are sure, you are certain that something is true or right ନିଶ୍ଚିତ, ନିଃସନ୍ଦେହ *I'm sure I've seen that man before.* ✪ ବିପରୀତ **unsure**

be sure to used to tell somebody to do something without forgetting ମନେ ରଖିବା *Be sure to water the plants.*

for sure without any doubt ନିଶ୍ଚିତ ଭାବେ, ନିଃସନ୍ଦେହରେ *I know for sure that he's coming to the party.*

make sure check something so that you are certain about it ସୁନିଶ୍ଚିତ କରିବା *Make sure you don't leave your bag on the bus.*

surely /'ʃɔ:li/ *adverb* a word that you use when you think that something must be true, or when you are surprised ନିଶ୍ଚୟ, ନିଶ୍ଚିତ ଭାବେ *Surely you know where your brother works!*

surf /sɜ:f/ *noun* (*no plural*) the white **foam** on the top of waves in the sea ସମୁଦ୍ର କୂଳରେ ଭାଙ୍ଗୁଥିବା ଢେଉର ଫେଣ

surface /ˈsɜ:fɪs/ *noun* **1** (*plural* **surfaces**) the outside part of something କୌଣସି ପଦାର୍ଥର ବାହାରଭାଗ ବା ଉପରିଭାଗ; ପୃଷ୍ଠ *A tomato has a shiny red surface.* **2** (*no plural*) the top of water ପାଣିର ଉପରିଭାଗ *She dived below the surface.*

surgeon /ˈsɜ:dʒən/ *noun* a doctor who does **operations**. A surgeon cuts somebody's body to take out or mend a part inside ଅସ୍ତ୍ରଚିକିତ୍ସକ, ଶଲ୍ୟ ଚିକିତ୍ସକ, ସର୍ଜନ *a heart surgeon*

surgery /ˈsɜ:dʒəri/ *noun* (*no plural*) the act of cutting somebody's body to take out or mend a part inside ଅସ୍ତ୍ରଚିକିତ୍ସା, ସର୍ଜରି *He needed surgery after the accident.*

surname /ˈsɜ:neɪm/ *noun* a name that all the members of your family share. Your surname is usually your last name କୁଳନାମ, ବଂଶଗତ ଉପାଧି *Her name is Megha Khanna. Khanna is her surname.* ➪ **name**[1] ର ଟିପ୍ପଣୀ ଦେଖନ୍ତୁ।

surplus /ˈsɜ:pləs/ *adjective* more than what is needed ବଳକା *surplus funds*

surprise[1] /səˈpraɪz/ *noun* **1** (*no plural*) the feeling that you have when something happens suddenly that you did not expect ବିସ୍ମୟ, ଆଶ୍ଚର୍ଯ୍ୟ *She looked at me in surprise when I told her the news* **2** (*plural* **surprises**) something that happens when you do not expect it ଅପ୍ରତ୍ୟାଶିତ ଘଟଣା। *Don't tell him about the birthday party—it's a surprise!*

take somebody by surprise happen when somebody does not expect it କାହାରିକୁ ଆଶ୍ଚର୍ଯ୍ୟାନ୍ୱିତ କରିବା *Your visit took me by surprise—I thought you were not in town.*

surprise[2] /səˈpraɪz/ *verb* (**surprises, surprising, surprised**) do something that somebody does not expect ବିସ୍ମିତ କରିବା, ଆଶ୍ଚର୍ଯ୍ୟାନ୍ୱିତ କରିବା *I arrived early to surprise her.*

surprised *adjective* if you are surprised, you feel or show surprise ଆଶ୍ଚର୍ଯ୍ୟାନ୍ୱିତ *I was surprised to see Asif yesterday—I thought he was in Canada.*

surprising *adjective* if something is surprising, it makes you feel surprised ବିସ୍ମୟକର *The news was surprising.*

surprisingly *adverb* ଅପ୍ରତ୍ୟାଶିତ ଭାବରେ *The exam was surprisingly easy.*

surrender /səˈrendə(r)/ *verb* (**surrenders, surrendering, surren-**

dered) stop fighting because you cannot win ଆତ୍ମସମର୍ପଣ କରିବା *After six hours on the roof, the man surrendered to the police.*

surround /səˈraʊnd/ *verb* (**surrounds, surrounding, surrounded**) be or go all around something ଘେରିଯିବା, ବେଷ୍ଟନ କରିବା *The lake is surrounded by trees.*

surroundings /səˈraʊndɪŋz/ *noun* (*plural*) everything around you, or the place where you live ପରିବେଶ, ପାରିପାର୍ଶ୍ୱିକ ଅବସ୍ଥା *The farm is in beautiful surroundings.*

survey /ˈsɜːveɪ/ *noun* (*plural* **surveys**) a study that asks questions about what people think or do ସର୍ବେକ୍ଷଣ କରିବା *We did a survey of people's favourite TV programmes.*

survive /səˈvaɪv/ *verb* (**survives, surviving, survived**) be alive after a difficult or dangerous time ବଞ୍ଚିରହିବା; (ବିପଦ ଆପଦରୁ) ବଞ୍ଚିଯିବା *Camels can survive for many days without water.*

survival /səˈvaɪvl/ *noun* (*no plural*) the state of being alive after a difficult or dangerous time ଜିବିତାବସ୍ଥା, ବଞ୍ଚିରହିବା ପ୍ରକ୍ରିୟା

survivor /səˈvaɪvə(r)/ *noun* a person who survives (ବିପଦଆପଦରୁ) ବଞ୍ଚିରହିବା ବ୍ୟକ୍ତି *The government sent help to the survivors of the earthquake.*

suspect /səˈspekt/ *verb* (**suspects, suspecting, suspected**) think that somebody has done something wrong but not be certain ସନ୍ଦେହ କରିବା; ଦୋଷୀ ବୋଲି ଅନୁମାନ କରିବା *They suspect Hemant of stealing the money.*

suspect /ˈsʌspekt/ *noun* a person who you think has done something wrong or illegal ଦୋଷୀ ବୋଲି ସନ୍ଦେହ କରାଯାଉଥିବା ବ୍ୟକ୍ତି *The police have arrested two suspects.*

suspend /səˈspend/ *verb* (**suspends, suspending, suspended**) **1** delay something for a certain period of time ବିଳମ୍ବିତ କରିବା, ସ୍ଥଗିତ ରଖିବା *Some trains to the city were suspended because of heavy rains.* **2** hang something ଟାଙ୍ଗିବା, ଝୁଲାଇବା *The swing was suspended from the branch of a tree.* **3** send someone away from school, college, job, position, etc. for a certain period of time as punishment ସାମୟିକ ଭାବେ କର୍ମଚାରୀଙ୍କୁ ବା ଛାତ୍ରଛାତ୍ରୀଙ୍କୁ ପଦଚ୍ୟୁତ ବା ନିଲମ୍ବିତ କରିବା *The student was suspended from college for two weeks.*

suspense /səˈspens/ *noun* (*no plural*) the feeling of uncertainty, worry or excitement caused while waiting for some event or news ଉତ୍କଣ୍ଠିତ ଓ ଅନିଶ୍ଚିତ ଅବସ୍ଥା

suspicion /səˈspɪʃn/ *noun* a feeling that somebody has done something wrong ସନ୍ଦେହ *When she saw a Rs 500 note in her son's bag, she was filled with suspicion.*

suspicious /səˈspɪʃəs/ *adjective* if you are suspicious, you do not believe somebody or something, or you feel that something is wrong ସନ୍ଦେହୀ, ସନ୍ଦେହପରାୟଣ, ସନ୍ଦିଗ୍ଧ *The police are suspicious of her story.*

suspiciously *adverb* ସନ୍ଦେହ କଲା ପରି, ସନ୍ଦେହରେ *'What are you doing here?' the woman asked suspiciously.*

swallow /ˈswɒləʊ/ *verb* (**swallows, swallowing, swallowed**) make food or drink move down your throat from your mouth ଢୋକିବା, ଗିଳିବା *I can't swallow these tablets without water.*

swam ଶବ୍ଦ **swim** ର ଏକ ଧାତୁରୂପ

swamp /swɒmp/ *noun* an area of soft wet ground ସନ୍ତସନ୍ତିଆ ଜମି, କାଦୁଆ ଜାଗା

swan /swɒn/ *noun* a big white bird with a very long neck. Swans live on rivers and lakes ହଂସ ✪ ହଂସ ଛୁଆକୁ **cygnet** କହନ୍ତି ।

swarm /swɔːm/ *noun* a big group of flying insects or people (ଉଡ଼ାକୀଟ–ପତଙ୍ଗ, ମଣିଷ ଇତ୍ୟାଦିଙ୍କ) ପଲ, ଦଳ *a swarm of bees*

sway /sweɪ/ *verb* (**sways, swaying, swayed**) move slowly from side to side ହଲିବା, ଦୋହଲିବା *The trees were swaying in the wind.*

swear /sweə(r)/ *verb* (**swears, swearing, swore** /swɔː(r)/, **has sworn** /swɔːn/) **1** make a serious promise ଶପଥ କରିବା, ରାଣ ପକେଇବା *He swears that he is telling the truth.* **2** say bad words ଅଭଦ୍ର ଭାଷା ପ୍ରୟୋଗ କରିବା *Why did he swear at Bobby like that?*

sweat /swet/ *noun* (*no plural*) drops of water that come out of your skin when you are hot or afraid ଝାଳ, ଘର୍ମ

sweat *verb* (**sweats, sweating, sweated**) have sweat coming out of your skin ଝାଳ ବହିବା, ଘର୍ମାକ୍ତ ହେବା *The room was so hot that everyone was sweating.*

sweaty *adjective* (**sweatier, sweatiest**) covered with sweat ଝାଳୁଆ, ଝାଳରେ ଓଦା ହୋଇଥିବା, ଘର୍ମାକ୍ତ *sweaty socks*

sweater /ˈswetə(r)/ *noun* a warm piece of clothing with sleeves that you wear on the upper part of your body. Sweaters are often made of wool ଶୀତଦିନ ପାଇଁ ପଶମ ବା ଉଲ୍‌ର ଜାମା, ସ୍ୱେଟର୍

sweep /swiːp/ *verb* (**sweeps, sweeping, swept** /swept/, **has swept**) **1** clean something with a **broom** ଝାଡୁ କରିବା, ଓଳାଇବା *I swept the floor.* **2** push something along or away quickly and strongly ଖୁବ୍ ଜୋର୍‌ରେ ଧସେଇ ନେଇଯିବା ବା ଭସାଇ ନେବା *The bridge was swept away by the floods.*

sweet[1] /swiːt/ *adjective* (**sweeter, sweetest**) **1** with the taste of sugar ମିଠା, ମଧୁର *Honey is sweet.* ✪ ବିପରୀତ **sour 1 2** pretty ସୁନ୍ଦର *What a sweet* *little girl!* **3** kind and gentle ଦୟାଶୀଳ ଓ କୋମଳ ସ୍ୱଭାବର *It was sweet of you to help me.* **4** with a good smell ସୁଗନ୍ଧଯୁକ୍ତ *the sweet smell of roses*

sweetly *adverb* in a pleasant kind of way ଆନନ୍ଦରେ ଓ କୋମଳ ଭାବରେ *She smiled sweetly.*

sweet² /swi:t/ *noun* **1** a small piece of sweet food. Chocolates and toffees are sweets ମିଠେଇ, ମିଠା ଖାଦ୍ୟ (ଚକ୍‌ଲେଟ୍ ଇତ୍ୟାଦି ମଧ୍ୟ) *He bought a packet of sweets for his children.* **2** a sweet food that you eat at the end of a meal ଭୋଜନ ଶେଷରେ ଖିଆ ଯାଉଥିବା ମିଠା ଖାଦ୍ୟ *Do you want any sweet?*

swell /swel/ *verb* (**swells, swelling, swelled, has swollen** /ˈswəʊlən/ ବା **has swelled**)

swell up become bigger or thicker than it usually is ଫୁଲିଯିବା *After he hurt his ankle, it began to swell up.*

swelling /ˈswelɪŋ/ *noun* a place on the body that is bigger or fatter than it usually is ଫୁଲିଯିବା *She has got a swelling on her head where she fell and hurt it.*

swift /swɪft/ *adjective* (**swifter, swiftest**) quick or fast ଦ୍ରୁତ, ଶୀଘ୍ର, କ୍ଷିପ୍ର, ତତ୍ପର *We made a swift decision.*

swiftly *adverb* ଦ୍ରୁତ ବା କ୍ଷିପ୍ର ଗତିରେ *She ran swiftly up the stairs.*

swim /swɪm/ *verb* (**swims, swimming, swam** /swæm/, **has swum** /swʌm/) move your body through water using your arms and legs ପହଁରିବା, ସନ୍ତରଣ କରିବା *Can you swim?* ○ *I swam across the lake.* ✪ ଖେଳ ଭାବରେ ପହଁରିବାର ଗତିବିଧିକୁ **go swimming** କହନ୍ତି *I go swimming every day.*

swim *noun* (*no plural*) ପହଁରା, ସନ୍ତରଣ *Let's go for a swim.*

swimmer *noun* a person who swims ପହଁରାଳି *He's a good swimmer.*

swimming *noun* (*no plural*) ପହଁରା, ସନ୍ତରଣ *Swimming is my favourite sport.*

swimming costume, swimsuit /swɪmsu:t/ *noun* a piece of clothing that a woman or girl wears for swimming ପହଁରିବା ପରିଧାନ

swimming pool *noun* a special place where you can swim ପହଁରିବା ପାଇଁ ବିଶେଷଭାବରେ ତିଆରି ପୋଖରୀ

swindle /ˈswɪndl/ *verb* (**swindles, swindling, swindled**) cheat someone to get something from them (ଟଙ୍କାପଇସା ଇତ୍ୟାଦି) ଠକି ନେବା *They swindled hundreds of rupees out of the merchant.*

swing¹ /swɪŋ/ *verb* (**swings, swinging, swung** /swʌŋ/, **has swung**) **1** hang from something and move backwards and forwards or from side to side through the air ଝୁଲି ଦୋହଲିବା; (ଦୋଳିରେ) ଝୁଲିବା *The monkey was swinging from a tree.* **2** make somebody or something move in this way ଦୋହଲାଇବା, ଝୁଲାଇ ଝୁଲାଇଯିବା *He swung his arms as he walked.*

swing² /swɪŋ/ *noun* a seat hung down from ropes or chains. Children sit on it to move backwards and forwards through the air ଦୋଳି

switch[1] /swɪtʃ/ *noun* (*plural* **switches**) a small thing that you press to stop or start something that runs on electricity for example a light ବିଦ୍ୟୁତ୍ ପ୍ରବାହକୁ ଚାଲୁ କରିବା ବା ବନ୍ଦ କରିବା ବୋତାମ, ସ୍ୱିଚ୍ *Where is the light switch?* ➪ ଚିତ୍ର ପାଇଁ **socket** ଦେଖନ୍ତୁ।

switch[2] /swɪtʃ/ *verb* (**switches, switching, switched**) change to something different or exchange with something else ବଦଳାଇବା, ଅଦଳବଦଳ କରିବା *I switched to another seat because I couldn't see the screen clearly.*

switch off press a switch to stop the flow of electricity to something ସ୍ୱିଚ୍‌ଟିପି ବିଦ୍ୟୁତ୍ ପ୍ରବାହ ବନ୍ଦ କରିବା *I switched the TV off.* ○ *Don't forget to switch off the lights!*

switch on press a switch to start the flow of electricity to something ସ୍ୱିଚ୍‌ଟିପି ବିଦ୍ୟୁତ୍‌ପ୍ରବାହ ଚାଲୁ କରିବା *Switch the radio on.*

switchboard /ˈswɪtʃbɔːd/ *noun* the place in a large office where somebody answers telephone calls and sends them to the right people ବଡ଼ ଅଫିସ ଇତ୍ୟାଦିରେ ଟେଲିଫୋନ ସଂଯୋଗ କରିବା ପାଇଁ ବହୁ ସ୍ୱିଚ୍ ଲାଗିଥିବା ଫଳକ ବା ଉପକରଣ

swollen ଶବ୍ଦ **swell** ର ଏକ ଧାତୁରୂପ

swollen /ˈswəʊlən/ *adjective* thicker or fatter than it usually is ଫୁଲିଯାଇଥିବା *a swollen ankle*

swoop /swuːp/ *verb* (**swoops, swooping, swooped**) fly down quickly to attack something (ଶିକାରୀ ପକ୍ଷୀ ପରି) ଝାମ୍ପମାରିବା *The bird swooped down to catch a fish.*

sword /sɔːd/ *noun* a long sharp knife for fighting ଖଣ୍ଡା, ଖଡ୍ଗ, ତରବାରି, ଅସି

swore, sworn ଶବ୍ଦ **swear** ର ଏକ ଧାତୁରୂପ

swum ଶବ୍ଦ **swim** ର ଏକ ଧାତୁରୂପ

swung ଶବ୍ଦ **swing**[1] ର ଏକ ଧାତୁରୂପ

syllable /ˈsɪləbl/ *noun* a part of a word that has one **vowel** sound when you say it. 'Swim' has one syllable and 'system' has two syllables ଶବ୍ଦରେ ଥିବା ପ୍ରତ୍ୟେକଟି ଏକକ ଧ୍ୱନି; ପଦାଂଶ ଶବ୍ଦାଂଶ

syllabus /ˈsɪləbəs/ *noun* (*plural* **syllabuses**) a list of all the things that you must study on a course ପାଠ୍ୟକ୍ରମ

symbol /ˈsɪmbl/ *noun* a mark, sign or picture that shows something ପ୍ରତୀକ ଚିହ୍ନ, ସଙ୍କେତ *+ and – are symbols for plus and minus in mathematics.* ○ *A dove is the symbol of peace.*

sympathetic /ˌsɪmpəˈθetɪk/ *adjective* if you are sympathetic, you show that you understand other people's feelings when they have problems ସହାନୁଭୂତିଶୀଳ *Everyone was very sympathetic when I was ill.* ✪ ବିପରୀତ **unsympathetic**

sympathetically *adverb* ସହାନୁଭୂତିଶୀଳ ଭାବରେ, ସହାନୁଭୂତିସହ *He smiled sympathetically.*

sympathize /ˈsɪmpəθaɪz/ *verb* (**sympathizes, sympathizing, sympathized**)

sympathize with somebody show that you understand somebody's feelings when they have problems

ସହାନୁଭୂତି ଦେଖାଇବା *I sympathize with you—I've got a lot of work too.*

sympathy /ˈsɪmpəθi/ *noun* (*no plural*) the ability to understand another person's feelings and problems ସହାନୁଭୂତି, ସମବେଦନା *She feels great sympathy for people who are ill and suffering.*

symptom /ˈsɪmptəm/ *noun* a change in your body that shows that you have an illness ରୋଗର ଶାରିରୀକ ବା ମାନସିକ ଲକ୍ଷଣ, ଚିହ୍ନ ବା ସୂଚନା *A sore throat is often a symptom of a cold.*

synagogue /ˈsɪnəɡɒɡ/ *noun* a building where Jewish people go to pray ଇହୁଦୀମାନଙ୍କର ମନ୍ଦିର ବା ପ୍ରାର୍ଥନା ସ୍ଥଳ

synthesis /ˈsɪnθəsɪs/ *noun* **1** (*plural* **syntheses** /ˈsɪnθəsiːz/) the act of combining separate ideas, beliefs, styles, etc.; the product of such a combination (ବିଭିନ୍ନ ଧାରଣା, ବିଶ୍ୱାସ, ଗଠଣ, ଶୈଳୀ ଇତ୍ୟାଦିର) ସମ୍ମିଶ୍ରଣ, ସଂଯୋଗ, ସଂଶ୍ଳେଷଣ; ଏହିପରି ସମ୍ମିଶ୍ରିତ ପଦାର୍ଥ, ଭାବଧାରା ଇତ୍ୟାଦି *the synthesis of modern and traditional values* **2** (*no plural*) the production of chemical substances in animals and plants either naturally or artificially ପଶୁ ଓ ଉଦ୍ଭିଦ ମଧ୍ୟରେ ପ୍ରାକୃତିକ ପ୍ରକ୍ରିୟାରେ ରାସାୟନିକ ପଦାର୍ଥର ସୃଷ୍ଟି; ଉଦ୍ଭିଦ ଓ ପଶୁଠାରେ ଥିବା ଉପାଦାନ କୃତ୍ରିମ ପ୍ରକ୍ରିୟାରେ ଉତ୍ପାଦନ *photosynthesis*

synthesizer /ˈsɪnθəsaɪzə(r)/ *noun* an electronic musical instrument that has keys like a piano and can produce different sounds ବହୁ ପ୍ରକାର ଧ୍ୱନି କରିପାରୁଥିବା ଇଲେକ୍‌ଟ୍ରନିକ୍ ବାଦ୍ୟଯନ୍ତ୍ରୀ ସିନ୍ଥେସାଇଜର ➪ ଚିତ୍ର ପାଇଁ **musical instrument** ଦେଖନ୍ତୁ।

synthetic /sɪnˈθetɪk/ *adjective* made by people, not natural କୃତ୍ରିମ *Nylon is a synthetic material, but wool is natural.*

syrup /ˈsɪrəp/ *noun* (*no plural*) a thick sweet liquid made with sugar and water or fruit juice ଚିନିସିରା *peaches in syrup*

system /ˈsɪstəm/ *noun* **1** a group of things or parts that work together ବହୁବ୍ୟକ୍ତି, ପଦାର୍ଥ ବା ଅଂଶମାନଙ୍କର ଏକକ ଭାବେ କାମ କରିବା ପଦ୍ଧତି, ପ୍ରଣାଳୀ ବା ବ୍ୟବସ୍ଥା *the railway system* ○ *We have a new computer system at work.* **2** a set of ideas or ways of doing something କିଛି କରିବାର ଭାବଧାରା ଓ ପ୍ରଣାଳୀ *What system of government do you have in your country?*

T t

tab /tæb/ *noun* a small piece of paper, cloth or metal that sticks out of an object to help you open, hold or identify it ଧରିବା, ଖୋଲିବା, ଚିହ୍ନଟ କରିବା ଇତ୍ୟାଦି ପାଇଁ କୌଣସି ପଦାର୍ଥରେ ଲଗାଯାଇଥିବା ପଟି ବା ନାମଫଳକ *You can open the can by pulling the metal tab.*

keep tabs on something or **somebody** keep a regular and close watch on someone or something କୌଣସି ବ୍ୟକ୍ତି ବା ପଦାର୍ଥ ଉପରେ ନିଘା ରଖିବା *His parents keep tabs on his movements.*

table /ˈteɪbl/ *noun* **1** a piece of furniture with a flat top on legs ମେଜ, ଟେବୁଲ୍ **2** a list of facts or numbers ତାଲିକା, ସାରଣୀ, ସରଣୀ *There is a table of population growth at the back of the book.*

set or **lay the table** put knives, forks, plates and other things on the table before you eat ଖାଇବା ପୂର୍ବରୁ ଟେବୁଲ ଉପରେ ଖାଇବା ବାସନକୁସନ ସଜାଇ ରଖିବା

tablecloth /ˈteɪblklɒθ/ *noun* a cloth that you put over a table when you have a meal ଖାଇବା ବେଳେ ଟେବୁଲ୍ ଉପରେ ପକା ଯାଉଥିବା କନା, ଟେବୁଲ୍ କ୍ଲଥ୍

tablespoon /ˈteɪblspuːn/ *noun* a big spoon that you use for eating and putting food on plates ଖାଇବା ବା ପରସିବା ଚାମଚ ➪ ଚିତ୍ର ପାଇଁ **cutlery** ଦେଖନ୍ତୁ।

tablet /ˈtæblət/ *noun* a small hard piece of medicine that you swallow ବଟିକା *Take two of these tablets before every meal.*

table tennis *noun* (*no plural*) a game for two or four players who use a flat round bat to hit a small light ball over a net on a big table; ping-pong ଘର ଭିତରେ ଏକ ନିର୍ଦ୍ଦିଷ୍ଟ ପ୍ରକାରର ଟେବୁଲ୍ ଉପରେ ଛୋଟ ବ୍ୟାଟ୍ ଓ ହାଲ୍‌କା ବଲ୍‌ରେ ଖେଳାଯାଉଥିବା ଖେଳ; ଟେବୁଲ୍ ଟେନିସ୍

tackle /ˈtækl/ *verb* (**tackles, tackling, tackled**) start to do a difficult job କୌଣସି ସମସ୍ୟା ବା ଅସୁବିଧାର ସମାଧାନ ପାଇଁ ଚେଷ୍ଟା କରିବା *I'm going to tackle my homework now.* ○ *How shall we tackle this problem?*

tactful /ˈtæktfl/ *adjective* careful not to say or do things that may make people unhappy or angry ଚତୁର, କୌଶଳୀ କାହାରିକୁ ଅସନ୍ତୁଷ୍ଟ ନକଲା ପରି କାମ କରୁଥିବା *He wrote me a tactful letter about the money I owe him.*

tadpole /ˈtædpəʊl/ *noun* the young one of a frog or toad that lives in water and has a small tail ବେଙ୍ଗଛୁଆ, ବେଙ୍ଗଫୁଲା

tag /tæg/ *noun* a small piece of paper or material fixed to something, that tells you about it; a label ଚିହ୍ନଟ ପାଇଁ ଲଗାଯାଇଥିବା ବନ୍ଧନୀ, ଚକତି ବା ଚିହ୍ନପତ୍ର; *I looked at the price tag to see the cost.*

tail /teɪl/ *noun* **1** the part that sticks out at the end of the body of an animal, a bird, fish, etc. ଲାଞ୍ଜ, ଲାଙ୍ଗୁଡ଼; ପୁଚ୍ଛ (ପଶୁର), (ପକ୍ଷୀର) *The dog wagged its tail.* **2** the part at the back of something ପଛପଟ, ପଶ୍ଚାଦ୍‌ଭାଗ *the tail of an aeroplane* **3 tails** (*plural*) the side of a coin that does not have the head of a person on it ଧାତୁ ମୁଦ୍ରାର ପଛପଟ ବା ମୁଣ୍ଡଚିତ୍ର ନଥିବା ପଟ ➪ **head[1]** ଠାରେ ଟିପ୍ପଣୀ ଦେଖନ୍ତୁ।

tailor /ˈteɪlə(r)/ *noun* a person whose job is to make clothes ଦରଜି

take /teɪk/ *verb* (**takes, taking, took** /tʊk/, **has taken** /ˈteɪkən/) **1** carry something along with you or go with somebody to another place ନେବା, ସାଙ୍ଗରେ ନେଇଯିବା *Take your coat with you—it's cold.* ○ *Cyrus took me to the station.* **2** put your hands or arms around something and hold it ଧରିବା *She took the baby in her arms.* **3** accept or receive something ଗ୍ରହଣ କରିବା, ନେବା *Take some advice from your father.* **4** need an amount of time to do something ସମୟ ନେବା *The journey took four hours.* **5** travel in a bus, train, etc. ଟ୍ୟାକ୍ସି, ବସ୍, ଟ୍ରେନ ଇତ୍ୟାଦିରେ ଯିବା *I took a taxi to the airport.* **6** eat or drink something ଖାଇବା *I took the medicine.* **7** steal something ଚୋରାଇନେବା *Somebody has taken my bike.*

take away remove something ଅପସାରଣ କରିବା, ନେଇଯିବା *I took the matchstick away from the child.*

take down write something that somebody says ଲେଖି ରଖିବା, ଲେଖି ନେବା *He took down my address.*

take off when an aeroplane takes off, it leaves the ground (ଉଡ଼ାଜାହାଜ ଇତ୍ୟାଦି) ଉଡ଼ିବା ପାଇଁ ଭୂମିରୁ ଉପରକୁ ଉଠିବା, ଉଡ଼ିଉଠିବା ✪ ବିପରୀତ **land[2]**

take something off remove clothes ଲୁଗାପଟା ଖୋଲିବା *Take your coat off.* ✪ ବିପରୀତ **put on**

take over look after a business, etc. when another person stops ଅକ୍ତିଆର ବା ଅଧିକାର କରିବା *Rohan took over the company when his father died.*

takeaway /ˈteɪkəweɪ/ *noun* (*plural* **takeaways**) a restaurant that sells hot food that you take out with you to eat somewhere else ପ୍ୟାକ୍ କରି ନେଇଯିବା ପାଇଁ ଖାଦ୍ୟ ବିକୁଥିବା ରେଷ୍ଟୁରାଣ୍ଟ ବା ଭୋଜନାଳୟ *a Chinese takeaway*

take-off *noun* the time when an aeroplane leaves the ground ଉଡ଼ାଜାହାଜ ଇତ୍ୟାଦିର ଭୂଇଁରୁ ଉଡ଼ିଉଠିବା ପ୍ରକ୍ରିୟା, ଟେକ୍‌ଅଫ୍ ✪ ବିପରୀତ **landing**

tale /teɪl/ *noun* a story ଗପ, ଗଳ୍ପ, କାହାଣୀ *fairy tales*

talent /ˈtælənt/ *noun* the natural ability to do something very well (କିଛି କାମ କରିବା ପାଇଁ) ବିଶେଷ ଗୁଣ ବା ସାମର୍ଥ୍ୟ, ନିପୁଣତା, ପ୍ରତିଭା, ଦକ୍ଷତା *Asha has a talent for drawing.*

talented *adjective* with a talent ନିପୁଣ, ପ୍ରତିଭାଶାଳୀ *a talented musician*

talk[1] /tɔːk/ *verb* (**talks, talking, talked**) speak to somebody; say words କଥାବାର୍ତ୍ତା ହେବା; କଥା କହିବା *She is* *talking to her brother on the telephone.* ○ *We talked about our holiday.*

talk² /tɔ:k/ *noun* **1** the act of talking with somebody about something କଥାବାର୍ତ୍ତା *Priya and I had a long talk about the problem.* ○ *The two countries are holding talks to try and increase their trade.* **2** a speech or **lecture** on a particular subject ବକ୍ତୃତା, ଭାଷଣ *Professor Rao gave an interesting talk on tribal art.*

talkative /ˈtɔ:kətɪv/ *adjective* a person who is talkative talks a lot ଗପୁଡ଼ି, କୁହାଳିଆ

tall /tɔ:l/ *adjective* (**taller, tallest**) **1** a person or thing that is tall goes up a long way ଡେଙ୍ଗା, ଲମ୍ବା (ବ୍ୟକ୍ତି); ଉଚ୍ଚା (ପାହାଡ଼, ଗଛ ଇତ୍ୟାଦି) *a tall tree* ○ *Ramesh is taller than his brother.* ✪ ବିପରୀତ **short 2** **2** you use 'tall' to say or ask how far it is from the bottom to the top of somebody or something ଉଚ୍ଚା *How tall are you?* ○ *She's five feet tall.* ➪ **high** ଦେଖନ୍ତୁ ।

tame /teɪm/ *adjective* (**tamer, tamest**) an animal or a bird that is tame is not afraid of people ପୋଷା, ଗୃହପାଳିତ ପଶୁପକ୍ଷୀ *a tame squirrel* ✪ ବିପରୀତ **wild**

tame *verb* (**tames, taming, tamed**) make a wild animal or bird tame ପୋଷା ମନେଇବା, ମଣ କରିବା

tan /tæn/ *noun* when you get a tan, your skin becomes brown because you have been in the hot sun for a long time ସୂର୍ଯ୍ୟତାପ ଯୋଗୁ ଚର୍ମରେ ହୋଇଥିବା ବାଦାମୀ ରଙ୍ଗ, ଟ୍ୟାନ୍

tanned *adjective* having a brown skin colour because you have been in the hot sun for a long time ସୂର୍ଯ୍ୟୋଦୀପ୍ତ ବାଦାମୀ ଚର୍ମ ଥିବା

tangle /ˈtæŋgl/ *verb* (**tangles, tangling, tangled**) mix or twist something like string or hair so that it is difficult to separate ସୂତା ବା ବାଳ ଛନ୍ଦିଛାନ୍ଦି ହୋଇ ଅଡୁଆ ହେବା, ଜଟ ହୋଇଯିବା, ଲଟେଇ ଯିବ, ଛଳ ପଡ଼ିଯିବା ✪ ବିପରୀତ **untangle**

tangled *adjective* ଅଡୁଆ ବା ଅଲରା ହୋଇଥିବା *The cat has been playing with my wool and now it's all tangled.*

tank /tæŋk/ *noun* **1** a container for a liquid or a gas ତରଳ ପଦାର୍ଥ ବା ବାଷ୍ପ ରଖିବା ଟାଙ୍କି, ଜଳ ଧାର, ତୈଳ ଧାର *a petrol tank* **2** a strong heavy vehicle with big guns. Tanks are used by armies in wars ଯୁଦ୍ଧରେ ବ୍ୟବହୃତ ଅସ୍ତ୍ରସଜ୍ଜିତ ଯାନ

tank 2

tanker /ˈtæŋkər/ *noun* **1** a ship that carries petrol or oil ଭୂଗର୍ଭ ତୈଳ ଇତ୍ୟାଦି ବହନ କରୁଥିବା ଜାହାଜ *an oil tanker* **2** a truck that carries liquids like water, petrol oil or gas ପାଣି, ପେଟ୍ରୋଲ, ବାଷ୍ପ, ଦୁଗ୍ଧ ପ୍ରଭୃତି ତରଳ ପଦାର୍ଥ ବହନ କରୁଥିବା ବାହାନ । ଯେଉଁଥିରେ ଇଞ୍ଜିନ ସହିତ ଟାଙ୍କି ସଂଯୁକ୍ତ ଥାଏ

tap¹ /tæp/ *noun* a thing that you turn to make something like water or gas come out of a pipe ପାଣିକଳ; ତରଳ ପଦାର୍ଥ ବା ବାଷ୍ପର ନିର୍ଗମ ନଳ *Turn the tap off*.

tap[2] /tæp/ *verb* (**taps, tapping, tapped**) hit or touch somebody or something quickly and lightly ହାତ ଦ୍ୱାରା ହାଲ୍କା ଭାବେ ମାରି ଅଳ୍ପ ଶବ୍ଦ କରିବା (କାନ୍ଧ, ଦୁଆର ଇତ୍ୟାଦିରେ) *She tapped me on the shoulder*.

tap *noun* ହାଲ୍କା ଆଘାତର ଶବ୍ଦ *They heard a tap at the door*.

tape /teɪp/ *noun* **1** a long thin piece of special plastic in a plastic box, that stores (**records**) sound, music or moving pictures so that you can listen or watch later. You use it in a **tape recorder** or a **video recorder** ଧ୍ୱନି, ସଙ୍ଗୀତ ବା ଚଳଚ୍ଚିତ୍ର ଲିପିବଦ୍ଧ ବା ରେକର୍ଡ଼୍ କରିବା ପାଇଁ ବ୍ୟବହୃତ ଚୁମ୍ବକ ଶକ୍ତିଥିବା ପ୍ଲାଷ୍ଟିକ ଟେପ୍ ବା ଫିତା *Will you play your new A.R. Rahman tape?* **2** a long thin piece of material or paper ଫିତା

tape *verb* (**tapes, taping, taped**) put (**record**) sound, music or moving pictures on tape so that you can listen or watch later ଧ୍ୱନି, ସଙ୍ଗୀତ ବା ଚଳଚ୍ଚିତ୍ର ରେକର୍ଡ଼୍ କରିବା *I taped the film that was on TV last night*.

tape measure *noun* (**tape, measuring tape** ମଧ୍ୟ) a long thin piece of metal, plastic or cloth for measuring things ମାପଫିତା

tape recorder *noun* (*plural* **tape recorders**) a machine that can put (**record**) sound or music on tape and play it again later ଧ୍ୱନି ବା ସଙ୍ଗୀତ ରେକର୍ଡ଼୍ କରିବା ଯନ୍ତ୍ର

tar /tɑ:(r)/ *noun* (*no plural*) a black substance that is thick and sticky when it is hot, and hard when it is cold. Tar is used for making roads ରାଳ, ଆଲକାତରା

target /ˈtɑ:gɪt/ *noun* a thing that you try to hit with a bullet, bomb or an arrow, for example (ଗୁଳି, ବୋମା, ତୀର ଇତ୍ୟାଦି ମାରିବାର) ଲକ୍ଷ୍ୟବସ୍ତୁ, ଲକ୍ଷସ୍ଥଳ; ଲକ୍ଷ୍ୟଫଳକ; ଟାର୍‌ଗେଟ୍ *The bomb hit its target*.

Tarmac /ˈtɑ:mæk/ *noun* a black substance used for making the surfaces of roads ରାସ୍ତାର ଚଟାଣ ବା ପୃଷ୍ଠ ତିଆରି କରିବାରେ ବ୍ୟବହୃତ ଭଙ୍ଗାପଥର ଓ ରାଳର ମିଶ୍ରଣ ✪ Tarmac ଶବ୍ଦ ଟ୍ରେଡ୍‌ମାର୍କ। ➪ **tar** ଦେଖନ୍ତୁ।

tart /tɑ:t/ *noun* a kind of pastry with fruit or jam on it ଫଳ, ଜ୍ୟାମ୍ ଇତ୍ୟାଦି ମିଶା କେକ୍ *Would you like a piece of apple tart?*

task /tɑ:sk/ *noun* a piece of work that you must do; a job (ଦିଆଯାଇଥିବା) କାମ, କାର୍ଯ୍ୟ *I was given the task of cleaning the floors*.

taste[1] /teɪst/ *noun* **1** (*no plural*) the power to know the quality of different foods and drinks when you put them into your mouth ସ୍ୱାଦଶକ୍ତି, ଆସ୍ୱାଦନ ଶକ୍ତି *When you have a cold, you often lose your sense of taste*. **2** (*plural* **tastes**) the feeling that a certain food or drink gives in your mouth ସ୍ୱାଦ *Sugar has a sweet taste and lemons have a sour taste*.

taste[2] /teɪst/ *verb* (**tastes, tasting, tasted**) **1** feel or know the quality of foods or drinks when you put them in your mouth ସ୍ୱାଦ ଜାଣିବା *Can you taste onions in this soup?* **2** eat or drink a little of something ଚାଖିବା *Taste this cheese to see if you like it.* **3** give a certain feeling when you put it in your mouth ସ୍ୱାଦହେବା ବା ଜାଣି ପାରିବା *Honey tastes sweet.*

tasty /ˈteɪsti/ *adjective* (**tastier, tastiest**) good to eat ସୁସ୍ୱାଦୁ *The sandwich was very tasty.*

tattered /ˈtætəd/ *adjective* old and in bad condition ପୁରୁଣା ଓ ଛିଣ୍ଡା *a tattered coat*

tattoo /təˈtuː/ *noun* (*plural* **tattoos**) a picture on somebody's skin, made with a needle and coloured liquid (ଦେହରେ) ଚିତାକୁଟା ଚିହ୍ନ ବା ଚିତ୍ର *He had a tattoo of a snake on his arm.*

taught ଶବ୍ଦ **teach** ର ଏକ ଧାତୁରୂପ

Taurus /ˈtɔːrəs/ *noun* the second sign of the **zodiac** ରାଶିଚକ୍ରର ଦ୍ୱିତୀୟ ରାଶି, ବୃଷରାଶି

tax /tæks/ *noun* (*plural* **taxes**) money that people have to pay to the government. People pay tax from the money they earn or when they buy things କର, ଖଜଣା, ଟିକସ, ଶୁଳ୍କ **tax** *verb* (**taxes, taxing, taxed**) make somebody pay tax କର ବସାଇବା

taxi /ˈtæksi/ *noun* a car that you can travel in if you pay the driver ଭଡ଼ା ମଟରଗାଡ଼ି, ଟ୍ୟାକ୍ସି *I took a taxi to the airport.*

tea /tiː/ *noun* **1** (*no plural*) a brown drink that you make with hot water and the dry leaves of a special plant ଚା', ଚାହା *Would you like a cup of tea?* **2** (*plural* **teas**) a cup of this drink କପେ ଚା' *Two teas, please.* **3** (*no plural*) the dry leaves that you use to make tea ଚା' ପତ୍ର,

tea bag *noun* (*plural* **tea bags**) a small paper bag with tea leaves inside. You dip it into a cup of hot water to make tea ଚା'ପତ୍ର ଥିବା ଛୋଟ ଛିଦ୍ରାଳ ଥଳି ବା ପ୍ୟାକେଟ୍ (ଯାହାକୁ ଗରମ୍ ପାଣିରେ ବୁଡ଼ାଇଲେ ଚା' ହୋଇଯାଏ) ,

teapot /ˈtiːpɒt/ *noun* a special pot for making and pouring tea ଚା' କେଟ୍ଲ

teach /tiːtʃ/ *verb* (**teaches, teaching, taught** /tɔːt/, **has taught**) give somebody lessons; tell or show somebody how to do something ପାଠ ପଢ଼ାଇବା, ଶିକ୍ଷାଦାନ କରିବା। *Mrs Bhatnagar is teaching me Sanskrit.* ○ *My mother taught me to drive.* ⇨ **learn** ଦେଖନ୍ତୁ।

teaching *noun* (*no plural*) the job of a teacher ପାଠ ପଢ଼ାଇବା କାମ, ଅଧ୍ୟାପନା

teacher /ˈtiːtʃə(r)/ *noun* a person whose job is to teach ଶିକ୍ଷକ *He's my English teacher.*

team /tiːm/ *noun* **1** a group of people who play a sport or a game together against another group ଖେଳାଳି ଦଳ, ଟିମ୍ *Which team do you play for?* **2** a group of people who work together ଏକାଠି ସଂଘବଦ୍ଧ ଭାବେ କାମ କରୁଥିବା ବ୍ୟକ୍ତିବୃନ୍ଦ *a team of doctors*

tear[1] /tɪə(r)/ *noun* a drop of water that comes from your eye when you cry ଲୁହ, ଅଶ୍ରୁ, ଲୋତକ

be in tears be crying କାନ୍ଦିବା *I was in tears at the end of the film.*

burst into tears suddenly start to cry ହଠାତ୍ କାନ୍ଦି ପକାଇବା *He read the letter and burst into tears.*

tear[2] /teə(r)/ *verb* (**tears, tearing, tore** /tɔː(r)/, **has torn** /tɔːn/) **1** pull something apart or make an untidy hole in something ଚିରିଦେବା, ଛିଣ୍ଡାଇଦେବା, କଣା କରିଦେବା *She tore her dress on a nail.* ○ *I tore the piece of paper in half.* ○ *I can't use this bag—it's torn.* **2** pull something roughly and quickly away from somebody or something ଛଡ଼ାଇ ନେବା; ଛିଣ୍ଡାଇଦେବା *I tore a page out of the book.* **3** come apart; break ଛିଣ୍ଡିଯିବା *Paper tears easily.*

tear up pull something into small pieces ଟିକିଟିକି କରି ଚିରିଦେବା *I tore up the letter and threw it away.*

tear[3] /tɪə(r)/ *noun* an untidy hole in something like paper or material ଚିରି କଣା ହୋଇଥିବା ସ୍ଥାନ *You've got a tear in your jeans.*

tease /tiːz/ *verb* (**teases, teasing, teased**) laugh at somebody or make jokes about them because you think it is funny ଚିଡ଼ାଇବା, ଥଟ୍ଟା କରିବା, ଟପରା କରିବା, ଚିଗୁଲେଇବା *People often tease me because I'm short.*

teaspoon /ˈtiːspuːn/ *noun* a small spoon that you use for putting sugar into tea, coffee or other drinks ➪ ଚିତ୍ର ପାଇଁ **cutlery** ଦେଖନ୍ତୁ।

technical /ˈteknɪkl/ *adjective* of or about the machines and materials used in science and in making things ଯାନ୍ତ୍ରିକ ପ୍ରୟୋଗ ବିଦ୍ୟା ସମ୍ବନ୍ଧୀୟ, ବୈଷୟିକ *technical knowledge*

technician /tekˈnɪʃn/ *noun* a person who works with machines or instruments ପ୍ରୟୋଗାତ୍ମକ କାମରେ ନିପୁଣ ବ୍ୟକ୍ତି; ଯନ୍ତ୍ରପାତିର କାରିଗର ବା ମିସ୍ତ୍ରୀ, ଟେକ୍ନିସିଆନ୍ *a laboratory technician*

technique /tekˈniːk/ *noun* a special way of doing something କୌଣସି କାମ କରିବାର ବିଧି ବା ଶୈଳୀ; ପ୍ରବିଧି *new techniques for building bridges*

technology /tekˈnɒlədʒi/ *noun* (*plural* **technologies**) the use of science for making machines, and using them to build and make things ଯନ୍ତ୍ରପାତି ତିଆରି କରିବା ବିଜ୍ଞାନ; ପ୍ରବିଧି *computer technology*

teddy bear, teddy /ˈtedi/ *noun* (*plural* **teddy bears, teddies**) a toy for children that looks like a bear ଭାଲୁ ଆକୃତିର ନରମ କଣ୍ଢେଇ

tedious /ˈtiːdiəs/ *adjective* very long and not interesting ଦୀର୍ଘକାଳ ବ୍ୟାପି ଓ ବିରକ୍ତିକର *a tedious journey*

teenager /ˈtiːneɪdʒə(r)/ *noun* a person who is between the ages of 13 and 19 ୧୩ ରୁ ୧୯ ବର୍ଷ ବୟସର ବ୍ୟକ୍ତି; ତରୁଣ ତରୁଣୀ, ଟିନ୍ଏଜର୍

teenage /ˈtiːneɪdʒ/ *adjective* ତରୁଣ ବା ତରୁଣୀ ବୟସର *a teenage boy*

teens /tiːnz/ *noun* (*plural*) the time when you are between the ages of 13 and 19 ୧୩ ରୁ ୧୯ ବର୍ଷ ବୟସ, କିଶୋର କିଶୋରୀ *She is in her teens.*

teeth ଶବ୍ଦ **tooth** ର ବହୁବଚନ

telecommunications /ˌtelɪkəˌmjuːnɪˈkeɪʃnz/ *noun* (*no singular*) the system of sending messages over a long distance with the help of radio, telephone, satellite, etc. ଟେଲିଫୋନ, ରେଡ଼ିଓ, ଉପଗ୍ରହ ଇତ୍ୟାଦି ଜରିଆରେ ଖବର ପଠାଇବା ପଦ୍ଧତି; ବେତାର ଯୋଗାଯୋଗ

telegram /ˈtelɪɡræm/ *noun* a message that you send very quickly by radio or by electric wires ଟେଲିଗ୍ରାମ୍, ତାର

telephone[1] /ˈtelɪfəʊn/ *noun* an instrument that you use for talking to somebody who is in another place ଟେଲିଫୋନ୍ *What's your telephone number?* ○ *Can I make a telephone call?* ✪ ସାଧାରଣତଃ **phone** ଶବ୍ଦର ବ୍ୟବହାର କରାଯାଇଥାଏ ।

telephone[2] /ˈtelɪfəʊn/ *verb* (**telephones, telephoning, telephoned**) use a telephone to speak to somebody ଟେଲିଫୋନ୍ କରିବା *I must telephone my parents.* ✪ ସାଧାରଣତଃ ଆମେ **phone** ବା **call** ଶବ୍ଦର ବ୍ୟବହାର କରୁ ।

telephone directory *noun* (*plural* **telephone directories**) a book of names, addresses and telephone numbers of people who live in a particular place ଲୋକମାନଙ୍କ ନାମ, ଠିକଣା ଓ ଟେଲିଫୋନ୍ ନମ୍ବର ଥିବା ବହି ବାଡାଏରି

telescope /ˈtelɪskəʊp/ *noun* a long round instrument with special glass inside it. You use it to make things that are a long way from you appear larger and nearer ଦୂରବୀକ୍ଷଣ ଯନ୍ତ୍ର ➪ ଚିତ୍ର ପାଇଁ **observatory** ଦେଖନ୍ତୁ ।

television /ˈtelɪvɪʒn/ *noun* **1** (*plural* **televisions**) (**television set** ମଧ୍ୟ) a machine with a screen that shows moving pictures with sound ଟେଲିଭିଜନ୍, ଟି.ଭି. (ଦୂର ସ୍ଥାନର ଖବର, ଖେଳ, ସିନେମା ଇତ୍ୟାଦି ଦେଖାଉଥିବା ଯନ୍ତ୍ର) **2** (*no plural*) programmes that you watch on television ଟେଲିଭିଜନ୍ କାର୍ଯ୍ୟକ୍ରମ *I watched television last night.* **3** (*no plural*) a way of sending pictures and sounds so that people can watch them on television ଟେଲିଭିଜନ କାର୍ଯ୍ୟକ୍ରମର ପ୍ରସାରଣ ପ୍ରକ୍ରିୟା ବା ପଦ୍ଧତି *satellite television* ✪ ଏହାର ସଂକ୍ଷିପ୍ତ ରୂପ ହେଲା **TV** ।

telex /ˈteleks/ *noun* **1** (*no plural*) a way of sending messages. You type the message on a special machine that sends it very quickly to another place by telephone ଟେଲିପ୍ରିଣ୍ଟରରେ ଟାଇପ୍‌କରା ସମ୍ବାଦ ଟେଲିଫୋନ ଲାଇନ୍ ଦ୍ୱାରା ଅନ୍ୟ ସ୍ଥାନକୁ ପଠାଇବା ପ୍ରକ୍ରିୟା ବା ପଦ୍ଧତି, ଟେଲେକ୍ସ **2** (*plural* **telexes**) a message that you send or receive in this way ଟେଲେକ୍ସ ଦ୍ୱାରା ପଠାଯାଉଥିବା ବା ପାଇଥିବା ସନ୍ଦେଶ

tell /tel/ *verb* (**tells, telling, told** /təʊld/, **has told**) **1** give information to somebody by speaking or writing; describe କହିବା ବା ଲେଖିବା; ବର୍ଣ୍ଣନା କରିବା *I told her my new address.* ○ *This book tells you how to make bread.* **2** say what somebody must do ନିର୍ଦ୍ଦିଷ୍ଟ କାମ କରିବାକୁ କହିବା ବା ଆଦେଶ ଦେବା *Our teacher told us to read this book.* ➪ **say** ଠାରେ ଟିପ୍ପଣୀ ଦେଖନ୍ତୁ ।

temper /ˈtempə(r)/ *noun* the way you feel at a particular time, mood ମାନସିକ ଅବସ୍ଥା, ମିଜାଜ୍; ସ୍ୱଭାବ, ପ୍ରକୃତି *She's in a bad temper this morning.*

lose your temper suddenly become angry ହଠାତ୍ ରାଗିଯିବା

temperate /ˈtempərət/ *adjective* (of climate) having mild temperatures; neither very hot nor very cold ନାତିଶୀତୋଷ୍ଣ, ନା ଅତି ଗରମ୍ ନା ଖୁବ୍ ଥଣ୍ଡା (ପାଗ, ଅଞ୍ଚଳ ଇତ୍ୟାଦି) *temperate zones of the world*

temperature /ˈtemprətʃə(r)/ *noun* a measure of how hot or cold somebody or something is (ସ୍ଥାନ, ଶରୀର ଇତ୍ୟାଦିର) ଉତ୍ତାପ, ଉଷ୍ଣତାର ପରିମାଣ *On a very hot day, the temperature reaches 40°C.* ○ *a high/low temperature*

have a temperature feel very hot because you are ill; have fever ଜ୍ୱର ଯୋଗୁଁ ଦେହ ଉଷୁମ ଲାଗିବା, ଜ୍ୱର ହେବା

take somebody's temperature see how hot somebody is using a special instrument called a **thermometer** ଥର୍ମୋମିଟର୍ ଦ୍ୱାରା ଜର ବା ଶରୀରର ଉତ୍ତାପ ମାପିବା

temple /ˈtempl/ *noun* a building where people go to pray and worship God ମନ୍ଦିର, ଦେବାଳୟ

temporary /ˈtemprəri/ *adjective* something that is temporary lasts for a short time ସ୍ଥାୟୀ, ଅସ୍ଥାୟୀ, ସାମୟିକ *I had a temporary job in the summer holidays.* ✪ ବିପରୀତ **permanent**

temporarily *adverb* ସାମୟିକ ଭାବରେ, ଅଳ୍ପ କାଳ ପାଇଁ *The road is temporarily closed for repairs.* ✪ ବିପରୀତ **permanently**

tempt /tempt/ *verb* (**tempts, tempting, tempted**) make somebody want to do something, especially something that is wrong କିଛି କାମ କରିବାକୁ (ବିଶେଷତଃ ଭୁଲ୍ କାମ) ଲୋଭ ଦେଖାଇବା; ଲୋଭ ହେବା *He tempted me to speak against you.* ○ *He saw the money on the table, and he was tempted to steal it.*

temptation /tempˈteɪʃn/ *noun* **1** (*plural* **temptations**) a thing that makes you want to do something wrong ପ୍ରଲୋଭନ; ପ୍ରଲୋଭିତ କରୁଥିବା ପଦାର୍ଥ **2** (*no plural*) a feeling that you want to do something that you know is wrong ଭୁଲ୍‌କାମ ବୋଲି ଜାଣି ସୁଦ୍ଧା ତା' କରିବାର ଇଚ୍ଛା *the temptation to eat another chocolate*

tempting *adjective* something that is tempting makes you want to do or have it ଲୋଭନୀୟ, ଲୋଭାତୁର *That cake looks very tempting!*

ten /ten/ *number* 10 ୧୦ ସଂଖ୍ୟା

tenant /ˈtenənt/ *noun* a person who pays money to live in or use a place ପ୍ରଜା, ରୟତ; ଭଡ଼ାଟିଆ

tend /tend/ *verb* (**tends, tending, tended**) usually do or be something ସାଧାରଣ ପ୍ରକ୍ରିୟାରେ କିଛି କରିବା, ଘଟିବା ବା ହେବା *Men tend to be taller than women.*

tendency /ˈtendənsi/ *noun* (*plural* **tendencies**) something that a person or thing often does କିଛି କରିବା ପାଇଁ ସାଧାରଣ ପ୍ରବୃତ୍ତି ବା ପ୍ରବଣତା *He has a tendency to be late.*

tender /ˈtendə(r)/ *adjective* **1** kind and gentle ଦୟାଶୀଳ ଓ କୋମଳ ସ୍ୱଭାବର *tender words* **2** food that is tender is soft and easy to cut or bite into କୋମଳ, ନରମ ✪ ବିପରୀତି **tough**

tenderly *adverb* in a kind and gentle way କୋମଳ ଭାବରେ *She held the child tenderly.*

tenderness *noun* (*no plural*) କୋମଳତା *a feeling of tenderness*

tennis /ˈtenɪs/ *noun* (*no plural*) a game for two or four players who hold **rackets** and hit a small ball over a net ଟେନିସ୍ ଖେଳ *Let's play tennis.*

tennis court *noun* a special place where you play tennis ଟେନିସ୍ ଖେଳର ପ୍ରାଙ୍ଗଣ

tense[1] /tens/ *adjective* (**tenser, tensest**) **1** worried because you are waiting for something to happen ଉତ୍କଣ୍ଠିତ, ଉଦ୍‌ବେଗଜନକ *I always feel very tense before exams.* **2** pulled tightly ଟାଣକରି ଟଣାଯାଇଥିବା ବା ଟାଣି ହୋଇଥିବା *tense muscles*

tense[2] /tens/ *noun* the form of a verb that shows if an action happens in the **past**, **present** or **future** (ବ୍ୟାକରଣରେ କ୍ରିୟାର କାଳ (ଅତୀତ, ବର୍ତ୍ତମାନ ବା ଭବିଷ୍ୟତ)

tension /ˈtenʃn/ *noun* the state of being tense ମାନସିକଭାର ବା ଉଦ୍‌ବେଗ *Tension can give you headaches.*

tent /tent/ *noun* a kind of a house made of cloth. You sleep in a tent when you go camping ତମ୍ବୁ, ଶିବିର *We put up our tent.*

tenth /tenθ/ *adjective*, *adverb*, *noun* **1** 10th ୧୦ମ **2** one of ten equal parts of something; $\frac{1}{10}$ (୧/୧୦ ଏକ ଦଶମାଂଶ) ଦଶ ଭାଗରୁ ଏକଭାଗ

term /tɜːm/ *noun* **1** the time between holidays when schools and colleges are open ସ୍କୁଲ୍ ଓ କଲେଜ୍‌ରେ ପାଠପଢ଼ାର ସମୟକାଳ *There will be exams at the end of the term.* **2** a word or group of words connected with a special subject କୌଣସି ବିଶେଷ ଭାବ ପ୍ରକାଶକ ଶବ୍ଦ ବା ବାକ୍ୟାଂଶ *a scientific term*

terminal /ˈtɜːmɪnl/ *noun* a building where people begin and end their journeys by bus, train, aeroplane or ship ବସ୍, ଟ୍ରେନ୍ ବା ଉଡ଼ାଜାହାଜର ଶେଷ ରହିବା ସ୍ଥାନ *Passengers for Chennai should go to Terminal 2.*

terrace /ˈterəs/ *noun* a flat place outside a house or restaurant ଘର ବା ଭୋଜନାଳୟ ପାଖରେ ଥିବା ସମତଳ ସିମେଣ୍ଟକରା ସ୍ଥାନ; ଚଉତରା *We had our lunch on the terrace.*

terrain /təˈreɪn/ *noun* an area of land ଭୂଭାଗ *the difficult terrain of the mountains*

terrible /ˈterəbl/ *adjective* very bad ଅତି ଖରାପ; ଭୟଙ୍କର *She had a terrible accident.* ○ *The food in that restaurant is terrible!*

terribly /ˈterəbli/ *adverb* **1** very ଅତି, ଖୁବ୍ *I'm terribly sorry!* **2** very badly ଖରାପ ବା ନିକୃଷ୍ଟ ଭାବରେ *He played terribly.*

terrific /təˈrɪfɪk/ *adjective* **1** very good, wonderful ଅତି ଭଲ; ଚମତ୍କାର

What a terrific idea! **2** very great ପ୍ରବଳ *a terrific storm*

terrify /ˈterɪfaɪ/ *verb* (**terrifies, terrifying, terrified, has terrified**) make somebody very frightened ଭୟଭୀତ କରିବା, ଆତଙ୍କିତ କରିବା, ଡରିଯିବା *Spiders terrify me!*

terrified *adjective* very frightened ଭୟଭୀତ, ଆତଙ୍କିତ *My sister is terrified of dogs.*

territory /ˈterətri/ *noun* (*plural* **territories**) the land that belongs to one country ଦେଶ ବା ରାଜ୍ୟର ଭୂଭାଗ *This island was once British territory.*

terror /ˈterə(r)/ *noun* (*no plural*) very great fear ଆତଙ୍କ, ଭୟ *He screamed in terror.*

terrorist /ˈterərɪst/ *noun* a person who frightens, hurts or kills people so that the government, etc. will do what he or she wants ଆତଙ୍କବାଦୀ, ସନ୍ତ୍ରାସବାଦୀ *The terrorists were caught placing a bomb inside the station.*

terrorism /ˈterərɪzəm/ *noun* (*no plural*) ଆତଙ୍କବାଦ, ସନ୍ତ୍ରାସବାଦ *an act of terrorism*

test /test/ *verb* (**tests, testing, tested**) **1** use or look at something carefully to find out how good it is or if it works well ପରୀକ୍ଷା ନିରୀକ୍ଷା କରିବା *The doctor tested my eyes.* **2** ask somebody questions to find out what they know or what they can do ପ୍ରଶ୍ନ ପଚାରି ପରୀକ୍ଷା କରିବା *The teacher tested us on our spelling.*

test *noun* **1** an examination to find out someone's knowledge or ability to do something ଜ୍ଞାନର ମାନ ଜାଣିବା ପାଇଁ କରାଯାଉଥିବା ପରୀକ୍ଷା *a maths test* ○ *a driving test* **2** an examination of a part of your body by a doctor to find out if it works well ଡାକ୍ତରଙ୍କ ଦ୍ୱାରା ଶରୀରର ପରୀକ୍ଷା *an eye test* **3** an experiment to find out if something works well କୌଣସି ପଦାର୍ଥର ମାନ ଜାଣିବା ପାଇଁ କରାଯାଉଥିବା ପରୀକ୍ଷା *Tests showed that the river is highly polluted.*

test tube *noun* a long thin glass tube that is used in chemistry and for other scientific experiments ବୈଜ୍ଞାନିକ ପରୀକ୍ଷାରେ ବ୍ୟବହୃତ କାଚନଳୀ, ଟେଷ୍ଟ୍ ଟ୍ୟୁବ୍

text /tekst/ *noun* **1** (*no plural*) the words in a book, newspaper or magazine (ବହି, ଖବରକାଗଜ, ପତ୍ରିକା ଇତ୍ୟାଦିର) ବିଷୟବସ୍ତୁ ସମ୍ବଳିତ ଲେଖା *This book has a lot of pictures but not much text.* **2** (*plural* **texts**) a book or a short piece of writing that you study (ବହି ଇତ୍ୟାଦିର) ଲେଖା *Read the text and answer the questions.*

textbook /ˈtekstbʊk/ *noun* a book that teaches you about something especially prescribed in a study programme (ପାଠ୍ୟପୁସ୍ତକ); ଅଧ୍ୟୟନ ପାଇଁ ଉଦ୍ଦିଷ୍ଟ ବହି *a biology textbook*

textile /ˈtekstaɪl/ *noun* any cloth produced in a factory କଳବୁଣା କନା; ବୁଣାଲୁଗା ଇତ୍ୟାଦି *He deals in cotton textiles.*

texture /ˈtekstʃə(r)/ *noun* the way that something feels when you touch it କୌଣସି ପଦାର୍ଥର ମସୃଣତା, ସୂକ୍ଷ୍ମତା, ଗଢ଼ଣ *Silk has a smooth texture.*

than /ðən; ðæn/ *conjunction, preposition* you use 'than' when you compare two people or things ଅପେକ୍ଷା, ଠାରୁ *I'm older than him.* ○ *We live less than a kilometre from the beach.*

thank /θæŋk/ *verb* (**thanks, thanking, thanked**) tell somebody that you are pleased because they gave you something or helped you ଧନ୍ୟବାଦ୍ ଦେବା *I thanked Tina for the present.*

no, thank you you use 'no, thank you' to politely say that you do not want something ଯଚା ଯାଉଥିବା ପଦାର୍ଥ ଗ୍ରହଣ ନ କରିବା ପାଇଁ କୁହା ଯାଉଥିବା ଖଣ୍ଡବାକ୍ୟ *'Would you like some more tea?' 'No, thank you.'* ✪ ଏ କ୍ଷେତ୍ରରେ **no, thanks** ମଧ୍ୟ କୁହାଯାଏ।

thank you, thanks you use 'thank you' or 'thanks' to tell somebody that you are pleased because they gave you something or helped you ଧନ୍ୟବାଦ୍ (କରିବା) *Thank you very much for the flowers.* ○ *'How are you?' 'I'm fine, thanks.'*

thanks *noun* (*plural*) words that show you are pleased because somebody gave you something or helped you ଧନ୍ୟବାଦ *Please give my thanks to your sister for her help.*

thankful /ˈθæŋkfl/ *adjective* happy that something good has happened କୃତଜ୍ଞ, ସନ୍ତୁଷ୍ଟ *I was thankful for a rest after the long walk.*

thankfully *adverb* you say 'thankfully' when you are pleased about something କୃତଜ୍ଞତାର ସହ; ଭାଗ୍ୟକୁ *There was an accident, but thankfully nobody was hurt.*

that[1] /ðæt/ *adjective*, *pronoun* (*plural* **those**) a word that you use to talk about a person or thing that is there or then ସେ, ସେଇଟା, ସେ ବ୍ୟକ୍ତି ଜଣକ *'Who is that boy in the garden?' 'That's my brother.'* ○ *She got married in 1998. At that time, she was a teacher.*

that[2] /ðæt/ *adverb* used to say how long, far, big, etc. something is ଏତେ, ସେତେ *The next village is ten kilometres from here. I can't walk that far.*

that[3] /ðæt/ *pronoun* which, who or whom ଯେକି, ଯିଏ, ଯାହା *A lion is an animal that lives in forests.* ○ *I'm reading the book (that) you gave me.*

that[4] /ðæt/ *conjunction* a word that you use to join two parts of a sentence ଯେ; ଯେଉଁଟି, ଯେଉଁମାନେ *Joe said (that) he was unhappy.* ○ *I'm sure (that) he will come.*

thatched cottage

thatch /θætʃ/ *noun* (*plural* **thatches**) dried straw that is used for making roofs ଚାଳ ବା ଛପର

thatched /θætʃt/ *adjective* ଚାଳ ଛାଉଥିବା *a thatched cottage*

thaw /θɔː/ *verb* (**thaws, thawing, thawed**) warm something that is frozen so that it becomes soft or liquid; get warmer so that it becomes soft or liquid ବରଫ ତରଳିବା ବା ତରଳାଇବା *The ice is thawing.*

the /ðə; ði; ðiː/ *article* **1** a word that you use before the name of somebody or something when it is clear which person or thing you mean ପୂର୍ବଲିଖିତ ବା ଜ୍ଞାତ ବ୍ୟକ୍ତି ବା ପଦାର୍ଥର ନାମ ପୂର୍ବରୁ ବ୍ୟବହୃତ ସୂଚକ ଶବ୍ଦ *The man you met at the door is a doctor.* ○ *The sun is shining.* **2** a word that you use before numbers and dates (ଚତୁର୍ଥ, ଦଶମ ଇତ୍ୟାଦି) ସଂଖ୍ୟା ବା ତିଥି ପୂର୍ବରୁ ବ୍ୟବହୃତ ଶବ୍ଦ *Monday the sixth of May* **3** a word that you use to talk about a group of people or things of the same kind ଏକ ବିଭାଗର ଏକ ବିଶେଷ ବ୍ୟକ୍ତି ବା ପଦାର୍ଥ ପୂର୍ବରୁ ବ୍ୟବହୃତ ଶବ୍ଦ *the French* ○ *Do you play the sitar?* **4** a word that you use before the names of rivers, seas, etc. and some countries ନଈ, ସମୁଦ୍ର, ପର୍ବତମାଳା ଇତ୍ୟାଦି ଓ ଅଳ୍ପ କିଛି ଦେଶଙ୍କ ନାମ ପୂର୍ବରୁ ବ୍ୟବହୃତ ଶବ୍ଦ *the Ganga* ○ *the Arabian Sea* ○ *the United States of America* ✪ ମନେ ରଖନ୍ତୁ! ଅଧିକାଂଶ ଦେଶର ନାମ ପୂର୍ବରୁ the ବ୍ୟବହୃତ ହୁଏନାହିଁ। *I went to France.* (*I went to the France* କୁହାଯାଏ ନାହିଁ)।

theatre /ˈθɪətə(r)/ *noun* a building where you go to see plays ଥିଏଟର୍, ରଙ୍ଗାଳୟ *I'm going to the theatre this evening.*

theft /θeft/ *noun* the act of taking something that is not yours; the act of stealing ଚୋରି *I told the police about the theft of my car.*

their /ðeə(r)/ *adjective* of them ତାଙ୍କର, ସେମାନଙ୍କର *What is their phone number?*

theirs /ðeəz/ *pronoun* something that belongs to them ତାଙ୍କ ଜିନିଷ *Our flat is smaller than theirs.*

them /ðəm/ *pronoun* (*plural*) **1** a word that shows more than one person, animal or thing ସେମାନେ, ସେଗୁଡ଼ିକ *I wrote them a letter and then I phoned them.* ○ *I'm looking for my keys. Have you seen them?* **2** him or her ସେ; ତାଙ୍କୁ *If anybody phones, tell them I'm busy.*

theme /θiːm/ *noun* something that you talk or write about ବିଷୟ, ବିଷୟବସ୍ତୁ (ବକ୍ତୃତା, ଲେଖା ଇତ୍ୟାଦିର) *The theme of his speech was 'Television and Children'.*

themselves /ðəmˈselvz/ *pronoun* (*plural*) a word that shows the same people, animals or things that you have just talked about ନିଜେ, ସ୍ୱୟଂ *They bought themselves a new car.*

by themselves 1 alone; without other people ନିଜେ ନିଜେ *The children went out by themselves.* **2** without help ଅନ୍ୟର ସାହାଯ୍ୟ ବିନା, ନିଜେ *They cooked dinner by themselves.*

then /ðen/ *adverb* **1** at that time ସେତେବେଳେ *I can't come next week. I will be on holiday then.* **2** next; after that ତା'ପରେ *We had dinner and then watched television.* **3** if that is true ତା'ହେଲେ *'I don't feel well.' 'Then why don't you go to the doctor's?'*

theory /ˈθɪəri/ *noun* (*plural* **theories**) an idea that tries to explain something ତତ୍ତ୍ୱ, ସିଦ୍ଧାନ୍ତ *There are a lot of different theories about how life began.*

therapy /ˈθerəpi/ *noun* (*plural* **therapies**) a way of helping people who are ill in their body or mind, usually without drugs ଚିକିତ୍ସା; ଚିକିତ୍ସା ପଦ୍ଧତି, ଚିକିତ୍ସା ପ୍ରକ୍ରିୟା *speech therapy*

there[1] /ðeə(r)/ *adverb* in, at or to that place ସେଠାରେ, ସେଠାକୁ, ସେଠି *Don't put the box there—put it here.* ○ *Have you been to Nashik? I'm going there next week.*

there[2] /ðeə(r)/ *pronoun* a word that you use with verbs like 'be', 'seem' and 'appear' to show that something is true or that something is happening କିଛି କଥା ସତ ବା କିଛି ଘଟଣା ଘଟୁଛି ବୋଲି ସୂଚାଇବାକୁ 'be', 'seem' ବା 'appear' ପରିକ୍ରିୟାପଦ ସହ ବ୍ୟବହୃତ ଶବ୍ଦ *There is a man at the door.* ○ *Is there a film on TV tonight?*

therefore /ˈðeəfɔː(r)/ *adverb* for that reason ତେଣୁ, ସେହି କାରଣରୁ *Sita was busy and therefore could not come to the meeting.*

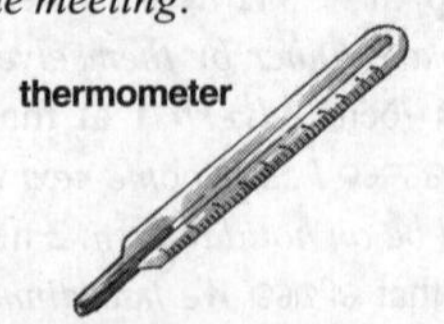

thermometer /θəˈmɒmɪtə(r)/ *noun* an instrument that shows how hot or cold something is ତାପ ମାନ ଯନ୍ତ୍ର, ଥର୍ମୋମିଟର

these /ðiːz/ *adjective*, *pronoun* (*plural*) a word that you use to talk about people or things that are here or now ଏ, ଏସବୁ *These books are mine.* ○ *Do you want these pencils?*

they /ðeɪ/ *pronoun* (*plural*) **1** the people, animals or things that the sentence is about ସେମାନେ, ସେଗୁଡ଼ିକ, ସେ ସବୁ *'Where are my keys?' 'They're on the table.'* **2** people in general ଲୋକମାନେ, ସେମାନେ *They say it will be cold this winter.*

they'd 1 = **they had 2** = **they would**

they'll = **they will**

they're = **they are**

they've = **they have**

thick /θɪk/ *adjective* (**thicker, thickest**) **1** far from one side to the other ମୋଟା, ଚଉଡ଼ା *The walls are very thick.* ○ *It's cold outside, so wear a thick coat.* ✪ ବିପରୀତ **thin 2** you use 'thick' to say or ask how far something is from one side to the other ଓସାରର, ଚଉଡ଼ାର *The ice is six centimetres thick.* **3** with a lot of people or things close together ଭରପୂର, ଘଞ୍ଚ *a thick forest* **4** if a liquid is thick, it does not flow easily ବହଳିଆ, ଘନ *This paint is too thick.* ✪ ବିପରୀତ **thin 5** difficult to see through ଘନ, ଯାହାକୁ ଭେଦି ଦେଖି ହେବନାହିଁ *thick fog*

thickly *adverb* **1** spread, cut, etc. in a way that there is a wide or deep layer of something ବହଳିଆ କରି *Spread the butter thickly on the toast.* **2** having a lot of people or things together ଘଞ୍ଚଭାବରେ *a thickly populated town*

thickness *noun* (*no plural*) ମୋଟେଇ, ସ୍ଥୁଳତା; ଘନତ୍ୱ *The wood is three centimetres in thickness.*

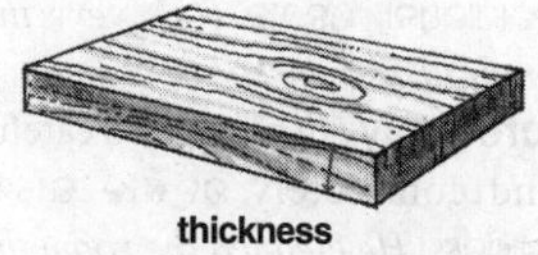

thickness

thicken /ˈθɪkən/ *verb* (**thickens, thickening, thickened**) become or make something thicker ଗାଢ଼ କରିବା ବା ହେବା। *The fog thickened in the evening.*

thief /θiːf/ *noun* (*plural* **thieves** /θiːvz/) a person who steals something ଚୋର *A thief stole my car.*

thigh /θaɪ/ *noun* the part of your leg above your knee ➪ ଚିତ୍ର ପାଇଁ **body** ଦେଖନ୍ତୁ।

thin /θɪn/ *adjective* (**thinner, thinnest**) **1** not far from one side to the other; not thick ଦୁର୍ବଳ, କ୍ଷୀଣ, ପତଳା *The walls in this house are very thin.* ○ *I cut the bread into thin slices.* **2** not fat ଅଳ୍ପ ଚଉଡ଼ା; ସରୁ, ପତଳା *He's tall and thin.* **3** If a liquid is thin, it flows easily like water ପାଣିଆ *The soup was very thin.* ✪ ବିପରୀତ **thick 4** not close together ଘଞ୍ଚ ହୋଇ ନଥିବା, ପତଳା *My father's hair is getting thin.*

thing /θɪŋ/ *noun* **1** an object ବସ୍ତୁ, ପଦାର୍ଥ *What's that red thing?* **2** an idea or subject ବିଷୟ, ଧାରଣା *We talked about a lot of things.*

think /θɪŋk/ *verb* (**thinks, thinking, thought** /θɔːt/, **has thought**) **1** use your mind ଭାବିବା, ଚିନ୍ତା କରିବା *Think before you answer the question.* **2** believe something ବିଶ୍ୱାସ କରିବା, ଭାବିବା *I think it's going to rain.* ○ *I think they live in Jhansi but I'm not sure.*

think about somebody or **something 1** have somebody or something in your mind କୌଣସି ବ୍ୟକ୍ତି, ପଦାର୍ଥ ଇତ୍ୟାଦି ବିଷୟରେ ଭାବିବା *I often think about that day.* **2** try to decide whether to do something or not କିଛି କରିବା ନ କରିବା ବିଷୟରେ ଭାବିବା ବା ବିଚାର କରିବା *Leela is thinking about leaving her job.*

think of somebody or **something 1** remember someone or something କାହାରି ବା କୌଣସି କଥା ଭାବିବା *I can't think of her name.* **2** have an opinion about somebody or something ମତାମତ ନିର୍ଣ୍ଣୟ କରିବା *What do you think of this music?* **3** try to decide whether to do something କିଛି କରିବା ନକରିବା ବିଷୟରେ ବିଚାର କରିବା *We're thinking of going to America.*

thinking /θɪŋkɪŋ/ *noun* (*no plural*) **1** the process of thinking about something ଭାବିବା ପ୍ରକ୍ରିୟା **2** ideas or opinions about or attitude towards something ମତ, ବିଚାର *His thinking is different from mine.*

third /θɜːd/ *adjective, adverb, noun* **1** 3rd ତୃତୀୟ (୩ୟ) **2** one of three equal parts of something; $\frac{1}{3}$ ତିନିଭାଗରୁ ଭାଗେ, ଏକ ତୃତୀୟାଂଶ; $\frac{୧}{୩}$

thirst /θɜːst/ *noun* (*no plural*) the feeling that you have when you want to drink something ଶୋଷ, ତୃଷା, ତୃଷ୍ଣା, ପିପାସା *Rahul quenched his thirst* *with a drink of water from the fridge.* ✪ ମନେ ରଖନ୍ତୁ ! 'I am thirsty' ର ପ୍ରୟୋଗ କରାଯାଏ। 'I have thirst' କହିବାଟ ଭୁଲ ହେବ।

thirsty /ˈθɜ:sti/ *adjective* (**thirstier, thirstiest**) if you are thirsty, you want to drink something ଶୋଷିଲା, ତୃଷାର୍ତ୍ତ *Salty food makes you thirsty.*

thirteen /ˌθɜ:ˈti:n/ *number* 13 ୧୩ ସଂଖ୍ୟା

thirteenth /ˌθɜ: ˈti:nθ/ *adjective, adverb, noun* 13th ୧୩ତମ

thirty /ˈθɜ:ti/ *number* **1** 30 ୩୦ ସଂଖ୍ୟା **2 the thirties** (*plural*) the numbers, years or temperatures between 30 and 39 ୩୦ ରୁ ୩୯ ପର୍ଯ୍ୟନ୍ତ ସଂଖ୍ୟା, ବର୍ଷ ବା ଉତ୍ତାପ

thirtieth /ˈθɜ:tiəθ/ *adjective, adverb, noun* 30th ୩୦ତମ

this¹ /ðɪs/ *adjective, pronoun* (*plural* **these**) a word that you use to talk about a person or thing that is near you ଏହା, ଏଇଟା, ଏହି, ଏ *Come and look at this photo.* ○ *This is my sister.* ○ *How much does this cost?*

this² /ðɪs/ *adverb* so ଏତେ *The other film was not this good.*

thorn /θɔ:n/ *noun* a sharp point that grows on a plant (ଗଛର) କଣ୍ଟା *Rose bushes have thorns.*

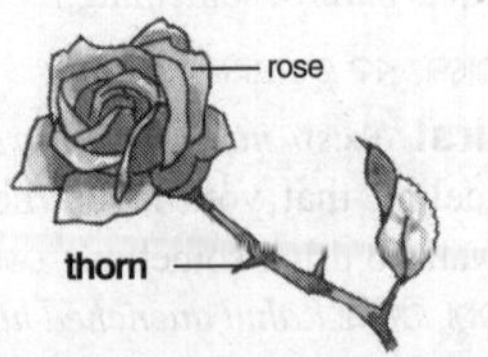

thorny /ˈθɔ:ni/ *adjective* (**thornier, thorniest**) full of thorns କଣ୍ଟକମୟ *a thorny bush*

thorough /ˈθʌrə/ *adjective* careful and complete ସମ୍ପୂର୍ଣ୍ଣରୂପେ ଓ ଯତ୍ନସହକାରେ କରାଯାଇଥିବା, ଯତ୍ନଶୀଳ *He's very thorough in his work.*

thoroughly /ˈθʌrəli/ *adverb* carefully and completely ଯତ୍ନଶୀଳ ଭାବେ ଓ ସମ୍ପୂର୍ଣ୍ଣରୂପେ *He cleaned the room thoroughly.*

those /ðəʊz/ *adjective, pronoun* (*plural*) a word that you use to talk about people or things that are there or then ସେ, ସେସବୁ, ସେଗୁଡ଼ିକ *I don't know those boys.* ○ *Her grandfather was born in 1850. In those days, there were no cars.* ○ *Can I have those?*

though¹ /ðəʊ/ *conjunction* in spite of something; although ଏହା ସତ୍ତ୍ୱେ; ଯଦିଓ *I was very cold, though I was wearing a coat.*

as though in a way that makes you think something ଯେମିତି *The house looks as though nobody lives there.*

though² /ðəʊ/ *adverb* however ପରନ୍ତୁ, ହେଲେହେଁ *I like him very much. I don't like his brother, though.*

thought¹ ଶବ୍ଦ **think** ର ଏକ ଧାତୁରୂପ

thought² /θɔ:t/ *noun* **1** (*no plural*) the act of thinking ଭାବିବା ପ୍ରକ୍ରିୟା *After a lot of thought, I decided not to take the job.* **2** (*plural* **thoughts**) an idea ଭାବନା *Have you had any thoughts about what you want to do when you leave school?*

thoughtful /ˈθɔːtfl/ *adjective* **1** if you are thoughtful, you are thinking deeply ଭାବନାପୂର୍ଣ୍ଣ, ଧ୍ୟାନରତ, ଚିନ୍ତାଶୀଳ *She listened with a thoughtful look on her face.* **2** a person who is thoughtful is kind, and thinks and cares about other people ବିଚାରଶୀଳ *It was very thoughtful of you to cook us dinner.*

thousand /ˈθaʊznd/ *number* 1,000 ୧୦୦୦ ସଂଖ୍ୟା *a thousand people* ○ *two thousand and fifteen*

thousandth /ˈθaʊznθ/ *adjective, adverb, noun* 1,000th ୧୦୦୦ତମ

thrash /θræʃ/ *verb* (**thrashes, thrashing, thrashed**) hit someone with a stick ବାଡ଼ିରେ ବାଡ଼େଇବା

thread /θred/ *noun* a long thin piece of cotton, wool, etc. that you use with a **needle** for sewing ସୂତା।

thread *verb* (**threads, threading, threaded**) put thread through the hole in a needle ଛୁଞ୍ଚିରେ ସୂତା ଗଳାଇବା

threat /θret/ *noun* **1** a warning that you will be hurt or punished if you do not do what somebody wants you to do ଧମକ, ଭୟ ପ୍ରଦର୍ଶନ **2** a person or thing that may damage or hurt somebody or something ସମ୍ଭବ୍ୟ କ୍ଷତିକାରକ ବ୍ୟକ୍ତି ବା ପଦାର୍ଥ *Pollution is a threat to the lives of animals and people.*

threaten /ˈθretn/ *verb* (**threatens, threatening, threatened**) **1** say that you will hurt somebody if they do not do what you want ଧମକାଇବା, ଭୟ ଦେଖାଇବା, ଡରାଇବା *They threatened to damage the building.* **2** seem ready to do something unpleasant କ୍ଷତି କରିବାର ଭୟ ଦେଖାଇବା। *The dark clouds threatened rain.*

threatening *adjective* expressing a threat of harm; expressing a sign of coming danger ହାନୀ କରିବାର ଧମକ ଥିବା; ବିପଦର ସଙ୍କେତ ଥିବା *He spoke in a threatening tone.*

three /θriː/ *number* 3 ୩ ସଂଖ୍ୟା

threw ଶବ୍ଦ **throw** ର ଏକ ଧାତୁରୂପ

thrill /θrɪl/ *noun* a sudden strong feeling of excitement ଉତ୍ତେଜନା, ଆବେଗ, ପୁଲକ, ଆନନ୍ଦ, ରୋମାଞ୍ଚ

thrill *verb* (**thrills, thrilling, thrilled**) make somebody feel excited ରୋମାଞ୍ଚିତ କରିବା, ପୁଲକିତ କରିବା

thrilled *adjective* very happy and excited ରୋମାଞ୍ଚିତ, ଆନନ୍ଦିତ *We are all thrilled that you have won the prize.*

thrilling *adjective* very exciting ଉତ୍ତେଜନା ପୂର୍ଣ୍ଣ; ରୋମାଞ୍ଚକର *a thrilling adventure*

throat /θrəʊt/ *noun* **1** the front part of your neck ତଣ୍ଟି, ଗଳଦେଶ ➪ ଚିତ୍ର ପାଇଁ **body** ଦେଖନ୍ତୁ। **2** the part inside your neck that takes food and air down from your mouth into your body କଣ୍ଠନଳୀ, ଗଳା, ତଣ୍ଟି *I've got a sore throat.*

throne /θrəʊn/ *noun* a special chair where a king or queen sits ସିଂହାସନ

throne

through /θruː/ *preposition*, *adverb* **1** from one side or end of something to the other side or end ଏପଟୁ ସେପଟକୁ, ମଧ୍ୟ ଦେଇ, ପାର ହେଇ *We drove through the tunnel.* ○ *What can you see through the window?* ○ *She opened the gate and we walked through.* **2** from the beginning to the end of something ମୂଳରୁ ଶେଷ ପର୍ଯ୍ୟନ୍ତ, ସାରା, ପୂରା *We travelled through the night.* **3** because of somebody or something ସାହାଯ୍ୟରେ *She got the job through her father.*

throughout /θruː'aʊt/ *preposition*, *adverb* **1** in every part of something ପୂରା *We painted the house throughout.* **2** from the beginning to the end of something ଆରମ୍ଭରୁ ଶେଷ ପର୍ଯ୍ୟନ୍ତ *They talked throughout the film.*

throw /θrəʊ/ *verb* (**throws, throwing, threw** /θruː/, **has thrown** /θrəʊn/) move your arm quickly to send something through the air ଫୋପାଡ଼ିବା, ଫିଙ୍ଗିବା *Throw the ball to Aman.*

throw something away or **out** put something in the dustbin because you do not want it ଅଦରକାରୀ ଜିନିଷ ଅଳିଆ ଡବାରେ ପକାଇ ଦେବା *Don't throw the box away.*

throw *noun* ନିକ୍ଷେପଣ, ଫୋପଡ଼ା *What a good throw!*

thrust /θrʌst/ *verb* (**thrusts, thrusting, thrust, has thrust**) push somebody or something suddenly and strongly ଠେଲିବା, ଧକ୍କା ମାରିବା *She thrust the money into my hand.*

thrust *noun* a strong push ଠେଲା, ଧକ୍କା

thud /θʌd/ *noun* the sound that a heavy thing makes when it hits something ଧଡ଼୍ ବା ଢ଼ପ୍ କରି ପଡ଼ିବାର ଶବ୍ଦ *The book hit the floor with a thud.*

thumb /θʌm/ *noun* the short thick finger at the side of your hand ହାତର ବୁଢ଼ା ଆଙ୍ଗୁଠି ➪ ଚିତ୍ର ପାଇଁ **finger** ଦେଖନ୍ତୁ।

thump /θʌmp/ *verb* (**thumps, thumping, thumped**) make a loud sound by hitting or beating hard ବାଡ଼େଇବା ବା ବାଡ଼େଇ ହେବାର ଶବ୍ଦ; ଧପ୍‌ଧପ୍ ଶବ୍ଦ *Her heart was thumping with fear.*

thunder /'θʌndə(r)/ *noun* (*no plural*) a loud noise in the sky when there is a storm ଘଡ଼ଘଡ଼ି, ବଜ୍ରଧ୍ୱନି ✪ ଆକାଶରେ ଘଡ଼ଘଡ଼ି ସହ ଦିଶୁଥିବା ବିଜୁଳିକୁ **lightning** କହନ୍ତି।

thunder *verb* (**thunders, thundering, thundered**) **1** make the sound of thunder ଘଡ଼ଘଡ଼ି ମାରିବା *It thundered all night.* **2** make a sound like thunder ଘଡ଼ଘଡ଼ି ପରି ଶବ୍ଦ କରିବା *The lorries thundered along the road.*

thunderstorm /'θʌndəstɔːm/ *noun* a storm with a lot of rain, thunder and lightning ଘଡ଼ଘଡ଼ି, ବିଜୁଳି ସହ ହେଉଥିବା ବର୍ଷାଝଡ଼

Thursday /'θɜːzdeɪ/ *noun* the fourth day of the week, next after Wednesday ଗୁରୁବାର

thus /ðʌs/ *adverb* **1** because of this ତେଣୁ, ଫଳରେ *He was very busy and was thus unable to come to the meeting.* **2** in this way ଏହିପରି, ଏମିତି *Hold the wheel in both hands thus.*

tick[1] /tɪk/ *noun* the sound that a clock or watch makes (ଘଣ୍ଟାର) ଟିକ୍ ଟିକ୍ ଶବ୍ଦ
tick *verb* (**ticks, ticking, ticked**) make this sound ଟିକ୍ ଟିକ୍ ଶବ୍ଦ କରିବା *The clock was ticking.*

tick[2] /tɪk/ *noun* a small mark like ✓, that shows that something is correct, for example ସଠିକତା ବା ଅଛି ବୋଲି ସୂଚାଉଥିବା (✓) ଚିହ୍ନ, ଟିକ୍ *Put a tick next to the correct answer.*
tick *verb* (**ticks, ticking, ticked**) make a mark like this ✓ next to something ଟିକ୍ ଚିହ୍ନ ✓ ଦେବା *Tick the right answer.*

ticket /ˈtɪkɪt/ *noun* a small piece of paper or card that you must buy to travel in a bus, train or an aeroplane or to go into a cinema, theatre or museum, for example ପ୍ରବେଶ ପତ୍ର, ଟିକେଟ୍, ଟିକଟ *a theatre ticket*

tickle /ˈtɪkl/ *verb* (**tickles, tickling, tickled**) touch somebody lightly with your fingers to make them laugh କୁତୁକୁତୁ କରିବା *She tickled the baby's feet.*

tide /taɪd/ *noun* the regular rise and fall in the level of the sea, which happens twice a day. Tides are caused by the pull of the moon and the sun (ସମୁଦ୍ରର) ଜୁଆର ଭଟ୍ଟା *The tide is coming in.* ○ *The tide is going out.* ✪ ସମୁଦ୍ର ପାଣି ଫୁଲି ଉଠିବା ଅବସ୍ଥାକୁ **high tide** (ଜୁଆର) କୁହାଯାଏ ଓ ଜୁଆର ଛାଡ଼ିଯିବାର ଅବସ୍ଥାକୁ **low tide** (ଭଟ୍ଟା) କୁହାଯାଏ।
tidal *adjective* connected with tides ଜୁଆର ଭଟ୍ଟା ସମ୍ବନ୍ଧୀୟ

tidy /ˈtaɪdi/ *adjective* (**tidier, tidiest**) with everything in the right place ପରିଚ୍ଛନ, ସୁଶୃଙ୍ଖଳ *Her room is very tidy.* ✪ ବିପରୀତ **untidy**
tidily *adverb* ସୁଶୃଙ୍ଖଳ ଭାବରେ, ସଜଡ଼ା ସଜଡ଼ି କରି, ସଜାଡ଼ି *Put the books back tidily when you've finished with them.*
tidiness *noun* (*no plural*) the state of being tidy ପରିଚ୍ଛନ୍ନତା
tidy *verb* (**tidies, tidying, tidied, has tidied**) make something tidy ପରିଚ୍ଛନ୍ନ କରିବା, ସଜଡ଼ା ସଜଡ଼ି କରିବା *I tidied up the house before my parents arrived.*

tie[1] /taɪ/ *noun* **1** a long thin piece of cloth that is worn round the collar of a shirt ଗଳାବନ୍ଧା ଟାଇ ➪ ଚିତ୍ର ପାଇଁ **suit** ଦେଖନ୍ତୁ। **2** a situation when two teams or players have the same number of points at the end of a game or competition ଖେଳର ଅମିମାଂସିତ ଅବସ୍ଥା (ଦୁଇ ପକ୍ଷର ସମାନ ଗୋଲ, ରନ୍ ବା ପଏଣ୍ଟ ପାଇବା ଅବସ୍ଥା) ଟାଇ *The match ended in a tie.* **3** something that holds people together ବନ୍ଧନ, ସମ୍ପର୍କ, ବୁଝାମଣା *Our school has ties with a school in Cuttack.*

tie[2] /taɪ/ *verb* (**ties, tying, tied, has tied**) **1** fasten two ends of string, rope, etc. together to hold somebody or something in place ବାନ୍ଧିବା *I tied a scarf round my neck.* ✪ ବିପରୀତ **untie** **2** end a game or competition with the same number of points for both teams or players ଖେଳ ଅମିମାଂସିତ ଭାବେ ଶେଷ ହେବା ବା ଶେଷ କରିବା *India tied with Spain for second place.*

tie somebody up put a piece of rope around somebody so that they cannot move କାହାରିକୁ ଦଉଡ଼ି ଇତ୍ୟାଦିରେ ବାନ୍ଧିବା *The robbers tied up the owner of the shop.*

tie something up put a piece of string or rope around something to hold it in place ଜିନିଷ ପତ୍ର ବାନ୍ଧିବା *I tied up the parcel with string.*

tiger /ˈtaɪɡə(r)/ *noun* a wild animal like a big cat, with yellow fur and black stripes. Tigers live in Asia ବ୍ୟାଘ୍ର, ବ୍ୟାଘ୍ର ➪ ଚିତ୍ର ପାଇଁ **camouflage** ଦେଖନ୍ତୁ।

✪ ବାଘୁଣୀକୁ **tigress** ଓ ବାଘ ଛୁଆକୁ **cub** କହନ୍ତି।

tight /taɪt/ *adjective* (**tighter, tightest**) **1** fixed firmly so that you cannot move it easily ଦୃଢ଼ ଭାବରେ ଧରାଯାଇଥିବା ବା ବନ୍ଧାଯାଇଥିବା, ଟାଇଟ୍ *a tight knot* ○ *I can't open this jar of jam—the lid is too tight.* **2** fitting closely to your body ଦେହରେ କଷିହୋଇ ବା ଭିଡ଼ି ହୋଇ ରହୁଥିବା, ଟାଇଟ୍ *These shoes are too tight.* ✪ ବିପରୀତ **loose**

tightly *adverb* କଷିକରି, ଭିଡ଼ିକରି *I tied the string tightly around the box.* ✪ ବିପରୀତ **loosely**

tighten /ˈtaɪtn/ *verb* (**tightens, tightening, tightened**) become tighter or make something tighter ଅଧିକ ଟାଇଟ୍ କରିବା, ଭିଡ଼ିଦେବା ବା ଦୃଢ଼ କରିବା *Can you tighten this screw?* ✪ ବିପରୀତ **loosen**

tightrope /ˈtaɪtrəʊp/ *noun* a rope or wire high above the ground. **Acrobats** walk along tightropes in a **circus** ଚାଲିବା ପାଇଁ ଭୂଇଁର ଉର୍ଦ୍ଧ୍ୱରେ ଟାଣ କରି ବନ୍ଧା ଯାଇଥିବା ଦଉଡ଼ି ବା ତାର (ସର୍କସ, ବାଉଁଶରାଣୀ ଖେଳ ଇତ୍ୟାଦିରେ)

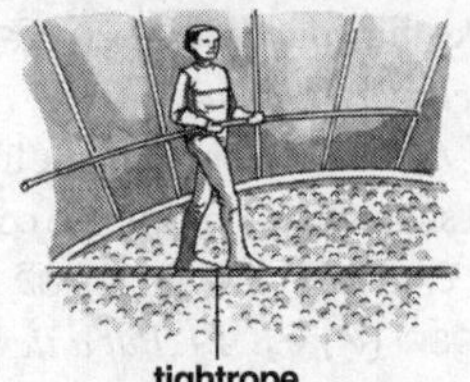

tightrope

tights /taɪts/ *noun* (*plural*) a thin piece of clothing that a woman or girl wears over her feet and legs ଅଣ୍ଟାରୁ ଗୋଡ଼ ଆଙ୍ଗୁଠି ପର୍ଯ୍ୟନ୍ତ ପିନ୍ଧାଯାଉଥିବା ମୋଜା ପରି ଚିପାବସ୍ତ୍ର (ଝିଅଙ୍କ ପାଇଁ) *a pair of tights*

tile /taɪl/ *noun* a flat square thing. We use tiles for covering roofs, walls and floors ଟାଇଲ୍

till /tɪl/ *conjunction* up to the time when ପର୍ଯ୍ୟନ୍ତ *Let's wait till the rain stops.*

till *preposition* **1** up to a certain time ପର୍ଯ୍ୟନ୍ତ *I'll be here till Monday.* **2** before ପୂର୍ବରୁ, ମଧ୍ୟରେ *He didn't arrive till six o'clock.* ✪ **'Till'** ଓ **'until'** ର ଅର୍ଥ ଏକା, କିନ୍ତୁ **until** ଟା ଆନୁଷ୍ଠାନିକ ବା ସାଧୁ ଭାଷାରେ, ବିଶେଷତଃ ବାକ୍ୟର ଆରମ୍ଭରେ ବ୍ୟବହୃତ ହୁଏ।

tilt /tɪlt/ *verb* (**tilts, tilting, tilted**) have one side higher than the other; move something so that it has one side higher than the other; slope or lean ଗୋଟିଏ ପଟକୁ ଢ଼ଳିବା ବା ଢ଼ଳାଇବା *She tilted the tray and all the glasses fell off.*

timber /ˈtɪmbə(r)/ *noun* (*no plural*) wood that we use for building and making things ଗୃହନିର୍ମାଣ ବା ବଢ଼େଇ କାମ ପାଇଁ ଉପଯୋଗୀ କାଠ

time[1] /taɪm/ *noun* **1** (*plural* **times**) a certain point in the day or night that you say in hours and minutes ସମୟ *'What time is it?' 'It's twenty past six.'* ○ *What's the time?* ○ *Can you tell me the times of trains to Kolkata, please?* **2** (*no plural*) all the seconds, minutes, hours, days, weeks, months and years ସମୟ, କାଳ (ସେକେଣ୍ଡ, ଘଣ୍ଟା ଦିନ, ସପ୍ତାହ, ମାସ, ବର୍ଷ ଇତ୍ୟାଦି) *Time passes quickly when you're busy.* **3** (*no plural*) an amount of time ନିର୍ଦ୍ଧାରିତ ସମୟକାଳ *They have lived here for a long time.* ○ *I haven't got time to help you now.* **4** (*plural* **times**) a certain moment or occasion ମୁହୂର୍ତ୍ତ; ଥର *I've seen this film four times.* **5** (*plural* **times**) certain years in history (ଇତିହାସ ଇତ୍ୟାଦିର) ସମୟକାଳ *In Akbar's times, not many people could read.*

at a time together; on one occasion ଏକାଥରେ, ଥରକେ *The lift can carry six people at a time.*

at times sometimes ବେଳେବେଳେ *A teacher's job can be very difficult at times.*

by the time when ଯେତେବେଳେ *By the time we arrived, they had eaten all the food.*

for the time being now, but not for long ବର୍ତ୍ତମାନ ପାଇଁ, ଅନ୍ୟ ବ୍ୟବସ୍ଥା କରିବା ପର୍ଯ୍ୟନ୍ତ *You can stay here for the time being, until you find a flat.*

have a good time enjoy yourself ମଉଜ କରିବା *Have a good time at the party!*

in time not late ଡେରି ନକରି, ନିର୍ଦ୍ଧାରିତ ସମୟ ଭିତରେ *If you hurry, you'll arrive in time for the film*

on time not late or early ଠିକ୍ ସମୟରେ *My train was on time.*

tell the time read the time from a clock or watch ଘଣ୍ଟା ଦେଖି ସମୟ କହିବା *Can your children tell the time?*

time[2] /taɪm/ *verb* (**times, timing, timed**) measure how much time it takes to do something ସମୟକାଳ ନିର୍ଦ୍ଧାରଣ କରିବା *We timed the journey—it took half an hour.*

times /taɪmz/ *noun* (*plural*) a word that you use to show how much bigger, smaller, more expensive, etc. one thing is than another thing କେତେ ଗୁଣ ସୂଚାଉଥିବା ଶବ୍ଦ; ଗୁଣନର ଥର; ଗୁଣ *This box is four times bigger than that one.*

times *preposition* multiplied by ଗୁଣନ *Three times four is twelve.*

timetable /ˈtaɪmteɪbl/ *noun* a list that shows the times when something will happen କିଛି ଘଟଣାର ସମୟ କ୍ରମ; ସମୟ ନିର୍ଘଣ୍ଟ *A train timetable shows when trains arrive and leave.* ○ *A school timetable shows when lessons start.*

timid /ˈtɪmɪd/ *adjective* shy and easily frightened ଡରକୁଳା

timidly *adverb* ଡରିଡରି, ଭୟାତୁର *She opened the door timidly and came in.*

tin /tɪn/ *noun* **1** (*no plural*) a soft white metal ଟିଣ **2** (*plural* **tins**) a metal container for food and drink that keeps it fresh ଧାତୁ ଡବା (ବିଶେଷତଃ ବାୟୁଶୂନ୍ୟ କରି ଖାଦ୍ୟପେୟ ସୁରକ୍ଷିତ ରଖିବା ପାଇଁ) *I opened a tin of beans.*

tinned *adjective* in a tin so that it will stay fresh; canned ବାୟୁଶୂନ୍ୟ ଧାତୁ ଡବାରେ ସୁରକ୍ଷିତ ଥିବା *tinned juice*

tin-opener *noun* a tool for opening tins ସିଲ୍ କରା ଟିଣଡବା ଖୋଲିବା ଉପକରଣ, ଟିନ୍ ଓପନର୍, କ୍ୟାନ ଓପନର

tiny /ˈtaɪni/ *adjective* (**tinier, tiniest**) very small ଅତି ଛୋଟ, କ୍ଷୁଦ୍ର *Ants are tiny insects.*

tip[1] /tɪp/ *noun* the pointed or thin end of something ମୁନିଆ ଅଗ; ଅଗ୍ରଭାଗ *the tips of your fingers*

tip[2] /tɪp/ *verb* (**tips, tipping, tipped**) give a small, extra amount of money to somebody who has done a job for you, for example a waiter ବକ୍ସିସ୍ ଦେବା *Do you tip hairdressers in your country?*

tip *noun* ବକ୍ସିସ୍ *I left a tip on the table.*

tip[3] /tɪp/ *noun* a small piece of advice ଛୋଟ ଉପଦେଶ *She gave me some useful tips on how to pass the exam.*

tiptoe /ˈtɪptəʊ/ *verb* (**tiptoes, tiptoeing, tiptoed**) walk quietly on your toes ଚୁପ୍‌ଚାପ୍ ଟିପେଇ ଟିପେଇ ଚାଲିବା *He tiptoed into the bedroom.*

tire /taɪər/ *verb* (**tires, tiring, tired**) feel that you need rest or sleep because you are tired; make someone feel tired ହାଲିଆ ହେବା; ହାଲିଆ କରିବା *Working for long hours on the computer can tire your eyes.*

tired /ˈtaɪəd/ *adjective* if you are tired, you need to rest or sleep ହାଲିଆ, କ୍ଳାନ୍ତ *I've been working all day and I'm really tired.* ○ *He's feeling tired.*

be tired of something have had or done too much of something, so that you do not want it any longer କିଛି କାମ କରି କରି ବିରକ୍ତ ହେବା ବା ଆଉ ସେ କାମ କରିବାକୁ ଇଚ୍ଛା ନ କରିବା *I'm tired of watching TV—let's go out.*

tiring *adjective* if something is tiring, it makes you tired ହାଲିଆ କରି ଦେଲାପରି *a tiring journey*

tissue /ˈtɪʃuː/ *noun* **1** a thin piece of soft paper that you use as a handkerchief ହାତମୁହଁ ପୋଛିବା ପାଇଁ ରୁମାଲ ଭାବରେ ବ୍ୟବହୃତ ପତଳା ଅବଶୋଷକ କାଗଜ *a box of tissues* **2** a mass of plant, animal or human cells that are similar in form and function and that make up an organ or a part of an organ ଶରୀର ଅଙ୍ଗପ୍ରତ୍ୟଙ୍ଗର ତନ୍ତୁ, ଉତକ *brain tissue*

title /ˈtaɪtl/ *noun* **1** the name of something, for example a book, film or picture (ବହି, ଫିଲ୍ମ, ଚିତ୍ର ଇତ୍ୟାଦିର) ନାମ, ଆଖ୍ୟା, ଶିରୋନାମା *What is the title of this poem?* **2** a word like 'Mr', 'Mrs' or 'Dr' that you put in front of a person's name (ବ୍ୟକ୍ତିଙ୍କ ନାମ ପୂର୍ବରୁ ଲଗା ଯାଉଥିବା) ଆଖ୍ୟା, ଉପାଧି, ପଦବୀ (ଶ୍ରୀ, ଶ୍ରୀମତୀ, ଡାଃ ଇତ୍ୟାଦି)

to[1] /tə; tu; tuː/ *preposition* **1** a word that shows where somebody or something is going, etc. ଯିବା ସ୍ଥାନ ସୂଚକ ଶବ୍ଦକୁ *She went to Amritsar.* ○ *Nawaz has gone to school.* ○ *I gave the book to Jasleen.* **2** a word that shows how many minutes before the hour ନିର୍ଦ୍ଦିଷ୍ଟ ଘଣ୍ଟା ପୂର୍ବରୁ ବାକିଥିବା ମିନିଟ୍ *It's two minutes to six.* **3** a word that shows the last or the highest time, price, etc. ପର୍ଯ୍ୟନ୍ତ *The museum is open from 9.30 a.m. to 5.30 p.m.* ○ *Jeans cost from Rs 300 to Rs 1,900.* **4** a word that shows how something changes ରୁ, ପର୍ଯ୍ୟନ୍ତ, ଆଡ଼କୁ *The sky changed from blue to grey.*

to and fro forwards and backwards ଇତସ୍ତତଃ, ଏଆଡ଼େ ସେଆଡ଼େ

to² /tə; tu/ a word that you use before verbs to make the **infinitive** ତୁମର୍ଥକ ପରିବର୍ତ୍ତେ ବ୍ୟବହୃତ ଶବ୍ଦ *I want to go home.* ○ *Don't forget to write.*

toad /təʊd/ *noun* an animal like a big frog, with a rough skin ଏକ ପ୍ରକାର ବଡ଼ ବେଙ୍ଗ

toast /təʊst/ *noun* (*no plural*) a thin piece of bread that has been heated to make it brown and crisp ନିଆଁ ଧାପରେ ସେକା ପାଉଁରୁଟି ଖଣ୍ଡ, ଟୋଷ୍ଟ *I had a slice of toast and jam for breakfast.*

toast *verb* (**toasts, toasting, toasted**) heat bread to make it brown and crisp ଟୋଷ୍ଟ କରିବା *Toast the slices lightly.*

toaster *noun* a machine for making toast ଟୋଷ୍ଟ କରିବା ଯନ୍ତ୍ର

tobacco /təˈbækəʊ/ *noun* (*no plural*) special dried leaves that people smoke in cigarettes, cigars and pipes ଧୂଆଁପତ୍ର

today /təˈdeɪ/ *adverb, noun* (*no plural*) **1** (on) this day ଆଜି *What shall we do today?* ○ *Today is Friday.* **2** (at) the present time; now ବର୍ତ୍ତମାନ, ଆଜିକାଲି *Students today have many courses to choose from.*

toddler /ˈtɒdlə(r)/ *noun* a young child who has just learnt to walk ଚାଲିବା ଆରମ୍ଭ କରୁଥିବା ଶିଶୁ

toe /təʊ/ *noun* **1** one of the five parts at the end of your foot ଗୋଡ଼ ଆଙ୍ଗୁଠି ➪ ଚିତ୍ର ପାଇଁ **body** ଦେଖନ୍ତୁ । **2** the part of a shoe or sock that covers the toes ପାଦ ଆଙ୍ଗୁଠିକୁ ଆବୃତ କରୁଥିବା ଜୋତା ବା ମୋଜାର ଅଂଶ

toenail /ˈtəʊneɪl/ *noun* the nail on your toe ପାଦ ଆଙ୍ଗୁଠିର ନଖ

toffee /ˈtɒfi/ *noun* (*plural* **toffees**) a hard brown sweet made from sugar, butter and water ଚିନି, ଲହୁଣି (ବଟର) ଓ ପାଣିରେ ତିଆରି ଟାଣ ମିଠେଇ, ଟଫି

together /təˈgeðə(r)/ *adverb* **1** with each other or close to each other ଏକ ସଙ୍ଗରେ, ଏକାଠି *They went to school together.* ○ *Stand with your feet together.* **2** so that they are joined to or mixed with each other ଯୋଡ଼ିକରି; ଏକାଠି, ଏକତ୍ର *Tie the ends of the rope together.* ○ *Mix the eggs and sugar together.*

toil /tɔɪl/ *verb* (**toils, toiling, toiled**) work very hard for a long time କଠିନ ପରିଶ୍ରମ କରିବା *They toiled all day in the fields.*

toilet /ˈtɔɪlət/ *noun* a large bowl-like thing that you use when you need to empty waste from your body. The room that it is in is also called a **toilet** ଶୌଚପାତ୍ର; ଶୌଚାଳୟ *I'm going to the toilet.*

token /ˈtəʊkən/ *noun* a piece of paper, plastic or metal that you use instead of money to pay for something କୌଣସି ପଦାର୍ଥର ବିଶେଷତଃ ଟଙ୍କାର ତୁଲ୍ୟବସ୍ତୁ (କାଗଜ, ପ୍ଲାଷ୍ଟିକ୍ ବା ଧାତୁ ଖଣ୍ଡ) *For buying milk we have to first take tokens from the counter.*

told ଶବ୍ଦ **tell** ର ଏକ ଧାତୁରୂପ

tolerant /ˈtɒlərənt/ *adjective* if you are tolerant, you let people do things although you may not like or understand them ସହିଷ୍ଣୁ, ସହନଶୀଳ

tolerance /ˈtɒlərəns/ *noun* (*no plural*) ସହନଶୀଳତା, ସହିଷ୍ଣୁତା *tolerance of other religions*

tolerate /ˈtɒləreɪt/ *verb* (**tolerates, tolerating, tolerated**) let people do something that you may not like or understand ସହିବା, ସହନ କରିବା *The teacher won't tolerate untidy work.*

tomato /təˈmɑːtəʊ/ *noun* (*plural* **tomatoes**) a soft red fruit that is cooked as a vegetable or eaten raw in salads ବିଲାତି ବାଇଗଣ, ଟମାଟୋ *tomato soup.*

tomb /tuːm/ *noun* a thing made of stone where a dead person's body is buried କବର

tomorrow /təˈmɒrəʊ/ *adverb, noun* (*no plural*) (on) the day after today ଆସନ୍ତାକାଲି *I'll see you tomorrow morning.* ○ *We are going home the day after tomorrow.*

ton /tʌn/ *noun* a measure of weight (= 1,016 kilograms) ଓଜନର ଏକ ମାପ (୧,୦୧୬ କିଲୋଗ୍ରାମ) ➪ **tonne** ଦେଖନ୍ତୁ ।

tone /təʊn/ *noun* the quality of a sound or of a voice କଣ୍ଠସ୍ୱରର ତାନ *I knew he was angry by the tone of his voice.*

tongue /tʌŋ/ *noun* the soft part inside your mouth that moves when you talk or eat ଜିଭ, ଜିହ୍ୱା

tonic /ˈtɒnɪk/ *noun* a medicine that helps you feel healthier and better ବଳକାରକ ଔଷଧ

tonight /təˈnaɪt/ *adverb, noun* (*no plural*) (on) the evening or night of today ଆଜି ରାତିରେ *I'm going to a party tonight.*

tonne /tʌn/ *noun* a measure of weight. There are 1,000 **kilograms** in a tonne ଓଜନର ଏକ ମାପ (୧,୦୦୦ କିଲୋଗ୍ରାମ) ➪ **ton** ଦେଖନ୍ତୁ ।

too /tuː/ *adverb* **1** also; as well ମଧ୍ୟ, ବି, ତା'ଛଡ଼ା *Green is my favourite colour but I like blue too.* **2** more than you want or need ଅତି, ଅତ୍ୟଧିକ *These shoes are too big.* ○ *She put too much sugar in my milk.*

took ଶବ୍ଦ **take** ର ଏକ ଧାତୁରୂପ

tool /tuːl/ *noun* a thing that you hold in your hand and use to do a

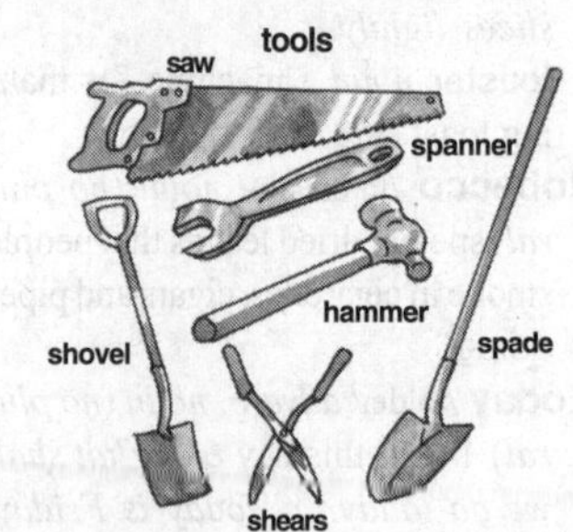

special job ଯନ୍ତ୍ରପାତି, ହତିଆର *Hammers and saws are tools.*

tooth /tu:θ/ *noun* (*plural* **teeth** /ti:θ/) **1** one of the hard white things in your mouth that you use for biting and chewing food ଦାନ୍ତ, ଦନ୍ତ *I brush my teeth after every meal.* ✪ ଦାନ୍ତ ଡାକ୍ତରକୁ **dentist** କହନ୍ତି । ଦାନ୍ତରେ କଣା ହୋଇଥିଲେ **dentist** ସେଥିରେ ଏକ ବିଶେଷ ପ୍ରକାର ପଦାର୍ଥ **filling** ପୂରାଇ ଭରଣ କରନ୍ତି (**fill it**) ବା ଦାନ୍ତଟା ଓପାଡ଼ି ଦିଅନ୍ତି (**take it out**). ଉପାଡ଼ି ଦାନ୍ତ ସ୍ଥାନରେ ନକଲି ଦାନ୍ତ (**false teeth**) ଲଗାଇଥାନ୍ତି । **2** one of the long sharp parts of a comb or a saw ପାନିଆ ବା କରତର ଦାନ୍ତ

toothache /ˈtu:θeɪk/ *noun* (*no plural*) a pain in your tooth ଦାନ୍ତବିନ୍ଧା *I've got toothache.*

toothbrush /tu:θbrʌʃ/ *noun* (*plural* **toothbrushes**) a small brush for cleaning your teeth ଦାନ୍ତଘଷା ବ୍ରସ୍, ଦାନ୍ତକାଠି, ଟୁଥ୍‌ବ୍ରସ୍ ➪ ଚିତ୍ର ପାଇଁ **brush** ଦେଖନ୍ତୁ ।

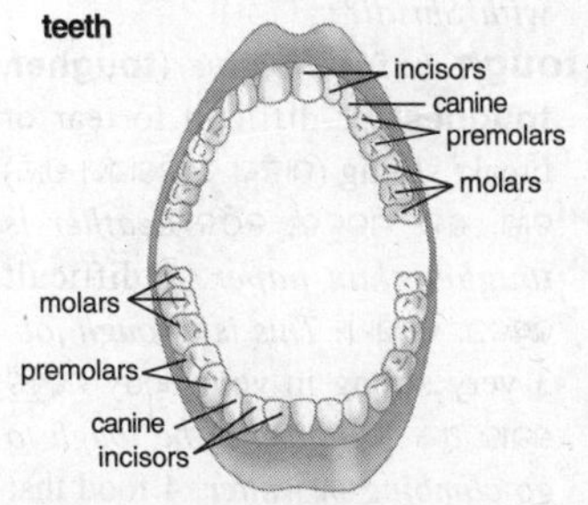

toothpaste /ˈtu:θpeɪst/ *noun* (*no plural*) a soft substance that you put on your toothbrush and use for cleaning your teeth ଦାନ୍ତଘଷା ପ୍ରଲେପ, ଟୁଥ୍‌ପେଷ୍ଟ

top[1] /tɒp/ *noun* **1** the highest part of something ଚୂଡ଼ା, ଶୀର୍ଷଦେଶ, ଶୀର୍ଷ *There's a fort at the top of the hill.* ✪ ବିପରୀତ **bottom 1** **2** a cover that you put on something to close it ଢାଙ୍କୁଣୀ, ଘୋଡ଼ଣୀ *Where's the top of this jar?* **3** a piece of clothing that you wear on the top part of your body ଦେହର ଉପରିଭାଗର ପୋଷାକ

on top on its highest part ଉପରେ *The cake had cream on top.*

on top of something on or over something କୌଣସି ପଦାର୍ଥର ଉପରେ *A tree fell on top of my car.*

top[2] /tɒp/ *adjective* highest ଉଚ୍ଚତମ (ପଦ, ଶ୍ରେଣୀ, ସ୍ଥାନ, ଗୁରୁତ୍ୱ ଇତ୍ୟାଦିରେ) *Put this book on the top shelf.* ✪ ବିପରୀତ **bottom**

top[3] /tɒp/ *noun* a toy that spins on a point when you turn it round very quickly with your hand or with the help of a string ନଟୁ, ଲଟୁ

topic /ˈtɒpɪk/ *noun* something that you talk, learn or write about; a subject (ଟକା, ଶିକ୍ଷା ବା ଲେଖାର) ବିଷୟ *The topic of the discussion was cartoon films.*

topple /ˈtɒpl/ *verb* (**topples, toppling, toppled**) become or make something unsteady and fall down ଟଳମଳ ହୋଇ ପଡ଼ିଯିବା *The cat leapt over the shelf and it toppled over.*

torch /tɔ:tʃ/ *noun* (*plural* **torches**) a small electric light that you can carry ଟର୍ଚ୍ଚଲାଇଟ୍

tore, **torn** ଶବ୍ଦ **tear**[2] ର ଧାତୁରୂପ

torrent /ˈtɒrənt/ *noun* a large amount of something, usually water, that comes out suddenly and forcefully ସ୍ରୋତ; ପାଣିର ସୁଅ; ପ୍ରବଳ ବର୍ଷା *The rain was coming down in torrents.*

tortoise /ˈtɔːtəs/ *noun* an animal with a hard shell on its back, that moves very slowly କଇଁଚ

toss /tɒs/ *verb* (**tosses, tossing, tossed**) **1** throw something quickly and without care ଫୋପାଡ଼ିବା, ଫିଙ୍ଗିବା *I tossed the paper into the bin.* **2** decide something by throwing a coin in the air and seeing which side shows when it falls ମୁଦ୍ରା ଉପରକୁ ଫିଙ୍ଗି ତା'ର ତଳେ ପଡ଼ିବାର ପଟ ଅନୁସାରେ କୌଣସି ବିଷୟର ନିଷ୍ପତ୍ତି କରିବା *We tossed a coin to see who would bat first.* **3** move quickly up and down or from side to side; make everything do this ଜୋର୍‌ରେ ଉପରତଳ ହେବା ବା ଏପଟ ସେପଟ ହୋଇ ଦୋହଲିବା; ଏହିପରି କରିବା *The boat tossed around on the big waves.*

total[1] /ˈtəʊtl/ *adjective* complete; if you count everything or everybody ସମ୍ପୂର୍ଣ୍ଣ; ମୋଟ *There was total silence in the classroom.* ○ *What was the total number of people at the meeting?*

totally *adverb* completely ସମ୍ପୂର୍ଣ୍ଣ ରୂପେ, ପୂରାପୂରି *I totally agree.*

total[2] /ˈtəʊtl/ *noun* the number you have when you add everything together ମୋଟ ସଂଖ୍ୟା ବା ପରିମାଣ; ଯୋଗଫଳ

touch[1] /tʌtʃ/ *verb* (**touches, touching, touched**) **1** put your hand or finger on somebody and something ଛୁଇଁବା, ସ୍ପର୍ଶ କରିବା *He touched me on the arm.* ○ *Don't touch the paint—it's still wet.* **2** be so close to another thing or person that there is no space in between ପରସ୍ପର ସହ ଛୁଇଁ ହୋଇଯିବା ବା ଲାଗିଯିବା *The two wires were touching.*

touch[2] /tʌtʃ/ *noun* **1** (*plural* **touches**) the act of touching somebody or something ସ୍ପର୍ଶ *I felt the touch of his hand on my arm.* **2** (*no plural*) the feeling in your hands and skin that tells you about something ସ୍ପର୍ଶଜ୍ଞାନ, ଛୁଇଁ ଜାଣିବା ଶକ୍ତି *He can't see, but he can read by touch.*

be or **keep in touch with somebody** meet, telephone or write to somebody often ଖବର ରଖିବା, ଯୋଗାଯୋଗ ରଖିବା *Are you still in touch with Shruti?*

tough /tʌf/ *adjective* (**tougher, toughest**) **1** difficult to tear or break; strong (ଭାଙ୍ଗିବା ବା ଛିଣ୍ଡାଇବା ପାଇଁ) ଟାଣ, ଶକ୍ତ, ମଜବୁଦ୍, କଠିନ *Leather is tougher than paper.* **2** difficult କଷ୍ଟକର, କଷ୍ଟସାଧ୍ୟ *This is a tough job.* **3** very strong in your body ମଜବୁତ ଶରୀର ଥିବା *You need to be tough to go climbing in winter.* **4** food that is tough is difficult to cut and eat କାଟିବାକୁ ବା ଖାଇବାକୁ ଟାଣ ହୋଇଥିବା ✪ ବିପରୀତ **tender**

tour /tʊə(r)/ *noun* a journey to see a lot of different places ଭ୍ରମଣ, ପର୍ଯ୍ୟଟନ,

ପରିଭ୍ରମଣ *We went on a tour of Himachal Pradesh.*

tour *verb* (**tours, touring, tour-ed**) ପର୍ଯ୍ୟଟନ ବା ପରିଭ୍ରମଣ ଯିବା *We toured Egypt for three weeks.*

tourism /ˈtʊərɪzəm/ *noun* (*no plural*) the business of arranging services for people who are on holiday ପର୍ଯ୍ୟଟନକାରୀଙ୍କ ଯିବାଆସିବା ଓ ରହିବା ଖାଇବା ସୁବିଧା କରାଇବା କାମ *This country earns a lot of money from tourism.*

tourist /ˈtʊərɪst/ *noun* a person who visits a place on holiday ପର୍ଯ୍ୟଟକ

tournament /ˈtʊənəmənt/ *noun* a sports competition with a lot of players or teams କ୍ରୀଡ଼ା ପ୍ରତିଯୋଗିତା *a tennis tournament*

tow /təʊ/ *verb* (**tows, towing, towed**) pull a car, etc. using a rope or chain ଗାଡ଼ି ଇତ୍ୟାଦିକୁ ଦଉଡ଼ି ବା ଶିକୁଳିରେ ବାନ୍ଧି ଟାଣିନେବା *My car was towed to a garage.*

towards /təˈwɔːdz/, **toward** /təˈwɔːd/ *preposition* **1** in the direction of somebody or something ଦିଗକୁ, ଆଡ଼କୁ, ଅଭିମୁଖେ *We walked towards the river.* **2** to somebody or something ପ୍ରତି *The people in the village have always been very friendly towards tourists.*

towel /ˈtaʊəl/ *noun* a piece of cloth that you use for drying yourself ଗାମୁଛା, ତଉଲିଆ, ଟାୱେଲ୍ *I washed my hands and dried them on a towel.*

tower /ˈtaʊə(r)/ *noun* a tall narrow building or a tall part of a building ଉଚ୍ଚ ସରୁ କୋଠା; କୋଠାର ମିନାର ପରି ଉଠିଥିବା ଅଂଶ *a church tower*

town /taʊn/ *noun* a place where there are many houses, offices, shops and other buildings ସହର, ନଗର, ଟାଉନ୍ *How many towns are there in this state?*

> ✪ ସହର **village** ଠାରୁ ବଡ଼, କିନ୍ତୁ **city** ଠାରୁ ସାନ।

toxic /ˈtɒksɪk/ *adjective* if something is toxic, it is poisonous or contains poison ବିଷାକ୍ତ *toxic gases*

toy /tɔɪ/ *noun* a thing for a child to play with ଖେଳନା

trace[1] /treɪs/ *noun* a mark or sign that shows that somebody has been in a place or that something has happened କୌଣସି ଘଟଣା ସ୍ଥଳରେ ରହିଯାଇଥିବା କାହାର କିଛି ଚିହ୍ନ, ଦାଗ ଇତ୍ୟାଦି *The police could not find any trace of the missing child.*

trace[2] /treɪs/ *verb* (**traces, tracing, traced**) **1** look for and find somebody or something ଚିହ୍ନ ଅନୁସରଣ କରି କୌଣସି ବ୍ୟକ୍ତି ଇତ୍ୟାଦିଙ୍କୁ ଖୋଜି ବାହାର କରିବା *The police have traced the stolen car.* **2** put a thin paper over a picture and draw over the lines to make a copy ଚିତ୍ର ଇତ୍ୟାଦି ଉପରେ ପତଳା କାଗଜ ପକାଇ ତାହାର ନକଲ କରିବା

track[1] /træk/ *noun* **1** a rough path or road ଚଲାବାଟ *We drove along a track through the woods.* **2 tracks** (*plural*) a line of marks that an animal, a person or vehicle makes on the ground ଭୂମି ଉପରେ ବ୍ୟକ୍ତି, ପଶୁ, ଯାନ ପ୍ରଭୃତିର ଉପସ୍ଥିତିର ଚିହ୍ନ *We saw tracks in the snow.* **3** the metal lines that a train runs on ରେଳପଥ **4** a special road for races ଦୌଡ଼ ପ୍ରତିଯୋଗିତା ପାଇଁ ପ୍ରସ୍ତୁତ ମାର୍ଗ, ଟ୍ରାକ୍

track² /træk/ *verb* (**tracks, tracking, tracked**) follow signs or marks to find somebody or something କୌଣସି ବ୍ୟକ୍ତି, ଯାନ ଇତ୍ୟାଦିର ଚିହ୍ନ ଅନୁକରଣ କରିବା

tractor /ˈtræktə(r)/ *noun* a big strong vehicle that people use on farms to pull heavy farm machines ହଳ କାମରେ ବ୍ୟବହୃତ ଯନ୍ତ୍ର, ଟ୍ରାକ୍ଟର

trade¹ /treɪd/ *noun* (*no plural*) the buying and selling of things ବାଣିଜ୍ୟ, ବେପାର, କିଣାବିକା *trade between Britain and India*

trade² /treɪd/ *verb* (**trades, trading, traded**) buy and sell things ବାଣିଜ୍ୟ ବା ବେପାର କରିବା, କିଣାବିକା କରିବା *India trades with many different countries.*

trademark /ˈtreɪdmɑːk/ *noun* a special mark or name that a company puts on the things it makes and that other companies must not use ବ୍ୟାପାର ବା ସ୍ୱତ୍ତ୍ୱ ଚିହ୍ନ ବା ନାମ; ଟ୍ରେଡ୍‌ମାର୍କ

tradition /trəˈdɪʃn/ *noun* something that people in a certain place have done or believed for a long time ପରମ୍ପରା, ପ୍ରଥା, ଐତିହ୍ୟ *In India, it's a tradition to light earthern lamps on Diwali.*

traditional *adjective* ପାରମ୍ପରିକ *traditional Gujarati food*

traditionally *adverb* ପାରମ୍ପରିକ ଭାବରେ *Driving trains was traditionally a man's job.*

traffic /ˈtræfɪk/ *noun* (*no plural*) all the cars, etc. that are on a road ରାସ୍ତାରେ ଯାଉଥିବା ଗାଡ଼ି, ମଟର, ମଣିଷ ଇତ୍ୟାଦି *There was a lot of traffic on the way to work this morning.*

traffic jam *noun* (*plural* **traffic jams**) a long line of cars, etc. on a road that cannot move or can move very slowly କୌଣସି ବାଧା ଯୋଗୁଁ ରାସ୍ତାରେ ଯାନବାହନ ଲାଇନ୍‌ମାରି ଅଟକି ଯିବା ବା ଅତି ଧୀର ଗତିରେ ଯିବା

traffic lights *noun* (*plural*) lights that change from red to orange to green to tell cars, etc. when to stop and start ଯାନ ଚଳାଚଳ ନିୟନ୍ତ୍ରଣ କରିବା ପାଇଁ ଛକ ଜାଗାରେ ଥିବା ରଙ୍ଗିନ୍ ଆଲୋକ (ଲାଲ୍, ନାରଙ୍ଗି ଓ ସବୁଜ) ଅବରୋଧକ ଲାଲବତୀ

tragedy /ˈtrædʒədi/ *noun* (*plural* **tragedies**) **1** a very sad thing that happens; ଦୁଃଖଦ ଘଟଣା *The child's death was a tragedy.* **2** a serious play with a sad ending ବିୟୋଗାନ୍ତକ ନାଟକ

tragic /ˈtrædʒɪk/ *adjective* very sad ଦୁଃଖଦ, ଦୁର୍ଦ୍ଦଶାପୂର୍ଣ୍ଣ *a tragic accident*

train¹ /treɪn/ *noun* carriages or wagons that are pulled by an engine along a railway line ରେଳଗାଡ଼ି, ଟ୍ରେନ୍ *I'm going to Pune by train.*

catch a train get on a train to go somewhere ଟ୍ରେନ୍‌ରେ ଚଢ଼ିବା *We caught the 7.15 train to Siliguri.*

✪ ଟ୍ରେନ୍‌ରେ ଚଢ଼ିବାକୁ **get on** କହନ୍ତି ଓ ଓହ୍ଲାଇବାକୁ **get off** କୁହାଯାଏ। **Goods train** ମାଲଗାଡ଼ିକୁ ବା **freight train** କୁହାଯାଏ ଓ ଯାତ୍ରିବାହୀ ଟ୍ରେନକୁ **passenger train** କହନ୍ତି।

train[2] /treɪn/ *verb* (**trains, training, trained**) **1** teach a person or an animal to do something ତାଲିମ୍ ଦେବା, ପ୍ରଶିକ୍ଷଣ ଦେବା *He was trained as a pilot*. **2** make yourself ready for something by studying or doing something a lot ଅଧ୍ୟୟନ କରି ବା ଅଭ୍ୟାସ କରି କୌଣସି କାମପାଇଁ ଉପଯୁକ୍ତ ହେବା *Anita is training to be a doctor*.

trainer /ˈtreɪnə(r)/ *noun* **1** a person who teaches other people to do a sport ଖେଳ ପ୍ରଶିକ୍ଷକ, କୋଚ୍ **2** a person who teaches animals to do something ପଶୁଙ୍କୁ ପ୍ରଶିକ୍ଷଣ ବା ତାଲିମ୍ ଦେଉଥିବା ବ୍ୟକ୍ତି

training /ˈtreɪnɪŋ/ *noun* (*no plural*) the process of learning a sport or job ପ୍ରଶିକ୍ଷଣ, ତାଲିମ୍ *She is in training for the Sports Day*.

traitor /ˈtreɪtə(r)/ *noun* a person who harms his or her country or friends to help another person or country ବିଶ୍ୱାସଘାତକ ବା କୃତଘ୍ନ ବ୍ୟକ୍ତି

tram /træm/ *noun* an electric bus that goes along rails in a town ଯାତ୍ରୀବାହୀ ବିଦ୍ୟୁତଚାଳିତ ଗାଡ଼ି ଯାହା ରାସ୍ତାରେ ଲଗାଯାଇଥିବା ରେଳ ଲାଇନ୍ ଉପରେ ଚାଲେ; ଟ୍ରାମ୍

trample /ˈtræmpl/ *verb* (**tramples, trampling, trampled**) walk on something and push it down with your feet ପାଦରେ ଦଳିବା, ଚିପିଦେବା *Don't trample on the flowers!*

tranquil /ˈtræŋkwɪl/ *adjective* calm and peaceful ଶାନ୍ତ, ପ୍ରଶାନ୍ତ, ଅବିଚଳିତ *the tranquil surroundings of the countryside*

tranquillity /træŋˈkwɪləti/ *noun* (*no plural*) ପ୍ରଶାନ୍ତି, ନିଃସ୍ତବ୍ଧତା

transaction /trænˈzækʃn/ *noun* a business deal କାରବାର *financial transactions*

transfer /trænsˈfɜː(r)/ *verb* (**transfers, transferring, transferred**) move somebody or something from one place to another ବ୍ୟକ୍ତିଙ୍କୁ ବା ପଦାର୍ଥକୁ ଏକ ସ୍ଥାନରୁ ଅନ୍ୟ ସ୍ଥାନକୁ ନେବା ବା ପଠାଇବା; (ଚାକିରିରେ) ବଦଳି କରିବା *My father was transferred to Kanpur*. ○ *I want to transfer Rs 5,000 to my bank account in Delhi*.

transfer /ˈtrænsfɜː(r)/ *noun* ବଦଳି; ହସ୍ତାନ୍ତର *Ravi wants a transfer to another town*.

transform /trænsˈfɔːm/ *verb* (**transforms, transforming, transformed**) change somebody or something so that they are or look completely different ରୂପାନ୍ତରିତ କରିବା, ବଦଳାଇ ନେବା, ପରିବର୍ତ୍ତିତ ହେବା *Electricity has transformed people's lives*.

transformation /ˈtrænsfəˈmeɪʃn/ *noun* a complete change ପରିବର୍ତ୍ତନ; ରୂପାନ୍ତର, ପରିବର୍ତ୍ତିତ

transistor /træn'zɪstə(r)/ *noun* a small part inside something electrical, for example a radio or television ରେଡିଓ, ଟେଲିଭିଜନ୍ ଇତ୍ୟାଦି ଭିତରେ ଲଗାଯାଉଥିବା ଛୋଟ ବିଦ୍ୟୁତ୍ ଅର୍ଦ୍ଧପରିବାହୀ ଉପକରଣ

transitive /'trænsətɪv/ *adjective* (in grammar) a transitive verb is one that has a direct object (ବ୍ୟାକରଣ) ସକର୍ମକ କ୍ରିୟା ➪ **intransitive** ଦେଖନ୍ତୁ ।

translate /træns'leɪt/ *verb* (**translates, translating, translated**) say or write in one language what somebody has said or written in another language ଅନୁବାଦ କରିବା, ଭାଷାନ୍ତର କରିବା *This letter is in Hindi—can you translate it into English for me?*

translation /træns'leɪʃn/ *noun* **1** (*no plural*) the process of translating something ଅନୁବାଦ *There was an error in translation.* **2** (*plural* **translations**) something that somebody has translated ଅନୁବାଦ କରାଯାଇଥିବା ଲେଖା *Two English translations of the play have been published.*

translator /træns'leɪtə(r)/ *noun* a person who translates ଅନୁବାଦକ

transmitter /træns'mɪtə(r)/ *noun* an equipment that sends out radio, television or other electrical signals ଧ୍ୱନି, ଚିତ୍ର, ସଙ୍କେତ ଇତ୍ୟାଦି ବିଦ୍ୟୁତଚୁମ୍ବକୀୟ ରଶ୍ମିଦ୍ୱାରା ପଠାଉଥିବା ଯନ୍ତ୍ର

transparent /træns'pærənt/ *adjective* if something is transparent, you can see through it ଆଲୋକ ଭେଦକରି ପାରୁଥିବା (ଅନ୍ୟ ପଟର ପଦାର୍ଥ ସ୍ପଷ୍ଟ ଦିଶୁଥିବା); ସ୍ୱଚ୍ଛ *Glass is transparent.*

transport /trænspɔːt/ *noun* (*no plural*) a way of carrying people or things from one place to another *road transport*

transport /'trænspɔːt/ *verb* (**transports, transporting, transported**) carry people or things from one place to another (ମଣିଷ ବା ପଦାର୍ଥ) ବହିବା; ପରିବହନ କରିବା *The goods were transported by air.*

trap /træp/ *noun* **1** a thing that you use for catching animals (ଜନ୍ତୁ ଧରିବାପାଇଁ ଯନ୍ତା, ଫାନ୍ଦ *The rabbit's leg was caught in a trap.* **2** a plan to trick somebody କାହାରିକୁ ଛଳନା କରି ଧରିବାର ଯୋଜନା ବା ବ୍ୟବସ୍ଥା *I knew the question was a trap, so I didn't answer it.*

trap *verb* (**traps, trapping, trapped**) **1** be forced to stay in a place or situation from which someone cannot escape ଅଚଳ ଅବସ୍ଥାରେ ବା ପଳାଇ ଯିବାର ଉପାୟ ନଥିବା ଅବସ୍ଥାରେ ପଡ଼ିବା *They were trapped in the burning building.* **2** catch or trick somebody or something କାହାକୁ ଛଳନା କରି ଧରିନେବା **3** catch an animal, bird, etc. in a trap ପଶୁପକ୍ଷୀଙ୍କୁ ଯନ୍ତାରେ ଧରିବା

travel /'trævl/ *verb* (**travels, travelling, travelled**) go from one place to another ଗୋଟିଏ ସ୍ଥାନରୁ ଅନ୍ୟ ସ୍ଥାନକୁ ଯିବା, ଯାତ୍ରା ବା ଭ୍ରମଣ କରିବା *I would like to travel round the world.* ○ *I travel to school by bus.*

travel *noun* (*no plural*) the action of travelling ଯାତ୍ରା, ଭ୍ରମଣ, ପରିଭ୍ରମଣ *My hobbies are music and travel.*

travel agency *noun* (*plural* **travel agencies**) a company that plans holidays and journeys for people ଲୋକମାନଙ୍କ ଯାତ୍ରାର ସୁବିଧା କରୁଥିବା ବ୍ୟବସାୟିକ ସଂସ୍ଥା, ଟ୍ରାଭ୍ଲ ଏଜେନ୍ସି, ଯାତ୍ରା ସେବା ସଂସ୍ଥା

travel agent *noun* a person who works in a travel agency ଟ୍ରାଭ୍ଲ ଏଜେନ୍ସିରେ କାମ କରୁଥିବା ବ୍ୟକ୍ତି, ଯାତ୍ରାସେବା ଯୋଗାଉଥିବା ବ୍ୟକ୍ତି

traveller /ˈtrævələ(r)/ *noun* a person who is travelling ଯାତ୍ରୀ; ଭ୍ରମଣକାରୀ; ପର୍ଯ୍ୟଟକ

tray /treɪ/ *noun* a flat thing with raised edges that you use for carrying food or drinks ଧାତୁ ବା କାଠ ନିର୍ମିତ ମଙ୍ଗଥିବା ଥାଳି, ଟ୍ରେ

tread /tred/ *verb* (**treads, treading, trod** /trɒd/, **has trodden** /ˈtrɒdn/) put your foot down ପାଦ ପକାଇବା, ପାଦରେ ମାଡ଼ିଦେବା *He trod on my foot.*

treasure /ˈtreʒə(r)/ *noun* gold, silver, jewels or other things that are worth a lot of money ସୁନା, ରୁପା, ହୀରାନୀଳା ଇତ୍ୟାଦି ଧନରତ୍ନ

treat[1] /triːt/ *verb* (**treats, treating, treated**) **1** behave in a certain way towards somebody or something ନିର୍ଦ୍ଦିଷ୍ଟ ବ୍ୟବହାର ବା ଆଚରଣ ପ୍ରଦର୍ଶନ କରିବା *How does your boss treat you?* **2** give medical care to make a sick person or animal well again ଚିକିତ୍ସା କରିବା *The doctor is treating him for stomach infection.*

treat[2] /triːt/ *noun* something very special that makes somebody happy ବିଶେଷ ଆନନ୍ଦଦାୟକ ଘଟଣା, ଆୟୋଜନ ଇତ୍ୟାଦି *My parents took me to the theatre as a treat for my birthday.*

treatment /ˈtriːtmənt/ *noun* **1** (*no plural*) the way that you behave towards somebody or something ବ୍ୟବହାର, ଆଚରଣ *Their treatment of the animals was very cruel.* **2** (*plural* **treatments**) the things that a doctor does to try to make a sick person well again ଚିକିତ୍ସା *treatment for sore throat*

treaty /ˈtriːti/ *noun* (*plural* **treaties**) an agreement between countries (ଦେଶ ଦେଶ ମଧ୍ୟରେ) ଚୁକ୍ତି, ସନ୍ଧି *The two countries signed a peace treaty.*

tree /triː/ *noun* a big tall plant with a trunk, branches and leaves ଗଛ, ବୃକ୍ଷ *a neem tree* ○ *Apples grow on trees.* ➪ ପୃଷ୍ଠା 584 ରେ ଚିତ୍ର ଦେଖନ୍ତୁ।

trek /trek/ *noun* a long difficult walk, usually over hills and mountains ଦୀର୍ଘ କଷ୍ଟସାଧ୍ୟ ପଦଯାତ୍ରା (ବିଶେଷତଃ ପାହାଡ଼ ପର୍ବତରେ)

trek *verb* (**treks, trekking, trekked**) go on a long and difficult journey in the mountains, especially on foot ଦୀର୍ଘ ସମୟ ପାହାଡ଼ ପର୍ବତରେ ଚାଲି ଚାଲି ଯିବା

tremble /ˈtrembl/ *verb* (**trembles, trembling, trembled**) shake, for example because you are cold, afraid or ill (ଥଣ୍ଡା, ଜର ବା ଭୟରେ) ଥରିବା, କମ୍ପିବା *She was trembling with fear.*

tremendous /trəˈmendəs/ *adjective* **1** very big or very great ଖୁବ ବଡ଼, ପ୍ରକାଣ୍ଡ; ଖୁବ୍ ବେଶୀ *The new trains travel at a tremendous speed.* **2** very good ଖୁବ୍ ଭଲ, ଚମତ୍କାର *The match was tremendous.*

trees

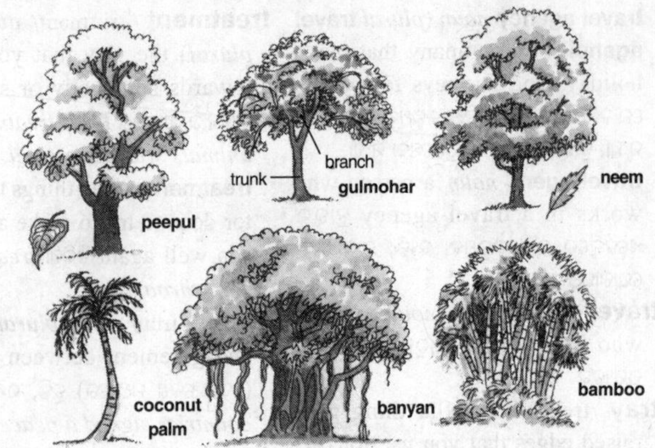

tremendously *adverb* very or very much ଖୁବ୍, ଚମତ୍କାର ଭାବରେ *The film was tremendously exciting.*

trend /trend/ *noun* a change to something different (ଘଟଣା, ମତ ବା ଫେସନ୍‌ର) ପରିବର୍ତ୍ତନ; ପରିବର୍ତ୍ତିତ ଢାଞ୍ଚା *new trends in fashion*

trial /ˈtraɪəl/ *noun* **1** the time when a person is in a **court of law** so that people (the **judge** and **jury**) can decide if he or she has done something wrong ଅଦାଲତରେ ମକଦ୍ଦମାର ବିଚାର **2** the act of using something to see if it is good or bad ଭଲ କି ମନ୍ଦ, ଜାଣିବା ପାଇଁ କୌଣସି ପଦାର୍ଥର ବ୍ୟବହାର ଦ୍ୱାରା ପରୀକ୍ଷା ନିରୀକ୍ଷା *the trial of a new system*

triangle /ˈtraɪæŋgl/ *noun* a shape with three straight sides and three angles ତ୍ରିଭୁଜ, ତ୍ରିକୋଣ କ୍ଷେତ୍ର ➪ ଚିତ୍ର ପାଇଁ **shape** ଦେଖନ୍ତୁ।

triangular /traɪˈæŋgjələ(r)/ *adjective* with the shape of a triangle ତିନି କୋଣିଆ, ତ୍ରିକୋଣାକାର, ତ୍ରିଭୁଜାକାର

tribe /traɪb/ *noun* a small group of people who have the same language and customs ଆଦିବାସୀ ଗୋଷ୍ଠୀ ବା ସମ୍ପ୍ରଦାୟ *the Mizo tribes of India*

tribal *adjective* ଆଦିବାସୀ ସମ୍ପ୍ରଦାୟର ବା ଏହା ସମ୍ବନ୍ଧୀୟ *tribal dances*

tributary /ˈtrɪbjətri/ *noun* (*plural* **tributaries**) a river or stream that flows into a larger river ଶାଖାନଦୀ

tribute /ˈtrɪbjuːt/ *noun* something that you do, say or give to show that you respect or admire somebody ଶ୍ରଦ୍ଧାଞ୍ଜଳି; ସମ୍ମାନ ପ୍ରଦର୍ଶନ *At the awards ceremony tribute was paid to those who had died in the war.*

trick[1] /trɪk/ *noun* **1** a clever plan that makes somebody believe something that is not true କୌଶଳ, ଫନ୍ଦି, ଫିକର, ଚାତୁରୀ *They played a trick on Minu.* **2** something clever that you have learnt to do ଚାତୁର୍ଯ୍ୟପୂର୍ଣ୍ଣ ଖେଳ ଇତ୍ୟାଦି *card tricks*

trick[2] /trɪk/ *verb* (**tricks, tricking, tricked**) do something that is not honest to get what you want from somebody ପ୍ରତାରଣା କରିବା ବା କୌଶଳ କରି ଅନ୍ୟାୟ ଉପାୟରେ ଅନ୍ୟକୁ ପରାସ୍ତ କରିବା, ଠକାଇବା *He tricked the old lady into giving him all her money.*

trickle /ˈtrɪkl/ *verb* (**trickles, trickling, trickled**) move slowly like a thin line of water ଟୋପା ଟୋପା ହୋଇ ଝରିବା *Tears trickled down her cheeks.*

trickle *noun* ବିନ୍ଦୁ ବିନ୍ଦୁ ହୋଇ ନିର୍ଗମନ *a trickle of blood*

tricky /ˈtrɪki/ *adjective* (**trickier, trickiest**) difficult; hard to do କଷ୍ଟକର *a tricky question*

tried, tries ଶବ୍ଦ **try** ର ଧାତୁରୂପ

trigger /ˈtrɪgə(r)/ *noun* the part of a gun that is pulled with a finger to fire it ବନ୍ଧୁକକୁ ଆଙ୍ଗୁଠିରେ ଟାଣି ଫୁଟାଇବାକୁ ବାହାରିଥିବା କାଠିପରି ଅଂଶ, ଟ୍ରିଗର୍

trim /trɪm/ *verb* (**trims, trimming, trimmed**) cut a small amount of something to make it tidy କୌଣସି ପଦାର୍ଥକୁ ଅଳ୍ପ କାଟି ଇଚ୍ଛାକୃତ ଆକାର ଦେବା, କତୁରିବା *He trimmed my hair.*

trim *noun* ସଜାଡ଼ିବା ବା ସମାନ କରିବା ପାଇଁ ଅଳ୍ପ କାଟିବା କାମ; ସଜ୍ଜିତ ଅବସ୍ଥା *My hair needs a trim.*

trip[1] /trɪp/ *noun* a short journey to a place and back again ଅଳ୍ପ ସମୟର ଭ୍ରମଣ ବା ପର୍ଯ୍ୟଟନ *We went on a trip to the mountains.*

trip[2] /trɪp/ *verb* (**trips, tripping, tripped**) hit your foot against something so that you fall or nearly fall ଝୁଣ୍ଟିବା, ଝୁଣ୍ଟି ପଡ଼ିଯିବା *She tripped over the step.*

triple /ˈtrɪpl/ *adjective* with three parts ତିନି ଅଂଶଥିବା *the triple jump*

triple *verb* (**triples, tripling, tripled**) become or make something three times bigger ତିନି ଗୁଣ କରିବା ବା ହେବା *Sales have tripled this year.*

triumph /ˈtraɪʌmf/ *noun* a great success; the act of winning ବଡ଼ ଧରଣର ସଫଳତା; ନିର୍ଣ୍ଣାୟକ ବିଜୟ *The race ended in triumph for the Indian team.*

triumphant /traɪˈʌmfənt/ *adjective* very successful, for example in a game or an election ଖୁବ୍ ସଫଳ; ବିଜୟରେ ଉଲ୍ଲସିତ *India emerged triumphant in their match against Sri Lanka.*

trod, trodden ଶବ୍ଦ **tread** ର ଧାତୁରୂପ

trolley /ˈtrɒli/ *noun* (*plural* **trolleys**) a thing on wheels that you use for carrying things ଜିନିଷପତ୍ର ନେବାପାଇଁ ଚକଲଗା ଛୋଟ ଠେଲାଗାଡ଼ି; ଟ୍ରଲି *a luggage trolley*

troops /tru:ps/ *noun* (*plural*) soldiers ସେନା, ସେନାବାହିନୀ

trophy /ˈtrəʊfi/ *noun* (*plural* **trophies**) a thing, for example a silver cup, that you get when you win a competition ପ୍ରତିଯୋଗିତାରେ ପୁରସ୍କାର ରୂପେ ଦିଆଯାଉଥିବା କପ୍ ଇତ୍ୟାଦି *a tennis trophy*

the tropics /ˈtrɒpɪks/ *noun* (*plural*) the very hot part of the world କର୍କଟ କ୍ରାନ୍ତି ଓ ମକର କାନ୍ତି ମଧ୍ୟରେ ଥିବା ଉଷ୍ଣମଣ୍ଡଳ ବା ଗ୍ରୀଷ୍ମ ମଣ୍ଡଳ; ବିଷୁବ ମଣ୍ଡଳ

tropical /ˈtrɒpɪkl/ *adjective* of or from the tropics ଉଷ୍ଣମଣ୍ଡଳ ବା ଗ୍ରୀଷ୍ମ ମଣ୍ଡଳ ସମ୍ବନ୍ଧୀୟ, ବିଷୁବ ମଣ୍ଡଳୀୟ *tropical fruit*

trot /trɒt/ *verb* (**trots, trotting, trotted**) run with short quick steps ଛୋଟ ଓ କ୍ଷୀପ୍ର ପଦକ୍ଷେପରେ ଦୌଡ଼ିବା *The horse trotted along the road.*

trouble[1] /ˈtrʌbl/ *noun* **1** (*plural* **troubles**) difficulty, problems or worry ଅସୁବିଧା, ସମସ୍ୟା, ଚିନ୍ତା *We had a lot of trouble finding the book you wanted.* **2** (*plural* **troubles**) a situation when people are fighting or arguing ଗୋଳମାଳ, ଗଣ୍ଡଗୋଳ *There was a lot of trouble after the football match last Saturday.* **3** (*no plural*) pain or illness କଷ୍ଟ; ବେମାରି *He's got heart trouble.*

get into trouble do something that brings problems because it is wrong ଅସୁବିଧାରେ ପଡ଼ିବା *You'll get into trouble if you park your car here.*

trouble[2] /ˈtrʌbl/ *verb* (**troubles, troubling, troubled**) worry somebody; bring somebody problems or pain କାହାରିକୁ ହଇରାଣ କରିବା; କାହାରିପାଇଁ ସମସ୍ୟା ସୃଷ୍ଟି କରିବା କାହାରିକୁ କଷ୍ଟଦେବା *I was troubled by the news.*

troublesome /ˈtrʌblsəm/ *adjective* that gives you trouble ହଇରାଣିଆ, ହଇରାଣ କରୁଥିବା; ଅଶାନ୍ତି ସୃଷ୍ଟି କରୁଥିବା, ଜଂଜାଳିଆ, ଝିଂଝଟିଆ *a troublesome child*

trough /trɒf/ *noun* a long open box that holds food or water for animals ପଶୁଙ୍କ ପାଇଁ ପାଣି ଓ ଖାଦ୍ୟ ରଖିବା ପାଇଁ ଲମ୍ବା ଅଣଓସାରିଆ କୁଣ୍ଡ

trousers /ˈtraʊzəz/ *noun* (*no singular*) a piece of clothing for your legs and the lower part of your body ମୁନା ପ୍ୟାଣ୍ଟ, ଫୁଲ ପ୍ୟାଣ୍ଟ, ଟ୍ରାଉଜର୍ସ *Your trousers are on the chair.* ➪ ଚିତ୍ର ପାଇଁ **suit** ଦେଖନ୍ତୁ। ✪ ମନେ ରଖନ୍ତୁ! ଇଂରାଜୀରେ **a pair of trousers** କୁହାଯାଏ (**a trousers** କୁ କୁହାଯାଏ ନାହିଁ)। *I bought a new pair of trousers.*

truck /trʌk/ *noun* a big vehicle for carrying heavy things ମାଲବାହୀ ମଟରଗାଡ଼ି, ଟ୍ରକ୍ *a truck driver*

true /tru:/ *adjective* **1** right or correct ଠିକ୍, ସତ, ଯଥାର୍ଥ *Is it true that you are leaving?* ○ *The Taj Mahal is in Agra: true or false?* **2** that really happened ସତରେ ପ୍ରକୃତରେ ଘଟିଥିବା *It's a true story.* **3** real ପ୍ରକୃତ *A true friend will always help you.* ✪ ଏହାର ବିଶେଷ୍ୟ ହେଲା **truth**। ✪ ବିପରୀତ **false 1**

come true happen in the way that you hoped ସତ ହେବା *Her dream came true.*

truly /ˈtru:li/ *adverb* really ପ୍ରକୃତରେ *I'm truly sorry.*

Yours truly words that you can use at the end of a formal letter ଔପଚାରିକ ଚିଠି ଶେଷରେ ଲେଖାଯାଉଥିବା ବାକ୍ୟାଂଶ

trumpet /ˈtrʌmpɪt/ *noun* a musical instrument that you blow ତୁରୀ ବା କାହାଳୀ ପରି ଏକ ବାଦ୍ୟଯନ୍ତ୍ର

trunk /trʌŋk/ *noun* **1** the thick part of a tree that grows up from the ground. Branches grow from the trunk ଗଛର ଗଣ୍ଡି ➪ ଚିତ୍ର ପାଇଁ **tree** ଦେଖନ୍ତୁ। **2** an elephant's long nose ହାତୀର ଶୁଣ୍ଢ ➪ ଚିତ୍ର ପାଇଁ **mammals** ଦେଖନ୍ତୁ। **3** a big strong box for carrying things when you travel ବଡ଼ ବାକ୍ସ

trunks /trʌŋks/ *noun* (*no singular*) short trousers that a man or boy wears for swimming ପୁରୁଷଙ୍କର ପହଁରା ପିନ୍ଧା ହାଫ୍‌ପ୍ୟାଣ୍ଟ

trust[1] /trʌst/ *noun* (*no plural*) the feeling you have that somebody or something will do what they should do; the feeling that somebody is honest and good ବିଶ୍ୱାସ, ପ୍ରତ୍ୟୟ, ଆସ୍ଥା *Put your trust in God.*

trust[2] /trʌst/ *verb* (**trusts, trusting, trusted**) feel sure that somebody or something will do what they should do; believe that somebody is honest and good ବିଶ୍ୱାସ କରିବା, ଆସ୍ଥା ରଖିବା, ନିର୍ଭର କରିବା *You can trust him with your money.*

truth /tru:θ/ *noun* (*no plural*) the state of being true; something that is true ସତ୍ୟତା; ସତକଥା *We need to find out the truth about what happened.*

truthful /ˈtru:θfl/ *adjective* **1** true ସତ *a truthful answer* **2** a person who is truthful tells the truth ସତ୍ୟବାଦୀ, ସଚ୍ଚୋଟ

truthfully *adverb* ସଚ୍ଚୋଟ ଭାବରେ, ସତ୍ୟନିଷ୍ଠ ଭାବରେ *You must answer me truthfully.*

try /traɪ/ *verb* (**tries, trying, tried, has tried**) **1** work hard to do something ଚେଷ୍ଟା କରିବା *I tried to remember her name but I couldn't.* **2** use or do something to find out if you like it ପରୀକ୍ଷା ବା ବ୍ୟବହାର କରି ଭଲମନ୍ଦ ଜାଣିବା *Have you ever tried Bengali food?*

try and do something try to do something ଚେଷ୍ଟାକରି କିଛି କାମ କରିବା *I'll try and come early tomorrow.*

try on put on a piece of clothing to see if you like it and if it fits you well ପୋଷାକ ପିନ୍ଧି ଠିକ୍ ମାପର କି ନୁହେଁ ଜାଣିବା ବା ଠିକ୍ ମାନୁଚି କି ନାହିଁ ଦେଖିବା *I tried the jeans on but they were too small.*

tub /tʌb/ *noun* a round container ଗୋଲିଆ କୁଣ୍ଡ *a tub of ice-cream* ➪ ଚିତ୍ର ପାଇଁ **water** ଦେଖନ୍ତୁ ।

tube /tju:b/ *noun* **1** a long thin pipe for liquid or gas ଲମ୍ବା ସରୁ ନଳୀ, ନଳୀ ଆକୃତିର ପଦାର୍ଥ, ପାଇପ୍, ଟ୍ୟୁବ୍ **2** a long thin soft container with a hole and a cap at one end ନଳାକୃତି ଠିପିଲଗା ଡବା (ଟୁଥ୍‌ପେଷ୍ଟ ଇତ୍ୟାଦିର) *a tube of toothpaste* ➪ ଚିତ୍ର ପାଇଁ **container** ଦେଖନ୍ତୁ ।

tube-well *noun* a pump usually operated by motor for bringing water up from underground ଭୂଗର୍ଭର ପାଣି ଉଠାଇବା ପାଇଁ ହାତମରା ବା ବିଦ୍ୟୁତ୍‌ଚାଳିତ ପମ୍ପ; ନଳକୂପ

tuck /tʌk/ *verb* (**tucks, tucking, tucked**) put or push the edges of something inside or under something else ଖୋଷିଦେବା *He tucked his shirt into his trousers.*

Tuesday /ˈtju:zdeɪ/ *noun* the second day of the week, next after Monday ମଙ୍ଗଳବାର

tug /tʌg/ *verb* (**tugs, tugging, tugged**) pull something hard and quickly ଜୋର୍‌ରେ ଟାଣିବା, ଛିଙ୍କିବା *I tugged at the rope and it broke.*

tug *noun* a sudden hard pull ଜୋର୍ ଝିଙ୍କା *The little girl gave my hand a tug.*

tuition /tjuˈɪʃn/ *noun* (*no plural*) the act of teaching one person or a very small group ପାଉଣା ନେଇ ଜଣଙ୍କୁ ବା ଅଳ୍ପ

ଛାତ୍ରଙ୍କୁ ଶିକ୍ଷାଦାନ, ଘରୋଇ ଶିକ୍ଷା, ଟ୍ୟୁସନ୍ *A lot of students take extra tuition before their exams.*

tulip /ˈtjuːlɪp/ *noun* a big brightly coloured flower shaped like a cup କପ୍ ଆକାରର ଉଜ୍ଜ୍ୱଳ ରଙ୍ଗର ଏକ ପ୍ରକାର ଫୁଲ, ଟ୍ୟୁଲିପ୍

tumble /ˈtʌmbl/ *verb* (**tumbles, tumbling, tumbled**) fall suddenly ହଠାତ୍ ଅଖାଡୁଆ ଭାବରେ ପଡ଼ିଯିବା *He tumbled down the steps.*

tumbler /ˈtʌmblə(r)/ *noun* a container like a glass with a flat bottom and straight sides (ପାଣି ଇତ୍ୟାଦି ପିଇବା ପାଇଁ ଥିବା) ଗିଲାସ

tummy /ˈtʌmi/ *noun* (*plural* **tummies**) (used especially by children) the part of your body between your chest and your legs; your stomach ପେଟ (ବିଶେଷତଃ ପିଲାଙ୍କ ଭାଷାରେ) *My tummy is full.*

tundra /ˈtʌndrə/ *noun* (*no plural*) the Arctic region where no trees grow as the soil below the surface of the ground is always frozen ସୁମେରୁ ଅଞ୍ଚଳର ବୃକ୍ଷହୀନ ବରଫାବୃତ ଅଞ୍ଚଳ, ତୁନ୍ଦ୍ରା ଅଞ୍ଚଳ

tune /tjuːn/ *noun* a group of musical notes that make a nice sound when you play or sing them together ସଙ୍ଗୀତର ସ୍ୱର, ସୁର, ରାଗିଣୀ *I know the tune but I don't know the words.*

tune *verb* (**tunes, tuning, tuned**) do something to a musical instrument so that it makes the right sounds ବାଦ୍ୟଯନ୍ତ୍ର ଠିକ୍ ସ୍ୱରରେ ବାନ୍ଧିବା, ଟ୍ୟୁନ୍ କରିବା *She tuned the piano.*

tunnel /ˈtʌnl/ *noun* a long hole under the ground or sea for a road or railway ରେଳ ବା ମଟର ରାସ୍ତା ପାଇଁ ଖୋଳା ଯାଇଥିବା ସୁଡ଼ଙ୍ଗ, ଟନେଲ୍

tunnel

turban /ˈtɜːbən/ *noun* a long piece of material that is wrapped around somebody's head ପଗଡ଼ି, ପାଗ

turn[1] /tɜːn/ *verb* (**turns, turning, turned**) **1** move round, or move something round a fixed central point ବୁଲିବା, ଘୂରିବା; ବୁଲାଇବା, ଘୁରାଇବା *The wheels are turning.* ○ *Turn the key.* ○ *She turned around and walked towards the door.* **2** move in a different direction ଭିନ୍ନ ଦିଗରେ ଯିବା, ନୂତନ ଦିଗକୁ ମୋଡ଼ିବା *Turn left at the traffic lights.* **3** become different ବଦଳିବା, ଭିନ୍ନ ପ୍ରକାରର ହୋଇଯିବା *The weather has turned cold.* **4** find a certain page in a book ପୃଷ୍ଠା ଓଲଟାଇବା; ପୃଷ୍ଠା ଓଲଟାଇ ନିର୍ଦ୍ଦିଷ୍ଟ ପୃଷ୍ଠା ବାହାର କରିବା *Turn to page 97.*

turn into something become different; change somebody or something into something different ପରିବର୍ତ୍ତିତ ହେବା *Water turns into ice when it gets very cold.*

turn off move the handle, switch, etc. that controls something, so that it stops (ହ୍ୟାଣ୍ଡେଲ୍, ମୋଡି ବା ସ୍ୱିଚ୍ ଚିପି କୌଣସି ଜିନିଷର ଚଳନ) ବନ୍ଦ କରିବା *Turn the tap off.* ○ *Turn off the television.*

turn on move the handle, switch, etc. that controls something, so that it starts (ହ୍ୟାଣ୍ଡେଲ, ସ୍ୱିଚ୍ ଇତ୍ୟାଦି ବୁଲାଇ ବା ଟିପି କୌଣସି ଜିନିଷ) ଚାଲୁ କରିବା *Could you turn the light on?*

turn over move so that the other side is on top ଓଲଟି ଯିବା, ଲେଉଟାଇବା *If you turn over the page, you'll find the answers on the other side.*

turn up arrive ପହଞ୍ଚିବା *Has David turned up yet?*

turn² /tɜːn/ *noun* **1** the act of turning something round ଘୂର୍ଣ୍ଣନ, ଆବର୍ତ୍ତନ *Give the screw a few turns.* **2** a change of direction ଦିଗ ପରିବର୍ତ୍ତନ *Take a left turn at the end of this road.* **3** the time when you can or should do something (କାମ କରିବାର) ପାଳି *It's your turn to do the cooking.*

take turns at something, take it in turns to do something do something one after the other (କିଛି କାମ) ପାଳିକରି କରିବା *You can't both use the computer at the same time. Why don't you take it in turns?*

turning /ˈtɜːnɪŋ/ *noun* a place where one road joins another road ରାସ୍ତାର ଛକ, ମୋଡ଼ *Take the first turning on the right.*

turnip /ˈtɜːnɪp/ *noun* a round white vegetable that grows under the ground ଓଲ୍‌କୋବି ବା ଶାଲ୍‌ଗମ୍ ଜାତୀୟ ଉଦ୍ଭିଦ ମୂଳ

turquoise /ˈtɜːkwɔɪz/ *noun* **1** a colour between blue and green ସବୁଜ ନୀଳ ବର୍ଣ୍ଣ **2** a precious stone of this colour ସବୁଜ ନୀଳ ରଙ୍ଗର ଏକ ଅସ୍ୱଚ୍ଛ ମୂଲ୍ୟବାନ୍ ପଥର

turtle /ˈtɜːtl/ *noun* an animal that lives in the sea and has a hard shell on its back କଇଁଛ, କଚ୍ଛପ, କୂର୍ମ

tusk /tʌsk/ *noun* a long pointed tooth that grows beside the mouth of an elephant ହାତୀ ଦାନ୍ତ ➪ ଚିତ୍ର ପାଇଁ **mammal** ଦେଖନ୍ତୁ

tutor /ˈtjuːtə(r)/ *noun* a teacher who teaches one person or a small group ଟ୍ୟୁସନ ମାଷ୍ଟ୍ର, ଘରୋଇ ଶିକ୍ଷକ

TV *abreviation* ଶବ୍ଦ **television** ର ସଂକ୍ଷିପ୍ତ ରୂପ

twelve /twelv/ *number* 12 ୧୨ ସଂଖ୍ୟା

twelfth /twelfθ/ *adjective, adverb, noun* 12th ୧୨ତମ, ଦ୍ୱାଦଶ

twenty /ˈtwenti/ *number* **1** 20 ୨୦ ସଂଖ୍ୟା **2 the twenties** (*plural*) the numbers, years or temperatures between 20 and 29 ୨୦ ରୁ ୨୯ ମଧ୍ୟସ୍ଥ ସଂଖ୍ୟା, ବର୍ଷ ବା ଉତ୍ତାପ

twentieth /ˈtwentiəθ/ *adjective, adverb, noun* 20th ୨୦ତମ

twice /twaɪs/ *adverb* two times ଦୁଇଥର, ଦି'ଥର *I have been to Darjiling twice.* ○ *He ate twice as much as I did.*

twig /twɪg/ *noun* a small thin branch of a tree ଗଛରେ ଛୋଟ ଡାଳ, ଶାଖା, ଡାଙ୍ଗ

twilight /ˈtwaɪlaɪt/ *noun* (*no plural*) the faint light or the time after the sun has gone down and before it gets completely dark (ଠିକ୍ ସୂର୍ଯ୍ୟାସ୍ତ ପରର) ଗୋଧୂଳି ଆଲୋକ, ମୁହଁ ଅନ୍ଧାର ସମୟ

twin /twɪn/ *noun* twins are two people who have the same mother and who were born at the same time ଯାଆଁଳା, ଯମଜ ସନ୍ତାନ *Ajay and Sanjay are twins.*

twinkle /ˈtwɪŋkl/ *verb* (**twinkles, twinkling, twinkled**) shine with a small bright light that comes and goes. Stars twinkle ଝକମକ ହେବା, ମିଞ୍ଜି ମିଞ୍ଜି ଜଳିବା ବା ଆଲୋକ ଦେବା

twist /twɪst/ *verb* (**twists, twisting, twisted**) **1** turn strongly ଜୋରରେ ମୋଡ଼ିବା *Twist the lid off the jar.* **2** change the shape of something by turning it in different directions; turn in many different directions ମୋଡ଼ିମାଡ଼ି ଅଙ୍କାବଙ୍କା କରିବା; (ରାସ୍ତା) ଅଙ୍କାବଙ୍କା ହୋଇଯିବା, ବାଟଭାଙ୍ଗି ଚାଲିଯିବା *She twisted the clay into strange shapes.* ○ *The path twists and turns through the forest.* **3** turn something like threads, etc. round and round each other ସୂତାର ଖିଅକୁ ପରସ୍ପର ଚାରିପଟେ ମୋଡ଼ିବା *They twisted the sheets into a rope and escaped through the window.*

twisted *adjective* if something is twisted, it is bent or turned in a way that its original shape is changed ବଙ୍କାଢଙ୍କା ହୋଇଥିବା, ମୋଡ଼ାମୋଡ଼ି ହୋଇଥିବା *twisted metal*

twitch /twɪtʃ/ *verb* (**twitches, twitching, twitched**) make a sudden quick movement with a part of your body (ଅଙ୍ଗ ବା ପେଶୀ) କ୍ଷଣିକ ଭାବେ ସଙ୍କୁଚିତ ହେବା, କ୍ଷଣିକ ପେଶୀସଂକୋଚନ ହେବା *Rabbits twitch their noses.*

two /tuː/ *number* 2 ୨ ସଂଖ୍ୟା

type¹ /taɪp/ *noun* a group of things or people that are the same in some way; a sort or kind ଏକା ଜାତୀୟ ଲୋକ ବା ପଦାର୍ଥ; ପ୍ରକାର *An almond is a type of nut.* ○ *What type of music do you like?*

type² /taɪp/ *verb* (**types, typing, typed**) make words on paper with a **typewriter** or **word processor** ଟାଇପ୍ ମେସିନ୍ ବା କମ୍ପ୍ୟୁଟର୍‌ର ୱାର୍ଡ ପ୍ରସେସର୍‌ରେ ଟାଇପ୍ କରିବା *Her secretary types all her letters.*

typewriter /ˈtaɪpraɪtə(r)/ *noun* a machine with keys that you use to make words on paper ଟାଇପମେସିନ୍, ଟାଇପ୍ ରାଇଟର *an electronic typewriter*

typical /ˈtɪpɪkl/ *adjective* if something is typical, it is a good example of its kind କୌଣସି ପଦାର୍ଥର ଉତ୍ତମ ନମୁନା ସଦୃଶ, ଠିକ୍ ପ୍ରକାରର *We saw a typical English house.*

typically *adverb* in a typical way ପ୍ରକାରଗତ ଭାବେ *She is typically Indian.*

tyrant /ˈtaɪrənt/ *noun* a person with a lot of power who rules a country or a kingdom in a cruel way ସ୍ୱେଚ୍ଛାଚାରୀ ଓ ନିଷ୍ଠୁର ଶାସକ

tyrannical /tɪˈrænɪkl/ *adjective* ସ୍ୱେଚ୍ଛାଚାରୀ ଓ ନିଷ୍ଠୁର *a tyrannical ruler*

tyre /ˈtaɪə(r)/ *noun* a circle of rubber around the outside of a wheel, for example on a car or bicycle ମଟରଗାଡ଼ି, ସାଇକେଲ୍, ଇତ୍ୟାଦିର ରବର ଚକ, ଟାୟାର୍ *I think we've got a flat tyre.* ➪ ଚିତ୍ର ପାଇଁ **car** ଦେଖନ୍ତୁ।

U u

UFO /ˌjuː efˈəʊ/ *noun* (*plural* **UFOs**) a strange object that some people think they have seen in the sky and that may have come from another planet ଅଚିହ୍ନା ଉଡ଼ନ୍ତା ଯାନ (ହୁଏତ ଅନ୍ୟ ଗ୍ରହ ନକ୍ଷତ୍ରରୁ ଆସିଥିବା); ୟୁ.ଏଫ୍.ଓ ✪ UFO ର ବିସ୍ତୃତ ରୂପ ହେଲା **unidentified flying object**।

ugly /ˈʌgli/ *adjective* (**uglier, ugliest**) not pleasant to look at ଅସୁନ୍ଦର *an ugly face*

umbrella /ʌmˈbrelə/ *noun* a thing that you hold over your head to keep you dry when it rains or to protect you from the hot sun ଛତା *It started to rain, so I put my umbrella up.*

umpire /ˈʌmpaɪə(r)/ *noun* a person who controls a tennis or cricket match ଟେନିସ୍ ବା କ୍ରିକେଟ୍ ଖେଳର ମିମାଂସାକାରୀ ପରିଚାଳକ

un- *prefix*

un- କିଛି ଶବ୍ଦ ପୂର୍ବରୁ ଲଗାଇଲେ ବିପରୀତ ଅର୍ଥ ବୁଝାଏ, ଯଥା

unhappy	= ଦୁଃଖିତ
untrue	= ଅସତ୍ୟ
undress	= ଦେହରୁ ଲୁଗାପଟା କାଢ଼ିବା

unable /ʌnˈeɪbl/ *adjective* not able to do something ଅସମର୍ଥ *Jai is unable to come to the meeting because he is ill.* ✪ ଏହାର ବିଶେଷ୍ୟ ପଦ ହେଲା **inability**।

unacceptable /ˌʌnəkˈseptəbl/ *adjective* if something is unacceptable, it is not allowed or approved of by most people ଅଗ୍ରହଣୀୟ *unacceptable behaviour* ✪ ବିପରୀତ **acceptable**

unattractive /ˌʌnəˈtræktɪv/ *adjective* not attractive or pleasant to look at ଅନାକର୍ଷକ *The pattern on the shirt is unattractive.*

unaware /ˌʌnəˈweə(r)/ *adjective* if you are unaware of something, you do not know about it ଅଜ୍ଞାତ, ଅଜଣା *I was unaware of the danger.* ✪ ବିପରୀତ **aware**

unbelievable /ˌʌnbɪˈliːvəbl/ *adjective* very surprising or difficult to believe ଅବିଶ୍ୱାସ, ବିଶ୍ୱାସଯୋଗ୍ୟ ହୋଇ ନଥିବା ✪ ବିପରୀତ **believable**

unbreakable /ʌnˈbreɪkəbl/ *adjective* that which cannot be broken ଅଭଙ୍ଗା, ଅଭଙ୍ଗୁର, ଭାଙ୍ଗୁ ନଥିବା *unbreakable glasses*

uncertain /ʌnˈsɜːtn/ *adjective* not sure; not decided ଅନିଶ୍ଚିତ *I'm uncertain about what to do.* ✪ ବିପରୀତ **certain**[1]

uncle /ˈʌŋkl/ *noun* the brother of your mother or father, or the husband of your aunt ମାମୁଁ, ଦଦେଇ, କକେଇ *Uncle Raj* ⇨ ଚିତ୍ର ପାଇଁ **family** ଦେଖନ୍ତୁ।

unclean /ʌnˈkliːn/ *adjective* dirty ଅପରିଷ୍କାର, ମଇଳା ✪ ବିପରୀତ **clean**[1]

uncomfortable /ʌnˈkʌmftəbl/ *adjective* not comfortable ଆରାମଦାୟକ ହୋଇନଥିବା, ଅଖାଡୁଆ, ଅସ୍ୱସ୍ତିକର *The chair was hard and uncomfortable.* ✪ ବିପରୀତ **comfortable**

uncomfortably *adverb* ଅସ୍ୱସ୍ତିକର ଭାବରେ *The room was uncomfortably hot.*

uncommon /ʌnˈkɒmən/ *adjective* not common; that you do not see, hear, etc. often ଅସାଧାରଣ *This bird is uncommon in India.* ✪ ବିପରୀତ **common**

unconscious /ʌnˈkɒnʃəs/ *adjective* if you are unconscious, you are in a state like sleep and you do not know what is happening ବେହୋସ୍, ଚେତନାଶୂନ୍ୟ, ଅଚେତ, ସଂଜ୍ଞାହୀନ *She was unconscious for three days after injuring her head.* ✪ ବିପରୀତ **conscious**

uncontrolled /ˌʌnkənˈtrəʊld/ *adjective* (emotions, behaviour, actions, etc.) that cannot be stopped, controlled or limited ନିୟନ୍ତ୍ରଣ କରି ହେଉନଥିବା, ଅସମ୍ଭାଳ *uncontrolled laughter* ○ *uncontrolled population growth*

uncover /ʌnˈkʌvə(r)/ *verb* (**uncovers, uncovering, uncovered**) take the cover off something ଘୋଡ଼ଣି ବା ଆବରଣ ଖୋଲିବା; ଗୁପ୍ତ ଯୋଜନା ଇତ୍ୟାଦି ଖୋଜି ଜାଣିବା *Uncover the pan and cook the soup for thirty minutes.* ○ *Police have uncovered a plot to kidnap the Chief Minister's son.*

under /ʌndə(r)/ *preposition, adverb* **1** in or to a place that is lower than or below something ତଳେ, ନିମ୍ନରେ *The cat is under the table.* ○ *The boat sailed under the bridge.* **2** less than something କମ୍ *If you are under 18, you are not allowed to drive a car.* **3** covered by something ତଳେ, ଭିତରେ *I'm wearing a vest under my shirt.* **4** controlled by somebody or something ନିୟନ୍ତ୍ରଣରେ, ଅଧୀନରେ *The team are playing well under their new captain.*

> **under-** *prefix*
>
> କିଛି ବିଶେଷ୍ୟ ଓ ବିଶେଷଣ ପୂର୍ବରୁ **under-** ଲଗାଇଲେ ନିମ୍ନଲିଖିତ ଅର୍ଥ ବାହାରିବ —
>
> **underground** = ମାଟିତଳ
> **undergrowth** = ବଡ଼ ଗଛ ତଳେ ବଢ଼ିଥିବା ବୁଦା
>
> **under-** କିଛି ବିଶେଷଣ ଓ କ୍ରିୟା' ପୂର୍ବରୁ ଲଗାଇଲେ ଅଯଥେଷ୍ଟ ଅର୍ଥ ବୁଝାଇବ, ଯଥା —
>
> **undercooked** = ହରସିଝା
> **underdeveloped** = ଅବିକଶିତ

undergo /ˌʌndəˈɡəʊ/ *verb* (**undergoes, undergoing, underwent** /ˌʌndəˈwent/, **has undergone** /ˌʌndəˈɡɒn/) if you undergo something, it happens to you ସହିବା, ଭୋଗିବା *My aunt is in hospital undergoing an operation.*

underground *adjective*/ˈʌndəɡraʊnd/, *adverb* under the ground ମାଟି ତଳର, ଭୂମିତଳେ ଥିବା *an underground car park*

underline /ˌʌndəˈlaɪn/ *verb* (**underlines, underlining, underlined**) draw a line under a word, sentence, etc. କୌଣସି ଶବ୍ଦ ବା ବାକ୍ୟ ତଳେ ଗାର ଦେବା, ଅଣ୍ଡର୍‌ଲାଇନ୍ କରିବା *<u>This sentence is underlined</u>.*

underneath /ˌʌndəˈniːθ/ *preposition, adverb* under or below something ତଳେ *The dog sat underneath the table.* ○ *She wore a black jacket with a red sweater underneath.*

understand /ˌʌndəˈstænd/ *verb* (**understands, understanding, understood** /ˌʌndəˈstʊd/, **has understood**) know what something means or why something happens ବୁଝିପାରିବା *I didn't understand what the teacher said.* ○ *He doesn't understand English.* ○ *I don't understand why you're so angry.*

understanding[1] /ˌʌndəˈstændɪŋ/ *adjective* if you are understanding, you listen to other people's problems and you try to understand them ବୁଝିବା ଶକ୍ତି ବା ବୁଦ୍ଧି ଥିବା *My parents are very understanding.*

understanding[2] /ˌʌndəˈstændɪŋ/ *noun* (*no plural*) the knowledge that you have about something ଜ୍ଞାନ *He's got a good understanding of computers.*

understood ଶବ୍ଦ **understand** ର ଏକ ଧାତୁରୂପ

underwater[1] /ˌʌndəˈwɔːtə(r)/ *adverb* below the surface of water ପାଣି ତଳେ *Can you swim underwater?*

underwater[2] /ˌʌndəˈwɔːtə(r)/ *adjective* living or working under the surface of water ଜଳ ମଧ୍ୟସ୍ଥ, ପାଣି ଭିତରେ ଥିବା *underwater creatures* ○ *an underwater camera*

underwear /ˈʌndəweə(r)/ *noun* (*no plural*) clothes that you wear next to your body, under your other clothes ଜାମାପଟା ତଳେ ପିନ୍ଧା ଯାଉଥିବା ପରିଧାନ, ଅନ୍ତର୍ବସ୍ତ୍ର

underweight /ˈʌndəˌweɪt/ *adjective* (of people) weighting less than the expected weight ସ୍ୱାଭାବିକ ଓଜନ ଠାରୁ କମ୍

underwent ଶବ୍ଦ **undergo** ର ଏକ ଧାତୁରୂପ

undo /ʌnˈduː/ *verb* (**undoes** /ʌnˈdʌz/, **undoing, undid** /ʌnˈdɪd/, **has undone** /ʌnˈdʌn/) open something that was tied or fixed ଖୋଲିବା, ଫିଟାଇବା *I undid the string and opened the parcel.* ○ *I can't undo these buttons.* ✪ ବିପରୀତ **do up**

undone *adjective* not tied or fixed ଖୋଲା, ବନ୍ଧା ହୋଇନଥିବା *Your shoelaces are undone.*

undress /ʌnˈdres/ *verb* (**undresses, undressing, undressed**) take clothes off yourself or another person ଲୁଗାପଟା ଖୋଲିବା *She undressed her baby.* ✪ ବିପରୀତ **dress**[2]

unearthly /ʌnˈɜːθli/ *adjective* strange, unnatural and a little scary ଅଦ୍ଭୁତ, ଅଲୌକିକ, ଅପାର୍ଥିବ *an unearthly scream*

at an unearthly hour very early in the morning ଅତି ସକାଳ ବା ରାତିଅଧିଆ ସମୟ *In order to catch the train to Jaipur, we had to get up at an unearthly hour of 3 a.m.*

uneasy /ʌnˈiːzi/ *adjective* worried that something is wrong ଅସ୍ୱସ୍ତିକର, ଅସ୍ୱଚ୍ଛଳ *She started to feel uneasy when her children didn't come home.*

uneasily *adverb* ଅସ୍ୱସ୍ତିକର ଭାବରେ *She looked uneasily around the room.*

unemployed /ˌʌnɪmˈplɔɪd/ *adjective* if someone is unemployed, they want a job but they do not have one ବେକାର, ବୃତ୍ତିହୀନ *Parul was unemployed for a year after leaving college.*

unemployment /ˌʌnɪmˈplɔɪmənt/ *noun* (*no plural*) the time when there are not enough jobs for the people who want to work ବେକାରୀ, କାମ ନଥିବା ଅବସ୍ଥା *If the factory closes down, unemployment in the town will increase.*

uneven /ʌnˈiːvn/ *adjective* not smooth or flat ଅସମତଳ, ଆବୁଡ଼ାଖବୁଡ଼ *We had to drive slowly because the road was so uneven.* ✪ ବିପରୀତ **even[1] 1**

unexpected /ˌʌnɪkˈspektɪd/ *adjective* surprising because you did not expect it ଅପ୍ରତ୍ୟାଶିତ, ଆଶା କରାଯାଉ ନଥିବା *an unexpected visit*

unexpectedly *adverb* ଅପ୍ରତ୍ୟାଶିତ ଭାବରେ *She arrived unexpectedly.*

unfair /ˌʌnˈfeə(r)/ *adjective* not treating people in the same way or in the right way ଅନ୍ୟାୟ, ପକ୍ଷପାତୀ *It was unfair to give chocolates to some of the children and not to the others.* ✪ ବିପରୀତ **fair[1] 1**

unfairly *adverb* ଅନ୍ୟାୟ ଭାବରେ *He left his job because the boss was treating him unfairly.* ✪ ବିପରୀତ **fairly 1**

unfamiliar /ˌʌnfəˈmɪliə(r)/ *adjective* that you do not know; strange ଅପରିଚିତ, ଅଜଣା *I woke up in an unfamiliar room.* ✪ ବିପରୀତ **familiar[1]**

unfashionable /ˌʌnˈfæʃnəbl/ *adjective* not fashionable ଅପ୍ରଚଳିତ ଲୋକପ୍ରିୟ ହୋଇନଥିବା *unfashionable clothes* ✪ ବିପରୀତ **fashionable**

unfasten /ʌnˈfɑːsn/ *verb* (**unfastens, unfastening, unfastened**) untie or open something ଖୋଲିବା *'You can unfasten your seat belts now,' said the pilot.* ✪ ବିପରୀତ **fasten**

unfit /ʌnˈfɪt/ *adjective* **1** not healthy or strong ବଳହୀନ, ଅସୁସ୍ଥ *She never takes any exercise—that's why she's so unfit.* **2** not good enough for something ଅନୁପଯୁକ୍ତ, ଅଯୋଗ୍ୟ *This house is unfit for people to live in.* ✪ ବିପରୀତ **fit[1]**

unfold /ʌnˈfəʊld/ *verb* (**unfolds, unfolding, unfolded**) spread or open something that is folded to make it flat; open out and become flat ଖୋଲିବା, ଖୋଲି ସମତଳ କରି ରଖିବା *Vijay unfolded the newspaper and started to read.* ○ *The sofa unfolds to make a bed.* ✪ ବିପରୀତ **fold[1]**

unfortunate /ʌnˈfɔːtʃənət/ *adjective* not lucky ଦୁର୍ଭାଗ୍ୟଜନକ *It's unfortunate that you were ill on your birthday.* ✪ ବିପରୀତ **fortunate**

unfortunately *adverb* it is unfortunate that ଦୁର୍ଭାଗ୍ୟବଶତଃ, ଦୁର୍ଭାଗ୍ୟକୁ *I would like to give you some money, but unfortunately I haven't got any.* ✪ ବିପରୀତ **fortunately**

unfriendly /ʌnˈfrendli/ *adjective* not friendly; not kind or helpful to other people ବନ୍ଧୁଭାବାପନ୍ନ ହୋଇନଥିବା; ଦୟାହୀନ, ଅସହଯୋଗୀ ✪ ବିପରୀତ **friendly**

ungrateful /ʌnˈgreɪtfl/ *adjective* if you are ungrateful, you do not show that you are grateful when somebody helps you or gives you something ଅକୃତଜ୍ଞ *Don't be so ungrateful! I spent all morning looking for this present.* ✪ ବିପରୀତ **grateful**

unhappy /ʌnˈhæpi/ *adjective* (**unhappier, unhappiest**) not happy; sad ଅସୁଖୀ; ଦୁଃଖୀ *He was very unhappy when he lost the match.* ✪ ବିପରୀତ **happy 1**

unhappily *adverb* ଅସୁଖୀ ବା ଦୁଃଖୀ ଭାବରେ, ଦୁଃଖରେ *'I failed the exam,' she said unhappily.*

unhappiness *noun* (*no plural*) ଦୁଃଖ *John has had a lot of unhappiness in his life.*

unhealthy /ʌnˈhelθi/ *adjective* (**unhealthier, unhealthiest**) **1** not well; often ill ଅସୁସ୍ଥ; ପୀଡ଼ିତ *an unhealthy child* **2** that can make you ill ଅସ୍ୱାସ୍ଥ୍ୟକର *unhealthy food* ✪ ବିପରୀତ **healthy**

unhelpful /ʌnˈhelpfl/ *adjective* a person or thing that is not helpful or useful; not willing to help somebody ସାହାଯ୍ୟ କରୁନଥିବା, ସୁବିଧା ଦେଉ ନଥିବା *The driver was rude and unhelpful.*

unhygienic /ˌʌnhaɪˈdʒiːnɪk/ *adjective* not clean and full of germs that cause disease ଅସ୍ୱାସ୍ଥ୍ୟକର, ଅପରିଷ୍କାର

unicorn /ˈjuːnɪkɔːn/ *noun* an animal in stories that is like a horse with a long straight horn on its forehead କିଂବଦନ୍ତୀରେ ବର୍ଣ୍ଣିତ ମୁଣ୍ଡରେ ଗୋଟିଏ ଶୃଙ୍ଗଥିବା ଘୋଡ଼ାପରି ପଶୁ, ୟୁନିକର୍ଣ୍ଣ

unicorn

uniform[1] /ˈjuːnɪfɔːm/ *noun* the special clothes that everybody in the same job, school, etc. wears କୌଣସି କାମ ବା ସ୍କୁଲ୍ ଇତ୍ୟାଦିର ବିଶେଷ ପୋଷାକ *Army officers wear dark green uniforms.*

uniform[2] /ˈjuːnɪfɔːm/ *adjective* something that is uniform remains the same at all times and in all cases ଏକାପରି, ସମାନ, ଅନୁରୂପ *uniform tax rates across the states*

unimportant /ˌʌnɪmˈpɔːtnt/ *adjective* not important ଅଦରକାରୀ, ଗୁରୁତ୍ୱପୂର୍ଣ୍ଣ ହୋଇ ନଥିବା *The boss said she would deal with unimportant issues later.*

uninhabited /ˌʌnɪnˈhæbɪtɪd/ *adjective* where nobody lives ଜନବସତିଶୂନ୍ୟ, ନିର୍ଜନ *an uninhabited island*

uninteresting /ʌnˈɪntrəstɪŋ/ *adjective* boring; not interesting ଦୃଷ୍ଟି ଆକର୍ଷକ ବା କୌତୁହଳଜନକ ହୋଇନଥିବା, ଅତି ସାଧାରଣ *I found the novel uninteresting.* ✪ ବିପରୀତ **interesting**

union /ˈjuːniən/ *noun* **1** (*plural* **unions**) a group of workers who have joined together to talk to their managers about things like pay and the way they work ଶ୍ରମିକ ସଂଘ *the trade union* **2** (*no plural*) the act of coming together ଏକତ୍ରୀକରଣ *The union of England and Scotland took place in 1707.*

union territory *noun* (*plural* **union territories**) (in India) an administrative division that is directly ruled by the central government (ଭାରତରେ) କେନ୍ଦ୍ରଶାସିତ ଅଞ୍ଚଳ

unique /ju'ni:k/ *adjective* not like anybody or anything else ଅଦ୍ୱିତୀୟ *That shop has some unique designs in shoes.*

unit /'ju:nɪt/ *noun* **1** one complete thing or group that may also be a part of something larger ସମ୍ପୂର୍ଣ୍ଣ ବିବେଚିତ ବସ୍ତୁ, ବ୍ୟକ୍ତି ବା ଗୋଷ୍ଠୀ; ଏକକ *The book has twelve units.* **2** a measurement ମାପର ଏକକ *A metre is a unit of length and a kilogram is a unit of weight.*

unite /ju'naɪt/ *verb* (**unites, uniting, united**) join together to become one; put two things together ଏକତ୍ରୀତ ହେବା; ସଂଘବଦ୍ଧ ହେବା; ସଂଯୁକ୍ତ କରିବା, ଯୋଡ଼ିବା *East and West Germany united in 1990.*

united *adjective* joined together ଏକତ୍ରୀତ, ସଂଘବଦ୍ଧ, ସଂଯୁକ୍ତ *the United States of America*

unity /'ju:nəti/ *noun* (*no plural*) the state of being together or working together ଏକତା *There is a great deal of unity among the students of our class.*

universal /ˌju:nɪ'vɜ:sl/ *adjective* of, by or for everybody ସାର୍ବଜନୀନ, ସର୍ବବ୍ୟାପୀ, ବିଶ୍ୱବ୍ୟାପୀ *This subject is of universal interest.*

universe /'ju:nɪvɜ:s/ *noun* (*no plural*) the earth, stars, planets and everything else in space ସମଗ୍ର ବିଶ୍ୱ, ବିଶ୍ୱର ସମସ୍ତ ବିଦ୍ୟମାନ ପଦାର୍ଥ

university /ˌju:nɪ'vɜ:səti/ *noun* (*plural* **universities**) a place where people go to study a subject at a higher level, after they have finished school ବିଶ୍ୱବିଦ୍ୟାଳୟ *My sister is at university studying Chemistry.* ○ *a list of universities in India* ✪ ବିଶ୍ୱବିଦ୍ୟାଳୟର କୌଣସି ପରୀକ୍ଷାରେ ବିଶେଷ ଉତ୍ତୀର୍ଣ୍ଣ ହେଲେ **degree** ପ୍ରାପ୍ତ ହୁଏ ।

unjust /ˌʌn'dʒʌst/ *adjective* not just; not fair or right ଅନ୍ୟାୟ *This tax is unjust because poor people have to pay as much as rich people.* ✪ ବିପରୀତ **just**[2]

unkind /ˌʌn'kaɪnd/ *adjective* not kind; cruel ନିର୍ଦ୍ଦୟ; ନିଷ୍ଠୁର *It was unkind of you to laugh at her dress.* ✪ ବିପରୀତ **kind**[1]

unknown /ˌʌn'nəʊn/ *adjective* **1** that you do not know ଅଜଣା, ଅଚିହ୍ନା, ଅପରିଚିତ *an unknown face* **2** not famous ଅନାମଧେୟ, ଅପ୍ରସିଦ୍ଧ *an unknown actor* ✪ ବିପରୀତ **known**

unless /ən'les/ *conjunction* if not; except if ନହେଲେ, ନତୁବା *You will be late unless you leave now.*

unlike /ˌʌn'laɪk/ *preposition* not like; different from ଅସଦୃଶ; ଅନ୍ୟ ଠାରୁ ଭିନ୍ନ *She is thin, unlike her sister who is quite fat.* ✪ ବିପରୀତ **like**[2] **1**

unlikely /ʌn'laɪkli/ *adjective* (**unlikelier, unlikeliest**) if something is unlikely, it will probably not happen ସମ୍ଭାବନା ନଥିବା, ଅସମ୍ଭାବ୍ୟ *It is unlikely that it will rain.* ✪ ବିପରୀତ **likely**

unload /ˌʌn'ləʊd/ *verb* (**unloads, unloading, unloaded**) take off or out the things that a car, lorry, ship or plane is carrying (ଗାଡ଼ି, ଜାହାଜ ଇତ୍ୟାଦିରୁ) ମାଲ ଓହ୍ଲାଇବା, ଜିନିଷପତ୍ର ଉତାରିବା ବା କାଢ଼ିବା *They unloaded the ship at the dock.* ✪ ବିପରୀତ **load² 1**

unlock /ˌʌnˈlɒk/ *verb* (**unlocks, unlocking, unlocked**) open something with a key ତାଲା ଖୋଲିବା। *I unlocked the door and went in.* ✪ ବିପରୀତ **lock²**

unlucky /ʌnˈlʌki/ *adjective* (**unluckier, unluckiest**) **1** if you are unlucky, something good does not happen to you because of bad luck ଭାଗ୍ୟହୀନ *She's unlucky—she plays very well but she never wins a game.* **2** something that is unlucky brings bad luck ଅମଙ୍ଗଳ ବା ଅଶୁଭ ସୂଚକ, ଅଶୁଭକର *Some people think that the number 13 is unlucky.* ✪ ବିପରୀତ **lucky**

unluckily *adverb* it is unlucky that ଦୁର୍ଭାଗ୍ୟବଶତଃ, ମନ୍ଦଭାଗ୍ୟ *Unluckily, I missed the bus.*

unmarried /ˌʌnˈmærid/ *adjective* not married; without a husband or wife ଅବିବାହିତ, କୁମାର, କୁମାରୀ

unnatural /ʌnˈnætʃrəl/ *adjective* **1** not made by nature, but by people ଅପ୍ରାକୃତିକ, କୃତ୍ରିମ **2** not normal or usual ଅସ୍ୱାଭାବିକ ✪ ବିପରୀତ **natural**

unnecessary /ˌʌnˈnesəsəri/ *adjective* not necessary; not needed ଅଦରକାରୀ, ଅପ୍ରୟୋଜନୀୟ ✪ ବିପରୀତ **necessary**

unofficial /ˌʌnəˈfɪʃl/ *adjective* that is not of or from the government or somebody who is important ବେସରକାରୀ; ଅନୌପଚାରିକ *an unofficial report* ○ *unofficial sources* ✪ ବିପରୀତ **official¹**

unpack /ˌʌnˈpæk/ *verb* (**unpacks, unpacking, unpacked**) take all the things out of a bag, suitcase, etc. ବାକ୍ସପତ୍ର ଖୋଲି ଜିନିଷ କାଢ଼ିବା *Have you unpacked your suitcase?* ✪ ବିପରୀତ **pack²**

unpleasant /ʌnˈpleznt/ *adjective* not pleasant; not nice ଅପ୍ରୀତିକର, ବିରକ୍ତିକର *There was an unpleasant smell of bad eggs.* ✪ ବିପରୀତ **pleasant**

unplug /ˌʌnˈplʌg/ *verb* (**unplugs, unplugging, unplugged**) take the electric plug of a machine out of a place in a wall (called a **socket**) where there is electricity ସକେଟ୍‌ରୁ ପ୍ଲଗ୍ କାଢ଼ି ବୈଦ୍ୟୁତିକ ପ୍ରବାହ ବନ୍ଦ କରିବା *Could you unplug the TV?* ✪ ବିପରୀତ **plug**

unpopular /ʌnˈpɒpjələ(r)/ *adjective* not popular; not liked by many people ଅପ୍ରୀୟ; ଜନତା ଦ୍ୱାରା ଅନାଦୃତ *He's unpopular at work because he talks too much.* ✪ ବିପରୀତ **popular**

unreasonable /ʌnˈriːznəbl/ *adjective* not fair or right; expecting too much ଆଯୌକ୍ତିକ; ଅତ୍ୟାଧିକ *The management decided not to agree to the unreasonable demands of the workers.* ✪ ବିପରୀତ **reasonable**

unreliable /ˌʌnrɪˈlaɪəbl/ *adjective* not reliable; that you cannot trust ନିର୍ଭରଯୋଗ୍ୟ ହୋଇନଥିବା, ବିଶ୍ୱାସଯୋଗ୍ୟ ହୋଇନଥିବା। *Don't lend her any money—she's very unreliable.* ○ *an unreliable car* ✪ ବିପରୀତ **reliable**

unsafe /ʌnˈseɪf/ *adjective* not safe; dangerous ଅସୁରକ୍ଷିତ; ବିପଜ୍ଜନକ *Don't climb on that wall—it's unsafe.* ✪ ବିପରୀତ **safe**[1]

unsatisfactory /ˌʌnˌsætɪsˈfæktəri/ *adjective* not satisfactory; not good enough ସନ୍ତୋଷଜନକ ହୋଇନଥିବା, ଆଶାରୂପ ହୋଇନଥିବା, ଅସନ୍ତୋଷଜନକ *Tina's work was unsatisfactory, so I asked her to do it again.* ✪ ବିପରୀତ **satisfactory**

unscrew /ˌʌnˈskruː/ *verb* (**unscrews, unscrewing, unscrewed**) open something by turning it, usually in the **anticlockwise** direction ସ୍କ୍ରୁ' ବୁଲାଇ ଖୋଲିବା; ସ୍କ୍ରୁ' ଘାଟିଥିବା ବୋତଲ ମୁହଁ ଇତ୍ୟାଦି ବୁଲାଇ ଖୋଲିବା ✪ ବିପରୀତ **screw**

unselfish /ʌnˈselfɪʃ/ *adjective* if you are unselfish, you care about other people's feelings and needs ନିଃସ୍ୱାର୍ଥପର ✪ ବିପରୀତ **selfish**

unstable /ʌnˈsteɪbl/ *adjective* something that is unstable may fall, move or change suddenly ଅଣଢଣିଆ, ପଡ଼ିଗଲା ପରି, ଟଳମଳ; ଅସ୍ଥିର, ସ୍ଥିରତା ନଥିବା *This bookshelf is unstable.* ○ *an unstable government* ✪ ବିପରୀତ **stable**[2]

unsteady /ʌnˈstedi/ *adjective* if something is unsteady, it moves or shakes, and seems that it might fall ଟଳମଳ, ପଡ଼ିଗଲାପରି *He felt undsteady for a few days after his illness.* ✪ ବିପରୀତ **steady 1**

unsuccessful /ˌʌnsəkˈsesfl/ *adjective* if you are unsuccessful, you have not been able to get what you wanted or do what you tried to do ଅସଫଳ, ବିଫଳ *I tried to repair the bike but I was unsuccessful.* ✪ ବିପରୀତ **successful**

unsuitable /ʌnˈsuːtəbl/ *adjective* not suitable; not right for somebody or something ଅନୁପଯୁକ୍ତ, ଅଯୋଗ୍ୟ *This film is unsuitable for children.* ✪ ବିପରୀତ **suitable**

unsure /ˌʌnˈʃʊə(r)/ *adjective* not sure ଅନିଶ୍ଚିତ, ଦୋଦୁଲ୍ୟମାନ *We were unsure what to do.* ✪ ବିପରୀତ **sure**

unsympathetic /ˌʌnˌsɪmpəˈθetɪk/ *adjective* not having any feelings or care for other people's problems ସହାନୁଭୂତି ନଥିବା ✪ ବିପରୀତ **sympathetic**

untidy /ʌnˈtaɪdi/ *adjective* (**untidier, untidiest**) not tidy; not with everything in the right place ଅପରିଷ୍କୃତ, ବିଶୃଙ୍ଖଳ, ଅପରିଚ୍ଛନ୍ନ *Your room is always so untidy!* ✪ ବିପରୀତ **tidy**

untidiness *noun* (*no plural*) ଅପରିଚ୍ଛନ୍ନତା, ଅନିର୍ମଳତା *I hate untidiness!*

untie /ʌnˈtaɪ/ *verb* (**unties, untying, untied, has untied**) **1** take off the string or rope that is holding something or somebody (ବନ୍ଧାଯାଇଥିବା ଜିନିଷର) ବନ୍ଧନ ଦଉଡ଼ି ଇତ୍ୟାଦି ଖୋଲିବା *I untied the parcel.* ✪ ବିପରୀତ **tie**[2] **1** **2** make a knot or bow loose ଫଉଡ଼ି

ଇତ୍ୟାଦିର ଗଣ୍ଠି ବା ଫାସ ଖୋଲିବା *Can you untie this knot?*

until /ən'tɪl/ *conjunction* up to the time when ପର୍ଯ୍ୟନ୍ତ *Stay in bed until you feel better.*

until *preposition* **1** up to a certain time (ନିର୍ଦ୍ଦିଷ୍ଟ ସମୟ) ପର୍ଯ୍ୟନ୍ତ *The shop is open until 6.30 p.m.* **2** before ପୂର୍ବରୁ *I can't come until tomorrow.* ⇨ **till** ଦେଖନ୍ତୁ।

unusual /ʌn'ju:ʒuəl/ *adjective* if something is unusual, it does not happen often or you do not see it often ଅସାଧାରଣ *It's unusual to see a cat without a tail.* ○ *What an unusual name!* ✪ ବିପରୀତ **usual**

unusually *adverb* ଅସାଧାରଣ ଭାବରେ *It was an unusually hot summer.*

unwell /ʌn'wel/ *adjective* not well; ill ଅସୁସ୍ଥ; ରୋଗଗ୍ରସ୍ତ ✪ ବିପରୀତ **well**[1]

unwilling /ʌn'wɪlɪŋ/ *adjective* if you are unwilling to do something, you are not ready or happy to do it ଅନିଚ୍ଛୁକ *He was unwilling to get some stamps for me from the post office.* ✪ ବିପରୀତ **willing**

unwillingly *adverb* ଅନିଚ୍ଛୁକ ଭାବରେ, ଇଚ୍ଛା ନଥିବା ସତ୍ତ୍ୱେ *She unwillingly paid for the extra cost.*

unwise /ˌʌn'waɪz/ *adjective* foolish; not wise ନିର୍ବୁଦ୍ଧିଆ, ବୋକା; ଅବିଜ୍ଞ, ଅନୁପଯୋଗୀ ✪ ବିପରୀତ **wise**

unwrap /ʌn'ræp/ *verb* (**unwraps, unwrapping, unwrapped**) take off the paper or cloth that is around something ଗୁଡ଼ିଆ ହୋଇଥିବା କାଗଜ ଇତ୍ୟାଦି ଖୋଲିବା, ଆବରଣ ଖୋଲିଦେବା *I unwrapped the parcel.* ✪ ବିପରୀତ **wrap1**

up /ʌp/ *preposition, adverb* **1** in or to a higher place ଉପରକୁ, ଉପରେ *We climbed up the mountain.* **2** from sitting or lying to standing (ବସିବା ବା ଶୋଇବା ଅବସ୍ଥାରୁ) ଠିଆହେବା ଅବସ୍ଥାକୁ *Stand up, please.* ○ *What time do you get up?* **3** in a way that is bigger, stronger, etc. (ଦର ଇତ୍ୟାଦି) ବଢ଼ିବା *The price of petrol is going up.* **4** so that it is finished ପୂରାପୂରି, ସମାପ୍ତ *Who used all the coffee up?* **5** towards and near somebody or something ପାଖକୁ *She came up to me and asked me the time.*

up to 1 as far as; until ପର୍ଯ୍ୟନ୍ତ *Up to now, she has worked very hard.* **2** as much or as many as ତାହାଠାରୁ ଅଧିକ ନୁହେଁ, ଯାଏଁ *Up to three hundred people came to the meeting.* **3** doing something ଉଦ୍ଦେଶ୍ୟରେ *What is that man up to?*

update /ˌʌp'deɪt/ *verb* (**updates, updating, updated**) make something more modern or add new things to it ଅଧୁନାତନ କରିବା *The information on the computer is updated every week.*

uphill /ˌʌp'hɪl/ *adverb* up, towards the top of a hill ପାହାଡ଼ ଉପରକୁ *It's difficult to ride a bicycle uphill.* ✪ ବିପରୀତ **downhill**

upon /ə'pɒn/ *preposition* on ଉପରେ ✪ **Upon** ସ୍ଥାନରେ ଆମେ ସାଧାରଣତଃ **on** ବ୍ୟବହାର କରୁ।

upper /'ʌpə(r)/ *adjective* higher than another; top ଉଚ୍ଚତର (ସ୍ଥାନ ବା ଅଂଶ); ଉପର *the upper lip* ✪ ବିପରୀତ **lower**[2]

upright /ˈʌpraɪt/ *adjective, adverb* standing straight up, not lying down ଭୂଲମ୍ବ, ସିଧାହୋଇ ଉପରକୁ ଉଠିଥିବା; ସିଧାହୋଇ *Put the ladder upright against the wall.*

uproot /ˌʌpˈruːt/ *verb* (**uproots, uprooting, uprooted**) pull a plant or tree out of the ground ଓପାଡ଼ିବା, ଉତ୍ପାଟନ କରିବା *The storm uprooted many trees in the city.*

upset /ʌpˈset/ *verb* (**upsets, upsetting, upset, has upset**) **1** make somebody feel unhappy or worried ବିରକ୍ତ କରିବା, ମାନସିକ ଅଶାନ୍ତି ଘଟାଇବା, ବିବ୍ରତ କରିବା *You upset Tilak when you said he was fat.* **2** make something go wrong ବିଗାଡ଼ିବା *The bad weather upset our plans for the weekend.* **3** knock something so that it turns over and things fall out ପକାଇ ଦେବା, ଓଲଟାଇବା; ଓଲଟି ପଡ଼ିବା *I upset a glass of water all over the table.*

upset /ˈʌpset/ *noun* an illness in your stomach ପେଟ ଗଣ୍ଡଗୋଳ *Seema has got a stomach upset.*

upset /ˌʌpˈset/ *adjective* **1** unhappy or worried ଦୁଃଖିତ, ବିବ୍ରତ *The children were very upset when their dog was ill.* **2** ill ଅସୁସ୍ଥ *I've got an upset stomach.*

upside down *adverb* with the top part at the bottom and the bottom part at the top ଓଲଟା ପର ଉପରକୁ *The picture is upside down.*

upstairs /ˌʌpˈsteəz/ *adverb* to or on a higher floor of a building ଉପର ମହଲାକୁ *I went upstairs to bed.* ✪ ବିପରୀତ **downstairs**

upstairs *adjective* ଉପର ମହଲାର *An upstairs window was open.* ✪ ବିପରୀତ **downstairs**

upwards /ˈʌpwədz/, **upward** /ˈʌpwəd/ *adverb* up; towards a higher place ଉପର ଆଡ଼କୁ; ଉଚ୍ଚତର ସ୍ଥାନକୁ *We climbed upwards, towards the top of the mountain.* ✪ ବିପରୀତ **downwards, downward**

upward *adjective* pointing, moving or increasing to a higher position or level ଊର୍ଦ୍ଧ୍ୱକୁ ପ୍ରସାରିତ ବା ନିକ୍ଷିପ୍ତ; ବଢୁଥିବା, ବର୍ଦ୍ଧନଶୀଳ *an upward glance* ○ *an upward trend of rising prices*

Uranus /ˈjʊərənəs/ *noun* (*no plural*) the seventh planet from the sun ସୌର ମଣ୍ଡଳର ସପ୍ତମ ଗ୍ରହ (ସୂର୍ଯ୍ୟଙ୍କ ଠାରୁ) ➪ ଚିତ୍ର ପାଇଁ **solar system** ଦେଖନ୍ତୁ।

urban /ɜːbən/ *adjective* of a town or city ସହର ସମ୍ବନ୍ଧୀୟ; ସହରର *urban areas* ➪ **rural** ଦେଖନ୍ତୁ।

urge /ɜːdʒ/ *verb* (**urges, urging, urged**) try hard to make somebody do something ପ୍ରରୋଚିତ କରିବା, ପ୍ରୋତ୍ସାହିତ କରିବା, ବାଧ୍ୟ କଲାପରି ଅନୁରୋଧ କରିବା *I urged him to stay for dinner.*

urge *noun* a strong feeling that you want to do something ପ୍ରବଳ ଇଚ୍ଛାଶକ୍ତି *I had a sudden urge to laugh.*

urgent /ɜːdʒənt/ *adjective* so important that you must do it or answer it quickly ଜରୁରୀ, ଅତି ପ୍ରୟୋଜନୀୟ *The doctor received an urgent telephone call.*

urgently *adverb* ଜରୁରୀ ଭାବରେ, ଅତି ଶୀଘ୍ର *I must see you urgently.*

us / əs/ *pronoun* (*plural*) me and another person or other people; me and you ଆମେ *We were pleased when she invited us to dinner.*

use[1] /juːz/ *verb* (**uses, using, used**) do a job with something ବ୍ୟବହାର କରିବା; ବ୍ୟବହୃତ ହେବା *Could I use your telephone?* ○ *Wood is used to make paper.*

use up use something until you have no more ବ୍ୟବହାର କରି ଶେଷ କରିବା *I've used up all the coffee, so I need to buy some more.*

use[2] /juːz/ *noun* **1** (*no plural*) the action of using something ବ୍ୟବହାର; ବ୍ୟବହାର କରିବା ପ୍ରକ୍ରିୟା *This pool is for the use of club members only.* **2** (*plural* **uses**) a purpose for which you use something ପ୍ରୟୋଗ, ଉପଯୋଗ *This tool has many uses.*

used[1] /juːzd/ *adjective* not new ପୁରୁଣା, ବ୍ୟବହୃତ *The garage sells used cars.*

used[2] /juːzd/ *adjective*

be used to something know something well because you have seen, heard, tasted or done it before *I'm used to walking because I haven't got a car.*

get used to something begin to know something well after a time ଅଭ୍ୟସ୍ତ ହେବା *I'm getting used to my new job.*

used to *modal verb* words that tell us about something that happened often or that was true in the past ଅତୀତରେ ଅଭ୍ୟସ୍ତ ଥିବା *I used to be afraid of dogs, but now I like them.* ➪ **modal verbs** ପାଇଁ ଟିପ୍ପଣୀ ଦେଖନ୍ତୁ ।

useful /ˈjuːsfl/ *adjective* good and helpful for doing something ଉପକାରୀ, ଦରକାରୀ *This bag will be useful for carrying my books.*

useless /ˈjuːsləs/ *adjective* not good for anything ଅଦରକାରୀ; ଅବ୍ୟବହାର ଯୋଗ୍ୟ *A car is useless without petrol.*

user /ˈjuːzə(r)/ *noun* a person who uses something ବ୍ୟବହାର କରୁଥିବା ବ୍ୟକ୍ତି *computer users*

user-friendly *adjective* easy to use and understand ସୁବିଧାରେ ବ୍ୟବହାର କରି ହେଉଥିବା *user-friendly computer programs*

usual /ˈjuːʒuəl/ *adjective* that happens most often ରୀତିମତ *It's not usual for children in Delhi to go to school on Saturdays.* ✪ ବିପରୀତ **unusual**

as usual as it happens most often ଅଭ୍ୟାସଗତ ଭାବେ, ପୂର୍ବପରି *Kajal was late, as usual.*

usually *adverb* ସାଧାରଣତଃ *We usually go to our grandparents' home for our holidays, but this year we are staying at home.*

utensil /juːˈtensl/ *noun* a container that is usually used in the kitchen ବାସନକୁସନ, ରାନ୍ଧିବା ପାତ୍ର

utilize /ˈjuːtəlaɪz/ *verb* (**utilizes, utilizing, utilized**) use a thing for doing something ବ୍ୟବହାର କରିବା, ବିନିଯୋଗ କରିବା, କାମରେ ଲଗାଇବା *Her students utilized their time well to complete their essays on time.*

utter[1] /ˈʌtə(r)/ *adjective* complete ସମ୍ପୂର୍ଣ୍ଣ, ଏକଦମ୍, ପୂରା *The room was in* *utter darkness and I couldn't see anything.*

utterly *adverb* completely or very ସମ୍ପୂର୍ଣ୍ଣ ଭାବରେ, ଏକେବାରେ, ପୂରାପୂରି *That's utterly impossible!*

utter[2] /ˈʌtə(r)/ *verb* (**utters, uttering, uttered**) say something or make a sound with your mouth କହିବା, ଉଚ୍ଚାରଣ କରିବା *He uttered a cry of pain.*

V v

V /viː/ *symbol* the number 5 in Roman numerals ରୋମାନ୍ ସଂଖ୍ୟା ୫

v, vs *abbreviation* ଶବ୍ଦ **versus** ର ସଂକ୍ଷିପ୍ତ ରୂପ *India v Sri Lanka* ○ *St Anthony School vs Kadambini School*

vacancy /ˈveɪkənsi/ *noun* (*plural* **vacancies**) a job that is available for somebody to do ଖାଲିଥିବା ଚାକିରି *We have a vacancy for a music teacher in our school.*

vacant /ˈveɪkənt/ *adjective* empty; with nobody in it ଶୂନ୍ୟ, ଖାଲି, ନିର୍ଜନ, କେହି ନଥିବା *a vacant house*

vacation /vəˈkeɪʃn/ *noun* **1** a holiday time when a university, school, court etc. is not open ଛୁଟିଦିନ, (ସ୍କୁଲ, କଲେଜ, କୋର୍ଟ ଇତ୍ୟାଦିର) ଛୁଟି ସମୟ *the summer vacation* **2** holiday ଅବକାଶ

vaccinate /ˈvæksɪneɪt/ *verb* (**vaccinates, vaccinating, vaccinated**) give a person or an animal a **vaccine** to protect them against a disease ରୋଗ ପ୍ରତିଷେଧକ ଟିକା ଦେବା

vaccination /ˌvæksɪˈneɪʃn/ *noun* the process of protecting a person or an animal against a disease with the help of a **vaccine** ଟିକା ଦାନ କାମ *vaccination against polio*

vaccine /ˈvæksiːn/ *noun* a substance that is given to a person or an animal to protect them from a disease (ରୋଗ ପ୍ରତିଷେଧକ) ଟିକା

vacuum /ˈvækjuəm/ *noun* a space with no air, gas or anything else in it କୌଣସି ପଦାର୍ଥ (ଯଥା : ପବନ, ବାଷ୍ପ ଇତ୍ୟାଦି) ନଥିବା ସ୍ଥାନ ବା ଅବସ୍ଥା; ଶୂନ୍ୟତା

vagabond /ˈvægəbɒnd/ *noun* a person without a home or job and who keeps travelling from one place to another ଚାକିରିବାକିରି ଓ ଘରଦ୍ୱାର ନଥିବା ବାରବୁଲା ଲୋକ *beggars and vagabonds sleeping on the pavement*

vague /veɪg/ *adjective* (**vaguer, vaguest**) not clear or not exact ଅସ୍ପଷ୍ଟ; ଅନିର୍ଦ୍ଦିଷ୍ଟ *I couldn't find the house because he gave me very vague directions.*

vaguely *adverb* ଅସ୍ପଷ୍ଟ ଭାବରେ *I vaguely remember what happened.*

vain /veɪn/ *adjective* (**vainer, vainest**) **1** too proud of what you can do or how you look ବୃଥାଗର୍ବୀ, ଅତି ଆତ୍ମାଭିମାନୀ ✪ ଏହାର ବିଶେଷ୍ୟ ପଦ ହେଲା **vanity**। **2** with no success; useless ଅସଫଳ, ତୁଚ୍ଛ *They made a vain attempt to contact him.*

in vain with no success ତୁଚ୍ଛାଟାରେ, ଅସଫଳ ଭାବରେ *I tried in vain to sleep.*

valid /ˈvælɪd/ *adjective* if something like a ticket or a cheque is valid, you can use it and other people will accept it କାର୍ଯ୍ୟକାରୀ, ଉପଯୋଗକ୍ଷମ, ବ୍ୟବହାରଯୋଗ୍ୟ *Your bus ticket is valid for one week.* ✪ ଏହାର ବିଶେଷ୍ୟ ପଦ ହେଲା **validity**।

valley /ˈvæli/ *noun* (*plural* **valleys**) an area of low land between two hills or mountains. A valley usually has a river flowing through it ଦୁଇ ପାହାଡ଼ ମଧ୍ୟସ୍ଥ ସମତଳ ଭୂମି ବା ନଦୀର ପାଣି ବହିଯାଉଥିବା ବିସ୍ତୀର୍ଣ୍ଣ ଅଞ୍ଚଳ; ଉପତ୍ୟକା *the Kashmir Valley*

valour /ˈvælə(r)/ *noun* (*no plural*) bravery; great courage ବୀରତ୍ୱ; ସାହସିକତା

valuable /ˈvæljuəbl/ *adjective* **1** worth a lot of money ମୂଲ୍ୟବାନ, ବହୁମୂଲ୍ୟ *Is this ring valuable?* **2** very useful ଅତି ଦରକାରୀ *valuable information*

value[1] /ˈvælju:/ *noun* **1** (*plural* **values**) the amount of money you can sell something for ମୂଲ୍ୟ, ଦାମ୍ *What is the value of this painting?* **2** (*no plural*) the quality of being useful or important ଉପଯୋଗିତା, ଗୁରୁତ୍ୱ *Their help was of great value.*

value[2] /ˈvælju:/ *verb* (**values, valuing, valued**) **1** think that something is very important ମୂଲ୍ୟବାନ୍ ବା ଗୁରୁତ୍ୱପୂର୍ଣ୍ଣ ବୋଲି ଭାବିବା *I value my freedom.* **2** say how much money something is worth ମୂଲ୍ୟାଙ୍କନ କରିବା, ଦର ନିର୍ଦ୍ଧାରଣ କରିବା *The antique watch was valued at Rs. 40,000.*

valve /vælv/ *noun* a device for controlling the flow of a liquid, air or gas, allowing it to move in one direction only ନଳଦ୍ୱାରା ପ୍ରବାହିତ ତରଳ ପଦାର୍ଥ ବା ବାଷ୍ପ ଗୋଟିଏ ପଟକୁ ଛାଡ଼ିବା ପାଇଁ ନଳରେ ଲଗା ଯାଇଥିବା ଉପକରଣ; ଭାଲ୍‌ଭ୍ *a radiator valve* ○ *valve of the heart*

van /væn/ *noun* a kind of big car or small lorry for carrying things ବଡ଼ କାର୍; ମାଲବାହୀ ଛୋଟ ବସ୍ ପରି ଗାଡ଼ି

vane /veɪn/ *noun* a thin, flat blade that is part of a machinery like a windmill or a fan ୱିଣ୍ଡ୍‌ମିଲ୍ (ବାୟୁଚାଳିତ) ପଙ୍ଖାକଳ ର ଡେଣା; ପଙ୍ଖାର ଡେଣା *the wooden vanes of the windmill*

vanilla /vəˈnɪlə/ *noun* (*no plural*) a substance used to add a special flavour to some foods, for example ice cream ଖାଦ୍ୟରେ ମିଶାଯାଉଥିବା ଭ୍ୟାନିଲା ଫଳର ସୁଗନ୍ଧ ଥିବା ପଦାର୍ଥ

vanish /ˈvænɪʃ/ *verb* (**vanishes, vanishing, vanished**) go away suddenly; disappear ହଠାତ୍ ଅନ୍ତର୍ଦ୍ଧାନ ବା ଅଦୃଶ୍ୟ ହେବା, ଉଭାନ୍ ହେବା *The thief ran into the crowd and vanished.*

vapour /ˈveɪpə(r)/ *noun* a gas that forms when you heat a liquid (ତରଳ ପଦାର୍ଥର) ବାଷ୍ପ, ବାମ୍ଫ, ଜଳୀୟ ବାଷ୍ପ *When you boil water, it changes into water vapour.*

variable[1] /ˈveəriəbl/ *adjective* that keeps changing ପରିବର୍ତ୍ତନଶୀଳ, ଅସ୍ଥିର *variable temperature*

variable[2] /ˈveəriəbl/ *noun* a situation, number or quantity that can change or be changed ପରିବର୍ତ୍ତିତ ହୋଇ ପାରୁଥିବା ଉପାଦାନ (ପରିସ୍ଥିତି, ସଂଖ୍ୟା ବା ପରିମାଣ)

variation /ˌveəriˈeɪʃn/ *noun* **1** a change or difference from the normal or usual ସାଧାରଣ ଅବସ୍ଥାରୁ ପରିବର୍ତ୍ତନ ବା ଭିନ୍ନତା *variations in the quality of paper* **2** a thing that is slightly different from the usual or normal ସାଧାରଣ ପ୍ରକାରରୁ ଭିନ୍ନ ହୋଇଥିବା ପଦାର୍ଥ *She tried the new variation of mango ice cream.*

varied, varies ଶବ୍ଦ **vary** ର ଧାତୁରୂପ

varied /ˈveərid/ *adjective* having different types of things, people, etc. in a way that is interesting ବିଭିନ୍ନ ପ୍ରକାରର *a varied selection of short stories*

variety /vəˈraɪəti/ *noun* **1** (*no plural*) if something has variety, it is full of different things or changes often ଭିନ୍ନ ଭିନ୍ନ ପ୍ରକାର, ନାନା ପ୍ରକାର *There's a wide variety of flowers you can choose from.* **2** (*plural* **varieties**) a kind of something that is different from others of the same kind (କୌଣସି ପଦାର୍ଥର) ଏକ ପ୍ରକାର *This variety of apple is very sweet.*

various /ˈveəriəs/ *adjective* many different ବିଭିନ୍ନ, ନାନାବିଧ, ବହୁ ପ୍ରକାରର *We sell this shirt in various colours and sizes.*

varnish /ˈvɑːnɪʃ/ *noun* (*no plural*) a clear paint with no colour, that you put on metal, wood, etc. to make it shine ଧାତୁ, କାଠ ଇତ୍ୟାଦି ଉପରେ ଲଗା ଯାଉଥିବା ଏକ ସ୍ୱଚ୍ଛ ଚକଚକିଆ ପ୍ରଲେପ ।

vary /ˈveəri/ *verb* (**varies, varying, varied, has varied**) be or become different from each other ପରିବର୍ତ୍ତିତ ହେବା, ପରିବର୍ତ୍ତନ କରିବା; ଭିନ୍ନ ଭିନ୍ନ ମାନ ବା ଦରର ହେବା *These tapes vary in price from Rs 40 to Rs 200.*

vase /vɑːz/ *noun* a pot into which you put cut flowers ଫୁଲଦାନି

vast /vɑːst/ *adjective* very big ଖୁବ୍‌ବଡ଼, ପ୍ରଶସ୍ତ *Australia is a vast country.*

vegetable /ˈvedʒtəbl/ *noun* a plant or part of a plant that we eat as food. Potatoes, carrots and beans are vegetables ପନିପରିବା, ପରିବା *vegetable soup*

vegetarian /ˈvedʒəˈteəriən/ *noun* a person who does not eat meat or fish ଆମିଷ ଖାଉନଥିବା ଲୋକ, ଶାକାହାରୀ ବ୍ୟକ୍ତି, ନିରାମିଶାଷି ବ୍ୟକ୍ତି

vehicle /ˈviːəkl/ *noun* anything that carries people or things from one place to another. Cars, buses and bicycles are all vehicles ଯାନବାହାନ

vein /veɪn/ *noun* one of the small tubes that carry blood from differ-

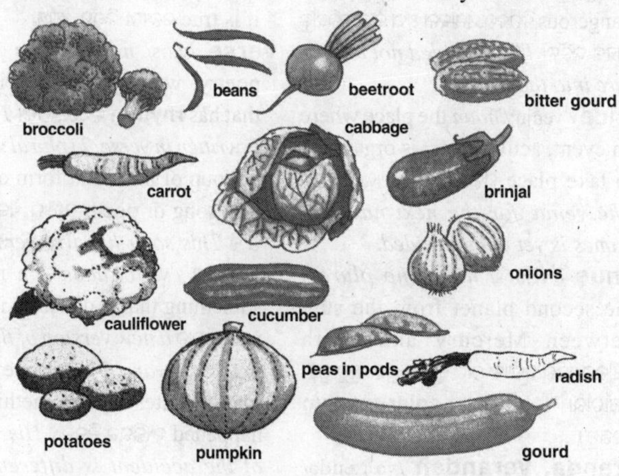

vegetables

ent parts of your body to your heart ଶରୀରର ବିଭିନ୍ନ ଅଙ୍ଗରୁ ହୃତପିଣ୍ଡକୁ ରକ୍ତ ବହନ କରୁଥିବା ଶିରା, ନାଡ଼ି ➪ **artery** ଦେଖନ୍ତୁ।

velvet /ˈvelvɪt/ *noun* (*no plural*) a cloth that is soft and thick on one side ଗୋଟେ ପଟ ନରମ ଓ ରୁମରୁମିଆ ହୋଇଥିବା କନା *red velvet curtains*

ventilate /ˈventɪleɪt/ *verb* (**ventilates, ventilating, ventilated**) allow air to move in and out a room, building, etc. (ଗୃହମଧ୍ୟରେ) ମୁକ୍ତ ଭାବରେ ବାୟୁ ସଞ୍ଚାଳନ କରିବା *ventilate the room*

ventilation /ˌventɪˈleɪʃn/ *noun* (*no plural*) the free movement of air in and out of a room or building (ଗୃହ ମଧ୍ୟରେ) ମୁକ୍ତ ବାୟୁ ସଞ୍ଚାଳନ *Rooms should have large windows for proper ventilation.*

venture /ˈventʃə(r)/ *verb* (**ventures, venturing, ventured**) do something which is new and could be dangerous ବିପଦର ସମ୍ଭାବନା ଥିବା କାମ କରିବାକୁ ସାହସ କରିବା *They decided not to venture into the water.*

venue /ˈvenjuː/ *noun* the place where an event, activity, etc. is organized to take place ଘଟଣା ବା କାର୍ଯ୍ୟକ୍ରମର ସ୍ଥଳ *The venue for the next national games is yet to be decided.*

Venus /ˈviːnəs/ *noun* (*no plural*) the second planet from the sun, between Mercury and Earth ସୌରମଣ୍ଡଳର ସୂର୍ଯ୍ୟଙ୍କ ଠାରୁ ଦ୍ୱିତୀୟ ଗ୍ରହ, ଶୁକ୍ର ଗ୍ରହ, କୁଆଁତାରା ➪ ଚିତ୍ର ପାଇଁ **solar system** ଦେଖନ୍ତୁ।

veranda, verandah /vəˈrændə/ *noun* a platform joined to the side of a house. Verandas usually have a roof and are open on the front ବାରନ୍ଦା, ବାରଣ୍ଡା *We often have our tea on the veranda.*

verb /vɜːb/ *noun* a word that tells you what somebody or something is or does. 'Go', 'sing', 'happen' and 'be' are all verbs (ବ୍ୟାକରଣରେ) କ୍ରିୟା

verdict /vɜːdɪkt/ *noun* the decision that the **jury** in a court of law takes at the end of a **trial**; a judgement (ମକଦ୍ଦମାରେ) ଜ୍ୟୁରିଙ୍କ ସିଦ୍ଧାନ୍ତ ବା ନିଷ୍ପତ୍ତି, ବିଚାରପତିଙ୍କ ରାୟ

verify /ˈverɪfaɪ/ *verb* (**verifies, verifying, verified, has verified**) check if something is true ସତ୍ୟତା, ବା ସଠିକତା ନିର୍ଣ୍ଣୟ କରିବା, ଯାଞ୍ଚ କରିବା

verification /ˌverɪfɪˈkeɪʃn/ *noun* (*no plural*) the act of checking and inspecting something to find out if it is true ସତ୍ୟତା ନିର୍ଣ୍ଣୟ, ଯାଞ୍ଚ

verse /vɜːs/ *noun* **1** (*no plural*) poetry; writing arranged in lines that has **rhythm** କବିତା, ପଦ୍ୟ *The play is written in verse.* **2** (*plural* **verses**) a group of lines that form one part of a song or poem ପଦ୍ୟର ଏକ ଅଂଶ ବା ପଂକ୍ତି *This song has five verses.*

version /ˈvɜːʃn/ *noun* **1** a form of something that is different in some way ପ୍ରକାର *a new version of the computer software* **2** what one person says or writes about something that happened ବ୍ୟକ୍ତିଗତ ବିବରଣ *His version of the accident is different from mine.*

versus /ˈvɜːsəs/ *preposition* on the other side in a sport; against ବନାମ, ବିପକ୍ଷରେ (ଖେଳିବା ମକଦ୍ଦମାରେ) *There's a good football match on TV tonight—England versus Brazil.* ✪ Versus ର ସଂକ୍ଷିପ୍ତ ରୂପ ହେଲା ବା **vs, v**।

vertebrate /ˈvɜːtɪbrət/ *noun* an animal that has a backbone to support its body ମେରୁଦଣ୍ଡ ଥିବା *Fish, reptiles, birds and mammals are vertebrates.* ✪ ବିପରୀତ **invertebrate**

vertical /ˈvɜːtɪkl/ *adjective* something that is vertical goes straight up, not from side to side ଭୂପୃଷ୍ଠରୁ ଭୂଲମ୍ବ ଭାବେ ଉପରକୁ ଉଠିଥିବା; ଭୂଲମ୍ବ, ଉର୍ଦ୍ଧ୍ୱାଧାର *a vertical line* ⇨ **horizontal** ଦେଖନ୍ତୁ।

very /ˈveri/ *adverb* you use 'very' before another word to make it stronger ଖୁବ୍, ଖୁବ୍ ବେଶି *Delhi is a very big city.* ○ *She speaks very softly.* ○ *I like chocolate very much.* ○ *I'm not very hungry.*

vessel /ˈvesl/ *noun* **1** a large ship or boat ବଡ଼ ଜାହାଜ ବା ନୌକା **2** a metal container for keeping liquids ତରଳ ପଦାର୍ଥ ରଖିବା ଧାତୁ ପାତ୍ର

vest /vest/ *noun* a piece of clothing that you wear under your other clothes on the top part of your body ଦେହର ଉପର ଭାଗରେ ପିନ୍ଧାଯାଉଥିବା ଭିତର ଜାମା, ଗେଞ୍ଜି

vet

vet /vet/, **veterinary surgeon** *noun* a doctor for animals ପଶୁଡାକ୍ତର, ପଶୁଚିକିତ୍ସକ

via /ˈvaɪə/ *preposition* **1** going through a place ବାଟେ, ବାଟଦେଇ *We flew from Delhi to Kolkata via Patna.* **2** by using something ଜରିଆରେ, ଦ୍ୱାରା, ରେ *I sent the letter via speed post.*

vibrate /vaɪˈbreɪt/ *verb* (**vibrates, vibrating, vibrated**) move very quickly from side to side or up and down କମ୍ପିତ ହେବା, ଥରିବା *The house vibrates every time a train goes past.*

vibration /vaɪˈbreɪʃn/ *noun* କମ୍ପନ *You can feel the vibrations from the engine when you are in the car.*

vice /vaɪs/ *noun* a bad habit or immoral quality in somebody ଖରାପ ବା ମନ୍ଦ ଗୁଣ, ଦୁର୍ଗୁଣ; ଅନୈତିକ ଅଭ୍ୟାସ *the vices of greed and jealousy* ⇨ **virtue** ଦେଖନ୍ତୁ।

> **vice-** *prefix*
>
> ପଦ ବା ମହତ୍ତ୍ୱରେ ଦ୍ୱିତୀୟ ସ୍ଥାନ ଦର୍ଶାଯାଉଥିବା ଉପସର୍ଗ— *The vice-captain leads the team when the captain is ill.* ○ *the vice-president*

victim /ˈvɪktɪm/ *noun* a person or an animal that is hurt or killed by somebody or something ନିପୀଡ଼ିତ ବ୍ୟକ୍ତି; ଶିକାର; ଦୁର୍ଦ୍ଦଶାଗ୍ରସ୍ତ ବା ମୃତ ବ୍ୟକ୍ତି, ହତାହତ ବ୍ୟକ୍ତି *The victims of the car accident were taken to hospital.*

victorious /vɪkˈtɔːriəs/ *adjective* successful in winning a battle, competition, etc. ଜୟଯୁକ୍ତ, ବିଜୟୀ *the victorious team*

victory /ˈvɪktəri/ *noun* (*plural* **victories**) success in a fight, game or war (ଯୁଦ୍ଧ, ଖେଳ ଇତ୍ୟାଦିର) ବିଜୟ, ସଫଳତା ✪ ବିପରୀତ **defeat**

video /ˈvɪdiəʊ/ *noun* (*plural* **videos**) **1** (**video recorder** ମଧ୍ୟ) a machine that puts television programmes on tape, so that you can watch them later ଟେଲିଭିଜନ କାର୍ଯ୍ୟକ୍ରମ ଇତ୍ୟାଦି ଟେପ୍‌ରେ ରେକର୍ଡ଼ କରି ରଖିପାରୁଥିବା ଯନ୍ତ୍ର *Have you got a video?* **2** tape in a box (called a **cassette**) that you put into a video recorder to show films, for example ଚଳଚ୍ଚିତ୍ର ବା ଗୀତ କ୍ୟାସେଟ୍ (ଯାହା ଟେଲିଭିଜନ୍ ମାଧ୍ୟମରେ ଘରେ ଦେଖାଯାଇ ପାରେ) *We stayed at home and watched a video.*

view /vjuː/ *noun* **1** what you can see from a certain place ଦୃଶ୍ୟ *There is a beautiful view of the mountains from our window.* **2** what you believe or think about something (କୌଣସି ବିଷୟରେ) ମତ, ବିଶ୍ୱାସ *What are your views on marriage?*

viewer /ˈvjuːə(r)/ *noun* **1** a person who watches television ଟେଲିଭିଜନ୍ ଦେଖଣାହାରୀ **2** a person who looks at something ଦର୍ଶକ

vigorous /ˈvɪgərəs/ *adjective* strong, active and full of energy ବଳିଷ୍ଠ, ସକ୍ରିୟ, ତେଜସ୍ୱୀ *vigorous exercises*

vigorously *adverb* ଜୋରରେ, ଉତ୍ସାହରେ *She shook my hand vigorously.*

village /ˈvɪlɪdʒ/ *noun* a small place in the countryside where people live. A village is smaller than a town ଗାଁ, ଗ୍ରାମ, ପଲ୍ଲୀ *a village in the mountains*

villager *noun* a person who lives in a village ଗ୍ରାମବାସୀ

villain /ˈvɪlən/ *noun* a bad person, usually in a book, play or film ଅନିଷ୍ଟସାଧକ ମନ୍ଦ ପ୍ରକୃତିର ବ୍ୟକ୍ତି; (ବହି, ନାଟକ, ସିନେମା ଇତ୍ୟାଦିର) ଖଳନାୟକ

vine /vaɪn/ *noun* a plant that grapes grow on ଅଙ୍ଗୁର ଲତା, ଦ୍ରାକ୍ଷାଲତା

vinegar /ˈvɪnɪgə(r)/ *noun* (*no plural*) a liquid with a strong sharp taste. You put it on food and use it for cooking (ଖାଦ୍ୟ ବା ରନ୍ଧନରେ ବ୍ୟବହୃତ) ଏକ ତୀବ୍ର ଅଠାଳିଆ ତରଳ ପଦାର୍ଥ, ଭିନେଗାର୍ *I added some oil and vinegar to the pieces of mango to make the pickle.*

violent /ˈvaɪələnt/ *adjective* a person or thing that is violent is very strong and dangerous and hurts people or damages things ହିଂସାତ୍ମକ (ବ୍ୟକ୍ତି); ପ୍ରଚଣ୍ଡ, ପ୍ରବଳ (ଘଟଣା) *a violent man* ○ *a violent storm*

violence /ˈvaɪələns/ *noun* (*no plural*) the act of being violent ହିଂସା, ହିଂସ୍ର ଆଚରଣ *Do you think there's too much violence on TV?*

violently *adverb* ହିଂସ୍ର ଭାବରେ; ତୀବ୍ର ଭାବରେ *Did she behave violently towards you?*

violet /ˈvaɪələt/ *noun* a small purple flower ନୀଳ-ବାଇଗଣୀ ରଙ୍ଗର ଏକ ଛୋଟ ଫୁଲ

violet *adjective* with a purple colour ନୀଳ-ବାଇଗଣୀ ରଙ୍ଗର *She wore a violet dress.*

violin /ˌvaɪəˈlɪn/ *noun* a musical instrument made of wood, with strings across it. You play a violin with a **bow** (ବାଦ୍ୟଯନ୍ତ୍ର) ବେହେଲା । ➪ ଚିତ୍ର ପାଇଁ **musical instrument** ଦେଖନ୍ତୁ ।

VIP /ˌviː aɪ ˈpiː/ *noun* a person who is famous or important ଅତି ବିଶିଷ୍ଟ ବ୍ୟକ୍ତି *The Prime Minister is a VIP.* ✪ VIP ର ବିସ୍ତୃତ ରୂପ ହେଲା **very important person**।

Virgo /ˈvɜːgəʊ/ *noun* the sixth sign of the **zodiac** ରାଶିଚକ୍ରର ଷଷ୍ଠରାଶି, କନ୍ୟାରାଶି

virtual /ˈvɜːtʃuəl/ *adjective* **1** being almost like or very near to what is being described ପ୍ରାୟତଃ, ବସ୍ତୁତଃ, କାର୍ଯ୍ୟତଃ; ପ୍ରକୃତ ନ ହେଲେବି ପ୍ରକୃତ ବ୍ୟକ୍ତି ବା ପଦାର୍ଥ ପରି *the virtual leader of the party* **2** made to appear or exist by using computer technology କମ୍ପ୍ୟୁଟର୍ ଦ୍ୱାରା ସୃଷ୍ଟ ବାସ୍ତବତା *a virtual classroom*

virtually *adverb* almost ପ୍ରାୟ *The two boys look virtually the same.*

virtue /ˈvɜːtʃuː/ *noun* **1** (*plural* **virtues**) a good habit or a high moral quality in somebody ଭଲଗୁଣ; ସାଧୁତା, ସଚ୍ଚୋଟତା ଇତ୍ୟାଦି ଗୁଣ *She possesses the virtues of patience and tolerance.* **2** (*no plural*) the condition of possessing high moral standards ଉଚ୍ଚ ନୈତିକ ମାନ *lead a life of virtue* ➪ **vice** ଦେଖନ୍ତୁ।

virus[1] /ˈvaɪrəs/ *noun* (*plural* **viruses**) a very small living thing that can make you ill ରୋଗଜନକ ଅତି ସୂକ୍ଷ୍ମ ଜୀବାଣୁ, ଭୂତାଣୁ *a flu virus*

virus[2] /ˈvaɪrəs/ *noun* (*plural* **viruses**) a program that is put into a computer to stop it from working properly or to destroy information that it contains କମ୍ପ୍ୟୁଟର୍ ପ୍ରୋଗ୍ରାମ୍ ମଧ୍ୟକୁ ଅବୈଧ ଭାବରେ ଛଡ଼ା ଯାଉଥିବା ଏକ ସ୍ୱୟଂ ସଂକ୍ରମିତ କୋଡ୍ ବା ପ୍ରୋଗ୍ରାମ୍ ଯାହା କମ୍ପ୍ୟୁଟର୍‌ର କାର୍ଯ୍ୟକ୍ରମ ଓ ଏଥିରେ ଗଚ୍ଛିତ ତଥ୍ୟ ନଷ୍ଟ କରିଦିଏ; କମ୍ପ୍ୟୁଟର୍ ଭାଇରସ୍

visa /ˈviːzə/ *noun* a special piece of paper or mark in your passport to show that you can go into a country କୌଣସି ଦେଶରେ ପ୍ରବେଶ କରିବା ପାଇଁ ପାସ୍‌ପୋର୍ଟ୍‌ରେ ଦିଆଯାଉଥିବା ଅନୁମତି

visible /ˈvɪzəbl/ *adjective* if something is visible, you can see it ଦେଖାଯାଉଥିବା, ଦୃଶ୍ୟମାନ *Stars are visible only at night.* ✪ ବିପରୀତ **invisible**

vision /ˈvɪʒn/ *noun* **1** (*no plural*) the power to see; sight ଦୃଷ୍ଟିଶକ୍ତି; ଦୃଶ୍ୟ *He wears glasses because he has poor vision.* **2** (*plural* **visions**) a picture or an idea that you have in your mind; a dream or plan that somebody has for a better future ମାନସିକ ଚିତ୍ର; ସ୍ୱପ୍ନରେ ଦେଖାଥିବା ଦୃଶ୍ୟ; ଉତ୍ତମ ଭବିଷ୍ୟତର ମାନସିକ ପରିକଳ୍ପନା *They have a vision of a world without war.*

visit /ˈvɪzɪt/ *verb* (**visits, visiting, visited**) go to see a person or place for a short time ଅଳ୍ପ ସମୟ ପାଇଁ କାହାରି ସାଙ୍ଗେ ଦେଖା କରିବାକୁ ଯିବା ବା କୌଣସି ସ୍ଥାନ ପରିଦର୍ଶନ କରିବା *She visited me in hospital.* ○ *Have you ever visited the Golden Temple in Amritsar?*

visit *noun* ପରିଦର୍ଶନ *This is my first visit to Bhubaneswar.*

pay somebody a visit go to see somebody କାହାରି ସାଙ୍ଗେ ଦେଖା କରିବାକୁ ଯିବା

visitor /ˈvɪzɪtə(r)/ *noun* a person who goes to see another person or a place for a short time ଅତିଥି; ଭ୍ରମଣକାରୀ *The old lady never has any visitors.* ○ *Thousands of visitors come to Jaipur every year.*

visual /ˈvɪʒuəl/ *adjective* of or about seeing ଆଖିରେ ଦେଖି ପାରିଲା ଭଳି; ଦୃଷ୍ଟି ସଂକ୍ରାନ୍ତ

Painting and cinema are visual arts.

vital /ˈvaɪtl/ *adjective* very important; that you must have or do ଅତି ପ୍ରୟୋଜନୀୟ, ଖୁବ୍ ଦରକାରୀ *It's vital that she see a doctor—she's very ill.*

vitamin /ˈvɪtəmɪn/ *noun* one of the things in food that you need to be healthy ଜୀବସାର, ଭିଟାମିନ୍ ବା ଭାଇଟାମିନ୍ *Oranges are full of vitamin C.*

vivid /ˈvɪvɪd/ *adjective* **1** with a strong bright colour ଉଜ୍ଜ୍ୱଳ ରଙ୍ଗର *vivid yellow* **2** that makes a very clear picture in your mind (ଭାବନା, ବର୍ଣ୍ଣନା ବା ଅନୁଭୂତି) ସୁସ୍ପଷ୍ଟ, ସତେଜ *I had a very vivid dream last night.*

vividly *adverb* ସ୍ପଷ୍ଟ ଭାବରେ *I remember my first day at school vividly.*

vixen /ˈvɪksn/ *noun* (*plural* **vixens**) a female fox ମାଈ କୋକିଶିଆଳି

vocabulary /vəˈkæbjələri/ *noun* (*plural* **vocabularies**) **1** all the words that somebody knows or uses ବ୍ୟକ୍ତି ଜାଣିଥିବା ଶବ୍ଦସମୂହ **2** all the words in a certain language ଭାଷାରେ ଥିବା ଶବ୍ଦସମୂହ **3** a list of words along with their meanings at the end of a lesson or book ବହି ଇତ୍ୟାଦିର ଶେଷରେ ଦିଆଯାଇଥିବା ଶବ୍ଦ ତାଲିକା ଓ ଶବ୍ଦାର୍ଥ *We have to learn this new vocabulary for homework.*

vocal /ˈvəʊkl/ *adjective* to do with the voice କଣ୍ଠସ୍ୱର ସମ୍ବନ୍ଧୀୟ, କଣ୍ଠସ୍ୱର ଦ୍ୱାରା ଉଚ୍ଚାରିତ *vocal music*

voice /vɔɪs/ *noun* the sounds that you make when you speak or sing କଣ୍ଠସ୍ୱର *Ratan has a very deep voice.*

at the top of your voice very loudly ଖୁବ୍ ବଡ଼ ପାଟିରେ *'Come here!' she shouted at the top of her voice.*

raise your voice speak very loudly ବଡ଼ ପାଟିରେ କହିବା

volcano /vɒlˈkeɪnəʊ/ *noun* (*plural* **volcanoes** ବା **volcanos**) a mountain with a hole at the top (called **crater**) through which fire, gas and hot liquid rock (called **lava**) sometimes come out ଆଗ୍ନେୟଗିରି *an active volcano*

volcanic *adjective* ଆଗ୍ନେୟଗିରି ସମ୍ବନ୍ଧୀୟ; ଆଗ୍ନେୟଗିରିରୁ ନିସୃତ *volcanic rocks*

volcano

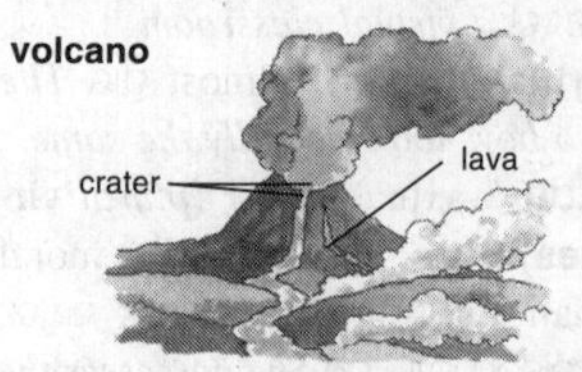

volleyball /ˈvɒlibɔːl/ *noun* (*no plural*) a game where two teams of six players try to hit a ball over a high net with their hands ଭଲିବଲ୍ ଖେଳ

volume /ˈvɒljuːm/ *noun* **1** (*no plural*) the amount of space that something fills, or the amount of space inside something କୌଣସି ବସ୍ତୁ ଦ୍ୱାରା ଅଧିକୃତ ସ୍ଥାନ ବା ଏଥିରେ ସମାହିତ ସ୍ଥାନ; ଆୟତନ *What is the volume of this box?* **2** (*no plural*) the amount of sound that something makes ଧ୍ୱନିର ପ୍ରବଳତା *I can't hear the radio. Can you turn the volume up?* **3** (*plural* **volumes**) a book, especially one of a set ବହିର ଏକ ଖଣ୍ଡ ବା ଗ୍ରନ୍ଥାବଳୀର ଏକ ଖଣ୍ଡ *That dictionary is in five volumes.*

voluntary /ˈvɒləntri/ *adjective* **1** if something is voluntary, you do it because you want to, not because you must ସ୍ୱେଚ୍ଛାକୃତ, ସ୍ୱତଃପ୍ରବୃତ୍ତ *She made a voluntary decision to leave the job.* **2** if work is voluntary, you are not paid to do it ଟଙ୍କା ପଇସା ନ ନେଇ ଇଚ୍ଛାକୃତ ଭାବେ କରାଯାଇଥିବା *He does voluntary work at a children's hospital.* ✪ ବିପରୀତ **involuntary**

voluntarily /ˈvɒləntrəli/ *adverb* because you want to, not because you must ସ୍ୱତଃ ପ୍ରବୃତ୍ତ ଭାବେ, ନିଜ ଇଚ୍ଛାରେ *She left the job voluntarily.*

volunteer /ˌvɒlənˈtɪə(r)/ *verb* (**volunteers, volunteering, volunteered**) say that you are willing to do something କିଛି କାମ କରିବା ପାଇଁ ସ୍ୱଇଚ୍ଛାରେ ଆଗେଇ ଆସିବା *I volunteered to do the dusting.*

volunteer *noun* a person who volunteers to do a job ସ୍ୱେଚ୍ଛାସେବକ ବା ସ୍ୱେଚ୍ଛାସେବିକା *They're asking for volunteers to help with the distribution of food.*

vomit /ˈvɒmɪt/ *verb* (**vomits, vomiting, vomited**) when someone vomits, food comes up from their stomach and out of their mouth ବାନ୍ତି କରିବା ✪ ସାଧାରଣତଃ ବାକ୍ୟାଂଶ **be sick** ର ପ୍ରୟୋଗ କରାଯାଏ ।

vote /vəʊt/ *verb* (**votes, voting, voted**) choose somebody or something by putting up your hand or writing on a piece of paper ଭୋଟ୍‌ଦେବା, ମତଦାନ କରିବା *Who did you vote for in the election?*

vote *noun* ଭୋଟ୍‌ଦାନ, ମତଦାନ, ଦିଆଯାଇଥିବା ଭୋଟ୍ *There were 96 votes for the plan, and 25 against.*

voter *noun* a person who votes ଭୋଟ୍‌ଦାତା, ଭୋଟ ଦେବାର ଅଧିକାରଥିବା ବ୍ୟକ୍ତି

vow /vaʊ/ *noun* a serious promise ପ୍ରତିଜ୍ଞା, ଶପଥ, ସଂକଳ୍ପ *take a vow*

vowel /ˈvaʊəl/ *noun* one of the letters *a*, *e*, *i*, *o* or *u*, or the sound that you make when you say it ସ୍ୱରବର୍ଣ୍ଣ ➪ **consonant** ଦେଖନ୍ତୁ ।

voyage /ˈvɔɪɪdʒ/ *noun* a long journey by boat or in space ଲମ୍ବା ଜଳଯାତ୍ରା; ମହାକାଶ ଯାତ୍ରା *a voyage from Mumbai to London*

vs ଶବ୍ଦ **versus** ର ସଂକ୍ଷିପ୍ତ ରୂପ

vulture /ˈvʌltʃə(r)/ *noun* a large bird with no feathers on its head or neck. It eats dead animals ଶାଗୁଣା, ଗୃଧ୍ର

W w

wade /weɪd/ *verb* (**wades, wading, waded**) walk through shallow water or mud with a lot of effort ପାଣି କାଦୁଅ ଇତ୍ୟାଦିରେ କଷ୍ଟରେ ଚାଲି ଚାଲି ଯିବା *Can we wade across the river, or is it too deep?*

wafer /ˈweɪfə(r)/ *noun* a thin light crisp biscuit ଏକ ପ୍ରକାର ଅତି ପତଳା ଓ ହାଲୁକା ବିସ୍କୁଟ୍

wag /wæg/ *verb* (**wags, wagging, wagged**) move or make something move from side to side or up and down (କୁକୁର ଲାଞ୍ଜ ହଲାଇଲା ପରି) ହଲିବା ବା ହଲାଇବା *My dog's tail wags when he's happy.*

wages /weɪdʒɪz/ *noun* (*plural*) the money that someone receives regularly for the work that they do ମଜୁରି, ପାରିଶ୍ରମିକ *low wages*

wagon /ˈwægən/ *noun* **1** a vehicle with four wheels that a horse pulls ଘୋଡ଼ା ଟଣା ଚାରିଚକିଆ ଗାଡ଼ି **2** a part of a train in which things like coal are carried ରେଳଗାଡ଼ିର ମାଲବୁହା ଡବା

wail /weɪl/ *verb* (**wails, wailing, wailed**) make a long sad cry or noise ଦୁଃଖରେ ବହୁ ସମୟ ରଡ଼ିଛାଡ଼ି କାନ୍ଦିବା *The little boy started wailing for his mother.*

waist /weɪst/ *noun* the part around the middle of your body ଅଣ୍ଟା ➪ ଚିତ୍ର ପାଇଁ **body** ଦେଖନ୍ତୁ।

wait[1] /weɪt/ *verb* (**waits, waiting, waited**) stay in one place until something happens or until somebody or something comes ଅପେକ୍ଷା କରିବା *If I'm late, please wait for me.* ○ *We've been waiting a long time.*

keep somebody waiting make somebody wait because you are late or busy କାହାରିକୁ ଅପେକ୍ଷା କରାଇବା *The doctor kept me waiting for half an hour.*

wait[2] /weɪt/ *noun* a time when you wait ଅପେକ୍ଷା *We had a long wait for the bus.*

waiter /ˈweɪtə(r)/ *noun* a man who brings food and drink to your table in a restaurant ଭୋଜନାଳୟରେ ବରାଦ ନେଇ ଖାଇବା ପିଇବା ଆଣୁଥିବା ବ୍ୟକ୍ତି; ପରିବେଷକ, ୱେଟର୍ ➪ **waitress** ଦେଖନ୍ତୁ।

waiting room *noun* a room where people can sit and wait, for example to see a doctor or to catch a train ବିଶ୍ରାମାଗାର, ଅପେକ୍ଷାଗାର

waitress /ˈweɪtrəs/ *noun* (*plural* **waitresses**) a woman who brings food and drink to your table in a restaurant ଭୋଜନାଳୟରେ ବରାଦ ନେଇ ଖାଇବାପିଇବା ଆଣୁଥିବା ମହିଳା, ପରିବେଷିକା ➪ **waiter** ଦେଖନ୍ତୁ।

wake /weɪk/ *verb* (**wakes, waking, woke** /wəʊk/, **has woken** /ˈwəʊkən/) **1** stop sleeping ନିଦରୁ ଉଠିବା *What time did you wake up this morning?* **2** make somebody stop sleeping ନିଦରୁ ଉଠାଇବା *The noise woke me up.* ○ *Don't wake the baby.* ✪ ସାଧାରଣତଃ ବାକ୍ୟାଂଶ **wake up** ର ପ୍ରୟୋଗ କରାଯାଏ।

walk[1] /wɔːk/ *verb* (**walks, walking, walked**) move on your legs, but not run ଚାଲିବା, ପଦଚାରଣ କରିବା *I usually walk to work.* ○ *We walked four kilometres today.*

walk² /wɔ:k/ *noun* a journey on foot ପଦଯାତ୍ରା *The beach is a short walk from our house.* ○ *I took the dog for a walk.*

go for a walk walk somewhere because you enjoy it ବୁଲିବା ପାଇଁ ଚାଲି ଚାଲି ଯିବା *It was a lovely day, so we went for a walk in the park.*

walker /ˈwɔ:kə(r)/ *noun* a person who walks or is walking ଚାଲିବା ବ୍ୟକ୍ତି ବା ଚାଲିଚାଲି ଯାଉଥିବା ବ୍ୟକ୍ତି

wall /wɔ:l/ *noun* **1** a side of a building or room କାନ୍ଥ *There's a picture on the wall.* ➪ ଚିତ୍ର ପାଇଁ **house** ଦେଖନ୍ତୁ। **2** a thing made of stones or bricks around a garden, field or town, for example ପାଚେରୀ *There's a high wall around the school.*

wallet /ˈwɒlɪt/ *noun* a small flat case for paper money, etc. that you can carry in your pocket ପକେଟ୍‌ରେ ରଖି ହେଲାପରି ଟଙ୍କାପଇସା ରଖିବା ଥଳି, ପର୍ସ, ୱାଲେଟ୍

wallpaper /ˈwɔ:lpeɪpə(r)/ *noun* (*no plural*) special paper that you use for covering the walls of a room ଘରର ଭିତର କାନ୍ଥରେ ଲଗାଯାଉଥିବା ଏକ ବିଶେଷ ପ୍ରକାରର କାଗଜ, ୱାଲ୍‌ପେପର୍

walnut /ˈwɔ:lnʌt/ *noun* a light-brown nut that grows inside a hard shell କଠିନ ଆବରଣ ଥିବା ଖାଇବାଯୋଗ୍ୟ ବାଦାମ୍, ଅଖରୋଟ୍ ➪ ଚିତ୍ର ପାଇଁ **nut** ଦେଖନ୍ତୁ।

walrus /ˈwɔ:lrəs/ *noun* (*plural* **walruses**) a large animal with two long outer teeth, that lives in the Arctic region ଉତ୍ତରମେରୁ ସାଗରର ଦୁଇଟି ଲମ୍ବା ଦାନ୍ତଥିବା ସ୍ତନ୍ୟପାୟୀ ଜୀବ, ୱାଲ୍‌ରସ୍

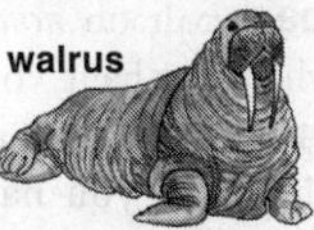
walrus

wander /ˈwɒndə(r)/ *verb* (**wanders, wandering, wandered**) walk slowly with no special plan ଉଦ୍ଦେଶ୍ୟହୀନ ଭାବରେ ବୁଲିବା *We wandered around the town until the shops opened.*

want /wɒnt/ *verb* (**wants, wanting, wanted**) **1** wish to have or do something (କୌଣସି ଜିନିଷ ପାଇବା ପାଇଁ ବା କୌଣସି କାମ କରିବା ପାଇଁ) ଇଚ୍ଛା କରିବା *Do you want a chocolate?* ○ *I want to go to Italy.* ○ *She wanted me to give her some money.* ✪ ଭଦ୍ରଭାବରେ କାହାକୁ କିଛି ଦେବାପାଇଁ ପଚାରିଲା ବେଳେ **'would like'** ର ପ୍ରୟୋଗ କରାଯାଏ। *Would you like a cup of tea?* **2** need something କିଛି ଦରକାର କରିବା *Your car wants a wash!*

war /wɔ:(r)/ *noun* a situation or time when two or more countries or groups of people are fighting ଯୁଦ୍ଧ, ସମର *the First World War.*

at war fighting ଯୁଦ୍ଧରତ, ଯୁଦ୍ଧ କରୁଥିବା ଅବସ୍ଥାରେ *The two countries have been at war for five years.*

ward /wɔ:d/ *noun* a big room in a hospital that has beds for patients ବହୁ ରୋଗୀଙ୍କ ପାଇଁ ଶଯ୍ୟାଥିବା ଡାକ୍ତରଖାନାର ବଡ଼ ପ୍ରକୋଷ୍ଠ

warden /ˈwɔ:dn/ *noun* a person whose job is to look after a place and the people in it ଭାରପ୍ରାପ୍ତ

ତତ୍ତ୍ୱାବଧାରକ, ୱାର୍ଡେନ୍ *the warden of a youth hostel*

wardrobe /ˈwɔːdrəʊb/ *noun* **1** a cupboard where you hang your clothes ଲୁଗାପଟା ରଖିବା ଆଲମାରି **2** a collection of clothes that you have ବ୍ୟକ୍ତିଙ୍କ ବସ୍ତ୍ରଭଣ୍ଡାର

warehouse /ˈweəhaʊs/ *noun* a big building where people keep things before they sell them ମାଲଗୋଦାମ *a furniture warehouse*

warm[1] /wɔːm/ *adjective* (**warmer, warmest**) **1** a little hot ଅଳ୍ପ ଗରମ୍, ଉଷ୍ମ *It's warm by the fire.* **2** that keeps you warm in cold weather ଗରମ (ଲୁଗା) *It's cold in Srinagar, so take some warm clothes with you.* **3** friendly and kind (ବ୍ୟବହାର) ହାର୍ଦ୍ଦିକ, ଉତ୍ସାହପୂର୍ଣ୍ଣ *My aunt is a very warm person.*

warm[2] /wɔːm/ *verb* (**warms, warming, warmed**)

warm up become warmer, or make somebody or something warmer ଗରମ ହେବା; ଗରମ କରିବା *I warmed up some soup for dinner.*

warm-blooded *adjective* an animal that is warm-blooded has a body temperature that does not change with the temperature of the surroundings ବାହାର ଉତ୍ତାପ ସହ ଦେହର ଉତ୍ତାପ ବଦଳୁ ନଥିବା (ପଶୁ); ସମୋଷ୍ଣ ରକ୍ତଧାରୀ *Birds and mammals are warm-blooded animals.* ✪ ବିପରୀତ **cold-blooded**

warmly /ˈwɔːmli/ *adverb* in a friendly way ହାର୍ଦ୍ଦିକ ଭାବେ *He thanked me warmly.* ✪ ବିପରୀତ **coldly**

warmth /wɔːmθ/ *noun* (*no plural*) **1** heat ଉଷ୍ମତା *the warmth of the sun* **2** friendliness and kindness ସୌହାର୍ଦ୍ଦ୍ୟ, ସ୍ନେହ *the warmth of his smile*

warn /wɔːn/ *verb* (**warns, warning, warned**) tell somebody about danger or about something bad that may happen (ଆସନ୍ନ ବିପଦ ବିଷୟରେ) ସତର୍କ କରିବା, ସାବଧାନ କରିବା *I warned him not to go too close to the fire.*

warning *noun* something that warns you ବିପଦ ସଂକେତ *There is a warning on every electricity pole.*

warrant /ˈwɒrənt/ *noun* a legal document that gives the police the authority to do something (ପୁଲିସ୍‌କୁ ଦିଆଯାଇଥିବା) ଅଧିକାରପତ୍ର *an arrest warrant*

warrior /ˈwɒriə(r)/ *noun* a soldier ସୈନିକ; ଯୋଦ୍ଧା

wary /ˈweəri/ *adjective*

wary of somebody or **something** careful because somebody or something might be dangerous or harmful ସତର୍କ, ସାବଧାନ *She told her son to be wary of strangers.*

was ଶବ୍ଦ **be** ର ଏକ ଧାତୁରୂପ

wash[1] /wɒʃ/ *verb* (**washes, washing, washed**) clean somebody, something or yourself with water ଧୋଇବା, ସଫା କରିବା *Have you washed the car?* ○ *Wash your hands before you eat.* ○ *He washes his clothes everyday.*

wash up clean the plates, knives, forks, etc. after a meal ବାସନପତ୍ର ମାଜିବା *I washed up after dinner.*

wash[2] /wɒʃ/ *noun* (*no plural*) the act of cleaning something with water ଧୋଇ ସଫା କରିବା କାମ *I gave the car a wash.*

have a wash wash yourself ଧୁଆଧୋଇ ହେବା *I had a quick wash.*

washbasin /ˈwɒʃbeɪsn/ *noun* a large bowl that has taps and is fixed to a wall, usually in the bathroom. This is used for washing your hands and face in ହାତମୁହଁ ଧୋଇବା ପାଇଁ କାନ୍ଥରେ ଲଗାଯାଇଥିବା କଳଲଗା ଆଧାର, ୱାସବେସିନ୍

washing /ˈwɒʃɪŋ/ *noun* (*no plural*) clothes that you need to wash or that you have washed ଧୁଆ ହେବାପାଇଁ ଥିବା ଲୁଗାପଟା; ଧୁଆଯାଇଥିବା ଲୁଗାପଟା *Shall I hang the washing outside to dry?* ○ *I've done the washing.*

washing machine *noun* (*plural* **washing machines**) a machine that washes clothes ଲୁଗାକଚା ଯନ୍ତ୍ର, ୱାଶିଂମେଶିନ୍

washing powder *noun* (*no plural*) soap powder for washing clothes ଲୁଗାଧୁଆ ସାବୁନଗୁଣ୍ଡ

wasn't = **was not**

wasp /wɒsp/ *noun* a small yellow and black insect that flies and can sting people ବିରୁଡ଼ି

wastage /ˈweɪstɪdʒ/ *noun* (*no plural*) the use of something in a careless way; the amount of something that is wasted କିଛି ଦ୍ରବ୍ୟର ଖାମଖିଆଲି ବ୍ୟବହାର; ନଷ୍ଟ ହୋଇଥିବା ଦ୍ରବ୍ୟର ପରିମାଣ

waste¹ /weɪst/ *verb* (**wastes, wasting, wasted**) use too much of something or not use something in a good way କିଛି ଦ୍ରବ୍ୟ ବେଶୀ ପରିମାଣରେ ବ୍ୟବହାର କରି ନଷ୍ଟ କରିବା *She wastes a lot of money on clothes she doesn't need.* ○ *He wasted his time in the evening—he didn't do any work.*

waste² /weɪst/ *noun* (*no plural*) **1** the act of not using something in a good way କ୍ଷୟ, ନଷ୍ଟପ୍ରାପ୍ତି *It's a waste to throw away all this food!* **2** things that people throw away because they are not useful ନଷ୍ଟ ଦ୍ରବ୍ୟ *A lot of waste from the factories goes into this river.*

waste³ /weɪst/ *adjective* that you do not want because it is not useful ନଷ୍ଟ ହୋଇଥିବା; ଅଦରକାରୀ

waste-paper basket *noun* (*plural* **waste-paper baskets**) a container in which you put things like paper that you do not want ଅଦରକାରୀ କାଗଜ ପକାଇବା ପାତ୍ର

watch¹ /wɒtʃ/ *noun* (*plural* **watches**) a thing that shows what time it is. You wear a watch on your wrist ହାତପିନ୍ଧା ଘଣ୍ଟା, ୱାଚ୍ ➪ **clock** ଠାରେ ଟିପ୍ପଣୀ ଦେଖନ୍ତୁ। ➪ ଚିତ୍ର ପାଇଁ **dial** ଦେଖନ୍ତୁ।

watch² /wɒtʃ/ *verb* (**watches, watching, watched**) look at somebody or something for some time to understand or know more about them ଜଗିବା, ସତର୍କ ଦୃଷ୍ଟି ରଖିବା *We watch that programme about birds on television every evening.* ○ *Watch how I do this.*

watch out be careful because of somebody or something dangerous (ବିପଦ ପାଇଁ) ସାବଧାନ ରହିବା *Watch out! There's a car coming.*

watch out for somebody or **something** look carefully, and be ready, for somebody or something dangerous କୌଣସି ବ୍ୟକ୍ତି, ବସ୍ତୁ ବା ଘଟଣା ପାଇଁ ସଜାଗ ରହିବା; ବିପଦର ସମ୍ମୁଖୀନ ହେବାକୁ ପ୍ରସ୍ତୁତ ରହିବା *Watch out for pieces of broken glass on the roads.*

watch³ /wɒtʃ/ *noun* (*no plural*) **keep watch** the action of looking out for danger (ବିପଦା ପାଇଁ) ଜଗି ରହିବା *The guard kept watch at the gate.*

watchman /ˈwɒtʃmən/ *noun* (*plural* **watchmen**) the person whose job is to guard a house, building or factory ଜଗୁଆଳି, ପ୍ରହରୀ

water¹ /ˈwɔːtə(r)/ *noun* (*no plural*) the clear liquid that falls as rain and is in rivers, lakes and seas. We use it for drinking, washing, etc. ପାଣି, ଜଳ

water² /ˈwɔːtə(r)/ *verb* (**waters, watering, watered**) give water to plants ଗଛରେ ପାଣି ଦେବା *Have you watered the plants?*

watercolour /ˈwɔːtəkʌlə(r)/ *noun* **1 watercolours** (*plural*) paints that are mixed with water, not oil, to make pictures ଚିତ୍ର ଆଙ୍କିବା ପାଇଁ ପାଣିରେ ମିଶା ଯାଉଥିବା ରଙ୍ଗ, ପାଣିରଙ୍ଗ **2** a picture that you make with these paints ପାଣିଘୋଳା ରଙ୍ଗରେ ଅଙ୍କିତ ଚିତ୍ର

waterfall /ˈwɔːtəfɔːl/ *noun* a place where a stream or river falls from a high place to a low place ଜଳପ୍ରପାତ

waterlogged /ˈwɔːtəlɒgd/ *adjective* an area that is waterlogged is so full of water that it cannot be used ଜଳମଗ୍ନ, ଜଳପୂର୍ଣ୍ଣ (ଅଞ୍ଚଳ) *waterlogged roads*

watermelon /ˈwɔːtəmelən/ *noun* a big round fruit with a thick green skin. It is red inside with a lot of black seeds ତରଭୁଜ ➪ ଚିତ୍ର ପାଇଁ **fruit** ଦେଖନ୍ତୁ।

waterproof /ˈwɔːtəpruːf/ *adjective* if something is waterproof, it does not let water go through it ଜଳରୋଧୀ, ଜଳରୋଧକ *a waterproof jacket*

water vapour *noun* the gas that is formed when water is heated ଜଳୀୟବାଷ୍ପ

wave¹ /weɪv/ *verb* (**waves, waving, waved**) **1** move your hand from side to side in the air to say hello or goodbye or to make a sign to somebody ହାତ ହଲାଇବା *She waved to me as the train left the station.* ○ *Who are you waving at?* **2** move up and down or from side to side ଦୋଳାୟିତ ହେବା *The flags were waving in the wind.*

wave² /weɪv/ *noun* **1** one of the raised lines of water that moves across the surface of the sea ଢେଉ, ତରଙ୍ଗ **2** a movement of your hand from side to side in the air, to say hello or goodbye or to make a sign to somebody (ଶୁଭେଚ୍ଛା ଜଣାଇବାକୁ ବା ବିଦାୟ ଦେବାପାଇଁ) ହାତ ହଲାଇବା କାମ **3** a gentle curve in hair ବାଳର ଢେଉ ବା କୁଞ୍ଚ **4** a movement like a wave on the sea, that carries heat, light, sound, etc. (ଉତ୍ତାପ, ଆଲୋକ, ଶବ୍ଦ ଇତ୍ୟାଦି) ତରଙ୍ଗ *radio waves*

wavy /ˈweɪvi/ *adjective* (**wavier, waviest**) something that is wavy has gentle curves in it ତରଙ୍ଗାୟିତ *She has wavy black hair.*

wax /wæks/ *noun* (*no plural*) a substance that is used for making candles ମହମ

way /weɪ/ *noun* **1** (*plural* **ways**) a road or path that you must follow to go to a place ବାଟ, ରାସ୍ତା, ପଥ, ମାର୍ଗ *Can you tell me the way to the station, please?* ○ *I lost my way and I had to look at the map.* **2** (*plural* **ways**) a direction, where somebody or something is going or looking ବାଟ, ଦିଗ, ଆଡ଼ *Come this way.* ○ *She was looking the other way.* **3** (*no plural*) the distance between two places ଦୂରତା, ଦୂରତ୍ୱ *It's a long way from Kashmir to Tamil Nadu.* **4** (*plural* **ways**) the method or style in which you do something ଶୈଳୀ, ଢଙ୍ଗ; ଉପାୟ, ପ୍ରଣାଳୀ *What is the best way to learn a language?*

give way break ଭାଙ୍ଗିଯିବା *The ladder gave way and the boy fell to the ground.*

give way to somebody or **something** stop and let somebody or something go before you ବାଟ ଛାଡ଼ିଦେବା *You must give way to traffic coming from the right.*

in the way in front of somebody so that you stop them from seeing something or moving ପ୍ରତିବନ୍ଧକ ବା ବାଧା ସୃଷ୍ଟି କରୁଥିବା *I couldn't see the television because Maya was in the way.*

on the way during the time when you are going somewhere ଯାଉଥିବା, ଅଗ୍ରସର ହେଉଥିବା *I stopped to have a drink on the way to the playground.*

out of the way not in a place where you stop somebody from moving or doing something ବାଟ ଛାଡ଼ିଦେବା, ବାଧା ଦେଉନଥିବା *Get out of the way! There's a car coming!*

way in the way to go into a building ପ୍ରବେଶ ଦ୍ୱାର *Here's the museum. Where's the way in?*

way of life the way people live ଜୀବନଶୈଳୀ, ଜୀବନଯାପନ ପ୍ରଣାଳୀ *Is the way of life in India different from that in America?*

way out the way to go out of a place ପ୍ରସ୍ଥାନ ପଥ *I can't find the way out.*

we /wiː/ *pronoun* (*plural*) I and another person or other people; you and I ଆମେ *John and I went out last night—we went to the theatre.* ○ *Are we late?*

weak /wiːk/ *adjective* (**weaker, weakest**) **1** not powerful or strong ଦୁର୍ବଳ *She felt very weak after her long illness.* ○ *a weak government* **2** that can break easily ଭାଙ୍ଗିପଡ଼ିବା ଅବସ୍ଥାରେ ଥିବା *The bridge was closed because it was too weak to carry heavy traffic.* **3** that you cannot see, taste, smell, hear or feel clearly ଅସ୍ପଷ୍ଟ (ଭଲଭାବରେ ଦିଶୁ ନଥିବା, ଚାଖି ବା ଶୁଙ୍ଘି ଜାଣି ହେଉନଥିବା, ଶୁଣି

ହେଉନଥିବା, ସ୍ପର୍ଶକରି ଜାଣି ହେଉନଥିବା) *weak light sound* ✪ ବିପରୀତ **strong**

weaken /ˈwi:kən/ *verb* (**weakens, weakening, weakened**) become less strong or make somebody or something less strong ଦୁର୍ବଳ ହେବା ବା କରିବା *He was weakened by the illness.* ✪ ବିପରୀତ **strengthen**

weakness /ˈwi:knəs/ *noun* **1** (*no plural*) the quality of not being strong ଦୁର୍ବଳତା *I have a feeling of weakness in my legs.* **2** (*plural* **weaknesses**) something that is wrong or bad in a person or thing (ଚରିତ୍ରର) ଦୁର୍ବଳତା ବା ଖରାପ ଗୁଣ ✪ ବିପରୀତ **strength**

wealth /welθ/ *noun* (*no plural*) a lot of money, land, etc. that someone has ଧନସମ୍ପତ୍ତି *He is a man of great wealth.*

wealthy *adjective* (**wealthier, wealthiest**) rich ଧନୀ *a wealthy family*

weapon /ˈwepən/ *noun* a thing that you use for fighting. Guns and swords are weapons ଅସ୍ତ୍ରଶସ୍ତ୍ର

wear¹ /weə(r)/ *verb* (**wears, wearing, wore** /wɔ:(r)/, **has worn** /wɔ:n/) have clothes, etc. on your body (ଲୁଗାପଟା, ଗହଣାପତ୍ର, ଇତ୍ୟାଦି) ପିନ୍ଧିବା *She was wearing a red dress.* ○ *I wear glasses.*

wear off become less strong ତୀବ୍ରତା କମିଯିବା; (ରଙ୍ଗ ଇତ୍ୟାଦି) ଛାଡ଼ିଯିବା *The pain is wearing off.*

wear out become thin or damaged because you have used it a lot; make something do this ବ୍ୟବହାର ଦ୍ୱାରା କ୍ଷୀଣ ବା ନଷ୍ଟ ହେବା; ଏହିପରି କରାଇବା *Children's shoes usually wear out very quickly.*

wear² /weə(r)/ *noun* (*no plural*) clothes for a particular purpose ବିଶେଷ ଉଦ୍ଦେଶ୍ୟରେ ବା ବିଶେଷ ଲୋକଙ୍କ ଦ୍ୱାରା ପିନ୍ଧିବା ପାଇଁ ଉଦ୍ଦିଷ୍ଟ ପୋଷାକ *sportswear* ○ *children's wear*

weary /ˈwɪəri/ *adjective* very tired because you have been working hard or doing something for a long time କ୍ଳାନ୍ତ, ଶ୍ରାନ୍ତ

weather /ˈweðə(r)/ *noun* (*no plural*) the amount of sunshine, rain, wind, etc. there is at a certain time, or how hot or cold it is ପାଣିପାଗ, ପାଗ *What was the weather like in Spain?* ○ *bad weather*

weave /wi:v/ *verb* (**weaves, weaving, wove** /wəʊv/, **has woven** /ˈwəʊvn/) make cloth by putting threads over and under one another on a **loom** ତନ୍ତରେ ଲୁଗା ବୁଣିବା, ବୟନ କରିବା *These scarves are woven in Jammu.*

weaver /ˈwi:və(r)/ *noun* a person who weaves cloth ତନ୍ତି, ବୟନକାରୀ, ଲୁଗା ବୁଣିବା ବ୍ୟକ୍ତି

web /web/ *noun* a thin net that a spider makes to catch insects ବୁଢ଼ିଆଣୀ ଜାଲ

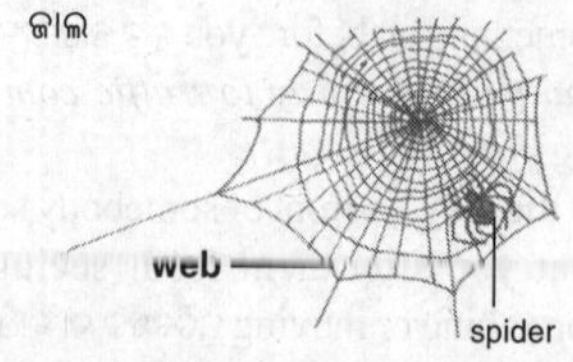

Web /web/ *noun* ➪ **world wide web** ଦେଖନ୍ତୁ ।

webbed /webd/ *adjective* an animal or a bird that has webbed feet has pieces of skin between its toes ପଦାଙ୍ଗୁଳି ମଝିରେ ସୂକ୍ଷ୍ମ ଚର୍ମ ବା ଝିଲ୍ଲୀଥିବା (ପଶୁ ବା ପକ୍ଷୀ) ➪ ଚିତ୍ର ପାଇଁ **goose** ଦେଖନ୍ତୁ ।

website /ˈwebsaɪt/ *noun* a place on the **web** where a company or an organization puts information about itself ୱେବ୍ ବା କମ୍ପ୍ୟୁଟର୍, ଇଣ୍ଟରନେଟ୍‌ରେ ଥିବା ସ୍ଥାନ ଯେଉଁଠାରେ କୌଣସି ସଂସ୍ଥା ନିଜ ବିଷୟରେ ସମସ୍ତ ତଥ୍ୟ ଅନ୍ୟମାନେ ଜାଣିବା ପାଇଁ ଲେଖି ରଖିଥାନ୍ତି; ୱେବ୍‌ସାଇଟ୍

wedding /ˈwedɪŋ/ *noun* a time when a man and a woman get married ବିବାହ, ବାହାଘର *Abdul and Rashida invited me to their wedding.* ○ *a wedding dress*

we'd **1** = **we had** **2** = **we would**

Wednesday /ˈwenzdeɪ/ *noun* the third day of the week, next after Tuesday ବୁଧବାର

weed /wi:d/ *noun* a wild plant that grows where you do not want it ବଣୁଆ ଘାସଗୁଳ୍ମ *The garden of the old house was full of weeds.*

week /wi:k/ *noun* **1** a time of seven days, either from Monday to Sunday or from Sunday to Saturday ସପ୍ତାହ *I'm going on holiday next week.* ○ *I play tennis twice a week.* ○ *I saw him two weeks ago.* ✪ **Fortnight** ହେଲା ଦୁଇ ସପ୍ତାହ କାଳ ବା ଏକ ପକ୍ଷ । **2** Monday to Friday or Monday to Saturday (କାମ କରିବାର ଦିନ) ସୋମବାରରୁ ଶୁକ୍ରବାର ବା ସୋମବାରରୁ ଶନିବାର *I work during the week but not on weekends.*

weekday /ˈwi:kdeɪ/ *noun* any day except Saturday and Sunday ଶନିବାର ଓ ରବିବାର ଛଡ଼ା ଅନ୍ୟ ଦିନ *I only work on weekdays.*

weekend /ˌwi:kˈend/ *noun* Saturday and Sunday ଶନିବାର ଓ ରବିବାର *What are you doing at the weekend?*

weekly /ˈwi:kli/ *adjective*, *adverb* that happens or comes every week or once a week ସାପ୍ତାହିକ *a weekly magazine*

weep /wi:p/ *verb* (**weeps, weeping, wept** /wept/, **has wept**) cry କାନ୍ଦିବା ✪ ଆମେ ସାଧାରଣତଃ **cry** ବ୍ୟବହାର କରୁ ।

weigh /weɪ/ *verb* (**weighs, weighing, weighed**) **1** measure how heavy somebody or something is, using a machine called **scales** ଓଜନ କରିବା *The shopkeeper weighed the tomatoes.* **2** have a certain amount of weight (ନିର୍ଦ୍ଦିଷ୍ଟ) ଓଜନର ହେବା *'How much do you weigh?' 'I weigh 55 kilos.'*

weight /weɪt/ *noun* **1** (*no plural*) the measure of how heavy somebody or something is ଓଜନ *Do you know the weight of the parcel?* **2** (*plural* **weights**) a piece of metal that you use on **scales** for measuring how heavy something is ଓଜନ କରିବାର ବଟକରା

lose weight become thinner and less heavy ଓଜନ କମିବା

put on weight become fatter and heavier ଓଜନ ବଢ଼ିବା

weird /wɪəd/ *adjective* (**weirder, weirdest**) very strange ଅଦ୍ଭୁତ *a weird dream*

welcome[1] /ˈwelkəm/ *adjective* if somebody or something is welcome, you are happy to have or see them ସାଦରେ ଗ୍ରହଣ କରୁଥିବା, ସ୍ୱାଗତ କରୁଥିବା, ଇପ୍ସିତ *The cool drink was welcome on such a hot day.*

be welcome to be allowed to do or have something ସ୍ୱାଗତ କରିବା, କିଛି କରିବା ପାଇଁ ଖୁସିରେ ଛାଡ଼ିଦେବା *If you come to Kochi again, you're welcome to stay with us.*

you're welcome polite words that you say when somebody has said 'thank you' ଧନ୍ୟବାଦ ପାଇଲା ପରେ ଦିଆ ଯାଉଥିବା ଶିଷ୍ଟ ଉତ୍ତର *'Thank you.' 'You're welcome.'*

welcome[2] /ˈwelkəm/ *verb* (**welcomes, welcoming, welcomed**) show that you are happy to have or see somebody or something ସ୍ୱାଗତ କରିବା, ପାଛୋଟି ଆଣିବା *He came to the door to welcome us.*

welcome *noun* ସ୍ୱାଗତ, ସାଦର ଅଭ୍ୟର୍ଥନା *They gave us a warm welcome when we arrived.*

welfare /ˈwelfeə(r)/ *noun* (*no plural*) the health and happiness of a person (ବ୍ୟକ୍ତି, ଗୋଷ୍ଠୀ ବା ସମାଜର) ମଙ୍ଗଳ, ସୁସ୍ୱାସ୍ଥ୍ୟ ଓ ସୁଖ *The school looks after the welfare of its students.*

well[1] /wel/ *adjective* (**better, best**) healthy; not ill ସୁସ୍ଥ, ସନ୍ତୋଷଜନକ *'How are you?' 'I am very well, thanks.'* ✪ ବିପରୀତ **unwell**

well[2] /wel/ *adverb* (**better, best**) **1** in a good or right way ଭଲ ବା ଠିକ୍ ଭାବରେ *You speak English very well.* ○ *These shoes fit her well.* ✪ ବିପରୀତ **badly 2** completely or very much ସମ୍ପୂର୍ଣ୍ଣ ଭାବରେ, ଭଲକରି *I don't know Anurag very well.* ○ *Shake the bottle well before you open it.*

as well as something and also ଆହୁରି ମଧ୍ୟ *She has a flat in Delhi as well as a house in Gurgaon.*

do well be successful ସଫଳ ହେବା, ଭଲ କରିବା *He did well in his exams.*

may or **might as well** words that you use to say that you will do something, often because there is nothing else to do (ଆଉ କିଛି କାମ ନଥିଲେ) ଏ କାମ ମଧ୍ୟ କରିପାର *If you've finished the work, you may as well go home.*

well done! words that you say to somebody who has done something good ଭଲ କାମ ପାଇଁ ପ୍ରଶଂସାସୂଚକ ଅଭିବ୍ୟକ୍ତି, ବାଃ, ବଢ଼ିଆ *'I got the job!' 'Well done!'*

well[3] /wel/ *noun* a deep hole that is dug in the ground for getting water or oil କୂଅ, କୂପ *an oil well*

we'll 1 = **we will 2** = **we shall**

well-known *adjective* famous ସୁପରିଚିତ, ପ୍ରସିଦ୍ଧ *a well-known writer*

well off *adjective* rich ବେଶ୍ ଧନୀ, ସ୍ୱଚ୍ଛଳ *They are very well off and they live in a big house.*

went ଶବ୍ଦ **go** ର ଏକ ଧାତୁରୂପ

wept ଶବ୍ଦ **weep** ର ଏକ ଧାତୁରୂପ

were ଶବ୍ଦ **be** ର ଏକ ଧାତୁରୂପ

we're = **we are**

weren't = **were not**

west /west/ *noun* (*no plural*) where the sun goes down in the evening ପଶ୍ଚିମ ଦିଗ, ସୂର୍ଯ୍ୟାସ୍ତର ଦିଗ *Which way is west?* ○ *They live in the west of the city.* ➪ ଚିତ୍ର ପାଇଁ **north** ଦେଖନ୍ତୁ।

west *adjective, adverb* ପଶ୍ଚିମ, ପଶ୍ଚିମ ଦିଗର, ପଶ୍ଚିମ ଦିଗକୁ *West London* ○ *The town is five kilometres west of here.*

western /'westən/ *adjective* in or of the west of a place ପଶ୍ଚିମ ଦିଗସ୍ଥ *The western parts of the country will be very hot.*

wet /wet/ *adjective* (**wetter, wettest**) **1** covered in water or another liquid; not dry ଓଦା *This towel is wet—can I have a dry one?* ○ *wet paint* **2** with a lot of rain ବହୁତ ବର୍ଷା ହୋଇଥିବା *a wet day* ✪ ବିପରୀତ **dry**[1]

we've = **we have**

whale /weɪl/ *noun* a very big animal that lives in the sea and looks like a fish ତିମି ମାଛ ➪ ଚିତ୍ର ପାଇଁ **mammal** ଦେଖନ୍ତୁ।

what /wɒt/ *pronoun, adjective* **1** a word that you use when you ask about somebody or something ପ୍ରଶ୍ନବାଚକ ଶବ୍ଦ: କଣ; କେଉଁ *What's your name?* ○ *What are you reading?* ○ *What time is it?* ○ *What kind of music do you like?* **2** the thing that କଣ *I don't know what this word means.* ○ *Tell me what to do.* **3** a word that you use to show surprise or other strong feelings ଆଶ୍ଚର୍ଯ୍ୟବାଚକ ଶବ୍ଦ: କ'ଣ ହେଲା ! *What a beautiful picture!*

what about? ... words that you use when you suggest something (ଏ ବିଷୟଟା) କଣ ହେଲା *What about going to the cinema tonight?*

what for? ... why?; for what use? କାହିଁକି, କୋଉ ଉଦ୍ଦେଶ୍ୟରେ *What's this machine for?*

whatever /wɒt'evə(r)/ *adjective* of any kind; any or every ଯେକୌଣସି (ଜିନିଷ), ଯାହାତାହା, ଯାହାକିଛି *He was very hungry, so he ate whatever food he could find.*

whatever *pronoun* **1** anything or everything ଯାହା, ଯାହାକିଛି, ଯାହା ସମ୍ଭବ *I'll do whatever I can to help you.* **2** used to say that it does not matter what ଯାହା ହେଲେ ବି, ସବୁକିଛି ସତ୍ତ୍ୱେ; ଯାହାକିଛି *Whatever you decide, I'll support you.*

what's 1 = **what is** 2 = **what has**

wheat /wi:t/ *noun* (*no plural*) a plant with seeds (called **grain**) that we can make into flour ଗହମ ➪ ଚିତ୍ର ପାଇଁ **grain** ଦେଖନ୍ତୁ।

wheel /wi:l/ *noun* a thing like a circle that turns to move something. Cars and bicycles have wheels ଚକ

wheel *verb* (**wheels, wheeling, wheeled**) push along a thing that has wheels ଚକଲଗା ଗାଡ଼ି ଇତ୍ୟାଦି ଗଡ଼ାଇ ନେବା *I wheeled my bicycle up the hill.*

wheelbarrow /'wi:lbærəʊ/ *noun* a small cart that has a wheel, and two handles that help you to carry things ଜିନିଷପତ୍ର ବା ଅଳିଆ ନେବାପାଇଁ ଏକ ଚକିଆ ଠେଲାଗାଡ଼ି

wheelbarrow

wheelchair /ˈwiːltʃeə(r)/ *noun* a chair with wheels for somebody who cannot walk ଚାଲିପାରୁ ନଥିବା ଲୋକଙ୍କୁ ବସାଇ ନେବାପାଇଁ ଦୁଇଚକିଆ ଚଉକି

when /wen/ *adverb* **1** at what time କେତେବେଳେ, କେବେ *When did she arrive?* ○ *I don't know when his birthday is.* **2** at the time when something happened or happens ଯେତେବେଳେ *I saw her in May, when she was in Chandigarh.*

when *conjunction* at the time that ଯେତେବେଳେ, ସମୟରେ *It was raining when we left school.* ○ *He came when I called him.*

whenever /wenˈevə(r)/ *conjunction* **1** at any time ଯେତେବେଳେ ବି, ଯେ କେଉଁ ସମୟରେ *Come and see us whenever you want.* **2** every time that ଯେତେବେଳେ ବି *Whenever I see her, she talks about movies.*

where /weə(r)/ *adverb, conjunction* **1** in or to what place କୋଉଠି; କେଉଁଠାକୁ; କେଉଁଠାରେ *Where do you live?* ○ *I asked her where she lived.* ○ *Where is she going?* **2** in which; at which ଯୋଉଠି, ଯେଉଁଠାରେ *This is the street where I live.*

whereas /ˌweərˈæz/ *conjunction* a word that you use between two different ideas କିନ୍ତୁ, ପରନ୍ତୁ *Lalit likes travelling, whereas I don't.*

wherever /weərˈevə(r)/ *adverb, conjunction* at, in or to any place ଯୋଉଠି ବି, ଯେକୌଣସି ଜାଗାରେ *Sit wherever you like.*

whether /ˈweðə(r)/ *conjunction* if ଦୁଇଟି ବିକଳ୍ପ ବିଷୟର ସୂଚକ; କି ନାହିଁ *She asked me whether I knew Bengali.* ○ *I don't know whether to go or not.*

which /wɪtʃ/ *adjective, pronoun* **1** what particular person or thing from a group of people or things କେଉଁ *Which colour do you like best—blue or green?* ○ *Which flat do you live in?* **2** a word that shows what particular person or thing ଯୋଉଟା, ଯେଉଁଟା *Did you read the poem (which) Radhika wrote?* **3** a word that you use to say more about something ଯେଉଁଟା, ଯୋଉଟା *Her new dress, which she bought in Mumbai, is beautiful.*

whichever /wɪtʃˈevə(r)/ *adjective, pronoun* any person or thing ଯେଉଁଟାବି; ଯାହାକୁ ବି *Here are two books—take whichever you want.*

while[1] /waɪl/ *conjunction* **1** during the time that; when (କିଛି କରୁଥିବା) ସମୟରେ; ଯେତେବେଳେ, ବେଳେ *The telephone rang while I was having a shower.* **2** at the same time as ଏକା ସମୟରେ, ବେଳେ *I listen to the radio while I'm eating my breakfast.*

while[2] /waɪl/ *noun* (*no plural*) some time କିଛି ସମୟ (ପାଇଁ) *Let's sit here for a while.* ○ *I'm going home in a while.*

whilst /waɪlst/ *conjunction* while ବେଳେ, ସମୟରେ *He waited whilst I looked for my keys.*

whine /waɪn/ *verb* (**whines, whining, whined**) make a long high sad sound (କୁକୁର ବା ଶିଶୁର) କରୁଣ କ୍ରନ୍ଦନ ବା ସେହିପରି ଶବ୍ଦ *The dog was whining outside the door.*

whip /wɪp/ *noun* a long piece of leather or rope with a handle ଚାବୁକ୍, କୋରଡ଼ା

whip *verb* (**whips, whipping, whipped**) **1** hit an animal or a person with a whip ଚାବୁକ୍‌ରେ ପିଟିବା *The rider whipped the horse to make it go faster.* **2** mix food very quickly with a fork, for example, until it is light and thick ଖାଦ୍ୟ ପଦାର୍ଥକୁ ଫେଣ୍ଟିବା ବା ଫେଣେଇବା *Whip up some eggs for the cake.*

whirl /wɜːl/ *verb* (**whirls, whirling, whirled**) move round and round very quickly ଜୋର୍‌ରେ ଘୂରିବା *The dancers whirled round the room.*

whisk /wɪsk/ *verb* (**whisks, whisking, whisked**) mix eggs or cream very quickly with a fork (ଅଣ୍ଡା ଇତ୍ୟାଦି) ଫେଣେଇବା

whisker /ˈwɪskə(r)/ *noun* one of the long hairs that grow near the mouth of cats, mice and other animals ବିଲେଇ ଇତ୍ୟାଦି ପଶୁଙ୍କର ନିଶ

whisky /ˈwɪski/ *noun* (*no plural*) a strong alcoholic drink ଏକ ପ୍ରକାର ମଦ

whisper /ˈwɪspə(r)/ *verb* (**whispers, whispering, whispered**) speak very quietly ଚୁପ୍‌ଚୁପ୍ କରି ବା ଫୁସ୍‌ଫୁସ୍ କରି କଥା କହିବା *He whispered so that he would not wake the baby up.*

whisper *noun* ନିମ୍ନ ସ୍ୱରର କଥାବାର୍ତ୍ତା; ମୃଦୁ ଶବ୍ଦ *She spoke in a whisper.*

whistle /ˈwɪsl/ *noun* **1** a small musical instrument that makes a long high sound when you blow it ସୁସୁରୀ, ହ୍ୱିସ୍ଲ *The referee blew his whistle to end the match.* **2** the long high sound that you make when you blow air out between your lips ଦୁଇ ଓଠ ସାହାଯ୍ୟରେ କରୁଥିବା ଶବ୍ଦ ବା ଧ୍ୱନି, ସିଟି, ସୁସୁରୀ **3** the sound made by something moving rapidly or by steam coming out of a small opening କୌଣସି ଜିନିଷ ଯାହାକି ଛୋଟ ରାସ୍ତା ଦେଇ ଶବ୍ଦ କରିଯାଏ *the whistle of the steam engine*

whistle *verb* (**whistles, whistling, whistled**) **1** make a long high sound by blowing air out between your lips or through a whistle ସିଟି ମାରିବା *She whistled to her dog.* **2** make a sound like something moving rapidly through the air or like steam coming out of a small opening କୌଣସି ଜିନିଷ ପକାଇ ଯାଉଥିବା ଏବଂ ଗୋଟିଏ ଛୋଟ ଜାଗାରୁ ହେଉଥିବା ଶବ୍ଦ *The bullets whistled past him.*

white /waɪt/ *adjective* (**whiter, whitest**) **1** with the colour of snow or milk ଧଳା, ଶ୍ୱେତ, ଶୁଭ୍ର **2** with light-coloured skin ଶ୍ୱେତ ଚର୍ମବିଶିଷ୍ଟ, ଗୋରା

white *noun* **1** (*no plural*) the colour of snow or milk ଧଳାବର୍ଣ୍ଣ *She was dressed in white.* **2** (*plural*

whites) a person with white skin ଗୋରା ଲୋକ

whitewash /ˈwaɪtwɒʃ/ *verb* (**whitewashes, whitewashing, whitewashed**) paint a house or wall white with a mixture of chalk and water ଘର ଧଉଳିବା *They whitewash their house every year.*

who /huː/ *pronoun* **1** which person or people କିଏ *Who is that girl?* ○ *I don't know who did it.* **2** a word that shows which person or people ଯେକି, ଯିଏ; ଯେଉଁମାନେ *He's the boy who invited me to this party.* ○ *The people (who) I met on holiday were very nice.*

who'd **1** = **who had** **2** = **who would**

whoever /huːˈevə(r)/ *pronoun* the person who; any person who ଯେ, ଯିଏ, ଯେ କେହି *Whoever broke the glass must pay for it.*

whole /həʊl/ *adjective* complete; with no parts missing ସମ୍ପୂର୍ଣ୍ଣ, ପୂରା *He ate the whole cake!* ○ *We are going to Cuttack for a whole month.*

whole *noun* (*no plural*) **1** all of something ସମସ୍ତ, ସାରା *I spent the whole of the weekend in bed.* **2** a thing that is complete ସମ୍ପୂର୍ଣ୍ଣ ପଦାର୍ଥ *Two halves make a whole.*

on the whole in general ମୋଟ ଉପରେ, ସବୁ କଥା ବିଚାର କଲାପରେ *On the whole, I think it's a good idea.*

who'll = **who will**

whom /huːm/ *pronoun* **1** which person or people କାହାକୁ *To whom did you give the money?* **2** a word that you use to say which person or people ଯାହାକୁ *She's the woman (whom) I met in Hyderabad.* **whom** ସ୍ଥାନରେ ଆମେ ସଧାରଣତଃ **who** ବ୍ୟବହାର କରୁ

who're = **who are**

who's **1** = **who is** **2** = **who has**

whose /huːz/ *adjective*, *pronoun* of which person କାହାର; ଯାହାର *Whose car is this?* ○ *That's the boy whose sister is a singer.*

who've = **who have**

why /waɪ/ *adverb* for what reason କାହିଁକି, କୋଉଥି ପାଇଁ *Why are you late?* ○ *I don't know why she's angry.*

wicked /ˈwɪkɪd/ *adjective* very bad ଖୁବ ଖରାପ, ଖଳ ପ୍ରକୃତିର *a wicked man*

wicket /ˈwɪkɪt/ *noun* in cricket, a set of three **stumps** with two small pieces of wood (called **bails**) lying across the top କ୍ରିକେଟ୍ ଖେଳରେ ପିଚ୍‌ର ଦୁଇ ପଟେ ପୋତା ଯାଉଥିବା ତିନୋଟି କରି ବାଡ଼ି ବା ଷ୍ଟମ୍ପ ଯାହା ଉପରେ ବେଲ୍ ରଖାଯାଏ, ୱିକେଟ୍

wide /waɪd/ *adjective* (**wider, widest**) **1** far from one side to the other ଚଉଡ଼ା, ପ୍ରଶସ୍ତ *a wide road* ✪ ବିପରୀତ **narrow** ✪ Wide ର ବିଶେଷ୍ୟ ପଦ ହେଲା **width**। **2** you use 'wide' to say or ask how far something is from one side to the other ଚଉଡ଼ା *The table was two metres wide.* ○ *How wide is the river?* **3** completely open ବିସ୍ଫାରିତ, ପୂରା ଖୋଲା *They watched the movie with their eyes wide with fear.*

wide *adverb* completely; as far or as much as possible ବଡ଼ କରି; ଏକେବାରେ *Open your mouth wide.* ○ *I'm wide awake!*

wide apart a long way from each other ପରସ୍ପର ଠାରୁ ବେଶ୍ ଦୂରରେ, ଛଡ଼ା ଛଡ଼ା *She stood with her feet wide apart.*

widely *adverb* **1** in a lot of different places or by a lot of people ବିସ୍ତୃତ ଭାବରେ; ବହୁ ଲୋକଙ୍କ ଦ୍ୱାରା *a widely travelled man* ○ *widely held beliefs* **2** to a large degree ବହୁ ଭାବରେ *views that vary widely*

widen /ˈwaɪdn/ *verb* (**widens, widening, widened**) become wider; make something wider ଚଉଡ଼ା ହେବା; ଚଉଡ଼ା କରିବା *They are widening the road.*

widespread /ˈwaɪdspred/ *adjective* if something is widespread, it is happening in many places ବ୍ୟାପ୍ତ; ବିସ୍ତୃତ *The disease is becoming more widespread.*

widow /ˈwɪdəʊ/ *noun* a woman whose husband is dead ବିଧବା

widower /ˈwɪdəʊə(r)/ *noun* a man whose wife is dead ସ୍ତ୍ରୀ ମରି ଯାଇଥିବା ବ୍ୟକ୍ତି

width /wɪdθ/ *noun* the measure of how far something is from one side to the other; the measure of how wide something is ଓସାର, ପ୍ରସ୍ଥ *The room is five metres in width.*

wife /waɪf/ *noun* (*plural* **wives** /waɪvz/) the woman that a man is married to ପତ୍ନୀ, ସ୍ତ୍ରୀ, ସହଧର୍ମିଣୀ ➪ **husband** ଦେଖନ୍ତୁ। ➪ ଚିତ୍ର ପାଇଁ **family** ଦେଖନ୍ତୁ।

wig /wɪg/ *noun* a covering for your head made of hair that is not your own ପରଚୁଳା, କୃତ୍ରିମ କେଶ

wild /waɪld/ *adjective* (**wilder, wildest**) **1** living or growing in forests, not with people ବଣୁଆ, ଜଙ୍ଗଲି *wild flowers* ○ *wild animals* ✪ ବିପରୀତ **tame 2** excited; not controlled ଅତି ଉତ୍ତେଜିତ, ବିଶୃଙ୍ଖଳ, ଉଚ୍ଛୃଙ୍ଖଳ *She was wild with anger.*

wildly *adverb* ଉଚ୍ଛୃଙ୍ଖଳ ଭାବରେ *She cheered wildly after her school's team won the match.*

wildlife /ˈwaɪldlaɪf/ *noun* (*no plural*) animals birds, insects etc. and plants that are wild and live in forests, not on farms or with people ବନ୍ୟ ପଶୁପକ୍ଷୀ, କୀଟପତଙ୍ଗ ସମୂହ

will[1] /wɪl/ *modal verb* **1** a word that is used for telling that something may happen in the future ଭବିଷ୍ୟତ ବାଚକ ସହାୟକ କ୍ରିୟା *Do you think she will come tomorrow?* **2** a word that you use when you agree or promise to do something ଇଚ୍ଛା ପ୍ରକାଶକ ଶବ୍ଦ *I'll carry your bag.* **3** a word that you use when you ask somebody to do something ପ୍ରଶ୍ନଭାବେ ଅନୁରୋଧ କରୁଥିବା ଶବ୍ଦ *Will you open the window, please?*

> ✪ 'Will' ବିପରୀତ ହେଲା **will not** ଓ ଯାହାର ସଂକ୍ଷିପ୍ତ ରୂପ ହେଲା **won't** — *They won't be there.*
> 'Will' ର ସଂକ୍ଷିପ୍ତ ରୂପ ହେଲା **'ll** ଯାହାର ବ୍ୟବହାର ପ୍ରାୟତଃ କରାଯାଏ —
> *You'll be late.*
> *He'll drive you to the station.*
> ➪ **modal verb** ପାଇଁ ଟିପ୍ପଣୀ ଦେଖନ୍ତୁ।

will² /wɪl/ *noun* **1** (*no plural*) the power of your mind that makes you choose, decide and do things ମାନସିକ ଶକ୍ତି *She has a very strong will and nobody can stop her from doing what she wants to do.* **2** (*no plural*) what somebody wants at a particular time ଇଚ୍ଛା ବା କାମନା *The man made him get into the car against his will.* **3** (*plural* **wills**) a piece of legal paper that says who will have your money, house, etc. when you die *My grandmother left me Rs 20,000 in her will.*

willing /ˈwɪlɪŋ/ *adjective* ready and happy to do something ଇଚ୍ଛୁକ *I'm willing to lend you some money.*
✪ ବିପରୀତ **unwilling**
willingly *adverb* ଇଚ୍ଛୁକ ଭାବରେ, ସ୍ୱଇଚ୍ଛାରେ *I'll willingly help you.*
willingness *noun* (*no plural*) ସମ୍ମତି, ଇଚ୍ଛା *willingness to help*

win /wɪn/ *verb* (**wins, winning, won** /wʌn/, **has won**) **1** be the best or the first in a game, race or competition (ଯୁଦ୍ଧ, ଖେଳ, ଦୌଡ଼ ଇତ୍ୟାଦିରେ) ଜିତିବା, ବିଜୟଲାଭ କରିବା *Who won the race?* ✪ ବିପରୀତ **lose 3** **2** receive something because you did well or tried hard ଉଦ୍ୟମ ଓ ଅଧ୍ୟବସାୟ ଫଳରେ ପାଇବା *I won a prize in the competition.* ○ *Who won the gold medal?*
winning *adjective* that wins a game, race or competition ଜିତିଥିବା, ବିଜୟୀ *the winning team*

wind¹ /wɪnd/ *noun* air that moves ପବନ, ବାୟୁ *The wind blew his hat off.* ○ *strong winds*
windy *adjective* (**windier, windiest**) with a lot of wind ପବନିଆ, ଜୋରରେ ପବନ ବହୁଥିବା *It's very windy today!*

wind² /waɪnd/ *verb* (**winds, winding, wound** /waʊnd/, **has wound**) **1** make something long go round and round another thing ଗୁଡ଼ାଇବା *The nurse wound the bandage around my arm.* **2** turn a key or handle to make something work or move (ଘଣ୍ଟା ଚାବି ଇତ୍ୟାଦି) ମୋଡ଼ିବା, ମୋଡ଼ି କାର୍ଯ୍ୟକାରୀ କରିବା *The clock will stop if you don't wind it up.* ○ *The driver wound his car window down.* **3** a road or river that winds has a lot of bends and turns ଅଙ୍କାବଙ୍କା ହୋଇଯିବା *The path winds through the forest.*
wind something up bring an activity or a meeting to an end ପରିସମାପ୍ତ କରିବା (ସଭା, ବକ୍ତୃତା ଇତ୍ୟାଦି)

windmill /ˈwɪndmɪl/ *noun* a tall building with long flat parts that turn in the wind ବାୟୁଚାଳିତ କଳ, ପବନ ଚକି

window /ˈwɪndəʊ/ *noun* an opening in a wall or in a car, for example, with glass in it ଝରକା *It was cold, so I closed the window.* ➪ ଚିତ୍ର ପାଇଁ **house** ଦେଖନ୍ତୁ।

windowpane /ˈwɪndəʊpeɪn/ *noun* a piece of glass in a window ଝରକା କାଚ

windowsill /ˈwɪndəʊsɪl/, **window ledge** /ˈwɪndəʊledʒ/ *noun* a shelf under a window ଝରକା ଚଉକାଠର ତଳପଟର ଥାକ ପରି ସ୍ଥାନ

windscreen /ˈwɪndskriːn/ *noun* the big window at the front of a car ମଟରଗାଡ଼ିର ଆଗରେ ଥିବା ପବନରୋଧି କାଚ ➪ ଚିତ୍ର ପାଇଁ **car** ଦେଖନ୍ତୁ।

windscreen wiper *noun* a thing that cleans rain and dirt off the windscreen while you are driving ମଟରଗାଡ଼ିର ସାମନା କାଚରୁ ବର୍ଷାପାଣି ପୋଛି ନେବାପାଇଁ ଥିବା ବୈଦ୍ୟୁତିକ ଉପକରଣ

windsurfing /ˈwɪndsɜːfɪŋ/ *noun* (*no plural*) the sport of moving over water on a special board with a sail ସେଲ୍‌ବୋର୍ଡ ବା ପାଲଲଗା ପଟା ଚଢ଼ି ପାଣି ଉପରେ ବିଚରଣ କରିବାର ଖେଳ ✪ ଏହି ଖେଳ ଖେଳିବାକୁ ଯିବାକୁ କହନ୍ତି **go windsurfing** *Have you been windsurfing?*

windsurfer /ˈwɪndsɜːfə(r)/ *noun* **1** a special board with a sail. You stand on it as it moves over the water ୱିଣ୍ଡସର୍ଫିଙ୍ଗ ପାଇଁ ଥିବା ପାଲ ଲଗା ପଟା ବା ସେଲ୍‌ବୋର୍ଡ **2** a person who rides on a board like this ୱିଣ୍ଡସର୍ଫିଙ୍ଗ କରୁଥିବା ବ୍ୟକ୍ତି

windsurfing

wine /waɪn/ *noun* an alcoholic drink made from grapes ଅଙ୍ଗୁର ମଦ

wing /wɪŋ/ *noun* the part of a bird, an insect or an aeroplane that helps it to fly ଡେଣା, ପକ୍ଷୀ ➪ ଚିତ୍ର ପାଇଁ **aircraft** ଓ **bird** ଦେଖନ୍ତୁ।

wink /wɪŋk/ *verb* (**winks, winking, winked**) close and open one eye quickly to make a friendly or secret sign ଆଖିମାରିବା, ସଙ୍କେତ ଭାବରେ ଗୋଟିଏ ଆଖି ବନ୍ଦ କରି ଖୋଲିବା *She winked at me.*

wink *noun* ଆଖିମରା, ଆଖିଠାର *He gave me a wink.*

winner /ˈwɪnə(r)/ *noun* a person or animal that wins a game, race or competition ବିଜେତା *The winner was given a prize.* ✪ ବିପରୀତ **loser**

winnow /ˈwɪnəʊ/ *verb* (**winnows, winnowing, winnowed**) blow air through grain to remove its outer covering କୁଲା ଇତ୍ୟାଦିରେ ଶସ୍ୟରୁ ଚଷୁ ଆଦି ପବନରେ ଉଡ଼ାଇ ସଫା କରିବା; ପାଛୁଡ଼ିବା *Farmers winnow out the husk from the grain.*

winter /ˈwɪntə(r)/ *noun* the coldest season of the year ଶୀତଋତୁ *In Shimla, it often snows in winter.*

wipe /waɪp/ *verb* (**wipes, wiping, wiped**) make something clean or dry with a cloth ପୋଛିବା, ପୋଛି ସଫା କରିବା *The waitress wiped the table.* ○ *I washed my hands and wiped them on a towel.*

wipe off take away something by wiping ପୋଛି କାଢ଼ି ନେବା, ସଫା କରିବା, ଲିଭାଇବା ଇତ୍ୟାଦି *She wiped the writing off the blackboard.*

wipe out destroy a place completely, or kill a lot of people ସମ୍ପୂର୍ଣ୍ଣରୂପେ

ଧ୍ୱଂସ କରିବା, ନିଶ୍ଚିହ୍ନ କରିବା *The floods wiped out many villages.*

wipe up take away liquid by wiping with a cloth କନା ଦ୍ୱାରା ତରଳ ପଦାର୍ଥ ପୋଛି ସଫା କରିବା

wire /ˈwaɪə(r)/ *noun* a long thin piece of metal ତାର *electrical wires*

wisdom /ˈwɪzdəm/ *noun* (*no plural*) the state of knowing and understanding a lot about many things; the state of being wise ଜ୍ଞାନ, ବିଜ୍ଞତା *Some people think that old age brings wisdom.*

wise /waɪz/ *adjective* (**wiser, wisest**) a person who is wise knows and understands a lot about many things ବିଜ୍ଞ, ଜ୍ଞାନୀ *a wise old man* ○ *You made a wise choice.* ✪ ବିପରୀତ **unwise**

wisely *adverb* ବିଜ୍ଞ ଭାବରେ, ବିଜ୍ଞତାର ସହ *Many people wisely stayed at home in the bad weather.*

wish¹ /wɪʃ/ *verb* (**wishes, wishing, wished**) **1** want something that is not possible or that probably will not happen ଇଚ୍ଛା କରିବା, କାମନା କରିବା *I wish I could fly!* ○ *I wish I had passed the exam!* **2** say that you hope somebody will have something କାହାରି ପାଇଁ ଶୁଭେଚ୍ଛା ଜଣାଇବା *I wished her a happy birthday.* **3** want to do or have something ବ୍ୟକ୍ତ କରିବା *I wish to see the manager.* ✪ ଆମେ ସାଧାରଣତଃ **want** ବା **would like** ବ୍ୟବହାର କରିଥାଉଁ।

wish² /wɪʃ/ *noun* (*plural* **wishes**) a feeling that you want to do or have something ଇଚ୍ଛା, କାମନା *I have no wish to go to his birthday party.*

best wishes words that you write at the end of a letter, before your name, to show that you hope somebody is well and happy ଚିଠି ଶେଷରେ ଲେଖା ଯାଉଥିବା ଶୁଭକାମନା ସୂଚକ ବାକ୍ୟାଂଶ *See you soon. Best wishes, Rupa*

wit /wɪt/ *noun* (*no plural*) the ability to speak or write in a clever or funny way ଚତୁର ଭାବରେ ବା ହସେଇଲା ପରି କହି ବା ଲେଖି ପାରିବା ଶକ୍ତି, ଚତୁରବୁଦ୍ଧି

witch /wɪtʃ/ *noun* (*plural* **witches**) a woman in stories who uses magic to do bad things ଗଳ୍ପରେ ବର୍ଣ୍ଣିତ ନାରୀ ଯିଏ ଗୁଣିଗାରେଡ଼ି ଦ୍ୱାରା ଅନିଷ୍ଟ କରେ; ଡାହାଣୀ

with /wɪð/ *preposition* **1** having or carrying ସହିତ; ଥିବା *a house with a garden* ○ *a woman with a suitcase* **2** a word that shows people or things are together ସହିତ, ସହ *I live with my parents.* ○ *Mix the flour with milk.* **3** using ଦ୍ୱାରା, ବ୍ୟବହାର କରି *I cut it with a knife.* **4** against ବିରୁଦ୍ଧରେ *I played tennis with my sister.* **5** because of ଯୋଗୁଁ *Her hands were blue with cold.*

withdraw /wɪðˈdrɔː/ *verb* (**withdraws, withdrawing, withdrew** /wɪðˈdruː/, **has withdrawn** /wɪðˈdrɔːn/) **1** take something out or away ଆଣିବା, କାଢ଼ିବା, ଉଠାଇ ଆଣିବା, ପ୍ରତ୍ୟାହାର କରିବା *I withdrew Rs 5,000 from my bank account.* **2** move back or away ପଛକୁ ଘୁଞ୍ଚିଯିବା, ଦୂରକୁ ଚାଲିଯିବା *The army withdrew from the town.*

wither /ˈwɪðə(r)/ *verb* (**withers, withering, withered**) if a plant withers, it becomes dry and dies

ଝାଉଁଳିଯିବା, ଝାଉଁଳି ପଡ଼ିବା *The plants withered in the hot sun.*

within /wɪˈðɪn/ *preposition* **1** inside ଭିତରେ, ମଧ୍ୟରେ *There are 400 flats within the boundary walls.* **2** before the end of (କୌଣସି କାମ ସରିବା) ପୂର୍ବରୁ, ଭିତରେ *I will be back within an hour.* **3** not further than (କୌଣସି ଦୂରତ୍ୱର) ଭିତରେ, ମଧ୍ୟରେ *We live within a kilometre of the station.*

without /wɪˈðaʊt/ *preposition* **1** not having, showing or using something ନଥାଇ, ନନେଇ, ବିନା *It's cold—don't go out without your coat.* ○ *coffee without sugar* **2** not being with somebody or something ଛାଡ଼ି, ନନେଇ *He left without me.*

without doing something not doing something କିଛି ନକରି ବା ନକହି *They left without saying goodbye.*

withstand /wɪðˈstænd/ *verb* (**withstands, withstanding, withstood** /wɪðˈstʊd/**, has withstood**) be strong enough not to be hurt or damaged in very difficult conditions ସହିବା, ସହ୍ୟ କରିବା *This building can withstand earthquakes.*

witness /ˈwɪtnəs/ *noun* (*plural* **witnesses**) **1** a person who sees something happen and can tell other people about it later କୌଣସି ଘଟଣା ନିଜେ ଦେଖିଥିବା ବ୍ୟକ୍ତି, ପ୍ରତ୍ୟକ୍ଷଦର୍ଶୀ *There were two witnesses to the accident.* **2** a person in a court of law who tells what he/she saw ସାକ୍ଷୀ, ଦେଖିଥିବା ଘଟଣା ବିଷୟରେ ବିଚାରାଳୟରେ ବୟାନ ଦେଉଥିବା ବ୍ୟକ୍ତି

witness *verb* (**witnesses, witnessing, witnessed**) see something happen ପ୍ରତ୍ୟକ୍ଷଦର୍ଶୀ ହେବା, ନିଜେ ଦେଖିବା *She witnessed an accident.*

witty /ˈwɪti/ *adjective* (**wittier, wittiest**) clever and funny ଭାବ ପ୍ରକାଶରେ ଚତୁର ଓ ମଜାଳିଆ *a witty answer*

wives ଶବ୍ଦ **wife** ର ବହୁବଚନ

wizard /ˈwɪzəd/ *noun* a man in stories who has magic powers ଗଳ୍ପରେ ବର୍ଣ୍ଣିତ ଅସାଧାରଣ ଶକ୍ତି ସମ୍ପନ୍ନ ବ୍ୟକ୍ତି, ଯାଦୁକର

wobble /ˈwɒbl/ *verb* (**wobbles, wobbling, wobbled**) move a little from side to side ଢ଼ଳ ଢ଼ଳ ହେବା, ଦୋଦୁଲ୍ୟମାନ ହେବା *That chair wobbles when you sit on it.*

woke, woken ଶବ୍ଦ **wake** ର ଧାତୁରୂପ

wolf /wʊlf/ *noun* (*plural* **wolves** /wʊlvz/) a wild animal like a big dog. Wolves live and hunt in groups (called **packs**) ଗଧିଆ ବା ହେଟା ଜାତୀୟ ବନ୍ୟ ପ୍ରାଣୀ, ଓ୍ୱଲଫ୍

woman /ˈwʊmən/ *noun* (*plural* **women** /ˈwɪmɪn/) an adult female human being ନାରୀ, ସ୍ତ୍ରୀଲୋକ *men, women and children*

won ଶବ୍ଦ **win** ର ଏକ ଧାତୁରୂପ

wonder¹ /ˈwʌndə(r)/ *verb* (**wonders, wondering, wondered**) ask yourself something; want to know something କୌଣସି ବିଷୟର କାରଣ ବିଷୟରେ ଭାବିବା; କୌତୁହଳୀ ହେବା *I wonder what that noise is.* ○ *I wonder why he didn't come.*

wonder² /ˈwʌndə(r)/ *noun* **1** (*no plural*) a feeling that you have when you see or hear something very strange, surprising or beautiful (ଅପ୍ରତ୍ୟାଶିତ, ଆଶ୍ଚର୍ଯ୍ୟଜନକ ବା ବିସ୍ମୟ ଚମତ୍କାର ବସ୍ତୁ ବା ଘଟଣା ଦେଖି ମନରେ ଜାତ ହେଉଥିବା

ଭାବନା) *The children looked up in wonder at the big elephant.* **2** (*plural* **wonders**) something that gives you this feeling ଆଶ୍ଚର୍ଯ୍ୟଜନକ ବା ବିସ୍ମୟକର ବସ୍ତୁ ବା ଘଟଣା *the wonders of modern medicine*

wonderful /ˈwʌndəfl/ *adjective* very good; excellent ଖୁବ୍ ଭଲ, ଚମତ୍କାର *What a wonderful present!* ○ *This food is wonderful!*

won't = **will not**

wood /wʊd/ *noun* **1** (*no plural*) the hard part of a tree କାଠ *The table is made of wood.* **2** (**woods** ମଧ୍ୟ) an area of land with trees. A wood is smaller than a forest ବଣ, ଜଙ୍ଗଲ *a walk in the woods*

wooden *adjective* made of wood କାଠରେ ତିଆରି *a wooden box*

woodcutter /ˈwʊdkʌtə(r)/ *noun* a person whose job is to cut down trees and sell the wood କାଠୁରିଆ

woodpecker /ˈwʊdpekə(r)/ *noun* a bird with a long beak that it uses to make holes in trees for its home and to look for insects କାଠହଣା ଚଢ଼େଇ

woodpecker

woodwork /ˈwʊdwɜːk/ *noun* (*no plural*) **1** things made of wood in a building or a room କାଠ କାମ, କାଠର କାରୁକାର୍ଯ୍ୟ **2** the skill or activity of making things from wood କାଠକାମ କରୁଥିବା ଲୋକଙ୍କୁ ବଢ଼ାଇ କୁହାଯାଏ ।

wool /wʊl/ *noun* (*no plural*) **1** the soft thick hair of sheep ମେଣ୍ଢା ଲୋମ **2** thread or cloth that is made from the hair of sheep ମେଣ୍ଢା ଲୋମରୁ ତିଆରି ସୂତା ବା ଲୁଗା, ଉଲ୍, ପଶମ *a ball of wool* ○ *This sweater is made of wool.*

woollen /ˈwʊlən/ *adjective* made of wool ଉଲ୍ ବା ପଶମରେ ତିଆରି *woollen socks*

woolly /ˈwʊli/ *adjective* made of wool, or like wool ଉଲ୍ ପରି ରୁମରୁମିଆ, ଲୋମଶ; ପଶମରେ ତିଆରି *a woolly mat*

word /wɜːd/ *noun* **1** (*plural* **words**) a sound that you make or a letter or group of letters that you write, that has a meaning ଶବ୍ଦ, ପଦ *What's the Sanskrit word for 'dog'?* ○ *Do you know the words of this song?* **2** (*no plural*) a promise ପ୍ରତିଶ୍ରୁତି *She gave me her word that she wouldn't tell anyone.*

have a word with somebody speak to somebody କାହାରି ସହ କଥାବାର୍ତ୍ତା ହେବା *Could I have a word with you?*

in other words used for saying something in a different way ଅନ୍ୟ ଭାବରେ, କହିଲେ, ଅର୍ଥାତ୍ *Saurabh doesn't like hard work—in other words, he's lazy!*

keep your word do what you promised ପ୍ରତିଶ୍ରୁତି ରକ୍ଷା କରିବା *Maya said she would come, and she kept her word.*

word processor *noun* (*plural* **word processors**) a small computer that you can use for writing letters, etc. ଲେଖା ଲେଖି କରିବା ପାଇଁ ଏକ ଛୋଟ କମ୍ପ୍ୟୁଟର୍, ୱାର୍ଡ୍ ପ୍ରୋସେସର୍

wore ଶବ୍ଦ **wear**[1] ର ଏକ ଧାତୁରୂପ

work[1] /wɜːk/ *noun* **1** (*no plural*) the act of doing or making something କାମ, କାର୍ଯ୍ୟ *Digging the garden is hard work.* **2** (*no plural*) the job that you do to earn money ରୋଜଗାର ପାଇଁ କରୁଥିବା କାମ; ଚାକିରି, ବୃତ୍ତି *I'm looking for work.* ○ *What time do you start work?* **3** (*plural* **works**) a book, painting or piece of music କୌଣସି ବହି, ଚିତ୍ର, ସଙ୍ଗୀତ; କୃତି *the works of Shakespeare* ○ *a work of art*

at work busy doing some work କାମ କରୁଥିବା, କାର୍ଯ୍ୟରତ *The group are at work on a new film.*

work[2] /wɜːk/ *verb* (**works, working, worked**) **1** do or make something; be busy କାମ କରିବା, ପରିଶ୍ରମ କରିବା; କାର୍ଯ୍ୟରତ ରହିବା *You will need to work harder if you want to top the exam.* **2** do something as a job and get money for it ଟଙ୍କା ଅର୍ଜନ ପାଇଁ ବୃତ୍ତି ଭାବରେ କାମ କରିବା *His sister works for the UN.* ○ *I work at the car factory.* **3** go correctly or do something correctly ଠିକ୍ ଭାବରେ କାମ କରିବା *We can't use the phone—it isn't working.* ○ *How does this computer work?* **4** make a thing do something (ଯନ୍ତ୍ର ଇତ୍ୟାଦି) କାମ କରାଇବା, ଚାଳନ କରାଇବା *Can you show me how to work this machine?* **5** have the result you wanted ଠିକ୍ କାମ କରିବା, ଉଦ୍ଦିଷ୍ଟ ଫଳ ପାଇବା *I think your plan will work.*

work out 1 have the result you wanted ଉଦ୍ଦିଷ୍ଟ ଫଳ ଦେବା, ସଫଳ ହେବା *I hope your plans work out.* **2** do exercises to keep your body strong and well ବ୍ୟାୟମ କରିବା *I work out every day.*

work something out find the answer to something ସମସ୍ୟାର ସମାଧାନ ବାହାର କରିବା, ପ୍ରଶ୍ନର ଉତ୍ତର ବାହାର କରିବା, ହିସାବ କରିବା *We worked out the cost of the holiday.*

workbook /ˈwɜːkbʊk/ *noun* a book where you write answers to questions, that you use when you are studying something ଛାତ୍ରମାନଙ୍କର ପଢ଼ା ବିଷୟର ପ୍ରଶ୍ନର ଉତ୍ତର ଲେଖିବା ବହି

worker /ˈwɜːkə(r)/ *noun* a person who does a particular kind of work କାମ କରୁଥିବା ବ୍ୟକ୍ତି, କର୍ମଚାରୀ, ଶ୍ରମିକ *factory workers*

working /ˈwɜːkɪŋ/ *adjective* **1** employed; having a job କାର୍ଯ୍ୟରେ ନିଯୁକ୍ତ, ଚାକିରି କରୁଥିବା *the problems of working women* **2** related to your job କାମ ସମ୍ବନ୍ଧୀୟ, କାମ ବିଷୟକ *working hours* ○ *working conditions*

workman /ˈwɜːkmən/ *noun* (*plural* **workmen**) a man who works with his hands to build or repair something ଶାରୀରିକ ଶ୍ରମ କରିବା ପାଇଁ ନିଯୁକ୍ତ ପୁରୁଷ, ଶ୍ରମିକ, କାରିଗର

worksheet /ˈwɜːkʃiːt/ *noun* a piece of paper where you write answers to questions while you are studying something ପାଠ ପଢ଼ିଲା ବେଳେ ନିର୍ଦ୍ଧାରିତ ପ୍ରଶ୍ନୋତ୍ତର ଲେଖିବା କାଗଜ

workshop /ˈwɜːkʃɒp/ *noun* a place where people make or repair things କାରଖାନା, କର୍ମଶାଳା

world /wɜːld/ *noun* (*no plural*) the earth with all its countries and people (ଦେଶ ଓ ଜନମାନବ ସମାହିତ) ପୃଥିବୀ, ବିଶ୍ୱ, ଦୁନିଆଁ

a map of the world ○ *Which is the biggest city in the world?*

world-famous *adjective* known everywhere in the world ବିଶ୍ୱପ୍ରସିଦ୍ଧ, ବିଶ୍ୱବିଖ୍ୟାତ *a world-famous writer*

worldwide /ˈwɜːldwaɪd/ *adjective* that you find everywhere in the world ବିଶ୍ୱବ୍ୟାପୀ *Pollution is a world-wide problem.*

World Wide Web (**the Web** ମଧ୍ୟ) *noun* (*no plural*) a system of computers that are interconnected and helps you get information from around the world on your computer ସବୁ କମ୍ପ୍ୟୁଟର୍ ଇଣ୍ଟରନେଟ୍‌ରେ ଗଚ୍ଛିତ ସବୁ ତଥ୍ୟ ପାଇ ପାରିବା ବ୍ୟବସ୍ଥା, ବିଶ୍ୱବ୍ୟାପୀ ତଥ୍ୟାଗାର, ୱେବ୍ ✪ World Wide Web ର ସଂକ୍ଷିପ୍ତ ରୂପ ହେଲା **www**।

worm /wɜːm/ *noun* a small creature with a long thin soft body and no legs. Worms live in the ground or inside other animals କ୍ଷୁଦ୍ର ମେରୁଦଣ୍ଡହୀନ ପ୍ରାଣୀ, ପୋକଜୋକ

worn ଶବ୍ଦ **wear**[1] ର ଏକ ଧାତୁରୂପ

worn out *adjective* **1** old and completely damaged because you have used it a lot ବ୍ୟବହାର ଦ୍ୱାରା ନଷ୍ଟ, ଘଷରା *I threw the shoes away because they were worn out.* **2** very tired ଖୁବ୍ କ୍ଲାନ୍ତ ବା ହାଲିଆ *He's worn out after his long journey.*

worried /ˈwʌrid/ *adjective* unhappy because you think that something bad will happen or has happened ଚିନ୍ତିତ, ବିବ୍ରତ *I'm worried about my brother—he looks ill.*

worry[1] /ˈwʌri/ *verb* (**worries, worrying, worried, has worried**) **1** feel that something bad will happen or has happened ଚିନ୍ତିତ ବା ବିବ୍ରତ ହେବା *I worried when my father didn't come home at the usual time.* ○ *Don't worry if you don't know the answer.* **2** make somebody feel that something bad will happen or has happened ଉଦ୍‌ବିଗ୍ନ କରାଇବା, ବିବ୍ରତ କରାଇବା *Pradip's illness is worrying his parents.*

worry[2] /ˈwʌri/ *noun* **1** (*no plural*) a feeling that something bad will happen or has happened ଚିନ୍ତା, ଉଦ୍‌ବିଗ୍ନତା, ଦୁଶ୍ଚିନ୍ତା *Her face showed signs of worry.* **2** (*plural* **worries**) a problem; something that makes you feel worried ସମସ୍ୟା; ବିବ୍ରତ କଲାପରି ବିଷୟ; ଚିନ୍ତା *I have a lot of worries.*

worse /wɜːs/ *adjective* (**bad, worse, worst** /wɜːst/) **1** more bad; less good ଅଧିକ ଖରାପ *The weather today is worse than yesterday.* ○ *Her English is bad but her Hindi is even worse.* **2** more ill ଅଧିକ ପୀଡ଼ିତ *If you get worse, you must go to the doctor's.*

worse *adverb* more badly ଅଧିକ ଖରାପ ଭାବରେ

worship /ˈwɜːʃɪp/ *verb* (**worships, worshipping, worshipped**) show that you believe in God or a god by praying ଈଶ୍ୱରଙ୍କୁ ବା ଦେବାଦେବୀଙ୍କୁ ପୂଜା କରିବା, ଉପାସନା କରିବା *Christians worship in a church.*

worship *noun* (*no plural*) ପୂଜା, ଉପାସନା, ଆରାଧନା *A temple is a place of worship.*

worst /wɜːst/ *adjective* (**bad, worse, worst**) most bad ସବୁଠାରୁ ଖରାପ *He's the worst player in the team!* ○ *the worst day of my life*

worst *adverb* most badly ସବୁଠାରୁ ଖରାପ ଭାବରେ *The captain played badly, but I played worst of all.*

worst *noun* (*no plural*) the most bad thing or person ସବୁଠାରୁ ଖରାପ ବ୍ୟକ୍ତି ବା ପଦାର୍ଥ *I'm the worst in the class at grammar.*

worth[1] /wɜːθ/ *adjective* **1** with a value of ନିର୍ଦ୍ଦିଷ୍ଟ ମୂଲ୍ୟର; ସମତୁଲ୍ୟ ମୂଲ୍ୟର *This house is worth a million!* **2** good or useful enough to do or have (ଦେଖିବା, ରଖିବା ଇତ୍ୟାଦି ପାଇଁ) ଯୋଗ୍ୟ, ଉପଯୁକ୍ତ *Is this film worth seeing?*

worth[2] /wɜːθ/ *noun* (*no plural*) value ମୂଲ୍ୟ, ଦାମ; ମହତ୍ତ୍ୱ, ଗୁଣ *This painting is of little worth.*

worthless /ˈwɜːθləs/ *adjective* with no value or use ମୂଲ୍ୟହୀନ, ଗୁଣହୀନ; କିଛି କାମର ହୋଇନଥିବା *A cheque is worthless if you don't sign it.*

worthwhile /ˌwɜːθˈwaɪl/ *adjective* good or useful enough for the time that you spend or the work that you do କରଣୀୟ, ପ୍ରୟୋଜନୀୟ, ସମୟ ଓ ଶ୍ରମର ଉଚିତ ବିନିଯୋଗ ହେଉଥିବା *The hard work was worthwhile because I passed the exam.*

worthy /ˈwɜːði/ *adjective* (**worthier, worthiest**) if you are worthy, you get a lot of respect and attention ପ୍ରଶଂସାଯୋଗ୍ୟ, ସମ୍ମାନାସ୍ପଦ, ସୁଯୋଗ୍ୟ *a worthy leader*

would /wʊd/ *modal verb* **1** used to say that something was planned in the past; 'will' ର ଅତୀତ କାଳ, ଅତୀତ ଯୋଜନା ସୂଚକ କ୍ରିୟାପଦ *He said he would come.* **2** a word that you use to talk about a situation or possibility that you imagine କଳ୍ପିତ ପରିସ୍ଥିତି ବା ସମ୍ଭାବନା ଅର୍ଥରେ ବ୍ୟବହୃତ କ୍ରିୟା *If I had lots of money, I would buy a big house.* **3** a word that you use to ask something in a polite way ଭଦ୍ର ଭାବରେ ପ୍ରଶ୍ନ କଲାବେଳେ ବ୍ୟବହୃତ କ୍ରିୟା *Would you close the door, please?*

would like want; words that you use when you ask or say something ପ୍ରଶ୍ନ ପଚାରିଲା ବେଳେ ବା ଇଚ୍ଛା ପ୍ରକାଶ କଲାବେଳେ ବ୍ୟବହୃତ କ୍ରିୟା ବାକ୍ୟାଂଶ *Would you like a cup of tea?* ○ *I would like to go to Singapore.*

> ✪ 'Would' ର ବିପରୀତ ହେଲା **would not** ଓ ଏହାର ସଂକ୍ଷିପ୍ତ ରୂପ ହେଲା **wouldn't** —
> *He wouldn't help me.*
> 'Would' ର ସଂକ୍ଷିପ୍ତ ରୂପ ହେଲା **'d** —
> *I'd like to meet her.*
> *They'd help if they had the time.*
> ⇨ **modal verb** ପାଇଁ ଟିପ୍ପଣୀ ଦେଖନ୍ତୁ।

would've = **would have**

wound[1] /wuːnd/ *verb* (**wounds, wounding, wounded**) hurt somebody ଆହତ କରିବା, ଆଘାତ ଦେବା, କ୍ଷତ କରିବା *The bullet wounded him in the leg.*

wound *noun* a place in your body where you have been injured by something like a gun or a knife କ୍ଷତ

wounded *adjective* with a lot of wounds କ୍ଷତବିକ୍ଷତ *a wounded soldier*

wound[2] ଶବ୍ଦ **wind**[2] ର ଏକ ଧାତୁରୂପ

wove, woven ଶବ୍ଦ **weave** ର ଏକ ଧାତୁରୂପ

wow /waʊ/ *interjection* a word that shows surprise and pleasure ଆଶ୍ଚର୍ଯ୍ୟ ଓ ଖୁସି ପ୍ରକାଶକ ଶବ୍ଦ; ବାଃ, ୱାଓ *Wow! What a lovely car!*

wrap /ræp/ *verb* (**wraps, wrapping, wrapped**) **1** put paper or other material around something to cover it completely କାଗଜ ଇତ୍ୟାଦିରେ ଗୁଡ଼ାଇବା *She wrapped the glass up in paper.* ✪ ବିପରୀତ **unwrap** **2** cover something or someone with cloth or other material to protect them ଘୋଡ଼ାଇ ଦେବା *The baby was wrapped in a blanket.*

wrapper /ˈræpə(r)/ *noun* a piece of paper or plastic that covers something like a sweet ପ୍ୟାକେଟ୍, ମିଠେଇ ଇତ୍ୟାଦି ଉପରେ ଲଗା ଯାଇଥିବା କାଗଜ ବା ପ୍ଲାଷ୍ଟିକ୍‌ର ଆବରଣ *Don't throw the toffee wrappers on the floor!*

wrapping /ˈræpɪŋ/ *noun* a piece of paper or plastic that covers a present or something that you buy ଉପହାର ଇତ୍ୟାଦି କିଣିଲା ବେଳେ ତା' ଉପରେ ଲଗାଯାଉଥିବା ଜରି କାଗଜ *I took the new shirt out of its wrapping.*

wrapping paper *noun* (*no plural*) special paper that you use for wrapping presents ଉପହାର ଗୁଡ଼ାଇବା ପାଇଁ ରଙ୍ଗୀନ ଜରିକାଗଜ; ପଠାଯାଉଥିବା ଜିନିଷ ଗୁଡ଼ାଇବା ପାଇଁ ମୋଟା କାଗଜ

wrath /rɒθ/ *noun* (*no plural*) very great anger ପ୍ରଚଣ୍ଡ କ୍ରୋଧ ବା ରାଗ

wreck /rek/ *noun* a ship, car or plane that has been very badly damaged in an accident ଧ୍ୱଂସପ୍ରାପ୍ତ ଜାହାଜ, ମଟରଗାଡ଼ି, ଉଡ଼ାଜାହାଜ ଇତ୍ୟାଦି, ଜାହାଜର ଧ୍ୱଂସପ୍ରାପ୍ତ *a shipwreck at sea*

wreck *verb* (**wrecks, wrecking, wrecked**) break or destroy something completely ସମ୍ପୂର୍ଣ୍ଣ ଭାବେ ଧ୍ୱଂସ କରିବା *The fire wrecked the hotel.*

wreckage /ˈrekɪdʒ/ *noun* (*no plural*) the broken parts of something that has been badly damaged ଧ୍ୱଂସପ୍ରାପ୍ତ ଦ୍ରବ୍ୟ, ଧ୍ୱଂସାବଶେଷ *the wreckage of the plane*

wrestle /ˈresl/ *verb* (**wrestles, wrestling, wrestled**) fight by trying to throw somebody to the ground. People often wrestle as a sport କୁସ୍ତିଲଢ଼ିବା

wrestler *noun* a person who wrestles as a sport କୁସ୍ତି ଲଢ଼ିବା ଲୋକ, ମଲ୍ଲ

wrestling *noun* (*no plural*) the sport where two people fight and try to throw each other to the ground କୁସ୍ତି, ମଲ୍ଲଯୁଦ୍ଧ *a wrestling match*

wretch /retʃ/ *noun* an unhappy or unfortunate person for whom you feel sorry ଭାଗ୍ୟହୀନ ବା ଦୁର୍ଭାଗା ବ୍ୟକ୍ତି, ଦୟାଯୋଗ୍ୟ ବ୍ୟକ୍ତି

wretched /ˈretʃɪd/ *adjective* very unhappy and miserable ଦୁଃଖୀ, ଦୀନହୀନ, ଦୁସ୍ଥ *wretched conditions*

wriggle /ˈrɪgl/ *verb* (**wriggles, wriggling, wriggled**) turn or move the body quickly from side to side, like a worm ଛାଟିପିଟି ହେବା, ମୋଡ଼ିଭିଡ଼ି ହେବା *The teacher told the children to stop wriggling.*

wring /rɪŋ/ *verb* (**wrings, wringing, wrung** /rʌŋ/, **has wrung**) press and twist something with your hands to make water come out ମୋଡ଼ି ଚିପୁଡ଼ିବା

He wrung the towel out and put it outside to dry.

wrinkle /ˈrɪŋkl/ *noun* a small line or fold in something, for example in the skin of the face କୁଞ୍ଚିତ ଚର୍ମ; ଅନ୍ୟ କୌଣସି ପଦାର୍ଥରେ ହୋଇଥିବା ଲୋଚାକୋଚା ଦାଗ *My grandmother has a lot of wrinkles.*

wrinkled *adjective* with a lot of wrinkles କୁଞ୍ଚିତ ଚର୍ମଥିବା; ଲୋଚାକୋଚା ହୋଇଥିବା

wrist /rɪst/ *noun* the part of your body where your arm joins your hand ମଣିବନ୍ଧା, ହାତର କବ୍‌ଜା ➪ ଚିତ୍ର ପାଇଁ **body** ଦେଖନ୍ତୁ।

write /raɪt/ *verb* (**writes, writing, wrote** /rəʊt/, **has written** /rɪtn/) make letters or words on paper using a pen or pencil ଲେଖିବା *Write your name at the top of the page.* ○ *He can't read or write.*

write down write something on paper, so that you can remember it (ମନେ ରଖିବା ପାଇଁ) ଲେଖି ପକାଇବା *I wrote down his telephone number.*

writer /ˈraɪtə(r)/ *noun* a person who writes books, stories, etc. ଲେଖକ *Charles Dickens was a famous writer.*

writing /ˈraɪtɪŋ/ *noun* (*no plural*) **1** the particular way in which a person writes ଲେଖା; ଲେଖିବା ଶୈଳୀ *I can't read your writing—it's so small.* **2** the activity of putting words on paper ଲେଖିବା କାମ ବା ପ୍ରକ୍ରିୟା *Writing is slower than telephoning.* **3** words that have been written, printed or painted on something ଲିଖିତ, ମୁଦ୍ରିତ ବା ଅଙ୍କିତ ଲେଖା *The agreement was put in writing.*

written ଶବ୍ଦ **write** ର ଏକ ଧାତୁରୂପ

wrong[1] /rɒŋ/ *adjective* **1** not true or not correct ଭୁଲ୍; ମିଛ *She gave me the wrong key, so I couldn't open the door.* ✪ ବିପରୀତ **right**[2] **2** bad, or not what the law allows ଖରାପ; ବେଆଇନ୍ *Stealing is wrong.* ✪ ବିପରୀତ **right**[2] **3** not the best, right or suitable ଅନୁପଯୁକ୍ତ, ଭୁଲ୍ *We're late because we took the wrong road.* ✪ **right**[2] **4** not as it should be, or not working well ଖରାପ, ଅସୁବିଧା *There's something wrong with my car—it won't start.*

wrong *adverb* not correctly; not right ଭୁଲ୍ ଭାବରେ, ଭୁଲ୍ କରି *You've spelt my name wrong.* ✪ ବିପରୀତ **right**[3]

go wrong 1 stop working well ଖରାପ ହୋଇଯିବା *The watch has gone wrong—can you mend it?* **2** not happen as you hoped or wanted ଇଚ୍ଛାମତେ ନ ହେବା, ଓଲଟ ପାଲଟ ହୋଇଯିବା, ବିଗିଡ଼ି ଯିବା *All our plans went wrong.*

wrong[2] /rɒŋ/ *noun* (*no plural*) things that are bad or not right ଖରାପ ବା ଅନ୍ୟାୟ କାମ *Babies don't know the difference between right and wrong.* ✪ ବିପରୀତ **right**[4]

wrongly /ˈrɒŋli/ *adverb* not correctly ଭୁଲ୍ ଭାବରେ *The letter didn't arrive because it was wrongly addressed.*

wrote ଶବ୍ଦ **write** ର ଏକ ଧାତୁରୂପ

wrung ଶବ୍ଦ **wring** ର ଏକ ଧାତୁରୂପ

WWW *abbreviation* ହେଲା **world wide web** ର ଏକ ସଂକ୍ଷିପ୍ତ ରୂପ

X x

X /eks/ *symbol* the number 10 in Roman numerals ରୋମାନ୍ ସଂଖ୍ୟା ୧୦

Xmas /ˈeksməs/ *noun* ର ସଂକ୍ଷିପ୍ତ ରୂପ **christmas** ✪ Xmas ଶବ୍ଦ କେବଳ ଲେଖାରେ ବ୍ୟବହାର କରାଯାଏ ।

X-ray *noun* a photograph of the inside of your body that is made by using a special light that you cannot see ଅସ୍ୱଚ୍ଛ ପଦାର୍ଥକୁ ଭେଦକରି ପାରୁଥିବା ବିଦ୍ୟୁତଚୁମ୍ବକୀୟ ରଶ୍ମି, ରଞ୍ଜନ ରଶ୍ମି; ରଞ୍ଜନ ରଶ୍ମି ଦ୍ୱାରା ନିଆଯାଇଥିବା ଦେହ ଭିତରର ଫଟୋ *The doctor took an X-ray of my arm to see if it was broken.*

X-ray *verb* (**X-rays, X-raying, X-rayed**) take a photograph using an X-ray machine ରଞ୍ଜନ ରଶ୍ମି ଯନ୍ତ୍ର ଦ୍ୱାରା ଫଟୋ ନେବା *She had her leg X-rayed.*

xylophone

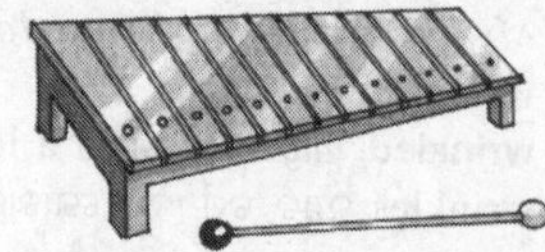

xylophone /ˈzaɪləfəʊn/ *noun* a musical instrument with metal or wooden bars that you hit with small hammers କାଠ ବା ଧାତୁ ପଟା ଖଞ୍ଜା, ବାଦ୍ୟଯନ୍ତ୍ର; କାଠତରଙ୍ଗ; ଧାତୁତରଙ୍ଗ

Y y

yacht /jɒt/ *noun* a large boat with **SAILS** that is used for trips or racing ପାଲଟଣା ବଡ଼ ଡଙ୍ଗା ➪ ଚିତ୍ର ପାଇଁ **sail** ଦେଖନ୍ତୁ ।

yard /jɑːd/ *noun* **1** a piece of hard ground next to a building, with a fence or wall around it ଘରକୁ ଲାଗିଥିବା ବାଡ଼ ବା କାନ୍ଥ ଘେରା ଜମି; ପ୍ରାଙ୍ଗଣ, ଅଗଣା *The children were playing in the school yard.* ○ *a farmyard* **2** a measure of length (= 0.914 of a metre) ଲମ୍ବର ଏକ ମାପକ (= ୦.୯୧୪ ମିଟର୍) ✪ 'Yard' ର ସଂକ୍ଷିପ୍ତ ରୂପ ହେଲା **yd** ।

yawn /jɔːn/ *verb* (**yawns, yawning, yawned**) open your mouth wide and breathe in, usually because you are tired or bored ହାଇ ମାରିବା

yawn *noun* ହାଇ, ହାଇମରା *'I'm going to bed now,' she said with a yawn.*

yeah /jeə/ *interjection* yes ହଁ ✪ Yeah ହେଲା ଏକ କଥିତ ଭାଷାର ଶବ୍ଦ ।

year /jɪə(r)/ *noun* **1** a time of 365 or 366 days, from 1 January to 31 December. A year has twelve **months** ୧ ବର୍ଷ: ୧ ଜାନୁଆରୀ ଠାରୁ ୩୧ ଡିସେମ୍ବର ପର୍ଯ୍ୟନ୍ତ ସମୟକାଳ (୧୨ମାସ, ୩୬୫ ବା ୩୬୬ ଦିନ) *Where are you going on holiday this year?* ○ *'In which year were you born?' 'In 1993.'* ➪ **leap year** ମଧ୍ୟ ଦେଖନ୍ତୁ । **2** any time of twelve months ଯେକୌଣସି ୧୨ ମାସର ବା ବର୍ଷକର ଅବଧି *I have known him for three years.* ○ *My son is five years old.* ○ *a two-year-old* ✪ ମନେ ରଖନ୍ତୁ ! ଇଂରାଜୀରେ *She's ten* ବା *She's ten years old* କହିବା ଠିକ୍ (*She's ten years.* ଟା ଠିକ୍ ନୁହେଁ) ।

all year round all through the year ବର୍ଷସାରା, ସାରା ବର୍ଷ *The swimming pool is open all year round.*

yearly /ˈjɪəli/ *adjective*, *adverb* that happens or comes every year or once a year ବାର୍ଷିକ *a yearly visit* ○ *We meet twice yearly.*

yeast /jiːst/ *noun* (*no plural*) a substance that is used for making bread rise ପାଉଁରୁଟି ଇତ୍ୟାଦି ବନାଇଲାବେଳେ ତାହାକୁ ଫୁଲାଉଥିବା ପଦାର୍ଥ; ଖମୀର, ୟିଷ୍ଟ

yell /jel/ *verb* (**yells, yelling, yelled**) shout loudly ଚିତ୍କାର କରିବା *'Look out!' she yelled as the car came towards them.*

yell *noun* ୟେଲ୍ ଚିତ୍କାର *He gave a yell of pain.*

yellow /ˈjeləʊ/ *adjective* with the colour of a ripe lemon or the middle part of the egg ହଳଦିଆ, ପୀତ *She was wearing a yellow shirt.*

yellow *noun* ହଳଦିଆ ରଙ୍ଗ *Yellow is my favourite colour.*

yes /jes/ *interjection* a word that you use for answering a question. You use 'yes' to agree, to say that something is true, or to say that you would like something ହଁ *'Have you got the key?' 'Yes, here it is.'* ○ *'Would you like some biscuits?' 'Yes, please.'*

yesterday /ˈjestədeɪ/ *adverb*, *noun* (*no plural*) (on) the day before today ଗତକାଲି *I saw Lara yesterday.* ○ *I sent the letter the day before yesterday.*

yet[1] /jet/ *adverb* **1** until now ଏପର୍ଯ୍ୟନ୍ତ *I haven't finished the book yet.* ○ *Have you seen that film yet?* ➪ **already** ର ଟିପ୍ପଣୀ ଦେଖନ୍ତୁ। **2** now; as early as this ବର୍ତ୍ତମାନ; ଏତିକିବେଳୁ *You don't need to go yet—it's only seven o'clock.*

as yet until now ବର୍ତ୍ତମାନ ପର୍ଯ୍ୟନ୍ତ *As yet, I haven't met her.*

yet again once more ପୁଣି ଥରେ *Mohan is late yet again!*

yet[2] /jet/ *conjunction* but; however ତଥାପି *We arrived home tired yet happy.*

yoghurt /ˈjɒɡət/ *noun* a thick liquid food made from milk to which a certain kind of bacteria has been added to make it sour ବସା ଦହିରୁ ପ୍ରସ୍ତୁତ ଖାଦ୍ୟ *flavoured yoghurt*

yolk /jəʊk/ *noun* the yellow part in an egg ଅଣ୍ଡାର କେଶର

you /juː/ *pronoun* **1** the person or people that someone is speaking to ତୁ, ତୁମେ, ଆପଣ; ତୁମେମାନେ, ଆପଣମାନେ *You are late.* ○ *I phoned you yesterday.* **2** any person; a person ଯେ କେହି ବ୍ୟକ୍ତି *You can buy stamps at a post office.*

you'd **1** = **you had** **2** = **you would**

you'll = **you will**

young[1] /jʌŋ/ *adjective* (**younger, youngest**) in the early part of life; not old ଯୁବାବସ୍ଥାରେ ଥିବା, ଅଳ୍ପ ବୟସ୍କ, ତରୁଣ *They have two young children.* ○ *You're younger than me.*
✪ ବିପରୀତ **old 1**

young[2] /jʌŋ/ *noun* (*plural*) baby animals ପଶୁ ପକ୍ଷୀଙ୍କ ଛୁଆ *Birds build nests for their young.*

the young *noun* (*plural*) children and young people ପିଲାମାନେ ଓ ତରୁଣ-ତରୁଣୀମାନେ *a television programme for the young*

youngster /ˈjʌŋstə(r)/ *noun* a young person ଅଳ୍ପବୟସ୍କ ବ୍ୟକ୍ତି

your /jɔː(r)/ *adjective* of you; belonging to you ତୋ'ର, ତୁମର, ଆପଣଙ୍କର *Where is your car?* ○ *Show me your hands.*

you're = **you are**

yours /jɔːz/ *pronoun* **1** something that belongs to you ତୋ'ର, ତୁମର, ଆପଣଙ୍କର *Is this pen yours or mine?* **2 Yours** a word that you write at the end of a letter ଚିଠି ଶେଷରେ ଲେଖା ଯାଉଥିବା ଶବ୍ଦ (ଯଥା: 'ଆପଣଙ୍କର') *Yours sincerely ...* ○ *Yours faithfully ...*

yourself /jɔːˈself/ *pronoun* (*plural* **yourselves** /jɔːˈselvz/) **1** a word that shows 'you' when I have just talked about you ନିଜକୁ ନିଜେ; ନିଜପାଇଁ; ନିଜେ *Did you hurt yourself?* ○ *Buy yourselves a drink.* **2** a word that makes 'you' stronger; 'you' ଶବ୍ଦକୁ ଶକ୍ତିଶାଳୀ କରିବାପାଇଁ ବ୍ୟବହୃତ ଶବ୍ଦ *Did you make this cake yourself?*

(all) by yourself, by yourselves **1** alone; without other people ଏକା, ଏକାକୀ; ଅନ୍ୟଙ୍କ ବିନା *Do you live by yourself?* **2** without help ବିନା ସାହାଯ୍ୟରେ *You can't carry all those bags by yourself.*

youth /ju:θ/ *noun* **1** (*no plural*) the part of your life when you are young ଯୌବନ କାଳ *He spent his youth in London.* ○ *She was very poor in her youth.* **2** (*plural* **youths**) a boy or young man ପୁଅପିଲା ବା ଯୁବକ

the youth *noun* (*plural*) young people ଯୁବା ବ୍ୟକ୍ତିମାନେ *the youth of this country*

you've = **you have**

yo-yo /ˈjəʊ jəʊ/ *noun* (*plural* **yo-yos**) a round toy with a string tied round its middle. You tie one end of the string to your finger and make the yo-yo go up and down the string ମଝିରେ ଘରାଥିବା ଦୁଇଟି ଚକତି ଯାହା ଘରାରେ ସୂତା ଗୁଡ଼ାଇ ହାତ ହଲାଇ ତାକୁ ଉପର ତଳେ କରିହୁଏ; ୟୋ ୟୋ

Z z

zebra /ˈzebrə/ *noun* an African wild animal like a horse, with black and white lines on its body କଳା ଓ ଧଳା ପଟାପଟା ଦାଗଥିବା ଗଧ ଓ ଅଶ୍ୱଜାତୀୟ ଆଫ୍ରିକା ଦେଶର ପଶୁ

zebra crossing *noun* a black and white path across a road. Cars must stop there to let people walk across the road safely ପଦଯାତ୍ରୀମାନେ ରାସ୍ତା ପାରହେବା ପାଇଁ ପଟାପଟା ଚିହ୍ନଥିବା ସ୍ଥାନ

zero /ˈzɪərəʊ/ *number* **1** (*plural* **zeroes**) the number '0' ସଂଖ୍ୟା **2** (*no plural*) the point that is equal to zero on a thermometer, etc. ଉତ୍ତାପ ଶୀତ ମାପର ଶୂନ୍ୟ ଡିଗ୍ରୀ *The temperature is five degrees below zero.*

zigzag /ˈzɪgzæg/ *noun* a line that goes sharply to the left ther the right and continues this way ଅଙ୍କାବଙ୍କା, ବଙ୍କାଟଙ୍କା, ଅସଳଖ

zip /zɪp/ *noun* a long metal or plastic thing with a small part that you pull to close and open things like clothes and bags ପୋଷାକ ଇତ୍ୟାଦିରେ ବୋତାମ ବଦଳରେ ଲଗାଯାଉଥିବା ଧାତୁ ବା ପ୍ଲାଷ୍ଟିକ୍‌ର ବନ୍ଧନୀ, ଜିପ୍

zip *verb* (**zips, zipping, zipped**)

zip up close something with a zip ଜିପ୍ ଟାଣି ବନ୍ଦ କରିବା *She zipped up her dress.*

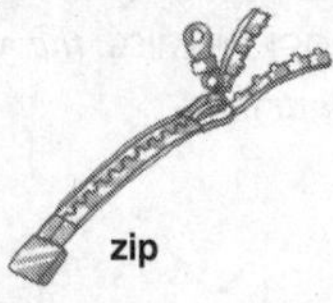
zip

zodiac /ˈzəʊdiæk/ (ମଧ୍ୟ *the zodiac*) *noun* a diagram of the positions of the sun, moon and planets, which is divided into twelve equal parts, each with a special name and symbol (the signs of the zodiac) ରାଶିଚକ୍ର, ଜ୍ୟୋତିଷ୍ଚକ୍ର

zone /zəʊn/ *noun* a place where something special happens ଅଞ୍ଚଳ *Do not enter the danger zone!*

zoo /zu:/ *noun* (*plural* **zoos**) a place where wild animals are kept so that people can see them and learn about them ଚିଡ଼ିଆଖାନା, ପଶୁଉଦ୍ୟାନ

zoo

zoology /zəʊˈɒlədʒi/ *noun* (*no plural*) the study of animals ପ୍ରାଣୀବିଜ୍ଞାନ ➪ **biology** ଓ **botany** ମଧ୍ୟ ଦେଖନ୍ତୁ ।

zoom /zu:m/ *verb* (**zooms, zooming, zoomed**) **1** move very fast ଶବ୍ଦକରି ଅତି ଦ୍ରୁତ ଗତିରେ ଯିବା *Arvind zoomed past in his car.* **2** (of prices, costs, etc.) to increase quickly and suddenly ଶିଘ୍ର ଏବଂ ହଠାତ୍ ବଢ଼ିଯିବା **3 zoom in/out** (of a camera) to make the picture of someone or something appear nearer or further away ଦୂରଜିନିଷକୁ ପାଖରେ ବଡ଼କରି ଦେଖିବା/ପାଖଜନିଷକୁ ସାନ କରି ଦେଖିବା

Zoom lens *noun* a camera **lens** that makes the picture of someone or something appear nearer or further away କ୍ୟାମେରାରେ ବ୍ୟବହୃତ କାଚ ଯେଉଁଥିରେ ଦୂରରେ ଥିବା ଜିନିଷ ପାଖରେ ବଡ଼ କରି ଦେଖାଯାଏ ଏବଂ ପାଖ ଜିନିଷ ସାନ ଦେଖାଯାଏ

Appendix 1
Numbers

Cardinal Numbers		Ordinal Numbers	
1	one	1st	first
2	two	2nd	second
3	three	3rd	third
4	four	4th	fourth
5	five	5th	fifth
6	six	6th	sixth
7	seven	7th	seventh
8	eight	8th	eighth
9	nine	9th	ninth
10	ten	10th	tenth
11	eleven	11th	eleventh
12	twelve	12th	twelfth
13	thirteen	13th	thirteenth
14	fourteen	14th	fourteenth
15	fifteen	15th	fifteenth
16	sixteen	16th	sixteenth
17	seventeen	17th	seventeenth
18	eighteen	18th	eighteenth
19	nineteen	19th	nineteenth
20	twenty	20th	twentieth
21	twenty-one	21st	twenty-first
22	twenty-two	22nd	twenty-second
30	thirty	30th	thirtieth
40	forty	40th	fortieth
50	fifty	50th	fiftieth
60	sixty	60th	sixtieth
70	seventy	70th	seventieth
80	eighty	80th	eightieth
90	ninety	90th	ninetieth
100	a/one hundred	100th	hundredth
101	a/one hundred and one	101st	hundred and first
200	two hundred	200th	two hundredth
1,000	a/one thousand	1,000th	thousandth
10,000	ten thousand	10,000th	ten thousandth
100,000	a/one hundred thousand	100,000th	hundred thousandth
1,000,000	a/one million	1,000,000th	millionth

Examples

635: six hundred and thirty-five • *5,498: five thousand, four hundred and ninety-eight* • *7,463: seven thousand, four hundred and sixty-three*

Appendix 2
Roman Numerals

I	=	1	XIV	=	14	XC	=	90
II	=	2	XV	=	15	C	=	100
III	=	3	XVI	=	16	CC	=	200
IV	=	4	XVII	=	17	CCC	=	300
V	=	5	XVIII	=	18	CD	=	400
VI	=	6	XIX	=	19	D	=	500
VII	=	7	XX	=	20	DC	=	600
VIII	=	8	XXX	=	30	DCC	=	700
IX	=	9	XL	=	40	DCCC	=	800
X	=	10	L	=	50	CM	=	900
XI	=	11	LX	=	60	M	=	1,000
XII	=	12	LXX	=	70	MM	=	2,000
XIII	=	13	LXXX	=	80			

Appendix 3
Fractions and Decimals

Fractions

$\frac{1}{2}$	a half
$\frac{1}{3}$	a/one third
$\frac{1}{4}$	a quarter
$\frac{1}{8}$	an/one eighth
$\frac{1}{10}$	a/one tenth
$\frac{1}{16}$	a/one sixteenth
$\frac{2}{5}$	two fifths
$1\frac{1}{2}$	one and a half
$3\frac{5}{6}$	three and five sixths

Decimals

0.1	(zero) point one
0.25	(zero) point two five
0.66	(zero) point six six
2.75	two point seven five
3.596	three point five nine six

Appendix 4
Mathematical Expressions

+	plus	5 + 7 = 12	*five plus seven equals twelve*
–	minus	10 – 3 = 7	*ten minus three equals seven*
×	times/multiplied by	5 × 6 = 30	*five times six equals thirty* OR *five sixes are thirty*
÷	divided by	20 ÷ 4 = 5	*twenty divided by four equals five*
=	equals		
≠	is not equal to		
>	is greater than		
≥	is greater than or equal to	9 > 6	*nine is greater than six*
<	is less than		
≤	is less than or equal to	5 < 7	*five is less than seven*
%	per cent		

Appendix 5
Temperatures: Celsius (Centigrade) and Fahrenheit

Celsius	Fahrenheit
–17.8°	0°
–10°	14°
0°	32°
10°	50°
20°	68°
30°	86°
40°	104°
50°	122°
60°	140°
70°	158°
80°	176°
90°	194°
100°	212°

To convert Celsius into Fahrenheit: multiply by 9, divide by 5, and add 32.
Example: 10°C × 9 = 90 ÷ 5 = 18 + 32 = 50°F

To convert Fahrenheit into Celsius: subtract 32, multiply by 5, and divide by 9.
Example: 86°F – 32 = 54 × 5 = 270 ÷ 9 = 30°C